THE PRENTICE-HALL SERIES IN MARKETING
Philip Kotler, Series Editor

ABELL/HAMMOND	Strategic Market Planning: Problems and Analytical Approaches
COREY	Industrial Marketing: Cases and Concepts, 3rd ed.
GREEN/TULL/ALBAUM	Research for Marketing Decisions, 5th ed.
KEEGAN	Global Marketing Management, 4th ed.
KOTLER	Marketing Management: Analysis, Planning, Implementations, and Control, 6th ed.
KOTLER/ANDREASEN	Strategic Marketing for Nonprofit Organizations, 3rd ed.
KOTLER	Principles of Marketing, 3rd ed.
LOVELOCK	Services Marketing: Text, Cases, and Readings
MYERS/MASSY/GREYSER	Marketing Research and Knowledge Development: An Assessment for Marketing Management
NAGLE	The Strategy and Tactics of Pricing: A Guide to Profitable Decision Making
RAY	Advertising and Communication Management
RUSSELL/VERRILL/LANE	Kleppner's Advertising Procedure, 10th ed.
STERN/EL-ANSARY	Marketing Channels, 3rd ed.
STERN/EOVALDI	Legal Aspects of Marketing Strategy: Antitrust and Consumer Protection Issues
URBAN/HAUSER	Design and Marketing of New Products

Sixth Edition

MARKETING

MANAGEMENT

Analysis, Planning, Implementation, and Control

PHILIP KOTLER

Northwestern University

Prentice-Hall International, Inc.

Sixth Edition
MARKETING MANAGEMENT: Analysis, Planning, Implementation, and Control
PHILIP KOTLER

Editorial/production supervision: Esther S. Koehn
Interior design: Janet Schmid
Manufacturing buyer: Barbara Kelly Kittle

Printed in the United States of America

10 9 8 7 6 5 4

ISBN 0-13-556267-8

Prentice-Hall of Australia Pty. Limited, *Sydney*
Prentice-Hall Canada Inc., *Toronto*
Prentice-Hall Hispanoamericana, S.A., *Mexico City*
Prentice-Hall of India Private Limited, *New Delhi*
Prentice-Hall of Japan, Inc., *Tokyo*
Simon & Schuster Asia Pte. Ltd., *Singapore*
Editora Prentice-Hall do Brasil, Ltda., *Rio de Janeiro*
Prentice-Hall, *Englewood Cliffs, New Jersey*

This book is dedicated
to my wife, Nancy,
with love

About the Author

PHILIP KOTLER is one of the world's leading authorities on marketing. He is the Harold T. Martin Professor of Marketing at the Kellogg Graduate School of Management, Northwestern University. He received his master's degree at the University of Chicago and his Ph.D. degree at M.I.T., both in economics. He did postdoctoral work in mathematics at Harvard and behavioral science at the University of Chicago.

Dr. Kotler is the author of *Principles of Marketing* and *Marketing: An Introduction*. His *Marketing for Nonprofit Organizations*, now in its third edition, is the best seller in that specialized area. Dr. Kotler's other books include *The New Competition*; *Marketing Professional Services*; *Marketing for Health Care Organizations*; *Strategic Marketing for Educational Institutions*; *High Visibility*; and *Marketing Model-Building*. In addition, he has written over eighty articles for leading journals, including the *Harvard Business Review*, *Journal of Marketing*, *Journal of Marketing Research*, *Management Science*, *Journal of Business Strategy*, and *Futurist*. He is the only three-time winner of the coveted Alpha Kappa Psi award for the best annual article published in the *Journal of Marketing*.

Dr. Kotler has served as chairman of the College on Marketing of the Institute of Management Sciences (TIMS); a director of the American Marketing Association; a trustee of the Marketing Science Institute; and a director of The MAC Group. He has consulted many major U.S. and foreign companies on marketing strategy.

In 1978, Dr. Kotler received the *Paul D. Converse Award* given by the American Marketing Association to honor "outstanding contributions to science in marketing." In 1983, he received the *Steuart Henderson Britt Award* as Marketer of the Year. In 1985, he was named the first recipient of the *Distinguished Marketing Educator Award*, a new award established by the American Marketing Association. In the same year, the Academy for Health Services Marketing established the *Philip Kotler Award for Excellence in Health Care Marketing* and nominated him as the first recipient. He also received the *Prize for Marketing Excellence* awarded by the European Association of Marketing Consultants and Sales Trainers.

Contents

Preface   xvii

PART I UNDERSTANDING MARKETING MANAGEMENT

1 Understanding the Critical Role of Marketing in Organizations and Society   1

THE CORE CONCEPTS OF MARKETING 3
Needs, Wants, and Demands 3   Products 4   Utility, Value, and Satisfaction 5
Exchange, Transactions, and Relationships 6   Markets 9   Marketing and Marketers 10
MARKETING MANAGEMENT 11
COMPANY ORIENTATIONS TOWARD THE MARKETPLACE 13
The Production Concept 13   The Product Concept 14   The Selling Concept 15
The Marketing Concept 17   The Societal Marketing Concept 28
THE RAPID ADOPTION OF MARKETING MANAGEMENT 29
In the Business Sector 29   In the Nonprofit Sector 29   In the International Sector 30
SUMMARY 30

2 Laying the Groundwork through Strategic Planning   33

CORPORATE STRATEGIC PLANNING 36
Corporate Mission 36   Strategic Business Unit Identification 38
Evaluating the Current Business Portfolio 40   Corporate New-Business Plan 46
BUSINESS STRATEGIC PLANNING 49
Business Mission 50
External Environment Analysis (Opportunity and Threat Analysis) 50
Internal Environment Analysis (Strength and Weakness Analysis) 52
Goal Formulation 55   Strategy Formulation 57
Program Formulation 59   Implementation 59   Feedback and Control 60
SUMMARY 62

3

The Marketing Management Process and Marketing Planning 65

THE MARKETING MANAGEMENT PROCESS 66
Analyzing Market Opportunities 66
Researching and Selecting Target Markets 69   Designing Marketing Strategies 71
Planning Marketing Programs 74
Organizing, Implementing, and Controlling the Marketing Effort 74
THE NATURE AND CONTENTS OF A MARKETING PLAN 76
Executive Summary 77   Current Marketing Situation 78
Opportunity and Issue Analysis 79   Objectives 81   Marketing Strategy 82
Action Programs 83   Projected Profit-and-Loss Statement 83   Controls 83
THE THEORY OF EFFECTIVE MARKETING-RESOURCE ALLOCATION 84
The Profit Equation 84   The Sales Equation 85
Profit-Optimization Planning 85   Profit Optimization 87
Long-run Profit Projection 90   Marketing-Mix Optimization 93
Marketing Allocation Optimization 96
SUMMARY 98

PART II   ANALYZING MARKETING OPPORTUNITIES

4

Marketing Information Systems and Marketing Research 101

CONCEPT AND COMPONENTS OF A MARKETING INFORMATION SYSTEM 102
INTERNAL REPORTS SYSTEM 103
The Order-Shipping-Billing Cycle 103   Improving the Timeliness of Sales Reports 103
Designing a User-Oriented Reports System 104
MARKETING INTELLIGENCE SYSTEM 105
MARKETING RESEARCH SYSTEM 107
Suppliers of Marketing Research 107   The Scope of Marketing Research 107
The Marketing Research Process 108
Characteristics of Good Marketing Research 120
Management's Use of Marketing Research 121
ANALYTICAL MARKETING SYSTEM 122
The Statistical Bank 122   The Model Bank 124
SUMMARY 131

5

Analyzing the Marketing Environment 134

ACTORS IN THE COMPANY'S MICROENVIRONMENT 136
Company 136   Suppliers 137   Marketing Intermediaries 137
Customers 139   Competitors 139   Publics 141
FORCES IN THE COMPANY'S MACROENVIRONMENT 143
Demographic Environment 143   Economic Environment 150
Physical Environment 151   Technological Environment 154
Political/Legal Environment 156   Socio/Cultural Environment 160
MAPPING A COMPANY'S MARKETING ENVIRONMENT, MARKETING SYSTEM, AND
    MARKETING STRATEGY 164
SUMMARY 170

6 Analyzing Consumer Markets and Buyer Behavior 173

A MODEL OF CONSUMER BEHAVIOR 174
MAJOR FACTORS INFLUENCING CONSUMER BEHAVIOR 175
Cultural Factors 174   Social Factors 177   Personal Factors 181
Psychological Factors 185
THE BUYING DECISION PROCESS 190
Buying Roles 190   Types of Buying Behavior 191
Researching the Buying Decision Process 193
Stages in the Buying Decision Process 194
SUMMARY 205

7 Analyzing Organizational Markets and Buyer Behavior 208

THE INDUSTRIAL MARKET 209
Who Is in the Industrial Market? 209
What Buying Decisions Do Industrial Buyers Make? 211
Who Participates in the Industrial Buying Process? 213
What Are the Major Influences on Industrial Buyers? 214
How Do Industrial Buyers Make Their Buying Decisions? 218
THE RESELLER MARKET 224
Who Is in the Reseller Market? 224
What Buying Decisions Do Resellers Make? 225
Who Participates in the Reseller Buying Process? 225
What Are the Major Influences on Reseller Buyers? 226
How Do Resellers Make Their Buying Decisions? 227
THE GOVERNMENT MARKET 227
Who Is in the Government Market? 227
What Buying Decisions Do Government Buyers Make? 228
Who Participates in the Government Buying Process? 228
What Are the Major Influences on Government Buyers? 229
How Do Government Buyers Make Their Buying Decisions? 229
SUMMARY 230

8 Analyzing Competitors 234

IDENTIFYING THE COMPANY'S COMPETITORS 235
Industry Concept of Competition 235   Market Concept of Competition 239
IDENTIFYING THE COMPETITORS' STRATEGIES 239
DETERMINING THE COMPETITORS' OBJECTIVES 241
ASSESSING THE COMPETITORS' STRENGTHS AND WEAKNESSES 243
ESTIMATING THE COMPETITORS' REACTION PATTERNS 246
DESIGNING THE COMPETITIVE INTELLIGENCE SYSTEM 248
SELECTING COMPETITORS TO ATTACK AND AVOID 250
Strong vs. Weak Competitors 250   Close vs. Distant Competitors 251
"Good" vs. "Bad" Competitors 252
BALANCING CUSTOMER AND COMPETITOR ORIENTATIONS 252
SUMMARY 254

PART III   RESEARCHING AND SELECTING TARGET MARKETS

9   Measuring and Forecasting Markets   256

MAJOR CONCEPTS IN DEMAND MEASUREMENT   256
A Multitude of Measures of Market Demand 257   Which Market to Measure? 257
A Vocabulary for Demand Management 259
ESTIMATING CURRENT DEMAND   264
Total Market Potential 264   Area Market Potential 265
Estimating Industry Sales and Market Shares 268
ESTIMATING FUTURE DEMAND   270
Survey of Buyers' Intentions 270   Composite of Sales-Force Opinions 272
Expert Opinion 273   Market-Test Method 273   Time-Series Analysis 273
Statistical Demand Analysis 275
SUMMARY   276

10   Identifying Market Segments, Selecting Target Markets, and Developing Market Positions   279

MARKET SEGMENTATION   281
The General Approach to Segmenting a Market 281
Patterns of Market Segmentation 283   Market Segmentation Procedure 283
Bases for Segmenting Consumer Markets 286   Bases for Segmenting Industrial Markets 295
Developing the Customer Segment Profile 296
Requirements for Effective Segmentation 298
MARKET TARGETING   298
Evaluating the Market Segments 298   Selecting the Market Segments 301
Other Considerations in Evaluating and Selecting Segments 304
PRODUCT POSITIONING   308
Identifying Potential Competitive Advantages 308
Choosing Competitive Advantages 312   Signaling the Competitive Advantage 313
SUMMARY   315

PART IV   DESIGNING MARKETING STRATEGIES

11   Marketing Strategies for Market Leaders, Challengers, Followers, and Nichers   318

MARKET-LEADER STRATEGIES   319
Expanding the Total Market 320   Defending Market Share 321
Expanding Market Share 327
MARKET-CHALLENGER STRATEGIES   330
Defining the Strategic Objective and Opponent(s) 333   Choosing an Attack Strategy 333
MARKET-FOLLOWER STRATEGIES   339
MARKET-NICHER STRATEGIES   342
SUMMARY   343

12 Marketing Strategies for Different Stages of the Product Life Cycle 347

THE CONCEPT OF THE PRODUCT LIFE CYCLE   347
Demand/Technology Life Cycle 347
The Product Life Cycle and Its Stages 349
Product-Category, Product-Form, and Brand Life Cycles 350
Other Shapes of the Product Life Cycle 350
Rationale for the Product Life Cycle 354
INTRODUCTION STAGE   355
Market Strategies in the Introduction Stage 355
GROWTH STAGE   358
Marketing Strategies in the Growth Stage 359
MATURITY STAGE   359
Marketing Strategies in the Mature Stage 360
DECLINE STAGE   362
Marketing Strategies during the Decline Stage 365
SUMMARY AND CRITIQUE OF THE PRODUCT LIFE-CYCLE CONCEPT   366
THE CONCEPT OF MARKET EVOLUTION   369
Stages in Market Evolution 369   Dynamics of Attribute Competition 372
SUMMARY   374

13 Marketing Strategies for the Global Marketplace 377

THE INTERNATIONAL PRODUCT LIFE CYCLE   379
APPRAISING THE INTERNATIONAL MARKETING ENVIRONMENT   381
The International Trade System 381   Economic Environment 382
Political-Legal Environment 383   Cultural Environment 385
Business Environment 386
DECIDING WHETHER TO GO ABROAD   386
DECIDING WHICH MARKETS TO ENTER   388
DECIDING HOW TO ENTER THE MARKET   389
Indirect Export 390   Direct Export 391   Licensing 391
Joint Ventures 392   Direct Investment 392   The Internationalization Process 392
DECIDING ON THE MARKETING PROGRAM   393
Product 395   Promotion 396   Price 397   Distribution Channels 398
DECIDING ON THE MARKETING ORGANIZATION   399
Export Department 399   International Division 399   Global Organization 400
SUMMARY   402

PART V   PLANNING MARKETING PROGRAMS

14 Developing, Testing, and Launching New Products and Services 405

THE NEW-PRODUCT-DEVELOPMENT DILEMMA   407
EFFECTIVE ORGANIZATIONAL ARRANGEMENTS   408
IDEA GENERATION   412
Sources of New-Product Ideas 412   Idea-Generating Techniques 413
IDEA SCREENING   415
Product-Idea Rating Devices 416

CONCEPT DEVELOPMENT AND TESTING   418
Concept Development 418   Concept Positioning 419   Concept Testing 419
MARKETING-STRATEGY DEVELOPMENT   420
BUSINESS ANALYSIS   421
Estimating Sales 421   Estimating Costs and Profits 425
PRODUCT DEVELOPMENT   428
MARKET TESTING   430
Consumer-Goods Market Testing 431   Industrial-Goods Market Testing 434
COMMERCIALIZATION   436
When (Timing) 436   Where (Geographical Strategy) 437
To Whom (Target-market Prospects) 437   How (Introductory Market Strategy) 437
THE CONSUMER-ADOPTION PROCESS   439
Concepts in Innovation Diffusion and Adoption 439
Stages in the Adoption Process 439   Individual Difference in Innovativeness 440
Role of Personal Influence 441
Influence of Product Characteristics on the Rate of Adoption 441
Influence of Organizational Buyers' Characteristics on the Rate of Adoption 442
SUMMARY   442

15 Managing Products, Product Lines, and Brands

445

WHAT IS A PRODUCT?   445
Core, Tangible, and Augmented Product 446   Product Hierarchy 447
Product Classifications 448
PRODUCT-MIX DECISIONS   451
PRODUCT-LINE DECISIONS   452
Product-Line Analysis 453   Product-Line Length 454
Line-Modernization Decision 457   Line-Featuring Decision 458
Line-Pruning Decision 458
INDIVIDUAL PRODUCT DECISIONS   458
Product-Attribute Decisions 458   Brand Decisions 463
Packaging and Labeling Decisions 471
SUMMARY   473

16 Managing Services

476

NATURE AND CLASSIFICATION OF SERVICES   477
CHARACTERISTICS OF SERVICES AND THEIR MARKETING IMPLICATIONS   478
Intangibility 478   Inseparability 479   Variability 479   Perishability 480
MARKETING STRATEGIES FOR SERVICE FIRMS   481
Managing Differentiation 483   Managing Service Quality 484
Managing Productivity 486
MANAGING PRODUCT SUPPORT SERVICES   489
Pre-sale Service Strategy 490   Postsale Service Strategy 491
SUMMARY   492

17 Designing Pricing Strategies and Programs

494

SETTING THE PRICE   495
Selecting the Pricing Objective 496   Determining Demand 499
Estimating Costs 501   Analyzing Competitors' Prices and Offers 503
Selecting a Pricing Method 503   Selecting the Final Price 510
ADAPTING THE PRICE   512

Geographical Pricing 512   Price Discounts and Allowances 513
Promotional Pricing 514   Discriminatory Pricing 515   Product-Mix Pricing 516
INITIATING AND RESPONDING TO PRICE CHANGES 517
Initiating Price Cuts 517   Initiating Price Increases 518
Buyers' Reactions to Price Changes 521   Competitors' Reactions to Price Changes 522
Responding to Price Changes 522
SUMMARY 525

18 Selecting and Managing Marketing Channels

528

THE NATURE OF MARKETING CHANNELS 529
Why Are Marketing Intermediaries Used? 529
Marketing-Channel Functions and Flows 530
Number of Channel Levels 532   Channels in the Service Sector 534
CHANNEL-DESIGN DECISIONS 534
Analyzing Consumer Needs for Service Outputs 534
Establishing the Channel Objectives and Constraints 535
Identifying the Major Channel Alternatives 536
Evaluating Major Channel Alternatives 538
CHANNEL-MANAGEMENT DECISIONS 540
Selecting Channel Members 540   Motivating Channel Members 541
Evaluating Channel Members 542   Modifying Channel Arrangements 542
CHANNEL DYNAMICS 545
Growth of Vertical Marketing Systems 545
Growth of Horizontal Marketing Systems 547
Growth of Multichannel Marketing Systems 548
Roles of Individual Firms in a Channel 550
Channel Cooperation, Conflict, and Competition 550
SUMMARY 551

19 Managing Retailing, Wholesaling, and Physical-Distribution Systems

554

RETAILING 554
Nature and Importance of Retailing 554   Types of Retailers 555
Retailer Marketing Decisions 564   Trends in Retailing 569
WHOLESALING 569
Nature and Importance of Wholesaling 569   Types of Wholesalers 571
Wholesaler Marketing Decisions 571   Trends in Wholesaling 574
PHYSICAL DISTRIBUTION 577
Nature of Physical Distribution 577   The Physical-Distribution Objective 578
Order Processing 579   Warehousing 580   Inventory 580
Transportation 581   Organizational Responsibility for Physical Distribution 583
SUMMARY 583

20 Designing Communication and Promotion Mix Strategies

587

THE COMMUNICATION PROCESS 588
STEPS IN DEVELOPING EFFECTIVE COMMUNICATIONS 591
Identifying the Target Audience 592   Determining the Communication Objectives 594
Designing the Message 596   Selecting the Communication Channels 601
Establishing the Total Promotion Budget 604   Deciding on the Promotion Mix 606
Measuring Promotion's Results 613
Managing and Coordinating the Marketing Communication Process 614
SUMMARY 615

21

Designing Effective Advertising Programs 617

SETTING THE ADVERTISING OBJECTIVES 618
DECIDING ON THE ADVERTISING BUDGET 620
DECIDING ON THE MESSAGE 622
Message Generation 622   Message Evaluation and Selection 624
Message Execution 625
DECIDING ON THE MEDIA 629
Deciding on Reach, Frequency, and Impact 629
Choosing Among Major Media Types 631   Selecting Specific Media Vehicles 633
Deciding on Media Timing 634
EVALUATING ADVERTISING EFFECTIVENESS 637
Communication-Effect Research 638   Sales-Effect Research 640
SUMMARY 642

22

Designing Sales Promotion and Public Relations Programs 645

SALES PROMOTION 645
Rapid Growth of Sales Promotion 646   Purpose of Sales Promotion 646
Major Decisions in Sales Promotion 647
Establishing the Sales Promotion Objectives 647   Selecting the Sales Promotion Tools 648
Developing the Sales Promotion Program 652
Pretesting the Sales Promotion Program 653
Implementing and Controlling the Sales Promotion Program 653
Evaluating the Sales Promotion Results 654
PUBLIC RELATIONS 655
Major Tools in Public Relations 657   Major Decisions in Marketing PR 658
SUMMARY 661

23

Managing the Sales Force 663

DESIGNING THE SALES FORCE 664
Sales-Force Objectives 665   Sales-Force Strategy 666
Sales-Force Structure 666   Sales-Force Size 670
Sales-Force Compensation 671
MANAGING THE SALES FORCE 673
Recruiting and Selecting Sales Representatives 673
Training Sales Representatives 675   Directing Sales Representatives 676
Motivating Sales Representatives 680   Evaluating Sales Representatives 683
PRINCIPLES OF PERSONAL SELLING 685
Salesmanship 685   Negotiation 690   Relationship Management 695
SUMMARY 698

PART VI ORGANIZING, IMPLEMENTING, AND CONTROLLING MARKETING EFFORT

24 Organizing and Implementing Marketing Programs 702

COMPANY ORGANIZATION 702
MARKETING ORGANIZATION 704
The Evolution of the Marketing Department 704
Ways of Organizing the Marketing Department 706   Market Management Organization 713
Marketing's Relations with Other Departments 716
Strategies for Building a Companywide Marketing Orientation 720
Introducing Marketing in Nonbusiness Organizations 722
MARKETING IMPLEMENTATION 724
Diagnostic Skills 725   Company Levels 725
Marketing Implementation Skills 725   Implementation-Evaluation Skills 726
SUMMARY 726

25 Evaluating and Controlling Marketing Performance 729

ANNUAL-PLAN CONTROL 730
Sales Analysis 731   Market-Share Analysis 731
Marketing Expense-to-Sales Analysis 734   Financial Analysis 735
Customer-Attitude Tracking 736   Corrective Action 737
PROFITABILITY CONTROL 738
Methodology of Marketing-Profitability Analysis 738
Determining the Best Corrective Action 740   Direct versus Full Costing 741
EFFICIENCY CONTROL 742
Sales-Force Efficiency 742   Advertising Efficiency 743
Sales Promotion Efficiency 743   Distribution Efficiency 743
STRATEGIC CONTROL 744
Marketing-Effectiveness Rating Review 744   The Marketing Audit 746
THE MARKETING CONTROLLER CONCEPT 753
SUMMARY 753

INDICES

Company Index 757

Name Index 761

Subject Index 767

Preface

"Marketing is too important to be left to the marketing department," states David Packard of Hewlett-Packard. And Professor Stephen Burnett of Northwestern adds: "In a truly great marketing organization, you can't tell who's in the marketing department. Everyone in the organization has to make decisions based on the impact on the customer."

Marketing is the business function that identifies unfulfilled needs and wants, defines and measures their magnitude, determines which target markets the organization can best serve, decides on appropriate products, services, and programs to serve these markets, and calls upon everyone in the organization to "think and serve the customer." From a societal point of view, marketing is the link between a society's material requirements and its economic patterns of response.

Yet, to many, marketing is seen narrowly as the art of finding clever ways to dispose of the company's products. Many people confuse marketing with subfunctions such as advertising and selling. But authentic marketing is not the art of selling what you make so much as knowing what to make! It is the art of identifying and understanding customer needs and coming up with solutions that satisfy the customers and produce profit for the stockholders. Market leadership is gained by creating customer satisfaction through product innovation, product quality, and customer service. If these are absent, no amount of advertising, sales promotion, or salesmanship can compensate.

William Davidow observed: "While great devices are invented in the laboratory, great products are invented in the Marketing Department." There is a wide chasm between an invention and an innovation. Too many wonderful laboratory products are greeted with yawns or laughs. The job of marketers is to "think customer" and to guide companies and non-profit organizations into developing offers that are meaningful and attractive to target customers.

The Current Marketing Environment

Market-oriented thinking is a necessity in today's competitive world. There are too many goods chasing too few customers. There are global gluts of steel, agricultural produce, automobiles, and many other products and services. Some companies are trying to expand the size of the market, but most are competing to enlarge their share of the existing market. As a result, there are winners and losers. The losers are those that bring nothing special to the market. We believe that if you can't bring something special to a market, you don't belong in it. The winners are those who carefully analyze needs, identify opportunities, and create value-rich offers for target customer groups that competitors can't match.

These are hard times for many companies. The United States foreign trade deficit is running at $170 billion a year. Many U.S. companies are losing to foreign competitors who come in with lower prices and often better products. The U.S. no longer holds a competitive edge in low, medium, or high-tech industries. Service industries are growing but cannot alone sustain rising incomes indefinitely.

Market thinkers must wrestle with several tough market challenges:

1. The low economic growth rates throughout the world with many major industries in the mature or decline stage of the product life cycle
2. The rise of global competitors such as Japan and Korea, which are capable of making high-quality products at lower costs
3. An international market that is moving toward greater protectionism
4. Foreign companies that receive subsidies from their government and use them to win business through lower prices
5. Many nations that are so debt-ridden and/or politically unstable that it is risky to do business with them
6. A great amount of price cutting and discounting in all industries resulting in an increasing number of buyers who "shop" for prices
7. Too much short-term focus by management and a fixation on buying other businesses rather than on building their existing businesses
8. Growing power of distributors to dictate terms to manufacturers
9. The splintering of the mass market into many micromarkets, each requiring tailored marketing
10. Increasing marketing costs due to the declining effectiveness of mass media and the rising costs of personal selling

Problems, properly analyzed, are also opportunities. Companies such as McDonald's, Procter & Gamble, Campbell's, and IBM have shown a capacity to adapt by staying close to their markets and reading the signs. They know that the marketplace, not the factory, ultimately determines which companies will succeed. Too many of our major auto companies, steel companies, electronics companies, and others didn't have their ears to the market and paid dearly—along with the rest of us—for their "marketing myopia."

Marketing thinking obviously isn't easy or it would be applied more successfully. Although it only takes a semester to learn marketing, it takes a lifetime to master it. Marketing problems, it turns out, do not exhibit the neat quantitative properties of many problems in the production, accounting, and finance areas. Psychological forces play a large role; marketing expenditures affect demand and costs simultaneously; marketing plans shape and interact with other business function plans. Marketing decisions must be made in the face of insufficient information about processes that are dynamic, lagged, stochastic, interactive, and downright difficult. However, this is not an argument for intuitive decision making. Rather it is an argument for improved strategic theory and sharper tools of analysis.

The Nature of This Book

Marketing Management has several major features:

1. *A managerial orientation*. This book focuses on the major decisions that marketing executives and top management face in their efforts to harmonize the objectives and resources of the organization with the needs and opportunities in the marketplace.

2. *An analytical approach*. This book presents a framework for analyzing recurrent problems in marketing management. Real company cases are introduced throughout the text to illustrate the marketing principles.

3. *A basic disciplines perspective*. This book draws on economics, behavioral science, and mathematics. *Economics* provides fundamental concepts and tools for seeking optimal results in the use of scarce resources. *Behavioral science* provides fundamental concepts and tools for understanding consumer and organizational buying behavior. *Mathematics* provides an exact language for expressing relationships among important variables.

4. *A universal approach*. This book applies marketing thinking to products and services, consumer and industrial markets, profit and nonprofit organizations, domestic and foreign companies, small and large firms, manufacturing and middlemen businesses, and low-tech and high-tech industries.

5. *Comprehensive and balanced coverage*. This book covers all the topics that an informed marketing manager needs to know. It covers the main issues faced in strategic, tactical, and administrative marketing.

Marketing Management, sixth edition, is organized into six parts. Part I develops the societal, managerial, and strategic underpinnings of marketing theory and practice. Part II presents concepts and tools for analyzing any market and marketing environment to discern opportunities. Part III presents principles for measuring and forecasting markets and carrying out segmenting, targeting, and positioning. Part IV examines issues in designing marketing strategies for companies in different market positions, global positions, and stages in the product life cycle. Part V deals with tactical marketing and how companies handle, or should handle, each element of the marketing mix—product, price, place, and promotion. Finally, Part VI examines the administrative side of marketing, namely, how firms organize, implement, and control marketing efforts.

Changes in the Sixth Edition

The sixth edition had the following objectives:

1. To update the statistics and analyze new forces in the environment
2. To strengthen the discussion of strategic marketing
3. To show recent company examples of creative market-oriented thinking
4. To stress the role of marketing planning, implementation, and control
5. To describe the growing use of computers, telecommunications, and other new technologies in improving marketing planning and performance

These objectives led to the following distinctive features in the sixth edition:

1. Two new chapters, specifically Chapter 8 (''Analyzing Competitors'') and Chapter 16 (''Managing Services'').
2. Several substantially revised chapters, specifically Chapters 1, 10, 12, 13, 15, 17, 18, and 19.
3. New and expanded material on relationship marketing, direct mail and telemarketing, systems selling, customer value analysis, customer segment profiles, benefit positioning, value chain analysis, customized marketing, vertical marketing, gap analysis, global strategies, multichannel marketing, retailer differentiation strategies, local area marketing, and marketing decision support systems.

Improved Pedagogical Aids

Pedagogical Aids for this edition of *Marketing Management* include:

1. A comprehensive, extensively revised Instructor's Manual which contains teaching formats, suggested syllabi, and transparency masters, as well as a complete section on integrating

supplementary material into the course such as cases, casebooks, readings, videos, and computer based material. It is available to adopters on request.

2. A Test Item File containing over 1,000 questions; it is also available on the PH Test Generator. Both are available to adopters on request.

3. A readings book, MARKETING MANAGEMENT AND STRATEGY, Fourth Edition by Philip Kotler and Keith K. Cox. Completely revised to reflect the sixth edition of *Marketing Management*, this best-selling collection of readings blends classic and recent articles.

4. Software applications, new to the sixth edition, are offered to suit every course.

- *Brandmaps* (Randall Chapman, Boston University) A sophisticated simulation for the IBM PC, designed to reflect product management of a number of individual brands. Available are a Student Manual, an Instructor's Manual, and a Box of Disks for the instructor.
- *Business Decision Making Using 1–2–3* (Albion/Hoff, Harvard Business School) Using a case study approach, this book/disk package is a thorough introduction to 1–2–3. Students analyze a marketing budgeting decision at Helene Curtis, Inc. An Instructor's Manual is available.
- *Marketing Management: Analysis Using Spreadsheets* (Laric/Stiff, University of Baltimore) This book/disk package offers adopters the TWIN spreadsheet program together with an applications disk. Includes templates for forecasting, budgeting, pricing, breakeven analysis, and much more. Compatible with Lotus 1–2–3 or TWIN.
- *Gradebook*: A program for recording, analyzing and displaying student grades is available to adopters on request.

5. Videos, like the software, are new to the sixth edition. Prentice Hall, in collaboration with various companies, offers videos ranging from ''In Search of Excellence: Management Action Program,'' to ''Competitive Strategy,'' the Enterprise Series, and others. A video catalog is available on request.

Acknowledgments

The sixth edition bears the imprint of many persons. My colleagues and associates at the J. L. Kellogg Graduate School of Management at Northwestern University continue to have an important impact on my thinking: James C. Anderson, Bobby J. Calder, Richard M. Clewett, Anne T. Coughlan, Dipak C. Jain, Lakshman Krishnamurthi, Sidney J. Levy, John F. Sherry, Jr., Louis W. Stern, Brian Sternthal, Alice Tybout, Naufel J. Vilcassim, and Andris A. Zoltners. I want to acknowledge the valuable research assistance of three Ph.D. students: Nirmalya Kumar, Laura Perrachio, and Mary Stansifer. Bruce Wrenn and Sy Saliba provided great help in preparing the Instructor's Manual. I benefited from the excellent secretarial assistance of Ruby Chan, Ellen Garbow, and Fred Lasky. I want to thank the Harold T. Martin family for the generous support of my chair at the Kellogg School. Completing the Northwestern team is my dean and longtime friend, Donald P. Jacobs, whom I want to thank for his continuous support of my research and writing efforts.

I am also indebted to the following colleagues at other universities whose reviews provided insightful suggestions: Mark Alpert, The University of Texas at Austin; Gregory Carpenter, Columbia University; C. William Emory, Washington University (St. Louis); Ralph Gaedeke, California State University—Sacramento; John Gottko, Oregon State University; Hal Johnson, Northern Illinois University; Leslie Kanuk, Baruch College; Hal Kassarjian, University of California at Los Angeles; Buck Matthews, Ohio State University; Robert Mika, Monmouth College; Nicholas Nugent, Boston College; Paul Prabhaker, SUNY at Buffalo; Arvind Rangaswamy, The Wharton School of the University of Pennsylvania; Robert Roe, University of Wyoming; Dean Siewers, Rochester Institute of Technology; Bruce Smackey, Lehigh University; Robert Spekman, University of Maryland; D. Sudharshan, University of Illinois; Linda Swayne, University of North Carolina—Charlotte; and Peter Wilton, University of California—Berkeley.

My thanks also go to my foreign-edition coauthors for their suggestions on the contents of the sixth edition:

- Bernard Dubois—Centre d'Enseignement Supérieur des Affairs (France)
- Peter Fitzroy and Robin Shaw—Monash University (Australia)
- Ronald E. Turner—Queen's University (Canada)

The talented staff at Prentice-Hall deserve praise for their role in shaping this edition. My editor, Whitney Blake, offered excellent advice and direction for the sixth edition. I also want to acknowledge the fine editorial work of Esther Koehn, college production editor; the creative graphic design of Janet Schmid; and the marketing research work of Paul Misselwitz.

The two four-color inserts, the Great Marketers picture essay and the Advertisement collection, were made possible by the cooperation of the companies whose marketers and advertisements are presented. That cooperation is greatly appreciated.

My overriding debt is to my wife, Nancy, who provided me the time, support, and inspiration needed to prepare this edition. It is truly our book.

PHILIP KOTLER
J. L. Kellogg Graduate School of Management
Northwestern University
Evanston, Illinois

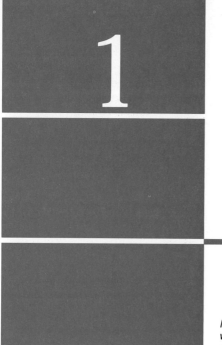

1 Understanding the Critical Role of Marketing in Organizations and Society

Marketing is so basic that it cannot be considered a separate function. It is the whole business seen from the point of view of its final result, that is, from the customer's point of view.

Peter Drucker

What makes a company excellent? This question exploded across America in the early 1980s, and for good reason. Several of America's blue-chip companies—Chrysler, International Harvester, Harley Davidson—were slipping badly in sales and profits. There were the normal problems—changing consumer tastes, rising material costs, falling prices. There were also some newer factors—foreign competition, particularly the invasion of high-quality products coming from Japan, Singapore, Hong Kong, Taiwan, and South Korea. Markets were undergoing dizzying rates of change, and yet many U.S. companies failed to acknowledge or respond to these changes. Like dinosaurs, they were flirting with extinction.

A handful of other American companies continued to rack up high and continuously improving sales and profits. Tom Peters and Bob Waterman interviewed forty-three high-performing companies—companies like Hewlett-Packard, Frito-Lay (PepsiCo), Procter & Gamble, 3M, Delta Airlines, McDonald's, Marriott—to find out what made them tick. They wrote up the results in what was to become the best-selling business book of all times—*In Search of Excellence*.[1] And what they found was that all of these companies shared a set of basic operating principles, among them a keen sense of customer ("stay close to the customer"), a keen sense of the market ("stick to your knitting"), and a high ability to motivate their employees to produce high quality and high value for the customers. Half of what they found relates to what marketers call the "marketing concept."

Since then Tom Peters has published a second book, *A Passion for Excellence*, offering further stories about companies doing wonderful and smart things to improve their customers' satisfaction.[2] He talks about Stew Leonard's supermarket in Norwalk, Connecticut, where Stew sits down with eight customers each Saturday for a few hours to

1

discuss how he can improve customer service; about the Limited Stores of Columbus, Ohio, which studies the clothing needs of specific groups of women and creates appropriate chain store systems (Limited, Limited Express, Victoria's Secret, Sizes Unlimited) to serve each group; about how IBM collects customer ratings of its sales and service people and gives awards to those IBM employees who satisfy the customers most.

In 1986, Frank "Buck" Rodgers, who served as IBM's marketing vice-president for fifteen years, wrote *The IBM Way*, in which he described the many steps IBM takes to ensure that the customer is king.[3] Rodgers is so dedicated to the marketing concept that when a special meeting was suddenly called at IBM headquarters that conflicted with an important appointment he had made with a customer in trouble, Rodgers chose to meet the customer! And his boss forgave him, saying, "You have the right priorities." Here are some of Rodgers's thoughts about IBM's marketing:

> At IBM, *everybody sells*! . . . Walk into the IBM building in New York or into any of its offices throughout the world and you'll get the idea. Every employee has been trained to think that the customer comes first—everybody from the CEO, to the people in finance, to the receptionists, to those who work in manufacturing.

> When I am asked, "What products does IBM sell?" I answer, "IBM doesn't sell products. It sells solutions.". . . An IBM marketing rep's success depends totally on his ability to understand a prospect's business so well that he can identify and analyze its problems and then come up with a solution that makes sense to the customer.

In no way are Buck Rodgers and Tom Peters saying that marketing is the only factor producing business success. But certainly, it is a key factor. And it must be understood not in the old sense of knowing how to make a sale (selling) but rather in the new sense of satisfying customer needs (marketing). It is not enough to produce state-of-the-art computers, as many now extinct computer companies have found out. Successful high-tech companies are the ones that have transformed themselves into marketing companies. That's the secret that Steve Jobs, who founded Apple Computer, learned, that he could not manage Apple as strictly a high-tech, engineering-oriented firm. And this realization sent him scurrying for the best marketing professional he could find, who turned out to be John Scully, then the head of the Pepsi-Cola Company. Scully agreed to leave the presidency of Pepsi-Cola to take over the challenge of converting Apple Computer from a product-driven to a market-driven company. To attract Scully to Apple, Jobs offered him $1 million for joining the company, $1 million a year, stock options, and other perquisites. Is this price too high to pay for a top marketing professional? Not really. Like a star football player, if Scully turns the company around, his salary will hardly be noticed in the income statement.

The high concern of today's companies over marketing is dramatically documented in a recent study in which senior managers of 250 major American corporations identified their number-one planning challenge to be "developing, improving, and implementing competitive marketing strategies"; "controlling costs" and "improving human resources" ran second and third.[4] As a further sign, the executive recruiting firm of Russell Reynolds Associates reported a 52 percent increase in demand for top executives with marketing backgrounds.[5] And Heidrick and Shruggles, Inc., another top recruiting firm, found that more top executives had come out of marketing than any other field; specifically, 31 percent of the Fortune 1000 CEOs had spent the bulk of their careers in marketing, up from 28 percent four years earlier.[6] This turn toward marketers, away from the 1970s preoccupation with financial executives, engineers, and lawyers, is highlighted by Chrysler's hiring of Lee Iacocca, the former president of Ford, to breathe new life into Chrysler. And Iacocca worked the miracle and laid out the challenge "If you can find a better car, buy it."

And the high concern about marketing is justified. No longer does the United States have the exclusive lead on quality, creativity, or capital. Today's companies survive by competing successfully in a global marketplace, not simply in their domestic market. Their domestic market is being invaded by skillful players such as Sony, Hitachi, Toshiba, Mercedes, Unilever, Beecham, Philips, and other major players from Japan, Europe, and elsewhere. And these players are capturing other markets around the world. U.S. companies must increasingly play an international game where the stakes are high and the prizes go to those who can best read customer wants and deliver the highest value to their target markets. And marketing skills will distinguish the amateur from the professional players in the global market.

We believe that stronger marketing will play an important role in launching a renewed era of economic activity and rising living standards. One marketing scholar defined *marketing* as "the creation and delivery of a standard of living." We take this as an inspired and insightful view of the marketing job.

This first chapter will describe the major concepts and philosophies underlying marketing thinking and practice, and we will come back to them again and again throughout the book. This chapter will answer the following specific questions:

- ■ What core concepts underlie the discipline of marketing?
- ■ What basic tasks are performed by marketing managers?
- ■ What is the marketing philosophy and how does it contrast with other philosophies of doing business?
- ■ What role does marketing play in different industries, in nonprofit organizations, and in different countries?

THE CORE CONCEPTS OF MARKETING

Marketing has been defined in various ways by different writers.[7] We like the following definition of marketing:

> **Marketing is a social and managerial process by which individuals and groups obtain what they need and want through creating and exchanging products and value with others.**

This definition of marketing rests on the following core concepts: *needs, wants, and demands*; *products*; *utility, value, and satisfaction*; *exchange, transactions, and relationships*; *markets*; *and marketing and marketers*. These concepts are illustrated in Figure 1-1 and discussed below.

Needs, Wants, and Demands
The starting point for the discipline of marketing lies in human needs and wants. People need food, air, water, clothing, and shelter to survive. Beyond this, people have a strong desire for recreation, education, and other services. They have strong preferences for particular versions of basic goods and services.

There is no doubt that people's needs and wants today are staggering. In a given year, 230 million Americans might purchase 67 billion eggs, 2 billion chickens, 5 million hair dryers, 133 billion domestic air travel passenger miles, and over 20 million lectures

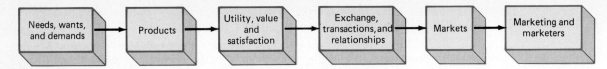

FIGURE 1-1
The Core Concepts of Marketing

by college English professors. These consumer goods and services create a demand for more than 150 million tons of steel, 4 billion pounds of cotton, and many other industrial goods. These are a few of the demands that get expressed in a $2 trillion economy.

A useful distinction can be drawn between needs, wants, and demands. *A human need is a state of felt deprivation of some basic satisfaction.* People require food, clothing, shelter, safety, belonging, esteem, and a few other things for survival. These needs are not created by their society or by marketers; they exist in the very texture of human biology and the human condition.

Wants are desires for specific satisfiers of these deeper needs. An American needs food and wants a hamburger, needs clothing and wants a Pierre Cardin suit, needs esteem and buys a Cadillac. In another society, these needs are satisfied differently: The Balinese satisfy their hunger with mangoes, their clothing needs with a loincloth, their esteem with a shell necklace. While people's needs are few, their wants are many. Human wants are continually shaped and reshaped by social forces and institutions such as churches, schools, families, and business corporations.

Demands are wants for specific products that are backed up by an ability and willingness to buy them. Wants become demands when backed up by purchasing power. Many persons want a Cadillac; only a few are able and willing to buy one. Companies must therefore measure not only how many people want their product but, more important, how many would actually be willing and able to buy it.

These distinctions shed light on the frequent charge by marketing critics that "marketers create needs" or "marketers get people to buy things they don't want." Marketers do not create needs; needs preexist marketers. Marketers, along with other influencers in the society, influence wants. They suggest to consumers that a Cadillac would satisfy a person's need for social status. Marketers do not create the need for social status but try to point out how a particular good would satisfy that need. Marketers try to influence demand by making the product attractive, affordable, and easily available.

Products People satisfy their needs and wants with products. We will define products broadly to cover *anything that can be offered to someone to satisfy a need or want.* Normally the word *product* brings to mind a physical object, such as an automobile, a television set, or a soft drink. And we normally use the expression *products and services* to distinguish between physical objects and intangible ones. But in thinking about physical products, their importance lies not so much in owning them as in using them to satisfy our wants. We don't buy a car to look at but because it supplies transportation service. We don't buy a microwave oven to admire but because it supplies a cooking service. Thus physical products are really vehicles that deliver services to us.

In fact, services are also supplied by other vehicles, such as *persons*, *places*, *activities*, *organizations*, and *ideas*. If we are bored, we can go to a nightclub and watch an entertainer (person); travel to a warm vacationland like Florida (place); engage in some physical exercise (activity); join a lonely hearts club (organization), or adopt a different philosophy about life (idea). In other words, services can be delivered through physical objects and other vehicles. We will use the term *product* to cover all vehicles that are capable of delivering satisfaction of a want or need. Occasionally we will use other terms for product, such as *offers*, *satisfiers*, or *resources*.

Manufacturers get into a lot of trouble by paying more attention to their products than to the services produced by these products. Manufacturers love their products but forget that customers buy them because they satisfy a need. People do not buy physical objects for their own sake. A tube of lipstick is bought to supply a service: helping the person look better. A drill bit is bought to supply a service: producing a needed hole. A physical object is a means of packaging a service. The marketer's job is to sell the benefits or services built into physical products, rather than just describe their features. Sellers who concentrate on the product instead of the customer's need are said to suffer from "marketing myopia."[8]

Utility, Value, and Satisfaction

How do consumers choose among the products that might satisfy a given need? To make the question concrete, suppose Tom Jones needs to travel three miles to work each day. Jones can visualize a number of products that will satisfy this need: walking, roller skates, a bicycle, a motorcycle, an automobile, a taxicab, and a bus. These alternatives constitute his *product choice set*. Assume that Jones would like to satisfy different needs in traveling to work, namely, speed, safety, ease, and economy. We call these his *need set*. Now each product has a different capacity to satisfy his various needs. Thus a bicycle will be slower, less safe, and more effortful than an automobile, but it will be more economical. Somehow Tom Jones has to decide on the most satisfying product.

The guiding concept is *utility*. Tom Jones will form an estimate of the utility of each product in satisfying his needs. He might rank the products from the most need-satisfying to the least need-satisfying. Utility is the consumer's estimate of the product's overall capacity to satisfy his or her needs.

We can ask Jones to imagine the characteristics of an *ideal product* for this task. Jones might answer that the *ideal product* would get him to his place of work in a split second, with absolute safety, no effort, and zero cost. Then the utility of each actual product would depend on how close it came to this ideal product.

To illustrate, suppose Jones is primarily interested in the speed and ease of getting to work. Figure 1-2 presents a product-space map showing where each actual product stands in its ability to satisfy these two needs. Also represented by a point is Jones's ideal product. The closer an actual product is to Jones's ideal product, the greater its utility to Jones. If Jones were offered any of these products at no cost, we would predict that he would choose the automobile. But now comes the rub. Since each product (except walking) involves a purchase price, he will not necessarily buy the automobile. The automobile costs substantially more than, say, a bicycle. Jones will have to give up more of other things (represented by the cost) to obtain the car. Therefore he will consider the product's utility and price before making a choice. He will choose the product that will produce the most utility per dollar if he is a rational, utility-maximizing person. He will try to maximize value, that is, utility per dollar. When we say that one product is a better *value* than another, we mean that it offers more for the price. Thus, while a Cadillac may offer more utility to a consumer (faster pickup, fewer repairs, etc.), it may represent less of a value in relation to, say, a Chevrolet.

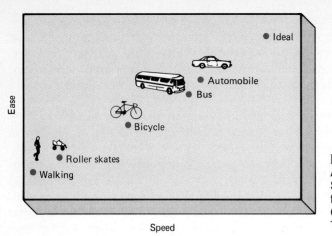

FIGURE 1-2
A Product-Space Map
Showing Alternative Choices
for Satisfying Two Needs
Connected with
Transportation

Today's consumer-behavior theorists have gone beyond narrow economic assumptions of how consumers form value in their mind and make product choices. We will look at modern theories of consumer choice behavior in Chapter 6. These theories are important to marketers because the whole marketing plan rests on assumptions about how customers make choices. Therefore the concepts of utility, value, and satisfaction are crucial to the discipline of marketing.

Exchange, Transactions, and Relationships

The fact that people have needs and wants and can place value on products does not fully define marketing. Marketing emerges when people decide to satisfy needs and wants through exchange. Exchange is one of four ways in which people can obtain products they want.

The first way is *self-production*. People can relieve hunger through hunting, fishing, or fruit gathering. They need not interact with anyone else. In this case there is no market and no marketing.

The second way is *coercion*. Hungry people can wrest or steal food from others. No benefit is offered to the others except that of not being harmed.

The third way is *begging*. Hungry people can approach others and beg for food. They have nothing tangible to offer except gratitude.

The fourth way is *exchange*. Hungry people can approach others and offer some resource in exchange, such as money, another good, or some service.

Marketing arises from this last approach to acquiring products. *Exchange is the act of obtaining a desired product from someone by offering something in return.* Exchange is the defining concept underlying marketing. For exchange to take place, five conditions must be satisfied:

1. There are at least two parties.
2. Each party has something that might be of value to the other party.
3. Each party is capable of communication and delivery.
4. Each party is free to accept or reject the offer.
5. Each party believes it is appropriate or desirable to deal with the other party.

If these conditions exist, there is a potential for exchange. Whether exchange actually takes place depends on whether the two parties can agree on *terms of exchange* that will leave them both better off (or at least not worse off) than before the exchange. This is the sense in which exchange is described as a value-creating process; that is, exchange normally leaves both parties better off than before the exchange.

Exchange must be seen as a process rather than as an event. Two parties are said to be engaged in exchange if they are negotiating and moving toward an agreement. If an agreement is reached, we say that a *transaction* takes place. Transactions are the basic unit of exchange. *A transaction consists of a trade of values between two parties.* We must be able to say: A gave X to B and received Y in return. Jones gave $400 to Smith and obtained a television set. This is a classic *monetary transaction*. Transactions, however, do not require money as one of the traded values. A *barter transaction* would consist of Jones's giving a refrigerator to Smith in return for a television set. A barter transaction can also consist of the trading of services instead of goods, as when lawyer Jones writes a will for physician Smith in return for a medical examination.

A transaction involves several dimensions: at least two things of value, agreed-upon conditions, a time of agreement, and a place of agreement. Usually a legal system arises to support and enforce compliance on the part of the transactors. Transactions can easily give rise to conflicts based on misinterpretation or malice. Without a "law of contracts," people would approach transactions with some distrust, and everyone would lose.

Businesses maintain records of their transactions and sort them by item, price, customer, location, and other variables. Sales analysis is the act of analyzing where the company's sales are coming from by product, customer, territory, and so on.

A *transaction* differs from a *transfer*. In a transfer, A gives X to B but does not receive anything tangible in return. When A gives B a gift, a subsidy, or a charitable contribution, we call this a transfer, not a transaction. It would seem that marketing should be confined to the study of transactions and not transfers. However, transfer behavior can also be understood through the concept of exchange. Typically the transferer has certain expectations upon giving a gift, such as getting back gratitude or seeing good behavior in the recipient. Professional fund-raisers are acutely aware of the "reciprocal" motives underlying donor behavior and try to provide benefits to the donors, such as thank-you notes, donor magazines, and special invitations to events. Marketers have recently broadened the concept of marketing to include the study of transfer behavior as well as transaction behavior.

In the most generic sense, the marketer is seeking to elicit some *behavioral response* from another party. A business firm wants a response called "buying," a political candidate wants a response called "voting," a church wants a response called "joining," a social-action group wants a response called "adopting the idea." Marketing consists of actions undertaken to elicit desired responses to some object from a target audience.

To effect successful exchanges, the marketer analyzes what each party expects to give and get. Simple exchange situations can be mapped by showing the two actors and the typical resource flows between them. Figure 1-3 shows five familiar exchange situations. The most familiar is the *commercial transaction*—a seller offers a good or service to a buyer for money. The second is the *employment transaction*—an employer offers wages and fringe benefits to an employee for the employee's productive services (made up of time, energy, and skill). The third is the *civic transaction*—a police force offers protective services to citizens for their taxes and cooperation. The fourth is the *religious transaction*—a church offers religious services to members for their contributions of money and

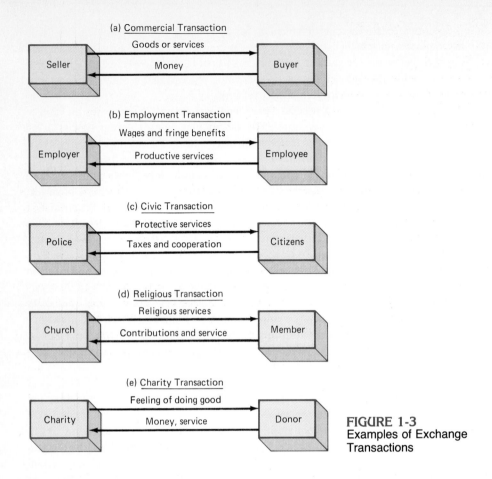

(a) Commercial Transaction

Seller → Goods or services → Buyer

Seller ← Money ← Buyer

(b) Employment Transaction

Employer → Wages and fringe benefits → Employee

Employer ← Productive services ← Employee

(c) Civic Transaction

Police → Protective services → Citizens

Police ← Taxes and cooperation ← Citizens

(d) Religious Transaction

Church → Religious services → Member

Church ← Contributions and service ← Member

(e) Charity Transaction

Charity → Feeling of doing good → Donor

Charity ← Money, service ← Donor

FIGURE 1-3
Examples of Exchange
Transactions

time. The fifth is the *charity transaction*—a charity organization offers gratitude and a feeling of doing good to donors for their contributions of money and time.

A marketer seeking to consummate a transaction examines what the other party wants. Suppose Caterpillar, the world's largest manufacturer of earth-moving equipment, researches the benefits that a typical construction company wants in buying earth-moving equipment. These benefits are listed at the top of the exchange map in Figure 1-4. A construction company wants high-quality equipment, a fair price, on-time delivery, good financing, and good service. This is the buyer's *want list* (or need set). The wants are not all equally important and may vary from buyer to buyer. One of Caterpillar's tasks is to discover the importance of these different wants of the buyer. At the same time, Caterpillar has a want list that is shown below the Caterpillar arrow in Figure 1-4. Caterpillar wants a good price for the equipment, on-time payment, and good word of mouth. If there is a sufficient match or overlap in the want lists, there is a basis for a transaction. Caterpillar's task is to formulate an offer that motivates the construction company to buy Caterpillar equipment. The construction company might in turn make a counteroffer. The process of trying to arrive at mutually agreeable terms is called *negotiation*. Negotiation leads to either mutually acceptable terms or a decision not to transact.

So far, we have explained the nature of *transaction marketing*. Transaction marketing is part of a larger idea, that of *relationship marketing*. Smart marketers try to build up

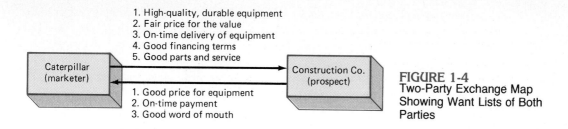

1. High-quality, durable equipment
2. Fair price for the value
3. On-time delivery of equipment
4. Good financing terms
5. Good parts and service

Caterpillar (marketer) → Construction Co. (prospect)

1. Good price for equipment
2. On-time payment
3. Good word of mouth

FIGURE 1-4
Two-Party Exchange Map
Showing Want Lists of Both
Parties

long-term, trusting, "win-win" relationships with customers, distributors, dealers, and suppliers. This is accomplished by promising and delivering high quality, good service, and fair prices to the other party over time. It is accomplished by strengthening the economic, technical, and social ties between members of the two organizations. The two parties grow more trusting, knowledgeable, and interested in helping each other. Relationship marketing cuts down on transaction costs and time; in the best cases, transactions move from being negotiated each time to being routinized.

The ultimate outcome of relationship marketing is the building of a unique company asset called a *marketing network*. A marketing network consists of the company and the firms with which it has built a solid, dependable business relationship. Increasingly, marketing is shifting from trying to maximize the profit on each individual transaction to maximizing beneficial relationships with other parties. The operating principle is "build good relationships and profitable transactions will follow."

Markets   The concept of exchange leads to the concept of a market.

> A *market* consists of all the potential customers sharing a particular need or want who might be willing and able to engage in exchange to satisfy that need or want.

Thus the size of the market depends on the number of persons who exhibit the need, have resources that interest others, and are willing to offer these resources in exchange for what they want.

Originally the term *market* stood for the place where buyers and sellers gathered to exchange their goods, such as a village square. Economists use the term *market* to refer to a collection of buyers and sellers who transact over a particular product or product class; hence the housing market, the grain market, and so on. Marketers, however, see the sellers as constituting the *industry* and the buyers as constituting the *market*. The relationship between the industry and the market is shown in Figure 1-5. The sellers and the buyers are connected by four flows. The sellers send goods and services and communications to the market; in return they receive money and information. The inner loop shows an exchange of money for goods; the outer loop shows an exchange of information.

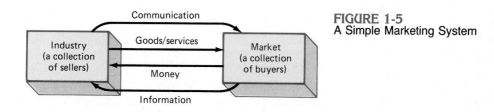

Communication
Goods/services

Industry (a collection of sellers)   Market (a collection of buyers)

Money
Information

FIGURE 1-5
A Simple Marketing System

Businesspeople use the term *markets* colloquially to cover various groupings of customers. They talk about *need markets* (such as the diet-seeking market); *product markets* (such as the shoe market); *demographic markets* (such as the youth market); and *geographic markets* (such as the French market). Or they extend the concept to cover noncustomer groupings as well, such as *voter markets*, *labor markets*, and *donor markets*.

The fact is that modern economies operate on the principle of division of labor where each person specializes in the production of something, receives payment, and buys needed things with this money. Thus modern economies abound in markets. The basic kinds of markets and the flows connecting them are shown in Figure 1-6. Essentially, manufacturers go to resource markets (raw-material markets, labor markets, money markets, and so on), buy resources, turn them into goods and services, and sell them to middlemen, who sell them to consumers. The consumers sell their labor, for which they receive money income to pay for the goods and services they buy. The government is another market that plays several roles. It buys goods from resource, manufacturer, and middlemen markets; it pays them; it taxes these markets (including consumer markets); and it returns needed public services. Thus each nation's economy and the whole world economy consist of complex interacting sets of markets that are linked through exchange processes.

Marketing and Marketers

The concept of markets brings us full circle to the concept of marketing. Marketing means human activity taking place in relation to markets. Marketing means working with markets to actualize potential exchanges for the purpose of satisfying human needs and wants.

If one party is more actively seeking an exchange than the other party, we call the first party a *marketer* and the second party a *prospect*. *A marketer is someone seeking a resource from someone else and willing to offer something of value in exchange.* The marketer is seeking a response from the other party, either to sell something or to buy something. The marketer, in other words, can be a seller or a buyer. Suppose several persons want to buy an attractive house that has just become available. Each would-be

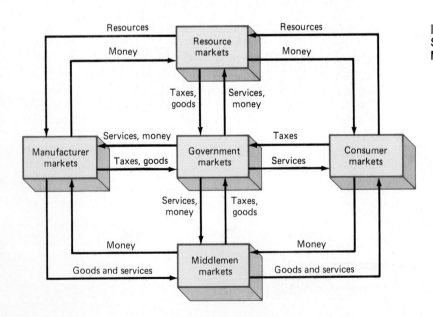

FIGURE 1-6
Structure of Flows in a
Modern Exchange Economy

buyer will try to market himself or herself to be the one the seller selects. These buyers are doing the marketing. In the event that both parties actively seek an exchange, we say that both of them are marketers and call the situation one of reciprocal marketing.

Having reviewed these concepts, we are ready to repeat our definition of marketing, that *marketing is a social and managerial process by which individuals and groups obtain what they need and want through creating and exchanging products and value with others.*

MARKETING MANAGEMENT

Coping with exchange processes calls for a considerable amount of work and skill. *Persons* become fairly adept at buying to meet their household needs. Occasionally they also undertake selling—selling their car, selling personal services. *Organizations* are more professional in handling exchange processes. They must attract resources from one set of markets, convert them into useful products, and trade them in another set of markets. *Nations* also plan and manage exchange relations with others. They search for beneficial trade relations with other nations. In this book we will focus on *organizational marketing* rather than on *person* or *nation* marketing.

Marketing management takes place when at least one party to a potential exchange gives thought to objectives and means of achieving desired responses from other parties. We will use the following definition of marketing (management) approved in 1985 by the American Marketing Association:

> *Marketing* (management) is the process of planning and executing the conception, pricing, promotion, and distribution of ideas, goods, and services to create exchanges that satisfy individual and organizational objectives.[9]

This definition recognizes marketing management as a process involving analysis, planning, implementation, and control; that it covers ideas, goods, and services; that it rests on the notion of exchange; and that the goal is to produce satisfaction for the parties involved.

Marketing management can occur in an organization in connection with any of its markets. Consider an automobile manufacturer. The vice-president of personnel deals in the *labor market*; the vice-president of purchasing, the *raw-materials market*; and the vice-president of finance, the *money market*. They must set objectives and develop strategies for achieving satisfactory results in these markets. Traditionally, however, these executives have not been called marketers, nor have they been trained in marketing. Instead marketing management is historically identified with tasks and personnel dealing with the *customer market*. We will follow this convention, although what we say about marketing applies to all markets.

Marketing work in the customer market is formally carried out by *sales managers, sales people, advertising and promotion managers, marketing researchers, customer-service managers, product managers, market managers, and the marketing vice-president.* Each job carries well-defined tasks and responsibilities. Many of these jobs involve managing particular marketing *resources* such as advertising, sales people, or marketing research. On the other hand, product managers, market managers, and the marketing vice-president manage *programs*. Their job is to analyze, plan, and implement programs that will produce a desired level and mix of transactions with target markets.

The popular image of the marketing manager is someone whose task is primarily to stimulate demand for the company's products. However, this is too limited a view of the diversity of marketing tasks performed by marketing managers. *Marketing management has the task of influencing the level, timing; and composition of demand in a way that will help the organization achieve its objectives*. Marketing management is essentially *demand management*.

The organization presumably forms an idea of a *desired level of transactions* with a target market. At times, the *actual demand level* may be below, equal to, or above the *desired demand level*. That is, there may be no demand, weak demand, adequate demand, excessive demand, and so on, and marketing management has to cope with these different states. Exhibit 1-1 distinguishes eight different states of demand and the corresponding tasks facing marketing managers.

EXHIBIT 1-1	Various States of Demand and the Corresponding Marketing Tasks

1. *Negative demand.* A market is in a state of negative demand if a major part of the market dislikes the product and may even pay a price to avoid it. People have a negative demand for vaccinations, dental work, vasectomies, and gall bladder operations. Employers feel a negative demand for ex-convicts and alcoholic employees. The marketing task is to analyze why the market dislikes the product and whether a marketing program consisting of product redesign, lower prices, and more positive promotion can change the market's belief and attitudes.

2. *No demand.* Target consumers may be uninterested or indifferent to the product. Thus farmers may not be interested in a new farming method, and college students may not be interested in foreign language courses. The marketing task is to find ways to connect the benefits of the product with the person's natural needs and interests.

3. *Latent demand.* Many consumers may share a strong need that cannot be satisfied by any existing product. There is a strong latent demand for harmless cigarettes, safer neighborhoods, and more-fuel-efficient cars. The marketing task is to measure the size of the potential market and develop effective goods and services that would satisfy the demand.

4. *Falling demand.* Every organization, sooner or later, faces falling demand for one or more of its products. Churches have seen their membership decline, and private colleges have seen their applications fall. The marketer must analyze the causes of market decline and determine whether demand can be restimulated through finding new target markets, changing the product's features, or developing more effective communication. The marketing task is to reverse the declining demand through creative *remarketing* of the product.

5. *Irregular demand.* Many organizations face demand that varies on a seasonal, daily, or even hourly basis, causing problems of idle capacity or overworked capacity. In mass transit, much of the equipment is idle during the off-peak hours and insufficient during the peak travel hours. Museums are undervisited during weekdays and overcrowded during weekends. Hospital operating rooms are overbooked early in the week and underbooked toward the end of the week. The marketing task, called *synchromarketing*, is to find ways to alter the time pattern of demand through flexible pricing, promotion, and other incentives.

6. *Full demand.* Organizations face full demand when they are pleased with their volume of business. The marketing task is to maintain the current level of demand in the face of changing consumer preferences and increasing competition. The organization must keep up or improve its quality and continually measure consumer satisfaction to make sure it is doing a good job.

7. *Overfull demand.* Some organizations face a demand level that is higher than they can or want to handle. Thus the Golden Gate Bridge carries a higher amount of traffic than is safe, and Yellowstone National Park is terribly overcrowded in the summertime. The marketing task, called *demarketing*, requires finding ways to reduce the demand temporarily or permanently. General demarketing seeks to discourage overall demand and consists of such steps as raising prices

Marketing managers cope with these tasks by carrying out *marketing research*, *planning*, *implementation*, and *control*. Within marketing planning, marketers must make decisions on target markets, market positioning, product development, pricing, channel of distribution, physical distribution, communication, and promotion. These marketing tasks will be analyzed in subsequent chapters of the book. Suffice it to say that marketing managers must acquire several skills to be effective in the marketplace.

COMPANY ORIENTATIONS TOWARD THE MARKETPLACE

We have described marketing management as the conscious effort to achieve desired exchange outcomes with target markets. Now the question arises, What philosophy should guide these marketing efforts? What weights should be given to the interests of the *organization*, the *customers*, and *society*? Very often these interests conflict. Clearly, marketing activities should be carried out under some well-thought-out philosophy of effective and responsible marketing.

There are five competing concepts under which organizations conduct their marketing activity.

The Production Concept

The production concept is one of the oldest concepts guiding sellers.

The *production concept* holds that consumers will favor those products that are widely available and low in cost. Managers of production-oriented organizations concentrate on achieving high production efficiency and wide distribution coverage.

The assumption that consumers are primarily interested in product availability and low price holds in at least two types of situations. The first is where the demand for a product exceeds supply, and therefore customers are more interested in obtaining the product than in its fine points. The suppliers will concentrate on finding ways to increase production. The second situation is where the product's cost is high and has to be brought down through increased productivity to expand the market. Texas Instruments provides a contemporary example of the production concept:[10]

> Texas Instruments, the Dallas-based electronics firm, is the leading American exponent of the "get-out-production, cut-the-price" philosophy that Henry Ford pioneered in the early 1900s to expand the automobile market. Ford put all of his talent into perfecting the mass production of automobiles to bring down their costs so that Americans could afford them. Texas Instruments puts all of its efforts into building production volume and improving technology in order to bring down costs. It uses its lower costs to cut prices and expand the market size. It goes after and usually achieves the dominant position in its markets. To Texas Instruments, marketing means one thing: bringing down the price to buyers. This orientation has also been a key strategy of many Japanese companies.

Some service organizations also follow the production concept. Many medical and dental practices are organized on assembly-line principles, as are some government agencies such as unemployment offices and license bureaus. While it results in handling many cases per hour, this type of management is open to charges of impersonality and consumer insensitivity.

The Product Concept

Other sellers are guided by the product concept.

The *product concept* holds that consumers will favor those products that offer the most quality, performance, and features. Managers in these product-oriented organizations focus their energy on making good products and improving them over time.

These managers assume that buyers admire well-made products, can appraise product quality and performance, and are willing to pay more for product "extras." Many of these managers are caught up in a love affair with their product and fail to appreciate that the market may be less "turned on" and may even be moving in a different direction. They say, "We make the finest men's tailored suits" or "We make the finest television sets" and wonder why the market doesn't appreciate this.

> There is a story about an office-files manufacturer complaining that his files should be selling better because they are the best in the world. "They can be dropped from a four-story building and not be damaged." "Yes," agreed his sales manager, "but our customers aren't planning to push them out of four-story buildings."

The Elgin National Watch Company provides a dramatic example of product-centered, rather than market-centered, thinking:

> Since its founding in 1864, the Elgin National Watch Company had enjoyed a reputation as one of America's finest watchmakers. Elgin placed its major emphasis on maintaining a superior product and merchandising it through a large network of leading jewelry and department stores. Its sales rose continuously until 1958, and thereafter its sales and market began to slip. What happened to undermine Elgin's dominant position?
>
> Essentially, Elgin's management was so enamored with fine, traditionally styled watches that it didn't notice the major changes taking place in the consumer watch market. Many consumers were losing interest in the idea that a watch needed superior timekeeping accuracy, had to carry a prestigious name, and last a lifetime. They expected a watch to tell time, look attractive, and not cost too much. Consumers had a growing desire for convenience (self-winding watches), durability (waterproof and shockproof watches), and economy (pin-lever watches). As for *channels*, an increasing number of watches were being sold through mass-distribution outlets and discount stores. Many Americans wanted to avoid the higher markups of the local jeweler, and also often bought on impulse when exposed to inexpensive watch displays. As for *competitors*, many had added lower-priced watches to their line and had begun to sell them through mass-distribution channels. Elgin's problem was that it had riveted its attention on a set of products instead of adapting to a rapidly changing market.

One of the most common manifestations of the product concept occurs with new products that a company invents. Management becomes enamored of the product and often loses perspective. It falls into the "better mousetrap fallacy," believing that a better mousetrap will cause people to beat a path to its door.[11] Consider the following example:[12]

In 1972, Du Pont researchers invented Kevlar, which it considers its most important new fiber since nylon. Kevlar has the same strength as steel with only one-fifth the weight. Du Pont asked its divisions to find applications for this new miracle fiber. Du Pont's executives imagined a huge number of applications and a billion-dollar market. Now, more than a decade later, Du Pont is still waiting for the bonanza. True, Kevlar is a very good fiber for bulletproof vests, but there isn't a really big market for bulletproof vests, so far. Kevlar is a promising fiber for sails, cords, and tires, and manufacturers are beginning to nibble. Eventually Kevlar may prove to be a miracle fiber, but it is taking longer than Du Pont expected.

Product-oriented companies go about designing their product in the wrong way. A General Motors executive said some years ago, "How can the public know what kind of car they want until we've invented it?" GM's perspective was that the company's designers and engineers would create a car, with emphasis on styling and durability. Then manufacturing would make it. Then the finance department would price it. Finally, marketing and sales would be called on to sell it. No wonder the car required such hard selling by the dealers! GM failed to ask customers what they wanted and never brought in the marketing people at the beginning to help figure out what kind of car would sell.

The product concept leads to "marketing myopia," an undue concentration on the product rather than the need. Railroad management thought that users wanted trains rather than transportation and overlooked the growing challenge of the airlines, buses, trucks, and automobiles. Slide rule manufacturers thought that engineers wanted slide rules rather than calculating capacity and overlooked the challenge of pocket calculators. Colleges assume that high school graduates want a liberal arts education and overlook the shift of preference to vocationally oriented education. Churches, symphonies, and the post office all assume that they are offering the public the right product and wonder why their sales falter. These organizations too often are looking into a mirror when they should be looking out of the window.

The Selling Concept

The selling concept (or sales concept) is another common approach many firms take to the market.

The *selling concept* holds that consumers, if left alone, will ordinarily not buy enough of the organization's products. The organization must therefore undertake an aggressive selling and promotion effort.

The concept assumes that consumers typically show buying inertia or resistance and have to be coaxed into buying more, and that the company has available a whole battery of effective selling and promotion tools to stimulate more buying.

The selling concept is practiced most aggressively with "unsought goods," those goods that buyers normally do not think of buying, such as insurance, encyclopedias, and funeral plots. These industries have perfected various sales techniques to locate prospects and hard-sell them on the benefits of their product.

Hard selling also occurs with sought goods, such as automobiles:[13]

> From the moment the customer walks into the showroom, the auto salesman "psychs him out." If the customer likes the floor model, he may be told that there is another customer about to buy it and that he should decide on the spot. If the customer balks at the price, the salesman offers to talk to the manager to get a special concession. The customer waits ten minutes and the salesman returns with "the boss doesn't like it but I got him to agree." The aim is to "work up the customer" to buy on the spot.

The selling concept is also practiced in the nonprofit area, by fund-raisers, college admissions offices, and political parties. A political party will vigorously sell its candidate to the voters as being a fantastic person for the job. The candidate stomps through voting precincts from early morning to late evening shaking hands, kissing babies, meeting donors, making breezy speeches. Countless dollars are spent on radio and television advertising, posters, and mailings. Any flaws in the candidate are concealed from the public because the aim is to get the sale, not worry about postpurchase satisfaction. After the election, the new official continues to take a sales-oriented view toward the citizens. There is little research into what the public wants and a lot of selling to get the public to accept policies that the politician or party wants.[14]

Most firms practice the selling concept when they have overcapacity. *Their aim is to sell what they make rather than make what they can sell.* In modern industrial economies, productive capacity has been built up to a point where most markets are buyer markets (i.e., the buyers are dominant), and sellers have to scramble hard for customers. Prospects are bombarded with television commercials, newspaper ads, direct mail, and sales calls. At every turn, someone is trying to sell something. As a result, the public identifies marketing with hard selling and advertising.

Therefore people are surprised when they are told that the most important part of marketing is not selling! Selling is only the tip of the marketing iceberg. Peter Drucker, one of the leading management theorists, puts it this way:

> There will always, one can assume, be need for some selling. *But the aim of marketing is to make selling superfluous.* The aim of marketing is to know and understand the customer so well that the product or service fits him and sells itself. Ideally, marketing should result in a customer who is ready to buy. All that should be needed then is to make the product or service available. . . .[15]

Thus selling, to be effective, must be preceded by several marketing activities such as needs assessment, marketing research, product development, pricing, and distribution. If the marketer does a good job of identifying consumer needs, developing appropriate products, and pricing, distributing, and promoting them effectively, these products will sell very easily. When Eastman Kodak designed its instamatic camera, when Atari designed its first video game, and when Mazda introduced its RX–7 sports car, these manufacturers were swamped with orders because they had designed the "right" product based on the marketing homework they had done.

Indeed, marketing based on hard selling carries high risks. It assumes that customers who are coaxed into buying the product will like it; and if they don't, they won't bad-mouth it to friends or complain to consumer organizations. And they will possibly forget their disappointment and buy it again. These are indefensible assumptions to make about buyers. One study showed that disappointed customers bad-mouth the product to eleven acquaintances, while satisfied customers may good-mouth the product to only three.

The Marketing Concept

The marketing concept is a business philosophy that arose to challenge the previous concepts. Although it has a long history, its central tenets did not fully crystallize until the mid-1950s.[16]

The *marketing concept* holds that the key to achieving organizational goals consists in determining the needs and wants of target markets and delivering the desired satisfactions more effectively and efficiently than competitors.

The marketing concept has been expressed in many colorful ways:

- "Find wants and fill them"
- "Make what will sell instead of trying to sell what you can make"
- "Love the customer and not the product"
- "Have it your way" (Burger King)
- "You're the boss" (United Airlines)
- "To do all in our power to pack the customer's dollar full of value, quality and satisfaction" (JC Penney)

Theodore Levitt drew a perceptive contrast between the selling and marketing concepts:

Selling focuses on the needs of the seller; marketing on the needs of the buyer. Selling is preoccupied with the seller's need to convert his product into cash; marketing with the idea of satisfying the needs of the customer by means of the product and the whole cluster of things associated with creating, delivering and finally consuming it.[17]

The marketing concept rests on four main pillars, namely, a *market focus*, *customer orientation*, *coordinated marketing*, and *profitability*. These are shown in Figure 1-7 where they are contrasted with a selling orientation. The selling concept takes an *inside-out* perspective. It starts with the factory, focuses on the company's existing products, and calls for heavy selling and promoting to produce profitable sales. The marketing concept takes an *outside-in* perspective. It starts with a well-defined market, focuses on customer needs, coordinates all the activities that will affect customers, and produces profits through creating

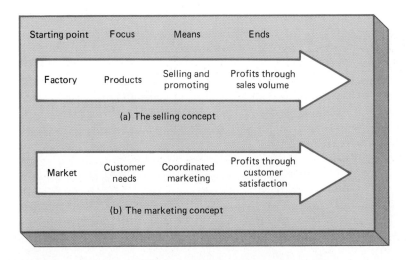

FIGURE 1-7
The Selling and Marketing Concepts Contrasted

customer satisfaction. In essence, the *marketing concept* is a *market-focused, customer-oriented, coordinated marketing effort* aimed at generating *customer satisfaction* as the key to satisfying *organizational goals*.

Here we examine how each pillar of the marketing concept contributes to more effective marketing.

Market Focus No company can operate in every market and satisfy every need. Nor can it even do a good job within one broad market: Even mighty IBM cannot offer the best solution for every computer customer need. Companies do best when they define the boundaries of their markets carefully. They do best when they prepare a tailored marketing program for each target market.

> An auto manufacturer can think of designing passenger cars, station wagons, sports cars, and luxury cars. But this thinking is less precise than defining a market target. One Japanese car maker is designing a car for the career woman, and it will have many features that male-dominated cars don't have. Another Japanese car maker is designing a car for the "town man," the young person who needs to get about town and park easily. In each case, the company has clarified a market target, and this will greatly influence the design of the car.

Customer Orientation A company can define its market carefully and still fail at customer-oriented thinking. Consider the following example:

> The chemists in a major chemical company invented a new substance that hardened into a pseudo-marble. Looking for an application, the marketing department thought that the substance could be used to produce elegant-looking bathtubs. They went ahead and created a few model bathtubs and rented space at a bathroom-furnishing trade show. They were hoping to convince bathtub manufacturers to produce bathtubs with the new material. Although manufacturers thought the new bathtubs were attractive, none signed up. The reason became obvious. The bathtub would have to be priced at $2,000; for this price, consumers could buy bathtubs made out of real marble or onyx. In addition, the bathtubs were so heavy that the bathroom floor would have to be reinforced at additional cost. Furthermore, most bathtubs were sold in the $500 range and few people were ready to spend $2,000. The chemical company had succeeded in developing a market focus but had failed to understand the customers.

Customer-oriented thinking requires the company to carefully define customer needs from the *customer point of view*, not from its own point of view. Every product involves trade-offs, and management cannot know what these are without talking to and researching customers. Thus a car buyer would like a high-performance car that never breaks down, one that is safe, attractively styled, and cheap. Since all of these virtues cannot be combined in one car, the car designers must make hard choices not on what pleases them but rather on what customers prefer or expect. The aim, after all, is to make a sale through meeting the customer's needs.

Why is it supremely important to satisfy the customer? Basically because a company's sales each period come from two groups: *new customers* and *repeat customers*. It is always more costly to attract new customers than to retain current customers. Therefore *customer retention* is more critical than *customer attraction*. The key to customer retention is *customer satisfaction*. A satisfied customer

1. Buys again
2. Talks favorably to others about the company

3. Pays less attention to competing brands and advertising
4. Buys other products that the company later adds to its line

One Japanese businessman recently told the author: "Our aim goes beyond satisfying the customer. Our aim is to *delight* the customer." In fact, this is a higher standard and a deeper quest and may be the secret of the great marketers. They go beyond meeting the mere expectations of the customer. When they delight a customer, the customer talks to even more acquaintances about the fine company. The delighted customers are more effective advertisers than advertisements placed in the media.

Now let us consider what happens when the company creates a dissatisfied customer. Whereas a satisfied customer tells three people about a good product experience, a dissatisfied customer gripes to eleven people. In fact, in one study, 13 percent of the people who had a problem with an organization complained about the company to more than twenty people.[18] Suppose each person who heard the bad story told eleven people, who told another eleven, and so on. Clearly, bad word of mouth travels further and faster than good word of mouth and can easily poison public opinion about the company.

Thus a company would be wise to check on customer satisfaction. But it cannot just rely on customers voluntarily complaining when they are dissatisfied. In fact, 96 percent of unhappy customers never tell the company.[19] This further emphasizes that companies must set up suggestion and other systems to *maximize the customers' opportunity to complain.* This is the only way a company can know how well it is doing. It is also a major way in which the company can learn how to do better. The 3M company claims that over two-thirds of its innovation ideas come from listening to customer complaints.

Listening is not enough. The company must respond constructively to the complaints.

Of the customers who register a complaint, between 54 and 70 percent will do business again with the organization if their complaint is resolved. The figure goes up to a staggering 95 percent if the customer feels that the complaint was resolved quickly. Customers who have complained to an organization and had their complaints satisfactorily resolved tell an average of five people about the treatment they received.[20]

When a company realizes that a loyal customer may account for a substantial sum of revenue over the years, it seems foolish to risk losing the customer by ignoring a grievance or quarreling over a small matter. For example, IBM makes every salesperson write a full report on each lost customer and all the steps taken to restore satisfaction.

A customer-oriented company would track its customer satisfaction level each period and set improvement goals. For example, the Chevrolet division of General Motors achieved a dealer/service satisfaction index of 79 (maximum 100) in 1984 and hopes to hit 90 by 1990. Its owner repurchase loyalty stood at 38 in 1984, and it wants to move this to 55 by 1990. If Chevrolet manages to increase customer satisfaction and loyalty, it does not have to worry even if its profits are down in a particular year: It is on the right track. If, on the other hand, its profits rise but its customer satisfaction keeps falling, it is on the wrong track. Profits could go up or down in a particular year for many reasons, including rising costs, falling prices, major investments, and so on, but the ultimate sign of a healthy company is that its customer satisfaction index is high and keeps rising. Customer satisfaction is the best indicator of the company's future profits. (See Exhibit 1-2.)

Coordinated Marketing   Unfortunately, not all the employees in a company are trained or motivated to pull together for the customer. An engineer at one company complained

EXHIBIT 1-2

The Secret of L. L. Bean's Profitability: Customer Satisfaction

One of the most successful mail-order houses is L. L. Bean, Inc., of Freeport, Maine, which specializes in clothing and equipment for rugged living. L. L. Bean has carefully blended its external and internal marketing programs. To its customers, it offers the following:

100% Guarantee

All of our products are guaranteed to give 100% satisfaction in every way. Return anything purchased from us at any time if it proves otherwise. We will replace it, refund your purchase price or credit your credit card, as you wish. We do not want you to have anything from L. L. Bean that is not completely satisfactory.

To motivate its employees to serve the customers well, it prominently displays the following poster around its offices:

What Is A Customer

A Customer is the most important person ever in this office . . . in person or by mail.

A Customer is not dependent on us . . . we are dependent on him.

A Customer is not an interruption of our work . . . he is the purpose of it. We are not doing a favor by serving him . . . he is doing us a favor by giving us the opportunity to do so.

A Customer is not someone to argue or match wits with. Nobody ever won an argument with a Customer.

A Customer is a person who brings us his wants. It is our job to handle them profitably to him and to ourselves.

SOURCE: Brochure and poster material from L. L. Bean, Inc., Freeport, Maine.

---

about the salespeople because they were "always protecting the customer and not thinking of the company's interests"! He went on to blast the customers for "always asking for too much." The following situation highlights the coordination problem:

> The marketing vice-president of a major airline wants to build up the airline's traffic share. His strategy is to build up customer satisfaction through providing better food, cleaner cabins, and better-trained cabin crews. Yet he has no authority in these matters. The catering department chooses food that keeps down food costs; the maintenance department uses cleaning services that keep down cleaning costs; and the personnel department hires people without regard to whether they are friendly and inclined to serve other people. Since these departments generally take a cost or production point of view, he is stymied in creating a high level of customer satisfaction.

Coordinated marketing means two things. First, the various marketing functions—sales force, advertising, marketing research, etc.—must be coordinated among themselves. Too often the sales force is mad at the marketing people for setting "too high a price" or "too high a quota"; or the advertising director and a brand manager cannot agree on the best advertising campaign for the brand. These marketing functions must be coordinated from the customer point of view.

Second, marketing must be well coordinated with the other departments in the company. Marketing does not work when it is merely a department; it only works when all employees appreciate how they impact on customer satisfaction. As David Packard of Hewlett-Packard put it: "Marketing is too important to be left to the marketing department!" IBM goes so far as to include in every one of its four hundred thousand job descriptions an explanation of how that job relates to serving the customer. An IBM factory manager knows that factory visits can sell a potential customer if the factory is clean and if he is proud to show the prospect how he runs his operations to ensure quality. IBM's accountants, purchasing agents, financial officers, and so forth, all know how their job is going to help customers, and they are trained and motivated in customer courtesy and responsiveness.

For this reason, the marketing concept requires the company to carry out *internal marketing* as well as *external marketing. Internal marketing is the task of successfully hiring, training, and motivating able employees to serve the customers well.* In fact, internal marketing must precede external marketing. It makes no sense to advertise the organization's services before it is ready to provide quality services. A story is told about how Bill Marriott, Jr., chairman of the Marriott hotels, interviews prospective managers:

Bill Marriott tells the prospect that the hotel chain wants to satisfy three groups: *customers*, *employees*, and *stockholders*. While all the groups are important, he asks in which order the groups should be satisfied. Most prospects say first satisfy the customers. Bill Marriott, however, reasons differently. First, the employees must be satisfied. If they love their jobs and feel a sense of pride in the hotel, they will serve the customers well. Satisfied customers will return frequently to the Marriott. This repeat business, in turn, results in high profits which satisfy the Marriott stockholders.

Bill Marriott is still saying that the customer is ultimately the key to profitability. He and others consider the typical organization chart—a pyramid with the president at the top, management in the middle, and front-line people (sales and service people, telephone operators, receptionists) at the bottom—to be obsolete. Master marketing companies know better; they invert the chart, as shown in Figure 1-8. At the top of the organization are the customers. Next in importance are the front-line people, who meet, serve, and satisfy the customers. Under them are the middle managers, whose job it is to support the front-line people so that they can serve the customers better. And finally, at the base is top management, whose job it is to support the middle managers so that they can support the

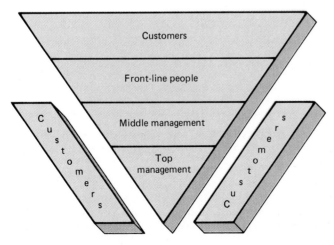

FIGURE 1-8
The "Correct" View of the Company Organization Chart

front-line people who make all the difference in whether the customers end up feeling satisfied with the company. We have added customers along the sides of the figure to indicate that all the managers in the company are personally involved in meeting and knowing customers.

Profitability The purpose of the marketing concept is to help organizations achieve their goals. In the case of private firms, the major goal is profit; in the case of nonprofit and public organizations, it is surviving and attracting enough funds to perform their work. Now the key is not to aim for profits as such but to achieve them as a byproduct of doing the job well. The General Motors executive who once said, "We're in the business of making money, not cars," is misplacing the emphasis. A company makes money by satisfying customer needs better than competitors can do. The job is not making money or cars but finding a profitable way to satisfy people's varied wants for personal transportation.

> The importance of satisfying customers is dramatically illustrated by Perdue Farms, a three-quarter-billion-dollar chicken business whose margins are 700 percent above the industry average and whose market shares in its major markets reach 50 percent. And the product is chicken!—a commodity if there ever was one. Yet its colorful founder, Frank Perdue, does not believe that "a chicken is a chicken is a chicken," nor do his customers. His theme is, "It takes a tough man to make a tender chicken," and he offers a money-back guarantee to dissatisfied customers. He is so devoted to producing quality chickens that his customers pay a premium to buy them. His attitude is that if one works toward superior product quality and business integrity, the profits, market share, and growth will take care of themselves.

This is not to say that marketers are unconcerned with profits. Quite the contrary, they are highly involved in analyzing the profit potential of different marketing opportunities. Whereas sales people commonly focus on means of achieving a certain volume of sales, marketing people focus on identifying profit-making opportunities. The following story vividly clarifies the difference between an order taker, a salesman, and a marketer:

> An American shoe company sent its financial officer to an African country to see if the company could sell its shoes there. After a week, the officer wired back: "The people here don't wear shoes. There is no market."
>
> The shoe company president decided to send its best salesman to the country to double-check on this. After a week, the salesman wired back: "The people here don't wear shoes. There is a tremendous market!"
>
> The shoe company president, wanting to be sure, sent its marketing vice-president to resolve this. After two weeks, the marketing vice-president wired back: "The people here don't wear shoes. However, they have bad feet and could benefit from wearing shoes. We would have to redesign our shoes, however, because they have smaller feet. We would have to invest in educating the people about the benefits of wearing shoes. We would need to gain the tribal chief's cooperation before we could begin. The people don't have any money, but they grow the sweetest pineapples I've ever tasted. I've estimated the potential sales over a three-year period and all of our costs, including selling the pineapples to a European supermarket chain that can pay us in dollars, and concluded that we could make a 20 percent return on our money. I say that we should go ahead."

Clearly, the marketing vice-president not only wore a marketing hat (he noticed a need and a way to satisfy it) but also a financial hat. He is in the business of creating customers profitably.

All four pillars of the marketing concept—market focus, customer orientation, coordinated marketing, and profitability—are admirably illustrated in the story of how SAS airline recovered its fortunes through the marvelous market-oriented leadership provided by its new president, Jan Carlzon (see Exhibit 1-3).

EXHIBIT 1-3

How Jan Carlzon "Marketized" SAS Airlines

When Jan Carlzon took over as president of Scandinavian Airlines (SAS) in 1980, the company was losing money. For some previous years, management had faced this problem by cutting costs. Carlzon saw this as the wrong solution: The company needed to find new ways to compete and build its revenue. SAS had been pursuing all travelers with no focus and no superior advantage to offer to anyone; in fact, it was seen as one of the least punctual carriers in Europe. Competition had increased so much that Carlzon had to figure out:

- Who are our customers?
- What are their needs?
- What must we do to win their preference?

Carlzon decided that the answer was to focus SAS's services on *frequently flying businesspeople* and their needs. But he recognized that other airlines were thinking the same way. They were introducing business class and were offering free drinks and other amenities. SAS had to find a way to do this better if it was to be the preferred air carrier for the frequent business traveler. The starting point was market research to find out what frequent business travelers wanted and expected in the way of airline service. Carlzon's goal was to find ways to be 1 percent better in one hundred details rather than 100 percent better in only one detail.

The market research showed that the number-one priority of business travelers was on-time arrival. Business travelers also wanted to check in fast and be able to retrieve their luggage fast. Carlzon appointed dozens of task forces to come up with ideas for improving these and other services. They came back with hundreds of projects, of which 150 were selected at an implementation cost of $40 million.

One of the key projects was to train a total customer orientation into all of SAS's personnel. Carlzon figured that the average passenger came into contact with five SAS employees on an average trip. Each interaction created "a moment of truth" about SAS. Given the 5 million passengers per year flying SAS, this amounted to 25 million moments of truth where the company either satisfied or dissatisfied its customers. To create the right customer attitudes within the company, SAS sent ten thousand front-line staff to service seminars for two days and twenty-five thousand managers to three-week courses. Carlzon regarded the front-line people who met the customers as the most important people in the company. As for managers, their role was to help the front-line people do their job well. And his role as president was to help the managers support the front-line employees.

The result: Within four months, SAS achieved the record as the most punctual airline system in Europe, and it has maintained this record. Check-in systems are much faster, including a service where travelers who are staying at SAS hotels can have their luggage sent directly to the airport and airplane for loading. SAS does a much faster job of unloading the luggage at landings as well. Another innovation is that SAS sells all tickets as business class unless the traveler wants economy class. The company's improved reputation among business flyers led to an increase in its full-fare traffic in Europe of 8 percent and its full-fare intercontinental travel of 16 percent, quite an accomplishment considering the price cutting that was taking place and zero growth in the air travel market.

Carlzon's impact on SAS illustrates the customer satisfaction and profits that a corporate leader can achieve when he creates a vision and target for his company that excites and gets the personnel to all swim in the same direction—namely, toward satisfying the target customers.

Besides SAS, how many companies have implemented the marketing concept? The answer is, too few. Only a handful of companies really stand out as master practitioners of the marketing concept: Procter & Gamble, IBM, Avon, McDonald's, General Foods, Marriott Hotels, Delta Airlines, General Electric, Caterpillar, and John Deere.

These companies not only focus on the customer but are organized to respond effectively to changing customer needs. Not only do they have well-staffed marketing departments but their other departments—manufacturing, finance, research and development, personnel, purchasing—all accept the concept that the customer is king. These organizations have a marketing culture that has deep roots in all of their departments and divisions.

Most companies have not arrived at full marketing maturity. They *think* they have marketing because they have a marketing vice-president, product managers, sales force, advertising budgets, and so on. *But a marketing department does not assure a market-oriented company.* The company has marketing operations, and yet it may fail to see the big picture and adapt to changing consumer needs and changing competition. International Harvester was on the verge of bankruptcy; Chrysler almost collapsed; and companies like Harley Davidson, Xerox, Singer, and Zenith, one-time leaders in their respective fields, all lost substantial market shares to Japanese competitors.

Most companies do not really grasp or embrace the marketing concept until driven to it by circumstances. Any of the following developments might prod them:

- **Sales decline.** When companies experience falling sales, they panic and start looking for answers. For example, newspapers have experienced falling circulation as more people turn to television news. Some publishers are realizing that they know very little about why people read newspapers and what they want out of newspapers. These publishers are commissioning consumer research and attempting to redesign newspapers to be contemporary, relevant, and interesting to readers.
- **Slow growth.** Slow sales growth will lead some companies to cast about for new markets. They realize that they need marketing know-how if they are to identify, evaluate, and select new opportunities successfully. Dow Chemical, wanting new sources of revenue, decided to enter consumer markets and invested heavily in acquiring marketing expertise to perform well in the markets.
- **Changing buying patterns.** Many companies operate in markets characterized by rapidly changing customer wants. These companies need more marketing know-how if they are to continue producing value for buyers.
- **Increasing competition.** Complacent companies may suddenly be attacked by powerful marketing companies and forced to learn marketing to meet the challenge. Thus American Telephone and Telegraph (AT&T) remained a regulated, marketing-naive company until the 1970s when other companies were suddenly allowed to sell telecommunications equipment to AT&T's customers. At this point, AT&T plunged into the marketing waters and hired the best marketers it could find to help it compete.[21]
- **Increasing market expenditures.** Companies may find their expenditures for advertising, sales promotion, marketing research, and customer service getting out of hand. Management then decides it is time to rationalize the marketing function.

In the course of converting to a market-oriented company, a company will face three hurdles—organized resistance, slow learning, and fast forgetting.

Organized Resistance   Some company departments, often manufacturing, finance, and R&D, do not like to see marketing built up because it threatens their power in the organization. The nature of the threat is illustrated in Figure 1-9. Initially, the marketing function is seen as one of several equally important business functions in a check-and-balance relationship [Fig. 1-9(a)]. A dearth of demand then leads marketers to argue that their function is somewhat more important than the others [Fig. 1-9(b)]. A few marketing enthusiasts go further and say marketing is the major function of the enterprise, for without customers, there would be no company. They put marketing at the center, with other business functions serving as support functions [Fig. 1-9(c)]. This view incenses the other managers, who do not want to think of themselves as working for marketing. Enlightened marketers clarify the issue by putting the customer rather than marketing at the center of

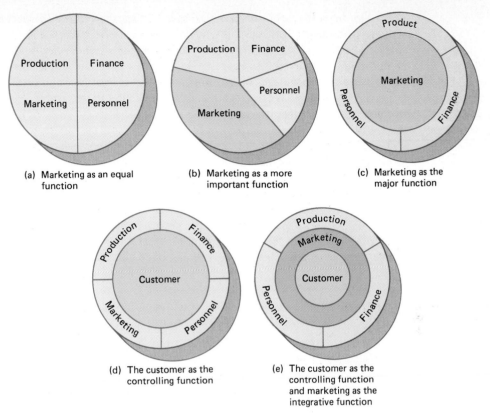

(a) Marketing as an equal function

(b) Marketing as a more important function

(c) Marketing as the major function

(d) The customer as the controlling function

(e) The customer as the controlling function and marketing as the integrative function

FIGURE 1-9
Evolving Views of Marketing's Role in the Company

the company [Fig. 1-9(d)]. They argue for a *customer orientation* in which all functions work together to sense, serve, and satisfy the customer. Finally, some marketers say that marketing still needs to command a central company position if customers' needs are to be correctly interpreted and efficiently satisfied [Fig. 1-9(e)].

The marketer's argument for the business concept shown in Figure 1-9(e) is as follows:

1. The assets of the firm have little value without the existence of customers.
2. The key task of the firm is therefore to attract and retain customers.
3. Customers are attracted through offers of high value and retained through satisfaction.
4. Marketing's task is to define an appropriate offer to the customer and to ensure the delivery of satisfaction.
5. The satisfaction actually received by the customer is affected by the performance of the other departments.
6. Marketing needs influence or control over these other departments if customers are to receive the expected satisfaction.

In spite of this argument, marketing is still being resisted in many quarters. The resistance is especially strong in industries where marketing is being introduced or proposed for the first time, such as in law offices, hospitals, or colleges. Colleges have to face the hostility of professors, and hospitals have to face the hostility of doctors, because each group thinks that "marketing" their services would be degrading. In the newspaper industry, the hostility of oldtimers is shown by one newspaper editor who wrote a diatribe entitled "Beware the 'Market' Thinkers."[22] This editor warned newspapers not to let marketers in because they do not understand the function of newspapers, which is to print news. Marketing is not the solution, he feels, to the national decline in newspaper readership. Marketers would destroy all that is good about today's newspapers.

Slow Learning In spite of some resistance, many companies manage to build up the marketing function in their organization. The company president gives enthusiastic support to the function; new job positions are created; outside marketing talent is hired; key members of management attend marketing seminars to gain a deeper understanding of marketing; the marketing budget is substantially increased; marketing planning and control systems are introduced. Even with these steps, however, the learning as to what marketing really is comes slowly. In the typical company, marketing enlightenment tends to pass through five separate stages. These stages are described and illustrated for the banking industry in Exhibit 1-4.

EXHIBIT 1-4

Five Stages in the Slow Learning of What Bank Marketing Is All About

Before the mid-1950s, bankers had little understanding or regard for marketing. Banks were supplying needed services. Bankers did not have to make a case for checking accounts, savings, loans, or safe-deposit boxes. The bank building was created in the image of a Greek temple, calculated to impress the public with the bank's importance and solidity. The interior was austere, and the tellers rarely smiled. One lending officer arranged his office so that a prospective borrower would sit across from his massive desk on a chair lower than his own. The office window was located behind the officer's back, and the sun would pour in on the hapless customer, who tried to explain why he or she needed a loan. This was the bank's posture before the age of marketing.

1. Marketing Is Advertising, Sales Promotion, and Publicity

Marketing came into banks in the late 1950s, not in the form of the "marketing concept" but in the form of the "advertising and promotion concept." Banks and other financial institutions were experiencing increased competition for savings. A few financial institutions decided to adopt the marketing weapons of the soap companies. They increased their budgets for advertising and sales promotion. By offering umbrellas, radios, and other "come-ons," they managed to attract new customer accounts. Their competitors were forced into adopting the same measures and scurried out to hire advertising agencies and sales promotion experts.

2. Marketing Is Smiling and a Friendly Atmosphere

The banks that first introduced modern advertising and promotion soon found their advantage dissipated by the rush of imitators. They also learned another lesson: Attracting people to a bank is easy; converting them into loyal customers is hard. These banks began to formulate a larger concept of marketing, that of trying to please the customer. Bankers had to learn to smile. The tellers had to be retrained. The bars had to be taken off the tellers' windows. The interior of the banks had to be redesigned to produce a warm, friendly atmosphere. Even the outside Greek-temple architecture had to be changed.

The first banks to implement these changes began to outperform their competitors in attracting and holding new customers. Their competitors, however, quickly figured out what was happening and rushed into similar programs of friendliness training and decor improvement. Soon all banks were so friendly that friendliness lost its potency as a determinant factor in bank choice.

| 3. Marketing Is Innovation | Banks had to search for a new basis for differential advantage. Some banks began to realize that they are in the business of meeting the evolving financial needs of their customers. These banks began to think in terms of continuous innovation of new and valued customer services, such as credit cards, Christmas savings plans, and automatic bank loans. Citibank, for example, today offers over 350 financial products to customers. |

A successful innovation provides the innovative bank with a competitive lead. Financial services, however, are easily copied, and advantages are short-lived. But if the same bank invests in continuous innovation, it can stay ahead of the other banks.

| 4. Marketing Is Positioning | What happens when all banks advertise, smile, and innovate? Clearly, they begin to look alike. They are forced to find a new basis for distinction. They begin to realize that no bank can be the best bank for all customers. No bank can offer all products. A bank must choose. It must examine its opportunities and "take a position" in the market. |

Positioning goes beyond image making. The image-making bank seeks to cultivate an image in the customer's mind as a large, friendly, or efficient bank. It often develops a symbol, such as a lion (Harris Bank in Chicago) or kangaroo (Continental Bank in Chicago) to dramatize its personality in a distinctive way. Yet the customer may see the competing banks as basically alike except for the chosen symbols. Positioning is an attempt to distinguish the bank from its competitors along real dimensions in order to be the preferred bank to certain segments of the market. Positioning aims to help customers know the real differences between competing banks so that they can match themselves to the bank that can provide them with the most satisfaction of their needs.

| 5. Marketing Is Marketing Analysis, Planning, and Control | There is a higher concept of bank marketing, which represents the ultimate essence of modern marketing. The issue is whether the bank has installed effective systems for marketing analysis, planning, and control. One large bank, which had achieved sophistication in advertising, friendliness, innovation, and positioning, nevertheless lacked good systems of marketing planning and control. Each fiscal year, commercial loan officers submitted their volume goals, usually 10 percent higher than the previous year's goals. They also requested a budget increase of 10 percent. No rationale or plans accompanied these submissions. Top management was satisfied with the officers who |

achieved their goals. One loan officer, judged to be a good performer, retired and was replaced by a younger man, who proceeded to increase the loan volume 50 percent the following year! The bank painfully learned that it had failed to conduct marketing research, to measure the potentials of its various markets, to require marketing plans, to set quotas, and to develop appropriate reward systems.

Fast Forgetting   Even after effective marketing is installed in an organization and matures through the various stages, management must fight a strong tendency to forget basic marketing principles. Management tends to forget marketing principles in the wake of marketing success. For example, a number of major American companies entered European markets in the 1950s and 1960s expecting to achieve outstanding success with their sophisticated products and marketing capabilities. A number of them failed, and a major reason is that they forgot the marketing maxim: *Know your target market and know how to satisfy it*. American companies came into these markets with their current products and advertising programs instead of redesigning them on the basis of what each market needed. For example, General Mills went into the British market with its Betty Crocker cake mixes only to have to withdraw a short time later. Their angel cake and devil's food cake sounded too exotic for British homemakers. And many potential customers felt that such perfect-looking cakes as those pictured on the Betty Crocker packages must be hard to make. American marketers failed to appreciate the major cultural variations between—and even within European countries—and the need to start where the target consumers are, not where their products are.

The Societal Marketing Concept

In recent years, some people have questioned whether the marketing concept was an appropriate organizational philosophy in an age of environmental deterioration, resource shortages, explosive population growth, world hunger, and poverty and neglected social services.[23] The question is whether companies that do an excellent job of sensing, serving, and satisfying individual consumer wants are necessarily acting in the best long-run interests of consumers and society. The marketing concept sidesteps the potential conflicts between *consumer wants*, *consumer interests*, and *long-run societal welfare*.

Consider the following criticisms:

> The fast-food hamburger industry offers tasty but not nutritious food. The hamburgers have a high-fat content, and the restaurants promote fries and pies, two products high in starch and fat. In satisfying consumer wants, they may be hurting consumer health.
>
> The American auto industry traditionally catered to the American demand for large automobiles, but meeting this desire resulted in high fuel consumption, heavy pollution, more fatal accidents to those in small cars, and higher auto purchase and repair costs.
>
> The soft-drink industry has catered to the American desire for convenience by increasing the share of one-way disposable bottles. However, the one-way bottle represents a great waste of resources in that approximately seventeen bottles are necessary where formerly one two-way bottle made seventeen trips before it was damaged; many one-way bottles are not biodegradable; and these bottles often litter the environment.
>
> The detergent industry catered to the American passion for whiter clothes by offering a product that polluted rivers and streams, killed fish, and injured recreational opportunities.

These situations called for a new concept that revised or replaced the marketing concept. Among the proposals are "the human concept," "the intelligent consumption concept," and "the ecological imperative concept," all of which get at different aspects of the same problem.[24] We propose calling it "the societal marketing concept."

> The *societal marketing concept* holds that the organization's task is to determine the needs, wants, and interests of target markets and to deliver the desired satisfactions more effectively and efficiently than competitors in a way that preserves or enhances the consumer's and the society's well-being.

The societal marketing concept calls upon marketers to balance three considerations in setting their marketing policies, namely, *company profits*, *consumer want satisfaction*, and *public interest*. Originally, companies based their marketing decisions largely on immediate company profit calculations. Then they began to recognize the long-run importance of satisfying consumer wants, and this introduced the marketing concept. Now they are beginning to factor in society's interests in their decision making. The societal marketing concept calls for balancing all three considerations. A number of companies have achieved notable sales and profit gains through adopting and practicing the societal marketing concept. Here is an example:

> Giant Food, Inc., a leading supermarket chain in the Washington, D.C., area, took the initiative during the consumerist era in the seventies and introduced unit pricing, open dating, and nutritional labeling. The company assigned home economists to its stores to help consumers buy and prepare food more intelligently. It invited Esther Peterson, formerly the president's adviser on consumer affairs, to join the board of directors and provide guidance on consumer-oriented retailing. According to a spokesman for the company, "These actions have improved Giant's goodwill immeasurably and have earned the admiration of leaders of the consumer movement."

THE RAPID ADOPTION OF MARKETING MANAGEMENT

Marketing management today is a subject of growing interest in all sizes and types of organizations within and outside the business sector in all kinds of countries.

In the Business Sector   In the business sector, marketing entered the consciousness of different companies at different times. General Electric, General Motors, Procter & Gamble, and Coca-Cola were among the leaders. Marketing spread most rapidly in consumer packaged goods companies, consumer durables companies, and industrial equipment companies—in that order. Producers of commodities such as steel, chemicals, and paper came later to marketing consciousness, and many still have a long way to go. Within the past decade consumer-service firms, especially airlines and banks, have moved toward modern marketing. Marketing is also beginning to excite the interest of insurance and stock brokerage companies, although they also have a long way to go in applying marketing effectively.

The most recent business groups to take an interest in marketing are professional service providers, such as lawyers, accountants, physicians, and architects. Professional societies, until recently, prohibited their members from engaging in price competition, client solicitation, and advertising. But the U.S. antitrust division recently ruled that these restraints are illegal. Accountants, lawyers, and other professional groups are now allowed to advertise and to price aggressively.

> The fierce competition engendered by the new limits on corporate growth is forcing accounting firms into aggressive new postures. . . . The accountants insist on referring to their efforts to drum up business as "practice development." But many of the activities that fall under this euphemism are dead ringers for what is called "marketing" in other fields. . . . Accountants speak of "positioning" their firms and of "penetrating" unexploited new industries. They compile "hit lists" of prospective clients and then "surround" them by placing their firms' partners in close social contact with the top executives of the target companies.[25]

In the Nonprofit Sector   Marketing is increasingly attracting the interest of nonprofit organizations such as colleges, hospitals, museums, and symphonies. Consider the following developments:

Of the nation's 3,000 private colleges, over 200 have closed their doors since 1965, unable to attract enough students or funds or both. Annual tuition alone at the top private colleges is now over $10,000. If college costs continue to climb at the current rate, the parents of a child born today will have to spend over $100,000 to pay for a bachelor's degree at one of the top private colleges.

Hospital costs continue to rise, leading to daily room rates in excess of $400 in some large hospitals. Many of the nation's 7,000 hospitals are experiencing underutilization, particularly in the maternity and pediatrics sections. Some experts have predicted the closing of 1,400–1,500 hospitals in the next ten years.

The Catholic Church drew as many as 55 percent of all adult Catholics under thirty years of age to church in a typical week in 1966. By 1975 the figure had fallen to 39 percent, and further declines in weekly attendance are expected.

Many performing arts groups cannot attract large enough audiences. Even those that have seasonal sellouts, such as the Lyric Opera Company of Chicago, face huge operating deficits each year.

Many flourishing nonprofit organizations of yesteryear—the YMCA, Salvation Army, Girl Scouts, and Women's Christian Temperance Union—have lost members and are busily revising their "product" to attract more members and donors.

These organizations have marketplace problems. Their administrators are struggling to keep them alive in the face of changing consumer attitudes and diminishing financial resources. Many organizations have turned to marketing as a major answer to their problems. Over 40 percent of the nation's hospitals now have a marketing director, in contrast with less than 1 percent a decade ago. U.S. government agencies are showing an increased interest in marketing. The U.S. Postal Service and Amtrak have developed and implemented marketing plans for their respective operations. The U.S. Army has an elaborate and well-researched marketing plan to attract recruits and is one of the top advertising spenders in the country. Other government agencies are now marketing antismoking campaigns, antidrug campaigns, and other public causes.[26]

In the International Sector

Marketing skills are improving in many companies around the world. In fact, several European and Japanese multinationals—companies like Nestlé, Beecham, Volvo, Unilever, Nixdorf, Toyota, and Sony—have in many cases understood marketing better and outperformed their U.S. competitors. Multinationals have introduced and spread modern marketing practices throughout the world. This has prodded smaller domestic companies in various countries to start looking into ways to strengthen their marketing muscle so they can compete effectively with the multinationals.

In socialist countries, marketing has traditionally had a bad name. However, various functions of marketing, such as marketing research, branding, advertising, and sales promotion, are now spreading rapidly. In the USSR, there are over one hundred state-operated advertising agencies and marketing research firms.[27] Several companies in Hungary and Romania have marketing departments, and several socialist universities teach marketing.[28] China is another socialist country showing a growing eagerness and openness to modern marketing ideas.

SUMMARY

Companies cannot survive today by simply doing a good job. They must do an excellent job if they are to succeed in markets characterized by slow growth and fierce competition at home and abroad. Consumer and business buyers face an abundance of choices in seeking to satisfy their needs and therefore look for excellence in quality or value or cost when they choose their suppliers. Recent studies have demonstrated that knowing and satisfying the customers with competitively superior offers is the key to profitable performance. And marketing is the company function charged with defining customer targets and the best way to satisfy their needs and wants competitively and profitably.

Marketing has its origins in the fact that humans are creatures of needs and wants. Needs and wants create a state of discomfort in people, which is resolved through acquiring products to satisfy these needs and wants. Since many products can satisfy a given need, product choice is guided by the concepts of utility, value, and satisfaction. These products are obtainable in several ways: self-production, coercion, begging, and exchange. Most modern societies work on the principle of exchange, which means that people specialize in producing particular products and trade them for the other things they need. They engage in transactions and relationship building. A market is a group of people who share a similar need. Marketing encompasses those activities that represent working with markets, that is, trying to actualize potential exchanges.

Marketing management is the conscious effort to achieve desired exchange outcomes with target markets. The marketer's basic skill lies in influencing the level, timing, and composition of demand for a product, service, organization, place, person, or idea.

Five alternative philosophies can guide organizations in carrying out their marketing work. The production concept holds that consumers will favor products that are affordable and available, and therefore management's major task is to improve production and distribution efficiency and bring down prices. The product concept holds that consumers favor quality products that are reasonably priced, and therefore little promotional effort is required. The selling concept holds that consumers will not buy enough of the company's products unless they are stimulated through a substantial selling and promotion effort. The marketing concept holds that the main task of the company is to determine the needs, wants, and preferences of a target group of customers and to deliver the desired satisfactions. Its four principles are market focus, customer orientation, coordinated marketing, and profitability. The societal marketing concept holds that the main task of the company is to generate customer satisfaction and long-run consumer and societal well-being as the key to satisfying organizational goals and responsibilities.

Interest in marketing is intensifying as more organizations in the business sector, the nonprofit sector, and the international sector recognize how marketing contributes to improved performance in the marketplace.

■ QUESTIONS

1. A managing director of a large company made the following statement: "To be successful in business, all you need is a customer. You don't need any of those tight little academic concepts of how to manage. You don't even need to solve all your problems or be efficient. All you need is to find out what you do right for the customer you've already got and do more of it." Assess the validity of this statement.

2. How does relationship marketing differ from "conventional" marketing? Does L. L. Bean practice relationship marketing? (See Exhibit 1-2.)

3. Discuss the difference between a *need* and a *want* as they might be expressed for computers. Why is such a distinction important to a computer manufacturer?

4. Hospitals have been experiencing a dramatic increase in the hiring of marketing talent and the size of marketing budgets. Likewise, hospital administrators are stating that their hospitals must be "market-driven" institutions. What has caused this greater interest in marketing and what does it mean for a hospital to be "market-driven"?

5. During the early 1980s, over 4,400 auto dealerships in the United States went out of business. William Turnbull, president of the National Automobile Dealers Association, stated that if the remaining dealers were to survive, they must change their orientation toward consumers. What might he have meant by that statement?

6. Does the marketing concept imply that marketers should confine themselves only to those wants and needs that consumers say they want to satisfy?

7. Is there a contradiction between marketing something that has negative demand and practicing the marketing concept?

8. Do all companies need to practice the marketing concept? Could you cite companies that do not need this orientation? Which companies need it most?

9. "Marketing is the science of actualizing the buying potentials of a market for a specific product." Does this definition reflect a product, selling, or marketing concept?

10. "Marketing is not simply the job of a group of people in the company who are responsible for selling the company's products. Every member of the firm should function as a marketer." What does it mean for a company recruiter, for example, to function as a marketer?

11. The five stages through which organizations pass as they develop an understanding of marketing were discussed in connection with the banking industry. Discuss them in the context of four-year private liberal arts colleges that are facing declining enrollment.

■ FOOTNOTES

1 Thomas J. Peters and Robert H. Waterman, Jr., *In Search of Excellence*: *Lessons from America's Best-Run Companies* (New York: Harper & Row, 1982).

2 Tom Peters and Nancy Austin, *A Passion for Excellence*: *The Leadership Difference* (New York: Random House, 1985).

3 F. G. "Buck" Rodgers, *The IBM Way: Insights into the World's Most Successful Marketing Organization* (New York: Harper & Row, 1985).

4 "Business Planning in the Eighties: The New Competitiveness of American Corporations," (Study conducted by Yankelovich, Skelly & White for Coopers and Lybrand, 1984).

5 See E. S. Ely, "Room at the Top: American Companies Turn to Marketers to Lead Them Through the '80s," *Madison Avenue*, September 1984, p. 57.

6 Ibid.

7 For other definitions, see footnote 9 below.

8 See Theodore Levitt's classic article, "Marketing Myopia," *Harvard Business Review*, July–August 1960, pp. 45–56.

9 Here are some other useful definitions of marketing (management):

Marketing **is the process of planning and executing the conception, pricing promotion, and distribution of ideas, goods, and services to create exchanges that satisfy individual and organizational objectives. (Official definition of the American Marketing Association).**

Marketing **is the process by which an organization relates creatively, productively, and profitably to the marketplace.**

Marketing **is the art of creating and satisfying customers at a profit.**

Marketing **is getting the right goods and services to the right people at the right places at the right time at the right price with the right communications and promotion.**

10 See "Texas Instruments Shows U.S. Business How to Survive in the 1980s," *Business Week*, September 18, 1978, pp. 66ff. But TI has not been entirely successful with this strategy, especially in launching watches and personal computers in the consumer market. See "When Marketing Failed at Texas Instruments," *Business Week*, June 22, 1981, pp. 91–94.

11 Emerson originated this advice: "If a man . . . makes a better mousetrap . . . the world will beat a path to his door." Several companies, however, have built better mousetraps. One was a laser mousetrap costing $1,500—and most of these companies failed. People do not automatically learn about new products, believe in their superiority, or willingly pay a higher price.

12 See Lee Smith, "A Miracle in Search of a Market," *Fortune*, December 1, 1980, pp. 92–98.

13 See Irving J. Rein, *Rudy's Red Wagon: Communication Strategies in Contemporary Society* (Glenview, Ill.: Scott, Foresman, 1972).

14 See Joseph McGinniss, *The Selling of the President* (New York: Trident Press, 1969); and the special political advertis-ing issue of the *Journal of Advertising*, Vol. 13, No. 3, 1984.

15 Peter F. Drucker, *Management: Tasks, Responsibilities, Practices* (New York: Harper & Row, 1973), pp. 64–65.

16 See John B. McKitterick, "What Is the Marketing Management Concept?" *The Frontiers of Marketing Thought and Action* (Chicago: American Marketing Association, 1957), pp. 71–82; Fred J. Borch, "The Marketing Philosophy as a Way of Business Life," *The Marketing Concept: Its Meaning to Management*, Marketing Series, No. 99 (New York: American Management Association, 1957), pp. 3–5; and Robert J. Keith, "The Marketing Revolution," *Journal of Marketing*, January 1960, pp. 35–38.

17 Levitt, "Marketing Myopia."

18 A research firm called Technical Assistance Programs (TARP) carried out a series of studies on customer behavior for the White House Office of Consumer Affairs during the Carter administration. The key results cited here are summarized in Karl Albrecht and Ron Zemke, *Service America!* (Homewood, Ill.: Dow-Jones Irwin, 1985), pp. 6–7.

19 Ibid.

20 Ibid.

21 See Bro Uttal, "Selling Is No Longer Mickey Mouse at AT&T," *Fortune*, July 17, 1978, pp. 98–104.

22 William H. Hornby, "Beware the 'Market' Thinkers," *Quill*, 1976, pp. 14ff.

23 See Lawrence P. Feldman, "Societal Adaptation: A New Challenge for Marketing," *Journal of Marketing*, July 1971, pp. 54–60; Martin L. Bell and C. William Emery, "The Faltering Marketing Concept," *Journal of Marketing*, October 1971, pp. 37–42; and Franklin S. Houston, "The Marketing Concept: What It Is and What It Is Not," *Journal of Marketing*, April 1986, pp. 81–87.

24 Leslie M. Dawson, "The Human Concept: New Philosophy for Business," *Business Horizons*, December 1969, pp. 29–38; James T. Rothe and Lissa Benson, "Intelligent Consumption: An Attractive Alternative to the Marketing Concept," *MSU Business Topics*, Winter 1974, pp. 29–34; and George Fisk, "Criteria for a Theory of Responsible Consumption," *Journal of Marketing*, April 1973, pp. 24–31.

25 Deborah Rankin, "How C.P.A.'s Sell Themselves," *New York Times*, September 25, 1977.

26 For further reading, see Philip Kotler and Alan R. Andreasen, *Strategic Marketing for Nonprofit Organizations* (Englewood Cliffs, N.J.: Prentice-Hall, 1987).

27 Thomas V. Greer, *Marketing in the Soviet Union* (New York: Holt, Rinehart & Winston, 1973).

28 Jacob Naor, "Towards a Socialist Marketing Concept—The Case of Romania," *Journal of Marketing*, January 1986, pp. 28–39.

2 Laying the Groundwork Through Strategic Planning

There are three types of companies: those who make things happen; those who watch things happen; those who wonder what happened.

Anonymous

In Chapter 1, we raised the question, "What makes a company excellent?" We found that a large part of the answer is that the company's employees are committed to creating and satisfying customers. We can now add a second part to the answer, namely, that excellent companies know how to adapt and respond to a continuously changing marketplace. They practice the art of *market-oriented strategic planning*. We define strategic planning as follows:

> **Strategic planning** is the managerial process of developing and maintaining a viable fit between the organization's **objectives** and **resources**, and its changing **market opportunities**. The aim of strategic planning is to shape and reshape the company's businesses and products so that they combine to produce satisfactory profits and growth.

Strategic planning and its collection of concepts and tools did not surface until the early 1970s. In the fifties and sixties, American management could pretty much get by with operations planning. With the steady growth of total demand, it was hard for even poor management to make a mess of their business. Then the turbulent seventies erupted. There was a succession of crises: Oil prices shot up following the Mideast War; material and energy shortages ensued, along with double-digit inflation; then economic stagnation and rising unemployment set in. Low-cost, high-quality foreign goods from Japan and elsewhere started to pour into the United States especially, taking share away from several U.S. stronghold industries such as steel, autos, motorcycles, watches, and cameras. Still later, U.S. business firms had to cope with a growing wave of deregulation in such key industries as telecommunications, transportation, energy, health care, law, and accounting. Firms that had played by the old rules now faced intense competition at home and abroad that challenged them to the core.

This succession of shock waves called for a new management planning process that would keep firms healthy in spite of upsets occurring in any one of their businesses or product lines. Three key ideas defined the new planning process. The first called for managing the company's businesses as an *investment portfolio*. Any financial portfolio manager would continuously monitor each investment vehicle in terms of whether more should be acquired, some should be sold, or all should be sold. The same principle applies to a company that operates several businesses, product lines, or products. The question is, Which business entities deserve to be *built*, *maintained*, *phased down* (harvested, milked), and *terminated*? This question is especially critical when a company no longer commands enough funds to feed all of its current businesses, as happened to many firms in the seventies. In this situation, it does not make sense for a company to cut down its support proportionately from all businesses. Each business has a different profit potential. A system is needed to assess future profit potential as a basis for reallocating the company's capital. Thus careful resource allocation to a portfolio of businesses is one key idea underlining strategic planning.

The second key idea calls for accurately assessing the *future profit potential* of each business. The firm can no longer operate safely on a one-year-at-a-time planning basis, nor can it plan for a longer period of time by naively extrapolating past business trends. The firm has to learn how to develop more analytical scenarios of future conditions in each market. It would be costly to stay in a market that the firm should abandon, or to abandon a market that the firm should actively stay in. It is not sufficient to use today's sales or profits as a guide to which businesses deserve backing. For example:

> If the Ford Motor Company used current profits as a guide to investment in the seventies, it would have continued to pour money into large cars, since the company was making the money at the time. But Ford's analysis showed that the profits on large cars would dry up, and therefore Ford needed to reallocate its funds to improving its compact cars, even though the company was currently losing money on compact cars.

The third key underlying strategic planning is that of *strategy*. For each of its businesses, the company must develop a "game plan" for achieving its long-run objectives. Furthermore, there is no one strategy that is optimal for all competitors in that business. Each company must determine what makes the most sense in the light of its *industry position* and its *objectives*, *opportunities*, and *resources*. Here are vastly different current game plans of four major companies operating in today's rubber tire industry:

> Goodyear Tire & Rubber Co., the world's No. 1 tiremaker, is pouring money into this industry in spite of the industry's slow growth, overcapacity, and price wars. Goodyear is investing heavily in plant modernization to lower costs and improve quality, in R&D to develop more-advanced tires, and in marketing to build up consumer and dealer preference. The result is an increased market share for Goodyear, but it will take a long time for this higher market share to translate into higher profits.[1]
>
> The French company Michelin, the world's No. 2 tiremaker, rose to its high place by leading the industry in innovation. Michelin introduced the steelbelted radial tire, a tire that lasted longer than its competitors'. Michelin's continuous innovation of better tires won it a "Cadillac" reputation for

high quality and allowed it to charge premium prices. Although Michelin has lately lowered its prices to gain market share, it still expects to maintain its leadership through technological innovation.[2]

Uniroyal, the fourth-ranked company in the tire industry, has chosen the route of diversification out of the tire business. Its strongest push will be in two nontire businesses, agricultural chemicals and fabricated plastic products, which together account for 33 percent of its sales but over 75 percent of its earnings. Uniroyal has divested its business units making fire hoses, inner tubes, and golf balls, but still has to figure out what to do with the core of the company, namely, the domestic tire division, which hangs like an albatross around its neck. Uniroyal is a major supplier of original equipment tires to General Motors, but because of the less than 2 percent growth in the tire industry and the intense price cutting, Uniroyal would be ready to sell its tire business if it could find a buyer.[3]

Armstrong Rubber Co., sixth among U.S. tiremakers, has decided to specialize in making tires almost entirely for the replacement market. It has shown great skill in picking and exploiting specialized niches, such as tires for recreational vehicles and farm equipment. "When you really excel in a market segment, you get paid for it," said Frank R. O'Keefe, Jr., Armstrong's president. O'Keefe has sharpened Armstrong's strategic planning process through which Armstrong identifies profitable market segments and its marketing planning process through which it pursues leadership in each chosen market segment.[4]

All of these companies exhibit varying adaptations to a rapidly changing environment. Each has adopted a different game plan: Goodyear is pressing for *cost reduction*; Michelin is pursuing *innovation*; Uniroyal prefers *diversification*; and Armstrong is practicing *niche-manship* by entering small but highly profitable markets. Each strategy can be successful under the right circumstances.

Marketing plays a critical role in the company's strategic planning process. According to a strategic planning manager at General Electric:

> . . . the marketing manager is the most significant functional contributor to the strategic planning process, with leadership roles in defining the business mission; analysis of the environmental, competitive, and business situations; developing objectives, goals, and strategies; and defining product, market, distribution, and quality plans to implement the business' strategies. This involvement extends to the development of programs and operating plans that are fully linked with the strategic plan.[5]

To understand strategic planning, we have to remember how the modern corporation is structured. Most corporations consist of three organizational levels: the *corporate level*, *business level*, and *product level*.[6] Corporate headquarters is responsible for designing a *corporate strategic plan* to guide the whole enterprise into a profitable future; it makes decisions on how much resource support to allocate to each business unit (division, subsidiary) as well as which new businesses to start. Each business unit in turn must develop a *business strategic plan* to carry that business unit into a profitable future, given the resources it has to work with from corporate headquarters. Finally, each product level (product line, brand) within a business unit needs to develop a *marketing plan* for achieving its objectives in its product market. These plans are then implemented at the various levels of the organization, results are monitored and evaluated, and corrective actions are taken. The whole planning, implementation, and control cycle is shown in Figure 2-1.

In this chapter, we will examine the major concepts and tools for carrying out corporate strategic planning and business strategic planning. In the next chapter, we will focus on marketing planning and the overall marketing management process.

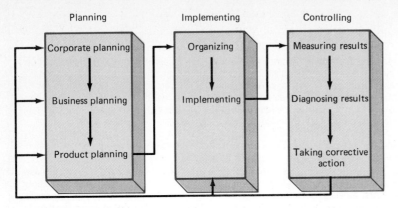

Planning   Implementing   Controlling

FIGURE 2-1
The Strategic Planning,
Implementation, and Control
Process

CORPORATE STRATEGIC PLANNING

Corporate headquarters has the responsibility for setting into motion the whole planning process. By preparing broad statements of mission, policy, and strategy, headquarters establishes the framework within which the individual business units prepare their business-level plans. Some corporations give a lot of freedom to their individual business units to set their own sales and profit goals and strategies; they only require that these business units turn in the promised performance. Other corporations set challenging goals for their business units but leave them the task of developing strategies for achieving these goals. Still other corporations set the goals and get heavily involved in the strategies of the individual business units.[7]

Regardless of which management style the corporation pursues, all corporations must carry out the following four planning activities (see Figure 2-2):

- Defining the corporate mission
- Identifying the company's strategic business units (SBUs)
- Analyzing and evaluating the current portfolio of businesses
- Identifying new business arenas to enter

We will examine each in turn.

Corporate Mission An organization exists to accomplish something in the larger environment. Its specific mission or purpose is usually clear at the beginning. Over time the mission may remain clear, but some managers may lose interest in it. Or the mission may remain clear but lose its relevance to the new conditions in the environment. Or the mission may become unclear as the organization grows and adds new products and markets. Recently,

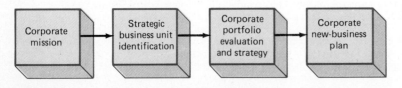

FIGURE 2-2
The Corporate Strategic
Planning Process

American Can put up its original business—canning—for sale; and Uniroyal is gradually moving out of the tire business. These companies are evidently redefining their mission.

When management senses that the organization is drifting, it must renew its search for purpose. According to Peter Drucker, it is time to ask some fundamental questions.[8] *What is our business? Who is the customer? What is value to the customer? What will our business be? What should our business be?* These simple-sounding questions are among the most difficult the company will ever have to answer. Successful companies continuously raise these questions and answer them thoughtfully and thoroughly.

The company's mission is shaped by five elements. The first is its *history*. Every company has a history of aims, policies, and achievements. In redefining its purpose, the organization must not depart too radically from its past history. It would not make sense for Harvard University, for example, to open two-year junior colleges, even if these colleges represented a growth opportunity. The second consideration is the *current preferences* of the management and owners. Those who direct the company have their personal goals and visions. If Sears's current management wants to serve higher-income consumers, this goal is going to influence Sears's mission statement. Third, *environmental factors* influence the organization's mission. The environment defines the main opportunities and threats that must be taken into account. The Girl Scouts of America would not get far in today's environment with their former purpose, ''to prepare young girls for motherhood and wifely duties.'' Fourth, the organization's *resources* make certain missions possible and others not. Piedmont Airlines would be deluding itself if it adopted the mission to become the world's largest airline. Finally, the organization should base its choice of purpose on its *distinctive competences*. McDonald's could probably enter the solar energy business, but this would not use its main competence—providing low-cost food and fast service to large groups of customers.

Organizations develop their mission statements in order to share them with their managers, employees, and in many cases, customers and various publics. A well-worked-out mission statement provides company personnel with a shared sense of opportunity, direction, significance, and achievement. The company mission statement acts as an ''invisible hand'' that guides geographically scattered employees to work independently and yet collectively toward realizing the organization's goals.

Writing a formal company mission statement is not easy. Some organizations will spend a year or two trying to prepare a satisfactory statement about the purpose of their firm. In the process they will discover a lot about themselves and their potential opportunities.

The mission statement should embody a number of characteristics to make it maximally useful. It should focus on certain *distinctive values*, rather than go after everything. The statement ''We want to produce the highest-quality products, offer the most service, achieve the widest distribution, and sell at the lowest prices,'' while sounding good, claims too much. It fails to supply guidelines when confronting tough value trade-offs.

The mission statement should define the *competitive domain* in which the corporation will operate. The domain can be spelled out by statements on scope:

■ *Industry scope.* The range of industries that the corporation will consider. Some corporations will operate in only one industry, some in only a set of related industries, some in only industrial goods, consumer goods, or services, and finally some in any industry. For example, Du Pont prefers to operate in the industrial market, whereas Dow is willing to operate in the industrial and consumer markets. 3M will get into almost any industry where it can see a profit at the end of the tunnel.

■ *Market segment scope.* The type of market or customers the corporation wishes to serve. Some corporations will only serve the upscale market in all their businesses (for example, Porsche only makes expensive cars, sunglasses, and other accessories). Gerber, for a long time, only served the baby market with its line of products.

■ *Vertical scope.* The degree to which the corporation will produce its own needed supplies internally. At one extreme are corporations that perform many of their activities internally, such as Ford, which owns its own rubber plantations, glass-manufacturing plants, and some steel foundries. At the other extreme are corporations with low or no vertical integration, such as the "hollow corporation" that consists of a person with a phone and a desk who contracts outside for every service including design, manufacture, marketing, and physical distribution.[9]

■ *Geographical scope.* The range of regions, countries, or country groups where the corporation wishes to operate. At one extreme are companies that operate in a specific city or state, and at the other extreme are multinationals like Unilever or Caterpillar which operate in almost every one of the world's 150-plus countries.

The company's mission statement should be *motivating.* Employees need to feel that their work is significant and contributes to people's lives. The mission should not be "to make profits." Profits are the result of accomplishing something useful *outside* the organization. When the prosaic task of producing fertilizer is reshaped into the larger idea of improving agricultural productivity to feed the world's hungry, a new sense of purpose comes over the employees. When the task of selling vacuum cleaners is transformed into the larger idea of creating a cleaner and healthier home environment, sales people feel more challenged. Profits are the reward to companies that do their basic job well.

The corporate mission statement should stress major *policies* that the company wants to honor. Policies define how employees should deal with customers, suppliers, distributors, competition, and other actors and publics. Policies narrow the range of individual discretion, so that the company acts consistently on important issues.

The company's mission statement should provide a vision and direction for the company for the next ten to twenty years. Missions are not revised every few years in response to every new turn in the economy. On the other hand, a company has to redefine its mission when it has lost credibility or no longer defines an optimal course for the company.

Strategic Business Unit Identification

Most companies, even small ones, operate several businesses. But these businesses may not all be obvious. A corporation with twelve operating divisions is not necessarily in twelve businesses. One division may in fact contain several businesses, as when the division produces different products for different customer groups. Sometimes two divisions may be so interrelated that they form a single business. Therefore companies must take the important step of identifying the businesses they are in, and managing each as a business.

Companies too often define their business in terms of a product they make. They will say they are in the "auto business" or the "slide rule business," and so on. But this definition of a business is myopic. In his "Marketing Myopia," Levitt advanced the thesis that market definitions of a business are superior to product definitions of a business.[10] He argued that a business must be viewed as a *customer-satisfying process*, not a *goods-producing process*. Products are transient, but basic needs and customer groups endure forever. A horse-carriage company will go out of business soon after the automobile is invented. But the same company, if it defines its purpose as that of providing transportation, will switch from making horse carriages to making cars. Levitt encouraged companies to shift their business-domain definition from a product to a market focus. Several examples are given in Table 2-1.

TABLE 2-1   Product-Oriented Versus Market-Oriented Definitions of a Business

Company	Product-Oriented Definition	Market-Oriented Definition
Revlon	We make cosmetics	We sell hope
Missouri-Pacific Railroad	We run a railroad	We are a people-and-goods mover
Xerox	We make copying equipment	We help improve office productivity
International Minerals and Chemicals	We sell fertilizer	We help improve agricultural productivity
Standard Oil	We sell gasoline	We supply energy
Columbia Pictures	We make movies	We market entertainment
Encyclopedia Britannica	We sell encyclopedias	We are in the information-production and distribution business
Carrier	We make air conditioners and furnaces	We provide a comfortable climate in the home

In developing a market-based definition of its business, management should avoid a definition that is too narrow or too broad. Consider a lead-pencil manufacturer. If it sees itself as a *small writing-instruments company*, it might expand into the production of pens and other small writing instruments. If it sees itself as a *writing-equipment company*, then it might also consider making typewriters and word-processing equipment. The broadest concept of its business is that it is a *communication company*, but this would be stretching things too far for a lead-pencil manufacturer.

> Holiday Inns, Inc., the world's largest hotel chain with over 300,000 rooms, fell into this trap. Some years ago it broadened its business definition from the ''hotel business'' to the ''travel industry.'' It acquired Trailways, Inc., the nation's second largest bus company, and Delta Steamship Lines Inc. But Holiday Inns did not manage these companies well and in 1978 divested Trailways and sought a buyer for Delta. Holiday Inns decided to stick to the ''hospitality industry'' and blanket this industry with alternative room and food systems.[11]

A business should be defined, according to Abell, in terms of three dimensions: the *customer groups* that will be served, the *customer needs* that will be met, and the *technology* that will satisfy these needs.[12] Consider, for example, a small company that designs incandescent lighting systems for television studios. Its customer group is television studios; the customer need is lighting; and the technology is incandescent lighting. This company's business domain is defined by the floating cell in Figure 2-3. This gives a very clear picture of the company's business.

This company might want to expand into additional businesses. For example, it could decide to make lighting for other customer groups, such as homes, factories, and offices. Or it could supply other services needed by television studios, such as heating, ventilation, or air conditioning. Or it could design other lighting technologies for television studios, such as infrared or ultraviolet lighting. Each of the company's businesses is defined by the intersection of the three dimensions. If this company expands into other cells, we say that it has widened its business domain.

Companies have to identify their businesses in order to manage them strategically. General Electric went through this grueling exercise some years ago and identified forty-nine *strategic business units* (SBUs). An SBU has three characteristics:

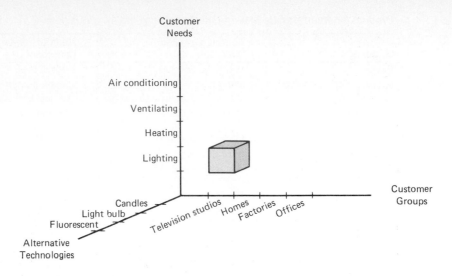

FIGURE 2-3
A Small Lighting Company's Current Definition of Its Business Domain

1. It is a single business or collection of related businesses that can be planned separately and, in principle, can stand alone from the rest of the company.
2. It has its own competitors, which it is trying to equal or surpass.
3. It has a manager who is responsible for strategic planning and profit performance and who controls most of the factors affecting profit.

Evaluating the Current Business Portfolio The purpose of identifying the corporation's strategic business units is to assign to these units strategic planning responsibilities. These units send their plans to the corporation, which approves them or sends them back for revision. The corporation reviews these plans in order to decide which of its SBUs to *build*, *maintain*, *harvest*, and *divest*. Senior management knows that its portfolio of businesses includes a number of "yesterday's has-beens" as well as "tomorrow's breadwinners." But it cannot rely on just impressions; it needs analytical tools for classifying its businesses by profit potential. In the past decade, several portfolio evaluation models have come into widespread use. Two of the best known are the Boston Consulting Group model and the General Electric model.[13]

Boston Consulting Group Approach The Boston Consulting Group (BCG), a leading management consulting firm, developed and popularized an approach known as the *growth-share matrix* shown in Figure 2-4. The eight circles represent the current sizes and positions of eight businesses making up a hypothetical company. The dollar-volume size of each business is proportional to the circle's area: Thus the two largest businesses are 5 and 6. The location of each business indicates its market growth rate and relative market share.

Specifically, the *market growth rate* on the vertical axis indicates the annual growth rate of the market in which the business operates; in the figure it ranges from 0 percent to 20 percent, although a larger range could be shown. A market growth rate above 10 percent is considered high.

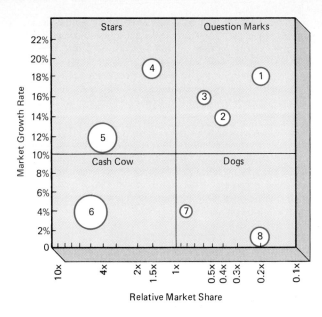

FIGURE 2-4
The Boston Consulting
Group's Growth-Share Matrix
SOURCE: B. Heldey, "Strategy and
the Business Portfolio," *Long Range
Planning*, February 1977, p. 12.
Reprinted with permission from *Long
Range Planning*, copyright 1977,
Pergamon Press, Ltd.

The horizontal axis, *relative market share*, refers to the SBU's market share relative to that of the largest competitor. It serves as a measure of the company's strength in the relevant market. A relative market share of 0.1 means that the company's SBU sales volume is only 10 percent of the leader's sales volume; and 10 means that the company's SBU is the leader and has ten times the sales of the next-strongest company in the market. Relative market share is divided into high and low share, using 1.0 as the dividing line. Relative market share is drawn in log scale, so that equal distances represent the same percentage increase.

The growth-share matrix is divided into four cells, each indicating a different type of business:

■ ***Question marks.*** Question marks are company businesses that operate in high-growth markets but have low relative market shares. Most businesses start off as a question mark in that the company tries to enter a high-growth market in which there is already a market leader. A question mark requires a lot of cash, since the company has to keep adding plant, equipment, and personnel to keep up with the fast-growing market, and additionally, it wants to overtake the leader. The term *question mark* is well chosen because the company has to think hard about whether to keep pouring money into this business or get out. The company in Figure 2-4 operates three question-mark businesses, and this may be too many. The company might be better off investing more cash in one or two of these businesses, instead of spreading its cash thinly over all three businesses.

■ ***Stars.*** If the question-mark business is successful, it becomes a star. A star is the market leader in a high-growth market. This does not necessarily mean that the star produces a positive cash flow for the company. The company must spend substantial funds to keep up with the high market growth and fight off competitors' attacks. Stars are usually profitable and become the company's future cash cows. In the illustration, the company has two stars. The company would justifiably be concerned if it had no stars.

■ ***Cash cows.*** When a market's annual growth rate falls to less than 10 percent, the star becomes a cash cow if it still has the largest relative market share. A cash cow produces a lot of cash for the company. The company does not have to finance a lot of capacity expansion because the market's growth rate has slowed down. And since the business is the market leader, it enjoys economies of scale and higher profit margins. The company uses its cash cow businesses to pay its bills and support the stars, question marks, and dogs, which tend to be cash hungry. In the illustration, however, the company has only one cash cow business and is therefore highly vulnerable. In the event this cash cow starts losing relative market share, the company has to pump enough money back into its cash cow to maintain market leadership. If instead it uses the throw-off cash to support its other businesses, its strong cash cow may decline into a weak cash cow.

■ *Dogs.* Dogs describe company businesses that have weak market shares in low-growth markets. They typically generate low profits or losses, although they may throw off some cash. The company in the illustration manages two dog businesses, and this may be two too many. The company should consider whether it is holding on to these dog businesses for good reasons (such as an expected turnaround in the market growth rate or a new chance at market leadership) or out of sentimental reasons. Dog businesses often take up more management time than they are worth and need to be phased down or out.

Having plotted its various businesses in the growth-share matrix, the company then determines whether its business portfolio is healthy. An unbalanced portfolio would have too many dogs or question marks and/or too few stars and cash cows.

The company's next task is to determine what objective, strategy, and budget to assign to each SBU. Four alternative objectives can be pursued:

■ *Build.* Here the objective is to increase the SBU's market share, even forgoing short-term earnings to achieve this objective. "Building" is appropriate for question marks whose shares have to grow if they are to become stars.

■ *Hold.* Here the objective is to preserve the SBU's market share. This objective is appropriate for strong cash cows if they are to continue to yield a large positive cash flow.

■ *Harvest.* Here the objective is to increase the SBU's short-term cash flow regardless of the long-term effect. This strategy is appropriate for weak cash cows whose future is dim and from whom more cash flow is needed. Harvesting can also be used with question marks and dogs.

■ *Divest.* Here the objective is to sell or liquidate the business because resources can be better used elsewhere. That is appropriate for dogs and question marks that are acting as a drag on the company's profits.

As time passes, SBUs change their position in the growth-share matrix. Successful SBUs have a life cycle. They start as question marks, become stars, then cash cows, and finally dogs toward the end of their life cycle. For this reason, companies should examine not only the current positions of their businesses in the growth-share matrix (as in a snapshot) but also their moving positions (as in a motion picture). Each business should be reviewed as to where it was last year, the year before, and so on, and where it will probably move next year, the year after, and so on. If the expected trajectory of a given business is not satisfactory, the company should ask its business's manager to propose a new strategy and the likely resulting trajectory. Thus the growth-share matrix becomes a planning framework for the strategic planners at company headquarters. They use it to try to assess each business and assign the most reasonable objective.

Although the portfolio in Figure 2-4 is basically healthy, wrong objectives or strategies could be assigned. The worst mistake would be to require all the SBUs to aim for the same growth rate or return level; the very point of SBU analysis is that each business has a different potential and requires its own objective. Additional mistakes would include

1. Leaving cash cow businesses with too little in retained funds, in which case they grow weak; or leaving them with too much in retained funds, in which case the company fails to invest enough in growth businesses.

2. Making major investments in dogs hoping to turn them around but failing each time.

3. Maintaining too many question marks and underinvesting in each, which amounts to throwing money away; question marks should either receive enough support to achieve segment dominance or be dropped.

General Electric Approach The appropriate objective to assign to an SBU cannot be determined solely on the basis of its position in the growth-share matrix. If additional factors are introduced, the growth-share matrix can be seen as a special case of a multifactor portfolio matrix that General Electric (GE) pioneered. This model is shown in Figure 2-5A, and seven businesses of a disguised company are plotted. This time the size of the circle represents the size of the relevant market rather than the size of the company's business. And the shaded part of the circle represents that business's market share. Thus the company's clutch business operates in a moderate-size market and enjoys approximately a 30 percent market share.

Each business is rated in terms of two major dimensions, *market attractiveness* and *competitive position*. These two factors make excellent marketing sense for rating a business. Companies will be successful to the extent that they go into attractive markets and possess the required mix of competitive business strengths to succeed in those markets. If one or the other is missing, the business will not produce outstanding results. Neither a strong company operating in an unattractive market nor a weak company operating in an attractive market will do very well.

The real issue, then, is to measure these two dimensions. To do this, the strategic planners must identify the factors underlying each dimension and find a way to measure them and combine them into an index. Table 2-2 illustrates sets of factors making up the two dimensions. (Each company has to decide on its list of factors.) Thus market attractiveness varies with the market's size, annual market growth rate, historical profit margins, and so on. And competitive position varies with the company's market share, share growth, product quality, and so on. Note that the two BCG factors, market growth rate and market share, are subsumed under the two major variables of the GE model. The GE model leads strategic planners to look at more factors involved in evaluating an actual or potential business than does the BCG model.

Table 2-2 shows a hypothetical rating for the hydraulic pumps business. Management rates each factor from 1 (very unattractive) to 5 (very attractive) to reflect how the business stands on that factor. In the illustration, the hydraulic pumps business is rated 4.00 on overall market size, indicating that the market size is pretty large (a 5.00 would be very large). Clearly, many of these factors require data and assessment from marketing personnel. The ratings are then multiplied by weights reflecting the factors' relative importance to arrive at the values, which are summed for each dimension. The hydraulic pumps business scored a 3.70 on market attractiveness and a 3.40 on competitive position, out of a maximum possible score of 5.00 for each. The analyst places a point in the multifactor matrix in Figure 2-5A representing this business and draws a circle around it whose size is proportional to the size of the market. The company's market share of approximately 14 percent is shaded in. Clearly, the hydraulic pumps business is in a fairly attractive part of the matrix.

In fact, the GE matrix is divided into nine cells, which in turn fall into three zones. The three cells at the upper left indicate strong SBUs in which the company should *invest/grow*. The diagonal cells stretching from the lower left to the upper right indicate SBUs

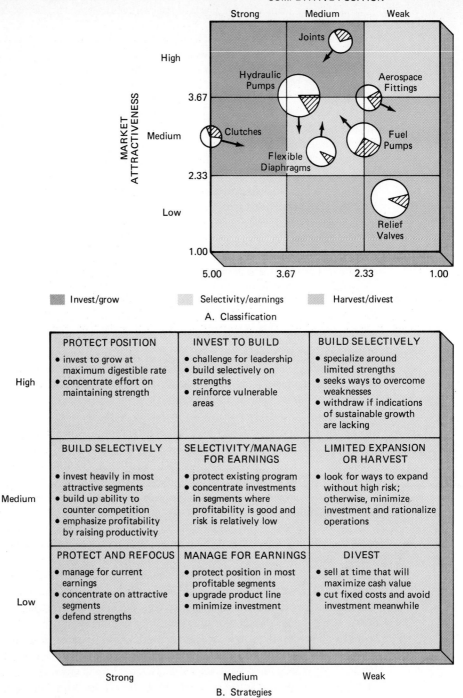

FIGURE 2-5
Market Attractiveness—Competitive Position Portfolio Classification and Strategies
SOURCE: Slightly modified and adapted with permission from *Analysis for Strategic Marketing Decisions* by George S. Day (St. Paul, Minn.: West Publishing, 1986), pp. 202 and 204.

TABLE 2-2
Factors Underlying Market Attractiveness and Competitive Position
in GE Multifactor Portfolio Model: Hydraulic Pumps Market

		Weight	Rating (1–5)	Value
Market Attractiveness	Overall market size	0.20	4.00	0.80
	Annual market growth rate	0.20	5.00	1.00
	Historical profit margin	0.15	4.00	0.60
	Competitive intensity	0.15	2.00	0.30
	Technological requirements	0.15	4.00	0.60
	Inflationary vulnerability	0.05	3.00	0.15
	Energy requirements	0.05	2.00	0.10
	Environmental impact	0.05	3.00	0.15
	Social/political/legal	Must be acceptable		
		1.00		3.70

		Weight	Rating (1–5)	Value
Competitive Position	Market share	0.10	4.00	0.40
	Share growth	0.15	2.00	0.30
	Product quality	0.10	4.00	0.40
	Brand reputation	0.10	5.00	0.50
	Distribution network	0.05	4.00	0.20
	Promotional effectiveness	0.05	3.00	0.15
	Productive capacity	0.05	3.00	0.15
	Productive efficiency	0.05	2.00	0.10
	Unit costs	0.15	3.00	0.45
	Material supplies	0.05	5.00	0.25
	R&D performance	0.10	3.00	0.30
	Managerial personnel	0.05	4.00	0.20
		1.00		3.40

SOURCE: Slightly modified from La Rue T. Hormer, **Strategic Management** (Englewood Cliffs, N.J.: Prentice-Hall, 1982), p. 310.

that are medium in overall attractiveness: The company should pursue *selectivity/earnings*. The three cells at the lower right indicate SBUs that are low in overall attractiveness: The company should give serious thought to *harvest/divest*. For example, the relief valves business represents an SBU with a small market share in a fair-size market that is not very attractive and in which the company has a weak competitive position: It is a fit candidate for harvest/divest.[14]

Management should also forecast the expected position of each SBU in the next three to five years given the current strategy. This involves analyzing where each product is in its product life cycle, as well as expected competitor strategies, new technologies, economic events, and so on. The results are indicated by the length and direction of the vectors in Figure 2-5A. For example, the hydraulic pumps business is expected to slightly decline in market attractiveness, and the clutches business is expected to strongly decline in the company's competitive position.

The final step is for management to decide what it wants to do with each business. Figure 2-5B outlines plausible strategy options for businesses in each cell. The strategy for each business has to be discussed and debated. The end result is that business and corporate management will, it is hoped, agree on the objectives and strategies for each business and the support funds necessary to achieve these objectives.

Marketing managers will find that their objective is not necessarily to build sales in certain SBUs. Their job might be to maintain the existing demand with fewer marketing dollars or to take cash out of the business and allow demand to fall. *Thus the task of marketing management is to manage demand or revenue to the target level negotiated with the corporate management.* Marketing contributes to assessing each SBU's sales and profit potential, but once the SBU's objective and budget are set, marketing's job is to carry out the plan efficiently and profitably.

Critique of Portfolio Models Other portfolio models have been developed and used, particularly the Arthur D. Little model and the Shell directional policy model.[15] The use of portfolio models has produced a number of benefits. The models have helped managers to think more futuristically and strategically, to understand the economics of their businesses better, to improve the quality of their plans, to communicate better between business and corporate management, to pinpoint information gaps and important issues, and to eliminate weaker businesses and strengthen their investment in more-promising businesses.

On the other hand, portfolio models must be used cautiously. They may lead the company to place too much emphasis on market-share growth and entry into high-growth businesses, to the neglect of managing the current businesses well. The results are sensitive to the ratings and weights and can be manipulated to produce a desired location in the matrix. Furthermore, since an averaging process is occurring, two or more businesses may end up in the same cell position but differ greatly in the underlying ratings and weights. A lot of businesses will end up in the middle of the matrix due to compromises in ratings, and this makes it hard to know what the appropriate strategy should be. Finally, the models fail to accommodate the synergies between two or more businesses, and this means that making decisions for one business at a time might be risky. Overall, however, portfolio models have improved the analytical and strategic capabilities of managers and permitted them to make tough decisions on a more data-oriented and hard-nosed basis than mere impressions would permit.

Corporate New-Business Plan

The company's plans for its existing businesses will allow it to project total sales and profits. Often, however, projected sales and profits will be less than what corporate management wants to achieve over the planning horizon. After all, the portfolio plan will include divesting some businesses, and these will need replacement. If there is a gap between future desired sales and projected sales, corporate management will have to develop or acquire new businesses to fill this strategic planning gap.

Figure 2-6 illustrates this strategic planning gap for a major manufacturer of cassette tape called Musicale (named disguised). The lowest curve projects the expected sales over the next ten years from the company's current portfolio of businesses. The highest curve describes the corporation's desired sales over the next ten years. Evidently the company wants to grow much faster than its current businesses will permit; in fact, it wants to double its size in ten years. How can it fill the strategic planning gap?

A company can fill the gap in three ways. The first is to identify further opportunities to achieve growth within the company's current businesses (*intensive growth opportunities*). The second is to identify opportunities to build or acquire businesses that are related to the company's current businesses (*integrative growth opportunities*). The third is to identify opportunities to add attractive businesses that are unrelated to the company's current businesses (*diversification growth opportunities*). The specific opportunities within each broad class are listed in Table 2-3 and discussed below.

Intensive Growth Corporate management should first review whether there are any further opportunities for improving the performance of its existing businesses. Ansoff has proposed

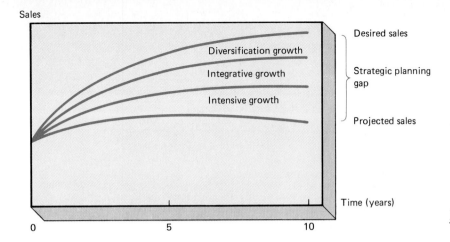

Sales

Desired sales

Diversification growth

Integrative growth

Strategic planning gap

Intensive growth

Projected sales

Time (years)

0   5   10

FIGURE 2-6
The Strategic Planning Gap

a useful framework for detecting new intensive growth opportunities. Called a *product/market expansion grid*, it is shown in Figure 2-7.[16] Management first considers whether it could gain more market share with its current products in their current markets (*market penetration strategy*). Then it considers whether it can find or develop new markets for its current products (*market development strategy*). Then it considers whether it can develop new products of potential interest to its current markets (*product development strategy*). (Later it will also review opportunities to develop new products for new markets—*diversification strategy*.) Let us examine the three major intensive growth strategies further.

Market penetration strategy   Here management looks for ways to increase the market share of its current products in their current markets. There are three major ways to do this. A company such as Musicale could try to encourage its current customers to buy and use more cassette tapes per period. This would make sense if most of its customers were infrequent buyers of tape and could be shown the benefits of using more tape for music recording or dictation. Or Musicale could try to attract the competitors' customers to switch to its brand. This would make sense if Musicale noticed a lot of weaknesses in the competitors' product or marketing program that it could exploit. Finally, Musicale could try to convince current nonusers of cassette tapes who resemble current users to start using tapes. This would make sense if there were a lot of people who still did not own tape recorders or tape players.

Market development strategy   Management should also look for new markets whose needs might be met by its current products. First, Musicale might try to identify potential user groups in the current sales areas whose interest in cassette tapes might be stimulated.

TABLE 2-3   Major Classes of Growth Opportunities

Intensive Growth	Integrative Growth	Diversification Growth
• Market penetration	• Backward integration	• Concentric diversification
• Market development	• Forward integration	• Horizontal diversification
• Product development	• Horizontal integration	• Conglomerate diversification

FIGURE 2-7
Three Intensive Growth
Strategies: Ansoff's Product/
Market Expansion Grid

If Musicale had been selling cassette tapes only to consumer markets, it might go after office and factory markets. Second, the company might seek additional distribution channels in its present locations. If it has been selling its tape only through stereo equipment dealers, it might add mass-merchandising channels. Third, the company might consider selling in new locations here or abroad. Thus if Musicale sold only in the eastern part of the United States, it could consider adding the western states or opening markets in Europe.

Product development strategy Next, management should consider some new-product development possibilities. It could develop new cassette tape features, such as a longer-playing tape and a tape that buzzes at the end of its play. It could develop other quality levels of tape, such as a higher-quality tape for fine music listeners and a lower-quality tape for the mass market. Or it could research an alternative technology to cassette tape that allows recording and dictating.

By examining all of these intensive growth strategies—deeper market penetration, broader market development, and new-product development—it is hoped that management will discover several ways to grow. Still, this may not be enough, in which case management must also examine integrative growth possibilities.

Integrative Growth Management should review each of its businesses to identify integrative growth possibilities. Often a business's sales and profits can be increased through integrating backward, forward, or horizontally within that business's industry. Figure 2-8 shows Musicale's core marketing system. Musicale might acquire one or more of its suppliers (such as plastic-material producers) to gain more profit or control (*backward integration strategy*). Or Musicale might acquire some wholesalers or retailers, especially if they are highly profitable (*forward integration strategy*). Finally, Musicale might acquire one or more competitors, providing that the government does not bar this move (*horizontal integration strategy*).

Through investigating possible integration moves, it is hoped that the company will discover additional sources of sales-volume increases over the next ten years. These new

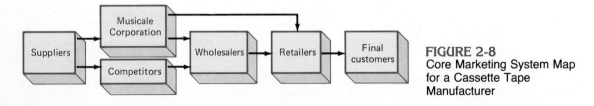

FIGURE 2-8
Core Marketing System Map
for a Cassette Tape
Manufacturer

sources may still not be enough to achieve the desired sales-growth level. In that case, the company must consider diversification moves.

Diversification Growth   Diversification growth makes sense when good opportunities can be found outside the present businesses. A good opportunity, of course, is one where the industry is highly attractive and the company has the mix of business strengths needed to be successful. Three types of diversification can be considered. The company could seek new products that have technological and/or marketing synergies with existing product lines, even though the products may appeal to a new class of customers (*concentric diversification strategy*). For example, Musicale might start a computer-tape manufacturing operation based on knowing how to manufacture cassette tape, well aware that it will be entering a new market and selling to a different class of customers. Second, the company might search for new products that could appeal to its current customers though technologically unrelated to its current product line (*horizontal diversification strategy*). For example, Musicale might go into the production of cassette holding trays, even though they require a different manufacturing process. Finally, the company might seek new businesses that have no relationship to the company's current technology, products, or markets (*conglomerate diversification strategy*). Musicale might want to consider such new business areas as personal computers, real estate office franchising, or fast-food services.

Thus we see that a company can systematically identify new business opportunities by using a marketing systems framework, first looking at ways to intensify its position in current product markets, then considering ways to integrate backward, forward, or horizontally in relation to its current businesses, and finally searching for profitable opportunities outside of its current businesses.

BUSINESS STRATEGIC PLANNING

Having examined the strategic planning tasks of corporate management, we can now look more closely at the strategic planning tasks facing business unit managers. The business strategic planning process consists of the following steps (also see Figure 2-9):

- ◼ Defining the business's mission
- ◼ Analyzing the external environment
- ◼ Analyzing the internal environment

FIGURE 2-9
The Business Strategic Planning Process

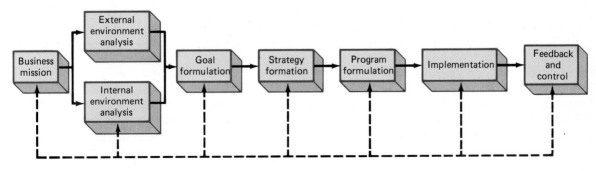

- Choosing business objectives and goals
- Developing business strategies
- Preparing program plans
- Implementing program plans
- Gathering feedback and exercising control

These steps are examined below.

Business Mission

We saw earlier that a corporation needs to develop a statement of its mission. Each business unit within the corporation similarly needs to define its specific mission within the broader corporate mission. Its mission statement should cover its *market segment scope* (target customer groups and needs), *industry scope*, *technology scope*, *vertical scope*, and *geographical scope*.

To illustrate, let us return to the business illustrated in Figure 2-3 that designed incandescent lighting systems for television studios. This business is clearly defined in terms of customer group (television studios) and customer need (lighting system). But it may need additional definition of its mission as a business. With regard to customer groups, will it go after all television studios or only those that can afford the finest, most-advanced lighting systems? With regard to customer needs, will it install and service the systems or merely sell them? With regard to vertical scope, will it manufacture its own lighting equipment or contract out the manufacturing to someone else? And will it sell the lighting through a direct sales force or through distributors? With regard to geographical scope, will it sell in one region, the whole country, or certain groups of countries in the world? Obviously, the business unit will need to spell out its business scope more clearly.

In addition, the mission should indicate the broad goals and values of the specific business, going beyond the corporate goals and values. Does this television lighting equipment business want to pursue growth, short-term profit, technological leadership, and so on? What policies does it want to have regarding customers, employees, and other important stakeholders? All of these matters require clarification in the mission statement.

External Environment Analysis (Opportunity and Threat Analysis)

The mission statement will help the business define its *environmental scanning* needs. The business manager now knows the parts of the environment to monitor and understand if the business is to achieve its objectives. For example, the television lighting equipment company needs to watch

- The growth rate in the number of television studios
- The level of television viewing as it affects the financial health of television studios and their ability to buy new equipment
- The strategies of current competitors as well as the entry of new competitors
- New technological developments that might affect present and future equipment
- Changes in laws and regulations that might affect equipment design or marketing
- New or changing distribution channels for selling lighting equipment
- Increases in supplier costs that might be passed on to equipment manufacturers

In general, the company has to monitor key *macroenvironment forces* (demographic/economic, technological, political/legal, and social/cultural) that affect its business. And it must monitor significant *microenvironment actors* (customers, competitors, distribution channels, suppliers) that affect its ability to earn profits in this marketplace.

EXHIBIT 2-1

Which Company Would Have the Greatest Competitive Advantage in Producing an Electric Car?

Suppose General Motors, General Electric, and Sears all became interested in developing and marketing an electric car. Which firm would enjoy the greatest competitive advantage? First consider the success requirements. The success requirements would include (1) having good relations with suppliers of metal, rubber, plastic, glass, and other materials needed to produce an automobile; (2) having skill in mass production and mass assembly of complicated pieces of equipment; (3) having a strong distribution capacity to store, show, and deliver automobiles to the public; and (4) having the confidence of buyers that the company is able to produce and service a good auto product.

Now General Motors has distinctive competences in all four of these areas. General Electric has distinctive competences in (1) supply and (2) production, but not in (3) distribution or (4) automobile reputation. It does have great know-how in electrical and electronic technology. Sears's major distinctive competence is its extensive retailing system, and it has some of the other competences through its wholly owned subsidiaries. All said, General Motors would enjoy the greatest differential advantage in the production and marketing of electric cars.

The business unit needs to categorize these environmental factors and set up a *marketing intelligence system* to track trends and important developments. Then, for each trend or development, the marketer should identify the obvious or not-so-obvious opportunities and threats.

Opportunities   One of the major purposes of environmental scanning is to discern new opportunities. We define a company marketing opportunity as follows:

> A *company marketing opportunity* is an attractive arena for company marketing action in which the company would enjoy a competitive advantage.

These opportunities should be classified according to their *attractiveness* and the *success probability* that the company would have with each opportunity (Figure 2-10). The company's success probability with a particular opportunity depends on whether its *business strengths* (i.e., *distinctive competences*) not only match the *key success requirements* for operating in the target market but also exceed those of its competitors. The best-performing company will be the one that can generate the greatest customer value and sustain it over time. Having competence is not enough. The company must bring superior competence in order to attain a *sustainable competitive advantage*. (See Exhibit 2-1.)

Looking at Figure 2-10, the best opportunities facing a TV lighting equipment company are those in the upper-left cell, and management should prepare plans to pursue one or more of these opportunities. The opportunities in the lower-right cell are too minor to consider. The opportunities in the upper-right cell and lower-left cell should be monitored in the event that any of them improve in their attractiveness and success probability.

Threats   Some of the developments in the external environment represent threats. We define an environmental threat as follows:

> An *environmental threat* is a challenge posed by an unfavorable trend or development in the environment that would lead, in the absence of purposeful marketing action, to the erosion of the company's or industry's position.

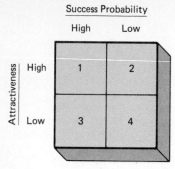

Success Probability

	High	Low
High	1	2
Low	3	4

Attractiveness

Opportunities

1. Company develops a more powerful lighting system
2. Company develops a much lower cost lighting system
3. Company develops a software disc to teach lighting fundamentals to TV studio personnel
4. Company develops a device for measuring the energy efficiency of any lighting system

FIGURE 2-10
Opportunity Matrix

The various identified threats should be classified according to their *seriousness* and *probability of occurrence*. Figure 2-11 shows a threat matrix and the location of several threats facing a TV lighting equipment company. The threats in the upper-left cell are major threats, since they can seriously hurt the company and they have a high probability of occurrence. For each of these threats, the company needs to prepare a contingency plan that spells out in advance what changes the company can make before or during the threat's occurrence. The threats in the lower-right cell are very minor and can be ignored. The threats in the upper-right and lower-left cells do not require contingency planning but need to be carefully monitored in the event that they grow more critical.

By assembling a picture of the major threats and opportunities facing a specific business, it is possible to characterize its overall attractiveness. Four outcomes are possible. An *ideal business* is one that is high in major opportunities and low in or devoid of major threats. A *speculative business* is high in both major opportunities and threats. A *mature business* is low in major opportunities and threats. Finally, a *troubled business* is low in opportunities and high in threats.

Internal Environment Analysis (Strength and Weakness Analysis)

It is one thing to discern attractive opportunities in the environment; it is another to have the necessary competencies to succeed in these opportunities. Each business needs to evaluate its strengths and weaknesses periodically. This can be done by using a form such as the one shown in Figure 2-12. Management—or an outside consultant—reviews the business's marketing, financial, manufacturing, and organizational competencies. Each factor is rated as to whether it is a major strength, minor strength, neutral factor, minor weakness, or major weakness. A company with strong

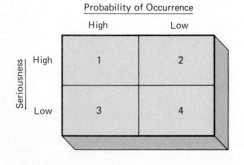

Probability of Occurrence

	High	Low
High	1	2
Low	3	4

Seriousness

Threats

1. Competitor develops a superior lighting system
2. Major prolonged economic depression
3. Higher costs
4. Legislation to reduce number of TV studio licenses

FIGURE 2-11
Threat Matrix

	Major Strength	Minor Strength	Neutral	Minor Weakness	Major Weakness	Hi	Med	Low
Marketing Strengths								
1. Company is well-known and highly regarded	___	___	___	___	___	___	___	___
2. Company has a strong relative market share	___	___	___	___	___	___	___	___
3. Good reputation for quality	___	___	___	___	___	___	___	___
4. Good reputation for service	___	___	___	___	___	___	___	___
5. Low manufacturing costs	___	___	___	___	___	___	___	___
6. Low distribution costs	___	___	___	___	___	___	___	___
7. Effective sales force	___	___	___	___	___	___	___	___
8. Effective R&D and innovation	___	___	___	___	___	___	___	___
9. Geographical advantage	___	___	___	___	___	___	___	___
10. Raw material advantage	___	___	___	___	___	___	___	___
Financial Strengths								
11. Low cost of capital	___	___	___	___	___	___	___	___
12. High availability	___	___	___	___	___	___	___	___
13. High profitability	___	___	___	___	___	___	___	___
14. Financial stability	___	___	___	___	___	___	___	___
Manufacturing Strengths								
15. New, well-equipped facilities	___	___	___	___	___	___	___	___
16. Strong economies of scale	___	___	___	___	___	___	___	___
17. Capacity to meet demand	___	___	___	___	___	___	___	___
18. Able and dedicated workforce	___	___	___	___	___	___	___	___
19. Ability to deliver on time	___	___	___	___	___	___	___	___
20. Technical and manufacturing skill	___	___	___	___	___	___	___	___
Organizational Strengths								
21. Enlightened, visionary leadership	___	___	___	___	___	___	___	___
22. Capable managers	___	___	___	___	___	___	___	___
23. Dedicated workers	___	___	___	___	___	___	___	___
24. Entrepreneurial orientation	___	___	___	___	___	___	___	___
25. Flexible and adaptable	___	___	___	___	___	___	___	___
26. Speedy response to changing conditions	___	___	___	___	___	___	___	___

FIGURE 2-12
Strengths and Weaknesses Analysis

marketing capability would show up with the ten marketing factors all rated as major strengths. By connecting the ratings vertically for a specific business, we can easily identify the business's major strengths and major weaknesses.

Of course, not all factors are equally important for succeeding in a business, or succeeding with a specific new marketing opportunity presented to this business. Therefore it is also necessary to rate the importance of each factor—high, medium, or low—for the business as a whole or for a particular marketing opportunity. When combining performance and importance levels, four possibilities emerge. They are illustrated in Figure 2-13. In cell A fall important factors where the business is performing poorly and therefore the business must strengthen these factors; hence "concentrate here." In cell B fall important factors where the business is already strong; hence "keep up the good work." In cell C fall unimportant factors where the business is performing poorly; these factors consequently

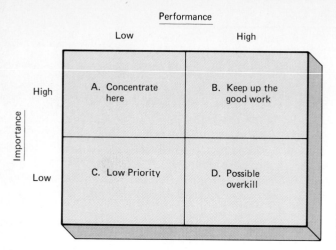

Performance

Low　　　　　High

High

Importance

Low

| A. Concentrate here | B. Keep up the good work |
| C. Low Priority | D. Possible overkill |

FIGURE 2-13
Performance-Importance Matrix

are of "low priority." In cell D fall unimportant factors where the business is strong; perhaps it is overinvesting in these factors at the cost of "possible overkill." An application of the analysis is shown in Chapter 16, Exhibit 16-1, p. 487.

This analysis tells us that even when a business has a major strength in a certain factor (i.e., a *distinctive competence*), that strength does not necessarily create a *competitive advantage*. First, it may not be a competence of any importance to the customers in that market. Second, even if it is, competitors may have the same strength level in that factor. What becomes important, then, is for the business to have relatively greater strength in that factor than its competitors. Thus two competitors may both enjoy low manufacturing costs, but the one with the lower of the manufacturing costs has a competitive advantage.

In examining its pattern of strengths and weaknesses, clearly the business does not have to correct all of its weaknesses (some are unimportant) or gloat about all of its strengths (again, some are unimportant). The big question is whether the business should limit itself to those opportunities where it now possesses the required strengths or should consider possibly better opportunities where it might have to acquire or develop certain strengths. For example, managers in Texas Instruments (TI) split between those who wanted TI to stick to industrial electronics where it had clear strength and those who urged the company to go into digital watches, personal computers, and other consumer products where it did not have the required marketing strengths. As it turned out, TI did poorly in these areas, but perhaps its mistake was not in going into these areas but rather not acquiring the required marketing strengths to do the job right.

Sometimes a business falters not because its departments lack strength but because they do not work well together. In one major electronics company, the engineers look down upon the sales people as "engineers who couldn't make it," and the sales people look down upon the service people as "sales people who couldn't make it." It is critically important to assess the quality of the interdepartmental working relationships as part of the internal environment audit. One company has solved this problem by conducting a survey each year asking each department to rate itself and each other department on its strengths and weaknesses. Its findings in the last survey are shown in Exhibit 2-2. Note that each department was seen as having some positive strengths, but there was also concern about some major weaknesses. Following these findings, the company undertakes programs to correct the departmental weaknesses and improve interdepartmental working relationships.

EXHIBIT 2-2

Assessing Interdepartmental Strengths and Weaknesses

A major computer manufacturer undertook an audit of its strengths and weaknesses by department. It asked each department (engineering, manufacturing, marketing, field sales, etc.) to evaluate the strengths and weaknesses of every other department. Here is what the company learned.

	Strengths	Weaknesses
Engineering	Skilled engineers Up to date in CAD/CAM	Overcosting Overdelays
Manufacturing	Produces good quality Can customize equipment Responsive to field needs	High cost Lack of cost reduction programs Union is inflexible
Field Sales	Good customer relations	Focuses on big orders, neglecting small orders Needs more training in benefit selling Conflict between home office and branches
Marketing	Competent Good programs for segments	Has not provided long-run strategy Planning is done in September instead of continuously Slow in filling product gaps

Goal Formulation

After the business unit has defined its mission and examined its external and internal environments, it is ready to set down specific objectives and goals. This stage is called *goal formulation* and indicates what the business unit wants to achieve in the planning period.

Very few businesses pursue only one objective. Most business units pursue a mix of objectives including *profitability*, *sales growth*, *market-share improvement*, *risk containment*, *innovativeness*, *reputation*, and so on. The business unit sets these objectives and *manages by objectives*. For this system to work, the business unit's various objectives should be hierarchical, quantitative, realistic, and consistent.

Because there are typically several objectives, they must be *hierarchically* arranged from the most to the least important. An excellent example of hierarchical objectives is provided by Interstate Telephone (name disguised), a strategic business unit of a larger company. This business unit has been earning only a 7.5 percent return on investment, too low to support its plans to expand and provide better service and equipment to customers. The business unit's mission is to provide good service to customers. Its current major objective is to increase its return on investment. From this objective follows a whole hierarchy of further objectives (see Figure 2-14).

There are two ways to increase return on investment: increase the total return and/or reduce the investment base. Interstate Telephone is not about to do the latter. To increase its return, Interstate Telephone can increase its billings and/or reduce its costs. To increase its billings, it can sell more equipment, increase the usage of present equipment, and

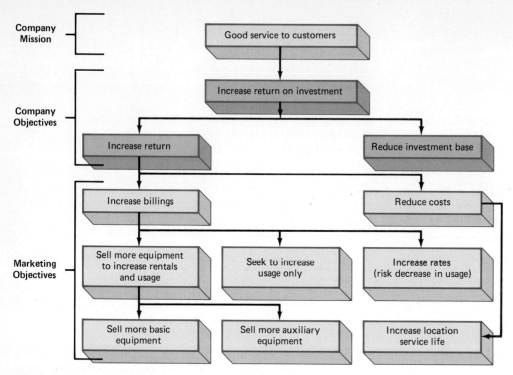

FIGURE 2-14
Hierarchy of Objectives for the Interstate Telephone Company
SOURCE: Adapted from Leon Winer, "Are You Really Planning Your Marketing?" *Journal of Marketing*, January 1965, p. 3. Published by the American Marketing Association.

increase its rates. Costs could be reduced by increasing the service life of rented telephone equipment. This could be accomplished by the better matching of rented equipment to actual customer needs. To the extent that Interstate sets increased billings as an objective, subsidiary objectives must be set for sales-force, advertising, and other marketing functions. For example, each sales district will be assigned a sales quota, which in turn must be broken down and assigned to individual sales representatives. In this way a major business objective is ultimately transformed into specific objectives for all employees.

To the extent possible, objectives should be stated *quantitatively*. The objective "increase the return on investment" is not as satisfactory as "increase the return on investment to 12 percent" or, even better, "increase the return on investment to 12 percent within two years." Managers use the term *goals* to describe objectives that are highly specific with respect to *magnitude* and *time*. Turning the objectives into concrete goals facilitates the process of management planning, implementation, and control.

A business has to choose *realistic* target levels for its objectives. The levels should come out of an analysis of its opportunities and competitive strengths, not out of wishful thinking.

Finally, the company's objectives need to be *consistent*. It is not possible to "maximize both sales and profits," or "achieve the greatest sales at the least cost," or "design the best product in the shortest possible time." These objectives are in a *trade-off* relationship. Here are some important trade-offs:

- Short-term profits versus long-term growth
- High profit margins versus high sales volume
- Deeper penetration of existing markets versus developing new markets
- Profit goals versus nonprofit goals
- High growth versus high stability

A business has to develop compatible goals or else they will cause confusion. Too often, senior management tells its line people to plan for the ''long run'' and then puts pressure on them to achieve ''high current profits.''

Strategy Formulation

Goals tell where a business wants to go; strategy answers how it plans to get there. Every business must tailor a strategy for achieving its goals. The strategy must then be refined into specific programs that are implemented efficiently and corrected if they are failing to achieve the objectives.

We saw at the beginning of this chapter (pp. 34–35) that competitors within an industry (here rubber tires) might pursue quite different strategies that are all reasonable, given that these competitors have different objectives, opportunities, and resources. Although one can list many types of strategies, Porter has condensed them into three generic types that provide a good starting point for strategic thinking:[17]

- *Overall cost leadership.* Here the business works hard to achieve the lowest costs of production and distribution so that it can price lower than its competitors and win a large market share. Firms pursuing this strategy must be good at engineering, purchasing, manufacturing, and physical distribution and need less skill in marketing. Texas Instruments is a leading practitioner of this strategy.
- *Differentiation.* Here the business concentrates on achieving superior performance in some important customer benefit area valued by the market as a whole. It can strive to be the service leader, the quality leader, the style leader, the technology leader, etc.; but it is hardly possible to be all of these things. The firm cultivates those strengths that will give it a differential performance advantage along some benefit line. Thus the firm seeking quality leadership must make or buy the best components, put them together expertly, inspect them carefully, and so on. This has been Canon's strategy in the copy machine field.
- *Focus.* Here the business focuses on one or more narrow market segments rather than going after the whole market. The firm gets to know the needs of these segments and pursues either cost leadership or some form of differentiation within the target segment. Thus Armstrong Rubber has specialized in making superior tires for farm equipment vehicles and recreational vehicles, and it keeps looking for new niches to serve.

According to Porter, those firms pursuing the same strategy directed to the same market or market segment constitute a *strategic group*. The firm that carries off that strategy best will make the most profits. Thus the lowest-cost firm of those pursuing a low-cost strategy will do the best. Porter suggests that firms that do not pursue a clear strategy—*middle-of-the-roaders*—do the worst. Thus Chrysler and International Harvester both came upon hard times because in their respective industries neither stood out as either lowest in cost, highest in perceived value, or best in serving some market segment. Middle-of-the-roaders try to be good on all strategic dimensions, but since strategic dimensions require different and often inconsistent ways to organize the firm, these firms end up being not particularly excellent at anything. (Exhibit 2-3 illustrates these principles for the truck manufacturing industry.)

EXHIBIT 2-3

Strategic Groups in the Truck Manufacturing Industry

The role of generic strategies and strategic groups can be illustrated by William Hall's research in the truck manufacturing industry. The accompanying figure shows how seven U.S. truck manufacturers were positioned some years ago in terms of their *relative delivered cost* (i.e., being a low-cost firm) and their *relative performance* (i.e., offering the most differentiated or desirable product and service). The percentages in the figure represent each manufacturer's rate of return on investment (ROI) in this industry.

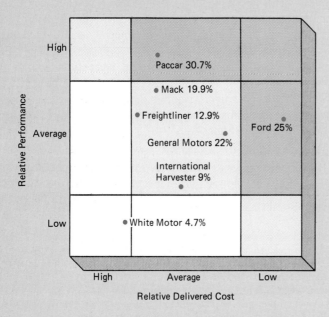

Relative Performance

High

Paccar 30.7%

Average

● Mack 19.9%

● Freightliner 12.9%

Ford 25%

General Motors 22%

International Harvester 9%

Low

● White Motor 4.7%

High   Average   Low

Relative Delivered Cost

Ford clearly has the lowest relative delivered cost, followed by General Motors. Although its trucks are average, Ford's low-cost leadership gives it the highest ROI (i.e., 25%) in its strategic group. Paccar, on the other hand, is the leader in the high-performance truck strategic group and commands a 31 percent ROI, compared with Mack's 20 percent.

At the other extreme is White Motor, whose trucks were below average in performance and high in manufactured cost. Not surprisingly, its rate of return was 4.7 percent, and White was subsequently purchased by Volvo, whose intent is to reposition it and strengthen its competitive effectiveness.

The four companies in the middle box are "middle-of-the-roaders" that try to be good at performance and cost but are not superior at either. Their rates of return are lower than those of the two leading firms, Ford and Paccar. As it turns out, Freightliner was subsequently purchased by Mercedes, and International Harvester's truck line was later reborn as Navistar.

In order for a middle-of-the-roader to improve its ROI, the company must make a clearer commitment to one of the three winning strategies. For example, International Harvester (IH) had three options. IH could invest in a more modern plant in a drive to become the low-cost firm. In this case, its major competitors would be Ford and General Motors, both of which make up the strategic group pursuing cost leadership. Alternatively, IH could try to improve the quality of its trucks and services so that it competed with Paccar and Mack, the strategic group pursuing profitability through product differentiation. This would be harder for IH because it takes years to build a better product and reputation, and Paccar is too well entrenched. Finally, IH might go after multiple niches within the trucking industry (this cannot be shown in the figure), becoming a leader in each niche through either low costs, product differentiation, or both. As it turned out, IH adopted the third strategy.

Program Formulation Once the business has developed its strategic ideas for attaining its goals, it must work out supporting programs for carrying out these strategies. Thus if the business has decided to attain technological leadership, it must run programs to strengthen its research and development department, gather intelligence on the newest technologies that might affect the business, develop leading edge products, train the sales force to understand the products and educate the customers, develop an advertising program to communicate its position as the technological leader, and so on. Since we will say much more about these programs later in the book, we will now turn to implementation.

Implementation Even if the firm has developed a clear strategy and well-thought-out supporting programs, they may not be enough. The firm may fail at implementation and control. According to the McKinsey Company, a leading consulting firm, strategic planning is not enough. Strategy is only one of seven elements that the best-managed companies exhibit.[18] The McKinsey 7–S framework is shown in Figure 2-15. The first three elements—strategy, structure, and systems—are considered the ''hardware'' of success. The next four—style, staff, skills, and shared values—are the ''software.''

Most management literature has emphasized the hardware elements. Thus a successful company is one that develops an appropriate *strategy* to reach its goals, builds an appropriate organizational *structure* to carry out this strategy, and equips the organization with effective *systems* of information, planning, control, and reward to get the job done. The key idea has been that strategy, not structure, is the starting point. The company must first decide on a strategy for achieving its objectives and must then develop an organizational structure and systems to carry out this strategy. Thus General Motors decides that it must start producing small cars to survive in the future, and its task is to reorganize to do this well. This makes more sense than if General Motors avoided this strategy largely because its current structure was not adapted to making small cars.

Consultants at McKinsey added the four software elements as a result of studying a large sample of excellently managed companies—IBM, P&G, Caterpillar, Delta, Mc-

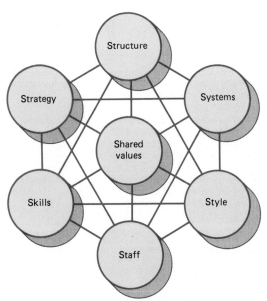

FIGURE 2-15
McKinsey 7–S Framework
SOURCE: Thomas J. Peters and Robert H. Waterman, Jr., *In Search of Excellence: Lessons from America's Best Run Companies.* Copyright © 1982 by Thomas J. Peters and Robert H. Waterman, Jr. Reprinted by permission of Harper & Row, Publishers.

Donald's, Levi Strauss, and so on—and discovering that their strengths went beyond strategy, structure, and systems. These organizations have four additional elements. The first is *style*, which means that employees in that company share a common style of behaving and thinking. Thus everyone at McDonald's smiles at the customer, and employees of IBM are very professional in their bearing and attire. The second element is *skills*, which means that employees have mastered those skills—such as financial analysis and marketing planning—that are needed to carry out the company's strategy. The third element is *staffing*, in that the company has hired able people, trained them well, and assigned the right jobs to exercise their talents. The fourth "soft" element is *shared values*, in that the employees of the firm share the same guiding values and missions. The well-managed company has a driving purpose and creed that everyone in the company knows and is proud to practice. Each successful company exhibits a distinct and widely shared culture that fits its strategy.[19]

Feedback and Control

The "software" of management will affect the firm's ability to implement its strategies and programs successfully. As the implementation occurs, the business needs to track the results and monitor new developments in the environment. The company can count on one thing: The environment will change during the planning period. And when it does, the company will be pressed to make appropriate adjustments in one or more of the component steps of the planning process if it is to achieve its objectives.

The extent of the required adjustments depends on the degree and speed of environmental change. Some environments are fairly stable from year to year in their economics, technology, law, culture, consumer wants, and competitive behavior. Other environments evolve slowly in a fairly predictable way. Still other environments are turbulent and change in major and unpredictable ways.

In turbulent environments, business units have to be ready to revise their programs, strategies, goals, or even mission in some cases. Some companies carry on continuous strategic planning in that they keep adapting their programs to changing conditions while holding to their core objectives and strategies. On the other hand, some dominant producers fail to recognize when their demand environment has changed from a stable to a turbulent one and they do not respond quickly enough. Consider what happened at GE's vacuum tube division:

> The president of General Electric called in the general manager of the vacuum tube division. The general manager expected to be congratulated because he had increased vacuum tube sales by 20 percent. Instead he was berated for keeping GE too long in the wrong business. GE's sales rose because some competitors left the vacuum tube business, not because of GE's competitive edge. In addition, transistor technology had just appeared and was making headway against vacuum tubes and bringing in new players such as Texas Instruments, Fairchild, and Transitron. In fact, the total market for devices that amplified weak electrical signals had grown by 30 percent during the same period, which meant that GE's market share of the total market had actually fallen. The manager was guilty of marketing myopia, focusing on vacuum tubes instead of the total range of technologies competing to serve the particular need. Some businesses are dead without the management really knowing it.

Another sad case of failing to adjust to new market factors occurred in the U.S. automobile industry:

The U.S. auto industry is central to a vast *business ecosystem* consisting of rubber, glass, and steel plants, petroleum refineries, gasoline stations, superhighways, the economy of Detroit, auto dealerships, auto repair and supply shops, and the incomes of millions of people. This business ecosystem had fairly stable characteristics for many years until the early 1970s, when a succession of "blows" left the industry reeling from shock: the oil crises, Nader's attack on automobile safety, government requirement for emission control, the advent of successful small foreign cars and tough competitors, and so on.

American car manufacturers were slow to respond to these environmental changes, in some cases either ignoring them or fighting them. When General Motors, Ford, and Chrysler finally started to make small cars to compete with the Japanese, they had already lost their leadership in the small-car market to Toyota, Volkswagen, Volvo, Datsun, and a host of other foreign manufacturers. As of today, the Japanese sell 49 percent of the 3.2 million small cars marketed in the United States.

Detroit's failure was in not reading the environmental signals early enough, not designing good small cars (where are the Vega and the Pinto today?), and not containing its labor and other costs. U.S. auto workers were paid $8 more an hour in wages and benefits than their Japanese counterparts and it took them thirty hours, as opposed to fifteen hours in Japan, to assemble a small car. The result is that Japanese car makers had a $2,500 cost edge over U.S. manufacturers.

Today U.S. companies are trying to respond to the challenge with (1) sourcing abroad, (2) strategic partnerships, (3) emphasis on quality, and (4) innovation. They used to say, "style is the only thing that counts." Today even styling for U.S. autos is done abroad, particularly in Italy. And small-car competition is likely to get worse, with Korean and Yugoslavian cars coming into the market at much lower prices than American or Japanese cars. To make matters worse, the Japanese continue to upgrade the size and quality of their cars, thus presenting stiff competition on America's medium- and large-size cars. The Big Three American firms are locked in a game of continuous catchup to their foreign competitors, a price they have to pay for years of arrogant leadership.

The sad fact is that U.S. car manufacturers missed their chance to lead in the rapidly growing small-car market. Small cars became a new opportunity for car manufacturers in a mature market. A new opportunity, like a window, stays open for only a short time. As the *strategic window* opened on small cars, U.S. manufacturers needed to jump in wholeheartedly and make the necessary investments. By waiting too long, the strategic window started to close, and U.S. car manufacturers came in too late to achieve leadership. Timing is crucial.[20]

A company's *strategic fit* with the environment will inevitably erode because the relevant environment will almost always change faster than the company's 7–S's. As a result, we find General Motors operating in mid-1980s environment with the leftovers of 1960s strategy, structure, systems, style, staff, skills, and shared values. The company is an efficient machine, but not an effective machine. As Peter Drucker pointed out long ago, it is more important *to do the right thing* (being effective) than *to do things right* (being efficient). Of course, the excellent company excels at both.

Once an organization starts losing its market position through failing to respond to critical events in its environment, it has but a limited number of possible counterstrategies. Thus General Motors can adopt one or more of the following strategies in connection with the small-car market:

1. *Fight harder*. General Motors can lower its small-car prices and boost its advertising expenditures, in an attempt to hold on to or regain share in the small-car market. General Motors would lose money doing this but would buy time to make more fundamental changes.

2. ***Develop a better product line.*** General Motors can invest heavily in designing better small cars noted for performance, quality, styling, features, or some other combination of desired attributes.

3. ***Lower its costs of production.*** General Motors can develop better factory-assembly layouts, make greater use of robotic equipment, and design lower-cost inventory systems (such as the "just-in-time" system used in Japan). It can source lower cost components from overseas as well as move some of its production overseas in search of lower costs. It can form a partnership with Japanese auto makers for the joint production or distribution of certain car models.

4. ***Reduce its level of involvement.*** General Motors can decide to slowly reduce its investment in small-car manufacture and move its resources into more profitable industries.

Thus each company needs to continuously review the level and type of investment needed to stay viable in a given industry. It must do its best to monitor the changing environment so that it does not suddenly become an obsolete organization, an economic dinosaur.

Organizations, especially large ones, have much inertia. They are set up to be efficient machines, and it is difficult to change one part without adjusting everything else. Yet organizations can be changed through leadership, probably in advance of a crisis but certainly in the midst of a crisis. The key to organizational survival is the organization's ability toward self-modification as the environment changes and calls for new behaviors. Adaptable organizations monitor the environment and make changes through anticipatory planning so as to maintain a fairly current strategic fit with the evolving environment.

SUMMARY

Excellent companies know how to adapt and respond to a continuously changing marketplace through the practice of market-oriented strategic planning. They know how to develop and maintain a viable fit between their objectives, resources, and opportunities. They carry out the strategic planning process at the corporate level, business level, and product level. The objectives developed at the corporate level move down to lower levels where business strategic plans and marketing plans are prepared to guide the company's activities. Strategic planning involves repeated cycles of planning, implementation, and control.

Corporate strategic planning involves four planning activities. The first is developing a clear sense of the company's mission in terms of its industry scope, customer segment scope, vertical scope, and geographical scope. A well-developed mission statement provides employees with a shared sense of direction, opportunity, significance, and achievement.

The second activity calls for identifying the company's strategic business units (SBUs). A business is best defined by its customer groups, customer needs, and technologies. SBUs are business units that can benefit from separate planning, face specific competitors, and be managed as profit centers.

The third activity calls for allocating resources to the various SBUs based on their industry attractiveness and company competitive strength. Several portfolio models, including those by the Boston Consulting Group and General Electric, are available to help determine which SBUs should be built, maintained, harvested, or divested.

The fourth activity calls for expanding present businesses and developing new ones to fill the strategic planning gap. The company can identify opportunities by considering intensive growth (market penetration, market development and product development); integrative growth (backward, forward, and horizontal integration); and diversification growth (concentric, horizontal, and conglomerate diversification).

Each SBU conducts its own business strategic planning, which consists of eight steps: defining the business's mission, analyzing the external environment, analyzing the internal environment, choosing business objectives and goals, developing business strategies, preparing program plans, implementing program plans, and gathering feedback and exercising control. All of these steps keep the SBU close to its environment and alert to new opportunities and problems. Furthermore, the SBU strategic plan provides the context for preparing market plans for specific products and services, which we will examine in the next chapter.

■ QUESTIONS

1. Define the competitive domain for Quaker Oats by discussing each of the four statements of scope for the company.

2. Joint venturing has become an increasingly popular method used by corporate strategists for competing in selected markets. What strategic motivations are behind the formation of joint ventures? Cite two examples of joint ventures to illustrate these motivations.

3. Portfolio models can be helpful to managers seeking to know whether the objective for an SBU should be to build, hold, harvest, or divest. However, research has shown that SBU managers tend to invest more than one might expect on the basis of the use of such models. What could account for this deviation from these prescriptive decision models?

4. Conduct a SWOT (strengths/weaknesses, opportunities/threats) analysis for Apple Computer.

5. Parker Bros., a marketer of traditional board games for adolescents, is concerned about the effect of the video-game market growth on the sale of its product line. How might the company's mission statement affect its response to such an environmental threat, and what counterstrategy might the company use to respond to this critical environmental change?

6. A local high school has operated a night school program with only marginal success for several years. Due to a recent tax referendum, the school board has decided it must either significantly increase night school enrollments or cancel the entire program. Suggest a statement of purpose for the night school program and a hierarchy of objectives based on the intention to increase enrollments.

7. An industrial-equipment company consists of the five strategic business units (SBUs) shown in the next column. Using the Boston Consulting Group portfolio analysis, determine whether the company is in a healthy condition. What future strategies should it consider?

SBU	Dollar Sales (in Millions)	Number of Competitors	Dollar Sales of the Top 3 (in Millions)	Market-Growth Rate
A	.5	8	.7, .7, .5	15%
B	1.6	22	1.6, 1.6, 1.0	18%
C	1.8	14	1.8, 1.2, 1.0	7%
D	3.2	5	3.2, .8, .7	4%
E	.5	10	2.5, 1.8, 1.7	4%

8. What is the major distinctive competence of (a) Sears; (b) Polaroid Company; (c) Procter & Gamble; (d) Ford Foundation?

9. "With more than 80 percent of the market already in its grasp, Campbell Soup Co. really doesn't need to increase its share of the $1.2 billion of condensed soup sold annually in food stores. What the company does need is to make folks hungrier for soup." What intensive-growth strategy is being pursued, and how might the company accomplish this objective?

10. An automotive-parts manufacturer produces three products: mufflers, filters, and silencers. The company is seeking new growth opportunities. Develop a product-market matrix showing some potential expansion opportunities for this manufacturer.

11. After decades as a marketer of personal-care products to men, Gillette, in the 1980s, began to move into the women's personal-care market with such products as Silkience hair products and Apri skin products. Describe Gillette's strategy, using Table 2-3 (Major Classes of Growth Opportunities) and Figure 2-7 (Intensive-Growth Strategies).

12. What kind of diversification-growth strategy is illustrated by (a) General Foods' acquisition of Burger Chef, a fast-food service chain; (b) Philip Morris's acquisition of Miller Brewing Company; (c) Mobil Oil's acquisition of Montgomery Ward?

■ FOOTNOTES

1 See "Goodyear: Will Staying No. 1 in Tires Pump Up Profits?" *Business Week*, July 12, 1982, pp. 85–88.

2 See "Michelin: Spinning Its Wheels in the Competitive U.S. Market," *Business Week*, December 1, 1980, pp. 119–24.

3 See "Uniroyal: Narrowing Choices As It Clings to the Tire Business," *Business Week*, June 11, 1979, pp. 74–76.

4 See "The Niche Pickers at Armstrong Rubber," *Fortune*, September 6, 1982, pp. 100–104.

5 Steve Harrell, in a speech at the Plenary Session of American Marketing Association's Educators' Meeting, Chicago, August 5, 1980.

6 Two points need to be made. First, these distinctions are not limited to corporations. Most organizations, including partnerships and nonprofit organizations, have three levels. There is a command center or group (headquarters), two or more businesses, and two or more products within each business. For example, a law firm may do corporate and personal work (two businesses) and, within corporate, handle franchising and antitrust work (two product lines). Second, large corporations may even have more organizational levels, such as groups, sectors, and divisions, all of which do planning. However, the most basic types of planning are done at the corporate, business, and product/market levels.

7 Currently, many companies are shrinking their corporate planning staffs and shifting strategic planning responsibilities to their operating division managers. Planning works best when it is done by the line people who have to carry out the plans, not by corporate planners; and the line people have picked up a lot of training in strategic planning in the last decade. See "The New Breed of Strategic Planner," *Business Week*, September 17, 1984.

8 See Peter F. Drucker, *Management: Tasks, Responsibilities and Practices* (New York: Harper & Row, 1973), Chap. 7.

9 See "The Hollow Corporation," *Business Week*, March 3, 1986, pp. 57–59.

10 Theodore Levitt, "Marketing Myopia," *Harvard Business Review*, July–August 1960, pp. 45–56.

11 See "Holiday Inns: Refining Its Focus to Food, Lodging and More Casinos," *Business Week*, July 21, 1980, pp. 100–104.

12 Derek Abell, *Defining the Business: The Starting Point of Strategic Planning* (Englewood Cliffs, N.J.: Prentice-Hall, 1980), Chap. 3.

13 See Derek Abell, *Strategic Market Planning: Problems and Analytical Perspectives* (Englewood Cliffs, N.J.: Prentice-Hall, 1979), Chaps. 4 and 5.

14 A hard decision must be made between harvesting and divesting a business. Harvesting a business will strip it of its long-run value, in which case it will be hard to find a buyer. Divesting, on the other hand, is facilitated by maintaining a business in a fit condition in order to attract a buyer.

15 See Peter Patel and Michael Younger, "A Frame of Reference for Strategy Development," *Long Range Planning*, April 1978, pp. 6–12; and S. J. Q. Robinson et al., "The Directional Policy Matrix—Tool for Strategic Planning," *Long Range Planning*, June 1978, pp. 8–15. A brief description of both models is found in Day, *Analysis for Strategic Marketing Decisions*, pp. 211–14.

16 Igor Ansoff, "Strategies for Diversification," *Harvard Business Review*, September–October 1957, pp. 113–24. The same matrix can be expanded into nine cells by adding modified products and modified markets. See S. C. Johnson and Conrad Jones, "How to Organize for New Products," *Harvard Business Review*, May–June 1957, pp. 49–62.

17 See Michael E. Porter, *Competitive Strategy: Techniques for Analyzing Industries and Competitors* (New York: Free Press, 1980), Chap. 2.

18 See Thomas J. Peters and Robert H. Waterman, Jr., *In Search of Excellence: Lessons from America's Best-Run Companies* (New York: Harper & Row, 1982), pp. 9–12. The same framework is used in Richard Tanner Pascale and Anthony G. Athos, *The Art of Japanese Management: Applications for American Executives* (New York: Simon & Schuster, 1981).

19 See Terrence E. Deal and Allan A. Kennedy, *Corporate Cultures: The Rites and Rituals of Corporate Life* (Reading, Mass.: Addison-Wesley, 1982); "Corporate Culture," *Business Week*, October 27, 1980, pp. 148–60; and Stanley M. Davis, *Managing Corporate Culture* (Cambridge, Mass.: Ballinger Publishing Co., 1984).

20 See Derek F. Abell, "Strategic Windows," *Journal of Marketing*, July 1978, pp. 21–26.

3

The Marketing Management Process and Marketing Planning

Plans are nothing; planning is everything.

Dwight D. Eisenhower

We saw in Chapters 1 and 2 that the *marketing concept* and *strategic planning* form the principal basis for managing the modern company in highly competitive markets. We saw that *corporate headquarters* has to evaluate its strategic business units continuously and assign appropriate objectives and funds to each. We saw that each *strategic business unit* in turn must carefully monitor its external and internal environments and develop a business strategic plan. Since each strategic business unit typically handles a number of products destined to a number of market segments, it must prepare marketing plans for each.

Marketing plans differ from *business strategic plans* in focusing more narrowly on a product/market and fleshing out the detailed marketing strategies and programs for achieving the product's objectives in that market. *The marketing plan is the central instrument for directing and coordinating the marketing effort.* Companies that want to improve their marketing effectiveness must learn how to create and implement sound marketing plans.

Our discussion of marketing planning will provide the reader with an overall framework for grasping the essentials of marketing management thinking. This chapter will answer three questions:

■ What are the major steps in the marketing management process?
■ What are the major components found in marketing plans?
■ What are the theoretical underpinnings that spell out how marketing efforts of various kind affect the company's sales and profits?

After this overview of marketing management and planning, we will examine more thoroughly in the subsequent chapters the steps involved in analyzing, planning, implementing, and controlling the marketing process.

65

THE MARKETING MANAGEMENT PROCESS

The relationship between the marketing departments in the various business units and the strategic planning department is shown in Figure 3-1. Each marketing department supplies information and recommendations (Step 1) to the strategic planning department for the latter's analysis and evaluation (Step 2). The strategic planning department then negotiates goals with each business unit (Step 3). Each business unit's marketing department then formulates marketing plans based on these goals (Step 4) and carries them out (Step 5). The results are evaluated by the strategic planning department, and the process recycles.

Thus each business unit relies on marketing as the main system for monitoring opportunities and developing marketing plans for achieving that business's objectives. In fact, the first step in business planning is the marketing step, for this defines the target market and reasonable sales goals and therefore the resources needed to achieve these goals. The role of the finance, purchasing, manufacturing, physical distribution, and personnel departments is to make sure that the proposed marketing plan can be supported with enough money, materials, machines, and manpower.

To carry out their responsibilities, marketing managers go through a process called the marketing management process. We define it as follows:

> The *marketing management process* consists of analyzing marketing opportunities, researching and selecting target markets, designing marketing strategies, planning marketing programs, and organizing, implementing, and controlling the marketing effort.

These steps are listed in Figure 3-2, along with the chapters in this book that will describe each step in detail. In this section, we will present an overview of these steps in the marketing management process. The steps will be illustrated in connection with the following situation:

Zeus, Inc. (name disguised) is a Fortune 500 company that operates in several industries, including chemicals, energy, typewriters, and some consumer goods. Each area is organized as an SBU. Corporate management is considering what to do with its Atlas typewriter division. At present, Atlas produces standard office electric typewriters that are comparable to the highly popular IBM Selectric typewriters but sell for less. The market for standard electric typewriters is showing slow growth, and this company's brand is dwarfed by the leader. On a growth-share matrix, this business would be called a dog. Zeus's corporate management wants Atlas's marketing group to produce a strong plan for this product line or else face being dropped as a division. Marketing management has to come up with a convincing marketing plan, sell corporate management on the plan, and then implement and control it.

Analyzing Market Opportunities

The first task facing Atlas's marketing management is to analyze the long-run opportunities in this market for improving its performance as a business division of Zeus, Inc. These managers recognize the abundance of opportunities in the burgeoning business-office-equipment field. The *office of the future* is a major investment frontier in the coming decades, just as the factory was the frontier in the past (the new robotic factory is, of course, another frontier). The U.S. economy is increasingly becoming a service economy, and there are more office workers than factory workers. Yet offices are often poorly organized in terms of such elementary tasks as typing, filing, storing, and transmitting information, especially in terms of the latest available technologies. Many manufacturers are active in this market and are seeking to provide integrated systems of typewriters,

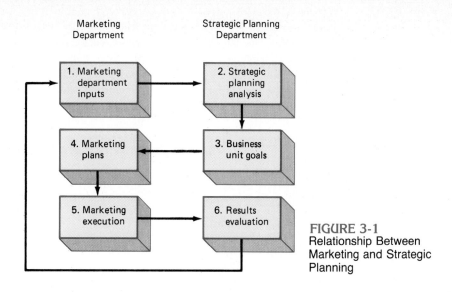

FIGURE 3-1
Relationship Between
Marketing and Strategic
Planning

microcomputers, copying and duplicating machines, facsimile transmission machines, electronic message systems, and the like. Among them are IBM, Xerox, Olivetti, and several Japanese companies. They are all engaged in developing office hardware and software that will increase office productivity, which is the chief buying motive of office-equipment purchasing agents. Xerox, in fact, sees itself not as a copying-machine company but as an office-productivity-improvement company.

Atlas's marketing management's long-run goal is to become a complete office equipment manufacturer. At the present time, however, it must come up with a plan to improve its typewriter product line. Even within typewriters, there are many opportunities. Atlas, for example, can scale down its office typewriter to a version for the home market and advertise it as an ''office quality'' home typewriter. But even larger opportunities lie in incorporating certain technological advances. Just as typing productivity increased greatly in the past when typewriters evolved from manual machines to electric machines and then to electric machines with automatic correction features, they are now evolving further. Atlas could design an electronic or ''smart'' typewriter, one of the hottest new products

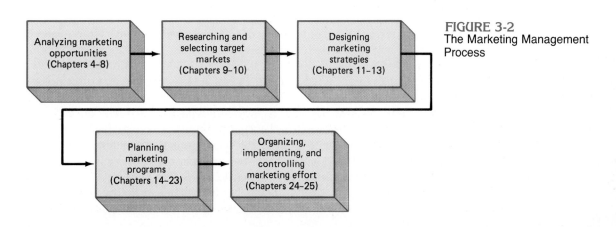

FIGURE 3-2
The Marketing Management
Process

in the office-equipment field. An electronic typewriter has only twenty-four moving parts compared with the roughly one thousand levers, springs, gears, and screws inside an electric typewriter; offers more characters; has a memory to carry the last few lines typed; can make automatic corrections; does not jam; and has a number of other useful features. Electronic typewriters are priced from several hundred to several thousand dollars and now include such entries as Smith Corona's Typetronic, Royal's 5010, Olivetti's ET121, and IBM's electronic Selectrics. Atlas can also consider designing a word processor, which would have more memory and text-editing capability than an electronic typewriter and sell for a few thousand dollars. Or Atlas can develop a whole computer work station like IBM's Displaywriter system that performs a large number of functions. Ultimately, Atlas can work on voice-activated typewriters, which only require oral dictation.

To identify and evaluate its opportunities, Atlas needs to build and operate a reliable marketing information system (Chapter 4). Marketing research is an indispensable ingredient of the modern marketing concept, in that companies can serve their customer markets well only by researching their needs and wants, their locations, their buying practices, and so on. There are different degrees of formal research that can be carried on by Atlas. At the very least, Atlas needs a good internal accounting system that speedily and accurately reports current sales by typewriter model, customer, industry and size, customer location, salesperson, and channels of distribution. In addition, Atlas's executives should be collecting continuous market intelligence on customers, competitors, dealers, and so on. The marketing people should conduct formal research by looking up information in secondary sources, running focus groups, and conducting telephone, mail, and personal surveys. If the collected data are well analyzed using advanced statistical methods and models, the company will probably gain useful information on how sales are affected by various marketing forces.

The purpose of Atlas's research is to gather significant and continuous information about Atlas's relevant marketing environment (Chapter 5). The marketing environment consists of a microenvironment and a macroenvironment. The company's *microenvironment* consists of all the actors who help or affect the company's ability to produce and sell typewriters, namely, suppliers, marketing intermediaries, customers, competitors, and publics of various sorts. Such questions arise as: What do customers want and look at in buying typewriters? What channels of distribution are growing and shrinking? Which suppliers are most efficient at making components? What are competitors doing?

Atlas's management also must stay on top of broad trends in the *macroenvironment*, namely, demographic, economic, physical, technological, political/legal, and social/cultural developments. It would be myopic to confine attention to the microenvironment and ignore larger changing forces in the society. Such questions arise as: What areas of the country are growing and shrinking? What is the economic outlook, and how will it affect sales of typewriters and the types purchased? What new technologies can be applied to improve typewriter efficiency? The large-scale forces can have a profound effect on Atlas's market.

To the extent that Atlas considers manufacturing a typewriter for the home, it needs to understand *consumer markets* and how they function (Chapter 6). It needs to know: How many households plan to buy new typewriters? Who buys and why do they buy? What are they looking for in the way of features and prices? Where do they shop? What are their images of existing competitors? What is the potential influence of price, advertising, sales promotion, personal selling, and so forth, on consumer brand choice decisions?

Atlas's main markets are *organizational buyers*, including professional firms, large corporations, government agencies, and so on (Chapter 7). Large organizations are staffed with professional purchasing agents, who are skilled at evaluating equipment and value.

Major equipment decisions are also made by buying committees consisting of different company personnel with different objectives and different degrees of influence on the final vendor decision. Selling to organizations usually involves personal selling through a sales force that is well trained to present the product and show how it can meet the customer's needs. Atlas needs to gain a full understanding of how organizational buyers buy.

Atlas must also pay close attention to identifying and monitoring its competitors (Chapter 8). Atlas can expect such surprise moves from its competitors as sudden price cuts, improved products, and new selling and promotion methods, all of which might cut into its market share. Atlas must anticipate its competitors' possible moves and know how to react quickly and decisively. Atlas may want to initiate some surprise moves of its own, in which case it needs to anticipate how its competitors will respond. The key lies in developing and maintaining a well-thought-out, up-to-date competitive intelligence system.

Researching and Selecting Target Markets

Now the firm is ready to research and select target markets. It needs to know how to measure the attractiveness of any given market (Chapter 9). This requires estimating the market's overall size, growth, and profitability. Marketers must understand the major techniques for measuring market potential and forecasting future demand. Each technique has certain advantages and limitations that must be carefully understood by marketers to avoid their misuse.

These market measures and forecasts become key inputs into deciding which markets and new products to focus on. Modern marketing practice calls for dividing the market into major market segments, evaluating them, selecting and targeting certain ones, and deciding on the company's positioning in each market (Chapter 10).

Market segmentation—the task of breaking the total market (which is often too large to serve) into segments that share common properties—can be done in a number of ways. Atlas can segment the typewriter market by *customer size* (large, medium, small), *customer buying criteria* (quality, price, service), *customer industry* (banks, professional firms, manufacturing companies), and so on.

Market segments can also be formed by crossing two or more variables. Figure 3-3 shows a segmentation of the typewriter market by two broad variables, namely, customer groups and customer needs (represented by different products). This particular framework is called a *product/market grid*. Marketing management can estimate, for each of the nine cells, the degree of market segment attractiveness and the company's degree of business

FIGURE 3-3
Product/Market Grid for Typewriters

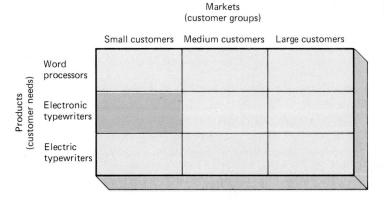

strength. Essentially Atlas seeks to determine which product/market cells, if any, best match the company's objectives and resources.

Suppose the most attractive segment for Atlas is the "small customer, electronic typewriter market" that is shaded in Figure 3-3. Even this market segment may be larger than the company can serve effectively, in which case *subsegmentation* can be undertaken. For example, Atlas might decide that its best opportunity lay in designing an inexpensive electronic typewriter whose features will have great appeal to small professional firms. In this way, Atlas will arrive at a clear idea of its *target market*.

Given that Atlas wants to pursue the "small customer, electronic typewriter market," it needs to develop a *positioning strategy* for that target market. Atlas needs to define how it wants to come across to buyers in relation to other competitors selling to that market. Should it be a "Cadillac" firm offering a superior product at a premium price with excellent service that is well advertised and aimed at the more affluent buyers? Or should Atlas build a simple low-price electronic typewriter aimed at the more price-conscious market?

Atlas needs to study carefully the positions taken by its major competitors in the same target market. Suppose companies position themselves in terms of their product quality and price. We can develop a *product-positioning map* (Figure 3-4) to describe the positions of four competitors currently selling to this market. The four competitors, A, B, C, and D, differ in sales volume as reflected by the sizes of the circles. Competitor A occupies the high-quality/high-price position in this market. Competitor B is perceived by the market to produce an average-quality product at an average price. Competitor C is known to sell a slightly below-average-quality product for a really low price. Competitor D is perceived as a "rip-off artist" because it sells a low-quality product for a high price.

Where should Atlas position itself in entering this market? It normally would not

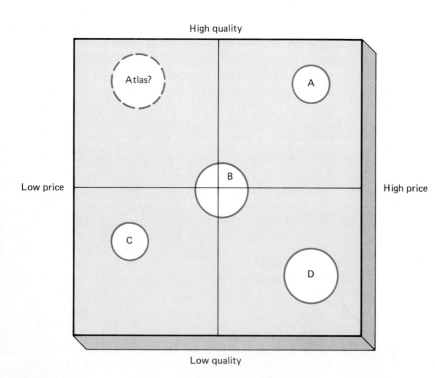

FIGURE 3-4
A Product-Positioning Map Showing Perceived Offers of Four Competitors and a Possible Position for Atlas

make sense to position itself against Competitor A because it would then have to fight a well-established company for the limited number of customers who want the best typewriter money can buy. However, if Competitor A is rendering poor service or underpromoting, Atlas may decide to attack A. Most marketing-oriented companies generally prefer not to attack an existing competitor (unless it is a weak one) but to find some important customer needs that competitors are not filling. For example, Atlas might give serious consideration to positioning itself in the high-quality/low-price quadrant (shown by the dotted circle). In this way, it would be "filling a hole" in the market. It must satisfy itself about three things, however. First, Atlas must find out from its engineers if they can build a high-quality typewriter that could sell at a low price and still make money. Second, Atlas must check whether there are a sufficient number of buyers who want a high-quality machine at a lower price. Formally yes, but price might contribute to snob appeal. Finally, Atlas must be able to convince buyers that its typewriter's quality and service are comparable to A's. Many buyers do not believe that lower-price units can be as good as higher-price units, so heavy promotional expenditures may be required.

The main point is that companies today must carefully choose not only their consumer targets but also their competitor targets. In an era of slow-growth markets, planning for the competitors is as important as planning for the consumers.

Designing Marketing Strategies

The marketing managers must refine the marketing strategy further and change it as time goes on. The marketing strategy spells out the game plan for attaining the business's objectives or product/market objectives. We define marketing strategy as follows:

> *Marketing strategy* **defines the broad principles by which the business unit expects to achieve its marketing objectives in a target market. It consists of basic decisions on total marketing expenditure, marketing mix, and marketing allocation.**

Marketing management must decide what level of *marketing expenditures* is necessary to achieve its marketing objectives. Companies typically establish their marketing budget at some conventional percentage of the sales goal. Companies entering a market try to learn what the marketing *budget-to-sales ratio* is for competitors. A particular company may spend more than the normal ratio in the hope of achieving a higher market share. Ultimately the company should analyze the marketing work required to attain a given sales volume or market share and then cost out this work; the result is the required marketing budget.

The company also has to decide how to divide the total marketing budget among the various tools in the *marketing mix*. Marketing mix is one of the key concepts in modern marketing theory.

> *Marketing mix* **is the set of marketing tools that the firm uses to pursue its marketing objectives in the target market.**

There are literally dozens of marketing-mix tools. McCarthy popularized a four-factor classification of these tools called the Four Ps: *product*, *price*, *place* (i.e., distribution), and *promotion*.[1] The particular marketing variables under each *P* are shown in Figure 3-5.

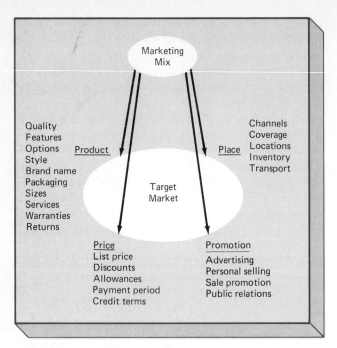

FIGURE 3-5
The Four Ps of the Marketing Mix

The company's marketing mix at time t for a particular product can be represented by the vector

$$(P_1, P_2, P_3, P_4)_t$$

where

P_1 = product quality, P_2 = price, P_3 = place, and P_4 = promotion.

If Atlas develops product quality at 1.2 (with 1.00 = average), prices it at $1,000, spends $30,000 a month on distribution and $20,000 a month on promotion, its marketing mix at time t is

$$(1.2, \$1,000, \$30,000, \$20,000)_t$$

One can see that a marketing mix is selected from a great number of possibilities. If product quality could take on one of two values, and product price is constrained to lie between $500 and $1,500 (to the nearest $100), and distribution and advertising expenditures are constrained to lie between $10,000 and $50,000 (to the nearest $10,000), then 550 (2 × 11 × 5 × 5) marketing-mix combinations are possible.

To complicate matters further, marketing-mix decisions must be made for both the channels and the final consumers. Figure 3-6 shows the company preparing an *offer mix* of products, services, and prices, and utilizing a *promotion mix* of sales promotion, advertising, sales force, public relations, direct mail, and telemarketing to reach the distribution channels and the final customers.

Not all marketing-mix variables can be adjusted in the short run. They vary in their adjustability. Typically, the firm can change its price, sales-force size, and advertising expenditures in the short run. It can only develop new products and modify its marketing

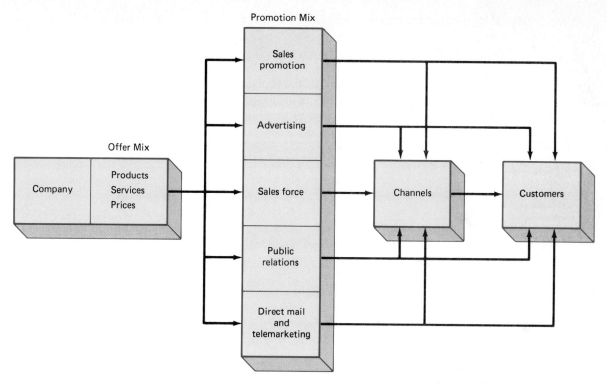

FIGURE 3-6
Marketing-Mix Strategy

channels in the long run. Thus the firm typically makes fewer period-to-period marketing-mix changes in the short run than the number of marketing-mix variables suggest.

Finally, marketers must decide on the *allocation* of the marketing dollars to the various products, channels, promotion media, and sales areas. How many dollars should support Atlas's electric versus electronic typewriters? Direct versus distributor sales? Direct mail advertising versus trade magazine advertising? East Coast markets versus West Coast markets? We can represent a distinct allocation in the following way: Suppose management sets product quality at 1.2, price at $1,000, a monthly distribution budget of $5,000, and a monthly advertising budget of $10,000 for product i selling to customer-type j in area k at time t. This is represented by the vector

$$(1.2, \$1,000, \$5,000, \$10,000)_{i,j,k,t}$$

To make these strategic allocations, marketing managers use the notion of *sales-response functions* (see p. 85) that show how sales would be affected by the amount of dollars put in each possible application.

After a product is launched under its initial marketing strategy, changes in strategy will be called for. Strategy will vary according to whether the firm plays the role of market leader, challenger, follower, or nicher (Chapter 11). Strategy will also have to be modified as the product passes through the major stages of the product/market life cycle, namely, introduction, growth, maturity, and decline (Chapter 12). Finally, strategy will have to take into account changing global market opportunities and challenges (Chapter 13).

**Planning
Marketing
Programs**

Marketers must not only formulate the broad strategies by which the business hopes to achieve its marketing objectives but also plan the supporting marketing-mix programs. Many well-conceived strategies fail when it comes to the development of specific marketing-mix tactics.

The detailed development of marketing-mix programs is best shown in the case of developing new products and services (Chapter 14). The new-product development process is a road strewn with land mines and booby traps. Too many products never come out of the laboratory, and of those that do, many fail in the marketplace, causing great expense to the company and a loss to society. The art of new-product development calls for organizing this process effectively and using distinct decision tools and controls at each stage of the process. Atlas, in designing a new electronic typewriter, will have to pay close attention to the various pitfalls involved in developing a successful new product.

The most basic marketing tool is *product*, which stands for the firm's tangible offer to the market, including the product features, packaging, branding, and servicing policies (Chapter 15). Thus Atlas manages a product line of typewriters that differ in features, quality, styling, and packaging. Atlas also provides various services, such as delivery, repair, and training (Chapter 16).

Another important marketing-decision tool is *price*, namely, the amount of money that customers have to pay for the product (Chapter 17). Atlas has to decide on wholesale and retail prices, discounts, allowances, and credit terms. Its price should be commensurate with the perceived value of the offer, or else buyers will turn to competitors in choosing their products.

Place stands for the various activities the company undertakes to make the product easily accessible and available to target consumers (Chapters 18 and 19). Atlas must identify, recruit, and link various middlemen and marketing facilitators so that its products and services are efficiently supplied to the target market. It must understand the various types of retailers, wholesalers, and physical distribution firms and how they make their decisions.

Promotion stands for the various activities the company undertakes to communicate its products' merits and to persuade target customers to buy them (Chapters 20–23). Thus Atlas has to buy advertising, set up sales promotions, arrange publicity, and dispatch sales people to promote its products.

**Organizing,
Implementing,
and Controlling
the Marketing
Effort**

The final step in the marketing management process is organizing the marketing resources and implementing and controlling the marketing plan. A plan is nothing "unless it degenerates into work."[2] Therefore the company must design a marketing organization that is capable of *implementing* the marketing plan (Chapter 24). In a small company, one person might carry out all of the marketing tasks: marketing research, selling, advertising, customer servicing, and so on. In large companies, several marketing specialists will be found. Thus Atlas has sales people, sales managers, marketing researchers, advertising personnel, product and brand managers, market-segment managers, and customer-service personnel.

Marketing organizations are typically headed by a marketing vice-president, who performs two tasks. The first is to coordinate the work of all the marketing personnel. Atlas's marketing vice-president must make sure, for example, that the advertising manager works closely with the sales-force manager so that the sales force is ready to handle inquiries generated by ads that are placed by the advertising department.

The marketing vice-president's other task is to work closely with the vice-presidents of finance, manufacturing, research and development, purchasing, and personnel to coordi-

Great Marketers

LEE IACOCCA

A **Great Salesman,** who convinced the United States Government to guarantee loans to save Chrysler, and who proved thereafter that he could inspire customers and employees to believe in the quality and future of Chrysler.

LESLIE WEXNER

A **Great Clothing Retailer,** who understood the advantages of focusing stores and services to serve distinct sets of customers as the key to satisfying their needs.

J.W. MARRIOT, JR.

A **Great Hospitality Services Marketer,** who showed that by treating both employees and guests with the same total dedication to satisfy their needs that he could build and sustain a great hotel chain.

CHARLES LAZARUS

A **Great Innovative Retailer,** who recognized the value of superspecialty retailing by launching Toys "R" Us to offer consumers broad and deep assortments in this category of shopping.

DAVID PACKARD

A **Great High Technology Marketer,** who worked hard to combine the best in research and development with marketing, who recognized that good marketing goes beyond the confines of the marketing department to involve the whole company.

FRANK PERDUE

A **Great Quality Marketer,** who took an ordinary unbranded class of product, chickens, and showed that it could be bred to exhibit such consistent quality that people would be willing to pay a premium for branded chicken.

AUGUST A. BUSCH III

A **Great Consumer Packaged Goods Marketer,** who consistently emphasized the importance of product quality and innovation, as well as distribution and advertising efficiency as the keys to marketing success in a highly competitive industry, with the result that Anhauser-Busch has led the worldwide brewing industry in brewing volume and sales since 1957.

FRANK "BUCK" RODGERS

A **Great Professional Marketer,** who as Vice President of Marketing at IBM set the highest standards for professional marketing and inspired others always to put the customer "first."

EDWIN LAND

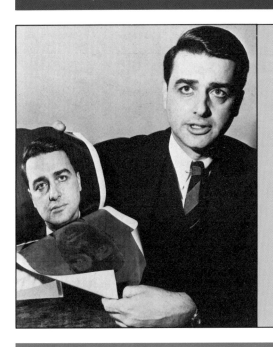

A **Great Innovator,** who carried out his conviction that instant photography is possible created the Polaroid Company. His inventions enabled photographers to see and enjoy results a moment after shooting and reshoot a scene which might otherwise be lost forever.

DAVID OGILVY

A **Great Advertising Genius,** who created memorable advertising copy and constantly researched and wrote about the principles of effective advertising.

A **Great Financial Services Discounter,** who applied the principles of high volume/low margin operations to the buying and selling of stock.

A **Great Direct Marketer,** who created The Sharper Image catalog devoted to high quality innovative goods and later opened stores to carry these same goods into major cities.

CALVIN KLEIN

A **Great Signature Marketer,** who designed his own line of clothing and licensed his name to other producers of high quality merchandise, making his name known and respected around the world.

RAY KROC

A **Great Fast-Food Retailer,** who grasped the advantages of food service standardization and convenience and applied franchising principles to create McDonald's, known around the world for servicing customers with quality, cleanliness, service, and value.

JAN CARLZON

A **Great Transportation Services Marketer,** who took a floundering airline and by choosing and focusing on a clear target market, researching its needs, and retraining the employees to think "customer," turned SAS into one of the best and most profitable airlines in Europe.

DANIEL YANKELOVICH

A **Great Marketing Researcher,** who created new ways to research customers, markets and broad social trends, and who has offered rich insights into the direction of American society.

nate company efforts to satisfy customers. Thus if Atlas's marketing people advertise its new electronic typewriter as a quality product, but R&D does not design a quality product or manufacturing fails to manufacture it carefully, then marketing will not deliver on its promise. The marketing vice-president's job is to make sure that all the company departments collaborate to fulfill the company's marketing promise to the customers.

The marketing department's effectiveness depends not only on how it is structured but also on how well its personnel are selected, trained, directed, motivated, and evaluated. There is a vast difference in the performance of a "turned-on" versus "turned-off" marketing group. The marketing personnel need constructive feedback on their marketing performance. Managers must meet with their subordinates periodically to review their performance, praise their strengths, point out their weaknesses, and suggest ways to correct them.

There are likely to be many surprises as marketing plans are implemented by the marketing organization. The company needs control procedures to make sure that the marketing objectives will be achieved (Chapter 25). Various managers will have to exercise control responsibilities in addition to their analysis, planning, and implementing responsibilities. Three types of marketing control can be distinguished: annual-plan control, profitability control, and strategic control.

Annual-plan control is the task of making sure that the company is achieving the sales, profits, and other goals that it established in its annual plan. The task breaks into four steps. First, management must state well-defined goals in the annual plan for each month, quarter, or other period during the year. Second, management must have ways to measure its ongoing performance in the marketplace. Third, management must determine the underlying causes of any serious gaps in performance. Fourth, management must decide on the best corrective action to take to close the gaps between goals and performance. It may call for improving the ways in which the plan is being implemented or even changing the goals.

Companies need to analyze periodically the actual *profitability* of their various products, customer groups, trade channels, and order sizes. This is not a simple task. A company's accounting system is seldom designed to report the real profitability of different marketing entities and activities. To measure the profit on different typewriter models, for example, Atlas's accountants have to estimate how much time the sales force spends promoting each model, how much advertising goes into each model, and so on. *Marketing profitability analysis* is the tool used to measure the profitability of different marketing activities. *Marketing efficiency studies* also need to be undertaken to study how various marketing activities could be carried on more efficiently.

From time to time, Atlas must stand back and critically reexamine its overall marketing game plan and decide whether it continues to make good *strategic* sense. Marketing is one of the major areas where rapid obsolescence of objectives, policies, strategies, and programs is a constant possibility. Giant companies such as Chrysler, International Harvester, Singer, and A&P all fell on hard times because they did not watch the changing marketplace and make the proper adaptations. Because of the rapid changes in the marketing environment, each company needs to reassess periodically its marketing effectiveness through a control instrument known as the *marketing audit*.

Figure 3-7 presents a grand summary of the marketing management process and the forces influencing the setting of company marketing strategy. The target customers stand in the center, and the company focuses its effort on serving and satisfying them. The company develops a marketing mix made up of the factors under its control, the four Ps—product, price, place, and promotion. To arrive at its marketing mix, the company

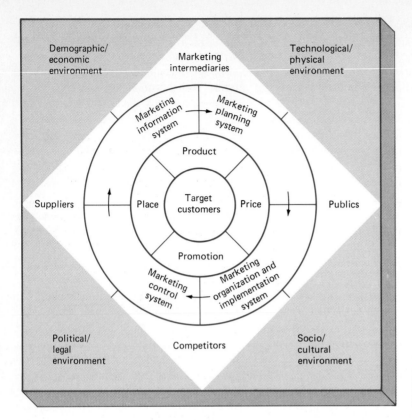

Demographic/economic environment

Technological/physical environment

Marketing intermediaries

Marketing information system

Marketing planning system

Product

Place — Target customers — Price

Suppliers

Publics

Promotion

Marketing control system

Marketing organization and implementation system

Political/legal environment

Competitors

Socio/cultural environment

FIGURE 3-7
Factors Influencing Company Marketing Strategy

manages four systems: a marketing information system, marketing planning system, marketing organizational system, and marketing control system. These systems are interrelated in that marketing information is needed to develop marketing plans, which in turn are implemented by the marketing organization, the results of which are reviewed and controlled.

Through these systems, the company monitors and adapts to the marketing environment. The company adapts to its microenvironment, consisting of marketing intermediaries, suppliers, competitors, and publics. And it adapts to the macroenvironment, consisting of demographic/economic forces, political/legal forces, technological/physical forces, and social/cultural forces. The company takes into account the actors and forces in the marketing environment in developing strategy and positioning an effective offer to the target market.

THE NATURE AND CONTENTS OF A MARKETING PLAN

We have just seen that one of the most important outputs of the marketing management process is the *marketing plan*. We may now ask, How does a marketing plan look?

Marketing plans will have several sections, varying with how much detail top management wants from its managers. Most marketing plans, particularly product and brand plans, will have the following sections: *executive summary, current marketing situation, opportunity and issue analysis, objectives, marketing strategy, action programs, projected profit-and-loss statement,* and *controls*. These sections and their purposes are listed in Table 3-1

TABLE 3-1   Contents of a Marketing Plan

Section	Purpose
I. Executive Summary	This presents an abbreviated overview of the proposed plan for quick management skimming.
II. Current Marketing Situation	This presents relevant background data on the market, product, competition, distribution, and macroenvironment.
III. Opportunity and Issue Analysis	This summarizes the main opportunities/threats, strengths/weaknesses, and issues facing the product that the plan must deal with.
IV. Objectives	This defines the goals the plan wants to reach in the areas of sales volume, market share, and profit.
V. Marketing Strategy	This presents the broad marketing approach that will be used to meet the plan's objectives.
VI. Action Programs	This answers **What** will be done? **Who** will do it? **When** will it be done? and **How much** will it cost?
VII. Projected Profit-and-Loss Statement	This summarizes the expected financial payoff from the plan.
VIII. Controls	This tells how the plan will be monitored.

and discussed in the following paragraphs. The plan sections will be illustrated with the following case:[3]

Zenith Corporation is a major producer of electronic consumer products, including television receivers, radios, and stereo equipment. Each product line is the responsibility of a product manager, who must prepare a long-range plan and an annual plan that would meet the financial objectives of the Zenith Corporation.

Currently Jane Melody is the product manager of Zenith's line of modular stereo systems, called the Allegro line. Each system consists of an AM–FM tuner/amplifier plus phonograph plus tape deck and separate speakers. Zenith offers thirteen different models that sell in the $150–$400 range. A modular stereo system differs on the one hand from stereo consoles, in which all of the components are built into one cabinet, and on the other hand from audio component systems, where consumers select unrelated but compatible components to make up the systems they want. Zenith also produces a line of stereo console units, but the console market is in a state of decline as consumers switch to smaller sound systems. Zenith does not produce audio components but has considered it from time to time. Zenith's main goal is to increase its market share and profitability in the modular-stereo-system market. As product manager, Jane Melody has to prepare a marketing plan to improve the performance of the Allegro line.

Executive Summary   The planning document should open with a short summary of the main goals and recommendations to be found in the body of the plan. Here is an abbreviated example:

The 1988 Allegro marketing plan seeks to generate a significant increase in company sales and profits over the preceding year. The profit target is set at $1.8 million. The sales-revenue target is set at $18 million, which represents a planned 9 percent sales gain over last year. This increase is seen as attainable through improved pricing, advertising, and distribution effort. The required marketing budget will be $2,290,000, a 14 percent increase over last year. . . . [More details follow]

The executive summary permits higher management to quickly grasp the major thrust of the plan. A table of contents should follow the executive summary.

Current Marketing Situation

This section of the plan presents relevant background data on the market, product, competition, distribution, and macroenvironment.

Market Situation Here data are presented on the served market. The size and growth of the market (in units and/or dollars) are shown for several past years in total and by market and geographical segments. Data are also presented on customer needs, perceptions, and buying behavior trends.

> The modular stereo market accounts for approximately $400 million, or 20 percent of the home stereo market. Sales are expected to be stable or declining over the next few years. . . . The primary buyers are upscale people who want to listen to good music but do not want to invest in expensive component equipment. They want to buy a complete system produced by a name they can trust. They want a system with good sound and whose looks fit the decor primarily of dens or living rooms.

Product Situation Here the sales, prices, contribution margins, and net profits are shown for each major product in the line for several past years.

> Table 3-2 shows an example of how product data might be presented for the modular stereo line. Row 1 shows the total industry sales in units growing at 5 percent annually until 1987, when demand declined slightly. Row 2 shows Zenith's market share hovering around 3 percent, although it reached 4 percent in 1986. Row 3 shows the average price for an Allegro stereo rising about 10 percent a year except the last year, when it rose 4 percent. Row 4 shows variable costs—materials, labor, energy—rising each year. Row 5 shows that the gross contribution margin per unit—the difference between price (row 3) and unit variable cost (row 4)—rose the first few years and remained at $100 in the latest year. Rows 6 and 7 show sales volume in units and dollars, and row 8 shows the total gross contribution margin, which rose until the latest year, when it fell. Row 9 shows that overhead remained constant during 1984 and 1985 and increased to a high level during 1986 and 1987, due to an explosion of manufacturing capacity. Row 10 shows net contribution margin, that is, gross contribution margin less overhead. Rows 11, 12, and 13 show marketing expenditures on advertising and promotion, sales force and distribution, and marketing research. Finally, row 14 shows net operating profit after marketing expenses. The picture is one of increasing profits until 1987, when they fell to about one-third of the 1986 level. Clearly Zenith's product manager needs to find a strategy for 1988 that will once again restore healthy growth in sales and profits to the product line.

Competitive Situation Here the major competitors are identified and are described in terms of their size, goals, market share, product quality, marketing strategies, and any other characteristics that are appropriate to understanding their intentions and behavior.

> Zenith's major competitors in the modular stereo system market are Panasonic, Sony, Magnavox, General Electric, and Electrophonic. Each competitor has a specific strategy and niche in the market. Panasonic, for example, offers thirty-three models covering the whole price range, sells primarily in department stores and discount stores, is a heavy advertising spender, and so on. It is out to dominate the market through product proliferation and price discounting. . . . [Similar descriptions are prepared for each of the other competitors.]

TABLE 3-2
Historical Product Data

Variable	Columns	1984	1985	1986	1987
1. Industry sales—in units		2,000,000	2,100,000	2,205,000	2,200,000
2. Company market share		0.03	0.03	0.04	0.03
3. Average price per unit $		200	220	240	250
4. Variable cost per unit $		120	125	140	150
5. Gross contribution margin per unit $	$(3 - 4)$	80	95	100	100
6. Sales volume in units	(1×2)	60,000	63,000	88,200	66,000
7. Sales revenue $	(3×6)	12,000,000	13,860,000	21,168,000	16,500,000
8. Gross contribution margin $	(5×6)	4,800,000	5,985,000	8,820,000	6,600,000
9. Overhead $		2,000,000	2,000,000	3,500,000	3,500,000
10. Net contribution margin $	$(8 - 9)$	2,800,000	3,985,000	5,320,000	3,100,000
11. Advertising and promotion $		800,000	1,000,000	1,000,000	900,000
12. Sales force and distribution $		700,000	1,000,000	1,100,000	1,000,000
13. Marketing research $		100,000	120,000	150,000	100,000
14. Net operating profit $	$(10 - 11 - 12 - 13)$	1,200,000	1,865,000	3,070,000	1,100,000

Distribution Situation   This section presents data on the number of stereo units sold in each distribution channel and the changing importance of each channel. Changes are noted in the power of distributors and dealers as well as in the prices and trade terms necessary to motivate them.

> Modular stereo sets are sold through a variety of distribution channels: department stores, radio/ TV stores, appliance stores, discount stores, furniture stores, music stores, audio specialty stores, and mail order. Zenith sells 37 percent of its sets through appliance stores, 23 percent through radio/TV stores, 10 percent through furniture stores, 3 percent through department stores, and the remainder through other channels. Zenith dominates in channels that are declining in importance, while it is a weak competitor in the faster-growing channels, such as discount stores. Zenith gives about a 30 percent margin to its dealers, which is similar to what other competitors give.

Macroenvironment Situation   This section describes broad macroenvironment trends— demographic, economic, technological, political/legal, social/cultural—that bear on this product line's future.

> About 50 percent of U.S. households now have stereo equipment. As the market approaches saturation, effort must be turned to convincing consumers to upgrade their equipment. . . . The economy is expected to remain in a weak state, which means people will postpone consumer- durables purchases. . . . The Japanese have designed new and more compact audio systems that pose a challenge to conventional stereo systems.

Opportunity and Issue Analysis

On the basis of the data describing the current marketing situation, the product manager needs to identify the major *opportunities/threats*, *strengths/weaknesses*, and issues the company faces with this product over the term of the plan.

Opportunities/Threats Analysis (O/T Analysis)   Here the manager identifies the main opportunities and threats facing the business. Opportunities and threats refer to outside factors that can affect the future of the business. They are written so as to suggest some possible actions that might be taken. The manager should rank the opportunities and threats so that the more important ones receive special attention.

The main *opportunities* facing Zenith's Allegro line are:

- Consumers are showing increased interest in more compact modular stereo systems, and Zenith should consider designing one or more compact models.
- Two major national department store chains are willing to carry the Allegro line if we will give them extra advertising support.
- A major national discount chain is willing to carry the Allegro line if we will offer a special discount for higher volume.

The main *threats* facing Zenith's Allegro line are:

- An increasing number of consumers who choose modular stereo systems are buying them in mass-merchandise and discount stores, in which we have weak representation.
- An increasing number of upscale consumers are showing a preference for component systems, and we do not have an audio component line.
- Some of our competitors have introduced smaller speakers with good-quality sound, and consumers seem to favor smaller speakers.
- The federal government may pass a more stringent product-safety law, which would entail some product redesign work on our part.

Strengths/Weaknesses Analysis (S/W Analysis) The manager should also identify company strengths and weaknesses. Strengths and weaknesses are inside factors, in contrast with opportunities and threats, which are outside factors. Company strengths point to certain strategies the company might be successful in using, while company weaknesses point to certain things the company needs to correct.

The main *strengths* of Zenith's Allegro line are:

- Zenith's name has excellent brand awareness and an image of high quality.
- Dealers who sell the Allegro line are knowledgeable and well trained in selling.
- Zenith has an excellent service network, and consumers know they will get quick repair service if needed.

The main *weaknesses* of Zenith's Allegro line are:

- The sound quality of Allegro is not demonstrably better than the sound quality of competing sets, and yet sound quality can make a big difference in brand choice.
- Zenith is budgeting only 5 percent of its sales revenue for advertising and promotion, while some major competitors are spending at twice that level.
- Zenith's Allegro line is not clearly positioned compared with Magnavox (''quality'') and Sony (''innovation''). Zenith needs a unique selling proposition. The current advertising campaign is not particularly creative or exciting.
- Zenith's brand is priced higher relative to other brands without being supported by a real perceived difference in quality. The brand loses the price-conscious buyer. The pricing strategy should be reevaluated.

Issues Analysis In this section, the company uses the findings of the O/T and S/W analyses to define the main issues that must be addressed in the plan. Decisions on these issues will lead to the subsequent setting of objectives, strategies, and tactics.

Zenith must consider the following basic *issues* with respect to the Allegro line:

- Should Zenith stay in the stereo-equipment business? Can it compete effectively? Or should it harvest or divest this product line?
- If Zenith stays in, should it continue with its present products, channels of distribution, and price and promotion policies, just making further refinements where possible?
- Or should Zenith switch to high-growth channels (such as discount stores), and can it do this and yet keep the loyalty of its traditional channels?
- Should Zenith go into more-intensive advertising and promotion to match competitors' expenditures, and will this lead to sufficient increases in market share and profitability?
- Or should Zenith pour money into R&D to develop advanced features, sound, and styling?

Objectives

At this point, management knows the issues and is faced with making some basic decisions about the objectives. These objectives will guide the subsequent search for strategies and action programs.

Two types of objectives must be set: financial and marketing.

Financial Objectives

Every company seeks certain financial objectives. The owners will be looking for a certain long-run rate of return on investment and know the profits they would like to achieve in the current year.

Zenith's management wants each business unit to deliver a certain rate of profit and return on investment. Furthermore it wants the Allegro line to grow stronger. The product manager sets the following financial objectives for the Allegro line:

- Earn an average rate of return on investment over the next five years of 20 percent after taxes.
- Produce net profits of $1,800,000 in 1988.
- Produce a cash flow of $2,000,000 in 1988.

Marketing Objectives

The financial objectives must be converted into marketing objectives. For example, if the company wants to earn $1,800,000 profit, and its target profit margin is 10 percent on sales, then it must set a goal of $18 million in sales revenue. If the company sets an average price of $260, it must sell 69,230 units. If it expects total industry sales to reach 2.3 million units, that is a 3 percent market share. To maintain this market share, the company will have to set certain goals for consumer awareness, distribution coverage, and so on. Thus the *marketing objectives* might read:

- Achieve total sales revenue of $18,000,000 in 1988, which represents a 9 percent increase from last year.
- Therefore achieve a sales volume in units of 69,230, which represents an expected market share of 3 percent.
- Expand consumer awareness of the Allegro brand from 15 percent to 30 percent over the planning period.
- Expand the number of distribution outlets by 10 percent.
- Aim for an average realized price of $260.

The set of objectives should meet certain criteria. First, each objective should be stated in an unambiguous and measurable form with a stated time period for accomplishment. Second, the various objectives should be internally consistent. Third, the objectives should be stated hierarchically, if possible, with lower objectives being clearly derived from higher objectives. Fourth, the objectives should be attainable but sufficiently challenging to stimulate maximum effort.

Marketing Strategy

The manager now outlines the broad marketing strategy, or "game plan." In developing a marketing strategy, a manager faces a multitude of possible choices. Each objective can be achieved in a number of ways. For example, the objective *increase the sales revenue by 9 percent* can be achieved by increasing the average price on all units, increasing the overall sales volume, and/or selling more of the higher-price units. Each of these objectives can in turn be achieved in a number of ways. The *overall sales volume* can be increased by increasing market growth and/or increasing market share. In turn, *increased market growth* can come about by convincing people to own more stereo systems per household or to replace their old systems more frequently. By going down the path of each objective, the manager can identify the major strategy options facing the product line.

Strategy formulation calls for making basic choices among these strategy options. The manager can write up a basic strategy statement in verbal form, such as the following:

> Zenith's basic strategy for Allegro is to aim at the upscale family, with particular emphasis on the woman buyer. The product line will be expanded by adding lower-price and higher-price units. The average price of the line will be raised 4 percent. A new and intensified advertising campaign will be developed to increase the perceived reliability of our brand in the consumer's mind. We will schedule a strong sales promotion program to attract increased consumer and dealer attention to our line. We will expand distribution to cover department stores but will avoid discount stores. We will put more funds into restyling the Allegro line so that it projects an image of high-quality sound and reliability.

Alternatively, the strategy statement can be presented in list form covering the major marketing tools:

STRATEGY STATEMENT

Target market:	Upscale households, with particular emphasis on female buyer.
Position:	The best-sounding and most-reliable modular stereo system.
Product line:	Add one lower-price model and two higher-price models.
Price:	Price somewhat above competitive brands.
Distribution outlets:	Heavy in radio/TV stores and appliance stores; increased effort to penetrate department stores.
Sales force:	Expand by 10 percent and introduce a national account-management system.
Service:	Widely available and quick service.
Advertising:	Develop a new advertising campaign, directed at the target market, that supports the positioning strategy; emphasize higher-price units in the ads; increase the advertising budget by 20 percent.
Sales promotion:	Increase the sales promotion budget by 15 percent to develop a point-of-purchase display and to participate to a greater extent in dealer trade shows.
Research & development:	Increase expenditures by 25 percent to develop better styling of Allegro line.
Marketing research:	Increase expenditures by 10 percent to improve knowledge of consumer-choice process and to monitor competitor moves.

In developing the strategy, the manager needs to discuss it with others whose cooperation will make the difference between failure and success. The product manager will see the purchasing and manufacturing people to make sure they are able to buy enough material and produce enough units to meet the planned sales-volume levels, the sales manager to obtain the planned sales-force support, and the financial officer to make sure enough funds will be available.

Action Programs

The strategy statement represents the broad marketing thrusts that the manager will use to achieve the business objectives. Each element of the marketing strategy must now be elaborated to answer: *What* will be done? *When* will it be done? *Who* will do it? *How much* will it cost? Here is an example for the sales promotion program:

Zenith's sales promotion program will be divided into two parts, one directed at dealers and the other at consumers. The dealer promotion program will consist of:

April. Zenith will participate in the Consumer Electronics Trade Show in Chicago. John Smith, dealer promotion director, will make the arrangements. The expected cost is $14,000.

August. A sales contest will be conducted, which will award three Hawaiian vacations to the three dealers producing the greatest percentage increase in sales of Allegro units. The contest will be handled by John Smith at a planned cost of $13,000.

The consumer promotion program will consist of:

February. Zenith will advertise in the newspapers that a free Anne Murray record album will be given to everyone buying an Allegro unit this month. Ann Morris, consumer promotion director, will handle this project at a planned cost of $5,000.

September. A newspaper advertisement will announce that consumers who listen to an Allegro store demonstration in the second week of September will have their names entered in a sweepstakes, the grand prizes to be ten Allegros. Ann Morris will handle this project at a planned cost of $4,000.

Projected Profit-and-Loss Statement

The action plans allow the product manager to assemble a supporting budget that is essentially a projected profit-and-loss statement. On the revenue side, it shows the forecasted sales volume in units and the average realized price. On the expense side, it shows the cost of production, physical distribution, and marketing, broken down into finer categories. The difference is projected profit. Higher management will review the budget and approve or modify it. If the requested budget is too high, the product manager will have to make some cuts. Once approved, the budget is the basis for developing plans and schedules for material procurement, production scheduling, manpower recruitment, and marketing operations.

Controls

The last section of the plan outlines the controls that will be applied to monitor the plan's progress. Typically the goals and budget are spelled out for each month or quarter. Higher management can review the results each period and spot businesses that are not attaining their goals. Managers of lagging businesses must explain what is happening and the actions they are taking to improve plan fulfillment.

Some control sections include contingency plans. A contingency plan outlines the steps that management would implement for specific adverse developments that might occur, such as a price war or a strike. The purpose of contingency planning is to encourage managers to give prior thought to some difficulties that might lie ahead.

THE THEORY OF EFFECTIVE MARKETING-RESOURCE ALLOCATION

Having examined how actual marketing plans are constructed, we will now describe some important tools and concepts that managers can use to improve their marketing planning. Planning can now be done on microcomputers using tailored computer programs. At companies such as Quaker Oats and General Mills, brand managers develop and estimate the cost of different marketing strategies, using computer programs in searching for the best plan. These computer programs utilize simple sales-and-profit equations and indicate how sales and profits would respond to different marketing-mix expenditures. We will illustrate these concepts in the following paragraphs.

The Profit Equation

Every marketing-mix strategy will lead to a certain level of profit. The profit can be estimated through a profit equation.

Profits (Z) by definition are equal to the product's revenue (R) less its costs (C):

$$Z = R - C \qquad (3\text{-}1)$$

Revenue is equal to the product's net price (P') times its unit sales (Q):

$$R = P'Q \qquad (3\text{-}2)$$

But the product's net price (P') is equal to its list price (P) less any allowance per unit (k) representing freight allowances, commissions, and discounts:

$$P' = P - k \qquad (3\text{-}3)$$

The product's costs can be conveniently classified into unit variable nonmarketing costs (c), fixed costs (F), and marketing costs (M):

$$C = cQ + F + M \qquad (3\text{-}4)$$

Substituting equations (3-2), (3-3), and (3-4) into (3-1) and simplifying,

$$Z = [(P - k) - c]\, Q - F - M \qquad (3\text{-}5)$$

where:
  Z = total profits
  P = list price
  k = allowance per unit (such as freight allowances, commissions, discounts)
  c = production and distribution variable cost (such as labor costs, delivery costs)
  Q = number of units sold
  F = fixed costs (such as salaries, rent, electricity)
  M = discretionary marketing costs

The expression $[(P - k) - c]$ is the *gross contribution margin per unit*—the amount the company realizes on the average unit after deducting allowances and the variable costs of producing and distributing the average unit. The expression $[(P - k) - c]Q$ is the *gross contribution margin*—the net revenue available to cover the fixed costs, profits, and discretionary marketing expenditures.

The Sales Equation

In order to use the profit equation for planning purposes, the product manager needs to model the determinants of sales volume (Q). The relation of sales volume to its determinants is specified in a sales equation (also called the sales-response function):

$$Q = f(X_1, X_2, \ldots, X_n, Y_1, Y_2, \ldots, Y_m) \tag{3-6}$$

where:

$(X_1, X_2, \ldots, X_n)$ = sales variables under the control of the firm
$(Y_1, Y_2, \ldots, Y_m)$ = sales variables not under the control of the firm

Y variables include such things as the cost-of-living index and the size and income of the served market. As these variables change, so does the market's buying rate. The manager has no influence over the Y variables but needs to estimate them for use in forecasting. We will assume that the manager has estimated Y variables and their effect on sales volume, which is conveyed by

$$Q = f(X_1, X_2, \ldots, X_n/Y_1, Y_2, \ldots, Y_m) \tag{3-7}$$

which says that sales volume is a function of the X variables, for given levels of the Y variables.

The X variables are the variables that the manager can set to influence the sales level. The X variables include the list price (P); allowances (k); variable cost (c) (to the extent that high variable costs reflect improved product quality, delivery time, and customer service); and marketing expenditures (M). Thus sales, as a function of the manager's controllable variables, is described by

$$Q = f(P, k, c, M) \tag{3-8}$$

We can make one additional refinement. The marketing budget, M, can be spent in several ways, such as advertising (A), sales promotion (S), sales force (D), and marketing research (R).

The sales equation is now

$$Q = f(P, k, c, A, S, D, R) \tag{3-9}$$

where the elements in the parentheses represent the marketing mix.

Profit-Optimization Planning

Suppose the manager wants to find a marketing mix that will maximize profits in the coming year. This requires having some idea of how each element in the marketing mix will affect sales. We will use the term *sales-response function* to describe the relationship between sales volume and a particular element of the marketing mix. Specifically, *the sales-response function forecasts the likely sales volume during a specified time period associated with different possible levels of a marketing-mix element, holding constant the other marketing-mix elements*. It should not be thought of as describing a relationship over time between the two variables. To the extent that managers have a good intuition for the relevant sales-response functions, they are in a position to formulate more effective marketing plans.

What are the possible shapes of sales-response functions? Figure 3–8 shows several possibilities. Figure 3-8(a) shows the well-known relationship between price and sales volume, known as the law of demand. The relationship states that more sales will occur, other things being equal, at lower prices. The illustration shows a curvilinear relationship, although a linear relationship is also possible.

Figure 3–8(b) shows four possible functional relationships between sales volume and marketing expenditures. Marketing expenditure function (*A*) is the least plausible: It states that sales volume is not affected by the level of marketing expenditures. It would mean that the number of customers and their purchasing rates are not affected by sales calls, advertising, sales promotion, or marketing research. Marketing expenditure function (*B*) states that sales volume grows linearly with marketing expenditures. In the illustration, the intercept is 0, but this is inaccurate if some sales would take place even in the absence of marketing expenditures.

Marketing expenditure function (*C*) is a concave function showing sales volume increasing throughout at a decreasing rate. It is a plausible description of sales response to sales-force-size increases. The rationale is as follows: If a field sales force consisted of one sales representative, that representative would call on the best prospects, and the marginal rate of sales response would be highest. A second sales rep would call on the next best prospects, and the marginal rate of sales response would be somewhat less. Successively hired sales reps would call on successively less responsive prospects, resulting in a diminishing rate of sales increase.

Marketing expenditure function (*D*) is an S-shaped function showing sales volume initially increasing at an increasing rate and then increasing at a decreasing rate. It is a plausible description of sales response to increasing levels of advertising expenditure. The rationale is as follows: Small advertising budgets do not buy enough advertising to create more than minimal brand awareness. Larger budgets can produce high brand awareness, interest, and preference, all of which might lead to increased purchase response. Very large budgets, however, may not produce much additional response because the target market is already highly familiar with the brand.

The occurrence of eventually diminishing returns to increases in marketing expendi-

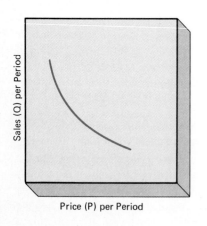

(a) Price function

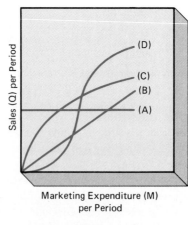

(b) Market expenditure functions

FIGURE 3-8
Sales-Response Functions

tures is plausible for the following reasons. First, there is an upper limit to the total potential demand for any particular product. The easier sales prospects buy almost immediately, leaving the more recalcitrant sales prospects. As the upper limit is approached, it becomes increasingly expensive to attract the remaining buyers. Second, as a company steps up its marketing effort, its competitors are likely to do the same, with the net result that each company experiences increasing sales resistance. And third, if sales were to increase at an increasing rate throughout, natural monopolies would result. A single firm would take over each industry. Yet we do not observe this happening.

How can marketing managers estimate the sales-response functions that apply to their business? Three methods are available. The first is the *statistical method*, where the manager gathers data on past sales and levels of marketing-mix variables and estimates the sales-response functions through statistical techniques. Several researchers have used this method with varying degrees of success, depending on the quantity and quality of available data and the stability of the underlying relationships.[4] The second is the *experimental method*, which calls for varying the marketing expenditure and mix levels in matched samples of geographical or other units and noting the resulting sales volume.[5] The experimental method produces the most reliable results but is not used extensively because of its complex requirements, high cost, and inordinate level of management resistance. The third is the *judgmental method*, where experts are asked to make intelligent guesses about the needed magnitudes. This method requires a careful selection of the experts and a defined procedure for gathering and combining their estimates, such as the Delphi method.[6] The judgmental method is often the only feasible one and can be quite useful. We believe that using the estimates of experts is better than forgoing formal analysis of profit optimization.

In estimating sales-response functions, some cautions have to be observed. The sales-response function assumes that other variables remain constant over the range of the function. Thus the company's price and competitors' prices are assumed to remain unchanged no matter what the company spends on marketing. Since this assumption is unrealistic, the sales-response function has to be modified to reflect competitors' probable responses. The sales-response function also assumes a certain level of company efficiency in spending marketing dollars. If the spending efficiency rises or falls, the sales-response function has to be modified. Also, the sales-response function has to be modified to reflect delayed impacts of expenditures on sales beyond one year. These and other characteristics of sales-response functions are spelled out in more detail elsewhere.[7]

Profit
Optimization

Once the sales-response functions are estimated, how are they used in profit optimization? Graphically, we introduce some further curves to find the point of optimal marketing expenditure. The analysis is shown in Figure 3-9. The sales-response function shown here is S-shaped, although the same analysis applies to any shape. First the manager subtracts all nonmarketing costs from the *sales-response function* to derive the *gross profit function*. Next, the marketing expenditure function is represented as a straight line starting at the origin and rising at the rate of one dollar of marketing expenditure for every ten dollars of the vertical axis. The marketing expenditure function is then subtracted from the *gross profit curve* to derive the *net profit curve*. The net profit curve shows positive net profits with marketing expenditures between M_L and M_U, which could be defined as the rational range of marketing expenditure. The net profit curve reaches a maximum of M. Therefore the marketing expenditure that would maximize net profit is M.

The graphical solution can also be carried out numerically or algebraically; indeed it

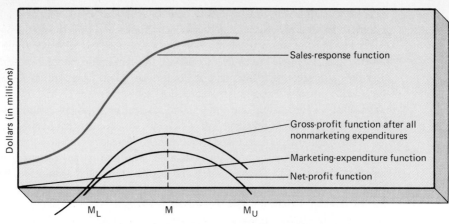

FIGURE 3-9
Relationship between Sales Volume, Marketing Expenditures, and Profits

has to be if sales volume is a function of more than one marketing-mix variable. Here we will present a numerical example of how it is done.

A Numerical Example   Jane Melody, the Allegro product manager at Zenith, also handles a small phonograph-record-cleaning machine that sells for $16. For some years, she has been using a low-price, low-promotion strategy. Last year she spent $10,000 on advertising and another $10,000 on sales promotion. Sales were 12,000 units, and profits were $14,000. Her boss thinks more profits could be made on this item. Ms. Melody is anxious to find a better strategy to increase profits.

Her first step is to visualize some alternative marketing-mix strategies. She imagines the eight strategies shown in the first three columns of Table 3-3 (the first strategy is the current one). They were formed by assuming a high and a low level for each of three marketing variables and elaborating all the combinations ($2^3 = 8$).

Her next step is to estimate the likely sales that would be attained with each marketing mix. She feels that the needed estimates are unlikely to be found through fitting historical data or through conducting experiments. She decides to ask the sales manager for his

TABLE 3-3   Marketing Mixes and Estimated Sales

Marketing Mix No.	Price (P)	Advertising (A)	Promotion (S)	Sales (Q)
1	$16	$10,000	$10,000	12,400
2	16	10,000	50,000	18,500
3	16	50,000	10,000	15,100
4	16	50,000	50,000	22,600
5	24	10,000	10,000	5,500
6	24	10,000	50,000	8,200
7	24	50,000	10,000	6,700
8	24	50,000	50,000	10,000

estimates, since he has shown an uncanny ability to be on target. Suppose he provides the sales estimates shown in the last column in Table 3–3.

The final step calls for determining which marketing mix maximizes profits, assuming the sales estimates are reliable. This calls for introducing a profit equation and inserting the different marketing mixes into this equation to see which maximizes profits.

Suppose fixed costs, F, are \$38,000; unit variable costs, c, are \$10; and the contemplated allowance off list price, k, is \$0. Then profit equation (3-5) reads:

$$Z = (P - 10)Q - 38{,}000 - A - S \qquad (3\text{-}11)$$

Thus profits are a function of the chosen price and the advertising and sales promotion budgets.

At this point the manager can insert each marketing mix and estimated sales level (from Table 3-3) into this equation. The resulting profits are #1(\$16,400), #2(\$13,000), #3(−\$7,400), #4(−\$2,400), #5(\$19,000), #6(\$16,800), #7(−\$4,200), and #8(\$2,000). Marketing-mix #5, calling for a price of \$24, advertising of \$10,000, and promotion of \$10,000, yields the highest expected profits (\$19,000).

The manager can take one more step. Some marketing mix not shown might yield a still higher profit. To check that possibility, the product manager can fit a sales equation to the data shown in Table 3-3. The sales estimates can be viewed as a sample from a larger universe of expert judgments concerning the sales equation $Q = f(P, A, S)$. A plausible mathematical form for the sales equation is the multiple exponential

$$Q = bP^p A^a S^s \qquad (3\text{-}12)$$

where:

b = a scale factor

p, a, s = price, advertising, and promotion elasticity, respectively

Using least-squares regression estimation (not shown), the manager finds that fitted sales equation to be

$$Q = 100{,}000\, P^{-2} A^{1/8} S^{1/4} \qquad (3\text{-}13)$$

This fits the sales estimates in Table 3-3 extremely well. Price has an elasticity of −2; that is, a 1 percent reduction in price, other things being equal, tends to increase unit sales by 2 percent. Advertising has an elasticity of 1/8, and promotion has an elasticity of 1/4. The coefficient 100,000 is a scale factor that translates the dollar magnitudes into sales-volume units.

The product manager now substitutes this sales equation for Q in the profit equation (3-11). This yields, when simplified:

$$Z = 100{,}000\, A^{1/8} S^{1/4}[P^{-1} - 10P^{-2}] - 38{,}000 - A - S \qquad (3\text{-}14)$$

Profits are shown to be strictly a function of the chosen marketing mix. The manager can insert any marketing mix (including those not shown in Table 3-3) and derive an estimate of profits. To find the profit-maximizing marketing mix, she applies standard calculus. The optimal marketing mix (P, A, S) is (\$20, \$12,947, \$25,894). Twice as much is spent on promotion as on advertising because its elasticity is twice as great. The product manager would forecast a sales volume of 10,358 units and profits of \$26,735. While other marketing mixes can produce higher sales, no other marketing mix can produce higher profits. Using this equation, the product manager has solved not only the optimum marketing mix but also the optimum marketing budget ($A + S = \$38,841$).

To facilitate profit-optimization planning, several companies have designed computer programs for use by marketing managers to identify and assess the impact of alternative marketing plans on profits and sales. The marketing manager sits at a computer terminal, requests the particular program, and proceeds to build and test a marketing expenditure plan. One computer program consists of four subprograms.[8] First the marketing manager retrieves the major statistics on the product for the past several years. This material is called the *historical base* and is similar to Table 3-2. She then instructs the computer to produce a *straightforward projection* of the major statistics for the next several years, using extrapolation. She then modifies any projections based on her knowledge, and the result is called the *profit-and-loss planning base*. This shows a normal "extrapolated" level of marketing expenditures, price, and sales, and the resulting profits. If the projected profits are satisfactory, the marketing manager can stop here. However, a fourth subprogram called a *marketing plan simulator* is available for trying out alternative marketing plans and estimating their sales and profits. The simulator incorporates an estimated sales equation. The marketing manager tests alternative marketing plans until she finds a satisfactory one.

Long-run Profit Projection

Computer programs have also been designed to help marketing managers build and test long-run strategies for the development of a product or market. The marketing manager may want to forecast, for a given product, the expected costs, prices, sales, profits, cash flow, and return on investment for the next several years as an indication of whether the particular product business should be built, maintained, harvested, or terminated. Table 3-4 shows the printout from one computer program for a ready-to-eat cereal product.

The first line shows that this projection is for a seven-year period. Details then appear on the undepreciated value of plant and equipment devoted to this product, current opportunity cost, working capital, and expected terminal salvage value.

TABLE 3-4
Sample Printout from Computer System

TIME HORIZON = 7			YEARS	
REMAINING UNDEPR. P&E INVEST. AT BEGIN. YR. 1	= 900000	DOLLARS		
REMAINING NO. OF YEARS OF P&E DEPRECIATION	= 3	YEARS		
REMAINING UNDEP. BLDG. INVEST. AT BEGIN. YR. 1	= 210000	DOLLARS		
REMAINING NO. OF YEARS OF BLDG. DEPRECIATION	= 21	YEARS		
DEPRECIATION HORIZON FOR P&E INVESTMENTS	= 10	YEARS		
DEPRECIATION HORIZON FOR BLDG. INVESTMENTS	= 30	YEARS		
OPPORTUNITY COST (AT BEGINNING OF PERIOD)	= 2.E + 06	DOLLARS		
WORKING CAPITAL	= 13	PCNT SALES		
SALVAGE VALUE (AT END OF PERIOD)	= 10	X EARNINGS		

	1	2	3	4
YEAR	RET.PRICE($)	RET.MAR.(PCNT)	WHOLE.PRICE($)	WHOLE.MAR.(PCNT)
1988	.577	18	.473	0
1989	.602	18	.494	0
1990	.621	18	.509	0
1991	.639	18	.524	0
1992	.659	18	.54	0
1993	.675	18	.554	0
1994	.698	18	.572	0
	5	6	7	8

TABLE 3-4 Continued

YEAR	FACTORY PRICE($)	VARIABLE MFG. COST($)	VARIABLE MFG. COST(PCNT)	VARIABLE MKTG COST(PCNT)
1988	.473	.191	40.4	5
1989	.494	.196	39.7	5
1990	.509	.202	39.7	5
1991	.524	.208	39.7	5
1992	.540	.214	39.6	5
1993	.554	.221	39.9	5
1994	.572	.227	39.7	5

	9	10	11	12
	CONTRIB. TO FIXED COSTS AND PROFIT		FIXED MAN.COST ($)	FIXED MKTG. COST ($)
YEAR	($)	(PCNT)		
1988	.258	54.6	915000	4.25E+06
1989	.273	55.3	971000	4.9E+06
1990	.282	55.3	1.028E+06	5.5E+06
1991	.29	55.3	1.31E+06	5.75E+06
1992	.299	55.4	1.386E+06	6.25E+06
1993	.305	55.1	1.471E+06	6.85E+06
1994	.317	55.3	1.824E+06	7.6E+06

	13	14	15
YEAR	P&E INVEST.	BLDG. INVEST.	DEPREC. EXPENSE
1987	850000	0	
1988	0	0	395000
1989	0	0	395000
1990	850000	1.E+06	395000
1991	0	0	213333
1992	0	0	213333
1993	850000	1.E+06	213333
1994	0	0	331666

	16	17	18	19
	INDEX OF	COMPANY	INDUSTRY	MARKET
YEAR	COMPANY SALES	SLS(UNITS)	SLS (UNITS)	SHARE
1988	1	3.E+07	1.166E+09	2.6
1989	1.1	3.3E+07	1.182E+09	2.8
1990	1.2	3.6E+07	1.198E+09	3
1991	1.3	3.9E+07	1.215E+09	3.2
1992	1.4	4.2E+07	1.23E+09	3.4
1993	1.5	4.5E+07	1.247E+09	3.6
1994	1.6	4.8E+07	1.265E+09	3.8

	20	21	22	23
YEAR	MKTG. EXP. (PCNT SLS)	P.A.T.(PCNT SLS)	P.A.T.($)	CSH FLOW(A.T.)
1987				−2.85E+06
1988	34.9	7.7	1.097245E+06	−353001
1989	35.1	8.4	1.370807E+06	1.493337E+06
1990	35	8.8	1.610162E+06	−110272
1991	33.1	9.9	2.014062E+06	1.953967E+06
1992	32.5	10.4	2.361914E+06	2.281351E+06
1993	32.5	10.4	2.591395E+06	667228
1994	32.7	9.9	2.723974E+06	2.722089E+06

CALCULATED INTERNAL RATE OF RETURN (AFTER TAXES) = 45   PCNT

SOURCE: Adapted from case material of the Harvard University Graduate School of Business Administration, prepared by Professors Derek Abell and Ralph Sultan, used by permission.

The rest of the printout shows the expected or planned year-to-year levels of important variables that will affect the internal rate of return. Column 1 shows the retail price per unit, which is expected to rise from $.58 to $.70 in the course of seven years. Column 2 shows that the retail margin for this product (18 percent) is not expected to change. Column 3 shows the resulting wholesale prices. Since this company will sell direct to the retailers, there is no wholesale margin (column 4), and the factory price (column 5) is the same as the wholesale price.

Column 6 shows estimated variable manufacturing costs, and they too are expected to rise over the period, from a present level of $.19 to $.23 in 1994. The ratio of variable manufacturing costs to factory prices is shown in column 7, followed by the planned ratio of variable marketing costs to factory prices (column 8). Subtracting variable manufacturing and marketing costs per unit from the price, the result is the contribution to fixed costs and profits, which is shown in dollar and percentage form in columns 9 and 10, respectively.

The next step calls for estimating fixed manufacturing costs and fixed marketing costs over the next seven years, which are shown in columns 11 and 12. The symbol $E + 06$ is computer printout shorthand and means that the reader should move the decimal place, in the associated number, six places to the right. Thus $1.028E + 06$ means $1,028,000. Columns 13 and 14 show the anticipated investments in plant, equipment, and building over the next seven years, and column 15 shows the estimated total depreciation expense.

We now arrive at the estimated sales and profits. Columns 16 and 17 show management's estimates of sales (in percentage and in unit terms, respectively) over the next seven years. The figures indicate that management expects company sales (in units) to rise at the rate of about 10 percent a year, on the basis of its planned levels of marketing expenditures. Column 18 presents management's estimates of industry sales for the next seven years.

The figures in column 19, market share, are derived by dividing estimated company sales (column 17) by estimated industry sales (column 18). We see that management expects market share to grow from 2.6 percent to 3.8 percent over a seven-year period. Column 20 expresses total marketing expenditures (columns 8 and 12) as a percent of sales, and this percentage is expected to fall. Examining this more closely, we see that management expects sales to rise faster than marketing expenditures; hence it is expecting increased marketing productivity.

Columns 21 and 22 show yearly profits after taxes in percentage and dollar terms. The computer program uses the following formula to calculate dollar profits after taxes:

$$Z = (1 - t)(mQ - F - D) \qquad (3\text{-}15)$$

where:

Z = profits after taxes
t = tax rate
m = contribution margin to fixed costs and profit
Q = sales in units
F = fixed manufacturing and marketing costs
D = depreciation

For example, the profits after taxes for 1988 are

$$(1 - .4967)[(\$.258)(30,000,000) - \$5,165,000 - \$395,000] = \$1,097,245$$

Column 23 shows the results of the conversion of *profits after taxes to cash flow after taxes*. The formula for cash flow is

$$L = Z + D - W - I \qquad (3\text{-}16)$$

where:

L = cash flow after taxes

Z = profits after taxes

D = depreciation

W = working capital in dollars (that is, working capital as a percent of sales, times wholesale price, times sales in units)

I = new investment expenditure

For example, the cash flow after taxes for 1988 is

$$\$1,097,245 + \$395,000 - [.13(\$.473)(30,000,000)] - 0 = -\$353,001$$

The computer now calculates the internal rate of return corresponding to the cash flow in column 23. This is found by taking the opportunity cost at the beginning of the period and searching for the interest rate that would discount the future cash flows so that the sum of the discounted cash flows is equal to the initial opportunity cost; this rate turns out to be 45 percent.

Thus a computer program enables the product manager to estimate the financial consequences of a particular strategy, environment, and set of costs. The manager can easily recalculate the profit impact of any alterations in the data or assumptions.

Marketing-Mix Optimization

The theory of profit optimization leads to finding the optimal total marketing expenditure level. Now we want to examine the issue of optimally dividing the marketing budget over the tools of the marketing mix. Clearly, the tools of the mix are partially substitutable for each other. A company that is seeking increased sales can achieve them by lowering the price or increasing the sales force, advertising budget, or promotion budget. The challenge is to find the optimal mix.

Assume that a product manager has identified advertising and promotion dollars as the two major elements of the marketing budget. In principle, the marketing budget can be divided in an infinite number of ways on these two items. This is shown in Figure 3-10(a). If there are no constraints on the level of advertising and promotion, then every point in the A–S plane shown in Figure 3-10(a) is a possible marketing mix. An arbitrary line drawn from the origin, called a constant-mix line, shows the set of all marketing mixes where the two tools are in a fixed ratio but where the budget varies. Another arbitrary line, called a constant-budget line, shows a set of varying mixes that would be affordable with a fixed marketing budget.

Associated with every possible marketing mix is a resulting sales level. Three sales levels are shown in Figure 3-10(a). The marketing mix (A_1S_2)—calling for a small budget and a rough equality between advertising and promotion—is expected to produce sales of Q_1. The marketing mix (A_2S_1) involves the same budget with more expenditure on advertising than on promotion; this is expected to produce slightly higher sales, Q_2. The mix (A_3S_3) calls for a larger budget but a relatively equal splitting between advertising and promotion and is expected to yield Q_3. Given the many possibilities, the marketer's job is to find the sales equation that predicts the Qs.

For a given marketing budget, the money should be divided among the various marketing tools in a way that gives the same marginal profit on the marginal dollar spent on each tool. A geometrical version of the solution is shown in Figure 3-10(b). Here we are looking down at the A–S plane shown in Figure 3-10(a). A constant-budget line is shown, indicating all the alternative marketing mixes that could be achieved with this budget.

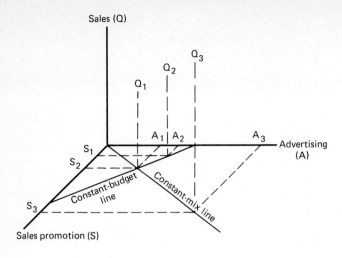

(a) Relation of sales to different marketing mixes of advertising and promotion

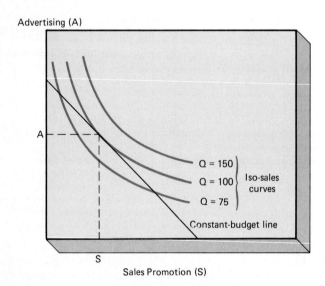

(b) Finding the optimal marketing mix for a given marketing budget

FIGURE 3-10
The Sales Function Associated with Two Marketing-Mix Elements

The curved lines are called *iso-sales curves*. An iso-sales curve shows the different mixes of advertising and personal selling that would produce a given level of sales. It is a projection into the *A–S* plane of the set of points resulting from horizontal slicing of the sales function shown in Figure 3-10(a) at a given level of sales. Figure 3-10(b) shows iso-sales curves for three different sales levels: 75, 100, and 150 units. Given the budget line, it is not possible to attain sales of more than 100 units. The optimum marketing mix is shown at the point of tangency between the budget line and the last-touching iso-sales curve above it. Consequently, the marketing mix (A^*S^*), which calls for somewhat more advertising than promotion, is the sales-maximizing (and in this case profit-maximizing) marketing mix.

Marketing managers carry beliefs in their heads about how specific pairs of marketing variables interact. Here are some of the more popular beliefs:

- Higher advertising expenditures reduce buyers' price sensitivity. Thus a company wishing to charge a higher price should spend more on advertising.
- Advertising expenditures have a greater sales impact on low-price products than high-price products.
- Better advertising copy positioning of a product reduces buyers' price sensitivity.
- Higher advertising expenditures reduce the total cost of selling. The advertising expenditures presell the customer, and sales representatives can spend their time answering objections and closing the sale.
- Higher product quality allows a disproportionately higher price to be charged.
- Higher prices leads buyers to impute higher product quality.
- Price cuts or increased sales effort places a strain on the distribution system and may require its enlargement or revision.
- Tighter credit terms require much greater selling and advertising effort to move the same volume of goods.

While many of these relationships hold true for many products, managers of particular products should be cautious. For example, Sasieni showed data on advertising elasticities for a number of brands and found that while some showed a more sensitive response at high prices, others were more sensitive at lower prices. He concluded that without a clear understanding of the nature of the advertising appeal and the structure of the market, a clear direction for such interactions could not be predicted a priori (Maurice Sasieni, "Pricing and Advertising for Profit," Paper presented at Pennsylvania State University, October 1981).

Marketing-mix variables interact not only with each other but also with nonmarketing variables in the firm. A manager cannot set the product's price and quality at any level he or she wishes. The chart below shows that the product's price and product quality are dependent on nonmarketing variables. Japanese companies are especially sensitive to the dependence of marketing variables on nonmarketing variables. The price they can charge depends on the company's productivity, which is influenced by personnel policies as well as investment decisions. Similarly, product quality is influenced by production reliability and technology, which in turn are influenced by personnel management and R&D investment. Thus marketers must not take price and product for granted but must influence those nonmarketing variables that will enable the company to drive down costs and produce higher-quality products.

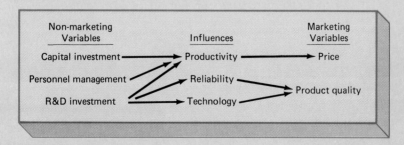

This analysis could be generalized to more than two marketing tools. Ferber and Verdoorn stated that "in an optimum position the additional sales obtained by a small increase in unit costs are the same for all nonprice instruments . . . ."[9]

Dorfman and Steiner went further and formalized the conditions under which price, promotion, and product quality would be optimized.[10] More recently, marketing scientists have investigated how various marketing-mix variables interact in their impact on sales, as Exhibit 3-1 shows.

Marketing
Allocation
Optimization

A final issue facing the marketing planner is to optimally allocate a given marketing budget to the various *target markets* (TMs). The TMs could be different sales territories, customer groups, or other market segments. With a given marketing budget and mix, it may be possible to increase sales and profits by shifting funds among different markets.

Most marketing managers allocate their marketing budgets to the various TMs on the basis of some percentage of actual or expected sales. Consider the following example:

> The marketing manager at the Guardian Oil Company (name disguised) estimates total gasoline sales volume (which combines regular and premium gasoline) and adds premium sales volume back to this figure to yield "profit gallons" (thus giving double weight to premium gasoline sales). The manager then takes the ratio of the advertising budget to the profit gallons to establish a figure for advertising dollars per profit gallon. This is called the prime multiplier. Each market receives an advertising budget equal to its previous year's profit gallons sold multiplied by the prime multiplier. Thus the advertising budget is allocated largely on the basis of last year's company sales in the territory.[11]

Unfortunately, size rules for allocating funds lead to inefficient allocations. They confuse "average" and "marginal" sales response. Figure 3-11(a) illustrates the difference between the two and indicates that there is no reason to assume they are correlated. The two dots in the figure show current marketing expenditures and company sales in two TMs. The company spends $3 million on marketing in both TMs. Company sales are $40 million in TM 1 and $20 million in TM 2. The average sales response to a dollar of marketing

FIGURE 3-11
Sales-Response Functions in Two Target Markets (TMs)

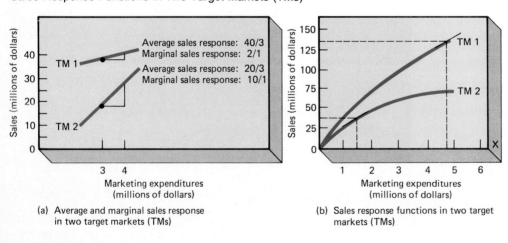

(a) Average and marginal sales response in two target markets (TMs)

(b) Sales response functions in two target markets (TMs)

effort is thus greater in TM 1 than in TM 2; it is 40/3 as opposed to 20/3, respectively. It might seem desirable to shift funds from TM 2 to TM 1, where the average response is greater. Yet the real issue is one of the marginal response. The marginal response is represented by the *slope* of the sales function through the points. A higher slope has been drawn for TM 2 than for TM 1. The respective slopes show that another $1 million in marketing expenditure would produce a $10 million sales increase in TM 2 and only a $2 million sales increase in TM 1. Evidently marginal response, not average response, should guide the allocation of marketing funds.

Marginal response is indicated along the sales-response function for each territory. Assume that a company is able to estimate TM sales-response functions. Suppose the sales-response functions for two TMs are those shown in Figure 3-11(b). The company wishes to allocate a budget of B dollars between the two TMs to maximize profits. When costs are identical for the two TMs, then the allocation that will maximize profits is the one that will maximize sales. The funds are optimally allocated when they exhaust the budget, and the marginal sales response is the same in both TMs. Geometrically, this means that the slopes of the tangents to the two sales-response functions at the optimal allocations will be equal. Figure 3-11(b) shows that a budget of $6 million would be allocated in the amounts of approximately $4.6 million to TM 1 and $1.4 million to TM 2 to produce maximum sales of approximately $180 million. The marginal sales response would be the same in both TMs.

The principle of allocating funds to TMs to equalize the marginal response is used in the planning technique called *zero-based budgeting*.[12] The manager of each TM is asked to formulate a marketing plan and estimate the expected sales for (say) three levels of marketing expenditure, such as 30 percent below the normal level, the normal level, and 30 percent above the normal level. An example is shown in Table 3-5, outlining what the Zenith marketing manager would do with each budget level and her estimate of Allegro sales volume. Then higher management reviews this response function against those of other product managers and gives serious consideration to shifting funds from TMs with low marginal responses to TMs with higher marginal responses.

Measuring sales-response functions can lead to substantial shifts in company marketing

TABLE 3-5   Illustration of Zero-based Marketing Budgeting

Budget (M)	Marketing Plan	Sales Forecast (Q)
$1,400,000	Maintain sales and market share in the short term by concentrating sales effort on largest chain stores, advertising only on TV, sponsoring two promotions a year, and carrying on only limited marketing research.	60,000 units
$2,000,000	Implement a coordinated effort to expand market share by contacting 80 percent of all retailers, adding magazine advertising, adding point-of-purchase displays, and sponsoring three promotions during the year.	70,000 units
$2,600,000	Seek to expand market size and share by adding two new product sizes, enlarging the sales force, increasing marketing research, and expanding the advertising budget.	90,000 units

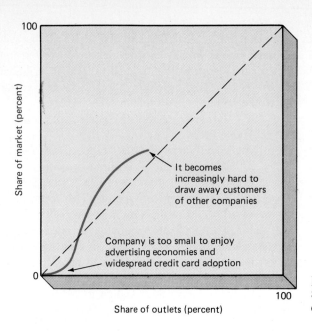

100

Share of market (percent)

It becomes
increasingly hard to
draw away customers
of other companies

Company is too small to enjoy
advertising economies and
widespread credit card adoption

0

100

Share of outlets (percent)

FIGURE 3-12
Share of Market as a Function
of Share of Outlets

strategy. A major oil company had located its service stations in every major U.S. city.[13] In many markets, it operated only a small percentage of the total stations. Company management began to question this broad location strategy. It decided to estimate how the company's market share in each city varied with its percentage share of marketing expenditures in each city (as measured by the share of outlets). A curve was fitted showing the share of outlets and share of markets in different cities. The resulting curve was S-shaped (see Figure 3-12). This showed that having a low percentage of stations in a city yielded an even lower percentage of market volume. The practical implication was clear: The company should either withdraw from its weak markets or build them up to, say, 15 percent of the competitive outlets. Instead of establishing a few outlets in each of many cities, the oil company should establish a large number of outlets in a smaller number of cities. In fact, this is what is happening. Most of the major oil companies in the past tried to be national companies. Today, each is concentrating regionally and trying to be the regional leader.

SUMMARY

Marketing plans focus more narrowly on a product/market and develop the detailed marketing strategies and programs for achieving the product's objectives in the market. Marketing plans are the central instrument for directing and coordinating the marketing effort.

The marketing planning process consists of five steps: analyzing market opportunities, researching and selecting target markets, designing marketing strategies, planning marketing programs, and organizing, implementing, and controlling the marketing effort. Each step is briefly described in this chapter and then examined in the following chapters.

Marketing planning results in a marketing plan document that contains, or should contain, the following sections: executive summary, current market situation, opportunity and issue analysis, objectives, marketing strategy, action programs, projected profit-and-loss statement, and controls.

To plan effectively, marketing managers must understand the key relationship between types of marketing-mix expenditures and their sales and profit consequences. These relationships are captured in a profit equation and a sales equation. Profit-optimization planning calls for finding the profit-maximizing plan. It involves determining the optimal marketing expenditure level, marketing mix, and marketing allocation.

▮ QUESTIONS

1. Using this chapter's contents and Table 3–1 as a guide, write a brief marketing plan for Apple Computer.

2. Various models have been developed to aid marketing managers in developing the marketing mix for their products. What properties should be included in the design of these models?

3. Marketing planning is difficult for toy companies because toys tend to be fads and toy companies must replace roughly 60 percent of their volume every year. Given the nature of this market, what would you do as a marketing manager for a toy company to generate long-term growth?

4. John Smith, Heinz's ketchup product manager, prepared the following marketing plan. Critique his procedure. What improvements can you suggest?

1. *Forecast of total market* This year's total market (23,600,000 cases) × recent growth rate (6%)	25,000,000 cases
2. *Forecast of market share*	28%
3. *Forecast of sales volume* (1 × 2)	7,000,000 cases
4. *Price to distributor*	$4.45 per case
5. *Estimate of sales revenue* (3 × 4)	$31,150,000
6. *Estimate of variable costs* Tomatoes and spices ($0.50) + bottles and caps ($1.00) + labor ($1.10) + physical distribution ($0.15)	$2.75 per case
7. *Estimate of contribution margin to* *cover fixed costs, profits, and* *marketing* ([4 − 6]3)	$11,900,000
8. *Estimate of fixed costs* Fixed charge $1 per case × 7 million cases	$7,000,000
9. *Estimate of contribution margin* *to cover profits and marketing* (7 − 8)	$4,900,000
10. *Estimate of target profit goal*	$1,900,000
11. *Amount available for marketing* (9 − 10)	$3,000,000
12. *Split of the marketing budget* Advertising Sales Promotion Marketing Research	$2,000,000 $ 900,000 $ 100,000

5. Opportunities/threats analysis is an important part of the marketing plan, designed to let management see what external factors it is facing and the possible action it might take. Develop an O/T analysis for the cigarette line of Philip Morris.

6. One marketing theorist maintains that "value rigidity" on the part of marketing managers poses a serious problem in the development of marketing plans. What might he mean by this assertion?

7. A marketer evaluates two marketing strategies and estimates their expected rates of return to be 8 percent and 12 percent, respectively. Which strategy should be chosen if this decision is to be made many times? Which strategy should be chosen if this decision is to be made only once?

8. Suppose the quantity sold (Q) of an item depends on the price charged (P), the level of advertising expenditure (A), and the level of distribution expenditure (D). Develop a sales-response equation (a) where the marginal effect of each marketing variable is uninfluenced by the levels of the other marketing variables; (b) where the marginal effect of each marketing variable is influenced by the levels of the other variables.

9. Suggest some equation forms that might be used to represent (a) a sales-response function when sales increase at a decreasing rate with marketing expenditures; (b) a sales-response function when sales increase at an increasing and then decreasing rate.

10. A firm wants to decide how much quality to build into a new machine tool. Illustrate diagrammatically the logic of determining the optimal quality level.

11. The brand manager in charge of a dry breakfast cereal has the following sales and expense statement:

Net Sales		100%
Manufacturing and shipping costs		
Fixed	12.9%	
Variable	39.6	
Total		52.5
All other expenses (excluding advertising and merchandising expenses)		
Distribution and delivery expenses	5.4	
Administrative and general expenses	4.0	
Sales people's expenses	3.5	
Market research	0.5	
Total		13.4
Available for advertising and merchandising and profit		34.1

Name several ways the brand manager can try to increase profits.

■ FOOTNOTES

1. E. Jerome McCarthy, *Basic Marketing: A Managerial Approach* (Homewood, Ill.: Richard D. Irwin, 1981), now in its ninth edition. Two alternative classifications are worth noting. Frey proposed that all marketing-decision variables could be categorized into two factors: the *offering* (product, packaging, brand, price, and service) and *methods and tools* (distribution channels, personal selling, advertising, sales promotion, and publicity). See Albert W. Frey, *Advertising*, 3rd ed. (New York: Ronald Press, 1961), p. 30. Lazer and Kelly proposed a three-factor classification: *goods and service mix, distribution mix*, and *communications mix*. See William Lazer and Eugene J. Kelly, *Managerial Marketing: Perspectives and Viewpoints*, rev. ed. (Homewood, Ill.: Richard D. Irwin, 1962), p. 413.

2. Peter F. Drucker, *Management: Tasks, Responsibilities, Practices* (New York: Harper & Row, 1973), p. 128.

3. This example is adapted with several changes and additions from "Zenith Radio Corporation; Allegro," a Harvard Business School case 9-575-062 prepared by Ed Popper under the supervision of Scott Ward, 1975.

4. For examples of empirical studies using fitted sales-response functions, see Doyle L. Weiss, "Determinants of Market Share," *Journal of Marketing Research*, August 1968, pp. 290–95; Donald E. Sexton, Jr., "Estimating Marketing Policy Effects on Sales of a Frequently Purchased Product," *Journal of Marketing Research*, August 1970, pp. 338–47; and Jean-Jacques Lambin, "A Computer On-Line Marketing Mix Model," *Journal of Marketing Research*, May 1972, pp. 119–26.

5. See Russell Ackoff and James R. Emshoff, "Advertising Research at Anheuser-Busch," *Sloan Management Review*, Winter 1975, pp. 1–15.

6. See Philip Kotler, "A Guide to Gathering Expert Estimates," *Business Horizons*, October 1970, pp. 79–87.

7. See Gary L. Lilien and Philip Kotler, *Marketing Decision Making: A Model Building Approach*, 2nd ed. (New York: Harper & Row, 1983).

8. See "Concorn Kitchens," in *Marketing Management Casebook*, ed. Harper W. Boyd, Jr., and Robert T. Davis (Homewood, Ill.: Richard D. Irwin, 1971), pp. 125–36.

9. Robert Ferber and P. J. Verdoorn, *Research Methods in Economics and Business* (New York: Macmillan, 1962), p. 535.

10. Robert Dorfman and Peter O. Steiner, "Optimal Advertising and Optimal Quality," *American Economic Review*, December 1954, pp. 826–36.

11. Donald C. Marschner, "Theory versus Practice in Allocating Advertising Money," *Journal of Business*, July 1967, pp. 286–302.

12. See Paul J. Stonich, *Zero-Base Planning and Budgeting: Improved Cost Control and Resource Allocation* (Homewood, Ill.: Dow-Jones-Irwin, 1977).

13. See John J. Cardwell, "Marketing and Management Science—A Marriage on the Rocks?" *California Management Review*, Summer 1968, pp. 3–12.

Marketing Information Systems and Marketing Research

We have seen the importance of starting marketing and strategic planning with an outside-inside point of view. Management needs to understand and monitor the larger marketing environment if it is to keep its products and marketing practices current. But how can management learn about changing customer wants, new-competitor initiatives, new modes of distribution, and so on? The answer is clear: Management must develop and maintain a marketing information system and have the skills of carrying out marketing research. This chapter will show how marketers collect and use marketing information about the relevant marketing environment. In the next four chapters, we will describe what marketing researchers have discovered about the overall marketing environment and, in particular, consumers, organizational buyers, and competitors.

In the long history of business enterprise, management has devoted most of its attention to managing *money*, *materials*, *machines*, and *men*. Management has paid less attention to the fifth critical resource of the firm: *information*. It is hard to find company executives who are highly satisfied with their marketing information. Their complaints include:

■ There is not enough marketing information of the right kind.
■ There is too much marketing information of the wrong kind.
■ Marketing information is so dispersed throughout the company that it takes a great effort to locate simple facts.
■ Marketing information is sometimes suppressed by subordinates when they believe it will reflect unfavorably on their performance.
■ Important information often arrives too late to be useful.
■ It is difficult to know whether the information is accurate.

Many companies have not yet adapted to the intensified information requirements for effective marketing in a modern economy. Three developments render the need for marketing information stronger than at any time in the past:

■ *From local to national to international marketing.* As companies expand their geographical market coverage, their managers need more market information than ever before.
■ *From buyer needs to buyer wants.* As buyers' incomes increase, they become more selective in their choice of goods. Sellers find it harder to predict buyers' response to different features, styles, and other attributes, and they turn to formal systems of market research.
■ *From price to nonprice competition.* As sellers increase their use of branding, product differentiation, advertising, and sales promotion, they require information on the effectiveness of these marketing tools.

The explosive information requirements have been met on the supply side by impressive new information technologies. The past thirty years have witnessed the emergence of the computer, microfilming, closed-circuit television, copy machines, tape recorders, facsimile transmitters, video recorders, videodisc players, and other devices that have revolutionized information handling. Nevertheless, business firms for the most part lack information sophistication. Many firms do not have a marketing research department. Many other firms have small marketing research departments whose work is limited to routine forecasting, sales analysis, and occasional surveys. Only a few firms have developed advanced marketing information systems that provide company management with up-to-date marketing information and analysis.

CONCEPT AND COMPONENTS OF A MARKETING INFORMATION SYSTEM

Every firm is the scene of many information flows of interest to marketing managers. Many companies are studying their executives' information needs and designing *marketing information systems* (MIS) to meet these needs. Instead of a plethora of unrelated data, an MIS combines various inputs and presents integrated reports. We define a marketing information system as follows:[1]

> A *marketing information system* is a continuing and interacting structure of people, equipment, and procedures to gather, sort, analyze, evaluate, and distribute pertinent, timely, and accurate information for use by marketing decision makers to improve their marketing planning, implementation, and control.

The marketing information system concept is illustrated in Figure 4-1. The box on the left shows the components of the marketing environment that marketing managers must monitor. Trends in the marketing environment are picked up and analyzed through four subsystems making up the marketing information system—*the internal reports system, marketing intelligence system, marketing research system*, and *analytical marketing system*. The information flows to marketing managers to help them in their marketing analysis, planning, implementation, and control. Their marketing decisions and communications then flow back to the market.

We will now describe each of the four major subsystems of the company's MIS.

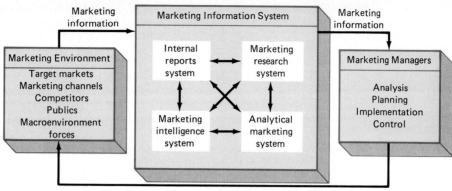

FIGURE 4-1
The Marketing Information System

INTERNAL REPORTS SYSTEM

The most basic information system used by marketing executives is the internal reports system. Included are reports on orders, sales, inventory levels, receivables, payables, and so on. By analyzing this information, marketing managers can spot important opportunities and problems.

The Order-
Shipping-Billing
Cycle

The heart of the internal reports system is the order-shipping-billing cycle. Sales representatives, dealers, and customers dispatch orders to the firm. The order department prepares multicopy invoices and sends them to various departments. Out-of-stock items are back ordered. Shipped items are accompanied by shipping and billing documents that are also multicopied and sent to various departments.

The company wants to perform these steps quickly and accurately. Sales representatives are expected to send in their orders every evening, in some cases immediately. The order department is designed to process them quickly. The warehouse is set up to send the goods out as soon as possible. And bills should go out as soon as possible. The computer is harnessed to expedite the order-shipping-billing cycle. Ringer and Howell reported a company study that resulted in reducing the time between the receipt and the execution of an order from sixty-two hours to thirty hours without any change in costs.[2]

Improving
the Timeliness
of Sales Reports

Marketing executives receive sales reports some time after the sales have taken place. In consumer-food companies, warehouse withdrawal reports are issued with fair regularity, but actual retail purchase reports take about two months, based on special store or consumer panel audits. In the auto industry, executives wait about ten days for their sales report; if sales are down, they will have to work harder and face ten sleepless nights until the next report. Many marketing executives complain that sales are not reported fast enough in their company.

Here are three companies that have designed timely and comprehensive sales-reporting systems:

■ *American Hospital Supply*. AHS supplied hospitals with computers so that the hospitals could enter orders that would go directly to the AHS sales department. The timely arrival of orders enabled AHS to cut inventories, improve customer service, and obtain better terms from suppliers for higher volumes. AHS achieved a great advantage over competitors and their market share soared.[3]

■ *Wrangler Womenswear*. Sales people at Wrangler Womenswear, a division of Blue Bell, Inc., can connect their portable computers to the corporate computer. The sales force can send and retrieve messages, enter orders and receive up-to-the-minute sales information. A salesperson can enter the average order in about half the time involved in writing out an order on paper.[4]

■ *Mead Paper*. Mead sales representatives can obtain on-the-spot answers to customers' questions about paper availability by dialing Mead Paper's computer center. The computer determines whether paper is available at the nearest warehouse and when it can be shipped; if it is not in stock, the computer checks the inventory at other nearby warehouses until one is located. If the paper is nowhere in stock, the computer determines where and when the paper can be produced. The sales representative gets an answer in seconds and thus has an advantage over competitors.

Designing a User-Oriented Reports System

In designing an advanced sales-information system, the company should avoid certain pitfalls. First, it is possible to create a system that delivers too much information. The managers arrive at their office each morning to face voluminous sales statistics, which they either ignore or spend too much time on. Second, it is possible to create a system that delivers information that is too current! Managers may end up overreacting to minor sales reversals.

The company's marketing information system should represent a cross between what managers think they need, what managers really need, and what is economically feasible. A useful step is the appointment of an *internal marketing information systems committee*, which interviews a cross section of marketing executives—product managers, sales managers, sales representatives, and so on—to discover their information needs. A useful set of questions is shown in Table 4-1. The MIS committee will want to pay special attention to strong desires and complaints. At the same time, the committee will wisely discount some of the information requests. Managers with a strong appetite for information will list many needs, failing to distinguish between *what is nice to know* and *what they need to know*. Other managers will be too busy to give the questionnaire serious thought and will omit many things they ought to know. This is why the information planning committee must take another step, that of determining what managers *need to know* to be able to make

TABLE 4-1   Questionnaire for Determining Marketing Information Needs

1. What types of decisions are you regularly called upon to make?
2. What types of information do you need to make these decisions?
3. What types of information do you regularly get?
4. What types of special studies do you periodically request?
5. What types of information would you like to get that you are not getting now?
6. What information would you want daily? Weekly? Monthly? Yearly?
7. What magazines and trade reports would you like to see routed to you on a regular basis?
8. What specific topics would you like to be kept informed of?
9. What types of data-analysis programs would you like to see made available?
10. What do you think would be the four most helpful improvements that could be made in the present marketing information system?

responsible decisions. For example, what do brand managers need to know in order to set the size of the advertising budget? Suppose they should know the degree of market saturation, the rate of sales decay in the absence of advertising, and the spending plans of competitors. The information system should be designed to provide the data needed for making the key marketing decisions.

MARKETING INTELLIGENCE SYSTEM

While the internal reports system supplies managers with *results data*, the marketing intelligence system supplies managers with *happenings data*. We define the *marketing intelligence system* as *the set of procedures and sources used by executives to obtain their everyday information about pertinent developments in the marketing environment.*

Executives scan the environment in four ways:[5]

- ■ *Undirected viewing.* General exposure to information where the manager has no specific purpose in mind.
- ■ *Conditioned viewing.* Directed exposure, not involving active search, to a more or less clearly identified area or type of information.
- ■ *Informal search.* A relatively limited and unstructured effort to obtain specific information or information for a specific purpose.
- ■ *Formal search.* A deliberate effort—usually following a preestablished plan, procedure, or methodology—to secure specific information or information relating to a specific issue.

Marketing executives carry on marketing intelligence mostly on their own by reading books, newspapers, and trade publications; talking to customers, suppliers, distributors, and other outsiders; and talking with other managers and personnel within the company. Yet this system is quite casual, and valuable information may be lost or arrive too late. Executives may learn of a competitive move, a new-customer need, or a dealer problem too late to make the best response.

Well-run companies take additional steps to improve the quality and quantity of marketing intelligence. First, they train and motivate the sales force to spot and report new developments. Sales representatives are the company's "eyes and ears." They are in an excellent position to pick up information missed by other means. Yet they are very busy and often fail to pass on significant information. The company must "sell" its sales force on their importance as intelligence gatherers and must emphasize this importance through their sales bonuses. The sales force should be provided with easy reports to fill out. Sales representatives should know the types of information that should go to different managers in their company. An innovative approach involves conducting focus groups with the sales force. The company can obtain valuable marketing information, involve a wide range of employees in customer problems, and stimulate thinking about customer needs.[6]

Second, the company motivates distributors, retailers, and other middlemen to pass along important intelligence. Consider the following example:[7]

Parker Hannifin Corporation, a major fluid power products manufacturer, has arranged with each distributor to forward to Parker's marketing research division a copy of all the invoices containing sales of their products. Parker analyzes these invoices to stay abreast of ultimate customer characteristics and to help its distributors improve their marketing programs.

Some companies appoint specialists to gather marketing intelligence. They send out "ghost shoppers" to monitor the presentations of retail personnel. Much can be learned about competitors through purchasing competitors' products; attending open houses and trade shows; reading competitors' published reports and attending stockholders' meetings; talking to competitors' former employees and present employees, dealers, distributors, suppliers, and freight agents; collecting competitors' ads; and reading the *Wall Street Journal, New York Times,* and trade association papers.

Third, the company purchases information from outside suppliers. The A. C. Nielsen Company sells bimonthly data based on a store audit of 1,300 supermarkets, 700 drugstores, and 150 mass merchandisers. The data include brand shares, retail prices, percentage of stores stocking the item, promotional efforts, and percentage of stock-out stores. Market Research Corporation of America sells reports (based on the purchase diaries of a representative panel of seventy-five hundred households scattered throughout the country) on weekly movements of brand shares, sizes, prices, and deals. Advertising Checking Bureau counts weekly newspaper advertising lineage in all U.S. daily and weekly newspapers to report on competitors' ads, advertising expenditures, and media mixes.

Fourth, some companies have established an internal *marketing information center* to collect and circulate marketing intelligence. The staff scans major publications, abstracts relevant news, and disseminates a news bulletin to marketing managers. It collects and files relevant information. The staff assists managers in evaluating new information. These services greatly improve the quality of information available to marketing managers. (See Exhibit 4-1.)

EXHIBIT 4-1 — A New Answer to Information Needs— Information Centers

Although the concept of an integrated management information system was widely discussed in the 1960s, few companies did anything to centralize and coordinate their information flows. Many managers complained that needed information was somewhere in the company but that it would take too long to find. There would be no one place to find a list of the data files available in the company.

Beginning in 1979, IBM recommended that its clients establish information centers as adjuncts of existing data-processing departments. Many of IBM's larger clients have now done this. Travelers Insurance Company, for example, opened its information center in December 1981 with ten consultants answering 200 calls for assistance a month. A year later, Travelers had twenty consultants handling 4,000 calls a month.

Managers have found these information centers to be real time savers. In one case, an insurance manager needed to know why customers in a certain part of the country were not renewing their insurance policies. The information center quickly drew data, analyzed these data, and demonstrated that the company's rates had become uncompetitive.

One of the main advantages of establishing an information center is that it leads the company for the first time to compile a list of what data files exist and where they are located, as well as what data gaps exist in terms of questions frequently asked by managers. In addition, these centers often provide a higher level of data analysis than busy executives can achieve by themselves. Montgomery and Weinberg see these centers performing many functions including data evaluation, data transformation into information, data transmission, data accumulation, data analysis, and pattern recognition.

SOURCES See "Helping Decision Makers Get at Data," *Business Week*, September 13, 1982, p. 118; and David B. Montgomery and Charles B. Weinberg, "Toward Strategic Intelligence Systems," *Journal of Marketing*, Fall 1979, pp. 41–57.

MARKETING RESEARCH SYSTEM

Besides internal reports information and marketing intelligence, marketing executives often need focused studies of specific problems and opportunities. They may need a market survey, a product-preference test, a sales forecast by region, or an advertising-effectiveness study. The managers themselves normally do not have the skill or time to obtain this information. They need to commission formal marketing research. We define *marketing research* as follows:

> *Marketing research* is the systematic design, collection, analysis, and reporting of data and findings relevant to a specific marketing situation facing the company.

Suppliers of Marketing Research

A company can obtain marketing research in a number of ways. Small companies can ask students or professors at a local college to design and carry out the project, or they can hire a marketing research firm. Large companies, in fact over 77 percent of them, have their own marketing research departments.[8] Marketing research departments consist of anywhere from one to several dozen researchers. The marketing research manager normally reports to the marketing vice-president and acts as a study director, administrator, company consultant, and advocate.

> Procter & Gamble assigns marketing researchers to each product operating division to conduct research for existing brands. There are two separate in-house research groups, one in charge of overall company advertising research and the other in charge of market testing. The staff of each group consists of marketing research managers, supporting specialists (survey designers, statisticians, behavioral scientists), and in-house field representatives to conduct and supervise interviewing. Each year, Procter & Gamble calls or visits over one million people in connection' with about one thousand research projects.

Companies normally budget marketing research at anywhere from .02 to 1 percent of company sales. Between 50 percent and 90 percent of this money is spent directly by the department, and the remainder is spent in buying the services of outside marketing research firms. Marketing research firms fall into three groups:

- *Syndicated-service research firms.* These firms gather periodic consumer and trade information which they sell for a fee to clients. Examples: A. C. Nielsen, SAMI.
- *Custom marketing research firms.* These firms are hired to carry out specific research projects. They participate in designing the study, and the report becomes the client's property.
- *Specialty-line marketing research firms.* These firms provide a specialized service to other marketing research firms and company marketing research departments. The best example is the field service firm, which sells field interviewing services to other firms.

The Scope of Marketing Research

Marketing researchers have steadily expanded their activities and techniques. Table 4-2 lists thirty-three marketing research activities and the percentage of companies carrying on each activity. The ten most common activities are *determination of market characteristics, measurement of market potentials, market-share analysis, sales analysis, studies of business trends, short-range forecasting, competitive-product studies, long-range forecasting, pricing studies, and testing of existing products.*[9]

TABLE 4-2   Research Activities of 599 Companies

Type of Research	Percent Doing
Advertising Research	
A. Motivation Research	47
B. Copy Research	61
C. Media Research	68
D. Studies of Ad Effectiveness	76
E. Studies of Competitive Advertising	67
Business Economics and Corporate Research	
A. Short-Range Forecasting (Up to 1 year)	89
B. Long-Range Forecasting (Over 1 year)	87
C. Studies of Business Trends	91
D. Pricing Studies	83
E. Plant and Warehouse Location Studies	68
F. Acquisition Studies	73
G. Export and International Studies	49
H. MIS (Management Information System)	80
I. Operations Research	65
J. Internal Company Employees	76
Corporate Responsibility Research	
A. Consumers "Right to Know" Studies	18
B. Ecological Impact Studies	23
C. Studies of Legal Constraints on Advertising and Promotion	46
D. Social Values and Policies Studies	39
Product Research	
A. New Product Acceptance and Potential	76
B. Competitive Product Studies	87
C. Testing of Existing Products	80
D. Packaging Research: Design or Physical Characteristics	65
Sales and Market Research	
A. Measurement of Market Potentials	97
B. Market Share Analysis	97
C. Determination of Market Characteristics	97
D. Sales Analysis	92
E. Establishment of Sales Quotas, Territories	78
F. Distribution Channel Studies	71
G. Test Markets, Store Audits	59
H. Consumer Panel Operations	63
I. Sales Compensation Studies	60
J. Promotional Studies of Premiums, Coupons, Sampling Deals, etc.	58

SOURCE: Reprinted from Dik Warren Twedt, ed., *1983 Survey of Marketing Research* (Chicago: American Marketing Association, 1983), p. 41.

These studies have benefited from increasingly sophisticated techniques. Table 4-3 shows the approximate decade in which various techniques came into consideration or use in marketing research. Many of them—such as questionnaire construction and area sampling—came along early and were quickly and widely applied by marketing researchers. Others—such as motivation research and mathematical methods—came in uneasily, with prolonged and heated debates among practitioners over their practical usefulness. But they, too, settled in the corpus of marketing research methodology.

The Marketing Research Process

Marketing research is undertaken to understand a marketing problem better. A brand manager at Procter & Gamble will commission three or four major marketing research studies annually. Marketing managers in smaller companies will order fewer marketing research studies. Nonprofit organizations increasingly find that they need marketing research. A hospital wants to know whether people in its service area have a positive attitude toward the hospital and its services. A college wants to determine what kind of image it has among high school counselors. A political organization wants to find out what voters think of the candidates.

Effective marketing research involves five steps: *defining the problem and research objectives*, *developing the research plan*, *collecting the information*, *analyzing the information*, and *presenting the findings* (see Figure 4-2). We will illustrate these steps with the following situation:

> American Airlines, one of the largest U.S. air carriers, is constantly looking for new ways to serve the needs of air travelers. Management would like to offer some new service that will give it a competitive advantage. Toward this end, a few managers convened in a brainstorming session and generated a number of ideas revolving around better food service, in-flight entertainment, newspaper and magazine availability, and so on. One manager came up with the idea of offering phone service to passengers who wished to make calls while riding 30,000 feet above the earth. The other managers got excited about this idea and agreed that it should be researched further. The marketing manager who suggested the idea then volunteered to do some preliminary research. He contacted a major telecommunications company to find out the cost of providing this service on B–747 coast-to-coast flights. The telecommunications company said that the device would cost the airline about $1,000 a flight. The airline could break even if it charged $25 a phone call and at least forty passengers made calls during the flight. The marketing manager then asked the company's marketing research manager to find out how air travelers would respond to this new service.

Defining the Problem and Research Objectives The first step in research calls for the marketing manager and marketing researcher to define the problem carefully and agree on the research objectives. Hundreds of things can be researched in any problem. Unless the problem is well defined, the cost of information gathering may well exceed the value of the findings. An old adage says, "A problem well defined is half solved."

Management must steer between defining the problem too broadly and defining it too narrowly. If the marketing manager tells the marketing researcher, "Find out everything you can about air travelers' needs," the manager will get much unneeded information and may not get the information he or she really needs. On the other hand, if the marketing manager says, "Find out if enough passengers aboard a B–747 flying between the East Coast and West Coast would be willing to pay $25 to call others so that American Airlines would break even on the cost of offering this service," this is too narrow a view of the problem. The marketing researcher at that point could say, "Why does American have to break even on the cost of the service itself? Why does it have to be priced at $25? The new service might attract enough new passengers to fly American so that even if they don't make enough phone calls, American will get its money back. Many travelers might fly American just because they like to know there is a phone aboard even if they probably won't use it."

The two managers worked further on the problem, and another issue arose. If the new service was successful, how fast could other airlines copy it? The history of airline marketing competition is replete with examples of new services that are so quickly copied by competitors that no airline gains a sustainable competitive advantage. Therefore it is important to determine the value of being first and how long the lead would be sustained.

The marketing manager and marketing researcher agreed to define the problem as follows: "Will offering an in-flight phone service create enough incremental preference

TABLE 4-3 Evolving Techniques in Marketing Research

Decade	Technique
Prior to 1910	Firsthand observation Elementary surveys
1910–20	Sales analysis Operating-cost analysis
1920–30	Questionnaire construction Survey technique
1930–40	Quota sampling Simple correlation analysis Distribution-cost analysis Store auditing techniques
1940–50	Probability sampling Regression methods Advanced statistical inference Consumer and store panels
1950–60	Motivation research Operations research Multiple regression and correlation Experimental design Attitude-measuring instruments Analysis of variance (ANOVA)
1960–70	Factor analysis and discriminant analysis Mathematical models Bayesian statistical analysis and decision theory Scaling theory Computer data processing and analysis Marketing simulation Information storage and retrieval
1970–80	Multidimensional scaling Econometric models Comprehensive marketing planning models Test-marketing laboratories Multiattribute attitude models
1980–	Conjoint analysis and trade-off analysis Causal analysis Computer controlled interviewing Uniform product code and optical scanners Canonical correlation

and profit for American Airlines to justify its cost against other possible investments that American might make?'' They then agreed on the following specific research objectives:

1. What are the main reasons why airline passengers might place phone calls while in flight instead of after landing?
2. What kinds of passengers would be the most likely to make phone calls during a flight?

FIGURE 4-2
The Marketing Research Process

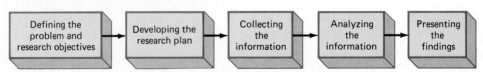

3. How many passengers on a typical long-distance B–747 flight are likely to make phone calls, and how will this be affected by price? What would be the best price to charge?
4. How many extra passengers might choose the American flight because of this new service?
5. How much long-term goodwill will this service add to American Airlines' image?
6. What is the relative importance of other factors, such as flight frequency, food, and baggage handling, in influencing air-carrier choice, and how important will phone service be relative to these other factors?

Not all research projects can be made this specific in its objectives. Three types of research projects can be distinguished. Some research is *exploratory*—i.e., to gather preliminary data to shed light on the real nature of the problem and possibly suggest some hypotheses or new ideas. Some research is *descriptive*—i.e., to describe certain magnitudes, such as how many people would make an in-flight phone call at $25 a call. Some research is *causal*—i.e., to test a cause-and-effect relationship, such as that a $20 charge as opposed to a $25 charge would increase the number of phone calls by at least 20 percent.

Developing the Research Plan   The second stage of marketing research calls for developing the most efficient plan for gathering the needed information. The marketing executive cannot simply say to the marketing researcher, "Find some passengers and ask them if they would use an in-flight phone service if it were available." The research plan should be designed professionally. At the same time, the marketing manager should know enough about marketing research to approve the research plan and budget and know how to interpret the findings.

The marketing manager should ask the marketing researcher to estimate the cost of the research plan before approving it. The purpose of the marketing research project is to help the company reduce its risks and improve its profits. Suppose the company estimates that launching the in-flight phone service without any marketing research would yield a long-term profit of $50,000. The manager also believes that the research will help him improve the promotional plan and make a long-term profit of $90,000. In this case, he should be willing to spend up to $40,000 on this research. If the research design would cost more than $40,000, he should decline it.[10]

Table 4-4 shows that designing a research plan calls for decisions on the *data sources*, *research approaches*, *research instruments*, *sampling plan*, and *contact methods*.

Data sources   The research plan can call for gathering secondary data, primary data, or both. *Secondary data consist of information that already exists somewhere, having been collected for another purpose.* Otherwise the researcher has to gather *primary data, which consist of original information for the specific purpose at hand.*

SECONDARY DATA   Researchers usually start their investigation by examining secondary data to see whether their problem can be partly or wholly solved without collecting

TABLE 4-4   Constructing the Research Plan

Data Sources	Research Approaches	Research Instruments	Sampling Plan	Contact Methods
Secondary data	Observation	Questionnaire	Sampling unit	Mail
Primary data	Survey	Mechanical instruments	Sample size	Telephone
	Experiment		Sampling procedure	Personal
	Focus groups			

costly primary data. Table 4-5 shows the rich variety of secondary-data sources available, including *internal sources* (company profit-and-loss statements, sales-call reports, prior-research reports), and *external sources* (government publications, on-line data banks, periodicals and books, and commercial services).[11]

In the American Airlines case, the researchers will find plenty of secondary data on the air travel market. The U.S. Civil Aeronautics Board publications provide data on the size, growth, and market shares of the various carriers. The Air Transport Association of

TABLE 4-5   Secondary Sources of Data

A. *Internal sources*
Internal sources include company profit-loss statements, balance sheets, sales figures, sales-call reports, invoices, inventory records, and prior-research reports.

B. *Government publications*
Statistical Abstract of the U.S., updated annually, provides summary data on demographic, economic, social, and other aspects of the American economy and society.
County and City Data Book, updated every three years, presents statistical information for counties, cities, and other geographical units on population, education, employment, aggregate and median income, housing, bank deposits, retail sales, etc.
U.S. Industrial Outlook provides projections of industrial activity by industry and includes data on production, sales, shipments, employment, etc.
Marketing Information Guide provides a monthly annotated bibliography of marketing information.
Other government publications include the *Annual Survey of Manufacturers*; *Business Statistics*; *Census of Manufacturers*; *Census of Population*; *Census of Retail Trade, Wholesale Trade, and Selected Service Industries*; *Census of Transportation*; *Federal Reserve Bulletin*; *Monthly Labor Review*; *Survey of Current Business*; and *Vital Statistics Report*.

C. *Periodicals and Books*
Business Periodicals Index, a monthly, lists business articles appearing in a wide variety of business publications.
Standard and Poor's Industry Surveys provides updated statistics and analyses of industries.
Moody's Manuals provide financial data and names of executives in major companies.
Encyclopedia of Associations provides information on every major trade and professional association in the U.S.
Marketing journals include the *Journal of Marketing*, *Journal of Marketing Research*, and *Journal of Consumer Research*.
Useful trade magazines include *Advertising Age*, *Chain Store Age*, *Progressive Grocer*, *Sales and Marketing Management*, and *Stores*.
Useful general business magazines include *Business Week*, *Fortune*, *Forbes*, and *Harvard Business Review*.

D. *Commercial Data*
A. C. Nielsen Company provides data on products and brands sold through retail outlets (Retail Index Services), data on television audiences (Media Research Services), magazine circulation data (Neodata Services, Inc.), etc.
Market Research Corporation of America provides data on weekly family purchases of consumer products (National Consumer Panel), data on home food consumption (National Menu Census), and data on 6,000 retail, drug, and discount retailers in various geographical areas (Metro Trade Audits).
Selling Areas-Marketing, Inc., provides reports on warehouse withdrawals to food stores in selected market areas (SAMI reports).
Simmons Market Research Bureau provides annual reports covering television markets, sporting goods, proprietary drugs, etc., giving demographic data by sex, income, age, and brand preferences (selective markets and media reaching them).
Burke Marketing Services, Inc. provides TV campaign testing in controlled marketing labs, marketing modeling, retail store audits, physiological measures of advertising stimuli, pre- and post-TV copy testing, and custom survey research.
Market Facts, Inc. provides consumer mail panel, market test store audit services, five shopping mall facilities, WATS telephone interviewing, and ad hoc survey research.
Other commercial research houses selling data to subscribers include the *Audit Bureau of Circulation*, *Audits and Surveys*, *Dun and Bradstreet*, *Opinion Research*, *Starch*, and *Arbitron Ratings Service*.

America has numerous studies in its library on the characteristics, carrier preferences, and behavior of air travelers. Similarly, various travel agencies have data that might throw light on how air travelers choose their carriers.

Secondary data provide a starting point for research and offer the advantages of lower cost and quicker availability. On the other hand, the data needed by the researcher might not exist, or the existing data might be dated, inaccurate, incomplete, or unreliable. In this case, the researcher will have to collect primary data at greater cost and longer delay, but probably with more relevance and accuracy.

PRIMARY DATA   Most marketing research projects involve some primary-data collection. Primary-data collection is more costly, but the data are usually more relevant to the issue at hand. The normal procedure is to interview some people individually and/or in groups to get a preliminary sense of how people feel about air carriers and particular services and, on the basis of the findings, develop a more formal and extensive interviewing approach and research instrument, debug it, and then carry it into the field. Here we present a fuller picture of the possible research approaches.

Research approaches   Primary data can be collected in four broad ways: observation, focus groups, surveys, and experiments.

OBSERVATIONAL RESEARCH   One way to gather fresh data is to observe the relevant actors and settings. The American Airlines researchers might hang around airports, airline offices, and travel agencies to hear how travelers talk about the different carriers and how agents handle the flight arrangement process. The researchers can fly on American and competitors' planes to observe the quality of in-flight service and hear consumer reactions. This exploratory research might yield some useful hypotheses about how travelers choose their air carriers.

FOCUS GROUP RESEARCH   A focus group is a gathering of six to ten persons who spend a few hours with a skilled interviewer to discuss a project, service, organization, or other marketing entity. The interviewer needs objectivity, knowledge of the subject matter and industry, and knowledge of group dynamics and consumer behavior; otherwise the results can be misleading. The participants are normally paid a small sum for attending. The meeting is typically held in pleasant surroundings (a home for example), and refreshments are served to increase the informality.

In the American Airlines example, the group interviewer may start with a broad question, such as "How do you feel when you are about to fly on an airplane?" Questions then move to how people feel about different airlines, different services, and in-flight telephone service. The interviewer encourages free and easy discussion among the participants, hoping that the group dynamics will reveal deep feelings and thoughts that are new to the researcher. At the same time, the interviewer "focuses" the discussion, and hence the name *focus-group interviewing*. The discussion is recorded through note taking or on audio or video tape and is subsequently studied to understand consumer attitudes and behavior.

Focus-group research is a useful exploratory step to take before designing a large-scale survey. It provides insight into consumer perceptions, attitudes, and satisfaction that will be important in defining the issues to be researched more formally. Consumer-goods companies interested in the appeal of specific products have been using focus groups for many years, and an increasing number of newspapers, law firms, hospitals, and public-service organizations are discovering their value. Yet, however useful they are, researchers must avoid generalizing the reported feelings of the people in the focus group(s) to the whole market, since the sample size is too small and the sample is not drawn randomly.[12]

SURVEY RESEARCH   Survey research stands midway between the exploratory nature of observational and focus group research and the rigor of experimental research. Generally speaking, observation and focus groups are best suited for exploratory research, surveys are best suited for descriptive research, and experiments are best suited for causal research. Companies undertake surveys to learn about people's knowledge, beliefs, preferences, satisfaction, and so on, and to measure these magnitudes in the population. Thus American Airlines researchers might want to survey how many people know American, have flown it, prefer it, and so on. We will say more about survey research when we move to research instruments, sampling plan, and contact methods.

EXPERIMENTAL RESEARCH   The most scientifically valid research is experimental research. Experimental research calls for selecting matched groups of subjects, subjecting them to different treatments, controlling extraneous variables, and checking whether observed response differences are statistically significant. To the extent that extraneous factors are eliminated or controlled, the observed effects can be related to the variations in the stimuli. The purpose of experimental research is to capture cause-and-effect relationships by eliminating competing explanations of the observed findings.

For example, American Airlines might introduce in-flight phone service on one of its regular flights from New York to Los Angeles at a price of $25 a phone call. On the same flight the following day, it announces the availability of this service at $15 a phone call. If the plane carried the same number of passengers on each flight, and the day of the week made no difference, then any significant difference in the number of calls made could be related to the price charged. The experimental design could be elaborated further by trying other prices, replicating the same price on a number of flights, and including other routes in the experiment. To the extent that the design and execution of the experiment eliminate alternative hypotheses that might explain the results, the research and marketing managers can have confidence in the conclusions.

Research instruments   Marketing researchers have a choice of two main research instruments in collecting primary data: the questionnaire and mechanical devices.

QUESTIONNAIRES   The questionnaire is by far the most common instrument in collecting primary data. Broadly speaking, a questionnaire consists of a set of questions presented to a respondent for his or her answers. The questionnaire is very flexible in that there are many ways to ask questions. Questionnaires need to be carefully developed, tested, and debugged before they are administered on a large scale. One can usually spot several errors in a casually prepared questionnaire (see Exhibit 4-2).

In preparing a questionnaire, the professional marketing researcher carefully chooses the questions and their form, wording, and sequence.

A common type of error occurs in the *questions asked*, that is, in including questions that cannot, would not, or need not be answered and in omitting questions that should be answered. Each question should be checked to determine whether it contributes to the research objectives. Questions that are merely interesting should be dropped because they lengthen the time required and try the respondent's patience.

The *form of the question* can influence the response. Marketing researchers distinguish between closed-end and open-end questions. *Closed-end questions* prespecify all the possible answers, and the respondent makes a choice among them. Table 4-6A shows the most common forms of closed-end questions.

EXHIBIT 4-2

A "Questionable" Questionnaire

Suppose an airline asked passengers the following questions. What do you think of each question? (Answer before reading the comment in italics.)

1. What is your income to the nearest hundred dollars?
   People don't necessarily know their income to the nearest hundred dollars, nor do they want to reveal their income that closely. Furthermore, a questionnaire should never open with such a personal question.

2. Are you an occasional or frequent flyer?
   How do you define frequent versus occasional flying?

3. Do you like this airline?
   Yes ( ) No ( )
   "Like" is a relative term. Besides, will people answer this honestly? Furthermore, is yes-no the best way to allow a response to the question? Why is the question being asked in the first place?

4. How many airline ads did you see on television last April? This April?
   Who can remember?

5. What are the most salient and determinant attributes in your evaluation of air carriers?
   What are "salient" and "determinant" attributes? Don't use big words on me.

6. Do you think it is right for the government to tax air tickets and deprive a lot of people of the chance to fly?
   Loaded question. How can one answer this biased question?

Open-end questions allow the respondent to answer in his or her own words. These questions take various forms; the main ones are shown in Table 4-6B. Generally speaking, open-end questions often reveal more because respondents are not constrained in their answers. Open-end questions are especially useful in the exploratory stage of research where the researcher is looking for insight into how people think rather than in measuring how many people think in a certain way. Closed-end questions, on the other hand, provide answers that are easier to interpret and tabulate.

Care should be exercised in the *wording of questions*. The researcher should use simple, direct, unbiased wording. The questions should be pretested with a sample of respondents before they are formally included.

Care should also be exercised in the *sequencing of questions*. The lead question should create interest when possible. Difficult or personal questions should be asked toward the end of the interview so that respondents do not become defensive. The questions should come up in a logical order. Classificatory data on the respondent are put last because they are more personal and less interesting to the respondent.

MECHANICAL INSTRUMENTS   Mechanical devices are less frequently used in marketing research. Galvanometers are used to measure the strength of a subject's interest or emotions aroused by an exposure to a specific ad or picture. The galvanometer picks up the minute degree of sweating that accompanies emotional arousal. The tachistoscope is a device that flashes an ad to a subject with an exposure interval that may range from less than one hundredth of a second to several seconds. After each exposure, the respondent describes everything he or she recalls. Eye cameras are used to study respondents' eye movements to see at what points their eyes land first, how long they linger on a given item, and so on. The audiometer is an electronic device that is attached to television sets in participating homes to record when the set is on and to which channel it is tuned.[13]

Sampling plan   The marketing researcher must design a sampling plan, which calls for three decisions:

1. *Sampling unit.* This answers *Who is to be surveyed*? The marketing research must define the target population that will be sampled. The particular sampling unit should be specified. The particular sampling unit is not always obvious. In the American Airlines survey, should the

TABLE 4-6
Types of Questions

A. Closed-End Questions		
Name	**Description**	**Example**
Dichotomous	A question offering two answer choices.	"In arranging this trip, did you personally phone American?" Yes ☐ No ☐
Multiple choice	A question offering three or more answer choices.	"With whom are you traveling on this flight?" No one ☐ Children only ☐ Spouse ☐ Business associates/ Spouse and friends/relatives ☐ children ☐ An organized tour group ☐
Likert scale	A statement with which the respondent shows the amount of agreement/disagreement.	"Small airlines generally give better service than large ones." Strongly Disagree Neither Agree Strongly disagree agree nor agree disagree 1 ☐ 2 ☐ 3 ☐ 4 ☐ 5 ☐
Semantic differential	A scale is inscribed between two bipolar words, and the respondent selects the point that represents the direction and intensity of his or her feelings.	**American Airlines** Large X · __ · __ · __ · __ · __ · __ Small Experienced __ · __ · __ · __ · __ · X · __ Inexperienced Modern __ · __ · __ · X · __ · __ · __ Old-fashioned
Importance scale	A scale that rates the importance of some attribute from "not at all important" to "extremely important."	"Airline food service to me is" Extremely Very Somewhat Not very Not at all important important important important important 1 __ 2 __ 3 __ 4 __ 5 __
Rating scale	A scale that rates some attribute from "poor" to "excellent."	"American's food service is" Excellent Very good Good Fair Poor 1 __ 2 __ 3 __ 4 __ 5 __
B. Open-End Questions		
Name	**Description**	**Example**
Completely unstructured	A question that respondents can answer in an almost unlimited number of ways.	"What is your opinion of American Airlines?"
Word association	Words are presented, one at a time, and respondents mention the first word that comes to mind.	"What is the first word that comes to your mind when you hear the following?" Airline _____ American _____ Travel _____
Sentence completion	Incomplete sentences are presented, one at a time, and respondents complete the sentence.	"When I choose an airline, the most important consideration in my decision is _____"
Story completion	An incomplete story is presented, and respondents are asked to complete it.	"I flew American a few days ago. I noticed that the exterior and interior of the plane had very bright colors. This aroused in me the following thoughts and feelings." **Now complete the story.**

TABLE 4-6 Continued

Name	Description	Example
Picture completion	A picture of two characters is presented, with one making a statement. Respondents are asked to identify with the other and fill in the empty balloon.	Fill in the empty balloon.
Thematic Apperception Tests (TAT)	A picture is presented, and respondents are asked to make up a story about what they think is happening or may happen in the picture.	Make up a story about what you see.

sampling unit be business travelers, vacation travelers, or both? Should travelers under twenty-one be interviewed? Should both husbands and wives be interviewed? Once this is determined, a sampling frame must be developed, namely, a way of giving everyone in the target population an equal or known chance of being sampled.

2. *Sample size.* This answers *How many people should be surveyed*? Large samples give more reliable results than small samples. However, it is not necessary to sample the entire target group or even a substantial portion to achieve reliable results. Samples of less than 1 percent of a population can often provide good reliability, given a creditable sampling procedure.

3. *Sampling procedure.* This answers *How should the respondents be chosen*? To obtain a representative sample, a probability sample of the population should be drawn. Probability sampling allows the calculation of confidence limits for sampling error. Thus one could conclude after the sample is taken that "the interval 5 to 7 trips per year has 95 chances in 100 of containing the true number of trips taken annually by air travelers in the Southwest." Three types of probability sampling are described in Table 4-7A. When the cost or time involved in probability sampling is too high, marketing researchers will take nonprobability samples. Table 4-7B describes three types of nonprobability sampling. Some marketing researchers feel that nonprobability samples can be very useful in many circumstances, even though the sampling error cannot be measured.

Contact methods   This answers *How should the subject be contacted*? The choices are telephone, mail, or personal interviews.

Telephone interviewing is the best method for gathering information quickly; the interviewer is also able to clarify questions if they are not understood. The two main drawbacks are that only people with telephones can be interviewed, and the interviews have to be short and not too personal.

The *mail questionnaire* may be the best way to reach individuals who would not give personal interviews or whose responses might be biased or distorted by the interviewers. On the other hand, mail questionnaires require simple and clearly worded questions, and the return rate is usually low and/or slow.

Personal interviewing is the most versatile of the three methods. The interviewer can ask more questions and can record additional observation about the respondent, such as dress and body language. Personal interviewing is the most expensive method and

TABLE 4-7   Types of Probability and Nonprobability Samples

A. Probability sample	
Simple random sample	Every member of the population has a known and equal chance of selection.
Stratified random sample	The population is divided into mutually exclusive groups (such as age groups), and random samples are drawn from each group.
Cluster (area) sample	The population is divided into mutually exclusive groups (such as blocks), and the researcher draws a sample of the groups to interview.
B. Nonprobability sample	
Convenience sample	The researcher selects the most accessible population members from which to obtain information.
Judgment sample	The researcher uses his or her judgment to select population members who are good prospects for accurate information.
Quota sample	The researcher finds and interviews a prescribed number of people in each of several categories.

requires more administrative planning and supervision. It is also subject to interviewer bias or distortion.

Personal interviewing takes two forms, *arranged interviews* and *mall intercept interviews*. In arranged interviews, respondents are randomly selected and are either telephoned or approached at their homes and asked to grant an interview. Often a small payment or incentive is presented to respondents in appreciation of their time, but the no-show rate can be high. Mall intercept interviews involve stopping people at a mall or street and requesting an interview. Mall interviews have the drawbacks of being nonprobability samples, and the interviews must be quite short.

Collecting the Information   The researcher must now arrange for collecting the data. This phase is generally the most expensive and the most liable to error. In the case of surveys, four major problems arise. Some respondents will not be at home and must be recontacted or replaced. Other respondents may refuse to cooperate. Still others may give biased or dishonest answers. Finally, some interviewers will occasionally be biased or dishonest.

In the case of experimental research, the researchers have to worry about matching the experimental and control groups, not influencing the participants by their presence, administering the treatments in a uniform way, and controlling for extraneous factors.

Data-collection methods are rapidly changing under the impact of modern telecommunications and electronics. Computers and electronic-communication hardware are causing a quiet revolution in marketing research. Some research firms now conduct their interviewing from a centralized location using a combination of *WATS lines, cathode-ray tubes (CRT)*, and *data-entry terminals*. Professional telephone interviewers sit in separate booths and draw telephone numbers at random from somewhere in the nation. In dialing the person whose number has been selected, the interviewers use WATS lines, which means that the research firm has prepaid the telephone company so that it can make a certain large number of long-distance calls. When the phone is answered, the interviewer asks the person a set of questions, reading them from the cathode-ray tube. The interviewer types the respondents' answers right into a computer, using the data-entry terminal. This procedure eliminates editing and coding, reduces the number of errors, saves time, and produces all the required statistics.

Other research firms have set up *interactive terminals* in shopping centers. Persons willing to be interviewed sit down at a terminal, read the questions from the CRT, and type in their answers. Most respondents enjoy this form of ''robot'' interviewing.[14] Exhibit 4-3 describes an even more recent and revolutionary breakthrough in ''electronic marketing research.''

Analyzing the Information The next step in the marketing research process is to extract pertinent findings from the data. The researcher tabulates the data and develops one-way and two-way frequency distributions. Averages and measures of dispersion are computed for the major variables. The researcher will attempt to apply some of the advanced statistical techniques and decision models in the analytical marketing system in the hope of discovering additional findings. (See pp. 122–31.)

EXHIBIT 4-3   The Marketer's Dream: Measuring Consumer Response to Ads

Several technical advances have recently permitted marketers to test the sales impact of ads and sales promotions. The advances include (1) the universal code on packages, (2) optical scanners, (3) electronic cash registers, (4) smart cards, (5) cable television, and (6) television viewing monitors. Here is how they work in concert.

A research firm, Information Resources, Inc., recruits a panel of supermarkets that are equipped with optical scanners and electronic cash registers. The store clerk passes the customer's goods over a light beam which reads the *universal code* on each package and records the brand, size, and price. Meanwhile the research firm has also recruited a panel of customers of these stores who have agreed to charge their grocery purchases with a special Shopper's Hotline ID card that has not only their name and bank account number but also personal information on household characteristics, lifestyle, income, and so on. These customers have also agreed to let their television-viewing habits be monitored by a black box in their television sets which records what is being watched, when, and by whom. All consumer panelists receive their programs through cable television. Now the key is that Information Resources, Inc., controls the advertising messages being sent out to the consumer panel members. The company can beam different messages, headlines, or promotions to different panel members. The research firm can then capture through the store purchase data which ads led to more purchasing and by what kinds of consumers. This research service, which Information Resources, Inc., calls BehaviorScan, makes it possible to evaluate consumer responses to various marketing stimuli with greater precision than ever.

Aside from this advanced service for advertisers, the retailers themselves have benefited greatly from simply the presence of optical scanner equipment which now accounts for half of all grocery store sales. Retailers can more quickly analyze the movement of goods for the purposes of improved inventory control and shelf space allocation, thus helping them improve the profitability of their store operations.

SOURCES See ''Big Brother Gets a Job in Market Research,'' *Business Week*, April 8, 1985, pp. 96–97; ''Wired Consumers: Market Researchers Go Hi-Tech to Hone Ads, Weed Out Flops,'' *Wall Street Journal*, January 23, 1986; and ''High-Tech Shocks in Ad Research,'' *Fortune*, July 7, 1986, pp. 58–62.

Presenting the Findings   The researcher should not try to overwhelm management with lots of numbers and fancy statistical techniques—this will lose them. The researcher should present major findings that are relevant to the major marketing decisions facing management. The study is useful when it reduces management's uncertainty concerning the right move to make.

Suppose the main survey findings for the American Airlines case show that

1. The chief reasons for using in-flight phone service are emergencies, urgent business deals, mix-ups in flight times, and so on. Making phone calls to pass the time would be rare. Most of the calls would be made by businesspeople on expense accounts.
2. About 5 passengers out of every 200 would make in-flight phone calls at a price of $25 a call; and about 12 would make calls at $15. Thus a charge of $15 would produce more revenue (12 × $15 = $180) than $25 a call (5 × $25 = $125). Still, that is far below the in-flight break-even cost of $1,000.
3. The promotion of in-flight phone service would win American about two extra passengers on each flight. The net revenue from these two extra passengers would be about $620, but that still would not help meet the break-even cost.
4. Offering in-flight service would strengthen the public's image of American Airlines as an innovative and progressive airline. However, it would cost American about $200 per flight to create this extra goodwill.

These findings, of course, could suffer from sampling error, and management may want to study the issue further. However, it looks as if in-flight phone service would add more to cost than to long-term revenue and should not be implemented at the present time. Thus a well-defined marketing research project has helped American's managers make a better decision than would probably have come out of "seat-of-the-pants" decision making.

Characteristics of Good Marketing Research

Having examined the major steps in the marketing research process, we can highlight five characteristics of good marketing research.

Scientific Method   Effective marketing research uses the principles of the scientific method: careful observation, formulation of hypotheses, prediction, and testing. An example follows.

> A mail-order house was suffering from a high rate (30 percent) of returned merchandise. Management asked the marketing research manager to investigate the causes of the high return rate. The marketing researcher examined the characteristics of returned orders, such as the geographical locations of the customers, the sizes of the returned orders, and the merchandise categories. One hypothesis was that the longer the customer waited for ordered merchandise, the greater the probability of its return. Statistical analysis confirmed this hypothesis. The researcher estimated how much the return rate would drop for a specific speedup of service. The company did this, and the prediction proved correct.[15]

Research Creativity   At its best, marketing research develops innovative ways to solve a problem. A classic example of research creativity is described below:

When instant coffee was first introduced, housewives complained that it did not taste like real coffee. Yet in blindfold tests, many of these same housewives could not distinguish between a cup of instant coffee and real coffee. This indicated that much of their resistance was psychological. The researcher decided to design two almost identical shopping lists, the only difference being that regular coffee was on one list and instant coffee on the other. The regular-coffee list was given to one group of housewives and the instant-coffee list was given to a different, but comparable, group. Both groups were asked to guess the social and personal characteristics of the woman whose shopping list they saw. The comments were pretty much the same with one significant difference: a higher proportion of the housewives whose list contained instant coffee described the subject as "lazy, a spendthrift, a poor wife, and failing to plan well for her family." These women obviously were imputing to the fictional housewife their own anxieties and negative images about the use of instant coffee. The instant-coffee company now knew the nature of the resistance and could develop a campaign to change the image of the housewife who serves instant coffee.[18]

Multiple Methods   Competent marketing researchers shy away from overreliance on any one method, preferring to adapt the method to the problem rather than the other way around. They also recognize the desirability of gathering information from multiple sources to give greater confidence.

Interdependence of Models and Data   Competent marketing researchers recognize that the facts derive their meaning from models of the problem. These models guide the type of information sought and therefore should be made as explicit as possible.

Value and Cost of Information   Competent marketing researchers show concern for measuring the value of information against its cost. Value/cost helps the marketing research department determine which research projects to conduct, which research designs to use, and whether to gather more information after the initial results are in.[17] The costs of research are typically easy to quantify, while the value is harder to anticipate. The value depends on the reliability and validity of the research findings and management's willingness to accept and act on its findings.

Management's Use of Marketing Research

In spite of the rapid growth of marketing research, many companies still fail to use it sufficiently or correctly. Several factors stand in the way of its greater utilization.

■ *A narrow conception of marketing research.* Many executives see marketing research as only a fact-finding operation. The marketing researcher is supposed to design a questionnaire, choose a sample, conduct interviews, and report results, often without being given a careful definition of the problem or of the decision alternatives before management. As a result, some of the fact finding fails to be useful. This reinforces management's idea of the limited good that can come from marketing research.

■ *Uneven caliber of marketing researchers.* Some executives view marketing research as little better than a clerical activity and reward it as such. Less-able marketing researchers are hired, and their weak training and deficient creativity lead to unimpressive results. The disappointing results reinforce management's prejudice against expecting too much from marketing research. Management continues to pay low salaries, perpetuating the basic difficulty.

■ *Late results.* Carefully designed marketing research can take a long time to carry out. The report may come too late in terms of when a decision has to be made.

■ *Occasional erroneous findings by marketing research.* Many executives want conclusive information from marketing research, although marketing phenomena are often too complex to yield conclusive findings. The problem is complicated by the low budgets given to marketing researchers to get the information. Executives become disappointed, and their opinion of the value of marketing research is lowered.

- ■ *Intellectual differences.* Intellectual divergences between the mental styles of line managers and marketing researchers often get in the way of productive relationships. The marketing researcher's report may seem abstract, complicated, and tentative, while what the line manager wants is concreteness, simplicity, and certainty. Yet in the more progressive companies, marketing researchers are increasingly being included as members of the brand management team, and their influence on marketing strategy is growing.

ANALYTICAL MARKETING SYSTEM

A growing number of organizations have added a fourth information service to help their marketing executives—an analytical marketing system. Today's marketing managers in such companies as General Foods and General Mills can sit down at their computer terminals and answer many questions based on stored data that were formerly inaccessible. Their computers store a bank of linked statistical and decision models that make up a *marketing decision support system*. Here we will examine the main statistical procedures and decision models in these decision support systems (see Figure 4-3).

The Statistical Bank

The *statistical bank is a collection of statistical procedures for extracting meaningful information from data*. It contains the usual statistical routines for calculating averages, measures of dispersion, and cross-tabulations of the data. In addition, the researcher can use various *multivariate statistical techniques* to discover important relationships in the data. The most important multivariate techniques are described below.[18]

Multiple Regression Analysis   Every marketing problem involves a set of variables. The marketing researcher is typically interested in one of these variables, such as sales, and seeks to understand the cause(s) of its variation over time and/or space. This variable is called the dependent variable. The researcher hypothesizes about other variables, called independent variables, whose variations over time or space might contribute to the variations in the dependent variable. Regression analysis is the technique of estimating an equation

FIGURE 4-3
Analytical Marketing System

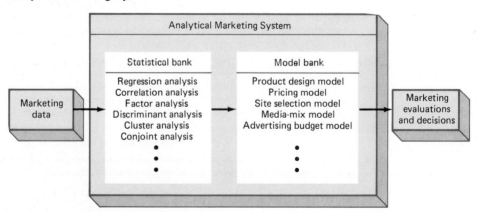

that shows the contribution of independent variables to variations in the dependent variable. When one independent variable is involved, the statistical procedure is called simple regression; when two or more independent variables are involved, the procedure is called multiple regression. An example of multiple regression is presented on page 275.

Discriminant Analysis   In many marketing situations, the dependent variable is classificatory rather than numerical. Consider the following situations:

- An automobile company wants to identify consumer traits associated with brand preferences for Chevrolet versus Ford.
- A detergent company wants to determine what consumer traits are associated with heavy, medium, and light usage of its brand.
- A retailing chain wants to be able to discriminate between potentially successful and unsuccessful store sites.

In these cases, the analyst visualizes two or more groups to which a person or object may belong. The challenge is to find discriminating variables that could be combined in a predictive equation to produce better-than-chance assignment of the entities to the groups. The technique for solving this problem is known as discriminant analysis. This analysis has been used to identify profiles of innovators, develop relevant criteria for market segmentation, and examine consumer brand preference behavior.[19]

Factor Analysis   One of the problems faced in many regression and discriminant studies is a high intercorrelation among the explanatory variables, which leads to biased estimates of the effect of these variables on the dependent variable(s). The ideal in multiple regression is to use variables that are truly independent, both in the sense that they influence but are not influenced by the dependent variable and in the sense that each independent variable is independent of the others. The simple correlation coefficients for all pairs of variables will reveal which variables are highly correlated. Factor analysis is a statistical procedure for trying to discover a few basic factors that may underlie and explain the correlations among a larger number of variables. In the marketing area, factor analysis has been used to determine the basic factors underlying attitudes toward air travel, alcoholic beverages, and television programs.

Cluster Analysis   Many marketing problems require the researcher to sort a set of objects into subgroups or clusters. The objects may be products, people, places, and so on. Thus the researcher might want to sort several automobile makes into major groups with as much likeness within groups and as much difference between groups as possible; automobiles within a group can be assumed to be most competitive with each other. Or the researcher might want to cluster people into subgroups, which is essentially what we mean by market segmentation. Or the researcher might want to cluster cities into groups so that test cities could be drawn that resemble each other. In all cases, the objects are described by multidimensional data, and the chosen clustering technique operates on the data to sort the objects into a prespecified number of groups.[20]

Conjoint Analysis   Conjoint analysis is used by marketers to determine how to design an appealing product for a target market. The marketer wants to decide what attributes to build in the product at what levels. Consumers are shown a set of hypothetical products (differing in attributes) and are asked to rank them. From these rankings, the researcher can determine the importance of each attribute and the most effective combination. Conjoint analysis has proved to be an increasingly useful marketing research tool with more than one thousand reported applications to date.[21]

The Model Bank   The *model bank is a collection of models that will help marketers develop better marketing decisions.* A model itself is a *set of variables and their interrelationships designed to represent some real system or process.* Models are built by management scientists (also called operations researchers), who apply scientific methodology to achieve understanding, prediction, or control over some management problem.

Although management science is a relative latecomer in marketing, it has already yielded useful models for new-product sales forecasting,[22] site selection,[23] sales-call planning,[24] media mix,[25] and marketing-mix budgeting.[26] Several models are being used by some large companies.[27]

Although marketing executives often lack the training to understand the mathematics of some of the more complex models, they certainly can grasp the central idea behind each type of model and can judge its relevance to their work. The major types of models are listed in Table 4-8 and discussed in the following paragraphs.

Descriptive Models   Descriptive models are designed to communicate, explain, or predict. They can be built at three levels of detail. A *macromodel* consists of a few variables and a set of relationships among them. An example would be a sales model consisting of a single equation with total sales as the dependent variable and national income, average price, and company advertising expenditures as the independent variables. They are derived by fitting the "best" possible equation to the set of variables.

A *microanalytic model* specifies more links between a dependent variable and its determinants. A good example is the DEMON model, in which the effect of advertising expenditures on sales is explained through a set of successive links between advertising expenditure, gross number of exposures, reach and frequency, advertising awareness, consumer trial, usage, and usage rate.[28]

A *microbehavioral model* creates hypothetical entities (consumers, dealers, and so on) who interact and produce a record of behavior, which is then analyzed. A good example is a consumer model built by Amstutz, in which a population of potential purchasers are exposed to weekly marketing stimuli, and some fraction of them purchase the product.[29]

Two descriptive models in the operations research literature are particularly germane

TABLE 4-8   A Classification of Models

I. According to Purpose	II. According to Techniques
A. Descriptive Models	A. Verbal Models
1. Markov-process model	B. Graphical Models
2. Queuing model	1. Logical-flow model
B. Decision Models	2. Network-planning model
1. Differential calculus	3. Causal model
2. Mathematical programming	4. Decision-tree model
3. Statistical decision theory	5. Functional-relationship model
4. Game theory	6. Feedback-systems model
	C. Mathematical Models
	1. Linear vs. nonlinear model
	2. Static vs. dynamic model
	3. Deterministic vs. stochastic model

to marketing-type problems. The first is the *Markov-process model*, which describes the probabilities of moving from any current state to any new state. Suppose there are three coffee brands, A, B, and C. Of those consumers who bought brand A last time, suppose 70 percent buy it again, 20 percent buy B, and 10 percent buy C. This information is represented in row one of Figure 4-4, along with probabilities associated with brands B and C. The brand-switching matrix provides information about

- ■ The *repeat-purchase rate* for each brand, indicated by the numbers in the diagonal starting at the upper left. Under certain assumptions, the repeat-purchase rate can be interpreted as a measure of brand loyalty.
- ■ The *switching-in* and *switching-out* rate for each brand, represented by the off-diagonal numbers.

If the switching rates remain constant, the matrix can be used to provide a conditional prediction as to where the market appears to be headed.[30]

Queuing models are also of interest to marketers. Queuing models describe waiting-line situations and answer two questions: What waiting time can be expected in a particular system? and How will this waiting time change if the system is altered? These questions are of interest to supermarkets, gasoline stations, airline ticket offices, and so on. Wherever customers wait, there is the danger that waiting time will become excessive, leading to the loss of some customers to competitors.

If the current system breeds long queues, the analyst can simulate the effects of different solutions. In the case of a supermarket, four possible attacks are possible. The supermarket can influence its customers to shop on less-busy days. The supermarket can employ baggers to aid the cashiers and thus reduce waiting time. More service channels can be added. Finally, some of the service channels can be specialized to handle smaller orders.

Decision Models Decision models assist managers in evaluating alternatives and finding a good solution. An *optimization model* is one for which mathematical routines exist for finding the best solution. A *heuristic model* is one for which computational routines exist to find a pretty good solution. The heuristic model may involve a much more complex statement of the problem. The analyst applies heuristics, defined as rules of thumb that shorten the time or work required to find a reasonably good solution. For example, in a model to determine good warehouse locations, the heuristic might be "Consider locations only in large cities." This may exclude a perfectly good location in a small city, but the savings in having to check far fewer cities may compensate for the omission.

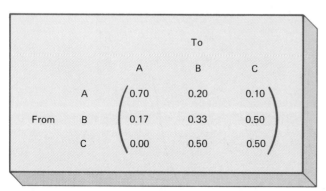

FIGURE 4-4
A Brand-Switching Matrix

Four optimization-type decision models are of particular relevance to marketing. The first is *differential calculus*, which is applied to well-defined mathematical functions to find the maximum or minimum value. Suppose a marketing analyst has determined the profit equation shown in Figure 4-5(a). The task is to find the best price—that is, the value of P that will maximize the value of Z. One approach is to graph the equation and examine it for the profit-maximizing price, here $150. A quicker procedure is to apply differential calculus to this equation without bothering to draw a graph.

The second type of decision model is *mathematical programming*. Here the decision maker's objective is expressed as some variable to be optimized subject to a set of explicitly expressed constraints. Consider the problem in Figure 4-5(b). It shows a profit function relating profits to the amount of funds spent on advertising and distribution. A dollar of advertising contributes $10 of profit, and a dollar of distribution contributes $20. A set of policy constraints is also introduced. First the marketing budget, as divided between advertising and distribution, should not exceed $100 (constraint 1). Of this, advertising should receive at least $40 (constraint 2) and no more than $80 (constraint 3); and distribution

FIGURE 4-5
Four Decision Models

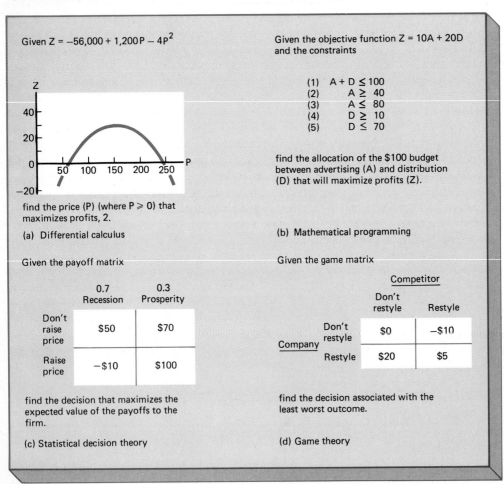

Given $Z = -56,000 + 1,200P - 4P^2$

find the price (P) (where $P \geq 0$) that maximizes profits, 2.

(a) Differential calculus

Given the objective function $Z = 10A + 20D$ and the constraints

(1)	$A + D \leq 100$
(2)	$A \geq 40$
(3)	$A \leq 80$
(4)	$D \geq 10$
(5)	$D \leq 70$

find the allocation of the $100 budget between advertising (A) and distribution (D) that will maximize profits (Z).

(b) Mathematical programming

Given the payoff matrix

	0.7 Recession	0.3 Prosperity
Don't raise price	$50	$70
Raise price	−$10	$100

find the decision that maximizes the expected value of the payoffs to the firm.

(c) Statistical decision theory

Given the game matrix

		Competitor	
		Don't restyle	Restyle
Company	Don't restyle	$0	−$10
	Restyle	$20	$5

find the decision associated with the least worst outcome.

(d) Game theory

should receive at least $10 (constraint 4) and no more than $70 (constraint 5). Because of the simplicity of this problem, the best marketing program can be found without invoking higher mathematics. Since distribution dollars are twice as effective as advertising dollars, it would make sense to spend all that is permitted within the constraints on distribution. This would be $70, leaving $30 for advertising. However, advertising must receive at least $40 according to constraint 2. Therefore the optimal marketing-mix allocation would be $40 for advertising and $60 for distribution; and with this solution, profits will be $10($40) + $20($60) = $1,600. In larger problems, the analyst would have to use specific mathematical procedures.

The third type of decision model is called *statistical decision theory* (or Bayesian decision theory). This model calls for (1) identifying major decision alternatives facing the firm, (2) distinguishing the events (states of nature) that might, with each possible decision, bring about a distinct outcome, (3) estimating the probability of each state of nature, (4) estimating the value (payoff) of each outcome to the firm, (5) determining the expected value of each decision, and (6) choosing the decision with the highest expected value. Consider this in relation to the problem in Figure 4-5(c). Suppose a product manager is trying to decide between raising a price or leaving it alone. The outcome will be affected by whether the economy slides into a recession, of which the product manager believes there is a 0.7 chance. If a recession occurs and the price is not raised, profits will be $50; but if the price is raised, there will be a loss of $10. On the other hand, if the economy is prosperous and prices are unchanged, the profits will be $70; and if prices had been raised, profits would have been $100. These estimates are summarized in the payoff matrix.

Statistical decision theory calls for the product manager to estimate the expected value of each decision. Expected value is the weighted mean of the payoffs, with the probabilities serving as the weights. The expected value associated with not raising the price is 0.7($50) + 0.3($70) = $56, while the expected value of raising the price is 0.7(−$10) + 0.3($100) = $23. Clearly, the extra gain with the best thing happening (a raised price and prosperity) is not worth the risk, and the product manager is better off leaving the price alone. This assumes that expected value is a satisfactory criterion for the firm to maximize. This criterion is sensible for a large firm that makes repeated decisions of this kind. It makes less sense for a smaller firm facing a major one-shot decision that could ruin it if things went wrong.[31] For more-complex problems, the options are represented in a decision tree [see Figure 4-6(d)].

Game theory is a fourth approach to evaluating decision alternatives. Like statistical decision theory, it calls for identifying the decision alternatives, uncertain variables, and the value of different outcomes. It differs from statistical decision theory in that the major uncertain variable is assumed to be a competitor, nature, or some other force that is malevolent. The probability is 1.00 that each actor will do what is in its best interest. Consider the example in Figure 4-5(d). An auto manufacturer is trying to decide whether to restyle its car. It knows that the competitor is also trying to make the same decision. The company estimates that if neither restyles, neither will gain anything over the normal rate of profit. If the company restyles and the competitor does not, the company will gain $20 over the competitor. (We will assume the competitor loses $20—that is, the gain to one company is a loss to the other.) If the company does not restyle and the competitor does, the company loses $10. Finally, if they both restyle, the company gains $5, and the competitor loses $5, because the company is assumed to be better at restyling.

A solution is possible if we assume that both opponents will want to take the course of action that will leave them *least worst off*. Called the *minimax criterion* (minimizing

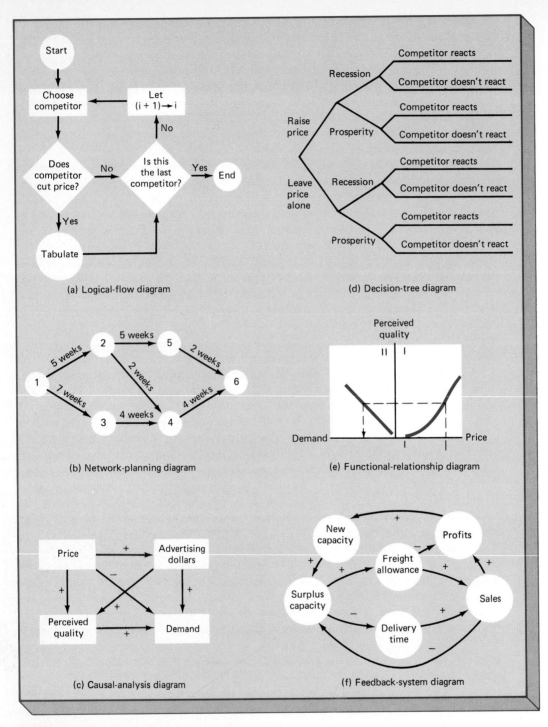

FIGURE 4-6
Six Graphical Models for Marketing Analysis

the maximum loss), it assumes that both opponents are conservative. This will lead the company to prefer the restyling alternative. It it does not restyle, it might lose as much as $10; if it does restyle, it will make at least $5. The competitor wants to restyle. If it does not restyle, it might lose as much as $20; if it does restyle, it will lose more than $5. Hence both opponents will decide to restyle, which leaves a $5 gain for the company and a $5 loss for the competitor. Neither opponent can gain by moving unilaterally to a different strategy.[32]

Verbal Models Models in which the variables and their relationships are described in prose are verbal models. Most of the great theories of individual, social, and societal behavior—theories such as those of Freud, Darwin, and Marx—are cast in verbal terms. Many models of consumer behavior are essentially in verbal-model form. Consider ". . . advertising should move people from *awareness* . . . to *knowledge* . . . to *liking* . . . to *preference* . . . to *conviction* . . . to *purchase*."[33]

Graphical Models Graphical models represent a useful step in the process of symbolizing a verbal model. Six graphical models can be distinguished.

Figure 4-6(a) shows a *logical-flow diagram*. A logical-flow diagram is a visual representation of a logical process or operation. The boxes in the diagram are connected in a sequential flow pattern and related through two operations. One of these is *branching*. Branching takes place when a question is posed at a certain step of the process, and its possible answers are depicted as alternative branches leading away from the box. The other operation is *looping*. Looping takes place if certain answers return the flow to an earlier stage. The flow diagram in Figure 4-6(a) describes a firm's efforts to determine how many competitors will cut their prices. The firm first considers competitor i and asks whether it is likely to cut its price. If the answer is yes, this result is tabulated, and then the firm asks whether there are any additional competitors to consider. If the answer is no, the firm goes directly to the next question. If there are more competitors to consider, the logical flow loops back to the first box; otherwise the flow ends. Logical-flow diagrams are coming into increasing use in marketing because of the clarity with which they illustrate a logical process.

Figure 4-6(b) shows a *network-planning diagram* (also called a critical-path diagram), which portrays the events that must occur to complete a project. The events, shown as circles, are connected by arrows indicating precedent relationships. In Figure 4-6(b), event 6 cannot occur until events 4 and 5 are completed; event 5 cannot occur until event 2 is completed; event 4 cannot occur until events 2 and 3 are completed; and so on. By estimating the completion time of each task (and sometimes the optimistic and pessimistic completion times), the analyst can find the earliest date to completion of the entire project. The network will contain a critical path that defines the earliest possible completion time; here it is fifteen weeks. Unless this critical path is shortened, there is no way to complete the project earlier. This diagram is the basis of planning, scheduling, and controlling projects, such as the development of a new product.

Figure 4-6(c) shows a *causal-analysis diagram*, which is used to portray the directions of influence of specific variables on each other. This diagram shows that price has a direct (negative) influence on demand and an indirect influence also through its positive effects on advertising dollars and perceived quality. A high price leads to high perceived quality and leads the company to spend more on advertising. Both of these in turn have a positive effect on demand. (Not shown is the fact that the resulting demand will have a feedback influence on advertising expenditures as well as on the perceived quality.) The value of causal-analysis diagrams is in exposing the complex relationships that the analyst must take into account. They remind us that single-equation relationships between variables may fail to capture the true causal relations among variables.

Figure 4-6(d) shows a *decision-tree diagram*, which portrays the decision alternatives and consequences found in a decision situation. A manager is trying to decide between raising the price and leaving it alone. The outcome will be influenced by whether the economy moves toward recession or prosperity and further by whether competitors react. The tree could be extended to show other contingencies related to buyer reactions, inventory situations, and so on. By adding payoffs and probabilities to the various branches of the tree, the best decision can be found by using statistical decision theory.

Figure 4-6(e) is a *functional-relationship diagram*, which portrays functional relationship(s) between two or more variables. Quadrant I shows a positive relationship between price and perceived quality. Quadrant II shows a positive relationship between perceived quality and demand. The two quadrants enable the analyst to trace the effect of a particular price, through perceived quality, on a particular demand level. Thus one can generate a demand function from knowledge of two other functions. Functional graphs can be used to portray sales-response functions, probability distributions, and many other relationships.

Figure 4-6(f) shows a *feedback-system diagram*, which portrays any system whose outputs return and influence subsequent outputs. This process should not be confused with looping in logical-flow diagrams, which merely returns the procedure to an earlier point without implying any influence on that point. The example shows the interactions among sales, profits, capacity, and marketing variables. Surplus capacity leads the company to offer higher freight allowances to customers and faster delivery time. These lead to higher sales. Increased sales lead to increased profits while drawing down surplus capacity. In the meantime, the higher freight allowances reduce profits. If the net effect is a gain in profits, that leads to additional investment in capacity; and the cycle continues. Thus feedback-system diagrams are useful devices for representing variables that have interactive properties and feedbacks.[34]

Graphical models have all the virtues that are found in "pictures." A graph strips the phenomenon of inessentials; it allows a viewer to grasp the whole and select which relationships to examine. For marketing analysts, graphs improve exposition, facilitate discussion, and guide analysis.

Mathematical Models Mathematical models can be classified in many ways. One distinction is between *linear* and *nonlinear models*. In a linear model, all the relationships between variables are expressed as straight lines. This means that a unit change in one variable has a constant marginal impact on a related variable. The advertising-sales relationship would be linear if every $100 increase in advertising created a $1,000 increase in sales, no matter how much had already been spent. This kind of increase is unlikely, however, because increasing or diminishing returns to advertising can be expected. It is also likely that other marketing inputs, such as price and sales-call time, do not relate to sales in a thoroughly linear way. The assumption of linearity is useful as a first approximation for mathematical convenience.

A second distinction can be drawn between *static* and *dynamic models*. A *static* model centers on the ultimate state (or solution) of a system, independent of time. A *dynamic* model brings time explicitly into its framework and allows the state of the system to be observed over time. The demand-supply diagram in beginning economics courses represents a static model of price determination in that it indicates where price and output will be in equilibrium without indicating the path of adjustment through time. Brand-switching models are dynamic in that they predict period-to-period changes in customer brand choices.

A third distinction can be drawn between *deterministic* and *stochastic* models. A *deterministic model* is one in which chance plays no role. The solution is determined by a set of exact relationships. The linear-programming model for determining blends (oils, animal feeds, candies) is deterministic because the relationships are exact and the cost data are known. A *stochastic model*, on the other hand, is one where chance or random variables are introduced explicitly. Brand-switching models are stochastic in that customers' brand choices are regulated by probabilities.

As management scientists enter more companies, they will provide a set of statistical procedures and decision models that will greatly enhance the marketing manager's skill in making better-informed decisions. The main need is that marketing managers and management scientists move rapidly toward understanding each other's needs and capabilities.[35]

SUMMARY

Marketing information is a critical element in effective marketing as a result of the trend toward national and international marketing, the transition from buyer needs to buyer wants, and the transition from price to nonprice competition. All firms have a marketing information system connecting the external environment with its executives, but the systems vary greatly in the level of sophistication. In too many cases, information is not available or comes too late or cannot be trusted. An increasing number of companies are not taking steps to improve their marketing information systems.

A well-designed market information system consists of four subsystems. The first is the internal reports system, which provides current data on sales, costs, inventories, cash flows, and accounts receivable and payable. Many companies have developed advanced computer-based internal reports systems to allow for speedier and more comprehensive information.

The second is the marketing intelligence system, which supplies marketing executives with everyday information about developments in the external marketing environment. Here a well-trained sales force, special intelligence personnel, purchased data from syndicated sources, and an intelligence office can improve the marketing intelligence available to company executives.

The third system is marketing research, which involves collecting information that is relevant to a specific marketing problem facing the company. The marketing research process consists of five steps: defining the problem and research objectives, developing the research plan, collecting the information, analyzing the information, and presenting the findings. Good marketing research is characterized by the scientific method, creativity, multiple methodologies, model building, and cost/benefit measures of the value of information.

The fourth system is the analytical marketing system, which consists of advanced statistical procedures and models to develop more rigorous findings from information.

Marketing scientists use descriptive or decision models and verbal, graphical, or mathematical models to come to grips with marketing problems.

■ QUESTIONS

1. The market for selling electronic data (e.g., Reuters selling commodities and securities quotes, and Dun and Bradstreet selling credit checks and business information to customers who access information on terminals and personal computers) is extremely competitive. What do you think are the "success requirements" that must be met by firms competing in this market?

2. A mail panel consists of large and nationally representative samples of households that have agreed to periodically participate in mail questionnaires, product tests, and telephone surveys. Under what circumstances would you use mail panels as part of the marketing research process described in this chapter?

3. Some research plans call for specifying at the design stage of the plan the multivariate statistical tools that will be used to analyze the data after they have been collected. Why would it be necessary to indicate these statistical techniques before the research approach and instruments have been designed?

4. For a model to prove useful to a marketing decision maker it first must be calibrated—values must be assigned to the model's parameters (the unknowns). What are some ways of calibrating models?

5. The uses of the computer for analyzing market research data are well known. What are some ways the computer can be helpful in collecting marketing research information?

6. Read Exhibit 4-3. The ACLU claims that this type of research invades the privacy of consumers. What do you think?

7. What might some research tasks be for the following areas: distribution decision, product decisions, advertising decisions, personal-selling decisions, pricing decisions?

8. You are a marketing director. Your boss wants to know how many stores carry your dry cereal. Since you sell through food brokers, you don't know the answer. She wants the answer in two days. What would you do?

9. (a) Suggest how a liquor company might estimate liquor consumption in a legally dry town. (b) Suggest how a research organization might estimate the number of people who read a specific magazine in doctors' offices. (c) Suggest six ways in which male respondents can be interviewed on their usage of hair tonics.

10. A manufacturer of automobiles is testing a new direct-mail approach B versus a standard approach A. An experiment is conducted in which each approach is tried out on random samples of size n (sample size $2n$ in total) from a large national mailing list. Suppose that $n = 100,000$, so that 200,000 is the total sample size of the experiment. During a three-month period, approach B has 761 sales and A has 753. What decision should be made? List the alternatives and the rationale of each.

11. Evaluate the following questions found in a consumer survey: (a) What is your husband's favorite brand of golf balls? (b) What TV programs did you watch last Monday? (c) How many pancakes did you make for your family last year? (d) Tell me your exact income. (e) Can you supply a list of your grocery purchases this month?

12. In obtaining estimates from company sales people, product managers, and other personnel, one must discourage estimates that are self-serving. Give some examples of self-serving estimates, and suggest how to combat this problem.

13. Some marketers are hostile toward mathematical model building in marketing. They will make the following statements: (a) We don't use models. (b) Models are unrealistic. (c) Anyone can build a model. (d) A model is useless unless you can get the data. How would you answer each objection?

■ FOOTNOTES

1 This definition is adapted from "Marketing Information Systems: An Introductory Overview," in *Readings in Marketing Information Systems*, ed. Samuel V. Smith, Richard H. Brien, and James E. Stafford (Boston: Houghton Mifflin, 1968), p. 7.

2 Jurgen F. Ringer and Charles D. Howell, "The Industrial Engineer and Marketing," in *Industrial Engineering Handbook* (2nd ed.), ed. Harold Bright Maynard (New York: McGraw-Hill, 1963), pp. 10, 102–3.

3 Catherine L. Harris, "Information Power: How Companies Are Using New Technologies to Gain a Competitive Edge," *Business Week*, October 14, 1985, pp. 108–14. Also see "Decision Systems for Marketers," *Marketing Communications*, March 1986, pp. 163–90.

4 Peter Finch, "How Computers Are Reshaping the Sales Process," *Business Marketing*, June 1985, pp. 108–18.

5 Francis Joseph Aguilar, *Scanning the Business Environment* (New York: Macmillan, 1967).

6 Eugene H. Fram, "How Focus Groups Unlock Market Intelligence: Tapping In-House 'Researchers,'" *Business Marketing*, December 1985, pp. 80–82.

7 James A. Narus and James C. Anderson, "Turn Your Industrial Distributors into Partners," *Harvard Business Review*, March–April 1986, pp. 66–71.

8 Dik Warren Twedt, ed., *1983 Survey of Marketing Research: Organization, Functions, Budget, Compensation* (Chicago: American Marketing Association, 1983).

9 Ibid.

10 For a discussion of the decision theory approach to the value of research, see Donald R. Lehmann, *Market Research and Analysis* (Homewood, Ill.: Richard D. Irwin, 1985), Chap. 2.

11 For an excellent annotated reference to major secondary sources of business and marketing data, see Thomas C. Kinnear and James R. Taylor, *Marketing Research: An Applied Approach* (New York, McGraw-Hill, 1983), pp. 134–39, 146–56, 169–84.

12 Amanda Bernett, "Once a Tool of Retail Marketers, Focus Groups Gain Wider Usage," *Wall Street Journal*, June 3, 1986.

13 An overview of mechanical devices is presented in Roger D. Blackwell, James S. Hensel, Michael B. Phillips, and Brian Sternthal, *Laboratory Equipment for Marketing Research* (Dubuque, Iowa: Kendall/Hunt Publishing Co., 1970), pp. 7–8. For newer devices, see Wally Wood, "The Race to Replace Memory," *Marketing and Media Decisions*, July 1986, pp. 166–67.

14 Selwyn Feinstein, "Computers Replacing Interviewers for Personnel and Marketing Tasks," *Wall Street Journal*, October 9, 1986, p. 35.

15 Horace C. Levinson, "Experiences in Commercial Operations Research," *Operations Research*, August 1953, pp. 220–39.

16 Mason Haire, "Projective Techniques in Marketing Research," *Journal of Marketing*, April 1950, pp. 649–56.

17 Donald R. Lehmann, *Market Research and Analysis* (Homewood, Ill.: Richard D. Irwin, 1985), pp. 35–36.

18 For an overview, see Kinnear and Taylor, *Marketing Research*, pp. 517–65.

19 William R. Dillon, Matthew Goldstein, and Leon G. Schiffman, "Appropriateness of Linear Discriminant and Multinomial Classification Analysis in Marketing Research," *Journal of Marketing Research*, February 1978, pp. 103–12; and Edward R. Bruning, Mary L. Kovacic, and Larry E. Oberdick, "Segmentation Analysis of Domestic Airline Passenger Markets," *Journal of Academy of Marketing Science*, Winter 1985, pp. 17–31.

20 Girish Punj and David W. Stewart, "Cluster Analysis in Marketing Research: Review and Suggestions for Application," *Journal of Marketing Research*, May 1983, pp. 134–48.

21 Philippe Cattin and Dick R. Wittink, "Commercial Use of Conjoint Analysis: A Survey," *Journal of Marketing*, Summer 1982, pp. 44–53; and Thomas M. Leigh, David B. MacKay, and John O. Summers, "Reliability and Validity of Conjoint Analysis and Self-explicated Weights: A Comparison," *Journal of Marketing Research*, November 1984, pp. 456–62.

22 See Glen L. Urban and John R. Hauser, *Design and Marketing of New Products* (Englewood Cliffs, N.J.: Prentice-Hall, 1980); Glen L. Urban and Gerald M. Katz, "Pre-Test-Market Models: Validation and Managerial Implications," *Journal of Marketing Research*, August 1983, pp. 221–34; and Fred S. Zufryden, "PROD II: A Model for Predicting from Tracking Studies," *Journal of Advertising Research*, April/May 1985, pp. 45–51.

23 T. E. Hlavac, Jr., and J.D.C. Little, "A Geographic Model of an Automobile Market," Working Paper No. 186–66 (Cambridge: Massachusetts Institute of Technology, Alfred P. Sloan School of Management, 1966); and Philippe A. Naert and Alain V. Bultez, "A Model of a Distribution Network Aggregate Performance," *Management Science*, June 1975, pp. 1102–12.

24 Leonard M. Lodish, "Callplan: An Interactive Salesman's Call Planning System," *Management Science*, December 1971, pp. 25–40; Arthur Meidan, "Optimizing the Number of Industrial Salespersons," *Industrial Marketing Management*, February 1982, pp. 63–74; and Andris A. Zoltners and Prabhakant Sinha, "Sales Territory Alignment: A Review and Model," *Management Science*, November 1983, pp. 1237–56.

25 See John D. C. Little and Leonard M. Lodish, "A Media Planning Calculus," *Operations Research*, January–February 1969, pp. 1–35.

26 John D. C. Little, "BRANDAID: A Marketing Mix Model, Structure, Implementation, Calibration, and Case Study," *Operations Research*, July–August 1975, pp. 628–73.

27 Applications of marketing models are examined in Jean-Claude Lerreche and David B. Montgomery, "A Framework for the Comparison of Marketing Models: A Delphi Study," *Journal of Marketing Research*, November 1977, pp. 487–98; and Randall L. Schultz and Andris A. Zoltners, eds., *Marketing Decision Models* (New York: Elsevier North Holland, 1981).

28 David B. Learner, "Profit Maximization through New-Product Marketing Planning and Control," in *Applications of the Sciences to Marketing Management*, ed. Frank M. Bass et al. (New York: John Wiley, 1968), pp. 151–67.

29 Arnold E. Amstutz, *Computer Simulation of Competitive Market Response* (Cambridge, Mass.: MIT Press, 1967).

30 David B. Montgomery and Adrian B. Rejans, "Stochastic Models of Consumer Choice Behavior," in *Consumer Behavior: Theoretical Sources*, ed. S. Ward and T. S. Robertson (Englewood Cliffs, N.J.: Prentice-Hall, 1973), pp. 521–76.

31 See Frank M. Bass, "Marketing Research Expenditures: A Decision Model," *Journal of Business*, January 1963, pp. 77–90; and Rex V. Brown, "Do Managers Find Decision Theory Useful?" *Harvard Business Review*, May–June 1970, pp. 78–89.

32 R. Duncan Luce and Howard Raiffa, *Games and Decisions* (New York: John Wiley, 1957), pp. 453–55.

33 Robert J. Lavidge and Gary A. Steiner, "A Model for Predictive Measurements of Advertising Effectiveness," *Journal of Marketing*, October 1961, pp. 59–62.

34 See Jay W. Forrester, "Modeling of Market and Company Interactions," in *Marketing and Economic Development*, ed. Peter D. Bennett (Chicago: American Marketing Association, 1965), pp. 353–64.

35 For an overview of statistical and decision models in marketing, see Gary L. Lilien and Philip Kotler, *Marketing Decision Making: A Model-Building Approach*, 2nd ed. (New York: Harper & Row, 1983). For an overview of computer applications in marketing, see John M. McCann, *The Marketing Workbench: Using Computers for Better Performance* (Homewood, Ill.: Dow Jones-Irwin, 1986).

5 Analyzing the Marketing Environment

It is useless to tell a river to stop running; the best thing is to learn how to sail in the direction it is flowing.

Anonymous

We have repeatedly emphasized that excellent companies take an *outside-inside* view of their business. These companies monitor the changing environment and continuously adapt their businesses to their best opportunities. In this and the next three chapters, we examine the world outside the firm and consider how to monitor and analyze it. In this chapter, we preview the key actors and forces operating in the firm's larger environment.

To the company's marketers falls the major responsibility for identifying major changes in the environment. The marketing environment is constantly spinning out new opportunities, in bad as well as in good years. Table 5-1 shows some of the great marketing success stories in the 1960s, 1970s, and early 1980s. Although the 1970s and early 1980s were years of slow growth, there were enough enterprising people around to create marvelous new businesses out of ideas that seem obvious in retrospect.

The marketing environment also spins out new threats—such as an energy crisis, a sharp rise in interest rates, a deep recession—and firms find their markets collapsing. Recent times have been marked by many sudden changes in the marketing environment, leading Drucker to dub it an *Age of Discontinuity*[1] and Toffler to describe it as a time of *Future Shock*.[2]

Company marketers need to continuously monitor the changing scene. They must use marketing intelligence and marketing research to track the changing environment. By erecting early warning systems, marketers will be able to revise marketing strategies in time to meet new challenges and opportunities in the environment.

What do we mean by the marketing environment? The marketing environment com-

TABLE 5-1
Great Marketing Successes

1960s	1970s		1980s
McDonald's	Miller Lite Beer	H&R Block	Atari Videogames
Honda Motorcycles	Perrier Water	Hanes L'eggs	Apple Computers
Playboy	Charlie Perfume	Intel's "Chip"	Computerland Stores
Avon Cosmetics	Club Mediterranee	Federal Express	Pocket TV
Levi Jeans (Levi Strauss)	Nautilus	Pac Man	Compact Disc Players
Crest Toothpaste (P&G)	Häagen-Dazs Ice Cream	Rubik Cube	Telephone-Answering Machines
Marlboro (Philip Morris)	Prince Tennis Racquets	Kruggerands	Automatic Teller Machines
BIC Pens	Adidas and Nike shoes	Tylenol	Camcorders
K-mart	Walkman (Sony)	Pampers (P&G)	
7–11 Convenience Stores	The Limited Stores	Mary Kay	
	Softsoap (Minnetonka)	Penthouse	
	Boeing 747	Microwave Ovens	
	Jovan Toiletries	Videorecorders	
	Texas Instrument Pocket Calculators		
	Tagamet (Smith, Klein & French)		

prises the "noncontrollable" actors and forces that impact on the company's markets and marketing. Specifically:

> A *company's marketing environment* consists of the external actors and forces that affect the company's ability to develop and maintain successful transactions and relationships with its target customers.

The actors and forces in a company's marketing environment are shown in Figure 5-1. We can distinguish between the company's microenvironment and macroenvironment. The *microenvironment* consists of the actors in the company's immediate environment that affect its ability to serve its markets: the company, suppliers, market intermediaries,

FIGURE 5-1
Major Actors and Forces in the Company's Marketing Environment

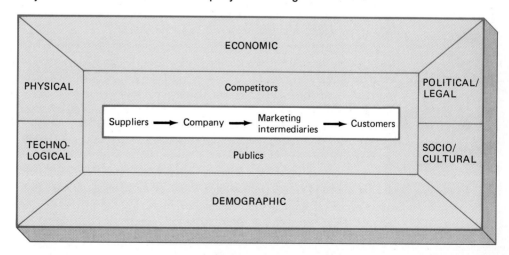

customers, competitors, and publics. The *macroenvironment* consists of the larger societal forces that affect all the actors in the company's microenvironment: the demographic, economic, physical, technological, political/legal, and socio/cultural forces. We will first examine the company's microenvironment and then its macroenvironment.

ACTORS IN THE COMPANY'S MICROENVIRONMENT

Every company's primary goal is to profitably serve and satisfy specific needs of chosen target markets. To carry out this task, the company links itself with a set of suppliers and a set of marketing intermediaries to reach its target customers. The *suppliers/company/ marketing intermediaries/customers* chain comprises the *core marketing system* of the company. The company's success will be affected by two additional groups, namely, a set of competitors and a set of publics. All the actors are shown in Figure 5-1. We will illustrate the role of these actors in the case of the Hershey Foods Corporation, a major U.S. manufacturer of chocolate candy and other food products. We will look at the company's candy line and its suppliers, marketing intermediaries, competitors, and publics.

Company   The Hershey Foods Corporation of Hershey, Pennsylvania, racks up over $1.8 billion of chocolate and confection sales each year. Its product line includes Hershey's Chocolate Bars, Hershey Kisses, Reese's candy, and several other items. Its marketing is handled by a large marketing and sales department consisting of brand managers, marketing researchers, advertising and sales promotion specialists, sales managers and sales representatives, and so on. The marketing department is responsible for developing marketing plans for all the existing products and brands as well as developing new products and brands.

Marketing management at Hershey, in formulating marketing plans, must take into account the other groups in the company, such as top management, finance, R&D, purchasing, manufacturing, and accounting. All of these groups constitute the *company's internal microenvironment*.

Hershey's *top management* consists of the president, the executive committee, and the board of directors. These higher levels of management set the company's mission, objectives, broad strategies, and policies. Marketing managers must make decisions within the context set by top management. Furthermore, their marketing proposals must be approved by top management before they can be implemented.

Marketing managers must also work closely with the functional departments. *Financial management* is concerned with the availability of funds to carry out the marketing plan; the efficient allocation of these funds to different products, brands, and marketing activities; the likely rates of return that will be realized; and the level of risk in the sales forecast and marketing plans. *Research and development management* focuses on researching and developing successful new products. *Purchasing* worries about obtaining sufficient supplies of raw materials (cocoa, sugar, and so on) as well as other productive inputs required to run this company. *Manufacturing* is responsible for acquiring sufficient productive capacity and personnel to meet production targets. *Accounting* has to measure revenues and costs to help marketing know how well it is achieving its profit objectives.

All of these departments have an impact on the marketing department's plans and actions. The various brand managers have to sell the manufacturing and finance department on their plans before presenting them to top management. If the manufacturing vice-president will not allocate enough production capacity, or the financial vice-president will not allocate money, the brand managers will have to revise their sales targets or bring the issue before top management. The many potential conflicts between marketing and the other functions mean that marketing has to negotiate with internal company groups in the course of designing and implementing its marketing plans (see pp. 716–20).

Suppliers

Suppliers are business firms and individuals who provide resources needed by the company and its competitors to produce goods and services. For example, Hershey must obtain cocoa, sugar, cellophane, paper, and various other materials to produce and package its candies. In addition, it must obtain labor, equipment, fuel, electricity, computers, and other factors of production. Hershey's purchasing department must decide which resources to make and which to buy outside. For "buy" decisions, Hershey's purchasing agents must develop specifications, search for suppliers, qualify them, and choose those who offer the best mix of quality, delivery reliability, credit, warranties, and low cost.

Developments in the "suppliers" environment can have a substantial impact on the company's marketing operations. Marketing managers need to watch price trends of their key inputs. Rising costs of sugar or cocoa may force Hershey to raise its prices or shrink its candy bar sizes, either step probably hurting Hershey's sales. Marketing managers are equally concerned with supply availability. Supply shortages, labor strikes, and other events can prevent fulfilling delivery promises and lose sales in the short run and damage customer goodwill in the long run. Many companies prefer to buy from multiple sources to avoid depending on any one supplier who might raise prices arbitrarily or limit supply. Company purchasing agents try to build long-term trusting relationships with key suppliers. In times of shortage, purchasing agents find that they have to "market" their company to suppliers in order to obtain preferential supplies.[3]

Supply planning has become more important and sophisticated in recent years. To the extent that companies can lower their supply costs and/or increase their product quality, they can gain a competitive advantage. Some companies are integrating backward so that they can make and control some of the key supplies that they need. Other companies are requiring their suppliers to move closer to their plants and practice "just-in-time production," that is, produce as the supplies are needed rather than for inventory. In this case, the suppliers must deliver the required quality, and this has led companies to work more closely with their suppliers on quality assurance programs taking place at the suppliers' sites. Companies are looking for suppliers whose quality and efficiency they can trust.

The marketing executive is a direct purchaser of certain services to support the marketing effort, such as advertising, marketing research, sales training, and marketing consulting. In going outside, the marketing executive evaluates different advertising agencies, marketing research firms, sales-training consultants, and marketing consultants. The executive has to decide which services to purchase outside and which to produce inside by adding specialists to the staff.

Marketing Intermediaries

Marketing intermediaries are firms that aid the company in promoting, selling, and distributing its goods to final buyers. They include middlemen, physical distribution firms, marketing service agencies, and financial intermediaries.

Middlemen

Middlemen are business firms that help the company find customers or close sales with them. They fall into two types, agent middlemen and merchant middlemen. *Agent middlemen*—such as agents, brokers, and manufacturers' representatives—find customers or negotiate contracts but do not take title to merchandise. Hershey, for example, might hire agents to find retailers in various South American countries and pay commission to these agents based on their success. The agents do not buy the candy; Hershey ships directly to the retailers. *Merchant middlemen*—such as wholesalers, retailers, and other resellers—buy, take title to, and resell merchandise. Hershey's primary method of marketing candy is to sell candy to wholesalers, large supermarket chains, and vending-machine operators, who in turn resell the candy to consumers at a profit.

Why does Hershey use middlemen at all? The answer is that middlemen are able to perform several marketing tasks more efficiently than Hershey can. As a manufacturer, Hershey is primarily interested in producing and rolling out large quantities of candy from its factory doors. The customer, on the other hand, is interested in finding one bar of candy in a convenient location, at a convenient time, with a related assortment of other goods sought by the consumer, and with an easy payment mechanism. The gap between the large quantities of candy that Hershey rolls out and the consumer's preferred way of buying candy must be overcome. Middlemen come into being to help overcome the *discrepancies* in quantities, place, time, assortment, and possession that would otherwise exist.

Specifically, middlemen create *place utility* by stocking Hershey candy where customers are located. They create *time utility* by staying open long hours so that customers can shop at their convenience. They create *quantity utility* by making candy available in single-bar purchases. They create *assortment utility* by collecting in one point other goods that consumers may seek on the same shopping trip. They create *possession utility* by transferring the candy bar to the consumer in an easy transaction format, namely, for a simple cash payment without the need for any billing. Hershey, to create the same utilities, would have to establish, finance, and operate a far-flung network of national stores and vending machines. Hershey, of course, finds it more efficient to work through established marketing channels.

Selecting and working with middlemen, however, is not a simple task. At one time the manufacturer had to contact and sell to numerous small independent middlemen. Today the manufacturer deals with fewer but larger middlemen organizations. An increasing share of all food distribution is in the hands of large corporate retail chains (such as Safeway and Jewel), large wholesalers, and franchised-sponsored voluntary chains (such as 7–11 and White Hen). To cite an extreme case, in Switzerland 70 percent of all food distribution is in the hands of two giant middlemen, Migros and the Coop. These groups have great power to dictate terms or else shut the manufacturer out of some large-volume markets. The manufacturer must work hard to get and maintain "shelf space." The manufacturer has to learn how to manage and satisfy members of its marketing channel or face diminishing support and maybe even exclusion.

Physical Distribution Firms   Physical distribution firms assist the company in stocking and moving goods from their original locations to their destinations. *Warehousing firms* store and protect goods before they move to the next destination. Every company has to decide how much storage space to build for itself and how much to rent from warehousing firms. *Transportation firms* consist of railroads, truckers, airlines, barges, and other freight-handling companies that move goods from one location to another. Every company has to decide on the most cost-effective modes of shipment, balancing such considerations as cost, delivery, speed, and safety (see Chapter 19).

Marketing Service Agencies   Marketing service agencies—marketing research firms, advertising agencies, media firms, and marketing consulting firms—assist the company in targeting and promoting its products to the right markets. The company faces a "make or buy" decision with respect to each of these services. Some large companies—such as Du Pont and Quaker Oats—operate their own in-house advertising agencies and marketing research departments. But most companies contract for the services of outside agencies. When a firm decides to buy outside services, it must carefully choose whom to hire, since the agencies vary in their creativity, quality, service, and price. The company has to review their performance periodically and must consider replacing those that no longer perform at the expected level.

Financial Intermediaries Financial intermediaries include banks, credit companies, insurance companies, and other companies that help finance and/or insure risk associated with the buying and selling of goods. Most companies and customers depend on financial intermediaries to finance their transactions. The company's marketing performance can be seriously affected by rising credit costs and/or limited credit. Each time the company needs major capital, it must develop a business plan and convince financial intermediaries of the plan's soundness. For these reasons, the company has to develop strong relationships with outside financial intermediaries.

Customers

A company links itself with suppliers and middlemen so that it can efficiently supply appropriate products and services to its target market. Its target market can be one (or more) of the following five types of customer markets:

- ■ *Consumer markets.* Individuals and households that buy goods and services for personal consumption.
- ■ *Industrial markets.* Organizations that buy goods and services needed for producing other products and services for the purpose of making profits and/or achieving other objectives.
- ■ *Reseller markets.* Organizations that buy goods and services in order to resell them at a profit.
- ■ *Government and nonprofit markets.* Government and nonprofit agencies that buy goods and services in order to produce public services or transfer these goods and services to others who need them.
- ■ *International markets.* Buyers found abroad, including foreign consumers, producers, resellers, and governments.

Hershey sells its products to a number of these customer markets. Its main customer market is resellers, which in turn sell Hershey candy to consumers. Another important group is institutional customers, namely, factories, hospitals, schools, government agencies, and other organizations that run cafeterias for their employees. Hershey also sells a substantial volume to foreign consumers, producers, resellers, and governments. Each customer market exhibits specific characteristics that warrant careful study by the seller. The major characteristics of *consumer market* and *business markets* (producers, resellers, and government and nonprofit agencies) will be examined in the following two chapters; foreign markets will be examined in Chapter 13.

Competitors

A company rarely stands alone in its effort to serve a given customer market. Its efforts to build an efficient marketing system to serve the market are matched by similar efforts on the part of others. The company's marketing system is surrounded and affected by a host of competitors. These competitors have to be identified, monitored, and outmaneuvered to capture and maintain customer loyalty.

The competitive environment consists not only of other companies but also of more basic things. The best way for a company to grasp the full range of its competition is to take the viewpoint of a buyer. What does a buyer think about that eventually leads to purchasing something? Suppose a person has been working hard and needs a break. The person asks, "What do I want to do now?" Among the possibilities that pop into his or her mind are socializing, exercising, and eating (see Figure 5-2). We will call these *desire competitors*. Suppose the person's most immediate need is to eat something. Then the question becomes, "What do I want to eat?" Different foods come to mind, such as potato chips, candy, soft drinks, and fruit. These can be called *generic competitors* in that they represent different basic ways to satisfy the same need. At this point, the person decides on candy and asks, "What type of candy do I want?" Different candy forms come to mind, such as chocolate bars, licorice, and sugar drops. They all represent *product form competitors* in that they are different forms for satisfying a desire for candy. Finally, the consumer decides on a chocolate bar and faces several brands, such as Hershey, Nestlé, and Mars. These are *brand competitors*.

In this way Hershey's marketers can determine all of the competitors standing in the way of selling more Hershey chocolate bars. Unfortunately, company executives tend to focus primarily on the brand competitors and on the task of building brand preference. Hershey wants to be thought of as the leading candy bar producer, and its executives spend their time trying to position its candy as the quality leader and a good value for the money. Hershey relies primarily on product quality, advertising, sales promotion, and universal distribution to build up its brand preference. Its competitive stance against Nestlé, Mars, and so on, may range from "live and let live" most of the time to occasional attacks on competitor positions. More often, however, the leading candy bar company is on the defensive against smaller companies that aggressively attack its position.

Candy bar companies are myopic if they focus only on their brand competitors. The real challenge is to expand their primary market, namely, the candy market, rather than simply fight for a larger share in a fixed-size market. Candy companies have to be concerned about megatrends in the environment, such as people eating less in general and eating less candy in particular, or even switching to other forms of candy, such as dietetic candy.

FIGURE 5-2
Four Types of Competition

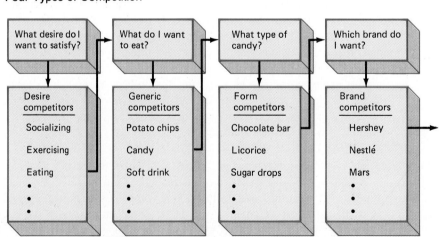

In too many industries, companies focus on the brand competitors and fail to exploit opportunities to expand the whole market or at least prevent it from eroding.

A basic observation about the task of competing effectively can now be summarized. A company must keep four basic dimensions in mind, which can be called the Four Cs of market positioning. It must consider the nature of the *Customers*, *Channels*, *Competition*, and its own characteristics as a *Company*. Successful marketing is a matter of achieving an effective alignment of the company with customers, channels, and competitors.

Publics

Not only does a company have to contend with competitors in seeking to satisfy a target market but it must also acknowledge a large set of publics that take an interest, whether welcome or not, in its methods of doing business. Because the actions of the company affect the interests of other groups, these groups become significant publics. We define a public as follows:

> A *public* is any group that has an actual or potential interest in or impact on a company's ability to achieve its objectives.

A public can facilitate or impede a company's ability to achieve its goals. The wise company takes concrete steps to manage successful relations with its key publics. Most companies operate public relations departments to plan constructive relations with various publics. These departments monitor the attitudes of the organization's publics and distribute information and communications to build goodwill. When negative publicity breaks out, these departments act as trouble-shooters. The best departments spend time counseling top management to adopt positive programs and to eliminate questionable practices so that negative publicity does not arise in the first place.

It would be a mistake for a company to leave public relations entirely in the hands of the public relations department. All the organization's employees are involved in public relations, from the chief executive officer who makes headlines in the press to the financial vice-president who addresses the financial community, to the field sales representatives who call on customers, to the telephone operators who answer the phones.

We believe that public relations is a broad marketing operation rather than a narrow communication operation.[4] A public is a group from which an organization wants some response, such as goodwill, favorable mentions, or donations of time or money. The organization must ask what that public is seeking that it could satisfy. It then plans a benefit bundle that builds goodwill.

Every company faces several important publics:

- ■ *Financial publics.* Financial institutions—banks, investment houses, stock brokerage firms, insurance companies—affect the company's ability to obtain funds. Hershey seeks the confidence of these groups by issuing upbeat annual reports, answering financial questions, and managing its money conservatively.
- ■ *Media publics.* Companies must cultivate the goodwill of media organizations, specifically newspapers, magazines, and radio and television stations. Hershey seeks more and better media coverage in the form of favorable news, features, and editorial comment.
- ■ *Government publics.* Companies need to take government developments into account in formulating marketing plans. Hershey's marketers must consult the company's lawyers about possible issues of product safety, truth in advertising, and so on. Hershey will join with other candy manufacturers to lobby against legislation that would hurt their interests.
- ■ *Citizen-action publics.* A company's marketing practices may be questioned by consumer organizations, environmental groups, minority groups, and others. For example, some consum-

erists have attacked candy as having little nutritional value, being high in calories, causing tooth decay, and so on. Hershey must choose between remaining silent or counterattacking with positive statements about candy's benefits. (See Exhibit 5-1 describing how consumerism affects company marketing practices.)

- ▪ **Local publics.** Every company faces local publics such as neighborhood residents and community organizations. Large companies usually appoint a community relations officer to deal with community issues, attend meetings, answer questions, and make contributions to worthwhile causes.

- ▪ **General public.** A company needs to be concerned with the general public's attitude toward its products and practices. While the general public does not act in an organized way toward the company, the public's image of the company affects its patronage. To build a strong "corporate citizen" image, Hershey will lend its officers to community fund drives, make substantial contributions to charity, and set up systems of consumer complaint handling.

- ▪ **Internal publics.** A company's internal publics include blue-collar workers, white-collar workers, managers, and the board of directors. Large companies develop newsletters and other forms of communication to inform and motivate its internal publics. When employees feel good about their company, this positive attitude spills over to external publics.

EXHIBIT 5-1

The Impact of Consumerism on Marketing Practices

Starting in the 1960s, American business firms found themselves the target of a growing consumer movement. Consumers had become better educated; products had become increasingly complex and hazardous; discontent with American institutions was widespread; influential writings by John Kenneth Galbraith, Vance Packard, and Rachel Carson accused big business of wasteful and manipulative practices; John Kennedy's presidential message of 1962 declared that consumers had the right to safety, to be informed, to choose, and to be heard; congressional investigations of certain industries proved embarrassing; and, finally, Ralph Nader appeared on the scene to crystallize many of the issues.

Since these early stirrings, many private consumer organizations have emerged, several pieces of consumer legislation have been passed, and several state and local offices of consumer affairs have been created. Furthermore, the consumer movement has acquired an international character, with much strength in Scandinavia and the Low Countries and a growing presence in France, Germany, and Japan.

But what is consumerism? *Consumerism is an organized movement of citizens and government to strengthen the rights and power of buyers in relation to sellers.* Consumerists' groups seek to increase the amount of consumer information, education, and protection. Consumerists have advocated—and in many cases won—such proposals as the right to know the true interest cost of a loan (*truth-in-lending*), the true cost per standard unit of competing brands (*unit pricing*), the basic ingredients in a product (*ingredient labeling*), the nutritional quality of food (*nutritional labeling*), the freshness of products (*open dating*), and the true benefits of a product (*truth-in-advertising*). They want the government to check on the safety of products that are potentially hazardous and to penalize companies that are careless. Some consumerists want companies to elect consumer representatives to their boards to introduce consumer considerations into business decision making.

The most successful consumer group is Ralph Nader's *Public Citizen*. Nader lifted consumerism to a major social force, first with his successful attack on unsafe automobiles (resulting in the passage of the National Traffic and Motor Vehicle Safety Act of 1962), and then through investigations into meat processing (resulting in the passage of the Wholesome Meat Act of 1967), truth-in-lending, auto repairs, insurance, and X-ray equipment.

At first a number of companies balked at the consumer movement. They resented the power of strong consumer leaders to point an accusing finger at their products and cause their sales to plummet, such as when Ralph Nader called the Corvair automobile unsafe, when Robert Choate accused breakfast cereals of providing "empty calories," and when Herbert S. Denenberg published a list showing the wide variation in premiums different insurance companies were charging for the same protection. Businesses resented consumer proposals that appeared to increase business costs more than they helped the consumer. They also felt that most consumers would not pay attention to unit pricing or ingredient labeling and that the doctrines of advertising substantiation, corrective advertising, and counter advertising would stifle advertising creativity.

Many other companies took no stand and simply went about their business. A few companies undertook a series of bold initiatives to show their endorsement of consumer aims. For example:

> Whirlpool Corporation responded by adopting a number of measures to improve customer information and services. It installed a toll-free corporate phone number for consumers to use if they were dissatisfied with their Whirlpool equipment or service. It expanded the coverage of its product warranties and rewrote them in basic English.

Several companies took the initiative in showing "we care" and in several cases enjoyed increased profits. Competitors were forced to emulate them, without, however, achieving the same impact enjoyed by these firms.

Currently, most companies have accepted consumerism in principle. They recognize the consumers' right to information and protection. Those who take a leadership role recognize that consumerism involves a total commitment by top management, new company policy guidelines, and training programs for all personnel. Several companies have established consumer affairs departments to help formulate policies and deal with "consumerist" problems.

Product managers today have to spend more time checking product ingredients and product features for safety, preparing safe packaging and informative labeling, substantiating their advertising claims, reviewing their sales promotion, developing clear and adequate product warranties, and so on. They have to work more closely with company lawyers.

Consumerism is actually the ultimate expression of the marketing concept. It compels company marketers to consider things from the consumers' point of view. It suggests consumer needs and wants that may have been overlooked by the firms in the industry. The resourceful manager will look for the positive opportunities created by consumerism rather than brood over its restraints.

(For an appraisal of the consumer movement in the United States, see Paul N. Bloom and Stephen A. Greyser, "The Maturity of Consumerism," *Harvard Business Review*, November–December 1981, pp. 130–39.)

Although companies must put their primary energy into effectively managing their relationships with their customers, distributors, and suppliers, their overall success will be affected by how other publics in the society view their activity. Companies would be wise to spend time monitoring all their publics, understanding their needs and opinions, and dealing with them constructively.

FORCES IN THE COMPANY'S MACROENVIRONMENT

The company and its suppliers, marketing intermediaries, customers, competitors, and publics all operate in a larger macroenvironment of forces and megatrends that shape opportunities and pose threats to the company. These forces represent "uncontrollables," which the company must monitor and respond to. There are six major forces, namely, demographic, economic, physical, technological, political/legal, and socio/cultural. We will examine the megatrends in each macroenvironment component and their implications for marketing in the coming years.

Demographic Environment
The first environmental fact of interest to marketers is population because people make up markets. Marketers are keenly interested in the size of the world's population; its geographical distribution; density; mobility trends; age distribution; birth, marriage,

and death rates; and racial, ethnic, and religious structure. We will examine the major demographic trends and their implications for marketing planning.[5]

Worldwide Explosive Population Growth   The world population is showing ''explosive'' growth. It totaled 5.0 billion in 1986 and is growing at 1.7 percent per year. At this rate, the world's population will reach 6.2 billion by A.D. 2000.

The world population explosion has been a major concern of governments and various groups throughout the world. Two factors underlie this concern. The first is the possible finiteness of the earth's resources to support this much human life, particularly at living standards that represent the aspiration of most people. *The Limits to Growth* presented an impressive array of evidence that unchecked population growth and consumption would eventually result in insufficient food supply, depletion of key minerals, overcrowding, pollution, and an overall deterioration in the quality of life.[7] One of its strong recommendations is the worldwide *social marketing* of birth control and family planning.[8]

The second cause for concern is that population growth is highest in countries and communities that can least afford it. The less-developed regions of the world currently account for 76 percent of the world population and are growing at 2 percent per year, whereas the population in the more developed regions of the world is growing at only 0.6 percent per year. In less-developed economies, the death rate has been falling as a result of modern medicine, while the birthrate has remained fairly stable. For these countries to feed, clothe, and educate the children and also provide a rising standard of living is out of the question. Furthermore, the poorer families have the most children, and this reinforces the cycle of poverty.

The explosive world population growth has great implications for business. A growing population means growing human needs, but it does not mean growing markets unless there is sufficient purchasing power. If the growing population presses too hard against the available food supply and resources, costs will shoot up and profit margins will be depressed.

Slowdown in U.S. Birthrate   A ''birth dearth'' has replaced the former ''baby boom'' in the United States. The U.S. population now stands at 239 million. It is projected to grow to 267 million by the year 2000. Yet despite the increase in the number of people, the rate of population growth has slowed considerably since the 1950s. The annual number of births peaked at 4.3 million in 1960 and, by the mid-1970s, fell to under 3.2 million births. Recently there has been a slight gain, to 3.6 million births. Population growth during this decade is expected to be less than 1 percent a year. Factors contributing to smaller families are the desire to improve personal living standards, the increasing desire of women to work outside the home, and the improved technology and knowledge of birth control.

The declining birthrate is a threat to some industries, a boon to others. It has created sleepless nights for executives in such businesses as children's toys, clothes, furniture, and food. For many years the Gerber Company advertised ''Babies are our business—our only business'' but quietly dropped this slogan some time ago. Gerber now sells life insurance to older folks, using the theme ''Gerber now babies the over-50's.'' Johnson & Johnson responded to the declining birthrate by wooing adults to switch to its baby powder, baby oil, and baby shampoo. Meanwhile industries such as hotels, airlines, and restaurants have benefited from the fact that young childless couples have more time and income for travel and dining out.

Aging of U.S. Population   Recent generations have been blessed with a declining death rate. Average life expectancy is 75 years, a 21-year increase since 1920. The life expectancy of males is 71 and females, 78. The rise in life expectancy and the declining birthrate are producing an aging U.S. population. The U.S. median age is now 31 and is forecast to reach 36 by the year 2000.[9]

Age-group populations show different rates of growth. The 15–24 age group will decrease by 14 percent in the 1985–95 decade. This forbodes a slowdown in the sales growth of motorcycles, baseball and football equipment, denim clothing, records, and college enrollment.

The 25–34 age group will decrease by 3 percent in the coming decade. This does not bode well for furniture manufacturers, vacation planners, life insurance companies, and tennis and ski equipment manufacturers, which market products to this group.

The 35–54 age group will undergo the greatest increase of all age groups in the coming decade, namely, 35 percent. Members of this group are well established in their work life and are a major market for large homes, new automobiles, and clothing.

The 55–64 age group will shrink by 6 percent in this decade. These ''empty-nesters,'' whose children have left home, will have more time and income on their hands. This group is a major market for eating out, travel, expensive clothes, golf, and other forms of recreation.

The over-65 age group will show the second largest increase in the coming decade, up by 18 percent. This group foretells a burgeoning demand for retirement homes and communities, campers, quieter forms of recreation (fishing, golf), single-portion food packaging, and medical goods and services (medicine, eyeglasses, canes, hearing aids, and convalescent homes). This group is becoming more self-centered, active, and more leisure oriented than the comparable group in past generations. They are willing to spend more money on themselves and not worry about leaving money to their children.

Companies that used to sell primarily to the youth market have responded to the graying of America by repositioning their products or introducing new ones. We saw that Johnson & Johnson had persuaded adults to use its baby oil and baby shampoo, and that Gerber now sells life insurance to older people. Wrigley introduced a stick-proof gum called Freedent for people who have dentures. And Helena Rubinstein produces a line of skin-care products for women over 50.

The Changing American Family   The character of the American family is changing as a result of later marriage, fewer children, more divorce, and more working wives. Specifically:

1. *Later marriage.* Although weddings might be ''in'' in the 1980s, the average age of couples marrying for the first time has been rising over the years and now stands at 24.1 years for males and 22.3 years for females. Fully 58.5 percent of women aged 20 to 24 had never married in 1985, up from 35.8 percent in 1970. The large numbers of never married women, combined with an increasing number of divorced and separated women, have led to a ''marriage crunch.''[10] This will lead to more single-adult households headed by women and will slow down sales of engagement and wedding rings, bridal outfits, and life insurance.

2. *Fewer children.* The average family size is shrinking. Couples with no children under 18 now make up 48 percent of all families. The newly married are also delaying childbearing longer. Of those families that have children, the mean number of children is 1.07, down from 3.5 in 1955. This indicates a slowed-down demand for baby food, toys, children's clothes, and other children's goods and services.

3. **Higher divorce rate.** The United States has the world's highest divorce rate, with about 50 percent of all marriages ending in divorce. This has created over a million single-parent families and the need for additional housing units, furniture, appliances, and other household products. About 79 percent of those divorced remarry, leading to the phenomenon of the "blended" family. Currently about 66 percent of all males and 61 percent of all females are married.

4. **More working wives.** Over 50 percent of all married women hold some kind of job. There is less stigma attached to working, a greater number of job opportunities, and new freedom resulting from birth-control acceptance. Working women are a market for better clothing, day-nursery services, home-cleaning services, and more frozen dinners. The growing number of working women means less viewing of the television soap operas and less reading of such women's magazines as *Good Housekeeping* and *Ladies' Home Journal*. Their incomes constitute 40 percent of their households' incomes and engender the purchase of higher-quality goods and services. Marketers of tires, automobiles, insurance, and travel service are increasingly directing their advertising to working women. All of this is accompanied by a shift in traditional roles and values of husbands and wives, with the husband assuming more domestic functions, such as shopping (over 40% of all grocery shopping trips) and child care. As a result, husbands are becoming more of a target market for food companies and household-appliance manufacturers and retailers.

The Rise of Nonfamily Households   The number of nonfamily households is increasing, from 19 percent of all households in 1970 to 28 percent in 1985, and possibly 30 percent in 1990. These households take several forms, each constituting a different market segment with special needs:

1. **Single-adult households.** Many young adults leave home early and move into apartments. In addition, many divorced and widowed people live alone. Altogether, nearly 21 million people live alone (24 percent of all households). By 1990, 45 percent of households will be single-person or single-parent households. They are the fastest-growing category of urban home seekers. The SSWD group (single, separated, widowed, divorced) need smaller apartments; inexpensive and smaller appliances, furniture, and furnishings; and food that is packaged in smaller sizes. Singles are a market for various services that enable singles to meet each other, such as singles bars, health clubs, tours, and cruises.

2. **Two-person cohabitor households.** There are 1 million households consisting of unmarried persons of the opposite sex sharing living quarters. (One sociologist observed that cohabitation is becoming more like the first stage of marriage.) And there are many more households consisting of two or more persons of the same sex sharing living quarters. Since their arrangements tend to be more temporary, these households are a market for inexpensive or rental furniture and furnishings.

3. **Group households.** Group households consist of three or more persons of the same or opposite sex living together and sharing expenses. Included are college students and certain secular and religious groups who live in communes.

Marketers should not get locked into thinking that the "typical American family" is their only target or even major target. They should consider the special needs of nonfamily households, since they are growing more rapidly than family households.

Geographical Shifts in Population   Americans are a mobile people, with approximately one out of six, or 40 million Americans, moving each year. Among the major mobility trends are the following:

1. **Movement of people to the Sunbelt states.** The South and the West accounted for 90 percent of the nation's population growth between 1980 and 1985. The South and the West now have 54 percent of the U.S. population, up from 45 percent in 1970. Major cities in the North, on the other hand, lost population between 1970 and 1984 (Detroit, 39 percent;

Pittsburgh, 29 percent; Philadelphia, 18.3 percent; Chicago, 12.6 percent; and New York, 10.2 percent). These regional population shifts interest marketers because of marked differences in regional expenditure patterns. Consumers in the West, for example, spend relatively less on food and relatively more on automobiles than those in the Northeast. The exodus to Sunbelt states will lessen the demand for warm clothing and home heating equipment and increase the demand for air conditioning.

2. *Movement from rural to urban areas.* People have been moving from rural to urban areas for over a century. In 1880, 70 percent of the nation's population lived in rural areas; at the present time, 75 percent live in urban areas. Cities show a faster pace of living, more commuting, higher incomes, and a greater variety of goods and services than can be found in the small towns and rural areas that dot America. The largest cities—New York, Los Angeles, Chicago—account for most of the sales of expensive furs, perfumes, luggage, and works of art; and these cities support the opera, ballet, and other forms of ''high culture.'' Recently, however, there has been a slight shift of population back to small towns and rural areas.

3. *Movement from the city to the suburbs.* Many persons live far away from their places of work, owing largely of the development of automobiles, major highways, and rapid rail and bus transit. Cities have become surrounded by suburbs, and these suburbs in turn by ''exurbs.'' The U.S. Census Bureau has created a separate population classification for sprawling urban concentrations: *Standard Metropolitan Statistical Areas* (SMSAs).[11] Out of a total of 318 SMSAs in 1980, 150 accounted for 86.9 percent of the total population, and these SMSA's constitute the primary market focus of firms. Companies use the SMSAs in researching the best geographical segments for their products, in planning on their geographical rollout strategy for new products, in deciding where to purchase advertising time or space, and so on. SMSA research shows, for example, that New Englanders smoke 29 percent more cigarettes than the national average; Chicagoans consume 22 percent more soft drinks; and New Yorkers use 19 percent more paper goods.

About 60 percent of the total metropolitan population now live in suburbs. Suburbs show more casual, outdoor living, greater neighbor interaction, higher incomes, and younger families. Suburbanites buy station wagons, home-workshop equipment, garden furniture, lawn and gardening tools and supplies, and outdoor-cooking equipment. Retailers have acknowledged the suburbs by building branch department stores and suburban shopping centers.

At the same time, marketers should recognize a recent countermove back to the central city, especially in cities where urban renewal has been successful. Young adults and older adults whose children have grown up are attracted by the superior cultural and recreational opportunities and are less interested in suburban commuting and gardening. This has led to new high-rise apartment construction and new retail outlets within the city.

Marketers must proceed cautiously when they develop their geographical marketing plans. Marketing researchers use several schemes to segment geographical markets—census tracts, standard metropolitan areas, Nielsen regions, media markets, and so forth. Garreau recently proposed a suggestive new segmentation scheme, which he calls ''The Nine Nations of North America.'' (See Exhibit 5-2.)

A Better-educated and White-collar Population   Seventy-three percent of Americans over twenty-five years of age have high school degrees. Nineteen percent of Americans have college degrees, and the percentage continues to rise. The rising number of educated people will increase the demand for quality products, books, magazines, and travel.

In 1985, the total labor force was 114.8 million people. Between 1960 and 1984, the number of white-collar workers rose from 43 to 55 percent, blue-collar workers declined from 37 to 29 percent, service workers increased from 12 to 13 percent, and farm workers declined from 8 to 3 percent. For the 1980s, the U.S. Bureau of Labor Statistics predicts the most growth in the following occupational categories: engineering, science, medicine, computers, social science, buying, selling, secretarial, construction, refrigeration, health service, personal service, and protection.

EXHIBIT 5-2

The Nine Nations of North America

Joel Garreau called upon marketers to stop viewing the United States as a "homogenous glob of humanity tied together by TV, WATS lines, and McDonald's outlets, but rather [to view it as] nine distinct regions or 'nations.' " His nine nations are shown on the accompanying map and described below.

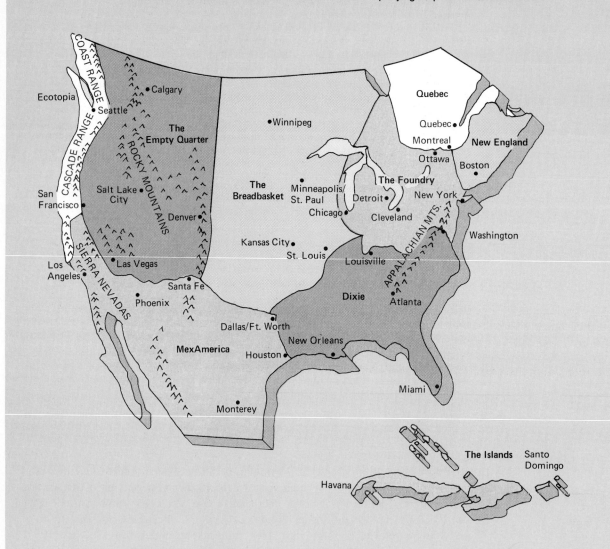

The Breadbasket. The integrating factor is the elemental simplicity of farming as a way of life.

Ecotopia. People here have an ethic of libertarian self-reliance and mystical relationship to the land.

The Foundry. Declining and gritty industrial cities with an ethic of heavy work with heavy machines. Hard work and yet hard times without work.

■ **The Empty Quarter.** An area of mining and power, with a land grab going on today.
■ **The Islands.** Latin American culture with Miami as its capital.
■ **MexAmerica.** Hispanic values of Catholicism, pride in family, and close community ties.
■ **New England.** Original boundaries of U.S. with traditional values.
■ **Dixie.** The southern culture provides a unifying history, language, food, dress, and charm.
■ **Quebec.** French speaking, it has a culture of its own.

Garreau argues that each region has its own ways of thinking, planning, and living, and marketers who ignore these differences can make big mistakes. Here are a few of his observations:

One of the reasons the U.S. auto industry was slow to react to imported cars was the industry's management base in Detroit. If auto executives lived in California, they would have seen the trend toward Japanese cars. But when they looked out of their windows in Detroit, all they saw were gas-guzzlers. They just didn't see Japanese cars as a problem.

Many of the regional labels businessmen use are obsolete or misleading. There are no such places as the "Sunbelt," or the "Midwest," or the "West Coast." Even state boundaries are meaningless in many regards. California is three states (MexAmerica, Ecotopia, and Empty Quarter), which is why it doesn't make any sense.

The notion of "suburb" and everything that term implies is strictly a Foundry phenomenon. Suburbs were formed in the Foundry because people wanted to get out of the decaying cities, and the people who stayed behind in the cities resented that. But in places like the Southwest, suburbs are an accepted fact of existence. Everything is a "suburb."

SOURCE Adapted from *The Nine Nations of North America* by Joel Garreau. Copyright 1981 by Joel Garreau. Reprinted by permission of Houghton Mifflin Company.

Changing Ethnic and Racial Population The U.S. population is 79 percent white, and blacks constitute another 12 percent. The Hispanic population has been growing fast and now stands at 16.9 million, with the largest subgroups being Mexicans, Puerto Ricans, and Cubans, in that order. The Asian population has also burgeoned, with the Chinese constituting the largest group, followed by the Filipinos, Japanese, Koreans, and Asian Indians, in that order. Hispanic and Asian consumers are concentrated in the far western and southern parts of the country, although some dispersal is taking place. Each population group has certain specific wants and buying habits. Several food, clothing, and furniture companies have directed their products and promotion to one or more of these groups.

Shift From a Mass Market to Micromarkets The effect of all these changes—smaller families, more nonfamily households, an aging population, the high growth rates of Hispanic, Oriental, and black consumers—is to transform the American marketplace from a *mass market* into more fragmented *micromarkets*, differentiated by age, sex, geography, life-style, ethnic background, education, and so on. Each group has strong preferences and consumer characteristics and is reached through increasingly differentiated media. Companies are abandoning the ''shotgun'' approach that aimed at a mythical ''average'' consumer and are increasingly designing their products and marketing programs for specific micromarkets.

These demographic trends are highly reliable for the short and intermediate run. There is little excuse for a company's being suddenly surprised by demographic developments. The Singer Company should have known for years that its sewing machine business would be negatively affected by small families and more working wives; yet it was slow in responding. Alert firms can identify the major demographic trends and determine the steps they should be taking to meet these changes.

Economic Environment

Markets consist of purchasing power as well as people. Total purchasing power is a function of current income, prices, savings, and credit availability. Marketers should be cognizant of major trends in the economic environment.

Slow Real-Income Growth   In 1984 American income per capita stood at $12,707. Although money income per capita kept rising, real income per capita for individuals had risen at only 1.4 percent annually for the 1973–83 decade. However, median household real income fell to $22,415 in 1984 from $23,584 in 1974. Real incomes had been hurt by several years of double-digit inflation and an unemployment rate between 6 and 10 percent. Household incomes had been reduced as an increasing number of households were headed by individuals and by the drop in the average age of the workers during the decade as the baby boomers entered the labor markets, often at relatively lower starting salaries. On the other hand, many "marrieds" had two-person incomes, and they were often better off.

In response to the real-income decline for households, many Americans turned to more cautious buying and changed their spending habits. Over the 1973–83 decade, individual consumer spending on food, gasoline and motor oil, and health-care services did not keep pace with the increase in prices for those categories. Consumers bought more store brands and generics and fewer national brands to save money. Many companies introduced economy versions of their products and turned to price appeals in their advertising messages. However, over the same period, spending outpaced inflation in home furnishings and equipment, entertainment, reading, eating out, and alcoholic beverages. It seems that in the face of lower real income, Americans were spending more judiciously on necessities while trying to improve the quality of their leisure time.[12]

Marketers should pay attention to income distribution as well as to average income. Income distribution in the United States is still pronouncedly skewed. At the top are *upper-class consumers*, whose expenditure patterns are not seriously affected by current economic events and who are a major market for goods (Rolls-Royces starting at $100,000) and services (round-the-world cruises starting at $10,000). There is a comfortable *middle class* that exercises some expenditure restraint but is able to afford expensive clothes, minor antiques, and a small boat or second home. The *lower class* must stick close to the basics of food, clothing, and shelter and must husband their resources carefully and try hard to save.

Marketers also have to note geographical income variations. A city like Phoenix is growing at a fast rate while Detroit is languishing. During the 1973–83 decade, per capita personal income in constant dollars increased at 1.9 percent annually for the South, compared with 0.8 percent annually for the Midwest. Marketers must focus their efforts on the geographical areas of greatest opportunity.

Lower Savings and High Debt   Consumer expenditures are affected by consumer savings and debt patterns. Eighty-eight percent of American spending units hold some liquid assets, the median amount being $2,850. Savings equaled 6.1 percent of disposable personal income in 1984. Americans hold their savings in the form of bank savings accounts, bonds and stocks, real estate, insurance, money market funds, and other assets. These savings are an important source of funds for financing major purchases.

Consumers can increase their purchasing power through borrowing. Consumer credit has been a major contributor to the rapid growth of the American economy, enabling people to buy more than their current income and savings allowed, thus creating more jobs and still more income and more demand. In 1984, outstanding consumer credit (including home mortgages) stood at $2.6 trillion, or $11,000 for every man, woman, and child in America. The ratio of consumer credit (not including mortgages) to disposable personal income stood at 22 percent in 1983. The cost of credit is currently running between 10 and 14 percent, much lower than in the early 1980s. Consumers are spending around twenty-one cents of every earned dollar to pay off existing debts. This retards the further growth of housing and other durable-goods markets that are heavily dependent on credit.

Changing Consumer Expenditure Patterns   Consumption expenditures in major goods and services categories have been changing over the years. Food, housing, household operations, and transportation use up two-thirds of household income. Over time, however, the food, clothing, and personal-care bills of households have been declining percentagewise while the housing, transportation, medical-care, and recreational bills have been increasing. Some of these changes were observed over a century ago by Ernest Engel, a German statistician who studied how people shifted their expenditures as their income rose. He observed that *as family income rises, the percentage spent on food declines, the percentage spent on housing and household operations remains constant, and the percentage spent on other categories* (*clothing, transportation, recreation, health, and education*) *and the percentage put into savings increase.* Engel's "laws" have generally been validated in subsequent budget studies.

Changes in such major economic variables as money income, cost of living, interest rates, and savings and borrowing patterns have an immediate impact on the marketplace. Companies whose products are highly income- and price-sensitive need to invest in sophisticated economic forecasting. Businesses do not have to be wiped out by a downturn in economic activity. With adequate forewarning, they can take the necessary steps to alter their products, reduce their costs, and ride out the economic storm.

Physical Environment   The 1960s witnessed a growing public concern over whether the physical environment was being irreparably damaged by the industrial activities of modern nations. Kenneth Boulding called the planet earth a spaceship that could run out of fuel if it failed to conserve and recycle its materials. The Erlichs in 1970 coined the term *eco-catastrophe* to symbolize the harmful impact of certain American business practices on the environment. The Meadowses in their 1972 book, *The Limits to Growth*, raised concerns about whether the world would run out of sufficient natural resources to maintain, let alone improve, current living standards.[13] Rachel Carson, in *Silent Spring*, pointed out the environmental damage to water, earth, and air caused by industrial activity of certain kinds.[14] Watchdog groups, such as the Sierra Club and Friends of the Earth, sprang up, and concerned legislators proposed various measures to protect the environment. (See Exhibit 5-3 for a discussion of the impact of the environmentalist movement on marketing.)

In contrast with those concerned about the quality of the environment are the "cornucopians." They argue that mankind, through its ability to innovate and substitute, has quickly overcome scarcities in the past. They therefore believe that there is no need to adopt any emergency governmental responses to scarcities, as the United States is not faced with any natural resources crisis.[15]

EXHIBIT 5-3
The Impact of Environmentalism on Marketing Decision Making

Whereas consumerists focus on whether companies are efficiently serving consumer material wants, environmentalists focus on the costs imposed on the environment in serving these needs and wants. *Environmentalism is an organized movement of concerned citizens and government to protect and enhance people's living environment.* Environmentalists are concerned with strip mining, forest depletion, factory smoke, billboards, and litter; with the loss of recreational opportunity; and with the increase in health problems caused by bad air, water, and chemically sprayed food.

Environmentalists are not against marketing and consumption; they simply want them to operate on more ecological principles. They think the goal of the marketing system should be to maximize life quality. And *life quality* means not only the quantity and quality of consumer goods and services but also the quality of the environment.

Environmentalists want environmental costs included in producer and consumer decision making. They favor using taxes and regulations to limit the true social costs of antienvironmental behavior. Requiring business to invest in antipollution devices, taxing nonreturnable bottles, and banning high-phosphate detergents are viewed as necessary to lead businesses and consumers to move in environmentally sound directions.

Environmentalists are more critical of marketing than are consumerists. They complain of too much wasteful packaging, whereas consumerists like the convenience of modern packaging. Environmentalists feel that advertising leads people to consume more than they need, whereas consumerists worry more about deception in advertising. Environmentalists dislike shopping centers, whereas consumerists welcome more stores.

Environmentalism has hit certain industries hard. Steel companies and public utilities have had to invest billions of dollars in pollution-control equipment and costlier fuels. The auto industry has had to introduce expensive emission-controls in cars. The soap industry has had to develop ways to reduce litter and increase biodegradability in its products. The gasoline industry has had to formulate low-lead and no-lead gasolines. These industries resent environmental regulations, especially when imposed too rapidly to allow the companies to make the proper adjustments. These companies have absorbed large costs and have passed them on to buyers.

Marketers' lives have become more complicated. Marketers have to check into the environmental consequences of the product, its packaging, and its production processes. They have to raise prices to cover environmental costs, even though this makes the product harder to sell. At the same time, many managers recognize the validity of respecting the environment and have introduced environmental criteria in their decision making on product ingredients, design, and packaging. Some companies direct their R&D toward finding ecologically superior products, as the major selling point of the product. Sears developed and promoted a phosphate-free laundry detergent; Pepsi-Cola developed a one-way, plastic soft-drink bottle that is biodegradable in solid-waste treatment; and American Oil pioneered no-lead and low-lead gasolines.

Marketers should be aware of the threats and opportunities associated with four trends in the physical environment.

Potential Shortages of Certain Raw Materials   The earth's materials consist of the infinite, the finite renewable, and the finite nonrenewable. An *infinite resource*, such as air, poses no immediate problem, although some groups see a long-run danger. Environmental groups have lobbied for a ban of certain propellants used in aerosol cans because of their potential damage to the ozone layer of air. Water is already a problem in some parts of the world.

Finite renewable resources, such as forests and food, have to be used wisely. Forestry companies are required to reforest timberlands in order to protect the soil and to ensure sufficient wood to meet future demand. Food supply can be a major problem in that the amount of arable land is relatively fixed, and urban areas are constantly encroaching on farmland.

Finite nonrenewable resources, such as oil, coal, and various minerals, pose a serious problem:

> . . . it would appear at present that the quantities of platinum, gold, zinc, and lead are not sufficient to meet demands . . . silver, tin, and uranium may be in short supply even at higher prices by the turn of the century. By the year 2050, several more minerals may be exhausted if the current rate of consumption continues.[16]

The marketing implications are many. Firms using increasingly scarce minerals face substantial cost increases. They may not find it easy to pass these cost increases on to consumers. Firms engaged in exploration and in research and development face an excellent opportunity to develop new sources or substitutes.

Unstable Cost of Energy One finite nonrenewable resource, oil, has created serious problems for the world economy. Oil prices shot up from $2.23 a barrel in 1970 to $34.00 a barrel in 1982, creating a frantic search for alternative energy forms. Coal became popular again, and companies searched for practical means to harness solar, nuclear, wind, and other forms of energy. In the solar energy field alone, hundreds of firms put out first-generation products to harness solar energy for heating homes and other uses. Other firms searched for ways to make a practical electric automobile, with a potential prize of billions going to the winner.

The search for alternative sources of energy, investment in more efficient ways to use it by firms, and increased exploration led to a slowing of the demand for oil, and there is now an oil glut. The price of oil plummeted in early 1986, falling to a low of $10 a barrel. The lower prices had an adverse effect on the oil exploration industry but considerably improved the bottom line for airlines. Not paying close attention to the effect on buying patterns resulting from changing energy costs can prove costly. Chrysler, which did not anticipate the popularity of the small car owing to higher gas prices, was stuck with huge inventories of large models, which led the company to bankruptcy. The lower gas prices are now leading the way to a comeback for the larger but more efficient automobile.

Increased Levels of Pollution Some industrial activity will inevitably damage the quality of the physical environment. Consider the disposal of chemical and nuclear wastes, the dangerous mercury levels in the ocean, the quantity of DDT and other chemical pollutants in the soil and food supply, and the littering of the environment with nonbiodegradable bottles, plastics, and other packaging materials.

The public's concern creates a marketing opportunity for alert companies. It creates a large market for pollution-control solutions such as scrubbers and recycling centers. It leads to a search for alternative ways to produce and package goods that do not cause environmental damage.[17]

Changing Role of Government in Environment Protection During the sixties and seventies, various government agencies played an active role in environmental protection. Ironically, their efforts often ran counter to efforts to increase employment, as when businesses were forced to buy expensive pollution-control equipment instead of more-advanced production equipment. The current administration recognizes this. Its environmental policy recommendations are thus based on two fundamental propositions, that the spirit, creativity, and personal drive of the individuals are the greatest resource of the country and that free markets rather than centralized controls will lead to the most efficient use of resources.

Based on these propositions, the administration seemed to be moving away from the earlier increased regulation and government intervention in environmental protection. It specifically recognized that "environmental protection regulations should be fashioned so that innovation and the substitution of progressively safer new products and technologies for old ones are not inhibited."[18] Thus it seems that business can expect a less-regulated environment to work in or at least a halt in the previous trend toward increasing government regulation.

Companies need to pay attention to the physical environment, in terms of obtaining needed resources and also of avoiding damage to the physical environment. Business can still expect strong controls from both government and pressure groups. Instead of opposing all forms of regulation, business should help develop acceptable solutions to the material and energy problems facing the nation.

Technological Environment

The most dramatic force shaping people's lives is technology. Technology has released such wonders as penicillin, open-heart surgery, and the birth-control pill. It has released such horrors as the hydrogen bomb, nerve gas, and the submachine gun. It has also released such mixed blessings as the automobile, video games, and white bread. One's attitudes toward technology depend on whether one is more enthralled with its wonders or its horrors.

Every new technology is a force for "creative destruction." Transistors hurt the vacuum-tube industry, xerography hurts the carbon-paper business, autos hurt the railroads, and television hurts the movies. Instead of old industries moving into the new, many fought or ignored them, and their businesses declined.

The economy's growth rate is affected by how many major new technologies are discovered. Unfortunately, technological discoveries do not arise evenly through time—the railroad industry created a lot of investment, and then there was a dearth until the auto industry emerged; later radio created a lot of investment, and then there was a dearth until television appeared. In the time between major innovations, the economy can stagnate. Some economists believe that the current economic flatness of the world economy will continue until a sufficient number of new major innovations emerge.

In the meantime, minor innovations fill the gap. Freeze-dried coffee probably made no one happier, and antiperspirant deodorants probably made no one wiser, but they do create new markets and investment opportunities.

Each technology creates major long-run consequences that are not always foreseeable. The contraceptive pill, for example, led to smaller families, more working wives, and larger discretionary incomes—resulting in higher expenditures on vacation travel, durable goods, and other things.

The marketer should watch the following trends in technology.

Accelerating Pace of Technological Change Many of today's common products were not available even one hundred years ago. Abraham Lincoln did not know automobiles, airplanes, phonographs, radio, or the electric light. Woodrow Wilson did not know television, aerosol cans, home freezers, automatic dishwashers, room air conditioners, antibiotics, or electronic computers. Franklin Delano Roosevelt did not know xerography, synthetic detergents, tape recorders, birth-control pills, or earth satellites. And John Kennedy did not know personal computers, digital wristwatches, videorecorders, or word processors.

Alvin Toffler, in his *Future Shock*, sees an accelerative thrust in the invention, exploitation, and diffusion of new technologies.[19] More ideas are being worked on; the time lag between new ideas and their successful implementation is decreasing rapidly; and the time between introduction and peak production is shortening considerably. Ninety percent of all the scientists who ever lived are alive today, and technology feeds upon itself.

In Toffler's later book, *The Third Wave*, he forecasts the emergence of the *electronic cottage* as a new way that work and play will be organized in society.[20] The advent of word-processing typewriters, telecopiers, personal computers, and audio and video links make it possible for many people to do their work at home instead of traveling to and from offices, which may be located thirty or more minutes away. Eventually people will find that the cost of installing and operating telecommunications equipment in the home will fall below the cost of commuting. As seen by Toffler, the electronic-cottage revolution will reduce the amount of auto pollution, bring the family closer together as a work unit, and create more home-centered entertainment and activity. It will have substantial impact on consumption patterns and marketing systems.

Unlimited Innovational Opportunities   Scientists today are working on a startling range of new technologies that will revolutionize our products and production processes. The most exciting work is being done in biotechnology, solid state electronics, robotics, and material sciences.[21] Scientists today are working on cancer cures, lung and liver cures, chemical control of mental illness, happiness pills, practical solar energy, practical electric cars, household robots, totally safe contraceptives, and nutritious foods that are nonfattening and tasty. In addition, scientists also speculate on fantasy products, such as small flying cars, single-person rocket belts, three-dimensional television, space colonies, and human clones. The challenge in each case is not only technical but commercial, namely, to develop practical affordable versions of these products.

High R&D Budgets   The United States leads the world in research and development spending. In 1985, R&D expenditures exceeded $107 billion with the annual percentage increase being 11.7 percent between 1980 and 1985.

The federal government supplied 47 percent of the 1985 total R&D funds. Almost 87 percent of the funds went to applied R&D. The remainder was spent on basic research, more than two-thirds of which took place in colleges and universities.

The five industries spending the most R&D money are aircraft and missiles, electrical equipment and communication, chemicals and allied products, machinery, and motor vehicles and other transportation. Industries that spend the least on R&D are lumber, wood products, furniture, textiles, apparel, and paper and allied products. Industries at the top range spend between 5 and 7 percent of their sales dollar on R&D, and those in the lowest range spend less than 1 percent of their sales dollar. The average company spends about 2 percent of its sales dollar on R&D. A recent study showed a high correlation between R&D expenditures and company profitability. Six companies—Merck, AT&T, Dow, Eastman Kodak, IBM, and Lilly—averaged 5.7 percent in their R&D expenditures-to-sales ratio, and their profitability averaged 15.3 percent of sales. Another six companies—Boeing, Chrysler, Goodyear, McDonnell-Douglas, Signal Companies, and United Technologies—averaged 3.5 percent in their R&D-to-sales ratio and were much less profitable.[22]

Today's research is conducted mostly in research laboratories by research teams rather than by lone inventors like Thomas Edison, Samuel Morse, or Alexander Graham Bell. Furthermore, the high cost of R&D and increased global competition has encouraged firms that traditionally compete with each other to establish cooperative R&D organizations.[23] The Microelectronics and Computer Technology Corporation is one such example. It was set up in 1983, with an annual budget of over $100 million and participation from twelve firms including Control Data, RCA, Digital Equipment, Honeywell, and Sperry.[24]

Managing company scientists is a major challenge. They resent too much cost control. They are often more interested in solving scientific problems than in coming up with marketable products. Companies are adding marketing people to R&D research teams, hoping to achieve a stronger marketing orientation.

Concentration on Minor Improvement Rather Than on Major Discoveries

As a result of the high cost of R&D, many companies are pursuing minor product improvements rather than gambling on major innovations. Even basic-research companies like Du Pont, Bell Laboratories, and Pfizer are proceeding cautiously. Many companies are content to put their money into copying competitors' products and making minor feature and style improvements. Much of the research is defensive rather than offensive. Increasingly, research directed toward major breakthroughs is being conducted by consortiums of companies, rather than by single companies.

Increased Regulation of Technological Change

As products become more complex, the public needs to be assured of their safety. Consequently, government agencies have expanded their powers to investigate and ban potentially unsafe products. Thus the federal Food and Drug Administration has issued elaborate regulations on testing new drugs, with the result that industry-research costs are higher, the time between idea and introduction has been lengthened from five to about nine years, and much drug research has been driven to countries with fewer regulations. Safety and health regulations have also increased in the areas of food, automobiles, clothing, electrical appliances, and construction. Marketers must be aware of these regulations when proposing, developing, and launching new products.

Technological change faces opposition from those who see it as threatening nature, privacy, simplicity, and even the human race. Various groups have opposed the construction of nuclear plants, high-rise buildings, and recreational facilities in national parks. They have called for *technological assessment* of new technologies before allowing their commercialization.

Marketers need to understand the changing technological environment and how new technologies can serve human needs. They need to work closely with R&D people to encourage more market-oriented research. They must be alert to the negative aspects of any innovation that might harm the users and create consumer distrust and opposition.

Political/ Legal Environment

Marketing decisions are substantially impacted by developments in the political/legal environment. This environment is composed of *laws*, *government agencies*, *and pressure groups* that influence and constrain various organizations and individuals in society. The main political trends and their implications for marketing management are discussed below.

Substantial Amount of Legislation Regulating Business

Legislation affecting business has steadily increased over the years. The legislation has a number of purposes. *The first is to protect companies from each other*. Business executives all praise competition but try to neutralize it when it touches them. If threatened, they show their teeth:

ReaLemon Foods, a subsidiary of Borden, held approximately 90 percent of the reconstituted lemon juice market until 1978. In that year, the Federal Trade Commission ruled that Borden had used a selective predatory pricing policy to run its major rivals out of business. They barred Borden from pricing its ReaLemon at "unreasonably" low levels. In 1983, this was modified to allow Borden to price anywhere above its variable costs without having to include its development and marketing costs.[25]

So laws are passed to define and prevent unfair competition. These laws are enforced by the Federal Trade Commission and the antitrust division of the Attorney General's office.

The second purpose of government regulation is to protect consumers from unfair business practices. Some firms, if left alone, would adulterate their products, tell lies in their advertising, deceive through their packages, and bait through their prices. Unfair consumer practices have been defined and are enforced by various agencies. Many managers see purple with each new consumer law, and yet a few have said that "consumerism may be the best thing that has happened . . . in the past twenty years."[26]

The third purpose of government regulation is to protect the larger interest of society against unbridled business behavior. It is possible for the gross national product to rise and the quality of life to fall. A major purpose of new legislation and/or enforcement is to charge businesses with the social costs created by their production processes or products.

The marketing executive needs a good working knowledge of the major laws protecting competition, consumers, and the larger interests of society. The main federal laws are listed in Table 5-2. The earlier laws dealt mainly with protecting competition; the later

TABLE 5-2   Milestone U.S. Legislation Affecting Marketing

Sherman Antitrust Act (1890)
Prohibits (a) "monopolies or attempts to monopolize" and (b) "contracts, combinations, or conspiracies in restraint of trade" in interstate and foreign commerce.

Federal Food and Drug Act (1906)
Forbids the manufacture, sale, or transport of adulterated or fraudulently labeled foods and drugs in interstate commerce. Supplanted by the Food, Drug, and Cosmetic Act, 1938; amended by Food Additives Amendment, 1958, and the Kefauver-Harris Amendment, 1962. The 1962 amendments deal with pretesting of drugs for safety and effectiveness and labeling of drugs by generic name.

Meat Inspection Act (1906)
Provides for the enforcement of sanitary regulations in meat-packing establishments and for federal inspection of all companies selling meats in interstate commerce.

Federal Trade Commission Act (1914)
Establishes the commission, a body of specialists with broad powers to investigate and to issue cease and desist orders to enforce Section 5, which declares that "unfair methods of competition in commerce are unlawful."

Clayton Act (1914)
Supplements the Sherman Act by prohibiting certain specific practices (certain types of price discrimination, tying clauses and exclusive dealing, intercorporate stockholdings, and interlocking directorates) "where the effect . . . may be to substantially lessen competition or tend to create a monopoly in any line of commerce." Provides that violating corporate officials could be held individually responsible; exempts labor and agricultural organizations from its provisions.

Robinson-Patman Act (1936)
Amends the Clayton Act. Adds the phrase "to injure, destroy, or prevent competition." Defines price discrimination as unlawful (subject to certain defenses) and provides the FTC with the right to establish limits on quantity discounts, to forbid brokerage allowances except to independent brokers, and to prohibit promotional allowances or the furnishing of services or facilities except where made available to all "on proportionately equal terms."

Miller-Tydings Act (1937)
Amends the Sherman Act to exempt interstate fair-trade (price fixing) agreements from antitrust prosecution. (The McGuire Act, 1952, reinstates the legality of the nonsigner clause.)

TABLE 5-2   Continued

Wheeler-Lea Act (1938)
Prohibits unfair and deceptive acts and practices regardless of whether competition is injured; places advertising of foods and drugs under FTC jurisdiction.

Antimerger Act (1950)
Amends Section 7 of the Clayton Act by broadening the power to prevent intercorporate acquisitions where the acquisition may have a substantially adverse effect on competition.

Automobile Information Disclosure Act (1958)
Prohibits car dealers from inflating the factory price of new cars.

National Traffic and Safety Act (1958)
Provides for the creation of compulsory safety standards for automobiles and tires.

Fair Packaging and Labeling Act (1966)
Provides for the regulation of the packaging and labeling of consumer goods. Requires manufacturers to state what the package contains, who made it, and how much it contains. Permits industries' voluntary adoption of uniform packaging standards.

Child Protection Act (1966)
Bans sale of hazardous toys and articles. Amended in 1969 to include articles that pose electrical, mechanical, or thermal hazards.

Federal Cigarette Labeling and Advertising Act (1967)
Requires that cigarette packages contain the statement "Warning: The Surgeon General Has Determined that Cigarette Smoking is Dangerous to Your Health."

Truth-in-Lending Act (1968)
Requires lenders to state the true costs of a credit transaction, outlaws the use of actual or threatened violence in collecting loans, and restricts the amount of garnishments. Established a National Commission on Consumer Finance.

National Environmental Policy Act (1969)
Establishes a national policy on the environment and provides for the establishment of the Council on Environmental Quality. The Environmental Protection Agency was established by "Reorganization Plan No. 3 of 1970."

Fair Credit Reporting Act (1970)
Ensures that a consumer's credit report would contain only accurate, relevant, and recent information and would be confidential unless requested for an appropriate reason by a proper party.

Consumer Product Safety Act (1972)
Establishes the Consumer Product Safety Commission and authorizes it to set safety standards for consumer products as well as exact penalties for failure to uphold the standards.

Consumer Goods Pricing Act (1975)
Prohibits the use of price maintenance agreements among manufacturers and resellers in interstate commerce.

Magnuson-Moss Warranty/FTC Improvement Act (1975)
Authorizes the FTC to determine rules concerning consumer warranties and provides for consumer access to means of redress, such as the "class-action" suit. Also expands FTC regulatory powers over unfair or deceptive acts or practices.

Equal Credit Opportunity Act (1975)
Prohibits discrimination in a credit transaction because of sex, marital status, race, national origin, religion, age, or receipt of public assistance.

Fair Debt Collection Practice Act (1978)
Makes it illegal to harass or abuse any person and make false statements or use unfair methods when collecting a debt.

Toy Safety Act (1984)
Gives the government the power to recall dangerous toys quickly when they are found.

---

laws, with protecting consumers. Marketing executives should know these federal laws and particularly the evolving court interpretations.[27] And they should know the state and local laws that affect their local marketing activity.

Several countries have gone further than the United States in the passage of strong consumerist legislation. Norway banned several forms of sales promotion, such as trading stamps, contests, and premiums, as being inappropriate or "unfair" instruments for the sellers to use in promoting their products. Thailand requires food processors selling national brands to market low-price brands also so that low-income consumers will also find economy brands on the shelves. In India, food companies need special approval to launch brands that duplicate what already exists on the market, such as another cola drink or brand of rice. These and other legislative developments have not surfaced prominently in the United States, but they suggest how far regulations could be pushed to constrain marketing practice.

The real issue raised by business legislation is, Where is the point reached when the costs of regulation exceed the benefits of regulation? The laws are not always administered fairly by those responsible for enforcing them. They may hurt many legitimate business firms and discourage new investment and market entry. They may also increase consumer costs. Although each new law may have a legitimate rationale, their totality may have the effect of sapping initiative and slowing down economic growth.

Changing Government Agency Enforcement   To enforce the laws, Congress established several federal regulatory agencies—the Federal Trade Commission, Food and Drug Administration, Interstate Commerce Commission, Federal Communications Commission, Federal Energy Regulation Commission, Civil Aeronautics Board, Consumer Products Safety Commission, Environmental Protection Agency, and Office of Consumer Affairs. These agencies can have a major impact on a company's marketing performance. Consider the following example:

> In 1973 the rotary-engine Mazda automobile had climbing sales. People were impressed by its smooth ride, low repair costs, and reduced air pollution. Then the Environmental Protection Agency issued a report stating that Mazda's fuel consumption was only eleven miles per gallon in city driving. Mazda executives objected, claiming seventeen to twenty-one miles per gallon. The charge stuck in the public's mind, however, and Mazda sales declined 39 percent in the first five months of 1974 as people became more concerned with fuel efficiency than with reduced air pollution.

These agencies are allowed some discretion in enforcing the laws. From time to time, they appear to be overzealous and capricious. The agencies are dominated by lawyers and economists, who often lack a practical sense of how business and marketing work.

During the early and middle 1980s, the degree of enforcement moderated under President Reagan, with a strong trend toward deregulation. The Justice Department relaxed its merger guidelines and a large number of megamergers resulted over the Reagan years. Instead of the old view that bigness is bad, the department when approving a merger considered whether the new entity resulting from the merger would be able to compete more effectively. There had been the opinion that tough antitrust laws were hampering U.S. firms from competing internationally. The administration also turned a blind eye toward most price and territorial arrangements between manufacturers and distributors. Business thus had relatively greater freedom in making economic decisions in the 1980s.[28]

Growth of Public-Interest Groups   Public-action committees (PACs) have increased in number and power during the past two decades. These groups lobby government officials and put pressure on business executives to pay more attention to consumer rights, women's rights, senior citizen rights, minority rights, and so on. Many companies have established public-affairs departments to study and deal with these groups and issues.

New laws and growing numbers of pressure groups have combined to put more restraints on marketers. Marketers have to clear their plans with the company's legal, public-relations, and public-affairs departments. Private marketing transactions have moved into the public domain. Salancik and Upah put it this way:

> There is some evidence that the consumer may not be king, nor even queen. The consumer is but a voice, one among many. Consider how General Motors makes its cars today. Vital features of the motor are designed by the United States government; the exhaust system is redesigned by certain state governments; the production materials used are dictated by suppliers who control scarce material resources. For other products, other groups and organizations may get involved. Thus, insurance companies directly or indirectly affect the design of smoke detectors; scientific groups affect the design of spray products by condemning aerosols; minority activist groups affect the design of dolls by requesting representative figures. Legal departments also can be expected to increase their importance in firms, affecting not only product design and promotion but also marketing strategies. At a minimum, marketing managers will spend less time with their research departments asking "What does the consumer want?" and more and more time with their production and legal people asking "What can the consumer have?"[29]

Socio/Cultural Environment

The society that people grow up in shapes their basic beliefs, values, and norms. They absorb, almost unconsciously, a world view that defines their relationship to themselves, to others, to nature, and to the universe. Here are some of the main cultural characteristics and trends of interest to marketers.

Core Cultural Values Have High Persistence

People in a given society hold many core beliefs and values that tend to persist. Thus most Americans still believe in work, in getting married, in giving to charity, and in being honest. Core beliefs and values are passed on from parents to children and are reinforced by the major institutions of society—schools, churches, business, and government.

People's secondary beliefs and values are more open to change. Believing in the institution of marriage is a core belief; believing that people ought to get married early is a secondary belief. Family-planning marketers could make more headway arguing that people should get married later than that they should not get married at all. Marketers have some chance of changing secondary values but little chance of changing core values.

Each Culture Consists of Subcultures

Each society contains subcultures, that is, various groups with shared values emerging from their special life experiences or circumstances. Episcopalians, teenagers, and Hell's Angels all represent subcultures whose members share common beliefs, preferences, and behaviors. To the extent that subcultural groups exhibit different wants and consumption behavior, marketers can choose subcultures as their target markets.

Secondary Cultural Values Undergo Shifts Through Time

Although core values are fairly persistent, cultural swings do take place. The advent in the 1960s of the "hippies," the Beatles, Elvis Presley, *Playboy* magazine, and other cultural phenomena had a major impact on young people's hair styles, clothing, sexual norms, and life goals. Today's young people are influenced by new heroes and fads; older symbols, such as the *playboy*, seem to be dying. One of the major new symbols is the "yuppies," who represent the much more careerist and conservative leanings of today's youth.

Marketers have a keen interest in anticipating cultural shifts in order to spot new marketing opportunities or threats. Several firms offer social/cultural forecasts in this connection. One of the best known is the Yankelovich Monitor, put out by the marketing research firm of Yankelovich, Skelly, & White. The Monitor interviews twenty-five hundred people each year and tracks thirty-five social trends, such as "anti-bigness," "mysticism," "living for today," "away from possessions," and "sensuousness." It describes the percentage of the population who share the attitude as well as the percentage who are antitrend. For example, the percentage of people who value physical fitness and well-being has been rising steadily over the years, especially in the under-thirty group, the young women and upscale group, and people living in the West. Marketers of foods, exercise equipment, and so on, will want to cater to this trend with appropriate products and communication appeals.

The major cultural values of a society are expressed in people's relationship to themselves, others, institutions, society, nature, and the cosmos.

People's relation to themselves People vary in the relative emphasis they place on self-gratification versus serving others. The move toward self-gratification was especially strong during the 1960s and 1970s. *Pleasure seekers* sought fun, change, and escape. Others sought *self-realization* and joined therapeutic or religious groups. The marketing implications of a "me-society" were many. People bought products, brands, and services as a means of self-expression. They bought "dream cars" and "dream vacations." They spent more time in health activities (jogging, tennis), in introspection, and in arts and crafts. The leisure industry (camping, boating, arts and crafts, sports) benefited from the growing number of self-gratifiers.

People's relation to others Recently some observers have pointed to a countermovement from a "me-society" to a "we-society." They think that more people want serious and long-lasting relationships with others, and not just to pursue their self-interest. Some recent advertising is shifting toward featuring people in groups enjoying sharing things with others. A Doyle Dane Bernbach survey showed a widespread concern among adults about social isolation and a strong desire for human contact.[30] This portends a bright future for "social support" products and services that enhance direct communication between human beings, such as health clubs, vacations, and games. It also suggests a growing market for "social surrogates," things that allow a person who is alone to feel that he or she is not, such as television, home video games, and computers.

People's relation to institutions People vary in their attitudes toward major organizations such as corporations, government agencies, and trade unions. Most people accept these institutions, although they may be critical of particular ones. By and large, people are willing to work for major organizations. There is, however, a decline in *institutional loyalty*. People are giving a little less to these institutions and trusting them less. The work ethic is eroding. Many see work not as a source of satisfaction but as necessary to earn the means to enjoy their nonwork hours.

Several marketing implications follow. Companies need to find new ways to win consumer confidence. They need to review their advertising communications to make sure that their messages are honest. They need to review their various activities to make sure that they are coming across as "good corporate citizens." More companies are turning to *social audits*[31] and to *public relations* to build a positive image with their publics. Drucker believes that "Social Responsibility of Business" in the years to come will no longer mean "Doing Good" or "Not Doing Harm."[32] It will eventually mean converting social problems into opportunities for profitable business.

People's relation to society People vary in their attitudes toward their society, from patriots who defend it to reformers who want to change it, to discontents who want to leave it. There is declining patriotism and stronger criticism and cynicism as to where the country and the world are going. Mitchell proposed the concept of *life ways* to distinguish ways people relate to their society. People fall into six life-way groups:

- ■ *Makers.* Makers are those who make the system work. They are the leaders and the up-and-comers. They are involved in worldly affairs, generally prosperous and ambitious. They are found in the professions and include the managers and proprietors of business.
- ■ *Preservers.* Preservers are people who are at ease with the familiar and are proud of tradition. They are a powerful force in promoting stability in a changing world.
- ■ *Takers.* Takers take what they can from the system. They live only marginally in the work world, finding their pleasures outside. They are attracted to bureaucracies and tenured posts.
- ■ *Changers.* Changers tend to be answer-havers; they commonly wish to change things to conform with their views. They are the critics, protestors, radicals, advocates, and complainers—and a significant segment of the doers. Their focus is chiefly outward.
- ■ *Seekers.* Seekers are the ones who search for a better grasp, a deeper understanding, a richer experience, a universal view. The pathways of their seeking and the rewards sought tend to be internal. They often originate and promulgate new ideas.
- ■ *Escapers.* Escapers have a drive to escape, to get away from it all. Escape takes many forms from dropping out to addiction to mental illness to mysticism.[33]

These types are found in all societies, and their relative size changes over time. Mitchell sees American society drifting toward a greater ratio of takers to makers, which does not augur well for future economic growth. He also sees an increasing ratio of escapers to changers, which means that society will become more conservative and self-indulgent.

Marketers can view life-way groups as market segments with specific symbolic and material needs. Makers are high achievers who collect success symbols, such as elegant homes, expensive automobiles, and fine clothes, whereas changers live more austerely, drive smaller cars, and wear simpler clothes. Escapers go in for motorcycles, chic clothes, surfing, and disco. In general, the consumption patterns of individuals will reflect their orientation toward society.

People's relation to nature   People vary in their attitude toward the physical world. Some feel subjugated by it, others feel harmony with it, and others seek mastery over it. A long-term trend has been people's growing mastery over nature through technology and the attendant belief that nature is bountiful. More recently, however, people have awakened to nature's fragility and finite supplies. People recognize that nature can be spoiled and destroyed by human activities.

People's love of nature is leading to more camping, hiking, boating, and fishing. Business has responded with hiking boots, tenting equipment, and other gear for nature enthusiasts. Tour operators are packaging more tours to wilderness areas. Food producers have found growing markets for "natural" products, such as natural cereal, natural ice cream, and health foods. Marketing communicators are using suggestive natural backgrounds in advertising their products.

People's relation to the universe   People vary in their beliefs about the origin of the universe and their place in it. Most Americans are monotheistic, although their religious conviction and practice have been waning through the years. Church attendance has fallen steadily, with the exception of certain evangelical movements reaching out to bring people back into organized religion. Some of the religious impulse has not been lost but has been redirected into a growing interest in Eastern religions, mysticism, the occult, and the human potential movement.

As people lose their religious orientation, they seek to enjoy their life on earth more fully. They seek goods and experiences that offer fun and pleasure. In the meantime, religious institutions start turning to marketers for help in reworking their appeals to compete against the secular attractions of modern society.

In summary, cultural values are showing the following long-run trends:

Other-centeredness - >	Self-fulfillment
Postponed gratification - >	Immediate gratification
Hard work - >	The easy life
Formal relationships - >	Informal, open relationships
Religious orientation - >	Secular orientation

Marketers should recognize that each trend is subject to exceptions. A long perspective on cultural change shows that much cultural change follows a model of long-term pendulum swings rather than one-way movements. Every force seems to breed a counterforce, and in many cases, the counterforce eventually becomes dominant.

From time to time, a "futurist" will come into prominence with a new list of trends that warrant attention. Exhibit 5-4 describes the ten "megatrends" identified by John Naisbitt.

EXHIBIT 5-4

Naisbitt's Megatrends: A Prominent Futurist Reports on Ten "Megatrends" of Great Import to Marketers

For the past fifteen years, John Naisbitt has been publishing the Trend Report, and several major corporations each pay over $15,000 a year to receive these reports. Naisbitt and his staff spot the trends through content analysis, namely, by counting the number of times hard-news items appear in major newspapers. The items fall into thirteen broad categories and over two hundred subcategories. In 1982, Naisbitt published a book based on his findings called *Megatrends: Ten New Directions Transforming Our Lives* (Warner Books, New York). Here are the ten megatrends Naisbitt found:

1. The American economy is undergoing a "megashift" from an industrial to an information-based society.

   ■ Today 13 percent of the total U.S. work force is employed in manufacturing, while 60 percent produce or process information.

2. As the society increases in high-tech, there will be high-touch reactions.

   ■ Teleconferencing, a high-technology innovation, has not yet caught on because people enjoy the high-touch of face-to-face meetings.

   ■ Many companies try to add high-touch to their high-tech to increase the latter's acceptance. Thus Apple Computer Co. chose the apple and a rainbow to symbolize its "user-friendly" nature.

3. The U.S. is moving away from isolation and self-sufficiency and recognizing its global interdependence. It is losing its dominance as an economic power.

   ■ Japan is number one in productivity. However, Japan is being challenged by Singapore, South Korea, and Brazil.

■ We need to begin thinking globally and acting locally. Illinois and Florida, for instance, are trading with countries around the globe.

4. U.S. corporate managers are beginning to think about the long term rather than the next quarter.

■ The short-term emphasis was due largely to pressure from shareholders and the fact that managers are rewarded for short-term performance rather than long-term planning.
■ American auto makers are suffering because of short-term behavior. which led to cutting costs at the expense of quality and durability.

5. We are beginning to build from the bottom up in our companies and are moving away from a centralized structure toward a decentralized structure.

■ In an industrial society, workers have to go to a central plant and work with others. In an information society, all one needs is a telephone and a typewriter.

6. We are returning to an emphasis on self-reliance and de-emphasizing help from institutions.

■ No longer are people content to devote their lives to corporations. There has been an entrepreneurial explosion.

7. Workers and consumers are demanding and getting a greater voice in government, in business, and in the marketplace.
8. The computer is smashing the corporate organizational chart. We are moving from hierarchies to networks.

■ People are forming networks to share ideas, information, and resources, and the networks often cut across hierarchies.
■ Information is power, and the people who have good access to information are increasing their influence in organizations.

9. Workers are moving from the North and Northeast to the South and Southwest.
10. People are demanding variety instead of "one size for all."

■ Only 7 percent of the population fits the old traditional family profile; i.e., working father, mother at home, two children.
■ Today there are 752 different models of cars and trucks, 2,500 types of light bulbs, and 200 different TV channels on cable networks.

Naisbitt summed it up with the last statement in his book: "My God what a fantastic time to be alive."

SOURCE John Naisbitt, *Megatrends: Ten New Directions Transforming Our Lives* (New York: Warner Books, 1982).

MAPPING A COMPANY'S MARKETING ENVIRONMENT, MARKETING SYSTEM, AND MARKETING STRATEGY

This chapter has described how a company must forge links with various parties to carry out its marketing work, and how these parties are all affected by major forces in the environment. We will use the Hershey Food Company to pull these ideas together and show the relationship between the company's marketing environment, marketing system, and marketing strategy.

Figure 5-3 shows the major components and flows in a candy company's marketing system. The diagram is divided into six elements:

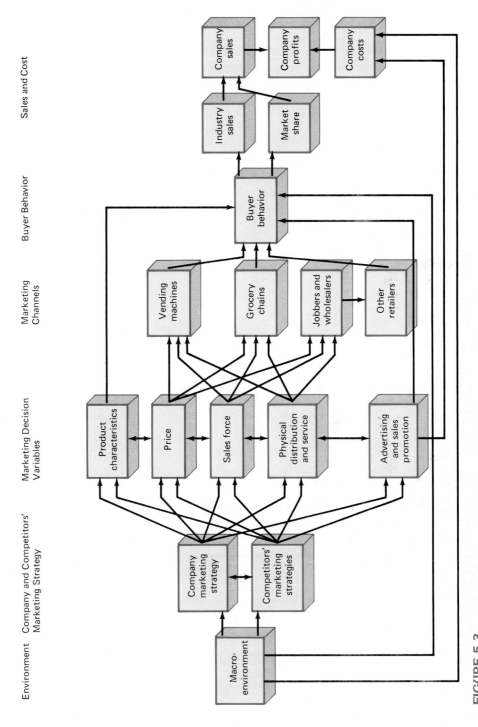

Environment | Company and Competitors' Marketing Strategy | Marketing Decision Variables | Marketing Channels | Buyer Behavior | Sales and Cost

FIGURE 5-3
Comprehensive Marketing System Map: Candy Company

1. The *environment* or, more precisely, those forces in the environment that affect candy demand and supply, such as population growth, per capita income, attitudes toward candy, and raw material availability and cost.
2. The *company's and competitors' marketing strategies.*
3. The *major marketing decision variables* in this market—product characteristics, price, sales force, physical distribution and service, and advertising and sales promotion.
4. The *major marketing channels* that the company uses for this product.
5. The *buyer-behavior model*, which shows customer response to the activities of the manufacturers and the distribution channels as well as to the environment.
6. The total *industry sales*, *company sales*, and *company costs*.

The various arrows show key flows in the marketing system. Let us select one element in Figure 5-3, the company marketing strategy box, and list on the right side of this box all the major marketing decisions made by the company (see Figure 5-4). There are two major types of decisions, trade decisions and consumer decisions. To influence the trade, the company sets the wholesale price, trade allowances, credit policy, and delivery policy. To influence consumers, the company decides on product characteristics, packaging characteristics, retail price, consumer deals, and consumer advertising.

The next step is to list on the left side of the box in Figure 5-3 the various inputs and influences on these decisions, which fall into one of three groups:

1. The company's long- and short-range goals for sales growth, return on sales, and return on investment.
2. Forecastable factors in the environment, such as population growth, disposable personal income, cultural factors, and the cost and supply outlook.

FIGURE 5-4

Input-Output Map of Company Marketing Decisions: Candy Company.

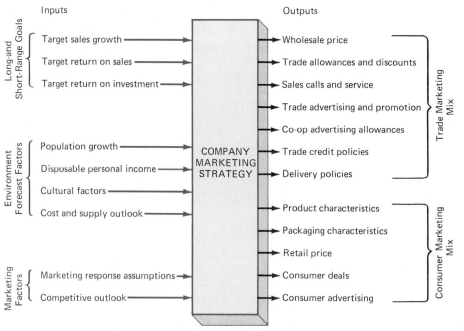

3. Assumptions about the sales effectiveness of different marketing instruments as well as expectations concerning competition.

Any input can be elaborated further. For example, it is possible to isolate four cultural factors that will have a significant effect on future candy consumption:

■ *Weight consciousness.* If Americans start abandoning the idea that "thin is beautiful," candy sales will rise substantially.
■ *Cavity consciousness.* As better toothpastes are developed, people will worry less about how sugar affects their teeth; on the other hand, some companies see cavity consciousness as an opportunity to develop a tasty, sugarless candy.
■ *Nutrition consciousness.* If publicity on the negative effects of refined sugar on human metabolism continues to grow, more people will steer away from candy.
■ *Cigarette consumption.* If people reduce their cigarette smoking, we can expect that candy, gum, and other oral gratifiers will replace cigarettes.

We can now trace how the company marketing strategy outputs feed into other parts of the system. Consider the output described as the trade marketing mix. This output becomes input into each of the distribution channels—for example, the grocery-chain model (see Figure 5-5). The trade marketing mix becomes the "handle" that the manufacturer uses to influence the retailer to provide favorable shelf facings and location, special displays and promotions, advertising, and in-stock maintenance.

The influence of the retailers' decisions on the final consumers is shown in Figure 5-6 along with influences coming from other parts of the marketing system. The various influences are classified into product and promotion factors (outputs coming from the company's marketing decisions), distribution channels factors, and environmental factors (outputs coming from the environmental model). These factors influence consumers' buying behavior and bring about a certain level of industry sales and company sales and company profits.

Ultimately, the marketing planner must estimate the quantitative relationships between various key elements. Figure 5-7 shows the estimated effect of a product characteristic—chocolate weight percentage—on the sales of one of its soft-center candy bars. The company would like to keep this percentage down because chocolate is expensive compared with the other ingredients that make up the soft center. Consumer tests, however, reveal that as the bar's chocolate content is reduced, the bar loses its appeal, and sales decline. The soft center begins to appear through the chocolate and leads consumers to feel that the

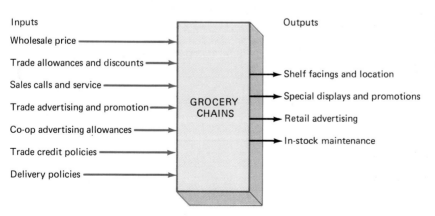

FIGURE 5-5
Input-Output Map of
Grocery-Chain Decisions:
Candy Company

Inputs
Wholesale price
Trade allowances and discounts
Sales calls and service
Trade advertising and promotion
Co-op advertising allowances
Trade credit policies
Delivery policies

GROCERY CHAINS

Outputs
Shelf facings and location
Special displays and promotions
Retail advertising
In-stock maintenance

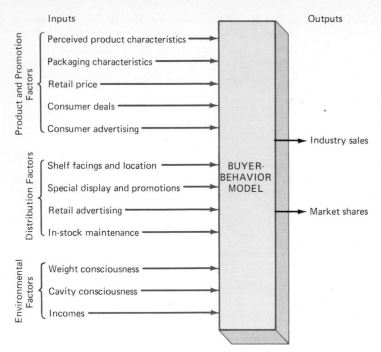

Inputs

Product and Promotion Factors
- Perceived product characteristics
- Packaging characteristics
- Retail price
- Consumer deals
- Consumer advertising

Distribution Factors
- Shelf facings and location
- Special display and promotions
- Retail advertising
- In-stock maintenance

Environmental Factors
- Weight consciousness
- Cavity consciousness
- Incomes

BUYER-BEHAVIOR MODEL

Outputs

→ Industry sales

→ Market shares

FIGURE 5-6
Input-Output Map of Buyer
Behavior: Candy Company

bar is poorly made. Furthermore, consumers desire more chocolate to offset the soft center. When the layer of chocolate gets too thick (above 35 percent of the bar's weight), consumer preference for the bar also falls. The consumers begin to think of it not as a soft-centered chocolate candy bar but as a chocolate bar with ''some stuff in it.'' They compare this bar with pure chocolate bars, and it suffers by comparison. Thus Figure 5-7 shows management's best estimate of how sales are affected by a specific product characteristic, here ''percentage chocolate.'' Any function that shows how sales are affected by a marketing variable under management's control is known as a *sales-response function*.

Given this sales-response function, what is the optimum percentage of chocolate? If the company wants to maximize sales, chocolate should constitute 35 percent of the candy bar's weight. Since the company is primarily interested in maximizing profit, however, management needs the ingredient-cost functions, as well as the sales-response function, to determine the profit-maximizing amount of chocolate.

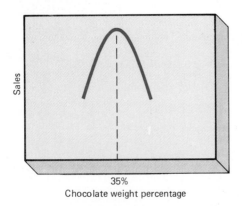

Sales

35%
Chocolate weight percentage

FIGURE 5-7
Functional Relationship Map:
Candy Company

Other functional relationships should be studied—the relationship between the amount spent on advertising and the resulting sales, the number of sales representatives and the resulting sales, and so on. At some point, the various functional relationships must be combined into a model for analyzing the sales and profit consequences of a proposed marketing plan. A useful device is shown in Figure 5-8

Quadrant 1 shows the assumed relationship between population and the total sales of chocolate-covered, soft-centered candy bars. The relationship shows that sales increase with population, but at a decreasing rate. The part of the curve describing candy consumption when the American population was under 240 million is derived through least-squares regression analysis. The part of the curve showing sales for future sizes of the U.S. population is extrapolated and is influenced by anticipated cultural and economic trends. The

FIGURE 5-8
Profit-Forecasting and Planning Map: Candy Company

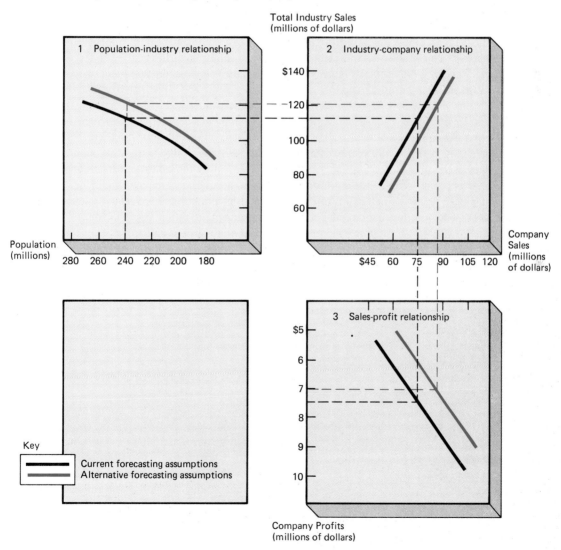

curve indicates that a population of 240 million consumes approximately $110 million of soft-centered candy bars.

The second quadrant shows the relationship between total sales of soft-centered candy bars and company sales. When industry sales are $110 million, Hershey enjoys sales of $75 million—that is, a market share of approximately 68 percent. The part of the curve toward the lower level of industry sales is derived from historical information; the part toward the higher levels of sales is extrapolated on the assumption of no dramatic changes in company and competitors' marketing efforts. The line indicates that the company expects its market share to fall slightly as total sales increase. For example, when industry sales are $140 million, the expectation of company sales is $90 million, or an estimated market share of 64 percent, as compared with 68 percent now.

The third quadrant shows a linear relationship between company sales and company profits. Current profits are $7.5 million on company sales of approximately $75 million, or 10 percent. If company sales rise to $105 million, the company expects profits of approximately $10.2 million—that is, 9.7 percent.

This graphical device allows the marketer to visualize the effect of a particular environment factor and marketing program on company sales and profits. Suppose the company expects a new antismoking campaign to favor candy bar sales and shift the curve in the first quadrant higher (see Figure 5-8). Furthermore, suppose the company plans to intensify its marketing effort to capture more market share. The anticipated effect on company market share can be seen by shifting the function in the second quadrant to the right, as shown in Figure 5-8. At the same time, the company's marketing costs increase and shift the sales-profit curve to the right, as shown in the third quadrant of Figure 5-8. What is the net effect of this complicated set of shifts? The result is that although sales have increased, profits have fallen. Apparently, the cost to the company of attaining a higher market share exceeds the profits on the extra sales. The company would be wise not to intensify its marketing effort unless this would have a stronger effect on sales and profits.

The four-quadrant model assists management in visualizing the impact of specific environmental assumptions and marketing plans on final sales and profits. It can be improved further by introducing more variables and representing their relationships in an overall mathematical model of the candy company's marketing system.

SUMMARY

The marketing environment is the place the company must start in searching for opportunities and monitoring threats. It consists of all the actors and forces that affect the company's ability to transact effectively with a target market. We can distinguish between the company's microenvironment and macroenvironment.

The company's microenvironment consists of the actors in the company's immediate environment that affect its ability to serve its markets; specifically, the company itself, suppliers, market intermediaries, customers, competitors, and publics. The company itself consists of several influential departments, all of which have an influence on marketing management's decision making. Suppliers, through their influence on the cost and availability of needed inputs, also have an influence on marketing decisions. The company converts these supplies into useful products and services and uses marketing intermediaries (middlemen, physical distribution facilitators, marketing service agencies, financial intermediaries) to help it find customers and deliver the goods. The target market itself may consist of consumers, producers, resellers, or government agencies, here or abroad. In carrying out its marketing task, the company faces several types of competitors: desire competitors, generic competitors, product-form competitors, and brand competitors. The company also has to deal with various publics that have an actual or potential interest in or impact on the company's ability to achieve its objectives: financial; media; government; citizen action; and local, general, and internal publics. All of these actors make up the company's microenvironment.

The company's macroenvironment consists of six major forces impinging on the company: demographic, economic, physical, technological, political/legal, and socio/cultural. The demographic environment shows a worldwide explosive population growth, a U.S. birthrate slowdown, an aging U.S. population, a changing American family, a rise of nonfamily households, geographical population shifts, a more-educated and white-collar population, a changing ethnic and racial population, and a shift from a mass market to micromarkets. The economic environment shows a slowdown in real-income growth, low savings and high debt, and changing consumer-expenditure patterns. The physical environment shows potential shortages of certain raw materials, unstable cost of energy, increased pollution levels, and a changing role of government in environmental protection. The technological environment exhibits accelerating technological change, unlimited innovational opportunities, high R&D budgets, concentration on minor improvements rather than on major discoveries, and increased regulation of technological change. The political/legal environment shows substantial business regulation, strong government agency enforcement, and the growth of public-interest groups. The socio/cultural environment shows long-run trends toward self-fulfillment, immediate gratification, the easy life, informal and open relationships, and a more secular orientation.

The interaction between the marketing environment and company marketing system and strategy is illustrated for a major candy company that produces a candy bar for the mass market.

■ QUESTIONS

1. The social environment is a major environmental force influencing marketing activities. How can marketing managers measure change in the social environment?

2. Counterfeit trade—the selling of illegal copies of a licensed product—costs legitimate businesses over $20 billion in lost sales annually. What steps can businesses take to reduce the costs from counterfeiting?

3. Marketers are concerned with both the number and the composition of U.S. households. In what ways would the composition of households influence marketers?

4. Teenagers spend over $45 billion annually on goods and services in the United States. In what ways is marketing to teenage consumers different from marketing to adult consumers?

5. During the early 1980s, a rash of product-tampering cases (beginning with the cyanide poisoning of Tylenol) struck food and drug marketers. What action can marketers take to minimize the threat of such catastrophic environmental events?

6. Develop a diagram showing the major publics of a privately owned hospital.

7. Videotex, also called Viewdata, is a two-way interactive system that allows a user to view a presentation over cable TV and then communicate a response via a home terminal to a computer over telephone lines. What implications does this new technology have for marketers?

8. Tell whether you would support or not support each of the following new legislative proposals (give your reasoning): (a) a bill to require companies in concentrated industries to go through federal hearings before each price boost; (b) a bill to allow auto makers to prevent dealers from selling outside their territories; (c) a bill to require manufacturers to grant wholesalers a bigger discount than they give to large retail chains; (d) a bill to protect independent retailers from price competition from a manufacturer that does its own retailing.

9. Lifestyle studies have shown a positive trend in the

attitude that "meal preparation should take as little time as possible." How might this attitude affect the sales of frozen vegetables?

10. A major alcoholic-beverage marketer is considering introducing an "adult" soft drink that would be a socially acceptable substitute for alcohol. What cultural factors could influence the introduction decision and subsequent marketing mix?

11. Discuss in some depth how the six macroenvironmental forces discussed in this chapter may affect the marketing of Coca-Cola in 1995.

12. Develop a comprehensive marketing system map of some company of your choice. Be sure to show the marketing-mix elements and the channels of distribution.

◼ FOOTNOTES

1 Peter Drucker, *Age of Discontinuity* (New York: Harper & Row, 1969).

2 See Alvin Toffler, *Future Shock* (New York: Bantam Books, 1970), p. 28.

3 This point is elaborated in Philip Kotler and Sidney J. Levy, "Buying Is Marketing, Too," *Journal of Marketing*, January 1973, pp. 54–59.

4 The interrelations between marketing and public relations are examined in Philip Kotler and William Mindak, "Marketing and Public Relations: Partners or Rivals," *Journal of Marketing*, October 1978, pp. 13–20.

5 For a discussion on use of demographic data in structuring marketing strategy, see Louis G. Pol, "Marketing and the Demographic Perspective," *Journal of Consumer Marketing*, Winter 1986, pp. 57–64.

6 Much of the statistical data in this chapter is drawn from the *Statistical Abstract of the United States*, 1986. Also see "America at Mid-decade," *American Demographics*, January 1986, pp. 24–29.

7 Donella H. Meadows, Dennis L. Meadows, Jorgen Randers, and William W. Behrens III, *The Limits to Growth* (New York: New American Library, 1972), p. 41.

8 See Eduardo Roberto, *Strategic Decision-Making in a Social Program: The Case of Family-Planning Diffusion* (Lexington, Mass.: Lexington Books, 1975).

9 See Harry Bacas, "Challenge to Business: America's Changing Face," *Nation's Business*, July 1984, pp. 18–25.

10 See "Too Late for Prince Charming?" *Newsweek*, June 2, 1986, pp. 54–61; and Joann S. Lublin, "Rise in Never-Marrieds Affects Social Customers and Buying Patterns," *Wall Street Journal*, May 28, 1986, p. 1.

11 An SMSA consists of a county or group of contiguous counties with a total population of at least 100,000 and a central city with a minimum population of 50,000 (or two close-together cities with a combined population of 50,000).

12 See David E. Bloom and Sanders D. Korenman, "The Spending Habits of American Consumers," *American Demographics*, March 1986, p. 23.

13 Meadows et al., *Limits to Growth*.

14 Rachel Carson, *Silent Spring* (Boston: Houghton Mifflin, 1962).

15 *Fifteenth Annual Report of the Council on Environmental Quality* (Washington, D.C.: Government Printing Office, 1984), p. 5.

16 *First Annual Report of the Council on Environmental Quality* (Washington, D.C.: Government Printing Office, 1970), p. 158.

17 See Karl E. Henion II, *Ecological Marketing* (Columbus, Ohio: Grid, 1976).

18 *Fifteenth Annual Report of the Council*, p. iv.

19 Toffler, *Future Shock*, pp. 25–30.

20 Alvin Toffler, *The Third Wave* (New York: Bantam Books, 1980).

21 For an excellent and comprehensive list of possible future products, see Charles Panat, *Breakthroughs* (Boston: Houghton Mifflin, 1980); and "Technologies for the '80s," *Business Week*, July 6, 1981, pp. 48ff.

22 "Corporate Growth, R&D, and the Gap Between," *Technology Review*, March–April 1978, p. 39.

23 "Cooperative R&D for Competitors," *Harvard Business Review*, November–December 1985, p. 60.

24 "Four Cities Vie for High-Tech Joint Venture," *Wall Street Journal*, May 12, 1983, p. 35.

25 "FTC to Relax Pricing Order against Borden," *Wall Street Journal*, March 2, 1983, p. 46.

26 Leo Greenland, "Advertisers Must Stop Conning Consumers," *Harvard Business Review*, July–August 1974, p. 18.

27 See Louis W. Stern and Thomas L. Eovaldi, *Legal Aspects of Marketing Strategy: Antitrust and Consumer Protection Issues* (Englewood Cliffs, N.J.: Prentice-Hall, 1984).

28 See Ann Reilly, "Reagan Turns a Cold Eye on Antitrust," *Fortune*, October 14, 1985, p. 31.

29 Extracts from Gerald R. Salancik and Gregory D. Upah, "Directions for Interorganizational Marketing" (Unpublished paper, School of Commerce, University of Illinois, Champaign, August 1978).

30 See Bill Abrams, " 'Middle Generation' Growing More Concerned with Selves," *Wall Street Journal*, January 21, 1982, p. 25.

31 See Raymond A. Bauer and Dan H. Fenn, Jr., "What Is a Corporate Social Audit?" *Harvard Business Review*, January–February 1973, pp. 37–48.

32 Peter F. Drucker, "Converting Social Problems into Business Opportunities: The New Meaning of Corporate Social Responsibility," *California Management Review*, Winter 1984, pp. 53–63.

33 Arnold Mitchell of the Stanford Research Institute, private publication.

6. Analyzing Consumer Markets and Buyer Behavior

There is an old saying in Spain: To be a bullfighter, you must first learn to be a bull.

Anonymous

Understanding the buying behavior of the target market is the essential task of marketing managers under the marketing concept. This chapter will explore the buying dynamics of consumers, and the next chapter will explore the buying dynamics of business buyers.

The consumer market consists of all the individuals and households that buy or acquire goods and services for personal consumption. In 1984, the American consumer market consisted of 238 million persons whose aggregate personal income was $3.0 trillion— the equivalent of $15,487 for each man, woman, and child. Every year, this market grows by several million persons and over $100 billion, representing one of the most lucrative consumer markets in the world.[1]

Consumers vary tremendously in age, income, educational level, mobility patterns, and taste. Marketers find it useful to distinguish different consumer groups or segments and to develop products and services tailored to their needs. If a market segment is large enough, some companies may set up special marketing programs to serve this market. Here are two examples of special consumer groups that managers are currently focusing on as important and growing market segments:

Hispanic consumers: A rapidly growing ethnic group in the U.S. is people of Hispanic origin: Mexicans, Cubans, Puerto Ricans, and Central/South Americans. According to census data, for the period 1980–85, the overall population increased 3.3 percent while the Hispanic population rose 16 percent to 16.9 million people. Hispanics are heavily concentrated in Los Angeles, Miami, New York, San Francisco, and Chicago. They are consumption-oriented and strongly prefer major brand name products. Advertisers, such as Philip Morris, Procter & Gamble, Anheuser Busch,

---

McDonald's, and Ford, spent $335.5 million dollars in 1985, a 17.2 percent increase over 1984, on Spanish language mass media. The result is that Hispanics favor certain brands over others and remain very loyal to these brands. Hispanics are far less likely than non-Hispanics to be adventurous shoppers. Rarely do they buy a new product "just to try something different." Placing a heavy emphasis on quality over price, Hispanic housewives throw away coupons that are perceived as food stamps. They do not use coupons because they are afraid they will look like cheapskates in front of their neighbors in the checkout aisles. Advertisers must be aware of the Hispanic subculture's beliefs, values, and customs in order to design successful marketing programs. At the same time, advertisers must pay attention to differences among major Hispanic groups. An appeal that might work with New York's Puerto Rican community can utterly fail with Miami's Cuban population.[2]

Older consumers: "Old age" in the U.S. officially begins on a person's sixty-fifth birthday, when work retirement usually occurs and social welfare benefits start flowing in. Older people make up 12 percent of the population and are the fastest-growing segment of the population. Marketers make two mistakes with respect to older consumers. They either ignore them as having little purchasing power or assume they are a homogeneous group. Older consumers spend 30 percent of the discretionary money in the marketplace and are less likely to be poor than the general population. Older consumers think of themselves as fifteen years younger and do not like to view themselves as retired and sedate; feeling elderly does not come until around the age of seventy-five. Many older people maintain an active lifestyle, traveling, shopping, and eating out. They are consumers of "yuppie" goods—cars, clothes, and jewelry—and have joined the fitness and nutrition trends, adding fiber, avoiding sugar, and buying more warm-up suits per capita than any other age group. Marketers should avoid promoting products to the older consumer that overemphasize age. Heinz launched a line of "senior foods," which failed because older people did not publicly want to call attention to their problem. Marketers who are trying to reach older consumers should favor television, since older consumers watch more television. At the same time, the main point is that older consumers fall into several segments, and the marketer must target carefully and study the specific characteristics of the target submarket.[3]

Other consumer submarkets—blacks,[4] young professionals,[5] women,[6]—could be similarly researched to see if focused marketing programs would make competitive sense.

The 238 million American consumers buy an incredible variety of goods and services. We will try to understand how consumers make their purchase choices among these goods and services.

A MODEL OF CONSUMER BEHAVIOR

In earlier times, marketers could understand consumers through the daily experience of selling to them. But the growth in the size of firms and markets has removed many marketing decision makers from direct contact with customers. Increasingly, managers have had to turn to consumer research for answers to the most important questions about any market—those shown below—called the Seven Os of the marketplace:

Who constitutes the market?	*Occupants*
What does the market buy?	*Objects*
Why does the market buy?	*Objectives*
Who participates in the buying?	*Organization*
How does the market buy?	*Operations*
When does the market buy?	*Occasions*
Where does the market buy?	*Outlets*

Of central interest is the question, How do consumers respond to various marketer-controlled stimuli? The company that understands how consumers will respond to different product features, prices, advertising appeals, and so on, will have an enormous advantage over its competitors. Therefore business and academic marketing researchers have invested much energy in researching the relationship between marketing stimuli and consumer response.

Their starting point is the stimulus-response model shown in Figure 6-1. This figure shows marketing and other stimuli entering the buyer's "black box" and producing the buyer's responses. The stimuli on the left are of two types. Marketing stimuli consist of the Four Ps: product, price, place, and promotion. Environmental stimuli consist of major forces and events in the buyer's macroenvironment: economic, technological, political, and cultural. All of these stimuli pass through the buyer's black box and produce the buyer's purchase decisions shown on the right: product choice, brand choice, dealer choice, purchase timing, and purchase amount.

The marketer's task is to understand what happens in the buyer's black box between the outside stimuli and purchase decisions. The buyer's black box has two components. First, the buyer's background characteristics have a major influence on how he or she reacts to the stimuli. Second, the buyer's decision processes influence the outcome. The first part of this chapter will examine how buyer background factors—cultural, social, personal and psychological—influence the person's buying behavior. The second part will examine how the buyer moves through a decision process to make purchasing choices.

MAJOR FACTORS INFLUENCING CONSUMER BEHAVIOR

Figure 6-1 indicates that a buyer's purchase decisions are highly influenced by the buyer's unique set of cultural, social, personal, and psychological factors. These factors are further elaborated in Figure 6-2. For the most part, they are "noncontrollable" by the marketer but must be taken into account. We want to examine each factor's influence on buying behavior. We will illustrate these influences for a hypothetical consumer named Linda Brown:

> Linda Brown is thirty-five, married, and a brand manager in a leading consumer-packaged-goods company. She received an M.B.A. some years before computers became available. Linda wants to expand her skill base and use a computer in her work and home. She is considering buying a personal computer but faces a great number of brand choices: IBM, Radio Shack, Apple, Texas Instruments, Compaq, and so on. Her choice will be influenced by many factors.

Cultural Factors   Cultural factors exert the broadest and deepest influence on consumer behavior. We will look at the role played by the buyer's culture, subculture, and social class.

Culture   Culture is the most fundamental determinant of a person's wants and behavior. Whereas lower creatures are largely governed by instinct, human behavior is largely learned. The child growing up in a society learns a basic set of values, perceptions, preferences, and behaviors through a process of socialization involving the family and other key institutions. Thus a child growing up in America is exposed to the following values: achievement and success, activity, efficiency and practicality, progress, material comfort, individualism, freedom, external comfort, humanitarianism, and youthfulness.[7]

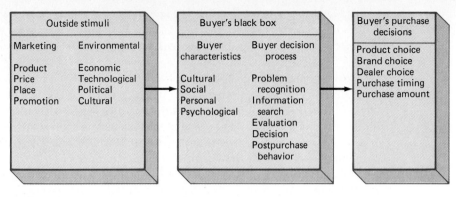

FIGURE 6-1
Model of Buyer Behavior

Linda Brown's interest in computers reflects her upbringing in an advanced technological society. Computers presuppose a whole set of consumer learnings and values. Linda knows what computers are; she knows how to read instructions on how to operate a computer; she knows that the society values computer expertise. In another culture, say a remote tribe in central Africa, a computer would mean nothing. It would simply be a curious piece of hardware, and there would be no buyers.

Subculture   Each culture consists of smaller subcultures that provide more specific identification and socialization for its members. Four types of subcultures can be distinguished. *Nationality groups* such as the Irish, Polish, Italians, and Puerto Ricans are found within large communities and exhibit distinct ethnic tastes and proclivities. *Religious groups* such as the Catholics, Mormons, Presbyterians, and Jews represent subcultures with specific cultural preferences and taboos. *Racial groups* such as the blacks and Orientals have distinct cultural styles and attitudes. *Geographical areas* such as the Deep South, California, and New England are distinct subcultures with characteristic lifestyles.

FIGURE 6-2
Detailed Model of Factors Influencing Behavior

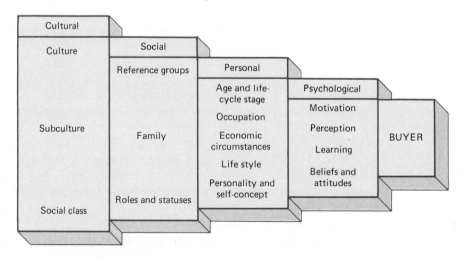

Linda Brown's interest in various goods will be influenced by her nationality, religion, race, and geographical background. These factors will influence her food preferences, clothing choices, recreation, and career aspirations. Her subculture identifications may influence her interest in a personal computer. She may come from a subculture that places a high value on being an ''educated person,'' and this helps explain her interest in computers.

Social Class   Virtually all human societies exhibit social stratification. Stratification sometimes takes the form of a caste system where the members of different castes are reared for certain roles and cannot change their caste membership. More frequently, stratification takes the form of social classes. *Social classes are relatively homogeneous and enduring divisions in a society, which are hierarchically ordered and whose members share similar values, interests, and behavior.* Social scientists have identified the seven social classes shown in Table 6-1.

Social classes have several characteristics. First, persons within each social class tend to behave more alike than persons from two different social classes. Second, persons are perceived as occupying inferior or superior positions according to their social class. Third, a person's social class is indicated by a number of variables, such as occupation, income, wealth, education, and value orientation, rather than by any single variable. Fourth, individuals can move from one social class to another—up or down—during their lifetime. The extent of this mobility varies according to the rigidity of social stratification in a given society.

Social classes show distinct product and brand preferences in such areas as clothing, home furnishings, leisure activities, and automobiles. Some marketers focus their efforts on one social class. Thus the Four Seasons restaurant in upper Manhattan focuses on upper-class customers, whereas Joe's Diner in lower Manhattan focuses on lower-class customers. The social classes differ in their media preferences, with upper-class consumers preferring magazines and books and lower-class consumers preferring television. Even within a media category such as TV, the social classes differ in their preferences. Upper-class consumers prefer news and drama, and lower-class consumers prefer soap operas and quiz shows. There are also language differences among the social classes. The advertiser has to compose copy and dialogue that ring true to the targeted social class.

Linda Brown comes from a middle- or upper-class background. Her family places a lot of value on education and becoming a professional such as a manager, lawyer, accountant, or physician. As a result, Linda has acquired good verbal and mathematical skills and is not daunted by computers, as someone from a less-educated background might be.

Social Factors

A consumer's behavior is also influenced by such social factors as reference groups, family, and social roles and statuses.

Reference Groups   Many groups influence a person's behavior. A person's *reference groups* consists of *all the groups that have a direct (face-to-face) or indirect influence on the person's attitudes or behavior.* Groups having a direct influence on a person are called *membership groups.* These are groups to which the person belongs and interacts. Some are *primary groups* with which there is fairly continuous interaction, such as family, friends, neighbors, and co-workers. Primary groups tend to be informal. A person also belongs to *secondary groups*, which tend to be more formal and where there is less continuous interaction: They include religious, professional, and trade union groups.

People are also influenced by groups in which they are not members. Groups to

1. **UPPER UPPERS (LESS THAN 1 PERCENT).** Upper uppers are the social elite who live on inherited wealth and have a well-known family background. They give large sums to charity, run the debutante balls, maintain more than one home, and send their children to the finest schools. They are a market for jewelry, antiques, homes, and vacations. They often buy and dress conservatively, not being interested in ostentation. While small as a group, they serve as a reference group for others to the extent that their consumption decisions trickle down and are imitated by the other social classes.

2. **LOWER UPPERS (ABOUT 2 PERCENT).** Lower uppers are persons who have earned high income or wealth through exceptional ability in the professions or business. They usually come from the middle class. They tend to be active in social and civic affairs and seek to buy the symbols of status for themselves and their children, such as expensive homes, schools, yachts, swimming pools, and automobiles. They include the nouveaux riches, whose pattern of conspicuous consumption is designed to impress those below them. The ambition of lower uppers is to be accepted in the upper-upper stratum, a status that is more likely to be achieved by their children than themselves.

3. **UPPER MIDDLES (12 PERCENT).** Upper middles possess neither family status nor unusual wealth. They are primarily concerned with "career." They have attained positions as professionals, independent businesspersons, and corporate managers. They believe in education and want their children to develop professional or administrative skills so that they will not drop into a lower stratum. Members of this class like to deal in ideas and "high culture." They are joiners and highly civic minded. They are the quality market for good homes, clothes, furniture, and appliances. They seek to run a gracious home, entertaining friends and clients.

4. **MIDDLE CLASS (31 PERCENT).** The middle class are average-pay white- and blue-collar workers who live on "the better side of town" and try to "do the proper things." Often, they buy products that are popular "to keep up with the trends." Twenty-five percent own imported cars while most are concerned with fashion, seeking "one of the better brand names." Better living means "a nicer home" in a "nice neighborhood on the better side of town" with "good schools." The middle class believes in spending more money on "worthwhile experiences" for their children and aiming them toward a college education.

5. **WORKING CLASS (38 PERCENT).** The working class consists of average-pay blue-collar workers and those who lead a "working class lifestyle," whatever their income, school background, or job. The working class depends heavily on relatives for economic and emotional support, for tips on job opportunities, for advice on purchases, and for assistance in times of trouble. A working class vacation means "staying in town," and "going away" means to a lake or resort no more than two hours away. The working class maintains sharp sex role division and stereotyping. Car preferences include standard size and larger cars, rejecting domestic and foreign compacts.

6. **UPPER LOWERS (9 PERCENT).** Upper lowers are working, not on welfare, although their living standard is just above poverty. They perform unskilled work and are very poorly paid, although they are striving toward a higher class. Often, upper lowers are educationally deficient. Although they fall near the poverty line financially, they manage to "present a picture of self-discipline" and "maintain some effort at cleanliness."

7. **LOWER LOWERS (7 PERCENT).** Lower lowers are on welfare, visibly poverty stricken, and usually out of work or have "the dirtiest jobs." They are seldom interested in finding a job and are permanently dependent on public aid or charity for income. Their homes, clothes, and possessions are "dirty," "raggedy," and "broken-down."

For further reading, see Richard P. Coleman, "The Continuing Significance of Social Class to Marketing," *Journal of Consumer Research*, December, 1983, pp. 265–80; and Richard P. Coleman and Lee P. Rainwater, *Social Standing in America*: *New Dimension of Class* (New York: Basic Books, 1978).

which a person would like to belong are called *aspirational groups*. For example, a teenager may hope one day to play for the Dallas Cowboys. A *dissociative group* is one whose values or behavior an individual rejects. The same teenager may want to avoid any relationship with the Hare Krishna cult group.

Marketers try to identify the reference groups of their target customers. People are significantly influenced by their reference groups in at least three ways. Reference groups expose an individual to new behaviors and lifestyles. They also influence the person's attitudes and self-concept because he or she normally desires to ''fit in.'' And they create pressures for conformity that may affect the person's actual product and brand choices.

The importance of reference-group influence varies among products and brands. Hendon asked two hundred consumers to specify which of their product and brand choices were strongly influenced by others.[8] He found that reference groups had a strong influence on both product and brand choice in the case of automobiles and color television. Reference groups had a strong influence on brand choice only in such items as furniture and clothing. And reference groups had a strong influence on product choice only in such items as beer and cigarettes.

Hendon also observed that reference group influence changes as products go through the product life cycle. When a product is introduced, the decision to buy it is heavily influenced by others, but the brand chosen is less influenced by others. In the market-growth stage, group influence is strong on both product and brand choice. In the product-maturity stage, brand choice but not product choice is heavily influenced by others. In the decline stage, group influence is weak in both product and brand choice.

Manufacturers of products and brands where group influence is strong must determine how to reach and influence the opinion leaders in the relevant reference groups. At one time, sellers thought that opinion leaders were primarily community social leaders whom the mass market imitated because of "snob appeal." But opinion leaders are found in all strata of society, and a specific person can be an opinion leader in certain product areas and an opinion follower in other areas. The marketer tries to reach the opinion leaders by identifying demographic and psychographic characteristics associated with opinion leadership, determining the media read by opinion leaders, and directing messages at the opinion leaders.

Group influence is strong for products that are visible to others whom the buyer respects. Linda Brown's interest in a computer and her attitudes toward various brands will be strongly influenced by some of her membership groups. Her co-workers' attitudes and brand choices will influence her. The more cohesive the group, the more effective its communication process, and the higher the person esteems it, the more influential it will be in shaping the person's product and brand choices.[9]

Family   Family members constitute the most influential primary reference groups shaping a buyer's behavior. We can distinguish between two families in the buyer's life. The *family of orientation* consists of one's parents. From parents a person acquires an orientation toward religion, politics, and economics and a sense of personal ambition, self-worth, and love.[10] Even if the buyer no longer interacts very much with his or her parents, the parents' influence on the unconscious behavior of the buyer can be significant. In countries where parents continue to live with their children, their influence can be substantial.

A more direct influence on everyday buying behavior is one's *family of procreation*, namely, one's spouse and children. The family is the most important consumer-buying organization in society, and it has been researched extensively.[11] Marketers are interested in the roles and relative influence of the husband, wife, and children in the purchase of a large variety of products and services.

Husband-wife involvement varies widely by product category. The wife has traditionally acted as the family's main purchasing agent, especially for food, sundries, and staple-clothing items. This is changing with the increased number of working wives and the husbands doing more family shopping. Convenience goods marketers would therefore make a mistake to think of women as the main or only purchasers of their products.

In the case of expensive products and services, husbands and wives engage in more joint decision making. The marketer needs to determine which member normally has the greater influence in choosing various products. Often it is a matter of who has more power or expertise than being husband or wife per se. The husband may be more dominant, or the wife may be, or they may have equal influence. Here are typical product patterns:

- ■ *Husband-dominant*: Life insurance, automobiles, television
- ■ *Wife-dominant*: Washing machines, carpeting, non-living-room furniture, kitchenware
- ■ *Equal*: Living-room furniture, vacation, housing, outside entertainment

At the same time, a family member's influence can vary with different subdecisions made within a product category. Davis found that the decision of "when to buy an automobile" was influenced primarily by the husband in 68 percent of the cases, primarily by the wife in 3 percent of the cases, and equally in 29 percent of the cases.[12] On the other hand, the decision of "what color of automobile to buy" was influenced primarily by the husband in 25 percent of the cases, by the wife in 25 percent of the cases, and equally in 50 percent of the cases. An automobile company would take these varying decision roles into account in designing and promoting its cars (see Exhibit 6-1 for more recent data on the influence of women car buyers).

In the case of Linda Brown's buying a personal computer, her husband will play an influencer role. He may like seeing her take up a new hobby, and he may also want to use the computer for certain applications related to his career. He may even have initiated the suggestion. His influence will depend on how strongly he makes the case for buying a computer and how much Linda values his opinion.

Roles and Statuses   A person participates in many groups throughout life—family, clubs, organizations. The person's position in each group can be defined in terms of *role* and

---

EXHIBIT 6-1

Women Become a More Important Market for Car Buying

Laurie Ashcraft, marketing research manager of Minnetonka, Inc., recently made the following observations at a Midwest marketing and research conference:

"Women in car ads have typically been shown sitting on the hood rather than behind the wheel. . . . It seems Detroit is always trying to catch up to changes in consumer demands. . . . And now, they're trying to catch up in their marketing to women. In 1980, women influenced 80 percent of new-car purchases and actually made 40 percent of these purchases. And the increase in car ownership by women has been a steady trend, jumping to 40 percent from 21 percent in 1972. . . . Some auto manufacturers are frantically trying to change their advertising to reflect the reality that women do more than pick out the color of the upholstery. . . . A study . . . revealed that 47 percent of women feel they are not being communicated with effectively in car ads. The women said car ads assume women to be primarily interested in appearance, underestimate women's car sense, and overestimate male influence on women drivers. . . . For example, 60 percent of service contracts are bought by women, and surveys have found that they should be approached differently than men since women are interested in aspects such as safety to a greater degree.

"Detroit and other top management suffer from inertia and cannot be easily persuaded that change is occurring. . . . Marketing decision makers are bringing too much of their own mind-set to the party."

SOURCES: Laurie Ashcraft, "Marketers Miss Their Target When They Eschew Research," *Marketing News*, January 7, 1983, p. 10. Also see J. Gilbert, "Marketing Cars to Women," *Madison Avenue*, August 1985, pp. 52–56.

---

status. With her parents, Linda Brown plays the role of daughter; in her family, she plays wife; in her corporation, she plays brand manager. A role consists of the activities that a person is expected to perform according to the persons around him or her. Each of Linda's roles will influence some of her buying behavior.

Each role carries a status reflecting the general esteem accorded to it by society. A Supreme Court justice has more status than a brand manager, and a brand manager has more status than an office clerk. People choose products that communicate their role and status in society. Thus company presidents drive Mercedes, wear expensive tailored suits, and drink Chivas Regal Scotch. Marketers are aware of the *status symbol* potential of products and brands. However, status symbols vary for different social classes and also geographically. Status symbols that are ''in'' in New York are jogging to work, fish and fowl, and cosmetic surgery for men; in Chicago, buying through catalogs, croissants and tacos, and car telephones; in Houston, elegant parties, caviar, and the ''preppy'' look; in San Francisco, sky diving, freshly made pasta, and Izod shirts.[13]

Personal Factors

A buyer's decisions are also influenced by his or her personal characteristics, notably the buyer's age and life-cycle stage, occupation, economic circumstances, lifestyle, and personality and self-concept.

Age and Life-Cycle Stage

People change the goods and services they buy over their lifetime. They eat baby food in the early years, most foods in the growing and mature years, and special diets in the later years. People's taste in clothes, furniture, and recreation is also age related.

Consumption is also shaped by the stage of the *family life cycle*. Nine stages of the family life cycle are listed in Table 6-2, along with the financial situation and typical product interests of each group. Marketers often define their target markets as certain life-cycle groups and develop appropriate products and marketing plans.

Some recent work has identified *psychological life-cycle stages*. Adults experience certain *passages* or *transformations* as they go through life.[14] Thus Linda Brown may move from being a satisfied brand manager and wife to being a dissatisfied person searching for a new career. This may have stimulated her interest in computers. Marketers should pay attention to the changing consumption interests that might be associated with these adult passages.

Occupation

A person's consumption pattern is also influenced by his or her occupation. A blue-collar worker will buy work clothes, work shoes, lunch boxes, and bowling recreation. A company president will buy expensive blue-serge suits, air travel, country club membership, and a large sailboat. Marketers try to identify the occupational groups that have an above-average interest in their products and services. A company can even specialize in producing products needed by a particular occupational group. Thus computer software companies will design different computer software for brand managers, engineers, lawyers, and physicians.

Economic Circumstances

Product choice is greatly affected by one's economic circumstances. People's economic circumstances consist of their *spendable income* (its level, stability, and time pattern), savings and assets (including the percentage that is liquid), *borrowing power*, and *attitude toward spending versus saving*. Thus Linda Brown can consider buying a personal computer if she has enough spendable income, savings, or

TABLE 6-2   An Overview of the Family Life Cycle and Buying Behavior

Stage in Family Life Cycle	Buying or Behavioral Pattern
1. Bachelor stage: young, single people not living at home.	Few financial burdens. Fashion opinion leaders. Recreation oriented. Buy: basic kitchen equipment, basic furniture, cars, equipment for the mating game, vacations.
2. Newly married couples: young, no children.	Better off financially than they will be in near future. Highest purchase rate and highest average purchase of durables. Buy: cars, refrigerators, stoves, sensible and durable furniture, vacations.
3. Full nest I: Youngest child under six.	Home purchasing at peak. Liquid assets low. Dissatisfied with financial position and amount of money saved. Interested in new products. Like advertised products. Buy: washers, dryers, TV, baby food, chest rubs and cough medicines, vitamins, dolls, wagons, sleds, skates.
4. Full nest II: Youngest child six or over.	Financial position better. Some wives work. Less influenced by advertising. Buy larger-sized packages, multiple-unit deals. Buy: many foods, cleaning materials, bicycles, music lessons, pianos.
5. Full nest III: Older married couples with dependent children.	Financial position still better. More wives work. Some children get jobs. Hard to influence with advertising. High average purchase of durables. Buy: new, more tasteful furniture, auto travel, unnecessary appliances, boats, dental services, magazines.
6. Empty nest I: Older married couples, no children living with them, head in labor force.	Home ownership at peak. Most satisfied with financial position and money saved. Interested in travel, recreation, self-education. Make gifts and contributions. Not interested in new products. Buy: vacations, luxuries, home improvements.
7. Empty nest II: Older married. No children living at home, head retired.	Drastic cut in income. Keep home. Buy: medical appliances, medical-care products that aid health, sleep, and digestion.
8. Solitary survivor, in labor force.	Income still good but likely to sell home.
9. Solitary survivor, retired.	Same medical and product needs as other retired group; drastic cut in income. Special need for attention, affection, and security.

SOURCES: William D. Wells and George Gubar, "Life-Cycle Concepts in Marketing Research," *Journal of Marketing Research*, November 1966, pp. 355–63, here p. 362. Also see Patrick E. Murphy and William A. Staples, "A Modernized Family Life Cycle," *Journal of Consumer Research*, June 1979, pp. 12–22; and Frederick W. Derrick and Alane E. Linfeld, "The Family Life Cycle: An Alternative Approach," *Journal of Consumer Research*, September 1980, pp. 214–17.

borrowing power and prefers spending to saving. Marketers of income-sensitive goods pay continuous attention to trends in personal income, savings, and interest rates. If economic indicators point to a recession, marketers can take steps to redesign, reposition, and reprice their products so they continue to appeal to target customers.

Lifestyle   People coming from the same subculture, social class, and even occupation may lead quite different lifestyles. Linda Brown, for example, can choose to live a "belonging" lifestyle, which is reflected in wearing conservative clothes, spending a lot of time with her family, helping her church. Or she can choose an "achiever" lifestyle, marked by working long hours on major projects and playing hard when it comes to travel and sports.

    A person's *lifestyle*, then, is the person's *pattern of living in the world as expressed in the person's activities, interests, and opinions.* Lifestyle portrays the "whole person" interacting with his or her environment. Lifestyle reflects something beyond the person's social class, on the one hand, or personality, on the other. If we know someone's social class, we can infer several things about the person's likely behavior but fail to see the person as an individual. If we know someone's personality, we can infer distinguishing psychological characteristics but not much about actual activities, interests, and opinions. Lifestyle attempts to profile a person's way of being and acting in the world. (See Exhibit 6-2.)

EXHIBIT 6-2

How Lifestyles are Identified

Researchers have worked hard to develop a lifestyle classification, based on *psychographic* measurements. A number of classifications have been proposed, two of which will be described here, namely, the AIO framework and the VALS framework.

The AIO Framework

In this approach, respondents are presented with long questionnaires seeking to measure their activities, interests, and opinions (AIO). The table below shows the major dimensions used to measure the AIO elements, as well as respondents' demographics.

Activities	Interests	Opinions	Demographics
Work	Family	Themselves	Age
Hobbies	Home	Social issues	Education
Social events	Job	Politics	Income
Vacation	Community	Business	Occupation
Entertainment	Recreation	Economics	Family size
Club membership	Fashion	Education	Dwelling
Community	Food	Products	Geography
Shopping	Media	Future	City size
Sports	Achievements	Culture	Stage in life cycle

SOURCE Joseph T. Plummer, "The Concept and Application of Life-Style Segmentation," *Journal of Marketing*, January 1974, p. 34.

Many of the questions are in the form of agreeing or disagreeing with such statements as

▮ I would like to become an actor.
▮ I enjoy going to concerts.
▮ I usually dress for fashion, not for comfort.
▮ I often have a cocktail before dinner.

The data are analyzed on a computer to find distinctive lifestyle groups. Using this approach, the Chicago-based advertising agency of Needham, Harper and Steers has identified ten major lifestyle types, to which they have given names:

FEMALE LIFESTYLE TYPES:
▮ Cathy, the contented housewife (18%)
▮ Candice, the chic suburbanite (20%)

- Eleanor, the elegant socialite (17%)
- Mildred, the militant mother (20%)
- Thelma, the old-fashioned traditionalist (25%)

MALE LIFESTYLE TYPES:

- Ben, the self-made businessman (17%)
- Scott, the successful professional (21%)
- Dale, the devoted family man (17%)
- Fred, the frustrated factory worker (19%)
- Herman, the retiring homebody (26%)

When developing an advertising campaign, the marketers explicate which lifestyle group(s) their product is aimed at and develop an ad appealing to the AIO characteristics of that lifestyle group(s).

The VALS Framework

Arnold Mitchell of SRI International developed a new classification of the American public into nine value lifestyle groups (VALS) based on analyzing the answers of 2,713 respondents to over 800 questions. The nine groups are described below, with the current estimated percentage of the U.S. adult population in each:

- Survivors (4%) are disadvantaged people who tend to be "despairing, depressed, withdrawn."
- Sustainers (7%) are disadvantaged people who are valiantly struggling to get out of poverty.
- Belongers (33%) are people who are conventional, conservative, nostalgic, and unexperimental, who would rather fit in than stand out.
- Emulators (10%) are ambitious, upwardly mobile, and status conscious; they want to "make it big."
- Achievers (23%) are the nation's leaders who make things happen, work within the system, and enjoy the good life.
- "I-am-me" (5%) are people who are typically young, self-engrossed, and given to whim.
- Experientials (7%) are people who pursue a rich inner life and want to directly experience what life has to offer.
- Societally conscious (9%) people have a high sense of social responsibility and want to improve conditions in society.
- Integrateds (2%) are people who have fully matured psychologically and combine the best elements of inner directedness and outer directedness.

The classification is based on the idea that individuals pass through a number of developmental stages, with each stage affecting the person's attitudes, behavior, and psychological needs. People pass from a need-driven stage (survivors and sustainers), into either an outer-directed hierarchy of stages (belongers, emulators, and achievers) or an inner-directed hierarchy of stages (I-am-me, experientials, societally conscious), with a few reaching an integrated stage.

Marketers pay little attention to need-driven segments of the population because they lack economic resources. The other groups are of greater interest and have some distinct demographic, occupational, and media characteristics. Thus a manufacturer of expensive luggage will want to know more about the characteristics of achievers and how to advertise effectively to them; a manufacturer of hot tubs will want to zero in on the experientials. A manufacturer of garbage disposals will direct different appeals to belongers versus societally conscious people. Over forty major corporations now subscribe to VALS and use the data to reach lifestyle groups more effectively.

SOURCES For further discussion of AIO, see William D. Wells, "Psychographics: A Critical Review," *Journal of Marketing Research*, May 1975, pp. 196–213; and Peter W. Bernstein, "Psychographics Is Still an Issue on Madison Avenue," *Fortune*, January 16, 1978, pp. 78–84. For further discussion of VALS, see Arnold Mitchell, *The Nine American Life Styles* (New York: Macmillan, 1983).

Marketers will search for relationships between their products and lifestyle groups. A personal-computer manufacturer might find that many target buyers have the value and lifestyles of an achiever, as described in Exhibit 6-2. The marketer may then aim the brand more clearly at the achiever lifestyle. Advertising copywriters can create advertising that is congruent with the symbols in this person's lifestyle:

> He lives in one of those modern high-rise apartments and the rooms are brightly colored. He has modern, expensive furniture, but not Danish modern. He buys his clothes at Brooks Brothers. He owns a good hi-fi. He skis. He has a sailboat. He eats Limburger and any other prestige cheese with his beer. He likes and cooks a lot of steak and would have a filet mignon for company. His liquor cabinet has Jack Daniels bourbon, Beefeater gin, and a good Scotch.[15]

The implications of the lifestyle concept are well stated by Boyd and Levy:

> Marketing is a process of providing customers with parts of a potential mosaic from which they, as artists of their own lifestyles, can pick and choose to develop the composition that for the time seems the best. The marketer who thinks about his products in this way will seek to understand their potential settings and relationships to other parts of consumer lifestyles, and thereby to increase the number of ways they fit meaningfully into the pattern.[16]

Personality and Self-Concept Each person has a distinct personality that will influence his or her buying behavior. By *personality*, we mean the *person's distinguishing psychological characteristics that lead to relatively consistent and enduring responses to his or her environment*. Personality is usually described in terms of such traits as self-confidence, dominance, autonomy, deference, sociability, defensiveness, and adaptability.[17] Personality can be a useful variable in analyzing consumer behavior provided that personality types can be classified and that strong correlations exist between certain personality types and product or brand choices. For example, a personal-computer company might discover that many prospects have high self-confidence, dominance, and autonomy. This suggests using these appeals in advertising personal computers.

Many marketers use a concept related to personality—a person's *self-concept* (or self-image). All of us carry around a complex mental picture of ourselves. For example, Linda Brown may see herself as highly accomplished and deserving the best. To that extent, she would favor a computer that projects the same qualities. If the IBM personal computer is promoted as a computer for those who want the best, then its brand image would match her self-image. Marketers should try to develop brand images that match the self-image of the target market.

The theory, admittedly, is not that simple. Linda's *actual self-concept* (how she views herself) differs from her ideal *self-concept* (how she would like to view herself) and from her *others-self-concept* (how she thinks others see her). Which self will she try to satisfy with the choice of a computer? Some marketers feel that buyers' choices will correspond more to their actual self-concepts, others to the ideal self-concept, and still others to the others-self-concept. As a result, self-concept theory has had a mixed record of success in predicting consumer responses to brand images.[18]

Psychological Factors A person's buying choices are also influenced by four major psychological factors—motivation, perception, learning, and beliefs and attitudes. We will explore each factor's role in the buying process.

Motivation We saw that Linda Brown became interested in buying a computer. Why? What is she really seeking? What needs is she trying to satisfy?

A person has many needs at any given time. Some needs are *biogenic*. They arise from physiological states of tension such as hunger, thirst, discomfort. Other needs are psychogenic. They arise from psychological states of tension such as the need for recognition, esteem, or belonging. Most of these needs will not be intense enough to motivate the person to act on them immediately. A need becomes a motive when it is aroused to a sufficient level of intensity. A motive (or drive) is a need that is sufficiently pressing to drive the person to act. Satisfying the need reduces the felt tension.

Psychologists have developed theories of human motivation. Three of the best known—the theories of Sigmund Freud, Abraham Maslow, and Frederick Herzberg—carry quite different implications for consumer analysis and marketing strategy.

Freud's theory of motivation   Freud assumes that the real psychological forces shaping people's behavior are largely unconscious. Freud sees the person as repressing many urges in the process of growing up and accepting social rules. These urges are never eliminated or perfectly controlled; they emerge in dreams, in slips of the tongue, in neurotic behavior.

Thus a person cannot fully understand his or her own motivations. If Linda Brown wants to purchase a personal computer, she may describe her motive as wanting a hobby or furthering her career. At a deeper level, she may be purchasing a computer to impress others. At a still deeper level, she may be buying the computer because it helps her feel smart and sophisticated.

When Linda looks at a particular computer, she will react not only to its stated capabilities but also to other cues. The computer's shape, size, weight, material, color, brand name, and case can all trigger certain emotions. The manufacturer, in designing the computer, should be aware of the impact of visual, auditory, and tactile elements in triggering consumer emotions that could stimulate or inhibit purchase.

The leading modern exponent of Freudian motivation theory in marketing is Ernest Dichter, who for over three decades has been interpreting buying situations and product choices in terms of underlying unconscious motives. Dichter calls his approach *motivational research*, and it consists of collecting "in-depth interviews" with a few dozen consumers to uncover their deeper motives triggered by the product. He uses various "projective techniques" to throw the ego off guard-techniques such as work association, sentence completion, picture interpretaion, and role playing.[19]

Motivation researchers have produced some interesting and occasionally bizarre hypotheses as to what may be in the buyer's mind regarding certain purchases. They have suggested that

- Consumers resist prunes because prunes are wrinkled looking and remind people of old age.
- Men smoke cigars as an adult version of thumb sucking. They like their cigars to have a strong odor in order to prove their masculinity.
- Women prefer vegetable shortening to animal fats because the latter arouse a sense of guilt over killing animals.
- A woman is very serious when baking a cake because unconsciously she is going through the symbolic act of giving birth. She dislikes easy-to-use cake mixes because the easy life evokes a sense of guilt.

Maslow's theory of motivation   Abraham Maslow sought to explain why people are driven by particular needs at particular times.[20] Why does one person spend considerable time and energy on personal safety and another on pursuing the esteem of others? His answer is that human needs are arranged in a hierarchy, from the most pressing to the least pressing. Maslow's hierarchy of needs is shown in Figure 6-3. In their order of

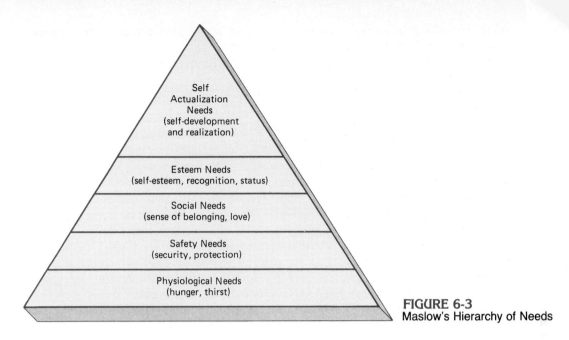

FIGURE 6-3
Maslow's Hierarchy of Needs

importance, they are *physiological* needs, *safety* needs, *social* needs, *esteem* needs, and *self-actualization* needs. A person will try to satisfy the most important needs first. When a person succeeds in satisfying an important need, it will cease being a motivator for the present time, and the person will try to satisfy the next-most-important need.

For example, a starving man (need 1) will not take an interest in the latest happenings in the art world (need 5), nor in how he is viewed or esteemed by others (need 3 or 4), nor even in whether he is breathing clear air (need 2). But as each important need is satisfied, the next-most-important need will come into play.

Maslow's theory helps the marketer understand how various products fit into the plans, goals, and lives of potential consumers. What light does Maslow's theory throw on Linda Brown's interest in buying a computer? We can guess that Linda has satisfied her physiological, safety, and social needs; they do not motivate her interest in computers. Her computer interest might come from a strong need for more esteem from others or from a higher need for self-actualization. She wants to actualize her potential as a creative person through learning to master the computer.

Herzberg's theory of motivation   Frederick Herzberg developed a "two-factor theory" of motivation, which distinguishes between dissatisfiers (factors that cause dissatisfaction) and satisfiers (factors that cause satisfaction).[21] For example, if an Apple computer did not come with a warranty, that would be a dissatisfier. Yet the presence of a product warranty would not act as a satisfier or motivator of Linda's purchase, since it is not a source of intrinsic satisfaction with the Apple computer. The Apple computer's fine-color graphics would be a satisfier and enhance Linda's enjoyment of the computer.

This theory of motivation has two implications. First, sellers should do their best to prevent dissatisfiers from affecting the buyer. These dissatisfiers might be a poor training manual or a poor service policy. While these things will not sell the computer, they might easily unsell the computer. Second, the manufacturer should carefully identify the major satisfiers or motivators of purchase in the computer market and be sure to supply them.

These factors will make the major difference as to which computer brand the customer buys.

Perception A motivated person is ready to act. How the motivated person acts is influenced by his or her perception of the situation. Two people in the same motivated state and objective situation may act quite differently because they perceive the situation differently. Linda Brown might see a fast-talking computer salesperson as aggressive and insincere. Another shopper might see the same salesperson as intelligent and helpful.

Why do people have different perceptions of the same situation? We start with the notion that all of us apprehend a stimulus object through *sensations*, that is, flows of information through our five senses: sight, hearing, smell, touch, and taste. However, each of us attends, organizes, and interprets this sensory information in an individual way. *Perception* can be defined as "the process by which an individual selects, organizes, and interprets information inputs to create a meaningful picture of the world."[22] Perception depends not only on the character of the physical stimuli but also on the relation of the stimuli to the surrounding field (the Gestalt idea) and on conditions within the individual.

People can emerge with different perceptions of the same stimulus object because of three perceptual processes: selective attention, selective distortion, and selective retention.

Selective attention People are exposed to a tremendous amount of daily stimuli. Looking at commercial stimuli alone, the average person may be exposed to over fifteen hundred ads a day. It is impossible for a person to attend to all of these stimuli. Most stimuli will be screened out. The real challenge is to explain what stimuli people will notice. Here are some findings:

- ■ *People are more likely to notice stimuli that relate to a current need.* Linda Brown will notice most computer ads because she is motivated to buy one; she will probably not notice stereo equipment ads.
- ■ *People are more likely to notice stimuli that they anticipate.* Linda Brown is more likely to notice computers than radios in a computer store because she did not expect the store to carry radios.
- ■ *People are more likely to notice stimuli whose deviations are large in relation to the normal size of the stimuli.* Linda Brown is more likely to notice an ad offering $100 off the list price of an Apple computer than one offering $5 off the list price.

Selective attention means that marketers have to work especially hard to attract consumer attention. Their messages will be lost on most people who are not in the market for the product. Even people who are in the market may not notice the message unless it stands out from the surrounding sea of stimuli. Ads that are larger, or use four colors where most ads are black and white, or are novel and provide contrast are more likely to be noticed.

Selective distortion Even stimuli that consumers attend to do not necessarily come across in the predicted way. Each person attempts to fit incoming information into his or her existing mind-set. Selective distortion describes the tendency of people to twist information into personal meanings. Thus Linda Brown may hear the salesperson mention some good and bad points about an IBM computer. If Linda has a strong leaning toward IBM, she is likely to distort the points in order to justify buying an IBM. People interpret information in a way that will support rather than challenge their preconceptions.

Selective retention People will forget much that they learn. They will tend to retain information that supports their attitudes and beliefs for chosen alternatives. Because of selective retention, Linda is likely to remember good points mentioned about the IBM and forget good points mentioned about competing computers. She remembers IBM's good points because she "rehearses" them more whenever she thinks about choosing a computer.

These three perceptual factors—selective exposure, distortion, and retention—mean that marketers have to work hard to get their messages through. That explains why marketers use so much drama and repetition in sending messages to their market.

Learning When people act, they learn. *Learning* describes *changes in an individual's behavior arising from experience.* Most human behavior is learned.

Learning theorists say that a person's learning is produced through the interplay of *drives*, *stimuli*, *cues*, *responses*, and *reinforcement.*

We saw that Linda Brown has a drive toward self-actualization. A *drive* is defined as a strong internal stimulus impelling action. Her drive becomes a *motive* when it is directed toward a particular drive-reducing *stimulus object*, in this case a computer. Linda's response to the idea of buying a computer is conditioned by the surrounding cues. Cues are minor stimuli that determine when, where, and how the person responds. Her husband's encouragement of her interest, seeing a computer in a friend's home, seeing computer ads and articles, hearing about a special sales price are all cues that can influence Linda's response to the impulse to buy a computer.

Suppose Linda buys a computer and chooses an IBM. If her experience is *rewarding*, she will use the computer more and more. Her response to computers will be reinforced.

Later on, Linda may want to buy a typewriter. She notices several brands, including one by IBM. Since she knows that IBM makes good computers, she infers that IBM also makes good typewriters. We say that she *generalizes* her response to similar stimuli.

A countertendency to generalization is *discrimination*. When Linda examines a typewriter made by Olivetti, she sees that it is lighter and more compact than IBM's typewriter. Discrimination means she has learned to recognize differences in sets of similar stimuli and can adjust her responses accordingly.

The practical importance of learning theory for marketers is that they can build up demand for a product by associating it with strong drives, using motivating cues, and providing positive reinforcement. A new company can enter the market by appealing to the same drives that competitors appeal to and providing similar cue configurations because buyers are more likely to transfer loyalty to similar brands than to dissimilar brands (generalization). Or it might design its brand to appeal to a different set of drives and offer strong cue inducements to switch (discrimination).

Beliefs and Attitudes Through acting and learning, people acquire their beliefs and attitudes. These in turn influence their buying behavior.

A *belief* is a *descriptive thought that a person holds about something*. Linda Brown may believe that an IBM personal computer has a larger memory, stands up well under rugged usage, and costs $2,000. These beliefs may be based on knowledge, opinion, or faith. They may or may not carry an emotional charge. For example, Linda Brown's belief that an IBM personal computer is heavier than an Apple might not matter to her decision.

Manufacturers, of course, are very interested in the beliefs that people carry in their heads about their products and services. These beliefs make up product and brand images, and people act on their images. If some of the beliefs are wrong and inhibit purchase, the manufacturer will want to launch a campaign to correct these beliefs.[23]

An *attitude* describes a person's *enduring favorable or unfavorable cognitive evaluations, emotional feelings, and action tendencies toward some object or idea.*[24] People have attitudes toward almost everything: religion, politics, clothes, music, food, and so on. Attitudes put them into a frame of mind of liking or disliking an object, moving toward or away from it. Thus Linda Brown may hold such attitudes as "Buy the best," "IBM makes the best computers in the world," and "Creativity and self-expression are among the most important things in life." The IBM computer is therefore salient to Linda because it fits well into her preexisting attitudes. A computer company can benefit greatly from researching the various attitudes people have toward the product and the company's brand.

Attitudes lead people to behave in a fairly consistent way toward similar objects. People do not have to interpret and react to every object in a fresh way. Attitudes economize on energy and thought. For this reason, attitudes are very difficult to change. A person's attitudes settle into a consistent pattern, and to change a single attitude may require major adjustments in other attitudes.

Thus a company would be well advised to fit its product into existing attitudes, rather than to try to change people's attitudes. There are exceptions, of course, where the great cost of trying to change attitudes might pay off.

Honda entered the U.S. motorcycle market facing a major decision. It could either sell its motorcycles to a small number of people already interested in motorcycles or try to increase the number interested in motorcycles. The latter would be more expensive because many people had negative attitudes toward motorcycles. They associated motorcycles with black leather jackets, switchblades, and crime. Honda took the second course and launched a major campaign based on the theme "You meet the nicest people on a Honda." Its campaign worked and many people adopted a new attitude toward motorcycles.

We can now appreciate the many forces acting on consumer behavior. A person's purchase choice is the result of the complex interplay of cultural, social, personal, and psychological factors. Many of these factors cannot be influenced by the marketer. They are useful, however, in identifying the buyers who might have the most interest in the product. Other factors are subject to marketer influence and clue the marketer on how to develop product, price, place, and promotion to attract strong consumer response.

THE BUYING DECISION PROCESS

Marketers have to go beyond the various influences on buyers and develop an understanding of how consumers actually make their buying decisions. Marketers must identify who makes the buying decision, the type of buying decision that is involved, and the steps in the buying process.

Buying Roles   For many products, it is fairly easy to identify the buyer. Men normally choose their tobacco, and women choose their pantyhose. On the other hand, other products involve a *decision-making unit* consisting of more than one person. Consider the selection of a family automobile. The suggestion to buy a new car might come from the oldest child. A friend might advise the family on the kind of car to buy. The husband might choose the make. The wife might have definite desires regarding the car's appearance.

The husband might make the final decision with the wife approving. The wife might end up using the car more than the husband does.

Thus we can distinguish several roles people might play in a buying decision:

- ■ **_Initiator._** The initiator is the person who first suggests the idea of buying the particular product or service.
- ■ **_Influencer._** An influencer is a person whose views or advice carries some weight in making the final decision.
- ■ **_Decider._** The decider is a person who ultimately determines any part of, or the entire, buying decision: whether to buy, what to buy, how to buy, or where to buy.
- ■ **_Buyer._** The buyer is the person who makes the actual purchase.
- ■ **_User._** The user is the person(s) who consumes or uses the product or service.

A company needs to identify these roles because they have implications for designing the product, determining messages, and allocating the promotional budget. If the husband decides on the car make, then the auto company will direct most of the advertising to reach husbands. The auto company might design certain car features to please the wife and place some ads in media reaching wives. Knowing the main participants and the roles they play helps the marketer fine-tune the marketing program.

Types of Buying Behavior

Consumer decision making varies with the type of buying decision. There are great differences between buying a toothpaste, a tennis racket, a personal computer, and a new car. The more complex and expensive decisions are likely to involve more buyer deliberation and more buying participants. Assael distinguished four types of consumer buying behavior based on the degree of buyer involvement in the purchase and the degree of differences among brands.[25] The four types are named in Table 6-3 and described below.

Complex Buying Behavior

Consumers go through complex buying behavior when they are highly involved in a purchase and aware of significant differences existing among brands. Consumers are highly involved in a purchase when it is expensive, bought infrequently, risky, and highly self-expressive. Typically the consumer does not know much about the product category and has much to learn. For example, a person buying a personal computer may not even know what attributes to look for. Many of the product features carry no meaning: "16K memory," "disc storage," "screen resolution," "BASIC language," and so on.

Four Types of Buying Behavior

	High Involvement	Low Involvement
Significant Differences between Brands	Complex buying behavior	Variety-seeking buying behavior
Few Differences between Brands	Dissonance-reducing buying behavior	Habitual buying behavior

SOURCE: Modified from Henry Assael, _Consumer Behavior and Marketing Action_ (Boston: Kent Publishing Co., 1987), p. 87. Copyright © 1987 by Wadsworth, Inc. Printed by permission of Kent Publishing Co., a division of Wadsworth, Inc.

This buyer will pass through a cognitive learning process characterized by first developing beliefs about the product, then attitudes, and then making a thoughtful purchase choice. The marketer of a high-involvement product must understand the information-gathering and evaluation behavior of high-involvement consumers. The marketer needs to develop strategies that assist the buyer in learning about the attributes of the product class, their relative importance, and the high standing of his brand on the more important attributes. The marketer needs to differentiate the features of his brand, use mainly print media and long copy to describe the brand's benefits, and enlist store sales personnel and the buyer's friends to influence the final brand choice.

Dissonance-Reducing Buying Behavior Sometimes the consumer is highly involved in a purchase but sees little difference in the brands. The high involvement is again based on the fact that the purchase is expensive, infrequent, and risky. In this case, the buyer will shop around to learn what is available but will buy fairly quickly because brand differences are not pronounced. The buyer may respond primarily to a good price or the convenience of purchasing at that time or place. An example might be in shopping for carpeting. Carpet buying is a high-involvement decision because it is expensive and relates to self-identification; yet the buyer is likely to consider most carpeting in a given price range to be the same.

After the purchase, the consumer might experience postpurchase dissonance because of noticing certain disquieting features of the carpet or hearing favorable things about other carpets. The consumer starts learning more things and seeks to justify his or her decision to reduce the dissonance. In this example, the consumer first acted, then acquired some new beliefs, and ended up with a set of attitudes. The major role of marketing communications in this case is to supply beliefs and evaluations that help the consumer feel good about his or her choice after the purchase.

Habitual Buying Behavior Many products are bought under conditions of low consumer involvement and the absence of significant brand differences. A good example is the purchase of salt. Consumers have little involvement in this product category. They go to the store and reach for the brand. If they keep reaching for the same brand, say, Morton salt, it is out of habit, not strong brand loyalty. There is good evidence that consumers have low involvement with most low-cost, frequently purchased products.

Consumer behavior in these cases does not pass through the normal belief/attitude/behavior sequence. Consumers do not search extensively for information about the brands, evaluate their characteristics, and make a weighty decision on which one to buy. Instead they are passive recipients of information as they watch television or see print ads. Ad repetition creates *brand familiarity* rather than *brand conviction*. Consumers do not really form an attitude toward a brand but select it simply because it is familiar. After purchase, they may not even evaluate it because they are not involved with the product. So the buying process is: brand beliefs formed by passive learning, followed by purchase behavior, which may or may not be followed by evaluation.

Marketers of low-involvement products with few brand differences find it effective to use price and sales promotions as an incentive to product trial, since buyers are not highly committed to any brand. In advertising a low-involvement product, a number of things should be observed. The ad copy should stress only a few key points. Visual symbols and imagery are important because they can easily be remembered and associated with the brand. The ad campaigns should go for high repetition with short-duration messages.

Television is more effective than print media because it is a low-involvement medium that is suitable for passive learning.[26] The advertising planning should be based on classical conditioning theory where the buyer comes to identify a certain product by a symbol that is repeatedly attached to it.

Marketers can also try to convert the low-involvement product into one of higher involvement. This can be accomplished by linking the product to some involving issue, as when Crest toothpaste is linked to keeping one's teeth healthy. Or the product can be linked to some involving personal situation, for instance, by advertising a coffee brand in the early morning when the consumer is looking for something to shake off sleepiness. Or the consumer can be drawn in by advertising that triggers strong emotions related to personal values or ego defense. Or an important feature might be added to an unimportant product, for instance, fortifying a plain, tasty drink with vitamins. It should be appreciated that these strategies at best raise consumer involvement from a low to a moderate level; in no way do they propel the consumer into complex buying behavior.

Variety-Seeking Buying Behavior Some buying situations are characterized by low consumer involvement but significant brand differences. Here consumers are often observed to do a lot of brand switching. An example occurs in purchasing cookies. The consumer has some beliefs, chooses a brand of cookies without much evaluation, and evaluates it during consumption. But the next time, the consumer may reach for another brand out of boredom or a wish for a different taste. Brand switching occurs for the sake of variety rather than dissatisfaction.

The marketing strategy is different for the market leader and the minor brands in this product category. The market leader will try to encourage habitual buying behavior by dominating the shelf space, avoiding out-of-stock conditions, and sponsoring frequent reminder advertising. Challenger firms, on the other hand, will encourage variety seeking by offering lower prices, deals, coupons, free samples, and advertising that features reasons for trying something new.

Researching the Buying Decision Process Companies need to research the buying decision process involved in their product category. Consumers can be asked when they first became acquainted with the product category, what their brand beliefs are, how involved they are with the product, how they make their brand choices, and how they rate their satisfaction after purchase.

Consumers, of course, will vary in the way they buy a given product. In buying a personal computer, some consumers will spend a great deal of time seeking information and making comparisons; others will go straight to a computer store, look at the brands, point to one, negotiate a price, and sign a contract. Thus consumers can be segmented in terms of *buying styles*—for instance, deliberate buyers versus impulsive buyers—and different marketing strategies can be directed at each segment.

How can marketers learn about the typical stages in the buying process for any given product? They can introspect about their own probable behavior, although this is of limited usefulness (*introspective method*). They can interview a small number of recent purchasers, asking them to recall the events leading to the purchase of the product (*retrospective method*). They can find some consumers who are contemplating buying the product and ask them to think out loud about going through the buying process (*prospective method*). Or they can ask a group of consumers to describe the ideal way to go about buying the product (*prescriptive method*). Each method results in a consumer-generated report of the steps in the buying process.

A report by a consumer who bought a computer is shown in Table 6-4. The buyer is a married male, who first got interested when his neighbor purchased a computer. He then developed a reason to justify purchasing one. A few days later, he saw an ad for an Apple computer. Two weeks later he dropped into a computer store just to browse. He liked the salesman, felt that he could afford a computer, and purchased one. The computer did not satisfy him completely, and an ad for a competitive brand made him feel a little dissonance. He was annoyed a few days later when his salesman did not seem very cooperative in answering some questions. The marketing analyst should collect reports from other consumers and attempt to identify one or more typical buying processes for that product.[27]

Stages in the Buying Decision Process

Based on examining many consumer reports of buying episodes, consumer-behavior researchers have proposed ''stage models'' of the buying process. Stage models are mostly relevant to complex decision making—i.e., buying expensive, high-involvement products. We will use the model shown in Figure 6-4, which shows the consumer as passing through five stages: *problem recognition*, *information search*, *evaluation of alternatives*, *purchase decision*, and *postpurchase behavior*. This model emphasizes that the buying process starts long before the actual purchase and has consequences long after the purchase. It encourages the marketer to focus on the *buying process* rather than on the *purchase decision*.[28]

This model implies that consumers pass through all five stages in buying a product. We saw that this is not the case, especially in low-involvement purchases. Consumers may skip or reverse some of these stages. Thus a woman buying her regular brand of toothpaste would go right from the need for toothpaste to the purchase decision, skipping information search and evaluation. However, we will use the model in Figure 6-4 because it shows the full range of considerations that arise when a consumer faces a highly involving new purchase.

To illustrate this model, we will allude again to Linda Brown and try to understand how she became interested in buying a personal computer and the stages she went through to make her final choice.

TABLE 6-4   Report of a Particular Consumer's Involvement in Buying a Computer

3/17 My neighbor just bought a computer. He says he finds it challenging. It would be nice to have a computer; I could keep my financial records on it.

3/19 Here's an ad for an Apple computer showing several applications that I would find interesting.

4/2 I don't have any plans this evening. I'll go over to Computerland and learn something about these computers.
Here comes a salesman.
He's very helpful. I'm pleased that he is not pressuring me to buy one.
I don't think I can afford a computer.
How much would it cost a month to finance?
I can afford it.
My wife also wants me to buy one. I'm impressed with the Apple. I'll buy it and take it home.

4/5 I didn't realize how much time it takes to master.
I wish the screen had eighty columns instead of forty.

4/6 Here's the new IBM advertised. It looks like it has some neat features.

4/8 My other neighbor wants to buy a computer. I told him the good and bad points about the Apple.

4/11 I phoned the computer salesman for some information about a sticky key. He wasn't helpful. He told me to call the service department.

FIGURE 6-4
Five-Stage Model of the Buying Process

Problem recognition → Information search → Evaluation of alternatives → Purchase decision → Postpurchase behavior

Problem Recognition   The buying process starts with the buyer's recognizing a problem or need. The buyer senses a difference between his or her actual state and a desired state. The need can be triggered by internal or external stimuli. In the former case, one of the person's normal needs—hunger, thirst, sex—rises to a threshold level and becomes a drive. From previous experience, the person has learned how to cope with this drive and is motivated toward a class of objects that he or she knows will satisfy the drive.

Or a need can be aroused by an external stimulus. Linda Brown passes a bakery, and the sight of freshly baked bread stimulates her hunger; she admires a neighbor's new car; or she watches a television commercial for a Jamaican vacation. All of these stimuli can lead her to recognize a problem or need.

The marketer needs to identify the circumstances that trigger the particular need or interest in consumers. The marketer should research consumers to find out *what kinds of felt needs or problems arose*, *what brought them about*, and *how they led to this particular product*.

Linda Brown might answer that her "busy season" at work had tapered off; she felt a need for a new hobby; and she was led to think of computers when a co-worker bought one. By gathering information from a number of consumers, the marketer can identify the more frequent stimuli that give rise to interest in the product category. The marketer can then develop marketing strategies that trigger consumer interest.

Information Search   An aroused consumer may or may not search for more information. If the consumer's drive is strong, and an affordable gratification object is at hand, the consumer is likely to buy the object then. If not, the consumer's need may simply be stored in memory. The consumer may undertake no further search, some further search, or a very active search for information bearing on the need.

If the consumer undertakes some search, we can distinguish between two levels. The milder search state is called *heightened attention*. Here Linda Brown simply becomes more receptive to information about computers. She pays attention to computer ads, computers purchased by friends, and conversation about computers.

Or Linda may go into *active information search* where she looks for reading material, phones friends, and engages in other search activities to learn about computers. How much search she undertakes depends on the strength of her drive, the amount of information she initially has, the ease of obtaining additional information, the value she places on additional information, and the satisfaction she gets from search. Normally the amount of consumer search activity increases as the consumer moves from decision situations of *limited problem solving* to *extensive problem solving*.

Of key interest to the marketer are the major information sources that the consumer will turn to and the relative influence each will have on the subsequent purchase decision. *Consumer information sources fall into four groups:*

- **Personal sources.** (Family, friends, neighbors, acquaintances)
- **Commercial sources.** (Advertising, salespersons, dealers, packaging, displays)
- **Public sources.** (Mass media, consumer-rating organizations)
- **Experiential sources.** (Handling, examining, using the product)

The relative amount and influence of these information sources varies with the product category and the buyer's characteristics. Generally speaking, the consumer receives the most information exposure about a product from commercial sources, that is, marketer-dominated sources. On the other hand, the most effective exposures come from personal sources. Each type of source may perform a somewhat different function in influencing the buying decision. Commercial information normally performs an informing function, and personal sources perform a legitimizing and/or evaluation function. For example, physicians often learn of new drugs from commercial sources but turn to other doctors for evaluation information.

Through gathering information, the consumer learns about the brands in the market and their features. The box at the far left of Figure 6-5 shows the *total set* of brands available to the consumer. Linda Brown will become acquainted with only a subset of these brands, which we will call the *awareness set*. Only some of these brands will meet Linda's initial buying criteria and make up the *consideration set*. As Linda gathers more information about these brands, only a few will remain as strong choices and make up the *choice set*. She makes her final decision from the choice set, based on the decision evaluation process she uses.[29]

The practical implication is that a company must "strategize" to get its brand into the prospect's awareness set, consideration set, and choice set. Otherwise the company has lost its opportunity to sell to the customer. The company must go further and learn which other brands remain in the consumer's choice set so that it knows its competition and can plan its appeals.

As for the consumer's information sources, the marketer should identify them carefully and evaluate their relative importance. Consumers should be asked how they first heard about the brand, what information came in later, and the relative importance of the different information sources. This information is critical for preparing effective communication for the target market.

FIGURE 6-5
Successive Sets Involved in Consumer Decision Making

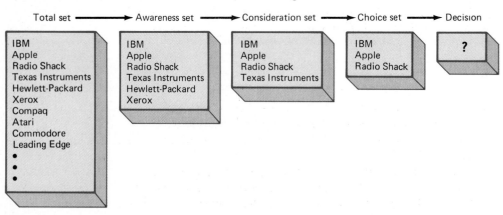

Evaluation of Alternatives We have seen how the consumer uses information to arrive at a brand choice set. The question is, How does the consumer process the information about the brand choices to make the final choice? Unfortunately, there is no simple and single evaluation process used by all consumers or even by one consumer in all buying situations. There are several decision evaluation processes. Most current models of the consumer evaluation process are cognitively oriented—that is, they see the consumer as forming product judgments largely on a conscious and rational basis.

Certain basic concepts will help us understand consumer evaluation processes. First, the consumer considers various *product attributes*. Each consumer sees a given product as a bundle of attributes. The attributes of interest to buyers in some familiar product classes are

- *Cheese.* Type, shape, consistency, appearance, texture, aging
- *Computers.* Memory capacity, graphics capability, software availability
- *Cameras.* Picture sharpness, camera speeds, camera size, price
- *Hotels.* Location, cleanliness, atmosphere, cost
- *Mouthwash.* Color, effectiveness, germ-killing capacity, price, taste/flavor
- *Brassieres.* Comfort, fit, life, price, style
- *Lipstick.* Color, container, creaminess, prestige factor, taste/flavor
- *Tires.* Safety, tread life, ride quality, price

Consumers will vary in which attributes of a product they deem relevant or salient. Consumers will pay the most attention to those attributes that are connected with their needs. The market for a product can often be segmented according to the attributes that are salient to different consumer groups.

Second, the marketer must not conclude that the salient attributes are the most important ones. Some of them may be salient because the consumer has just been exposed to a commercial message mentioning them or has had a problem involving them, hence making these attributes "top-of-the-mind." Furthermore, nonsalient attributes might include some that the consumer forgot but whose importance would be recognized when mentioned. Marketers should be more concerned with attribute importance than attribute salience. They should try to find the *importance weights* that consumers attach to the salient attributes.[30]

Third, the consumer is likely to develop a set of *brand beliefs* about where each brand stands on each attribute. The set of beliefs held about a particular brand is known as the *brand image*. The consumer's beliefs may be at variance with the true attributes owing to his or her particular experience and the effect of selective perception, selective distortion, and selective retention.

Fourth, the consumer is assumed to have a *utility function* for each attribute.[31] The utility function describes how the consumer expects product satisfaction to vary with different levels of each attribute. For example, Linda Brown may expect her satisfaction from a computer to increase with its memory capacity, graphics capability, and software availability; and to decrease with its price. If we combine the attribute levels where the utilities are highest, they make up Linda's ideal computer. The expected utility from actual computers in the marketplace will vary below the maximum utility that would be derived from an ideal computer.

Fifth, the consumer arrives at attitudes (judgments, preferences) toward the brand alternatives through some *evaluation procedure*. Consumers have been found to apply different evaluation procedures to make a choice among multiattribute objects.[32]

We will illustrate these concepts in connection with Linda Brown's buying a computer. Suppose Linda Brown has narrowed her choice set to four computers (A, B, C, D). Assume that she is primarily interested in four attributes: memory capacity, graphics capability, software availability, and price. Table 6-5 shows her beliefs about how each brand rates on the four attributes. Linda rates brand A as follows: memory capacity, 10 on a 10-point scale; graphics capability, 8; software availability, 6; and price, 4 (somewhat expensive). Similarly, she has beliefs about how the other three computers rate on these attributes. The marketer would like to be able to predict which computer Linda will buy.

Clearly, if one computer dominated the others on all the criteria, we could predict that Linda would choose it. But her choice set consists of brands that vary in their appeal. If Linda wants memory capacity above everything, she should buy A; if she wants the best graphics capability, she should buy B; if she wants the best software availability, she should buy C; if she wants the lowest-price computer, she should buy D. Some buyers will buy on only one attribute, and we can easily predict their choice.

Most buyers will consider several attributes but place different weights on them. If we knew the importance weights that Linda Brown assigned to the four attributes, we could more reliably predict her computer choice.

Suppose Linda assigned 40 percent of the importance to the computer's memory capacity, 30 percent to its graphics capability, 20 percent to its software availability, and 10 percent to its price. To find Linda's perceived value for each computer, her weights are multiplied by her beliefs about each computer. This leads to the following perceived values:

$$\text{Computer A} = 0.4(10) + 0.3(8) + 0.2(6) + 0.1(4) = 8.0$$
$$\text{Computer B} = 0.4(8) + 0.3(9) + 0.2(8) + 0.1(3) = 7.8$$
$$\text{Computer C} = 0.4(6) + 0.3(8) + 0.2(10) + 0.1(5) = 7.3$$
$$\text{Computer D} = 0.4(4) + 0.3(3) + 0.2(7) + 0.1(8) = 4.7$$

We would predict that Linda, given her weights, will favor computer A.

This model is called the *expectancy value model* of consumer choice.[33] It is one of several possible models describing how consumers go about evaluating alternatives. (See Exhibit 6-3.) As noted earlier, marketers should interview computer buyers to find out how they actually evaluate brand alternatives.

Suppose most computer buyers say they form their preferences using the expectancy-value process described above. Knowing this, a computer manufacturer can do a number

TABLE 6-5   A Consumer's Brand Beliefs about Computers

Computer	Attribute			
	Memory Capacity	**Graphics Capability**	**Software Availability**	**Price**
A	10	8	6	4
B	8	9	8	3
C	6	8	10	5
D	4	3	7	8

Note: Each attribute is rated from 0 to 10, where 10 represents the highest level on that attribute. Thus computer A has the highest memory capacity. The consumer is assumed to normally want more of each attribute. Price is indexed, however, in a reverse manner, with a 10 representing the lowest price, since a consumer prefers a low price to a high price.

EXHIBIT 6-3

The text described the *expectancy-value model* of how consumers might evaluate alternatives. It can be stated more formally as follows:

$$A_{jk} = \sum_{i=1}^{n} W_{ik}B_{ijk} \qquad (6\text{–}1)$$

where:
A_{jk} = consumer k's attitude score for brand j
W_{ik} = the importance weight assigned by consumer k to attribute i
B_{ijk} = consumer k's belief as to the amount of attribute i offered by brand j
n = the number of important attributes in the selection of a given brand

Essentially, a consumer's beliefs about a brand's attributes are multiplied by the respective importance weights and summed to derive an attitude score. Here are some other models.

Ideal-brand Model   This model says that the consumer holds an image of the ideal brand and compares actual brands with this ideal. The closer an actual brand comes to this ideal, the more it will be preferred.

Suppose Linda Brown does not value memory capacity beyond a certain point because she has no use for it, and it adds to cost. And suppose she has a certain price in mind as ideal. Suppose her ideal levels of the four attributes are not (10, 10, 10, 10) as in the expectancy value model but (6, 10, 10, 5). We would calculate how dissatisfied she would be with each brand according to the formula

$$D_{jk} = \sum_{i=1}^{n} W_{ik}|B_{ijk} - I_{ik}| \qquad (6\text{–}2)$$

where D_{jk} is consumer k's *dissatisfaction* with brand j, and I_{ik} is consumer k's *ideal level* of attribute i. Other terms remain the same. The lower the D, the more favorable consumer k's attitude toward brand j. For example, if there were a brand whose attributes were all at the ideal levels, the term $|B_{ijk} - I_{jk}|$ would disappear, and the dissatisfaction would be zero. Here is Linda Brown's dissatisfaction score with each brand:

$$\text{Computer A} = 0.4\,|\,10-6\,| + 0.3\,|\,8-10\,| + 0.2\,|\,6-10\,| + 0.1\,|\,4-5\,| = 3.1$$
$$\text{Computer B} = 0.4\,|\,8-6\,| + 0.3\,|\,9-10\,| + 0.2\,|\,8-10\,| + 0.1\,|\,3-5\,| = 1.7$$
$$\text{Computer C} = 0.4\,|\,6-6\,| + 0.3\,|\,8-10\,| + 0.2\,|\,10-10\,| + 0.1\,|\,5-5\,| = 0.6$$
$$\text{Computer D} = 0.4\,|\,4-6\,| + 0.3\,|\,3-10\,| + 0.2\,|\,7-10\,| + 0.1\,|\,8-5\,| = 3.8$$

In this case, Linda Brown would have the strongest preference (i.e., least dissatisfaction) with computer C.

To use the ideal-brand model, the marketer would interview a sample of buyers and ask them to describe their ideal brands. The marketer will obtain three classes of response. Some consumers will have clear pictures of their ideal brand. Other consumers will mention two or more ideals that would satisfy them. The remaining consumers will have trouble defining an ideal brand and would find a wide range of brands equally acceptable.

Conjunctive Model   Some consumers will evaluate alternatives by establishing minimum attribute levels that acceptable brands must possess. They will only consider the brands that exhibit a *conjunction* of all the minimum requirements. Thus Linda Brown might consider only computers that score better than (7, 6, 7, 2) on memory, graphics, software, and price, respectively. These cutoffs eliminate brands A, C, D from further consideration. Conjunctive evaluation in the extreme could eliminate all brands. A consumer might not purchase any computer because no brand meets his or her minimal requirements. Note that conjunctive evaluation does not pay attention to how high an attribute level is as long as it exceeds the minimum. A high level of one attribute does not compensate for a below-minimum level of another attribute.

Disjunctive Model Linda Brown might want to consider only computers that exceed specified levels on one or a few attributes, regardless of their standing on the other attributes. She might decide that she will consider only computers that have strong memory (> 9) *or* graphics (> 9). According to Table 6-5, Linda is left with computers A and B as choices. The model is noncompensatory in that high scores on the other variables have no bearing on keeping them in the choice set.

Lexicographic model Another noncompensatory process occurs if Linda Brown arranges the attributes in order of importance and compares the brands on the first important attribute. If one brand is superior on the most important attribute, it becomes her choice. If two or more brands are tied on this attribute, Linda considers the second most important attribute; she continues this process until one brand remains. Suppose Linda "prioritizes" the attributes in the following order: price, software, memory, graphics. She looks at price and finds brand D dominates. At this point she has determined that brand D is her preferred computer.

Determinance Model This model says that an attribute might be important to the customer, but not influence his or her choice if all the products possessed the same amount of that attribute. Thus Linda Brown might highly value computer speed, but if all four computers were equally fast, it would not help decide among them. Ironically, many products are at parity on the important attributes, and it is the less important attributes that often determine product choice. The marketing researcher must identify the determinant attributes, not simply the important ones.

Marketing Implications The preceding models indicate that buyers can form their product preferences in several ways. A particular buyer, on a particular buying occasion, facing a particular product class, might be a conjunctive buyer, disjunctive buyer, or some other type. The same buyer might be a conjunctive buyer for large-ticket purchases and a disjunctive buyer for small-ticket items. Or the same buyer, in buying a large-ticket item, might behave first like a conjunctive buyer to eliminate many alternatives and then make a final choice as an ideal brand buyer. When we realize that a market is made up of many buyers, we need to identify the major buying styles.

The marketer might find that the majority of consumers in that market use one particular evaluation procedure. The marketer can then try to make his brand salient to consumers who are using that evaluation procedure.

SOURCE: For additional discussion of these models, see Paul E. Green and Yoram Wind, *Multiattribute Decisions in Marketing: A Measurement Approach* (Hinsdale, Ill.: Dryden Press, 1972), Chap. 2. Also see James H. Myers and Mark I. Alpert, "Determinant Buying Attitudes: Meaning and Measurement," *Journal of Marketing*, October 1968, pp. 13–20.

of things to influence buyer decisions. The marketer of computer C, for example, could apply the following strategies to influence people like Linda Brown to show a greater interest in the marketer's brand:[34]

- **Modifying the computer.** The marketer could redesign his brand so that it offers more memory or other characteristics that this type of buyer desires. This is called *real repositioning*.
- **Altering beliefs about the brand.** The marketer could try to alter buyers' beliefs of where his brand stands on key attributes. This is especially recommended if buyers underestimate brand C's qualities. It is not recommended if buyers are accurately evaluating brand C; exaggerated claims would lead to buyer dissatisfaction and bad word of mouth. Attempting to alter beliefs about the brand is called *psychological repositioning*.
- **Altering beliefs about the competitors' brands.** The marketer could try to change buyers' beliefs about where competitive brands stand on different attributes. This may make sense where buyers mistakenly believe a competitor's brand has more quality than it actually has. This is called *competitive depositioning* and is often carried out through running a comparison ad.
- **Altering the importance weights.** The marketer could try to persuade buyers to attach more importance to the attributes in which the brand excels. The marketer of brand C can tout the benefits of choosing a computer with great software availability, since C is superior in this attribute.

■ *Calling attention to neglected attributes*. The marketer could try to draw the buyer's attention to neglected attributes. If brand C is a highly portable computer, the marketer might tout the benefit of portability.

■ *Shifting the buyer's ideals*. The marketer could try to persuade buyers to change their ideal levels for one or more attributes. The marketer of brand C might try to convince buyers that computers with a large memory are more likely to jam and that a moderate-size memory is more desirable.

Purchase Decision   In the decision evaluation stage, the consumer forms preferences among the brands in the choice set. The consumer may also form a purchase intention and lean toward buying the most preferred brand. However, two factors can intervene between the purchase intention and the purchase decision. These factors are shown in Figure 6-6.[35]

The first factor is the *attitudes of others*. Suppose Linda Brown's husband feels strongly that Linda should buy the lowest-priced computer (D) to keep down expenses. As a result, Linda's "purchase probability" for computer A will be somewhat reduced. The extent to which another person's attitude will reduce one's preferred alternative depends on two things: (1) the intensity of the other person's negative attitude toward the consumer's preferred alternative and (2) the consumer's motivation to comply with the other person's wishes.[36] The more intense the other person's negativism, and the closer the other person is to the consumer, the more the consumer will revise downward his or her purchase intention. The converse is also true: A buyer's preference for a brand will increase if someone he or she likes favors the same brand. The influence of others becomes complex when several people close to the buyer hold contradictory opinions and the buyer would like to please them all.

Purchase intention is also influenced by *unanticipated situational factors*. The consumer forms a purchase intention on the basis of such factors as expected family income, expected price, and expected benefits from the product. When the consumer is about to act, *unanticipated situational factors* may erupt to change the purchase intention. Linda Brown might lose her job, some other purchase might become more urgent, or a friend might report disappointment in that computer brand. Thus preferences and even purchase intentions are not completely reliable predictors of purchase behavior.

A consumer's decision to modify, postpone, or avoid a purchase decision is heavily influenced by *perceived risk*. Many purchases involve some *risk taking*.[37] Consumers cannot be certain about the purchase outcome. This produces anxiety. The amount of perceived risk varies with the amount of money at stake, the amount of attribute uncertainty, and the amount of consumer self-confidence. A consumer develops certain routines for reducing risk, such as decision avoidance, information gathering from friends, and preference for national brand names and warranties. The marketer must understand the factors that provoke

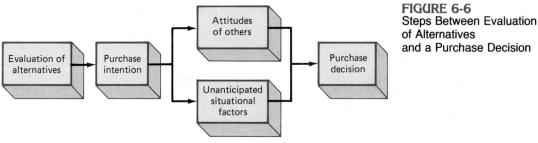

FIGURE 6-6
Steps Between Evaluation
of Alternatives
and a Purchase Decision

a feeling of risk in consumers and provide information and support that will reduce the perceived risk.

A consumer who decides to execute a purchase intention will be making up to five *purchase subdecisions*. Thus Linda Brown will make a *brand decision* (brand A), *vendor decision* (dealer 2), *quantity decision* (one computer), *timing decision* (weekend), and *payment-method decision* (credit card). The decisions are not necessarily made in this order. Furthermore, purchases of everyday products, in contrast, involve fewer of these decisions and much less buyer deliberation. Thus in buying cigarettes, Linda gives little thought to the vendor or payment method. We deliberately chose a product that involves extensive problem solving—here personal computers—to illustrate the full range of behavior that might arise in buying something.

Postpurchase Behavior After purchasing the product, the consumer will experience some level of satisfaction or dissatisfaction. The consumer will also engage in postpurchase actions and product uses of interest to the marketer. The marketer's job does not end when the product is bought but continues into the postpurchase period.

Postpurchase satisfaction After purchasing a product, a consumer may detect a flaw. Some buyers will not want the flawed product, others will be indifferent to the flaw, and some may even see the flaw as enhancing the value of the product. Flaws can sometimes be dangerous to consumers. For example, in the case of the Ford Pinto, Ford persisted in marketing this flawed product for several years and finally had to recall it in response to public pressure.[38]

What, in general, determines whether the buyer is highly satisfied, somewhat satisfied, somewhat dissatisfied, or highly dissatisfied with a purchase? The buyer's satisfaction is a function of the closeness between the buyer's product *expectations* (E) and the product's *perceived performance* (P), that is, $S = f(E,P)$.[39] If the product matches expectations, the consumer is satisfied; if it exceeds them, the consumer is highly satisfied; if it falls short, the consumer is dissatisfied.

Consumers form their expectations on the basis of messages they receive from sellers, friends, and other information sources. If the seller exaggerates the benefits, consumers will experience *disconfirmed expectations*, which lead to dissatisfaction. The larger the gap between expectations and performance, the greater the consumer's dissatisfaction. Here the consumer's coping style comes into play. Some consumers magnify the gap when the product is not perfect, and they are highly dissatisfied. Other consumers minimize the gap and are less dissatisfied.[40]

This theory suggests that the seller should make product claims that faithfully represent the product's likely performance so that buyers experience satisfaction. Some sellers might even understate performance levels so that consumers experience higher-than-expected satisfaction with the product.

Festinger and Bramel believe that the most nonroutine purchase will unavoidably involve some postpurchase dissonance:

> When a person chooses between two or more alternatives, discomfort or dissonance will almost inevitably arise because of the person's knowledge that while the decision he has made has certain advantages, it also has some disadvantages. That dissonance arises after almost every decision, and further, that the individual will invariably take steps to reduce this dissonance.[41]

Postpurchase actions The consumer's satisfaction or dissatisfaction with the product will influence subsequent behavior. If the consumer is satisfied, then he or she will exhibit a higher probability of purchasing the product on the next occasion. The satisfied consumer will also tend to say good things about the product and the company to others. According to marketers: "Our best advertisement is a satisfied customer."[42]

A dissatisfied consumer responds differently. The dissatisfied consumer will try to reduce the dissonance because a human being strives "to establish internal harmony, consistency, or congruity among his opinions, knowledge, and values."[43] Dissonant consumers will resort to one or two courses of action. They may try to reduce the dissonance by *abandoning* or *returning* the product, or they may try to reduce the dissonance by seeking information that might *confirm* its high value (or avoiding information that might confirm its low value). In the case of Linda Brown, she might return the computer, or she might seek information that would make her feel better about the computer.

Marketers should be aware of the full range of ways in which consumers handle dissatisfaction (see Figure 6-7). Consumers have a choice between taking and not taking any action. If the former, they can take public action or private action. Public actions include complaining to the company, going to a lawyer, or complaining to other groups that might help the buyer get satisfaction, such as business, private, or government agencies. Or the buyer might simply stop buying the product, utilizing the *exit option*. Alternatively, the consumer may choose to use the *voice option*.[44] In all these cases, the seller loses something in having done a poor job of satisfying the customer.[45]

Marketers can take steps to minimize the amount of consumer postpurchase dissatisfaction. Computer companies can send a letter to new computer owners congratulating them

FIGURE 6-7
How Customers Handle Dissatisfaction
SOURCE: Ralph L. Day and E. Laird Landon, Jr., "Toward a Theory of Consumer Complaining Behavior," in *Consumer and Industrial Buying Behavior*, ed. Arch G. Woodside, Jagdish N. Sheth, and Peter D. Bennett (New York: Elsevier North-Holland, 1977), p. 432.

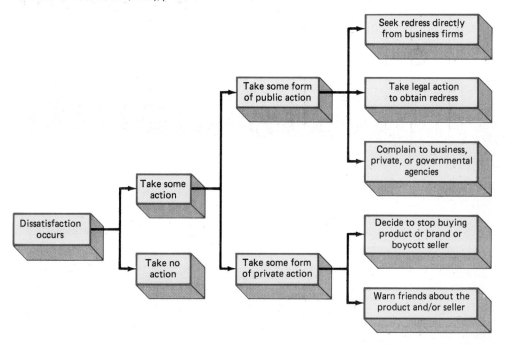

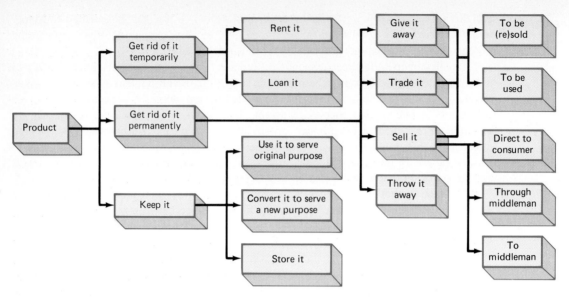

FIGURE 6-8
How Customers Use or Dispose of Products
SOURCE: Jacob Jacoby, Carol K. Berning and Thomas F. Dietvorst, "What about Disposition?" *Journal of Marketing*, July 1977, p. 23.

on having selected a fine computer. They can place ads showing satisfied brand owners. They can solicit customer suggestions for improvements and list the location of available services. They can write instruction booklets that are dissonance reducing. They can send owners a magazine containing articles describing new computer applications. Postpurchase communications to buyers have been shown to result in fewer product returns and order cancellations.[46] In addition, they can provide good channels for customer complaining and arrange for speedy redress of customer grievances.

Postpurchase use and disposal   There is one more step in the postpurchase behavior of buyers that marketers should watch, namely, how the buyers use and dispose of the product (see Figure 6-8). If consumers find a new use for the product, that should interest the marketer because this use can be advertised. If consumers put the product away in their closet or throw it out, this indicates that the product is not very satisfying, and word of mouth would not be strong. If they sell or trade the product, this will depress new-product sales. All said, the marketer needs to study product use and disposal for clues to possible problems and opportunities.[47]

Understanding consumer needs and buying processes is essential to building effective marketing strategies. By understanding how buyers go through problem recognition, information search, evaluation of alternatives, the purchase decision, and postpurchase behavior, marketers can pick up many clues as to how to meet buyer needs. By understanding the various participants in the buying process and the major influences on their buying behavior, marketers can design effective marketing programs for their target markets.

SUMMARY

Consumer markets and consumer buying behavior have to be understood before sound marketing plans can be developed.

The consumer market buys goods and services for personal consumption. It is the ultimate market for which economic activities are organized. The market consists of many submarkets, such as black consumers, young adult consumers, and elderly consumers. In analyzing a consumer market, one needs to know the occupants, the objects, and the buyers' objectives, organization, operations, occasions, and outlets.

The buyer's behavior is influenced by four major factors: cultural (culture, subculture, and social class); social (reference groups, family, and roles and statuses); personal (age and life-cycle stage, occupation, economic circumstances, lifestyle, and personality and self-concept); and psychological (motivation, perception, learning, and beliefs and attitudes). All of these provide clues as to how to reach and serve the buyer more effectively.

Before planning its marketing, a company needs to identify its target consumers and the type of decision process they go through. While many buying decisions involve only one decision maker, other decisions may involve several participants, who play such roles as initiator, influencer, decider, buyer, and user. The marketer's job is to identify the other buying participants, their buying criteria, and the amount of influence they have on the buyer. The marketing program should be designed to appeal to and reach the other key participants as well as the buyer.

The amount of buying deliberateness and the number of buying participants increase with the complexity of the buying situation. Marketers must plan differently for four types of consumer buying behavior: complex buying behavior, dissonance-reducing buying behavior, habitual buying behavior, and variety-seeking buying behavior. These four types are based on whether the consumer has high or low involvement in the purchase and whether there are many or few significant differences among the brands.

In complex buying behavior, the buyer goes through a decision process consisting of problem recognition, information search, evaluation of alternatives, purchase decision, and postpurchase behavior. The marketer's job is to understand the buyer's behavior at each stage and what influences are operating. This understanding allows the marketer to develop a significant and effective marketing program for the target market.

■ QUESTIONS

1. Some U.S., Japanese, and European car companies are trying to design ''chameleon cars,'' or cars that will change ''personality'' to fit the personality of the consumer who is using the car. In what ways can a car adapt to its driver, and will consumers desire such a feature?

2. Although technological advances have resulted in ''better sound for less money'' for home audio equipment, the fastest-growing segment of the market is the ''high-end''—the most-expensive equipment. What explains this phenomenon?

3. Some marketers are studying consumer behavior by using a form of ethnographic research—observing the behavior of consumers in their own homes. How might such an approach provide more valuable insights to consumer behavior than survey methods? Give three examples of products that might benefit from such research, citing specific observational techniques to be used.

4. Many marketers use taste tests to help predict the behavior of consumers regarding a new food product. What are some of the dangers of using taste-test information as a predictor of consumer behavior?

5. Jovan has introduced Andron, a cologne containing pheromones—a chemical believed to evoke an aphrodisiac response in members of the opposite sex who

are near the wearer of the cologne. What factors are operating to influence a potential purchaser of this product?

6. "A person will tend to buy the brand in the product class whose image is most congruent with his or her self-image." Is a person's self-image a highly reliable predictor of his or her brand choice?

7. Apply the five different roles in the decision process to your decision regarding a college.

8. A friend of yours plans to buy a new car. He prefers foreign makes and his choice has narrowed down to Volkswagen, Toyota, and Volvo. He looks for three things in a car: economy, quality, and roominess, and he values them at 5, 3, and 2, respectively. He rates Volkswagen at 8, 8, and 2 on the three attributes;

Toyota, 3, 5, and 9; and Volvo, 5, 8, and 7. Predict the car he is most likely to buy and least likely to buy if he evaluates cars according to the expectancy-value model.

9. Suppose Linda Brown, the consumer discussed in this chapter, purchased a personal computer. Discuss the information-search stage of the buying decision process for her subsequent purchase of computer software.

10. Develop a map showing the structure of purchase decisions made by potential buyers of paint. Indicate how a paint company such as Du Pont can determine points at which advertising might favorably affect Du Pont's share of the market.

11. Describe the consumer market for briefcases, using the "Seven Os" framework described in this chapter.

■ FOOTNOTES

1 *Statistical Abstract of the United States*, 1986.

2 See "Special Report: Marketing to Hispanics," *Advertising Age*, February 27, 1986, pp. 11–51.

3 See Hank Gilman, "Marketers Count Older Consumers as Balance of Buying Power Shifts," *Wall Street Journal*, April 23, 1986, p. 37; Ken Dychtwald, "The Senior Boom," *Hospital Forum*, May/June, 1985, pp. 63–66; and Peter Petre, "Marketers Mine for Gold in the Old," *Fortune*, March 31, 1986, pp. 70–78.

4 See Ronald Alsop, "Firms Still Struggle to Devise Best Approach to Black Buyers," *Wall Street Journal*, October 25, 1984, pp. 35; "Black Broadcast: The Market," *Television/Radio Age*, February 1986, pp. A3–A18; and Ken Snickle, "The Image Makers," *Black Enterprise*, December 1985, pp. 44–52.

5 See Stephen Kindel, "The Last Yuppie Story You Will Ever Have to Read," *Forbes*, February 25, 1985, pp. 134–36; and Stewart Alter, "Yuppie Pursuit: It's Too Trivial for Marketers," *Advertising Age*, July 18, 1985, p. 3.

6 See "Special Report: Marketing to Women," *Advertising Age*, April 2, 1984, pp. 9–36; and Alladi Venkatesh, "Changing Roles of Women—A Life-Style Analysis," *Journal of Consumer Behavior*, September 1980, pp. 189–97.

7 See Leon G. Schiffman and Leslie Lazar Kanuk, *Consumer Behavior*, 2nd ed. (Englewood Cliffs, N.J.: Prentice-Hall, 1983), pp. 404–20.

8 See Donald W. Hendon, "A New Empirical Look at the Influence of Reference Groups on Generic Product Category and Brand Choice: Evidence from Two Nations," in *Proceedings of the Academy of International Business: Asia-Pacific Dimension of International Business* (Honolulu, College of Business Administration, University of Hawaii, December 18–20, 1979), pp. 752–61.

9 See Linda L. Price and Lawrence F. Feick, "The Role of Interpersonal Sources in External Search: An Informational Perspective," in *Advances in Consumer Research*, ed. Thomas C. Kinnear, XI (1984), 250; and David Brinberg and Linda Plimpton, "Self-Monitoring and Product Conspicuousness on Reference Group Influence," in *Advances in Consumer Research*, ed. Richard Lutz, XIII (1986), 297–300.

10 See George Moschis, "The Role of Family Communication in Consumer Socialization of Children and Adolescents," *Journal of Consumer Research*, March 1985, pp. 898–913.

11 See Rosann L. Spiro, "Persuasion in Family Decision Making," *Journal of Consumer Research*, March 1983, pp. 393–402; Lawrence H. Wortzel, "Marital Roles and Typologies as Predictors of Purchase Decision Making for Everyday Household Products: Suggestions for Research," in *Advances in Consumer Research*, ed. Jerry C. Olson, VII (1980), 212–15.

12 See Harry L. Davis, "Dimensions of Marital Roles in Consumer Decision-Making," *Journal of Marketing Research*, May 1970, pp. 168–77.

13 See "Flaunting Wealth: It's Back in Style," *U.S. News & World Report*, September 21, 1981, pp. 61–64; and John Brooks, *Showing Off in America: From Conspicuous Consumption to Parody Display* (Boston: Little, Brown, 1978).

14 See Lawrence Lepisto, "A Life Span Perspective of Consumer Behavior," in *Advances in Consumer Research*, ed. Elizabeth Hirshman and Morris Holbrook, XII (1985), 47.

15 Sidney J. Levy, "Symbolism and Life Style," in *Toward Scientific Marketing*, ed. Stephen A. Greyser (Chicago: American Marketing Association, 1964), pp. 140–50.

16 Harper W. Boyd, Jr., and Sidney J. Levy, *Promotion: A Behavioral View* (Englewood Cliffs, N.J.: Prentice-Hall, 1967), p. 38.

17 See Harold H. Kassarjian and Mary Jane Sheffet, "Personality and Consumer Behavior: An Update," in *Perspectives in Consumer Behavior*, ed. Harold H. Kassarjian and Thomas S. Robertson (Glenview, Ill.: Scott, Foresman, 1981), pp. 160–80.

18 See M. Joseph Sirgy, "Self-Concept in Consumer Behavior: A Critical Review, *Journal of Consumer Research*, December 1982, pp. 287–300.

19 See Ernest Dichter, *Handbook of Consumer Motivations* (New York: McGraw-Hill, 1964).

20 Abraham H. Maslow, *Motivation and Personality* (New York: Harper & Row, 1954), pp. 80–106.

21 See Frederick Herzberg, *Work and the Nature of Man* (Cleveland: William Collins Publishers, 1966); Henk Thierry and

Agnes M. Koopman-Iwerna, "Motivation and Satisfaction," in *Handbook of Work and Organizational Psychology*," ed. P. J. Drenth (New York: John Wiley, 1984), pp. 141–42.

22 Bernard Berelson and Gary A. Steiner, *Human Behavior: An Inventory of Scientific Findings* (New York: Harcourt Brace Jovanovich, 1964), p. 88.

23 See Alice M. Tybout, Bobby J. Calder, and Brian Sternthal, "Using Information Processing Theory to Design Marketing Strategies," *Journal of Marketing Research*, February 1981, pp. 73–79.

24 See David Krech, Richard S. Crutchfield, and Egerton L. Ballachey, *Individual in Society* (New York: McGraw-Hill, 1962), Chap. 2.

25 See Henry Assael, *Consumer Behavior and Marketing Action* (Boston: Kent Publishing, 1987), Chap. 4, for a full discussion of these four types of consumer buying behavior. An earlier classification of three types of consumer buying behavior—extensive problem solving, limited problem solving, and routinized response behavior—is found in John A. Howard and Jagdish N. Sheth, *The Theory of Buyer Behavior* (New York: John Wiley, 1969), pp. 27–28.

26 Herbert E. Krugman, "The Impact of Television Advertising: Learning without Involvement," *Public Opinion Quarterly*, Fall 1965, pp. 349–56.

27 See James R. Bettman, *Information Processing Theory of Consumer Behavior* (Reading, Mass.: Addison-Wesley, 1979).

28 Marketing scholars have developed several models of the consumer buying process. The most prominent models are those of Howard and Sheth, *Theory of Buyer Behavior*; Francesco M. Nicosia, *Consumer Decision Processes* (Englewood Cliffs, N.J.: Prentice-Hall, 1966); and James F. Engel, Roger D. Blackwell, and Paul W. Miniard, *Consumer Behavior*, 5th ed. (New York: Holt, Rinehart & Winston, 1986).

29 Originally, Howard and Sheth suggested the term *evoked set* to describe the set of alternatives that the buyer considers. (See Howard and Sheth, *Theory of Buyer Behavior*, p. 26.) We believe that the set of brands of interest to the consumer keeps changing as information comes in, and it is more useful to distinguish different sets as he or she goes through the buying decision process. See Chem L. Narayana and Rom J. Markin, "Consumer Behavior and Product Performance: An Alternative Conceptualization," *Journal of Marketing*, October 1975, pp. 1–6.

30 James H. Myers and Mark L. Alpert, "Semantic Confusion in Attitude Research: Salience vs. Importance vs. Determinance," in *Advances in Consumer Research* (Proceedings of the Seventh Annual Conference of the Association of Consumer Research, October 1976), IV, pp. 106–10.

31 Some progress has been made in attempting to measure individual and market utility functions. See Exhibit 14-3, pp. 422–24.

32 See Paul E. Green and Yoram Wind, *Multiattribute Decisions in Marketing: A Measurement Approach* (Hinsdale, Ill.: Dryden Press, 1973), Chap. 2; and Leigh McAlister, "Choosing Multiple Items from a Product Class," *Journal of Consumer Research*, December 1979, pp. 213–24.

33 This model was developed by Martin Fishbein in "Attitudes and Prediction of Behavior," in *Readings in Attitude Theory and Measurement*, ed. Martin Fishbein (New York: John Wiley, 1967), pp. 477–92. For a critical review of this model, see Paul W. Miniard and Joel B. Cohen, "An Examination of the Fishbein-Ajzen Behavioral-Intentions Model's Concepts and Measures," *Journal of Experimental Social Psychology*, May 1981, pp. 309–39.

34 See Harper W. Boyd, Jr., Michael L. Ray, and Edward C. Strong, "An Attitudinal Framework for Advertising Strategy," *Journal of Marketing*, April 1972, pp. 27–33; Richard E. Petty and John T. Cacioppo, *Attitudes and Persuasion: Classic and Contemporary Approaches* (Dubuque, Iowa: W. C. Brown Company, 1981), pp. 60–86.

35 See Jagdish N. Sheth, "An Investigation of Relationships among Evaluative Beliefs, Affect, Behavioral Intention, and Behavior," in *Consumer Behavior: Theory and Application*, ed. John U. Farley, John A. Howard, and L. Winston Ring (Boston: Allyn & Bacon, 1974), pp. 89–114.

36 See Fishbein, "Attitudes and Prediction."

37 See Raymond A. Bauer, "Consumer Behavior as Risk Taking," in *Risk Taking and Information Handling in Consumer Behavior*, ed. Donald F. Cox (Boston: Division of Research, Harvard Business School, 1967); James W. Taylor, "The Role of Risk in Consumer Behavior," *Journal of Marketing*, April 1974, pp. 54–60; and Arniram Gafin and George W. Torrance, "Risk Attitude and Time Preference in Health," *Management Science*, April 1981, pp. 440–51.

38 See Philip Kotler and Murali K. Mantrala, "Flawed Products: Consumer Responses and Marketer Strategies," *Journal of Consumer Marketing*, Summer 1985, pp. 27–36.

39 See Priscilla A. La Barbera and David Mazursky, "A Longitudinal Assessment of Consumer Satisfaction/Dissatisfaction: The Dynamic Aspect of the Cognitive Process," *Journal of Marketing Research*, November 1983, pp. 393–404.

40 See Ralph L. Day, "Modeling Choices among Alternative Responses to Dissatisfaction," in *Advances in Consumer Research*, ed. Thomas C. Kinnear, XI, (1984), 496–99.

41 Leon Festinger and Dana Bramel, "The Reactions of Humans to Cognitive Dissonance," in *Experimental Foundations of Clinical Psychology*, ed. Arthur J. Bachrach (New York: Basic Books, 1962), pp. 251–62.

42 See Barry L. Bayus, "Word of Mouth: The Indirect Effects of Marketing Efforts," *Journal of Advertising Research*, June/July 1985, pp. 31–39.

43 Leon Festinger, *A Theory of Cognitive Dissonance* (Stanford, Calif.: Stanford University Press, 1957), p. 260; and Everett M. Rogers, *Diffusion of Innovations* (New York: Free Press, 1983), pp. 185–88.

44 See Albert O. Hirschman, *Exit, Voice, and Loyalty* (Cambridge, Mass.: Harvard University Press, 1970).

45 See Mary C. Gilly and Richard W. Hansen, "Consumer Complaint Handling as a Strategic Marketing Tool," *Journal of Consumer Marketing*, Fall 1985, pp. 5–16.

46 See James H. Donnelly, Jr., and John M. Ivancevich, "Post-Purchase Reinforcement and Back-Out Behavior," *Journal of Marketing Research*, August 1970, pp. 399–400.

47 See Jacob Jacoby, Carol K. Berning, and Thomas F. Dietvorst, "What about Disposition?" *Journal of Marketing*, July 1977, p. 23.

7

Analyzing Organizational Markets and Buyer Behavior

Companies don't make purchases; they establish relationships.

Charles S. Goodman

Business organizations not only sell; they also buy vast quantities of raw materials, manufactured parts, installations, accessory equipment, supplies, and business services. There are over 14 million organizations buying goods and services. Companies that sell steel, computers, nuclear-power plants, and other goods need to understand the business buyers' needs, resources, policies, and buying procedures. They must take into account several considerations not normally found in consumer marketing:

- Organizations buy goods and services to satisfy a variety of goals: making profits, reducing costs, meeting employee needs, and meeting social and legal obligations.
- More persons typically participate in organizational buying decisions than in consumer buying decisions, especially in procuring major items. The decision participants usually have different organizational responsibilities and apply different criteria to the purchase decision.
- The buyers must heed formal purchasing policies, constraints, and requirements established by their organizations.
- The buying instruments, such as requests for quotations, proposals, and purchase contracts, add another dimension not typically found in consumer buying.

Webster and Wind define *organizational buying* as ''the decision-making process by which formal organizations establish the need for purchased products and services, and identify, evaluate, and choose among alternative brands and suppliers.''[1] No two companies buy in the same way, yet the seller hopes to identify enough uniformities in organizational buying behavior to improve the task of marketing strategy planning.

In this chapter, we will look at three organizational markets: industrial markets, reseller markets, and government markets. Industrial buyers buy goods and services to aid them in producing other goods and services. Resellers buy goods and services to resell at a profit. Government agencies buy goods and services to carry out mandated governmental functions. We will examine five questions about each market: *Who is in the market? What buying decisions do buyers make? Who participates in the buying process? What are the major influences on the buyers? How do the buyers make their buying decisions?*

THE INDUSTRIAL MARKET

Who Is in the Industrial Market?
The *industrial market* (also called the producer or business market) consists of all the individuals and organizations that acquire goods and services that enter into the production of other products or services that are sold, rented, or supplied to others.

The major types of industries making up the industrial market are agriculture, forestry, and fisheries; mining; manufacturing; construction; transportation; communication; public utilities; banking, finance, and insurance; and services.

More dollars and items are involved in sales to industrial buyers than to consumers. For a simple pair of shoes to be produced and sold, hide dealers must sell hides to tanners, who sell leather to shoe manufacturers, who sell shoes to wholesalers, who in turn sell shoes to retailers, who finally sell them to consumers. Each party in the chain of production and distribution has to buy many other goods and services as well, and this explains why more industrial buying occurs than consumer buying.

Industrial markets have certain characteristics that contrast sharply with consumer markets.[2] These characteristics are described below.

Fewer Buyers   The industrial marketer normally deals with far fewer buyers than does the consumer marketer. Goodyear Tire Company's fate critically depends on getting an order from one of the big three U.S. auto makers. But when Goodyear sells replacement tires to consumers, it faces a potential market of 112 million American car owners.

Larger Buyers   Many industrial markets are characterized by a high buyer concentration ratio; that is, a few large buyers account for most of the purchasing. In such industries as motor vehicles, telephone and telegraph, cigarettes, aircraft engines and engine parts, and organic fibers, the top four manufacturers account for over 70 percent of total production.

Close Supplier-Customer Relationship   Because of the smaller customer base and the importance and power of the larger customers over the suppliers, we observe a close relationship between customers and sellers in the industrial markets. Suppliers are frequently expected to customize their offerings to individual customer needs. Sales go to those suppliers who closely cooperate with the buyer on technical specifications and delivery requirements, such as just-in-time production. Suppliers are increasingly expected to attend special seminars held by the industrial customer to become familiar with the buyer's quality and procurement requirements.

Geographically Concentrated Buyers   More than half of the nation's industrial buyers are concentrated in seven states: New York, California, Pennsylvania, Illinois, Ohio, New Jersey, and Michigan. Industries such as petroleum, rubber, and steel show an even greater geographical concentration. Most agricultural output comes from a relatively few states.

This geographical concentration of producers helps to reduce the costs of selling to them. At the same time, industrial marketers should monitor the regional shifts of certain industries to the Sunbelt states, such as when textiles moved out of New England to the southern states.

Derived Demand   The demand for industrial goods is ultimately derived from the demand for consumer goods. Thus animal hides are purchased because consumers buy shoes, purses, and other leather goods. If the demand for these consumer goods slackens, so will the demand for all the industrial goods entering into their production. For this reason, the industrial marketer must closely monitor the buying patterns of the ultimate consumer and those environmental factors that affect them.[3]

Inelastic Demand   The total demand for many industrial goods and services is not much affected by price changes. Shoe manufacturers are not going to buy much more leather if the price of leather falls. Nor are they going to buy much less leather if the price of leather rises unless they can find satisfactory leather substitutes. Demand is especially inelastic in the short run because producers cannot make many changes in their production methods. Demand is also inelastic for industrial goods that represent a small percentage of the item's total cost. For example, an increase in the price of metal eyelets for shoes will barely affect the total demand for metal eyelets. At the same time, producers may switch their sources of eyelets in response to price differences.

Fluctuating Demand   The demand for industrial goods and services tends to be more volatile than the demand for consumer goods and services. This is especially true of the demand for new plants and equipment. A given percentage increase in consumer demand can lead to a much larger percentage increase in the demand for plant and equipment necessary to produce the additional output. Economists refer to this as the *acceleration principle*. Sometimes a rise of only 10 percent in consumer demand can cause as much as a 200 percent rise in industrial demand in the next period; and a 10 percent fall in consumer demand may cause a complete collapse in the demand for investment goods. This sales volatility has led many industrial marketers to diversify their products and markets to achieve more-balanced sales over the business cycle.

Professional Purchasing   Industrial goods are purchased by professionally trained purchasing agents, who spend their work lives learning how to buy better. Many belong to the National Association of Purchasing Managers (NAPM), which seeks to improve the effectiveness and status of professional buyers. Their professional approach and greater ability to assimilate technical details leads to a more rational buying decision. This means that industrial marketers have to provide a greater amount of specific performance and technical data about their product.

Several Buying Influences   More people typically influence business buying decisions than consumer buying decisions. Buying committees consisting of technical experts and even senior management are common in the purchase of major goods. Consequently, industrial marketers have to hire well-trained sales representatives and often use sales teams to deal with the well-trained buyers. Although advertising, sales promotion, and publicity play an important role in the industrial promotional mix, personal selling serves as the main selling tool.

Miscellaneous Characteristics   Here are some additional characteristics of industrial buying:

- ■ *Direct purchasing.* Industrial buyers often buy directly from producers rather than through middlemen, especially those items that are technically complex and/or expensive.
- ■ *Reciprocity.* Industrial buyers often select suppliers who also buy from them. An example of this reciprocity would be a paper manufacturer who buys needed chemicals from a chemical company that is buying a considerable amount of its paper. Reciprocity is illegal if there is coercive use of pressure by one of the parties and it results in reduced competition. Noncoercive reciprocity is legal provided it is supported by elaborate records of purchases and sales to and from other parties.[4]
- ■ *Leasing.* Many industrial buyers lease their equipment instead of buying it. This happens with computers, shoe machinery, packaging equipment, heavy-construction equipment, delivery trucks, machine tools, and sales-force automobiles. The lessee gains a number of advantages: conserving capital, getting the seller's latest products, receiving better servicing, and gaining some tax advantages. The lessor often ends up with a larger net income and the chance to sell to customers who might not have been able to afford outright purchase.[5]

What Buying Decisions Do Industrial Buyers Make?

The industrial buyer faces many decisions in making a purchase. The number of decisions depends on the type of buying situation.

Major Types of Buying Situations   Robinson and others distinguish three types of buying situations, which they call *buyclasses*.[6] They are the straight rebuy, modified rebuy, and new task.

Straight rebuy   The straight rebuy describes a buying situation where the purchasing department reorders on a routine basis (e.g., office supplies, bulk chemicals). The buyer chooses from suppliers on its "approved list," giving weight to its past buying satisfaction with the various suppliers. The "in" suppliers make an effort to maintain product and service quality. They often propose automatic reordering systems so that the purchasing agent will save reordering time. The "out" suppliers attempt to offer something new or to exploit dissatisfaction so that the industrial buyer will consider buying some amount from them. Out-suppliers try to get their foot in the door with a small order and then try to enlarge their "purchase share" over time.

Modified rebuy   The modified rebuy describes a situation where the buyer wants to modify product specifications, prices, delivery requirements, or other terms. The modified rebuy usually involves additional decision participants on both the buyers' and the sellers' sides. The in-suppliers become nervous and have to put their best foot forward to protect the account. The out-suppliers see it as an opportunity to make a "better offer" to gain entry into the account.

New task   The new task faces a purchaser buying a product or service for the first time (e.g., custom-built office building, new weapon system). The greater the cost and/or risk, the larger the number of decision participants; and the greater their information seeking, the longer the time to decision completion.[7] The new-task situation is the marketer's greatest opportunity and challenge. The marketer tries to reach as many key buying influences as possible and provide helpful information and assistance. Because of the complicated selling involved in the new task, many companies use a special sales force, called a *missionary sales force*, consisting of their best sales people.

New-task buying passes through several stages, each with its own requirements and challenges to the marketer. Ozanne and Churchill have applied an innovation diffusion perspective to the new task, identifying the stages as *awareness*, *interest*, *evaluation*, *trial*, and *adoption*.[8] They found that information sources varied in effectiveness at each stage. Mass media were the most important during the initial awareness stage, whereas salespeople had their greatest impact at the interest stage. Technical sources were the most important during the evaluation stage. These findings provide clues to the marketer as to efficient communications to use at different stages of the new-task buying process.

Major Subdecisions Involved in the Buying Decision   The buyer makes the fewest decisions in the straight rebuy and the most in the new-task situation. In the new-task situation, the buyer has to determine *product specifications*, *price limits*, *delivery terms and times*, *service terms*, *payment terms*, *order quantities*, *acceptable suppliers*, and the *selected supplier*. Different decision participants influence each decision, and the order in which these decisions are made varies.

The Role of Systems Buying and Selling   Many buyers prefer to buy a total solution to their problem and not make many separate decisions. This is called *systems* buying; it originated in government practices in buying major weapons and communication systems. Instead of making separate purchases and putting all the components together, the government would solicit bids from prime contractors, who would assemble the package or system. The winning prime contractor would be responsible for bidding and assembling the subcomponents. The prime contractor would thus provide a *turnkey solution*, so called because the buyer simply had to turn one key to get everything that was wanted.

Sellers have increasingly recognized that buyers like to purchase in this way and have adopted the practice of *systems selling* as a marketing tool. Systems selling can take different forms. The supplier might sell a set of interlocking products; thus a glue supplier sells not only glue but glue applicators and dryers as well. The supplier might sell a system of production, inventory control, distribution, and other services to meet the buyer's need for a smooth-running operation. Another variant is systems contracting, where a single supply source provides the buyer with his entire requirement of MRO (maintenance, repair, operating) supplies. The customer benefits from reduced costs as the inventory is shifted to the seller. Savings also result from reduced time spent on supplier selection, and price protection over the term of the contract. The marketer benefits from lower operating costs because of a steady demand and reduced paperwork.[9]

Systems selling is a key industrial marketing strategy in bidding to build large-scale industrial projects, such as dams, steel factories, irrigation systems, sanitation systems, pipelines, utilities, and even new towns. Companies such as Bechtel, Fluor, and other project engineering firms must compete on price, quality, reliability, and other attributes to win awards. The award often goes to the firm that best meets the customer's real needs. Consider the following:

> The Indonesian government requested bids to build a cement factory near Jakarta. An American firm made a proposal that included choosing the site, designing the cement factory, hiring the construction crews, assembling the materials and equipment, and turning over the finished factory to the Indonesian government. A Japanese firm, in outlining its proposal, included all of these services plus hiring and training the workers to run the factory, exporting the cement through their trading companies, using the cement to build some needed roads out of Jakarta, and using the cement to build some new office buildings in Jakarta. Although the Japanese proposal involved more money, its appeal was greater and they won the contract. Clearly, the Japanese viewed the problem not as one of just building a cement factory (the narrow view of systems selling) but of running it in a way that would contribute to the country's economy. They saw themselves not as an engineering project firm but as an economic development agency. They took the broadest view of the customer's needs. This is true systems selling.

Who Participates in the Industrial Buying Process?

Who does the buying of the trillions of dollars' worth of goods and services needed by the industrial market? A number of studies have been done to answer that question. Purchasing agents are more influential in straight rebuy and modified rebuy situations, whereas other organizational members are more influential in new-buy situations. Engineering personnel usually have greatest influence over the product selection decision, whereas purchasing agents dominate the supplier selection decision.[10] This indicates that in new-buy situations, the industrial marketer must first direct product information to the engineering personnel. In rebuy situations and at supplier selection time in new-buy situations, communications should be directed primarily at the purchasing agent.

Webster and Wind call the decision-making unit of a buying organization the *buying center*, defined as "all those individuals and groups who participate in the purchasing decision-making process, who share some common goals and the risks arising from the decisions."[11]

The buying center includes all members of the organization who play any of six roles in the purchase decision process:[12]

- *Users.* Users are the members of the organization who will use the product or service. In many cases, the users initiate the buying proposal and help define the product specifications.
- *Influencers.* Influencers are persons who influence the buying decision. They often help define specifications and also provide information for evaluating alternatives. Technical personnel are particularly important as influencers.
- *Deciders.* Deciders are persons who have the power to decide on product requirements and/or on suppliers.
- *Approvers.* Approvers are persons who must authorize the proposed actions of deciders or buyers.
- *Buyers.* Buyers are persons with formal authority for selecting the supplier and arranging the terms of purchase. Buyers may help shape product specifications, but they play their major role in selecting vendors and negotiating. In more complex purchases, the buyers might include high-level officers participating in the negotiations.
- *Gatekeepers.* Gatekeepers are persons who have the power to prevent sellers or information from reaching members of the buying center. For example, purchasing agents, receptionists, and telephone operators may prevent salespersons from talking to users or deciders.

Within any organization, the buying center will vary in size and composition for different classes of products. More decision participants will be involved in buying a computer than in buying paper clips. The industrial marketer has to figure out: *Who are the major decision participants? In what decisions do they exercise influence? What is their level of influence? And what evaluation criteria does each decision participant use?* Consider the following example:

The American Hospital Supply Corporation sells nonwoven disposable surgical gowns to hospitals. It tries to identify the hospital personnel who participate in this buying decision. The decision participants turn out to be the vice-president of purchasing, the operating-room administrator, and the surgeons. Each party plays a different role. The vice-president of purchasing analyzes whether the hospital should buy disposable gowns or reusable gowns. If the findings favor disposable gowns, then the operating-room administrator compares various competitors' products and prices and makes a choice. This administrator considers the gown's absorbency, antiseptic quality, design, and cost and normally buys the brand that meets the functional requirements at the lowest cost. Finally, surgeons influence the decision retroactively by reporting their satisfaction with the particular brand.

When a buying center includes many participants, the industrial marketer will not have the time or resources to reach all of them. Smaller companies concentrate on reaching the *key buying influences*. Larger companies go for *multilevel in-depth selling* to reach as many decision participants as possible. Their sales people virtually "live" with the customer when it is a major account with recurrent sales.

Industrial marketers must periodically review their assumptions on the roles and influence of different decision participants. For example, for years Kodak's strategy for selling X-ray film to hospitals was to sell through lab technicians. The company did not notice that the decision was increasingly being made by professional administrators. As its sales declined, Kodak finally grasped the change in buying practices and hurriedly changed its market targeting strategy.

What Are the Major Influences on Industrial Buyers?

Industrial buyers are subject to many influences when they make their buying decisions. Some marketers assume that the most important influences are economic. They see the buyers as favoring the supplier who offers the lowest price, or best product, or most service. This view suggests that industrial marketers should concentrate on offering strong economic benefits to buyers.

Other marketers see buyers responding to personal factors such as favors, attention, or risk avoidance. A study of buyers in ten large companies concluded that

> corporate decision-makers remain human after they enter the office. They respond to "image"; they buy from companies to which they feel "close"; they favor suppliers who show them respect and personal consideration, and who do extra things "for them"; they "over-react" to real or imagined slights, tending to reject companies which fail to respond or delay in submitting requested bids.[13]

Industrial buyers actually respond to both economic and personal factors. Where there is substantial similarity in supplier offers, industrial buyers have little basis for rational choice. Since they can satisfy the purchasing requirements with any supplier, these buyers can place more weight on the personal treatment they receive. On the other hand, where competing products differ substantially, industrial buyers are more accountable for their choice and pay more attention to economic factors.

Webster and Wind have classified the various influences on industrial buyers into four main groups: environmental, organizational, interpersonal, and individual.[14] These groups are shown in Figure 7-1 and described below.

Environmental Factors Industrial buyers are heavily influenced by factors in the current and expected economic environment, such as the level of primary demand, the economic outlook, and the cost of money. In a recession economy, industrial buyers reduce their investment in plant, equipment, and inventories. Industrial marketers can do little to stimulate total demand in this environment. They can only fight harder to increase or maintain their share of demand.

Companies that fear a shortage of key materials are willing to buy and hold larger inventories. They will sign long-term contracts with suppliers to ensure a steady flow of materials. Du Pont, Ford, Chrysler, and several other major companies regard *supply planning* as a major responsibility of their purchasing executives.

Industrial buyers are also affected by technological, political, and competitive developments in the environment. The industrial marketer has to monitor all of these environmental forces, determine how they will affect buyers, and try to turn problems into opportunities.

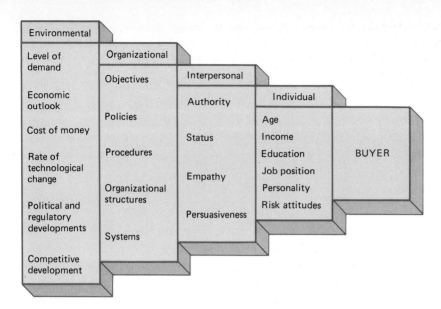

FIGURE 7-1
Major Influences on Industrial Buying Behavior

Each buying organization has specific objectives, policies, procedures, organizational structure, and systems. The industrial marketer has to know these as well as possible. Such questions arise as: How many people are involved in the buying decision? Who are they? What are their evaluation criteria? What are the company's policies and constraints on the buyers?

The industrial marketer should be aware of the following organizational trends in the purchasing area:

■ *Purchasing-department upgrading.* Purchasing departments often occupy a low position in the management hierarchy, in spite of managing often more than half of the company's costs. However, recent bouts with inflation and shortages have led many companies to upgrade their purchasing departments. Several large corporations have elevated the heads of purchasing to vice-presidential levels. Caterpillar and some other companies have combined several functions—such as purchasing, inventory control, production scheduling, and traffic—into a high-level function called *material management.* ''New-wave'' materials managers are actively building new supply sources. Many companies are looking for top talent, hiring M.B.A.'s, and offering higher compensation. This means that industrial marketers must correspondingly upgrade their sales personnel to match the caliber of the new buyers.

■ *Centralized purchasing.* In multidivisional companies, most purchasing is carried out by separate divisions because of their differing needs. Recently companies have started to recentralize some of the purchasing. Headquarters identifies materials purchased by several divisions and considers buying them centrally. This gives the company more purchasing clout. The individual divisions can buy from another source if they can get a better deal, but in general, centralized purchasing produces substantial savings for the company. For the industrial marketer, this development means dealing with fewer and higher-level buyers. Instead of the seller's regional sales forces selling at separate plant locations, the seller may use a *national account sales force* to deal with the corporate buyer. National account selling is challenging and demands a sophisticated sales force and marketing planning effort.[15]

■ *Long-term contracts.* Industrial buyers are increasingly initiating or accepting long-term contracts with trusted suppliers. For example, General Motors wants to buy from fewer suppliers who are willing to locate close to its plants and produce high-quality components. Another aspect involves companies supplying *electronic order exchange* systems to their customers. The customer can type orders directly on the computer, and these go by modem to the supplier.

Many hospitals order directly from American Hospital Supply in this way, and many bookstores order from Follett's in this way.

■ **Purchasing-performance evaluation.** More companies are setting up incentive systems to reward purchasing managers for good buying performance, in much the same way that sales personnel receive bonuses for good selling performance. These systems will lead purchasing managers to increase their pressure on sellers for the best terms.

The emergence of just-in-time production systems promises to have a major impact on organizational purchasing policies. Its ramifications are described in Exhibit 7-1.

EXHIBIT 7-1

Just-In-Time Production Changes the Face of Organizational Buying

Over the past two decades, American markets have been bombarded with foreign products. Japanese market-share gains have been especially pronounced in such industries as steel, office equipment, electronics, and automobiles. As American business started studying the reasons for Japanese success in manufacturing, it discovered several concepts including just-in-time (JIT), early supplier involvement, value analysis, quality circles, total quality control, and flexible manufacturing.

JIT in particular promises to produce significant change in the relationship between suppliers and their industrial customers. The goal of JIT is zero inventory with 100 percent quality. It means that materials arrive at the customer's factory exactly at the time they are needed. It does not mean that the customer shifts inventory to the supplier, as this would not reduce total system costs; instead it calls for a synchronization between supplier and customer production schedules so that inventory buffers are unnecessary. Effective implementation of JIT should result in reduced inventory and lead times and increased quality, productivity, and adaptability to changes.

In a survey of two thousand purchasing executives in 1986, 59 percent indicated that their firm had used or planned to use JIT. General Motors, through its JIT programs, reduced inventory-related costs from $8 billion to $2 billion.

Industrial marketers need to be aware of the changes that JIT will bring about in the purchasing practices of organizations. They must position themselves to exploit the opportunities that JIT will create. The following are the major features and implications of JIT:

■ **Strict quality control.** Maximum cost savings from JIT are achieved if preinspected goods are received by the buyer. The buyers thus expect that suppliers have strict quality-control procedures such as SPC (statistical process control) or TQC (total quality control). This means that suppliers need to work closely with the industrial customer and satisfy the latter that they can ship products that meet the quality standards.

■ **Frequent and reliable delivery.** Daily delivery is frequently the only way to avoid inventory buildup. Increasingly, customers are specifying delivery dates rather than shipping dates, with penalties for not meeting them. Apple even penalizes for early delivery, while Kasle Steel has around-the-clock deliveries to the General Motors plant in Buick City. This means that suppliers must develop reliable transportation arrangements.

■ **Closer location.** Since JIT involves frequent delivery, a location closer to the customer can be an advantage for the supplier. A close location results in more efficiency in delivering smaller lots and greater reliability in inclement weather. Kasle Steel set up its blanking mill within Buick City to serve the General Motors plant there. This means that an industrial marketer may have to make large commitments to major customers.

■ **Telecommunication.** New technologies of communication permit suppliers to establish computerized purchasing systems that are hooked up to their customers. One large customer requires that suppliers make their inventory figures and prices available on the system. It allows for just-in-time on-line ordering as the computer looks for the lowest prices where inventory is available. This reduces transaction costs but puts pressure on industrial marketers to keep prices very competitive.

■ **Stable production schedules.** Under JIT, customers provide their production schedule to the supplier so that the delivery is made on the day the materials are required. International Harvester provides one of its suppliers with a six-month forecast and a firm twenty-day order. If any last-minute changes are made, International Harvester is billed for the additional costs. This will help reduce the uncertainty and costs faced by the industrial suppliers.

■ **Single sourcing.** JIT implies that the buying and selling organizations work closely together to reduce costs. This often translates into the industrial customer's awarding a long-term contract to only one supplier who can be trusted. This makes payoffs high for the winning supplier, and very difficult for other competitors to subsequently get the contract. Contracts are almost automatically renewed provided the supplier met delivery schedules and maintained quality. Single sourcing is increasing rapidly under JIT. Thus while General Motors still uses more than 3,500 suppliers, Toyota, which has totally adopted JIT, uses less than 250. In the United States, Harley Davidson reduced its supplier base from 320 to 180 in two years.

■ **Value analysis.** The major objectives of JIT are to reduce costs and improve quality, and value analysis is critical to accomplishing those objectives. To reduce costs of its product, a customer must not only reduce its own costs but also get its suppliers to reduce their costs. Thus some large manufacturers hold VA seminars for their suppliers. Suppliers with a strong VA program have a competitive edge, as they can contribute to their customers' VA program.

■ **Early supplier involvement.** Industrial buyers are increasingly realizing that industrial marketers are experts in their field and should be brought into the design process. Industrial marketers must have qualified personnel who can participate in customers' design teams. In 1986, a survey of one thousand purchasing executives found that the major criteria for selecting suppliers to participate in design teams were quality, prior delivery performance, recommendations by the customer's engineering department, and prior value-analysis assistance.

■ **Close relationship.** All the above features of JIT help to forge a close relationship between the industrial customer and the industrial marketer. To make JIT successful, they coordinate their efforts to maximally satisfy the customer's needs. Under JIT, the supplier is viewed as a work station that is located away from the customer's manufacturing site. To be successful, the supplier has to customize its offering for the particular industrial customer. In return, the supplier wins the contract for a specific term. Because of the time invested by the parties, locational decisions, and telecommunication hookups, the transaction-specific investments are high. Since switching costs for the industrial customer are high, these customers are extremely selective in choosing suppliers. A major implication is that U.S. industrial marketers must improve their skill in *relationship marketing* as compared with *transaction marketing*. Profit maximization over the entire relationship rather than over each transaction should be the objective. Otherwise the supplier may lose the customer for good.

For further information, see G. H. Manoochehri, "Suppliers and the Just-In-Time Concept," *Journal of Purchasing and Materials Management*, Winter 1984, pp. 16–21; Somerby Dowst, "Buyers Say VA Is More Important Than Ever," *Purchasing*, June 26, 1986, pp. 64–83; Ernest Raia, "Just-in-Time USA," *Purchasing*, February 13, 1986, pp. 48–62; Eric K. Clemons and F. Warren McFarlan, "Telecom: Hook Up or Lose Out," *Harvard Business Review*, July–August 1986, pp. 91–97; and Somerby Dowst and Ernest Raia, "Design Team Signals for More Supplier Involvement," *Purchasing*, March 27, 1986, pp. 76–83.

Interpersonal Factors   The buying center usually includes several participants with different statuses, authority, empathy, and persuasiveness. The industrial marketer is not likely to know what kind of group dynamics will take place during the buying process, although whatever information he or she can discover about the personalities and interpersonal factors would be useful.

Individual Factors   Each participant in the buying decision process has personal motivations, perceptions, and preferences. These are influenced by the participant's age, income, education, professional identification, personality, and attitudes toward risk. Buyers definitely exhibit different buying styles. Some of the younger, better-educated buyers are "computer freaks" and make rigorous analyses of competitive proposals before choosing a supplier. Other buyers are "tough guys" from the "old school" and play off the sellers:

A good example of a cagey buyer is [the] vice-president in charge of purchasing for Rheingold's big New York brewery. . . . Using the leverage of hundreds of millions of cans a year, like many other buyers, he takes punitive action when one company slips in quality or fails to deliver. "At one point American started talking about a price rise," he recalls. "Continental kept its mouth shut. . . . American never did put the price rise into effect, but anyway, I punished them for talking about it." For a three-month period he cut the percentage of cans he bought from American.[16]

Industrial marketers must know their customers and adapt their tactics to known environmental, organizational, interpersonal, and individual influences on the buying situation.

How Do Industrial Buyers Make Their Buying Decisions?

Industrial buyers do not buy goods and services for personal consumption or utility. They buy things to make money, or to reduce operating costs, or to satisfy a social or legal obligation. A steel company will add another furnace if it sees a chance to make more money. It will computerize its accounting system to reduce the costs of doing business. It will add pollution-control equipment to satisfy legal requirements.

To buy the needed goods, industrial buyers move through a purchasing or procurement process. Robinson et al. have identified eight stages of the industrial buying process and called them *buyphases*.[17] These stages are shown in Table 7-1. All eight stages apply to a new-task buying situation, and some of them to the other two types of buying situations. This model is called the *buygrid* framework. We will describe the eight steps for the typical new-task buying situation.

Problem Recognition   The buying process begins when someone in the company recognizes a problem or need that can be met by acquiring a good or a service. Problem recognition can occur as a result of internal or external stimuli. Internally, the most common events leading to problem recognition are the following:

- The company decides to develop a new product and needs new equipment and materials to produce this product.
- A machine breaks down and requires replacement or new parts.
- Some purchased material turns out to be unsatisfactory, and the company searches for another supplier.
- A purchasing manager senses an opportunity to obtain better prices or quality.

TABLE 7-1   Major Stages (Buyphases) of the Industrial Buying Process in Relation to Major Buying Situations (Buyclasses)

		Buy Classes		
		New Task	Modified Rebuy	Straight Rebuy
Buy Phases	1. Problem recognition	Yes	Maybe	No
	2. General need description	Yes	Maybe	No
	3. Product specification	Yes	Yes	Yes
	4. Suppliers' search	Yes	Maybe	No
	5. Proposal solicitation	Yes	Maybe	No
	6. Supplier selection	Yes	Maybe	No
	7. Order-routine specification	Yes	Maybe	No
	8. Performance review	Yes	Yes	Yes

SOURCE: Adapted from Patrick J. Robinson, Charles W. Faris, and Yoram Wind, *Industrial Buying and Creative Marketing* (Boston: Allyn & Bacon, 1967), p. 14.

Externally, the buyer may get some new ideas at a trade show, or see an ad, or receive a call from a sales representative who offers a better product or a lower price. Industrial marketers can therefore stimulate problem recognition by developing ads, calling on prospects, and so on.

General Need Description   Having recognized a need, the buyer proceeds to determine the general characteristics and quantity of the needed item. For standard items, this is not much of a problem. For complex items, the buyer will work with others—engineers, users, and so on—to define the general characteristics. They will want to rank the importance of reliability, durability, price, and other attributes desired in the item.

The industrial marketer can render assistance to the buying company in this phase. Often the buyer is not aware of the benefits of different product features. An alert marketer can help buyers define their companies' needs.

Product Specifications   Now the buying organization proceeds to develop the item's technical specifications. A *product value-analysis* engineering team will be put to work on the problem. *Product value analysis*, which General Electric pioneered in the late forties, is *an approach to cost reduction in which components are carefully studied to determine if they can be redesigned or standardized or made by cheaper methods of production.* The team will examine the high-cost components in a given product—usually 20 percent of the parts account for 80 percent of the costs. The team will also look for product components that are overdesigned in that they will last longer than the product itself. Table 7-2 lists the major questions that are raised in product value analysis. The team will decide on the optimal product characteristics and specify them accordingly. Tightly written specifications will allow the buyer to refuse merchandise that fails to meet the intended standards.

Sellers, too, can use product value analysis as a tool for breaking into an account. By demonstrating a better way to make an object, an out-supplier can turn a straight rebuy situation into a new-task situation and break into the account.

Supplier Search   The buyer now tries to identify the most appropriate vendors. The buyer can examine trade directories, do a computer search, or phone other companies for recommendations. Some vendors will not qualify because they lack the required production capacity or have a poor reputation for delivery and service. Those who appear to qualify

TABLE 7-2	Questions Asked in Product Value Analysis
	1. Does the use of the item contribute value?
	2. Is its cost proportionate to its usefulness?
	3. Does it need all its features?
	4. Is there anything better for its intended use?
	5. Can a usable part be made by a lower-cost method?
	6. Can a standard product be found that will be usable?
	7. Is the product made on proper tooling, considering the quantities that are used?
	8. Will another dependable supplier provide it for less?
	9. Is anyone buying it for less?

SOURCE: Albert W. Frey, *Marketing Handbook*, 2nd ed. (New York: Ronald Press, 1965), section 27, p. 21. Copyright © by John Wiley & Sons.

may be visited to examine their production facilities and meet their personnel. The buyer will end up with a short list of qualified suppliers.

The newer the buying task and the more complex and expensive the item, the greater the amount of time buyers will spend in searching for, and qualifying, suppliers. A survey of purchasing managers in the electronics industry found that their major information sources, in order of importance, were[18]

1. Internal information such as purchasing records, other departments, and purchasing directories
2. Salespersons' telephone calls and personal visits
3. External information such as investigations of vendors' facilities, outside purchasing managers, credit and financial reports, and members of the local purchasing chapter
4. External information such as journal advertisements, journal articles, mail advertisements, catalogs, telephone directories, and trade shows

The supplier's task is to get listed in major directories, develop a strong advertising and promotion program, build a good reputation in the marketplace, and identify buyers who are looking for new suppliers.

Proposal Solicitation   The buyer will now invite qualified suppliers to submit proposals. Some suppliers will send only a catalog or a sales representative. Where the item is complex or expensive, the buyer will require a detailed written proposal from each potential supplier. The buyer will eliminate some and ask the remaining suppliers to make formal presentations.

Thus industrial marketers must be skilled in researching, writing, and presenting proposals. Their proposals should be marketing documents, not just technical documents. Their oral presentations should inspire confidence. They should position their company's capabilities and resources so that they stand out from the competition.

Supplier Selection   In this stage, the members of the buying center will review the proposals and move toward supplier selection. They will perform a vendor analysis to select supplier(s). They will consider not only the technical competence of the various suppliers but also their ability to deliver the item on time and provide necessary services. The buying center will often draw up a list of the desired supplier attributes and their relative importance. A survey of purchasing managers listed the following attributes in order of importance:[19]

1. Delivery capability
2. Quality
3. Price
4. Repair service
5. Technical capability
6. Performance history
7. Production facilities
8. Aid and advice
9. Control systems
10. Reputation
11. Financial position
12. Attitude toward buyer
13. Bidding compliance
14. Training aids
15. Progress communications
16. Management and organization
17. Packaging capability
18. Moral/legal issues
19. Geographic location
20. Labor relations record

The members of the buying center will rate the suppliers against these attributes and will identify the most attractive suppliers. They often use a supplier evaluation model such as the one shown in Table 7-3.

TABLE 7-3 An Example of Vendor Analysis

Attributes	Rating Scale				
	Unacceptable (0)	Poor (1)	Fair (2)	Good (3)	Excellent (4)
Technical and production capabilities					x
Financial strength			x		
Product reliability					x
Delivery reliability			x		
Service capability					x
Total score: $4 + 2 + 4 + 2 + 4 = 16$					
Average score: $16/5 = 3.2$					

Note: This vendor shows up as strong, except on two attributes. The purchasing agent has to decide how important the two weaknesses are. The analysis could be redone using importance weights for the five attributes.

SOURCE: Adapted from Richard Hill, Ralph Alexander, and James Cross, *Industrial Marketing*, 4th ed. (Homewood, Ill.: Richard D. Irwin, Copyright 1975), pp. 101–4.

Lehmann and O'Shaughnessy found that the relative importance of different attributes varies with the type of buying situation.[20] For *routine-order products*, they found that delivery reliability, price, and supplier reputation are highly important. For *procedural-problem products*, such as a dry copying machine, the three most important attributes are technical service, supplier flexibility, and product reliability. Finally, for *political-problem products* that stir rivalries in the organization, the most important attributes are price, supplier reputation, product reliability, service reliability, and supplier flexibility.

The buying center may attempt to negotiate with the preferred suppliers for better prices and terms before making the final selection. The marketer can counter the request for a lower price in a number of ways. The marketer can cite the value of the services the buyer now receives, especially where these services are superior to those offered by competitors. The marketer may be able to show that the "life-cycle costs" of using its product is lower than that of competitors, even if its purchase price is higher. Other more innovative ways may also be used to counter intense price competition. Consider the following example:[21]

> Lincoln Electric has instituted the "Guaranteed Cost Reduction Program" for its distributors. Under this program, whenever a customer requests a distributor to lower prices on Lincoln equipment to match Lincoln's competitors, the company and the particular distributor guarantee that during the coming year, they will find cost reductions in the customer's plant that meet or exceed the price difference between Lincoln's products and the competition's. Lincoln sales representative and the distributor then get together, and after surveying the customer's operations, identify and help to implement possible cost reductions. If an independent audit at the end of the year does not reveal the promised cost reductions, Lincoln Electric and the distributor make good the difference, with Lincoln paying 70 percent and the distributor the rest.

Buying centers must also decide on how many suppliers they want to work with. Many buyers prefer multiple sources of supply so that they will not be totally dependent on one supplier in case something goes wrong and also so that they will be able to compare the prices and performance of the various suppliers. The buyer will normally place most of the order with one supplier, and less with other suppliers. For example, a buyer using three suppliers may buy 60 percent of the needed quantity from the prime supplier and 30 and 10 percent, respectively, from the two other suppliers. The *prime supplier* will make an effort to protect its prime position, while the *secondary suppliers* will try to expand their supplier share. In the meantime, *out-suppliers* will attempt to get their foot in the door by making an especially low price offer and will then work hard to increase their share of the customer's business.

Order-Routine Specification   The buyer now writes the final order with the chosen supplier(s), listing the technical specifications, the quantity needed, the expected time of delivery, return policies, warranties, and so on. In the case of MRO items (maintenance, repair, and operating items), buyers are increasingly moving toward *blanket contracts* rather than *periodic purchase orders*. Writing a new purchase order each time stock is needed is expensive. Nor does the buyer want to write fewer and larger purchase orders, because this means carrying more inventory. A blanket contract establishes a long-term relationship where the supplier promises to resupply the buyer as needed on agreed price terms over a specified period of time. The stock is held by the seller; hence the name *stockless purchase plan*. The buyer's computer automatically teletypes an order to the seller when stock is needed. Blanket contracting leads to more single-source buying and the buying of more items from that single source. This locks the supplier in tighter with the buyer and makes it difficult for out-suppliers to break in unless the buyer becomes dissatisfied with the in-supplier's prices, quality, or service.[22]

Performance Review   In this stage the buyer reviews the performance of the particular supplier(s). Three methods are used. The buyer may contact the end users and ask for their evaluations. Or the buyer may rate the supplier on several criteria using a weighted point method. Or the buyer may aggregate the cost of poor performance to come up with an adjusted cost of purchase, including price.[23] The performance review may lead the buyer to continue, modify, or drop the supplier. The supplier's job is to monitor the same variables that buyers and end users use to rate the supplied items.

We have described the buying stages that would operate in a new-task buying situation. In the modified rebuy or straight rebuy situation, some of these stages would be compressed or bypassed. Each stage represents a narrowing of the number of supplier alternatives. Cardozo has used the buying stages to come up with a model to yield the probability that a supplier *i* will get the order for a product *j* from a particular buyer. To use the model, industrial marketers must[24]

1. Specify the decisions to be included in the sequence for a particular situation
2. Estimate probabilities of outcomes favorable to them for each decision in the sequence
3. Multiply those probabilities together to compute the overall probability of purchase or repurchase

The eight-stage buyphase model represents the major steps in the industrial buying process. In any real situation, further steps can occur. The industrial marketer needs to model each situation individually. Each buying situation involves a particular flow of work, and this *buyflow* can provide many clues to the marketer. A buyflow map for the purchase of a computer is shown in Figure 7-2. The map shows eight different company employees (represented by desk symbols) who were involved in this buying decision. Three suppliers were involved, as well as other outside influences (shown in the diamond-shaped figures). Finally, fifteen different events (shown as circles) led to placing the order with one of the suppliers.

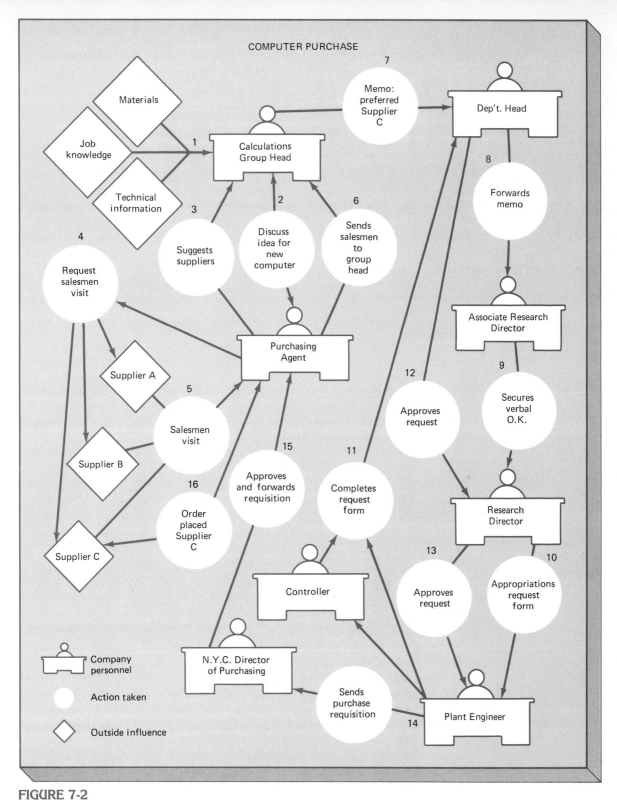

FIGURE 7-2
Map of Company Events in the Purchase of a Computer
SOURCE: "Who Makes the Purchasing Decision?" Reprinted from October 31, 1966, issue of *Marketing Insights,*
copyright © 1966 by Advertising Publications, Inc., Chicago, Illinois.

Clearly, industrial marketing is a challenging area. The key is to know the user's needs, the buying participants, the buying criteria, and the buying procedures. With this knowledge, the industrial marketer can proceed to design marketing plans for selling to different types of customers. (See Exhibit 7-2.)

THE RESELLER MARKET

Who Is in the Reseller Market? The *reseller market* consists of *all the individuals and organizations that acquire goods for the purpose of reselling or renting them to others at a profit.* Instead of producing form utility, resellers produce time, place, and possession utility. The reseller market includes nearly 416,000 wholesaling establishments employing 5,355,000 persons, and 1,923,200 retailing establishments employing 14,000,000 persons. Both sectors account for over 14.7 percent of the national income. Resellers are more geographically dispersed than producers but more concentrated than consumers.

Resellers purchase goods for resale and goods and services for conducting their operations. The latter are bought by resellers in their role as "producers." We will confine the discussion here to the goods they purchase for resale.

Resellers handle a vast variety of products for resale, indeed everything produced except the few classes of goods that producers sell directly to final customers, such as heavy or complex machinery, customized products, and products sold on a direct-mail or a door-to-door basis. With these exceptions, most products are sold to final buyers through selling intermediaries.

Suppliers should view resellers as purchasing agents for their customers, not selling agents for the suppliers. Suppliers will be successful to the extent they can help resellers serve their customers better.

| What Buying Decisions Do Resellers Make? | Resellers must make the following purchasing decisions: *What assortment to carry?* *What vendors to buy from?* and *What prices and terms to negotiate?* The assortment decision is primary and positions the reseller in the marketplace. Wholesalers and retailers can choose one of four assortment strategies: |

- ▪ *Exclusive assortment.* Carrying the line of only one manufacturer
- ▪ *Deep assortment.* Carrying a product family in depth, drawing on many producers' outputs
- ▪ *Broad assortment.* Carrying several product lines that fall within the normal scope of the reseller's type of business
- ▪ *Scrambled assortment.* Carrying many unrelated product lines

Thus a camera store might carry only Kodak cameras (exclusive assortment); many brands of cameras (deep assortment); cameras, tape recorders, radios, and stereophonic equipment (broad assortment); or the last plus stoves and refrigerators (scrambled assortment). The reseller's chosen assortment will influence its customer mix, marketing mix, and supplier mix.

Resellers confront three types of buying situations.

The *new-item situation* describes the situation where the reseller is offered a new item. The reseller will give a yes-no answer depending on how profitable the item looks. This differs from the new-task situation faced by producers who definitely have to purchase the needed item from someone.

The *best-vendor situation* faces the reseller who needs an item and must determine the best supplier. This occurs (1) when the reseller does not have the space to carry all the available brands and (2) when the reseller is seeking someone to produce a private brand. Resellers such as Sears and the A&P sell a substantial number of items under their own name; therefore much of their buying operation consists of vendor selection.

The *better-terms situation* arises when the reseller wants to obtain better terms from current suppliers. Legally, suppliers are prevented, under the Robinson-Patman Act, from granting different terms to different resellers in the same reseller class unless they reflect cost differences, distress sales, or other special conditions. Nevertheless, resellers will press their suppliers for preferential treatment, such as more service, easier credit terms, and larger-volume discounts.

| Who Participates in the Reseller Buying Process? | Who does the buying for wholesale and retail organizations? In small "mom and pop" firms, the owner usually takes care of merchandise selection and buying. In large firms, buying is a specialized function and full-time job. Buying is carried out in different ways by department stores, supermarkets, drug wholesalers, and so on, and differences can even be found within each reseller type. |

Consider supermarkets. In the corporate headquarters of a supermarket chain, specialist buyers (sometimes called merchandise managers) will be responsible for developing brand assortments and listening to new-brand presentations by salespersons. In some chains, these buyers have the authority to accept or reject new items. In many chains, however, they are limited to screening "obvious rejects" and "obvious accepts"; otherwise they must bring new items to the chain's buying committee for approval. Borden found that the buyer's recommendation carries a lot of influence in the committee decision.[25]

Even when an item is accepted by a chain-store buying committee, individual stores in the chain may not carry it. According to one supermarket chain executive: "No matter what the sales representatives sell or buyers buy, the person who has the greatest influence on the final sale of the new item is the store manager.'' In the nation's chain and independent supermarkets, two-thirds of the new items accepted at the warehouse are ordered on the store manager's own decision, and only one-third represent forced distribution.[26]

Thus producers face a major challenge in trying to get new items into stores. They offer the nation's supermarkets between 150 and 2,510 new items each week, and store space does not permit more than 10 percent to be accepted.

Several studies have attempted to rank the acceptance criteria used by buyers, buying committees, and store managers. A. C. Nielsen Company asked store managers to rank on a three-point scale the importance of different elements in influencing their decision to accept a new item.[27] The results are shown below:

Evidence of consumer acceptance	2.5
Advertising/promotion	2.2
Introductory terms and allowances	2.0
Why item was developed	1.9
Merchandising recommendations	1.8

Thus sellers stand the best chance when they can report strong evidence of consumer acceptance, present a well-designed advertising and sales promotion plan, and provide strong financial incentives to the retailer. On the other hand, Montgomery found the two most important elements in new-product acceptance to be company reputation and perceived product newness.[28]

The role of supermarket buyers, buying committees, and store managers characterizes, with some variation, the buying organizations of other reseller enterprises. Large department-store chains use buyers who specialize by line of merchandise and have a lot of authority to select the merchandise to be featured. The buyers are aided by assistant buyers, who carry out a preliminary search and also do the clerical tasks involved in ordering. The buyers may perform other functions such as demand forecasting, stock control, and merchandising. Individual store managers or their staff usually have some freedom with respect to which goods to order as well as which to display prominently.

What Are the Major Influences on Reseller Buyers?

Resellers are influenced by the same factors—environmental, organizational, interpersonal, and individual—shown earlier in Figure 7-1. The seller has to note these influences and develop strategies that help resellers make money or reduce their costs.

The individual buyer's buying style should be taken into account. Dickinson has distinguished seven buyer types:[29]

- ■ *Loyal buyer.* This buyer remains loyal to a source year after year.
- ■ *Opportunistic buyer.* This buyer selects those vendors who will further his or her long-term interests and drives the best bargain possible.
- ■ *Best-deal buyer.* This buyer selects the best deal available at a given point in time.
- ■ *Creative buyer.* This buyer tells the seller what he or she wants in the way of a product, services, and prices.
- ■ *Advertising buyer.* This buyer attempts to obtain advertising money as part of every deal.

TABLE 7-4 Vendor Marketing Tools Used with Resellers

Cooperative advertising, where vendor agrees to pay a portion of the retailer's advertising costs for the vendor's product.

Preticketing, where the vendor places a tag on each product listing its price, manufacturer, size, identification number, and color; these tags help the reseller reorder merchandise as it is sold.

Stockless purchasing, where the vendor carries the inventory and delivers goods to the reseller on short notice.

Automatic reordering systems, where the vendor supplies forms and computer links for the automatic reordering of merchandise by the reseller.

Advertising ads, such as glossy photos, broadcast scripts.

Special prices for storewide promotion.

Return and exchange privileges for the reseller.

Allowances for merchandise markdowns by the reseller.

Sponsorship of in-store demonstrations.

- *The chiseler.* This buyer constantly negotiates extra concessions in price. He or she accepts the vendor offering the greatest discount from the price he or she feels that other vendors might charge.
- *Nuts-and-bolts buyer.* This buyer selects merchandise that is the best constructed.

How Do Resellers Make Their Buying Decisions? For new items, resellers use roughly the same buying process described for the industrial buyer. For standard items, resellers simply reorder goods when the inventory gets low. The orders are placed with the same suppliers as long as their terms, goods, and services are satisfactory. Resellers will try to renegotiate prices if their margins erode owing to rising operating costs. In many retail lines, the profit margin is so low (1 to 2 percent on sales in supermarkets for example) that a sudden drop in sales or a rise in operating costs will drive profits into the red.

Resellers are improving their buying skills over time. They are mastering the principles of demand forecasting, merchandise selection, stock control, space allocation, and display. They are learning to measure profit-per-cubic-foot rather than only profit per product.[30] They are making increased use of computers to keep current inventory figures, compute economic order quantities, prepare orders, and generate printouts of dollars spent on vendors and products. They can easily tell whether carrying a particular product is profitable.

Thus vendors are facing increasingly sophisticated buying on the part of resellers, and this accounts for some of the shifting of power from manufacturers to resellers. Vendors need to understand the resellers' changing requirements and to develop competitively attractive offers that help resellers serve their customers better. Table 7-4 lists several marketing tools used by vendors to improve their offer attractiveness to resellers.

THE GOVERNMENT MARKET

Who Is in the Government Market? The *government market* consists of *governmental units—federal, state, and local— that purchase or rent goods for carrying out the main functions of government.* In 1983, governmental units purchased over one trillion dollars worth of products and services, or 30 percent of the gross national product, making the government the nation's largest customer.[31] The federal government accounts for approximately 58 percent of the total dollars spent by government at all levels.

What Buying Decisions Do Government Buyers Make?

Government buying is based on acquiring products and services that the voters and their representatives establish as necessary to carry out public objectives. Government agencies buy an amazing range of products and services. They buy bombers, sculpture, chalkboards, furniture, toiletries, clothing, materials-handling equipment, fire engines, mobile equipment, and fuel. In 1983, federal, state, and local governmental units spent approximately $229 billion for defense, $189 billion for education, $122 billion for public welfare, $66 billion for natural resources, $60 billion for health and hospitals, $46 billion for highways, and smaller sums for postal service, space research, and housing and urban renewal. The mix of expenditures varied with the particular type of governmental unit, with defense looming large in the federal budget (37 percent) and education looming large in the state and local budgets (35 percent). No wonder the government market represents a tremendous market for any producer or reseller.

Each item that the government buys requires further decisions on how much to buy, where to buy it, how much to pay, and what services to require. These decisions are made on the basis of trying to minimize *taxpayer cost*. Normally, government buyers will favor the lowest-cost bidders that can meet stated specifications. Parenthetically, the *nonprofit market*—which we have not described—overlaps with the government market and has many of the same buying characteristics. (See Exhibit 7-3.)

Who Participates in the Government Buying Process?

Who does the buying of the over one trillion dollars of goods and services? Government buying organizations are found at the federal, state, and local levels. The federal level is the largest, and its buying units operate in the civilian and military sectors.

The *federal civilian buying establishment* consists of seven categories (examples of each category are in parentheses): departments (Commerce), administration (General Services Administration), agencies (Federal Aviation Agency), boards (Railroad Retirement Board), commissions (Federal Communications Commission), the executive office (Office of Management and Budget), and miscellaneous (Tennessee Valley Authority).

No single federal agency contracts for all the government's requirements, and no single buyer in any agency purchases all that agency's needs for any single item of supplies, equipment, or services. Many agencies control a substantial percentage of their own buying, particularly for industrial products and specialized equipment. At the same time, the General Services Administration plays a major role in centralizing the procurement of commonly

---

EXHIBIT 7-3

The Institutional Market—A Fourth Type of Organizational Buying Market

The institutional market consists of schools, hospitals, nursing homes, prisons, and other institutions that must provide goods and services to people in their care. Included also are companies that must feed their employees. Many of these institutions are characterized by low budgets and captive clienteles. A hospital purchasing agent has to decide on the quality of food to buy for the patients. The buying objective is not profit, since the food is provided to the patients as part of the total service package. The basic objective is not cost minimization either, because patients served with poor food in a hospital will complain to others and hurt the hospital's reputation. The hospital purchasing agent has to find institutional-food vendors whose quality meets or exceeds a certain minimum standard and whose prices are low. Many food vendors set up a separate division to sell to institutional buyers because of their special buying needs and characteristics.

---

used items in the civilian section (office furniture and equipment, vehicles, fuels, and so on) and in developing standardized buying procedures for the other agencies.

Federal military buying is carried out by the Defense Department, largely through the Defense Logistics Agency and the U.S. Army, Navy, and Air Force. The Defense Logistics Agency procures and distributes supplies used by all military services in an effort to reduce costly duplication. It purchases through six Defense Supply Centers, which specialize in construction, electronics, fuel, personnel support, industrial, and general supplies. The trend has been toward ''single managers'' for major product classifications. Each service branch procures equipment and supplies in line with its own mission; for example, the Army Department operates offices for acquiring its own material, vehicles, medical supplies and services, and weaponry.

State and local buying agencies include school districts, highway departments, hospitals, housing agencies, and many others. Each has its own buying procedures that sellers have to master.

The various government agencies may all be potential targets for the supplier who wishes to sell to this large market. However, the supplier should review the agencies for purchasing patterns. The agencies tend to differ in quality requirements and the amount of direct marketing efforts needed to make a sale. Some agencies buy standardized items while others buy mostly customized items. The supplier should target those agencies and buying centers that match the supplier's strengths and objectives.[32]

What Are the Major Influences on Government Buyers?

Government buyers are influenced by environmental, organizational, interpersonal, and individual factors. A unique thing about government buying is that it is monitored closely by outside publics. One watchdog is Congress, and certain congressmen have made a career out of exposing government extravagance and waste. Another watchdog is the Office of Management and Budget, which checks on government spending and seeks to improve spending efficiency. Many private watchdog groups also watch government agencies to monitor how they spend the public's money.

Because spending decisions are subject to public review, government organizations get involved in considerable paperwork. Elaborate forms must be filled out and signed before purchases are approved. The level of bureaucracy is high, and marketers have to find ways to ''cut through the red tape.''

Noneconomic criteria are playing a growing role in government buying. Government buyers are asked to favor depressed business firms and areas, small-business firms, and business firms that avoid racial, sex, or age discrimination. Sellers need to keep these factors in mind when deciding whether to pursue government business.

How Do Government Buyers Make Their Buying Decisions?

Government buying practices appear complex and often frustrating to suppliers. Suppliers have registered a variety of complaints about government purchasing procedures. These complaints included excessive paperwork, bureaucracy, needless regulations, emphasis on low bid prices, decision-making delays, frequent shifts in procurement personnel, and excessive policy changes. Yet the ins and outs of selling to the government can be mastered in a short time. The government is generally helpful in disseminating information about its buying needs and procedures. Government is often as anxious to attract new suppliers as the suppliers are to find government customers. For example, the Small Business Administration prints a booklet, *U.S. Government Purchasing, Specifications, and Sales Directory*, listing thousands of items most frequently purchased by government and cross-referenced by the agencies most frequently buying them. The Government Printing Office prints *Commerce Business Daily*, which lists current defense procurements estimated to exceed $15,000 and civilian agency procurements expected to exceed $10,000, as well as recent contract awards, which can provide leads to subcontracting markets. The federal government publicizes its needs through formal advertisements in media such as the *Commerce Business Daily* and through invitations for bids (IFBs) sent to firms on established mailing lists. The General Services Administration operates business service centers in several major cities, whose staffs provide a complete education on the way government agencies buy and the steps that suppliers should follow. Various trade magazines and associations provide information on how to reach schools, hospitals, highway departments, and other government agencies.

Government buying procedures fall into two types: the *open bid* and the *negotiated contract*. Open-bid buying means that the government procurement office invites bids from qualified suppliers for carefully described items, generally awarding a contract to the lowest bidder. The supplier must consider whether it can meet the specifications and accept the terms. For commodities and standard items, such as fuel or school supplies, the specifications are not a hurdle. They may be a hurdle, however, for nonstandard items. The government procurement office is usually required to award the contract to the lowest bidder on a winner-take-all basis. In some cases, allowance is made for the supplier's superior product or reputation for completing contracts.

In negotiated-contract buying, the agency works with one or more companies and directly negotiates a contract covering the project and terms. This type of buying occurs primarily with complex projects, often involving major research-and-development costs and risks and/or where there is little effective competition. Contracts can have countless variations, such as *cost-plus pricing*, *fixed price*, and *fixed price-and-incentive* (the supplier earns more if costs are reduced). Contract performance is open to review and renegotiation if the supplier's profits appear excessive.

Government contracts won by large companies give rise to substantial subcontracting opportunities for small companies. Thus government purchasing activity creates derived demand in the producer market. Subcontracting firms, however, must be willing to place performance bonds with the prime contractor, thereby assuming some of the risk.

Many companies that sell to the government have not manifested a marketing orientation—for a number of reasons. Total government spending is determined by elected officials rather than by marketing effort to develop this market. The government's procurement policies have emphasized price, leading the suppliers to invest considerable effort in bringing their costs down. Where the product's characteristics are carefully specified, product differentiation is not a marketing factor. Nor are advertising and personal selling of much consequence in winning bids on an open-bid basis.

More companies, however, are now establishing separate government marketing departments. J. I. Case, Eastman Kodak, and Goodyear are examples. These companies are preparing their bids more scientifically, initiating projects that anticipate government needs rather than just responding to government initiatives, gathering competitive intelligence, and producing stronger communications to describe the company's competence.

SUMMARY

Business markets consist of all the individuals and organizations that buy goods for purposes of further production, resale, or redistribution. Businesses (including government and nonprofit organizations) are a market for raw and manufactured materials and parts, installations, accessory equipment, and supplies and services.

The industrial market buys goods and services for the purpose of increasing sales, cutting costs, or meeting social and legal requirements. Compared with the consumer market, the industrial market consists of fewer buyers, larger buyers, and more geographically concentrated buyers; the demand is derived, relatively inelastic, and more fluctuating; and the purchasing is more professional and more buying influences are involved. Industrial buyers make decisions that vary with the buying situation or buyclass. Buyclasses consist of three types: straight rebuys, modified rebuys, and new tasks. The decision-making unit of a buying organization, the buying center, consists of persons who play any of six roles: users, influencers, buyers, deciders, approvers, and gatekeepers. The industrial marketer needs to know: Who are the major participants? In what decisions do they exercise influence? What is their relative degree of influence? and What evaluation criteria does each decision participant use? The industrial marketer also needs to understand the major environmental, organizational, interpersonal, and individual influences operating in the buying process. The buying process itself consists of eight stages called buyphases: problem recognition, general need description, product specification, supplier search, proposal solicitation, supplier selection, order-routine specification, and performance review. As industrial buyers become more sophisticated, industrial marketers must upgrade their marketing capabilities.

The reseller market consists of individuals and organizations that acquire and resell goods produced by others. Resellers have to decide on their assortment, suppliers, prices, and terms. They face three types of buying situations: new items, new vendors, and new terms. In small wholesale and retail organizations, buying may be carried on by one or a few individuals; in larger organizations, by a whole purchasing department. In a modern supermarket chain, the major participants include headquarters buyers, storewide buying committees, and individual store managers. With new items, the buyers go through a buying process similar to the one shown for industrial buyers; and with standard items, the buying process consists of routines for reordering and renegotiating contracts.

The government market is a vast one that annually purchases over a trillion dollars worth of products and services—for the pursuit of defense, education, public welfare, and other public needs. Government buying practices are highly specialized and specified, with open bidding and/or negotiated contracts characterizing most of the buying. Government buyers operate under the watchful eye of Congress, the Bureau of the Budget, and several private watchdog groups. Hence they tend to fill out more forms, require more signatures, and respond more slowly in placing orders.

■ QUESTIONS

1. A research lab discovered a new method of detecting minute vibrations in objects. A venture capital firm was considering financing the development of this new technique into a production model but required that market research be undertaken to (a) determine the market for application of the technique, and (b) develop specifications for the equipment that would fit the needs of customers in the market. Develop a research plan that accomplishes these objectives.

2. How might the buying decision for a computer system differ between a university and a manufacturer of automobile replacement parts?

3. You are a wholesale-distributor for chemicals. What types of concerns would you have in distributing products for manufacturer-suppliers like Celanese and Dow?

4. Discuss the major influences affecting how U.S. airlines buy airplane seats.

5. General Electric has begun to market a factory automation planning service along with CAD/CAM and robotic products in an attempt to sell fully automated factories-of-the-future to other manufacturers. Discuss the factors that will determine the success or failure of such a venture.

6. Farm-equipment dealers act as resellers for the products sold to them by equipment manufacturers. When

International Harvester faced bankruptcy in the early 1980s, what marketing policies could it have used to prevent these resellers from abandoning it to carry a competing line of equipment?

7. How do the buying influences on the government buyer differ from those on the producer or reseller buyer?

8. Describe some of the major characteristics of commercial-services firms (finance, insurance, and real estate) as a market for goods and services.

9. There are several important institutional markets: hospitals, educational institutions, welfare organizations, and the like. Discuss the characteristic buying needs and buying organization for, say, educational institutions.

10. What types of assortment strategies are used by the following types of businesses? (a) bicycle shop, (b) sports shop, (c) pawn shop, (d) Salvation Army store, and (e) discount store.

11. A home-decorating service plans to buy a paint-mixing machine. Four machines are available:

Evoked Set	Price	Number of Speeds	Size (in Ounces)	Quietness Level*
1	$30	10	32	3
2	$22	7	30	4
3	$25	5	48	5
4	$22	5	30	4

* A score of 5 represents the least noise.

Which machine(s) would this company prefer if its decision making could be explained by (a) a conjunctive model using cutoff points of less than $28, with at least 5 speeds, weighing 32 ounces, and with a quietness level equal to or greater than 4; (b) a disjunctive model based on criteria of at least 8 speeds or at least 48 ounces; and (c) a lexicographic model with an importance ordering of least cost, size, speeds, and quietness. (See Exhibit 6-3 for discussion of these models.)

▮▮ FOOTNOTES

1 Frederick E. Webster, Jr., and Yoram Wind, *Organizational Buying Behavior* (Englewood Cliffs, N.J.: Prentice-Hall, 1972), p. 2.

2 However, for an argument that consumer and industrial marketing do not differ substantially, see Edward F. Fern and James R. Brown, "The Industrial/Consumer Marketing Dichotomy: A Case of Insufficient Justification," *Journal of Marketing*, Spring 1984, pp. 68–77.

3 See William S. Bishop, John L. Graham, and Michael H. Jones, "Volatility of Derived Demand in Industrial Markets and Its Management Implications," *Journal of Marketing*, Fall 1984, pp. 95–103.

4 See Louis W. Stern and Thomas L. Eovaldi, *Legal Aspects of Marketing Strategy* (Englewood Cliffs, N.J.: Prentice-Hall, 1984).

5 See Russell Hindin, "Lease Your Way to Corporate Growth," *Financial Executive*, May 1984, pp. 20–25.

6 Patrick J. Robinson, Charles W. Faris, and Yoram Wind, *Industrial Buying and Creative Marketing* (Boston: Allyn & Bacon, 1967).

7 See Peter Boyle, Arch G. Woodside, and Paul Mitchell, "Organizations Buying in New Task and Rebuy Situations," *Industrial Marketing Management*, February 1979, pp. 7–11.

8 Urban B. Ozanne and Gilbert A. Churchill, Jr., "Five Dimensions of the Industrial Adoption Process," *Journal of Marketing Research*, 1971, pp. 322–28.

9 Marsha A. Schiedt, Frederick T. Trawick, and John E. Swan, "Impact of Purchasing Systems Contracts on Distributors and Producers," *Industrial Marketing Management*, October 1982, pp. 283–89.

10 See Donald W. Jackson, Jr., Janet E. Keith, and Richard K. Burdick, "Purchasing Agents' Perceptions of Industrial Buying Center Influence: A Situational Approach," *Journal of Marketing*, Fall 1984, pp. 75–83.

11 Webster and Wind, *Organizational Buying Behavior*, p. 6.

12 Ibid., pp. 78–80.

13 See Murray Harding, "Who Really Makes the Purchasing Decision?" *Industrial Marketing*, September 1966, p. 76. This point of view is further developed in Ernest Dichter, "Industrial Buying Is Based on Same 'Only Human' Emotional Factors that Motivate Consumer Market's Housewife," *Industrial Marketing*, February 1973, pp. 14–16.

14 Webster and Wind, *Organizational Buying Behavior*, pp. 33–37.

15 See Thomas H. Stevenson and Albert L. Page, "The Adoption of National Account Marketing by Industrial Firms," *Industrial Marketing Management*, VIII (1979), 94–100; and Benson P. Shapiro and Rowland T. Moriarty, *National Account Management: Emerging Insights* (Cambridge, Mass.: Marketing Science Institute, March 1982).

16 Walter Guzzardi, Jr., "The Fight for 9/10 of a Cent," *Fortune*, April 1961, p. 152.

17 Robinson, Faris, and Wind, *Industrial Buying*.

18 See William A. Dempsey, "Vendor Selection and the Buying Process," *Industrial Marketing Management*, VII (1978), 257–67.

19 Ibid.

20 See Donald R. Lehmann and John O'Shaughnessy, "Difference in Attribute Importance for Different Industrial Products," *Journal of Marketing*, April 1974, pp. 36–42.

21 See James A. Narus and James C. Anderson, "Turn Your Industrial Distributors Into Partners," *Harvard Business Review*, March–April 1986, pp. 66–71.

22 See Leonard Groeneveld, "The Implications of Blanket Contracting for Industrial Purchasing and Marketing," *Journal of Purchasing*, November 1972, pp. 51–58; and H. Lee Mathews, David T. Wilson, and Klaus Backhaus, "Selling

to the Computer Assisted Buyer,'' *Industrial Marketing Management*, VI (1977), 307–15.

23 See C. David Wieters and Lonnie L. Ostrom, ''Supplier Evaluation as a New Marketing Tool,'' *Industrial Marketing Management*, VIII (1979), 161–66.

24 See Richard N. Cardozo, ''Modelling Organizational Buying as a Sequence of Decisions,'' *Industrial Marketing Management*, XII (1983), 75–81.

25 Neil H. Borden, Jr., *Acceptance of New Food Products by Supermarkets* (Boston: Division of Research, Graduate School of Business Administration, Harvard University, 1968).

26 Robert W. Mueller and Franklin H. Graf, ''New Items in the Food Industry, Their Problems and Opportunities'' (Special report to the Annual Convention of the Supermarket Institute, Cleveland, May 20, 1968), p. 2.

27 Ibid., p. 5.

28 David B. Montgomery, *New Product Distribution: An Analysis of Supermarket Buyer Decisions* (Cambridge, Mass.: Marketing Science Institute, March 1973).

29 Roger A. Dickinson, *Buyer Decision Making* (Berkeley, Calif.: Institute of Business and Economic Research, 1967), pp. 14–17.

30 See Robert D. Buzzell, *Product Profitability Measurement and Merchandising Decisions* (Boston: Harvard University Press, 1965).

31 See *Statistical Abstract of the United States, 1986*, for these and other data.

32 See Warren H. Suss, ''How to Sell to Uncle Sam,'' *Harvard Business Review*, November–December 1984, pp. 136–44.

8

Analyzing Competitors

Marketing is merely a civilized form of warfare in which most battles are won with words, ideas, and disciplined thinking.

Albert W. Emery

Having an understanding of customers is not enough today. In the Soaring Sixties, companies could ignore their competitors because most markets were growing. In the Turbulent Seventies and Flat Eighties, companies realized that sales gains would largely come by wresting share away from competitors. As a result, today's companies are starting to pay as much attention to tracking their competitors as to understanding their target customers.

This explains why we hear so much current talk about "marketing warfare," "competitive intelligence systems," and similar themes.[1] Yet not all companies are investing enough in monitoring their competitors. Some companies think they know their competitors just through the daily act of competing with them; they do not see the need for a formal competitive intelligence system. Other companies think they can never know their competitors, so why collect information? Sensible companies, however, appreciate the value of tracking their competitors and are designing intelligence systems for this purpose.

The fact is that knowing one's competitors is critical to effective marketing planning. The company should constantly compare its products, prices, channels, and promotion with those of its close competitors. In this way, it can discern areas of potential competitive advantage and disadvantage. The company can launch more precise attacks on its competitors as well as prepare stronger defenses against attacks.

But what do companies need to know about their competitors? At least five things:

1. Who are our *competitors*?
2. What are their *strategies*?
3. What are their *objectives*?

4. What are their *strengths and weaknesses*?
5. What are their *reaction patterns*?

We will now examine how this information helps shape the company's marketing strategy.

IDENTIFYING THE COMPANY'S COMPETITORS

Normally, it would seem a simple task for a company to identify its competitors. Coca-Cola knows that Pepsi-Cola is its major competitor; and General Motors knows that Ford is a major competitor. But the range of a company's actual and potential competitors is much broader. Companies must avoid "competitor myopia." A company is more likely to be "buried" by its latent competitors than its current ones. Here are four levels of competitors, based on a broadening of the concept of *product substitution*:

1. A company can see its competitors as other companies offering a similar product and services to the same customers at similar prices. Thus Buick might see its major competitors to be Ford, Toyota, Honda, Renault, and other manufacturers of moderate price automobiles. But it would not see itself as competing with Mercedes, on the one hand, or Yugo automobiles, on the other.
2. A company can see its competitors more broadly as all companies making the same product or class of products. Here Buick would see itself as competing against all other automobile manufacturers.
3. A company can see its competitors even more broadly as all companies manufacturing products that supply the same service. Here Buick would see itself competing against not only other automobile manufacturers but also manufacturers of motorcycles, bicycles, and trucks.
4. A company can see its competitors still more broadly as all companies that compete for the same consumer dollars. Here Buick would see itself competing with companies that sell major consumer durables, foreign vacations, new homes, major home repairs, and so on.

Now we will consider more specifically identifying the company's competitors from the *industry* point of view and the *market* point of view.

Industry Concept of Competition
Here we want to focus on industry-level definitions of competition because they are widely used and constitute an important part of the analysis that must be done to identify competitors.

An *industry* is defined as *a group of firms that offer a product or class of products that are close substitutes of each other*. Normally, we talk about the auto industry, the oil industry, the pharmaceutical industry, and so on. Economists define "close substitutes" as products with a *high cross-elasticity of demand*. Thus if the price of one product rises and causes the demand for another product to rise, the two products are close substitutes. For example, if the price of coffee rises and this leads people to switch to tea, coffee and tea are substitutes, even though they are physically different products. Sometimes the cross-elasticity of demand is not revealed immediately following a price change, since consumers do not all notice the change when it takes place and also need time to adjust their purchase mix. For example, if the price of automobile transportation rose considerably, some people would switch to public transportation, but this would take time.

A company must strive to understand the competitive pattern in its industry if it hopes to be an effective "player." Economists have formulated a useful framework to understand industry dynamics. The framework is shown in Figure 8-1. Essentially it says that understanding the competitive dynamics of an industry must start with understanding the basic conditions underlying *demand and supply*. These conditions in turn influence the *industry structure*. Industry structure in turn influences *industry conduct*, such as product development, pricing, and advertising strategy. Industry conduct then shapes *industry performance*, such as the industry's efficiency, growth, and employment.

Here we will examine the main factors determining industry structure.

Number of Sellers and Degree of Differentiation The starting point for describing any industry is to specify whether there are one, few, or many sellers and whether the product is homogeneous or highly differentiated. These characteristics are extremely important and give rise to five well-known industry structure types. They are shown and described in Exhibit 8-1.

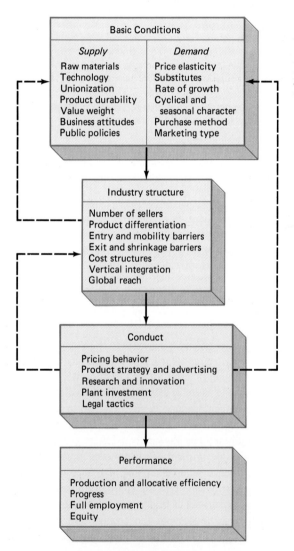

FIGURE 8-1
A Model of Industrial Organization Analysis
SOURCE: Adapted from F. M. Scherer, *Industrial Market Structure and Economic Performance*, 2nd ed. (Chicago: Rand McNally, 1980), p. 4.

EXHIBIT 8-1

Five Industry Structure Types

	One Seller	Few Sellers	Many Sellers
Undifferentiated Product	Pure monopoly	Pure oligopoly	Pure competitive
Differentiated Product		Differentiated oligopoly	Monopolistic competitive

■ **Pure monopoly.** A pure monopoly exists when only one firm provides a certain product or service in a certain country or area (U.S. Post Office, local electricity company). This monopoly might be the result of a regulatory edict, a patent, a license, scale economies, or other factors. An unregulated monopolist that sought to maximize profits would charge a high price, do little or no advertising, and offer minimal service, since customers have to buy its product in the absence of close substitutes. If there are partial substitutes and some danger of imminent competition, the pure monopolist might invest in more service and technology to act as entry barriers to new competition. A regulated monopoly, on the other hand, would normally be required to charge a lower price and provide more service as a matter of public interest.

■ **Pure oligopoly.** A pure oligopoly consists of a few companies producing essentially the same commodity (oil, steel, etc.). A company would find it hard to charge anything other than the going price except to the extent that it can differentiate its services. If the competitors match each other on services, then the only way to gain a competitive advantage is through achieving lower costs. Lower costs are achieved through pursuing a volume strategy that is supported by large-scale efficient manufacturing and strong experience economies.

■ **Differentiated oligopoly.** A differentiated oligopoly consists of a few companies producing products that are partially differentiated (autos, cameras, etc.). The differentiation can occur along lines of quality, features, styling, or services. Each competitor may seek leadership along one of these major attributes, attract the customers favoring that attribute, and charge a premium for that attribute.

■ **Monopolistic competition.** A monopolistic competitive industry consists of many competitors able to differentiate their offers in whole or part (restaurants, beauty shops). Many of the competitors tend to focus on market segments where they can meet customer needs in a superior way and command a price premium.

■ **Pure competition.** A pure competitive industry consists of many competitors offering the same product and service (stock market, commodity market). Since there is no basis for differentiation, competitors' prices will be the same. No competitor will advertise unless advertising could create psychological differentiation (cigarettes, beer); in this case, it would be more proper to describe the industry as monopolistically competitive. Sellers will enjoy different profit rates only to the extent that they can achieve lower costs in production or distribution.

Although the competitive structure of an industry can be described by any of the five types in Exhibit 8-1 at a particular point in time, the competitive structure can change over time. Consider the case where a company innovates a radically different product, such as Sony innovating the Walkman. Sony is a monopolist at first, but soon many other companies enter offering slightly different versions of the product, leading to a monopolistically competitive structure. When demand growth slows down, a "shakeout" occurs and the industry structure might turn into a differentiated oligopoly. Eventually the products might be seen as essentially the same with price being the only characteristic of buyer interest; in this case, the industry is now virtually a pure oligopoly.

Entry and Mobility Barriers   Ideally, firms should be free to enter industries that show attractive profits. Their entry would lead to more supply and ultimately bring down profits to a normal rate of return. Ease of entry prevents current firms from extracting excess profits in the long run. However, industries differ greatly in the ease with which they can be entered. Thus it is easy to open a new restaurant but difficult to enter the auto industry. The major barriers to entry include *high capital requirements; economies of scale; patents and licensing requirements; scarcity of locations, raw materials, or distributors; reputational requirements; and so on*. Some of these barriers are intrinsic to certain industries, and others are put up by the single or combined actions of the incumbent firms who know that new competitors will hurt their sales and profits. Even after a firm enters an industry, it might face mobility barriers when it tries to enter certain more attractive parts of the industry.

Exit and Shrinkage Barriers   Ideally, firms should be free to exit industries in which profits are unattractive, but they often face exit barriers.[2] Among the exit barriers are *legal or moral obligations to customers, creditors, and employees; government restrictions; low salvage value of assets due to overspecialization or obsolescence; lack of alternative opportunities; high vertical integration; emotional barriers; and so on.* Many firms persevere in an industry as long as they manage to cover all their variable costs and some or all of their fixed costs. Their presence, however, dampens profits for everyone. It is in the interest of companies that want to stay in this industry to lower the exit barriers for others. They can offer to buy other firms' assets, meet customer obligations, and so on. Even if some firms cannot be induced to exit, they may be induced to shrink in size. But here, too, there are *shrinkage barriers* that the more aggressive firms can try to help remove.[3]

Cost Structures   Each industry will have a certain cost mix that will drive much of its strategic conduct. For example, making steel involves heavy manufacturing and raw material costs, whereas making toys involves heavy distribution and marketing costs. The firms in an industry will pay the greatest attention to their greatest costs and will "strategize" to reduce or discipline these costs. Thus the steel company with the most modern plant will have a great advantage over the other steel companies.

Vertical Integration   In some industries, companies will find it advantageous to integrate backward and/or forward. A good example is the oil industry where major oil producers carry on oil exploration, oil drilling, oil refining, and chemical manufacture as part of their operation. Vertical integration often effects lower costs and also more control over the value-added stream. In addition, these firms can manipulate their prices and costs in different segments of their business to earn profits where taxes are lowest. To this extent, firms that are not able to integrate vertically operate at a disadvantage.

Global Reach   Some industries are highly local (such as lawn care) and others are *global industries* (such as oil, aircraft engines, cameras). Companies in global industries need to compete on a global basis if they are to enjoy economies of scale and keep up with the latest advances in technology.[4]

Product segmentation	Children/Teens	Age 19–35	Age 36+
Plain toothpaste	Colgate-Palmolive Procter & Gamble	Colgate-Palmolive Procter & Gamble	Colgate-Palmolive Procter & Gamble
Toothpaste with fluoride	Colgate-Palmolive Procter & Gamble	Colgate-Palmolive Procter & Gamble	Colgate-Palmolive Procter & Gamble
Gel	Colgate-Palmolive Procter & Gamble Lever Bros.	Colgate-Palmolive Procter & Gamble Lever Bros.	Colgate-Palmolive Procter & Gamble Lever Bros.
Striped	Beecham	Beecham	
Smoker's toothpaste		Topol	Topol

Customer segmentation

FIGURE 8-2

Product/Market Battlefield Map for Toothpaste

SOURCE: William A. Cohen, *Winning on the Marketing Front: The Corporate Manager's Game Plan* (New York: John Wiley & Sons, Inc., 1986), p. 63.

Market Concept of Competition

Instead of looking at companies making the same product (the industry approach), we can look at companies that are trying to satisfy the same customer need or serve the same customer group. A typewriter manufacturer normally sees its competition as other typewriter manufacturers. From a customer need point of view, however, the customer really wants ''writing ability.'' This need can be satisfied by pencils, pens, computers, and so on. Similarly, a dog-collar manufacturer aims its products at a customer group called ''dog owners.'' Therefore its competitors are other manufacturers of products aimed at dog owners. In general, the market concept of competition opens the company's eyes to a broader set of actual and potential competitors and stimulates more long-run strategic market planning.

The key to identifying competitors is to link industry and market analysis through mapping the *product/market battlefield*. Figure 8-2 illustrates the product/market battlefield map in the toothpaste market according to product types and customer age groups. We see that P&G and Colgate-Palmolive occupy nine segments; Lever Brothers, three; Beecham, two; and Topol, two. If Topol wanted to enter other segments, it would need to estimate the market size of each segment, the market shares of the current competitors in each segment, and their current capabilities, objectives, and strategies. Evidently each product/market segment would pose different entry barriers, however attractive the segment is.

IDENTIFYING THE COMPETITORS' STRATEGIES

There is a close relationship between who the company's competitors are and the strategies that other firms are pursuing. *The more that one firm's strategy resembles another firm's strategy, the more they compete.* In most industries, the competitors can be sorted into groups that pursue different strategies. A *strategic group* is *a group of firms in an industry following the same or a similar strategy along key dimensions.*[5]

To illustrate, suppose a company wants to enter the major appliance industry and identify the key strategic groups. Suppose the company determines that two important strategic dimensions of this industry are *quality image* and *vertical integration*. It develops the chart shown in Figure 8-3 and discovers that there are four strategic groups. Strategic group A consists of one competitor, Maytag. Strategic group B consists of three major competitors, General Electric, Whirlpool, and Sears. Strategic group C consists of four other firms, and strategic group D consists of two firms.

Some important insights emerge from this strategic group identification. First, the height of the entry barriers differ for each strategic group. A new company would find it easiest to enter Group D because it requires minimal investment in vertical integration and in quality components and reputation. Conversely, the company would find it hardest to enter Group A or Group B. Second, if the company successfully enters one of the groups, the members of that group become its key competitors. Thus if the company enters Group B, it will need strength primarily against General Electric, Whirlpool, and Sears. It would need to enter with some additional strategic advantages if it hopes to

FIGURE 8-3
Strategic Groups in the Major Appliance Industry

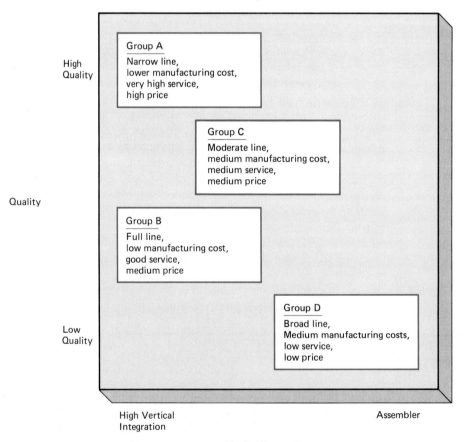

TABLE 8-1 Comparison of Strategic Profiles of Texas Instruments and Hewlett-Packard

	Texas Instruments	Hewlett-Packard
Business strategy	Competitive advantage in large standard markets based on long-run cost position	Competitive advantage in selected small markets based on unique, high-value products
Marketing	High volume/low price Rapid growth	High value/high price Controlled growth
Manufacturing	Experience curve cost driven Vertical integration	Delivery and quality Limited vertical integration
R&D	Design to cost	Features and quality Design to performance
Financial	Aggressive Full utilization	Conservative No debt
Human resources	Competitive Individual incentives	Cooperative Companywide incentives

succeed. One reason is that the members of a strategic group typically attract the same target customers insofar as they present the same appeals to the market.

Although competition is most intense within a strategic group, there is also rivalry among the groups as well. In the first place, some of the strategic groups may appeal to overlapping customer groups. For example, major appliance manufacturers with different strategies will nevertheless all go after apartment home builders. In the second place, the customers may not see much difference in all the offers. In the third place, each group might want to expand its market scope, especially if they are all fairly equal in size and power and the mobility barriers between groups are low.

Figure 8-3 used only two dimensions to identify strategic groups within the industry. Other dimensions would include level of technological sophistication, geographical scope, manufacturing methods, and so on. In fact, each competitor would need to be more fully profiled than two dimensions alone would suggest. Table 8-1 contrasts two major electronics firms, Texas Instruments and Hewlett-Packard, in greater depth. Clearly, each has a different strategic makeup and therefore appeals to somewhat different customer segments. The company has to collect even more detailed information about each competitor. It needs to know each competitor's product quality, features, and mix; customer services; pricing policy; distribution coverage; sales-force strategy; and advertising and sales promotion programs. The same applies to the details of each competitor's R&D, manufacturing, purchasing, financial, and other strategies.

DETERMINING THE COMPETITORS' OBJECTIVES

Having identified the main competitors and their strategies, we must ask, What is each competitor seeking in the marketplace? What drives each competitor's behavior?

A useful initial assumption is that competitors will strive to maximize their profits and choose their actions accordingly. Even here, companies differ in the weights they put on short-term versus long-term profits. It might even be said that some companies orient their thinking around "satisficing" rather than "maximizing." They have target profit goals and are satisfied in achieving them, even if more profits could have been produced by other strategies and exertions.

An alternative assumption is that each competitor has a mix of objectives with different weights. We would want to know the relative weights that a competitor places on current profitability, market-share growth, cash flow, technological leadership, service leadership, and so on. Knowing a competitor's weighted mix of objectives allows us to know whether the competitor is satisfied with its current financial results, how it might react to different types of competitive attack, and so on. For example, a competitor that pursues low-cost leadership will react much more strongly to a manufacturing process breakthrough by another competitor than to an advertising step-up by the same competitor.

That competitors' goals can differ sharply is well illustrated by contrasting U.S. and Japanese firms:

> U.S. firms operate largely on a short-run profit maximization model, largely because their current performance is judged by stockholders who might lose confidence, sell their stock, and cause the company's cost of capital to rise. Japanese firms operate largely on a market-share maximization model. They need to provide employment for more than 100 million people in a resource-poor country. Japanese firms have lower profit requirements because most of the capital comes from banks that seek regular interest payments rather than high returns at somewhat higher risks. As a result, Japanese firms can charge lower prices and show more patience in building and penetrating markets. Thus competitors who are satisfied with lower profits have an advantage over their opponents.

A competitor's objectives are shaped by many things, including its size, history, current management, and economics. If the competitor is part of a larger company, we would like to know whether it is being run for growth or cash or being milked by the parent firm. If the business unit is not central to the parent's enterprise (for example, if it is a dumping ground for excess capacity or is used to exploit distribution channels), we could

FIGURE 8-4
Market Battlefield Map for Microcomputers
SOURCE: Rothschild, *How to Gain (and Maintain) the Competitive Advantage*, p. 72.

	Domestic	Quasi-International	Multinational Corporations
Specialist			IBM DEC
Quasi-Specialist			Honeywell Fujitsu
Multi-Industry	Zenith		Sperry Hitachi Siemens Toshiba

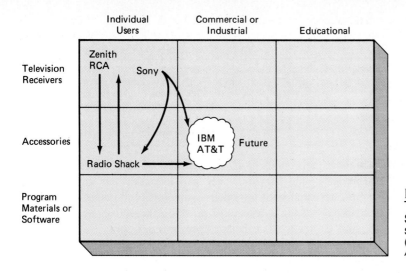

FIGURE 8-5
The Changing Television
Scene
SOURCE: Rothschild, *How to Gain
(and Maintain) the Competitive
Advantage*, p. 23.

attack it more successfully than if it were the centerpiece in the competitor's empire. Rothschild contends that the worst competitor to attack is the competitor for whom this is the only or major business and that has a global operation.[6] This is illustrated in the market battlefield map in Figure 8-4. It would make no sense to attack IBM in the microcomputer business because it is a multinational specialist; but attacking Zenith would make sense because computers are only one of the company's businesses and Zenith operates only domestically.

A company must also monitor its competitors' objectives with respect to attacking new product/market segments. Figure 8-5 shows a product/market battlefield map for the television industry. It shows the present locations of major competitors as well as their likely moves into other segments. The evidence indicates, among other things, that Zenith will be moving into television accessories for individual users, and that Radio Shack will move its accessories business into the commercial market. The incumbents in these segments are therefore forewarned and, it is hoped, forearmed.

ASSESSING THE COMPETITORS' STRENGTHS AND WEAKNESSES

Can the various competitors carry out their strategies and reach their goals? This depends on each competitor's resources and capabilities. The company needs to identify each competitor's strengths and weaknesses accurately.

As a first step, a company needs to gather key data on each competitor's business over the past few years. The main variables are (1) *sales*, (2) *market share*, (3) *profit margin*, (4) *return on investment*, (5) *cash flow*, (6) *new investment*, and (7) *capacity utilization*. Admittedly, some of this information will be hard to collect. For example, industrial goods companies find it hard to estimate competitors' market shares because they do not have the same syndicated data services that are available to consumer packaged goods companies (such as Nielsen). Nevertheless, any information they can find will help them form a better estimate of each competitor's strengths and weaknesses. This kind of information helped a company decide who to challenge in the programmable controls market:

> A company recently made a decision to enter the programmable controls market. It knew it would face three entrenched competitors, namely, Allen Bradley, Texas Instruments, and Gould. Its research showed that Allen Bradley enjoyed an excellent reputation in the industry for technological leadership; Texas Instruments enjoyed low costs and engaged in bloody battles for market share; and Gould did a good job but not a particularly distinguished job. The company concluded that its best target was Gould.

Companies normally learn about their competitors' strengths and weaknesses through secondary data, personal experience, and hearsay. They can increase their knowledge by conducting primary marketing research with customers, suppliers, and dealers. Table 8-2 shows the results of a company's hiring a research firm that asked customers to rate its three competitors, A, B, and C, on five attributes. Competitor A turns out to be well known and is viewed as producing high-quality products that are sold by a good sales force. However, competitor A is poor in providing product availability and technical assistance. Competitor B is good across the board and excellent in product availability and sales force. Competitor C rates poor to fair on most attributes. This information suggests that our company could attack competitor A on product availability and technical assistance, and competitor C on almost anything, but competitor B has no outstanding weakness.

The research findings summarized in Table 8-2 would, in fact, be more comprehensive. First, the company itself must be included in the competitor ratings. The management in one company was shocked when it learned that customers rated it in the bottom third of competitors on most attributes. Second, the cell ratings would show more details. Obviously, not every buyer thought that competitor B had good quality; this is an average perception. Behind it might lie the finding that 20 percent said excellent, 40 percent said good, 30 percent said fair, and 10 percent said poor. It would be interesting to know what customer types did not share the general view of competitor B's product quality. Third, customers should also rate additional variables not shown, such as price, management quality, and manufacturing capability.

There are additional marketing variables that should be competitively tracked, such as:

■ *Share of market.* A measure of the sales share that the competitor has of relevant market.
■ *Share of mind.* A measure of the percentage of customers who named the competitor in answering the question, "Name the first company that comes to mind in this industry."
■ *Share of heart.* A measure of the percentage of customers who named the competitor in answering the question, "Name the company from whom you would prefer to buy the product."

TABLE 8-2   Customers' Ratings of Competitors on Key Success Factors

	Customer Awareness	Product Quality	Product Availability	Technical Assistance	Selling Staff
A	E	E	P	P	G
B	G	G	E	G	E
C	F	P	G	F	F

Note: E = excellent, G = good, F = fair, P = poor.

TABLE 8-3 Market Share, Mind Share, and Heart Share

	Market Share			Mind Share			Heart Share		
	1985	1986	1987	1985	1986	1987	1985	1986	1987
A	50%	47%	44%	60%	58%	54%	45%	42%	39%
B	30%	34%	37%	30%	31%	35%	44%	47%	53%
C	20%	19%	19%	10%	11%	11%	11%	11%	8%

There is an interesting relationship among these three measures. Table 8-3 shows these numbers for the same three competitors listed in Table 8-2. Competitor A enjoys the highest market share, but it is falling. A partial explanation is provided by the fact that its mind share and its heart share are also falling. This slip in customer awareness and preference is probably because competitor A, although providing a good product, is not providing good product availability and technical assistance. Competitor B, on the other hand, is steadily gaining in market share, and this is probably due to strategies that are increasing its mind share and heart share. Competitor C seems to be stuck at a low level of market share, mind share, and heart share, given its poor product and marketing attributes. We could generalize as follows: *Companies that make steady gains in mind share and heart share will inevitably make gains in market share and profitability.* What is important, then, is not whether the company made high or low profits in a particular year (so many factors could affect this), but *whether the company has been steadily building up customer awareness and customer preference.*

Among the other measures that a company should track about its competitors are their financial strengths and weaknesses. The financial situation of a competitor is revealed by examining five key ratios:[7]

1. *Liquidity ratio.* This indicates whether the competitor can meet short-term financial obligations without much of a problem when they fall due.
2. *Leverage-capital structure ratio.* This indicates whether the competitor has the ability to fulfill its long-term commitments to its debtholders. This could be a problem for the competitor if its capital structure has too much long-term debt in relation to its shareholders' equity.
3. *Profitability ratio.* This indicates whether the competitor is generating a reasonable level of profits. It can be tracked by such measures as return on total assets, return on equity, or profit margin.
4. *Turnover ratio.* This indicates whether the competitor is utilizing its assets efficiently. It is measured by dividing its sales by its average assets during the period. A low turnover would dampen the profitability ratio.
5. *Common-stock security ratio.* This tells us whether the stock market has high or low confidence in the company. It is measured by movements in earnings per share or market-to-book value.

The profitability and turnover ratios can be combined in a chart that shows the financial profile of the key competitors—specifically, how much money is coming from operating margin versus asset turnover. (See Exhibit 8-2.)

Finally, in searching for competitors' weaknesses, we should try to identify any assumptions they make about their business and the market that are no longer valid. Some companies believe they produce the best quality in the industry when this is no longer true. Many companies are victims of conventional wisdom such as "Customers prefer full-line companies," "The sales force is the only important marketing tool," "Customers

EXHIBIT 8-2

Du Pont Profitability Chart

A company's return on operating assets (ROA) is a function of its *operating margin* and its *operating asset turnover*. It is possible for companies to earn the same ROA in vastly different ways. The accompanying figure shows three competitors, A, B, and C, and their ROAs. Competitors A and B both earn a 20 percent ROA, but in quite different ways. Competitor A earns it through a low margin but a high turnover; competitor B earns it through a high margin and a low turnover. Competitor C turns over its assets at approximately the same rate as competitor A but has a much lower margin, thereby achieving only a 10 percent ROA. The industry as a whole averages 15 percent, consisting of a 15 percent margin and an asset turnover of 1.00.

A company will naturally want to increase its margin and/or its turnover in order to increase its ROA. The accompanying figure shows competitor C as hoping to move to C' (a higher ROA) through increasing its operating margin by more than the decline in its asset turnover.

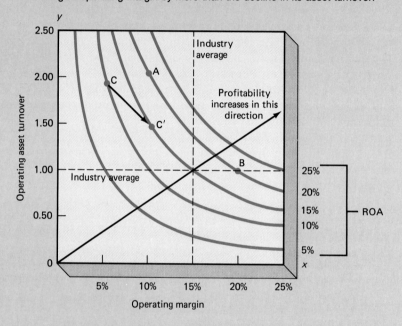

SOURCE: Adapted from William L. Sammon, Mark A. Kurland, and Robert Spitalnic, *Business Competitor Intelligence* (New York: John Wiley, 1984).

value service more than price.'' If we know that a competitor is operating on a major wrong assumption, we can take advantage of it.

ESTIMATING THE COMPETITORS' REACTION PATTERNS

A competitor's objectives and strengths/weaknesses go a long way toward explaining its likely moves, and reactions to company moves such as a price cut, a promotion step-up, or a new-product introduction. In addition, each competitor has a certain philosophy of doing business, a certain internal culture, and certain guiding beliefs. One needs a deep understanding of a given competitor's mentality to have hope of anticipating how the competitor may react or proact.

Here are some common reaction profiles found among competitors:

1. *The laid-back competitor.* Some competitors do not react quickly or strongly to a given competitor move. They may feel that their customers are loyal; they may be harvesting the business; they may be slow in noticing the initiative; they may lack the funds to react. The firm must try to assess the reasons for the competitors' laid-back behavior.

2. *The selective competitor.* A competitor might react to only certain types of assaults and not others. It might always respond to price cuts in order to signal that these are futile. But it might not respond to advertising expenditure increases, believing these to be less threatening. Knowing what a key competitor reacts to gives the company a clue as to the most feasible types of attack.

3. *The tiger competitor.* This company reacts swiftly and strongly to any assault on its terrain. Thus P&G does not let a new detergent come easily into the market. A tiger competitor is signaling that another firm had better avoid any attack because the defender is going to fight to the finish if attacked. It is always better to attack a sheep than a tiger.

4. *The stochastic competitor.* Some competitors do not exhibit a predictable reaction pattern. Such a competitor might or might not retaliate on any particular occasion, and there is no way to foresee what it will do based on its economics, history, or anything else.

Some industries are characterized by relative accord among the competitors and others by constant fighting. Bruce Henderson, founder of the Boston Consulting Group, thinks that much depends on the industry's "competitive equilibrium." Here are some of his observations about the likely state of competitive relations:[8]

1. *If competitors are nearly identical and make their living in the same way, then their competitive equilibrium is unstable.*
   There is likely to be perpetual conflict in industries where competitive ability is at parity. This would describe "commodity industries" where sellers have not found any major way to differentiate their costs or their offers. In such cases, the competitive equilibrium would be upset if any firm lowers its price. This is a strong temptation, especially for a competitor with overcapacity. This explains why price wars frequently break out in these industries.

2. *If a single major factor is the critical factor, then competitive equilibrium is unstable.*
   This would describe industries where cost differentiation opportunities exist through economies of scale, advanced technology, experience curve learning, etc. In such industries, any company that achieves a cost breakthrough can cut its price and win market share at the expense of other firms who could only defend their market shares at great cost. Price wars frequently break out in these industries as a function of cost breakthroughs.

3. *If multiple factors may be critical factors, then it is possible for each competitor to have some advantage and be differentially attractive to some customers. The more the multiple factors that may provide an advantage, the more the number of competitors who can coexist. Each competitor has his competitive segment defined by the preference for the factor trade-offs that he offers.*
   This would describe industries where many opportunities exist for differentiating quality, service, convenience, and so on. If customers also place different values on these factors, then many firms can coexist through niching.

4. *The fewer the number of competitive variables that are critical, the fewer the number of competitors.*
   If only one factor is critical, then no more than two or three competitors are likely to coexist. Conversely, the larger the number of competitive variables, the larger the number of competitors, but each is likely to be smaller in its absolute size.

5. *A ratio of 2 to 1 in market share between any two competitors seems to be the equilibrium point at which it is neither practical nor advantageous for either competitor to increase or decrease share.*

On the basis of this, Henderson proposed three rules for dealing with competitors:

1. Be sure that your rival is fully aware of what he can gain if he cooperates and what it will cost him if he does not.
2. Avoid any action which will arouse your competitor's emotions, since it is essential that he behave in a logical, reasonable fashion.
3. Convince your opponent that you are emotionally dedicated to your position and are completely convinced that it is reasonable.

DESIGNING THE COMPETITIVE INTELLIGENCE SYSTEM

We have described the main types of information that company decision makers need to know about their competitors. This information must be collected, interpreted, disseminated, and used. While the cost in money and time of gathering competitive intelligence is high, the cost of not gathering it is higher. Yet the company must design its competitive intelligence system in a cost-effective way. There are four main steps:

1. *Setting up the system.* The first step calls for identifying vital types of competitive information, identifying the best sources of this information, and assigning a person who will manage the system and its services.
2. *Collecting the data.* Here the data are collected on a continuous basis from the field (sales force, channels, suppliers, market research firms, trade associations) and from published data (government publications, speeches, articles). The company has to develop effective ways of acquiring needed information about competitors without violating legal or ethical standards (see Exhibit 8-3).
3. *Evaluating and analyzing.* In this step, the data are checked for validity and reliability, interpreted, and organized in an appropriate way.
4. *Disseminating and responding.* Here key information is sent to relevant decision makers, and inquiries from managers about competitors are answered.

EXHIBIT 8-3

Intelligence Gathering: Snooping on Competitors

Competitive intelligence gathering has grown dramatically as more and more companies need to be aware of what their competitors are doing. Such well-known companies as Ford, Westinghouse, General Electric, Gillette, Revlon, Del Monte, General Foods, Kraft, and J. C. Penney are among those that are busy snooping on their competitors.

A recent article in *Fortune* lists over twenty techniques companies use to collect their own intelligence. The techniques fall into four major categories:

Getting Information from Recruits and Competitors' Employees. Companies can obtain intelligence through job interviews or from conversations with competitors' employees. According to *Fortune*:

When they interview students for jobs, some companies pay special attention to those who have worked for competitors, even temporarily. Job seekers are eager to impress and often have not been warned about divulging what is proprietary. They sometimes volunteer valuable information . . . Several companies now send teams of highly trained technicians instead of personnel executives to recruit on campus.

Companies send engineers to conferences and trade shows to question competitors' technical people. Often conversations start innocently—just a few fellow technicians discussing processes and problems . . . [yet competitors'] engineers and scientists often brag about surmounting technical challenges, in the process divulging sensitive information.

Companies sometimes advertise and hold interviews for jobs that don't exist in order to entice competitors' employees to spill the beans. . . . Often applicants have toiled in obscurity or feel that their careers have stalled. They're dying to impress somebody.

In probably the hoariest tactic in corporate intelligence gathering, companies hire key executives from competitors to find out what they know.

Getting Information from People Who Do Business with Competitors. Key customers can keep the company informed about competitors—they might even be willing to request and pass along information on competitors' products. For example, a while back Gillette told a large Canadian account the date on which it planned to begin selling its new Good News disposable razor in the U.S. . . . The Canadian distributor promptly called Bic and told it about the impending product launch. Bic put on a crash program and was able to start selling its razor shortly after Gillette did.

Intelligence can also be gathered by infiltrating customers' business operations:

Companies may provide their engineers free of charge to customers. . . . The close, cooperative relationship that the engineers on loan cultivate with the customer's design staff often enables them to learn what new products competitors are pitching.

Getting Information from Published Materials and Public Documents. Keeping track of seemingly meaningless published information can provide competitor intelligence. For example, the types of people sought in help wanted ads can indicate something about a competitor's technological thrusts and new product development. Government agencies are another good source. For example:

Although it is often illegal for a company to photograph a competitor's plant from the air . . . there are legitimate ways to get the photos. . . . Aerial photos often are on file with the U.S. Geological Survey or Environmental Protection Agency. These are public documents, available for a nominal fee.

Companies can obtain valuable information from government agencies under the Freedom of Information Act, or they can use specialized firms to obtain such information discreetly.

Getting Information by Observing Competitors or Analyzing Physical Evidence. Companies can get to know competitors better by buying their products or examining other physical evidence.

Companies increasingly buy competitors' products and take them apart to . . . determine costs of production and even manufacturing methods.

In the absence of better information on market share and the volume of product that competitors are shipping, companies have measured the rust on rails of railroad sidings to their competitors' plants or have counted the tractor-trailers leaving loading bays.

Some companies even buy their competitors' garbage:

Once it has left the competitor's premises, refuse is legally considered abandoned property. While some companies now shred the paper coming out of their design labs, they often neglect to do this for almost-as-revealing refuse from the marketing or public relations departments.

Though most of these techniques are legal and some might be considered shrewd competitiveness, many involve questionable ethics. The company should take advantage of publicly available information, but responsible companies avoid practices that might be considered illegal or unethical. A company does not have to break the law or violate accepted codes of ethics to get intelligence information, and the benefits gained from using such techniques are not worth the risks.

SOURCE: Based on Steven Flax, "How to Snoop on Your Competitors," *Fortune*, May 14, 1984, pp. 29–33.

TABLE 8-4   Competitor Profile Information

	Competitor A	Competitor B	Competitor C
Descriptors (product line, market segments, sales, market shares, profit margin, ROI, new investment, capacity utilization, etc.)			
Strategies (R&D, manufacturing, marketing, financial, personnel) (Within marketing: products, price, distribution, and promotion strategies)			
Objectives (marketing, financial, etc.)			
Strengths/weaknesses			
Reaction patterns			
Marketing implications			

With this system, company managers will receive timely information about competitors in the form of phone calls, bulletins, newsletters, and reports. In addition, managers can contact the department when they need an interpretation of a sudden move by a competitor, or when they need to know a competitor's weaknesses and strengths or how a competitor will respond to a contemplated company move. The competitive information can be organized in a form similar to that shown in Table 8-4. In fact, this table shows what each manager should know about his or her competitors in each product market.

In smaller companies that cannot afford to set up a formal competitive intelligence office, a useful step would be to assign specific executives to watch specific competitors. Thus a manager who used to work for a competitor would closely follow all developments connected with that competitor; he or she would be the "in-house" expert on that competitor. In this way, any manager who needs to know the thinking of a specific competitor could contact the corresponding in-house expert.

SELECTING COMPETITORS TO ATTACK AND AVOID

Given good competitive intelligence support, managers will find it easier to formulate their competitive strategies. They will have a better sense of whom they can effectively compete with in the market. They have already determined who their major competitors are through their prior decisions on customer targets, distribution channels, and marketing-mix strategy. These decisions determine the strategic group to which they belong.

The manager must now decide which competitor to compete against most vigorously. This manager's choice will be aided by conducting a *customer value analysis*, which will reveal his or her company's strengths and weaknesses relative to various competitors. (Exhibit 8-4 describes the methodology of customer value analysis.) The company can focus its attack on one of several classes of competitors as described below.

Strong vs. Weak Competitors — Most companies prefer to aim their shots at their weak competitors. This requires fewer resources and time per share point gained. But in the process, the firm may achieve little in the way of improved capabilities. The firm should also compete with strong competitors because, by competing with them, the firm will have to keep up

EXHIBIT 8-4

Customer Value Analysis: the Key to Competitive Advantage

In the search for competitive advantage, one of the most important marketing steps that a company can take is to carry out a *customer value analysis*. The aim of a customer value analysis is to determine what benefits the customers in a target market segment want and how they perceive the relative value of competing suppliers' offers. The major steps in customer value analysis are as follows:

1. ***Identify the major attributes that customers value.*** Various people in the company will have their ideas on what customers value. Senior management will say quality and service, salespeople will say price, and so on. Their lists will generally be short and not in full agreement. Therefore it is essential to ask the customers themselves what functions and performance levels they look for in choosing a product and vendors. Different customers will mention different features/benefits. If the list gets overly long, the researcher can remove redundant attributes. Still, the final list of attributes that customers value may run as high as ten or twenty items.

2. ***Assess the customer ratings of the importance of different attributes.*** Here again company personnel will have varying opinions on the importance that customers attach to the different attributes. R&D will see design as important, manufacturing will see cost as important, and sales people will see price as important. But it is the customers who must supply their ratings or rankings of the importance of the different attributes. If the customers diverge much in their ratings, they should be clustered into different customer segments.

3. ***Assess the company's and competitors' performances on different attributes against their rated importance.*** Here the customers are asked where they see each competitor's performance on each attribute. Ideally, the company's own performance should be high on the attributes that customers value most and low on the attributes that customers value least. Two pieces of bad news would be (a) the company's performance ranks high on some minor attributes—a case of "overkill"; (b) the company's performance ranks low on some major attributes—a case of "underkill." The company must also examine how each competitor ranks on the attributes that are important to customers.

4. ***Examine how customers in a specific segment rate the company's performance against a specific major competitor on an attribute-by-attribute basis.*** The key to gaining competitive advantage is to take each customer segment and examine how the company's offer compares with that of its major competitor. If the company's offer exceeds the competitor's offer on all important attributes, the company can charge a higher price, thereby earning higher profits, or it can charge the same price and gain more market share. However, if the company finds that it performs at a lower level on some important attributes than does its major competitor, it must invest in strengthening those attributes or finding other important attributes where it can build even more of a lead on the competitor. Investments can take two forms. If the company's performance is really inferior on an important attribute, it needs to improve it in real terms. If the company's attribute standing is on par with the competitor's but has not been adequately or persuasively communicated to customers, the company must improve its marketing communication program rather than the attribute.

5. ***Monitor changing customer attributes and importance ratings over time.*** Although customer values are fairly stable in the short run, they will probably change as competing technologies and features become available and as customers face different economic climates. A company that assumes that customer values will remain stable is flirting with danger. The company must periodically redo its studies of customer values and competitors' standings if it wants to be strategically effective.

with the state-of-the-art. Furthermore, even strong competitors have some weaknesses, and the firm may prove to be a worthy competitor.

Close vs. Distant Competitors Most companies will compete with those competitors that resemble them the most. Thus Chevrolet competes more against Ford than against Jaguar. At the same time, the company should avoid trying to "destroy" the close competitor. Porter cites two cases of counterproductive "victories":[9]

Bausch and Lomb in the late 1970s moved aggressively against other soft lens manufacturers with great success. However, this led one after another competitor to sell out to larger firms such as Revlon, Johnson & Johnson, and Schering-Plough, with the result that Bausch and Lomb now faced much larger competitors.

A specialty rubber manufacturer attacked another specialty rubber manufacturer as its mortal enemy and took away share. The damage to the other company allowed the specialty divisions of the large tire companies to move more quickly into specialty rubber markets, using them as a dumping ground for excess capacity.

In each case, the company's success in hurting its closest rival brought in tougher competitors to contend with.

"Good" vs. "Bad" Competitors Porter argues that every industry contains "good" and "bad" competitors.[10] A company would be smart to support the good competitors and attack the bad competitors.

Good competitors have a number of characteristics: They play by the rules of the industry, they make realistic assumptions about the industry's growth potential, they set prices in a reasonable relation to costs, they favor a healthy industry, they limit themselves to a portion or segment of the industry, they motivate others to lower costs or improve differentiation, and they accept the general location of their share and profits. Bad competitors, on the other hand, violate the rules: They try to buy share rather than earn it, they take large risks, they invest in overcapacity, and in general, they upset the industrial equilibrium. For example, IBM finds Cray Research to be a good competitor because it plays by the rules, sticks to its segment, and does not attack IBM's core markets; but IBM finds Fujitsu to be a bad competitor because it attacks IBM in its core markets with subsidized prices and little differentiation. The implication is that "good" companies in an industry should try to configure an industry that consists of only good competitors. Through careful licensing, selective retaliation, and coalitions, they can shape the industry so that (1) the competitors are not seeking to destroy each other and behave irrationally, (2) they follow the rules, (3) each differentiates somewhat, and (4) they try to earn share rather than buy it.

Behind this is a larger point, that a company really needs and benefits from competitors. The existence of competitors confers such strategic benefits as the following: (1) They lower the antitrust risk, (2) they may increase total demand, (3) they lead to more differentiation, (4) they provide a cost umbrella for the less-efficient producers, (5) they share the cost of market development and legitimize a new technology, (6) they improve bargaining power versus labor or regulators, and (7) they may serve less-attractive segments.

BALANCING CUSTOMER AND COMPETITOR ORIENTATIONS

We have stressed the importance of a company watching its competitors closely. The question now arises, Is it possible to spend too much time and energy tracking competitors, to the detriment of a customer orientation? The answer is yes! A company can become so competitor-centered that it loses even its more important customer focus.[11]

> Consider the myopia of many mid-to-up-market hotel chains fighting each other and trying to figure out each other's moves while their customers went about searching for cheaper accommodations. These hotels not only missed the consumer yearnings but also missed the new emerging competitors by focusing only or predominantly on existing major competitors.

A *competitor-centered company* is one whose moves are basically dictated by competitors' actions and reactions. The company spends a great deal of time tracking competitors' moves and market shares on a market-by-market basis. It sets its course based on data such as the following:

COMPETITOR-CENTERED COMPANY

Situation

- ▪ Competitor W is going all out to crush us in Miami.
- ▪ Competitor X is improving its distribution coverage in Houston and hurting our sales.
- ▪ Competitor Y has cut its price in Denver and we lost three share points.
- ▪ Competitor Z has introduced a new service feature in New Orleans and our customers are starting to switch their business to this competitor.

Solutions

- ▪ We will withdraw from the Miami market because we cannot afford to fight this battle.
- ▪ We will increase our advertising expenditure level in Houston.
- ▪ We will meet competitor Y's price cut in Denver.
- ▪ We will increase our sales promotion budget in New Orleans.

Now this mode of strategy planning has some pluses and minuses. On the positive side, the company develops a fighter orientation. It trains its marketers to be on a constant alert, watching for weaknesses in its own position, and watching for competitors' weaknesses. On the negative side, the company exhibits too much of a reactive pattern. Rather than carrying out a consistent customer-oriented strategy, it determines its moves based on its competitors' moves. As a result, it does not move in a predetermined direction toward a goal. It does not know where it will end up, since so much depends on what the competitors decide to do.

A *customer-centered company*, in contrast, would focus more on customer developments in formulating its strategies. It would pay more attention to the following types of data:

CUSTOMER-CENTERED COMPANY

Situation

- ▪ The total market is growing at 4 percent annually.
- ▪ The fastest-growing segment is the quality-sensitive segment; it is growing at 8 percent annually.
- ▪ The deal-prone customer segment is also growing, but these customers do not stay with any supplier very long.
- ▪ A growing number of customers have expressed an interest in a twenty-four-hour hotline, which no one in the industry offers.

Solutions

- ▪ We will focus more effort on reaching and satisfying the quality segment of the market; our plan will be to buy better components, improve our quality control, and shift our advertising theme to quality.
- ▪ We will avoid cutting prices and making deals because we do not want the kind of customer that buys this way.
- ▪ We will investigate the costs and share-gain potential of a twenty-four-hour hotline and install it if it looks promising.

Competitor-centered \ Customer-centered	No	Yes
No	Product orientation	Customer orientation
Yes	Competitor orientation	Market orientation

FIGURE 8-6
Shifting Company Orientations

Clearly, the customer-centered company is in a better position to identify new opportunities and set a strategy course that makes long-run sense. By watching customer needs evolve, it can decide what customer groups and what emerging needs are the most important to serve, given its resources and objectives.

In practice, today's companies must watch both their customers and their competitors. The caution is that they must not let competitor watching blind them to customer focusing. Figure 8-6 shows that companies have moved through four orientations over the years. In the first stage, companies paid little attention to either customers or competitors; they were *product-oriented*. In the second stage, they started to pay attention to customers; they were *customer-oriented*. In the third stage, they started to pay attention to competitors; they became *competitor-oriented*. In today's stage, they need to pay balanced attention to both, which we call practicing a *market orientation*.

SUMMARY

To prepare an effective marketing strategy, a company must consider its competitors as well as its actual and potential customers. This is especially necessary in slow-growth markets because sales can only be gained by winning them away from competitors.

A company's competitors include those seeking to satisfy the same customers and customer needs and making similar offers to them. A company, however, should also pay attention to its latent competitors who may offer new or other ways to satisfy the same needs. The company should try to identify its competitors by using both an industry and a market-based analysis.

The company needs to gather information on competitors' strategies, objectives, strengths/weaknesses, and reaction patterns. The company needs to know each competitor's strategies in order to identify its closest competitors and take the proper steps. The company should know the competitor's objectives in order to anticipate further moves and reactions. Knowing the competitors' strengths and weaknesses will permit the company to refine its own strategy to take advantage of the competitor limitations while avoiding engagement where the competitor is strong. Knowing the competitor's typical reaction pattern helps the company choose and time its moves.

Competitive intelligence needs to be collected, interpreted, and disseminated continuously. Company marketing executives should be able to obtain full and reliable information about any competitor that has a bearing on a decision.

As important as a competitive orientation is in today's markets, companies should not overdo their focus on competitors. Companies are more likely to be hurt by emerging consumer needs and latent competitors than by their existing competitors. Companies that manage to factor in a good balance of consumer and competitor considerations are practicing a true market orientation.

◼ QUESTIONS

1. Discuss the four levels of competition for Pepsi based on a broadening of the concept of product substitution.
2. Contrast the industry and market concept of competition for the category "lawn care." Design and discuss a product/market battlefield map for this category.
3. Mobility barriers are factors that protect members of a strategic group from incursion by firms outside the group. What are some sources of mobility barriers? That is, what factors can deter movement between strategic groups in an industry by making such movement costly for invading firms?
4. Why is the concept of strategic groups useful to marketing strategists?
5. Set up a chart similar to Table 8-2 which compares the obstetrics/maternity programs for three competing hospitals. (a) How would you arrive at the appropriate dimensions for comparison? (b) How would you determine each hospital's ratings on those dimensions? (c) Which hospital has a competitive advantage? (d) Devise a strategy to capitalize on the advantage that you have indicated exists.
6. Competition in the pasta market is primarily on a regional instead of a national basis. What explanation would you give for this phenomenon? If you were a marketing manager for one of these pasta companies, what would you do to try to make your brand nationally dominant?
7. Despite being the first entrant in the home videocassette recorder market, having several technological advantages, and having an overall cost/benefit advantage, Sony's Beta format is no longer a major force in the market. What happened? Use relevant concepts of competition discussed in this chapter in your analysis.
8. Listed below are several company strengths as might be seen by a manager conducting an internal audit. How might these strengths be translated into customer benefits which would give the company a competitive advantage?
   a. Innovative product features
   b. Broad distribution
   c. Lower costs and prices
   d. Broad product line
   e. Strong technical service
9. A headline for an article in *Business Week* read "Forget Satisfying the Consumer—Just Outfox the Other Guy." Debate the merits of this advice.

◼ FOOTNOTES

1. See Al Ries and Jack Trout, *Marketing Warfare* (New York: McGraw-Hill, 1986); William L. Sammon, Mark A. Kurland, and Robert Spitalnic, *Business Competitor Intelligence* (New York: Ronald Press, 1984); and Leonard M. Fuld, *Competitor Intelligence: How to Get It—How to Use It* (New York: John Wiley, 1985).
2. See Kathryn Rudie Harrigan, "The Effect of Exit Barriers upon Strategic Flexibility," *Strategic Management Journal*, I (1980), 165–76.
3. See Michael E. Porter, *Competitive Advantage* (New York: Free Press, 1985), pp. 225, 485.
4. See Michael E. Porter, *Competitive Strategy* (New York: Free Press, 1980), Chap. 13.
5. George Foster, *Financial Statement Analysis* (Englewood Cliffs, N.J.: Prentice-Hall, 1986).
6. William E. Rothschild, *How to Gain (and Maintain) the Competitive Advantage* (New York: McGraw-Hill, 1984), Chap. 5.
7. Porter, *Competitive Strategy*, Chap. 7.
8. The following list has been drawn from various Bruce Henderson writings, including "The Unanswered Questions, The Unsolved Problems" (Unpublished paper delivered in a speech at Northwestern University in 1986); *Henderson on Corporate Strategy* (New York: Mentor, 1982); and "Understanding the Forces of Strategic and Natural Competition," *Journal of Business Strategy*, Winter 1981, pp. 11–15.
9. Porter, *Competitive Advantage*, pp. 226–27.
10. Ibid., Chap 6.
11. See Alfred R. Oxenfeldt and William L. Moore, "Customer or Competitor: Which Guidelines for Marketing?" *Management Review*, August 1978, pp. 43–48.

9

Measuring and Forecasting Markets

Forecasting is hard, particularly of the future.

Anonymous

Forecasting is like trying to drive a car blindfolded and following directions given by a person who is looking out of the back window.

Anonymous

Having examined the tools for analyzing customer markets and competitive forces, we are now ready to consider how the company can choose *attractive markets* and develop *winning strategies* for operating in these markets. Some companies face a large number of market opportunities and they need to evaluate and compare them before making market choices.

In examining the criteria for market attractiveness in Chapter 2, page 40–41, we saw that two definitive criteria are *market size* and *market growth*. Clearly, companies want to enter and/or stay in markets of sufficient size and growth, at least sufficient in relation to the company's size and growth objectives. Therefore marketing managers need to know how to estimate market size and growth. Such questions arise as: How large is the total market? How large is the target market? How large are different geographical and customer segments? What will the market size be in the next several years? How well is the company doing in relation to its sales potential? Market measurement and forecasting skills are an essential requirement for formulating marketing objectives and plans.

The first part of this chapter will look at major concepts in demand measurement. The second and third parts will describe major methods for estimating current demand and future demand, respectively.

MAJOR CONCEPTS IN DEMAND MEASUREMENT

Managers need to define carefully what they mean by market demand. We will present several distinctions that will help managers talk more precisely about market demand.

A Multitude of Measures of Market Demand

As part of their ongoing planning, companies prepare a great number of market-size estimates. Figure 9-1 shows *ninety* different types of demand estimates that a company can make. Demand can be measured for six different *product levels* (product item, product form, product line, company sales, industry sales, national sales); five different *space levels* (customer, territory, region, U.S.A., world); and three different *time levels* (short-range, medium-range, and long-range).

Each type of demand measurement serves a specific purpose. Thus a company might make a short-range forecast of the total demand for a particular product item to provide a basis for ordering raw materials, planning production, and scheduling short-run financing. Or it might make a long-range forecast of regional demand for its major product line to provide a basis for considering market expansion.

Which Market to Measure?

Marketers talk about *potential markets*, *available markets*, *served markets*, and *penetrated markets*. To clarify these terms, let us start with the notion that a *market* is *the set of all actual and potential buyers of a product*. The *size* of a market then hinges on the number of buyers who might exist for a particular market offer. Those who are in the market would have three characteristics: *interest*, *income*, and *access*.

Let us apply this to the market for motorcycles. We will ignore companies that purchase motorcycles and concentrate on the consumer market. We must first estimate the number of consumers who have a potential *interest* in owning a motorcycle. To do this, we could contact a random sample of consumers and pose the following question: "Would you have a strong interest in owning a motorcycle?" If one person out of ten says yes, we can assume that 10 percent of the total number of consumers would constitute the potential market for motorcycles. The *potential market* is the set of consumers who profess some level of interest in a defined market offer.

Consumer interest is not enough to define a market. Potential consumers must have enough *income* to afford the product. They must be able to answer the following question positively: "Can you afford to purchase a motorcycle?" The higher the price, the fewer the number of people who can answer this question positively. The size of a market is a function of both interest and income.

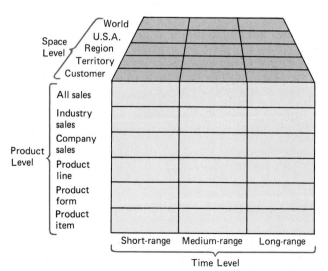

FIGURE 9-1
Ninety Types of Demand
Measurement (6 × 5 × 3)

Access barriers further reduce market size. If motorcycles are not distributed in a certain area because they are too costly to ship in, potential consumers in that area are not available to marketers. The *available market* is the set of consumers who have interest, income, and access to a particular market offer.

For some market offers, the company may restrict sales to certain groups. A particular state might ban the sale of motorcycles to anyone under twenty-one years of age. The remaining adults constitute the *qualified available market*—the set of consumers who have interest, income, access, and qualifications for the particular market offer.

The company now has the choice of going after the whole qualified available market or concentrating on certain segments. The *served market* (also called the *target market*) is the part of the qualified available market the company decides to pursue. The company, for example, may decide to concentrate its marketing and distribution effort on the East Coast. The East Coast becomes its served market.

The company and its competitors will end up selling a certain number of motorcycles in its served market. The *penetrated market* is the set of consumers who have already bought the product.

Figure 9-2 brings the preceding concepts together with some hypothetical numbers. The bar on the left of the figure illustrates the ratio of the potential market—all interested persons—to the total population, here 10 percent. The bar on the right illustrates several breakdowns of the potential market. The available market—those who have interest, income, and access—is 40 percent of the potential market. The qualified available market—those who can meet the legal requirements—is 20 percent of the potential market (or 50 percent of the available market). The company is concentrating its efforts on 10 percent of the potential market (or 50 percent of the qualified available market). Finally, the company and its competitors have already penetrated 5 percent of the potential market (or 50 percent of the served market).

These definitions of a market are a useful tool for marketing planning. If the company is not satisfied with current sales, it can consider a number of actions. It can try to attract a larger percentage of buyers from its served market. It can lower the qualifications of

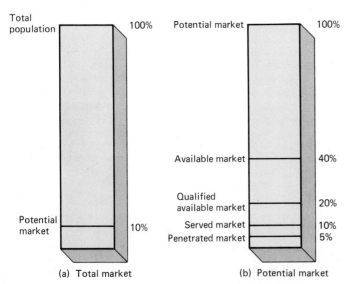

Total population

100%

Potential market

10%

(a) Total market

Potential market

100%

Available market 40%

Qualified available market 20%

Served market 10%

Penetrated market 5%

(b) Potential market

FIGURE 9-2
Levels of Market Definition

potential buyers. It can expand to other available markets, such as the West Coast. It can lower its price to expand the size of the available market. Ultimately, the company can try to expand the potential market by a major advertising campaign to convert noninterested consumers into interested consumers. This is what Honda did when it ran its successful campaign on the theme "You meet the nicest people on a Honda."

A Vocabulary for Demand Management

The field of demand measurement is filled with a confusing number of terms. Company executives talk of forecasts, predictions, potentials, estimates, projections, goals, targets, quotas, and budgets. Many of these terms are redundant. The major concepts in demand measurement are *market demand* and *company demand*. Within each, we distinguish between a *demand function*, a *forecast*, and a *potential*.

Market Demand

In evaluating marketing opportunities, the first step is to estimate total market demand. It is not a simple concept, however, as the following definition makes clear:

> *Market demand* for a *product* is the *total volume* that would be *bought* by a defined *customer group* in a defined *geographical area* in a defined *time period* in a defined *marketing environment* under a defined *marketing program*.

There are eight elements in this definition:

- **Product.** Market demand measurement requires defining the scope of the product class. A tin-can manufacturer has to define whether its market is all metal-can users or all container users. It depends on how the manufacturer views its opportunities for penetrating adjacent markets.
- **Total volume.** Market demand can be measured in terms of physical volume, dollar volume, or relative volume. The U.S. market demand for automobiles may be described as 10 million cars or $100 billion. The market demand for automobiles in the Greater Chicago area can be expressed as 3 percent of the nation's total demand.
- **Bought.** In measuring market demand, it is important to define whether "bought" means the volume ordered, shipped, paid for, received, or consumed. For example, a forecast of new housing for the next year usually means the number of units that will be ordered, not the number that will be completed (called housing starts).
- **Customer group.** Market demand may be measured for the whole market or for any segment(s). Thus a steel producer may make separate estimates of the volume to be bought by the construction industry and by the transportation industry.
- **Geographical area.** Market demand should be measured with reference to well-defined geographical boundaries. A forecast of next year's passenger automobile sales will vary depending on whether the boundaries are limited to the United States or include Canada and/or Mexico.
- **Time period.** Market demand should be measured with reference to a stated period of time. One can talk about the market demand for the next calendar year, for the coming five years, or for the year 2000. The longer the forecasting interval, the more tenuous the forecast. Every forecast is based on a set of assumptions about environmental and marketing conditions, and the chance that some of these assumptions will not be fulfilled increases with the length of the forecast period.
- **Marketing environment.** Market demand is affected by a host of uncontrollable factors. Every forecast of demand should explicitly list the assumptions made about the demographic, economic, technological, political, and cultural environment. Demographic and economic forecasting are well developed, technological forecasting is coming into its own, but political and cultural forecasting are still in their infancy. Much interest in the whole subject of predicting future environments is being stimulated by futurists. At the same time, Levitt has cautioned:

"The easiest kind of expert to be is the specialist who predicts the future. It takes only two things: imagination and a good command of the active verb."[1]

■ *Marketing program.* Market demand is also affected by controllable factors, particularly marketing programs developed by the sellers. Demand in most markets will show some elasticity with respect to industry price, promotion, product improvements, and distribution effort. Thus a market demand forecast requires assumptions about future industry prices, product features, and marketing expenditures.

The most important thing to realize about total market demand is that it is not a fixed number but a function. For this reason it is also called the *market demand function* or *market response function*. The dependence of total market demand on these conditions is illustrated in Figure 9-3(a). The horizontal axis shows different possible levels of industry marketing expenditure in a given time period. The vertical axis shows the resulting demand level. The curve represents the estimated level of market demand associated with varying levels of industry marketing expenditure. Some base sales (called the *market minimum*) would take place without any demand-stimulating expenditures. Higher levels of industry marketing expenditures would yield higher levels of demand, first at an increasing rate, then at a decreasing rate. Marketing expenditures beyond a certain level would not stimulate much further demand, thus suggesting an upper limit to market demand called the *market potential*.

The distance between the market minimum and the market potential shows the overall *marketing sensitivity of demand.* We can think of two extreme types of markets, the *expansible* and the *nonexpansible*. An expansible market, such as the market for racquetball, is quite affected in its total size by the level of industry-marketing expenditures. In terms of Figure 9-3(a), the distance between Q_1 and Q_2 is relatively large. A nonexpansible market, such as the market for opera, is not much affected by the level of marketing expenditures; the distance between Q_1 and Q_2 is relatively small. Organizations selling in a nonexpansible market can accept the market's size (the level of *primary demand*) and direct their marketing resources to winning a desired market share (the level of *selective demand*).

It is important to emphasize that the *market demand function* is *not* a picture of market demand over *time*. Rather, the curve shows alternative current forecasts of market

FIGURE 9-3
Market Demand

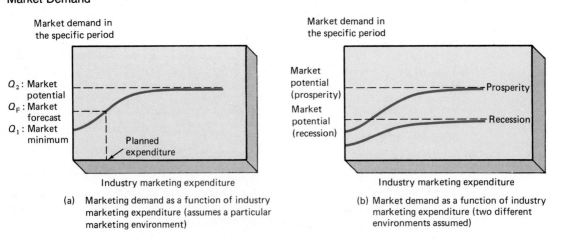

(a) Marketing demand as a function of industry marketing expenditure (assumes a particular marketing environment)

(b) Market demand as a function of industry marketing expenditure (two different environments assumed)

demand associated with alternative possible levels of industry marketing effort in the current period.

Market Forecast Only one level of industry marketing expenditure will actually occur. The market demand corresponding to this level is called the *market forecast*.

Market Potential The market forecast shows expected market demand, not maximum market demand. For the latter, we have to visualize the level of market demand for a very ''high'' level of industry marketing expenditure, where further increases in marketing effort would have little effect in stimulating further demand. *Market potential is the limit approached by market demand as industry marketing expenditures approach infinity, for a given environment.*

The phrase ''for a given environment'' is crucial in the concept of market potential. Consider the market potential for automobiles in a period of recession versus a period of prosperity. The market potential is higher during prosperity. In other words, market demand is income-elastic. The dependence of market potential on the environment is illustrated in Figure 9-3(b). Thus the analyst distinguishes between the position of the market demand function and movement along it. Companies cannot do anything about the position of the market demand function; that is determined by the marketing environment. However, companies influence their particular location on the function when they decide how much to spend on marketing.

Company Demand We are now ready to define company demand. *Company demand* is the company's *share of market demand*. In symbols:

$$Q_i = s_i Q \qquad (9\text{-}1)$$

where:

Q_i = company i's demand
s_i = company i's market share
Q = total market demand

Company demand, like market demand, is a function—called the *company demand function* or *sales-response function*—and is subject to all the determinants of market demand plus the determinants of *company market share*.

But what influences company market share? The most popular theory is that the *market shares* of various competitors will be proportional to their *marketing-effort shares*. This normal expectation can be called *the fundamental theorem of market-share determination* and is expressed:

$$s_i = \frac{M_i}{\Sigma M_i} \qquad (9\text{-}2)$$

where:

M_i = company i's marketing effort

Consider the simple case where two identical firms are selling the same product but spending different amounts on marketing: $60,000 and $40,000, respectively. Using equation (9-2), company one's market share is predicted to be 60 percent:

$$s_i = \frac{\$60,000}{\$60,000 + \$40,000} = 0.60$$

If company one is not enjoying a 0.60 market share, additional factors must be operating. Suppose the companies differ in the *effectiveness* with which they spend marketing dollars. Then equation (9-2) can be revised to read

$$s_i = \frac{\alpha_i M_i}{\Sigma \alpha_i M_i} \qquad (9\text{-}3)$$

where:

α_i = marketing effectiveness of a dollar spent by company i (with $\alpha = 1.00$ for average effectiveness)

$\alpha_i M_i$ = company i's effective marketing effort

Suppose that company one spends its marketing funds less effectively than company two, with $\alpha_1 = 0.90$ and $\alpha_2 = 1.20$. Then company one's market share would be 53 percent:

$$s_i = \frac{0.90(\$60,000)}{0.90(\$60,000) + 1.20(\$40,000)} \cong 0.53$$

Equation (9-3) assumes a strict proportionality between market share and effective marketing effort share. Yet if there are grounds for expecting diminishing returns as one firm's effective effort increases relative to the industry's effective effort, equation (9-3) should be modified to reflect this expectation. One way to reflect diminishing returns is through the use of a marketing-effort elasticity exponent that is less than unity:

$$s_i = \frac{(\alpha_i M_i)^{e_{m_i}}}{\Sigma (\alpha_i M_i)^{e_{mi}}} \qquad \text{where } 0 < e_{m_i} < 1 \qquad (9\text{-}4)$$

where:

e_{m_i} = elasticity of market share with respect to company i's effective marketing effort

Assume that the marketing-effort elasticity is 0.8 for all companies. As a result, company one's market share would be

$$s_i = \frac{[(0.90)(\$60,000)]^{0.8}}{[(0.90)(\$60,000)]^{0.8} + [(1.20)(\$40,000)]^{0.8}} \cong 0.50$$

Thus company one's estimated market share is revised to reflect diminishing returns. Although company one is spending 60 percent of the marketing funds in the industry, its market share is only 50 percent because of lower spending efficiency and diminishing returns.

A further improvement can be introduced by breaking up each company's marketing effort into its major components and separately expressing the effectiveness and elasticity of each marketing component. The equation becomes

$$s_{it} = \frac{R_{it}{}^{e_{Ri}} P_{it}{}^{-e_{Pi}} (\alpha_{it} A_{it})^{e_{Ai}} (d_{it} D_{it})^{e_{Di}}}{\Sigma [R_{it}{}^{e_{Ri}} P_{it}{}^{-e_{Pi}} (\alpha_{it} A_{it})^{e_{Ai}} (d_{it} D_{it})^{e_{Di}}]} \qquad (9\text{-}5)$$

where:

s_{it} = company i's estimated market share at time t

R_{it} = quality rating of company i's product in year t

P_{it} = price of company i's product in year t

A_{it} = advertising and promotion costs of company i in year t

D_{it} = distribution and sales-force costs of company i in year t

α_{it} = advertising-effectiveness index for company i at time t

d_{it} = distribution-effectiveness index for company i at time t

$\left.\begin{matrix} e_{Ri}, e_{Pi}, \\ e_{Ai}, e_{Di} \end{matrix}\right\}$ = elasticities of quality, price, advertising, and distribution, respectively, of company i

Thus equation (9-5) reflects four major influences on a company's market share: *marketing expenditures*, *marketing mix*, *marketing effectiveness*, and *marketing elasticity*. Although this would seem to be a great deal, the expression could be further refined (we will not do this here) to take into account (1) *geographical allocation of marketing expenditures*, (2) *carry-over effects of past marketing expenditures*, and (3) *synergistic effects of marketing-mix variables*.[2]

Company Forecast   Company demand describes estimated company sales at alternative levels of company marketing effort. It remains for management to choose one of the levels.[3] The chosen level of marketing effort will produce an expected level of sales, called the company sales forecast:

> The *company sales forecast* is the expected level of company sales based on a chosen marketing plan and an assumed marketing environment.

The company sales forecast is represented graphically in the same way as the market forecast was in Figure 9-3(a): substitute company sales for the vertical axis and company marketing effort for the horizontal axis.

Too often the sequential relationship between the company forecast and the company marketing plan is confused. One frequently hears that the company should develop its marketing plan on the basis of its sales forecast. The forecast-to-plan sequence is valid if *forecast* means an estimate of national economic activity or if company demand is nonexpansible. The sequence is not valid, however, where market demand is expansible, or where *forecast* means an estimate of company sales. The company sales forecast does not establish a basis for deciding what to spend on marketing; quite the contrary, the sales forecast is the *result* of an assumed marketing expenditure plan.

Two other concepts are worth mentioning in relation to the company forecast.

> A *sales quota* is the sales goal set for a product line, company division, or sales representative. It is primarily a managerial device for defining and stimulating sales effort.

Management sets sales quotas on the basis of the company forecast and the psychology of stimulating its achievement. Generally, sales quotas are set slightly higher than estimated sales to stretch the sales force's effort.

The other concept is a *sales budget*.

> A *sales budget* is a conservative estimate of the expected volume of sales and is used primarily for making current purchasing, production, and cash-flow decisions.

The sales budget considers the sales forecast and the need to avoid excessive risk. Sales budgets are generally set slightly lower than the company forecast.

Company Potential   Company sales potential is *the limit approached by company demand as company marketing effort increases relative to competitors*. The absolute limit of company demand is, of course, the market potential. The two would be equal if the company achieved 100 percent of the market—that is, if the company became a monopolist. In most cases, company sales potential is less than market potential, even when company marketing expenditures increase considerably relative to competitors. The reason is that each competitor has a hard core of loyal buyers who are not very responsive to other companies' efforts to woo them away.

ESTIMATING CURRENT DEMAND

We are now ready to examine practical methods for estimating current market demand. Marketing executives will want to estimate *total market potential*, *area market potential*, and *total industry sales and market shares*.

Total Market Potential   Total market potential is the maximum amount of sales (in units or dollars) that might be available to all the firms in an industry during a given period under a given level of industry marketing effort and given environmental conditions. A common way to estimate it is as follows:

$$Q = nqp \tag{9-6}$$

where:

Q = total market potential
n = number of buyers in the specific product/market under the given assumptions
q = quantity purchased by an average buyer
p = price of an average unit

Thus if there are 100 million buyers of books each year, and the average book buyer buys three books a year, and the average price is $4, then the total market potential for books is $1.2 billion (= 100,000,000 × 3 × $4).

The most difficult component to estimate in (9-6) is n, the number of buyers in the specific product/market. One can always start with the total population in the nation, say 238,000,000 people. This can be called the *suspect pool*. The next step is to eliminate groups that obviously would not buy the product. Let us assume that illiterate people, children under twelve, and persons with poor eyesight do not buy books, and they constitute 20 percent of the population. Then only 80 percent of the population, or 190,400,000 people, would be in the *prospect pool*. We might do further research and find that persons of low income and low education do not read books, and they constitute over 30 percent of the prospect pool. Eliminating them, we arrive at a *hot prospect pool* of approximately 133,280,000 book buyers. We would use this number of potential buyers in formula (9-6) for calculating total market potential.

A variation on formula (9-6) is known as the *chain ratio method*. The chain ratio method involves multiplying a base number by several adjusting percentages. Suppose a brewery is interested in estimating the market potential for a new dietetic beer. An estimate can be made by the following calculation:[4]

$$
\left.\begin{matrix} \text{Demand} \\ \text{for the} \\ \text{new} \\ \text{dietetic} \\ \text{beer} \end{matrix}\right\} = \left\{\begin{matrix} \text{Population} \times \text{Personal discretionary income per capita} \times \\ \text{Average percentage of discretionary income spent on} \\ \text{food} \times \text{Average percentage of amount spent on food that} \\ \text{is spent on beverages} \times \text{Average percentage of amount} \\ \text{spent on beverages that is spent on alcoholic beverages} \\ \times \text{Average percentage of amount spent on alcoholic bev-} \\ \text{erages that is spent on beer} \times \text{Expected percentage of} \\ \text{amount spent on beer that will be spent on dietetic beer.} \end{matrix}\right.
$$

Area Market Potential

Companies face the problem of selecting the best territories and allocating their marketing budget optimally among these territories. Therefore they need to estimate the market potential of different territories. Two major methods are available: the *market-buildup method*, which is used primarily by business marketers, and the *multiple-factor index method*, which is used primarily by consumer marketers.

Market-buildup Method

The market-buildup method calls for identifying all the potential buyers in each market and estimating their potential purchases. The market-buildup method is straightforward if we have a list of all potential buyers *and* a good estimate of what each will buy. Unfortunately one or both are usually lacking.

Consider a machine-tool company that wants to estimate the area market potential for its wood lathe in the Greater Boston area.

The first step is to identify all potential buyers of lathes in the Boston area. The lathe is of no purchase interest to households and many other types of buyers, such as hospitals, retailers, and farmers. The market consists primarily of manufacturing establishments, specifically, those that have to shape or ream wood as part of their operation.

The company could compile a list from a directory of all manufacturing establishments in the Greater Boston area. Then it might estimate the number of lathes each industry might purchase based on the number of lathes per thousand employees or per $1 million of sales in that industry.

An efficient method of estimating area market potentials makes use of the Standard Industrial Classification System (S.I.C.) developed by the U.S. Bureau of the Census. The S.I.C. classifies all manufacturing into 20 major industry groups, each having a two-digit code. Thus #25 is furniture and fixtures, and #35 is machinery except electrical. Each major industry group is further subdivided into about 150 industry groups designated by a three-digit code (#251 is household furniture, and #252 is office furniture). Each industry is further subdivided into approximately 450 product categories designated by a four-digit code (#2521 is wood office furniture, and #2522 is metal office furniture). For each four-digit S.I.C. number, the Census of Manufacturers provides the number of establishments subclassified by location, number of employees, annual sales, and net worth.

To use the S.I.C., the lathe manufacturer must first determine the four-digit S.I.C. codes that represent products whose manufacturers are likely to require lathe machines. For example, lathes will be used by manufacturers in S.I.C. #2511 (wood household furniture), #2521 (wood office furniture), and so on. To get a full picture of all four-digit S.I.C. industries that might use lathes, the company can use three methods. It can determine the S.I.C. codes of past customers. It can go through the S.I.C. manual and check off all the four-digit industries that in its judgment would have an interest in lathes. It can mail

TABLE 9-1   Market-Buildup Method Using S.I.C. Codes (Hypothetical Lathe Manufacturer—
Boston Area)

	1	2	3	4
S.I.C.	Annual Sales (in Millions $)	Number of Establish- ments	Potential Number of Lathe Sales per $1 Million Customer Sales	Market Potential (1 × 2 × 3)
2511	$1	6	10	60
	5	2	10	100
2521	1	3	5	15
	5	1	5	25
				200

questionnaires to a wide range of companies inquiring about their interest in wood lathes.

The company's next task is to determine an appropriate base for estimating the number of lathes that will be used in each industry. Suppose customer industry sales are the most appropriate base. For example, in S.I.C. #2511, ten lathes may be used for every $1 million worth of sales. Once the company estimates the rate of lathe ownership relative to the customer industry's sales, it can compute the market potential.

Table 9-1 shows a hypothetical computation for the Boston area involving two S.I.C. codes. In #2511 (wood household furniture) there are six establishments with annual sales of $1 million and two establishments with annual sales of $5 million. It is estimated that ten lathes can be sold in this S.I.C. code for every $1 million in customer sales. Since there are six establishments with annual sales of $1 million, they account for $6 million in sales, which is a potential of 60 lathes (6 × 10). The other figures in the table are similarly computed. Altogether, it appears that the Greater Boston area has a market potential for 200 lathes.

The company can use the same method to estimate the market potential for other areas in the country. Suppose the market potentials for all the markets add to 2,000 lathes. Then the Boston market contains 10 percent of the total market potential. This might warrant the company's allocating 10 percent of its marketing expenditures to the Boston market. In practice, the lathe manufacturer needs additional information about each market, such as the extent of market saturation, the number of competitors, the market growth rate, and the average age of existing equipment.

If the company decides to sell lathes in Boston, it must know how to identify the best-prospect companies. In the old days, sales reps called on companies door to door; this was called *bird-dogging* or *smokestacking*. "Cold calls" are far too costly today. The company should get a list of the companies in Boston, qualify them, and then use direct mail or phone calls to reach the best prospects. The lathe manufacturer can use *Dun's Market Identifiers*, which lists twenty-seven key facts for over 3,250,000 establishments in the United States and Canada.[5]

Multiple-factor Index Methods   Consumer companies also have to estimate area market potentials. Because their customers are so numerous, they cannot list them. The method most commonly used is a straightforward *index method*. A drug manufacturer, for example, might assume that the market potential for drugs is directly related to population. If the state of Virginia has 2.28 percent of the U.S. population, the company might assume that Virginia would be a market for 2.28 percent of total drugs sold.

A single factor, however, is rarely a complete indicator of sales opportunity. Regional drug sales are also influenced by per capita income and the number of physicians per 10,000 people. This makes it desirable to develop a multiple-factor index with each factor assigned a specific weight.

One of the best-known multiple-factor indices of area demand is the "Annual Survey of Buying Power" published by *Sales and Marketing Management*.[6] The index reflects the relative consumer buying power in the different regions, states, and metropolitan areas of the nation. *Sales and Marketing Management*'s index of the relative buying power of an area is given

$$B_i = 0.5y_i + 0.3r_i + 0.2p_i \qquad (9\text{-}7)$$

where:

B_i = percentage of total national buying power found in area i
y_i = percentage of national disposable personal income originating in area i
r_i = percentage of national retail sales in area i
p_i = percentage of national population located in area i

For example, suppose Virginia has 2.00 percent of the U.S. disposable personal income, 1.96 percent of U.S. retail sales, and 2.28 percent of U.S. population. The buying-power index for Virginia would be

$$0.5(2.00) + 0.3(1.96) + 0.2(2.28) = 2.04$$

Thus 2.04 percent of the nation's drug sales might be expected to take place in Virginia.

The manufacturer recognizes that the weights used in the buying-power index are somewhat arbitrary. They apply mainly to consumer goods that are neither low-priced staples nor high-priced luxury goods. Other weights can be assigned if more appropriate. Furthermore, the manufacturer would want to adjust the market potential for additional factors, such as competitors' presence in that market, local promotional costs, seasonal factors, and local market idiosyncrasies.

Many companies will compute additional area indices as a guide to allocating marketing resources. Suppose the company is reviewing the eight cities listed in Table 9-2. The

TABLE 9-2   Indices of Category Development, Brand Development, and Market Opportunity

Territory	Percent of Total U.S. Population (1)	Percent of Total Sales of Product Category (2)	Percent of Total Sales of Brand A (3)	Category Development Index (4) = (2 ÷ 1)	Brand Development Index (5) = (3 ÷ 1)	Market Opportunity Index (6) = (4 ÷ 5)
Seattle	1.23	2.71	3.09	221	252	0.88
Portland	1.02	2.17	2.48	212	242	0.88
Los Angeles	5.54	10.41	6.74	188	122	1.54
Boston	2.18	3.85	3.49	177	160	1.11
San Francisco	3.66	6.41	7.22	175	198	0.88
Toledo	0.79	0.81	0.97	102	123	0.83
Albuquerque	0.79	0.81	1.13	102	143	0.71
Baltimore	2.67	3.00	3.12	113	117	0.97

first three columns show the percentage of total U.S. population, category sales, and brand A sales, respectively, in these eight cities. Column 4 shows the *category development index*, which is the ratio of consumption intensity to population intensity. Seattle, for example, has a category development index of 221 because it accounts for 2.71 percent of the nation's consumption of this category, while it has only 1.23 percent of the nation's population. Column 5 shows the *brand development index*, which is the ratio of brand consumption intensity to population intensity. For Seattle, the brand development index is 252 because Seattle consumes 3.09 percent of this brand and has only 1.23 percent of the nation's population. Column 6 shows the *market opportunity index*, which is the ratio of category development to brand development. This ratio is 0.88 for Seattle, indicating that the company's brand is more developed in Seattle than in other cities. Seattle is an area of low (incremental) opportunity in that the company brand is highly developed in Seattle. In Los Angeles, the market opportunity index stands at 1.54, indicating a high opportunity area. However, companies should not put all of their money in the high market opportunity areas; other factors should be considered.

After the company decides on the city-by-city allocation of its budget, it can refine each city allocation down to *census tracts* or *ZIP-code centers*. Census tracts are small areas about the size of a neighborhood, and ZIP-code centers (which were designed by the U.S. Post Office Department) are larger areas, often the size of small towns. Information on population size, median family income, and other characteristics is available for each type of unit. Marketers have found that these data are extremely useful for identifying high-potential retail areas within large cities or for buying mailing lists to use in direct-mail campaigns.[7] Exhibit 9-1 describes how U.S. Census data are now incorporated into geocoding systems for improved customer identification and targeting.

Estimating Industry Sales and Market Shares

Besides estimating total potential and area potential, a company needs to know the actual industry sales taking place in its market. This means that it must identify its competitors and estimate their sales.

The industry's trade association will often collect and publish total industry sales, although not listing individual company sales separately. In this way, each company can evaluate its performance against the whole industry. Suppose a company's sales are increasing 5 percent a year, and industry sales are increasing 10 percent. This company is actually losing its relative standing in the industry.

Another way to estimate sales is to buy reports from a marketing research firm that audits total sales and brand sales. For example, A. C. Nielsen Company audits retail sales in various product categories in supermarkets and drugstores and sells this information to interested companies. In this way, a company learns total product-category sales as well as brand sales. It can compare its performance with the total industry and/or any particular competitor to see whether it is gaining or losing.

Industrial goods marketers typically have a harder time estimating industry sales and market shares than do consumer goods marketers. The former have no Nielsen's or other regular syndicated services on which to rely. Distributors typically will not supply information about how much of competitors' products they are selling. Industrial goods marketers therefore have to live with less knowledge of their market share results or be ingenious. Some industrial goods marketers simply want to know whether they are gaining or losing share relative to their leading competitor rather than relative to the whole market. They can then concentrate on estimating the sales of one competitor and make some progress.

EXHIBIT 9-1

Geocoding: A New Technique For Identifying the Best Market Targets

In recent years, several new business information services have been offered to marketing planners that link U.S. Census data on a zip-code basis with lifestyle patterns. Among the leading services are PRIZM (by Claritas), Cluster Plus (by Donnelley Marketing Information Services), and Acorn (C.A.C.I., Inc.). These data services can help marketing planners identify the best geographical areas (zip-code areas) in which to concentrate their marketing efforts. We will use the PRIZM system to show how geocoding works.

The PRIZM designers have picturesquely classified all U.S. zip-code markets into forty clusters, such as "blue blood estates," "money and brains," "furs and station wagons," "shotguns and pickups," and "tobacco roads." The clusters were formed by manipulating eight characteristics. For example, "blue blood estates" are characterized by

- A medium household density per square mile
- A suburban complexion
- A high degree of homogeneity of the residents
- A white ethnicity
- A heavy family orientation
- A college graduate makeup
- A white-collar makeup
- A single-unit housing pattern

On the other hand, the cluster "single city blues" is characterized by a high household density, city location, mixed population, white with minorities, many singles and couples, some college, white/blue collar mix, and multiunit housing. Each of the other thirty-eight zip clusters has a unique combination of characteristics.

To illustrate how geocoding works, we can draw from a recent publication of the Seventh Day Adventists who are seeking to identify the best zip-code areas for recruiting new members. Their working hypothesis is that they would have the best chance attracting new members from zip-code areas that resemble the ones that now contain most current members. Using their home addresses, all Seventh Day Adventists were coded into one of the forty zip clusters. In examining the data, the researchers found that the "Hispanic mix" zip cluster had the highest *index of concentration* of Seventh Day Adventists. Specifically, while the Hispanic mix cluster accounted for only 3.393 percent of the U.S. population, it accounted for 12.706 percent of all Seventh Day Adventists. By dividing the latter number by the former, and multiplying by 100, they found that the "Hispanic mix" zip cluster had an index of concentration of 375. This suggests that this type of zip area has a high potential for further members and deserves focused marketing, including the opening in these areas of new Seventh Day Adventist churches, door-to-door recruitment, and direct-mail campaigns. On the other hand, the zip cluster with the lowest potential for Seventh Day Adventist recruitment was "nonmobile married couples, old homes, farm areas," whose index of concentration was only 16. Using this methodology, all forty zip-cluster areas could be ranked, and those whose index of concentration exceeded 100 would be the most attractive areas for recruitment.

The zip-cluster areas are also linked with other data banks showing product preferences, lifestyle characteristics, and so on. For example, the "Hispanic mix" zip cluster has product preferences for high-quality dresses, tequila, nonfilter cigarettes, lip gloss, and so on, and this information, plus lifestyle information, can help the religious marketers in their communication and recruitment efforts.

We have deliberately illustrated the geocoding methodology in an unusual application: religious recruitment. More normally, geocoding is used by manufacturers, retailers, and others to identify the best zip clusters to target based on where their current customers live.

SOURCES Thomas Moore, "Different Folks, Different Strokes," *Fortune*, September 16, 1985, pp. 65–68; "PRIZM-Guided Retail Plan Yields Dynamic Results," *Direct Marketing*, November 1985, p. 116; Hugh M. Cannon and Gerald Linda, "Beyond Media Imperatives: Geodemographic Media Selection," *Journal of Advertising Research*, June/July 1982, pp. 31–36; and "Marketing Firm Slices U.S. into 240,000 Parts to Spur Clients' Sales," *Wall Street Journal*, November 3, 1986, p. 1. The illustration was taken from *The North American Division Marketing Program, Vol. 1: Profiling Adventist Members and Baptisms*, published in mimeograph form, 1986.

They can determine how many work shifts the competitor is operating, or sample typical customers to see what they are buying from the company and the leading competitor.

ESTIMATING FUTURE DEMAND

We are now ready to examine methods of estimating future demand. Very few products or services lend themselves to easy forecasting. Cases of easy forecasting generally involve a product whose absolute level or trend is fairly constant and a situation where competitive relations are nonexistent (public utilities) or stable (pure oligopolies). In most markets, total demand and company demand are not stable, and good forecasting becomes a key factor in company success. Poor forecasting can lead to overly large inventories, costly price markdowns, or lost sales due to being out of stock. The more unstable the demand, the more critical is forecast accuracy, and the more elaborate is forecasting procedure.

Forecasting methods range from the crude to the highly sophisticated. Many technical aspects fall within the province of experts. Yet marketing managers need to be familiar with the major forecasting methods. They need to understand each method's advantages and limitations.

Companies commonly use a three-stage procedure to arrive at a sales forecast. They make an *environmental forecast*, followed by an *industry forecast*, followed by a *company sales forecast*. The environmental forecast calls for projecting inflation, unemployment, interest rates, consumer spending and saving, business investment, government expenditures, net exports, and other environmental magnitudes and events of importance to the company. (See Exhibit 9-2.) The end result is a forecast of *gross national product*, which is then used, along with other environmental indicators, to forecast industry sales. Then the company derives its sales forecast by assuming that it will win a certain market share.

All forecasts are built on one of three information bases: *what people say*, *what people do*, or *what people have done*. The first basis—*what people say*—involves surveying the opinions of buyers or those close to them, such as salespeople or outside experts. It encompasses three methods: surveys of buyer intentions, composites of sales-force opinions, and expert opinion. Building a forecast on *what people do* involves another method, that of putting the product into a market test to indicate buyer response. The final basis—*what people have done*—involves analyzing records of past buying behavior or using time-series analysis or statistical demand analysis.

Survey
of Buyers'
Intentions

Forecasting is the art of anticipating what buyers are likely to do under a given set of conditions. That suggests that the buyers should be surveyed. Surveys are especially valuable if the buyers have clearly formulated intentions, will carry them out, and will describe them to interviewers.

In regard to *major consumer durables*, several research organizations conduct periodic surveys of consumer buying intentions. These organizations ask questions like the following:

Do you intend to buy an automobile within the next six months?					
0.00	0.20	0.40	0.60	0.80	1.00
No chance	Slight possibility	Fair possibility	Good possibility	High probability	Certain

Methods of Environmental Forecasting

The key to organizational survival and growth is the firm's ability to adapt its strategies to a rapidly changing environment. This puts a large burden on management to anticipate future events correctly. The price can be enormous when a mistake is made. For example, Montgomery Ward lost its leadership in the chain-store retailing field after World War II because its chairman, Sewell Avery, bet on a stagnant economy while its major competitor, Sears, bet on an expanding economy. That is why a growing number of companies carry out *environmental forecasting*.

How do firms develop environmental forecasts? Large firms have planning departments that develop long-run forecasts of key environmental factors affecting their markets. General Electric, for example, has a large staff of forecasters who study worldwide forces that affect its operations. GE makes its forecasts available to GE divisions and also sells certain forecasts to other firms.

Smaller firms can buy forecasts from several types of suppliers. *Marketing research firms* can develop a forecast by interviewing customers, distributors, and other knowledgeable parties. *Specialized forecasting firms* produce long-range forecasts of particular macroenvironmental components, such as the economy, the population, natural resources, or technology. Finally, there are *futurist research firms* that produce speculative scenarios. Among the latter are the Hudson Institute, the Futures Group, and the Institute for the Future.

Here are some methodologies used to produce environmental forecasts:

- ■ *Expert opinion.* Knowledgeable people are selected and asked to assign importance and probability ratings to various possible future developments. The most refined version, the Delphi method, puts experts through several rounds of event assessment, where they keep refining their assumptions and judgments.
- ■ *Trend extrapolation.* Researchers fit best-fitting curves (linear, quadratic, or S-shaped growth curves) through past time series to use for extrapolation. This method can be very unreliable in that new developments can completely alter the future direction.
- ■ *Trend correlation.* Researchers correlate various time series in the hope of identifying leading and lagging indicators that can be used for forecasting. The National Bureau of Economic Research has identified twelve of the best-looking economic indicators, and their values are published monthly in the *Survey of Current Business*.
- ■ *Dynamic modeling.* Researchers build sets of equations that attempt to describe the underlying system. The coefficients in the equations are fitted through statistical means. Econometric models of more than three hundred equations, for example, are used to forecast changes in the U.S. economy.
- ■ *Cross-impact analysis.* Researchers identify a set of key trends (those high in importance and/ or probability). The question is then put: "If event A occurs, what will be the impact on all other trends?" The results are then used to build sets of "domino chains," with one event triggering others.
- ■ *Multiple scenarios.* Researchers build pictures of alternative futures, each internally consistent and having a certain probability of occurring. The major purpose of the scenarios is to stimulate contingency planning.
- ■ *Demand/hazard forecasting.* Researchers identify major events that would greatly affect the firm. Each event is rated for its *convergence* with several major trends taking place in society. It is also rated for its *appeal* to each major public in the society. The higher the event's convergence and appeal, the higher its probability of occurring. The highest-scoring events are then researched further.

This is called a *purchase probability scale*. In addition, the various surveys inquire into the consumer's present and future personal finances, and expectations about the economy. The various bits of information are combined into a *consumer sentiment measure* (Survey Research Center of the University of Michigan) or a *consumer confidence measure*

(Sindlinger and Company). Consumer durable-goods producers subscribe to these indices in the hope of anticipating major shifts in consumer buying intentions so that they can adjust their production and marketing plans accordingly.[8]

In the realm of *industrial buying*, various agencies carry out buyer intention surveys regarding plant, equipment, and materials. The better known among these are McGraw-Hill Research of New York and Opinion Research Corporation of Princeton. Most of the estimates have been within a 10 percent error band of the actual outcomes.

Various industrial firms conduct their own surveys of customer buying intentions:

> National Lead's marketing research personnel periodically visit a carefully selected sample of 100 companies and interview the manufacturer's technical research director, sales manager, and purchasing director, in that order. The technical research director is asked about the rate of incorporation of titanium in the manufacturer's various products; the sales manager is questioned about the sales outlook for the company's products that incorporate titanium; and the purchasing director is queried about the total amount of titanium his company plans to purchase in relation to past purchases. On the basis of these interviews and supplementary information, National's marketing research department estimates the market demand for titanium and prepares a "most favorable" forecast and a "least favorable" forecast. There are also indirect benefits. National Lead's analysts learn of new developments and modes of thinking that would not be apparent through secondary data. Their visits also promote National's image as a company that is concerned about buyers' needs. Another advantage of this method is that it yields subestimates for various industries and territories in the process of building an aggregate estimate.[9]

In summary, the value of a buyers' intentions survey increases to the extent that the buyers are few, the cost of effectively reaching them is small, they have clear intentions, they follow out their original intentions, and they are willing to disclose their intentions. As a result, it is of value for industrial products, for consumer durables, for product purchases where advanced planning is required, and for new products where past data do not exist.

Composite of Sales-Force Opinions

Where buyer interviewing is impractical, the company will ask its sales representatives for estimates. An example is the Pennwalt Corporation:

> In August, the field sales personnel are provided with tabulating cards to prepare their sales forecasts for the upcoming year. Individual cards are prepared for each product sold to each major customer, showing the quantity shipped to the customer in the previous six months. Each card also provides space in which the field salesmen post their forecasts for the coming year. Additional tab cards are also supplied for those customers who were not sold in the current six-month period but who were customers in the prior year; and finally, blank cards are provided for submitting forecasts of sales to new customers. Salesmen fill in their forecasts (on the basis of current prices) using informed judgment; in some divisions, they are in a position to substantiate their forecasts by obtaining purchase estimates from their customers.[10]

Few companies use their sales force's estimates without some adjustments. Sales representatives are biased observers. They might be congenitally pessimistic or optimistic, or they might go to one extreme or another because of a recent sales setback or success. Furthermore, they are often unaware of larger economic developments and do not know how their company's marketing plans will influence future sales in their territory. They might deliberately underestimate demand so that the company will set a low sales quota. They might not have the time to prepare careful estimates or might not consider it worthwhile.

In the light of these adverse factors, why are sales-force estimates used at all? There is the possibility that the over-and-under errors cancel out. Or a consistent bias in the forecast of individual sales representatives might be recognized and adjusted before aggregating the individual sales forecasts.

The company could supply certain aids or incentives to the sales force to encourage better estimating. The sales representatives might receive a record of their past forecasts compared with their actual sales, and also a set of company assumptions on the business outlook. Some companies will summarize individual forecasting records and distribute them to the sales force. A tendency for sales representatives to produce ultraconservative estimates to keep down their sales quota can be countered by basing territorial advertising and promotional expenditures on each sales representative's estimate.

Assuming these biases can be countered, a number of benefits can be gained by involving the sales force in forecasting. Sales representatives might have better insight into developing trends than any other single group. Through participating in the forecasting process, the sales representatives might have greater confidence in their sales quotas and more incentive to achieve them.[11] Also, a "grassroots" forecasting procedure provides estimates broken down by product, territory, customer, and sales representatives.

Expert Opinion

Companies can also obtain forecasts by turning to experts. Experts include dealers, distributors, suppliers, marketing consultants, and trade associations. Thus auto companies survey their dealers periodically for their forecasts of short-term demand. Dealer estimates, however, are subject to the same strengths and weaknesses as sales-force estimates.

Many companies buy economic and industry forecasts from well-known economic forecasting firms, such as Data Resources, Wharton Econometric, and Chase Econometric. These forecasting specialists are in a better position than the company to prepare economic forecasts because they have more data available and more forecasting expertise.

Occasionally companies will assemble a special group of experts to make a particular kind of forecast. The experts are asked to exchange views and come up with a group estimate (*group-discussion methods*). Or they are asked to supply their estimates individually, and the analyst combines them in a single estimate (*pooling of individual estimates*). Or they are asked to supply individual estimates and assumptions that are reviewed by a company analyst, revised, and followed by further rounds of estimating (*Delphi method*).[12]

An interesting variant of the expert-opinion method has been used by Lockheed Aircraft Corporation. A group of Lockheed executives pose as different major customers. In a hardheaded way, they evaluate Lockheed's offer in relation to competitors' offers. A decision on what and where to buy is made for each customer. The purchases from Lockheed are totaled to see how well Lockheed's offer is likely to succeed in the marketplace.

Market-Test Method

Where buyers do not plan their purchases carefully or are very erratic in carrying out their intentions or where experts are not very good guessers, a direct market test is desirable. A direct market test is especially desirable in forecasting the sales of a new product or of an established product in a new channel of distribution or territory. Market testing is discussed in Chapter 14.

Time-Series Analysis

Many firms prepare their forecasts on the basis of past sales. The assumption is that past data capture causal relations that can be uncovered through statistical analysis. These causal relations can be used to predict future sales.

A time series of a product's past sales (Y) can be analyzed into four major components.

The first component, *trend* (T), is the result of basic developments in population, capital formation, and technology. It is found by fitting a straight or curved line through past sales.

The second component, *cycle* (*C*), captures the wavelike movement of sales. Many sales are affected by swings in general economic activity, which tends to be somewhat periodic. The cyclical component can be useful in intermediate-range forecasting.

The third component, *season* (*S*), refers to a consistent pattern of sales movements within the year. The term *season* describes any recurrent hourly, weekly, monthly, or quarterly sales pattern. The seasonal component may be related to weather factors, holidays, and trade customs. The seasonal pattern provides a norm for forecasting short-range sales.

The fourth component, *erratic events* (*E*), includes strikes, blizzards, fads, riots, fires, war scares, and other disturbances. These erratic components are by definition unpredictable and should be removed from past data to see the more normal behavior of sales.

Time-series analysis consists of decomposing the original sales series, *Y*, into the components, *T*, *C*, *S*, and *E*. Then these components are recombined to produce the sales forecast.[13] Here is an example:

An insurance company sold 12,000 new ordinary life insurance policies this year. It would like to predict next year's December sales. The long-term trend shows a 5 percent sales growth rate per year. This alone suggests sales next year of 12,600 (= 12,000 × 1.05). However, a business recession is expected next year and will probably result in total sales achieving only 90 percent of the expected trend-adjusted sales. Sales next year will more likely be 11,340 (= 12,600 × 0.90). If sales were the same each month, monthly sales would be 945 (= 11,340/12). However, December is an above-average month for insurance-policy sales, with a seasonal index standing at 1.30. Therefore December sales may be as high as 1,228.5 (= 945 × 1.3). No erratic events, such as strikes or new insurance regulations, are expected. Therefore the best estimate of new policy sales next December is 1,228.5.

For a company that has hundreds of items in its product line and wants to produce efficient and economical short-run forecasts, a newer time-series technique called *exponential smoothing* is available. In its simplest form, exponential smoothing requires only three pieces of information: this period's actual sales, Q_t; this period's smoothed sales, $\overline{Q}_t$; and a smoothing parameter, α. The sales forecast for next period's sales is given by

$$\overline{Q}_{t+1} = \alpha Q_t + (1 - \alpha)\overline{Q}_t \tag{9-8}$$

where:
$\overline{Q}_{t+1}$ = sales forecast for next period
α = the smoothing constant, where $0 \leq \alpha \leq 1$
Q_t = current sales in period t
$\overline{Q}_t$ = smoothed sales in period t

Suppose the smoothing constant is 0.4, current sales are $50,000, and smoothed sales are $40,000. Then the sales forecast is

$$\overline{Q}_{t+1} = 0.4(\$50,000) + 0.6(\$40,000) = \$44,000$$

In other words, the sales forecast is always between (or at an extreme of) current sales and smoothed sales. The relative influence of current and smoothed sales depends on the smoothing constant, here 0.4. Thus the sales forecast "tracks" actual sales.

For each of its products, the company determines an initial level of smoothed sales and a smoothing constant. The initial level of smoothed sales can simply be average sales for the last few periods. The smoothing constant is derived by trial-and-error testing of different smoothing constants between zero and one to find the constant that produces the best fit of past sales. The method can be refined to reflect seasonal and trend factors by adding two more constants.[14]

Statistical Demand Analysis Time-series analysis treats past and future sales as a function of time, rather than of any real demand factors. Numerous real factors affect the sales of any product. *Statistical demand analysis* is a set of statistical procedures designed to discover the most important real factors affecting sales and their relative influence. The factors most commonly analyzed are price, income, population, and promotion.

Statistical demand analysis consists of expressing sales (Q) as a dependent variable and trying to explain sales as a function of a number of independent demand variables $X_1, X_2, \ldots, X_n$; that is,

$$Q = f(X_1, X_2, \ldots, X_n) \qquad (9\text{-}9)$$

Using a technique called multiple-regression analysis, various equation forms can be statistically fitted to the data in the search for the best predicting variables and equation.

For example, Palda found that the following demand equation gave a fairly good fit to the historical sales of Lydia Pinkham's Vegetable Compound between the years 1908 and 1960:[15]

$$Y = -3649 + 0.665X_1 + 1180 \log X_2 + 774X_3 + 32X_4 - 2.83X_5 \qquad (9\text{-}10)$$

where:

Y = yearly sales in thousands of dollars

X_1 = yearly sales (lagged one year) in thousands of dollars

X_2 = yearly advertising expenditures in thousands of dollars

X_3 = a dummy variable, taking on the value of 1 between 1908 and 1925 and 0 from 1926 on

X_4 = year (1908 = 0, 1909 = 1, and so on)

X_5 = disposable personal income in billions of current dollars

The five independent variables on the right account for 94 percent of the yearly variation in the sale of Lydia Pinkham's Vegetable Compound between 1908 and 1960. To use it as a sales-forecasting equation for 1961, it would be necessary to insert figures for the five independent variables. Sales in 1960 should be put in X_1; the log of the company's planned advertising expenditures for 1961 should be put in X_2; 0 should be put in X_3; the numbered year corresponding to 1961 should be put in X_4; and estimated 1961 disposable personal income should be put in X_5. The result of multiplying these numbers by the respective coefficients and summing them gives a sales forecast (Y) for 1961.

Basically, demand equations are derived by fitting the "best" equation to historical or cross-sectional data. The coefficients of the equation are estimated according to the *least squares* criterion. According to this criterion, the best equation is the one that *minimizes the sum of the squared deviations of the actual from the predicted observations*. The equation can be derived through the use of standard formulas. The closer the fit, the more useful the equation, all other things being equal.

Computers have rendered statistical demand analysis an increasingly popular approach to forecasting. The user, however, should be wary of five problems that might diminish the validity or usefulness of a statistical demand equation: too few observations, too much correlation among the independent variables, violation of normal distribution assumptions, two-way causation, and emergence of new variables not accounted for.

SUMMARY

To carry out their responsibilities, marketing managers need various estimates of current and future demand. Quantitative measurements are essential for the analysis of market opportunity, the planning of marketing programs, and the control of marketing effort. The firm may prepare several estimates of demand, varying in the level of product aggregation, the time dimension, and the space dimension.

A market consists of the set of actual and potential consumers of a market offer. The size of the market depends on how many people have interest, income, and access to the market offer. Marketers must know how to distinguish between the potential market, available market, qualified available market, served market, and penetrated market.

Marketers must also distinguish between market demand and company demand, and within these, between potentials and forecasts. Market demand is a function, not a single number, and as such is highly dependent on the level of other variables.

A major task is estimating current demand. Total demand can be estimated through the chain-ratio method, which involves multiplying a base number by successive percentages. Area market demand can be estimated by the market-buildup method (for industrial markets) and the multiple-factor index method (for consumer markets). In the latter case, geodemographic coding systems are proving a boon to marketers. Actual industry sales require identifying the relevant competitors and using some method of estimating the sales of each. Finally, companies are interested in estimating the market shares of competitors to judge their relative performance.

For estimating future demand, the company can use seven major forecasting methods: buyer intentions surveys, composite of sales-force opinion, expert opinion, market tests, time-series analysis, leading indicators, and statistical demand analysis. These methods vary in their appropriateness with the purpose of the forecast, the type of product, and the availability and reliability of data.

QUESTIONS

1. What kinds of information can be derived from standard industrial classifications for demand forecasting? What are some limitations of SIC analysis?

2. What evaluative dimensions would you use to compare the various forecasting methods?

3. Using the dimensions you developed in question 2, compare the following forecasting methods: sales-force composite opinions, market testing, exponential smoothing, regression models.

4. One use of forecasts is as an input into the development of marketing strategy. However, integrating forecasts, goals, and strategies can be a complex and "politicized" process. Suggest some guidelines to achieve a better link between forecasts, goals, and strategies.

5. Describe the difference between the potential market, available market, served market, and penetrated market for a Rolls Royce Silver Spirit.

6. List some expansible and nonexpansible markets. Can you think of any markets that may previously have been considered nonexpansible but have been expanded? What caused the unexpected expansion to occur?

7. A manufacturer of women's hair products (home permanents, hair rinses, shampoos, and so on) wants to determine the relative market potential for its products in each county of the United States. What factors are most likely to belong in a weighted index of potential?

8. A chemical company wants to estimate the demand for sulfur next year. One use of sulfur is in manufacturing sulfuric acid. Another use of sulfur is in polishing new cars. Auto maker C is a customer of this manufacturer. What ratios have to be linked to go from auto maker C's new-car production to its impact on the chemical company's sulfur sales?

9. An automotive manufacturer is developing its sales forecast for next year. The company forecaster has estimated sales for six different environment-strategy combinations:

Sales Forecast		
High Marketing Budget	**Medium Marketing Budget**	**Low Marketing Budget**
Recession 15	12	10
Normal 20	16	14

The forecaster believes that there is a 0.20 probability of recession and an 0.80 probability of normal times. He also believes the probabilities of a high, medium, and low company marketing budget are 0.30, 0.50, and 0.20, respectively. How might he arrive at a single point forecast? What assumptions are being made?

10. A motorboat company located in Washington State plans to open additional retail outlets in several counties on the Columbia River and Puget Sound. Using market opportunity indexes, recommend in which counties the outlets should be located.

County	Population	Sales of Motorboats (in dollars)	Sales of Company's Boats (in dollars)
Clark	161,300	2,800,000	186,200
Klickitat	13,400	140,000	38,000
Cowlitz	72,000	455,000	72,000
Snohamish	261,700	2,835,000	361,000
Pacific	16,200	1,750,000	836,000
Skagit	56,200	2,310,000	155,000
Total in counties	580,800	10,290,000	1,648,200
Total in state	3,583,400	35,000,000	3,800,000

11. Suppose a company's past sales are: 10, 12, 15, 12, 11, 13, 18, 20. The company forecaster uses an exponential smoothing equation with $a = 0.4$ and initial $Q_t = 10$. Estimate the exponentially smoothed sales that would be predicted for the third period on.

12. A beverage company wants to use multiple regression to explain state-to-state variations in the consumption of soft drinks. (a) What independent variable should be tested? (b) If the fitted regression equation "explains" most of the state-to-state variation in sales, does it follow that it indicates relative market potential by state?

13. A marketing researcher sought a multiple-regression equation to explain past sales in an industry. Industry data on the dependent and independent variables went back only five years. The following equation was fitted:

$$Y = 5,241 + 31X_1 + 12X_2 + 50X_3$$

where:

Y = yearly sales in thousands of dollars

X_1 = U.S. disposable personal income in billions of dollars

X_2 = U.S. population in millions of households

X_3 = time, in years (1983 = 0)

The marketing researcher was pleased that this equation accounted for 98 percent of the yearly variations in industry sales. List any reservations you have about using this equation to forecast industry sales.

■ FOOTNOTES

1 Theodore Levitt, "The New Markets—Think Before You Leap," *Harvard Business Review*, May–June 1969, pp. 53–68, here p. 53.

2 See Gary Lilien and Philip Kotler, *Marketing Decision Making: A Model-Building Approach* (New York: Harper & Row, 1983). Also see David E. Bell, Ralph L. Keeney, and John D. C. Little, "A Market Share Theorem," *Journal of Marketing Research*, May 1975, pp. 136–41.

3 The theory of choosing the best level of marketing effort is described in Chapter 3, pp 84–98.

4 See Russell L. Ackoff, *A Concept of Corporate Planning* (New York: Wiley-Interscience, 1970), pp. 36–37.

5 Dun's Market Identifiers (DMI), Dun & Bradstreet, New York, 1982.

6 For a helpful exposition on using this survey and three other surveys published by *Sales and Marketing Management*, see "Putting the Four to Work," *Sales Management*, October 28, 1974, pp. 13ff.

7 See Bob Stone, *Successful Direct Marketing Methods*, 2nd ed. (Chicago: Crain Books, 1979).

8 The consumer pollsters include the Survey Research Center at the University of Michigan; Sindlinger & Company of Norwood, Pa.; The Conference Board, Inc., and the Commercial Credit Corporation. For a discussion, see "How Good Are Consumer Pollsters?" *Business Week*, November 9, 1969, pp. 108–10.

9 Adapted from *Forecasting Sales*, Business Policy Study No. 106 (New York: National Conference Board, 1963), pp. 31–32.

10 Ibid., p. 25.

11 See Jacob Gonik, "Tie Salesmen's Bonuses to Their Forecasts," *Harvard Business Review*, May–June 1978, pp. 116–23.

12 See Norman Dalkey and Olaf Helmer, "An Experimental Application of the Delphi Method to the Use of Experts," *Management Science*, April 1963, pp. 458–67. Also see

Roger J. Best, "An Experiment in Delphi Estimation in Marketing Decision Making," *Journal of Marketing Research*, November 1974, pp. 447–52.

13 See Ya-Lun Chou, *Statistical Analysis with Business and Economic Applications*, 2nd ed. (New York: Holt, Rinehart & Winston, 1975), Chap. 2. For computer programs, see Julius Shiskin, *Electronic Computers and Business Indicators* (New York: National Bureau of Economics Research, 1957). For an application, see Robert L. McLaughlin, "The Break-through in Sales Forecasting," *Journal of Marketing*, April 1963, pp. 46–54.

14 See Nick T. Thomopoulos, *Applied Forecasting Methods for Management* (Englewood Cliffs, N.J.: Prentice-Hall, 1980), pp. 186–93. For another interesting method, the Box-Jenkins method, also see pp. 214–44.

15 Kristian S. Palda, *The Measurement of Cumulative Advertising Effects* (Englewood Cliffs, N.J.: Prentice-Hall, 1964), pp. 67–68.

10 Identifying Market Segments, Selecting Market Targets, and Developing Market Positions

Small is beautiful. Less is more.

E. F. Schumacher

Never follow the crowd.

Bernard M. Baruch

A company that decides to operate in some broad market—whether consumer, industrial, reseller, or government—recognizes that it normally cannot serve all the customers in that market. The customers are too numerous, widely scattered, and varied in their buying requirements. Some competitors will be in a better position to serve particular customer segments of that market. The firm, instead of competing everywhere, often against superior odds, needs to identify the most attractive market segments that it can serve effectively.

The heart of modern *strategic marketing* can be described as *STP* marketing—namely, *segmenting, targeting, and positioning.* This does not obviate the importance of *LGD* marketing—lunch, golf, and dinner—but rather provides the broader framework for strategic success in the marketplace.

Sellers have not always held this view of market strategy. Their thinking passed through three stages:

■ **Mass marketing.** Here the seller engages in the mass production, mass distribution, and mass promotion of one product for all buyers. This market strategy was epitomized by Henry Ford, who offered the Model T Ford to all buyers. They could have "the car in any color as long as it is black." The traditional argument for mass marketing is that it will lead to the lowest costs and prices and create the largest potential market.

■ **Product-variety marketing.** Here the seller produces several products that exhibit different features, styles, qualities, sizes, and so on. They are designed to offer variety to buyers rather than to appeal to different market segments. General Motors practices this market strategy in that many of its cars go under different names—Pontiac, Buick, Oldsmobile, etc.—and exhibit only slight differences in features and style. The traditional argument for product-variety marketing is that customers have different tastes and their tastes change over time. Customers also seek variety.

■ **Target marketing.** Here the seller distinguishes the major market segments, targets one or more of these segments, and develops products and marketing programs tailored to each selected segment. Volkswagen, Mercedes, and Porsche represent automobile companies that have targeted clear customer segments. Ford, with its larger product line, nevertheless tends to create concept cars—such as the Mustang and Thunderbird—that are often targeted to specific groups.

Today's companies are finding it increasingly unrewarding to practice mass marketing or product-variety marketing. Mass markets are becoming "de-massified." They are dissolving into hundreds of *mini-markets* characterized by different life-style groups pursuing different products in different distribution channels and attending to different communication channels. According to Arbeit:

> All advertisers will be forced to design products that fit with the multiplicity of channels, with a multiplicity of retail outlets, and with a multiplicity of discrete consumer target audiences.
>
> McDonald's understands the great lesson of the 1980's—that marketing in the 80's is guerrilla warfare. You can no longer fly over in your network B–52's and drop coherent, heavy messages, saturating communities with what you want to say, and hope for a response. Guerrilla warfare marketing in the 80's means that the battles for the heart and mind and pocketbook of the consumer will be won on a block-by-block, store-by-store, purchase-by-purchase basis.[1]

Companies are increasingly embracing target marketing. Target marketing helps sellers identify marketing opportunities better. The sellers can develop the right offer for each target market. They can adjust their prices, distribution channels, and advertising to reach the target market efficiently. Instead of scattering their marketing effort ("shotgun" approach), they can focus it on the buyers with whom they have the greatest chance of satisfying ("rifle" approach).

Target marketing calls for three major steps (Figure 10-1). The first is *market segmentation*, the act of dividing a market into distinct groups of buyers who might require separate products and/or marketing mixes. The company identifies different ways to segment the market and develops profiles of the resulting market segments. The second step is *market targeting*, the act of developing measures of segment attractiveness and selecting one or more market segments to enter. The third step is *product positioning*, the act of establishing a viable competitive positioning of the firm and its offer in each target market. This chapter will describe the principles and methods of market segmentation, market targeting, and market positioning.

FIGURE 10-1
Steps in Market Segmentation, Targeting, and Positioning

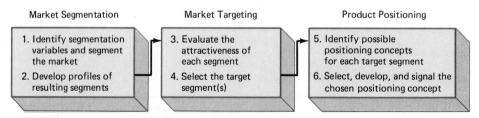

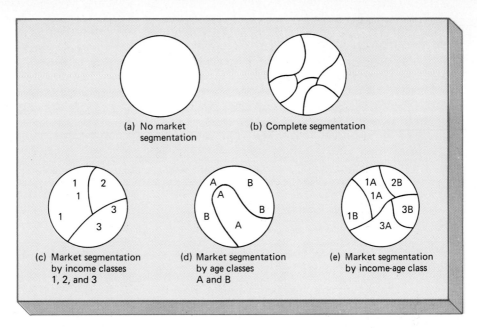

FIGURE 10-2
Different Segmentations of a Market

MARKET SEGMENTATION

Markets consist of buyers, and buyers differ in one or more respects. They may differ in their wants, resources, geographical locations, buying attitudes, and buying practices. Any of these variables can be used to segment a market.

The General Approach to Segmenting a Market

Figure 10-2(a) shows a market of six buyers. Each buyer is potentially a separate market because of unique needs and wants. Ideally, a seller might design a separate product and/or marketing program for each buyer. For example, airframe producers such as Boeing and McDonnell-Douglas face only a few major airline customers and customize their product for each. This ultimate degree of market segmentation, called *customized marketing*, is illustrated in Figure 10-2(b) and Exhibit 10-1.

Most sellers will not find it worthwhile to "customize" their product to satisfy each specific buyer. Instead the seller identifies broad classes of buyers who differ in their product requirements and/or marketing responses. For example, the seller may discover that income groups differ in their wants. In Figure 10-2(c), a number (1, 2, or 3) is used to identify each buyer's income class. Lines are drawn around buyers in the same income class. Segmentation by income results in three segments, the most numerous segment being income class 1.

On the other hand, the seller may find pronounced differences between younger and older buyers. In Figure 10-2(d), a letter (A or B) is used to indicate each buyer's age. Segmentation by age class results in two segments, each with three buyers.

Now income and age may both count heavily in influencing the buyer's behavior toward the product. In this case, the market can be divided into five segments: 1A, 1B,

EXHIBIT 10-1

Customized Marketing: It's Coming Back

In early markets, many sellers made their goods for specific customers. Tailors made a different garment for each woman; and shoemakers made a special pair for shoes for each pair of feet. These craftsmen did not produce for inventory but for order because they did not know what size or materials their customers would want. Even today some people will order customized suits, shirts, and shoes to fit their individual requirements. But generally, the advent of mass production led producers to produce standard-size goods for inventory, and this spelled the end of many "job shops."

Today customized marketing is coming back, in a form that Stanley Davis calls *mass customization*. This is a strange oxymoron, like "jumbo shrimp," "permanent change," and so on, but it well describes new marketing possibilities opened up by advances in manufacturing technology. *Mass customization is the ability to prepare on a mass basis individually designed products to meet each customer's requirements*. Here are some examples.

As a result of General Motors' Saturn project, American car buyers will be able to walk into a GM dealership, sit down at a computer terminal, and select the car's color, engine, seat material, radio, and so on. Their order will be transmitted to the auto plant, which will then produce the desired car.

In Japan, home buyers can sit down with a sales representative at a computer terminal and design their home. They can choose from twenty thousand different standardized parts, make the rooms as large or small as they want, and design the overall layout. The information is sent electronically to the factory where the parts are put together on an assembly line stretching one-third of a mile long. The prefabricated modules are delivered to the site within thirty days, and the room and walls are assembled in one day. The finishing touches take another thirty days, and the family can then move into its customized home.

There are some men's clothing stores in Japan that can custom-tailor suits without any tailors! The customer is measured electronically, and the information travels to a cutting shop where laser equipment directs the cutting and sewing of the cloth. The customer comes back the next day to pick up his custom-tailored suit. Another development is an electronic mirror that superimposes images of various suits on the customer's body in different colors, styles, and materials. After the customer finds a pleasing combination, the information is sent electronically to the factory to cut that suit.

Customization permits people to participate in producing exactly what they want. That people enjoy this is demonstrated in a number of situations. Salad bars are becoming increasingly popular in restaurants because they permit people to "compose" their own salads. Similarly, certain ice-cream parlors allow people to make their own sundaes.

Services as well as products can be customized. Jack Whittle predicts the following scenario for financial services:

> The customer will enter an institution, sit down at a selling module, and be counseled by a highly qualified professional . . . The counselor and the customer will work together from a computer terminal to build and price a financial relationship. For example, the customer might inquire about opening up a deposit relationship. The counselor asks a number of basic questions: Does the customer want to earn interest? Write checks? Transfer money between accounts occasionally? Obtain a loan? Depending on the customer's responses, the desired services will be configured and priced based upon the customer's individualized needs.

In general, as the cost of customization falls and approaches the cost of segmentation, more companies will turn to customized marketing.

SOURCES See Stanley M. Davis, *Future Perfect* (Reading, Mass.: Addison-Wesley, 1987); Jack W. Whittle, "Beyond Segmentation: Customized Products for Individuals," *American Banker*, January 22, 1986, p. 4; and Philip Kotler, "Prosumers: A New Type of Consumer," *Futurist*, September–October 1986, pp. 24–28.

2B, 3A, and 3B. Figure 10-2(e) shows that segment 1A contains two buyers, and the other segments contain one buyer. As a market is segmented using more characteristics, the seller achieves finer precision but at the price of multiplying the number of segments and thinning out the populations in the segments.

Patterns of Market Segmentation

In the preceding illustration, the market was segmented by income and age, resulting in different *demographic segments*. Suppose, instead, buyers are asked how much they want of two product attributes (say, *sweetness* and *creaminess* in the case of ice cream). The result is the identification of different *preference segments* in the market. Three different patterns can emerge:

■ **Homogeneous preferences.** Figure 10-3(a) shows a market where all the consumers have roughly the same preference. The market shows no *natural segments*, at least as far as the two attributes are concerned. We would predict that existing brands would be similar and located in the center of the preferences.

■ **Diffused preferences.** At the other extreme, consumer preferences may be scattered throughout the space [Figure 10-3(b)], showing that consumers differ in what they want from the product. If one brand exists in the market, it is likely to be positioned in the center to appeal to the most people. A brand in the center minimizes the sum of total consumer dissatisfaction. A new competitor could locate next to the first brand and fight for market share. Or the competitor could locate in a corner to win over a customer group that was not satisfied with the center brand. If several brands are in the market, they are likely to be positioned throughout the space and show real differences to match consumer-preference differences.

■ **Clustered preferences.** The market might reveal distinct preference clusters, called *natural market segments* [Figure 10-3(c)]. The first firm in this market has three options. It might position itself in the center hoping to appeal to all the groups (undifferentiated marketing). It might position itself in the largest market segment (concentrated marketing). It might develop several brands, each positioned in a different segment (differentiated marketing). Clearly, if it developed only one brand, competition would enter and introduce brands in the other segments.

Market Segmentation Procedure

We have seen that market segments can be identified by applying successive variables to subdivide a market. As an illustration:

> An airline is interested in attracting nonflyers (segmentation variable: *user status*). Nonflyers consist of those who fear flying, those who are indifferent, and those who are positive toward flying (segmentation variable: *attitude*). Among those who feel positive are people with higher incomes who can afford to fly (segmentation variable: *income*). The airline may decide to target higher-income people who have a positive attitude toward flying but simply have not flown.

The question arises, Is there a formal procedure for identifying the major segments in a market? The answer is yes, and several research firms regularly conduct formal segmentation

FIGURE 10-3
Basic Market-Preference Patterns

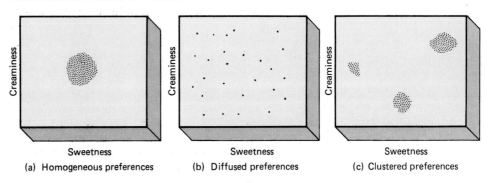

(a) Homogeneous preferences   (b) Diffused preferences   (c) Clustered preferences

studies in which the major market segments are systematically revealed. The procedure consists of three steps:

1. **Survey stage.** The researcher conducts informal interviews and focus groups with consumers to gain insight into their motivations, attitudes and behavior. Based on these findings, the researcher prepares a formal questionnaire that is administered to a sample of consumers to collect data on
   - ■ Attributes and their importance ratings
   - ■ Brand awareness and brand ratings
   - ■ Product usage patterns
   - ■ Attitudes toward the product category
   - ■ Demographics, psychographics, and mediagraphics of the respondents

   The sample should be large in order to gather enough data to profile each segment accurately. If the researcher guesses that there are, say, four segments, and generally two hundred interviews are desired per segment, then the questionnaire might be administered to eight hundred consumers.

2. **Analysis stage.** The researcher applies *factor analysis* to the data to remove highly correlated variables. Then the researcher applies *cluster analysis* to create a specified number of maximally different segments. Each cluster is internally homogeneous and externally very different from every other cluster. (For these techniques, see p. 103.)

3. **Profiling stage.** Each cluster is now profiled in terms of its distinguishing attitudes, behavior, demographics, psychographics, and media consumption habits. Each segment can be given a name based on a dominant distinguishing characteristic. Thus in a study of the leisure market, Andreasen and Belk found six market segments:[2]
   - ■ The passive homebody
   - ■ The active sports enthusiast
   - ■ The inner-directed self-sufficient
   - ■ The culture patron
   - ■ The active homebody
   - ■ The socially active

   They found, for example, that the culture patron is the best target for both theater and symphony subscriptions. The socially active can also be drawn to symphonies (though not theaters) in order to satisfy social needs.

This market segmentation procedure must be reapplied periodically because market segments change. At any point in time, the companies in an industry operate on an assumed segmentation. For example, Henry Ford assumed that only price mattered. General Motors later outpaced Ford because it started to design cars that recognized different income and preference groups in the market. Still later, Volkswagen and the Japanese automakers recognized the growing importance of car size and fuel economy as consumer choice attributes. Very often, the way in which a new company successfully breaks into an entrenched market is by discovering new segmentation possibilities in the market. The company transcends the current segmentation thinking assumed by the incumbents.

One way to discover new segments is to investigate the current sequence of variables that consumers look at on their way to choosing a product. In the 1960s, most car buyers first decided on the manufacturer and then on one of its car divisions. This is shown in Figure 10-4(a) as a *brand-dominant hierarchy*. Thus a buyer might favor General Motors cars and, within this set, Pontiac. Today many buyers decide first on the nation from which they want to buy a car [see Figure 10-4(b)]. Thus a growing number of buyers first decide that they want to buy a Japanese car, and then they may have a second-level preference for, say, Toyota followed by a third-level preference for Cressida. Now behind the emergence of a *nation-dominant hierarchy* is a deeper attribute, namely, quality, and the perception that nations differ in the quality of cars they produce. Had U.S. auto makers

FIGURE 10-4
Hierarchy of Attributes in the Auto Market

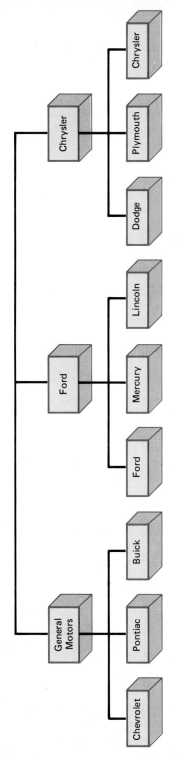

a. Brand-dominated hierarchy (1960s)

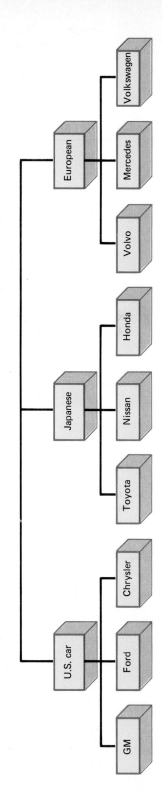

b. Nation-dominant hierarchy (1980s)

understood that the switch to Japanese cars was based on the growing importance of quality and value to the American car-buying public, they would not have relied on "Buy American" campaigns so much as on more rapidly improving the quality of their cars. The lesson is that a company must be alert to changes in the consumers' hierarchy of attributes in order to move with changing consumer priorities.

The hierarchy of attributes can be used to distinguish current customer segments. Those buyers who first decide on price are price-dominant; those who first decide on the type of the car (sports, passenger, station wagon, etc.) are type-dominant; those who first decide on the car brand are brand-dominant; and so on. One can go further and identify those who are type/price/brand dominant, in that order, as making up a segment; those who are quality/service/type dominant as making up another segment; and so on. Each segment may have distinct demographics, psychographics, and media graphics. This is called *market-partitioning theory*. The Hendry Corporation of New York has built a successful brand-forecasting system based on identifying the primary partitioning attributes used by buyers.[3]

Bases for Segmenting Consumer Markets

Here we want to look at variables that are commonly used to segment consumer markets (later we will look at industrial markets). The variables fall into the two broad groups shown in Figure 10-5. Some researchers try to form segments by looking at *consumer characteristics* independent of the particular product of interest. They commonly use a variety of geographic, demographic, and psychographic characteristics. Then they see whether these customer segments show different responses to the product. For example, they might examine the differing attitudes of "yuppies," "blue collars," and other groups toward American cars.

Other researchers try to form segments by looking at *consumer responses* to the product, such as benefits sought, use occasions, and brand loyalties. Once the segments are formed, the researcher then sees whether different consumer characteristics are associated with each segment. For example, the researcher might examine whether people who want "quality" versus "low price" in buying an automobile differ in their geographic, demographic, and psychographic makeup.

We will now comment on the major variables shown in Table 10-1 and describe how they are used to segment markets.

Geographic Segmentation Geographic segmentation calls for dividing the market into different geographical units such as nations, states, regions, counties, cities, or neighborhoods. The company can decide to operate in one or a few geographic areas or operate in

FIGURE 10-5
Two Major Approaches to Segmentation

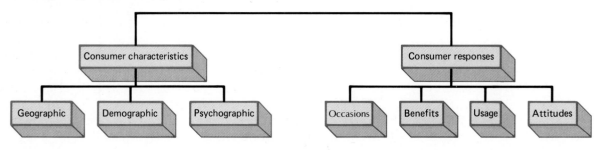

TABLE 10-1 Major Segmentation Variables for Consumer Markets

Variable	Typical Breakdowns
Geographic	
Region	Pacific, Mountain, West North Central, West South Central, East North Central, East South Central, South Atlantic, Middle Atlantic, New England
County size	A, B, C, D
City or SMSA size	Under 5,000; 5,000–20,000; 20,000–50,000; 50,000–100,000; 100,000–250,000; 250,000–500,000; 500,000–1,000,000; 1,000,000–4,000,000; 4,000,000 or over
Density	Urban, suburban, rural
Climate	Northern, southern
Demographic	
Age	Under 6, 6–11, 12–19, 20–34, 35–49, 50–64, 65+
Sex	Male, female
Family size	1–2, 3–4, 5+
Family life cycle	Young, single; young, married, no children; young, married, youngest child under 6; young, married, youngest child 6 or over; older, married, with children; older, married, no children under 18; older, single; other
Income	Under $5,000; $5,000–$10,000; $10,000–$15,000; $15,000–$20,000; $20,000–$25,000; $25,000–$30,000; $30,000–$50,000; $50,000 and over
Occupation	Professional and technical; managers, officials, and proprietors; clerical, sales; craftsmen, foremen; operatives; farmers; retired; students; housewives; unemployed
Education	Grade school or less; some high school; high school graduate; some college; college graduate
Religion	Catholic, Protestant, Jewish, other
Race	White, black, Oriental
Nationality	American, British, French, German, Scandinavian, Italian, Latin American, Middle Eastern, Japanese
Psychographic	
Social class	Lower lowers, upper lowers, working class, middle class, upper middles, lower uppers, upper uppers
Lifestyle	Straights, swingers, longhairs
Personality	Compulsive, gregarious, authoritarian, ambitious
Behavioral	
Occasions	Regular occasion, special occasion
Benefits	Quality, service, economy
User status	Nonuser, ex-user, potential user, first-time user, regular user
Usage rate	Light user, medium user, heavy user
Loyalty status	None, medium, strong, absolute
Readiness stage	Unaware, aware, informed, interested, desirous, intending to buy
Attitude toward product	Enthusiastic, positive, indifferent, negative, hostile

all but pay attention to variations in geographic needs and preferences. For example, General Foods' Maxwell House ground coffee is sold nationally but is flavored regionally. Its coffee is flavored stronger in the West than in the East. Campbell Soup Company recently appointed local area market managers and gave them budgets to study local markets and to adapt Campbell's products and promotions to local conditions.[4] Some companies even subdivide major cities into smaller geographic areas:

R. J. Reynolds Company has subdivided Chicago into three distinct submarkets. In the North Shore area, Reynolds promotes its low-tar brands because residents are better educated and concerned about health. In the blue-collar Southeast area, Reynolds promotes Winston because this area is conservative. In the black South Side, Reynolds promotes the high menthol content of Salem, using the black press and billboards heavily.

Demographic Segmentation   Demographic segmentation consists of dividing the market into groups on the basis of demographic variables such as age, sex, family size, family life cycle, income, occupation, education, religion, race, and nationality. Demographic variables are the most popular bases for distinguishing customer groups. One reason is that consumer wants, preferences, and usage rates are often highly associated with demographic variables. Another is that demographic variables are easier to measure than most other types of variables. Even when the target market is described in nondemographic terms (say, a personality type), the link back to demographic characteristics is necessary in order to know the size of the target market and how to reach it efficiently.

Here we will illustrate how certain demographic variables have been applied to market segmentation.

Age and life-cycle stage   Consumer wants and capacities change with age. Even six-month-old infants differ from three-month-old infants in their consumption potential. Alabe Products, a toy manufacturer, realized this and designed different toys for babies as they move through various stages from three months to one year. Crib Jiminy is to be used when babies begin to reach for things, Talky Rattle when they first grasp things, and so on. This segmentation strategy means that parents and gift givers can more easily find the appropriate toy by considering the baby's age.

General Foods applied age segmentation strategy to dog food. Many dog owners know that their dog's food needs change with age. So General Foods formulated four types of canned dog food: Cycle 1 for puppies, Cycle 2 for adult dogs, Cycle 3 for overweight dogs, and Cycle 4 for older dogs. General Foods managed to grab a large market share through this creative segmentation strategy.

Nevertheless, age and life cycle can be tricky variables. For example, the Ford Motor Company used buyers' ages in developing its target market for its Mustang automobile; the car was designed to appeal to young people who wanted an inexpensive sporty automobile. But Ford found that the car was being purchased by all age groups. It then realized that its target market was not the chronologically young but the psychologically young.

The Neugartens' research indicates that age stereotypes need to be carefully guarded against:

Age has become a poor predictor of the timing of life events, as well as a poor predictor of a person's health, work status, family status, and therefore, also, of a person's interests, preoccupations, and needs. We have multiple images of persons of the same age: there is the 70-year-old in a wheelchair and the 70-year-old on the tennis court. Likewise, there are 35-year-olds sending children off to college and 35-year-olds furnishing the nursery for newborns, producing in turn, first-time grandparenthood for persons who range in age from 35 to 75.[5]

Sex   Sex segmentation has long been applied in clothing, hairdressing, cosmetics, and magazines. Occasionally other marketers will notice an opportunity for sex segmentation. The cigarette market provides an excellent example. Most cigarette brands are smoked by men and women alike. Increasingly, however, feminine brands like Eve and Virginia

Slims have been introduced, accompanied by appropriate flavor, packaging, and advertising cues to reinforce the female image. Today it is as unlikely that men will smoke Eve as it is that women will smoke Marlboros. Another industry that is beginning to recognize the potential for sex segmentation is the automobile industry. In the past, cars were designed to appeal primarily to males. With more women car owners, however, some manufacturers are studying the opportunity to design cars with features appealing to women.

Income Income segmentation is another longstanding practice in such product and service categories as automobiles, boats, clothing, cosmetics, and travel. Other industries occasionally recognize its possibilities. For example, Suntory, the Japanese liquor company, introduced a scotch selling for $75 to attract drinkers who want the very best.

At the same time, income does not always predict the best customers for a given product. One would think that manual workers would buy Chevrolets and managers would buy Cadillacs. Yet many Chevrolets are bought by managers (often as a second car), and some Cadillacs are bought by manual workers (such as highly paid plumbers and carpenters). Manual workers were among the first purchasers of color television sets; it was cheaper for them to buy these sets than to go to movies and restaurants. Coleman drew a distinction between the "underprivileged" segments and the "overprivileged" segments of each social class.[6] The most economical cars are not bought by the really poor, Coleman pointed out, but rather by "those who think of themselves as poor relative to their status aspirations and to their needs for a certain level of clothing, furniture, and housing which they could not afford if they bought a more expensive car." On the other hand, medium-priced and expensive cars tend to be purchased by the overprivileged segments of each social class.

Multiattribute demographic segmentation Most companies will segment a market by combining two or more demographic variables. For example, a major bank identified age and income as the two major demographic variables for segmenting its retail customers. Figure 10-6 shows three age breakdowns and three income breakdowns. A number of things should be noted. First, the age breakdowns could be finer: People who are in their early forties can differ substantially from those in their late fifties with respect to financial needs, yet they are lumped together. The fact that the middle cell is subdivided into two cells acknowledges that differences exist between young middle-age people and preretired

FIGURE 10-6
Age and Income Segmentation of a Bank's Retail Customers

		Age		
		Under 39	40–65	Over 65
Income	Below $16,000	Young, low income	Middle-aged, lower income	Retired, low income
	$16,000–44,000	Young, middle income	Middle-aged middle income / Pre-retired, middle income	Retired, middle income
	Above $44,000	Young, high income	Middle-aged high income	Retired, high income

people. Second, income must be supplemented by an asset category. For example, some retired people have low incomes but high assets, and others may have high incomes but low assets. Nevertheless, this demographic segmentation scheme provides a starting point by which the bank can create different offers for different customer groups.

The "young, high income" segment shown at the lower left of Figure 10-6 would include the so-called yuppie segment, namely, *young, upwardly mobile urban professionals*. Defined demographically, yuppies are age 25–39, high income, upscale professional, city address. Defined psychographically, they are thought to favor tennis, skiing, and sailing as sports; enjoy gourmet foods and wines; participate in fashion, art, and cultural events; and like foreign travel. However, demographics and psychographics are not always tightly linked. It turns out that many persons who would be defined demographically as yuppies but who live in the Midwest as opposed to New England favor golf, hunting, and fishing; prefer "junk" food and beer; and score low in art and cultural interests. Thus a bank would have to decide whether it wants to reach demographically defined yuppies or psychographically defined yuppies because it makes a big difference in the bank's offer and communication mix.

Psychographic Segmentation   In psychographic segmentation, buyers are divided into different groups on the basis of their social class, lifestyle, and/or personality characteristics. People within the same demographic group can exhibit very different psychographic profiles.

Social class   We described the seven American social classes in Chapter 6, p. 197, and showed that social class has a strong influence on the person's preferences in cars, clothing, home furnishings, leisure activities, reading habits, retailers, and so on. Many companies design products and/or services for specific social classes, building in those features that appeal to the target social class.

Lifestyle   We also saw in Chapter 6 that people's interest in various goods is influenced by their lifestyles, and in fact the goods they consume express their lifestyle. Marketers of various products and brands are increasingly segmenting their markets by consumer lifestyles:

Volkswagen has designed lifestyle automobiles: a car for "the good citizen" emphasizing economy, safety, and ecology; and a car for the "car freak" emphasizing handling, maneuverability, and sportiness. A research firm classified auto buyers into six types: "auto philes," "sensible centrists," "comfort seekers," "auto cynics," "necessity drivers," and "auto phobes."

Manufacturers of women's clothing have followed Du Pont's advice and are designing different clothes for the "plain woman," the "fashionable woman," and the "manly woman."

Cigarette companies develop brands for the "defiant smoker," the "casual smoker," and the "careful smoker."

The President's Commission on American Outdoors divided Americans into five recreational lifestyle clusters: "health-conscious sociables," "get-away actives," "excitement-seeking competitives," "fitness driven" and "unstressed and unmotivated."

Companies making cosmetics, alcoholic beverages, and furniture are seeking opportunities in lifestyle segmentation. At the same time, lifestyle segmentation does not always work; Nestlé introduced a special brand of decaffeinated coffee for "late nighters," and it failed.

Personality   Marketers have also used personality variables to segment markets. They endow their products with *brand personalities* that correspond to *consumer personalities*. In the late fifties, Fords and Chevrolets were promoted as having different personalities.

Ford buyers were identified as "independent, impulsive, masculine, alert to change, and self-confident, while Chevrolet owners were conservative, thrifty, prestige-conscious, less masculine, and seeking to avoid extremes."[7] Evans investigated the validity of these descriptions by subjecting Ford and Chevrolet owners to the Edwards Personal Preference test, which measured needs for achievement, dominance, change, aggression, and so on. Except for a slightly higher score on dominance, Ford owners' scores were not significantly different from those of Chevrolet owners. Evans concluded that "the distributions of scores for all needs overlap to such an extent that [personality] discrimination is virtually impossible." Work subsequent to Evans on a wide variety of products and brands has occasionally revealed personality differences. Westfall found some evidence of personality differences between the owners of convertibles and nonconvertibles, with owners of the former appearing to be more active, impulsive, and sociable.[8] Shirley Young, the director of research for a leading advertising agency, reported developing successful market segmentation strategies based on personality traits in such product categories as women's cosmetics, cigarettes, insurance, and liquor.[9]

Behavioral Segmentation   In behavioral segmentation, buyers are divided into groups on the basis of their knowledge, attitude, use, or response to a product. Many marketers believe that behavioral variables are the best starting point for constructing market segments.

Occasions   Buyers can be distinguished according to occasions when they develop a need, purchase a product, or use a product. For example, air travel is triggered by occasions related to business, vacation, or family. An airline can specialize in serving people for whom one of these occasions dominates. Thus charter airlines serve people who fly for a vacation.

Occasion segmentation can help firms expand product usage. For example, orange juice is usually consumed at breakfast. An orange juice company can try to promote drinking orange juice on other occasions, such as lunch, dinner, or midday. Certain holidays— Mother's Day and Father's Day for example—were promoted partly to increase the sale of candy and flowers. The Curtis Candy Company promoted the "trick-or-treat" custom at Halloween, with every home ready to dispense candy to eager little callers knocking at their doors.

Instead of looking for product-specific occasions, a company can look at the major occasions that mark life's passages to see whether they are accompanied by certain needs that can be met by product and/or service bundles. Sometimes called "critical event segmentation," the occasions include marriage, separation, divorce; acquisition of a home; injury or illness; change in employment or career; retirement; death of a family member; and so on. Among the providers that have emerged to offer services on these critical occasions are marriage counselors, employment counselors, and bereavement counselors.

Benefits   A powerful form of segmentation is the classification of buyers according to the different benefits that they seek from the product. Yankelovich applied benefit segmentation to the purchase of watches. He found that "approximately 23 percent of the buyers bought for lowest price, another 46 percent bought for durability and general product quality, and 31 percent bought watches as symbols of some important occasion."[10] The better-known watch companies at the time focused almost exclusively on the third segment by producing expensive watches, stressing prestige, and selling through jewelry stores. The U.S. Time Company decided to focus on the first two segments by creating Timex

TABLE 10-2   Benefit Segmentation of the Toothpaste Market

Benefit Segments	Demographics	Behavioristics	Psychographics	Favored Brands
Economy (low price)	Men	Heavy users	High autonomy, value oriented	Brands on sale
Medicinal (decay prevention)	Large families	Heavy users	Hypochondriac, conservative	Crest
Cosmetic (bright teeth)	Teens, young adults	Smokers	High sociability, active	Macleans, Ultra Brite
Taste (good tasting)	Children	Spearmint lovers	High self-involvement, hedonistic	Colgate, Aim

SOURCE: Adapted from Russell J. Haley, "Benefit Segmentation: A Decision Oriented Research Tool," *Journal of Marketing*, July 1963, pp. 30–35.

watches and selling them through mass merchandisers. This segmentation strategy led to its becoming one of the world's largest watch companies.

Benefit segmentation requires determining the major benefits that people look for in the product class, the kinds of people who look for each benefit, and the major brands that deliver each benefit. One of the most successful benefit segmentations was reported by Haley, who studied the toothpaste market (see Table 10-2). Haley's research uncovered four benefit segments, seeking economy, protection, cosmetic, and taste benefits, respectively. Each benefit-seeking group had particular demographic, behavioristic, and psychographic characteristics. For example, decay-prevention seekers had large families, were heavy toothpaste users, and were conservative. Each segment also favored certain brands. A toothpaste company can use these findings to clarify which benefit segment it is appealing to, the characteristics of that segment, and the major competitive brands. The company can also search for a new benefit and launch a brand that delivers it.

Benefit segmentation usually implies that a company should focus on satisfying one benefit group. Thus Crest toothpaste offered the benefit of "anticavity protection" and became extremely successful. "Anticavity protection" became its *unique selling proposition*. A unique selling proposition (USP) is stronger than just a unique proposition (UP). Too many companies develop a unique proposition and forget selling. For example, a purple toothpaste is unique, but it probably won't sell.

Actually a company has more choices. The choices are

- Single benefit positioning
- Primary and secondary benefit positioning
- Double benefit positioning
- Triple benefit positioning

For example, Beecham promotes its Aquafresh toothpaste as offering three benefits: "anticavity protection," "better breath," and "whiter teeth." Clearly, many people want all three benefits, and the challenge is to convince them that the brand delivers all three. Beecham hit upon the solution by creating a toothpaste that squeezed out in three colors simultaneously, thus visually confirming the three benefits. In the process, Beecham "countersegmented"; that is, it attracted three segments instead of one. In a time when segments are becoming very small, companies are trying to develop a positioning that bridges a number of segments.

Generally speaking, however, as companies try to say that their brand is superior in several ways to competitors' brands, they risk both disbelief and a loss of clear positioning. Nevertheless, people generally want *benefit bundles*. Companies that can identify clear benefit bundle segments that are unsatisfied by any current offerings have a great opportunity.

User status Many markets can be segmented into nonusers, ex-users, potential users, first-time users, and regular users of a product. High-market-share companies are particularly interested in converting potential users into actual users, while smaller firms will try to get users of competitive brands to switch to their brand. Potential users and regular users require different marketing approaches.

Social marketing agencies pay close attention to user status. Drug rehabilitation agencies sponsor rehabilitation programs to help regular users quit the habit. They sponsor talks by ex-users to discourage young people from trying drugs.

Usage rate Markets can also be segmented into light-, medium-, and heavy-user groups of the product (called *volume segmentation*). Heavy users are often a small percentage of the market but account for a high percentage of total consumption. Some data on usage rates for popular consumer products are shown in Figure 10-7. Using beer as an example, the chart shows that 68 percent of the panel members did not drink beer. The 32 percent who did were divided into two groups. The lower 16 percent were light users and accounted for only 12 percent of total beer consumption. The heavy half accounted for 88 percent of the total consumption—that is, for over seven times as much consumption as the light users. Thus a beer company would prefer to attract one heavy user to its brand over several light users. Most beer companies target the heavy beer drinker, using appeals such as Schaefer's "The one beer to have when you're having more than one."

The heavy users of a product often have common demographics, psychographics, and media habits. In the case of heavy beer drinkers, their profile shows the following characteristics: More of them are in the working class compared with light beer drinkers; they fall between the ages of twenty-five and fifty (instead of under twenty-five and over fifty); they watch television more than three and one-half hours per day (instead of under

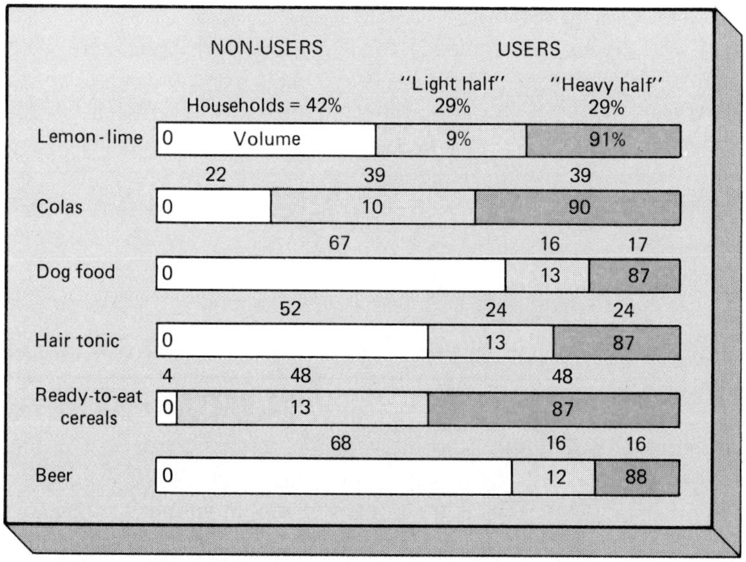

FIGURE 10-7
Annual Purchase Concentration in Several Product Categories
SOURCE: Dik Warren Twedt, "How Important to Marketing Strategy Is the 'Heavy User'?" *Journal of Marketing*, January 1974, p. 72.

two hours); and they prefer to watch sports programs.[11] Profiles like this one can assist the marketer in developing price, message, and media strategies.

Social marketing agencies often face a heavy-user dilemma. A family-planning agency would normally target families who have the most children, but these families are also the most resistant to birth-control messages. The National Safety Council would target unsafe drivers, but these drivers are the most resistant to safe-driving appeals. The agencies must consider whether to go after a few highly resistant heavy offenders or many less-resistant light offenders.

Loyalty status   A market can also be segmented by consumer loyalty patterns. Consumers can be loyal to brands (Schlitz), stores (Sears), and other entities. We will deal here with brand loyalty. Suppose there are five brands: A, B, C, D, and E. Buyers can be divided into four groups according to their loyalty status:[12]

- *Hard-core loyals*. Consumers who buy one brand all the time. Thus a buying pattern of A, A, A, A, A, A represents a consumer with undivided loyalty to brand A.
- *Soft-core loyals*. Consumers who are loyal to two or three brands. The buying pattern A, A, B, B, A, B represents a consumer with a divided loyalty between A and B.
- *Shifting loyals*. Consumers who shift from favoring one brand to another. The buying pattern A, A, A, B, B, B would suggest a consumer who is shifting brand loyalty from A to B.
- *Switchers*. Consumers who show no loyalty to any brand. The buying pattern A, C, E, B, D, B would suggest a nonloyal consumer who is either *deal prone* (buys the brand on sale) or *variety prone* (wants something different).

Each market consists of different numbers of the four types of buyers. A brand-loyal market is one with a high percentage of the buyers showing hard-core brand loyalty. Thus the toothpaste market and the beer market seem to be fairly high brand-loyal markets. Companies selling in a brand-loyal market have a hard time gaining more market share, and companies that enter such a market have a hard time getting in.

A company can learn a great deal by analyzing loyalty patterns in its market. It should study the characteristics of its own hard-core loyals. Colgate finds that its hard-core loyals are more middle class, have larger families, and are more health conscious. This pinpoints the target market for Colgate.

By studying its soft-core loyals, the company can pinpoint which brands are most competitive with its own. If many Colgate buyers also buy Crest, Colgate can attempt to improve its positioning against Crest, possibly using direct-comparison advertising.

By looking at customers who are shifting away from its brand, the company can learn about its marketing weaknesses. As for nonloyals, the company can attract them by putting its brand on sale.

The company should be aware that what appear to be brand-loyal purchase patterns may reflect *habit*, *indifference*, a *low price*, or the *nonavailability* of other brands. The concept of brand loyalty has some ambiguities and must be used carefully.

Buyer readiness stage   At any time, people are in different stages of readiness to buy a product. Some people are unaware of the product; some are aware; some are informed; some are interested; some are desirous of buying; and some intend to buy. The relative numbers make a big difference in designing the marketing program. Suppose a health agency wants women to take an annual Pap test to detect cervical cancer. At the beginning, most women are unaware of the Pap test. The marketing effort should go into high-aware-ness-building advertising using a simple message. If successful, the advertising should then dramatize the benefits of the Pap test and the risks of not taking it, in order to move more women into the stage of desire. Facilities should be readied for handling the large number of women who may be motivated to take the examination. In general, the marketing program must be adjusted to the changing number of people in each buyer-readiness stage.

Attitude People in a market can be classified by their degree of enthusiasm for the product. Five attitude classes can be distinguished: enthusiastic, positive, indifferent, negative, and hostile. Door-to-door workers in a political campaign use the voter's attitude to determine how much time to spend with the voter. They thank enthusiastic voters and remind them to vote; they reinforce those who are positively disposed; they try to win the votes of indifferent voters; they spend no time trying to change the attitudes of negative and hostile voters. To the extent that attitudes are correlated with demographic descriptors, the organization can increase its efficiency in locating the best prospects.

Bases for Segmenting Industrial Markets

Industrial markets can be segmented using many of the same variables employed in consumer market segmentation, such as geography, benefits sought, and usage rate. Yet there are also some new variables. Bonoma and Shapiro proposed the classification of segmentation variables for the industrial market shown in Table 10-3. They add that the demographic variables are the most important, followed by the operating variables . . . down to the personal characteristics of the buyer.

The table lists major questions that industrial marketers should ask in determining which customers they want to serve. In going after segments instead of the whole market,

TABLE 10-3   Major Segmentation Variables for Industrial Markets

Demographic
- *Industry*: which industries that buy this product should we focus on?
- *Company size*: what size companies should we focus on?
- *Location*: what geographical areas should we focus on?

Operating Variables
- *Technology*: what customer technologies should we focus on?
- *User/non-user status*: should we focus on heavy, medium, light users or non-users?
- *Customer capabilities*: should we focus on customers needing many services or few services?

Purchasing Approaches
- *Purchasing function organization*: should we focus on companies with highly centralized or decentralized purchasing organizations?
- *Power structure*: should we focus on companies that are engineering-dominated, financially-dominated, etc.
- *Nature of existing relationships*: should we focus on companies with which we have strong existing relationships or simply go after the most desirable companies?
- *General purchase policies*: should we focus on companies that prefer leasing? service contracts? systems purchases? sealed bidding?
- *Purchasing criteria*: should we focus on companies that are seeking quality? service? price?

Situational Factors
- *Urgency*: should we focus on companies that need quick and sudden delivery or service?
- *Specific application*: should we focus on certain applications of our product rather than all applications?
- *Size of order*: should we focus on large or small orders?

Personal Characteristics
- *Buyer-seller similarity*: should we focus on companies whose people and values are similar to ours?
- *Attitudes toward risk*: should we focus on risk-taking or risk-avoiding customers?
- *Loyalty*: should we focus on companies that show high loyalty to their suppliers?

SOURCE: Adapted from Thomas V. Bonoma and Benson P. Shapiro, *Segmenting the Industrial Market* (Lexington, Mass.: Lexington Books, 1983).

the company has a much better chance of delivering real value and receiving a premium price for its close attention to the needs of those segments. Thus a rubber tire company should decide which *industries* it wants to serve, noting the following differences:

> Automobile manufacturers seeking original equipment tires vary in their requirements, with luxury car manufacturers wanting a much higher grade tire than standard car manufacturers. And the tires needed by aircraft manufactuers have to meet much higher safety standards than tires needed by farm tractor manufacturers.

Within a chosen target industry, a company can further segment by *customer size*. The company might set up separate systems for dealing with large and small customers. For example, Steelcase, a major manufacturer of office furniture, divides its customers into two groups:

- ■ *Major accounts.* Accounts such as IBM, Prudential, and Standard Oil are handled by national account managers working with field district managers.
- ■ *Dealer accounts.* Smaller accounts are handled through field sales personnel working with franchised dealers who sell Steelcase products.

Within a certain target industry and customer size, the company can segment by *purchase criteria*:

> Government laboratories, university laboratories, and industrial laboratories typically differ in their purchase criteria for instruments. Government laboratories need low prices (because they have difficulty getting funds to buy instruments) and service contracts (because they can easily get money to maintain instruments). University laboratories need equipment that requires little continuous service because they do not have service people on their payroll. Industrial laboratories need equipment that is highly reliable because they cannot afford downtime.

In general, industrial companies do not focus on one segmentation variable but generally apply multiattribute segmentation. This is illustrated in Figure 10-8 for an aluminum company:

> The aluminum company first undertook *macrosegmentation* consisting of three steps.[13] It looked at which end-use market to serve: automobile, residential, or beverage containers. Choosing the residential market, it determined the most attractive product application: semifinished material, building components, or aluminum mobile homes. Deciding to focus on building components, it next considered the best customer size to serve and chose large customers.
>
> The second stage consisted of *microsegmentation* within the large-customer building-components markets. The company saw customers falling into three groups—those who bought on price, those who bought on service, and those who bought on quality. Because the aluminum company had a high-service profile, it decided to concentrate on the service-motivated segment of the market.

Developing the Customer Segment Profile Each customer segment that a company becomes interested in should be profiled in some detail. It is not enough to consider, say, price-sensitive customers versus quality-sensitive customers. We need further segment descriptors, such as their demographics, psychographics, mediagraphics, attitudes, and behavior. As an example, Smythe reported a benefit segmentation study of coffee drinkers.[14] They were asked to assign importance ratings to twenty-five product attributes. The data were factor-analyzed, and three

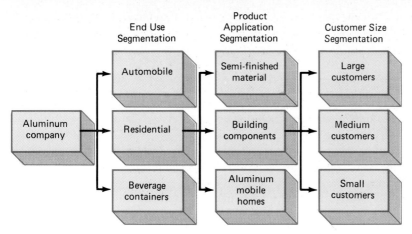

End Use Segmentation

Product Application Segmentation

Customer Size Segmentation

FIGURE 10-8
Three-Step Segmentation of the Aluminum Market
SOURCE: Based on an example in E. Raymond Corey, "Key Options in Market Selection and Product Planning," *Harvard Business Review*, September–October 1975, pp. 119–28.

clear segments emerged based on different needs for coffee. The segments were named decaffeinated, non-decaffeinated, and ground. Table 10-4 shows a partial profile of the three customer segments. They were approximately equal in size but quite different in benefits desired, use frequency, and demographics. In finding that, for example, decaffeinated coffee drinkers were older, widowed, etc., this did not mean that no decaffeinated coffee drinkers were younger, married, etc. It only meant that decaffeinated coffee drinkers were on the average older, widowed, etc. In fact, if there were no average demographic differences among the three groups, then demographic characteristics would be omitted from the profiles.

Clearly, the marketer's hope is to find quite different profiles for the segments. In the best case, the segments will differ psychographically and have different demographics

TABLE 10-4 Coffee Market Segment Profiles

| Name | Segment | | |
	Decaffeinated	**Non-Decaffeinated**	**Ground**
Size	35%	33%	32%
Distinguishing Benefits Desired	Decaffeinated	Not decaffeinated	Not prepared quickly
	Not make me nervous	Wake up	Not convenient package
	Prepared quickly	Convenient package	Not easy to prepare
	Not wake up	Well-known brand	Special equipment
	Concentrated form	Easy to prepare	Not concentrated form
Frequency of Use	Light users	Medium users	Heavy users
Type Usage	Instant	Both	Ground
Brand Usage	Sanka	Maxwell House	Hills Bros.
	Brim	Folger's	All others
	Taster's Choice		
	Nescafé		
	High Pont		
Demographics	Older	Average age	Younger
	Widowed	Divorced	Married
	Lower income	Average income	Higher income
	More minorities	More minorities	Fewer minorities

SOURCE: Robert J. Smythe, *Market Segmentation*, a pamphlet published by NFO Research, Inc., Toledo, Ohio (no date).

and mediagraphics. Thus the results would indicate that a decaffeinated coffee brand such as Sanka should be placed into heavy distribution where older, widowed, etc., people are found, and the brand should be advertised mostly in media read by people who are older, widowed, etc.

Requirements for Effective Segmentation

There are many ways to segment a market. Not all segmentations, however, are effective. For example, buyers of table salt could be divided into blond and brunette customers. But hair color is not relevant to the purchase of salt. Furthermore, if all salt buyers buy the same amount of salt each month, believe all salt is the same, and want to pay the same price, this market would be minimally segmentable from a marketing point of view.

To be maximally useful, market segments must exhibit the following characteristics:

- ■ **Measurability.** The degree to which the size and purchasing power of the segments can be measured. Certain segmentation variables are difficult to measure. An illustration would be the size of the segment of teenage smokers who smoke primarily to rebel against their parents.
- ■ **Substantiality.** The degree to which the segments are large and/or profitable enough. A segment should be the largest possible homogeneous group worth going after with a tailored marketing program. It would not pay, for example, for an automobile manufacturer to develop cars for persons who are shorter than four feet.
- ■ **Accessibility.** The degree to which the segments can be effectively reached and served. Suppose a perfume company finds that heavy users of its brand are single women who are out late at night and frequent bars. Unless this group lives or shops at certain places and is exposed to certain media, they will be difficult to reach.
- ■ **Actionability.** The degree to which effective programs can be formulated for attracting and serving the segments. A small airline, for example, identified seven market segments, but its staff was too small to develop separate marketing programs for each segment.

MARKET TARGETING

Market segmentation reveals the market segment opportunities facing the firm. The firm now has to evaluate the various segments and decide how many and which ones to serve. We will look at the tools for segment evaluation and selection below.

Evaluating the Market Segments

The firm, in evaluating different market segments, must look at three factors, namely (1) segment size and growth, (2) segment structural attractiveness, and (3) company objectives and resources.

Segment Size and Growth   The first question that a company should ask is whether a potential segment has the right size and growth characteristics. The "right size" is a relative matter. Large companies prefer segments with large sales volumes and often overlook or avoid small segments; small segments are not worth bothering with. Small companies in turn avoid large segments because they require too much in resources and are too attractive to the larger firms.

Segment growth is normally a desirable characteristic, since companies generally want growing sales and profits. At the same time, competitors will more rapidly enter growing segments and depress their profitability.

Segment Structural Attractiveness   A segment might have desirable size and growth characteristics and still not be attractive from a profitability point of view. Porter has identified five forces that determine the intrinsic long-run attractiveness of a whole market or any segment within it.[15] His five-force model is shown in Figure 10-9. The diagram shows a market consisting of nine segments (three customer groups times three possible products). The middle segment is being analyzed for its structural attractiveness. The company has to appraise the impact on long-run profitability of five groups: *industry competitors*, *potential entrants*, *substitutes*, *buyers*, and *suppliers*. The five threats they pose are as follows:

1. ***Threat of intense segment rivalry.*** A segment is unattractive if it already contains numerous, strong, or aggressive competitors. The picture is even worse if the segment is stable or declining, if capacity additions are done in large increments, if fixed costs are high, if exit barriers are high, or if competitors have high stakes in staying in the segment. These conditions will lead to frequent price wars, advertising battles, and new-product introductions and will make it expensive for the companies to compete.

2. ***Threat of new entrant.*** A segment is unattractive if it is likely to attract new competitors who will bring in new capacity, substantial resources, and a drive for market-share growth. The question boils down to whether new entrants can easily get in. They will find it hard if there are high barriers to entry coupled with sharp retaliation from incumbent firms. The lower the barriers to entry or willingness to retaliate, the less attractive the segment.

    A segment's attractiveness varies with the height of the entry and exit barriers.[16] The most attractive segment from the viewpoint of industry profits is one in which entry barriers

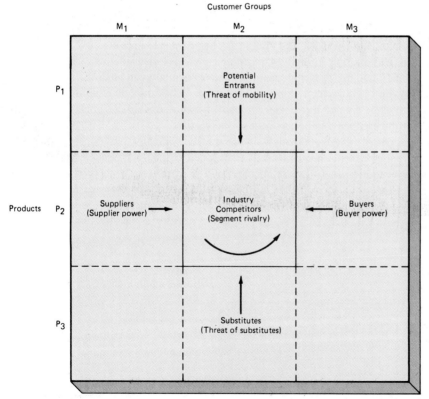

FIGURE 10-9
Five Forces Determining Segment Structural Attractiveness
SOURCE: Adapted with permission of the Free Press, a Division of Macmillian, Inc. from *Competitive Advantage: Creating and Sustaining Superior Performance* by Michael E. Porter, p. 235. Copyright © 1985 by Michael E. Porter.

are high and exit barriers are low (see Figure 10-10). Few new firms can enter the industry and poor-performing firms can easily exit. When both entry and exit barriers are high, profit potential is high but is usually accompanied by more risk because poorer-performing firms stay in and fight it out. When entry and exit barriers are both low, then firms easily enter and leave the industry, and the returns are stable and low. The worst case is when entry barriers are low and exit barriers are high: here firms enter during good times but find it hard to leave during bad times. The result is chronic overcapacity and depressed earnings for all.

3. ***Threat of substitute products.*** A segment is unattractive if there exist actual or potential substitutes for the product. Substitutes place a limit on the potential prices and profits that can be earned in a segment. The company has to watch closely the price trends in the substitutes. If technology advances or competition increases in these substitute industries, prices and profits in the segment are likely to fall.

4. ***Threat of growing bargaining power of buyers.*** A segment is unattractive if the buyers possess strong or increasing bargaining power. Buyers will try to force prices down, demand more quality or services, and set competitors against each other, all at the expense of seller profitability. Buyers' bargaining power grows when they become more concentrated or organized, when the product represents a significant fraction of the buyers' costs, when the product is undifferentiated, when the buyers' switching costs are low, when the buyers' are price-sensitive because of low profits, or when the buyers can integrate backward. In defense, sellers might select buyers who possess the least power to negotiate or switch suppliers. A better defense consists of developing superior offers that buyers cannot refuse.

5. ***Threat of growing bargaining power of suppliers.*** A segment is unattractive if the company's suppliers—raw material and equipment suppliers, public utilities, banks, trade unions, etc.— are able to raise prices or reduce the quality or quantity of ordered goods and services. Suppliers tend to be powerful when they are concentrated or organized, when there are few substitutes, when the supplied product is an important input, when the switching costs are high, and when the suppliers can integrate forward. The best defense is to build good relations with suppliers and have multiple supply sources.

Company Objectives and Resources   Even if a segment has positive size and growth characteristics and is structurally attractive, the company needs to consider its own objectives and resources in relation to that segment. Some attractive segments can be dismissed because they do not mesh with the company's long-run objectives. They may be tempting segments in themselves, but they do not move the company forward toward its goals. At worst, they would divert the company's energy from its main goals.

Even if the segment fits the company's objectives, the company must consider whether it possesses the requisite skills and resources to succeed in that segment. Each segment has certain success requirements. The segment should be dismissed if the company lacks one or more necessary competences and is in no position to acquire the necessary competences. But even if the company possesses the requisite competences, this is not enough. If it is really to win in that market segment, it needs to develop some superior advantages

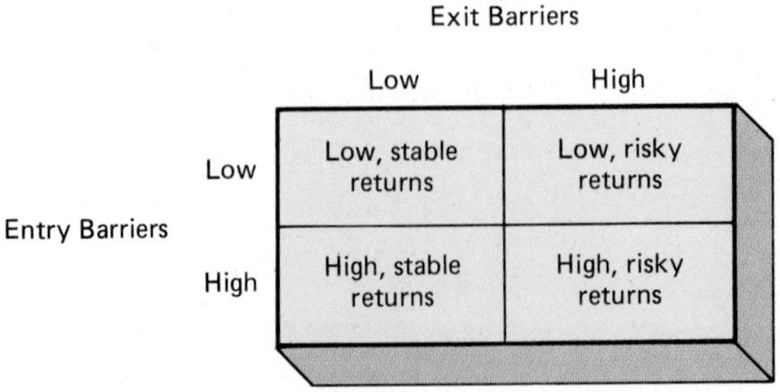

FIGURE 10-10
Barriers and Profitability

	Exit Barriers	
	Low	High
Entry Barriers — Low	Low, stable returns	Low, risky returns
Entry Barriers — High	High, stable returns	High, risky returns

to the competition. It should not enter markets or market segments where it cannot produce some form of superior value.

Selecting the Market Segments   As a result of evaluating different segments, the company hopes that it will find one or more market segments worth entering. The company must now decide which and how many segments to enter. Here the company can consider five possible market coverage patterns, those shown in Figure 10-11.

Single-segment Concentration   In the simplest case, the company selects a single segment to concentrate on. The company might have a natural match to this segment's success requirements; it might have very limited funds and can operate only in one segment; it might be a segment with no other competitor; it might be a segment that is a logical launching pad for further segment expansion.

Several examples of *concentrated marketing* can be cited. Volkswagen has concentrated on the small-car market, Hewlett-Packard on the high-price calculator market, and Richard D. Irwin on the economics and business texts market. Through concentrated marketing, the firm achieves a strong market position in the segment owing to its greater knowledge of the segment's needs and the special reputation it builds. Furthermore, the firm enjoys many operating economies through specializing its production, distribution, and promotion. If it niches well in the segment, the firm can earn a high return on its investment.

At the same time, concentrated marketing involves higher than normal risks. The particular market segment can turn sour; for example, when young women suddenly stopped buying sportswear, it caused Bobbie Brooks's earnings to go deeply into the red. Or a competitor may decide to enter the same segment. For these reasons, many companies prefer to operate in more than one segment.

Selective Specialization   Here the firm selects a number of segments, each of which is objectively attractive and matches the firm's objectives and resources. There may be little or no synergy between the segments, but each segment promises to be a money maker. This strategy of *multisegment coverage* has the advantage over *single-segment coverage* of divesifying the firm's risk. Even if one segment becomes unattractive, the firm can continue to earn money in other segments.

FIGURE 10-11
Five Patterns of Market Coverage
SOURCE: Adapted from Derek F. Abell, *Defining the Business: The Starting Point of Strategic Planning* (Englewood Cliffs, N.J.: Prentice-Hall, 1980), Chap. 8, pp. 192–196.

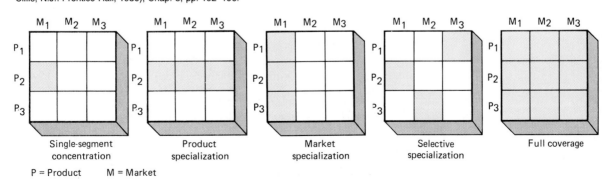

| | Single-segment concentration | Product specialization | Market specialization | Selective specialization | Full coverage |

P = Product   M = Market

Product Specialization   Here the firm concentrates on making a certain product that it sells to a variety of customer groups. An example would be a microscope manufacturer that sells microscopes to university laboratories, government laboratories, and commercial laboratories. The firm is prepared to make different microscopes for these different customer groups but avoids getting into the production of any other instruments that laboratories might use. Through this strategy, the firm builds up a strong reputation in the specific product area. The downside risk would occur if the product—here microscopes—is supplanted by an entirely new technology for magnifying small objects.

Market Specialization   Here the firm concentrates on serving many needs of a particular customer group. An example would be a firm that carries an array of products for university laboratories, including microscopes, oscilloscopes, bunsen burners, chemical flasks, and so on. The firm gains a strong reputation for specializing in serving this customer group and becomes a channel agent for all the new products that this customer group could feasibly use. The downside risk would occur if this customer group—here university laboratories—suddenly find that their budgets have been cut and they reduce their purchases from this market specialized firm.

Full Market Coverage   Here a firm attempts to serve all customer groups with all the products that they might need. Only large firms can undertake a full market coverage strategy. Examples would include IBM (computer market), General Motors (vehicle market), and Coca-Cola (drink market).

Large firms can cover a whole market in two broad ways, namely, through undifferentiated marketing or differentiated marketing.

Undifferentiated marketing   The firm might ignore market segment differences and go after the whole market with one market offer.[17] It focuses on what is common in the needs of buyers rather than on what is different. It designs a product and a marketing program that will appeal to the broadest number of buyers. It relies on mass distribution and mass advertising. It aims to endow the product with a superior image in people's minds. An example of undifferentiated marketing is the Coca-Cola Company's early marketing of only one drink in one bottle size in one taste to suit all.

Undifferentiated marketing is defended on the grounds of cost economies. It is seen as "the marketing counterpart to standardization and mass production in manufacturing."[18] The narrow product line keeps down production, inventory, and transportation costs. The undifferentiated advertising program keeps down advertising costs. The absence of segment marketing research and planning lowers the costs of marketing research and product management.

Nevertheless, a growing number of marketers have expressed strong doubts about this strategy. Gardner and Levy, while acknowledging that "some brands have very skillfully built up reputations of being suitable for a wide variety of people," noted that

> in most areas audience groupings will differ, if only because there are deviants who refuse to consume the same way other people do. . . . It is not easy for a brand to appeal to stable lower-middle-class people and at the same time to be interesting to sophisticated, intellectual upper-middle-class buyers. . . . It is rarely possible for a product or brand to be all things to all people.[19]

The firm practicing undifferentiated marketing typically develops an offer aimed at the largest segments in the market. When several firms do this, the result is intense competition for the largest segments and undersatisfaction of the smaller ones. Thus the American auto industry for a long time produced only large automobiles. The further result is that the larger segments may be less profitable because they attract disproportionately heavy competition. Kuehn and Day have called this tendency to go after the largest market segment the "majority fallacy."[20] The recognition of this fallacy has led firms into increased interest in the smaller segments of the market.

Differentiated marketing Here the firm operates in most segments of the market but designs tailored programs for each significantly different segment. General Motors claims to do this when it says that it produces a car for every "purse, purpose, and personality." And IBM offers many hardware and software variations to different segments in the computer market.

A growing number of firms have adopted differentiated marketing. Here is an excellent example:[21]

> Edison Brothers operates nine hundred shoe stores that fall into four different chain categories, each appealing to a different market segment. Chandler's sells higher-priced shoes. Baker's sells moderate-priced shoes. Burt's sells shoes for budget shoppers, and Wild Pair is oriented to the shopper who wants very stylized shoes. Within three blocks on State Street in Chicago are found Burt's, Chandler's, and Baker's. Putting the stores near each other does not hurt them because they are aimed at different segments of the women's shoe market. This strategy has made Edison Brothers the country's largest retailer of women's shoes.

Differentiated marketing typically creates more total sales than undifferentiated marketing. "It is ordinarily demonstrable that total sales may be increased with a more diversified product line sold through more diversified channels."[22] However, it also increases the costs of doing business. The following costs are likely to be higher:

- *Product modification costs.* Modifying a product to meet different market segment requirements usually involves some R&D, engineering, and/or special tooling costs.
- *Production costs.* It is usually more expensive to produce, say, ten units of ten different products than one hundred units of one product. The longer the production setup time for each product and the smaller the sales volume of each product, the more expensive it becomes. On the other hand, if each model is sold in sufficiently large volume, the higher costs of setup time may be quite small per unit.
- *Administrative costs.* The company has to develop separate marketing plans for the separate segments of the market. This requires extra marketing research, forecasting, sales analysis, promotion, planning, and channel management.
- *Inventory costs.* It is generally more costly to manage inventories of differentiated products than an inventory of only one product. The extra costs arise because more records must be kept and more auditing must be done. Furthermore, each product must be carried at a level that reflects basic demand plus a safety factor to cover unexpected variations in demand. The sum of the safety stocks for several products will exceed the safety stock required for one product.
- *Promotion costs.* Differentiated marketing involves trying to reach different market segments with different advertising. This leads to lower usage rates of individual media and the loss of quantity discounts. Furthermore, since each segment may require separate creative advertising planning, promotion costs are increased.

Since differentiated marketing leads to both higher sales and higher costs, nothing can be said in advance regarding the profitability of this strategy. Some firms find that they have *oversegmented* their market and offer too many brands. They would like to

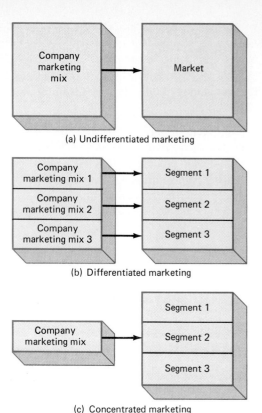

FIGURE 10-12
Three Alternative Market Selection Strategies

(a) Undifferentiated marketing

(b) Differentiated marketing

(c) Concentrated marketing

manage fewer brands, with each appealing to a broader customer group. Called ''counterseg-mentation'' or ''broadening the base,'' they seek a larger volume for each brand.[23] Johnson & Johnson, for example, as we mentioned in an earlier chapter, broadened its target market for its baby shampoo to include adults. And Beecham launched its Aquafresh toothpaste to attract three benefit segments, those seeking fresh breath, whiter teeth, and cavity protection.

Figure 10-12 summarizes the differences between undifferentiated marketing, differentiated marketing, and concentrated marketing.

Other Considerations in Evaluating and Selecting Segments

Three other considerations must be taken into account in evaluating and selecting segments.

Segment Interrelationships and Supersegments   In selecting more than one segment to serve, the company should pay close attention to *segment interrelationships* on the cost, performance, or technology side. Two or more segments might provide a joint opportunity for exploitation because of common technology, manufacturing, distribution channels, logistics, and so on. For example, a company that has a sales force that sells carburetors to Detroit auto makers might ask its sales force to sell fuel pumps as well. This company would have lower sales-force costs for selling carburetors to Detroit than another company that only sold carburetors to Detroit.

When the joint costs of operating in two (or more) segments simultaneously is less

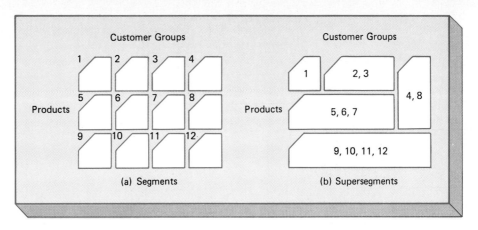

FIGURE 10-13
Segments and Supersegments

than the cost of operating in the two segments independently, *economies of scope* are said to exist. Economies of scope can be just as important as economies of scale. Companies should attempt to identify and operate in *supersegments* rather than in isolated segments. Figure 10-13 shows how twelve single segments can be regrouped into five supersegments based on certain synergies, such as using the same raw materials, manufacturing facilities, or distribution channels. The firm would be wise to choose a supersegment rather than a single segment within the supersegment; otherwise it might be at a competitive disadvantage with those firms that have locked into that supersegment.

Segment-by-Segment Invasion Plans   Even if the firm plans to move into a supersegment, it is wise to enter one segment at a time and conceal its grand plan. The competitors must not know to what segment(s) the firm will move next. This situation is illustrated in Figure 10-14. Three firms, A, B, and C, have specialized in adapting computers systems to the needs of transportation companies—specifically, airlines, railroads, and trucking companies. Company A has specialized in meeting all the computer needs of airlines. Company B has specialized in selling large computer systems to all three transportation sectors. Company C recently entered this market and has specialized in tailoring and selling value-added microcomputers to trucking companies. The question is, Where should Company C move next? The arrows have been added to the chart to show the planned sequence of market segment invasions unknown to Company C's competitors. Company C will start offering midsize computers to trucking companies; then to allay Company B's concern about its large computer business with trucking companies being attacked, Company C moves into offering microcomputers tailored to railroad needs. Later it offers midsize computers to railroads. Finally it launches a full attack on Company B's large computer position in trucking companies. Of course, its planned sequence is provisional in that much depends on the segment moves of the other competitors over time.

   Unfortunately, too many companies fail to develop a long-term invasion plan in which they have plotted the sequence and timing of market segment entries. Pepsi-Cola is an exception in that its attack on Coca-Cola was thought through in grand-plan terms, first attacking Coca-Cola in the grocery market, then in the vending machine market, then in the fast-food market, and so on. Japanese firms also plot their invasion sequence. They

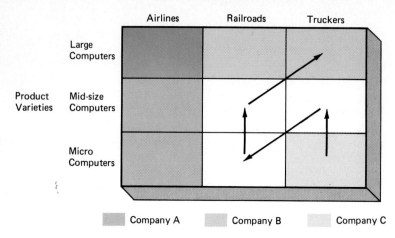

Customers Groups

Airlines   Railroads   Truckers

Product Varieties

Large Computers

Mid-size Computers

Micro Computers

■ Company A   ■ Company B   ■ Company C

FIGURE 10-14
A Segment-by-Segment Invasion Plan

first gain a foothold in a market—say Toyota brings a small car into the market—and then they expand with more cars, then larger cars, and eventually luxury cars. American firms turn blue when a Japanese firm enters the market, knowing that the Japanese firm will not stop at the first segment but will use it as a launching pad for successive invasions.

The question of who will dominate a segment is also raised by Figure 10-14. For example, both Company A and Company B compete in selling large computers to airlines. Company A is a specialist in large computers and probably enjoys lower costs through its higher volume. Company B specializes in all the computer needs of airlines and has the advantage of knowing airlines and their people better. The issue boils down to which is a greater advantage for operating in that segment.

Detailed Segment Analysis   In choosing a segment, the company must make sure that it fully understands that segment. A useful analytical tool for doing this is illustrated in Figure 10-15, which shows the market for the product line of a steel-fabricating company. Stage 1 shows a segmentation of this market, using customer groups and product varieties. The customer groups consist of contractors in general, electrical, and plumbing lines. The product mix consists of three products sold to contractors: pipe hangers, concrete inserts, and electrical supports. This joint segmentation results in nine market segments. A dollar figure in each cell represents the company's sales in that segment.

Company sales in the nine segments provide no indication of their relative profit potential. The latter depends on market demand, company costs, and competitive trends in each submarket. Stages 2 and 3 show how one product submarket, the electrical contractor market for concrete inserts, can be analyzed in depth.

Stage 2 estimates present and future sales in the submarket. The vertical axis accommodates estimates of industry sales, company sales, and company market share. The horizontal axis is used to project future sales and market shares. The company plans to initially sell $200,000 worth of goods, or one-fourth of total estimated industry sales. By the third year, the company expects to capture a 30 percent share of this submarket.

Stage 3 probes deeper into the marketing thinking behind the sales forecasts of stage 2. The horizontal axis shows the promotional mix that the company plans to use to stimulate the sale of concrete inserts to electrical contractors. The vertical axis shows the distribution

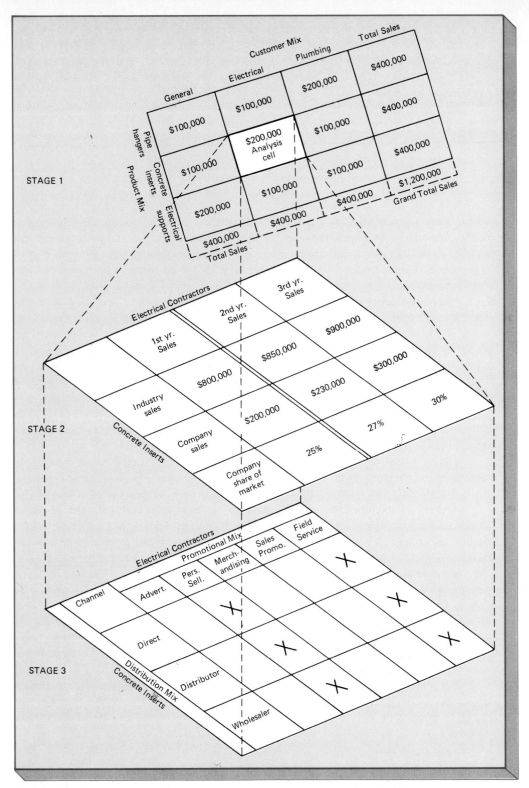

FIGURE 10-15
Analyzing the Worth of Different Market Segments for Steel-Fabricated Products
SOURCE: Adapted from an unpublished paper by Rhett W. Butler, Northwestern University, 1964.

mix that the company plans to use to move concrete inserts into the hands of electric contractors. The actual promotion-distribution mix could be detailed by placing budget figures (funds and personnel) in the relevant cells. The company will use all three types of distribution and rely mainly on personal selling and field service for stimulating sales to electrical contractors.

This analysis allows the marketing strategist to select strategies and evaluate their long-run profit potential.[24]

PRODUCT POSITIONING

Within each segment, the company needs to develop a product-positioning strategy. It needs to describe to customers how the company differs from current and potential competitors. *Positioning* is *the act of designing the company's image and value offer so that the segment's customers understand and appreciate what the company stands for in relation to its competitors.*

Many positions are available to a firm. It might go after the "low-price position," "high-quality position," "high-service position," "advanced-technology position," and so on. Essentially the firm is trying to establish a competitive advantage that it hopes will appeal to a substantial number of the segment's customers. (See Exhibit 10-2.)

Positioning would seem to put the firm in a subsegment of its chosen market segment. Thus the firm that goes after the "high-quality position" will attract the "high-quality customer segment" within the broader market. But here we can distinguish between a *segment* and a *niche* within a segment. Thus if the segment being served consists of electrical contractors who want concrete inserts, our firm has niched (or positioned) itself to serve the high-quality oriented customers within this segment.

The advantage of solving the *positioning problem* is that it enables the company to solve the *marketing-mix problem*. The marketing mix—product, price, place, and promotion—is essentially the working out of the tactical details of the positioning strategy. Thus a firm that seizes upon the "high-quality position" knows that it must put out high-quality products, charge a high price, distribute through high-class dealers, and advertise in high-quality magazines. This is the only way to project a consistent and believable high-quality image.

Some firms will find it easy to choose their positioning strategy. Thus a firm that is well known for quality in other segments will go for this position in a new segment as long as there is a sufficient number of quality-oriented buyers. But in many cases, two or more firms will go after the same positioning. Then each will have to seek further differentiation, such as "high quality for a lower cost" or "high quality with more technical service." Another way of saying this is that each firm must build a unique bundle of competitive advantages that appeal to a substantial group within the segment.

The positioning task consists of three steps: identifying a set of possible competitive advantages to exploit, selecting the right one(s), and effectively signaling to the market the firm's positioning concept.

Identifying Potential Competitive Advantages A company differentiates itself from competitors by bundling competitive advantages. Porter describes competitive advantage as follows:

Competitive advantage grows out of value a firm is able to create for its buyers that exceeds the firm's cost of creating it. Value is what buyers are willing to pay, and superior value stems from offering lower prices than competitors for equivalent benefits or providing unique benefits that more than offset a higher price. There are two basic types of competitive advantage: cost leadership and differentiation.[25]

EXHIBIT 10-2

Positioning Theme Parks

Here is an example of market positioning using perceptual maps. A theme park company wants to build a new theme park in the Los Angeles area to take advantage of the substantial number of tourists who come to Los Angeles with the idea of seeing Disneyland and other tourist attractions in the area. At least seven theme parks now operate in the Los Angeles area. Management feels that the existing theme parks are quite expensive: A family of four will pay $50 for a day at Disneyland. Management believes it could develop a less-expensive theme park that would appeal to the segment of cost-conscious tourists. Management, however, needs to know how consumers view the seven existing theme parks in terms of the various satisfactions they seek in a theme park, including low cost.

The company's marketing researcher used the following procedure to develop a perceptual map of Los Angeles' seven major tourist attractions. The marketing researcher presented consumers with a series of triads (such as the triad "Bush Gardens, Japanese Deer Park, and Disneyland") and asked them to choose the two most similar attractions and the two least similar attractions in each triad. A statistical analysis led to the accompanying perceptual map.

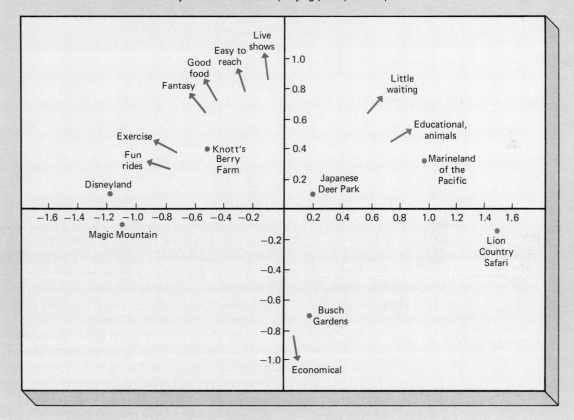

This map contains two features. There are seven dots representing the seven major tourist attractions in the Los Angeles area. The closer any two attractions are, the more similar they are; thus Disneyland and Magic Mountain are perceived as similar, whereas Disneyland and Lion Country Safari are perceived as very dissimilar. The map also contains nine satisfactions that people look for in tourist attractions, indicated by arrows. The standing of each tourist attraction on each attribute can be read. For example, Marineland of the Pacific is perceived by consumers as involving the "least waiting time" because it is farthest along the imaginary line of the "little waiting" arrow, while Magic Mountain is perceived as involving the most waiting time. Consumers think of Busch Gardens as the most economical attraction and Knott's Berry Farm as the most expensive attraction. Evidently the theme park company will face Busch Gardens as a major competitor if it decides to build a theme park to appeal to cost-conscious tourists. At the same time, management will pay attention to all the other satisfactions consumers seek as it figures out a product concept for the theme park and its positioning strategy in relation to the other theme parks in the Los Angeles area.

The analysis can be improved further by preparing a separate perceptual map for each market segment instead of one map for the total market. Each market segment is likely to perceive the products and benefits somewhat differently. The marketer really wants to know how its target market(s) perceives the product alternatives.

Clearly, every product needs a positioning strategy so that its place in the total market can be communicated. Professor Wind has identified six alternative bases for constructing a product-positioning strategy. They are listed below and hypothetically illustrated for the case of theme parks:

■ *Positioning on specific product features.* Disneyland can advertise itself as the largest theme park in the world. Largeness is a product feature that indirectly implies a benefit, namely, the most entertainment options.

■ *Positioning on benefits, problem solution, or needs.* Knott's Berry Farm can position itself as a theme park for people seeking a fantasy experience.

■ *Positioning for specific usage occasions.* Japanese Deer Park can position itself for the tourist who can spend only an hour and wants to catch some quick entertainment.

■ *Positioning for user category.* Magic Mountain can advertise itself as the theme park for "thrill seekers," thus defining itself through a user category.

■ *Positioning against another product.* Lion Country Safari can advertise that it has a greater variety of animals than the Japanese Deer Park.

■ *Product class dissociation.* Marineland of the Pacific can position itself not as a "recreational theme park" but as an "educational institution," thus putting itself into another product class than the expected one.

SOURCES See Robert V. Stumpf, "The Market Structure of the Major Tourist Attractions in Southern California," *Proceedings* of the 1976 Sperry Business Conference (Chicago: American Marketing Association, pp. 101–6); and Yoram J. Wind, *Product Policy*: *Concepts*, *Methods*, and *Strategy* (Reading, Mass.: Addison-Wesley, 1982), pp. 79–81.

Porter proposed the *value chain* as the major tool for identifying potential competitive advantages (see Figure 10-16). Every firm is a collection of activities that are performed to design, produce, market, deliver, and support its product. The value chain disaggregates a firm into nine strategically relevant activities in order to understand the behavior of costs in the specific business and industry and the existing and potential sources of differentiation. The nine value activities consist of five primary activities and four support activities.

The primary activities represent the sequence of bringing materials into the business, operating on them, sending them out, marketing them, and servicing them. The support activities occur throughout all of these primary activities. Thus procurement represents the purchasing of various inputs for each primary activity, only a fraction of which are handled by the purchasing department. Technology development occurs in every primary activity, only a fraction of which are done in the R&D department. Human resource management also occurs in all departments. The firm's infrastructure covers the overhead of general

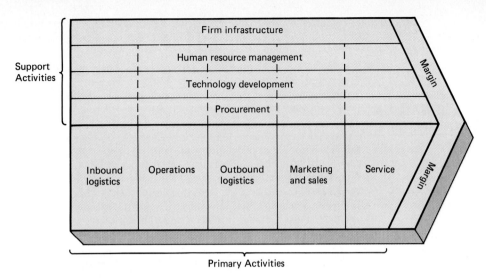

FIGURE 10-16
The Generic Value Chain
SOURCE: Porter, *Competitive Advantage*, p. 37.

management, planning, finance, accounting, and legal and government affairs that are borne by all the primary and support activities.

The firm's task is to examine its costs and performance in each value activity and to look for improvements. It should estimate its competitors' costs and performances as benchmarks. To the extent that it can do better than its competitors, it has achieved a competitive advantage.

The firm needs to look for competitive advantages beyond its own value chain, into the value chains of its suppliers, distributors, and ultimately customers. Thus the company might help a major supplier reduce its costs and thereby pass on the savings to the company; or it might help customers perform some activity better or cheaper to win their loyalty.

Clearly, the value chain provides the firm with a comprehensive framework for systematically searching for ways to provide superior value to customers. Whether it produces few or many ideas depends on the nature of the industry to some extent. The Boston Consulting Group recently proposed a new matrix in which it distinguished four types of industries (see Figure 10-17). The two dimensions are the size of the competitive advantage

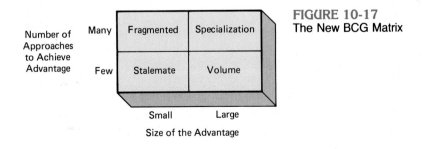

FIGURE 10-17
The New BCG Matrix

and the number of approaches to achieving advantage. The four industry types are as follows:

- ■ *Volume industry.* A volume industry is one in which companies can gain only a few, but rather large, advantages. An example would be the construction equipment industry where a company can strive for the low-cost position or the highly differentiated position and win "big" on either basis. Here profitability is correlated with company size and market share.
- ■ *Stalemated industry.* A stalemated industry is one in which there are few potential advantages and each of them is small. An example would be the steel industry where it is hard to differentiate the product or its manufacturing cost (under a certain technology). The companies can try to hire better salespeople, entertain more lavishly, etc., but these are small advantages. Here profitability is unrelated to company market share.
- ■ *Fragmented industry.* A fragmented industry is one in which companies face many opportunities for differentiation, but each is of small import. Restaurants are an example in that restaurants can differentiate themselves in many ways but not end up gaining a large share of the market. Profitability is not related to restaurant size: Both small and large restaurants can be profitable or unprofitable.
- ■ *Specialized industry.* A specialized industry is one in which companies face many opportunities for differentiation, and each can have a high payoff. An example would be companies making specialized machinery for selected market segments. Some small companies can be as profitable as some large companies.

Thus not every company will face a plethora of cost or performance opportunities for gaining competitive advantage. Some companies will find many minor advantages available, but all are highly imitable and therefore perishable. The solution for these companies is to identify new potential advantages continually and move them out one by one to keep the competitors off balance. That is, these companies need to "routinize" the innovation process, expecting not so much to achieve a major permanent advantage but rather to discover many little ones that can be introduced sequentially to win market share.

Choosing Competitive Advantages   Suppose a company has been fortunate enough to discover several potential competitive advantages through its value chain analysis. Some could be ruled out because they are too slight, too costly to develop, or too inconsistent with the company's profile. Suppose four advantages remain and the company needs a framework for selecting the one that makes the most sense to develop. Table 10-5 shows a systematic way to evaluate several potential advantages and choose the right one.

In the example, the company compares its standing on four atttributes—technology, cost, quality, and service—with the standing of its major competitor. Both companies

TABLE 10-5   Method for Competitive Advantage Selection

(1)	(2)	(3)	(4)	(5)	(6)	(7)
Competitive Advantage	Company Standing (1–10)	Competitor Standing (1–10)	Importance of Improving Standing (H-M-L)*	Affordability and Speed (H-M-L)	Competitor's Ability to Improve Standing (H-M-L)	Recommended Action
TECHNOLOGY	8	8	L	L	M	HOLD
COST	6	8	H	M	M	MONITOR
QUALITY	8	6	L	L	H	MONITOR
SERVICE	4	3	H	H	L	INVEST

*H = High; M = Medium; L = Low

stand at 8 on technology (1 = low score, 10 = high score), which means they both have good technology. There is a question about whether the company can gain much by improving its technology further, especially against the cost of doing this. The competitor has a better standing on cost (8 instead of 6), and this can hurt the company if the market becomes more price-sensitive. The company offers higher quality than its competitor (8 instead of 6). Finally, both companies offer below-average service.

It would seem that the company should go after cost or service to improve its market appeal relative to the competitor. However, other considerations arise. The first is: How important are improvements in each of these attributes to the target customers? Column 4 indicates that improvements in cost and service would be of high importance to customers. Next: Can the company afford to make the improvements and how fast can it complete them? Column 5 shows that improving service would have high affordability and speed. But would the competitor also be able to improve service if the company started to do this? Column 6 shows that the competitor's ability to improve service is low, perhaps because the competitor does not believe in service or is strapped for funds. Column 7 then shows the appropriate actions to take with respect to each attribute. The one that makes the most sense for the company is to invest in improving its service. Service is important to customers; the company can afford to improve its service and do it fast; and the competitor probably cannot catch up. Thus we see that this type of reasoning process can help the company choose the best competitive advantage.

Signaling the Competitive Advantage Companies must take specific steps to build and advertise their competitive advantage and not assume that it will automatically be apparent to the market. Thus a company that decides to build service superiority should go about quietly hiring and training more service people, and then broadcast its service capabilities and its superiority in this attribute: "Company X . . . the service leader."

Positioning the company calls for concrete action, not just talk. The company must manifest its chosen market position through deeds and words. It must avoid three major positioning errors:

1. *Underpositioning.* Some companies discover that buyers have only a vague idea of what the company stands for. They see it as just another company.
2. *Overpositioning.* Buyers may see a company too narrowly. Thus a consumer might think that the Steuben company only makes fine glass in the range of $1,000 and up when in fact it makes affordable fine glass starting around $50.
3. *Confused positioning.* Buyers could have a confused image of a company. Car buyers, when asked about Chrysler cars, might give quite different impressions, some saying that Chrysler cars are well engineered and others saying they are poorly engineered, some saying that they handle well, others saying they handle poorly, etc.

Ries and Trout, who were early proponents of the positioning concept, see positioning as primarily a communication strategy rather than a total marketing-mix strategy. Yet they make some fine points about what it takes to develop and signal a company or a product's position in the marketplace. Their thinking is described in Exhibit 10-3.

Now that we have examined the major steps and tools involved in segmenting, targeting, and positioning, we can move to identifying, in the next three chapters, appropriate competitive strategies for companies finding themselves in different leadership positions in the market, in different stages of the product life cycle, and in different international engagements.

EXHIBIT 10-3

"Positioning" According to Ries and Trout

The word *positioning* was popularized in 1972 by two advertising executives, Al Ries and Jack Trout, in a series of articles in *Advertising Age* called "The Positioning Era." Later they wrote a book called *Positioning: The Battle for Your Mind*. Ries and Trout see positioning as a creative exercise done with an existing product. Here is their definition:

> Positioning starts with a product. A piece of merchandise, a service, a company, an institution, or even a person. . . . But positioning is not what you do to a product. Positioning is what you do to the mind of the prospect. That is, you position the product in the mind of the prospect.

Ries and Trout argue that current products generally have a position in the minds of consumers. Thus Hertz is thought of as the world's largest auto rental agency, Coca-Cola as the world's largest soft-drink company, Porsche as one of the world's best sports cars, and so on. These brands own those positions and it would be hard for a competitor to steal these positions. A competitor has only three strategy options.

One strategy is to strengthen and leverage its own current position in the minds of consumers. Thus Avis took its second position in the auto rental business and made a strong point about it: "We're number two. We try harder." This is believable to the consumer. And 7–Up capitalized on the fact that it was not a cola soft drink by advertising itself as the Uncola.

The second strategy is to search for a new unowned position that is valued by enough consumers and to grab it. They call it "Cherchez le créneau," or "Look for the hole." Find the hole in the market and fill it. Thus Milky Way wanted to strengthen its market share against Hershey. Its marketers noticed that most candy bars are eaten within a minute once they are opened, but Milky Way lasts longer. So they went after the position "lasts longer," which no competitor owned. As another example, United Jersey Bank was searching for a way to compete against the giant New York banks such as Citibank and Chase. Its marketers noticed that giant banks were usually slower in arranging loans. They positioned United Jersey as "the fast-moving bank," and their success rested on actually making themselves a "fast-moving bank."

The third strategy is to deposition or reposition the competition. Most U.S. buyers of dinnerware thought that Lenox china and Royal Dalton both came from England. Royal Dalton put out ads showing that Lenox china was made in New Jersey but theirs came from England. In a similar vein, Stolichnaya vodka attacked Smirnoff and Wolfschmidt vodka by pointing out that these brands were made, respectively, in Hartford (Connecticut) and Lawrenceberg (Indiana), but "Stolichnaya is different. It is Russian." As a final example, Wendy's famous commercial where a seventy-year-old woman named Clara looks at a competitor's hamburger and says, "Where's the beef?" shows how an attack can destabilize the consumer's confidence in the leader.

Essentially, Ries and Trout outline how similar brands can acquire some distinctiveness in an "overcommunicated society" where there is so much advertising that consumers screen out most of the messages. A consumer may know only about seven soft drinks even though there are many more on the market. Even then, the mind often knows them in the form of a *product ladder*, such as Coke/Pepsi/RC Cola or Hertz/Avis/National. Ries and Trout note that the second firm usually enjoys half the business of the first firm, and the third firm enjoys half the business of the second firm. Furthermore, the top firm is remembered best.

People tend to remember *number one*. For example, when we are asked, "Who was the first person to successfully fly alone over the Atlantic ocean?" we will answer, "Charles Lindbergh." When we are asked, "Who was the second person to do this?" we draw a blank. This is why companies fight for the number-one position. But Ries and Trout point out that the "size" position can be held by only one brand. What counts is to achieve a number-one position along some valued attribute, not necessarily "size." Thus 7–Up is the number-one Uncola, Porsche is the number-one small sports car, and Dial is the number-one deodorant soap. The marketer should identify an important attribute or benefit that can convincingly be won by the brand. In this way, brands get hooked into the mind in spite of the incessant advertising bombardment reaching consumers.

A fourth strategy that Ries and Trout do not mention can be called the "exclusive club strategy." It can be developed by a company when a number-one position along some meaningful attribute cannot be achieved. A competitor can promote the idea that it is one of the Big Three, Big Eight, and so on. The Big Three idea was invented by the third-largest auto firm, Chrysler, and the Big Eight idea was invented by the eighth-largest accounting firm. (The market leader never invents this concept.) The implication is that those in the club are the "best." Thus a Fortune 500 company financial officer feels safe in choosing any of the Big Eight accounting firms for auditing; but if the officer chose some other firm and something went wrong, he or she could be criticized for straying out of the Big Eight.

Ries and Trout essentially deal with the psychology of positioning or repositioning a current brand in the consumer's mind. They acknowledge that the positioning strategy might call for changes in the product's name, price, and packaging, but these are "cosmetic changes done for the purpose of securing a worthwhile position in the prospect's mind." Other marketers would add more emphasis to *real positioning* where they work up every tangible aspect of a new product to capture a position. Psychological positioning must be supported by real positioning; it is not just a mind game.

See Al Ries and Jack Trout, *Positioning: The Battle for Your Mind* (New York: Warner Books, 1982).

SUMMARY

Sellers can take three approaches to a market. Mass marketing is the decision to mass-produce and mass-distribute one product and attempt to attract all kinds of buyers. Product-variety marketing is the decision to produce two or more market offers differentiated in style, features, quality, sizes, and so on, and designed to offer variety to the market and distinguish the seller's products from competitors' products. Target marketing is the decision to distinguish the different groups that make up a market and to develop corresponding products and marketing mixes for each target market. Sellers today are moving away from mass marketing and product differentiation toward target marketing because the latter is more helpful in spotting market opportunities and developing effective products and marketing mixes.

The key steps in target marketing are market segmentation, market targeting, and product positioning. Market segmentation is the act of dividing a market into distinct groups of buyers who might merit separate products and/or marketing mixes. The marketer tries different variables to see which reveal the best segmentation opportunities. For consumer marketing, the major segmentation variables are geographic, demographic (age and life-cycle stage, sex, income), psychographic (social class, lifestyle, personality), and behavioral (occasions, benefits, user status, usage rate, loyalty status, buyer readiness stage, attitude). Industrial markets can be segmented by demographic variables, operating variables, purchasing approaches, situational factors, and personal characteristics. For each potential segment, a customer segment profile is developed. The effectiveness of the segmentation analysis depends on arriving at segments that are measurable, substantial, accessible, and actionable.

Next, the seller has to target the best market segment(s). To do this, the seller must first evaluate the profit potential of each segment. This is a function of segment size and growth, segment structural attractiveness (according to Porter's five-force model), and company objectives and resources. Then the seller must decide how many segments to cover. The seller can ignore segment differences (undifferentiated marketing), develop different market offers for several segments (differentiated marketing), or go after one or a few market segments (concentrated marketing). The market coverage decision will be influenced by such factors as company resources, product and market homogeneity, product life-cycle stage, and competitive marketing strategies. In choosing target segments, marketers need to be aware of segment interrelationships and potential segment roll-out plans.

This market targeting determines the company's competitors. The company must research the competitors' positions and decide on its best positioning. Positioning is the act of designing the company's image and value offer so that the segment's customers understand and appreciate what the company stands for in relation to its competitors. The positioning tasks consists of three steps: identifying possible competitive advantages to exploit, selecting the right ones, and effectively signaling to the market the firm's chosen position. The company's product-positioning strategy will then enable it to take the next step, namely, plan its competitive marketing strategies.

■ QUESTIONS

1. Evaluate the pros and cons of "regionalized" marketing, or segmenting markets on a geographic basis.

2. Use Porter's five forces for determining segment structural attractiveness to evaluate the "light" beer segment of the beer market.

3. How might the personal computer market be segmented? Develop a segment-by-segment invasion plan for Compaq, a manufacturer of IBM-compatible personal computers. Develop a position strategy statement for Compaq.

4. The choice of a base for segmenting consumer markets depends on its relevance for differentiating the buying patterns of consumer groups in a particular market. What might be a relevant base(s) for segmenting the market for banking and other financial services?

5. By making slight changes in the product and its packaging, cigarette manufacturers have been able to make what is essentially the same product appeal to a wide variety of consumer segments. In what ways has the smoking public been segmented, and how have cigarette makers positioned their products to these markets via product and package design and advertising messages?

6. Choose a consumer service and discuss how the market for such a service is segmented.

7. Market segments can be developed by cross-classifying pertinent variables. What problems arise in trying to cross-classify more than a few variables?

8. Suggest a useful way to segment the markets for the following products: (a) household detergents, (b) animal feeds, (c) household coffee, (d) automobile tires.

9. A camera manufacturer wants to develop a benefit segmentation of the camera market. Suggest some major benefit segments.

10. The Quaker Oats Company produces a dry breakfast cereal called Life. Life's brand manager wants to identify different market segments for the cereal. The segments are formed by using wife's age, family size, and city size. Rank the segments from the most important to the least important.

11. A clock manufacturer recognizes that it is basically in the time-measurement business. It wants to segment the time-measurement market in order to identify new opportunities. Identify the major segments in this market.

■ FOOTNOTES

1 Stephen P. Arbeit, "Confronting the Crisis in Mass Marketing," *Viewpoint,* II (1982), 2, 9.

2 Alan R. Andreasen and Russell W. Belk, "Predictors of Attendance at the Performing Arts," *Journal of Consumer Research,* September 1980, pp. 112–120.

3 See Manohar U. Kalwani and Donald G. Morrison, "A Parsimonious Description of the Hendry System," *Management Science,* January 1977, pp. 467–77.

4 See "Marketing's New Look: Campbell Leads a Revolution in the Way Consumer Products Are Sold," *Business Week,* January 26, 1987, pp. 64–69.

5 *American Demographics,* August 1986.

6 Richard P. Coleman, "The Significance of Social Stratification in Selling," in *Marketing: A Maturing Discipline,* ed. Martin L. Bell (Chicago: American Marketing Association, 1961), pp. 171–84.

7 Quoted in Franklin B. Evans, "Psychological and Objective Factors in the Prediction of Brand Choice; Ford versus Chevrolet," *Journal of Business,* October 1959, pp. 340–69.

8 Ralph Westfall, "Psychological Factors in Predicting Product Choice," *Journal of Marketing,* April 1962, pp. 34–40.

9 Shirley Young, "The Dynamics of Measuring Unchange," in *Attitude Research in Transition,* ed. Russell I. Haley (Chicago: American Marketing Association, 1972), pp. 61–82.

10 See Daniel Yankelovich, "New Criteria for Market Segmentation," *Harvard Business Review,* March–April 1964, pp. 83–90, here p. 85.

11 Frank M. Bass, Douglas J. Tigert, and Ronald T. Lonsdale, "Market Segmentation: Group versus Individual Behavior," *Journal of Marketing Research,* August 1968, p. 276.

12 This classification was adapted from George H. Brown, "Brand Loyalty—Fact or Fiction?" *Advertising Age,* June 1952–January 1953, a series.

13 Wind and Cardozo suggest that industrial segmentation should proceed by first developing macrosegments and then microsegments. See Yoram Wind and Richard Cardozo, "Industrial Market Segmentation," *Industrial Marketing Management,* III (1974), 153–66. For other views, see Thomas V. Bonoma and Benson P. Shapiro, *Segmenting the Industrial Market* (Lexington, Mass.: Lexington Books, 1983); and James D. Hlavacek and B. C. Ames, "Segmenting Industrial and High-Tech Markets," *Journal of Business Strategy,* Fall 1986, pp. 39–50.

14 Robert J. Smythe, *Market Segmentation*, a pamphlet published by NFO Research, Inc., Toledo, Ohio (no date).

15 Michael E. Porter, *Competitive Advantage* (New York: Free Press, 1985), pp. 4–8 and 234–36.

16 Michael E. Porter, *Competitive Strategy* (New York: Free Press, 1980), pp. 22–23.

17 See Wendell R. Smith, "Product Differentiation and Market Segmentation as Alternative Marketing Strategies," *Journal of Marketing*, July 1956, pp. 3–8; and Alan A. Roberts, "Applying the Strategy of Market Segmentation," *Business Horizons*, Fall 1961, pp. 65–72.

18 Smith, Product Differentiation," p. 4.

19 Burleigh Gardner and Sidney Levy, "The Product and the Brand," *Harvard Business Review*, March–April 1955, p. 37.

20 Alfred A. Kuehn and Ralph L. Day, "Strategy of Product Quality," *Harvard Business Review*, November–December 1962, pp. 101–2.

21 Natalie McKelvy, "Shoes Make Edison Brothers a Big Name," *Chicago Tribune*, February 23, 1979.

22 Roberts, "Applying the Strategy of Market Segmentation," p. 66.

23 Alan J. Resnik, Peter B. B. Turney, and J. Barry Mason, "Marketers Turn to 'Countersegmentation,' " *Harvard Business Review*, September–October, 1979, pp. 100–106.

24 For further discussion of this general approach, see William J. Crissy and Frank H. Mossman, "Matrix Models for Marketing Planning: An Update and Expansion," *MSU Business Topics*, Autumn 1977, pp. 17–26.

25 Porter, *Competitive Advantage*, Chap. 2.

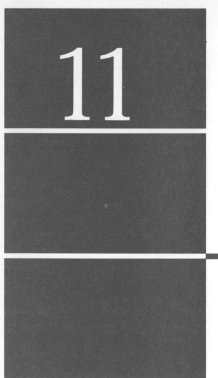

11 Marketing Strategies for Market Leaders, Challengers, Followers, and Nichers

"Cheshire Puss," she [Alice] began . . . "would you please tell me which way I ought to go from here?" "That depends on where you want to get to," said the cat.

Lewis Carroll

A rough sea makes a great captain.

Anonymous

We are now ready to examine, in this and the next two chapters, the problem of designing winning marketing strategies that take into account competitors' strategies, changing phases of the product life cycle, and global opportunities and challenges.

Competitors in a particular target market will, at any point in time, differ in their objectives and resources, and hence in their strategies. Some firms will be large, others small. Some will have great resources, others will be strapped for funds. Some will go for leadership, others for followership. In general, firms will occupy different competitive positions in the target market.

The management consulting firm of Arthur D. Little sees firms as occupying one of six competitive positions in their industry:[1]

- **Dominant.** This firm controls the behavior of other competitors and has a wide choice of strategic options.
- **Strong.** This firm can take independent action without endangering its long-term position and can maintain its long-term position regardless of competitors' actions.
- **Favorable.** This firm has a strength that is exploitable in particular strategies and has more than average opportunity to improve its position.
- **Tenable.** This firm is performing at a sufficiently satisfactory level to warrant continuing in business, but it exists at the sufferance of the dominant company and has a less-than-average opportunity to improve its position.
- **Weak.** This firm has unsatisfactory performance but an opportunity exists for improvement and it must change or else exit.
- **Nonviable.** This firm has unsatisfactory performance and no opportunity for improvement.

Every firm or business unit can recognize itself in one of these competitive positions. The business unit's competitive position, along with its stage in the product life cycle, will help it decide whether to invest, maintain, harvest, or exit from the industry.

We will develop a different classification of competitive positions in this chapter. Much can be gained by classifying firms by the role they play in the target market, that of leading, challenging, following, or niching. Suppose a market is occupied by the firms shown in Figure 11-1. Forty percent of the market is in the hands of a *market leader*, the firm with the largest market share. Another 30 percent is in the hands of a *market challenger*, a runner-up firm that is fighting hard for an increased market share. Another 20 percent is in the hands of a *market follower*, another runner-up firm that is willing to maintain its market share and not rock the boat. The remaining 10 percent is in the hands of *market nichers*, firms that serve small market segments not being pursued by larger firms.

We will argue on the following pages that different marketing challenges and strategies face market leaders, challengers, followers, and nichers.

MARKET-LEADER STRATEGIES

Most industries contain one firm that is acknowledged as the market leader. This firm has the largest market share in the relevant product market. It usually leads the other firms in price changes, new-product introductions, distribution coverage, and promotional intensity. The leader may or may not be admired or respected, but other firms acknowledge its dominance. The leader is an orientation point for competitors, a company to either challenge, imitate, or avoid. Some of the best-known market leaders are General Motors (autos), Kodak (photography), IBM (computers), Xerox (copying), Procter & Gamble (consumer packaged goods), Caterpillar (earth-moving equipment), Coca-Cola (soft drinks), Sears (retailing), McDonald's (fast food), and Gillette (razor blades).

Unless a dominant firm enjoys a legal monopoly, its life is not altogether easy. It must maintain a constant vigilance. Other firms keep challenging its strengths or trying to take advantage of its weaknesses. The market leader can easily miss a turn in the road and plunge into second or third place. A product innovation may come along and hurt the leader (e.g., Tylenol's nonaspirin painkiller taking over the lead from Bayer aspirin). The leader might spend conservatively, expecting hard times, while a challenger spends liberally (Montgomery Ward's loss of its retail dominance to Sears after World War II). The dominant firm might look old-fashioned against new and peppier rivals (*Playboy* magazine's fall to second place in newsstand circulation after *Penthouse*). The dominant firm's costs might rise excessively and hurt its profits (Food Fair's decline, resulting from poor cost control).

Dominant firms want to remain number one. This calls for action on three fronts. First, the firm must find ways to expand total market demand. Second, the firm must

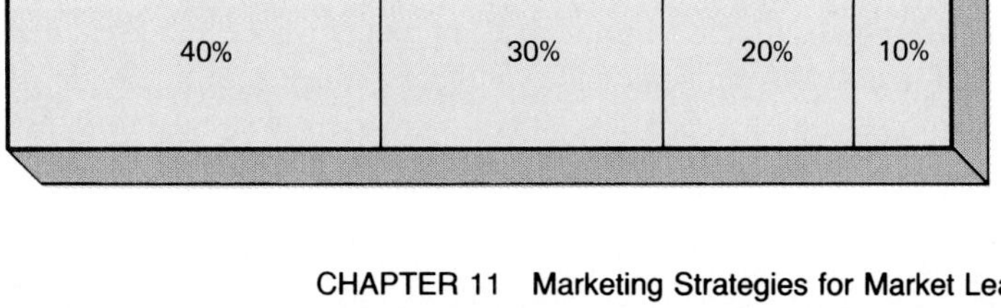

Market Leader	Market Challenger	Market Follower	Market Nichers
40%	30%	20%	10%

FIGURE 11-1
Hypothetical Market Structure

protect its current market share through good defensive and offensive actions. Third, the firm can try to increase its market share further, even if market size remains constant.

Expanding the Total Market

The dominant firm normally gains the most when the total market expands. If Americans increase their picture taking, Kodak stands to gain the most because it sells over 70 percent of the country's film. If Kodak can convince more Americans to buy cameras and take pictures, or take pictures on other occasions besides holidays, or take more pictures on each occasion, Kodak would benefit considerably. In general, the market leader should look for *new users*, *new uses*, and *more usage* of its products.

New Users

Every product class has the potential for attracting buyers who are unaware of the product or who are resisting it because of its price or lack of certain features. A manufacturer can search for new users among three groups. For example, a perfume manufacturer can try to convince women who do not use perfume to use perfume (*market-penetration strategy*), or convince men to start using perfume (*new-market strategy*), or sell perfume in other countries (*geographical-expansion strategy*).

One of the great success stories in developing a new class of users is that of Johnson & Johnson's baby shampoo, the leading brand of baby shampoo. The company became concerned about future sales growth when the birthrate slowed down. Its marketers noticed that other family members occasionally used the baby shampoo for their own hair. Management decided to develop an advertising campaign aimed at adults. In a short time, Johnson & Johnson baby shampoo became the leading brand in the total shampoo market.

In another case, Boeing faced a sharp decline in orders for B–747 jumbo jets when the airlines had acquired enough aircraft to serve existing demand. Boeing concluded that the key to more B–747 sales was to help the airlines attract more people to flying. Boeing analyzed potential flying segments and concluded that the working class did not fly much. Boeing encouraged the airlines and the travel industry to create and sell charter travel packages to unions, churches, and lodges.

New Uses

Markets can be expanded through discovering and promoting new uses for the product. For example, the average American eats dry breakfast cereal three mornings a week. Cereal manufacturers would gain if they could promote cereal eating on other occasions during the day. Thus some cereals are promoted as snacks to increase their use frequency.

Du Pont's nylon provides a classic story of new-use expansion. Every time nylon became a mature product, some new use was discovered. Nylon was first used as a synthetic fiber for parachutes; then as a fiber for women's stockings; later as a major material in women's blouses and men's shirts; still later, it entered automobile tires, seat upholstery, and carpeting.[2] Each new use started the product on a new life cycle. Credit goes to Du Pont's continuous R&D program to find new uses.

In even more cases, customers deserve credit for discovering new uses. Vaseline petroleum jelly started out as a lubricant in machine shops, and over the years users have reported many new uses for the product, including use as a skin ointment, a healing agent, and a hair dressing.

Arm & Hammer, the baking-soda manufacturer, had a product whose sales had been on a downward slide for 125 years! Baking soda had a number of uses, but no single use was advertised. Then the company discovered that some consumers were using it as a refrigerator deodorant. It launched a heavy advertising and publicity campaign focusing on this single use and succeeded in getting half the homes in America to place an open box of baking soda in their refrigerator. A few years later, Arm & Hammer discovered consumers who used it to quell kitchen grease fires, and it promoted this use with great results.

The company's task is to monitor customers' uses of the product. This applies to industrial products as well as consumer products. Von Hippel's studies show that most new industrial products were originally suggested by customers rather than by company R&D laboratories.[3] This highlights the importance of marketing research as a contributor to company growth and profits.

More Usage A third market-expansion strategy is to convince people to *use more of the product per use occasion*. If a cereal manufacturer convinces consumers to eat a full bowl of cereal instead of half a bowl, total sales will increase. Procter & Gamble advises users that its Head & Shoulders shampoo is more effective with two applications instead of one per shampoo.

A creative example of a company stimulating higher usage per occasion is the Michelin Tire Company (French). Michelin wanted French car owners to drive their cars more miles per year—thus leading to more tire replacement. It conceived the idea of rating French restaurants on a three-star system. It reported that many of the best restaurants were in the south of France, leading many Parisians to consider weekend drives to the south of France. Michelin also published guidebooks with maps and sights along the way to further entice travel.

Defending Market Share While trying to expand total market size, the dominant firm must continuously defend its current business against enemy attacks. The leader is like a large elephant being attacked by a swarm of bees. The largest and nastiest bee keeps buzzing around the leader. Coca-Cola must constantly maintain its guard against Pepsi-Cola; Gillette against Bic; Kodak against Fuji; Hertz against Avis; McDonald's against Burger King; General Motors against Ford.

Sometimes there are several large dangerous bees. AT&T has to defend its telecommunications business against the former Bell regional companies, the connect companies (MCI, Sprint), domestic and foreign equipment producers (Motorola, Toshiba), and computer firms moving into telecommunications (IBM, Apple, etc.). Clearly, it cannot defend all of its territory and needs to decide where to draw the battle lines.

What can the market leader do to defend its terrain? Twenty centuries ago, Sun Tzu told his warriors: "One does not rely on the enemy not attacking, but relies on the fact that he himself is unassailable." The most constructive response is *continuous innovation*. The leader refuses to be content with the way things are and leads the industry in new-product ideas, customer services, distribution effectiveness, and cost cutting. It keeps increasing its competitive effectiveness and value to customers. The leader applies the "military principle of the offensive": The commander exercises initiative, sets the pace, and exploits enemy weaknesses. The best defense is a good offense.

The dominant firm, even when it does not launch offensives, must at least guard all of its fronts and not leave any exposed flanks. It must keep its costs down, and its prices must be consonant with the value the customers see in the brand. The leader must "plug holes" so that attackers do not jump in. Thus a consumer-packaged-goods leader will produce its brands in several sizes and forms to meet varying consumer preferences and hold on to as much scarce dealer shelf space as possible. And IBM decided to produce personal computers partly in order to block others from getting entrenched and stronger.

The cost of "plugging holes" can be high. But the cost of abandoning a losing product/market segment can be higher! General Motors did not want to lose money by making small cars, but it is losing more now because it allowed Japanese car makers to come in strong in the U.S. market. Kodak abandoned the 35mm camera market because its 35mm camera was losing money, but the Japanese figured out a way to make these cameras easy to operate and they are now replacing cheaper Kodak cameras at a fast rate.

The real answer is that the market leader must look carefully into which terrains are important to defend even at a cost, and which can be given up with little risk. The leader cannot defend all of its positions in the whole market; it must concentrate its resources where they count. The aim of defensive strategy is to reduce the probability of attack, divert attacks to less-threatening areas, and lessen their intensity. Any attack is likely to hurt profits. But the defender's form and speed of response can make an important difference in the profit consequences. Researchers are currently exploring the most appropriate forms of response to price and other attacks. (See Exhibit 11-1 for an interesting model called Defender.)

The intensified competition that has taken place worldwide in recent years has sparked management's interest in models of military warfare, particularly as described in the writings of Sun-Tsu, Mushashi, von Clausewitz, and Liddell-Hart.[4] Leader companies, like leader nations, have been advised to protect their interests with such strategies as "brinkmanship," "massive retaliation," "limited warfare," "graduated response," "diplomacy of violence," and "threat systems." There are, in fact, six military defense strategies that a dominant firm can use. They are illustrated in Figure 11-2 and described below.[5]

Position Defense   The most basic idea of defense is to build an impregnable fortification around one's territory. The French built the famous Maginot line in peacetime to protect its territory against possible future German invasion. But this fortification, like all static defense maneuvers, failed. Simply defending one's current position or products is a form of *marketing myopia*. Henry Ford's myopia about his Model-T brought an enviably healthy company with $1 billion in cash reserves at its zenith to the brink of financial ruin. Even such death-defying brands as Coca-Cola and Bayer aspirin cannot be relied on by their companies as the main sources of future growth and profitability. Coca-Cola today, in spite of producing nearly half the soft drinks of the world, has aggressively moved into the wine market, has acquired fruit-drink companies, and has diversified into desalinization equipment and plastics. Clearly, leaders under attack would be foolish to put all their resources into building fortifications around their current product.

Flanking Defense   The market leader should not only guard its territory but also erect some flanks or outposts to serve as a defensive corner to protect a weak front or possibly as an invasion base for counterattacking if necessary. Here is a good example of a flanking defense:

> The defensive stance taken by Chicago-based Jewel Food Stores is instructive. The company believes that the supermarket will continue to remain a dominant force but is flanking its position by strengthening its food-retailing-assortment mix to meet new challenges. The fast-food boom has been met by offering a wide assortment of instant and frozen meals and the discount-food challenge by promoting generic lines; Jewel's various supermarkets are being tailored to suit local demands for such items as fresh bakery products and ethnic foods. And the company is

taking no chances with some institutional developments. It has set up the Jewel-T division, which is a network of "box" discount stores patterned after pioneer Aldi. Watching a sudden turnaround in the competitive position of "independence," Jewel's Star Market division in New England promptly began moving into franchising the following year. To hedge the "combination store" challenge, it integrated a large number of its supermarkets with its Osco Drug Stores, using both side-by-side and fully integrated designs.

EXHIBIT 11-1

Defensive Strategies According to the Defender Model

For several years, Professors Hauser, Shugan, and Gaskin have been building and testing a model called Defender. The model makes the following assumptions:

1. Consumers share the same perceptions of the products in the market and their relative strengths. (Thus all consumers see Tylenol as high in gentleness per dollar but low in effectiveness per dollar, Excedrin as high in effectiveness but low in gentleness, etc.)
2. Consumers differ in their preferences for various product characteristics. (Thus some consumers value gentleness more than effectiveness, others show the reverse preference).
3. Consumers vary in the number of brands they know and will consider.
4. Consumers' choices are affected by product features, price, distribution, advertising, and promotion. (Each marketing tool's effect on sales response is plausibly represented.)

The Defender model can be illustrated with the history of *Datril*'s price attack on the market leader, *Tylenol*. Tylenol had gained a large market share based on its perceived gentleness (no stomach upsets) and was earning outstanding profits. Along came an attacker, Bristol-Myers, which introduced the same product, Datril, and advertised it as "just as good as Tylenol, only cheaper." If consumers believed this, Datril would make deep inroads into Tylenol's market share. How should Tylenol defend itself?

The researchers examined the possible defensive measures available to Tylenol, using the Defender model, and came to the following conclusions:

1. The defender should lower its prices, especially if the market is unsegmented. If the market is segmented, the price might be raised in some of the less-vulnerable segments. (The best pricing strategy is independent of what should be done with distribution and advertising; once chosen, however, the pricing strategy will affect distribution and advertising.)
2. The defender should reduce its expenditures on distribution; specifically it should drop marginal retailers who are no longer profitable to serve.
3. The defender should improve its strong product features even more rather than try to improve along the lines of the attacker's strong product features.
4. The defender should spend less on awareness-building advertising and direct more on repositioning-building advertising.

These conclusions are subject to further qualifications given the restrictive assumptions on which the model was based. For example, price and positioning are interrelated strategically. In some cases, price cuts encourage price wars. To avoid such destructive competition, it is often best to differentiate products in order to compete on product benefits, not price.

What did Tylenol actually do to defend itself from Datril's attack? Tylenol quickly cut its price to match Datril's, and later added the Extra Strength Tylenol brand to capture consumers' interest in effectiveness. Through these steps, Tylenol preserved its position as market leader and prevented Datril from making much of an inroad.

SOURCES John R. Hauser and Steve M. Shugan, "Defensive Marketing Strategy," *Marketing Science*, Fall 1983, pp. 319–60; and John R. Hauser and S. P. Gaskin, "Application of the 'DEFENDER' Consumer Model," *Marketing Science*, Fall 1984, pp. 327–51.

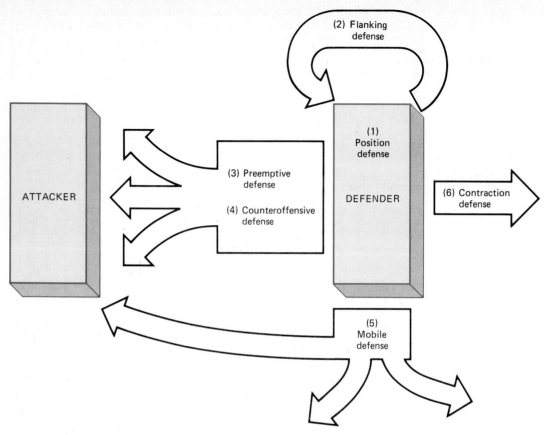

FIGURE 11-2
Defense Strategies

The flanking position is of little value if it is so lightly held that an enemy could pin it down with a small force while its main formations swing past unmolested. This was precisely General Motors' and Ford's mistake when they halfheartedly designed the Vega and Pinto compacts some years ago to ward off the small-car attacks launched by the Japanese and European car makers. Unfortunately for everyone, the American compacts were poorly made, and they failed to retard the purchase of foreign compacts. A careful assessment of any potential threat must be made, and if indicated, a relatively serious commitment should be made to flanking the threat.

Preemptive Defense   A more aggressive defense maneuver is to actually launch an offense against the enemy *before* it starts an offense against the company. The company cuts down the enemy before the latter strikes. Preemptive defense assumes that an ounce of prevention is worth more than a pound of cure. For example, a company could launch an attack against a competitor whose market share is approaching some dangerous level. When Chrysler's market share began rising from 12 to 18 percent some years ago, one rival marketing executive was overheard to say, "If they [Chrysler] go to 20 percent, it will be over our dead bodies."

Or a company could wage guerrilla action across the market—hitting one competitor here, another there—and keep everyone off balance. Or the preemptive defense could assume the proportions of a grand market envelopment, as practiced by Seiko with its twenty-three hundred watch models distributed worldwide. Or it could resemble the sustained frontal barrage of the Texas Instruments type. Sustained high-pressure strategies aim at retaining the initiative at all times and keeping the competition always on the defensive.

Sometimes the preemptive strike is waged psychologically rather than actually carried out. The market leader sends out *market signals* to dissuade competitors from attacking.[6] A major U.S. pharmaceutical firm is the leader in a certain drug category. Every time it learns that a competitor is about to build a factory to produce that drug, the company leaks the news that it is considering cutting the drug price and building another plant. This intimidates the competitor, who decides against entering that product arena. Meanwhile the leader never gets to cutting its price or adding another plant. Of course, this bluff can work only a few times.

Companies fortunate enough to enjoy strong market assets—high brand loyalty, technological leadership, and so on—would probably find it disadvantageous to pursue too broad a preemptive strategy. They have the capacity to weather some punishment, and some may even prefer to entice the opponents into expensive and costly attacks that will not pay off (they hope) in the long run. Heinz let Hunt's carry out its massive attack in the ketchup market without much counteroffensive; and in the end, this proved very costly to Hunt's.[7] Standing firm in the face of an attack, however, calls for great confidence in the ultimate superiority of the company's market offer.

Counteroffensive Defense When a market leader is attacked in spite of its flanking and even preemptive maneuvers, it must respond with a counterattack on the opponent. The leader cannot remain passive in the face of a competitor's price cut, promotion blitz, product improvement, or sales-territory invasion. The leader has the strategic choice of meeting the attacker's spearhead frontally, or maneuvering against the attacker's flank, or launching a pincer movement to cut off the attacking formations from their base of operation.

> Clearasil, the market leader in the acne medications market, suddenly found itself under a powerful promotional attack by Oxy-5. Clearasil retaliated with a stepped-up counterpromotion of its own.

Sometimes market-share erosion is so rapid that a head-on counterattack is necessary. But a defender enjoying some strategic depth can often weather the initial attack and riposte effectively at the opportune moment. In many situations, it may be worth some minor setbacks to allow the offensive to develop fully (and be understood) before countering. This may seem a dangerous strategy of "wait and see," but there are sound reasons for not barreling into a counteroffensive.

A better retort to an offensive is for the defender to pause and identify a chink in the attacker's armor, namely, a segment gap in which a viable counteroffensive can be launched. Cadillac designed its Seville as an alternative to the Mercedes and pinned its hope on offering a smoother ride and more creature comforts than Mercedes was willing to design.

When a market leader's territory is attacked, an effective counterattack is to invade the attacker's main territory so that it will have to pull back some of its troops to defend its territory. One of Northwest Airlines' most profitable routes is Minneapolis to Atlanta.

A small carrier launched a deep fare cut and advertised it heavily to expand its share in this market. Northwest retaliated by cutting its fares on the Minneapolis/Chicago route, which the other airline depended on for its major revenue. With its major revenue source hurting, the other airline restored its Minneapolis/Atlanta fare to a normal level.

Mobile Defense   Mobile defense involves more than the leader's aggressively defending its current territory. Mobile defense consists of the leader's stretching its domain over new territories that can serve as future centers for defense and offense. It spreads to these new territories not so much through normal brand proliferation as through innovation activity on two fronts, namely, market broadening and market diversification. These moves generate ''strategic depth'' for the firm, which enables it to weather continual attacks and to launch retaliatory strikes.

Market broadening calls upon a company to shift its focus from the current product to the underlying generic need and to get involved in R&D across the whole range of technology associated with that need. Thus ''petroleum'' companies are asked to recast themselves into ''energy'' companies. Implicitly, this demands that they dip their research fingers into the oil, coal, nuclear, hydroelectric, and chemical industries. But this market-broadening strategy should not be carried too far or it would fault two fundamental military principles—the *principle of the objective* (''pursue a clearly defined and attainable objective'') and the *principle of mass* (''concentrate your efforts at a point of the enemy's weakness''). The objective of being in the energy business is too broad. The energy business is not a single need but a whole range of needs (heating, lighting, propelling, and so on). That leaves very little in the world that is not potentially the energy business. Furthermore, too much broadening would dilute the company's mass in the competitive theater today, and survival today must surely take precedence over the grand battles imagined for some tomorrow. The error of *marketing myopia* would be replaced by *marketing hyperopia*, a condition where vision is better for distant than for near objects.

Reasonable broadening, however, makes sense. Armstrong Cork exemplified a successful market-broadening strategy by redefining its domain from ''floor covering'' to ''decorative room covering'' (including walls and ceilings). By recognizing the customer's need to create a pleasant interior through various covering materials, Armstrong Cork expanded into neighboring businesses that were synergistically balanced for growth and defense.

Market diversification into unrelated industries is the other alternative to generating ''strategic depth.'' When U.S. tobacco companies like Reynolds and Philip Morris acknowledged the growing curbs on cigarette smoking, they were not content with position defense or even with looking for new substitutes for the cigarette; instead they moved quickly into new industries such as beer, liquor, soft drinks, and frozen food.

Contraction Defense   Large companies sometimes recognize that they can no longer defend all of their territory. Their forces are spread too thin, and competitors are nibbling away on several fronts. The best course of action then appears to be planned contraction (also called strategic withdrawal). Planned contraction is not market abandonment but rather giving up the weaker territories and reassigning forces to stronger territories. Planned contraction is a move to consolidate one's competitive strength in the market and concentrate mass at pivotal positions.

In the slow-growth 1980s, an increasing opportunity seems to be emerging for profitable strategy in their eliminating or fusing fragmented market segments. Westinghouse cut its number of refrigerator models from forty to the thirty that accounted for 85 percent of sales. General Motors standardized its auto engines and now offers fewer options. Campbell's Soup, Heinz, General Mills, Del Monte, and Georgia-Pacific are among those companies that have significantly pruned their product lines in recent years. Once again we find the underlying principle is concentration of mass if the desegmentation opportunity permits.

Expanding Market Share

Market leaders can also try to improve their profitability through increasing their market share further. In many markets, one share point is worth tens of millions of dollars. A one-share point gain in coffee is worth $48 million and in soft drinks, $120 million! No wonder normal competition has turned into marketing warfare.

Some years ago, the Strategic Planning Institute launched a study called *Profit Impact of Marketing Strategies* (PIMS), which sought to identify the most important variables impacting on profits. It gathered data from over six hundred business units in a variety of industries and identified the most important variables associated with profitability. The key variables included market share, product quality, and a few others.

They found that *profitability* (measured by pretax ROI) rises curvilinearly with *relative market share*,[8] as shown in Figure 11-3(a).[9] According to a PIMS report, "The average ROI for business with under 10 percent market share was about 9 percent. . . . On the average, a difference of 10 percentage points in market share is accompanied by a difference of about 5 points in pretax ROI." The PIMS study shows that businesses with market shares above 40 percent earn an average ROI of 30 percent, or three times that of those with shares under 10 percent.[10]

These findings have led many companies to adopt the objective of expanding their market share, since this would produce not only more *profit dollars* but also more *profitability* (return on investment). General Electric, for example, has decided that it wants to be at

FIGURE 11-3
Relationship between Market Share and Profitability
SOURCE: Strategic Planning Institute (The PIMS Program), 955 Massachusetts Avenue, Cambridge, Mass. 02139.

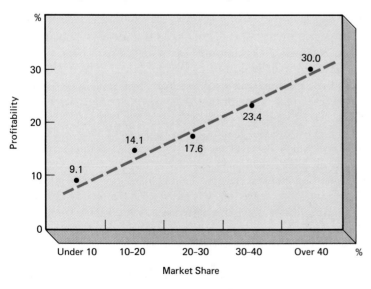

(a) Linear relationship according to PIMS studies

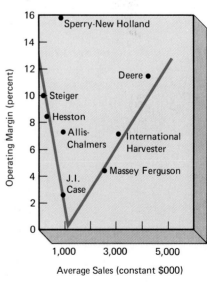

(b) V-shaped relationship

least number one or two in each of its markets or else get out. GE divested its computer business and its air-conditioning business because it could not achieve top-dog position in these industries. Cynics have concluded that GE does not really want to stay in markets where it has to compete!

Various critics have attacked the PIMS study as either weak or spurious. Hamermesh and his colleagues reported finding numerous successful low-share businesses.[11] Woo and Cooper identified forty low-share businesses that enjoyed pretax ROIs of 20 percent or more; they were characterized as having high relative product quality, medium-to-low prices relative to high quality, narrow product lines, and low total costs.[12] Most of these companies made frequently purchased industrial components or supplies and seldom changed their products.

Some industry studies have yielded a V-shaped relationship between market share and profitability. Figure 11-3(b) shows a V-curve for agricultural equipment firms. The industry leader, Deere & Company, earns a high return. However, Hesston and Sperry–New Holland, small specialty firms, also earn high returns. J. I. Case and Massey-Ferguson are trapped in the valley, and International Harvester commands a substantial market share but earns lower returns. Thus such industries have one or a few highly profitable leaders, several profitable small and more-focused firms, and a large number of medium-sized firms with poorer profit performance. According to Roach:

> The large firms on the V-curve tend to address the entire market, achieving cost advantages and high market share by realizing economies of scale. The small competitors reap high profits by focusing on some narrower segment of the business and by developing specialized approaches to production, marketing, and distribution for that segment. Ironically, the medium-sized competitors at the trough of the V-curve are unable to realize any competitive advantage and often show the poorest profit performance. Trapped in a strategic ''No Man's Land,'' they are too large to reap the benefits of more focused competition, yet too small to benefit from the economies of scale that their larger competitors enjoy.[13]

How can the two graphs in Figure 11-3 be reconciled? The PIMS findings argue that profitability increases as a business gains share relative to its competitors in its *served market*. The V-shaped curve ignores market segments and looks at a business's profitability relative to its size in the total market. Thus Mercedes earns high profit because it is a high-share company in its served market of luxury cars even though it is a low-share company in the total auto market. And it has achieved this high share in its served market because it does other things right, such as producing high relative product quality and achieving high asset turnover, good cost control, and so on.

Companies must not think, however, that gaining increased market share will automatically improve their profitability. Much depends on their strategy for gaining increased market share. The cost of buying higher market share may far exceed its revenue value. There are three factors the company should consider before blindly pursuing increased market share.

The first factor is the possibility of provoking antitrust action. Jealous competitors are likely to cry ''monopolization'' if a dominant firm makes further inroads on market share. This rise in risk would cut down the attractiveness of pushing market-share gains too far. Thus IBM would have to carefully consider the antitrust risk of plotting further market-share gains. Yet IBM is very tempted to attack DEC's strong position in the minicomputer market. According to a former IBM marketing strategist quoted in *Business Week*:

IBM's "management committee approved plans for a so-called competitive-analysis task force that . . . targeted DEC. IBM even set up a "war room" at marketing headquarters . . . with maps and lists of target areas. The management committee authorized a specially trained force of up to 1,300 salespeople . . . to win the scientific and engineering accounts that favor midrange machines.[14]

The second factor is economic cost. Figure 11-4 shows the possibility that profitability might begin to fall with still further gains in market share after some level short of 100 percent. In the illustration, the firm's *optimal market share* is 50 percent, and if the firm pursues a still larger share, this is apt to come at the expense of profitability. This is consistent with the PIMS findings in that PIMS did not show what happens to profitability for different levels within the over 40 percent category. Basically, the cost of gaining further market share might exceed the value. The cost of making further gains in market share after a large market share has been achieved may rise fast and reduce profitability. A company that has (say) 60 percent of the market must recognize that the "holdout" customers may dislike the company, be loyal to competitive suppliers, have unique needs, or prefer dealing with smaller suppliers. Furthermore, the competitors are likely to fight harder to defend their falling market share. The cost of legal work, public relations, and lobbying rises with market share. In general, pushing for higher market share is less justified when there are few scale or experience economies, unattractive market segments exist, buyers want multiple sources of supply, and exit barriers are high. The leader may be better off concentrating on expanding market size rather than fighting for further increases in market share. Some dominant marketers have even gained by selectively decreasing their market share in weaker areas.[15]

The third factor is that companies may pursue the wrong marketing-mix strategy in their bid for higher market share and therefore not increase their profit. While certain marketing-mix variables are more effective in building market share, their use does not necessarily lead to higher profits. (See Exhibit 11-2.) Higher shares tend to produce higher profits under two conditions:

■ *Unit costs fall with increased market share.* Unit costs fall because the leader enjoys cost economies of scale by running larger plants and because it goes down the cost experience curve faster. This means that one effective marketing strategy for gaining profitable increases in market share is to fanatically pursue the lowest costs in the industry and pass the cost

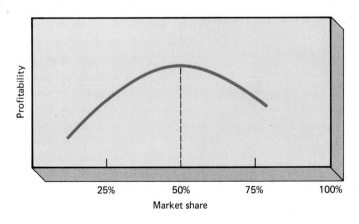

FIGURE 11-4
The Concept of an Optimal Market Share

The Impact of Different Marketing-Mix Variables on Market Share

Some light on the impact of different marketing variables on market share was shed by Buzzell and Wiersema, drawing on the PIMS (Profit Impact of Management Strategies) data base. They found that companies showing market-share gains typically outperformed their competitors in three areas: new-product activity, relative product quality, and marketing expenditures. Specifically:

1. Share-gaining companies typically developed and added more new products to their line.
2. Companies that increased their product quality relative to competitors' enjoyed greater share gains than those whose quality ratings remained constant or declined.
3. Companies that increased their marketing expenditures faster than the rate of market growth typically achieved share gains. Increases in sales-force expenditures were effective in producing share gains for both industrial and consumer markets. Increased advertising expenditures produced share gains mainly for consumer-goods companies. Increased sales promotion expenditures were effective in producing share gains for all kinds of companies.
4. Companies that cut their prices more deeply than competitors did not achieve significant market-share gains, contrary to expectations. Presumably enough rivals met the price cuts partly, and others offered other values to the buyers, so that buyers did not switch as much to the price cutter.

The reported study did not investigate whether the market-share gains were worth the cost of achieving them. Evidently companies are able to "buy" a higher market share, but the real issue is whether it will lead to higher profits sooner or later.

SOURCE Based on Robert D. Buzzell and Frederik D. Wiersema, "Successful Share-Building Strategies," *Harvard Business Review*, January–February, 1981, pp. 135–44.

savings to customers through lower prices. That was Henry Ford's strategy for selling autos in the 1920s and Texas Instruments' strategy for selling transistors in the 1960s.

■ *The company offers a superior-quality product and charges a premium price that more than covers the cost of offering higher quality.* Crosby, in his book *Quality Is Free*, claims that building more quality into a product does not cost the company much more because the company saves in less scrappage, after-sales servicing, and so on.[16] But its products are so desired that consumers pay a large premium over cost. This strategy for profitable market-share growth is pursued by IBM, Caterpillar, and Michelin, among others.

All said, market leaders who stay on top have learned the art of expanding the total market, defending their current territory, and increasing their market share profitably. Exhibit 11-3 details the specific principles that two great companies—Procter & Gamble and Caterpillar—use to maintain and expand their leadership in their respective markets.

MARKET-CHALLENGER STRATEGIES

The firms that occupy second, third, and lower ranks in an industry can be called runner-up or trailing firms. Some are quite large in their own right, such as Colgate, Ford, Montgomery Ward, Avis, Westinghouse, and Pepsi-Cola. These runner-up firms can adopt one of two postures. They can attack the leader and other competitors in an aggressive bid for

EXHIBIT 11-3

How Two Great Companies—Procter & Gamble and Caterpillar—Maintain Their Market Leadership

The principles of maintaining market leadership are admirably illustrated by companies such as Procter & Gamble, Caterpillar, IBM, McDonald's, and Hertz, all of which have shown a remarkable ability to protect their market shares against repeated attacks by able challengers. Their success is based not on doing one thing well but on doing everything well. They do not allow any weaknesses to develop. We will examine the basics behind Procter & Gamble's and Caterpillar's success.

Procter & Gamble   P&G is widely regarded as the nation's most skilled marketer of consumer packaged goods. It sells the number-one brand in each of eight important categories: disposable diapers (Pampers), detergents (Tide), toilet tissue (Charmin), paper towels (Bounty), fabric softeners (Downy), toothpaste (Crest), shampoo (Head & Shoulders), and mouthwash (Scope). (See "P&G Up Against Its Wall," *Fortune*, February 23, 1981, pp. 49–54). Its market leadership rests on several principles:

- ▪ *Customer knowledge.* P&G studies its customers—both final consumers and the trade—through continuous marketing research and intelligence gathering. It provides a toll-free 800 number to permit customers to call P&G directly with any comments or complaints about P&G products.

- ▪ *Long-term outlook.* P&G takes its time to analyze an opportunity and prepare the best product, and it then commits itself for the long-run to make this product a success. It is still trying to perfect its Pringles potato chips in spite of the many reverses in this product's fortune.

- ▪ *Product innovation.* P&G is an active product innovator and benefit segmenter. It launches brands offering new consumer benefits rather than me-too brands backed by heavy advertising. P&G spent ten years researching and developing the first effective anticavity toothpaste, Crest. It spent several years researching the first effective over-the-counter antidandruff shampoo, Head & Shoulders. The company thoroughly tests its new products with consumers, and only when real preference is indicated does it launch them in the national market.

- ▪ *Quality strategy.* P&G designs products of above-average quality. Once launched, it makes a continuous effort to improve the product's quality over time. When they announce "new and improved," they mean it. This is in contrast to some companies that, after establishing the quality level, rarely improve it, and to other companies that reduce the quality in an effort to squeeze out more profit.

- ▪ *Product flanking.* P&G produces its brands in several sizes and forms to satisfy varying consumer preferences. This gives its brand more shelf space and prevents competitors from moving in to satisfy unmet needs in the market.

- ▪ *Multibrand strategy.* P&G is the originator of the art of marketing several brands in the same product category. For example, it produces ten brands of laundry detergents, each positioned somewhat differently in the consumer's mind. The trick is to design brands that meet different consumer wants and that compete against specific competitors' brands. Each brand manager runs the brand independently of the other brand managers and competes for company resources. Having several brands on the shelf, the company "locks up" shelf space and gains more clout with distributors.

- ▪ *Brand-extension strategy.* P&G will often use its strong brand names to launch new products. For example, the Ivory brand has been extended from a soap to include liquid soap and a detergent. Launching a new product under a strong existing brand name gives it more instant recognition and credibility with much less advertising outlay.

- ▪ *Heavy advertising.* P&G is the nation's largest consumer-packaged-good advertiser, spending over $872 million in 1984. It never stints on spending money to create strong consumer awareness and preference.

- ▪ *Aggressive sales force.* P&G has a top-flight field sales force, which is very effective in gaining shelf space and retailer cooperation in point-of-purchase displays and promotions.

- ▪ *Effective sales promotion.* P&G has a sales promotion department to counsel its brand managers on the most effective promotions to achieve particular objectives. The department studies the results of consumer and trade deals and develops an expert sense of their effectiveness under varying circumstances. At the same time, P&G prefers to minimize the use of sales promotion, preferring to rely on advertising to build long-term consumer preference.

- **Competitive toughness.** P&G carries a big stick when it comes to constraining aggressors. P&G is willing to spend large sums of money to outpromote new competitive brands and prevent them from gaining a foothold in the market.
- **Manufacturing efficiency.** P&G's reputation as a great marketing company is matched by its greatness as a manufacturing company. P&G spends large sums of money developing and improving production operations to keep its costs among the lowest in the industry.
- **Brand-management system.** P&G originated the brand-management system, in which one executive is responsible for each brand. The system has been copied by many competitors but frequently without the success that P&G has achieved through perfecting its system over the years.

Thus P&G's market leadership is not based on doing one thing well but on the successful orchestration of all the factors that count in market leadership.

Caterpillar Since the 1940s, Caterpillar has dominated the construction-equipment industry. Its tractors, crawlers, and loaders, painted in the familiar yellow, are a common sight at any construction area and account for 50 percent of the world's sales of heavy construction equipment. Caterpillar has managed to retain leadership in spite of charging a premium price for its equipment and being challenged by a number of able competitors, including John Deere, Massey-Ferguson, J. I. Case, and Komatsu. Several principles combine to explain Caterpillar's success:

- **Premium-product quality.** Caterpillar produces high-quality equipment known for its reliability. Reliability is a key buyer consideration in the purchase of heavy industrial equipment. Caterpillar designs its equipment with a heavier gauge of steel than necessary, to convince buyers of its superior quality.
- **Extensive-and-efficient-dealership system.** Caterpillar maintains the largest number of independent construction-equipment dealers in the industry. Its 260 dealers are located throughout the world and carry a complete line of Caterpillar equipment. Caterpillar dealers can focus all of their attention on Caterpillar equipment and do not need to carry other lines. Competitors' dealers, on the other hand, normally lack a full line and have to carry complementary, noncompeting lines. Caterpillar can choose the best dealers among those applying (a new Caterpillar dealership costs the franchisee $5 million) and spends the most money in training, servicing, and motivating them.
- **Superior service.** Caterpillar has built a worldwide parts and service system second to none in the industry. Caterpillar can deliver replacement parts and service anywhere in the world within a few hours of equipment breakdown. This service level is hard for competitors to match without a substantial investment. Any competitor duplicating the service level would only neutralize Caterpillar's advantage rather than gain any net advantage.
- **Superior parts management.** Thirty percent of Caterpillar's sales volume and over 50 percent of its profit come from the sale of replacement parts. Caterpillar has developed a superior parts-management system to keep margins high in this end of the business.
- **Premium price.** Caterpillar is able to charge a premium of 10 to 20 percent over comparable competitors' equipment because of the extra value perceived by buyers.
- **Full-line strategy.** Caterpillar produces a full line of construction equipment to enable customers to do one-stop buying.
- **Good financing.** Caterpillar arranges generous financial terms to customers buying its equipment. This is important because of the large sums of money involved.

Recently Caterpillar has been experiencing difficulties because of the depressed market conditions and the cutthroat competition. Its specific problem is Komatsu, Japan's number-one construction firm, which adopted the internal slogan "Encircle Caterpillar." Komatsu studies and attacks market niches, continuously enlarges its product line and improves its product quality, and prices its equipment 10 to 15 percent lower. Caterpillar tells buyers that Komatsu's lower prices reflect lower quality, but not all buyers believe this. Caterpillar sorely needs to reevaluate and redesign its competitive strategies for the next decade.

further market share (market challengers). Or they can play ball and not rock the boat (market followers). Dolan found that competitive rivalry is most intense in industries with high fixed costs, high inventory costs, and stagnant primary demand.[17] We will now examine the competitive attack strategies available to market challengers.[18]

Defining the Strategic Objective and Opponent(s)	A market challenger must first define its strategic objective. The military "principle of objective" holds that "every military operation must be directed toward a clearly defined, decisive, and attainable objective." The strategic objective of most market challengers is to increase their market shares, thinking that this will lead to greater profitability (subject to the preceding caveats on pp. 327–30). Deciding on the objective, whether it is to crush the competitior or reduce its share, interacts with the question

of who the competitor is. Unlike war, where the enemy is "given," the business firm in most cases is able to choose its opponent. Basically, an aggressor can choose to attack one of three types of firms:

- ▪ **It can attack the market leader.** This is a high-risk but potentially high-payoff strategy and makes good sense if the leader is not a "true leader" and is not serving the market well. The "terrain" to examine closely is consumer need or dissatisfaction. If a substantial area is unserved or poorly served, it offers a great strategic target. Miller's campaign in the beer market was successful because it pivoted initially on discovering many consumers who wanted a "lighter" beer. The alternative strategy is to out-innovate the leader across the whole segment. Thus Xerox took the copy market away from 3M by developing a better copying process (dry copying instead of wet copying).
- ▪ **It can attack firms of its own size that are not doing the job and that are underfinanced.** Both consumer satisfaction and innovation potential need to be examined minutely. Even a frontal attack might work if the other firm's resources are limited.
- ▪ **It can attack small local and regional firms that are not doing the job and are underfinanced.** Several of the major beer companies grew to their present size not by stealing each other's customers so much as by gobbling up the "small fry," or "guppies."

Thus the issue of choosing the opponent and choosing the objective interact. If the attacking company goes after the market leader, its objective may be to wrest a certain share. Thus Bic is under no illusion that it could topple Gillette in the razor market—it is simply seeking a larger share. If the attacking company goes after a small local company, its objective may be to drive that company out of existence. The important principle remains: "Every military operation must be directed toward a clearly defined, decisive, and attainable objective."

Choosing an Attack Strategy	Given clear opponents and objectives, how do military strategists view their major options in attacking an enemy? The starting point is known as the "principle of mass," which holds that "superior combat power must be concentrated at the critical

time and place for a decisive purpose." We can make progress by imagining an opponent who occupies a certain market territory. We distinguish the five possible attack strategies shown in Figure 11-5 and discussed below.

Frontal Attack

An aggressor is said to launch a frontal (or "head-on") attack when it masses its forces right up against those of its opponent. It attacks the opponent's strengths rather than its weaknesses. The outcome depends on who has the greater strength and endurance. In a pure frontal attack, the attacker matches its opponent's product, advertising, price, and so on. Recently the second-place razor-blade manufacturer in Brazil decided to go after Gillette, the market leader. Management was asked if it was offering the consumer a better blade. "No," was the reply. "A lower price?" "No." "A better package?" "No." "A cleverer advertising campaign?" "No." "Better allowances to the trade?" "No." "Then how do you expect to take share away from Gillette?" "Sheer determination" was the reply. Needless to say, its offensive failed.

For a pure frontal attack to succeed, the aggressor needs a strength advantage over the competitor. The "principle of force" says that the side with the greater manpower

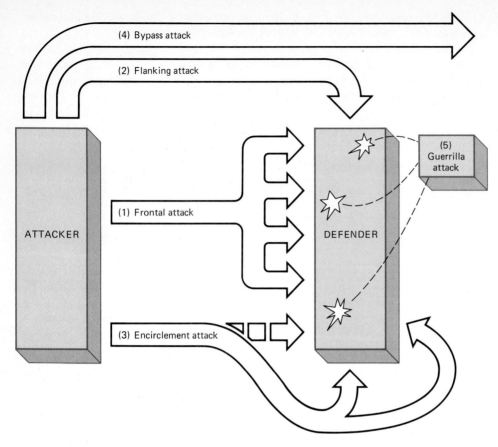

FIGURE 11-5
Attack Strategies

(resources) will win the engagement. This rule is modified if the defender has greater firing efficiency through enjoying a terrain advantage (such as holding a mountaintop). The military dogma is that for a frontal attack to succeed against a well-entrenched opponent or one controlling the "high ground," the attacking forces must deploy at least a 3:1 advantage in combat firepower. If the aggressor has a smaller force or poorer firepower than the defender, a frontal attack amounts to a suicide mission and makes no sense. RCA, GE, and Xerox learned this the hard way when they launched frontal attacks on IBM, overlooking its superior defensive position.

As an example of a successful pure frontal attack and the resources it required, consider S. C. Johnson & Son's entry into the shampoo market with its new Agree brand.[19] In 1977, with what Forbes described as "almost Japanese-like thoroughness," S. C. Johnson first raided Colgate and others for experienced executives. Then it blitzed the market with a $14 million promotion that included 30 million sample bottles of its new hair conditioner, Agree. That about equaled the industry's total promotion on hair conditioners. It grabbed 15 percent of the market in its first year, wrested from such giants as Gillette's Toni, Breck, and Clairol. (By 1979, its share was 20 percent.) Then, in 1978, it invaded the shampoo market, reportedly spending $30 million in marketing costs in the summer of that year. It ended up with a 6 percent share of that market.

As an alternative to a pure frontal attack, the aggressor may launch a modified frontal attack, the most common being to cut its price vis-à-vis the opponent's. Such attacks can take two forms. The more usual ploy is to match the leader's offer on other counts and beat it on price. This can work if the market leader does not retaliate by cutting price, too, and if the competitor convinces the market that its product is equal to the competitor's or, that at a lower price, it is a real value.

> Helene Curtis is a master practitioner of the somewhat risky strategy of convincing the market that its product is equal in quality to the higher-priced products of competitors.[20] Curtis makes no bones about its approach—making budget imitations of leading high-priced brands and promoting them with blatant comparative advertising campaigns: "We do what theirs does for less than half the price" is the message. In 1972 Curtis had a meager 1 percent share of the shampoo market for its five Suave shampoos. Its new strategy was launched in 1973. By 1976, it had overtaken Procter & Gamble's Head & Shoulders and Johnson & Johnson's Baby Shampoo to lead the market in volume. Its share hit 16 percent in 1979.

The other form of price-aggressive strategy is one in which the attacker invests heavily in research to achieve lower production costs and then attacks competitors on a price basis. Texas Instruments has had brilliant success in using the price weapon strategically. It invests heavily in R&D and moves very rapidly down the experience curve. The Japanese, too, launch frontal attacks on the basis of cost-related price cutting, and this is one of the most viable bases on which a sustained frontal-attack strategy can be founded.

Flank Attack   An enemy's army is strongest where it expects to be attacked. It is necessarily less secure in its flanks and rear. Its weak spots (blind sides), therefore, are natural points of attack for the enemy. The major principle of modern offensive warfare is "concentration of strength against weakness." The aggressor will act as if it will attack the strong side to tie up the defender's troops but will launch the real attack at the side or rear. This "turning" maneuver catches the defending army off guard. Flank attacks make excellent marketing sense and are particularly attractive to the aggressor possessing fewer resources than the opponent. If the aggressor cannot overwhelm the defender with brute strength, it can outmaneuver the defender with subterfuge.

A flank attack can be directed against a competitor along two strategic dimensions— geographical and segmental. A geographical attack consists of the aggressor's spotting areas in the country or the world in which the opponent is not performing at high levels. For example, some of IBM's rivals chose to set up strong branches in medium- and smaller-sized cities, which are relatively neglected by IBM. According to a Honeywell field sales manager:

> Out in the rural areas, we are relatively better off than in the cities. We have been quite successful in these areas because our sales force does not meet the ten plus to one ratio it hits in the cities where IBM concentrates its people. Thus, ours must be a concentration game.[21]

The other, and potentially more powerful, flanking strategy is to spot uncovered market needs not being served by the leaders:

> German and Japanese auto makers chose not to compete with American auto makers by producing large, flashy, gas-guzzling automobiles, even though these were supposedly the preference of American buyers. Instead they recognized an unserved consumer segment that wanted small,

fuel-efficient cars. They moved vigorously to fill this hole in the market, and to their satisfaction and Detroit's surprise, American taste for smaller, fuel-efficient cars grew to be a substantial part of the market.

"Discovering," so to speak, the "light" beer segment, Miller Brewing Company pivoted on this unserved gap in the market and vigorously developed it into a huge breach across the whole industry's front and propelled itself from seventh place in the industry to a very close second in five years.

A flanking strategy is another name for identifying shifts in market segments—which are causing gaps to develop that are not being served by the industry's product profile—and rushing in to fill the gaps and develop them into strong segments. Instead of a bloody battle between two or more companies trying to serve the same market, flanking leads to a fuller coverage of the varied needs of the whole market. Flanking is in the best tradition of the modern marketing philosophy, which holds that the purpose of marketing is to "discover needs and serve them." Flank attacks have a higher probability of being successful than frontal attacks. This is also borne out in military history. In his penetrating analysis of the thirty most important conflicts of the world from the Greek wars up to World War I (which embraced more than 280 campaigns), Liddell-Hart concluded that in only six campaigns did decisive results follow strategies of direct head-on assault.[22] The strategy of "the indirect approach" has overwhelming support from history as the most effective and economic form of strategy.

Encirclement Attack   The pure flanking maneuver was defined as pivoting on a gap in the existing market coverage of the competitors. The encirclement maneuver, on the other hand, is an attempt to capture a wide slice of the enemy's territory through a "blitzkrieg" attack. Encirclement involves launching a grand offensive on several fronts, so that the enemy must protect its front, sides, and rear simultaneously. The aggressor may offer the market everything the opponent offers and more, so that the offer is unrefusable. Encirclement makes sense as a strategy where the aggressor commands resources superior to those of the opponent and believes that the encirclement will be complete and swift enough to break the opponent's will to resist. Here are two examples:

Seiko's attack on the watch market illustrates an encirclement strategy.[23] For several years, Seiko has been acquiring distribution in every major watch outlet and overwhelming its competitors and consumers with an enormous variety of constantly changing models. In the United States, it offers some four hundred models, but its marketing clout is backed by the some twenty-three hundred models it makes and sells worldwide. "They hit the mark on fashion, features, user preferences, and everything else that might motivate the consumer," says an admiring vice-president of a U.S. competitor.

An encirclement attack does not always work, as Hunt's found out when it tried to blitz Heinz's brand of ketchup in a grab for increased market share. In 1963 Hunt's, with a 19 percent share of the ketchup market, launched a major encirclement attack on Heinz to go after Heinz's 27 percent market share. Hunt's rolled out a number of marketing attacks simultaneously. It introduced two new flavors of ketchup (pizza and hickory) to disrupt the consumers' traditional taste preference for Heinz and also to capture more retail shelf space. It lowered its price to 70 percent of Heinz's price. It offered heavy trade allowances to the retailers. It raised its advertising budget to over twice the level of Heinz's. This marketing program meant that Hunt's would lose money while the battle raged but would make it up if it attracted enough brand switchers. The strategy failed to work. The Heinz brand continued to enjoy consumer preference; as a result, not enough Heinz users tried the Hunt's brand, and most of those who did returned to the Heinz brand. By the mid-1970s, Heinz had increased its share to over 40 percent.

Hunt's debacle underscores our core proposition that segmentation opportunity is fundamental to choosing the axis for an indirect approach. If empty niches do not now exist or cannot be created by segment diffusion tactics, then what is a flank attack in the mind of the aggressor peters out into a plain frontal attack in the marketplace. As such, it would require the 3:1 advantage in combat firepower to succeed.

Bypass Attack The bypass is the most indirect of assault strategies and eschews any belligerent move directed against the enemy's existing territory. It means bypassing the enemy and attacking easier markets to broaden one's resources base. This offers three lines of approach: diversifying into *unrelated products*, diversifying into new *geographical markets* for existing products, and leapfrogging into *new technologies* to supplant existing products.

Colgate's impressive turnaround utilized the first two principles.[24] In the United States, Colgate has always struggled in Procter & Gamble's shadow. In heavy-duty detergents, P&G's Tide routed Colgate's Fab by almost 5:1. In dishwashing liquids, P&G had almost twice Colgate's share. In soaps, too, Colgate trailed far behind. When David Foster took over as CEO in 1971, despite its $1.3 billion in sales, Colgate still had the reputation as a stodgy marketer of soap and detergent. By 1979 Foster had transformed the company into a $4.3 billion conglomerate, capable of challenging P&G if necessary. Foster's real achievement was in recognizing that any head-on battle with P&G was futile. "They outgunned us 3 to 1 at the store level," said Foster, "and had three research people to our one." Foster's strategy was simple—increase Colgate's lead abroad and bypass P&G at home by diversifying into non–P&G markets. A string of acquisitions followed in textiles and hospital products, cosmetics, and a range of sporting goods and food products. The outcome: In 1971, Colgate was underdog to P&G in about half of its business. By 1976, in three-fourths of its business, it was either comfortably placed against P&G or did not face it at all.

Technological leapfrogging is a bypass strategy used often in high-tech industries. Instead of imitating the competitor's product and engaging in a costly frontal attack, the challenger patiently researches and develops the next technology and, when satisfied about its superiority, launches an attack, thus shifting the battleground to its territory, where it has an advantage. Intellevision's attack strategy on Atari in the video game market was precisely to bypass Atari's state-of-the-art and attack when it had discovered a superior technology.

Guerrilla Attack Guerrilla attack is another option available to market aggressors, especially smaller undercapitalized ones. Guerrilla warfare consists of making small, intermittent attacks on different territories of the opponent, with the aim of harassing and demoralizing the opponent and eventually securing permanent footholds. The military rationale was stated by Liddell-Hart:

> The more usual reason for adopting a strategy of limited aim is that of awaiting a change in the balance of force—a change often sought and achieved by draining the enemy's force, weakening him by pricks instead of risking blows. The essential condition of such a strategy is that the drain on him should be disproportionately greater than on oneself. The object may be sought by raiding his supplies; by local attacks which annihilate or inflict disproportionate loss on parts of his force: by bringing him into unprofitable attacks; by causing an excessively wide distribution of his force; and, not least, by exhausting his moral and physical energy.[25]

The guerrilla attacker will use both conventional and unconventional means to attack the opponent. These would include selective price cuts, intense promotional bursts, and occasional legal actions. The key is to focus the attack on a narrow territory:

Diamond Crystal Salt had less than a 5 percent share of the national salt market compared with Morton's 50 percent. There is no way that it could compete with Morton on a broad front. Diamond decided to focus its attack against Morton in its own core regional market and launched an aggressive marketing campaign. It managed to build a 3:1 lead over Morton.

EXHIBIT 11-4

Some Specific Attack Strategies Available to Challengers

Several specific attack strategies are available to the market challenger who is seeking an advantage vis-à-vis competition:

1. **Price-discount strategy.** A major attack strategy for challengers is to offer buyers a product comparable to the leader's at a lower price. (See Figure 17-1, p. 495. Leader in cell 1, challenger in cell 2.) The Fuji Corporation used this strategy to attack Kodak's preeminence in the photographic-paper field. Its paper is of comparable quality and is priced 10 percent lower than Kodak's. Kodak chose not to lower its price, with the result that Fuji achieved strong market-share inroads. Texas Instruments is the prime practitioner of price cutting. It will offer a comparable-quality product and cut its price progressively to gain market share and still lower costs of production. Texas Instruments willingly forgoes profits in the first few years in a drive to gain unchallenged market leadership. It did this with transistors and hand calculators and seemed bent on doing this in the personal computer market. For a price-discount strategy to work, three assumptions must be fulfilled. First, the challenger must convince buyers that its product and service are comparable to the leader's. Second, the buyers must be sensitive to the price difference and feel comfortable about turning their back on existing suppliers. Third, the market leader must refuse to cut its price in spite of the competitor's attack.

2. **Cheaper-goods strategy.** Another strategy is to offer the market an average- or low-quality product at a much lower price. (See Figure 17-1, p. 495. Leader in cell 1, challenger in cell 5 or 9.) This works when there is a sufficient segment of buyers who are interested only in price. Firms that get established through this strategy, however, may be attacked by "cheaper-goods" firms whose prices are even lower. In defense, they try to upgrade their quality gradually over time.

3. **Prestige-goods strategy.** A market challenger can launch a higher-quality product and charge a higher price than the leader. (See Figure 17-1, p. 495. Leader in cell 1, challenger goes to northwest of cell 1.) Mercedes gained on Cadillac in the American market by offering a car of even higher quality and higher price. Some prestige-goods firms later roll out lower-price products to take advantage of their charisma.

4. **Product-proliferation strategy.** The challenger can go after the leader by launching a large number of product versions, thus giving buyers more options. Hunt went after Heinz's leadership in the ketchup market by creating several new ketchup flavors and bottle sizes in contrast with Heinz's reliance on one flavor of ketchup, sold in a limited number of bottle sizes.

5. **Product-innovation strategy.** The challenger may pursue product innovation to attack the leader's position. Polaroid and Xerox are companies whose success is based on continuously introducing outstanding innovations in the camera and copying fields, respectively. Miller rose to second place in the beer industry by successfully launching a light beer and introducing "pony-sized" bottle for lighter beer drinkers. The public often gains most from challenger strategies oriented toward product innovation.

6. **Improved-services strategy.** The challenger might find ways to offer new or better services to customers. IBM achieved its success by recognizing that customers were more interested in the software and the service than in the hardware. Avis's famous attack on Hertz, "We're only second. We try harder," was based on promising and delivering cleaner cars and faster service than Hertz.

7. **Distribution-innovation strategy.** A challenger might discover or develop a new channel of distribution. Avon became a major cosmetics company by perfecting door-to-door selling instead of battling other cosmetic firms in conventional stores. U.S. Time Company achieved great success by selling its low-price Timex watches through mass-merchandise channels instead of jewelry stores.

8. **Manufacturing-cost-reduction strategy.** The challenger might seek to achieve lower manufacturing costs than its competitors through more efficient purchasing, lower labor costs, and more modern production equipment. The company can use its lower costs to price more aggressively in order to gain market share. This strategy has been the key to the successful Japanese invasion of various world markets.

9. **Intensive advertising promotion.** Some challengers attack the leader by increasing their expenditures on advertising and promotion. When Hunt went after Heinz in the ketchup market, it built its annual spending level to $6.4 million as against Heinz's $3.4 million. Miller Beer similarly outspent Budweiser in its attempt to achieve first place in the U.S. beer market. Substantial promotional spending, however, is usually not a sensible strategy unless the challenger's product or advertising message exhibits some superiority over competition.

A challenger rarely succeeds in improving its market share by relying on only one strategy element. Its success depends on designing a total strategy that will improve its position over time.

Normally, guerrilla warfare is practiced by a smaller firm against a larger one. It is a case of David attacking Goliath. Not able to mount a frontal or even an effective flanking attack, the smaller firm launches a barrage of short promotional and price attacks in random corners of the larger opponent's market in a manner calculated to gradually weaken the opponent's market power. Even here, the attacker has to decide between launching a few major attacks or a continual stream of minor attacks. Military dogma holds that a continual stream of minor attacks usually creates more cumulative impact, disorganization, and confusion in the enemy than a few major ones. In line with this, the guerrilla attacker would find it more effective to attack small, isolated, weakly defended markets rather than major stronghold markets like New York, Chicago, and Los Angeles, where the defender is better entrenched and more willing to retaliate quickly and decisively.

It would be a mistake to think of a guerrilla campaign as only a "low-resource" strategy alternative available to financially weak challengers. Conducting a continual guerrilla campaign can be expensive, although admittedly less expensive than a frontal, encirclement, or even flanking attack. Furthermore, guerrilla war is more a preparation for war than a war itself. Ultimately it must be backed by a stronger attack if the aggressor hopes to "beat" the opponent. Hence in terms of resources, guerrilla warfare is not necessarily a cheap operation.

The preceding attack strategies are very broad. The challenger must put together a total strategy consisting of several specific strategies. Exhibit 11-4 lists several specific marketing strategies for attacking competitive positions. Exhibit 11-5 details how two well-known challenger companies, Pepsi-Cola and Yamaha, attacked the leaders in their respective industries.

MARKET-FOLLOWER STRATEGIES

Some years ago, Professor Levitt wrote an article entitled "Innovative Imitation" in which he argued that a strategy of *product imitation* might be as profitable as a strategy as *product innovation*.[26] After all, the innovator bears the huge expense of developing the new product, getting it into distribution, and informing and educating the market. The reward for all this work and risk is normally market leadership. However, another firm

EXHIBIT 11-5

How Two Challengers—Pepsi-Cola and Yamaha—Gained Share on Their Respective Market Leaders

Pepsi-Cola Attacks Coca-Cola   Before World War II, Coca-Cola dominated the American soft-drink industry. There was no second-place firm worth mentioning. "Pepsi raised hardly a flicker of recognition in Coke's consciousness." Pepsi-Cola was a newer drink, costing less to manufacture and with a less satisfactory taste than Coke's. Its major selling point was more drink for the same price. Pepsi emphasized this in its advertising, "Twice as much for a nickel, too." Its plain bottle carried a paper label that often got dirty in transit, adding to the impression that it was a second-class soft drink.

During World War II, Pepsi and Coke both enjoyed increased sales as they followed the flag around the world. After the war, Pepsi's sales started to fall relative to Coke's. A number of factors contributed to Pepsi's problems, including poor image, poor taste, poor packaging, and poor quality control. Furthermore Pepsi had to raise its prices to cover rising costs, and it became less of a bargain than before. Morale was quite low at Pepsi toward the end of the 1940s.

At this point, Alfred N. Steele came to the presidency of Pepsi-Cola with a great reputation for merchandising. He and his staff recognized that the main hope lay in transforming Pepsi from a cheap imitation of Coke to a first-class soft drink. They recognized that this turnaround would take several years. They conceived of a grand offensive against Coke that would take place in two phases. In the first phase, which lasted from 1950 to 1955, the following steps were taken: First, Pepsi's taste was improved. Second, the bottle and other corporate symbols were redesigned and unified. Third, the advertising campaign was redesigned to upgrade Pepsi's image. Fourth, Steele decided to concentrate on the take-home market, which Coke had neglected. Finally, Steele singled out twenty-five cities for a special push for market share.

By 1955, all of Pepsi's major weaknesses had been overcome, sales had climbed substantially, and Steele was ready for the next phase. The second phase consisted of mounting a direct attack on Coke's "on-premise" market, particularly the vending machine and cold-bottle segments, which were growing fast. Another decision was to introduce new-size bottles that offered convenience to customers in the take-home and cold-bottle markets. Finally, Pepsi offered to finance its bottlers who were willing to buy and install Pepsi vending machines. These actions during 1955 to 1960 led to considerable sales growth for Pepsi. Within one decade, Pepsi's sales had grown fourfold.

Yamaha Attacks Honda   In the early 1960s, Honda had established itself as the number-one motorcycle brand in the United States. Its lightweight machines with their great eye appeal, the slogan "You Meet the Nicest People on a Honda," and an aggressive sales organization and distribution network combined to greatly expand the total motorcycle market. Yamaha, another Japanese manufacturer, decided to enter the market against Honda. Its first step was to study Honda's major weaknesses, which included several dealers who had grown rich and lazy, abrupt management changes, discouragement of franchise-seeking dealers, and failure to promote the mechanical features of its motorcycles. Yamaha offered franchises to the best of the Honda-rejected franchises and used an enthusiastic sales force to train and motivate these dealers. It improved its motorcycle to the point that it could claim and demonstrate the motorcycle's mechanical superiority. It spent liberally on advertising and sales promotion programs to build buyer awareness and dealer enthusiasm. When motorcycle safety became a big issue, Yamaha designed superior safety features and advertised them extensively. These strategies propelled Yamaha into a clear second position in an industry swarming with over fifty manufacturers.

But then Yamaha's president, Hisao Koike, launched an all-out effort to take first place away from Honda. Yamaha adopted the slogan "Take the Lead" and launched several new models in an encirclement attack. The plan was ill conceived and Yamaha became burdened by inventories and had to lay off two thousand workers. Koike was removed as president and the "kamikaze attack" was withdrawn.

SOURCES Alvin Toffler, "The Competition That Refreshes," *Fortune*, May 1961. Also see "Pepsi Takes on the Champ," *Business Week*, June 12, 1978, pp. 88–97.

can come along, copy or improve the new product, and launch it. Although this firm probably will not overtake the leader, the follower can achieve high profits because it did not bear any of the innovation expense.

Not all runner-up companies will challenge the market leader. The effort to draw away the leader's customers is never taken lightly by the leader. If the challenger's lure is lower prices, improved service, or additional product features, the leader can quickly match these to diffuse the attack. The leader probably has more staying power in an all-out battle. A hard fight might leave both firms worse off, and this means the challenger must think twice before attacking. Unless the challenger can launch a preemptive strike—in the form of a substantial product innovation or distribution breakthrough—it often prefers to follow rather than attack the leader.

Patterns of "conscious parallelism" are common in capital-intensive homogeneous-product industries, such as steel, fertilizers, and chemicals. The opportunities for product differentiation and image differentiation are low; service quality is often comparable; price sensitivity runs high. Price wars can erupt at any time. The mood in these industries is against short-run grabs for market share because that strategy only provokes retaliation. Most firms decide against stealing each other's customers. Instead they present similar offers to buyers, usually by copying the leader. Market shares show a high stability.

This is not to say that market followers are without strategies. A market follower must know how to hold current customers and win a fair share of new customers. Each follower tries to bring distinctive advantages to its target market—location, services, financing. The follower is a major target of attack by challengers. Therefore the market follower must keep its manufacturing costs low and its product quality and services high. It must also enter new markets as they open up. Followship is not the same as being passive or a carbon copy of the leader. The follower has to define a growth path, but one that does not create competitive retaliation. Three broad followership strategies can be distinguished:

- **Following closely.** Here the follower emulates the leader in as many market-segmentation and marketing-mix areas as possible. The follower almost appears to be a challenger, but if it does not radically block the leader, no direct conflict will occur. Some followers may even be described as parasitic in that they put very little into stimulating the market, hoping to live off the market leader's investments.
- **Following at a distance.** Here the follower maintains some differentiation but follows the leader in terms of major market and product innovations, general price levels, and distribution. This follower is quite acceptable to the market leader, who may see little interference with its market plans and may be pleased that the follower's market share helps the leader avoid charges of monopolization. The distant follower may achieve its growth through acquiring smaller firms in the industry.
- **Following selectively.** This company follows the leader quite closely in some ways and sometimes goes its own way. The company may be quite innovative, and yet it avoids direct competition and follows many strategies of the leader where advantages are apparent. This company often grows into the future challenger.

There is a specific form of followership that is highly parasitic and is on the increase in global markets. These are firms that produce copies, or "knockoffs," of globally popular products. Many Apple personal computers that were not produced by Apple are being sold in Far East markets; and a Rolex watch that is hard to distinguish from a real $7,000 Rolex can be bought in Hong Kong for $25. In some cases, the parasitic producer uses a close-sounding name and modifies a slight feature. In either case, the brand leader faces a major threat and must figure out a way of policing or defeating these "followers."

MARKET-NICHER STRATEGIES

Almost every industry includes smaller firms that specialize in parts of the market where they avoid clashes with the majors. These smaller firms occupy market niches that they serve effectively through specialization and which the majors are likely to overlook or ignore. Market niching is of interest not only to small companies but also to smaller divisions of larger companies that are unable to achieve a major standing in that industry. These firms try to find one or more market niches that are safe and profitable. An ideal market niche would have the following characteristics:

- The niche is of sufficient size and purchasing power to be profitable.
- The niche has growth potential.
- The niche is of negligible interest to major competitors.
- The firm has the required skills and resources to serve the niche effectively.
- The firm can defend itself against an attacking major competitor through the customer goodwill it has built up.

The key idea in nichemanship is specialization. The firm has to specialize along market, customer, product, or marketing-mix lines. Here are several specialist roles open to a market nicher:

- *End-user specialist.* The firm specializes in serving one type of end-use customer. For example, a law firm can specialize in the criminal, civil, or business law markets.
- *Vertical-level specialist.* The firm specializes at some vertical level of the production-distribution cycle. For example, a copper firm may concentrate on producing raw copper, copper components, or finished copper products.
- *Customer-size specialist.* The firm concentrates on selling to either small-, medium- or large-size customers. Many nichers specialize in serving small customers who are neglected by the majors.
- *Specific-customer specialist.* The firm limits its selling to one or a few major customers. Many firms sell their entire output to a single company, such as Sears or General Motors.
- *Geographic specialist.* The firm sells only in a certain locality, region, or area of the world.
- *Product or product-line specialist.* The firm produces only one product line or product. Within the laboratory-equipment industry are firms that produce only microscopes, or even more narrowly, only lenses for microscopes.
- *Product-feature specialist.* The firm specializes in producing a certain type of product or product feature. Rent-a-Wreck, for example, is a California car-rental agency that rents only "beat-up" cars.
- *Job-shop specialist.* The firm manufactures customized products as ordered by the customer.
- *Quality/price specialist.* The firm operates at the low or high end of the market. For example, Hewlett-Packard specializes in the high-quality, high-price end of the hand-calculator market.
- *Service specialist.* The firm offers one or more services not available from other firms. An example would be a bank that takes loan requests over the phone and hand-delivers the money to the customer.
- *Channel specialist.* The firm specializes in serving only one channel of distribution. For example, a soft-drink company decided to make a very large size soft drink available only in gas stations.

Computer companies are among the newest converts to the "end user" type of niche marketing, but they call it *vertical marketing*. For years, computer companies fought to sell general hardware and software systems horizontally across many markets, and the price battles got rougher. Smaller companies started to specialize by vertical slices—law firms, medical practices, banks, etc.—studying the specific hardware and software needs of their target group and designing high-value-added products that had a competitive advantage over more general products. Their sales forces were trained to understand and service the particular vertical market. Computer companies also worked with independent *value-added resellers* (VARS), who customized the computer hardware and software for individual clients or customer segments and earned a price premium in the process.[27]

Niching carries a major risk in that the market niche may dry up or be attacked. That is why *multiple niching* is preferable to *single niching*. By developing strength in two or more niches, the company increases its chances for survival. Even some large firms prefer a multiple-niche strategy to serving the total market. One large law firm has developed a national reputation in the three areas of mergers and acquisitions, bankruptcies, and prospectus development, and it does little else.

The main point is that firms with low shares of the total market can be profitable too, and smart niching is one of the main answers. Recently two McKinsey consultants, Clifford and Cavanagh, carefully identified over two dozen highly successful midsize companies in order to probe into their success factors.[28] They found that in virtually all cases, these companies niched within the larger market rather than going after the whole market. One example is A. T. Cross, which niched itself in the high-price pen and pencil market with its famous gold writing instruments that every executive owns or wants to own. Instead of manufacturing all types of writing instruments, it has stuck to the high-price niche and enjoyed great sales growth and profit. Of course, the consultants discovered other common features shared by successful midsize companies, including offering high value, charging a premium price, creating new experience curves, and shaping a strong corporate culture and vision.

We can see that small firms have many opportunities to serve customers in profitable ways. Many small firms discover good niches through blind luck, although good opportunities can be detected and developed in a more systematic manner. Exhibit 11-6 describes the major entry strategies used by several companies that entered markets occupied by incumbents. Most of the companies chose a niching strategy.

SUMMARY

Marketing strategies are highly dependent on whether the company is a market leader, challenger, follower, or nicher.

A market leader faces three challenges: expanding the total market, protecting market share, and expanding market share. The market leader is interested in finding ways to expand the total market because it is the chief beneficiary of any increased sales. To expand market size the leader looks for new users of the product, new uses, and more usage. To protect its existing market share, the market leader has several defenses: position defense, flanking defense, preemptive defense, counteroffensive defense, mobile defense, and contraction defense. The most-sophisticated leaders cover themselves by doing everything right, leaving no openings for competitive attack. Leaders can also try to increase their market share. This makes sense if profitability increases at higher market-share levels and the company's tactics will not invite antitrust action.

A market challenger is a firm that aggressively tries to expand its market share by attacking the leader, other runner-up firms, or smaller firms in the industry. The challenger can choose from a variety of attack strategies, including a frontal attack, flanking attack, encirclement attack, bypass attack, and guerrilla attack.

A market follower is a runner-up firm that chooses not to rock the boat, usually out of fear that it stands to lose more than it might gain. The follower is not without a strategy, however, and seeks to use its particular competences to participate actively in the growth of the market. Some followers enjoy a higher rate of return on equity than the leaders in their industry do.

A market nicher is a smaller firm that chooses to operate in some part of the market that is specialized and is unlikely to attract the larger firms. Market nichers often become specialists in some end use, vertical level, customer size, specific customer, geographic area, product or product line, product feature, job-shop approach, quality/price level, service, or channel. Multiple niching is preferable to single niching in order to reduce a risk. Many of the most profitable small and medium-size firms owe their success to a niching strategy.

■ QUESTIONS

1. Briefly discuss the strategies used by market leaders, challengers, followers, and nichers in the personal computer market.

2. Describe a market-nicher strategy for a small firm competing in the home refrigerator market.

3. Describe how Coca-Cola or McDonald's has used and

could use the market-leader strategies listed in this chapter.

4. Describe how Pepsi-Cola or Burger King has used and could use the market-challenger strategies listed in this chapter.

5. Hewlett-Packard, a market leader in the top end of

the hand-held calculator market, has found itself in a squeeze between aggressively promoted portable computers and less-expensive calculators with increasingly sophisticated features. What market-leader strategy would you recommend for Hewlett-Packard?

6. What are some of the marketing principles that General Motors used to maintain its four decades of leadership in the U.S. auto industry?

7. IBM is one of the best marketing companies in the world. List the principles upon which its market leadership rests.

8. Although Caterpillar is an extremely strong company, it has some vulnerabilities. Name some potential threats to Caterpillar.

9. Briefly critique the following marketing strategy statement: "The company will offer the best product and best service at the lowest price."

10. Suggest a strategy for a new small firm entering the photocopying market.

11. Comment on the following statements made about the appropriate marketing strategy of smaller firms: (a) "The smaller firm should concentrate on pulling away the larger firm's customers, while the larger firm should concentrate on stimulating new customers to enter the market." (b) "Larger firms should pioneer new products, and smaller ones should copy them."

■ FOOTNOTES

1 See Robert V. L. Wright, *A System for Managing Diversity* (Cambridge, Mass.: Arthur D. Little, December 1974).

2 See Jordan P. Yale, "The Strategy of Nylon's Growth," *Modern Textiles Magazine*, February 1964, pp. 32ff. Also see Theodore Levitt, "Exploit the Product Life Cycle," *Harvard Business Review*, November–December 1965, pp. 81–94.

3 See Eric von Hippel, "A Customer-Active Paradigm for Industrial Product Idea Generation" (Unpublished working paper, Sloan School of Management, MIT, Cambridge, Mass., May 1977).

4 Sun Tsu, *The Art of War* (London: Oxford University Press, 1963); Miyamoto Mushashi, *A Book of Five Rings* (Woodstock, N.Y., Overlook Press, 1974); Carl von Clausewitz, *On War* (London: Routledge & Kegan Paul, 1908); and B. H. Liddell-Hart, *Strategy* (New York: Praeger, 1967).

5 These six defense strategies, as well as the five attack strategies described on pages 330–39, are taken from Philip Kotler and Ravi Singh, "Marketing Warfare in the 1980s," *Journal of Business Strategy*, Winter 1981, pp. 30–41.

6 See Michael E. Porter, *Competitive Strategy* (New York: Free Press, 1980), Chap. 4.

7 See "The H. J. Heinz Company (A)," Harvard Business School Case 9–569–011 M-357. Also see page 336 of this text.

8 *Relative market share* is the business's market share in its served market relative to the combined market share of its three leading competitors, expressed as a percentage. For example, if this business has 30 percent of the market and its three largest competitors have 20 percent, 10 percent, and 10 percent: 30/(20 + 10 + 10) = 75%.

9 Sidney Schoeffler, Robert D. Buzzell, and Donald F. Heany, "Impact of Strategic Planning on Profit Performance," *Harvard Business Review*, March–April 1974, pp. 137–45; and Robert D. Buzzell, Bradley T. Gale, and Ralph G. M. Sultan, "Market Share—A Key to Profitability," *Harvard Business Review*, January–February 1975, pp. 97–106.

10 See Buzzell et al., "Market Share," pp. 97, 100. The results represent a "best fit" to the data. There was some variance around the data; for example, some low-share competitors were highly profitable, and some high-share companies had low profits. But the regression was statistically significant.

It also held up in more recent PIMS studies where the data base now includes over 2,600 business units in a wider range of industries.

11 Richard G. Hamermesh, M. J. Anderson, Jr., and J. E. Harris, "Strategies for Low Market Share Businesses," *Harvard Business Review*, May–June 1978, pp. 95–102.

12 Carolyn Y. Woo and Arnold C. Cooper, "The Surprising Case for Low Market Share," *Harvard Business Review*, November–December 1982, pp. 106–13. Also see their "Market-Share Leadership—Not Always So Good," *Harvard Business Review*, January–February 1984, pp. 2–4.

13 John D. C. Roach, "From Strategic Planning to Strategic Performance: Closing the Achievement Gap," *Outlook*, published by Booz, Allen & Hamilton, New York, Spring 1981, p. 21. This curve assumes that pretax return on sales is highly correlated with profitability and that company revenue is a surrogate for market share. Michael Porter, in his *Competitive Strategy*, p. 43, shows a similar V-shaped curve that makes the same point.

14 *Business Week*, November 17, 1986, p. 155.

15 Philip Kotler and Paul N. Bloom, "Strategies for High Market-Share Companies," *Harvard Business Review*, November–December 1975, pp. 63–72. Also see Michael E. Porter, *Competitive Advantage* (New York: Free Press, 1985), pp. 221–26.

16 Philip B. Crosby, *Quality Is Free* (New York: McGraw-Hill, 1979).

17 See Robert J. Dolan, "Models of Competition: A Review of Theory and Empirical Evidence" in *Review of Marketing*, ed. Ben M. Enis and Kenneth J. Roering (Chicago: American Marketing Association, 1981), pp. 224–34.

18 For additional reading, see C. David Fogg, "Planning Gains in Market Share," *Journal of Marketing*, July 1974, pp. 30–38; and Bernard Catry and Michel Chevalier, "Market Share Strategy and the Product Life Cycle," *Journal of Marketing*, October 1974, pp. 29–34.

19 See "Stopping the Greasies," *Forbes*, July 9, 1979, p. 121.

20 "A 'Me-Too' Strategy That Paid Off," *Fortune*, August 27, 1979, p. 86.

21 Quoted in "Honeywell Information Systems" (case available from the Intercollegiate Case Clearing House, Soldiers Field, Boston, 1975), pp. 7–8.

22 Liddell-Hart, *Strategy*, p. 161.

23 See "Seiko's Smash," *Business Week*, June 5, 1978, p. 89.

24 See "The Changing of the Guard," *Fortune*, Sept. 24, 1979; and "How to Be Happy Though No. Two," *Forbes*, July 15, 1976, p. 36.

25 Liddell-Hart, *Strategy*, p. 335.

26 Theodore Levitt, "Innovative Imitation," *Harvard Business Review*, September–October 1966, pp. 63ff.

27 See Bro Uttal, "Pitching Computers to Small Business," *Fortune*, April 1, 1985, pp. 95–104.

28 Donald K. Clifford and Richard E. Cavanagh, *The Winning Performance: How America's High- and Midsize Growth Companies Succeed* (New York: Bantam Books, 1985).

12

Marketing Strategies
for Different Stages
of the Product Life Cycle

This is one of the saddest days of my life, a sad one for me, for our employees, officers, and directors; indeed, it is sad for the American public. Apparently, there is just not the need for our product in today's scheme of living.
Martin Ackerman, president of *The Saturday Evening Post*

During a product's life, a company will normally reformulate its marketing strategy several times. Not only are economic conditions changing and competitors launching new assaults but, in addition, the product is passing through new stages in the role that it plays in its market. Consequently the company needs to plan for a succession of strategies appropriate to each stage in the product's life cycle. The company must think about how to extend the product's life and profitability in the face of knowing that it will not last forever.

In this chapter, we will discuss the concept of the product life cycle, the appropriate marketing strategies for each stage, and the concept of market evolution and its implications for marketing planning.

THE CONCEPT OF THE PRODUCT LIFE CYCLE

The product life cycle (PLC) is an important concept in marketing that provides insights into a product's competitive dynamics. At the same time, the concept can prove misleading if not carefully used. To fully understand PLC, we will first describe its parent concept, the *demand/technology life cycle*.[1]

Demand/
Technology
Life Cycle

Marketing thinking should not begin with a product or even a product class, but rather with a need. The product exists as one solution among many to meet a need. For example, the human race has a need for "calculating power," and this need has grown over the centuries with the expansion of trade. The changing need level

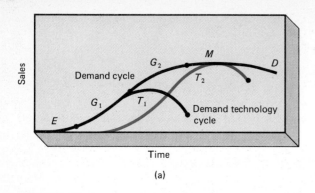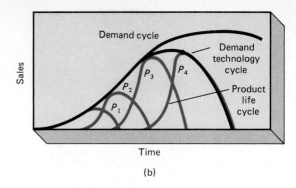

(a)   (b)

FIGURE 12-1
Demand-Technology-Product Life Cycles
SOURCE: H. Igor Ansoff, *Implanting Strategic Management* (Englewood Cliffs, N.J.: Prentice-Hall, 1984), p. 41.

is described by a *demand life-cycle curve*, the highest curve shown in Figure 12-1(a). There is a stage of *emergence* (E), followed by stages of *accelerating growth* (G_1), *decelerating growth* (G_2), *maturity* (M), and *decline* (D). In the case of "calculating power," the maturity and decline stage may not have set in yet. In the case of another need, say the need for "personal transportation" the need may be in a mature or declining stage in certain advanced countries.

Now a need is satisfied at the time by some technology. The need for "calculating power" was first satisfied by finger counting; later by abacuses; still later by slide rules, adding machines, hand calculators, and computers. Each new technology normally satisfies the need in a superior way. Each exhibits a *demand-technology life cycle*, shown by the curves (T_1 and T_2) under the demand cycle curve in Figures 12-1(a). Each demand-technology life cycle shows an emergence, rapid growth, slower growth, maturity, and then decline.

Within a given demand-technology cycle, there will appear a succession of product forms that satisfy the specific need at the time. Thus the hand calculator provided a new technology offering "calculating power." In the beginning, it took the product form of a rather large plastic box with a small screen and numerical keys, and it could perform only four tasks: adding, subtracting, multiplying, and dividing. This form lasted a few years and was succeeded by smaller-size hand calculators that could perform even more mathematical operations. Today's product forms include hand calculators no larger than the size of a business card. Figure 12-1(b) shows a succession of *product forms life cycles*, P_1, P_2, P_3, P_4. Later we will show that each product form contains a set of brands with their own *brand life cycles*.

The import of these distinctions is that if a company only concentrates on its own brand life cycle, it is missing the bigger picture and may wake up one day to find its whole business destroyed. Thus a manufacturer of simple slide rules may see its competitors as other manufacturers of simple slide rules (brand competitors) or even more-complex slide rules (different product forms), but it should actually be worrying about a new technology taking over (hand calculators), which will kill slide rules.

The same point can be made about the fate of vacuum tubes. Vacuum tubes were a technology for meeting the need for "amplifying weak electrical signals," and many product form improvements were made over the years. Yet their life was ended by the innovation of a new technology, namely, solid-state technology. The leading vacuum tube companies such as General Electric and RCA failed to make a transition to the new technology, and this is how newcomers such as Texas Instruments, Fairchild, and Transitron got their start.

The key point is that a company must decide what demand-technology to invest in and when to transit to a new demand-technology. Ansoff calls a demand-technology a *strategic business area (SBA)*, namely, "a distinctive segment of the environment in which the firm does or may want to do business."[2] The problem today is that many firms operate in turbulent markets with rapidly changing technologies and cannot invest in or master all the technologies. They are put in the position of having to bet on which demand-technology will win. They can bet heavily on one new technology or bet lightly on several. In the latter case, they are not likely to become the leader. The pioneering firm that bets heavily on the winning technology is likely to capture and hold leadership. Thus a crucial issue facing firms is the choice of the strategic business area in which they will "play the game." And a subsequent question is how to manage that area and whether the answer is to establish a *strategic business unit (SBU)* to manage each *strategic business area (SBA)*.

The Product Life Cycle and Its Stages

With this background, we can now focus on the product life cycle, which is what marketing people spend most of their time managing. The product life cycle is an attempt to recognize *distinct stages* in the *sales history* of the product. Corresponding to these stages are distinct opportunities and problems with respect to marketing strategy and profit potential. By identifying the stage that a product is in, or may be headed toward, companies can formulate better marketing plans.

To say that a product has a life cycle is to assert four things:

- Products have a limited life.
- Product sales pass through distinct stages, each posing different challenges to the seller.
- Product profits rise and fall at different stages of the product life cycle.
- Products require different marketing, financial, manufacturing, purchasing, and personnel strategies in the different stages of their life cycle.

Most discussions of product life cycle (PLC) portray the sales history of a typical product as following an S-shaped curve. (See Figure 12-2.) The curve is typically divided into four stages, known as *introduction*, *growth*, *maturity*, and *decline*:[3]

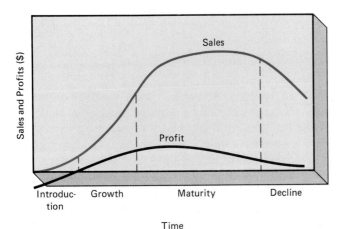

FIGURE 12-2
Sales and Profit Life Cycles

- **Introduction.** A period of slow sales growth as the product is introduced in the market. Profits are nonexistent in this stage because of the heavy expenses of product introduction.
- **Growth.** A period of rapid market acceptance and substantial profit improvement.
- **Maturity.** A period of a slowdown in sales growth because the product has achieved acceptance by most of the potential buyers. Profits stabilize or decline because of increased marketing outlays to defend the product against competition.
- **Decline.** The period when sales show a strong downward drift and profits erode.

Designating where each stage begins and ends is somewhat arbitrary. Usually the stages are marked where the rates of sales growth or decline become pronounced. Polli and Cook proposed an operational measure based on a normal distribution of percentage changes in real sales from year to year.[4]

Studies by Buzzell[5] of grocery food products and Polli and Cook[6] of consumer nondurables showed that the S-shaped PLC concept holds up well for many product categories. Those planning to use this concept must investigate the extent to which the PLC concept describes product histories in their industry. They should check the normal sequence of stages and the average duration of each stage. Cox found that a typical ethical drug spanned an introductory period of one month, a growth stage of six months, a maturity stage of fifteen months, and a very long decline stage—the last because of manufacturers' reluctance to drop drugs from their catalogs. These stage lengths must be reviewed periodically. Intensifying competition is leading to shortening PLCs over time, which means that products must make their profits in a shorter period.

Product-Category, Product-Form, and Brand Life Cycles

The PLC concept can be used to analyze a product category (cigarettes), a product form (plain filter cigarettes), or a brand (Philip Morris regular nonfilter). (See Figure 12-3.) The PLC concept has a different degree of applicability in each case:

- *Product categories* have the longest life cycles. The sales of many product categories stay in the mature stage for an indefinite duration, since they are highly population related. Some major product categories—cigars, newspapers, coffee, movies—seem to have entered the decline stage of the PLC.[7] Meanwhile some others—microcomputers, videocassettes, cordless telephones—are clearly in the introductory or growth stage.
- *Product forms* tend to exhibit the standard PLC histories more faithfully than do product categories. Thus manual typewriters went through the stages of introduction, growth, maturity, and decline; now electric typewriters are showing a similar history as electronic typewriters start replacing them.
- *Brands* tend to show the shortest PLC history. A Nielsen study found that in the past the life expectancy of a new brand was approximately three years, and the signs are that it is growing shorter.[8] At the same time, some very old brands—such as Arm & Hammer Baking Soda, Ivory Soap, Jell-O—are still going strong.

Other Shapes of the Product Life Cycle

Not all products exhibit an S-shaped PLC. Researchers have identified anywhere from six to seventeen different PLC patterns.[9] Three common patterns are shown in Figure 12-4. Figure 12-4(a) shows a "growth-slump-maturity" pattern, often characteristic of new small kitchen appliances. For example, the sales of slow cookers grew rapidly between 1970 and 1976, then slid to half of their 1976 level by 1979, and thereafter stabilized or "petrified" at that level. The petrified level is held up by late adopters buying the product for the first time and early adopters replacing the product.

The "cycle-recycle" pattern in Figure 12-4(b) often describes the sales of new drugs. The pharmaceutical company aggressively promotes its new drug, and this produces the

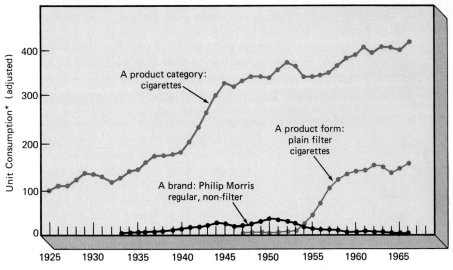

*Number of cigarettes per $100 of constant dollar nondurable consumption

FIGURE 12-3
PLCs for a Product Category, Product Form, and Brand
SOURCE: Rolando Polli and Victor Cook, "Validity of the Product Life Cycle," *Journal of Business*, October 1969, p. 389. The University of Chicago Press. Copyright © 1969 by The University of Chicago Press.

first cycle. Later sales slump and the company decides to give the drug another promotion push, which produces a second cycle usually of smaller magnitude and duration.

Still another common pattern is the "scalloped" PLC in Figure 12-4(c). Here sales show a succession of life cycles based on the discovery of new-product characteristics, uses, or users. Nylon's sales, for example, show a scalloped pattern because of the many new uses—parachutes, hosiery, shirts, carpeting—discovered over time.[10]

Exhibit 12-1 describes some of the major factors that shape the PLC for a specific product.

FIGURE 12-4
Some Common Product Life-Cycle Patterns

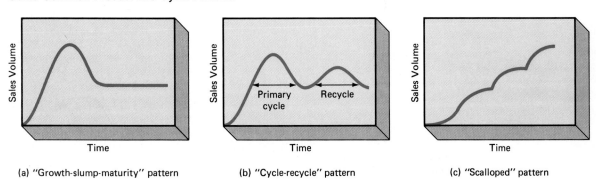

(a) "Growth-slump-maturity" pattern

(b) "Cycle-recycle" pattern

(c) "Scalloped" pattern

Goldman and Muller have presented some interesting observations on factors influencing the shape and duration of product-specific life cycles. First consider the shape that an ideal product life cycle would exhibit. It is shown below:

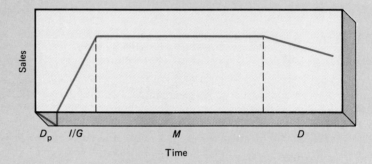

This shape is ideal for the following reasons:

■ The product development period (D_p) is short, and therefore the company's product development costs are low.

■ The introduction/growth period (I/G) is short, and therefore sales reach their peak quite soon, which means early maximum revenue.

■ The maturity period (M) lasts quite long, which means the company enjoys an extended period of profits.

■ The decline (D) is very slow, which means that profits fall gradually rather than suddenly.

A firm that is considering launching a new product should forecast the PLC shape based on factors that influence the length of each stage:

■ *Development time* is shorter and less costly for routine products than for high-tech products. Thus new perfumes, new snacks, and so on, do not involve much development time, whereas high-tech products require much R&D and engineering time and cost.

■ *Introduction and growth time* will be short under the following conditions:
  ■ The product does not require setting up a new infrastructure of channel institutions, transportation, services, or communication.
  ■ The dealers will rapidly accept and promote the new product.
  ■ Consumers have an interest in the product, will adopt it early, and will give it favorable word of mouth.

■ These conditions apply to many familiar consumer products. They are less valid for many high-tech products, which therefore require longer introduction/growth periods.

■ *Maturity time* will last long to the extent that consumer tastes and product technology are fairly stable and the company maintains leadership in the market. Companies make the most money by riding out a long maturity period. If the maturity period is short, the company may not recover its full investment.

■ The *decline time* is long if consumer tastes and product technology change only slowly. The more brand loyal the consumers, the slower the rate of decline. The lower the exit barriers, the faster some firms will exit, and this will slow down the rate of decline for the firms remaining in the industry.

Given these factors, we can see why many high-tech firms fail. They face highly unattractive PLCs. The worst type of PLC would look like this:

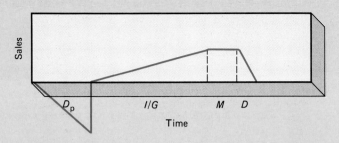

The development time is long, and the development cost is steep; the introduction/growth time is long; the maturity period is short; and the decline is fast. Many high-tech firms must invest a great amount of time and cost to develop their product; they find that it takes a long time to introduce it to the market; the market does not last long; and the decline is steep, due to the rapid technological change.

SOURCE: Arieh Goldman and Eitan Muller, "Measuring Shape Patterns of Product Life Cycles; Implications for Marketing Strategy," (Unpublished paper, Hebrew University of Jerusalem, Jerusalem School of Business Administration), August 1982.

Style, Fashion, and Fad Life Cycles There are three categories of product life cycles that should be distinguished from the others, those pertaining to styles, fashions, and fads. (See Figure 12-5.)

A *style* is a basic and distinctive mode of expression appearing in a field of human endeavor. For example, styles appear in homes (colonial, ranch, Cape Cod); clothing (formal, casual, funky); and art (realistic, surrealistic, abstract). Once a style is invented, it may last for generations, going in and out of vogue. A style exhibits a cycle showing several periods of renewed interest.

A *fashion* is a currently accepted or popular style in a given field. For example, jeans are a fashion in today's clothing, and "country western" is a fashion in today's popular music. Fashions pass through four stages.[11] In the *distinctiveness stage*, some

FIGURE 12-5
Style, Fashion, and Fad Life Cycles

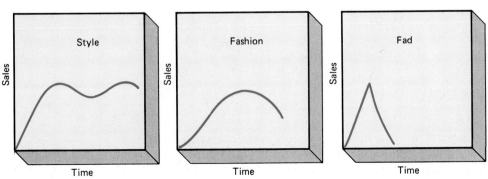

consumers take an interest in something new to set themselves apart from other consumers. The products may be custom-made or produced in small quantities by some manufacturer. In the *emulation stage*, other consumers take an interest out of a desire to emulate the fashion leaders, and additional manufacturers begin to produce larger quantities of the product. In the *mass-fashion stage*, the fashion has become extremely popular and manufacturers have geared up for mass production. Finally, in the *decline stage*, consumers start moving toward other fashions that are beginning to catch their eye.

Thus fashions tend to grow slowly, remain popular for a while, and decline slowly. The length of a fashion cycle is hard to predict. Wasson believes that fashions come to an end because they represent a purchase compromise, and consumers start looking for missing attributes. For example, as automobiles become shorter, they become less comfortable, and then a growing number of buyers start wanting longer cars. Furthermore, too many consumers adopt the fashion, thus turning others away. Reynolds suggests that the length of a particular fashion cycle depends on the extent to which the fashion meets a genuine need, is consistent with other trends in the society, satisfies societal norms and values, and does not meet technological limits as it develops.[12] Robinson, however, sees fashions as living out inexorable cycles regardless of economic, functional, or technological changes in society.[13] Sproles has recently reviewed and compared several theories of fashion cycles.[14]

Fads are fashions that come quickly into the public eye, are adopted with great zeal, peak early, and decline very fast. Their acceptance cycle is short, and they tend to attract only a limited following. They often have a novel or capricious aspect, as when people start buying "pet rocks" or run naked and "streak." Fads appeal to people who are searching for excitement or who want to distinguish themselves from others or have something to talk about to others. Fads do not survive because they do not normally satisfy a strong need or at least do not satisfy it well. It is difficult to predict whether something will be only a fad, and if so, how long it will last—a few days, weeks, or months. The amount of media attention it receives, along with other factors, will influence its duration.

Rationale for the Product Life Cycle	Earlier we described the S-shaped PLC concept without providing a rationale in marketing terms. The theory of the diffusion and adoption of innovations provides the underlying rationale. (See pp. 439–42.) When a new product is launched, the company has to stimulate awareness, interest, trial, and purchase. This takes time,

and in the introductory stage only a few persons ("innovators") will buy it. If the product is satisfying, larger numbers of buyers ("early adopters") are drawn in. The entry of competitors into the market speeds up the adoption process by increasing the market's awareness and by causing prices to fall. More buyers come in ("early majority") as the product is legitimized. Eventually the growth rate decreases as the number of potential new buyers approaches zero. Sales become steady at the replacement purchase rate. Eventually sales decline as new-product classes, forms, and brands appear and divert buyer interest from the existing product. Thus the product life cycle is explained by normal developments in the diffusion and adoption of new products.

The PLC concept provides a useful framework for developing effective marketing strategies in different stages of the product life cycle. We now turn to these stages and consider the appropriate marketing strategies.

INTRODUCTION STAGE

The introduction stage starts when the new product is first distributed and made available for purchase. It takes time to fill the dealer pipelines and roll out the product in several markets; so sales growth is apt to be slow. Such well-known products as instant coffee, frozen orange juice, and powdered coffee creamers lingered for many years before they entered a stage of rapid growth. Buzzell identified several causes for the slow growth of many processed food products: delays in the expansion of production capacity; technical problems ("working out the bugs"); delays in making the product available to customers, especially in obtaining adequate distribution through retail outlets; and customer reluctance to change established behavior patterns.[15] In the case of expensive new products, sales growth is retarded by additional factors, such as the small number of buyers who can afford the new product.

In this stage, profits are negative or low because of the low sales and heavy distribution and promotion expenses. Much money is needed to attract distributors and "fill the pipelines." Promotional expenditures are at their highest ratio to sales "because of the need for a high level of promotional effort to (1) inform potential consumers of the new and unknown product, (2) induce trial of the product, and (3) secure distribution in retail outlets."[16]

There are only a few competitors, and they produce basic versions of the product, since the market is not ready for product refinements. The firms focus their selling on those buyers who are the readiest to buy, usually higher-income groups. Prices tend to be on the high side because "(1) costs are high due to relatively low output rates, (2) technological problems in production may have not yet been fully mastered, and (3) high margins are required to support the heavy promotional expenditures which are necessary to achieve growth."[17]

Marketing Strategies in the Introduction Stage In launching a new product, marketing management can set a high or a low level for each marketing variable, such as price, promotion, distribution, and product quality. Considering only price and promotion, management can pursue one of the four strategies shown in Figure 12-6.

A *rapid-skimming strategy* consists of launching the new product at a high price and a high promotion level. The firm charges a high price in order to recover as much gross profit per unit as possible. It spends heavily on promotion to convince the market

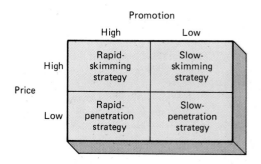

FIGURE 12-6
Four Introductory Marketing Strategies

of the product's merits even at the high price level. The high promotion acts to accelerate the rate of market penetration. This strategy makes sense under the following assumptions: (1) a large part of the potential market is unaware of the product; (2) those who become aware are eager to have the product and able to pay the asking price; (3) the firm faces potential competition and wants to build up brand preference.

A *slow-skimming strategy* consists of launching the new product at a high price and low promotion. The purpose of the high price is to recover as much gross profit per unit as possible, and the low level of promotion keeps marketing expenses down. This combination is expected to skim a lot of profit from the market. This strategy makes sense when (1) the market is limited in size; (2) most of the market is aware of the product; (3) buyers are willing to pay a high price; and (4) potential competition is not imminent.

A *rapid-penetration strategy* consists of launching the product at a low price and spending heavily on promotion. This strategy promises to bring about the fastest market penetration and the largest market share. This strategy makes sense when (1) the market is large; (2) the market is unaware of the product; (3) most buyers are price sensitive; (4) there is strong potential competition; and (5) the company's unit manufacturing costs fall with the scale of production and accumulated manufacturing experience.

A *slow-penetration strategy* consists of launching the new product at a low price and low level of promotion. The low price will encourage rapid product acceptance; and the company keeps its promotion costs down in order to realize more net profit. The company believes that market demand is highly price elastic but minimally promotion elastic. This strategy makes sense when (1) the market is large; (2) the market is highly aware of the product; (3) the market is price sensitive; and (4) there is some potential competition.

A company, especially the *market pioneer*, must not choose one of these strategies arbitrarily; rather the strategy must be the carefully chosen first step in a grand plan for life-cycle marketing. If the pioneer chooses its initial strategy to make a "killing," it will sacrifice long-run revenue for short-run gain. Market pioneers have the best chance of retaining market leadership if they play their cards right. (See Exhibit 12-2.) The pioneer should visualize the various product markets that it could initially enter, knowing that it cannot enter all of them. Suppose market segmentation analysis reveals the product market segments shown in Figure 12-7. The pioneer should analyze the profit potential of each market singly and in combination and decide on a market expansion strategy. Thus the pioneer in Figure 12-7 plans to launch its initial product in product market P_1M_1, then take the same product into a second market (P_1M_2), then surprise competition by developing

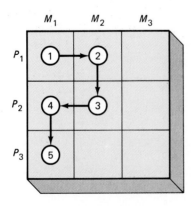

FIGURE 12-7
Long-Range Product/Market Expansion Strategy (P_1 = product i; M; = market j)

The Market Pioneer "Advantage"

Firms that pioneer new markets typically develop sustainable competitive advantages. One has only to think of Campbell's, Coca-Cola, Eastman Kodak, Hallmark, and Xerox. Of course there are exceptions, such as Bowmar (hand calculators), Reynolds (ballpoint pens), and Osborne (portable computers), which were quickly overtaken by later entrants.

William Robinson and Claes Fornell studied a broad range of mature consumer and industrial goods businesses and found that market pioneers generally enjoy a substantially higher market share than late entrants:

	Average Market Share	
	Consumer Goods	**Industrial Goods**
Pioneer	29%	29%
Early Follower	17%	21%
Late Entrant	13%	15%

In the PIMS data, a business is classified as (1) one of the *pioneers* in first developing such products or services, or (2) an *early follower* of the pioneer(s) in a still growing dynamic market, or (3) a *later entrant* into a more established market position.

Why do market pioneers gain a sustainable competitive advantage? First, pioneers tend to have higher product quality and broader product lines than late entrants. Second, they gain a brand-name advantage because being first is an effective way to secure a position in the consumer's mind. This is especially important in markets where consumers buy out of habit.

Pioneers are *not* found to have important direct cost savings. While cost savings are roughly 1 to 2 percent, the associated market-share impact is less than one share point. In these mature markets, patents and trade secrets do not benefit pioneers. Thus these sustainable competitive advantages are typically developed in the marketplace, and not in the patent office.

SOURCES: William T. Robinson and Claes Fornell, "Sources of Market Pioneer Advantages in Consumer Goods Industries," *Journal of Marketing Research*, August 1985, pp. 305–17; and Robinson and Fornell, "Market Pioneering and Sustainable Market Share Advantages," PIMSletter, #39, Strategic Planning Institute, 1986.

a second product for the second market (P_2M_2), then take the second product back into the first market (P_2M_1), and then launch a third product for the first market (P_3M_1). If this game plan works, the market-pioneer firm will own a good part of the first two market segments and serve them with two or three products. Naturally, this game plan may be altered as time passes and new factors emerge. But at least the firm has thought ahead about how it wants to evolve in this new market.

By looking ahead, the pioneer knows that competition will enter sooner or later and cause prices and its market share to fall. The questions are, When will this happen? and What should the pioneer do at each stage? Frey has described the stages of the competitive cycle that the pioneer has to anticipate (See Figure 12-8.)[18] Initially, the pioneer is the sole supplier, having 100 percent of the production capacity and, of course, all the sales of the product. The second stage, competitive penetration, starts when a new competitor

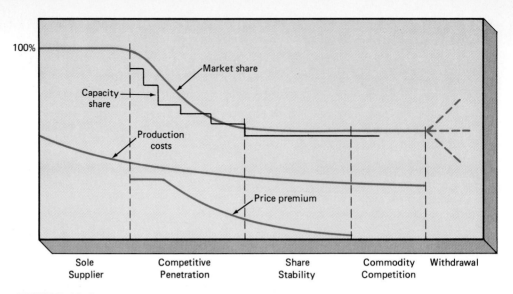

FIGURE 12-8
Stages of the Competitive Cycle
SOURCE: John B. Frey, "Pricing Over the Competitive Cycle," speech presented at the 1982 Marketing Conference, © 1982, The Conference Board, New York.

has built production capacity and begins commercial sales. Other competitors enter as well, and the leader's share of production capacity and of sales fall.

Subsequent competitors often enter the market at a lower price than the leader's due to perceived risks and uncertainties in their quality. As time goes on, the perceived relative values associated with the leader decline, causing a decline in the leader's price premium.

Capacity tends to be overbuilt during the rapid growth stages, so that when a cyclical slowdown occurs, industry overcapacity drives down margins to more "normal" levels. New competitors become reluctant to enter, and those already in try to solidify their positions. This leads to the third stage, share stability, in which capacity shares and market shares tend to stabilize.

This period of share stability is followed by a period in which the product has turned into a commodity and buyers no longer pay a price premium, and the suppliers earn only an average rate of return. At this point, one or more firms may withdraw. The pioneer, which is still likely to own the dominant share, may decide to build share further as others leave or may give up share and gradually withdraw. As the pioneer passes through the various stages of this competitive cycle, it must formulate new pricing and marketing strategies if it is to succeed.

GROWTH STAGE

The growth stage is marked by a rapid climb in sales. The early adopters like the product, and middle-majority consumers start following their lead. New competitors enter the market, attracted by the opportunities for large-scale production and profit. They introduce new-product features, and this further expands the market. The increased number of competitors leads to an increased number of distribution outlets, and factory sales jump just to fill the distribution pipeline.

Prices remain where they are or fall only slightly insofar as demand is increasing quite rapidly. Companies maintain their promotional expenditures at the same or at a slightly raised level to meet competition and continue educating the market. Sales rise much faster, causing a decline in the promotion-sales ratio.

Profits increase during this stage as promotion costs are spread over a larger volume, and unit manufacturing costs fall faster than price declines owing to the "experience-curve" effect.

The rate of growth eventually changes from an accelerating rate to a decelerating rate. Firms have to watch for the onset of the decelerating rate in order to prepare new strategies.

Marketing Strategies in the Growth Stage

During this stage, the firm uses several strategies to sustain market growth as long as possible:

- ■ The firm improves product quality and adds new product features and improved styling.
- ■ The firm adds new models and flanker products.
- ■ It enters new market segments.
- ■ It enters new distribution channels.
- ■ It shifts some advertising from building product awareness to bringing about product conviction and purchase.
- ■ It lowers prices at the right time to attract the next layer of price-sensitive buyers.

The firm that pursues these market-expanding strategies will strengthen its competitive position. But this improvement comes at additional cost. The firm in the growth stage faces a trade-off between high market share and high current profit. By spending a lot of money on product improvement, promotion, and distribution, it can capture a dominant position. It forgoes maximum current profit in the hope of making even greater profits in the next stage.

MATURITY STAGE

At some point a product's rate of sales growth will slow down, and the product will enter a stage of relative maturity. This stage normally lasts longer than the previous stages, and it poses formidable challenges to marketing management. *Most products are in the maturity stage of the life cycle*, *and therefore most of marketing management deals with the mature product.*

The maturity stage can be divided into three phases. In the first phase, *growth maturity*, the sales-growth rate starts to decline. There are no new distribution channels to fill, although some laggard buyers still enter the market. In the second phase, *stable maturity*, sales become level on a per capita basis because of market saturation. Most potential consumers have tried the product, and future sales are governed by population growth and replacement demand. In the third phase, *decaying maturity*, the absolute level of sales now starts to decline, and customers start moving toward other products and substitutes.

The slowdown in the rate of sales growth creates overcapacity in the industry. This overcapacity leads to intensified competition. Competitors scramble to find and enter niches.

They engage in frequent markdowns and off-list pricing. They increase their advertising and trade and consumer deals. They increase their R&D budgets to develop product improvements and flanker products. They make deals to supply private brands. These steps mean some profit erosion. A shakeout period begins and the weaker competitors start dropping out. The industry eventually consists of well-entrenched competitors whose basic drive is to gain competitive advantage.

Marketing Strategies in the Mature Stage

Some companies give up on mature products, feeling there is little they can do. They think the best thing is to conserve their money and spend it on newer products in the development pipeline. This ignores the low success rate of new products and the high potential that many old products still have. Many industries widely thought to be mature—autos, motocycles, television, watches, cameras—were proved otherwise by the Japanese, who found ways to offer new values to customers. Seemingly moribund brands like Jell-O, Ovaltine, and Arm & Hammer Baking Soda have had major sales revivals several times, through the exercise of marketing imagination. Marketing managers should not ignore or passively defend aging or "dog-eared" products. A good offense is the best defense. Marketers should systematically consider strategies of market, product, and marketing-mix modification.

Market Modification

The company should seek to expand the market for its brand by working with the two factors that make up sales volume:

$$\text{Volume} = \text{Number of brand users} \times \text{Usage rate per user}$$

We will examine each factor in turn.

The company can try to expand the number of brand users in three ways:

- **Convert nonusers.** The company can try to convert nonusers into users of the product category. For example, the key to the growth of air-freight service is the constant search for new users to whom air carriers can demonstrate the benefits of using air freight over ground transportation.
- **Enter new market segments.** The company can try to enter new market segments—geographic, demographic, and so on—that use the product but not the brand. For example, Johnson & Johnson successfully promoted its baby shampoo to adult users.
- **Win competitors' customers.** The company can work to attract competitors' customers to try or adopt the brand. For example, Pepsi-Cola is constantly coaxing Coca-Cola users to switch to Pepsi-Cola, throwing out one challenge after another.

Volume can also be increased by getting current brand users to increase their annual usage of the brand. There are three strategies:

- **More frequent use.** The company can try to get customers to use the product more frequently. For example, orange juice marketers try to get people to drink orange juice on occasions other than breakfast time.
- **More usage per occasion.** The company can try to interest users in using more of the product each time it is used. Thus a shampoo manufacturer might indicate that the shampoo is more effective with two rinsings than one.
- **New and more varied uses.** The company can try to discover new uses for the product and convince people to make more varied use of it. A common practice of food manufacturers, for example, is to list several recipes on their packages to broaden the consumers' awareness of all the uses of the product.

Product Modification   Managers also try to turn sales around by modifying the product's characteristics in a way that will attract new users and/or more usage from current users. The product relaunch can take several forms.

A strategy of *quality improvement* aims at increasing the functional performance of the product—its durability, reliability, speed, taste. A manufacturer can often overtake its competition by launching the "new and improved" machine tool, automobile, television set, or detergent. Grocery manufacturers call this a "plus" launch and promote a new additive or advertise something as "stronger," "bigger," or "better." This strategy is effective to the extent that the quality can be improved, the buyers believe the claim of improved quality, and a sufficient number of buyers want higher quality.

A strategy of *feature improvement* aims at adding new features (e.g., size, weight, materials, additives, accessories) that expand the product's versatility, safety, or convenience. For example, the addition of power to hand lawn mowers increased the speed and ease of cutting grass. Manufacturers then worked on engineering better safety features. Some manufacturers have added conversion features so that a power lawn mower doubles as a snow plow. Stewart outlined five advantages of feature improvement:

■ New features build a company image of progressiveness and leadership.
■ New features can be adapted quickly, dropped quickly, and often made optional at very little expense.
■ New features can win the loyalty of certain market segments.
■ New features can bring the company free publicity.
■ New features generate sales-force and distributors' enthusiasm.[19]

The chief disadvantage is that feature improvements are highly imitable; unless there is a permanent gain from being first, the feature improvement may not pay.

A strategy of *style improvement* aims at increasing the aesthetic appeal of the product. The periodic introduction of new car models amounts to style competition rather than quality or feature competition. In the case of packaged-food and household products, companies introduce color and texture variations and often restyle the package, treating it as an extension of the product. The advantage of a style strategy is that it might confer a unique market identity and secure a loyal following. Yet style competition has some problems. First, it is difficult to predict whether people—and which people—will like a new style. Second, style changes usually mean discontinuing the old style, and the company risks losing some customers who liked the old style.

Marketing-mix Modification   The product manager should also try to stimulate sales through modifying one or more marketing-mix elements. Here is a list of key questions that marketing managers should ask about the nonproduct elements of the marketing mix in their search for ways to stimulate the sales of a mature product:

■ *Prices.* Would a price cut attract new triers and users? If so, should the list price be lowered, or should prices be lowered through price specials, volume or early-purchase discounts, freight absorption, or easier credit terms? Or would it be better to raise the price to suggest more quality?
■ *Distribution.* Can the company obtain more product support and display in the existing outlets? Can more outlets be penetrated? Can the company get the product into some new types of distribution channels?

- **Advertising.** Should advertising expenditures be increased? Should the advertising message or copy be changed? Should the media vehicle mix be changed? Should the timing, frequency, or size of ads be changed?
- **Sales promotion.** Should the company step up sales promotion—trade deals, cents-off, rebates, warranties, gifts, and contests?
- **Personal selling.** Should the number or quality of sales people be increased? Should the basis for sales-force specialization be changed? Should sales territories be revised? Should sales-force incentives be revised? Can sales-call planning be improved?
- **Services.** Can the company speed up delivery? Can it extend more technical assistance to customers? Can it extend more credit?

Years ago, Gosta Mickwitz speculated on the elasticity of different marketing-mix tools at different stages of the product life cycle.[20] For mature products, he held that the impact of marketing-mix tools ranked in this order (from high to low): price, advertising and sales promotion, product quality, and service. His distinctions, however, were not fine enough. For example, what is the relative effectiveness of advertising versus sales promotion in the case of mature products? Many marketers argue that sales promotion has more impact than advertising because consumers have reached an equilibrium in their buying habits and preferences, and psychological persuasion (advertising) is not as effective as financial persuasion (sales promotion deals) in breaking this equilibrium. Hence many consumer-packaged-goods companies spend over 50 percent of their total promotion budget on sales promotion to support mature products. Yet there are also voices taking exception to this. Seymour Banks, a former vice-president at Leo Burnett, says that brands should be managed as capital assets. Advertising is wrongly treated as an expense rather than a capital investment. Branch managers like to use sales promotion because its effects are more currently visible to their superiors, but they are actually hurting the brand's long-run profit performance.

A major problem with marketing-mix modifications is that they are highly imitable by competition, especially price reductions and additional services. The firm may not gain as much as expected, and in fact, all firms may experience profit erosion as they step up their marketing attacks on each other.

Exhibit 12-3 presents a framework for finding ideas for rebuilding the sales of mature products.

DECLINE STAGE

The sales of most product forms and brands eventually decline. The sales decline may be slow, as in the case of oatmeal cereal; or rapid, as in the case of the Edsel automobile. Sales may plunge to zero, or they may petrify at a low level and continue for many years at that level.

Sales decline for a number of reasons, including technological advances, consumer shifts in tastes, and increased domestic and foreign competition. All of these lead to overcapacity, increased price cutting, and profit erosion.

As sales and profits decline, some firms withdraw from the market. Those remaining may reduce the number of product offerings. They may drop smaller market segments and weaker trade channels. They may cut the promotion budget and reduce their prices further.

EXHIBIT 12-3

Breaking Through the "Mature Product" Syndrome

Recently General Foods (GF) flew in six M.B.A. marketing teams—Chicago, Columbia, Michigan, North-western, Stanford, and Wharton—to compete with proposals for helping GF expand its sales of one of its mature products, Kool-Aid. The student teams had been supplied earlier with forty-two pages of data on this product/market. Each team had twenty minutes to present its proposal. Wharton and Stanford proposed that the product be aimed at young teenagers in addition to children; Northwestern, Michigan, and Columbia suggested targeting parents as a market; and Chicago proposed a new type of packaging. Clearly, these were drawn from a universe of possible ideas, and each had to be backed by a convincing execution strategy.

Managers of mature products need a systematic framework for identifying possible "breakthrough" ideas. Professor John A. Weber of Notre Dame developed the following framework, which he calls "Gap Analysis," to guide the search for growth opportunities:

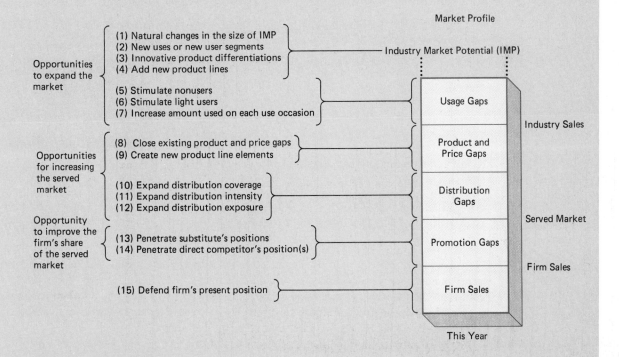

The key idea is to identify possible gaps in the product line, distribution, usage, competition, and so on. Market structure analysis would prompt the following questions about Kool-Aid:

1. **Natural changes in the size of industry market potential.** Will current birthrates and demographics favor more consumption of Kool-Aid? How will the economic outlook affect Kool-Aid consumption?

2. **New uses or new user segments.** Can Kool-Aid be made to appeal to teenagers, young adult singles, young adult parents, etc.?

3. **Innovative product differentiations.** Can Kool-Aid be made in different versions such as low-cal, super-sweet, etc.?

4. **Add new product lines.** Can the Kool-Aid name be used to launch a new soft-drink line?

Unfortunately, most companies have not developed a well-thought-out policy for handling their aging products. Sentiment plays a role:

> But putting products to death—or letting them die—is a drab business, and often engenders much of the sadness of a final parting with old and tried friends. The portable, six-sided pretzel was the first product The Company ever made. Our line will no longer be our line without it.[21]

Logic also plays a role. Management believes that product sales will improve when the economy improves, or when the marketing strategy is revised, or when the product is improved. Or the weak product may be retained because of its alleged contribution to the sales of the company's other products. Or it may be that its revenue covers out-of-pocket costs, and the company has no better way of using the money.

Unless strong reasons for retention exist, carrying a weak product is very costly to the firm. The cost is not just the amount of uncovered overhead and profit. Financial accounting cannot adequately convey all the hidden costs: The weak product may consume a disproportionate amount of management's time; it often requires frequent price and inventory adjustment; it generally involves short production runs in spite of expensive setup times; it requires both advertising and sales-force attention that might better be diverted to making the "healthy" products more profitable; its very unfitness can cause customer misgivings and cast a shadow on the company's image. The biggest cost may well lie in the future. By not being eliminated at the proper time, weak products delay the aggressive search for replacement products; they create a lopsided product mix, long on "yesterday's breadwinners" and short on "tomorrow's breadwinners"; they depress current profitability and weaken the company's foothold on the future.

A company faces a number of tasks and decisions to handle its aging products.

Identifying the Weak Products   The first task is to establish a system for identifying weak products. Six steps are involved:[22]

- The company appoints a product-review committee with representatives from marketing, manufacturing, and finance.
- This committee develops a system for identifying weak products.
- The controller's office supplies data for each product showing trends in market size, market share, prices, costs, and profits.
- This information is analyzed by a computer program that identifies dubious products. The criteria include the number of years of sales decline, market-share trends, gross profit margin, and return on investment.
- The dubious products are reported to those managers responsible for them. The managers fill out rating forms showing where they think sales and profits will go, with and without any changes in marketing strategy.
- The product-review committee examines this information and makes a recommendation for each dubious product—leave it alone, modify its marketing strategy, or drop it.

Determining Marketing Strategies   Some firms will abandon declining markets earlier than others. Much depends on the level of the *exit barriers*.[23] The lower the exit barriers, the easier it is for firms to leave the industry, and the more tempting it is for the remaining firms to remain and attract the customers of the withdrawing firms. The remaining firms will enjoy an increase in sales and profits. Thus a firm must decide whether to stay in the market until the end. For example, Procter & Gamble remained in the declining liquid-soap business until the end and made good profits as the others withdrew.

In a study of company strategies in declining industries, Harrigan distinguished five decline strategies open to the firm:

- Increasing the firm's investment (to dominate or strengthen its competitive position).
- Maintaining the firm's investment level until the uncertainties about the industry are resolved.
- Decreasing the firm's investment level selectively, by sloughing off the unpromising customer groups, while simultaneously strengthening the firm's investment posture within the lucrative niches of enduring customer demands.
- Harvesting (or milking) the firm's investment to recover cash quickly, regardless of the resulting investment posture.
- Divesting the business quickly by disposing of its assets as advantageously as possible.[24]

The appropriate decline strategy is a function of the industry's relative attractiveness and the company's competitive strength in that industry. For example, a company that finds itself in an unattractive industry and yet has competitive strength should consider shrinking selectively. However, if it finds itself in an attractive industry and has competitive strength, it should consider increasing or maintaining its investment level. Procter & Gamble on a number of occasions has taken disappointing brands that were in strong markets and attempted to *restage* them:

> P&G had launched a hand cream called Wondra that claimed to be less oily and was packaged in an inverted bottle so the cream would flow out from the bottom. Although initial sales were high, repeat purchases were disappointing. Consumers complained that the bottom got sticky and that "not oily" suggested it wouldn't work well. P&G carried out two restagings: First, it reintroduced Wondra in an upright bottle, and later, it reformulated the ingredients so they would work better. Sales then picked up.

P&G spokespersons have at times claimed that there is no such thing as a product life cycle, and they point to Ivory, Camay, and many other "dowager" brands that are still thriving.

If the company were choosing between *harvesting* and *divesting*, its strategies would be quite different. Harvesting calls for gradually removing costs from a product or business while trying to maintain sales as high as possible. The first costs to cut are R&D costs and plant and equipment investment. The company might also reduce product quality, not replace retiring sales force, eliminate certain services, and reduce its advertising expenditures. It would like to undertake these cost-reducing steps without tipping off customers, competitors, and employees that it is slowly pulling out of the business. If customers knew this, they would switch suppliers; if competitors knew this, they would tell customers; if employees knew this, they would seek new jobs elsewhere. Thus harvesting is an ethically ambivalent strategy, and it is also difficult to execute effectively. Yet many mature products warrant this strategy. Harvesting can substantially increase the company's cash flow during the period that it lasts, providing that sales do not utterly collapse. This happens when the company has successfully cut its costs without causing sales to fall any faster than before.[25]

The effect of harvesting a business is to make it eventually worthless. On the other hand, if the firm had decided instead to divest the business, it might have looked for a buyer. In this case, it would have tried to increase the attractiveness of the business, not run it down. Therefore the company must think carefully about whether to harvest or divest the weakening business unit.

The Drop Decision   When a company decides to drop a product, it faces further decisions. If the product has strong distribution and residual goodwill, the company can probably sell it to a smaller firm:

Jeffrey Martin, Inc., bought several "worn-out" brands from Purex Corporation, including *Cuticura*, *Bantron*, and *Doan's Pills*, and turned them around. Two Minnesota businessmen bought the *Ipana* toothpaste name and formula from Bristol-Myers; with no promotion, they sold $250,000 in the first seven months of operation.

If the company cannot find any buyers, it must decide whether to liquidate the brand quickly or slowly. It must also decide on how much parts inventory and service to maintain to service past customers.

SUMMARY AND CRITIQUE OF THE PRODUCT LIFE-CYCLE CONCEPT

Table 12-1 summarizes the characteristics, marketing objectives, and marketing strategies of the four stages of the PLC. Not all marketers would agree with all strategies, but they represent a consensus of what most marketers would advise.

Some marketers have prescribed more specific strategies during each stage of the PLC. Figure 12-9 shows a more elaborate analysis for grocery-product marketing, based on the assumption that many brands exhibit a cycle-recycle PLC.

The PLC concept is used by many managers to interpret product and market dynamics. Its real usefulness varies in different decision-making situations. As a *planning tool*, the

TABLE 12-1

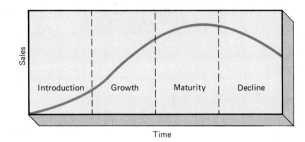

CHARACTERISTICS

	Introduction	Growth	Maturity	Decline
Sales	Low sales	Rapidly rising sales	Peak sales	Declining sales
Costs	High cost per customer	Average cost per customer	Low cost per customer	Low cost per customer
Profits	Negative	Rising profits	High profits	Declining profits
Customers	Innovators	Early adopters	Middle majority	Laggards
Competitors	Few	Growing number	Stable number beginning to decline	Declining number

MARKETING OBJECTIVES

	Create product awareness and trial	Maximize market share	Maximize profit while defending market share	Reduce expenditure and milk the brand

STRATEGIES

Product	Offer a basic product	Offer product extensions, service, warranty	Diversify brands and models	Phase out weak items
Price	Use cost-plus	Price to penetrate market	Price to match or beat competitors	Cut price
Distribution	Build selective distribution	Build intensive distribution	Build more intensive distribution	Go selective: phase out unprofitable outlets
Advertising	Build product awareness among early adopters and dealers	Build awareness and interest in the mass market	Stress brand differences and benefits	Reduce to level needed to retain hardcore loyals
Sales Promotion	Use heavy sales promotion to entice trial	Reduce to take advantage of heavy consumer demand	Increase to encourage brand switching	Reduce to minimal level

SOURCES This table was assembled by the author from several sources: Chester R. Wasson, *Dynamic Competitive Strategy and Product Life Cycles* (Austin, Tex; Austin Press, 1978); John A. Weber, "Planning Corporate Growth with Inverted Product Life Cycles," *Long Range Planning*, October 1976, pp. 12–29; and Peter Doyle, "The Realities of the Product Life Cycle," *Quarterly Review of Marketing*, Summer 1976, pp. 1–6.

FIGURE 12-9
PLC Marketing for Grocery Products

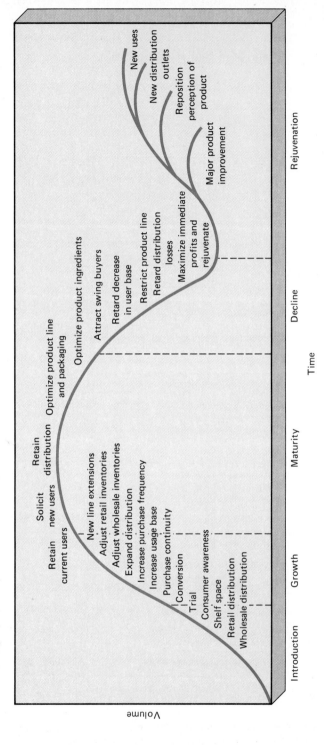

PLC concept characterizes the main marketing challenges in each stage and suggests major alternative marketing strategies the firm might pursue. As a *control tool*, the PLC concept allows the company to compare product performance against similar products in the past. As a *forecasting tool*, the PLC concept is less useful because sales histories exhibit diverse patterns, and the stages are of varying duration.

PLC theory has its share of critics. Critics claim that life-cycle patterns are too variable, as evidenced by the several shapes that the PLCs of different products have shown. They charge that the stages do not have predictable durations. In other words, PLCs lack what living organisms have, namely, a fixed sequence of stages and a fixed length of each stage. They even charge that the marketer can seldom tell what stage the product is in. A product may appear to be mature when actually it has only reached a temporary plateau in the growth stage prior to another upsurge. Finally, they charge that the PLC pattern is an artifact of the marketing strategies used rather than an inevitable course that sales have to follow:

> Suppose a brand is acceptable to consumers but has a few bad years because of other factors— for instance, poor advertising, delisting by a major chain, or entry of a "me-too" competitive product backed by massive sampling. Instead of thinking in terms of corrective measures, management begins to feel that its brand has entered a declining stage. It therefore withdraws funds from the promotion budget to finance R&D on new items. The next year the brand does even worse, panic increases. . . . Clearly, the PLC is a dependent variable which is determined by marketing actions; it is not an independent variable to which companies should adapt their marketing programs.[26]

In other words, product sales do not follow a natural and inevitable cycle, as living organisms do. The PLC is the result, not the cause, of the marketing strategies chosen by the firm. Thus if a brand's sales are declining, management should not conclude that the brand is inevitably in the decline stage of its life cycle. If it starts withdrawing funds from the brand, it will create a self-fulfilling prophecy that the brand is at the end of its life. Instead management should examine all the ways it could try to stimulate sales: modifying the customer mix, the brand's positioning, or the marketing mix. Only when management cannot identify a promising turnaround strategy might it draw the conclusion that the brand is in the decline stage of its life cycle. Then it must decide what to do.

Furthermore the best marketing strategy to follow in a given stage of the PLC is not necessarily the one prescribed in the PLC charts. Companies should pursue original strategies at each stage, not the ones everyone else is using.

THE CONCEPT OF MARKET EVOLUTION

The PLC focuses on what is happening to a particular product or brand rather than on what is happening to the overall market. It yields a product-oriented picture rather than a market-oriented picture. The demand/technology life cycle mentioned earlier reminds us to take a broader look at what is happening in the market as a whole. Firms need a way to anticipate the evolutionary path of a market as it is affected by new needs, competitors, technology, channels, and other developments.

Stages in Market Evolution   A market evolves through four stages: emergence, growth, maturity, and decline. We will describe and illustrate these stages next.

Emergence Stage   Before a market materializes, it exists as a *latent market*. A latent market consists of people who share a similar need or want for something that does not yet exist. For example, people have wanted a means of more rapid calculation than can be provided by a paper and pencil. Until recently, as we noted earlier, this need was imperfectly satisfied through abacuses, slide rules, and large adding machines.

Suppose an entrepreneur recognizes this need and imagines a technological solution in the form of a small, hand-size electronic calculator. He now has to determine the product attributes, specifically *physical size* and *number of arithmetic functions*. Being market oriented, he interviews potential buyers and asks them to state their preferred levels on each attribute.

Suppose consumer preferences are those shown in Figure 12-10(a). Evidently target customers differ greatly in their preferences. Some want a four-function calculator (adding, subtracting, multiplying, and dividing), and others want more functions (calculating percentages, square roots, logs, and so forth). Some want a small hand calculator and others want a large one. When buyer preferences scatter evenly in a market, it is called a *diffused-preference market*.

The entrepreneur's problem is to design an optimal product for this market.[27] He has three options:

■ The new product can be designed to meet the preferences of one of the corners of the market (*a single-niche strategy*).

■ Two or more products can be simultaneously launched to capture two or more parts of the market (*a multiple-niche strategy*).

■ The new product can be designed for the middle of the market (*a mass-market strategy*).

FIGURE 12-10
Market-Space Diagrams

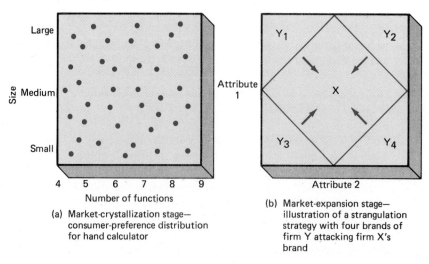

(a) Market-crystallization stage—
consumer-preference distribution
for hand calculator

(b) Market-expansion stage—
illustration of a strangulation
strategy with four brands of
firm Y attacking firm X's
brand

For small firms, a single-niche market strategy makes the most sense. A small firm has insufficient resources for capturing and holding the mass market. Larger firms would enter and clobber the small firm. Its best bet is to develop a specialized product and capture a corner of the market that will not attract competitors for a long time.

If the firm is large, it makes sense to go after the mass market by designing a product that is "medium" in size and number of functions. A product in the center minimizes the sum of the distances of existing preferences from the actual product. A hand calculator designed for the mass market will minimize total dissatisfaction.

We will assume that the pioneer firm is large and designs its product for the mass market. It launches the product and the *emergence stage* begins.

Growth Stage If sales are good, new firms will enter the market, ushering in a *market growth stage*. An interesting question is, Where will a second firm enter the market, assuming that the first firm established itself in the center? The second firm has three options:

- It can locate its brand in one of the corners (*a single-niche strategy*).
- It can locate its brand next to the first competitor (*a mass-market strategy*).
- It can launch two or more products in different unoccupied corners (*a multiple-niche strategy*).

If the second firm is small, it will avoid head-on competition with the pioneer and launch its brand in one of the market corners. If the second firm is large, it might launch its brand in the center against the pioneer firm. The two firms can easily end up sharing the mass market almost equally. Or a large second firm can implement a multiniche strategy.

> Procter & Gamble will occasionally enter a market containing a large, entrenched competitor, and instead of launching a me-too product or single-segment product, it introduces a succession of products aimed at different segments. Each entry creates a loyal following and takes some business away from the major competitor. Soon the major competitor is surrounded, its revenue is weakened, and it is too late to launch new brands in outlying segments. P&G, in a moment of triumph, then launches a brand against the major segment. This is called an encirclement strategy and is illustrated in Figure 12-10(b).

Maturity Stage Each firm entering the market will go after some position, locating either next to a competitor or in some unoccupied segment. Eventually the competitors cover and serve all the major market segments. In fact, they go further and invade each other's segments, reducing everyone's profits in the process. As the market's growth slows down, the market splits into finer and finer segments and a condition of high market fragmentation occurs. This is illustrated in Figure 12-11(a), with the letters representing different companies supplying various segments. Note that two segments are unserved because they are too small to yield a profit.[28]

This, however, is not the end of the evolution of a market. The condition of market fragmentation is often followed by a period of market consolidation, caused by the emergence of a new attribute that has cogent market appeal. The new attribute may not cause the market to expand so much as to shift market shares. Market consolidation took place in the toothpaste market when P&G introduced its new fluoride toothpaste, Crest, which effectively retarded dental decay. Suddenly other toothpaste brands that claimed whitening

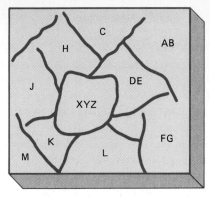

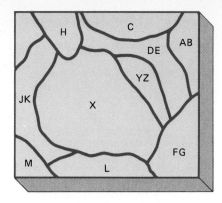

(a) Market-fragmentation stage　　　　　　(b) Market-reconsolidation stage

FIGURE 12-11
Market-Fragmentation and Market-Reconsolidation Stages

power, cleaning power, sex appeal, taste, and mouthwash effectiveness were pushed into the corners because consumers primarily wanted a dental-protection toothpaste. P&G's Crest won a lion's share of the market, as shown by the X territory in Figure 12-11(b).

But even a consolidated market condition will not last. Other companies will copy the successful brand, and the market will eventually become fragmented again. Mature markets swing between market fragmentation and market consolidation. The fragmentation is brought about by competition, and the consolidation is brought about by innovation.

Decline Stage　Eventually the market demand for the present products will begin to decline. Either the total need level declines or a new technology starts replacing the old. Thus an entrepreneur might introduce an effective mouth-spray substitute that is superior to toothpaste. In this case, the old technology will eventually disappear and a new demand-technology life cycle will emerge.

Dynamics
of Attribute
Competition
Thus markets emerge and evolve through several stages. Consider the evolution of the paper towel market. Originally, homemakers used only cotton and linen dish cloths and towels in their kitchens. A paper company, looking for new markets, developed paper towels to compete with cloth towels. This development crystallized a new market. Other paper manufacturers entered and expanded the market. The number of brands proliferated and created market fragmentation. Industry overcapacity led manufacturers to search for new features. One manufacturer, hearing consumers complain that paper towels were not absorbent, introduced "absorbent" paper towels and increased its market share. This market consolidation did not last long because competitors came out with their versions of absorbent paper towels. The market became fragmented again. Then another manufacturer heard consumers express a wish for a "superstrength" paper towel and proceeded to introduce one. It was soon copied by other manufacturers. Another manufacturer introduced a "lint-free" paper towel, which was subsequently copied. Thus paper towels evolved from a simple product to one with various absorbencies, strengths, and applications. Market evolution was driven by the forces of innovation and competition.

Competition in a market produces a continuous round of discovered new-product attributes. If a new attribute succeeds, then several competitors soon offer it, and it loses its determinance. To the extent that most banks are now "friendly," friendliness no longer influences consumer choice of a bank. To the extent that most airlines serve in-flight meals, meals are no longer a basis for air-carrier choice. *Customer expectations are progressive*. This underlines the strategic importance of a company's maintaining the lead in innovating other attributes. Each new attribute, if successful, creates a competitive advantage for the firm, leading to temporarily higher-than-average market share and profits. The market leader must learn to *routinize* the innovation process.

A crucial question is, Can a firm look ahead and anticipate the succession of attributes that are likely to be high in demand and technologically feasible over time? How can the firm discover new attributes? There are four approaches.

The first approach employs an *empirical process* to identify new attributes. The company asks consumers what benefits they would like added to the product and their desire level for each. The firm also examines the cost of developing each attribute and likely competitive responses. It decides to develop those attributes promising the highest incremental profit.

The second approach sees attribute search as an *intuitive process*. Entrepreneurs get hunches and go into product development without much marketing research. Natural selection determines the winners and the losers. If a manufacturer has intuited an attribute that the market wants, that manufacturer is considered smart, although from another perspective, it was only luck. This theory offers no guidance as to how to visualize new attributes.

A third approach says that new attributes emerge through a *dialectical process*. Any valued attribute gets pushed to an extreme form through the competitive process. Thus blue jeans, starting out as an inexpensive clothing article, over time became fashionable and more expensive. This unidirectional movement, however, contains the seeds of its own destruction. Eventually some manufacturer will discover a new cheap material for pants, and consumers will flock to buy it. The message of dialectical theory is that innovators should not march with the crowd but rather head in the opposite direction toward market segments that are suffering from increasing neglect.

A fourth approach holds that new attributes emerge through a *needs-hierarchy process* (see Maslow's theory, pp. 186–87). On this theory, we would predict that the first automobiles would provide basic transportation and be designed for safety. At a later time, automobiles would start appealing to social acceptance and status needs. Still later, automobiles would be designed to help people "fulfill" themselves. The innovator's task is to assess when the market is ready to satisfy a higher-order need.

The actual unfolding of new attributes in a market is more complex than any simple theories would suggest. We should not underestimate the role of technological and societal processes in influencing the emergence of new attributes. For example, the strong consumer interest in compact-size television sets remained unmet until miniaturization technology was sufficiently developed. Technological forecasting attempts to predict the timing of future technological developments that will permit new-attribute offers to consumers. The societal factor also plays a major role in shaping attribute evolution. Developments such as inflation, shortages, environmentalism, consumerism, and new lifestyles create consumer disequilibrium and lead consumers to reevaluate product attributes. For example, inflation increases the desire for a smaller car, and car safety increases the desire for a heavier car. The innovator must use marketing research to guage the demand potency of different attributes in order to determine the company's best move vis-à-vis competition.

SUMMARY

Products and markets have life cycles that call for changing marketing strategies over time. Every new need follows a demand life cycle that passes through the stages of emergence, accelerating growth, decelerating growth, maturity, and decline. Each new technology that emerges to satisfy that need exhibits a demand-technology life cycle. Particular product forms of a given technology also show a life cycle, as do brands within that product form.

The sales history of many products follows an S-shaped curve consisting of four stages. The *introduction* stage is marked by slow growth and minimal profits as the product is pushed into distribution. During this stage, the company has to decide between the four strategies of rapid skimming, slow skimming, rapid penetration, or slow penetration. If successful, the product enters a *growth* stage marked by rapid sales growth and increasing profits. During this stage, the company attempts to improve the product, enter new market segments and distribution channels, and reduce its prices slightly. There follows a *maturity* stage in which sales growth slows down and profits stabilize. The company seeks innovative strategies to renew sales growth, including market, product, and marketing-mix modification. Finally, the product enters a *decline* stage in which little can be done to halt the deterioration of sales and profits. The company's task during this period is to identify the truly weak products; develop for each one a strategy of continuation, focusing, or milking; and finally phase out weak products in a way that minimizes the hardship to company profits, employees, and customers.

Not all products pass through an S-shaped PLC. Some products show a growth-slump-maturity pattern, others a cycle-recycle shape, and still others a scalloped shape. Some investigators have discovered over a dozen PLC shapes, including those describing styles, fashions, and fads. PLC theory has been criticized on the grounds that companies cannot predict the shapes in advance, or know what stage they are in within a given shape, or predict the duration of the stages. Also, PLCs are the result of chosen marketing strategies rather than of an inevitable sales history that is independent of the chosen marketing strategies.

Product life-cycle theory must be broadened by a theory of market evolution. The theory of market evolution holds that new markets *emerge* when a product is created to satisfy an unmet need. The innovator usually designs a product for the mass market. Competitors enter the market with similar products leading to *market growth*. Later growth slows down and the market enters *maturity*. The market undergoes increasing *fragmentation* until some firm introduces a powerful new attribute that *consolidates* the market into fewer and larger segments. This stage does not last, because competitors copy the new attributes. There is a cycling back and forth between market consolidation based on innovation and fragmentation based on competition. The market for the present technology will ultimately *decline* upon the discovery of superior technologies.

Companies must try to anticipate new attributes that the market wants. Profits go to those who introduce new and valued benefits early. The search for new attributes can be based on empirical work, intuition, dialectical reasoning, or needs-hierarchy reasoning.

Market-evolution theory shifts marketers' attention from specific brand PLCs to the evolution of the overall market. Each brand tells only a limited story about the opportunities and evolution of the market. Successful marketing comes through creatively visualizing the market's evolutionary potential.

QUESTIONS

1. Discuss the demand/technology life cycle for home entertainment.

2. Conduct a "Gap-Analysis" (see Exhibit 12-3) for Ocean Spray Cranberry Juice.

3. Select a personal-care product that you believe is in the maturity stage of its PLC. Discuss the competitive strategies used by the brands in this product category. Have all the strategies been equally effective? Why or why not?

4. Packaging strategies were not included in Table 12-1 as one of the marketing areas where changes would be made over the course of a PLC. Would you expect changes in packaging to coincide with PLC stages? If so, what would they be? If not, why not?

5. Levi Strauss's income declines during the 1980s caused the company to wonder if the denim jean market was in the decline stage of its PLC. If this is true, what strategies could Levi Strauss pursue to increase profits?

6. What should be the focus for marketing research studies at each stage of the PLC?

7. Develop a long-range marketing plan for a new line of electric can openers, indicating for each stage in the product life cycle the major objective and the likely policy on price, quality, advertising, personal selling, and channels.

8. As a product passes through the successive stages of its product life cycle, both its rate of sales growth and its rate of return on investment change. Using these two variables as axes, develop a diagram showing the typical trajectory of these variables over the product life cycle.

9. Discuss the changes in the promotion level and mix in the different stages of the product life cycle.

10. Select an actual fad and a fashion product and plot their respective product life-cycle patterns on one graph. How do they differ from each other?

11. What is the difference between a product life-cycle analysis of the product class "paper towels" and the market-evolution analysis of them found in the chapter?

FOOTNOTES

1 This discussion of demand/technology cycles is drawn from H. Igor Ansoff, *Implanting Strategic Management* (Englewood Cliffs, N.J.: Prentice-Hall, 1984), pp. 37–44.

2 Ibid., p. 38.

3 Some authors distinguish additional stages. Wasson suggested a stage of competitive turbulence between growth and maturity. See Chester R. Wasson, *Dynamic Competitive Strategy and Product Life Cycles* (Austin, Tex.: Austin Press, 1978). Maturity describes a stage of sales growth slowdown, and saturation describes a stage of flat sales after sales have peaked.

4 Rolando Polli and Victor Cook, "Validity of the Product Life Cycle," *Journal of Business*, October 1969, pp. 385–400.

5 Robert D. Buzzell, "Competitive Behavior and Product Life Cycles," in *New Ideas for Successful Marketing*, ed. John S. Wright and Jac L. Goldstucker (Chicago: American Marketing Association, 1966), pp. 46–68.

6 Polli and Cook, "Validity of the Product Life Cycle."

7 For some prescriptions, see Richard G. Hamermesh and Steven B. Silk, "How to compete in Stagnant Industries," *Harvard Business Review*, September–October 1979, pp. 161–68.

8 The *Nielsen Researcher*, No. 1 (Chicago: A. C. Nielsen Co., 1968).

9 See William E. Cox, Jr., "Product Life Cycles as Marketing Models," *Journal of Business,* October 1967, pp. 375–84; John E. Swan and David R. Rink, "Fitting Market Strategy to Varying Product Life Cycles," *Business Horizons*, January–February 1982, pp. 72–76; and Gerald J. Tellis and C.

Merle Crawford, "An Evolutionary Approach to Product Growth Theory," *Journal of Marketing*, Fall 1981, pp. 125–34.

10 Jordan P. Yale, "The Strategy of Nylon's Growth," *Modern Textiles Magazine*, February 1964, pp. 32ff. Also see Theodore Levitt, "Exploit the Product Life Cycle," *Harvard Business Review*, November–December 1965, pp. 81–94.

11 Chester R. Wasson, "How Predictable Are Fashion and Other Product Life Cycles?" *Journal of Marketing*, July 1968, pp. 36–43.

12 William H. Reynolds, "Cars and Clothing: Understanding Fashion Trends," *Journal of Marketing*, July 1968, pp. 44–49.

13 Dwight E. Robinson, "Style Changes: Cyclical, Inexorable and Foreseeable," *Harvard Business Review*, November–December 1975, pp. 121–31.

14 George B. Sproles, "Analyzing Fashion Life Cycles—Principles and Perspective," *Journal of Marketing*, Fall 1981, pp. 116–24.

15 Buzzell, "Competitive Behavior," p. 51.

16 Ibid.

17 Ibid., p. 52.

18 John B. Frey, "Pricing Over the Competitive Cycle" (Speech presented at the 1982 Marketing Conference, The Conference Board, New York).

19 John B. Stewart, "Functional Features in Product Strategy," *Harvard Business Review*, March–April 1959, pp. 65–78.

20 Gosta Mickwitz, *Marketing and Competition* (Finland: Centraltryckeriet, Kelsing & Fors, 1959).

21 R. S. Alexander, "The Death and Burial of 'Sick Products,'" *Journal of Marketing*, April 1964, p. 1.

22 See Philip Kotler, "Phasing Out Weak Products," *Harvard Business Review*, March–April 1965, pp. 107–18; Paul W. Hamelman and Edward M. Mazze, "Improving Product Abandonment Decisions," *Journal of Marketing*, April 1972, pp. 20–26; and Richard T. Hise, A. Parasuraman, and R. Viswanathan, "Product Elimination: The Neglected Management Responsibility," *Journal of Business Strategy*.

23 See Kathryn Rudie Harrigan, "The Effect of Exit Barriers upon Strategic Flexibility," *Strategic Management Journal*, I (1980), 165–76.

24 Kathryn Rudie Harrigan, "Strategies for Declining Industries," *Journal of Business Strategy*, Fall 1980, p. 27.

25 See Philip Kotler, "Harvesting Strategies for Weak Products," *Business Horizons*, August 1978, pp. 15–22; and Laurence P. Feldman and Albert L. Page, "Harvesting: The Misunderstood Market Exit Strategy," *Journal of Business Strategy*, Spring 1985, pp. 79–85.

26 Nariman K. Dhalla and Sonia Yuspeh, "Forget the Product Life Cycle Concept!" *Harvard Business Review*, January–February 1976, pp. 102–12, here p. 105.

27 This problem is trivial if consumers' preferences are concentrated at one point. If there are distinct clusters of preference, the entrepreneur can design a product for the largest cluster or for the cluster that the company can serve best.

28 For simplicity, the product space is drawn with two attributes. Actually, more attributes come into being as the market evolves. The product space grows from a two-dimensional to an N-dimensional space, which unfortunately cannot be drawn.

13 Marketing Strategies for the Global Marketplace

A traveller without knowledge is a bird without wings.

Sa'di, Gulistan (1258)

Ford's "world truck" has a European-made cab, a North American built chassis, is assembled in Brazil and imported into the U.S. for sale.

In former times, American companies paid little attention to international trade. If they could pick up some extra sales through export, this might be OK. But the big market was at home and was teeming with opportunities. The home market was much safer. Managers did not need to learn another language, deal with strange and volatile currencies, face political and legal uncertainties and harassments, or redesign their products to suit quite different customer needs and expectations.

Today the situation is radically different. The home market is no longer rich in opportunity. Various foreign firms are aggressively entering other countries with their products. And what is worse, these firms have also entered the U.S. market, offering in many cases higher-quality products and more value. The American firm that stays at home in order to play safe might not only lose its last chance to enter other markets but also face losing its home market.

The daily headlines tell about the almost complete victory of the Japanese in the consumer electronics market and motorcycle markets; the gains of Japanese, German, Swedish, and even Korean car imports in the U.S. market; about the French firm Bic's successful attacks on Gillette; on Nestlé's gains in the coffee and candy markets; and on the loss of textile and shoe markets to Third World imports. Such names as Sony, Honda, Nestlé, Perrier, Norelco, Mercedes-Benz, and Volkswagen have become household words. Other products that appear to be produced by American firms are really produced by foreign multinationals: Bantam Books, Baskin-Robbins Ice Cream, Capitol Records, Kiwi Shoe Polish, Lipton Tea, and Saks Fifth Avenue. America is also attracting huge foreign investments in tourist and real estate ventures, notably Japanese land purchases in Hawaii, Kuwait's resort development off the South Carolina coast, and Arab purchases of Manhattan office buildings—and one offer by a Saudi Arabian sheik to buy the Alamo for his son. Few American industries are safe any longer from the flails of foreign competition.

Although some companies would like to stem the tide of foreign imports through protectionism, this is only a temporary palliative and in the long run would raise the cost of living and protect inefficient firms. The only answer is that more American firms must learn to move abroad and increase their competitiveness. Several American firms have demonstrated their effectiveness at global marketing: Coca-Cola is a household word in almost every country; McDonald's has some of its biggest sales abroad; IBM, Ford, Gillette, Kodak, Kellogg, Boeing, Xerox, Goodyear, and dozens of other American firms have made the world their market. But there are not enough like them. (See Exhibit 13-1.)

The fact is that the United States has been losing its overall position in world trade. It is running a $150 billion annual trade deficit. It is therefore not surprising that the U.S. government is aggressively encouraging U.S. firms to venture abroad. As it turns out, a mere five U.S. manufacturers account for 17 percent of all manufacturing exports; and one thousand U.S. manufacturers (out of three hundred thousand) account for 60 percent of all manufacturing exports. The U.S. Department of Commerce provides information, consultation, preferential financing, and so on, to all firms interested in overseas marketing. In fact, Commerce Department officials target certain firms that they think should consider foreign trade and present the case for it.

And export promotion drives are not confined to the United States. Every country in the world is trying to get its business firms to internationalize, or at least to start exporting. West Germany, the United Kingdom, and the Benelux and Scandinavian countries are now subsidizing marketing programs in their firms.[1] Denmark pays more than half the salary of marketing consultants to help small and medium-size companies get into exports. Many countries go further and subsidize their companies by granting preferential land and energy costs, and they even supply outright cash so that they can charge lower prices than their competitors.

EXHIBIT 13-1

U.S. and Other Multinationals

The United States, in spite of its exports adding up to only 11 percent of its GNP, is still the world's largest exporting nation in absolute dollars. Among American companies deriving more than 55 percent of their revenue from abroad in 1985 are Pan Am World Airways (74 percent), Exxon (71 percent), Mobil (59 percent), Gillette (57 percent), CPG International (56 percent), American Brands (56 percent), and Dow Chemical (55 percent). Several American oil companies, TWA, ITT, Dow, American Cyanamid, Control Data, Firestone, and Deere earn over half of their profits abroad. In several cases, these companies earn a higher rate of return on their foreign sales than on their domestic sales.

At the same time, U.S. companies are much less dependent on foreign trade than are the companies in many other countries. Small countries such as Hong Kong, Singapore, and the Benelux and Scandinavian countries must of necessity sell more than half of their output abroad in order to pay for needed imports and support high employment. Some of these countries have spawned formidable multinationals such as Royal Dutch/Shell and Philips (the Netherlands), Volvo and Saab (Sweden), and Nestlé (Switzerland) to support their exports. Larger-population countries such as the United Kingdom, West Germany, and Japan, of course, boast major multinationals such as Mercedes, Siemens, British Petroleum, Unilever, Nippon Steel, and Mitsubishi.

Ironically, while the need of companies to go abroad is higher, so are the risks. There are several major problems weighing on management's minds when they think of going abroad:

1. *Huge foreign indebtedness.* Many countries of the world that would otherwise be attractive markets have accumulated such high foreign indebtedness that they cannot even pay the interest on their foreign debt. Among these countries are Mexico, Brazil, Poland, and Romania.

2. *Unstable governments.* High indebtedness, high inflation, and high unemployment in several countries have resulted in highly unstable governments that expose foreign firms to the risks of expropriation, nationalization, limits to profit repatriation, and so on.

3. *Exchange instability.* High indebtedness and political instability force a country's currency to depreciate, or at least add a lot of volatility to the currency's value. The result is that foreign investors hesitate to hold much of the foreign currency, and this limits trade.

4. *Foreign government entry requirements.* Governments are placing more regulations on foreign firms, such as requiring joint ownership with the majority share going to the domestic partner; a high level of nationals hired for management; technological transfer of trade secrets; and limits on profit repatriation.

5. *Tariffs and other trade barriers.* Governments often impose unreasonably high tariffs against imports in order to "subsidize" or protect their own industries. They also resort to invisible trade barriers such as withholding or slowing down import approval and requiring adjustments in imported products to meet their standards.

6. *Corruption.* Officials in several countries require bribes in order to cooperate. They often award business to the highest briber rather than the best bidder. U.S. managers are prohibited by the Foreign Corrupt Practices Act of 1977 from paying bribes, whereas competitors from Europe and elsewhere are under no such limitation.

7. *Technological pirating.* A company locating its plant abroad worries about foreign managers learning how to make its product and breaking away to compete openly or clandestinely. This has happened in such diverse areas as machinery, electronics, chemicals, and pharmaceuticals.

8. *High cost of product and communication adaptation.* A company going abroad must study each foreign market carefully, become sensitive to its economics, politics, and culture, and make some adaptations in its products and communications to suit foreign tastes. Otherwise it might make some serious blunders. (See Exhibit 13-2.) It will bear higher costs and must be more patient in waiting for its profits to materialize.

One might conclude that companies are doomed whether they stay at home or go abroad. We would argue that companies selling "global products" have no choice but to internationalize their operations. And they must do so before the window closes on them, since firms from other countries are globalizing and achieving scale economies. This does not mean that the small or medium-size firms must operate in over one hundred countries to succeed. These firms can practice global nichemanship, as many Scandinavian and Benelux companies do. Japan and West Germany have been particularly successful in entering and operating in foreign markets. A study of successful multinationals would help firms in various countries proceed intelligently through the tangle of international business.

THE INTERNATIONAL PRODUCT LIFE CYCLE

The reason why domestic companies must pay attention to foreign markets lies in the phenomenon of the *international product life cycle*. First, foreign markets offer domestic manufacturers a way to extend their product's life cycle after domestic demand is saturated. Second, foreign companies will eventually learn to make the same products at possibly

EXHIBIT 13-2

Some Examples of Global Marketing Blunders

- Hallmark cards bombed in France. The French dislike syrupy sentiment and prefer writing their own cards.
- The Ronnie McDonald promotion of McDonald's failed in Japan. White face means death.
- Philips only began to earn a profit in Japan after it had reduced the size of its coffeemakers to fit into the smaller Japanese kitchens and its shavers to fit the smaller Japanese hands.
- Coca-Cola had to withdraw the two-liter bottle in Spain after discovering that few Spaniards owned refrigerators with large enough compartments.
- General Foods' Tang initially failed in France because it was positioned as a substitute for orange juice at breakfast. The French drink little orange juice and almost none at breakfast.
- Kellogg's Pop-Tarts failed in Britain because the percentage of British homes with toasters was significantly lower than in the United States and the product was too sweet for British tastes.
- Crest initially failed in Mexico when it used the U.S. campaign. Mexicans did not believe in or care about the decay prevention benefit, nor did scientifically oriented advertising appeal to them.
- General Foods squandered millions trying to introduce Japanese consumers to packaged cake mixes. The company failed to note that only 3 percent of Japanese homes were equipped with ovens.

less cost and bring them into the domestic market to compete with domestic firms. According to Wells, "Many products go through a trade cycle, during which the United States is initially an exporter, then loses its export markets and may finally become an importer of the product."[2] The four stages are

- *U.S. export strength.* An innovation is launched in the United States and succeeds because of the huge market and the highly developed infrastructure. Eventually U.S. producers start exporting the product to other countries.
- *Foreign production starts.* As foreign manufacturers become familiar with the product, some of them start producing it for their market. They do this under licensing or joint venture arrangement or simply by copying the product. The government may abet their efforts by imposing tariffs or quotas on imports of the product.
- *Foreign production becomes competitive in export markets.* By now, foreign manufacturers have gained production experience, and with their lower costs, they start exporting the product to other countries.
- *Import competition begins.* The foreign manufacturers' growing volume and lower costs lead them to start exporting the product to the United States in direct competition with U.S. producers.

Thus the product has moved from a *new product* (stage 1) to a *mature product* (stage 2) to a *standardized product* (stages 3 and 4). The implication is that a U.S. manufacturer's sales in the home market will eventually decline as foreign markets start producing the product and ultimately export it to the United States. The U.S. manufacturers' best defense is to become global marketers. U.S. firms should open production and distribution facilities in other countries with large markets and/or lower costs. Global marketers are able to stretch the product life cycle of any product form by taking it to the countries that are getting ready to use it.[3]

We will now examine the six basic decisions that a company faces in considering international marketing. (See Figure 13-1.)

APPRAISING THE INTERNATIONAL MARKETING ENVIRONMENT

A company has to learn many things before deciding whether to sell abroad. The company has to acquire a thorough understanding of the international marketing environment. The international marketing environment has undergone significant changes in the past two decades, creating both new opportunities and new problems. The following are the most significant changes:

■ The internationalization of the world economy reflected in the rapid growth of world trade and investment

■ The gradual erosion of U.S. international dominance and competitiveness, marked by its huge annual foreign trade deficit

■ The rising economic power of Japan and several Far Eastern countries in world markets

■ The growth of global brands in autos, food, clothing, electronics, and many other categories

■ Rising trade barriers put up to protect domestic markets against foreign competition

■ The gradual opening up of major new markets, namely, China, Eastern Europe, and the Arab countries

■ The severe debt problems of several countries, such as Mexico and Poland, along with the increasing fragility of the international financial system

■ The increasing use of barter and countertrade to support international transactions

■ Movement in many countries toward "privatizing" publicly owned companies in order to make them more efficient

■ Increased forming of strategic alliances between major international companies from different countries—e.g., General Motors and Toyota, AT&T and Olivetti, GTE and Fujitsu, and Corning and Ciba-Geigy

■ Substantial speedup of international transportation, communication, and financial transactions

The International Trade System   A company seeking to do business abroad needs to understand the international trade system. In attempting to sell to another country, a firm will face various trade restrictions. The most common is the *tariff*, which is a tax levied by the foreign government against designated imported products. The tariff may be designed to raise revenue (revenue tariff) or to protect domestic firms (protective tariff). The exporter might also face a *quota*, which sets limits on the amount of goods that the importing country will accept in certain product categories. The purpose of the quota is to conserve on foreign exchange and protect local industry and employment. An *embargo* is the ultimate form of quota in that

FIGURE 13-1
Major Decisions in International Marketing

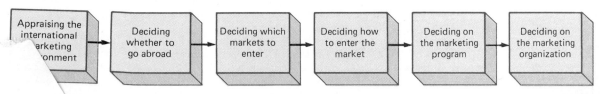

imports in prescribed categories are totally banned. Trade is also discouraged by *exchange control*, which regulates the amount of available foreign exchange and its exchange rate against other currencies. The company might also confront *nontariff barriers*, such as discrimination against American company bids, and product standards that discriminate against American product features. For example, the Dutch government bars tractors that run faster than ten miles an hour, which means that most American-made tractors are barred.

At the same time, certain forces seek to liberalize and foster trade between nations, or at least between some nations. The General Agreement on Tariffs and Trade (GATT) is an international agreement that has reduced the level of tariffs throughout the world on six different occasions. Today, however, GATT seems unable to preserve low tariffs against a growing wave of protectionism.

Several countries have formed *economic communities*, the most important of which is the European Economic Community (EEC, also known as the Common Market). The EEC's members are the major Western European nations, and they are striving to reduce tariffs within the community, reduce prices, and expand employment and investment. EEC has taken the form of a *customs union*, which is a *free-trade area* (no tariffs facing the members) that imposes a uniform tariff for trade with nonmember nations. The next move would be an *economic union* in which all members would operate under the same trade policies. While EEC has facilitated trade between the countries within the Common Market, it has retarded the trade with countries outside the Common Market. Since EEC's formation, other economic communities have been formed, notably the Latin American Integration Association (LAIA), the Central American Common Market (CACM), and the Council for Mutual Economic Assistance (CMEA) (Eastern European countries).

Each national market has unique features that must be grasped. A nation's readiness for different products and services and its attractiveness as a market to foreign firms depend on its economic, political-legal, cultural, and business environment.

Economic Environment

In considering foreign markets, the international marketer must study each country's economy. Three characteristics reflect the country's attractiveness as an export market.

The first is the size of the country's *population*. All other things being equal, large countries are more attractive to exporters than small countries. Thus Turkey, with its 50 million people, is a more attractive market for pharmaceutical products than Hungary, with its 10 million people.

The second is the country's *industrial structure*. The country's industrial structure shapes its product and service requirements, income levels, employment levels, and so on. Four types of industrial structure can be distinguished:

1. *Subsistence economies.* In a subsistence economy, the vast majority of people engage in simple agriculture. They consume most of their output and barter the rest for simple goods and services. They offer few opportunities for exporters.

2. *Raw-material-exporting economies.* These economies are rich in one or more natural resources but poor in other respects. Much of their revenue comes from exporting these resources. Examples are Chile (tin and copper), Zaire (rubber), and Saudi Arabia (oil). These countries are good markets for extractive equipment, tools and supplies, materials-handling equipment, and trucks. Depending on the number of foreign residents and wealthy native rulers and landholders, they are also a market for Western-style commodities and luxury goods.

3. *Industrializing economies.* In an industrializing economy, manufacturing is beginning to account for between 10 and 20 percent of the country's gross national product. Examples

include India, Egypt, and the Philippines. As manufacturing increases, the country relies more on imports of textile raw materials, steel, and heavy machinery and less on imports of finished textiles, paper products, and automobiles. The industrialization creates a new rich class and a small but growing middle class, both demanding new types of goods, some of which can be satisfied only by imports.

4. *Industrial economies.* Industrial economies are major exporters of manufactured goods and investment funds. They trade manufactured goods among themselves and also export them to other types of economies in exchange for raw materials and semifinished goods. The large and varied manufacturing activities of these industrial nations and their sizable middle class make them rich markets for all sorts of goods.

These four structural types are not necessarily chronological. Many developing countries are characterized by a *dual economy* where a subsistence sector coexists with a type 2 or type 3 modern sector.

The third economic characteristic is the country's *income distribution*. Income distribution is related to a country's industrial structure but is also affected by the political system. The international marketer distinguishes countries with five different income-distribution patterns: (1) very low family incomes, (2) mostly low family incomes, (3) very low, very high family incomes, (4) low, medium, high family incomes, and (5) mostly medium family incomes. Consider the market for Lamborghinis, an automobile costing more than $50,000. The market would be very small in countries with type 1 or type 2 income patterns. The largest single market for Lamborghinis turns out to be Portugal (income pattern 3), the poorest country in Europe, but one with enough wealthy status-conscious families to afford them.

Income distribution is not an accurate indicator of development in countries where an important subsistence sector has a noncash income that is not easily quantifiable in standard terms. Other measurements used increasingly are the energy and food consumption indices and the percentage of labor force in industrial employment.

Political-Legal Environment

Nations differ greatly in their political-legal environment. A company should consider four factors in deciding whether to do business in a particular country.

Attitudes Toward International Buying

Some nations are very receptive, indeed encouraging, to foreign firms, and others are very hostile. As an example of the former, Mexico for a number of years has been attracting foreign investment by offering investment incentives and site-location services. On the other hand, India in the past required the exporter to cope with import quotas, blocked currencies, local management requirements, and so on. IBM and Coca-Cola decided to leave India because of all the "hassles."

Political Stability

The country's future stability is another issue. Governments change hands, sometimes quite violently. Even without a change, a regime may decide to respond to new popular feelings. The foreign company's property might be expropriated; or its currency holdings might be blocked; or import quotas or new duties might be imposed. Where political instability is high, international marketers may still find it profitable to do business in that country, but the situation will affect their mode of entry. They will prefer export marketing to direct foreign investment. They will keep their foreign stocks low. They will convert their currency rapidly. As a result, the people in the host country pay higher prices, have fewer jobs, and get less-satisfactory products.

Monetary Regulations   Sellers want to realize profits in a currency of value to them. In the best situation, the importer can pay either in the seller's currency or in hard world currencies. Short of this, sellers might accept a blocked currency if they can buy other goods in that country that they need or that they can sell elsewhere for a needed currency. In the worst case, they have to take their money out of the host country in the form of relatively unmarketable products that they can sell elsewhere only at a loss. (For a description of various countertrade practices, see Exhibit 13-3.) Besides currency restrictions, a fluctuating exchange rate also creates high risks for the exporter.

Government Bureaucracy   A fourth factor is the extent to which the host government runs an efficient system for assisting foreign companies: quick licensing procedures, efficient customs handling, adequate market information, and other factors conducive to doing busi-

---

EXHIBIT 13-3

How the Nations of the World Have Been Moving Back to Barter

Most international trade involves a cash transaction. The buyer agrees to pay the seller in cash within a certain stated time period. Yet many nations today lack sufficient hard currency to pay for their purchases from other nations. They want to offer other items in payment, and this has led to a growing practice called countertrade. Approximately 40 percent of trade with Communist-block nations is handled through countertrade. Less-developed countries are also pressing for more countertrade agreements when they buy. Although most companies dislike countertrade deals, they may have no choice if they want the business.

Countertrade takes several forms:

- *Barter.* Barter involves the direct exchange of goods, with no money and no third party involved. For example, the West Germans agreed to build a steel plant in Indonesia in exchange for Indonesian oil.
- *Compensation deal.* Here the seller receives some percentage of the payment in cash and the rest in products. A British aircraft manufacturer sold planes to Brazil for 70 percent cash and the rest in coffee.
- *Buyback arrangement.* The seller sells a plant, equipment, or technology to another country and agrees to accept as partial payment products manufactured with the equipment supplied. For example, a U.S. chemical company built a plant for an Indian company and accepted partial payment in cash and the remainder in chemicals to be manufactured at the plant.
- *Counterpurchase.* The seller receives full payment in cash but agrees to spend a substantial amount of money in that country within a stated time period. For example, Pepsi-Cola sells its cola syrup to the USSR for rubles and agrees to buy USSR vodka at a certain rate for sale in the United States.

More-complex countertrade deals involve more than two parties. For example, Daimler-Benz agreed to sell thirty trucks to Romania and accept in exchange 150 Romanian-made jeeps, which it sold in Ecuador for bananas, which in turn it sold to a West German supermarket chain for deutschmarks. Through this circuitous transaction, Daimler-Benz finally achieved payment in German currency. Various barter houses and countertrade specialists have emerged to assist the parties to these transactions. Everyone agrees that international trade would be more efficient if carried out in cash, but too many nations lack sufficient hard currency. Sellers have no choice but to learn the intricacies of countertrade, which is a growing phenomenon in world trade. (For further reading, see John W. Dizard, "The Explosion of International Barter," *Fortune*, February 7, 1983; and Leo G. B. Welt, *Trade without Money: Barter and Countertrade* [New York: Harcourt Brace Jovanovich, 1984].)

Megamarketing: Breaking into Blocked Markets

It is one thing to want to do business in a particular country and another to be allowed in on reasonable terms. The problem of entering *blocked markets* calls for a *megamarketing* approach, defined as "the strategic coordination of economic, psychological, political, and public relations skills to gain the cooperation of a number of parties in order to enter and/or operate in a given market."* Pepsi-Cola faced this problem in seeking to enter the Indian market:

> After Coca-Cola was asked to leave India, Pepsi began to lay plans to enter this huge market. Pepsi worked with an Indian business group to seek government approval for its entry over the objections of both domestic soft-drink companies and anti-multinational legislators. Pepsi saw the solution as requiring making an offer that the Indian government would find it hard to refuse. Pepsi offered to help India export its agro-based products in a volume that would more than cover the cost of importing soft-drink concentrate. Pepsi also promised to focus considerable selling effort on rural areas to help in their economic development. Pepsi further offered to transfer food processing, packaging, and water treatment technology to India. Clearly, Pepsi's strategy was to bundle a set of benefits that would win the support of various interest groups in India.

Thus Pepsi's marketing problem was not the normal 4 Ps of operating in a market, but rather the problem of getting in. Pepsi faced a 6 P marketing problem, with "politics" and "public opinion" constituting the two additional Ps. Winning over the government and the public to gain admission is a much tougher challenge.

Once in, a multinational must be on its best behavior, since it is under great scrutiny and critics abound. This task calls for well-thought-out *civic positioning* of the multinational. Olivetti, for example, enters new markets by building housing for workers, generously supporting local arts and charities, and hiring and training indigenous managers. In this way, it hopes to realize long-run profits by accepting high short-run costs.

* Philip Kotler, "Megamarketing," *Harvard Business Review*, March–April 1986, pp. 117–24.

ness. American companies have found it especially frustrating to do business with Eastern Bloc countries or the People's Republic of China. An American executive even reported frustration in Portugal after his third month of waiting in Lisbon for the Ministry of International Trade to act on a proposal. A common shock to Americans is the extent to which impediments to trade disappear if a suitable payment (bribe) is made to some official(s). (See Exhibit 13-4 above.)

Cultural Environment   Each nation has its own values, customs, and taboos. Foreign businesspeople, if they are to be effective, must drop their ethnocentrism and try to understand the culture and business practices of their hosts, who often act on different concepts of time, space, and etiquette.

The way foreign consumers think about and use certain products must be checked out by the seller before planning the marketing program. Here is a sampling of some of the surprises in the consumer market:

> The average Frenchman uses almost twice as many cosmetics and beauty aids as does his wife.
>
> The Germans and the French eat more packaged, branded spaghetti than the Italians.
>
> Italian children like to eat a bar of chocolate between two slices of bread as a snack.
>
> Women in Tanzania will not give their children eggs for fear of making them bald or impotent.

Business Environment Business norms and behavior also vary from country to country. Business executives need to be briefed on these before negotiating in another country. Here are some examples of business behavior at variance with U.S. business behavior:

> Arab businessmen are accustomed to talking business in close physical proximity with other persons—in fact, almost nose to nose. They sometimes will take your hand and hold it as a sign of friendship. If the American business executive retreats, the Arab is offended.
>
> In face-to-face communications, Japanese business executives rarely say no to an American business executive. Americans are frustrated and don't know where they stand. Americans come to the point quickly. Japanese business executives find this offensive.
>
> In France, wholesalers don't care to promote a product. They ask their retailers what they want and deliver it. If an American company builds its strategy around the French wholesaler cooperating in promotions, it is likely to fail.

Each country (and even regional groups within each country) has cultural and business traditions, preferences, and taboos that the marketer must study.[4]

DECIDING WHETHER TO GO ABROAD

Not all companies need to venture into foreign markets in order to survive. Many companies are local businesses—restaurants, cleaning establishments, food manufacturers—and they simply must market well in the local marketplace. Other companies, however, operate in *global industries*, which Porter defines as industries "in which the strategic positions of competitors in major geographic or national markets are fundamentally affected by their overall global positions."[5] Thus IBM must organize globally if it is to gain purchasing, manufacturing, logistical, and marketing advantages. Firms in a global industry must compete on a worldwide, coordinated basis if they are to succeed.

Companies become involved in international marketing in one of two ways. Someone—a domestic exporter, a foreign importer, a foreign government—solicits the company to sell abroad. Or the company starts to think on its own about going abroad. It might face overcapacity or see better marketing opportunities in other countries than at home.

Before going abroad, the company should try to define its *international marketing objectives and policies*. First, it should decide *what proportion of foreign to total sales* it will seek. Most companies start small when they venture abroad. Some plan to stay small, seeing foreign operations as a small part of their business. Other companies will have more-grandiose plans, seeing foreign business as ultimately equal to, or even more important than, their domestic business.

Second, the company must choose between marketing in a *few countries* or *many countries*. The Bulova Watch Company made the latter choice and expanded into over one hundred countries. It spread itself too thin, made profits in only two countries, and lost around $40 million. Generally speaking, it makes sense to operate in fewer countries with a deeper commitment and penetration in each. Ayal and Zif argued that a company should enter fewer countries when[6]

- Market entry and market control costs are high
- Product and communication adaptation costs are high
- Population and income size and growth are high in the initial countries chosen
- Dominant foreign firms can establish high barriers to entry

Third, the company must decide on the *types of countries* to consider. Country attractiveness is influenced by the product, geographical factors, income and population, political climate, and other factors. The seller may have a predilection for certain groups of countries or parts of the world. Kenichi Ohmae, for example, argues that only the "triad powers"—United States, Europe, and Japan—are worth pursuing as markets. (See Exhibit 13-5.)

EXHIBIT 13-5

Should Multinationals Restrict Their Trade to the Triad Markets?

Some trade strategists have argued that it is not worthwhile for multinationals to bother building markets in the Third World; the lucrative markets exist in the United States, Europe, and Japan. Kenichi Ohmae, the head of McKinsey's office in Tokyo, argues this view in his *Triad Power*. He notes that

> opportunities are great in booming states such as California, which is bigger than Brazil (in economic terms), and Texas, whose gross state product is bigger than the combined GNP of the Association of Southeast Asian Nations.

He goes on to say:

> The "triad" of Japan, Europe, and U.S. represents not only the major and fastest growing market for most products, but also an increasingly homogeneous one. Gucci bags, Sony Walkmans and McDonald's hamburgers are seen on the streets of Tokyo, Paris and New York.

Ohmae would advise multinationals to pull out of low-income countries and put more resources in the triad markets. He also thinks multinationals make a mistake rushing to Third World countries to produce components just because the wages are lower. Low wages do not necessarily spell lower costs if the labor is inefficient or product quality is poorer. With growing automation, labor costs are becoming smaller anyway.

Ohmae also sees multinationals taking too much time to introduce their new products into foreign markets. As a result, swift competitors copy their products and capture leadership in these foreign markets. His solution: A multinational should form longstanding strategic alliances (licenses, joint ventures, consortia, etc.) with companies that operate in each triad market so that the multinational could introduce its new products in all triad markets simultaneously and establish market leadership. This strategy would provide a sufficient size market to justify larger initial plant investment and lower unit costs. In addition, the multinational need not worry about being kept out by trade barriers, since its partners would be "insiders" in the foreign markets.

While Ohmae's position makes short-run sense—i.e., profits are likely to be better in the triad regions—it can spell a disastrous policy for the world economy in the long run. Although the triad markets possess most of the world's purchasing power, they do not represent most of the world's latent demand. The triad markets are rich but mature: Companies have to strain their creativity to find growth opportunities in these markets. In contrast, the unmet needs of the developing world represent an ocean of opportunity. They are huge potential markets for food, clothing, shelter, consumer electronics, appliances, and other goods that triad markets take for granted. Unless purchasing power is somehow put into the Third World, the industrial world will remain saddled with excess productive capacity and a very slow growth rate; and the developing economies will be stuck with excess consumer needs that they are unable to satisfy. Somehow various governments and multinationals must find ways to link these two worlds together dynamically and synergistically in a win-win relationship.

SOURCE See Kenichi Ohmae, *Triad Power* (New York: Free Press, 1985).

DECIDING WHICH MARKETS TO ENTER

Suppose a company has assembled a list of potential export markets. How does it choose among them? Many companies opt for selling to neighboring countries because they understand them better and they present lower distribution and control costs. Thus it is not surprising that the U.S.'s largest market is Canada, or that Swedish companies first sold their goods to their Scandinavian neighbors. At other times, *psychic proximity* rather than *geographical proximity* determines choices. Consider the following example:

> CMC's market research in the computer field revealed that England, France, West Germany, and Italy offer us significant markets. England, France, and Germany are about equal-size markets, while Italy represents about two thirds the potential of any one of those countries. . . . Taking everything into consideration, we decided to set up first in England because its market for our products is as large as any and its language and laws are similar to ours. England is different enough to get your feet wet, yet similar enough to the familiar U.S. business environment so that you do not get in over your head.[7]

Yet one can question whether the reason for selecting England—the compatibility of its language and culture—should have been given this prominence. The candidate countries should be initially rated on three major criteria, namely, *market attractiveness*, *competitive advantage*, and *risk*. Here is an example:

> The International Hough Company manufactures mining equipment and is evaluating China and four Eastern European countries as possible market opportunities. It first rates the market attractiveness of each country, looking at such indicators as GNP/capita, work force in mining, imports of machinery, and population growth. It then rates its own potential competitive advantage in each country, looking at such indicators as prior business dealings, whether it would be a low-cost producer, and whether its senior management can work comfortably in that country. Finally it rates the risk level of each country, looking at such indicators as political stability, currency stability, and repatriation rules. (See Exhibit 13-6.) By indexing, weighing, and combining the various numbers, it arrives at the picture shown in Figure 13-2. China appears to present the best opportunity insofar as it rates high on market attractiveness and competitive advantage, and low on risk. Romania, on the other hand, ranks low on market attractiveness, medium on competitive advantage, and high on risk.

This approach provides an initial ranking of the candidate countries according to their overall attractiveness. China is first, followed by Czechoslovakia and East Germany. International Hough must now prepare a financial analysis of these three countries to see what it could expect to earn on its investment. It could turn out that none of the countries promise a sufficient return, or that they all do. Five steps are involved in estimating the probable rate of return on investment:[8]

1. **Estimate of current market potential.** The first step is to estimate total industry sales in each market. This task calls for using published data and primary data collected through company surveys.
2. **Forecast of future market potential and risk.** The firm also needs to forecast future industry sales, a difficult task. It requires predicting economic and political developments and their impact on industry sales.
3. **Forecast of sales potential.** Estimating the company's sales requires forecasting its probable market share based on its competitive advantage, another difficult task.
4. **Forecast of costs and profits.** Costs will depend on the company's contemplated entry strategy. If it exports or licenses, its costs will be spelled out in the contracts. If it locates manufacturing

EXHIBIT 13-6

Assessing Country Risk

The daily news is so filled with reports of unstable governments and faltering economies that business firms are of course hesitant to put their investment at risk in another country. If seemingly secure governments like the Shah's regime in Iran and Marcos's regime in the Philippines could topple, can any country be trusted? Since 1960, over fifteen hundred companies were expropriated in 511 separate actions by seventy-six nations. Even short of expropriation, a company could lose its investment because of strikes, currency devaluation, blocked currency, and so on.

Analysts distinguish between two types of country risk. The first is *asset protection/investment recovery risk*, which arises from direct action taken by the government or the people that results in destroying, expropriating, or limiting transfer of invested resources. The second is *operational profitability/ cash flow risk*, which arises from economic downturns, currency depreciation, strikes, and so on. Some analysts think of the former risk as political risk and the latter risk as economic risk, but both types often intermingle.

No wonder then that companies are large buyers of *political risk assessment reports*. Supplied by a number of specialist firms, they include Business International's (BI) Country Assessment Service, which surveys seventy-one countries twice a year; BERI, which surveys forty-five countries three times a year; and Frost & Sullivan's World Political Risk Forecasts, which summarizes sixty countries monthly. Using somewhat different models and measurement techniques, these services come up with numerical ratings showing each country's current risk level and, in some cases, their expected risk level three years from now.

Many companies find these estimates interesting, but inadequate. They measure the *macro-risk* affecting all foreign companies but not the *micro-risk* facing any particular company or industry. For example, a country may present little macro-risk but may be planning to nationalize foreign oil companies. Consequently companies need to supplement macro-risk estimates with other methods of gaining insight into the risk they would face. General Motors and Caterpillar use advisory councils of prominent foreign experts. Gulf Oil has its own political risk assessment office staffed with area experts. Many companies send their senior officers on periodic grand tours to various countries where they have or are planning major investments to talk to government officials and their own staff about recent and expected developments.

SOURCES For further reading, see Stephan Kobrin, "Political Risk: A Review and Reconsiderations," *Journal of International Business Studies*, November 1980; R. J. Rummel and D. A. Heenan, "How Multinationals Analyze Political Risk," *Harvard Business Review*, January–February 1978; and Louis Kraar, "The Multinationals Get Smarter about Political Risks," *Fortune*, March 24, 1980.

facilities in the country, its cost estimation will require understanding local labor conditions, taxes, trade practices, and so on. The company subtracts estimated costs from estimated sales to derive company profits for each year of the planning horizon.

5. ***Estimate of rate of return on investment.*** The forecasted income stream should be related to the investment stream to derive the implicit rate of return. This should be high enough to cover (1) the company's normal target return on its investment and (2) the risk of marketing in that country.

DECIDING HOW TO ENTER THE MARKET

Once a company decides to target a particular country, it has to determine the best mode of entry. Its broad choices are *indirect exporting*, *direct exporting*, *licensing*, *joint ventures*, and *direct investment*. Each succeeding strategy involves more commitment, risk, control, and profit potential. The five market-entry strategies are shown in Figure 13-3 and examined on the following pages.

Market Attractiveness

	High	Medium	Low	
H	China			
M		Czech.		**L**
L	East Germany			
H		Poland		
M			Romania	**H**
L				

Competitive Advantage

Risk

FIGURE 13-2
Evaluating Which Markets to Enter

Indirect Export   The normal way to become involved in a foreign market is through export. *Occasional exporting* is a passive level of involvement where the company exports from time to time on its own or in response to unsolicited orders from abroad. *Active exporting* takes place when the company makes a commitment to expand exports to a particular market. In either case, the company produces all of its goods in the home country. It may or may not adapt them to the foreign market. Exporting involves the least change in the company's product lines, organization, investments, or mission.

Companies typically start with *indirect exporting*, that is, they work through independent middlemen. Four types of middlemen are available to the company:

- **Domestic-based export merchant.** This middleman buys the manufacturer's product and sells it abroad on its own account.
- **Domestic-based export agent.** This agent seeks and negotiates foreign purchases for a commission. Included in the group are trading companies.
- **Cooperative organization.** A cooperative organization carries on exporting activities on behalf of several producers and is partly under their administrative control. This form is often used by producers of primary products—fruits, nuts, and so on.
- **Export-management company.** This middleman agrees to manage a company's export activities for a fee.

Indirect export has two advantages. First, it involves less investment. The firm does not have to develop an export department, an overseas sales force, or a set of foreign contacts.

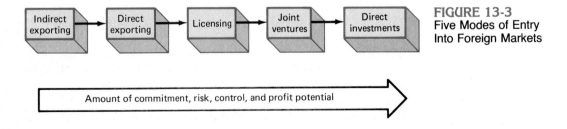

FIGURE 13-3
Five Modes of Entry
Into Foreign Markets

Second, it involves less risk. International-marketing middlemen bring know-how and services to the relationship, and the seller will normally make fewer mistakes.

Direct Export
Companies eventually undertake handling their own exports. The investment and risk are somewhat greater, but so is the potential return. The company can carry on direct exporting in several ways:

- **Domestic-based export department or division.** An export sales manager with some clerical assistants carry on the actual selling and draw on market assistance as needed. It might evolve into a self-contained export department performing all the activities involved in export and operating as a profit center.
- **Overseas sales branch or subsidiary.** An overseas sales branch allows the manufacturer to achieve greater presence and program control in the foreign market. The sales branch handles sales distribution and may handle warehousing and promotion as well. It often serves as a display center and customer-service center.
- **Traveling export sales representatives.** The company can send home-based sales representatives abroad at certain times to find business.
- **Foreign-based distributors or agents.** Foreign-based distributors would buy and own the goods; foreign-based agents would sell the goods on behalf of the company. They may be given exclusive rights to represent the manufacturer in that country or only general rights.

Licensing
Licensing represents a simple way for a manufacturer to become involved in international marketing. The licensor enters an agreement with a licensee in the foreign market, offering the right to use a manufacturing process, trademark, patent, trade secret, or other item of value for a fee or royalty. The licensor gains entry into the market at little risk; the licensee gains production expertise or a well-known product or name without having to start from scratch. Gerber introduced its baby foods in the Japanese market through a licensing arrangement. Coca-Cola carried out its international marketing by licensing bottlers around the world—or, more technically, franchising bottlers—and supplies them with the syrup needed to produce the product.

Licensing has potential disadvantages in that the firm has less control over the licensee than if it had set up its own production facilities. Furthermore, if the licensee is very successful, the firm has forgone profits, and if and when the contract ends, it might find that it has created a competitor. To avoid creating a future competitor, the licensor usually supplies some ingredients or components needed in the product. But the main hope is for the licensor to lead in innovation so that the licensee will continue to depend on this licensor.

Companies can enter foreign markets working with others on other bases than licensing them. A company can sell a *management contract* in which it offers to manage a hotel, an airport, a hospital, or other organization in return for a fee. In this case, the firm is exporting a service instead of a product. Management contracting is a low-risk method of getting into a foreign market, and it yields income from the beginning. The arrangement is especially attractive if the contracting firm is given an option to purchase some share in the managed company within a stated period. On the other hand, the arrangement is not sensible if the company can put its scarce management talent to better uses or if there are greater profits to be made by undertaking the whole venture. Management contracting prevents the company from setting up its own operations for a period of time.

Another entry method is *contract manufacturing*, where the firm engages local manufacturers to produce the product. When Sears opened department stores in Mexico and

Spain, Sears found qualified local manufacturers to produce many of the products it sells. Contract manufacturing has the drawback of less control over the manufacturing process and the loss of potential profits on manufacturing. On the other hand, it offers the company a chance to start faster, with less risk, and with the opportunity to form a partnership or buy out the local manufacturer later.

Joint Ventures

In joint ventures, foreign investors join with local investors to create a local business in which they share joint ownership and control. The foreign investor may buy an interest in a local company, a local company may buy an interest in an existing operation of a foreign company, or the two parties may form a new business venture.

A jointly owned venture may be necessary or desirable for economic or political reasons. The firm may lack the financial, physical, or managerial resources to undertake the venture alone. Or the foreign government may require joint ownership as a condition for entry.

Joint ownership has certain drawbacks. The partners may disagree over investment, marketing, or other policies. Where many American firms like to reinvest earnings for growth, local firms often like to take out these earnings. Where American firms accord a large role to marketing, local investors may rely only on selling. Furthermore, joint ownership can hamper a multinational company from carrying out specific manufacturing and marketing policies on a worldwide basis.[9]

Direct Investment

The ultimate form of foreign involvement is investment in foreign-based assembly or manufacturing facilities. As a company gains experience in export, and if the foreign market appears large enough, foreign production facilities offer distinct advantages. First, the firm may secure cost economies in the form of cheaper labor or raw materials, foreign-government investment incentives, freight savings, and so on. Second, the firm will gain a better image in the host country because it creates jobs. Third, the firm develops a deeper relationship with government, customers, local suppliers, and distributors, enabling it to adapt its products better to the local marketing environment. Fourth, the firm retains full control over the investment and therefore can develop manufacturing and marketing policies that serve its long-term international objectives.

The main disadvantage is that the firm exposes a large investment to risk, such as blocked or devalued currencies, worsening markets, or expropriation. The firm will find it expensive to reduce or close down its operations, since the host country may require substantial severance pay to the employees. The firm, however, has no choice but to accept these risks if it wants to operate in the host country.

The Internationalization Process

Many companies show a distinct preference for one mode of entry. One company might prefer exporting because this minimizes its risk. Another company might prefer licensing because this is an easy way to make money. Another company might favor direct investment because it wants full control without having to satisfy any partner. Yet insisting on one mode of entry is too limiting. Some countries will not permit imports of certain goods, nor allow direct investment, but will only accept a joint-owned venture with a foreign national. Consequently, companies must learn and master all of these entry methods. Even though a company might have preferences, it needs to optimally adapt to each situation. Most sophisticated multinationals manage several different entry modes simultaneously.

The problem facing most countries is that not enough of their companies participate in any international trade. This keeps the country from earning sufficient foreign exchange to pay for the goods it needs to import. Consequently, governments have turned to aggressive export promotion. Yet export promotion programs rarely achieve their goals. They are not based on a deep understanding of the process by which companies become internationalized.

Johanson and his associates have studied the "internationalization process" among Swedish companies.[10] They see internationalization as a changing attitude that takes place within a company as a result of a series of incremental decisions, which leads to some learning and increased confidence in further trade. They see firms moving through four stages:

1. No regular export activities
2. Export via independent representatives (agents)
3. Establishment of one or more sales subsidiaries
4. Establishment of production facilities abroad

The first problem is how to get companies to move from stage 1 to stage 2. This is helped by studies of what types of firms have moved into exporting and how they made their first export decision.[11] Most firms handle their first export opportunity by working with an independent agent, usually in a country with low *psychic distance*, that is, low psychic barriers to entry. If this works out well, the company engages further agents to enter additional countries. At some point the company establishes an export department to manage its agent relationships. Later the company finds that certain export markets are large enough to be better handled by their own sales force, and they replace the agent with a sales subsidiary in those countries. This increases their commitment and risk but also increases their earnings potential. To manage these sales subsidiaries, they replace the export department with an international department. If certain markets continue to be large and stable, or if the host country insists on local production, they take the next step of locating production facilities in those markets, representing a still larger commitment and still larger potential earnings. By this time, they are well on their way to operating as a multinational company and reconsidering how best to organize and manage their global operations.

DECIDING ON THE MARKETING PROGRAM

Companies that operate in one or more foreign markets must decide how much to adapt their marketing mix to local conditions. At one extreme are companies that use a *standardized marketing mix worldwide*. Standardization of the product, advertising, distribution channels, and other elements of the marketing mix promises the lowest costs because no major changes have been introduced. At the other extreme is the idea of a *customized marketing mix*, where the producer adjusts the marketing-mix elements to each target market, bearing more costs but hoping for a larger market share and return. Between these two extremes, many possibilities exist. The debate is described more fully in Exhibit 13-7. Here we will examine potential adaptations that firms might make of their product, promotion, price, and distribution as they enter foreign markets.

EXHIBIT 13-7

Global Standardization or Customization?

Traditional supporters of the marketing concept hold that consumers vary in their needs and that marketing programs will be more effective if tailored to each customer target group. Since this applies within a country, it should apply even more cogently in foreign markets where economic, political, and cultural conditions vary widely.

Yet many multinationals are bothered by what they see as an excessive amount of adaptation. Consider Gillette:

> Gillette sells over eight hundred products in more than two hundred countries. It has fallen into a situation where different brand names are used for the same product in different countries, and where the same brand is formulated differently in different countries. Gillette's Silkience shampoo is called Soyance in France, Sientel in Italy, and Silience in Germany; and its formula is the same in some cases but varies in other cases. Its advertising messages and copy are also varied because each Gillette country manager proposes several changes that he or she thinks will increase sales. Headquarters management feels at a loss to think that they might know more about the local situation than their country managers.

As a result, Gillette and other companies have been anxious to impose more standardization, globally or at least regionally. They see this as a way to save costs and to build up global brand power.

And along have come the British advertising firm of Saatchi & Saatchi and Professor Theodore Levitt of Harvard to help them. Saatchi & Saatchi won several new advertising accounts on the strength of their claim that they could build single advertising campaigns that would work globally. Meanwhile Professor Levitt supplied the intellectual rationale for global standardization. He wrote:

> The world is becoming a common marketplace in which people—no matter where they live—desire the same products and lifestyles. Global companies must forget the idiosyncratic differences between countries and cultures and instead concentrate on satisfying universal drives.

Levitt believes that new communication, transportation, and travel technologies have created a more homogeneous world market. People around the world want the same basic things—things that make life easier and increase their discretionary time and buying power. This convergence of needs and wants has created global markets for standardized products.

According to Levitt, traditional multinational corporations focus on differences between specific markets and falsely assume that the marketing concept means giving people what they say they want. They cater to superficial differences and produce a proliferation of highly customized products rather than questioning whether differing preferences can be changed to accept standardized products. Customization results in less efficiency and higher prices to consumers.

In contrast, the global corporation sells more or less the same product the same way to all consumers to take advantage of the lower costs resulting from standardization. It focuses on similarities across world markets and aggressively works to "sensibly force suitably standardized products and services on the entire globe." It customizes products and marketing programs to meet local preferences only when these preferences cannot be changed or avoided. These global marketers realize substantial economies through standardization of production, distribution, marketing, and management. Thus they can translate efficiencies from standardization into greater value for consumers by offering high quality and more-reliable products at lower prices:

> If the price is low enough, they will take highly standardized world products, even if these aren't exactly what mother said was suitable, what immemorial custom decreed was right, or what market research fabulists asserted was preferred.

Levitt would advise an auto company to make a world car, a shampoo company to make a world shampoo, and a construction company to make a world tractor. In fact, some companies have successfully marketed global products: Coca-Cola, McDonald's hamburgers, A. T. Cross pens and pencils, Sony Walkmans, and so on. Some products are more global and require less adaptation on the whole.

Yet even in these cases, some adaptation takes place. Coca-Cola is less sweet or less carbonated in certain countries; McDonald's uses chili sauce instead of ketchup on its hamburgers in Mexico; and Cross pens and pencils have different advertising copy and messages in some countries.

Professor Levitt assumes that global standardization will save a lot of cost, will lead to lower prices, and will cause more goods to be snapped up by price-sensitive consumers. But this begs the question. A company really needs to think in terms of incremental revenue versus incremental cost. Thus the Mattel Company faced a decision about whether to change Barbie Doll's face to a Japanese one when introducing Barbie to Japan. It had to estimate whether the revenue from the extra sales it might gain would more than cover the extra costs of product retooling and redoing the ad copy. If yes, then Mattel should make the changes. In fact it did, and Barbie's sales shot up significantly.

Rather than assuming in advance that the company's product can be introduced as is in another country, the company should review all possible adaptation elements and determine which adaptations would add more revenue than cost. The adaptation elements include the following:

Product features	Colors	Advertising themes
Name	Materials	Advertising media
Labeling	Prices	Advertising execution
Packaging	Sales promotion	

One study of company adaptation programs showed that companies made one or more adaptations in 80 percent of their foreign-directed products and that the average product underwent four out of eleven adaptations. It should also be recognized that some host countries require adaptations, independently of whether the company wants to make them. The French do not allow children to be used in ads; the Germans ban the use of the word "best" to describe a product; and so on.

Thus global standardization is not an all-or-nothing proposition, but a matter of degree. Companies are certainly justified in looking for more standardization, regionally if not globally. Goodyear, for example, is trying to bring regional uniformity into its logos, corporate advertising, and product lines in continental Europe so that it will have a more coherent presence. Resistance typically arises from country managers because regional standardization puts more power in the hands of the regional manager and less in each country manager. And country managers may have been excessive in the changes they ask for. Yet, all said, companies must remember that while standardization might save some costs, competitors are always ready to offer more of what the customers in each country want, and the company might pay dearly for replacing long-run marketing thinking with short-run financial thinking. Global marketing, yes; global standardization, not necessarily.

SOURCES Theodore Levitt, "The Globalization of Markets," *Harvard Business Review*, May–June 1983, pp. 92–102. For an example of the work involved in building a single global campaign, see "Playtex Kicks Off a One-Ad-Fits-All Campaign," *Business Week*, December 16, 1985, pp. 48–49.

Product

Keegan distinguished five adaptation strategies of product and promotion to a foreign market (Figure 13-4).[12] We will now examine the three product strategies, and later we will look at the two promotion strategies.

Straight extension means introducing the product in the foreign market without any change. Top management instructs its marketing people: "Take the product as it is and find customers for it." The first step, however, should be to determine whether the foreign consumers use that product. Deodorant usage among men ranges from 80 percent in the United States to 55 percent in Sweden to 28 percent in Italy to 8 percent in the Philippines. Many Spaniards do not use such common products as butter and cheese.

Straight extension has been successful with cameras, consumer electronics, many machine tools, and so on, but a disaster in other cases. General Foods introduced its standard powdered Jell-O in the British market only to find that British consumers prefer the solid wafer or cake form. Campbell Soup lost an estimated $30 million in introducing its condensed soups in England by failing to explain that consumers should add water; the consumers saw the small-size cans and thought they were expensive. Straight extension is

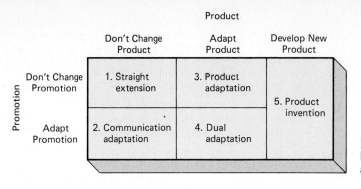

Product

| | Don't Change Product | Adapt Product | Develop New Product |

Promotion

| Don't Change Promotion | 1. Straight extension | 3. Product adaptation | 5. Product invention |
| Adapt Promotion | 2. Communication adaptation | 4. Dual adaptation | |

FIGURE 13-4
Five International Product and Promotion Strategies

tempting because it involves no additional R&D expense, manufacturing retooling, or promotional modification. But it can be costly in the long run.

One way to increase its utility is to use market research to discover possible new applications for the product in foreign markets. Variations in product use are common in developing countries. In Nigeria, for instance, Swiss-made embroidered fabrics are purchased for both male and female clothing, whereas the European market is restricted to the female segment.

Product adaptation involves altering the product to meet local conditions or preferences. Heinz varies its baby-food products: In Australia it sells a baby food made from strained lamb brains; and in the Netherlands, a baby food made from strained brown beans. General Foods blends different coffees for the British (who drink their coffee with milk), the French (who drink their coffee black), and Latin Americans (who want a chicory taste).

An important variant of product adaptation responds to the *basic-needs* concept in developing economies. Pharmaceutical companies such as Ciba-Geigy have set up a specific product line for these markets, distinguished by a narrower and more-focused range (stressing, for example, antibiotics) and by ''no-frills'' packaging, allowing a reduced price. This concept, close to a branded generics line, is equally applicable to other areas, such as the food and beverage industry.

Product invention consists of creating something new. This can take two forms. *Backward invention* is the reintroducing of earlier product forms that happen to be well adapted to the needs of a country. The National Cash Register Company reintroduced its crank-operated cash register, which could sell at half the cost of a modern cash register, and sold substantial numbers in the Orient, Latin America, and Spain. This illustrates the existence of *international product life cycles* where countries stand at different stages of readiness to accept a particular product. *Forward invention* is creating a brand new product to meet a need in another country. There is an enormous need in less-developed countries for low-cost, high-protein foods. Companies such as Quaker Oats, Swift, and Monsanto are researching the nutrition needs of these countries, formulating new foods, and developing advertising campaigns to gain product trial and acceptance. Product invention is a costly strategy, but the payoffs might also be great.

Promotion   Companies can either adopt the same promotion strategy they used in the home market or change it for each local market.

Consider the message. The company can change the message at three different levels. The company can use one message around the world by varying only the language, name, and colors. Exxon used "Put a tiger in your tank" with minor variations and gained international recognition. Colors were changed to avoid taboos in other countries. Purple is associated with death in most of Latin America; white is a mourning color in Japan; and green is associated with jungle sickness in Malaysia. Even names and headlines have to be modified. In Germany, *mist* means "manure," and *scotch* (scotch tape) means "schmuck"; in Spain, Chevrolet's *Nova* translates as *no va*, which means "it doesn't go"! An Electrolux vacuum cleaner ad, translated from Swedish into English was run in a Korean magazine reading "Nothing sucks like Electrolux." And a laundry soap ad claiming to wash "really dirty parts" was translated in French-speaking Quebec to read "a soap for washing 'private parts.' "

The next possibility is to use the same theme but adapt it to the values of each local market:

> A Camay soap commercial showed a beautiful woman bathing. In Venezuela, a man was seen in the bathroom; in Italy and France, only a man's hand was seen; and in Japan, the man waited outside.

Finally, some companies encourage their ad agencies to make a full adaptation to the local market, including changing the theme. The Schwinn Company uses a pleasure theme for its bicycles in the United States and a safety theme in Scandinavia. Kraft uses different ads for Cheez Whiz in different countries, given that household penetration is 95 percent in Puerto Rico where the cheese is put on everything, 65 percent in Canada where it is spread on toast in the morning breakfast, and 35 percent in the United States where it is considered a junk food.

The use of media also requires international adaptation because media availability varies from country to country. TV advertising time is very limited in Europe, ranging from four hours a day in France to none in the Scandinavian countries. Advertisers must buy time months in advance and have little control over when their ads will be broadcast. The rapid growth of VCR usage in Europe has cut further into the size of TV audiences. Another medium, magazines, varies in its effectiveness; magazines play a major role in Italy and a minor one in Austria. Newspapers have a national reach in the United Kingdom, but the advertiser can only buy local newspaper coverage in Spain.

Price   Multinationals face a number of problems in setting their international prices. In setting a global pricing policy, companies have three choices:

1. *Setting a uniform price everywhere.* Thus Coca-Cola might want to charge forty cents everywhere in the world. But this would be too high a price in poor countries and not high enough in rich countries.
2. *Setting a market-based price in each country.* Here Coca-Cola would charge what each country would bear. But this ignores differences in the actual cost from country to country.
3. *Setting a cost-based price in each country.* Here Coca-Cola would use a standard markup of its costs everywhere. But this might price Coca-Cola out of the market in certain countries where its costs are high.

Regardless of their choice, companies' foreign prices are likely to be higher than their domestic prices (unless they decide to subsidize the price). The reason lies in the *price escalation phenomenon.* A Gucci handbag may sell for $60 in Italy and $240 in the United States. Why? Gucci has to add the cost of transportation, tariffs, importer margin, wholesaler margin, and retailer margin to its factory price. Depending on these added costs, as well as the currency fluctuation risk, the product may have to sell for two to five times as much in another country to make the same profit for the manufacturer.

Another problem involves the company's setting a *transfer price* for goods that it ships to its foreign subsidiaries. Consider the following:

> The Swiss pharmaceutical company Hoffman-LaRoche charged its Italian subsidiary only $22 a kilo for librium in order to make high profits in Italy where the corporate taxes were lower. It charged its British subsidiary $925 per kilo for the same librium in order to make high profits at home instead of in Britain where the corporate taxes were high. The British Monopoly Commission sued Hoffman-LaRoche for back taxes and won.

If the company charges too high a price to a subsidiary, it ends up paying higher tariff duties, although it may pay lower income taxes in the foreign country. If the company charges too low a price to its subsidiary, it can be charged with *dumping*. Dumping is indicated when a company either charges less than its costs or less than it charges in its home market. Thus Zenith accused Japanese television manufacturers of dumping their TV sets on the U.S. market. When the U.S. Customs Bureau finds evidence of dumping, it can levy a dumping tariff. Various governments are watching for abuses and often force companies to charge the *arm's-length price*, namely, the price charged by other competitors for the same or similar product.

Last but not least, many multinationals are plagued by the *gray market* problem. For example:

> Minolta sold its cameras to dealers in Hong Kong for a lower price than in Germany because of lower transportation costs and tariffs. The Hong Kong dealers worked on smaller margins than the German retailers, who preferred high markups to high volume. Minolta's cameras ended up selling at retail for $174 in Hong Kong and $270 in Germany. Some Hong Kong wholesalers noticed this price difference and shipped Minolta cameras to German dealers for less than they were paying the German distributor. The German distributor couldn't sell his stock and complained to Minolta.

Very often a company finds some enterprising distributors buying more than they can sell in their own country and transshipping goods to another country in competition with the established distributor in order to take advantage of price differences. Multinationals try to prevent gray markets by policing the distributors, or by raising their prices to lower-cost distributors, or by altering the product characteristics for different countries.

Distribution Channels

The international company must take a *whole-channel* view of the problem of distributing its products to the final users. Figure 13-5 shows the three major links between the seller and the ultimate user. The first link, *seller's international marketing headquarters*, consists of its export department or international division making decisions on channels and other marketing-mix elements. The second link, *channels between nations*, gets the products to the borders of the foreign nations. It consists of decisions on the types of intermediaries (agents, trading companies, etc.), the type of transportation (air, sea, etc.), and the financing and risk arrangements. The third link, *channels within foreign nations*, gets the products from their foreign entry point to the final buyers and users. Too many American manufacturers think their job is done once the product leaves their hands. They should pay attention to how the product moves within the foreign country.

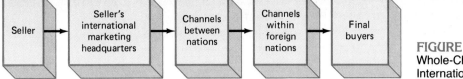

FIGURE 13-5
Whole-Channel Concept for
International Marketing

Within-country channels of distribution vary considerably from country to country. There are striking differences in the *number* and *types of middlemen* serving each foreign market. To get soap into Japan, Procter & Gamble has to work through what is probably the most complicated distribution system in the world. It must sell to a *general wholesaler*, who sells to a *basic product specialty wholesaler*, who sells to a *specialty wholesaler*, who sells to a *regional wholesaler*, who sells to a *local wholesaler*, who finally sells to *retailers*. All of these distribution levels may result in the doubling or tripling of the consumers' price over the importer's price.[13] If P&G takes the same soap to tropical Africa, the company might sell to an *import wholesaler*, who sells to several *jobbers*, who in turn sell to *petty traders* (mostly women) established in local markets.

Another difference lies in the *size and character of retail units* abroad. Where large-scale retail chains dominate the U.S. scene, most foreign retailing is in the hands of many small independent retailers. In India, millions of retailers operate tiny shops or sell in open markets. Their markups are high, but the real price is brought down through price haggling. Supermarkets could conceivably bring down prices, but they are difficult to start because of many economic and cultural barriers.[14] People's incomes are low, and they must shop daily for small amounts and are limited to whatever quantity can be carried home on foot or on a bicycle. Also, there is a lack of storage and refrigeration space to keep food for several days. Packaging costs are kept low in order to keep the prices low. In India, cigarettes are often bought singly (instead of in packs). Breaking bulk remains an important function of middlemen and helps perpetuate the long channels of distribution that are a major obstacle to the expansion of large-scale retailing in developing countries.

DECIDING ON THE MARKETING ORGANIZATION

Companies manage their international marketing activities in at least three ways.

Export Department A firm normally gets into international marketing by simply shipping out the goods. If its international sales expand, the company organizes an export department consisting of a sales manager and a few assistants. As sales increase further, the export department is expanded to include various marketing services so that the company can go after business more aggressively. If the firm moves into joint ventures or direct investment, the export department will no longer be adequate to manage international operations.

International Division Many companies become involved in several international markets and ventures. A company might export to one country, license to another, have a joint-ownership venture in a third, and own a subsidiary in a fourth. Sooner or later it will create an international division to handle all its international activity. The international division is headed by an international-division president, who set goals and budgets and is responsible for the company's growth to the international market.

International divisions are organized in a variety of ways. The international division's corporate staff consists of specialists in marketing, manufacturing, research, finance, planning, and personnel; they will plan for, and provide services to, various operating units. The operating units may be organized according to one or more of three principles. They may be *geographical organizations*. Reporting to the international-division president may be regional vice-presidents for North America, Latin America, Europe, Africa, the Middle East, and the Far East. Reporting to the regional vice-presidents are country managers who are responsible for a sales force, sales branches, distributors, and licensees in the respective countries. Or the operating units may be *world product groups*, each with an international vice-president responsible for worldwide sales of each product group. The vice-presidents may draw on corporate-staff area specialists for expertise on different geographical areas. Finally, the operating units may be *international subsidiaries*, each headed by a president. The various subsidiary presidents report to the president of the international division.

Many multinationals shift between these three types of organizations because each creates some problems. The history of Westinghouse's international operations is illustrative:[15]

Before 1960, Westinghouse had several fairly autonomous foreign subsidiaries that were loosely linked through an international division. To achieve more coordination, Westinghouse established in 1960 a strong international division with regional and country managers. However, several of Westinghouse's product groups found it frustrating to work through the international division and they pressed for global control over planning and implementation. The corporation acceded in 1971 and disbanded the international division and gave 125 division managers worldwide responsibility. However, the results were not uniformly good. It turned out that many product groups did not pay sufficient attention to the international opportunities, since most of their business was domestic; they lacked international expertise; and they failed to coordinate their international operations with each other. Not surprisingly, Westinghouse established a matrix organization in 1979 consisting of an international vice-president who managed four regional managers, who in turn managed country managers, along with an overlay of international managers from the various product groups. The matrix solution promised to be sensitive both to local area needs and to global product strategy but at greater cost and some management conflict along the way.

Global Organization

Several firms have passed beyond the international-division stage and become truly global organizations. They stop thinking of themselves as national marketers who venture abroad and start thinking of themselves as global marketers. The top corporate management and staff are involved in the planning of worldwide manufacturing facilities, marketing policies, financial flows, and logistical systems. The global operating units report directly to the chief executive or executive committee, not to the head of an international division. Executives are trained in worldwide operations, not just domestic or international. Management is recruited from many countries; components and supplies are purchased where they can be obtained at the least cost; and investments are made where the anticipated returns are greatest.

Major companies must go more global if they hope to compete. As foreign companies successfully invade the U.S. market, U.S. companies will have to move more aggressively into foreign markets. (See Exhibit 13-8.)

EXHIBIT 13-8

The World's Champion Marketers: The Japanese?

Few dispute that the Japanese have performed an economic miracle since World War II. In a relatively short time, they have achieved global market leadership in industries thought to be "mature" and dominated by impregnable giants: autos, motorcycles, watches, cameras, optical instruments, steel, shipbuilding, pianos, zippers, radios, television, video recorders, hand calculators, and so on. Japanese firms are currently moving into the number-two position in computers and construction equipment and making strong inroads into the chemical, rubber tires, pharmaceutical, and machine-tool industries. They are building a stronger position in designer clothing and cosmetics, and slowly moving into aircraft manufacture.

Many theories have been offered to explain Japan's global successes. Some point to its unique business practices, such as lifetime employment, quality circles, consensus management, and just-in-time production. Others point to the supportive role of government policies and subsidies, the existence of powerful trading companies, and businesses' easy access to bank financing. Still others view Japan's success as based on low wage rates, unfair dumping policies, protected markets, and almost zero defense industry costs.

One of the main keys to Japan's performance is its skill in marketing-strategy formulation and implementation. The Japanese came to the United States to study marketing and went home understanding its principles better than many U.S. companies did. The Japanese know how to select a market, enter it in the right way, build their market share, and protect their leadership position against competitors' attacks.

Selecting Markets The Japanese government and companies work hard to identify attractive global markets. They favor industries that require high skills, high labor intensity, and only small quantities of natural resources: Candidates include consumer electronics, cameras, watches, motocycles, and pharmaceuticals. They prefer product markets that are in a state of technological evolution. They identify product markets where consumers are dissatisfied. They look for industries where the market leaders are complacent or underfinanced.

Entering Markets The Japanese send study teams into the target country to spend several weeks or several months evaluating the market and figuring out a strategy. They may enter by first selling their products to a private brander, such as an American department store or manufacturer. Later they will introduce their own brand—a low-price stripped-down product, or a product as good as the competitions' but priced lower, or a product exhibiting higher quality or new features or designs. The Japanese proceed to line up good distribution in order to provide quick service to their customers. They rely on advertising to bring their products to the public's attention. A key characteristic of their entry strategy is to build market share rather than early profits. The Japanese are patient capitalists who are willing to wait even a decade before realizing their profits.

Building Market Share Once Japanese firms gain a market foothold, they direct their energies toward expanding their market share. They rely on product-development strategies and market-development strategies. They pour money into product improvement, product upgrading, and product proliferation so that they can offer more and better things than the competition. They spot new opportunities through market segmentation, and they sequence market development across a number of countries, pushing toward building a network of world markets and production locations.

Protecting Market Share Once the Japanese achieve market domination, they find themselves in the role of defenders rather than attackers. The Japanese defense strategy is a good offense through continuous product development and refined market segmentation. Japanese firms use two market-oriented principles to maintain their leadership. The first is "zero customer feedback time" whereby they survey recent customers to find out how they like the product and what improvements they would suggest. The second is "zero product improvement time" whereby they add worthwhile product improvements continuously so that the product remains the leader.

Responding to the Japanese Competitors Although U.S. and European firms were slow to respond to Japanese inroads, most of them are now mounting counteroffensive. IBM is adding new products, automating its factories, sourcing components from abroad, and entering strategic partnerships with others. Black & Decker is closing product line gaps, increasing product quality, streamlining manufacturing, and pricing more aggres-

Many multinationals have evolved from narrow *ethnocentric* thinking where they view things only from their culture to *polycentric* thinking where they view things from the perspective of the host culture. Still, a polycentric orientation means a highly decentralized approach to building global sales. Polycentric multinationals give a high degree of autonomy to their managers abroad. Their managers work hard to be good citizens in the host country and they advocate local production, product and marketing adaptations, and so on, to win local favor. Yet the multinational's fate might depend more on its ability to shape a global competitive strategy and capture system-level advantages through design production/marketing coordination and some degree of standardization. To succeed in this, planning and power must be more centralized at the regional and headquarters level. Today's multinationals are increasingly reestablishing more centralized control through *geocentric* planning, or at least *regiocentric* planning.[16]

SUMMARY

Companies today can no longer afford to pay attention only to their domestic market, no matter how large it is. Many industries are global industries, and those firms that operate globally achieve lower costs and higher brand awareness. Protectionist measures can only slow down the invasion of superior goods; the best company defense is a sound global offense.

At the same time, global marketing is risky because of fluctuating exchange rates, unstable governments, protectionist barriers, high product and communication adaptation costs, and several other factors. Yet the international product life cycle provides support for the notion that comparative advantage in many industries will move from high-cost to low-cost countries, and companies therefore cannot simply stay domestic and expect to maintain their markets. Given the potential gains and risks of international marketing, companies need a systematic way to make their international marketing decisions.

The first step is to understand the international marketing environment, particularly the international trade system. In considering a particular foreign market, its economic, political-legal, and cultural characteristics must be assessed. Second, the company must consider what proportion of foreign to total sales it will seek, whether it will do business in a few or many countries, and what types of countries it wants to enter. The third step is to decide which particular markets to enter, and this calls for evaluating the probable rate of return on investment against the level of risk. Fourth, the company has to decide how to enter each attractive market. Many companies start as indirect or direct exporters and then move to licensing, joint ventures, and finally direct investment; this company evolution has been called the internationalization process. Companies must next decide on the extent to which their products, promotion, price, and distribution should be adapted to individual foreign markets. Finally, the company must develop an effective organization for pursuing international marketing. Most firms start with an export department and graduate to an international division. A few pass to a global organization, which means that top management thinks and plans a global strategy for the company.

◼ QUESTIONS

1. "The benefits for trading in the U.S. domestic market far outweigh the risks involved in doing business overseas." Discuss this statement citing specific examples in industry to support your arguments.

2. Select one of the following companies—Procter & Gamble, McDonald's, or Hyundai—and analyze its strategies in reaching its overseas markets. How might the company have increased its effectiveness?

3. "While cigarette sales decline or stagnate in many industrialized nations . . . the Third World is where the growth is. Tobacco companies operate unburdened by many of the restraints they face in the West." Discuss the pros and cons of this "marketing opportunity."

4. Compare and contrast features of the markets in Brazil and West Germany for a line of food processors.

5. The U.S. Congress passed the Foreign Corrupt Practices Act, which attempts to curb bribery by prohibiting firms from making or authorizing payments, offers, promises, or gifts for the purpose of "corruptly" influencing actions by governments or their officials in order to obtain or retain business for a company. The act has been criticized as an expression of cultural/moral ethnocentrism and as a deterrent to effective marketing practices overseas. What do you think is the proper stance for the U.S. government to take?

6. Discuss the relevant aspects of the political-legal environment that might affect K-mart's decision to open retail outlets in Italy.

7. What product-strategy possibilities might Hershey's consider in marketing its chocolate bars in South American countries?

8. Which type of international marketing organization would you suggest for the following companies? (a) Huffy bicycles in planning to sell three models in the Far East; (b) a small manufacturer of toys about to market its products in Europe; and (c) Dodge in contemplating selling its full line of cars and trucks in Kuwait.

9. A U.S. heavy-equipment manufacturer operating in Western Europe has been using Americans as sales people. The company feels that it could reduce its costs by hiring and training nationals for sales people. What are the advantages and disadvantages of using Americans versus nationals for selling abroad?

10. A large American company decided to enter the French tire market some years ago. The company produced tires for medium-sized trucks designed to meet the official rear-axle weight. Its subsequent experience was bad, with many of its tires blowing out. The company acquired a poor image in France as a result. What went wrong?

11. Select one of the following nations—Italy, Japan, or the USSR—and describe its marketing institutions and practices.

◼ FOOTNOTES

1 See "European States Subsidize Marketing Aid," *Business Marketing*, November 1986, pp. 27–28.

2 Louis T. Well, Jr., "A Product Life Cycle for International Trade?" *Journal of Marketing*, July 1968, pp. 1–6. The original formulation was stated in Raymond Vernon, "International Investment and International Trade in the Product Cycle," *Quarterly Journal of Economics*, May 1966, pp. 190–207.

3 The international product life cycle describes past developments in such markets as office machinery, consumer durables, and synthetic materials. Some critics feel that it has less validity today because multinational enterprises now operate vast global networks through which they may innovate new products anywhere in the world and move them through various countries not necessarily in the sequence predicted by the original formulation of the international PLC. See Ian H. Giddy, "The Demise of the Product Cycle Model in International Business Theory," *Columbia Journal of World Business*, Spring 1978, p. 92; and Raymond Vernon, "The Product Cycle Hypothesis in a New International Environment," *Oxford Bulletin of Economics and Statistics*, November 1979, pp. 255–67.

4 See David A. Ricks, Marilyn Y. C. Fu, and Jeffery S. Arpan, *International Business Blunders* (Columbus, Ohio: Grid, 1974). For an account of negotiating styles in different countries, see Gavin Kennedy, *Negotiate Anywhere!* (London: Hutchinson Business, 1985).

5 Michael E. Porter, *Competitive Strategy* (New York: Free Press, 1980), p. 275.

6 Igal Ayal and Jehiel Zif, "Market Expansion Strategies in Multinational Marketing," *Journal of Marketing*, Spring 1979, pp. 84–94.

7 James K. Sweeney, "A Small Company Enters the European Market," *Harvard Business Review*, September–October 1970, pp. 127–28.

8 See David S. R. Leighton, "Deciding When to Enter International Markets," in *Handbook of Modern Marketing*, ed. Victor P. Buell (New York: McGraw-Hill, 1970), Sec. 20, pp. 23–28.

9 However, see J. Peter Killing, "How to Make a Global Joint Venture Work," *Harvard Business Review*, May–June 1982, pp. 120–27.

10 See Jan Johanson and Finn Wiedersheim-Paul, "The Internationalization of the Firm," *Journal of Management Studies*, October 1975, pp. 305–22.

11 See Stan Reid, "The Decision Maker and Export Entry and Expansion," *Journal of International Business Studies*, Fall 1981, pp. 101–12; Igal Ayal, "Industry Export Performance: Assessment and Prediction," *Journal of Marketing*, Summer 1982, pp. 54–61; and Somkid Jatusripitak, *The Exporting Behavior of Manufacturing Firms* (Ann Arbor, Mich.: UMI Press, 1986).

12 Warren J. Keegan, *Multinational Marketing Management*, 3rd ed. (Englewood Cliffs, N.J.: Prentice-Hall, 1984), pp. 317–24.

13 See William D. Hartley, "How Not to Do It: Cumbersome Japanese Distribution System Stumps U.S. Concerns," *Wall Street Journal*, March 2, 1972.

14 See Arieh Goldman, "Outreach of Consumers and the Modernization of Urban Food Retailing in Developing Countries," *Journal of Marketing*, October 1974, pp. 8–16.

15 See Christopher A. Bartlett, "How Multinational Organizations Evolve," *Journal of Business Strategy*, Summer 1982, pp. 20–32.

16 See Yoram Wind, Susan P. Douglas, and Howard V. Perlmutter, "Guidelines for Developing International Marketing Strategies," *Journal of Marketing*, April 1973, pp. 14–23.

14 Developing, Testing, and Launching New Products and Services

Nothing in this world is so powerful as an idea whose time has come.

Victor Hugo

An extremely important responsibility of the marketing group is to help the company identify new market needs and opportunities and respond to them with appropriate and effective product solutions. This must be done, and done successfully, if for no other reason than some existing products in the company's portfolio are in, or will shortly enter, the decline stage. Replacement products and businesses must be found in order to maintain or build the company's sales. Furthermore, customers want new products, and competitors will do their best to supply them. A Booz, Allen & Hamilton survey reported that seven hundred companies expect that 31 percent of their profits will come from new products introduced in the next five years.[1]

A company can add new products in two ways: *acquisition* and *new-product development.* The acquisition route can take three forms. The company can search for and buy other companies; this is how Beatrice Foods and Litton Industries grew. The company can buy patents from other companies. Or the company can buy a license or franchise from another company to make that company's products or services. In all three cases, the company does not develop new products but simply acquires the rights to existing ones.

The new-product route can take two forms. The company can develop new products in its own laboratories. Or it can contract with independent researchers or new-product-development agencies to develop specific products for the firm.

Many companies pursue growth through both acquisition and new-product development. Their management feels that the best opportunities might lie in acquisition at certain times and new-product development at other times, and they want to be skilled at both.

405

This chapter will focus on new-product development as a growth strategy because of the heavy role that marketing plays in finding, developing, and launching successful new products. "New products" for our purposes will include *original products*, *improved products*, *modified products*, and *new brands* that the firm develops through its own R&D efforts. We will also be concerned with whether consumers see them as "new."

Booz, Allen & Hamilton identified six categories of new products in terms of their newness to the company and to the marketplace.[2] Figure 14-1 shows these categories and the percentage of products appearing in each category over the past five years. The categories are

- *New-to-the-world products.* New products that create an entirely new market
- *New-product lines.* New products that allow a company to enter an established market for the first time
- *Additions to existing product lines.* New products that supplement a company's established product lines
- *Improvements in/revisions to existing products.* New products that provide improved performance or greater perceived value and replace existing products
- *Repositionings.* Existing products that are targeted to new markets or market segments
- *Cost reductions.* New products that provide similar performance at lower cost

A company usually pursues a mix of these new products. An important finding is that only 10 percent of all new products are truly innovative or new to the world. These products involve the greatest cost and risk because they are new to both the company and the marketplace.

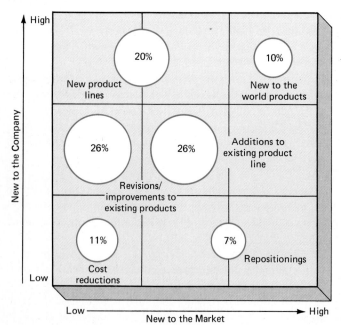

FIGURE 14-1
Types of New Products
SOURCE: New Products Management for the 1980s (New York: Booz, Allen & Hamilton, 1982).

THE NEW-PRODUCT-DEVELOPMENT DILEMMA

Given the intense competition in most industries today, companies that fail to develop new products are exposing themselves to great risk. Their existing products are vulnerable to changing consumer needs and tastes, new technologies, shortened product life cycles, and increased domestic and foreign competition.

At the same time, new-product development can be very risky. Texas Instruments lost $660 million before withdrawing from the home computer business; RCA lost $575 million on its ill-fated videodisc players; Ford lost $350 million on its ill-fated Edsel; Du Pont lost an estimated $100 million on its synthetic leather called Corfam; and the French Concorde aircraft will never recover its investment. Here are several consumer-packaged-goods products, launched by sophisticated companies, that failed in the marketplace:

Red Kettle soup (Campbell)	Vim tablet detergent (Lever)
Knorr soup (Best)	Post dried fruit cereal (General Foods)
Cut toothpaste (Colgate)	Gablinger's beer (Rheingold)
Flavored ketchups (Hunt's)	Resolve analgesic (Bristol-Myers)
Babyscott diapers (Scott)	Mennen E deodorant (Mennen)

One study found that the new-product failure rate was 40 percent for consumer products, 20 percent for industrial products, and 18 percent for services.[3] The failure rate for new consumer products is especially disturbing.

Why do many new products fail? There are several factors. A high-level executive might push a favorite idea through in spite of negative marketing research findings. Or the idea is good, but the market size is overestimated. Or the actual product is not designed as well as it should be. Or it is incorrectly positioned in the market, not advertised effectively, or overpriced. Sometimes new-product development costs are higher than expected, or the competitors fight back harder than expected.

Successful new-product development may even be more difficult to achieve in the future for the following reasons:

- *Shortage of important new-product ideas in certain areas.* Some scientists think there are too few feasible new technologies with the investment potential that was provided by automobiles, television, computers, xerography, and wonder drugs in times past.
- *Fragmented markets.* Keen competition is leading to increasingly fragmented markets. Companies have to aim new products at smaller market segments rather than the mass market, and this means lower sales and profits for each product.
- *Social and governmental constraints.* New products have to satisfy public-interest criteria such as consumer safety and ecological compatibility. Government requirements have slowed down innovation in the drug industry and have complicated product-design and advertising decisions in such industries as industrial equipment, chemicals, automobiles, and toys.
- *Costliness of the new-product-development process.* A company typically has to generate many new-product ideas in order to finish with a few good ones. Furthermore, the company has to face rising R&D, manufacturing, and marketing costs.
- *Capital shortage.* Some companies with good ideas cannot raise the funds needed to research them. Venture capital has, in recent years, become much more cautious.
- *Shortened time span to completion.* Many competitors are likely to get the same idea at the same time, and the victory often goes to the swiftest. Alert companies have to compress development time by using computer-aided design and manufacturing techniques, joint partners,

early concept tests, and advanced marketing planning. Japanese companies see the challenge as "achieving better quality at a cheaper price at a faster speed than competitors."[4]

■ **Shorter life spans for successful products.** When a new product is successful, rivals are so quick to imitate it that the new product's life cycle is considerably shortened. Thus IBM finds dozens of imitators offering IBM-compatible personal computers; and Apple finds foreign "knockoffs" of its computers being sold in the Far East.

The answer to successful new-product introductions lies in two directions. First, the company must establish an effective organization for handling the new-product-development process. Second, it must employ the best tools and concepts in each stage of the new-product-development process. We will look at each in turn.

EFFECTIVE ORGANIZATIONAL ARRANGEMENTS

Top management is ultimately accountable for the new-product-success record. It cannot simply ask the new-product manager to come up with great ideas. New-product-development work requires top management to define the business domains and product categories that the company wants to emphasize. In one food company, the new-product manager spent thousands of dollars researching a new snack idea only to hear the president say, "Drop it. We don't want to be in the snack business."

Top management must establish specific criteria for new-product-idea acceptance, especially in large multidivisional companies where all kinds of projects bubble up as favorites of various managers. The criteria can vary with the specific *strategic role* the product is expected to play. Booz, Allen & Hamilton identified six major strategic roles that companies set for their new products (percentages show the portion of recent products playing each role):

■ Maintain position as a product innovator (46 percent)
■ Defend a market-share position (44 percent)
■ Establish a foothold in a future new market (37 percent)
■ Preempt a market segment (33 percent)
■ Exploit technology in a new way (27 percent)
■ Capitalize on distribution strengths (24 percent)[5]

Thus the Gould Corporation established some years ago the following acceptance criteria for new products aimed at exploiting a technology in a new way: (1) the product can be introduced within five years; (2) the product has a market potential of at least $50 million and a 15 percent growth rate; (3) the product will provide at least 30 percent return on sales and 40 percent on investment; and (4) the product will achieve technical or market leadership.

A major decision facing top management is how much to budget for new-product development. R&D outcomes are so uncertain that it is difficult to use normal investment criteria for budgeting. Some companies solve this problem by encouraging and financing as many projects as possible, hoping to hit a few winners. Other companies set their R&D budget by applying a conventional percentage-to-sales figure or by spending what the competition spends. Still other companies decide how many successful new products they need and work backward to estimate the required R&D investment.

Booz, Allen & Hamilton has conducted several studies of how many new-product ideas it takes to yield one successful product. (See Exhibit 14-1 for a summary of one study's main findings.) Fifteen years ago it took fifty-eight new-product ideas to yield one good one. Booz, Allen & Hamilton's latest study shows that companies are now able to turn one out of seven new-product ideas into a successful new product. Figure 14-2 shows the decay curve for new-product ideas. Booz, Allen & Hamilton concluded that many companies have learned to handle prescreening and planning more effectively and are putting money only on the best ideas instead of using a shotgun approach.

EXHIBIT 14-1

Key Findings on New-Product-Management Activity

Here are some key findings from a Booz, Allen & Hamilton study of new-product-management activity. The information comes from a mail survey of seven hundred consumer and industrial companies and lengthy interviews with 150 new-product executives.

1. Management achieved success with 65 percent of the products they launched.
2. Companies were able to develop one successful product out of every seven they researched.
3. Ten percent of the new products were "new to the world," and 20 percent were "new-product lines." Yet these high-risk products represented 60 percent of the "most successful" new products.
4. New-product spending had become more efficient, in that successful entries accounted for 54 percent of total new-product expenditures, up from 30 percent in 1968.
5. Successful new-product companies don't spend more on R&D and marketing, as a percentage of sales, than unsuccessful ones.
6. The median company introduced 5 new products in the period 1976–1981; that number is expected to double over the next five years.
7. Managers expect new products to increase company sales growth by one-third over the next five years, while the portion of total company profits generated by new products is expected to be 40 percent.

SOURCE *New Products Management for the 1980s* (New York: Booz, Allen & Hamilton, 1982).

Table 14-1 shows how a company can work out the investment cost of new-product development. The new-products manager at a large consumer-packaged-goods company reviewed the results of sixty-four new-product ideas his company considered. Only one in four ideas, or sixteen, passed the idea-screening stage, and it cost $1,000 per idea reviewed at this stage. Half of these ideas, or eight, survived the concept-testing stage, at a cost of $20,000 each. Half of these, or four, survived the product-development stage. Half of these, or two, did well in the test market, at a cost of $500,000 each.[6] When these two ideas were launched, at a cost of $5,000,000 each, only one was highly successful. Thus the one successful idea had cost the company $5,721,000 to develop. In the process, sixty-three other ideas fell by the wayside. Therefore the total cost for developing one successful new product was $13,984,400. Unless the company can improve the pass ratios and reduce the costs at each stage, it will have to budget nearly $14,000,000 for each successful new idea it hopes to find. If top management wants four successful new products in the next few years, it will have to budget at least $56,000,000 (= 4 × $14,000,000) for new-product development.

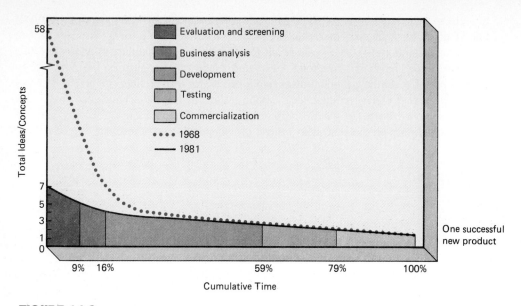

FIGURE 14-2
Mortality of New-Product Ideas
SOURCE: New Products Management for the 1980s (New York: Booz, Allen & Hamilton, 1982).

A key factor in new-product-development work is to establish effective organizational structures. Companies handle new-product development in several ways:[7]

■ **Product managers.** Many companies assign responsibility for new-product ideas to their product managers. In practice, this system has several faults. Product managers are usually so busy managing their product lines that they give little thought to new products other than brand modifications or extensions; they also lack the specific skills and knowledge needed to critique and develop new products.

■ **New-product managers.** General Foods and Johnson & Johnson have new-product managers who report to group-product managers. This position professionalizes the new-product function; on the other hand, new-product managers tend to think in terms of product modifications and line extensions limited to their product market.

■ **New-product committees.** Most companies have a high-level management committee charged with reviewing and approving new-product proposals.

■ **New-product departments.** Large companies often establish a new-product department headed by a manager who has substantial authority and access to top management. The department's

TABLE 14-1   Estimated Cost of Finding One Successful New Product
(Starting with Sixty-Four New Ideas)

Stage	Number of Ideas	Pass Ratio	Cost per Product Idea	Total Cost
1. Idea screening	64	1:4	$ 1,000	$ 64,000
2. Concept test	16	1:2	20,000	320,000
3. Product development	8	1:2	200,000	1,600,000
4. Test marketing	4	1:2	500,000	2,000,000
5. National launch	2	1:2	5,000,000	10,000,000
			$5,721,000	$13,984,000

major responsibilities include generating and screening new ideas, working with the R&D department, and carrying out field testing and commercialization.

- ■ *New-product venture teams.* The 3M Company, Dow, Westinghouse, and General Mills often assign major new-product-development work to venture teams. A venture team is a group brought together from various operating departments and charged with bringing a specific product or business into being. They are "intrapreneurs" relieved of their other duties, given a budget, a time frame, and a "skunkworks" setting. (See Exhibit 14-2.)

EXHIBIT 14-2

3M's Approach to Innovation

Certain American companies have earned an outstanding reputation for successful and continuous innovation. Heading most lists is the Minneapolis-based 3M Company. 3M's immodest goal is to have each of its forty divisions generate at least 25 percent of its income from products introduced within the preceding five years! And more astonishing, they succeed. Each year the company launches more than one hundred new products.

The key centers on 3M's innovation-driven and supported corporate culture. 3M encourages everyone, not just its engineers, to become "product champions." Anyone who is hot about an idea is encouraged to do some homework to find out what knowledge exists, where the product would be developed in the company, whether it is patentable, and how profitable it might be. If the idea finds support, a venture team is formed with volunteer representatives from R&D, manufacturing, sales, marketing, and legal. Each team is headed by an "executive champion" who nurtures the team and protects it from bureaucratic intrusion. If a "healthy-looking product" is developed, the team stays with it and markets it. If the product fails, each team member nevertheless returns to his or her previous level. Some teams have tried three or four times to make a success out of an idea, and in several cases have succeeded.

Each year 3M hands out its "Golden Step" awards to venture teams whose new product earned more than $2 million in U.S. sales or $4 million in worldwide sales within three years of its commercial introduction. All said, "intrapreneurship" is the name of the game at 3M, a game that more companies are seeking to play.

Where companies have poor records of new-product success, the cause often is traceable to the lack of organizational teamwork. The traditional model of innovation calls for the R&D department to get a bright idea and research it, then have an engineering team design it and the design turned over to the manufacturing department to produce, and then over to sales to sell. But this "serial" model of innovation led to many problems. The manufacturing people would often send the design back to the engineers saying they could not produce it at the targeted cost; the engineers would then spend time redesigning the product. When the sales force later showed the product to customers, they would realize that it could not be sold at the targeted price, since consumer needs and wants were not met. The sales people would be mad at the engineers, the R&D people would call the sales force a bunch of incompetents who could not sell, and mutual blaming would be rife.

The solution is clear. Effective product development requires closer teamwork among design, manufacturing, and marketing from the beginning. The product idea must be researched from a marketing point of view, and a marketing person must follow and advise on the idea throughout its development. Design engineers and manufacturing people must jointly work on the design so that the prototype passes smoothly into manufacture. Studies of Japanese companies show that their new-product success is due in large part to building in much more teamwork in product development from the beginning.

According to the Booz, Allen & Hamilton study, the most successful innovating companies have made a consistent commitment of resources to new-product development, have designed a new-product strategy that is linked to their strategic planning process, and have established formal and sophisticated organizational arrangements for managing the new-product-development process.[8]

We are now ready to look at the major management challenges at each stage of the new-product-development process. Eight stages are involved: *idea generation*, *screening*, *concept development and testing*, *marketing strategy*, *business analysis*, *product development*, *market testing*, *and commercialization*.

IDEA GENERATION

The new-product-development process starts with the search for ideas. The search should not be casual. Top management should define the products and markets to emphasize. It should state the new-product objective, whether it is high cash flow, market-share domination, or some other objective. It should state how much effort should be devoted to developing original products, modifying existing products, and copying competitors' products.

Sources of New-Product Ideas

New-product ideas can come from many sources: customers, scientists, competitors, company sales people, channel members, and top management.

The marketing concept suggests that *customers' needs and wants* are the logical place to start in the search for new-product ideas. Hippel has shown that the highest percentage of ideas for new industrial products originate with customers.[9] Companies can identify customers' needs and wants through direct customer surveys, projective tests, focused group discussion, and suggestion and complaint letters from customers. Many idea hunters find the best ideas by asking customers to describe their problems with current products rather than by asking them for new-product ideas directly.

Technical companies rely on their *scientists* for new-product ideas. Companies in the chemical, electronics, and pharmaceutical industries, such as Du Pont, Bell Laboratories, and Merck, rely on scientists for new ideas.

Companies can find new ideas by monitoring their *competitors'* products. They can learn from distributors, suppliers, and sales representatives what competitors are doing. They can find out what customers like and dislike in their competitors' new products. They can buy their competitors' products, take them apart, build better ones. Their competitive strategy is one of *product imitation* and *improvement* rather than *product innovation*. The Japanese are masters of this strategy in that they have licensed or copied many Western products and found ways to improve them.

Company *sales representatives* and *middlemen* are a particularly good source of new-product ideas. They have firsthand exposure to customers' needs and complaints. They are often the first to learn of competitive developments. An increasing number of companies are training and rewarding their sales representatives, distributors, and dealers for finding new ideas. For example: Bill Keefer, chairman of Warner Electric Brake and Clutch, requires his sales force to list on each monthly call report the three best potential product ideas they heard about on customer visits. He reads these ideas each month and pens notes to his engineers, manufacturing executives, and so on, to follow up the better ideas.

Top management can be another major source of new-product ideas. Some company leaders, such as Edwin H. Land, former CEO of Polaroid, take personal responsibility for technological innovation in their companies. This is not always constructive, as when a top executive pushes through a pet idea without thoroughly researching market size or interest. This happened when Land pushed forward his Polavision project (instant-developed movies), which ended as a major product failure because the market became more interested in videotapes as a way to film action.

New-product ideas can come from other sources as well, including inventors, patent attorneys, university and commercial laboratories, industrial consultants, advertising agencies, marketing research firms, and industrial publications.

While ideas can come in from many sources, their chance of receiving serious attention often depends on someone in the organization taking the role of *product champion*. Unless someone is personally enthusiastic about the product idea and willing to advocate it strongly, the idea is not likely to receive serious consideration.

Idea-Generating Techniques

Really good ideas come out of inspiration, perspiration, and techniques. A number of "creativity" techniques can help individuals and groups generate better ideas.

Attribute Listing This technique calls for first listing the major attributes of an existing product and then modifying each attribute in the search for an improved product. Consider a screwdriver.[10] Its attributes: a round, steel shank; a wooden handle, manually operated; and torque provided by twisting action. Now a group is asked to propose attribute modifications to improve product performance or appeal. The round shank could be made hexagonal so that a wrench could be applied to increase the torque; electric power could replace manual power; the torque could be produced by pushing. Osborn suggested that useful ideas can be stimulated by putting the following questions to an object and its attributes: *put to other uses? adapt? magnify? minify? substitute? rearrange? reverse? combine?*[11]

Forced Relationships Here several objects are listed, and each object is considered in relation to every other object. Recently an office-equipment manufacturer wanted to design a new desk for executives. Several objects were listed—a desk, television set, clock, computer, copying machine, bookcase, and so on. The result was a fully electronic desk with a console resembling that found in a pilot cockpit.

Morphological Analysis *Morphology* means structure, and this method calls for identifying the structural dimensions of a problem and examining the relationships among them. Suppose the problem is described as that of "getting something from one place to another via a powered vehicle." The important dimensions are the type of vehicle (cart, chair, sling, bed); the medium in which the vehicle operates (air, water, oil, hard surface, rollers, rails); the power source (pressed air, internal-combustion engine, electric motor, steam, magnetic fields, moving cables, moving belt). Then the imagination is let loose on every combination. A cart-type vehicle powered by an internal-combustion engine and moving over hard surfaces is the automobile. The hope is to find some novel combinations.[12]

Need/problem Identification The preceding creativity techniques do not require consumer input to generate ideas. Need/problem identification, on the other hand, starts with the consumer. Consumers are asked about needs, problems, and ideas. For example, they can be asked about problems they have in using a particular product or product category. The

Landis Group, a marketing research firm, uses this technique. For a given product category, it interviews about one thousand respondents and asks whether they are "completely satisfied," "slightly dissatisfied," "moderately dissatisfied," or "extremely dissatisfied." If they have any degree of dissatisfaction, the respondents describe their problems and complaints in their own words. For example, in a study of users of English muffins, 15 percent expressed some dissatisfaction, and the largest problems were muffins that were not precut, were too dry or soft, or had poor taste. The demographics revealed that the most dissatisfied users were in the 19–29 age group with low incomes. This information can be used by an existing competitor or a new entrant to improve the product and target the most dissatisfied groups. The various problems would be rated for their *seriousness*, *incidence*, and *cost of remedying* to determine which product improvements to make.

The technique can be used in reverse. Consumers receive a list of problems and tell which products come to mind as having each problem.[13] Thus the problem: "The package of _____ doesn't fit well on the shelf" might lead consumers to name dog foods and dry breakfast cereals. A food marketer might think of entering these markets with a smaller-size package.

Hippel recommends that industrial marketers can identify new-product ideas best by working with *lead users* rather than *average users* of the product class. Lead users are individuals and companies that have more-advanced needs and face them years before the majority of the other users. Thus the Allen-Bradley Company, a leading programmable controls manufacturer, would pick up "breakthrough" ideas by researching the needs of its most-advanced customers.[14]

Brainstorming Group creativity can be stimulated through brainstorming, a technique developed by Alex Osborn. Brainstorming sessions are held when a company needs a lot of ideas. The usual group consists of six to ten people. It is not a good idea to include too many experts in the group, because they tend to look at a problem in a rigid way. The problem should be specific. The sessions, preferably held in the morning, should last about an hour. The chairperson starts with, "Remember, we want as many ideas as possible—the wilder the better, and remember, no *evaluation*." The ideas start flowing, one idea sparks another, and within an hour over a hundred or more new ideas may find their way into the tape recorder. For the conference to be maximally effective, Osborn laid down four guidelines:

- *Criticism is ruled out.* Negative comments on ideas must be withheld until later.
- *Freewheeling is welcomed.* The wilder the idea, the better; it is easier to tame down than to think up.
- *Quantity is encouraged.* The greater the number of ideas, the more the likelihood of useful ideas.
- *Combining and improving ideas is encouraged.* Participants should suggest how ideas of others can be joined into still newer ideas.[15]

Synectics William J. J. Gordon felt that Osborn's brainstorming session produced solutions too quickly, before a sufficient number of perspectives had been developed. Gordon decided to define the problem so broadly that the group would have no inkling of the specific problem.

One of the problems was to design a vaporproof method of closing vaporproof suits worn by workers who handled high-powered fuels.[16] Gordon kept the specific problem a secret and sparked a discussion of the general notion of ''closure,'' which led to images of different closure mechanisms, such as birds' nests, mouths, or thread. As the group exhausted the initial perspectives, Gordon gradually introduced facts that defined the problem further. When the group was getting close to a good solution, Gordon described the problem. Then the group started to refine the solution. These sessions would last a minimum of three hours, for Gordon believed that fatigue played an important role in unlocking ideas. Gordon described five principles underlying the synectics method:

- **Deferment.** Look first for viewpoint rather than solutions.
- **Autonomy of object.** Let the problem take on a life of its own.
- **Use of the commonplace.** Take advantage of the familiar as a springboard to the strange.
- **Involvement/detachment.** Alternate between entering into the particulars of the problem and standing back from them, in order to see them as instances of a universal.
- **Use of metaphor.** Let apparently irrelevant, accidental things suggest analogies that are sources of new viewpoints.[17]

IDEA SCREENING

The purpose of idea generation is to create a large number of ideas. The purpose of the succeeding stages is to *reduce* the number of ideas to an attractive practicable few. The first idea-pruning stage is screening.

In screening the ideas, the company must avoid two types of errors. A DROP–*error* occurs when the company dismisses an otherwise good idea. The easiest thing to do is to put down other people's ideas. (See Figure 14-3.) Some companies shudder when they look back at some ideas they dismissed:

> Xerox saw the novel promise of Chester Carlson's copying machine; IBM and Eastman Kodak did not see it at all. RCA was able to envision the innovative opportunity of radio; the Victor Talking Machine Company could not. Henry Ford recognized the promise of the automobile; yet only General Motors realized the need to segment the automobile market into price and performance categories, with a model for every classification, if the promise was to be fully achieved. Marshall Field understood the unique market development possibilities of installment buying; Endicott Johnson did not, calling it ''the vilest system yet devised to create trouble.'' And so it has gone.[18]

If a company makes too many DROP–errors, its standards are too conservative.

A GO–error occurs when the company permits a poor idea to move into development and commercialization. We can distinguish three types of product failures that ensue. An *absolute product failure* loses money, its sales do not cover variable costs. A *partial product failure* loses money, but its sales cover all the variable costs and some of the fixed costs. A *relative product failure* yields a profit, but one that is less than the company's normal or target rate of return.

The purpose of screening is to spot and drop poor ideas as early as possible. The rationale is that product-development costs rise substantially with each successive develop-

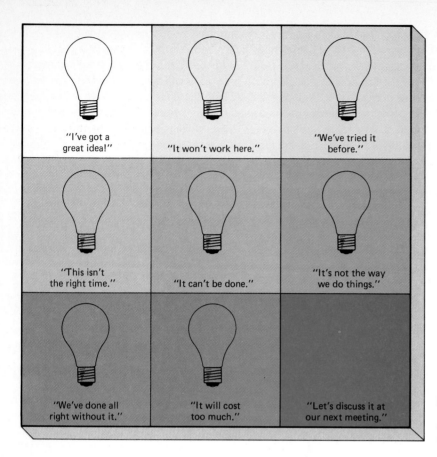

FIGURE 14-3
Forces Fighting New Ideas
SOURCE: Jerold Panas, Young &
Partners, Inc.

ment stage. When products reach later stages, management often feels that they have invested so much in developing the product that it should be launched to recoup some of the investment. But this is letting good money chase bad money, and the real solution is to not let poor product ideas get this far.

Product-Idea Rating Devices   Most companies require their executives to write up new-product ideas on a standard form that can be reviewed by a new-product committee. The write-up describes the product idea, the target market, and the competition, and it roughly estimates the market size, product price, development time and costs, manufacturing costs, and rate of return.

Even when the idea looks good, the question should be raised, Is the product appropriate for this company? That is, Does it mesh well with this company's objectives, strategies, and resources? Figure 14-4 shows a set of questions that should be put to each new-product idea. Ideas that do not satisfy one or more of these questions are dropped.

The ideas that survive can be rated using the weighted index method shown in Table 14-2. The first column lists factors required for the successful launching of the product in the marketplace. In the next column, management assigns weights to these factors to reflect

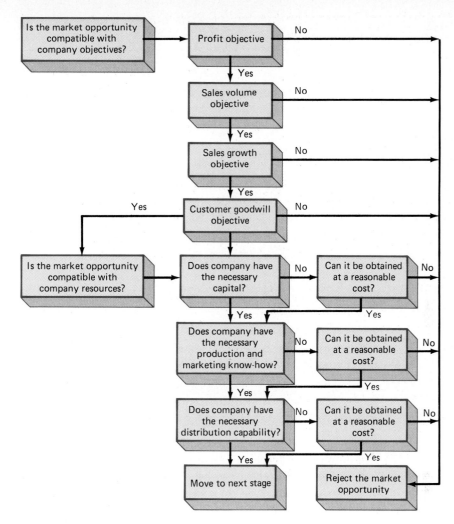

FIGURE 14-4
Evaluating a Market Opportunity in Terms of the Company's Objectives and Resources

their relative importance. Thus management believes marketing competence will be very important (0.20) and purchasing and supplies competence will be of minor importance (0.05). The next task is to rate the company's competence on each factor on a scale from 0.0 to 1.0. Here management feels that its marketing competence is very high (0.9) and its location and facilities competence low (0.3). The final step is to multiply the importance of each success factor by the company competence level to obtain an overall rating of the company's ability to launch this product successfully into the market. Thus if marketing is an important success factor, and this company is very good at marketing, the overall rating of the product idea will be increased. In the example the product idea scored 0.72, which places it at the high end of the "fair idea" level.

TABLE 14-2
Product-Idea-Rating Device

Product Success Requirements	Relative Weight (A)	Company Competence Level (B)											Rating (A × B)
		0.0	0.1	0.2	0.3	0.4	0.5	0.6	0.7	0.8	0.9	1.0	
Company personality and goodwill	0.20							√					0.120
Marketing	0.20										√		0.180
Research and development	0.20								√				0.140
Personnel	0.15							√					0.090
Finance	0.10										√		0.090
Production	0.05									√			0.040
Location and facilities	0.05				√								0.015
Purchasing and supplies	0.05										√		0.045
Total	1.00												0.720*

* Rating scale: 0.00–0.40 poor; 0.41–0.75 fair; 0.76–1.00 good. Present minimum acceptance rate: 0.70.

SOURCE: Adapted with modifications from Barry M. Richman, "A Rating Scale for Product Innovation," *Business Horizons*, Summer 1962, pp. 37–44.

This basic rating device can be refined further.[19] Its purpose is to promote more systematic product-idea evaluation—it is not supposed to make the decision for management.

CONCEPT DEVELOPMENT AND TESTING

Attractive ideas need to be developed into finer product concepts if they are to be tested. We can distinguish between a product idea, a product concept, and a product image. A *product idea* is an idea for a possible product that the company can see offering to the market. A *product concept* is an elaborated version of the idea expressed in meaningful consumer terms. A *product image* is the particular picture that consumers acquire of an actual or potential product.

Concept Development

We will illustrate concept development with the following situation. A large food processor gets the idea of producing a powder to add to milk to increase its nutritional level and taste. This is a product idea. Consumers, however, do not buy product ideas; they buy product concepts.

Any product idea can be turned into several product concepts. First, the question can be asked, Who is to use this product? The powder can be aimed at infants, children, teenagers, young or middle-aged adults, or senior citizens. Second, What primary benefit should be built into this product? Taste, nutrition, refreshment, energy? Third, What is the primary occasion for this drink? Breakfast, midmorning, lunch, midafternoon, dinner, late evening? By asking these questions, a company can form several product concepts:

- ■ *Concept 1.* An *instant breakfast drink* for adults who want a quick nutritional breakfast without preparing a breakfast.
- ■ *Concept 2.* A *tasty snack drink* for children to drink as a midday refreshment.
- ■ *Concept 3.* A *health supplement* for senior citizens to drink in the late evening before retiring.

Concept Positioning

Each concept requires positioning so that its real competition can be understood. An *instant breakfast drink* would compete against bacon and eggs, breakfast cereals, coffee and pastry, and other breakfast alternatives. A *tasty snack drink* would compete against soft drinks, fruit juices, and other tasty thirst quenchers. The product concept, and not the product idea, defines the product's competition.

Let us look at the instant breakfast drink concept further. Figure 14-5(a) is a *product-positioning map* showing where an instant breakfast drink stands in relation to other breakfast products, using the two dimensions of cost and preparation time. An instant breakfast drink offers the buyer low cost and quick preparation. Its nearest competitor is cold cereal; its most distant competitor is bacon and eggs. These contrasts can be utilized in communicating and promoting the concept to the market.

The concept also has to be positioned against existing brands in the product category. Figure 14-5(b) shows the positions of three other instant breakfast drinks. The company needs to decide how much to charge and how calorific to make its drink if these are salient attributes to buyers. The new brand could be positioned in the medium-price, medium-calorie market or in the low-price, low-calorie market. The new brand would gain distinctiveness in either position, as opposed to positioning next to another brand and fighting for share of market. This decision requires researching the size of alternative preference segments in the market.

Concept Testing

Concept testing calls for testing these concepts with an appropriate group of target consumers. The concepts may be presented symbolically or physically. At this stage, a word and/or picture description suffices, although the reliability of a concept test increases, the more concrete and physical the stimulus. The consumers are presented with an elaborated version of each concept. Here is concept 1:

> A powdered product that is added to milk to make an instant breakfast that gives the person all the breakfast nutrition needed along with good taste and high convenience. The product would be offered in three flavors, chocolate, vanilla, and strawberry, and would come in individual packets, six to a box, at $.79 a box.

FIGURE 14-5
Product and Brand Positioning

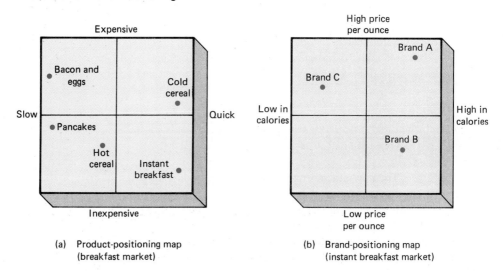

(a) Product-positioning map (breakfast market)

(b) Brand-positioning map (instant breakfast market)

Consumers are asked to respond to the following questions about the concept:

1. Are the benefits clear to you and believable?

   This measures the concept's *communicability* and *believability*. If the scores are low, the concept must be refined or revised.

2. Do you see this product as solving a problem or filling a need for you?

   This measures the *need level*. The stronger the need, the higher the expected consumer interest.

3. Do other products currently meet this need and satisfy you?

   This measures the *gap level* between the new product and existing products. The greater the gap, the higher the expected consumer interest. The need level can be multiplied by the gap level to produce a *need-gap score*. The higher the need-gap score, the higher the expected interest. A high need-gap score means that the consumer sees the product as filling a strong need *and* is not satisfied with available alternatives.

4. Is the price reasonable in relation to the value?

   This measures *perceived value*. The higher the perceived value, the higher the expected consumer interest.

5. Would you (definitely, probably, probably not, definitely not) buy the product?

   This measures *purchase intent*. We would expect it to be high for consumers who answered the previous three questions positively.

6. Who would use this product and how often would it be used?

   This provides a measure of *user targets* and *purchase frequency*.

The marketer now summarizes the sampled respondents' answers to judge whether the concept has a broad enough and strong enough consumer appeal. The need-gap levels and purchase intent levels can be checked against norms for the product category to see whether the concept appears to be a winner, a long shot, or a loser. One food manufacturer rejects any concept that draws a definitely-will-buy score of less than 40 percent. If the concept looks good, the information also tells the company what products this new product would replace, what consumers are the best targets, and so on.

Concept development and testing methodology applies to any product, service, or idea, such as an electric car, a new machine tool, a new banking service, or a new health plan. Too many managers think their job is done when they get a product idea. They think the task is to turn the idea into a physical product and sell it. But as Theodore Levitt put it, "Everybody sells intangibles in the marketplace, no matter what is produced in the factory." They forget that all selling is *concept selling*.[20] Later the product encounters all kinds of problems in the marketplace that would have been avoided if the company had done a good job of concept development and testing. (For some advanced methods of concept development and testing, see Exhibit 14-3.)

MARKETING-STRATEGY DEVELOPMENT

The new-product manager will have to develop a preliminary marketing-strategy statement for introducing this product into the market. The marketing strategy will undergo further refinement in subsequent stages.

The marketing-strategy statement consists of three parts. The first part describes the size, structure, and behavior of the target market, the planned product positioning, and the sales, market share, and profit goals sought in the first few years. Thus:

> The target market for the instant breakfast drink is families with children who are receptive to a new, convenient, nutritious, and inexpensive form of breakfast. The company's brand will be positioned at the higher-price, higher-quality end of the market. The company will aim initially to sell 500,000 cases, or 10 percent of the market, with a loss in the first year not exceeding $1.3 million dollars. The second year will aim for 700,000 cases, or 14 percent of the market, with a planned profit of $2.2 million dollars.

The second part of the marketing-strategy statement outlines the product's planned price, distribution strategy, and marketing budget for the first year:

> The product will be offered in a chocolate flavor in individual packets of six to a box at a retail price of $.79 a box. There will be forty-eight boxes per case, and the case's price to distributors will be $24. For the first two months, dealers will be offered one case free for every four cases bought, plus cooperative-advertising allowances. Free samples will be distributed door to door. Coupons with $.10 off will be advertised in newspapers. The total sales promotion budget will be $2,900,000. An advertising budget of $6,000,000 will be split between national and local 50:50. Two-thirds will go into television and one-third into newspapers. Advertising copy will emphasize the benefit concepts of nutrition and convenience. The advertising-execution concept will revolve around a little boy who drinks instant breakfast and grows strong. During the first year, $100,000 will be spent on marketing research to buy store audits and consumer panel information to monitor the market's reaction and buying rates.

The third part of the marketing-strategy statement describes the planned long-run sales and profit goals and marketing-mix strategy over time:

> The company intends to ultimately capture 25 percent market share and realize an after-tax return on investment of 12 percent. To achieve this, product quality will start high and be further improved over time through technical research. Price will initially be set at a skimming level and lowered gradually to expand the market and meet competition. The total promotion budget will be boosted each year about 20 percent, with the initial advertising/sales promotion split of 63:37 evolving eventually to 50:50. Marketing research will be reduced to $60,000 per year after the first year.

BUSINESS ANALYSIS

Once management develops the product concept and a marketing strategy, it can evaluate the business attractiveness of the proposal. Management must review the sales, cost, and profit projections to determine whether they satisfy the company's objectives. If they do, the product concept can move to the product-development stage. As new information comes in, the business analysis will undergo further revision.

Estimating Sales   Management needs to estimate whether sales will be high enough to return a satisfactory profit to the firm. Management should examine the sales history of similar products and should survey market opinion. Ultimately, management should prepare estimates of minimum and maximum sales to learn the range of risk.

Sales-estimation methods depend on whether they deal with a one-time purchased product, an infrequently purchased product, or a frequently purchased product. Figure 14-6(a) illustrates the product life-cycle sales that can be expected for one-time purchased products. Sales rise at the beginning, peak, and later approach zero as the number of potential buyers is exhausted. If new buyers keep entering the market, the curve will not go down to zero.

EXHIBIT 14-3

Measuring Consumer Preferences for Alternative Product Concepts through Conjoint Analysis

Consumer preferences for alternative product concepts can be measured through conjoint analysis. Two approaches to data collection can be used, the full profile approach and the pairwise approach. We will illustrate these methods below.

Full Profile Approach

Green and Wind have illustrated the full profile approach in connection with developing a new carpet-cleaning agent for home use. Suppose the new-product marketer is considering the following five design elements:

■ Three package designs (a, b, c—see figure)
■ Three brand names (K2R, Glory, Bissell)
■ Three prices ($1.19, $1.39, $1.59)
■ A possible Good Housekeeping seal (Yes, No)
■ A possible money-back guarantee (Yes, No)

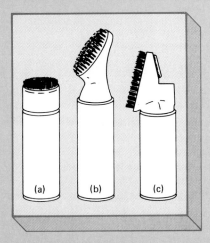

(a)   (b)   (c)

Experimental Design Used in Spot-Remover Product Evaluation   Altogether, the marketer can form 108 possible product concepts ($3 \times 3 \times 3 \times 2 \times 2$). It would be too much to ask consumers to rank or rate all of these concepts. A sample of, say, 18 contrasting product concepts can be chosen, and consumers would find it easy enough to rank them from the most preferred to the least preferred. The accompanying chart shows how one consumer ranked the eighteen product concepts.

This consumer ranked product concept 18 the highest, thus preferring package design C, the name Bissell, a price of $1.19, a Good Housekeeping seal, and a money-back guarantee.

Now suppose 100 consumers provide their rankings. A statistical program will analyze these rankings and derive a utility function measured for each attribute. Suppose the derived utility functions are those shown in the following illustration.

Results of Computer Analysis of Experimental Data   From these utility functions, we can derive a number of conclusions. Package B is the most favored, followed by C and then A; in fact, A has hardly any utility. The preferred names are Bissell, K2R, and Glory, in that order. The consumer's utility varies inversely with price. A Good Housekeeping seal is preferred, but it does not add that much utility and may not be worth the bother of obtaining it. A money-back guarantee is strongly preferred. Putting these results together, we can see that the most desirable offer would be package design B, with the brand name Bissell, selling at the price of $1.19, with a Good Housekeeping seal and a money-back guarantee. Thus we see how conjoint analysis can help the new-product researcher develop and test the attractiveness of alternative product concepts.

One Consumer's Ranking of 18 Stimulus Combinations

Card	Package Design	Brand Name	Price	Good Housekeeping Seal?	Money-Back Guarantee?	Respondent's Evaluation (rank number)
1	A	K2R	$1.19	No	No	13
2	A	Glory	1.39	No	Yes	11
3	A	Bissell	1.59	Yes	No	17
4	B	K2R	1.39	Yes	Yes	2
5	B	Glory	1.59	No	No	14
6	B	Bissell	1.19	No	No	3
7	C	K2R	1.59	No	Yes	12
8	C	Glory	1.19	Yes	No	7
9	C	Bissell	1.39	No	No	9
10	A	K2R	1.59	Yes	No	18
11	A	Glory	1.19	No	Yes	8
12	A	Bissell	1.39	No	No	15
13	B	K2R	1.19	No	No	4
14	B	Glory	1.39	Yes	No	6
15	B	Bissell	1.59	No	Yes	5
16	C	K2R	1.39	No	No	10
17	C	Glory	1.59	No	No	16
18	C	Bissell	1.19	Yes	Yes	1*

* Highest ranked.

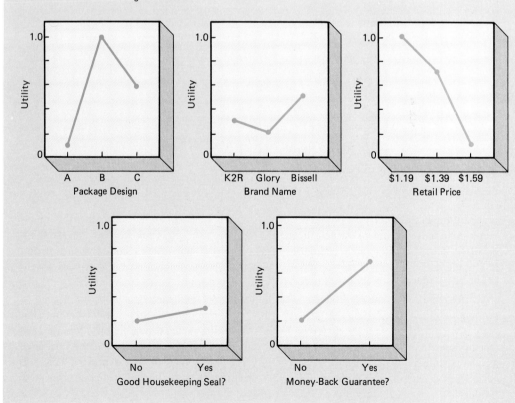

An alternative approach to data collection is the pairwise approach (also called trade-off approach). Consumers are asked to indicate their preferences for attribute levels, with two attributes taken at a time. The following table shows how a consumer filled in six trade-off matrices:

One Respondent's Trade-Off Data
(Rank Orders of Preference)

	Top Speed			Seating Capacity			Months of Warranty		
	130	100	70	2	4	6	60	12	3
Price									
$8,000	1	2	5	2	1	3	1	3	4
$12,000	3	4	6	5	4	6	2	5	6
$16,000	7	8	9	8	7	9	7	8	9
Top speed									
130 MPH				2	1	3	1	2	5
100 MPH				5	4	6	3	4	6
70 MPH				8	7	9	7	8	9
Seating capacity									
2							2	5	8
4							1	4	7
6							3	6	9

Look at the upper left matrix, which shows three car prices and three top car speeds. The consumer placed a *1* in the most preferred cell; here it is for a car priced at $8,000 with a top speed of 130 miles. The consumer placed a *2* in the next preferred cell, showing that he would prefer to pay $8,000 and give up some top speed. The consumer ranked the remaining combinations, each time showing the trade-off he would make. The other matrices were similarly filled in by the consumer. By collecting the numbers from many consumers, the researcher can derive the utility functions for each attribute: price, top speed, seating capacity, and months of warranty. These utility functions will help the researcher figure out the most ideal car to design.

SOURCE: The full profile example was taken from Paul E. Green and Yoram Wind, "New Ways to Measure Consumers' Judgments," *Harvard Business Review* (July–August, 1975), pp. 107–17. Copyright © 1975 by the President and Fellows of Harvard College; all rights reserved. The pairwise example was adapted from Richard M. Johnson, "Trade-off Analysis of Consumer Values," *Journal of Marketing Research*, May 1974, pp. 121–27.

Infrequently purchased products, such as automobiles, toasters, and industrial equipment, exhibit replacement cycles dictated either by their physical wearing out or their obsolescence associated with changing styles, features, and tastes. Sales forecasting for this product category calls for separately estimating first-time sales and replacement sales. [See Figure 14-6(b).]

Frequently purchased products, such as consumer and industrial nondurables, have product life-cycle sales resembling Figure 14-6(c). The number of first-time buyers initially increases and then decreases as fewer are left (assuming a fixed population). Repeat purchases occur soon, providing that the product satisfies some fraction of people who become steady customers. The sales curve eventually falls to a plateau representing a level of steady repeat-purchase volume; by this time the product is no longer in the class of new products.

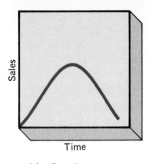

(a) One-time
    purchased product

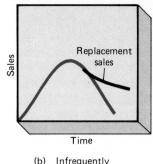

(b) Infrequently
    purchased product

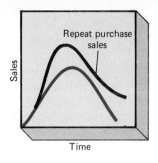

(c) Frequently
    purchased product

FIGURE 14-6
Product Life-Cycle Sales for Three Types of Products

Estimating First-Time Sales The first task, regardless of the type of product, is to estimate first-time purchases of the new product in each period. Three examples of methods for estimating first-time purchases are shown in Exhibit 14-4.

Estimating Replacement Sales To estimate replacement sales, management has to research the *survival-age distribution* of its product. The low end of the distribution indicates when the first replacement sales will take place. The actual timing of replacement will be influenced by the customer's economic outlook, cash flow, and product alternatives as well as the company's prices, financing terms, and sales effort. Since replacement sales are difficult to estimate before the product is in actual use, some manufacturers base their decision to launch a new product solely on their estimate of first-time sales.

Estimating Repeat Sales For a frequently purchased new product, the seller has to estimate repeat sales as well as first-time sales. That is because the unit value of frequently purchased products is low, and repeat purchases take place soon after the introduction. A high rate of repeat purchasing means that customers are satisfied; sales are likely to stay high even after all first-time purchases take place. The seller should note the percentage of repeat purchases that take place in each *repeat-purchase class*: those who buy once, twice, three times, and so on. Some products and brands are bought a few times and dropped. It is important to estimate whether the repeat-purchase ratio is likely to rise or fall, and at what rate, with deeper repeat-purchase classes.[21]

Estimating Costs and Profits After preparing the sales forecast, management can estimate the expected costs and profits of this venture. The costs are estimated by the R&D, manufacturing, marketing, and finance departments. Table 14-3 illustrates a five-year projection of sales, costs, and profits for the instant breakfast drink product.

Row 1 shows the projected sales revenue over the five-year period. The company expects to sell $11,889,000 (approximately 500,000 cases at $24 per case) in the first year. Sales are expected to rise around 28 percent in each of the next two years, increase by 47 percent in the fourth year, and then slow down to 15 percent growth in the fifth year. Behind this sales projection is a set of assumptions about the rate of market growth, the company's market share, and the factory-realized price.

EXHIBIT 14-4

Estimating First-Time Purchases of New Products— Three Examples

Medical Equipment A medical-equipment manufacturer developed a new instrument for analyzing blood specimens. The company identified three market segments—hospitals, clinics, and unaffiliated laboratories. For each segment, management defined the minimum-size facility that would buy this instrument. Then it estimated the number of facilities in each segment. It reduced the number by the estimated purchase probability, which varied from segment to segment. It then summed the remaining number of potential customers and called this the *market potential. Market penetration* was then estimated, based on the planned advertising and personal selling per period, the rate of favorable word of mouth, the price of the machine, and the activity of competitors. These two estimates were multiplied to estimate new-product sales.

Room Air Conditioners Models of epidemics (sometimes called contagion models) provide a useful analogy to the new-product diffusion process. Bass has used an epidemic equation to forecast sales of new appliances, including room air conditioners, refrigerators, home freezers, black-and-white television, and power lawn mowers.[*] He used sales data for the first few years of product introduction to estimate sales for the subsequent years, until replacement demand became a major factor. His sales projection for room air conditioners fit the pattern of actual sales with a coefficient of determination, $R^2 = 0.92$. The predicted time of peak was 8.6 years as against an actual time of peak of 7.0 years. The predicted magnitude of peak was 1.9 million as against an actual peak of 1.8 million.

Consumer Nondurables Fourt and Woodlock developed a first-time sales model that they tested with several new consumer-nondurable products.[†] Their observation of new-product market-penetration rates showed that (1) cumulative sales approached a limiting penetration level of less than 100 percent of all households and (2) the successive increments of gain declined. Their equation is

$$q_t = r\bar{q}(1 - r)^{t-1} \qquad (14\text{-}1)$$

where:

q_t = percentage of total U.S. households expected to try the product in period t
r = rate of penetration of untapped potential
$\bar{q}$ = percentage of total U.S. households expected to eventually try the new product
t = time period

Assume that it is estimated that 40 percent of all households will eventually try a new product ($\bar{q} = 0.4$). Furthermore, in each period 30 percent of the remaining new-buyer potential is penetrated ($r = 0.3$) The percentages of U.S. households trying the product in the first four periods are:

$$q_1 = r\bar{q}(1 - r)^{1-1} = (0.3)(0.4)(0.7^0) = 0.120$$
$$q_2 = r\bar{q}(1 - r)^{2-1} = (0.3)(0.4)(0.7^1) = 0.084$$
$$q_3 = r\bar{q}(1 - r)^{3-1} = (0.3)(0.4)(0.7^2) = 0.059$$
$$q_4 = r\bar{q}(1 - r)^{4-1} = (0.3)(0.4)(0.7^3) = 0.041$$

As time moves on, the incremental trial percentage moves toward zero. To estimate dollar sales from new buyers in any period, the estimated trial rate for any period is multiplied by the total number of U.S. households times the expected first-purchase expenditure per household of the product.

[*] Frank M. Bass, "A New Product Growth Model for Consumer Durables," *Management Science*, January 1969, pp. 215–17.
[†] Louis A. Fourt and Joseph N. Woodlock, "Early Prediction of Market Success for New Grocery Products," *Journal of Marketing*, October 1960, pp. 31–38.

TABLE 14-3
Projected Five-Year Cash-Flow Statement (in Thousands of Dollars)

	Year 0	Year 1	Year 2	Year 3	Year 4	Year 5
1. Sales revenue	0	11,889	15,381	19,654	28,253	32,491
2. Cost of goods sold	0	3,981	5,150	6,581	9,461	10,880
3. Gross margin	0	7,908	10,231	13,073	18,792	21,611
4. Development costs	−3,500	0	0	0	0	0
5. Marketing costs	0	8,000	6,460	8,255	11,866	13,646
6. Allocated overhead	0	1,189	1,538	1,965	2,825	3,249
7. Gross contribution	−3,500	−1,281	2,233	2,853	4,101	4,716
8. Supplementary contribution	0	0	0	0	0	0
9. Net contribution	−3,500	−1,281	2,233	2,853	4,101	4,716
10. Discounted contribution (15%)	−3,500	−1,113	1,691	1,877	2,343	2,346
11. Cumulative discounted cash flow	−3,500	−4,613	−2,922	−1,045	1,298	3,644

Row 2 shows the *cost of goods sold*, which hovers around 33 percent of sales revenue. This cost is found by estimating the average cost of labor, ingredients, and packaging per case.

Row 3 shows the expected *gross margin*, which is the difference between sales revenue and cost of goods sold.

Row 4 shows anticipated *development costs* of $3.5 million. The development costs consist of three components. The first is the *product-development cost* of researching, developing, and testing the physical product. The second is the *marketing research costs* of fine tuning the marketing program and assessing the market's likely response. It covers the estimated costs of package testing, in-home placement testing, name testing, and test marketing. The third is the *manufacturing-development costs* of new equipment, new or renovated plant, and inventory investment.

Row 5 shows the estimated *marketing costs* over the five-year period to cover advertising, sales promotion, and marketing research and an amount allocated for sales-force coverage and marketing administration. In the first year, marketing costs stand at 67 percent of sales, and by the fifth year are estimated to run at 42 percent of sales.

Row 6 shows the *allocated overhead* to this new product to cover its share of the cost of executive salaries, heat, light, and so on.

Row 7, the *gross contribution*, is found by subtracting the preceding three costs from the gross margin. Years 0 and 1 involve losses, and thereafter the gross contribution becomes positive and is expected to run as high as 15 percent of sales by the fifth year.

Row 8, *supplementary contribution*, is used to list any change in income from other company products caused by the introduction of the new product. It has two components. *Dragalong income* is additional income on other company products resulting from adding this product to the line. *Cannibalized income* is the reduced income on other company products resulting from adding this product to the line.[22]

Row 9 shows the *net contribution*, which in this case is the same as the gross contribution.

Row 10 shows the *discounted contribution*, namely, the present value of each future contribution discounted at 15 percent per annum. For example, the company will not receive $4,716,000 until the fifth year, which means that it is worth only $2,346,000 today if the company can earn 15 percent on its money.[23]

Finally, row 11 shows the *cumulative discounted cash flow*, which is the cumulation of the annual contributions in row 10. This cash flow is the key series on which management bases its decision on whether to go forward into product development or drop the project. Two things are of central interest. The first is the *maximum investment exposure*, which is the highest loss that the project can create. We see that the company will be in a maximum loss position of $4,613,000 in year 1; this will be the company's loss if it terminates the project. The second is the *payback period*, which is the time when the company recovers all of its investment including the built-in return of 15 percent. The payback period here is approximately three and a half years. Management therefore has to decide whether it can expose itself to a maximum investment loss of $4.6 million and wait three and a half years for payback.

Companies use other financial measures to evaluate the merit of a new-product proposal. The simplest is break-even analysis, where management estimates how many cases of the product the company would have to sell to break even with the given price and cost structure. If management believed that the company could sell at least the break-even number of cases, it would normally move the project into product development.

The most complex method is *risk analysis*. Here three estimates (optimistic, pessimistic, and most likely) are obtained for each uncertain variable affecting profitability under an assumed marketing environment and marketing strategy for the planning period. The computer simulates possible outcomes and computes a rate-of-return probability distribution, showing the range of possible rates of returns and their probabilities.[24]

PRODUCT DEVELOPMENT

If the product concept passes the business test, it moves to R&D and/or engineering to be developed into a physical product. Up to now it has existed only as a word description, a drawing, or a very crude mock-up. This step calls for a large jump in investment, which dwarfs the idea-evaluation costs incurred in the earlier stages. This stage will answer whether the product idea can be translated into a technically and commercially feasible product. If not, the company's accumulated investment will be lost except for any useful information gained in the process.

The R&D department will develop one or more physical versions of the product concept. It hopes to find a prototype that satisfies the following criteria: (1) the consumers see it as embodying the key attributes described in the product-concept statement; (2) the prototype performs safely under normal use and conditions; (3) the prototype can be produced for the budgeted manufacturing costs.

Developing a successful prototype can take days, weeks, months, or even years. Designing a new commercial aircraft, for example, will take several years of development work. Even developing a new taste formula can take time. For example, the Maxwell House Division of General Foods discovered that consumers wanted a brand of coffee that was "bold, vigorous, deep tasting." Its laboratory technicians spent over four months working with various coffee blends and flavors to formulate a corresponding taste. It turned out to be too expensive to produce, and the company "cost reduced" the blend to meet the target manufacturing cost. This compromised the taste, however, and the new coffee brand did not do well in the market.

The lab scientists must not only design the required functional characteristics but also know how to communicate the psychological aspects through *physical cues*. This requires knowing how consumers react to different colors, sizes, weights, and other physical cues. In the case of a mouthwash, a yellow color supports an "antiseptic" claim (Listerine), a red color supports a "refreshing" claim (Lavoris), and a green color supports a "cool" claim (Micrin). Or to support the claim that a lawn mower is powerful, the lab people have to design a heavy frame and a fairly noisy engine. Marketers need to supply lab people with information on what attributes are sought by consumers and how consumers judge whether these attributes are present.

When the prototypes are ready, they must be put through rigorous functional and consumer tests. The *functional tests* are conducted under laboratory and field conditions to make sure that the product performs safely and effectively. The new aircraft must fly; the new snack food must be shelf stable; the new drug must not create dangerous side effects. Functional product testing of new drugs now takes years of laboratory work with animal subjects and then human subjects before the drugs obtain Federal Drug Administration approval. In the case of equipment testing, consider the Bissell Company's experience testing a combination electric vacuum and floor scrubber:

> . . . four were left with the research and development department for continued tests on such things as water lift, motor lift, effectiveness in cleaning, and dust bag design. The other eight were sent to the company's advertising agency for tests by a panel of fifty housewives. The research and development department found some serious problems in their further tests of the product. The life of the motor was not sufficiently long, the filter bag did not fit properly, and the scrubber foot was not correct. Similarly, the consumer tests brought in many consumer dissatisfactions that had not been anticipated; the unit was too heavy, the vacuum did not glide easily enough, and the scrubber left some residue on the floor after use.[25]

Consumer testing can take a variety of forms, from bringing consumers into a laboratory to test the product to giving them samples to use in their homes. *In-home product-placement tests* are common with products ranging from ice cream flavors to new appliances. When Du Pont developed its new synthetic carpeting, it installed free carpeting in several homes in exchange for the homeowners' willingness to report their likes and dislikes about synthetic carpeting. Consumer-preference testing draws on a variety of techniques, such as simple ranking, paired comparisons, and rating scales, each with its own advantages and biases (see Exhibit 14-5).

EXHIBIT 14-5

Methods for Measuring Consumer Preferences

Suppose a consumer is shown three items—*A*, *B*, and *C*. They might be three automobiles or advertisements or names of political candidates. There are three methods—simple rank ordering, paired comparison, and monadic rating—for measuring an individual's preferences for these items.

The *simple rank order* method asks the consumer to rank the three items in order of preference.

The consumer might respond with $A > B > C$. This method does not reveal how intensely the consumer feels about each item. The consumer may not like any one of them very much. Nor does it indicate how much the consumer prefers one object to another. Also, this method is difficult to use when there are many objects.

The *paired comparison* method calls for presenting a set of items to the consumer, two at a time, asking which one is preferred in each pair. Thus the consumer could be presented with the pairs *AB*, *AC*, and *BC* and say that he or she prefers *A* to *B*, *A* to *C*, and *B* to *C*. Then we could conclude that $A > B > C$. Paired comparisons offer two major advantages. First, people find it easy to state their preference between items taken two at a time. The second advantage is that the paired comparison method allows the consumer to concentrate intensely on the two items, noting their differences and similarities.

The *monadic rating* method asks the consumer to rate his or her liking of each product on a scale. Suppose the following seven-point scale is used:

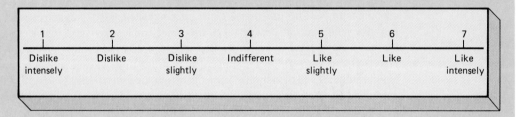

1	2	3	4	5	6	7
Dislike intensely	Dislike	Dislike slightly	Indifferent	Like slightly	Like	Like intensely

Suppose the consumer returns the following ratings: $A = 6$, $B = 5$, $C = 3$. This yields more information than the previous methods. We can derive the individual's preference order (i.e., $A > B > C$) and even know the qualitative levels of his or her preference for each and the rough distance between preferences. This method is also easy for respondents to use, especially when there is a large set of objects to evaluate.

MARKET TESTING

After management is satisfied with the product's functional performance, the product is ready to be dressed up with a brand name, packaging, and a preliminary marketing program to test it in more-authentic consumer settings. (Branding and packaging decisions are discussed in Chapter 15.) The purpose of market testing is to learn how consumers and dealers react to handling, using, and repurchasing the actual product and how large the market is.

Not all companies choose the route of market testing. A company officer of Revlon, Inc., stated:

> In our field—primarily higher-priced cosmetics not geared for mass distribution—it would be unnecessary for us to market test. When we develop a new product, say an improved liquid makeup, we know it's going to sell because we're familiar with the field. And we've got 1,500 demonstrators in department stores to promote it.

Most companies, however, know market testing can yield valuable information about buyers, dealers, marketing program effectiveness, market potential, and other matters. The main issues are, How much market testing? and What kind?

The amount of market testing is influenced by the *investment cost* and *risk* on the one hand, and the *time pressure* and *research cost* on the other. High investment/risk products deserve to be market tested so as not to make a mistake; the cost of the market tests will be an insignificant percentage of the project cost. High-risk products—those that create new-product categories (first instant breakfast) or have novel features (first fluoride toothpaste)—warrant more market testing than modified products (another toothpaste brand). But the amount of market testing may be severely reduced if the company is under great pressure to introduce its brand because the season is just starting or because competitors are about to launch their brands. The company may prefer the risk of a product failure to the risk of losing distribution or market penetration on a highly successful product. The cost of market testing will also affect how much is done and what kind.

Market-testing methods differ in testing consumer versus industrial products.

Consumer-Goods Market Testing

In testing consumer products, the company aims to estimate four variables, namely, *trial*, *first repeat*, *adoption*, and *purchase frequency*. The company hopes to find all of these at high levels. In some cases, it will find many consumers trying the product but few rebuying it, showing a lack of product satisfaction. Or it might find high first-time repurchase but then a rapid wear-out in the repeat purchase rate. Or it might find high permanent adoption but low frequency of purchase (as with gourmet frozen foods) because the buyers use the product only on special occasions.

In testing the trade, the company wants to learn how many and what types of dealers will handle the product, under what terms, and with what shelf-position commitments.

The major methods of consumer-goods market testing, from the least to the most costly, are described in the following paragraphs.

Sales-Wave Research   In sales-wave research, consumers who initially try the product at no cost are reoffered the product, or a competitor's products, at slightly reduced prices. They may be reoffered the product as many as three to five times (sales waves), the company noting how many consumers selected that company's product again and their reported level of satisfaction. Sales-wave research can also include exposing consumers to one or more advertising concepts in rough form to see what impact the advertising has on repeat purchase.

Sales-wave research enables the company to estimate the repeat-purchase rate under conditions where consumers spend their own money and choose among competing brands. The company can also gauge the impact of alternative advertising concepts on producing repeat purchases. Finally, sales-wave research can be implemented quickly, conducted under relative competitive security, and carried out without needing to develop final packaging and advertising.

On the other hand, sales-wave research does not indicate the trial rates that would be achieved with different sales promotion incentives, since the consumers are preselected to try the product. Nor does it indicate the brand's power to gain distribution and favorable shelf position from the trade.

Simulated Store Technique   The simulated store technique (also called "laboratory test markets," "purchase laboratories," or "accelerated test marketing") calls for finding thirty to forty shoppers (at a shopping center or elsewhere) and inviting them to a brief screening of some television commercials. Included are a number of well-known commercials and some new ones, and they cover a range of products. One commercial advertises the new product, but it is not singled out for attention. The consumers are given a small amount of money and invited into a store where they may use the money to buy any items or keep the money. The company notes how many consumers buy the new product and competing brands. This provides a measure of the commercial's relative effectiveness in producing trial against competing commercials. The consumers are reconvened and are asked the reasons for their purchases or nonpurchases. Some weeks later they are reinterviewed by phone to determine product attitudes, usage, satisfaction, and repurchase intention and are offered an opportunity to repurchase any products.

This method has several advantages, including the measuring of advertising effectiveness and trial rates (and repeat rates if extended), speedy results, and competitive security. The results are usually incorporated into mathematical models to project ultimate sales levels. Marketing research firms that offer this service have reported surprisingly accurate predictions of sales levels of products that are subsequently launched in the market.[26]

Controlled Test Marketing   Several research firms have arranged a controlled panel of stores that have agreed to carry new products for a certain fee. The company with the new product specifies the number of stores and geographical locations it wants. The research firm delivers the product to the participating stores and controls shelf location, number of facings, displays and point-of-purchase promotions, and pricing, according to prespecified plans. Sales results can be audited both from shelf movement and from consumer diaries. The company can also test small-scale advertising in local newspapers during the test.

Controlled testing (also called ''minimarket testing'') allows the company to test the impact of in-store factors and limited advertising on consumers' buying behavior without involving consumers directly. A sample of consumers can be interviewed later to gather their impressions of the product. The company does not have to use its own sales force, give trade allowances, or ''buy'' distribution. On the other hand, controlled test marketing does not challenge the company to sell the trade on carrying the new product. This technique also exposes the product to competitors.

Test Markets   Test markets are the ultimate way to test a new consumer product in a situation resembling the one that would be faced in a full-scale launching of the product. The company usually works with an outside research firm to locate a few representative test cities in which the company's sales force will try to sell the trade on carrying the product and giving it good shelf exposure. The company will put on a full advertising and promotion campaign in these markets similar to the one that would be used in national marketing. It is a chance to do a dress rehearsal of the total plan. Test marketing can cost the company several hundred thousand dollars, depending on the number of cities tested, the duration of the test, and the amount of data the company wants to collect. Exhibit 14-6 shows the major decisions called for in test marketing.

Test marketing can yield several benefits. Its primary benefit is to yield a *more reliable forecast of future sales*. If product sales fall below target levels in the test market, the company must drop or modify the product or the marketing program.

A second benefit is the *pretesting of alternative marketing plans*. Some years ago Colgate-Palmolive used a different marketing mix in each of four cities to market a new soap product. The four approaches were (1) an average amount of advertising coupled with free samples distributed door to door, (2) heavy advertising plus samples, (3) an average amount of advertising linked with mailed redeemable coupons, and (4) an average amount of advertising with no special introductory offer. The third alternative generated the best profit level, although not the highest sales level.

Through test marketing, the company may discover a product fault that escaped attention in the product-development stage. It may pick up valuable clues to distribution-

EXHIBIT 14-6

Decisions Facing Management in Setting Up Test Markets

1. **How many test cities?** Most tests use between two and six cities, with an average of four. A larger number of cities should be used (1) the greater the maximum possible loss and/or the probability of loss from going national, (2) the greater the number of contending/marketing strategies and/or the greater the uncertainty surrounding which is best, (3) the greater the regional differences, and (4) the greater the chance of calculated test-market interference by competitors.

2. **Which cities?** No city is a perfect microcosm of the nation as a whole. Some cities, however, typify aggregate national or regional characteristics better than others, such as Syracuse, Dayton, Peoria, and Des Moines. Each company develops its own test-city selection criteria. One company looks for test cities that have diversified industry, good media coverage, cooperative chain stores, average competitive activity, and no evidence of being overtested. Additional test-city selection criteria may be introduced because of the special characteristics of the product. Patio Foods, in testing a new line of frozen Mexican dinners, selected cities according to the incidence of travel to Mexico, the existence of a Spanish-language press, and good retail sales of prepared chili and frozen Chinese food.

3. **Length of test?** Test markets last anywhere from a few months to several years. The longer the product's average repurchase period, the longer the test period necessary to observe repeat-purchase rates. On the other hand, the period should be cut down if competitors are rushing to the market.

4. **What information?** Management must decide on the type of information to collect in relation to its value and cost. *Warehouse shipment data* will show gross inventory buying but will not indicate weekly sales at retail. *Store audits* will show actual retail sales and competitors' market shares but will not reveal the characteristics of the buyers of the different brands. *Consumer panels* will indicate which people are buying which brands and their loyalty and switching rates. *Buyer surveys* will yield in-depth information about consumer attitudes, usage, and satisfaction. Among other things that can be researched are trade attitudes, retail distribution, and the effectiveness of advertising, promotion, and point-of-sale material.

5. **What action to take?** If the test markets show a high trial and high repurchase rate, this indicates a GO–decision. If the test markets show a high trial and a low repurchase rate, the customers are not satisfied, and the product should be redesigned or dropped. If the test markets show a low trial and a high repurchase rate, the product is satisfying, but more people have to try it; this means increasing advertising and sales promotion. Finally, if the trial and repurchase rates are both low, then the product should be dropped.

level problems. And the company may gain better insight into the behavior of different market segments.

In spite of the benefits of test marketing, some experts question its value. Achenbaum lists the following concerns:

■ There is the problem of obtaining a set of markets that is reasonably representative of the country as a whole.

■ There is the problem of translating national media plans into local equivalents.

■ There is the problem of estimating what is going to happen next year based on what has happened in this year's competitive environment.

■ There is the problem of competitive knowledge of your test and of deciding whether any local counteractivities are representative of what competition will do nationally at a later date.

■ There is the problem of extraneous and uncontrollable factors such as economic conditions and weather.[27]

Achenbaum contends that test marketing's main value lies not in sales forecasting but in learning about unsuspected problems and opportunities connected with the new product. He points to the large number of products that failed after successful test-market results. Some large companies are skipping the test-marketing stage and relying on other market-testing methods.[28] (However, see Exhibit 14-7.)

Industrial-Goods Market Testing

New industrial goods typically undergo extensive *product testing* in the labs to measure performance, reliability, design, and operating cost. Following satisfactory results, many companies will commercialize the product by listing it in the catalog and turning it over to the sales force. Today, however, an increasing number of companies are turning to *market testing* as an intermediate step. Market testing can indicate the product's perfor-

---

EXHIBIT 14-7

Not "Whether to Test" But "How to Test"— That Is the Question: The Case of New Coke

In May 1985, the Coca-Cola Company made what now appears to have been a spectacular marketing blunder. After ninety-nine successful years, it set aside its longstanding rule—"Don't mess with Mother Coke"—and dropped its original formula Coke! In its place came New Coke with a sweeter, smoother taste. The company boldly announced the exciting new taste with a flurry of advertising and publicity.

At first, New Coke sold well. But sales soon went flat. Coke began receiving more than fifteen hundred phone calls and many sacks of mail each day from angry consumers. A group called Old Cola Drinkers staged protests, handed out T-shirts, and threatened to start a class-action suit unless Coca-Cola brought back the old formula or made it public. Business analysts and the media debated the decision, and some marketing experts predicted that New Coke would be the "Edsel of the Eighties."

In mid-July 1985, after just two months, the Coca-Cola Company brought old Coke back. Called Coke Classic, it was sold side by side with New Coke on supermarket shelves. The company said that New Coke would remain its "flagship" brand, but consumers had a different idea. By the end of 1985, Classic was outselling New Coke in supermarkets by two to one. By mid-1986, the company's two largest fountain accounts, McDonald's and Kentucky Fried Chicken, had returned to serving Coke Classic in their restaurants. Thus Coke Classic again became the company's main brand and New Coke became the also-ran.

But why was New Coke introduced in the first place? And what went wrong? Many analysts blame the blunder on poor marketing research.

In the early 1980s, though Coke was still the leading soft drink, it was slowly losing market share to Pepsi. For years, Pepsi had successfully mounted the "Pepsi Challenge," a series of televised taste tests showing that consumers preferred the sweeter taste of Pepsi. By early 1985, though Coke led in the overall market, Pepsi led in share of supermarket sales by 2 percent. (That doesn't sound like much, but 2 percent of the huge soft-drink market amounts to $600 million in retail sales!) Coca-Cola had to do something to stop the erosion of its market share. The solution appeared to be a change in Coke's taste.

Coca-Cola began the largest new-product research project in the company's history. It spent over two years and $4 million on research before settling on a new formula. It conducted some two hundred thousand taste tests—thirty thousand on the final formula alone. In the blind tests, 60 percent of consumers chose the new Coke over the old, and 52 percent chose it over Pepsi. Research showed that New Coke would be a winner and the company introduced it with confidence. So what happened?

Looking back, Coke's marketing research appears to have been too narrowly focused. The research looked only at taste; it did not explore how consumers felt about dropping the old Coke and replacing it with a new version. As one expert noted, the research consisted mostly of "blind comparisons, which took no account of the total product . . . name, history, packaging, cultural heritage, image—a rich mix of tangible and intangible." To many people, Coke stands beside baseball, hotdogs, and apple pie as an American institution. It represents the very fabric of America. The company failed to measure these deep emotional ties, but Coke's symbolic meaning was more important to many consumers than its taste. More complete concept testing would have detected these strong emotions.

Coke's managers may also have used poor judgment in interpreting the research findings and planning strategies around them. For example, they took the finding that 60 percent of consumers preferred New Coke's taste to mean that the new product would win in the marketplace. But test results also showed that 40 percent still wanted the old Coke. By dropping the old Coke, the company trampled on the taste buds of its large core of loyal Coke drinkers who did not want a change. The company might have been wiser to leave the old Coke alone and introduce New Coke as a brand extension, as was later done successfully with Cherry Coke.

Furthermore, the New Coke should not have gone national immediately. Too much was at stake. New Coke should have been introduced regionally to see how well it did in repeat sales.

Some observers thought that Coke's managers had pulled off a smart move rather than a marketing blunder. Supermarkets chains would have resisted adding another Coke flavor on their shelves. By first withdrawing its original Coke and then reintroducing it, the company got two brands on the shelf, quite a coup in the bitter struggle for shelf space.

Based on numerous sources, including Betsy D. Gelb and Gabriel M. Gelb, "New Coke's Fizzle—Lessons for the Rest of Us," *Sloan Management Review*, Fall 1986; "Coke 'Family' Sales Fly as New Coke Stumbles," *Advertising Age*, January 17, 1986, pp. 1ff; and Scott Scredon and Marc Frons, "Coke's Man on the Spot: The Changes Goizueta Is Making Outweigh the Spectacular Blunder," *Business Week*, July 29, 1985, pp. 56–61. The quoted material is from Jack Honomichl, "Missing Ingredients in 'New' Coke's Research," *Advertising Age*, July 22, 1985, pp. 1ff.

mance under actual operating conditions; the key buying influences; how different buying influences react to alternative prices and sales approaches; the market potential; and the best market segments.

Test marketing is not typically used in the case of industrial products. It is too expensive to produce a sample of Concordes or new mainframe computers, let alone put them up for sale in a select market to see how well they sell. Industrial buyers will not buy durable goods without assurances of service and parts. Furthermore, marketing research firms have not built the test-market systems that are found in consumer markets. Therefore industrial-goods manufacturers have to use other methods to research the market's interest in a new industrial product.

The most common method is a *product-use test*, similar to the in-home–use test for consumer products. The manufacturer selects some potential customers, who agree to use the new product for a limited period. The manufacturer's technical people observe how these customers use the product, a practice that often exposes unanticipated problems of safety and servicing and clues the manufacturer about customer training and servicing requirements. After the test, the customer is asked to express purchase intent and other reactions.

A second common market-test method is to introduce the new industrial product at *trade shows*. Trade shows draw a large number of buyers, who view new products in a few concentrated days. The manufacturer can see how much interest buyers show in the new product, how they react to various features and terms, and how many express purchase intentions or place orders. The disadvantage is that trade shows reveal the product to competitors; therefore the manufacturer should be ready to launch the product at that point.

The new industrial product can also be tested in *distributor and dealer display rooms*, where it may stand next to the manufacturer's other products and possibly competitors' products. This method yields preference and pricing information in the normal selling atmosphere for the product. The disadvantages are that the customers may want to place orders that cannot be filled, and those customers who come in might not be representative of the target market.

Controlled or *test marketing* has been used by some manufacturers. They produce a limited supply of the product and give it to the sales force to sell in a limited set of geographical areas that will be given promotional support, printed catalog sheets, and so on. In this way, management can learn what might happen under full-scale marketing and make a more informed decision about launching.

COMMERCIALIZATION

Market testing presumably gives management enough information to make a final decision about whether to launch the new product. If the company goes ahead with commercialization, it will face its largest costs to date. The company will have to contract for manufacture or build or rent a full-scale manufacturing facility. The size of the plant will be a critical decision variable. The company can build a plant smaller than that called for by the sales forecast, to be on the safe side. That is what Quaker Oats did when it launched its 100 percent Natural breakfast cereal. The demand so exceeded the company's sales forecast that for about a year it could not supply enough product to the stores. Although it was gratified with the response, the low forecast cost it a considerable amount of lost profits.

Another major cost is marketing. To introduce a major new consumer packaged good into the national market, the company may have to spend between $10 million and $50 million in advertising and promotion in the first year. In the introduction of new food products, marketing expenditures typically represent 57 percent of sales during the first year.

When (Timing)   In commercializing a new product, *market entry timing* can be critical. Suppose a company has almost completed the development work on its new product and hears about a competitor nearing the end of its development work. The company faces three choices:

1. **First entry.** The first firm entering a market usually enjoys "first mover advantages" consisting of locking up some key distributors and customers and gaining reputational leadership. On the other hand, if the product is rushed to the market before it is thoroughly debugged, the company can acquire a flawed image.
2. **Parallel entry.** The firm might decide to time its entry with the competitor. If the competitor is rushing to launch, the company does the same so that it can neutralize the competitor's gaining of first-mover advantages. If the competitor is taking time, the company might also take time, using it to refine its product. The company might want the promotional costs of launching to be borne by both of them.
3. **Late entry.** The firm might deliberately delay its launch until after the competitor has entered. There are three potential advantages. The competitor will have borne the cost of educating the market. The competitor's product may reveal faults that the late entrant can avoid. And the company can learn how big the market might be.

The timing decision involves other considerations as well. If the new product replaces another product of the company, the company might want to delay the introduction until the old product's stock is drawn down. If the product is highly seasonal, the new product might be held back until the right season. All said, market entry timing deserves careful thought.[29]

**Where
(Geographical
Strategy)**

The company must decide whether to launch the new product in a *single locality*, a *region*, *several regions*, the *national market*, or the *international market*. Few companies have the confidence, capital, and capacity to launch new products into full national distribution. They will develop a *planned market rollout* over time. Small companies, in particular, will select an attractive city and put on a blitz campaign to enter the market. They will enter other cities one at a time. Large companies will introduce their product into a whole region and then move to the next region. Companies with national distribution networks, such as auto companies, will launch their new models in the national market unless there are production shortages.

In rollout marketing, the company has to rate the alternative markets for their attractiveness. The candidate markets can be listed as rows, and rollout attractiveness criteria can be listed as columns. The major rating criteria are *market potential*, *company's local reputation*, *cost of filling the pipeline*, *quality of research data in that area*, *influence of area on other areas*, and *competitive penetration*. In this way, the company determines the prime markets and develops a geographical rollout plan.

The factor of competitive presence is very important. Suppose McDonald's wants to launch a new chain of fast-food pizza parlors. Suppose Shakey's, a formidable competitor, is strongly entrenched on the East Coast. Another pizza chain is entrenched on the East Coast but is weak. The Midwest is the battleground between two other chains. The South is open, but Shakey's is planning to move in. We can see that McDonald's faces quite a complex decision in choosing a rollout strategy.

**To Whom
(Target-market
Prospects)**

Within the rollout markets, the company must target its distribution and promotion to the best prospect groups. Presumably the company has already profiled the prime prospects on the basis of earlier market testing. Prime prospects for a new consumer product would ideally have the following characteristics: They would be early adopters; they would be heavy users; they would be opinion leaders and would talk favorably about the product; and they could be reached at a low cost.[30] Few groups have all of these characteristics. The company can rate the various prospect groups on these characteristics and target to the best prospect group. The aim is to generate high sales as soon as possible to motivate the sales force and attract other new prospects.

**How
(Introductory
Market Strategy)**

The company must develop an action plan for introducing the new product into the rollout markets. It must allocate the marketing budget among the marketing-mix elements and sequence the various activities. For example:

> In May 1986, Polaroid launched its new Spectra instant camera with a $40 million first-year advertising budget. Billboard ads were put up in twenty-five markets as part of a teaser campaign, followed by a saturation print and television campaign aiming to generate twenty-five exposures for 90 percent of Spectra's target audience.

To sequence and coordinate the many activities involved in launching a new product, management can use various network-planning techniques, such as critical path scheduling (see pages 128–29).

A summary of the various steps and decisions in the new-product-development process is presented in Figure 14-7.

FIGURE 14-7
Summary of the New-Product-Development Decision Process

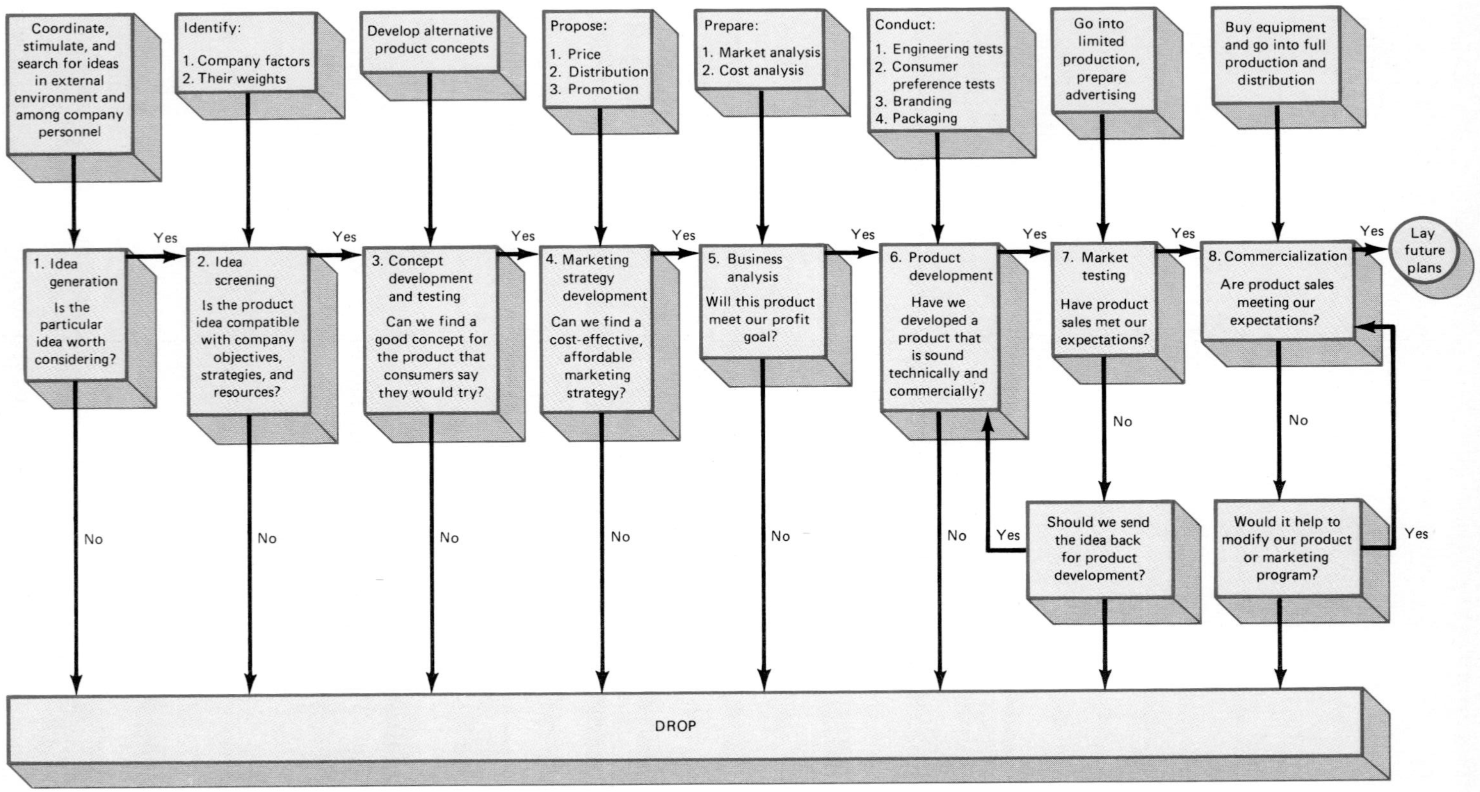

THE CONSUMER-ADOPTION PROCESS

The *consumer-adoption process* begins where the *firm's innovation process* leaves off. It describes how potential customers learn about new products, try them, and adopt or reject them. Management must understand this process in order to build an effective strategy for early market penetration. The *consumer-adoption process* is later followed by the *consumer-loyalty process*, which is the concern of the established producer.

Years ago, new-product marketers used a *mass-market approach* in launching their product. They would distribute the product everywhere and advertise it to everyone on the notion that most people are potential buyers. The mass-market approach, however, has two drawbacks: It calls for heavy marketing expenditures, and it involves many wasted exposures to people who are not potential consumers. These drawbacks led to a second approach, *heavy-user target marketing*, where the product is initially aimed at the heavy users. This approach makes sense, provided heavy users are identifiable and among the first to try the new product. But even within the heavy-user group, consumers differ in their interest in new products and brands; many heavy users are quite loyal to their existing brands. Certain heavy users are earlier adopters than others. Many new-product marketers now aim at those consumers who are likely to be the earlier adopters. According to *early-adopter theory*:

■ Persons within a target market differ in the amount of elapsed time between their exposure to a new product and their trial.
■ Early adopters share some traits that differentiate them from late adopters.
■ Efficient media exist for reaching early-adopter types.
■ Early adopters tend to be opinion leaders and helpful in "advertising" the new product to other potential buyers.

We now turn to the theory of innovation diffusion and consumer adoption, which provides clues to identifying early adopters.

Concepts in Innovation Diffusion and Adoption

An *innovation* refers to any good, service, or idea that is *perceived* by someone as new. The idea may have a long history, but it is an innovation to the person who sees it as new.

Innovations take time to spread through the social system. Rogers defines *diffusion process* as "the spread of a new idea from its source of invention or creation to its ultimate users or adopters."[31] The *adoption process*, on the other hand, focuses on "the mental process through which an individual passes from first hearing about an innovation to final adoption." *Adoption* is the decision of an individual to become a regular user to a product.

We will now examine the main generalizations drawn from hundreds of studies of how people accept new ideas.

Stages in the Adoption Process

Adopters of new products have been observed to move through the following five stages:

■ *Awareness.* The consumer becomes aware of the innovation but lacks information about it.
■ *Interest.* The consumer is stimulated to seek information about the innovation.

- **Evaluation.** The consumer considers whether it would make sense to try the innovation.
- **Trial.** The consumer tries the innovation on a small scale to improve his or her estimate of its value.
- **Adoption.** The consumer decides to make full and regular use of the innovation.

This progression suggests that the new-product marketer should think about how to facilitate consumer movement through these stages. An electric-dishwasher manufacturer might discover that many consumers are stuck in the interest stage; they do not move to the trial stage because of their uncertainty and the large investment cost. But these same consumers would be willing to use an electric dishwasher on a trial basis for a small monthly fee. The manufacturer should consider offering a trial-use plan with option to buy.

Individual Difference in Innovativeness

People differ markedly in their readiness to try new products. Rogers defines a person's *innovativeness* as "the degree to which an individual is relatively earlier in adopting new ideas than the other members of his social system." In each product area, there are apt to be "consumption pioneers" and early adopters. Some women are the first to adopt new clothing fashions or new appliances, such as the microwave oven; some doctors are the first to prescribe new medicines; and some farmers are the first to adopt new farming methods.

And other individuals adopt new products much later. People can be classified into the adopter categories shown in Figure 14-8. The adoption process is represented as a normal distribution when plotted over time. After a slow start, an increasing number of people adopt the innovation, the number reaches a peak, and then it diminishes as fewer nonadopters remain. Innovators are defined as the first $2\frac{1}{2}$ percent of the buyers to adopt a new idea; the early adopters are the next $13\frac{1}{2}$ percent who adopt the new idea; and so forth.

Rogers sees the five adopter groups as differing in their value orientations. Innovators are *venturesome*; they are willing to try new ideas at some risk. Early adopters are guided

FIGURE 14-8
Adopter Categorization on the Basis of Relative Time of Adoption of Innovations
SOURCE: Redrawn from Everett M. Rogers, *Diffusion of Innovations* (New York: Free Press, 1962), p. 162.

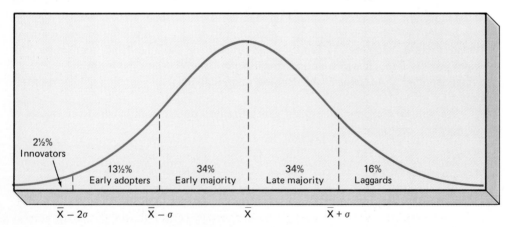

Time of adoption of innovations

by *respect*; they are opinion leaders in their community and adopt new ideas early but carefully. The early majority are *deliberate*; they adopt new ideas before the average person, although they rarely are leaders. The late majority are *skeptical*; they adopt an innovation only after a majority of people have tried it. Finally, laggards are *tradition bound*; they are suspicious of changes, mix with other tradition-bound people, and adopt the innovation only because it has now taken on a measure of tradition itself.

This adopter classification suggests that an innovating firm should research the demographic, psychographic, and media characteristics of innovators and early adopters and should direct communications specifically to them. Identifying early adopters is not always easy. No one has demonstrated the existence of a general personality trait called innovativeness. Individuals tend to be innovators in certain areas and laggards in others. We can think of a businessman who dresses conservatively but who delights in trying unfamiliar cuisines. The marketer's challenge is to identify the characteristics of likely early adopters in its product area. For example, studies show that innovative farmers are likely to be better educated and more efficient than noninnovative farmers. Innovative housewives are more gregarious and usually higher in social status than noninnovative housewives. Certain communities tend to have more people who are early adopters. Rogers offered the following hypotheses about early adopters:

> The relatively earlier adopters in a social system tend to be younger in age, have higher social status, a more favorable financial position, more specialized operations, and a different type of mental ability from later adopters. Earlier adopters utilize information sources that are more impersonal and cosmopolite than later adopters and that are in closer contact with the origin of new ideas. Earlier adopters utilize a greater number of different information sources than do later adopters. The social relationships of earlier adopters are more cosmopolite than for later adopters, and earlier adopters have more opinion leadership.[32]

Role of Personal Influence

Personal influence plays a large role in the adoption of new products. Personal influence describes the effect of product statements made by one person on another's attitude or purchase probability. According to Katz and Lazarsfeld:

> About half of the women in our sample reported that they had recently made some change from a product or brand to which they were accustomed to something new. The fact that one third of these changes involved personal influences indicates that there is also considerable traffic in marketing advice. Women consult each other for opinions about new products, about the quality of different brands, about shopping economies and the like.[33]

Although personal influence is an important factor, its significance is greater in some situations and for some individuals than for others. Personal influence is more important in the evaluation stage of the adoption process than in the other stages. It has more influence on late adopters than early adopters. And it is more important in risky situations than in safe situations.

Influence of Product Characteristics on the Rate of Adoption

The characteristics of the innovation affect its rate of adoption. Some products catch on almost overnight (e.g., frisbees), whereas others take a long time to gain acceptance (e.g., diesel-engine autos). Five characteristics are especially important in influencing the rate of adoption of an innovation. We will consider these characteristics in relation to the rate of adoption of personal computers for home use.

The first is the innovation's *relative advantage*—the degree to which it appears superior to existing products. The greater the perceived relative advantage of using a personal computer, say, in preparing income taxes and keeping financial records, the more quickly the personal computer will be adopted.

The second characteristic is the innovation's *compatibility*—the degree to which it matches the values and experiences of the individuals in the community. Personal computers, for example, are highly compatible with the lifestyles found in upper-middle-class homes.

Third is the innovation's *complexity*—the degree to which it is relatively difficult to understand or use. Personal computers are complex and will therefore take a longer time to penetrate into home use.

Fourth is the innovation's *divisibility*—the degree to which it may be tried on a limited basis. The availability of rentals of personal computers with an option to buy increases their rate of adoption.

The fifth characteristic is the innovation's *communicability*—the degree to which the results of its use are observable or describable to others. The fact that personal computers lend themselves to demonstration and description helps them diffuse faster in the social system.

Other characteristics influence the rate of adoption, such as initial costs, ongoing costs, risk and uncertainty, scientific credibility, and social approval. The new-product marketer has to research all these factors and give the key ones maximum attention in designing the new-product and marketing program.[34]

Influence of Organizational Buyers' Characteristics on the Rate of Adoption

Organizations can also be classified as to their readiness to try and adopt a new product. Thus the producer of a new teaching method would want to identify the schools that have a high adoption probability. The producer of a new piece of medical equipment would want to identify hospitals that have a high adoption probability. Adoption is associated with variables in the organization's environment (community progressiveness, community income), the organization itself (size, profits, pressure to change), and the administrators (education level, age, cosmopoliteness). Once a set of useful indicators are found, they can be used to identify the best target organizations.

SUMMARY

Organizations are increasingly recognizing the necessity and advantages of regularly developing new products and services. Their more mature and declining products must be replaced by newer products.

New products, however, can fail. The risks of innovation are as great as the rewards. The key to successful innovation lies in developing better organizational arrangements for handling new-product ideas and developing sound research and decision procedures at each stage of the new-product-development process.

The new-product-development process consists of eight stages: idea generation, idea screening, concept development and testing, marketing strategy development, business analysis, product development, market testing, and commercialization. The purpose of each stage is to decide whether the idea should be further developed or dropped. The company wants to minimize the chances that poor ideas will move forward and good ideas will be rejected.

With regard to new products, consumers respond at different rates, depending on the consumer's characteristics and the product's characteristics. Manufacturers try to bring their new products to the attention of potential early adopters, particularly those with opinion-leader characteristics.

1. The declining pool of college-age youth has led to a decreasing enrollment for a midwestern university. The institution offers a liberal arts program at the undergraduate level with professional schools in business and education at the graduate and undergraduate levels. What new-product services might be developed? How might the university test and launch these new services?

2. Seek out examples of new services development in one of the following areas and discuss its success or failure in light of the concepts presented in this chapter: (a) financial services, (b) health-care delivery, (c) electronic or rapid mail delivery.

3. Procter & Gamble has several patent filings pending: (a) a new plaque-removing oral rinse; (b) a disposable, elasticized diaper insert that can be used with either regular or disposable diapers; (c) a laundry product that both washes and softens clothes. Can you suggest two new-product ideas with supporting arguments that would establish some probability for success?

4. Devise a list of questions that management should answer prior to developing a new product or service. Organize the questions according to the following areas: market opportunity, competition, production, patents, distribution, finance. Would the development and testing of a new service differ from that of a new product?

5. A food company develops a new salad-dressing powder that is mixed with water. The company is trying to compete against another company that has a powdered dressing that is mixed with oil and vinegar. Discuss different methods of concept testing this new product.

6. Polaroid, an acknowledged leader in photographic technology, introduced an "instant movie" system, Polavision, with substantial promotional expenditures to retailers and consumers. Polaroid spent $60 million in the first two years after introduction of the product, yet the product never gained wide acceptance. Given Polaroid's previous record of new-product successes, how can you explain Polavision's failure?

7. A candy-store chain is seeking ideas for a new sales promotion campaign. Show how morphological analysis might be used to generate a large number of ideas for a campaign.

8. (a) Expected profit and risk are two dimensions for determining whether to introduce a new product nationally. Can you develop a diagram using these two dimensions to show how critical limits might be set up by a firm before a market test to guide its decision after the test? (b) Suppose a firm finds that test-market results are borderline and concludes that the product would probably yield a below-average return. It has sunk a lot of money into the development of the product. Should it introduce the product nationally or drop it? (c) State the two opposing risks that a firm faces when it bases its new-product decision on test-market results. How can it reduce these risks? (d) In the test marketing of Colgate's new soap (described in the text), the third marketing mix yielded the best profit level. Does this mean that it should be adopted when the product is launched nationally?

9. A school furniture manufacturer wants to develop a line of lightweight chairs for elementary school classrooms. Recommend steps for researching, developing, and testing these chairs.

10. A company president asked the new-product manager what a proposed new product would earn if launched. "Profits of three million dollars in five years." Then the president asked whether the product might fail. "Yes." "What would we lose if the product fails?" "One million dollars." "Forget it," said the president. Do you agree with the president's decision?

FOOTNOTES

1 *New Products Management for the 1980s* (New York: Booz, Allen & Hamilton, 1982).

2 Ibid.

3 David S. Hopkins and Earl L. Bailey, "New Product Pressures," *Conference Board Record*, June 1971, pp. 16–24.

4 See "High-Speed Management for the High-Tech Age," *Fortune*, March 5, 1984, pp. 62–68.

5 *New Products Management for the 1980s.*

6 In a sample of 228 frequently purchased consumer products that were test marketed in 1977, 64.5 percent were not launched nationally. See Nielsen Marketing Service, "New Product Success Ratios," *Nielsen Researcher*, 1979, pp. 2–9.

7 See David S. Hopkins, *Options in New-Product Organization* (New York: Conference Board, 1974).

8 A good review of other studies of factors associated with new-product success is found in Modesto A. Maidique and Billie Jo Zirger, "A Study of Success and Failure in Product Innovation: The Case of the U.S. Electronics Industry," *IEEE Transactions on Engineering Management*, November 1984, pp. 192–203.

9 Eric A. von Hippel, "Users as Innovators," *Technology Review*, January 1978, pp. 3–11.

10 See John E. Arnold, "Useful Creative Techniques," in *Source Book for Creative Thinking*, ed. Sidney J. Parnes and Harold F. Harding (New York: Scribner's, 1962), p. 255.

11 See Alex F. Osborn, *Applied Imagination*, 3rd ed. (New York: Scribner's, 1963), pp. 286–87.

12 See Edward M. Tauber, "HIT: Heuristic Ideation Technique—A Systematic Procedure for New Product Search," *Journal of Marketing*, January 1972, pp. 58–70; and Charles L. Alford and Joseph Barry Mason, "Generating New Product Ideas," *Journal of Advertising Research*, December 1975, pp. 27–32.

13 See Edward M. Tauber, "Discovering New Product Opportunities with Problem Inventory Analysis," *Journal of Marketing*, January 1975, pp. 67–70.

14 Eric von Hippel, "Learning from Lead Users," in *Marketing in an Electronic Age*, ed. Robert D. Buzzell (Cambridge: Harvard Business School Press, 1985), pp. 308–17.

15 Osborn, *Applied Imagination*, p. 156.

16 John W. Lincoln, "Defining a Creativeness in People," in *Source Book for Creative Thinking*, Parnes and Harding, pp. 274–75.

17 Ibid., p. 274.

18 Mark Hanan, "Corporate Growth through Venture Management," *Harvard Business Review*, January–February 1969, p. 44.

19 See John T. O'Meara, Jr., "Selecting Profitable Products," *Harvard Business Review*, January–February 1961, pp. 110–18.

20 Theodore Levitt, "Marketing Intangible Products and Product Intangibles," *Harvard Business Review*, May–June 1981, p. 95.

21 See Robert Blattberg and John Golanty, "Tracker: An Early Test Market Forecasting and Diagnostic Model for New Product Planning," *Journal of Marketing Research*, May 1978, pp. 192–202.

22 See Roger A. Kerin, Michael G. Harvey, and James T. Rothe, "Cannibalism and New Product Development," *Business Horizons*, October 1978, pp. 25–31.

23 The present value (V) of a future sum (I) to be received t years from today and discounted at the interest rate (r) is given by $V = I_t/(1 + r)^t$. Thus $4,716/(1.15)^5 = $2,346.

24 See David B. Hertz, "Risk Analysis in Capital Investment," *Harvard Business Review*, January–February 1964, pp. 96–106.

25 Ralph Westfall and Harper W. Boyd, Jr., *Cases in Marketing Management* (Homewood, Ill.: Richard D. Irwin, 1961), p. 365.

26 The best-known systems are Yankelovich's "Laboratory Test Market," Elrick and Lavidge's "Comp," and Management Decision Systems' "Assessor." For a description of "Assessor," see Alvin J. Silk and Glen L. Urban, "Pre-Test Marketing Evaluation of New Packaged Goods: A Model and Measurement Methodology," *Journal of Marketing Research*, May 1978, pp. 171–91. For a recent assessment, see Allan D. Shocker and William G. Hall, "Pretest Market Models: A Critical Evaluation," *Journal of Product Innovation Management*, 3 (1986), 86–107.

27 Alvin A. Achenbaum, "The Purpose of Test Marketing," in *The Marketing Concept in Action*, ed. Robert M. Kaplan (Chicago: American Marketing Association, 1964), p. 582.

28 See "Spotting Competitive Edges Begets New Product Success," *Marketing News*, December 21, 1984, p. 4. Also see "Testing Time for Test Marketing," *Fortune*, October 29, 1984, pp. 75–76; and Jay E. Klompmaker, G. David Hughes, and Russell I. Haley, "Test Marketing in New Product Development," *Harvard Business Review*, May–June 1976, pp. 128–38.

29 See Robert J. Thomas, "Timing—The Key to Market Entry," *Journal of Consumer Marketing*, Summer 1985, pp. 77–87.

30 Philip Kotler and Gerald Zaltman, "Targeting Prospects for a New Product," *Journal of Advertising Research*, February 1976, pp. 7–20.

31 The following discussion leans heavily on Everett M. Rogers, *Diffusion of Innovations* (New York: Free Press, 1962).

32 Rogers, *Diffusion of Innovations*, p. 192.

33 Elihu Katz and Paul F. Lazarsfeld, *Personal Influence* (New York: Free Press, 1955), p. 234.

34 For a recent summary of the literature, see Hubert Gatignon and Thomas S. Robertson, "A Propositional Inventory for New Diffusion Research," *Journal of Consumer Research*, March 1985, pp. 849–67.

15

Managing Products, Product Lines, and Brands

In the factory, we make cosmetics; in the store, we sell hope.

Charles Revson

We are now ready to examine each marketing-mix element in some detail. We will begin with product, the most important marketing-mix element. First we ask, *What is a product?* It turns out that *product* is a complex concept, which has to be carefully defined. Then we will examine the major decisions involved in managing the *product mix*, a *product line* within the product mix, and *individual products* and *brands* within the product line.

WHAT IS A PRODUCT?

We define product as follows:

> A *product* is anything that can be offered to a market for attention, acquisition, use, or consumption that might satisfy a want or need.

Most products we think of are *physical products*, such as automobiles, toasters, shoes, eggs, and books. But products also include *services* (sometimes called service products), such as haircuts, concerts, and vacations. We can also think of *persons* as products. Barbra Streisand can be marketed, not in the sense that we "buy" her, but in the sense that we give her attention, buy her records, and attend her concerts. A *place* like Hawaii can be marketed, in the sense of either buying some land in Hawaii or taking a vacation there. An *organization* like the American Red Cross can be marketed, in the sense that we feel positive toward it and will support it. Even an *idea* can be marketed, such as

445

family planning or safe driving, in the sense that we might adopt the behavior associated with the idea. Thus we say that products consist broadly of anything that can be marketed, including physical objects, services, persons, places, organizations, and ideas.

Core, Tangible, and Augmented Product

In developing a product, the product planner needs to think about the product on three levels. The most fundamental level is the *core product*, which answers the question, What is the buyer really buying? Every product is really the packaging of a want-satisfying service. A woman buying lipstick is not simply buying lip color. Charles Revson of Revlon, Inc., recognized this early: "In the factory, we make cosmetics; in the store, we sell hope." Theodore Levitt pointed out that "purchasing agents do not buy quarter-inch drills; they buy quarter-inch holes." And supersalesman Elmer Wheeler would say, "Don't sell the steak—sell the sizzle." The marketer's job is to uncover the needs hiding under every product and to sell *benefits*, not *features*. The core product stands at the center of the total product, as illustrated in Figure 15-1.

The product planner has to turn the core product into a *tangible product*. Lipsticks, computers, educational seminars, and political candidates are all tangible products. Tangible products may have as many as five characteristics: a *quality level*, *features*, *styling*, a *brand name*, and *packaging*.

> Even a service may have all five characteristics. The U.S. Income Tax Advisory Service exhibits a certain quality level in that government tax advisers have a certain level of competence. The service has certain features, such as being available at no charge and usually requiring some waiting time. The service has a certain style, such as being brief, cursory, and impersonal. The service has a formal name, that of Federal Income Tax Advisory Service. Finally, the service is packaged within branch offices located in various cities.

Finally, the product planner may offer additional services and benefits that make up an *augmented product*. IBM's success is partly traceable to its skillful augmentation of its tangible product—the computer. While its competitors were busy touting the hardware

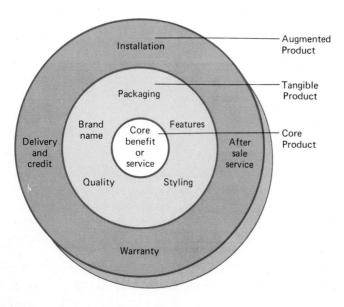

FIGURE 15-1
Three Levels of Product

features of its computers to buyers, IBM recognized that customers were more interested in efficient software, quick repairs, guarantees, and so on. IBM sold a working system, not just computer hardware.

Product augmentation leads the marketer to look at the buyer's total *consumption system*: "The way a purchaser of a product performs the total task of whatever it is that he or she is trying to accomplish when using the product."[1] In this way, the marketer will recognize many opportunities for augmenting its offer in a competitively effective way. According to Levitt:

> The *new competition* is not between what companies produce in their factories, but between what they add to their factory output in the form of packaging, services, advertising, customer advice, financing, delivery arrangements, warehousing, and other things that people value.[2]

Consider the competition today among major companies selling expensive CT-scanners to hospitals. These scanners range in price from half a million to a few million dollars each. The equipment requires specially designed facilities, intensive staff training, and many other things. General Electric Medical Systems, the market-share leader, sees itself as not only selling an expensive piece of equipment but also providing the following services: installation, operator training, twenty-four-hour repair service, warranties, special financing arrangements, and so on. Not only is GE selling an augmented product, but it goes one step further and *customizes the augmented product* for each buyer. Some hospitals may not need all the surrounding services. GE Medical Services tailors its terms to the wish list of each buyer. Companies that customize, rather than standardize, the augmented product have the best chance of winning customers in the long run. (See Exhibit 15-1.)

Product Hierarchy

Each product is related to certain other products. Product hierarchies stretch from basic needs to particular items that might satisfy those needs. We can identify seven levels of the product hierarchy. Here they are defined and illustrated for life insurance:

1. *Need family.* The core need that underlies the product family. Example: security.
2. *Product family.* All the product classes that can satisfy a core need with more or less effectiveness. Example: savings and income.
3. *Product class.* A group of products within the product family that are recognized as having a certain functional coherence. Example: financial instruments.
4. *Product line.* A group of products within a product class that are closely related because they function in a similar manner, or are sold to the same customer groups, or are marketed through the same types of outlets, or fall within given price ranges. Example: life insurance.
5. *Product type.* Those items within a product line that share one of several possible forms of the product. Example: term life.
6. *Brand.* The name associated with one or more items in the product line that is used to identify the source or character of the item(s). Example: Prudential.
7. *Item.* A distinct unit within a brand or product line that is distinguishable by size, price, appearance, or some other attribute. The item is called a stockkeeping unit, or product variant. Example: Prudential renewable term insurance.

Another example: The need "hope" gives rise to a product family called toiletries and a product class within that family called cosmetics, of which one line is lipstick, which has different product forms, such as tube lipstick, which is offered as a brand called Revlon in a particular type, such as "frosted."

Two other terms frequently arise. A *product system* is a group of diverse but related

EXHIBIT 15-1

Marketing Strategies for "Commodities"

The word *commodity* describes products and services that are highly standardized; such items as sulfuric acid, cement, steel, and chickens come to mind. If a product class is perceived by buyers to be homogeneous, then buyers will buy it from whoever charges the lowest price.

A seller has only two lines of defense. One is to claim that the items in the class are not all identical; there is enough variation in quality or performance to justify slight price differences. Thus certain steel companies make their steel with higher-quality consistency, and when this matters to buyers, they will pay more for this company's steel. Furthermore, the history of steel making is replete with examples of innovating higher grades of "steel" and steel with new properties. And clearly, Frank Perdue has shown that all chickens are not the same. He goes to great pains to produce a consistently higher-quality chicken and gets a 15 percent price premium from convinced customers.

A company has a second line of defense even when the items in a class are nearly identical. The seller can differentiate the offer surrounding the product. Instead of thinking that the company is selling a "commodity," the company must see itself as handling an "undifferentiated product" waiting to be turned into a "differentiated offer." Dermot Dunphy, the CEO of Sealed Air Corporation, the firm that pioneered plastic bubble wrap, puts it emphatically:

> The lesson to be learned is that no matter how commonplace a product may appear, it does not have to become a commodity. Every product, every service can be differentiated.*

Levitt and others have pointed out hundreds of ways that an offer can be augmented, including offering more reliable delivery, training, technical assistance, longer payment terms, and so on.† Part of the answer lies in recognizing that buyers have different needs and are therefore attracted to different offers. Thus some buyers carry very little inventory and instead phone in a lot of emergency orders. A seller can specialize in supplying customers on an emergency basis and charging a premium price for this service.

The real challenge is to identify customers' needs that are not being met and for which those customers would pay a premium. IBM has clearly shown the value that buyers place on *better service* when products are roughly comparable. And Marlboro cigarettes has shown the value that buyers put on *image* when products are roughly comparable. Some "commodity" companies get a higher price from their customers simply on the strength of the *personal relationship* with the salesperson on whom they know they can rely.

* Speech to a sales meeting of Sealed Air Corporation, March 19, 1984.
† Theodore Levitt, "Marketing Success Through Differentiation—of Anything," *Harvard Business Review*, January–February 1980.

items that function in a compatible manner. For example, the Nikon Company sells a basic 35mm camera along with an extensive set of lenses, filters, and other options that constitute a product system. A *product mix* (or product assortment) is the set of all products and items that a particular seller makes available to the buyers.

Product Classifications

Marketers have traditionally classified products into different types on the basis of varying product characteristics. The thought is that each product type has an appropriate marketing-mix strategy. Exhibit 15-2 presents the major classifications of consumer and industrial goods and their marketing strategy implications.

With this background, we are ready to examine the major product decisions companies make regarding the product mix, product lines, and individual products.

EXHIBIT 15-2   Product Classifications and Their Marketing Strategy Implications

Durable Goods, Nondurable Goods, and Services

Products can be classified into three groups according to their durability or tangibility:

- ■ *Nondurable goods.* Nondurable goods are tangible goods that normally are consumed in one or a few uses. Examples include beer, soap, and salt. Since these goods are consumed fast and purchased frequently, the appropriate strategy is to make them available in many locations, charge only a small markup, and advertise heavily to induce trial and build preference.

- ■ *Durable goods.* Durable goods are tangible goods that normally survive many uses. Examples include refrigerators, machine tools, and clothing. Durable products normally require more personal selling and service, command a higher margin, and require more seller guarantees.

- ■ *Services.* Services are activities, benefits, or satisfactions that are offered for sale. Examples include haircuts and repairs. Services are intangible, inseparable, variable, and perishable. As a result, they normally require more quality control, supplier credibility, and adaptability. (For further discussion of services, see Chapter 16.)

Consumer-Goods Classification

Consumers buy a vast number of goods. A useful way to classify these goods is on the basis of *consumer shopping habits* because they have implications for marketing strategy. We can distinguish between convenience, shopping, specialty, and unsought goods.

Convenience goods. Goods that the customer usually purchases frequently, immediately, and with the minimum of effort in comparison and buying. Examples include tobacco products, soap, and newspapers.

Convenience goods can be further divided into staples, impulse goods, and emergency goods. *Staples* are goods that consumers purchase on a regular basis. For example, one buyer might routinely purchase Heinz ketchup, Crest toothpaste, and Ritz crackers. *Impulse goods* are purchased without any planning or search effort. These goods are normally available in many places because consumers do not normally look for them. Thus candy bars and magazines are placed next to checkout counters because shoppers may not have thought of buying them. *Emergency goods* are purchased when a need is urgent—umbrellas during a rainstorm, boots and shovels during the first winter snowstorm. Manufacturers of emergency goods will place them in many outlets so they will not lose the sale when the customer needs these goods.

Shopping goods. Goods that the customer, in the process of selection and purchase, characteristically compares on such bases as suitability, quality, price, and style. Examples include furniture, clothing, used cars, and major appliances.

Shopping goods can be divided into homogeneous and heterogeneous goods. The buyer sees homogeneous shopping goods as similar in quality but different enough in price to justify shopping comparisons. The seller has to "talk price" to the buyer. But in shopping for clothing, furniture, and more heterogeneous goods, product features are often more important to the consumer than the price. If the buyer wants a pin-striped suit, the cut, fit, and look are likely to be more important than small price differences. The seller of heterogeneous shopping goods must therefore carry a wide assortment to satisfy individual tastes and must have well-trained sales personnel to provide information and advice to customers.

Specialty goods. Goods with unique characteristics and/or brand identification for which a significant group of buyers are habitually willing to make a special purchasing effort. Examples would include specific brands and types of fancy goods, cars, hi-fi components, photographic equipment, and men's suits.

A Mercedes, for example, is a specialty good because buyers are willing to travel far to buy a Mercedes. Specialty goods do not involve the buyer in making comparisons; the buyer only invests time to reach the dealers carrying the wanted products. The dealers do not need convenient locations; however, they must let prospective buyers know their locations.

Unsought goods. Goods that the consumer does not know about or knows about but does not normally think of buying. New products, such as smoke detectors and food processors, are unsought goods until the consumer is made aware of them through advertising. The classic examples of known but unsought goods are life insurance, cemetery plots, gravestones, and encyclopedias.

By their very nature, unsought goods require a lot of marketing effort in the form of advertising and personal selling. Some of the most sophisticated personal-selling techniques have developed from the challenge of selling unsought goods.

Industrial-Goods Classification

Organizations buy a vast variety of goods and services. A useful industrial-goods classification would suggest appropriate marketing strategies in the industrial market. Industrial goods can be classified in terms of *how they enter the production process and their relative costliness*. We can distinguish three groups: materials and parts, capital items, and supplies and services.

Materials and parts. Goods that enter the manufacturer's product completely. They fall into two classes: raw materials, and manufactured materials and parts.

Raw materials in turn fall into two major classes: *farm products* (e.g., wheat, cotton, livestock, fruits, and vegetables) and *natural products* (e.g., fish, lumber, crude petroleum, iron ore). Each is marketed somewhat differently. *Farm products* are supplied by many producers, who turn them over to marketing intermediaries, who provide assembly, grading, storage, transportation, and selling services. Farm products are somewhat expandable in the long run, but not in the short run. Farm products' perishable and seasonal nature gives rise to special marketing practices. Their commodity character results in relatively little advertising and promotional activity, with some exceptions. From time to time, commodity groups will launch campaigns to promote the consumption of their product—such as potatoes, prunes, or milk. And some producers even brand their product—such as Sunkist oranges and Chiquita bananas.

Natural products are highly limited in supply. They usually have great bulk and low unit value and require substantial transportation to move them from producer to user. There are fewer and larger producers who often market them directly to industrial users. Because the users depend on these materials, long-term supply contracts are common. The homogeneity of natural materials limits the amount of demand-creation activity. Price and delivery reliability are the major factors influencing the selection of suppliers.

Manufactured materials and parts are exemplified by *component materials* (e.g., iron, yarn, cement, wires) and *component parts* (e.g., small motors, tires, castings). *Component materials* are usually fabricated further—for example, pig iron is made into steel, and yarn is woven into cloth. The standardized nature of component materials usually means that price and supplier reliability are the most important purchase factors. *Component parts* enter the finished product completely with no further change in form, as when small motors are put into vacuum cleaners and tires are added on automobiles. Most manufactured materials and parts are sold directly to industrial users, with orders often placed a year or more in advance. Price and service are the major marketing considerations, and branding and advertising tend to be less important.

Capital items. Goods that enter the finished product partly. They include two groups: installations and accessory equipment.

Installations consist of *buildings* (e.g., factories and offices) and *fixed equipment* (e.g., generators, drill presses, computers, elevators). Installations are major purchases. They are usually bought directly from the producer, with the typical sale being preceded by a long negotiation period. The producers use a top-notch sales force, which often includes sales engineers. The producers have to be willing to design to specification and to supply postsale services. Advertising is used but is much less important than personal selling.

Accessory equipment comprises *portable factory equipment and tools* (e.g., hand tools, lift trucks) and *office equipment* (e.g., typewriters, desks). These types of equipment do not become part of the finished product. They simply help in the production process. They have a shorter life than installations but a longer life than operating supplies. Although some accessory-equipment manufacturers sell direct, more often they use middlemen because the market is geographically dispersed, the buyers are numerous, and the orders are small. Quality, features, price, and service are major considerations in vendor selection. The sales force tends to be more important than advertising, although the latter can be used effectively.

Supplies and services. Items that do not enter the finished product at all.

Supplies are of two kinds: *operating supplies* (e.g., lubricants, coal, typing paper, pencils) and *maintenance and repair items* (paint, nails, brooms). Supplies are the equivalent of convenience goods in the industrial field because they are usually purchased with a minimum effort on a straight rebuy basis. They are normally marketed through intermediaries because of the great number of customers, their geographical dispersion, and the low unit value of these goods. Price and service are important considerations because suppliers are quite standardized, and brand preference is not high.

Business services include *maintenance and repair services* (e.g., window cleaning, typewriter repair) and *business advisory services* (e.g., legal, management consulting, advertising). Maintenance and repair services are usually supplied under contract. Maintenance services are often provided by small producers, and repair services are often available from the manufacturers of the original equipment. Business advisory services are normally new task-buying situations, and the industrial buyer will choose the supplier on the basis of the supplier's reputation and personnel.

Thus we see that a product's characteristics will have a major influence on marketing strategy. At the same time, marketing strategy will also depend on other factors, such as the product's stage of the life cycle, the strategies of competitors, and the economic climate.

SOURCE For definitions, see *Marketing Definitions*: *A Glossary of Marketing Terms* (Chicago: American Marketing Association, 1960).

PRODUCT-MIX DECISIONS

We will first consider product-mix decisions. A company's product mix is defined as follows:

A *product mix* (also called *product assortment*) is the set of all product lines and items that a particular seller offers for sale to buyers.

Avon's product mix consists of three major product lines: cosmetics, jewelry, and household items. Each product line consists of several sublines: for example, cosmetics breaks down into lipstick, rouge, powder, and so on. Each line and subline has many individual items.

Altogether, Avon's product mix includes 1,300 items. A large supermarket handles as many as 10,000 items; a typical K-Mart stocks 15,000 items; and General Electric manufactures as many as 250,000 items.

A company's product mix will have a certain width, length, depth, and consistency. These concepts are illustrated in Table 15-1 in connection with selected Procter & Gamble consumer products.

The *width* of P&G's product mix refers to how many different product lines the company carries. Table 15-1 shows a product-mix width of five lines. (In fact, P&G produces many additional lines—hair care products, health care products, personal hygiene products, beverages, food, and so on.)

The *length* of P&G's product mix refers to the total number of items in its product mix. In Table 15-1, it is thirty-two. We can also talk about the average length of a line at P&G. This is obtained by dividing the total length (here 32) by the number of lines (here 5), or 6.4. The average product line at P&G, as represented in Table 15-1, consists of 6.4 brands.

TABLE 15-1
Product-Mix Width and Product-Line Length Shown for Procter & Gamble Products

← Product-Mix Width →				
Detergents	**Toothpaste**	**Bar Soap**	**Disposable Diapers**	**Coffee**
Ivory Snow 1930	Gleem 1952	Ivory 1879	Pampers 1961	Folger's 1963
Dreft 1933	Crest 1955	Camay 1927	Luvs 1975	Instant Folger's 1963
Tide 1946	Denquel 1985	Lava 1928		High Point Instant 1975
Joy 1949		Kirk's 1930		Folger's Flaked Coffee 1977
Cheer 1950		Zest 1952		Folger's Decaffeinated 1984
Oxydol 1952		Safeguard 1963		
Dash 1954		Coast 1974		
Cascade 1955				
Duz 1956				
Ivory Liquid 1957				
Gain 1966				
Dawn 1972				
Era 1972				
Bold 3 1976				
Solo 1979				

(vertical axis label: Product Line-Length)

The *depth* of P&G's product mix refers to how many variants are offered of each product in the line. Thus if Crest comes in three sizes and two formulations (regular and mint), Crest has a depth of six. By counting the number of variants within each brand, the average depth of P&G's product mix can be calculated.

The *consistency* of the product mix refers to how closely related the various product lines are in end use, production requirements, distribution channels, or some other way. P&G's product lines are consistent insofar as they are consumer goods that go through the same distribution channels. The lines are less consistent insofar as they perform different functions for the buyers.

These four dimensions of the product mix provide the handles for defining the company's product strategy. The company can expand its business in four ways. The company can add new product lines, thus widening its product mix. Or the company can lengthen its existing product lines to become a more full-line company. Or the company can add more product variants to each product and thus deepen its product mix. Finally, the company can pursue more product-line consistency or less, depending on whether it wants to acquire a strong reputation in a single field or participate in several fields.

Product-mix planning is largely the responsiblity of the company's strategic planners. They must assess, with information supplied by the company marketers, which product lines to grow, maintain, harvest, and divest. We have already reviewed the various analytical approaches to this task in Chapter 2.

PRODUCT-LINE DECISIONS

A product mix is made up of various product lines. We define a product line as follows:

> **A *product line* is a group of products that are closely related because they function in a similar manner, are sold to the same customer groups, are marketed through the same types of outlets, or fall within given price ranges.**

Each product line within a company is usually managed by some executive. In General Electric's Consumer Appliance Division, there are product-line managers for refrigerators, stoves, washing machines, dryers, and other appliances. At Northwestern University, there are separate academic deans for the medical school, law school, business school, engineering school, music school, speech school, journalism school, and liberal arts.

Product-Line Analysis Product-line managers have two important information needs. First, they must know the sales and profits of each item in the line. Second, they must know how their product line compares with competitors' product lines in the same markets.

Product-line Sales and Profits Each item in a product line contributes differently to total sales and profits. The product-line manager needs to know the percentage of total sales and profits contributed by each item in the line. An example of a five-item product line is shown in Figure 15-2.

The first item in the product line accounts for 50 percent of total sales and 30 percent of total profits. The first two items account for 80 percent of total sales and 60 percent of total profits. If these two items were suddenly hurt by a competitor, the product line's sales and profitablity would collapse. A high concentration of sales in a few items means line vulnerability. These items must be carefully monitored and protected. At the other end, the last item constitutes only 5 percent of the product line's sales and profits. The product-line manager may even want to consider dropping this slow seller from the line.

Product-line Market Profile The product-line manager must also review how the product line is positioned against competitors' product lines. Consider a paper company with a product line consisting of paper board.[3] Two of the major attributes of paper board are paper weight and finish quality. Paper weight is usually offered at standard levels of 90, 120, 150, and 180 weight. Finish quality is offered at three standard levels. Figure 15-3 is a product map showing the location of the various product-line items of Company X and four competitors, A, B, C, and D. Competitor A sells two product items in the extra-high weight class ranging from medium to low finish quality. Competitor B sells four items that vary in weight and finish quality. Competitor C sells three items in which the greater their weight, the greater their finish quality. Competitor D sells three items, all

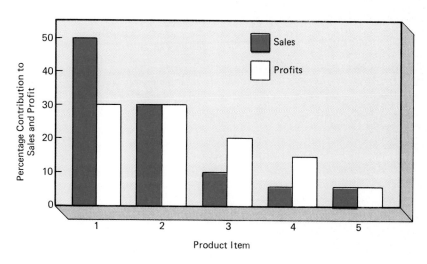

FIGURE 15-2
Product-Item Contributions to a Product Line's Total Sales and Profits

lightweight but varying in finish quality. Finally, Company X offers three items that vary in weight and vary between low and medium finish quality.

This product-item mapping is useful for designing product-line marketing strategy. It shows which competitors' items are competing against Company X's items. For example, Company X's low-weight/medium-quality paper competes against competitor D's paper. But its high-weight/medium-quality paper has no direct competitor. The map reveals locations for possible new-product items. For example, no manufacturer offers a high-weight/low-quality paper. If Company X determines there is a strong unmet demand and can produce this paper and price it right, it should add this item to its line.

Another benefit of product mapping is that it identifies market segments according to their paper-buying preferences. Figure 15-3 shows the types of paper, by weight and quality, preferred by the general printing industry, the point-of-purchase display industry, and the office-supply industry, respectively. The map shows that Company X is well positioned to serve the needs of the general printing industry but is less effective in serving the other two industries and should consider bringing out more paper types that meet these needs.

Product-Line Length

One of the major issues facing product-line managers is the optimal length (the number of items) of the product line. The line is too short if the manager can increase profits by adding items; the line is too long if the manager can increase profits by dropping items.

The issue of product-line length is influenced by company objectives. Companies that want to be positioned as full-line companies and/or are seeking high market share and market growth will carry longer lines. They are less concerned when some items fail to contribute to profits. Companies that are keen on high profitability will carry shorter lines consisting of "cherry-picked" items.

Product lines tend to lengthen over time. Excess manufacturing capacity will put pressure on the product-line manager to develop new items. The sales force and distributors will also pressure for a more complete product line to satisfy their customers. The product-line manager will want to add items to the product line in pursuit of greater sales and profits.

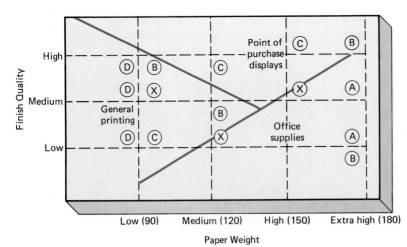

FIGURE 15-3
Product Map for a Paper-Product Line
SOURCE: Benson P. Shapiro, *Industrial Product Policy: Managing the Existing Product Line* (Cambridge, Mass.: Marketing Science Institute, September 1977), p. 101.

But as items are added, several costs rise: design and engineering costs, inventory-carrying costs, manufacturing-changeover costs, order-processing costs, transportation costs, and new-item promotional costs. Eventually someone calls a halt to the mushrooming product line. Top management may freeze things because of insufficient funds or manufacturing capacity. Or the controller may question the line's profitability and call for a study. The study will probably show a large number of money-losing items, and they will be pruned from the line in a major effort to increase profitability. A pattern of undisciplined product-line growth followed by massive product pruning will repeat itself many times.

A company can systematically enlarge the length of its product line in two ways: by stretching its line and by filling its line.

Line-stretching decision. Every company's product line covers a certain part of the total range offered by the industry as a whole. For example, BMW automobiles are located in the medium-high price range of the automobile market. *Line stretching* occurs when a company lengthens its product line beyond its current range. The company can stretch its line downward, upward, or both ways.

Downward stretch Many companies initially locate at the high end of the market and subsequently stretch their line downward. Here are two examples:

Caterpillar. For years, Caterpillar has been the dominant supplier of tractors above 100 horsepower (with five models), while John Deere has dominated the lower-horsepower end of the market (with three models). In the early 1970s, each company invaded the other's market segment. Caterpillar teamed up with a Japanese supplier to build a lighter tractor. Deere went for a high-end stretch by designing its first large tractor. Caterpillar moved toward the low end to participate in a growing market segment that it had been neglecting.

IBM. IBM historically operated in the large-mainframe end of the computer market, leaving minicomputer manufacture to other firms, such as Digital Equipment and Data General. However, the slowdown in growth of the large-batch-oriented data-processing units had led IBM to enter minicomputer manufacture as an avenue to further growth. IBM's interest in minicomputers was further stimulated by its growing interest in computer networks and distributed data-processing systems. This in turn led IBM to stretch further downward into manufacturing microcomputers, in which it became the major force.

Companies often add models to the lower end of their line in order to advertise their brand as starting at a low price. Thus Sears may advertise room air conditioners "starting at $240," and General Motors may advertise a new Chevrolet at $6,000. These "fighter" or "promotional" models are used to draw in customers on a price basis. The customers, upon seeing the better models, often decide to trade up. This strategy must be used carefully. The "promotional" brand, although stripped, must be up to the brand's quality image. The seller must be sure to have the promotional model in stock when it is advertised. Consumers must not feel they were "baited and switched."

A company might stretch downward for any of the following reasons:

- The company is attacked at the high end and decides to counterattack by invading the low end.
- The company finds that slower growth is taking place at the high end.
- The company initially entered the high end to establish a quality image and intended to roll downward.
- The company adds a low-end unit to plug a market hole that would otherwise attract a new competitor.

In making a downward stretch, the company faces some risks. The new low-end item might *cannibalize* higher-end items, leaving the company worse off. Consider the following:

> Ford introduced the small-size Falcon in 1959 to attract economy-car buyers. But many of its buyers were those who would have bought the standard-size Ford. In effect, Ford reduced its own profit margin by failing to design its car for a segment that was really different from that of loyal Ford buyers.

Or the low-end item might provoke competitors to counteract by moving into the higher end. Or the company's dealers may not be willing or able to handle the lower-end products because they are less profitable or dilute their image. Harley Davidson's dealers neglected the small motorcycles that Harley finally designed to compete with the Japanese.

One of the major miscalculations of several American companies has been their unwillingness to plug holes in the lower end of their markets. General Motors resisted building smaller cars, and Xerox resisted building smaller copying machines. Japanese companies spotted a major opening and moved in quickly.

Upward stretch Companies in the lower end of the market might contemplate entering the higher end. They may be attracted by a higher growth rate, higher margins, or simply the chance to position themselves as full-line manufacturers.

An upward-stretch decision can be risky. Not only are the higher-end competitors well entrenched, but they may counterattack by entering the lower end of the market. Prospective customers may not believe that the newcomer can produce quality products. Finally, the company's sales representatives and distributors may lack the talent and training to serve the higher end of the market.

Two-way stretch Companies in the middle range of the market may decide to stretch their line in both directions. Texas Instruments' strategy in the hand-calculator market illustrates this. Before Texas Instruments (TI) entered this market, the market was dominated primarily by Bowmar at the low-price/low-quality end and Hewlett-Packard at the high-price/high-quality end. (See Figure 15-4.) TI introduced its first calculators in the medium-price/medium-quality end of the market. Gradually it added more machines

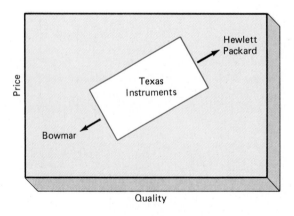

FIGURE 15-4
Two-Way Product-Line Stretch in the Hand-Calculator Market.

at each end. It offered better calculators at the same price as, or at lower prices than, Bowmar, ultimately destroying it; and it designed high-quality calculators selling at lower prices than Hewlett-Packard calculators, taking away a good share of HP's sales at the high end. This two-way stretch won TI early market leadership in the hand-calculator market.

Line-filling decision   A product line can also be lengthened by adding more items within the present range of the line. There are several motives for line filling: reaching for incremental profits; trying to satisfy dealers who complain about lost sales because of missing items in the line; trying to utilize excess capacity; trying to be the leading full-line company; and trying to plug holes to keep out competitors.

Line filling is overdone if it results in cannibalization and customer confusion. The company needs to differentiate each item in the consumer's mind. Each item should possess a *just noticeable difference*. According to Weber's law, customers are more attuned to relative than to absolute difference.[4] They will perceive the difference between boards two and three feet long and boards twenty and thirty feet long, but not between boards twenty-nine and thirty feet long. The company should make sure that new-product items have a noticeable difference.

The company should check that the proposed item meets a market need and is not being added simply to satisfy an internal company need. The famous Edsel automobile, on which Ford lost $350 million, met Ford's internal positioning needs but not the market's needs. Ford noticed that Ford owners would trade up to General Motors products like Oldsmobile or Buick rather than step up to Ford's Mercury or Lincoln. Ford decided to create a steppingstone car to fill its line. The Edsel was created, but it failed to meet a market need because many similar cars were available to the same buyers, and many buyers were beginning to buy smaller cars.

Once the product-line manager decides to add another item to sell at a certain price, the design task is turned over to the company engineers. The planned price will dictate how the item is designed, rather than the design dictating the price that will be charged.

Line-Modernization Decision

In some cases, product-line length is adequate, but the line needs to be modernized. For example, a company's machine tools may have a 1920s look and lose out to newer-styled competitors' lines.

The issue is whether to overhaul the line piecemeal or all at once. A piecemeal approach allows the company to see how customers and dealers take to the new style before changing the whole line. Piecemeal modernization is less draining on the company's cash flow. A major disadvantage of piecemeal modernization is that it allows competitors to see changes and start designing their own line.

In rapidly changing high-tech products, product modernization is a must. Although Apple personal computers are less than a decade old, the line has already migrated through Apple 1, Apple 2, Apple 3, Lisa, and McIntosh. Competitors are constantly upgrading the equipment, and each company must defend itself by designing a new generation of equipment to replace the current line. Companies plan product improvements to induce *customer migration* to higher-valued, higher-priced items. A major issue is timing the product improvements so they do not come out too early (thus damaging sales of the current product line) or too late (after competition has established a strong reputation for more-advanced equipment).

Line-Featuring Decision

The product-line manager typically selects one or a few items in the line to feature. Sometimes managers feature promotional models at the low end of the line to serve as "traffic builders." Thus Sears will announce a special low-priced sewing machine to attract people. And Rolls-Royce announced an economy model selling for only $49,000—in contrast to its high-end model selling for $108,000—to bring people into its showrooms. Once the customers arrive, sales people may try to influence them to buy at the high end of the line.

At other times, managers will feature a high-end item to lend class to the product line. Stetson promotes a man's hat selling for $150, which few people buy but which acts as a "flagship" or "crown jewel" to enhance the whole line.

Sometimes a company finds one end of its line selling well and the other end poorly. The company may try to boost demand for the slower sellers, especially if the slower sellers are produced in a separate factory that is idled by the lack of demand. This situation faced Honeywell when its medium-sized computers were not selling as well as its large computers. But things are not this simple. It could be argued that the company should promote the items that sell well rather than try to prop up weak demand.

Line-Pruning Decision

Product-line managers must periodically review items for pruning. There are two occasions for pruning. One is when the product line includes deadwood that is depressing profits. The weak items can be identified through sales and cost analysis. RCA cut down its color television sets from 69 to 44 models, and a chemical company cut down its products from 217 to the 93 with the largest volume, the largest contribution to profits, and the greatest long-term potential. Many companies that have implemented major prunings have achieved stronger long-term profits.

The other occasion for product pruning is when the company lacks production capacity to produce all of the items demanded in their desired quantities. The manager should examine the profit margins and concentrate on producing the higher-margin items, dropping some of the low-margin or losing items. Companies typically shorten their lines in periods of tight demand and lengthen their lines in periods of slow demand.

INDIVIDUAL PRODUCT DECISIONS

We will now look at decisions pertaining to developing and marketing the individual product. We will look at the following product decisions: *product attributes, branding,* and *packaging and labeling.* Other marketing decisions, such as pricing, distribution, advertising, and promotion, will be examined in the following chapters.

Product-Attribute Decisions

The process of developing a product concept involves defining the benefits that a product will offer. The benefits are communicated and delivered by tangible product attributes, such as *quality, features,* and *design.* These attributes must be modified over the product's life cycle to remain competitive.

To improve sales or profits, the quality might be raised or lowered, features might be added or withdrawn, and the styling might be changed. We want to look at the issues involved in each decision.

Product quality.   The theme of quality has become extremely important to consumers and companies. American consumers have been impressed with the product quality found in Japanese autos and electronics and in European autos, apparel, and food.[5]

Here are two examples of differing concerns with quality:

> A Japanese firm imported Oster blenders and sold them through twenty-five hundred stores in Japan. The Japanese firm complained about receiving 2 percent returns because the agitator blade rusted. It told the American manufacturer that it would not accept more than ½ of 1 percent returns and that the manufacturer needed to use a higher grade of stainless steel for Japan than that used in the United States. The U.S. manufacturer acceded and in time introduced the better blade in the United States as well.
>
> The Mitsubishi company acquired Motorola's Quasar division which manufactured television receivers. Motorola had experienced 141 defects in every 100 sets; Mitsubishi reduced this to 6 per 100. Buyer complaints fell to one-tenth their previous level and the company's warranty liability also dropped to one-tenth.

Finally, today U.S. manufacturers are responding strongly to the growing demand for quality. Ford is an excellent example of a company that mounted a quality drive and is reaping the benefits in increased market share and profitability. More companies are building in quality and taking pains to communicate it to their target buyers.

The term *quality* is used in two different ways. Engineers typically use it to mean "conformance to requirements," namely, the ability of a product to perform as specified. Thus a blood analyzer machine has "quality" if it meets the stated performance criteria such as analyzing so many blood samples per minute, having less downtime than one day a year, and lasting six years. A hospital, after buying a blood analyzer with this promised quality, can complain about the machine's quality if one or more of these specifications are not met.

Quality is used in a second sense to mean "level of performance." Thus while two blood analyzers might both have quality in the first sense—i.e., each delivers its own promised performance—one might have "higher quality" in that it delivers more performance along attributes valued by most buyers. It is in the second sense in which we say that a Mercedes is a higher-quality car than a Chevette; it drives faster, handles better, lasts longer, and so on. And those people who value higher "quality" will pay more for products designed with higher quality.

Thus the manufacturer has two tasks in developing a product. It has to decide on the quality level, that is, how high the performance criteria (e.g., durability, speed, reliability, etc.) will be. And the manufacturer has to deliver the promised quality. In deciding how much quality to go for, the manufacturer must take a marketing point of view. It must study how consumer preferences vary over different performance attributes and how competitor's products are positioned with respect to attribute levels. This allows the manufacturer to identify a position in the quality spectrum that it can fill that will attract a sufficient number of buyers.

The quality level must not only be built in; it must be adequately communicated. Quality is communicated by choosing those physical signs and cues that people normally associate with a certain quality level. Here are some examples:

A designer of fine fur coats sews in expensive silk linings knowing that women will partly judge the fur's quality by the lining's quality.

A lawn mower manufacturer designs its lawn mower to be louder than necessary because buyers think "noisy" lawn mowers are more "powerful."

A truck manufacturer undercoats the chassis not because it needs undercoating but because undercoating suggests concern for quality.

A car manufacturer makes cars with good-slamming doors because many buyers slam the doors in the showroom as a test of how well the car is built.

Ford designed its Mustang to be a "sports car" and communicated this by the car's styling, bucket seats, and leather steering wheel. Yet it was not a true sports car in terms of performance. On the other hand, the BMW is a true sports car, but BMW failed to design it to look like a sports car.

Quality is also communicated through other elements of the marketing mix. A high price usually signals a premium-quality product by buyers. The product's quality image is also affected positively or negatively by the packaging, distribution, advertising, or promotion. Here are some cases where a brand's quality image was hurt:

■ A well-known brand of frozen foods lost its elite image by being put on sale too often.
■ A premium beer hurt its image when it switched from bottles to cans.
■ A highly regarded brand of television receiver lost its quality image when mass-merchandise outlets started to carry it.

Thus the quality of the packaging, channels, promotion, and so on, must collectively communicate and support the brand's image.

Beyond this, the manufacturer's reputation also contributes to the perception of quality. Certain companies are sticklers for quality; consumers expect any P&G product or IBM product to be good. Finally, consumers' perceptions are also affected by the product's country of origin. Japanese products, at one time considered shoddy, today are all perceived to have high quality even when not justified. Italian clothing is always assumed to be well made and stylish. On the other hand, Chrysler had a problem selling its Mexican-made cars not because they were not well made but because of the perception that Mexican-manufactured products are not up to American standards.

Most products are established initially at one of four quality levels: low, average, high, and superior. The question is, Does higher product quality produce higher profitability? The Strategic Planning Institute, which runs the PIMS studies, went into its data base and found a significantly positive correlation between relative product quality and return on investment, other variables held constant [See Figure 15–5(a)]. In a subsample of 525 midsize business units, those with low relative product quality earned about 17 percent; medium quality, 20 percent; and high quality, 27 percent. Thus the high-quality business units earned 60 percent more than the low-quality business units. They earned more because their premium quality enabled them to charge a premium price, they benefited from more repeat purchasing and consumer loyalty, and their costs of delivering more quality were not much higher than for business units producing low quality.

At the same time, one should not leap to the conclusion that the firm should design the highest quality possible. There are diminishing returns to still higher quality in that fewer buyers will be willing to pay for it. They will complain about certain products being "over-engineered." A person who drives ten blocks to work does not need a Rolls-

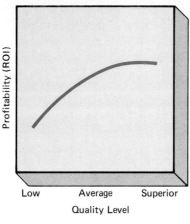

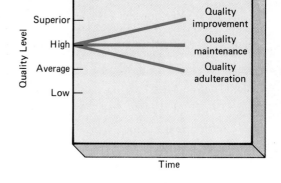

(a) Relationship between product quality and profitability (return on investment — ROI)

(b) Three strategies for managing product quality through time

FIGURE 15-5
Brand-Quality Strategies and Profitability

Royce. The manufacturer must choose a quality level with a target market segment in mind and an understanding of the quality levels of competitive products.

A company must also decide how to manage product quality through time. Three strategies are illustrated in figure 15–5(b). The first, where the manufacturer invests in continuous research and development to improve the product, usually produces the highest return and market share. Procter & Gamble is a major practitioner of product-improvement strategy, which when combined with the high initial product quality, helps explain its leading position in many markets. The second strategy is to maintain product quality. Many companies leave their quality unaltered after its initial formulation unless glaring faults or opportunities occur. The third strategy is to reduce product quality through time. Some companies cut the quality to offset rising costs, hoping the buyers will not notice any difference. Others reduce the quality deliberately in order to increase their current profits, although this often hurts their long-run profitability.

Product features   Any product can be offered with varying features. A "stripped-down" or "bare-bones" model is the starting point, one without any "extras." The company can create higher-level models by adding one or more features. In the case of an automobile, the buyer can order electric windows, automatic transmission, air conditioning, stereo radio, and so on. The automobile manufacturer needs to decide which standard features to offer and which to make optional. Each feature has a chance of capturing the fancy of additional buyers.

Features are a competitive tool for differentiating the company's product from competitors' products. Some companies are extremely innovative in adding new features to their product. The Japanese have an excellent record for improving 35mm cameras through new features such as autofocusing and built-in flash. Their automobiles, calculators, wristwatches, videorecorders, and so on, acquire continuous product enhancements. Being the first producer to introduce a needed and valued new feature is one of the most effective ways to compete.

How can a company identify new features and decide which ones to add to its product? The answer is that the company should periodically contact buyers after they have had a chance to use the product and should ask them a series of questions:

■ How do you like the product?

■ Are there any features that could be added that would improve the product in your mind? What are they? How much would you have paid for each feature?

■ How do you feel about the following features other customers mentioned? (A list would be shown.) For each feature that interests you, how much would you have paid?

This will provide the company with a rich list of feature ideas. The next task is to decide which ones are worth adding. As a first step, the company should calculate, for each potential feature, its *customer value* versus its *company cost*. Suppose an auto manufacturer is considering the three possible improvements shown in Table 15–2. Adding "rear window defrosting" would cost the company $10 per car to add at the factory level. But the average customer said this feature was worth $20. The company could therefore generate $2 of incremental customer satisfaction for $1 in incremental company cost. Looking at the other two features, it appears that "power steering" would create the most customer satisfaction per dollar of company cost.

These criteria are only a starting point, but they do help eliminate some features that customers value minimally in relation to the company cost. Other considerations must come in, of course, to make the final choices.

Product design. Another way to add product distinctiveness is through design. Some companies have outstanding reputations for design distinctiveness, such as Herman Miller in modern furniture, Olivetti in office machines, Bang & Olufsen in home stereo equipment, and Datsun and Mazda in the design of sports cars. They are the exceptions rather than the rule, since most companies lack a "design touch." Their products are prosaically styled. Many cars look the same, many toasters look the same, many television sets look the same. Yet design can be one of the most powerful competitive weapons in a company's marketing arsenal.

Design is a larger concept than style. *Style* describes the appearance of a product. A camera can be done in metal or plastic, look plain or high-tech, be black or any other color. Styles can be eye-catching or yawn-producing. A great or unusual style will grab attention. But this does not mean that an attractive style contributes to the product's performance, and in some cases it might even impair the product's performance. A chair may look sensational and be extremely uncomfortable.

This is where design comes in. *Design* follows the maxim "form follows function." Good design contributes to a product's usefulness as well as its attractiveness. In fact, a

TABLE 15-2   Measuring Customer Effectiveness Value

Feature	Company Cost (1)	Customer Value (2)	Customer Effectiveness (3 = 2 ÷ 1)
Rear window defrosting	$10	$ 20	2
Cruise control	$60	$ 60	1
Power steering	$60	$180	3

good designer considers functionality, aesthetics, human factors (ergonomics), ease of service and repair, ease of manufacture, and costs of materials and tooling.

Unfortunately, many managers confuse style with design and underinvest in one or both. Numbers-oriented managers resist investing in anything as nebulous as design. Some designers are to blame because they do not pay sufficient attention to cost or they produce designs that are too novel for the market to accept. A design audit instrument to measure a company's design sensitivity and effectiveness would help management gauge whether it is adding value through design.[6]

Several companies are now waking up to design's importance:

> General Motors' Cadillac division recently hired Pininfarina, an Italian automobile design firm, to redesign the Cadillac, which had acquired a stodgy image compared with European-designed cars such as the Mercedes, Jaguar, and Saab.
>
> The British Design Council reports that some of its design projects not only have helped British companies increase their sales by 100 percent or more and cut manufacturing costs by 50 percent, but have also helped nearly bankrupt companies turn around and vigorously compete with Japanese and West German firms.

All said, good design can attract attention, improve performance, cut costs, and communicate value to the intended target market.

Brand Decisions

In developing a marketing strategy for individual products, the seller has to confront the issue of branding. Branding can add great value to a product and is therefore an intrinsic aspect of product strategy.

First, we should become familiar with the language of branding. Here are some key definitions:[7]

- **Brand.** A name, term, sign, symbol, or design, or a combination of them, which is intended to identify the goods or services of one seller or group of sellers and to differentiate them from those of competitors.
- **Brand name.** That part of a brand which can be vocalized—the utterable. Examples are Avon, Chevrolet, Disneyland, American Express, and UCLA.
- **Brand mark.** That part of a brand which can be recognized but is not utterable, such as a symbol, design, or distinctive coloring or lettering. Examples are the Playboy bunny and the Metro-Goldwyn-Mayer lion.
- **Trademark.** A brand or part of a brand that is given legal protection because it is capable of exclusive appropriation. A trademark protects the seller's exclusive rights to use the brand name and/or brand mark.
- **Copyright.** The exclusive legal right to reproduce, publish, and sell the matter and form of a literary, musical, or artistic work.

Branding poses challenging decisions to the marketer. The key decisions are shown in Figure 15-6 on page 464 and discussed below.

Branding decision

The first decision is whether the company should put a brand name on its product. Historically, most products went unbranded. Producers and middlemen sold their goods directly out of barrels, bins, and cases, without any supplier identification. The earliest signs of branding were in the efforts of medieval guilds to require craftsmen to put trade marks on their products to protect themselves and consumers against inferior quality. In the fine arts, too, branding began with artists signing their works.

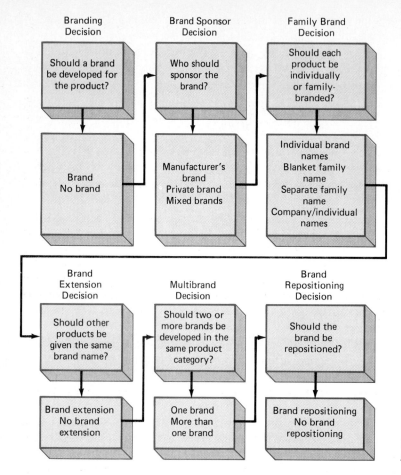

FIGURE 15-6
An Overview of Branding Decisions

In the United States the earliest brand promoters were the patent-medicine makers. Branding's real growth occurred after the Civil War with the growth of national firms and national advertising media. Some of the early brands still survive, such as Borden's Condensed Milk, Quaker Oats, Vaseline, and Ivory Soap.

Branding has become so strong that today hardly anything goes unbranded. Salt is packaged in distinctive manufacturers' containers, oranges are stamped with growers' names, common nuts and bolts are packaged in cellophane with a distributor's label, and automobile components—spark plugs, tires, filters—bear separate brand names from the auto makers.

In some cases, there has been a return to "no branding" of certain staple consumer goods and pharmaceuticals. In 1977, the Jewel Food Stores, a large Chicago-based supermarket chain, introduced a forty-item "generic" line. *Generics* are unbranded, plainly packaged, less-expensive versions of common products purchased in supermarkets, such as spaghetti, paper towels, and canned peaches. They offer standard or lower quality at a price that may be as much as 30 to 50 percent lower than nationally advertised brands and 10 to 15 percent lower than retailer private label items. The lower price is made possible by lower-quality ingredients, lower-cost labeling and packaging, and minimal advertising. Nevertheless, generics are sufficiently satisfying so that over 70 percent of consumers who have purchased generics said they would buy them again. Generic products in the food, household goods, and pharmaceutical industries present a major challenge to high-priced brands and weaker brands.

National brands have fought generics in a number of ways. Ralston-Purina increased its quality and targeted pet owners who identified strongly with their pets and cared most about quality. Procter & Gamble introduced its Banner paper products, a line offering less quality than its higher lines but greater quality than generics at a competitive price. Other companies simply have cut their price to compete with generics. Still, generics have steadily increased their share of market (as measured by percentage of dollar sales) from 1.1 percent in 1979 to 4.1 percent in 1982.[8]

Why do sellers prefer to brand their products when it clearly involves a cost—packaging, labeling, legal protection—and a risk if the product should prove unsatisfying to the user? It turns out that branding gives the seller several advantages.

First, the brand name makes it easier for the seller to process orders and track down problems. Thus Anheuser-Busch receives an order for one hundred cases of Michelob eight-ounce beer instead of an order for ''some of your better beer.'' Furthermore, the seller finds it easier to trace the order if it is misshipped or to determine why the beer was rancid if consumers complain.

Second, the seller's brand name and trademark provide legal protection of unique product features, which would otherwise be copied by competitors.

Third, branding gives the seller the opportunity to attract a loyal and profitable set of customers. Brand loyalty gives sellers some protection from competition and greater control in planning their marketing mix.

Fourth, branding helps the seller segment markets. Instead of P&G's selling a simple detergent, it can offer eight detergent brands, each formulated somewhat differently and aimed at specific benefit-seeking segments.

Fifth, good brands help build the corporate image. By carrying the company's name, they help advertise the quality and size of the company.

There is evidence that distributors want brand names as a means of making the product easier to handle, identifying suppliers, holding production to certain quality standards, and increasing buyer preference. Consumers want brand names to help them identify quality differences and shop more efficiently. In the Soviet Union, consumers look for identification marks on television receivers to find out which factory produced them, since the factories have different reputations for reliability.

Brand-sponsor decision In deciding to brand a product, the manufacturer has several options with respect to brand sponsorship. The product may be launched as a *manufacturer-owned brand*. Or it may be launched as a *licensed name brand* (See Exhibit 15–3.) Or the manufacturer may sell the product to middlemen, who put on a *private brand* (also called middlemen brand, distributor brand, or dealer brand). Or the manufacturer may produce some output under its own name and some that is sold under private labels. Kellogg's, John Deere & Company, and IBM produce virtually all of their output under their own brand names. Hart Schaffner & Marx sells a lot of its manufactured clothes under licensed names such as Christian Dior, Pierre Cardin, and Johnny Carson. Whirlpool produces output both under its own name and under distributors' names.

EXHIBIT 15–3

Licensing Brand Names for Royalties

A manufacturer or retailer may take years and spend millions to develop consumer preference for a new brand name. Or it can "rent" names that already hold magic for consumers. Names or symbols created by other manufacturers, the names of well-known people, characters from popular movies and books—for a fee, any of these can give a product an instant and proven brand name.

Name and character licensing has become a big business in recent years. Manufacturers pay out almost $1 billion each year to use popular names and characters on their products, and these products generate almost $20 billion each year in retail sales.

Clothing sellers are the largest users of licensing. Producers and retailers pay large royalties to adorn their products with the names of fashion innovators. Bill Blass, Calvin Klein, Pierre Cardin, Gucci, Halston, and others license their names or initials for items ranging from blouses to ties and linens to luggage. Such names can be expensive—in 1981, Pierre Cardin reaped a reported $50 million in royalties on products that generated about $1 billion of wholesale business for 540 licensees. In recent years, designer labels have become so common that many retailers are dropping them in favor of their own store brands in order to regain exclusivity, pricing freedom, and higher margins.

Sellers of children's toys, games, food, and other products also do a lot of name and character licensing. The list of characters attached to children's clothing, toys, school supplies, linens, dolls, lunchboxes, cereals, and other items is almost endless—from such classics as Disney, Peanuts, and Flintstones characters to E. T. and the latest Star Wars heroes. And from the ageless Raggedy Ann and Andy to Pac Man, the Shirt Tales, Cabbage Patch, and Pound Puppies.

Licensed names or characters can quickly make a new product familiar and can set it apart from competitors' products. Customers choosing between two similar products will most likely reach for the one containing a familiar name. In fact, consumers often seek out products that carry their favorite names or characters.

Almost everyone is getting into licensing these days. Harley Davidson is licensing its name to toys and even chocolate and cologne. Porche is licensing its name to skis, sunglasses, and other products needing an instant prestige image. And Maxim's is licensing its name to products ranging from tuxedos to prune juice.

For further reading, see John A. Quelch, "How to Build a Product Licensing Program," *Harvard Business Review*, May–June 1985, pp. 186ff.

Manufacturers' brands tend to dominate the American scene. Consider such well-known brands as Campbell's Soup and Heinz Tomato Ketchup. In recent times, however, large retailers and wholesalers have developed their own brands. The private-label tires of Sears and J. C. Penney are as well known today as the manufacturers' brands of Goodyear, Goodrich, and Firestone. Sears has created several names—Diehard batteries, Craftsman tools, Kenmore appliances—that command brand preference and even brand insistence. An increasing number of department stores, service stations, clothiers, drugstores, and appliance dealers are launching private labels.

Why do middlemen bother with sponsoring their own brands? They have to hunt down qualified suppliers who can deliver consistent quality. They have to order large quantities and tie up their capital in inventories. They have to spend money promoting their private label; Sears spent $747 million on major advertising in 1984. They have to take the chance that if their private-label product is not good, the customer will develop a negative attitude toward their other products.

In spite of these potential disadvantages, middlemen develop private brands because they can be profitable. They can often locate manufacturers with excess capacity who will produce the private label at a low cost. Other costs, such as advertising and physical distribution, may also be low. This means that the private brander is able to charge a lower price and often make a higher profit margin. The private brander may be able to develop some strong store brands that draw traffic into its stores.

The competition between manufacturers' and middlemen's brands is called the *battle of the brands*. In this confrontation, middlemen have many advantages. Retail shelf space is scarce, and many manufacturers, especially the newer and smaller ones, cannot introduce products into distribution under their own name. Middlemen take special care to maintain the quality of their brands, thus building consumers' confidence. Many shoppers know that the private-label brand is often manufactured by one of the larger manufacturers anyway. Middlemen's brands are often priced lower than comparable manufacturers' brands, thus appealing to budget-conscious shoppers, especially in times of inflation. Middlemen give more prominent display to their own brands and make sure they are better stocked. As a result, the former dominance of manufacturers' brands is weakening. Some marketing commentators predict that middlemen's brands will eventually knock out all but the strongest manufacturers' brands.

Manufacturers of national brands are very frustrated. Their inclination is to spend a lot of money on consumer-directed advertising and promotion to maintain strong brand preference. Their price has to be somewhat higher to cover this promotion. At the same time, the mass distributors put considerable pressure on them to put more of their promotional money into trade allowances and deals if they want adequate shelf space. Once manufacturers start giving in, they have less to spend on consumer promotion, and their brand leadership starts slipping. This is the national brand manufacturers' dilemma.

Family-brand decision Manufacturers who brand their products face several further choices. At least four brand-name strategies can be distinguished:

1. *Individual brand names.* This policy is followed by Procter & Gamble (Tide, Bold, Dash, Cheer, Gain, Oxydol, Duz) and Genesco, Inc. (Jarman, Mademoiselle, Johnson & Murphy, and Cover Girl).
2. *A blanket family name for all products.* This policy is followed by Heinz and General Electric.
3. *Separate family names for all products.* This policy is followed by Sears (Kenmore for appliances, Kerrybrook for women's clothing, and Homart for major home installations).
4. *Company trade name combined with individual product names.* This policy is followed by Kellogg's (Kellogg's Rice Krispies and Kellogg's Raisin Bran).

Competitors within the same industry will often adopt different brand-name strategies. In the soap industry, Procter & Gamble favors individual brand names. P&G will use its name with new products during the first six weeks of television promotion and then de-emphasize it. P&G wants each product to make it on its own. Colgate, on the other hand, makes much use of the phrase "the Colgate family" to help its individual products along.

What are the advantages of an individual brand-names strategy? A major advantage is that the company does not tie its reputation to the product's acceptance. If the product fails or comes across as having lower quality, it does not compromise the manufacturer's name. A manufacturer of expensive watches or high-quality foods can introduce lower-quality lines without diluting its high-quality brand names. The individual-brand-names strategy permits the firm to search for the best name for each new product. A new name permits the building of new excitement and conviction.

Using a blanket family name for all products also has some advantages. The cost of introducing the product is less because there is no need for "name" research or for heavy advertising expenditures to create brand-name recognition and preference. Furthermore, sales will be strong if the manufacturer's name is good. Thus Campbell's introduces new soups under its brand name with extreme simplicity and instant recognition. On the other hand, Phillips in Europe used its name on all of its products, but since its products vary greatly in quality, most people expect only average quality in a Phillips product. That hurts sales of its superior products; here is a case where individual branding might be better, or the company might avoid putting its own name on its weaker products.

Where a company produces quite different products, it may not be appropriate to use one blanket family name. Swift and Company developed separate family names for its hams (Premium) and fertilizers (Vigoro). When Mead Johnson developed a diet supplement for gaining weight, it created a new family name, Nutriment, to avoid confusion with its family-brand weight-reducing products, Metrecal. Companies will often invent different family brand names for different quality lines within the same product class. Thus A&P sells a first grade, second grade, and third grade set of brands—Ann Page, Sultana, and Iona, respectively.

Finally, some manufacturers want to associate their company name along with an individual brand name for each product. The company name legitimizes, and the individual name individualizes, the new product. Thus Quaker Oats in *Quaker Oats Cap'n Crunch* taps the company's reputation in the breakfast-cereal field, and Cap'n Crunch individualizes and dramatizes the new product.

The brand name should not be a casual afterthought but an integral reinforcer of the product concept. Among the desirable qualities for a brand name are the following:

1. *It should suggest something about the product's benefits.* Examples: Coldspot, Beautyrest, Craftsman, Accutron.
2. *It should suggest product qualities such as action or color.* Examples: Duz, Sunkist, Spic and Span, Firebird.
3. *It should be easy to pronounce, recognize, and remember.* Short names help. Examples: Tide, Crest, Puffs.
4. *It should be distinctive.* Examples: Mustang, Kodak, Exxon.

Marketing research firms have developed elaborate name-research procedures, including *association tests* (what images come to mind?), *learning tests* (how easily is the name pronounced?), *memory tests* (how well is the name remembered?), and *preference tests* (which names are preferred?). One of the best-known specialists in the "name game" is NameLab, Inc., which uses a technique known as constructional linguistics to help clients find effective names. NameLab is responsible for such recent product names as Acura, Compaq, and Zapmail. There are even computer programs available to help firms find names.

Many firms strive to build a unique brand name that will eventually become identified with the product category. Such brand names as Frigidaire, Kleenex, Levis, Jell-O, Scotch Tape, and Fiberglas have succeeded in this way. However, their very success may threaten the exclusive rights to the name. Cellophane and shredded wheat are now names in the common domain.

Brand-extension decision *A brand-extension strategy is any effort to extend a successful brand name to launch new or modified products or lines.* After Quaker Oats' success with Cap'n Crunch dry breakfast cereal, the company used the brand name and cartoon character to launch a line of ice cream bars, T-shirts, and other products. Armour used its Dial brand name to launch a variety of new products that would not easily have obtained distribution without the strength of the Dial name. Honda Motor Company used its name to launch its new power lawn mower.

As a strategy, brand extension appears to offer a number of advantages. The company can use a strong brand name to give a new product instant recognition. The company saves all the advertising cost involved in familiarizing consumers with a new name.

At the same time, brand extension strategy involves some risk. Such brand extensions as Bic pantyhose and Life Savers gum met early deaths. The brand name might be put on a product that disappoints the consumer and hurts the consumer's regard for the company's other products. The brand name may be inappropriate to the new product, even if it is well made and satisfying. And the brand name may lose its special positioning in the consumer's mind through its overuse. Ries and Trout call this the "line-extension" trap.[9] They do not think that the Scott Paper Company helped itself by naming its various paper products ScotTowels, ScotTissues, Scotties, Scotkins, and BabyScott diapers. The Scot name acquired less meaning and each of its products went without a personality compared with its rivals such as Charmin, Bounty, and Pampers.

Multibrand decision   In multibrand strategy, the seller develops two or more brands in the same product category. This marketing practice was pioneered by P&G when it introduced Cheer detergent as a competitor for its already successful Tide. Although Tide's sales dropped slightly, the combined sales of Cheer and Tide were higher. P&G now markets eight detergent brands.

Manufacturers adopt multibrand strategies for several reasons. First, manufacturers can gain more shelf space, thus increasing the retailer's dependence on their brands. Second, few consumers are so loyal to a brand that they will not try another. The only way to capture the "brand switchers" is to offer several brands. Third, creating new brands develops excitement and efficiency within the manufacturer's organization. Managers in P&G and General Motors compete to outperform each other. Fourth, a multibrand strategy positions each brand to capture a different market segment.

In deciding whether to introduce another brand, the manufacturer should consider such questions as the following:

- Can a unique story be built for the new brand?
- Will the unique story be believable?
- How much will the new brand cannibalize the manufacturer's other brands versus competitors' brands?
- Will the cost of product development and promotion be covered by the sales of the new brand?

A major pitfall in introducing a number of multibrand entries is that each may obtain only a small share of the market, and none may be particularly profitable. The company will have dissipated its resources over several brands instead of building a few brands to a highly profitable level. These companies should weed out the weaker brands and establish tighter screening procedures for choosing new brands. Ideally, a company's brands should cannibalize the competitors' brands and not each other. Or at least the net profits or net cash flow with the multibrand strategy should be larger even if some cannibalism occurs.[10]

Brand-repositioning decision However well a brand is initially positioned in a market, the company may have to reposition it later. A competitor may have launched a brand next to the company's brand and cut into its market share. Or customer preferences may have shifted, leaving the company's brand with less demand.

A classic story of successful brand repositioning is the campaign developed by Seven-Up. Seven-Up was one of many soft drinks and was bought primarily by older people who wanted a bland, lemon-flavored drink. Research indicated that while a majority of soft-drink consumers preferred a cola, they did not prefer it all the time, and many other consumers were noncola drinkers. Seven-Up went for leadership in the noncola market by executing a brilliant campaign, calling itself the Uncola. The Uncola was featured as a youthful and refreshing drink, the one to reach for instead of a cola. Seven-Up created a new way for consumers to view the soft-drink market, as consisting of colas and uncolas, with Seven-Up leading the uncolas.

The problem of repositioning a brand can be illustrated for Hamm's beer. Figure 15-7 shows beer brand perceptions and taste preferences on two attributes: lightness and mildness. The dots show the perceived positions of the brands, and the circles represent locations of consumer preference. The larger circles represent more-intense preference. This map reveals that Hamm is not meeting the preferences of any distinct segment.

To remedy this problem, Hamm needs to identify the best preference cluster in which to reposition. Preference cluster #1 would be a poor choice because Schlitz and Budweiser are serving this segment. Preference cluster #2 seems like a good choice because of its size and the presence of only one competitor, Miller. Preference cluster #9 would be another possibility, although it is relatively small. Hamm can also think about a long-shot repositioning toward the supercluster #3, #5, and #8 or the supercluster #4 and #6.

Management must weigh two factors in making its choice. The first is the cost of shifting the brand to that segment. The cost includes changing the product's qualities, packaging, advertising, and so on. In general, the repositioning cost rises with the repositioning distance. The more radically the brand image has to be modified, the greater the required investment. Hamm would need more money to reposition its brand in segment #8 than in segment #2. Hamm would be better off creating a new brand for segment #8 than repositioning its present brand.

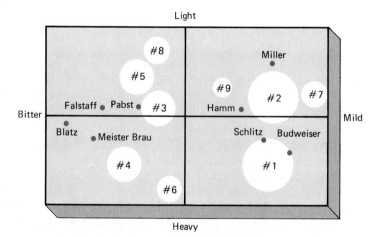

FIGURE 15-7
Distribution of Perceptions
and Preferences in the Beer
Market

The other factor is the revenue that would be earned by the brand in the new position. The revenue depends on the number of consumers in the preference segment, their average purchase rate, the number and strength of competitors in that segment, and the price charged by brands in that segment. Hamm must make its choice by comparing the likely revenues and costs of each repositioning alternative.

Packaging and Labeling Decisions

Many physical products going to the market have to be packaged and labeled.

Packaging Packaging can play a minor role (e.g., inexpensive hardware items) or a major role (e.g., cosmetics). Some packages—such as the Coke bottle and the L'eggs container—are world famous. Many marketers have called packaging a fifth P, along with price, product, place, and promotion. Most marketers, however, treat packaging as an element of product strategy.

We define *packaging* as *the activities of designing and producing the container or wrapper for a product.* The container or wrapper is called the package. The package may include up to three levels of material. The *primary package* is the product's immediate container. Thus the bottle holding Old Spice After-Shave Lotion is the primary package. The *secondary package* refers to material that protects the primary package and is discarded when the product is about to be used. The cardboard box containing the bottle of after-shave lotion is a secondary package and provides additional protection and promotion opportunity. The *shipping package* refers to packaging necessary for storage, identification, or transportation. Thus a corrugated box carrying six dozen of Old Spice After-Shave Lotion is a shipping package. Finally, *labeling* is part of packaging and consists of printed information that describes the product, appearing on or with the package.

In recent times, packaging has become a potent marketing tool. Well-designed packages can create convenience value for the consumer and promotional value for the producer. Various factors have contributed to packaging's growing use as a marketing tool:

- **Self-service.** An increasing number of products are sold on a self-service basis at supermarkets and discount houses. The package must now perform many of the sales tasks. It must attract attention, describe the product's features, give the consumer confidence, and make a favorable overall impression.
- **Consumer affluence.** Rising consumer affluence means consumers are willing to pay a little more for the convenience, appearance, dependability, and prestige of better packages.
- **Company and brand image.** Companies are recognizing the power of well-designed packages to contribute to instant consumer recognition of the company or brand. Every film buyer immediately recognizes the familiar yellow packaging of Kodak film.
- **Innovational opportunity.** Innovative packaging can bring large benefits to consumers and profits to producers. Toothpaste pump dispensers have captured 12 percent of the toothpaste market because for many consumers, they are more convenient and less messy. Chesebrough-Ponds increased its overall nail-polish sales by 22 percent after introducing its novel Aziza Polishing Pen for nails. Kraft is testing retort pouches, which are foil-and-plastic containers, as a successor to cans. The first companies to put their soft drinks in pop-top cans and their liquid sprays in aerosol cans attracted many new customers. Now wine makers are experimenting with pop-top cans and bag-in-the-carton forms of packaging.

Developing an effective package for a new product requires a multitude of decisions. The first task is to establish the *packaging concept.* The packaging concept is a definition of what the package should basically *be* or *do* for the particular product. Should the main function(s) of the package be to offer superior product protection, introduce a novel dispensing method, suggest certain qualities about the product or the company, or something else?

> General Foods developed a new dog-food product in the form of meatlike patties. Management decided that the unique and palatable appearance of these patties demanded maximum visibility. *Visibility* was defined as the basic packaging concept, and management considered alternatives in this light. It finally narrowed down the choice to a tray with a film covering.

Decisions must be made on further elements of package design—*size, shape, materials, color, text,* and *brand mark.* Decisions must be made on much text or little text, cellophane or other transparent films, a plastic or a laminate tray, and so on. The various packaging elements must be harmonized. Size suggests certain things about materials, colors, and so on. The packaging elements must also be harmonized with decisions on pricing, advertising, and other marketing elements.

After the packaging is designed, it must be put through a number of tests. *Engineering tests* are conducted to ensure that the package stands up under normal conditions; *visual tests,* to ensure that the script is legible and the colors harmonious; *dealer tests,* to ensure that dealers find the packages attractive and easy to handle; and *consumer tests,* to ensure favorable consumer response.

In spite of these precautions, a packaging design occasionally gets through with some basic flaw:

> Sizzl-Spray, a pressurized can of barbecue sauce developed by Heublein, . . . had a potential packaging disaster that was discovered in the market tests. . . . ''We thought we had a good can, but fortunately we first test marketed the product in stores in Texas and California. It appears as soon as the cans got warm they began to explode. Because we hadn't gotten into national distribution, our loss was only $150,000 instead of a couple of million.''[11]

Developing effective packaging for a new product may cost a few hundred thousand dollars and take from a few months to a year. The importance of packaging cannot be overemphasized, considering the several functions it performs in attracting and satisfying customers. Companies must pay attention, however, to the growing societal concerns about packaging and make decisions that serve society's interests as well as immediate customer and company objectives.

Labeling   Sellers will also design labels for their products. The label may be a simple tag attached to the product or an elaborately designed graphic that is part of the package. The label might carry only the brand name or a great deal of information. Even if the seller prefers a simple label, the law may require additional information.

Labels perform several functions, and the seller has to decide which ones to use. At the very least, the label *identifies* the product or brand, such as the name Sunkist stamped on oranges. The label might also *grade* the product; thus canned peaches are grade-labeled A, B, and C. The label might *describe* several things about the product: who made it, where it was made, when it was made, what it contains, how it is to be used, and how to use it safely. Finally, the label might *promote* the product through its attractive graphics. Some writers distinguish between identification labels, grade labels, descriptive labels, and promotional labels.

Labels of well-known brands eventually become outmoded and need freshening up. The label on Ivory soap has been redone eighteen times since the 1890s, with gradual changes in the size and design of the letters. The label on Orange Crush soft drink was substantially changed when its competitors' labels began to picture fresh fruits, thereby pulling in more sales. Orange Crush developed a label with new symbols to suggest freshness and much stronger and deeper colors.

There has been a long history of legal concerns surrounding labels. Formerly labels could mislead customers or fail to describe important ingredients or fail to include sufficient safety warnings. As a result, several federal and state laws were enacted to regulate labeling, the most prominent being the Fair Packaging and Labeling Act of 1966. Labeling practices have been affected in recent times by *unit pricing* (stating the price per unit of standard measure), *open dating* (stating the expected shelf life of the product), and *nutritional labeling* (stating the nutritional values in the product). Sellers should make sure that their labels contain all the required information before launching new products.

SUMMARY

Product is the first and most important element of the marketing mix. Product strategy calls for making coordinated decisions on product mixes, product lines, individual products, and service products.

Each product offered to customers can be looked at on three levels. The core product is the essential service that the buyer is really buying. The tangible product is the features, styling, quality, brand name, and packaging that constitute the tangible product. The augmented product is the tangible product plus the various services accompanying it, such as warranty, installation, service maintenance, and free delivery.

Several schemes have been proposed for classifying products. For example, all products can be classified according to their durability (nondurable goods, durable goods, and services). Consumer goods are usually classified according to consumer shopping habits (convenience, shopping, specialty, and unsought goods). Industrial goods are classified according to how they enter the production process (materials and parts, capital items, and supplies and services).

Most companies handle more than one product, and then product mix can be described as having a certain width, length, depth, and consistency. The four dimensions of the product mix are the tools for developing the company's product strategy. The various lines making up the product mix have to be periodically evaluated for profitability and growth potential. The company's better lines should receive disproportionate support; weaker lines should be phased down or out; and new lines should be added to fill the profit gap.

Each product line consists of product items, which should be evaluated. The product-line manager should study the sales and profit contributions of each item in the product line as well as the way the items are positioned against competitors' items. This provides information needed for making several product-line decisions. Line stretching involves the question of whether a particular line should be extended downward, upward, or both ways. Line filling raises the question of whether additional items should be added within the present range of the line. Line modernization raises the question of whether the line needs a new look and whether the new look should be installed piecemeal or all at once. Line featuring raises the question of which items to feature in promoting the line. Line pruning raises the question of how to detect and remove weaker product items from the line.

Companies have to develop brand policies for the individual product items in their lines. They must decide on product attributes (quality, features, design), whether to brand at all, whether to do manufacturing or private branding, whether to use family brand names or individual brand names, whether to extend the brand name to new products, whether to put out several competing brands, and whether to reposition any of the brands.

Physical products require packaging decisions to create such benefits as protection, economy, convenience, and promotion. Marketers have to develop a packaging concept and test it functionally and psychologically to make sure it achieves the desired objectives and is compatible with public policy. Physical products also require labeling for identification and possible grading, description, and promotion of the product. U.S. laws require sellers to present certain minimum information on the label to inform and protect consumers.

■ QUESTIONS

1. Compare and contrast the market-positioning strategies for the IBM PC, the Apple Macintosh, and the Atari 520ST.

2. Develop a two-dimensional product-line map for the Macintosh and IBM PC. Determine if there are locations on your map for new-product items and suggest how these might be positioned.

3. "Several companies are planning to put their brand names on fresh food, and many of their initial forays will be in produce." Discuss the problems that the companies might face, and suggest how these problems might be overcome.

4. By refusing to review a lower-court decision, the U.S. Supreme Court said, in effect, that Parker Bros.' game "Monopoly" was a generic trademark. The ruling was based on a market survey of buyers' motivations submitted by the makers of another board game, "Antimonopoly," which revealed that 65 percent of the people surveyed would buy Monopoly if it were produced by any manufacturer. What implications does this ruling have for trademark protection by marketers?

5. Both North American Watch (marketers of Piaget, Corum, and Concord brands) and Timex have changed from advertising their products as accurate timepieces to promoting them as jewelry that tells time. What changes have taken place in the core, tangible, and augmented product, and what are the respective companies' chances for success with the new strategy?

6. Define the primary want-satisfying purpose(s) of the following goods: (a) cars; (b) bread; (c) oil; (d) pillows; (e) pens; (f) novels; (g) textbooks; (h) uniforms; (i) detergents.

7. Offer a definition of the basic business of each of the following large companies: (a) General Motors; (b) Bayer's (maker of aspirin); (c) Massachusetts Investors Trust (a mutual fund); (d) Sears; and (e) *Time* magazine.

8. Most firms prefer to develop a diversified product line to avoid overdependence on a single product. Yet there are certain advantages that accrue to the firm that produces and sells one product. Name them.

9. "As a firm increases the number of its products arithmetically, management's problems tend to increase geometrically." Do you agree?

10. Does the ranking of a company's products according to their relative profit contribution indicate the best way to allocate the marketing budget to these products? If yes, how should the budget be allocated to the products? If no, why?

11. A marketing consultant advised a large consumer packaged goods company that its product line should consist of (1) a top-quality national brand, (2) private-label brands for supermarket chains, and (3) a generic brand. Discuss the advantages and risks of this product-line strategy.

■ FOOTNOTES

1 See Harper W. Boyd, Jr., and Sidney J. Levy, "New Dimensions in Consumer Analysis," *Harvard Business Review,* November–December 1963, pp. 129–40.

2 Theodore Levitt, *The Marketing Mode* (New York: McGraw-Hill, 1969), p. 2.

3 This illustration is found in Benson P. Shapiro, *Industrial Product Policy: Managing the Existing Product Line* (Cambridge, Mass.: Marketing Science Institute, September 1977), pp. 3–5, 98–101.

4 See Steuart Henderson Britt, "How Weber's Law Can Be Applied to Marketing," *Business Horizons*, February 1975, pp. 21–29.

5 "Research Suggests Consumers Will Increasingly Seek Quality," *Wall Street Journal*, October 15, 1981.

6 See Philip Kotler, "Design: A Powerful but Neglected Strategic Tool," *Journal of Business Strategy*, Fall 1984, pp. 16–21. Also see Robert A. Abler, "The Value-Added of Design," *Business Marketing*, September 1986, pp. 96–103.

7 The first four definitions can be found in *Marketing Definitions: A Glossary of Marketing Terms* (Chicago: American Marketing Association, 1960).

8 For further reading, see Brian F. Harris and Roger A. Strang, "Marketing Strategies in the Age of Generics," *Journal of Marketing,* Fall 1985, pp. 70–81.

9 Al Ries and Jack Trout, *Positioning: The Battle for Your Mind* (New York: McGraw-Hill, 1981).

10 See Mark B. Taylor, "Cannibalism in Multibrand Firms," *Journal of Business Strategy*, Spring 1986, pp. 69–75.

11 "Product Tryouts: Sales Tests in Selected Cities Help Trim Risks of National Marketing," *Wall Street Journal*, August 10, 1962.

Managing Services

There are no such things as service industries. There are only industries whose service components are greater or less than those of other industries. Everybody is in service.

Theodore Levitt

Marketing developed initially in connection with selling physical products such as toothpaste, cars, steel, and equipment. Yet one of the major megatrends in America has been the phenomenal growth of services. Service jobs now account for 77 percent of total employment and 70 percent of GNP. Service jobs not only include persons working in service industries (hotels, airlines, banks, etc.) but also persons providing services within product-based industries (corporate lawyers, medical staff, trainers, etc.). As a result of rising affluence, more leisure, and the growing complexity of products that require servicing, the United States has become the world's first service economy. This has led to a growing interest in the special problems of marketing services.[1] We will look at the issues here.

Service industries are quite varied. The *government sector*, with its courts, employment services, hospitals, loan agencies, military services, police and fire departments, post office, regulatory agencies, and schools, is in the service business. The *private nonprofit sector*, with its museums, charities, churches, colleges, foundations, and hospitals, is in the service business. A good part of the *business sector*, with its airlines, banks, computer service bureaus, hotels, insurance companies, law firms, management consulting firms, medical practices, motion picture companies, plumbing-repair companies, and real estate firms, is in the service business. Many workers in the *manufacturing sector* are really service providers, such as the computer operators, accountants, and legal staff.

Not only are there traditional service industries but new types keep popping up all the time:

For a fee, there are now companies that will balance your budget, babysit your philodendron, wake you up in the morning, drive you to work, or find you a new home, job, car, wife, clairvoyant, cat feeder, or gypsy violinist. Or perhaps you want to rent a garden tractor? A few cattle? Some original paintings? Or maybe some hippies to decorate your next cocktail party? If it is business services you need, other companies will plan your conventions and sales meetings, design your products, handle your data processing, or supply temporary secretaries or even executives.[2]

In this chapter, we will examine the nature of services and their great variety. We will describe how the major characteristics of services affect their marketing; how service firms can increase their differentiation, quality, and productivity; and how product companies can manage their customer support services more effectively.

NATURE AND CLASSIFICATION OF SERVICES

We define a service as follows:

A *service* is any act or performance that one party can offer to another that is essentially intangible and does not result in the ownership of anything. Its production may or may not be tied to a physical product.

A company's offer to the marketplace usually includes some services. The service component can be a minor or a major part of the total offer. In fact, the offer can range from a pure good on the one hand to a pure service on the other. Four categories of offer can be distinguished:

1. *A pure tangible good.* Here the offer consists primarily of a tangible good such as soap, toothpaste, or salt. No services accompany the product.
2. *A tangible good with accompanying services.* Here the offer consists of a tangible good accompanied by one or more services to enhance its consumer appeal. For example, an automobile manufacturer sells an automobile with a warranty, service and maintenance instructions, and so on. Levitt observes that "the more technologically sophisticated the generic product (e.g., cars and computers), the more dependent are its sales on the quality and availability of its accompanying customer services (e.g., display rooms, delivery, repairs and maintenance, application aids, operator training, installation advice, warranty fulfillment). In this sense, General Motors is probably more service intensive than manufacturing intensive. Without its services, its sales would shrivel."[3]
3. *A major service with accompanying minor goods and services.* Here the offer consists of a major service along with some additional services and/or supporting goods. For example, airline passengers are buying transportation service. They arrive at their destinations without anything tangible to show for their expenditure. However, the trip includes some tangibles, such as food and drinks, a ticket stub, and an airline magazine. The service requires a capital-intensive good called an airplane for its realization, but the primary item is a service.
4. *A pure service.* Here the offer consists primarily of a service. Examples include psychotherapy and massages. The psychoanalyst gives a pure service, with the only tangible elements consisting of an office and couch.

As a consequence of this varying goods-to-service mix, it is difficult to generalize about services unless some further distinctions are made.

First, services vary as to whether they are *people-based* or *equipment-based*. Equipment-based services vary in turn depending on whether they are automated or monitored by unskilled or skilled operators. People-based services also vary by whether they are provided by unskilled, skilled, or professional workers. Figure 16-1 shows several industries that cluster in each group.

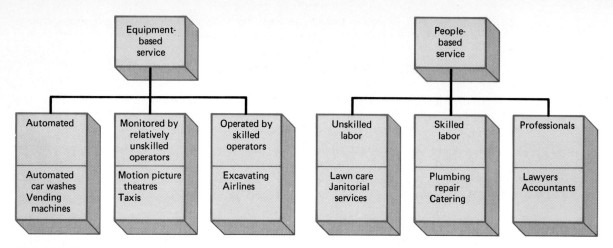

FIGURE 16-1
Types of Service Businesses
SOURCE: Adapted by permission of the *Harvard Business Review*. An exhibit from "Strategy Is Different in Service Businesses," by Dan R. E. Thomas (July–August 1978). Copyright © 1978 by The President and Fellows of Harvard College; all rights reserved.

Some, but not all, services require the *client's presence*. Thus brain surgery involves the client's presence, but a car repair does not. If the client must be present, the service provider has to be considerate of his or her needs. Thus beauty shop operators will invest in their shop's decor, play background music, and engage in light conversation with the client.

Services differ as to whether they meet a *personal* need (personal services) or a *business* need (business services). Physicians will price physical examinations differently for private patients versus company employees on a retainer. Service providers typically develop different marketing programs for personal and business markets.

Finally, *service providers differ in their objectives* (profit or nonprofit) and *ownership* (private or public). These two characteristics, when crossed, produce four quite different types of service organizations. Clearly, the marketing programs of a private investor hospital will differ from those of a private charity hospital or a Veterans' Administration hospital.[4]

CHARACTERISTICS OF SERVICES
AND THEIR MARKETING IMPLICATIONS

Services have four major characteristics that greatly affect the design of marketing programs.

Intangibility Services are intangible. Unlike physical products, they cannot be seen, tasted, felt, heard, or smelled before they are bought. The person getting a "face lift" cannot see the result before the purchase, and the patient in the psychiatrist's office cannot predict the outcome.

To reduce uncertainty, the buyers will look for signs or evidence of the service quality. They will draw inferences about the quality of the service from the place, people, equipment, communication material, symbols, and price that they see.

Therefore the service provider's task is to "manage the evidence," to "tangibilize the intangible.''[5] Whereas product marketers are challenged to add abstract ideas, service marketers are challenged to put physical evidence on their abstract offers.

Consider a bank that wants to convey the idea that its service is quick and efficient. It could "tangibilize" this positioning strategy through a number of tools:

1. *Place.* The bank's physical setting must connote quick and efficient service. The bank's exterior and interior should have clean lines. The layout of the desks and the traffic flow should be planned carefully. Queues should not seem overly long. Customers waiting for a loan officer should have plenty of seating. The background music should reinforce the concept of efficient service.
2. *People.* The bank's personnel should be busy. They should wear appropriate clothing, not be dressed in blue jeans or other apparel that would lead to negative inferences about the personnel and service.
3. *Equipment.* The bank's equipment—computers, copying machines, desks—should look "state-of-the art." A customer would think twice if all the typewriters were 1940-vintage Remingtons.
4. *Communication material.* The bank's communication material should suggest efficiency. Pamphlets should have clean lines and avoid clutter. Photos should be chosen carefully. Lending proposals should be typed neatly. Ads should communicate the bank's positioning.
5. *Symbols.* The bank should choose a name and symbol for its service. For example, it can adopt the name "Mercury Service" and use the Greek god Mercury as a pictorial symbol.
6. *Price.* The bank's pricing of its various services can be kept simple and clear at all times.

Inseparability

Services are typically produced and consumed at the same time. This is not true of physical goods that are manufactured, put into inventory, sold later, and consumed still later. If the service is rendered by a person, then the person is part of the service. Since the client is also present as the service is being produced, provider-client interaction is a special feature of services marketing. Both the provider and the client affect the service outcome.

In the case of entertainment and professional services, buyers are highly interested in who the provider is. It is not the same service if an announcer at a Kenny Rogers concert says that Rogers is indisposed and will be replaced by Marie Osmond, or if someone says that a legal defense will be supplied by John Nobody because F. Lee Bailey is unavailable. When clients have strong provider preferences, price is used to ration the limited supply of the preferred provider's time.

Several strategies exist for getting around this limitation. The service provider can learn to work with larger groups. Psychotherapists have moved from one-on-one therapy to small-group therapy to groups of over three hundred people in a large hotel ballroom getting "therapized." The service provider can learn to work faster—the psychotherapist can spend thirty minutes with each patient instead of fifty minutes and can see more patients. The service organization can train more service providers and build up client confidence, as H&R Block has done with its national network of trained tax consultants.

Variability

Services are highly variable, as they depend on who provides them and when and where they are provided. A Dr. Christiaan Barnard heart transplant was believed to be of higher quality than one performed by a recent M.D. And Dr. Barnard's heart transplants varied with his energy and mental set at the time of each operation. Service buyers are aware of this high variability and frequently talk to others before selecting a service provider.

Service firms can take two steps toward quality control. The first is investing in good personnel selection and training. Airlines, banks, and hotels spend substantial sums to train their employees in providing good service. One should find the same friendly and helpful personnel in every Hyatt Hotel. Variability can be reduced by training the service providers in appropriate responses to each customer situation. Figure 16-2 diagrams how service station attendants are expected to deal with customers.

The second step is monitoring customer satisfaction through suggestion and complaint systems, customer surveys, and comparison shopping so that poor service can be detected and corrected.[6]

Perishability　Services cannot be stored. The reason many doctors charge patients for missed appointments is that the service value existed only at the point when the patient should have shown up. The perishability of services is not a problem when demand is steady, because it is easy to staff the services in advance. When demand fluctuates, service firms

FIGURE 16-2
Part of a Task Breakdown Chart for the Job of Service Station Attendant
Note: Diamond-shaped figures represent possible conditions; rectangles represent actions.
SOURCE: Reprinted, by permission of the publisher, from JOB ANALYSIS: METHODS AND APPLICATIONS, by Ernest J. McCormick, p. 100 © 1979 AMACOM, a division of American Management Associations, New York. All rights reserved.

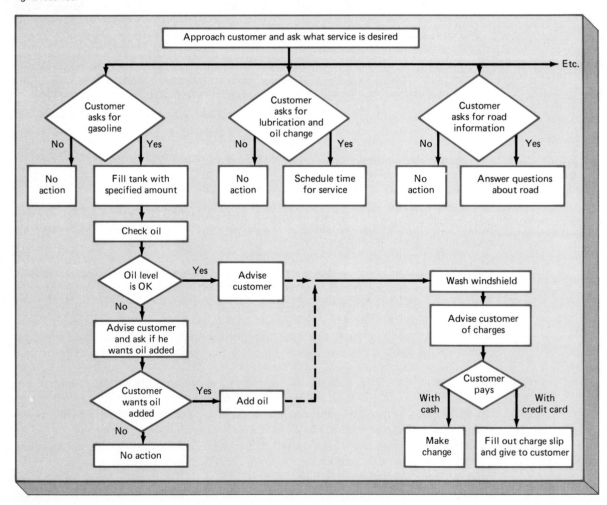

have difficult problems. For example, public transportation companies have to own much more equipment because of rush-hour demand than they would if demand were even throughout the day.

Sasser has described several strategies for producing a better match between demand and supply in a service business.[7]

On the demand side:

- *Differential pricing* will shift some demand from peak to off-peak periods. Examples include low early-evening movie prices and weekend discount prices for car rentals.
- *Nonpeak demand can be cultivated*. McDonald's opened its Egg McMuffin breakfast service, and hotels developed their minivacation weekends.
- *Complementary services* can be developed during peak time to provide alternatives to waiting customers, such as cocktail lounges to sit in while waiting for a table and automatic tellers in banks.
- *Reservation systems* are a way to manage the demand level, and airlines, hotels, and physicians employ them extensively.

On the supply side:

- *Part-time employees* can be hired to serve peak demand. Colleges add part-time teachers when enrollment goes up, and restaurants call in part-time waitresses when needed.
- *Peak-time efficiency routines* can be introduced. Employees perform only essential tasks during peak periods. Paramedics assist physicians during busy periods.
- *Increased consumer participation* in the tasks can be encouraged, as when consumers fill out their own medical records or bag their own groceries.
- *Shared services* can be developed, as when several hospitals share medical-equipment purchases.
- *Facilities for future expansion* can be developed, as when an amusement park buys surrounding land for later development.

MARKETING STRATEGIES FOR SERVICE FIRMS

Until recently, service firms lagged behind manufacturing firms in their use of marketing. George and Barksdale surveyed four hundred service and manufacturing firms and concluded that

> in comparison to manufacturing firms, service firms appear to be: (1) generally less likely to have marketing-mix activities carried out in the marketing department, (2) less likely to perform analysis in the offering area, (3) more likely to handle their advertising internally rather than go to outside agencies, (4) less likely to have an overall sales plan, (5) less likely to develop sales training programs, (6) less likely to use marketing research firms and marketing consultants, and (7) less likely to spend as much on marketing when expressed as a percentage of gross sales.[8]

There are several reasons why service firms neglected marketing in the past. Many service businesses are small (shoe repair, barbershops) and do not use formal management or marketing techniques. There are also service businesses (law and accounting firms) that formerly believed it was unprofessional to use marketing. Other service businesses (colleges, hospitals) faced so much demand until recently that they saw no need for marketing.

Furthermore, service businesses are more difficult to manage using only a *traditional marketing* approach. In a product business, the product is fairly standardized and sits on a shelf, waiting for the customer to reach for it. In a service business, the customer confronts a service provider whose service quality is less certain and more variable. The service outcome is influenced not only by the service provider but by the whole "backroom" production process, which is subject to high variation because it is more labor-intensive. Gronroos has argued that service marketing requires not only 4P traditional marketing but two other marketing thrusts, namely, internal marketing and interactive marketing.[9]

Internal marketing means that the service firm must effectively train and motivate its customer contact employees, as well as all the supporting service personnel, to work as a team to provide customer satisfaction. Everyone must practice a customer orientation or else a high and consistent level of service will not be forthcoming. It is not enough to have a marketing department doing traditional marketing while the rest of the company goes its own way. Berry has argued that the biggest contribution the marketing department can make is to be "exceptionally clever in getting everyone else in the organization to practice marketing."[10] Consider the following example:

Many of the seven thousand U.S. hospitals are rushing to put in *guest relations programs* to train and motivate physicians, nurses, and other employees in hospitality. Radford Community Hospital is among the latest of several hospitals to add a further wrinkle—a "Guaranteed Services" program. Radford set up a fund of $10,000 out of which it would pay patients who have a justified complaint ranging from cold food to overlong waits in the emergency room. The "hook" is that any money not paid out of the fund at the end of the year will be divided among the hospital's employees. This added a tremendous incentive for the staff to treat the patients well. If there are one hundred employees and no patients have to be paid by the end of the year, each employee gets a $100 bonus. In the first six months, the hospital only had to pay out $300 to patients.

Interactive marketing means that the perceived service quality is highly dependent on the quality of the buyer/seller interaction. Whereas in product marketing, the product quality is fairly independent of how it is obtained, in services marketing, the service quality is enmeshed with the service deliverer. This is conspicuously true of professional services.[11] The customer judges service quality not only by its *technical quality* (e.g., was the surgery successful?) but also by its *functional quality* (e.g., did the surgeon show concern and inspire confidence?).[12] Professionals cannot assume that they will satisfy the patient simply because they provide a good technical service. Therefore the professional has to master the skills of interactive marketing.

In fact, there are some services for which the customer cannot even judge the technical quality after they have been received! Figure 16-3 arrays various products and services according to their difficulty of evaluation.[13] At the left are goods high in *search qualities*, namely, characteristics that the buyer can evaluate before purchase. In the middle are goods and services high in *experience qualities*, namely, characteristics that the buyer can evaluate after purchase. At the right are goods and services high in *credence qualities*, namely, characteristics that the buyer normally finds hard to evaluate even after consumption. Since services are generally higher in experience and credence qualities, consumers will generally rely more on word of mouth than on service firm advertising; and they will put more weight on cues such as price, physical facilities, and personnel.

As services competition intensifies, more marketing sophistication will be needed. One of the main agents of change will be product marketers who move into service industries. Sears moved into services marketing years ago—insurance, banking, income tax consulting, car rentals. Xerox Corporation operates a major sales-training business (Xerox Learning), and Gerber Products runs nursery schools and insurance companies.[14]

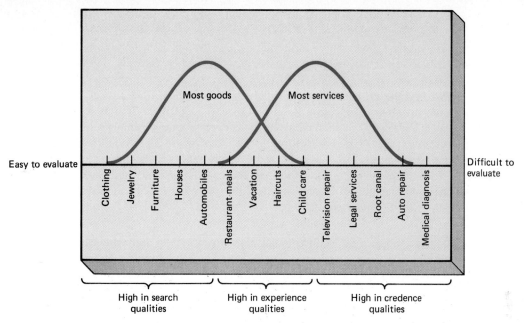

FIGURE 16-3
Continuum of Evaluation for Different Types of Products
SOURCE: Valarie A. Zeithaml, "How Consumer Evaluation Processes Differ between Goods and Services," in *Marketing of Services*, ed. James H. Donnelly and William R. George (Chicago: American Marketing Association, 1981).

Service companies face three tasks, those of increasing their *competitive differentiation*, *service quality*, *and productivity*. Although these interact and to some extent compete, we will examine each separately.

Managing
Differentiation

Service marketers frequently complain about the difficulty of differentiating their services from those of competitors. The deregulation of several major service industries—communications, transportation, energy, banking—precipitated intense price competition. The early success of People's Express airline showed that many commuters cared more about travel costs than service. The great success of Charles Schwab in the discount brokerage service showed that many customers had little loyalty to the more-established brokerage houses when they could save money. To the extent that customers view a service as fairly homogeneous, they care less about the provider than the price.

The solution to price competition is to develop a differentiated offer and image. The service company can add *innovative features* to distinguish its offer. What the customer expects is called the *primary service package*, and to this can be added *secondary service features*. In the airline industry, various carriers have introduced such innovations as movies on board, advanced seating, merchandise for sale, air-to-ground telephone service, and frequent-flyer award programs to augment the offer. Braniff at one time introduced sparsely costumed cabin crews, and Singapore Airlines added a piano bar. Airlines today talk about adding suit-pressing and shoe-shining services, a library of best-selling books, laptop computers, and so on.

The only problem is that most service innovations are easily copied. Few of them are preemptive in the long run. Still, the service company that regularly researches and develops service innovations will gain a succession of temporary advantages over its competitors, and through earning an innovative reputation, may retain customers who want to go with the best. Thus Citicorp enjoys the reputation as a *lead innovator* in the banking industry in aggressively creating or furthering such innovations as automatic teller machines, nationwide banking, broad-spectrum financial accounts and credit cards, and floating prime rates.

Service companies can also work on differentiating their image, specifically through symbols and branding. The Harris Bank of Chicago adopted the lion as its symbol and uses it on its stationery, in its advertising, and even as stuffed animals offered to new depositors. As a result, "The Harris Lion" is well known and confers an image of strength to the bank. Several hospitals have attained "megabrand" reputations for being the best in their field, such as the Mayo Clinic, Massachusetts General, and Sloane-Kettering. Any of these hospitals could locate satellite clinics in other cities and attract patients on the strength of their "brand power."

Managing Service Quality

One of the major ways to differentiate a service firm is to deliver consistently higher quality service than competitors. The key is to meet or exceed the target customers' service quality expectations. Their expectations are formed by their past experiences, word of mouth, and service firm advertising. The customers choose providers on this basis, and after receiving the service, they compare the *perceived service* with the *expected service*. If the perceived service falls below the expected service, customers lose interest in the provider. If the perceived service meets or exceeds their expectations, they are apt to use the provider again.

Therefore the service provider needs to identify target customers' wants in the way of service quality. Unfortunately, service quality is harder to define and judge than product quality. It is harder to get agreement on the quality of a haircut than on the quality of a hair dryer. Yet customers will make judgments about service quality, and service providers need to know customer expectations in order to design effective services.

Clearly, customers will be satisfied if they get what they want, when they want it, where they want it, and how they want it. Still, it is necessary to research the specific customer criteria for any specific service. Thus bank customers may expect on a trip to a bank that they will not wait in line more than five minutes, that the teller will be courteous, knowledgeable, and accurate, and that the computer will not break down. Service providers must do their best to identify the expectations of their target customers with respect to each specific service.

This does not mean that the service provider will be able to meet the customers' wishes. The service provider faces trade-offs between customer satisfaction and company profitability. What is important is that the service provider clearly defines and communicates the service level that will be provided, so that the employees know what they must deliver and the attracted customers know what they will get.

Parasuraman, Zeithaml, and Berry formulated a service quality model that highlights the main requirements for a service provider delivering the expected service quality.[15] The model, shown in Figure 16-4, identifies five gaps that cause unsuccessful service delivery. They are described below:

1. *Gap between consumer expectation and management perception.* Management does not always perceive correctly what customers want or how customers judge the service components. Thus hospital administrators might think that patients judge hospital service by the food quality, whereas patients may be more concerned with nurse responsiveness.

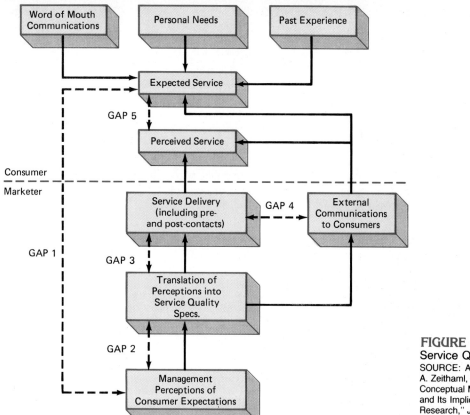

FIGURE 16-4
Service Quality Model
SOURCE: A. Parasuraman, Valarie A. Zeithaml, and Leonard L. Berry, "A Conceptual Model of Service Quality and Its Implications for Future Research," *Journal of Marketing*, Fall 1985, p. 44.

2. **Gap between management perception and service quality specifications.** Management might not set quality standards or very clear ones; or they might be clear but unrealistic; or they might be clear and realistic but management might not be fully committed to enforcing this quality level. For example, an airline's management may want phones to be answered within ten seconds of ringing but not provide enough operators nor do much about it when service falls below this level.

3. **Gap between service quality specifications and service delivery.** Many factors affect service delivery. The personnel might be poorly trained or overworked. Their morale might be low. There might be equipment breakdowns. Those handling operations typically drive for efficiency, and sometimes this runs counter to a drive for customer satisfaction. Consider the cross-pressures on the bank teller who is told by the operations department to work fast and by the marketing department to be courteous and friendly to each customer.

4. **Gap between service delivery and external communications.** Consumer expectations are affected by promises made by the service provider's communications. If a resort hotel's brochure shows a gorgeous room but the guest arrives and finds the room to be cheap and tacky looking, then the fault lies in the expectations created by the external communications.

5. **Gap between perceived service and expected service.** This gap results when one or more of the previous gaps occur. It becomes clear why service providers have a hard time delivering the expected service quality.

The same researchers developed a list of the major *determinants of service quality*. They found that consumers use basically similar criteria regardless of the type of service. The criteria are listed below:

1. *Access.* The service is easy to access in convenient locations at convenient times with little waiting.
2. *Communication.* The service is described accurately in the consumer's language.
3. *Competence.* The employees possess the required skill and knowledge.
4. *Courtesy.* The employees are friendly, respectful, and considerate.
5. *Credibility.* The company and employees are trustworthy and have the customer's best interests at heart.
6. *Reliability.* The service is performed with consistency and accuracy.
7. *Responsiveness.* The employees respond quickly and creatively to customers' requests and problems.
8. *Security.* The service is free from danger, risk, or doubt.
9. *Tangibles.* The service tangibles correctly project the service quality.
10. *Understanding/knowing the customer.* The employees make an effort to understand the customer's needs and provide individual attention.

Various studies of excellently managed service companies show that they share a number of common practices with respect to service quality. Among them are the following:

1. *A history of top management commitment to quality.* Companies such as Marriott, Disney, Delta, and McDonald's have thorough commitments to quality. Their management looks not only at financial performance on a monthly basis but also at service performance. Ray Kroc of McDonald's insisted on continually measuring each McDonald's outlet on its conformance to QSCV, namely, quality, service, cleanliness, and value. Franchisers that failed to conform were dropped.
2. *The setting of high standards.* The best service providers set high service quality standards. Swissair, for example, aims for 96 percent or more of its passengers rating its service as good or superior; otherwise it takes action.
3. *Systems for monitoring service performance.* The top service firms audit service performance, both their own and competitors', on a regular basis. They use a number of devices to measure performance: *comparison shopping, ghost shopping, customer surveys,* and *suggestion and complaint forms.* General Electric sends out seven hundred thousand response cards a year to households to rate its service people's performance. Citibank checks continuously on measures of ART, namely, accuracy, responsiveness, and timeliness. It does "ghost shopping" to check on its employees' delivering good service. Exhibit 16-1 outlines a useful system for rating the various elements of the service bundle and identifying what actions are required.
4. *Satisfying the employees as well as the customers.* Excellently managed service companies believe that employee relations will reflect on customer relations. Management creates an environment of employee support and rewards for good service performance. Management regularly audits employees' satisfaction with their jobs.

Exhibit 16-2 illustrates how one great service marketer, Disney, combines a number of excellent practices that provide a continuing high level of customer satisfaction with its theme parks.

Managing Productivity

Service firms are under great pressure to increase productivity. Since the service business is highly labor intensive, costs have been rising rapidly. There are six approaches to improving service productivity.

The first is to have service providers work harder or more skillfully for the same pay. Working harder is not a likely solution, but working more skillfully can occur through better selection and training procedures.

EXHIBIT 16-1

Rating Services by Importance and Performance

Services can be usefully rated according to their *customer importance* and *company performance*. In the accompanying figure, part (a) shows how customers rated fourteen service elements (attributes) of an automobile dealer's service department on importance and performance.

Importance was rated on a four-point scale of "extremely important," "important," "slightly important," and "not important." Dealer performance was rated on a four-point scale of "excellent," "good," "fair," and "poor." For example, "Job done right the first time" received a mean importance rating of 3.83 and a mean performance rating of 2.63, indicating that customers felt it was highly important but was not being performed well.

The ratings of the fourteen elements are displayed in part (b) of the figure and are divided into four sections. Quadrant A shows important service elements that are not being performed at the desired levels; they include elements 1, 2, and 9. The dealer should concentrate on improving the service department's performance on these elements. Quadrant B shows important service elements where the department is performing well; its job is to maintain the high performance. Quadrant C shows minor service elements that are being delivered in a mediocre way but do not need any attention, since they are not very important. Quadrant D shows that a minor service element, "Send out maintenance notices," is being performed in an excellent manner, a case of possible overkill. Measuring service elements according to their importance and performance tells marketers where to focus their efforts.

Attribute number	Attribute description	Mean importance rating*	Mean performance rating†
1	Job done right the first time	3.83	2.63
2	Fast action on complaints	3.63	2.73
3	Prompt warranty work	3.60	3.15
4	Able to do any job needed	3.56	3.00
5	Service available when needed	3.41	3.05
6	Courteous and friendly service	3.41	3.29
7	Car ready when promised	3.38	3.03
8	Perform only necessary work	3.37	3.11
9	Low prices on service	3.29	2.00
10	Clean up after service work	3.27	3.02
11	Convenient to home	2.52	2.25
12	Convenient to work	2.43	2.49
13	Courtesy buses and cars	2.37	2.35
14	Send out maintenance notices	2.05	3.33

*Ratings obtained from a four-point scale of "extremely important," "important," "slightly important," and "not important."

†Ratings obtained from a four-point scale of "excellent," "good," "fair," and "poor." A "no basis for judgment" category was also provided.

(a)

(b)

SOURCE: John A. Martilla and John C. James, "Importance-Performance Analysis," *Journal of Marketing*, January 1977, pp. 77–79.

The second is to increase the quantity of service by surrendering some quality. Doctors working for HMOs have moved toward handling more patients and giving less time to each patient.

The third is to "industrialize the service" by adding equipment and standardizing

EXHIBIT 16-2

Walt Disney Enterprises—A Highly Responsive Organization

Service companies—hotels, hospitals, colleges, banks, and others—are increasingly recognizing that their marketing mix consists of five Ps, that is, product, price, place, promotion, people. And people may be the most important P! The organization's employees are in constant contact with consumers and can create good or bad impressions.

Organizations are eager to learn how to "turn on" their inside people (employees) to serve their outside people (customers). Here is what the Disney organization does to market "positive customer attitudes" to its employees:

1. The personnel staff at Disney extends a special welcome to new applicants. Those who are hired are given written instructions on what to expect—where to report, what to wear, and how long each training phase will be.

2. On the first day, new employees report to Disney University for an all-day orientation session. They sit four to a table, receive name tags, and enjoy coffee, juice, and pastry while they introduce themselves and get acquainted. The result is that each new employee immediately knows three other people and feels part of a group.

3. The employees are introduced to the Disney philosophy and operations through the latest audiovisual presentations. They learn that they are in the entertainment business. They are "cast members" whose job it is to be enthusiastic, knowledgeable, and professional in serving Disney's "guests." Each division is described, and the new employees learn how they will each play a role in producing the "show." Then they are treated to lunch, tour the park, and are shown the recreational area set aside for the employees' exclusive use. That area consists of a lake, recreation hall, picnic area, boating and fishing facilities, and a large library.

4. The next day, the new employees report to their assigned jobs, such as security hosts (police), transportation hosts (drivers), custodial hosts (street cleaners), or food and beverage hosts (restaurant workers). They will receive a few days of additional training before they go "on stage." When they have learned their function, they receive their "theme costumes" and are ready to go on stage.

5. The new employees receive additional training on how to answer questions guests frequently ask about the park. When they don't have the answer, they can dial switchboard operators who are armed with thick fact books and stand ready to answer any question.

6. The employees receive a Disney newspaper called *Eyes and Ears*, which features news of activities, employment opportunities, special benefits, educational offerings, and so on. Each issue contains a generous number of pictures of smiling employees.

7. Each Disney manager spends a week each year in "cross-utilization," namely, giving up the desk and heading for the front line, such as taking tickets, selling popcorn, or loading or unloading rides. In this way, management stays in touch with running the park and maintaining quality service to satisfy the millions of visitors. All managers and employees wear name badges and address each other on a first-name basis, regardless of rank.

8. All exiting employees answer a questionnaire on how they felt about working for Disney and any dissatisfactions they might have. In this way, Disney's management can measure its success in producing employee satisfaction and ultimately customer satisfaction.

No wonder the Disney people are so successful in satisfying their "guests." Management's attention to its employees helps the latter feel important and personally responsible for the "show." The employees' sense of "owning this organization" spills over to the millions of visitors with whom they come in contact.

SOURCE: See N. W. Pope, "Mickey Mouse Marketing," *American Banker*, July 25, 1979; and "More Mickey Mouse Marketing," *American Banker*, September 12, 1979.

production. Levitt recommended that companies adopt a "manufacturing attitude" toward producing services as represented by McDonald's assembly-line approach to fast-food retailing, culminating in the "technological hamburger."[16] Commercial dishwashing, jumbo jets, multiple-unit motion picture theatres—all represent technological expansions of service.

The fourth is to reduce or make obsolete the need for a service by inventing a product solution, the way television substituted for out-of-home entertainment, the wash-and-wear shirt reduced the need for commercial laundry, and certain antibiotics reduced the need for tuberculosis sanitariums.

The fifth is to design a more effective service. How-to-quit-smoking clinics and jogging may reduce the need for expensive medical services later on. Hiring paralegal workers reduces the need for expensive legal professionals.

The sixth is to give customers incentives to substitute company labor with their own labor. For example, business firms that sort their own mail before delivering it to the post office pay lower postal rates.

Companies must avoid pushing productivity so hard that it reduces perceived quality. Some productivity steps, by standardizing quality, increase customer satisfaction. Other productivity steps lead to too much standardization and rob the customer of customized service. Burger King successfully challenged McDonald's with its "Have It Your Way" campaign, where customers could get a "customized" hamburger sandwich even though this reduced Burger King's productivity somewhat.

MANAGING PRODUCT SUPPORT SERVICES

Thus far we have focused our attention on service industries. No less important are product-based industries that must provide a service bundle to their customers. Manufacturers of equipment—small appliances, office machines, tractors, mainframes, airplanes—all have to provide the buyers with *product support services*. In fact, product support service is becoming a major arena in the battle for competitive advantage.

Firms that provide high-quality service will undoubtedly outperform their less-service-oriented competitors. Table 16-1 provides evidence of this. The Strategic Planning Institute selected several industries and, within each, sorted out the top third and the bottom third of the business units according to customer ratings of "relative perceived service quality." The table shows that the high-service businesses managed to charge more, grow faster, and make more profits on the strength of their superior service quality. Clearly, manufacturers have to think through their presale and postsale service strategy.

TABLE 16-1   Contribution of Service Quality to Relative Performance

	Low-third in service quality	High-third in service quality	Difference in % points
Price index relative to competition	−2%	7%	+ 9%
Change in market share per annum	−2%	6%	+ 8%
Sales growth per annum	8%	17%	+ 9%
Return on sales	1%	12%	+11%

SOURCE: Strategic Planning Institute, Cambridge, Mass.

Pre-sale Service Strategy   An equipment manufacturer must design its equipment and service to meet the expectations of its target customers. Granted, the manufacturer cannot meet the customers' ideal of equipment that performs fast and at low cost, never breaks down, and lasts forever. The manufacturer can only promise a certain level of performance on these buyer objectives. The implied level of performance becomes the manufacturer's positioning strategy vis-à-vis competitors. For example:

> Caterpillar has achieved a lead over many competitors by guaranteeing forty-eight-hour delivery of parts anywhere in the world—or else the customer gets the parts free.

Therefore a necessary step requires the manufacturer to survey its target customers to identify the main services that they value and their relative importance. For example, Canadian buyers of industrial equipment ranked twelve service elements in the following order of importance:[17]

1. Delivery reliability
2. Prompt quotation
3. Technical advice
4. Discounts
5. After-sales service
6. Sales representation
7. Ease of contact
8. Replacement guarantee
9. Wide range of manufacturer
10. Pattern design
11. Credit
12. Test facilities

These importance rankings suggest that the seller should at least match or exceed competition on delivery reliability, prompt quotation, technical advice, and other services deemed most important by the customers.

This research helps companies decide on the service mix that will best augment their equipment offer. In the case of expensive equipment, such as medical imaging equipment, manufacturers have to offer at a minimum

1. *Architectural services* to design the special facility housing the equipment
2. *Installation services* to install the equipment
3. *Training services* for the staff to operate the equipment
4. *Equipment maintenance and repair services*
5. *Financing services*

Competitors vie to go beyond the minimum to offer secondary service-pluses. One major office furniture company, Herman Miller, offers buyers the Herman Miller promise:

1. Five-year product warranties
2. Quality audits after project installation
3. Guaranteed move-in dates
4. Trade-in allowances on systems products

Herman Miller's competitors then have to compose their own service mix promises.

Companies need to plan their product design and service mix decisions in tandem. Design and quality assurance managers should be part of the new-product team from the beginning. Products often can be designed to reduce the amount of required servicing. The Canon home copier uses a disposable toner cartridge that greatly reduces the need for service calls. Kodak and 3M are designing equipment that allows the user to ''plug in'' to a central diagnostic facility that performs tests, locates the trouble, and fixes the equipment over the telephone lines. Thus a key to successful service strategy is to design the products so that they rarely break down, and if they do, they are easily and rapidly fixable with minimal service expense.

Postsale Service Strategy

Equipment manufacturers must decide how they want to offer after-sales service to customers, including maintenance and repair services, training services, and the like. They have three alternatives:

1. The manufacturer could provide these services.
2. The manufacturer could make arrangements with distributors and dealers to provide these services.
3. The manufacturer could leave it to third parties to provide these services.

Consider the case of ''maintenance and repair services.'' Manufacturers usually start out adopting the first alternative. They want to stay close to the equipment and know its problems. They also find it expensive to train others, and this takes time. They also discover that they can make good money running the ''parts and service business.'' As long as they are the only supplier of the needed parts, they can charge a premium price. In fact, many equipment manufacturers price their equipment lower in order to sell it and compensate for this by the money they receive in the ''parts and service'' business. Some equipment manufacturers make over half of their profits in after-sale service. This also explains why competitors emerge who make the same or similar parts and sell them to customers or middlemen for less. Manufacturers warn customers of the danger of using non-manufacturer-made parts, but they are not always convincing.

Over time, manufacturers switch more of the maintenance and repair service to authorized distributors and dealers. These middlemen are closer to the customers, operate in more locations, and can offer quicker if not better service. The manufacturer still makes a profit on selling the parts but leaves the servicing cost to them.

Still later, independent third-party service firms emerge. Over 40 percent of the auto service work is now done outside the franchised automobile dealerships, by independent garages and chains such as Midas Muffler, Sears, and Penney's. Independent service organizations have emerged to handle mainframes, telecommunications equipment, and a variety of other equipment lines. They typically offer lower cost and/or faster service than the manufacturer or authorized middlemen.

Ultimately, some large customers take over responsibility for handling their own maintenance and repair services. Thus a company with several hundred personal computers, printers, and related equipment might find it cheaper to have its own service personnel on site.

Lele has noted the following major trends in the product support area:[18]

1. Equipment manufacturers are building more reliable and more easily fixable equipment. This is partly due to the shift from electromechanical equipment to electronic equipment which has fewer breakdowns and is more repairable. Also, companies are adding modularity and disposable elements that facilitate self-servicing.
2. Customers are becoming more sophisticated about buying product support services and are pressing for ''services unbundling.'' They want separate prices quoted for each service element and the right to shop for the service elements they want.

3. Customers increasingly dislike having to deal with a multitude of service providers handling their different types of equipment. Some third-party service organizations now service a greater range of equipment.[19]

4. Service contracts are an "endangered species." Because of the increase in disposable and/or never-fail equipment, customers are less inclined to pay anywhere from 2 to 10 percent of the purchase price every year for a service.

5. Customer service choices are increasing rapidly, and this is holding down prices and profits on service. Equipment manufacturers have to increasingly figure out how to make money on pricing their equipment independent of service contracts.

SUMMARY

As the United States moves increasingly toward a service economy, marketers need to know more about marketing service products. Services are activities or benefits that one party can offer to another that are essentially intangible and do not result in the ownership of anything. Services are intangible, inseparable, variable, and perishable. Each characteristic poses problems and requires strategies. Marketers have to find ways to "tangibilize" the intangible; to increase the productivity of providers who are inseparable from the product; to standardize the quality in the face of variability; and to influence demand movements and supply capacities better in the face of service perishability.

Service industries have typically lagged behind manufacturing firms in adopting and using marketing concepts, but this is now changing. Services marketing strategy calls for not only external marketing but also internal marketing to motivate the employees and interactive marketing to create skills in the service providers. Customers will use technical and functional criteria to judge the quality of services. To succeed, service marketers must create competitive differentiation, offer high service quality, and find ways to increase service productivity.

Even product-based companies must provide and manage a service bundle for their customers; in fact, their services bundle may be more critical than the product in winning customers. The service mix includes presale services such as technical advice and dependable delivery, as well as postsale services such as prompt repair and personnel training. The marketer has to decide on the mix, quality, and source of various product support services that customers require.

■ QUESTIONS

1. What is interactive marketing? What is its function? What is its importance and relevance to the marketing of services?

2. Discuss the factors that contributed to the adoption of marketing concepts and practices by service industries.

3. Select an airline and suggest how it might increase its competitive differentiation, service quality, and productivity.

4. The following terms used by the health-care industry were reported by *Marketing News*:

   ■ Advertising and public relations are referred to as "improved community awareness."

   ■ Marketing research becomes "needs assessment."

   ■ Salesmanship is called "persuasive interpersonal communication."

   ■ Sales or advertising success may be described as "improved community utilization."

   What does this "Unmarket Speak" suggest about the health-care industry's perceptions of marketing? How should marketing professionals relate to these attitudes and perceptions?

5. Computer software technology is moving rapidly to develop "Expert Systems." These are software programs that capture a person's expertise in a given area and make it available on a computer for a fraction of the original cost. What are the implications for service industries?

6. Select any nearby firm offering a service. Survey its target customers. Identify the main services that these customers value and the relative importance to them. (Describe your methodology in your answer.) Develop a list of recommendations from your findings.

7. What is the role of the marketer's personal values in the marketing of a social cause? Should he or she bring only technical competence to the problem?

8. Discuss the differences and similarities that exist between services and tangible goods marketing.

9. Identify the core, tangible, and augmented product (Chapter 15) provided by (a) the U.S. Navy, (b) organized religion (c) a life insurance company.

10. A Florida hospital located in a high-growth city would like to build name recognition and a reputation of concern for health-care needs among new arrivals to the city. Devise a telephone information service that would meet this objective.

■ FOOTNOTES

1 See G. Lynn Shostack, "Breaking Free from Product Marketing," *Journal of Marketing*, April 1977, pp. 73–80; Leonard L. Berry, "Services Marketing Is Different," *Business*, May–June 1980, pp. 24–30; Eric Langeard, John E. G. Bateson, Christopher H. Lovelock, and Pierre Eiglier, *Services Marketing: New Insights from Consumers and Managers* (Cambridge, Mass.: Marketing Science Institute, 1981); and Karl Albrecht and Ron Zemke, *Service America! Doing Business in the New Economy* (Homewood, Ill.: Dow-Jones-Irwin, 1985).

2 "Services Grow While the Quality Shrinks," *Business Week*, October 30, 1971, p. 50.

3 Theodore Levitt, "Production-Line Approach to Service," *Harvard Business Review*, September–October 1972, pp. 41–42.

4 Further classifications of services are described in Christopher H. Lovelock, *Services Marketing* (Englewood Cliffs, N.J.: Prentice-Hall, 1984).

5 See Theodore Levitt, "Marketing Intangible Products and Product Intangibles," *Harvard Business Review*, May–June 1981, pp. 94–102; and Berry, "Services Marketing Is Different," pp. 24–29.

6 For a good discussion of quality-control systems at the Marriott Hotel chain, see G. M. Hostage, "Quality Control in a Service Business," *Harvard Business Review*, July–August 1975, pp. 98–106.

7 See W. Earl Sasser, "Match Supply and Demand in Service Industries," *Harvard Business Review*, November–December 1976, pp. 133–40.

8 William R. George and Hiram C. Barksdale, "Marketing Activities in the Service Industries," *Journal of Marketing*, October 1974, p. 65.

9 Christian Gronroos, "A Service Quality Model and Its Marketing Implications," *European Journal of Marketing*, 18,

No. 4. (1984), 36–44. Gronroos's model is one of the most thoughtful contributions to service marketing strategy.

10 Leonard Berry, "Big Ideas in Services Marketing," *Journal of Consumer Marketing*, Spring 1986, pp. 47–51.

11 See Philip Kotler and Paul N. Bloom, *Marketing Professional Services* (Englewood Cliffs, N.J.: Prentice-Hall, 1984).

12 Gronroos, "Service Quality Model," pp. 38–39.

13 See Valarie A. Zeithaml, "How Consumer Evaluation Processes Differ between Goods and Services," in *Marketing of Services*, ed. James H. Donnelly and William R. George (Chicago: American Marketing Association, 1981).

14 The argument that product-based companies face substantial opportunities in the service sector is presented in Irving D. Canton, "Learning to Love the Service Economy," *Harvard Business Review*, May–June 1984, pp. 89–97.

15 A. Parasuraman, Valarie A. Zeithaml, and Leonard L. Berry, "A Conceptual Model of Service Quality and Its Implications for Future Research." *Journal of Marketing*, Fall 1985, pp. 41–50.

16 Levitt, "Production-Line Approach to Service," pp. 41–52. Also see Theodore Levitt, "The Industrialization of Service," *Harvard Business Review*, September–October 1976, pp. 63–74.

17 Peter G. Banting, "Customer Service in Industrial Marketing: A Comparative Study," *European Journal of Marketing*, 10, No. 3 (1976), 140.

18 Milind M. Lele, "How Service Needs Influence Product Strategy," *Sloan Management Review*, Fall 1986, pp. 63–70.

19 However, see Ellen Day and Richard J. Fox, "Extended Warranties, Service Contracts, and Maintenance Agreement—A Marketing Opportunity?" *Journal of Consumer Marketing*, Fall 1985, pp. 77–86.

17

Designing Pricing Strategies and Programs

There ain't no brand loyalty that two-cents-off can't overcome.

Anonymous

All profit organizations and many nonprofit organizations face the task of setting a price on their products or services. Price goes by many names:

> Price is all around us. You pay *rent* for your apartment, *tuition* for your education, and a *fee* to your physician or dentist. The airline, railway, taxi, and bus companies charge you a *fare*; the local utilities call their price a *rate*; and the local bank charges you *interest* for the money you borrow. The price for driving your car on Florida's Sunshine Parkway is a *toll*, and the company that insures your car charges you a *premium*. The guest lecturer charges an *honorarium* to tell you about a government official who took a *bribe* to help a shady character steal *dues* collected by a trade association. Clubs or societies to which you belong may make a special *assessment* to pay unusual expenses. Your regular lawyer may ask for a *retainer* to cover her services. The ''price'' of an executive is a *salary*, the price of a salesperson may be a *commission*, and the price of a worker is a *wage*. Finally, although economists would disagree, many of us feel that *income taxes* are the price we pay for the privilege of making money.[1]

How are prices set? Through most of history, prices were set by buyers and sellers negotiating with each other. Sellers would ask for a higher price than they expected to receive, and buyers would offer less than they expected to pay. Through bargaining, they would arrive at an acceptable price.

Setting one price for all buyers is a relatively modern idea. It was given impetus by the development of large-scale retailing at the end of the nineteenth century. F. W. Woolworth, Tiffany and Co., John Wanamaker, J. L. Hudson, and others advertised a ''strictly one-price policy'' because they carried so many items and supervised so many employees.

Through most of history, price has operated as the major determinant of buyer choice.

This is still true in poorer nations, among poorer groups, and with commodity-type products. However, nonprice factors have become relatively more important in buyer-choice behavior in recent decades. Yet price still remains one of the most important elements determining company market share and profitability.

Price is the only element in the marketing mix that produces revenue; the other elements produce costs. Furthermore, pricing and price competition was rated as the number-one problem facing marketing executives in the mid-1980s.[2] Yet many companies do not handle pricing well. The most common mistakes are: Pricing is too cost oriented; price is not revised often enough to capitalize on market changes; price is set independently of the rest of the marketing mix rather than as an intrinsic element of market-positioning strategy; and price is not varied enough for different product items and market segments.

Companies handle pricing in a variety of ways. In small companies, prices are often set by top management rather than by the marketing or sales department. In large companies, pricing is typically handled by divisional and product-line managers. Even here, top management sets the general pricing objectives and policies and often approves the prices proposed by lower levels of management. In industries where pricing is a key factor (aerospace, railroads, oil companies), companies will often establish a pricing department to set prices or assist others in determining appropriate prices. This department reports either to the marketing department, finance department, or top management. Others who exert an influence on pricing include sales managers, production managers, finance managers, and accountants.

In this chapter, we will look at three major pricing-decision problems facing sellers. The first is how to set prices on a product for the first time. The second is how to adapt a product's price over time and space to meet varying circumstances and opportunities. The third is how to initiate and respond to competitive price changes.

SETTING THE PRICE

Pricing is a problem when a firm has to set a price for the first time. This happens when the firm develops or acquires a new product, when it introduces its regular product into a new distribution channel or geographical area, and when it regularly enters bids on new contract work.

The firm must decide where to position its product on quality and price. Figure 17-1 shows nine possible price-quality strategies. The diagonal strategies 1, 5, and 9 can all coexist in the same market; that is, one firm offers a high-quality product at a high price,

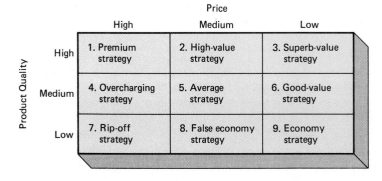

Price

	High	Medium	Low
High	1. Premium strategy	2. High-value strategy	3. Superb-value strategy
Medium	4. Overcharging strategy	5. Average strategy	6. Good-value strategy
Low	7. Rip-off strategy	8. False economy strategy	9. Economy strategy

Product Quality

FIGURE 17-1
Nine Marketing-Mix Strategies on Price/Quality

another firm offers an average-quality product at an average price, and still another firm offers a low-quality product at a low price. All three competitors can coexist as long as the market consists of three groups of buyers, those who insist on quality, those who insist on price, and those who balance the two considerations.

Positioning strategies 2, 3, and 6 represent ways to competitively attack the diagonal positions. Thus strategy 2 says, "Our product has the same high quality as product 1 but we charge less." Strategy 3 says the same thing and offers an even greater saving. If quality-sensitive customers believe these competitors, they will sensibly buy from them and save money (unless firm 1's product has acquired snob appeal).

Positioning strategies 4, 7, and 8 amount to overpricing the product in relation to its value. The customers will feel "taken" and will probably complain or spread bad word-of-mouth about the company. These strategies should be avoided by professional marketers.

The firm has to consider many factors in setting its pricing policy. In the following paragraphs, we will describe a six-step procedure for price setting: (1) selecting the pricing objective, (2) determining demand, (3) estimating costs, (4) analyzing competitors' prices and offers, (5) selecting a pricing method, and (6) selecting the final price.

Selecting the Pricing Objective

The company first has to decide what it wants to accomplish with the particular product. If the company has selected its target market and market positioning carefully, then its marketing-mix strategy, including price, will be fairly straightforward. For example, if a recreational-vehicle company wants to produce a luxurious truck camper for the affluent-customer segment, this implies charging a high price. Thus pricing strategy is largely determined by the prior decision on market positioning.

At the same time, the company may pursue additional objectives. The clearer a firm is about its objectives, the easier it is to set price. Each possible price will have a different impact on such objectives as profits, sales revenue, and market share. This is shown in Figure 17-2 for a hypothetical product. If the company wants to maximize pretax profits,

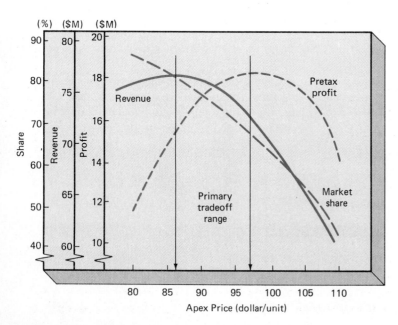

FIGURE 17-2
Relation Between Price, Revenue, Market Share, and Profits
SOURCE: *Decision Making in Marketing* (New York: The Conference Board, 1971). Figure is by Franz Edelman.

it should charge $97. If it wants to maximize sales revenue, it should charge $86. If it wants to maximize market share, it should set an even lower price.

We will examine six major business objectives that a company can pursue through its pricing, namely, survival, maximum current profit, maximum current revenue, maximum sales growth, maximum market skimming, and product-quality leadership.

Survival Companies set survival as their major objective if plagued with overcapacity, intense competition, or changing consumer wants. To keep the plant going and the inventories turning over, they will often cut prices. Profits are less important than survival. Troubled companies such as Chrysler and International Harvester in the past resorted to large price-rebate programs in order to stay alive. As long as their prices covered variable costs and some fixed costs, they were able to continue in business. However, survival is only a short-run objective. In the long run, the firm must find a way to add value in the market or face extinction.

Maximum Current Profit Many companies want to set a price that will maximize current profits. They estimate the demand and costs associated with alternative prices and choose the price that will produce the maximum current profit, cash flow, or rate of return on investment. (See Exhibit 17-1 for the theory of profit-maximization pricing.)

There are some problems associated with adopting the current profit maximization objective. It assumes that the firm has knowledge of its demand and cost functions when in reality they are difficult to estimate. Also, the company is emphasizing current financial performance rather than long-run performance. Finally, the company is ignoring the effects of other marketing-mix variables, competitors' reactions, and legal restraints on price.

Maximum Current Revenue Some companies will set a price that will maximize sales revenue. When the cost function is difficult to estimate because of joint and indirect costs, revenue maximization requires only estimating the demand function. This objective is also simpler to implement insofar as the sales force will be paid a commission on sales revenue. Many managers believe that revenue maximization will lead in the long run to profit maximization and market-share growth.

Maximum Sales Growth Other companies want to achieve maximum sales growth. They believe that higher sales volume will lead to lower unit costs and higher long-run profit. They set the lowest price, assuming the market is price sensitive. This is called *market penetration pricing*. Texas Instruments (TI) is a prime practitioner of market-penetration pricing. TI will build a large plant, set its price as low as possible, win a large market share, experience falling costs, and cut its price further as costs fall.

The following conditions favor setting a low price: (1) the market is highly price sensitive, and a low price stimulates more market growth; (2) production and distribution costs fall with accumulated production experience; and (3) a low price discourages actual and potential competition.

Maximum Market Skimming Many companies favor setting high prices to "skim" the market. Du Pont is a prime practitioner of *market-skimming pricing*. With each innovation—cellophane, nylon, teflon, and so on—it estimates the highest price it can charge given the comparative benefits of its new product versus the available substitutes. The company sets a price that makes it just worthwhile for some segments of the market to adopt the

EXHIBIT 17-1

Finding the Price that Will Maximize Current Profits

Economists have worked out a simple model for pricing to maximize current profits. The model assumes that the firm has knowledge of its demand and cost functions for the product in question. The demand function describes the estimated quantity (Q) that would be purchased per period at various prices (P) that might be charged. Suppose the firm determines through statistical demand analysis that its *demand equation* is

$$Q = 1,000 - 4P \qquad (17-1)$$

This equation expresses the law of demand—less will be bought per period at higher prices.

The cost function describes the total cost (C) of producing any quantity per period (Q). In the simplest case, the total cost function is described by the linear equation $C = F + cQ$ where F is total fixed cost and c is unit variable cost. Suppose the company estimated the following *cost equation* for its product:

$$C = 6,000 + 50Q \qquad (17-2)$$

Management is almost in a position to determine the current profit-maximizing price. It needs only two more equations, both definitional. First, *total revenue* (R) is equal to price times quantity sold—that is,

$$R = PQ \qquad (17-3)$$

Second, *total profits* (Z) is the difference between total revenue and total cost—that is,

$$Z = R - C \qquad (17-4)$$

The company can now determine the relationship between profits (Z) and price (P) by starting with the profit equation (17-4) and going through the following derivation:

$$Z = R - C$$
$$Z = PQ - C$$
$$Z = PQ - (6,000 + 50Q)$$
$$Z = P(1,000 - 4P) - 6,000 - 50(1,000 - 4P)$$
$$Z = 1,000P - 4P^2 - 6,000 - 50,000 + 200P$$
$$Z = -56,000 + 1,200P - 4P^2$$

Total profits turn out to be a second-degree function of price. It is a hatlike figure (a parabola), and profits reach their highest point ($34,000) at a price of $150. The optimal price of $150 can be found by drawing the parabola with some sample prices and locating the high point, or by using calculus.

new material. Each time sales slow down, Du Pont lowers the price to draw in the next price-sensitive layer of customers. In this way, Du Pont skims a maximum amount of revenue from the various segments of the market. As another example, Polaroid also practices market skimming. It first introduces an expensive version of a new camera and gradually introduces simpler, lower-priced models to draw in new segments.

Market skimming makes sense under the following conditions: (1) a sufficient number of buyers have a high current demand; (2) the unit costs of producing a small volume are not so much higher that they cancel the advantage of charging what the traffic will bear; (3) the high initial price will not attract more competitors; (4) the high price supports the image of a superior product.

Product-Quality Leadership A company might aim to be the product-quality leader in the market. It will charge a high price to cover the high product quality and high R&D cost. Caterpillar is a prime example of a firm pursuing product-quality leadership. It builds high-quality construction equipment and offers excellent service, with the result that it is able to price its equipment at a premium.

Determining Demand

Each price that the company might charge will lead to a different level of demand and will therefore have a different impact on its marketing objectives. The relation between the current price charged and the resulting current demand is captured in the familiar *demand schedule*. [See Figure 17-3(a).] The demand schedule shows the number of units the market will buy in a given time period at alternative prices that might be charged during the period. In the normal case, demand and price are inversely related, that is, the higher the price, the lower the demand (and conversely).

In the case of prestige goods, the demand curve is sometimes positively sloped. A perfume company found that by raising its price, it sold more perfume rather than less! Consumers take the higher price to signify a better or more exclusive perfume. However, if too high a price is charged, the level of demand will be lower.

Factors Affecting Price Sensitivity The demand curve shows the market's overall reaction to alternative prices that might be charged. It sums the reactions of many individuals who have different price sensitivities. The important first step is to understand the factors that affect buyers' price sensitivity. Nagle has identified nine factors:[3]

1. *Unique value effect.* Buyers are less price-sensitive when the product is more unique.
2. *Substitute awareness effect.* Buyers are less price-sensitive when they are less aware of substitutes.
3. *Difficult comparison effect.* Buyers are less price-sensitive when they cannot easily compare the quality of substitutes.
4. *Total expenditure effect.* Buyers are less price-sensitive the lower the expenditure is as a ratio to their income.

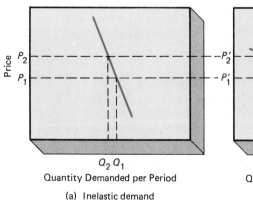

(a) Inelastic demand

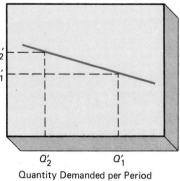

(b) Elastic demand

FIGURE 17-3
Inelastic and Elastic Demand

5. **End-benefit effect.** Buyers are less price-sensitive the less the expenditure is to the total cost of the end product.
6. **Shared cost effect.** Buyers are less price-sensitive when part of the cost is borne by another party.
7. **Sunk investment effect.** Buyers are less price-sensitive when the product is used in conjunction with assets previously bought.
8. **Price-quality effect.** Buyers are less price-sensitive when the product is assumed to have more quality, prestige, or exclusiveness.
9. **Inventory effect.** Buyers are less price-sensitive when they cannot store the product.

Methods of Estimating Demand Schedules   Most companies make some attempt to measure their demand schedules. In researching the demand schedule, the investigator needs to make assumptions about competitive behavior. There are two ways to estimate demand. One is to assume that competitors' prices remain constant regardless of the price charged by the company. The other is to assume that competitors charge a different price for each price the company might set. We will assume the former and defer the question of competitors' price reactions until later.

To measure a demand schedule requires varying the price. This can be done in a laboratory setting asking subjects how many units of a product they would buy at different possible prices.[4] Bennett and Wilkinson used an in-store method of estimating the demand schedule. They systematically varied the prices of several products sold in a discount store and observed the results.[5]

In measuring the price/demand relationship, the market researcher must control or allow for other factors that might affect demand. If a company raised its advertising budget at the same time that it lowered its price, we would not know how much of the increased demand was due to the lower price and how much to the increased advertising. Economists show the impact of nonprice factors on demand by shifts of the demand curve rather than movements along the demand curve. Nagle has presented an excellent summary of the various methods used to measure price sensitivity and demand.[6]

Price Elasticity of Demand   Marketers need to know how responsive demand would be to a change in price. Consider the two demand curves in Figure 17-3. In (a), a price increase from P_1 to P_2 leads to a relatively small decline in demand from Q_1 to Q_2. In (b), the same price increase leads to a substantial drop in demand from Q'_1 to Q'_2. If demand hardly changes with a small change in price, we say the demand is inelastic. If demand changes considerably, we say demand is elastic. Specifically, the price elasticity of demand is given by the following formula:[7]

$$\text{Price elasticity of demand} = \frac{\% \text{ Change in quantity demanded}}{\% \text{ Change in price}}$$

Suppose demand falls by 10 percent when a seller raises the price by 2 percent. Price elasticity of demand is therefore -5 (the minus sign confirms the inverse relation between price and demand). If demand falls by 2 percent with a 2 percent increase in price, then elasticity is -1. In this case, the seller's total revenue stays the same: The seller sells fewer items but at a higher price that preserves the same total revenue. If demand falls by 1 percent when price is increased by 2 percent, then elasticity is $-\frac{1}{2}$. The less elastic the demand, the more it pays for the seller to raise the price.

What determines the price elasticity of demand? Demand is likely to be less elastic under the following conditions: (1) there are few or no substitutes or competitors: (2) buyers do not readily notice the higher price; (3) buyers are slow to change their buying habits and search for lower prices; (4) buyers think the higher prices are justified by quality improvements, normal inflation, and so on.

If demand is elastic rather than inelastic, sellers will consider lowering their price. A lower price will produce more total revenue. This makes sense as long as the costs of producing and selling more do not increase disproportionately.

Various studies of price elasticity have been reported. For example, the price elasticity of housing, 0.5; refrigerators, -1.07 to -2.06; and automobiles, -0.6 to -1.1.[8] But one must be careful in using these estimates. Price elasticity depends on the magnitude and direction of the contemplated price change. It may be negligible with a small price change and substantial with a large price change. It may differ for a price cut versus a price increase. Finally, long-run price elasticity is apt to differ from short-run elasticity. Buyers may continue with their current supplier after a price increase because they do not notice the increase, or the increase is too small, or they are distracted by other concerns, or find choosing a new supplier takes time, but they may eventually switch suppliers. In this case, demand is more elastic in the long run than in the short run. Or the reverse may happen: Buyers drop a supplier after being notified of a price increase but return later. The distinction between short-run and long-run elasticity means that sellers will temporarily be unaware of the total effect of their price change.[9]

Estimating Costs

Demand largely sets a ceiling to the price that the company can charge for its product.

And company costs set the floor. The company wants to charge a price that covers all of its costs of producing, distributing, and selling the product, including a fair return for its effort and risk.

Types of Costs

A company's costs take two forms, fixed and variable. *Fixed costs* (also known as overhead) are costs that do not vary with production or sales revenue. Thus a company must pay bills each month for rent, heat, interest, executive salaries, and so on, whatever the company's output. Fixed costs go on irrespective of the production level.

Variable costs vary directly with the level of production. For example, each hand calculator produced by Texas Instruments (TI) involves a cost of plastic, microprocessing chips, packaging, and the like. These costs tend to be constant per unit produced. They are called variable because their total varies with the number of units produced.

Total costs consist of the sum of the fixed and variable costs for any given level of production. Management wants to charge a price that will at least cover the total production costs at a given level of production.

Cost Behavior at Different Levels of Production Per Period

To price intelligently, management needs to know how its costs vary with different levels of production.

First take the case where a company such as TI has built a fixed-size plant to produce 1,000 hand calculators per day. Figure 17-4(a) shows the typical U-shaped behavior of the short-run average cost curve (SRAC). The cost per unit is high if few units are produced per day. As production approaches 1,000 units per day, average cost falls. The reason is that the fixed costs are spread over more units, with each one bearing a smaller fixed cost. TI can try to produce more than 1,000 units per day but at increasing costs. Average cost increases after 1,000 units because the plant becomes inefficient: Workers have to

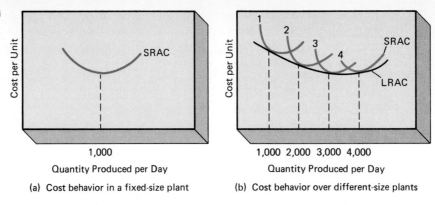

(a) Cost behavior in a fixed-size plant   **(b)** Cost behavior over different-size plants

FIGURE 17-4
Cost per Unit at Different Levels of Production per Period

queue for machines, machines break down more often, and workers get in each other's way.

If TI believes that it could sell 2,000 units per day, it should consider building a larger plant. The plant will use more efficient machinery and work arrangements, and the unit cost of producing 2,000 units per day will be less than the unit cost of producing 1,000 units per day. This is shown in the long-run average cost curve in Figure 17-4(b). In fact, a 3,000-capacity plant would be even more efficient, according to Figure 17-4(b). But a 4,000-daily production plant would be less efficient because of increasing diseconomies of scale: There are too many workers to manage, paperwork slows things down, and so on. Figure 17-4(b) indicates that a 3,000-daily production plant is the optimal size to build if demand is strong enough to support this level of production.

Cost Behavior as a Function of Accumulated Production   Suppose TI runs a plant that produces 3,000 hand calculators per day. As TI gains experience producing hand calculators, it learns how to do it better. The workers learn shortcuts, the flow of materials is improved, procurement costs are cut, and so on. The result is that average cost tends to fall with accumulated production experience. This is shown in Figure 17-5. Thus the average cost of producing the first 100,000 hand calculators is $10 per calculator. When the company has produced the first 200,000 calculators, the average cost has fallen to $9. After its accumulated production experience doubles again to 400,000, the average cost is $8. This decline in the average cost with accumulated production experience is called the *experience curve* (sometimes *learning curve*).

Now suppose three firms compete in this industry, TI, A, and B. TI is the lowest-cost producer at $8, having produced 400,000 units in the past. If all three firms sell the calculator for $10, TI makes $2 profit per unit, A makes $1, and B breaks even. The smart move for TI would be to lower its price to $9. This will drive B out of the market, and even A will consider leaving. TI will pick up the business that would have gone to B (and possibly A). Furthermore, price-sensitive customers will enter the market at the lower price. TI's costs will drop still further and faster and more than restore its profits, even at a price of $9. TI has used this aggressive pricing strategy repeatedly to gain market share and drive others out of the industry.

Experience curve pricing nevertheless carries some major risks. The aggressive pricing

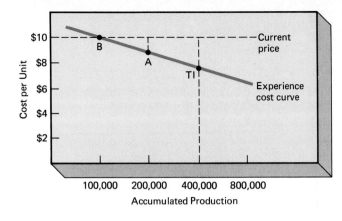

FIGURE 17-5
Cost per Unit as a Function
of Accumulated Production:
The Experience Curve

might give the product a cheap image: This might have happened with TI's personal computers where it ran the price down from $950 in 1980 to $99 by 1983. The strategy also assumes that the competitors are weak and not willing to fight it out. Finally, the strategy leads the company into building more plants to meet the demand while a competitor can be innovating a lower-cost technology and starting at lower costs than the market leader who is still operating on the old experience curve.

Most experience curve pricing has focused on the behavior of manufacturing costs. But all costs, including marketing costs, are subject to learning improvements. Thus if three firms are each investing a large sum of money trying out telemarketing, the firm that has used it the longest can be expected to have the lowest telemarketing costs, assuming that telemarketing costs fall with experience. This firm can charge a little less for its product and still earn the same return, all other costs being equal.

Analyzing Competitors' Prices and Offers

While market demand might set a ceiling and costs set a floor to pricing, competitors' prices and possible price reactions help the firm establish where its prices might be set. The company needs to learn the price and quality of each competitor's offer.

This can be done in several ways. The firm can send out comparison shoppers to price and compare competitors' offers. The firm can acquire competitors' price lists and buy competitors' equipment and take it apart. The firm can ask buyers how they perceive the price and quality of each competitor's offer.

Once the company is aware of competitors' prices and offers, it can use them as an orienting point for its own pricing. If the firm's offer is similar to a major competitor's offer, then the firm will have to price close to the competitor or lose sales. If the firm's offer is inferior, the firm will not be able to charge as much as the competitor does. If the firm's offer is superior, the firm can charge more than the competitor. The firm must be aware, however, that competitors might change their prices in response to the firm's price. Basically, the firm will use price to position its offer vis-à-vis competitors.

Selecting a Pricing Method

Given the demand schedule, the cost function, and competitors' prices, the company is now ready to select a price. The price will be somewhere between one that is too low to produce a profit and one that is too high to produce any demand. Figure 17-6 summarizes the three major considerations in price setting. Product costs set a floor to the price. Competitors' prices and the prices of substitutes provide an orienting point that

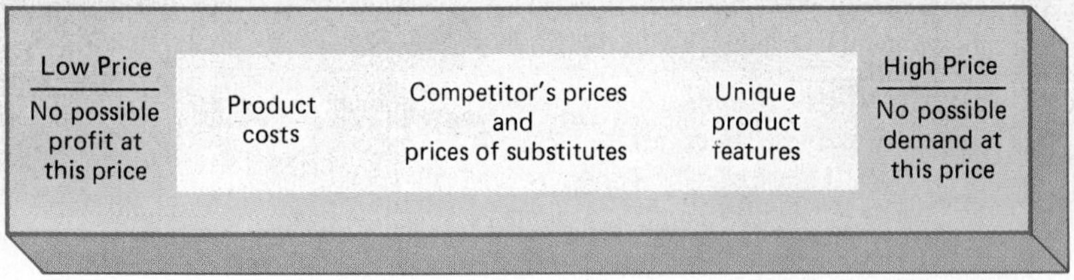

Low Price				High Price
No possible profit at this price	Product costs	Competitor's prices and prices of substitutes	Unique product features	No possible demand at this price

FIGURE 17-6
Major Considerations in Setting a Price

the company has to consider in setting its price. Unique product features in the company's offer establish the ceiling on its price.

Companies resolve the pricing issue by selecting a pricing method that includes one or more of these three considerations. They hope that the pricing method will then lead to a specific price. We will examine the following price-setting methods: markup pricing, target return pricing, perceived-value pricing, going-rate pricing, and sealed-bid pricing.

Markup Pricing   The most elementary pricing method is to add a standard markup to the cost of the product. Construction companies submit job bids by estimating the total project cost and adding a standard markup for profit. Lawyers, accountants, and other professionals typically price by adding a standard markup to their costs. Some sellers tell their customers they will charge their cost plus a specified markup; for example, aerospace companies price this way to the government.

To illustrate markup pricing, suppose a toaster manufacturer had the following costs and sales expectations:

Variable cost	$ 10
Fixed costs	$300,000
Expected unit sales	50,000

Therefore the manufacturer's unit cost is given by

$$\text{Unit cost} = \text{Variable cost} + \frac{\text{Fixed costs}}{\text{Unit sales}} = \$10 + \frac{\$300,000}{50,000} = \$16$$

Now assume the manufacturer wants to earn a 20 percent markup on sales. The manufacturer's markup price is given by

$$\text{Markup price} = \frac{\text{Unit cost}}{(1 - \text{Desired return on sales})} = \frac{\$16}{1 - .2} = \$20$$

The manufacturer would charge dealers $20 per toaster and make a profit of $4 per unit. The dealers in turn will mark up the toaster. If dealers want to earn 50 percent on sales, they will mark up the toaster to $40. This is equivalent to a cost markup of 100 percent (= $20/20).

Markups vary considerably among different goods. Some common markups (on price, not cost) in supermarkets are 9 percent on baby foods, 14 percent on tobacco products,

20 percent on bakery products, 27 percent on dried foods and vegetables, 37 percent on spices and extracts, and 50 percent on greeting cards.[10] Quite a lot of dispersion is found around the averages. Within the spices and extracts category, for example, markups on retail price range from a low of 19 percent to a high of 56 percent. Markups are generally higher on seasonal items (to cover the risk of not selling), specialty items, slower-moving items, items with high storage and handling costs, and demand-inelastic items.

Does the use of standard markups to set prices make logical sense? Generally, no. Any pricing method that ignores current demand and competition is not likely to lead to the optimal price. Suppose the toaster manufacturer above charged $20 but only sold 30,000 toasters instead of 50,000. Then the manufacturer's unit cost would have been higher, since the fixed costs are spread over fewer units, and its realized percentage markup on sales would have been lower. Markup pricing only works if that price actually brings in the expected level of sales.

Still, markup pricing remains popular for a number of reasons. First, sellers have more certainty about costs than about demand. By tying the price to cost, sellers simplify their own pricing task; they do not have to make frequent adjustments as demand changes. Second, where all firms in the industry use this pricing method, their prices tend to be similar. Price competition is therefore minimized, which it would not be if firms paid attention to demand variations when they priced. Third, many people feel that cost-plus pricing is fairer to both buyers and sellers. Sellers do not take advantage of buyers when the latter's demand becomes acute; yet the sellers earn a fair return on their investment.

Target Return Pricing Another cost-oriented pricing approach is *target return pricing*. The firm tries to determine the price that would yield the target rate of return on investment. Target pricing is used by General Motors, which prices its automobiles to achieve a 15 to 20 percent profit on its investment. This pricing method is also used by public utilities that are constrained to make a fair return on their investment.

Suppose the toaster manufacturer above has invested $1,000,000 in the business and wants to set price to earn a 20 percent return, namely, $200,000. The target return price is given by the following formula:

$$\text{Target return price} = \text{Unit cost} + \frac{\text{Desired return} \times \text{Invested capital}}{\text{Unit sales}}$$

$$= \$16 + \frac{.20 \times \$1,000,000}{50,000} = \$20$$

The manufacturer will realize this 20 percent return of investment providing its costs and estimated sales turn out to be accurate. But what if sales do not reach 50,000 units? The manufacturer can prepare a *break-even chart* to learn what would happen at other sales levels. Figure 17-7 shows the break-even chart. Fixed costs are $300,000 regardless of sales volume. Variable costs are superimposed on the fixed costs and rise linearly with volume. The total revenue curve starts at zero and rises linearly with each unit sold. The slope of the total revenue curve reflects the price of $20 per unit.

The total revenue and total cost curves cross at 30,000 units. This is the *break-even volume*. It can be verified by the following formula:

$$\text{Break-even volume} = \frac{\text{Fixed cost}}{\text{Price} - \text{Variable cost}} = \frac{\$300,000}{\$20 - \$10} = 30,000$$

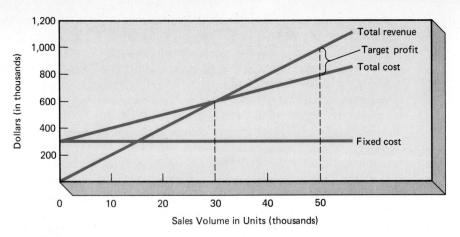

FIGURE 17-7
Break-even Chart for Determining Target Return Price and Break-Even Volume

The manufacturer, of course, is hoping that the market will buy 50,000 units at $20, in which case it earns $200,000 on its $1,000,000 investment. But much depends on the price elasticity and competitors' prices. Unfortunately, target return pricing tends to ignore these considerations. The manufacturer should consider different prices and estimate their probable impacts on sales volume and profits. The manufacturer should also search for ways to lower its fixed and/or variable costs, because this will lower its required break-even volume.

Perceived-Value Pricing   An increasing number of companies are basing their price on the product's *perceived value*. They see the buyers' perception of value, not the seller's cost, as the key to pricing. They use the nonprice variables in the marketing mix to build up perceived value in the buyers' minds. Price is set to capture the perceived value.[11]

Perceived-value pricing fits in well with modern product-positioning thinking. A company develops a product concept for a particular target market with a planned quality and price. Then management estimates the volume it hopes to sell at this price. This indicates the needed plant capacity, investment, and unit costs. Management then figures out whether the product will yield a satisfactory profit at the planned price and cost. If the answer is yes, the company goes ahead with product development. Otherwise the company drops the idea.

Two major practitioners of perceived-value pricing are Du Pont and Caterpillar. When Du Pont developed its new synthetic fiber for carpets, it demonstrated to carpet manufacturers that they could afford to pay Du Pont as much as $1.40 per pound for the new fiber and still make their current profit. Du Pont calls this the *value-in-use price*. Du Pont recognized, however, that pricing the new material at $1.40 per pound would leave the market indifferent. So it set the price lower than $1.40, the amount depending on the rate of market penetration it wanted. Du Pont did not use its unit-manufacturing cost to set the price but only to judge whether there was enough profit to go ahead in the first place.

Caterpillar uses perceived value to set prices on its construction equipment. It might price a tractor at $100,000, although a similar competitor's tractor might be priced at $90,000. And Caterpillar will get more sales than the competitor! When a prospective customer asks a Caterpillar dealer why he should pay $10,000 more for the Caterpillar tractor, the dealer answers:

$ 90,000 is the tractor's price if it is only equivalent to the competitor's tractor
+ $ 7,000 is the price premium for superior durability
+ $ 6,000 is the price premium for superior reliability
+ $ 5,000 is the price premium for superior service
+ $ 2,000 is the price premium for the longer warranty on parts

$110,000 is the price to cover the value package
− $ 10,000 discount

$100,000 final price

This stunned customer learns that although he is being asked to pay a $10,000 premium for the Caterpillar tractor, he is in fact getting a $10,000 discount! He ends up choosing the Caterpillar tractor because he is convinced that the lifetime operating costs of the Caterpillar tractor will be smaller.

The key to perceived-value pricing is to accurately determine the market's perception of the offer's value. Sellers with an inflated view of the value of their offer will overprice their product. Or they might underestimate the perceived value and charge less than they could. Market research is needed to establish the market's perception of value as a guide to effective pricing. Methods for estimating perceived value are described in Exhibit 17-2. Methods for establishing a price around the estimated perceived value are described in Exhibit 17-3.

Going-Rate Pricing   In *going-rate pricing*, the firm bases its price largely on competitors' prices, with less attention paid to its own cost or demand. The firm might charge the same, more, or less than its major competitor(s). In oligopolistic industries that sell a commodity such as steel, paper, or fertilizer, firms normally charge the same price. The smaller firms "follow the leader." They change their prices when the market leader's

EXHIBIT 17-2

Methods for Estimating Perceived Value—An Illustration

Three companies, A, B, and C, produce rapid-relay switches. Industrial buyers are asked to examine and rate the respective companies' offers. Here are three alternative methods:

- **Direct price-rating method.** Here the buyers estimate a price for each switch that they think reflects the total value of buying the switch from each company. For example, they may assign $2.55, $2.00, and $1.52, respectively.
- **Direct perceived-value-rating method.** Here the buyers allocate 100 points to the three companies to reflect the total value of buying the switch from each company. Suppose they assign 42, 33, and 25, respectively. If the average market price of a relay switch is $2.00, the three firms could charge, respectively, $2.55, $2.00, and $1.52, to reflect the variation in perceived value.
- **Diagnostic method.** Here the buyers rate the three offers on a set of attributes. They allocate 100 points to the three companies with regard to each attribute. They also allocate 100 points to reflect the relative importance of the attributes. Suppose the results are as follows:

Importance Weight	Attribute	Products		
		A	B	C
25	Product durability	40	40	20
30	Product reliability	33	33	33
30	Delivery reliability	50	25	25
15	Service quality	45	35	20
100	(Perceived value)	(41.65)	(32.65)	(24.9)

By multiplying the importance weights against each company's ratings, we find that Company A's offer is perceived to be above average (at 42), Company B's offer is average (at 33), and Company C's offer is below average (at 25).

Company A can set a high price for its switches because it is perceived to offer more. If it wants to price proportionally to its perceived value, it can charge around $2.55 (= $2.00 for an average quality switch $\times \frac{42}{33}$). If all three companies set their price proportional to their perceived value, they will all enjoy some market share, since they all offer the same value-to-price.

If a company prices at less than its perceived value, it will gain a higher-than-average market share because buyers will be getting extra value for their money. This is illustrated in the accompanying figure.

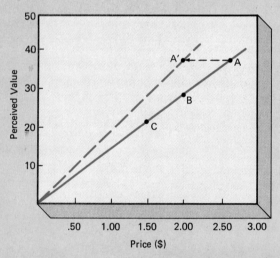

The three offers, A, B, and C, initially lie on the same value/price line. Respective market shares will depend on the relative density of ideal points (not shown) surrounding the three locations. Now suppose Company A lowers its price to A'. Its value/price will be on a higher line (the dashed line), and it will pull market share away from both B and C, particularly B because it offers more value at the same price as B. In self-defense, B will either lower its price or try to raise its perceived value by adding more service, quality, communication, and so on. If the cost of doing this is less than the loss in revenue that would result from a lower price, B should strengthen its perceived value.

prices change rather than when their own demand or cost changes. Some firms may charge a slight premium or slight discount, but they preserve the amount of difference. Thus minor gasoline retailers usually charge a few cents less than the major oil companies, without letting the difference increase or decrease.

EXHIBIT 17-3

Methods for Establishing a Price around a Perceived Value

Companies cannot always depend on their customers' recognizing the value of their offer against their competitors' offers. Sophisticated industrial companies use a tool called *economic value to the customer* (EVC) to build up their customers' perception of value. EVC is calculated by comparing their product's total costs against the benefits of the product the customer is currently using (reference product). This is a particularly effective way of analyzing pricing policy for industrial goods where the purchase price represents only a portion of the lifetime costs to the customer.

We illustrate in the accompanying figure how EVC is determined by looking at two industrial products, "Y" and "Z," being developed to compete with product "X" currently being used by the customer.

New product "Y" performs the same function as the reference product "X," but its start-up and postpurchase costs are only $400, yielding a $300 savings. Because the customer's current product "X" has life-cycle costs of $1,000, the economic value that product "Y" offers the customer is $600 ($1,000 minus $400). Thus the customer will be willing to pay up to $600 for product "Y."

New product "Z" has more features or performance characteristics than product "X" or "Y." These extra features of "Z" have a perceived incremental value of $300 for the customer when compared with the reference product. So compared with the current product, product "Z" saves $100 in postpurchase costs and has an incremental value of $300, resulting in an economic value of $700 to the customer. Thus "Z" provides a higher EVC than "Y" despite its higher postpurchase costs, because it provides additional customer value.

The firm should set its price at a point between its costs and the EVC, as perceived by the customer. So if the firm decided to price product "Y" at $400, it could make a case to the customer that its product yields a savings of $200 compared with the reference product "X," despite the purchase price being higher by a hundred dollars. The firm's profit depends on its cost of supplying "Y." If "Y" costs $250 to supply, the firm will make $150 (= $400 − $250).

The firm can use EVC to determine which market segments to enter. It should enter those market segments where its price will leave the segment's customers with more economic value than they are getting from their current product.

SOURCE: This exhibit has been condensed by the author from John L. Forbis and Nitin T. Mehta, "Economic Value to the Customer," *McKinsey Staff Paper* (Chicago: McKinsey & Co., February 1979), pp. 1–10.

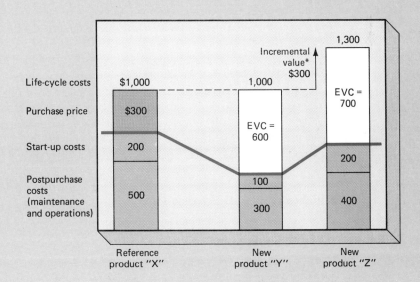

Going-rate pricing is quite popular. Where costs are difficult to measure, or competitive response is uncertain, firms feel that the going price represents a good solution. The going price is thought to reflect the industry's collective wisdom as to the price that would yield a fair return and not jeopardize industrial harmony.

Sealed-Bid Pricing   Competitive-oriented pricing also dominates where firms bid for jobs. The firm bases its price on expectations of how competitors will price rather than on a rigid relation to the firm's costs or demand. The firm wants to win the contract, and this requires pricing lower than the other firms.

Yet the firm cannot set its price below a certain level. It cannot price below cost without worsening its position. On the other hand, the higher it sets its price above its costs, the lower its chance of getting the contract.

The net effect of the two opposite pulls can be described in terms of the *expected profit* of the particular bid. (See Table 17-1.) Suppose a bid of $9,500 would yield a high chance of getting the contract, say .81, but only a low profit, say $100. The expected profit with this bid is therefore $81. If the firm bid $11,000, its profits would be $1,600, but its chance of getting the contract might be reduced, say to .01. The expected profit would be only $16. One logical bidding criterion would be to bid the price that would maximize the expected profit. According to Table 17-1, the best bid would be $10,000, for which the expected profit if $216.

Using expected profit as a criterion for setting price makes sense for the large firm that makes many bids. In playing the odds, the firm will achieve maximum profits in the long run. The firm that bids only occasionally or needs a particular contract badly will not find it advantageous to use the expected-profit criterion. The criterion, for example, does not distinguish between a $1,000 profit with a 0.10 probability and a $125 profit with a 0.80 probability. Yet the firm that wants to keep production going would prefer the second contract to the first.

Selecting the Final Price   The purpose of the previous pricing methods is to narrow the price range from which to select the final price. In selecting the final price, the company must consider some additional factors.

Psychological Pricing   Sellers should consider the psychology of prices and not only their economics. Many consumers use price as an indicator of quality. When Fleischmann raised the price of its gin from $4.50 to $5.50 a fifth, its liquor sales went up, not down. Image pricing is especially effective with ego-sensitive products such as perfumes and expensive cars. A $100 bottle of perfume may contain $10 worth of scent, but people are willing to pay $100 because this price suggests something special.

TABLE 17-1   Effect of Different Bids on Expected Profit

Company's Bid	Company's Profit	Probability of Getting Award with This Bid (Assumed)	Expected Profit
$ 9,500	$ 100	0.81	$ 81
10,000	600	0.36	216
10,500	1,100	0.09	99
11,000	1,600	0.01	16

A study of the relationship between price and quality perceptions of cars found the relationship to be operating in a reciprocal manner.[12] Higher-priced cars were perceived to possess (unwarranted) high quality. Higher-quality cars were likewise perceived to be higher priced than they actually were. When alternative sources of information such as physical differences and store image are available, price becomes an insignificant indicator of quality.[13] However, when other signals are not available, price is important as a quality signal.

Sellers often manipulate *reference prices* in pricing their product. Buyers carry in their minds a reference price when looking at a particular product. The reference price might have been formed by noticing current prices, past prices, or the buying context. For example, a seller could put its product next to an expensive one to imply that the seller's product belongs to the same class. Department stores will sell women's clothing in separate departments differentiated by price; clothing found in the more expensive department is assumed to be of better quality. Reference price thinking is also created by stating a high manufacturer's suggested price, or by indicating that the product was priced much higher originally, or by pointing to a competitor's high price.

Many sellers believe that prices should end in an odd number. Newspaper ads are dominated by prices ending in odd numbers. Thus a stereo amplifier is priced at $299 instead of $300. Many customers see this as a price in the $200 range rather than $300 range. Another explanation is that odd endings convey the notion of a discount or bargain. But if a company wants a high-price image instead of a low-price image, it should avoid the odd-ending tactic.

The Influence of Other Marketing-Mix Elements on Price   The final price must also take into account the brand's quality and advertising relative to competition. Farris and Reibstein examined the relationship between relative price, relative quality, and relative advertising for 227 consumer businesses and found the following results:[14]

1. Brands with average relative quality but high relative advertising budgets were able to charge premium prices. Consumers apparently were more willing to pay higher prices for known products than for unknown products.
2. Brands with high relative quality and high relative advertising obtained the highest prices. Conversely, brands with low quality and low advertising charged the lowest prices.
3. The positive relationship between high prices and high advertising held most strongly in the later stages of the product life cycle, for market leaders, and for low-cost products.

Company Pricing Policies   The contemplated price should be checked for consistency with company pricing policies. Many companies set up a pricing department to develop pricing policies and establish or approve pricing decisions. Their aim is to make sure that the salespeople quote prices that are reasonable to customers and profitable to the company.

Impact of Price on Other Parties   Management must also consider the reactions of other parties to the contemplated price. How will the *distributors* and *dealers* feel about it? Will the *company sales force* be willing to sell at that price or will they complain that it is too high? How will *competitors* react to this price? Will *suppliers* raise their prices when they see the company's price? Will the *government* intervene and prevent this price from being charged? In the last case, marketers need to know the laws affecting price and make sure that their pricing policies are defensible.

ADAPTING THE PRICE

Companies do not set a single price but set a pricing structure that covers different products and items in the line and reflects variations in geographical demand and costs, market-segment intensity of demand, purchase timing, and other factors. We will examine the following price adaptation strategies: geographical pricing, price discounts and allowances, promotional pricing, discriminatory pricing, and product-mix pricing.

Geographical Pricing

Geographical pricing involves the company in deciding how to price its products to customers located in different parts of the country. Should the company charge higher prices to distant customers to cover the higher shipping costs and thereby risk losing their business? Or should the company charge the same to all customers regardless of location? Companies have evolved five different approaches to geographical pricing strategy, and they are described and illustrated in Exhibit 17-4.

EXHIBIT 17-4

Five Geographical Pricing Strategies

We will examine five major geographical pricing strategies in connection with the following hypothetical situation:

> The Peerless Paper Company is located in Atlanta, Georgia, and sells paper products to customers all over the United States. The cost of freight is high and affects from whom customers buy their paper. Peerless wants to establish a geographical pricing policy. Management is trying to think through how to price a $100 order to three specific customers: customer A (Atlanta), customer B (Bloomington, Indiana), and customer C (Compton, California).

FOB Origin Pricing   Peerless can ask each customer to pay the shipping cost from the Atlanta factory to the specific destination. All three customers would pay the same factory price of $100, with customer A paying, say, $10 additional shipping, customer B paying $15 additional, and customer C paying $25 additional. Called FOB origin pricing, it means that the goods are placed free on board a carrier, at which point the title and responsibility passes to the customer, who pays the freight from the factory to the destination.

Advocates of FOB pricing feel that it is the most equitable way to allocate freight charges because each customer picks up its own cost. The disadvantage, however, is that Peerless will be a high-cost firm to distant customers. If Peerless's main competitor is in California, this competitor will outsell Peerless in California. In fact, the competitor will outsell Peerless in most of the West while Peerless will dominate the East. A vertical line could be drawn on a map connecting the cities where the two companies' price plus freight will just be equal. Peerless will have the price advantage east of this line, and its competitor will have the price advantage west of this line.

Uniform Delivered Pricing   Uniform delivered pricing is the exact opposite of FOB pricing. Here the company charges the same price plus freight to all customers regardless of their location. It is called "postage stamp pricing" after the fact that the U.S. government sets a uniform delivered price on first-class mail anywhere in the country. The freight charge is set at the average freight cost. Suppose this is $15. Uniform delivered pricing therefore results in a high charge to the Atlanta customer (who pays $15 freight instead of $10) and a subsidized charge to the Compton customer (who pays $15 instead of $25). The Atlanta customer would prefer to buy paper from another local paper company that uses FOB origin pricing. On the other hand, Peerless has a better chance to win the California customer.

Other advantages are that uniform delivered pricing is relatively easy to administer and allows the firm to maintain a nationally advertised price.

Zone Pricing   Zone pricing falls between FOB origin pricing and uniform delivered pricing. The company establishes two or more zones. All customers within a zone pay the same total price; and this price is higher in the more distant zones. Peerless might set up an East zone and charge $10 freight to all customers in this zone, a Midwest zone and charge $15, and a West zone and charge $25. In this way, the customers within a given price zone receive no price advantage from the company; thus a customer in Atlanta and a customer in Boston pay the same total price to Peerless. The complaint, however, is that the Atlanta customer is subsidizing the freight cost of the Boston customer. In addition, a customer just on the west side of the line dividing the East and Midwest pays substantially more than one just on the east side of the line, although they may be within a few miles of each other.

Basing-Point Pricing   Basing-point pricing allows the seller to designate some city as a basing point and charge all customers the freight cost from that city to the customer location regardless of the city from which the goods are actually shipped. For example, Peerless might establish Chicago as the basing point and charge all customers $100 plus the appropriate freight from Chicago to their destination. This means that Atlanta customers pay the freight cost from Chicago to Atlanta even though the goods may be shipped from Atlanta. They are paying a "phantom charge." In its favor, using a basing-point location other than the factory raises the total price to customers near the factory and lowers the total price to customers far from the factory.

   If all the sellers used the same basing-point city, delivered prices would be the same for all customers, and price competition would be eliminated. Such industries as sugar, cement, steel, and automobiles used basing-point pricing for years, but this method is less popular today because of adverse court ruling charging collusive pricing by competitors. Some companies establish multiple basing points to create more flexibility. They would quote freight charges from the basing-point city nearest to the customer.

Freight Absorption Pricing   The seller who is anxious to do business with a particular customer or geographical area might absorb all or part of the actual freight charges in order to get the business. Sellers might reason that if they can get more business, their average costs will fall and more than compensate for the extra freight costs. Freight-absorption pricing is used for market penetration and also to hold on to increasingly competitive markets.

Price Discounts and Allowances

Most companies will modify their basic price to reward customers for certain acts, such as early payment, volume purchases, and off-season buying. These price adjustments—called discounts and allowances—are described below.

Cash Discounts   A cash discount is a price reduction to buyers who pay their bills promptly. A typical example is "2/10, net 30," which means that payment is due within thirty days but the buyer can deduct 2 percent from the cost by paying the bill within ten days. The discount must be granted to all buyers meeting these terms. Such discounts are customary in many industries and serve the purpose of improving the sellers' liquidity and reducing credit collection costs and bad debts.

Quantity Discounts   A quantity discount is a price reduction to buyers who buy large volumes. A typical example is "$10 per unit for less than 100 units; $9 per unit for 100 or more units." Quantity discounts must be offered to all customers and must not exceed the cost savings to the seller associated with selling large quantities. These savings include reduced expenses of selling, inventory, and transportation. They may be offered on a noncumulative basis (on each order placed) or a cumulative basis (on the number of units ordered over a given period). Discounts provide an incentive to the customer to buy more from a given seller rather than buying from multiple sources.

Functional Discounts   Functional discounts (also called trade discounts) are offered by the manufacturer to trade-channel members if they will perform certain functions such as selling, storing, and record keeping. Manufacturers may offer different functional discounts to different trade channels because of the varying services they perform, but manufacturers must offer the same functional discounts within each trade channel.

Seasonal Discounts   A seasonal discount is a price reduction to buyers who buy merchandise or services out of season. Seasonal discounts allow the seller to maintain steadier production during the year. Ski manufacturers will offer seasonal discounts to retailers in the spring and summer to encourage early ordering. Hotels, motels, and airlines will offer seasonal discounts in their slower selling periods.

Allowances   Allowances are other types of reductions from the list price. For example, *trade-in allowances* are price reductions granted for turning in an old item when buying a new one. Trade-in allowances are most common in the automobile industry and are also found in some other durable-goods categories. *Promotional allowances* are payments or price reductions to reward dealers for participating in advertising and sales-support programs.

Promotional Pricing   Under certain circumstances, companies will temporarily price their products below the list price and sometimes even below cost. Promotional pricing takes several forms.

■ *Loss leader pricing.* Here supermarkets and department stores drop the price on well-known brands to generate store traffic. But manufacturers typically disapprove of their brands being used as loss leaders because this can dilute the brand image as well as cause complaints from other retailers who charge the normal price. Manufacturers have tried to restrain middlemen from loss-leader pricing through retail price maintenance laws, but these laws have been revoked.

■ *Special event pricing.* This will be used by sellers in certain seasons to draw in more customers. Thus linens are promotionally priced every January to attract shopping-weary customers into the stores.

■ *Cash rebates.* Consumers are offered cash rebates to get them to buy the manufacturer's product within a specified time period. The rebate can help the manufacturer clear inventories without having to cut the list price. Auto manufacturers have resorted to rebates a number of times to stimulate sales. The initial rebates were effective, but when repeated, they seemed to lose their effectiveness. They may have given a price break to those who intended to buy a car without stimulating others to think about buying a car. Rebates also appear in consumer packaged goods marketing. They stimulate sales without costing the company as much as would cutting the price. The reason is that many buyers buy the product but never get around to mailing in the coupon for a refund.

■ *Low-interest financing.* This is another tool for stimulating sales without lowering the price. Auto makers resorted to announcing 3 percent financing and in one case 0 percent financing for short periods to attract customers. Since many auto buyers finance their auto purchases, low-interest financing is appealing.[15] Other ways to reduce the "cost" to the auto buyer are through offering *free maintenance* or *longer product warranties.*

■ *Psychological discounting.* This involves putting an artificially high price on a product and then offering it at substantial savings; for example, "Was $359, Now $299." Illegitimate discount tactics are fought by the Federal Trade Commission and Better Business Bureaus. On the other hand, discounts from normal prices are a legitimate form of promotional pricing.

The difficulty with promotional pricing tactics is that if they work, competitors copy them rapidly, and they lose their effectiveness for the individual company; if they do not work, they waste company money that could have been put into longer-impact marketing tools, such as building up product quality and service and improving the product image through advertising.

Discriminatory Pricing

Companies will often modify their basic price to accommodate differences in customers, products, locations, and so on. *Discriminatory pricing* describes the situation where the company sells a product or service at two or more prices that do not reflect a proportional difference in costs. Discriminatory pricing takes several forms:

- ■ *Customer-segment pricing.* Here different customer groups are charged different prices for the same product or service. Museums will charge a lower admission fee to students and senior citizens.
- ■ *Product-form pricing.* Here different versions of the product are priced differently but not proportionately to their respective costs. SCM Corporation prices its most-expensive Proctor-Silex steam/dry iron at $54.95, $5 above its next-most-expensive iron. The top model has a light that signals when the iron is ready. Yet the extra feature costs less than $1 to make. As another example, Evian prices an eight-ounce bottle of its mineral water at 56 cents. Evian takes the same water and packages an ounce of it in a moisturizer spray for $5. Through image pricing, Evian manages to charge $5 an ounce for what is nothing more than water.
- ■ *Image pricing.* Some companies will price the same product at two different levels based on image differences. Thus a perfume manufacturer can put the perfume in one bottle, give it a name and image, and price it at $10 an ounce; and in a fancier bottle with a different name and image and price it at $30 an ounce.
- ■ *Location pricing.* Here different locations are priced differently even though the cost of offering each location is the same. A theater varies its seat prices because of audience preferences for certain locations.
- ■ *Time pricing.* Here prices are varied seasonally, by the day, and even by the hour. Public utilities vary their energy rates to commercial users by time of day and weekend versus weekday.

For price discrimination to work, certain conditions must exist. First, the market must be segmentable, and the segments must show different intensities of demand. Second, members of the segment paying the lower price should not be able to turn around and resell the product to the segment paying the higher price. Third, competitors should not be able to undersell the firm in the segment being charged the higher price. Fourth, the cost of segmenting and policing the market should not exceed the extra revenue derived from price discrimination. Fifth, the practice should not breed customer resentment and ill will. Sixth, the particular form of price discrimination should not be illegal.

With the current deregulation taking place in certain industries, such as airlines and trucks, companies in these industries have increased their use of discriminatory pricing. Consider the price discrimination introduced by airlines:

> The passengers on a plane bound from Cleveland to Miami may be paying as many as eleven different fares for the same flight. Those who checked carefully are benefiting from the heated-up competition between Eastern, United, and three other airlines flying this route. Many of the fares are aimed at segments of the market. The eleven possible fares are (1) $218 for first class, (2) $168 for standard economy class, (3) $136 for night coach, (4) $134 for weekend excursion, (5) $130 for Job Corps volunteers, (6) $128 for midweek excursion, (7) $118 for group-excursion tour, (8) $112 for military personnel, (9) $112 for youth fares, (10) $103 for weekend fares, and (11) $95 for charter.

Product-Mix Pricing   Price-setting logic has to be modified when the product is part of a product mix. In this case, the firm searches for a mutual set of prices that maximize the profits on the total product mix. Pricing is difficult because the various products have demand and cost interrelationships and are subject to different degrees of competition. We can distinguish six situations.

Product-line Pricing   Companies normally develop product lines rather than single products. For example, Panasonic offers five different color video sound cameras, ranging from a simple one weighing 4.6 pounds to a complex one weighing 6.3 pounds that includes auto focusing, fade control, and two-speed zoom lens. Each successive camera in the line offers additional features, permitting *premium pricing*. Management must decide on the *price steps* to establish between the various cameras. The price steps should take into account cost differences between the cameras, customer evaluations of the different features, and competitors' prices. If the price difference between two successive cameras is small, buyers will buy the more-advanced camera, and this will increase company profits if the cost difference is smaller than the price difference. If the price difference is large, customers will buy the less-advanced cameras.

In many lines of trade, sellers use well-established *price points* for the products in their line. Thus men's clothing stores might carry men's suits at three price levels: $150, $220, and $310. The customers will associate low-, average-, and high-quality suits with the three price ''points.'' Even if the three prices are all moderately raised, men will normally buy suits at their preferred price point. The seller's task is to establish perceived-quality differences that lend support to the price differences.

Optional-feature Pricing   Many companies offer optional products or features along with their main product. The automobile buyer can order electric window controls, defoggers, and light dimmers. However, pricing these options is a sticky problem. Automobile companies have to decide which items to build into the price and which ones to offer as options. General Motors' normal pricing strategy is to advertise a stripped-down model for $8,000, to pull people into the showrooms, and devote most of the showroom space to a display of feature-loaded cars at $10,000 or up. The economy model is stripped of so many comforts and conveniences that most buyers will reject it. When GM launched its new front-wheel drive J-cars in the spring of 1981, it took a clue from the Japanese auto makers and included in the sticker price a number of useful features previously sold only as options. Now the advertised price represented a well-equipped car. Unfortunately, however, the price was high and many car shoppers balked.

Restaurants face a similar pricing problem. Restaurant customers can order liquor in addition to the meal. The seller needs to price the optional items. Management can price these options high to make them independently profitable or price them low to act as a traffic builder. Many restaurants price their liquor high and their food low. The food revenue covers the food and other costs of operating the restaurant, and the liquor produces the profit. This explains why waiters press hard to get customers to order drinks. Other restaurants will price their liquor low and food high to draw in a drinking crowd.

Captive-product Pricing   Companies in certain industries produce products that must be used with the main product. Examples of captive products are razor blades and camera film. Manufacturers of the main products (razors and cameras) often price them low and set high markups on the supplies. Thus Kodak prices its cameras low because it makes its money on selling film. Those camera makers who do not sell film have to price their cameras higher in order to make the same overall profit.

There is a danger, however, in pricing the captive product too high. Caterpillar, for example, makes high profits in the aftermarket by putting a high price on its parts and service. It marks up its equipment by 30 percent and its parts sometimes by 300 percent. This has given rise to "pirates" who make copies of these parts and sell them to "shady tree" mechanics who install them, sometimes without passing on the cost savings to the customers. Meanwhile Caterpillar loses these sales. Caterpillar attempts to control this by exhorting equipment owners to use only authorized dealers if they want guaranteed performance. But clearly the problem is created by the high markups that manufacturers put on their aftermarket products in the first place.

Two-part Pricing   Service firms often charge a fixed fee plus a variable usage fee. Thus a telephone user has to pay a minimum monthly fee plus charges for calls beyond the minimum number. Amusement parks charge an admission fee plus fees for rides over a certain minimum. The service firm faces a problem similar to captive-product pricing, namely, how much to charge for the basic service and how much for the variable usage. The fixed fee should be low enough to induce usage of the service, and the profit can be made on the variable usage fees.

Byproduct Pricing   In producing processed meats, petroleum products, and other chemicals, there are often byproducts. If the byproducts have no value and are in fact costly to dispose of, this will affect the pricing of the main product. The manufacturer will seek a market for these byproducts and should accept any price that covers more than the cost of disposing of them. If the byproducts have value to some customer group, then they should be priced on their value. Any income earned on the byproducts will make it easier for the company to charge a lower price on its main product if forced to by competition.

Product-bundling Pricing   Sellers will often combine a set of their products and offer the set at a reduced price. Thus an auto manufacturer might offer an option package at less than the cost of buying all the options separately. A theater company will price a season subscription at less than the cost of buying all the performances separately. Since customers may not have planned to buy all the components, the savings on the price bundle must be substantial enough to induce them to buy the bundle.[16]

INITIATING AND RESPONDING TO PRICE CHANGES

After developing their price strategies and structures, companies will face occasions when they will want to cut or raise prices.

Initiating Price Cuts   Several circumstances might lead a firm to cut its price, even though this might provoke a price war. One circumstance is *excess capacity*. Here the firm needs additional business and cannot generate it through increased sales effort, product improvement, or other alternative measures. In the late 1970s, various companies abandoned "follow-the-leader pricing" and turned to "aggressive pricing" to boost their sales. But in initiating a price cut in an industry with high fixed costs, high contribution margins, and excess capacity, a price cut may lead to a price war as competitors try to hold on to their market share.

Another circumstance is *falling market share* in the face of vigorous price competition. Several American industries—automobiles, consumer electronics, cameras, watches, and steel—have been losing market share to Japanese competitors. Zenith, General Motors, and other American companies have resorted to more-aggressive pricing action. General Motors, for example, cut its subcompact car prices by 10 percent on the West Coast, where Japanese competition is strongest.

Companies will also initiate price cuts in a *drive to dominate the market through lower costs.* Either the company starts with lower costs than its competitors or it initiates price cuts in the hope of gaining market share, which would lead to falling costs through larger volume. People Express waged an aggressive low-price strategy and gained a large market share. But this strategy also involves high risks. The three traps are

1. *Low-quality trap.* Consumers will assume that the quality is below that of the higher-priced competitors.
2. *Fragile market-share trap.* A low price buys market share but not market loyalty. Customers will shift to the next lower-price firm that comes along.
3. *Shallow pockets trap.* The higher-priced competitors may cut their prices and have longer staying power because of deeper cash reserves.

People Express and, some years earlier, Freddie Laker's discount transatlantic airline both fell into these traps.

Companies will consider cutting prices in a period of economic *recession.* Fewer consumers are willing to buy higher-priced versions of a product. Exhibit 17-5 shows that there are several ways in which sellers can adjust their price and marketing mix in the face of a declining demand situation.

Initiating Price Increases

Many companies have had to raise prices in recent years. They do this knowing that the price increases will be resented by customers, dealers, and the company's own sales force. Yet a successful price increase can increase profits considerably. For example, if the company's profit margin is 3 percent of sales, a 1 percent price increase will increase profits by 33 percent if sales volume is unaffected. This is illustrated below where we assume that a company charged $10 and sold 100 units and had costs of $970,

EXHIBIT 17-5

Analyzing the Marketing-Mix Alternatives Facing a Firm in an Economic Recession

Here we will describe an actual but disguised situation involving two competing appliance manufacturers. Company A's appliances are perceived to be of higher quality and higher prices than Company B's appliances. The perceived positions of the two brands are shown in Figure (a) along the dimensions of *perceived value* and *price.* Note that the two brands lie on the same value-to-price line. This means that consumers feel they would get approximately the same value per dollar whether they bought brand A or B. Those who want more total value would buy A if they could afford it. Those who want to spend less would buy B.

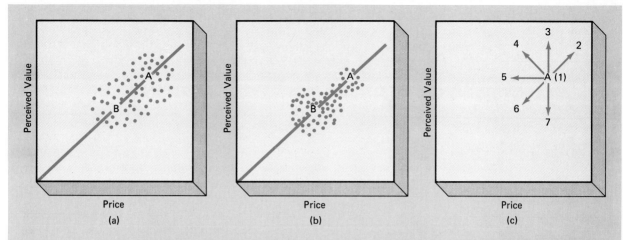

The dots in Figure (a) represent the preferences of potential buyers for value/price combinations. Buyers whose preferences are nearest to A will buy A; the same goes for B. Clearly each brand has a substantial market, and both are likely to enjoy good market shares.

An economic recession now occurs. It shifts buyer preferences toward the cheaper appliance B. [See Figure (b).] The number of buyers who are willing to buy the higher-price appliance diminishes. If Company A does nothing about this, its market share will shrink.

Company A must identify its marketing alternatives and choose among them. At least seven marketing alternatives exist. They are illustrated in Figure (c) and described below.

Strategic Options	Reasoning	Consequences
1. Maintain price and perceived value. Engage in selective customer pruning.	Firm has high customer loyalty. It is willing to lose poorer customers to competitors.	Smaller market share. Lower profitability.
2. Raise price and perceived value.	Raise price to cover rising costs. Improve offer quality to justify higher prices.	Smaller market share. Maintained profitability.
3. Maintain price and raise perceived value.	It is cheaper to maintain price and raise perceived value.	Smaller market share. Short-term decline in profitability. Long-term increase in profitability.
4. Cut price partly and raise perceived value.	Must give customers some price reduction but stress higher value of offer.	Maintained market share. Short-term decline in profitability. Long-term maintained profitability.
5. Cut price fully and maintain perceived value.	Discipline and discourage price competition.	Maintained market share. Short-term decline in profitability.
6. Cut price fully and reduce perceived value.	Discipline and discourage price competition and maintain profit margin.	Maintained market share. Maintained margin. Reduced long-term profitability.
7. Maintain price and reduce perceived value.	Cut marketing expenses to combat rising costs.	Smaller market share. Maintained margin. Reduced long-term profitability.

Here we want to make a few observations:

- Company A should think seriously about launching an economy model located close to Company B's model so that it can capture the increased number of economy-minded customers (a modification of alternative 6). By offering both a prestige and an economy model, Company A can hold or increase its market share.

leaving a profit of $30, or 3 percent on sales. By raising its price by ten cents (1 percent price increase), it boosted its profits by 33 1/3 percent, assuming the same sales volume:

	Before	After	
Price	$ 10	$10.10	(a 1% price increase)
Units sold	100	100	
Revenue	$1,000	$1,010	
Costs	−970	−970	
Profit	$ 30	$ 40	(a 33⅓% profit increase)

A major circumstance provoking price increases is the occurrence of *cost inflation*. Rising costs unmatched by productivity gains squeeze profit margins and lead companies to regular rounds of price increases. Companies often raise their prices by more than the cost increase in anticipation of further inflation or government price controls; this is called *anticipatory pricing*. Companies hesitate to make long-run price commitments to customers, fearing that cost inflation will erode their profit margins.

Another factor leading to price increases is *overdemand*. When a company cannot supply all of its customers' needs, it can raise its prices, put customers on allocation, or both. The "real" price can be increased in several ways, each with a different impact on buyers. The following price adjustments are common:

■ *Adoption of delayed quotation pricing.* The company decides not to set its final price until the product is finished or delivered. Delayed quotation pricing is prevalent in industries with long production lead times, such as industrial construction and heavy-equipment manufacture.

■ *Use of escalator clauses.* The company requires the customer to pay today's price and all or part of any inflation increase that takes place before delivery. An escalator clause in the contract bases price increases on some specified price index, such as the cost-of-living index. Escalator clauses are found in many contracts involving industrial projects of long duration.

■ *Unbundling of goods and services.* The company maintains its price but removes or prices separately one or more elements that were part of the former offer, such as free delivery or installation. IBM, for example, now offers training as a separately priced service. Many restaurants have shifted from dinner pricing to a la carte pricing. A joke in Argentina is that the current price of a car no longer includes the tires and steering wheel.

■ *Reduction of discounts.* The company reduces its normal cash and quantity discounts and instructs its sales force not to offer off-list pricing to get the business.

Sometimes the issue is whether to raise the price sharply on a one-time basis or to raise it by small amounts several times.

> U.S. Gypsum faced this problem when it fell into an oversold position on wallboard, fully recognizing that it would catch up with demand in six months and move to an undersold position. The issue was whether to put through a sharp price increase followed by a sharp price decrease six months later, or a small price increase followed by a small price decrease six months later. It chose the former because dealers were more concerned with availability than price and would make good money even at the higher price.

In passing price increases on to the customers, the company needs to avoid acquiring the image of price gouger. Customer memories are long, and they will turn against the price gougers when the market softens. The price increases should be supported with company communications explaining to customers why prices are being increased. The company's sales force should help customers find ways to economize.

It should be added that there are other ways to meet high costs or demand without raising prices. The possibilities include the following:

- Shrinking the amount of product instead of raising the price. (For example, at one time Hershey Foods maintained its fifteen-cent candy bar but trimmed its size. Nestlé, on the other hand, maintained the old size but raised the price to twenty cents.)
- Substituting less-expensive materials or ingredients. (For example, many candy bar companies substituted synthetic chocolate for real chocolate to fight the price increases in cocoa. Auto manufacturers have replaced metal with plastic wherever possible.)
- Reducing or removing product features to reduce cost. (For example, Sears engineered down a number of its appliances so they could be priced competitively with those sold in discount stores.)
- Removing or reducing product services, such as installation, free delivery, or long warranties.
- Using less-expensive packaging material or promoting larger units to keep down the relative cost of packaging.
- Reducing the number of sizes and models offered.
- Creating new economy brands or generic foods. (For example, the Jewel Food Stores introduced 170 generic items selling at 10 to 30 percent less than national brands to offer to price-conscious consumers.)

The best action to take is not always obvious. Quaker Oats produces the successful cereal called Quaker Oats Natural, which contains several ingredients, such as almonds and raisins, whose prices jumped during the inflation. Quaker Oats saw two choices, namely, raising the price or cost-reducing the contents by including fewer almonds and raisins or finding cheaper substitutes. It wanted to avoid tampering with the product and raised the price. But the price elasticity was high, and sales fell. This forced it to reconsider ways to cost-reduce the contents, knowing that this would involve a great risk.

Buyers' Reactions to Price Changes

Any price change will certainly affect buyers, competitors, distributors, and suppliers and may interest government as well. Here we will consider buyers' reactions.

Customers do not always put a straightforward interpretation on price changes.[17]

A price cut can be interpreted in the following ways: The item is about to be replaced by a later model; the item has some fault and is not selling well; the firm is in financial trouble and may not stay in business to supply future parts; the price will come down even further and it pays to wait; or the quality has been reduced.

A price increase, which would normally deter sales, may carry some positive meanings to the buyers: The item is very "hot" and may be unobtainable unless it is bought soon; the item represents an unusually good value; or the seller is greedy and is charging what the traffic will bear.

Buyers' reactions to price changes also vary with their perception of the product's cost in relation to their total expenditures. Buyers are most price sensitive to products that cost a lot and/or are bought frequently, whereas they hardly notice higher prices on small items that they buy infrequently. In addition, buyers are normally less concerned with the product's *price* than the *total costs* of obtaining, operating, and servicing the product. A seller can charge more than the competition and still get the business if the customer can be convinced that the total costs are lower.

Competitors' Reactions to Price Changes

A firm contemplating a price change has to worry about competitors' as well as customers' reactions. Competitors are very likely to react where the number of firms is small, the product is homogeneous, and the buyers are highly informed.

How can the firm anticipate the likely reactions of its competitors? Assume that the firm faces one large competitor. The competitor's reaction can be estimated from two vantage points. One is to assume that the competitor reacts in a set way to price changes. In this case, its reaction can be anticipated. The other is to assume that the competitor treats each price change as a fresh challenge and reacts according to self-interest at the time. In this case, the company will have to figure out what lies in the competitor's self-interest at the time. The competitor's current financial situation should be researched, along with recent sales and capacity, customer loyalty, and corporate objectives. If the competitor has a market-share objective, it is likely to match the price change. If it has a profit-maximization objective, it may react on some other strategy front, such as increasing the advertising budget or improving the product quality. The task is to read the competitor's mind by using inside and outside sources of information.

The problem is complicated because the competitor can put different interpretations on, say, a company price cut: The competitor can surmise that the company is trying to steal the market, that the company is doing poorly and trying to boost its sales, or that the company wants the whole industry to reduce prices to stimulate total demand.

When there are several competitors, the company must estimate each competitor's likely reaction. If all competitors behave alike, this estimate amounts to an analysis of a typical competitor. If the competitors do not react uniformly because of critical differences in size, market shares, or policies, then separate analyses are necessary. If some competitors will match the price change, there is good reason to expect that the rest will also match it. Exhibit 17-6 shows how a major chemical company analyzed the probable reactions of various parties to a contemplated price reduction.

Responding to Price Changes

Here we reverse the question and ask how a firm should respond to a price change initiated by a competitor. In markets characterized by high product homogeneity, the firm has little choice but to meet a competitor that cuts its price. The firm should search for ways to differentiate its own augmented product, but if it cannot find any, it will have to meet the price reduction.

When a competitor raises its price in a homogeneous product market, the other firms may not match it. They will comply if the price increase will benefit the industry as a whole. But if one firm does not think that it or the industry would gain, its noncompliance can make the leader and the others rescind the price increases.

In nonhomogeneous product markets, a firm has more latitude in reacting to a competitor's price change. Buyers choose the vendor on a multiplicity of considerations: service, quality, reliability, and other factors. These factors desensitize buyers to minor price differences.

EXHIBIT 17-6

How a Large Chemical Company Assessed Likely Competitors' Reactions to a Contemplated Price Cut and Used Decision Theory to Guide its Decision Making

A large chemical company had been selling a plastic substance to industrial users for several years and enjoyed a 40 percent market share. The management became worried about whether its current price of one dollar per pound could be maintained for much longer. The main source of concern was the rapid buildup of capacity by its three competitors and the possible attraction of further competitors by the current price. Management saw that the key to the problem of possible oversupply lay in further market expansion. The key area for market expansion lay in an important segment of the market that was closely held by a substitute plastic product produced by six firms. This substitute product was not as good, but it was priced lower. Management saw a possible solution in displacing the substitute product in the recalcitrant segment through a price reduction. If it could penetrate this segment, there was a good chance it could also penetrate three other segments, which had resisted the displacement.

The first task was to develop a decision model for the problem. This required defining the objectives, price alternatives, and key uncertainties. The chosen objective was to maximize the present value of future profits over the next five years. Management considered four price alternatives: maintaining the price at one dollar, or reducing the price to ninety-three, eighty-five, and eighty cents. The key uncertainties were:

- How much penetration in the key segment would take place without a price reduction?
- How would the six firms producing the substitute plastic react to each possible price reduction?
- How much key-segment penetration would take place for each possible price reaction by the suppliers of the substitute plastic?
- How much would key segment penetration speed up penetration of the other segments?
- If the key segment was not penetrated, what is the probability that the company's competitors would initiate price reduction soon?
- How would a price reduction affect the decision of existing competitors to expand their capacity and potential competitors to enter the industry?

The data-gathering phase consisted in asking sales personnel to place subjective probabilities on the possible states of the key uncertainties. For example, one question asked for the probability that the producers of the substitute product would retaliate if the company reduced its price to ninety-three cents per pound. On the average, the sales personnel felt that there was a 5 percent probability of a full match, a 60 percent probability of a half match, and a 35 percent probability of no retaliation. They were also asked for probabilities if price were reduced to eighty-five and to eighty cents. The sales personnel indicated, as expected, that the probability of retaliation increased with the size of the price reduction.

The next step was to estimate the payoff associated with each price alternative. A decision-tree analysis revealed over four hundred possible outcomes. For this reason, the estimation of expected payoffs was programmed on a computer. The results indicated that all price reductions had a higher expected payoff than no price reduction, and a price reduction to eighty cents had the highest expected payoff. To check the sensitivity of these results, they were recomputed for alternative assumptions about the rate of market growth and the cost of capital. The ranking of the strategies was not affected by the change in assumptions. The analysis confirmed the desirability of a price reduction.

SOURCE: See Paul E. Green, "Bayesian Decision Theory in Pricing Strategy," *Journal of Marketing,* January 1963, pp. 5–14:

Before reacting, the firm needs to consider the following issues: (1) Why did the competitor change the price? Is it to steal the market, to utilize excess capacity, to meet changing cost conditions, or to lead an industrywide price change? (2) Does the competitor plan to make the price change temporary or permanent? (3) What will happen to the company's market share and profits if it does not respond? Are other companies going to respond? and (4) What are the competitor's and other firms' responses likely to be to each possible reaction?

Market leaders frequently face aggressive price cutting by smaller firms trying to build market share. Using price, Fuji attacks Kodak, Bic attacks Gillette, and Datril attacks Tylenol. IBM's personal computers are under great attack today from much lower priced computers such as Leading Edge and Amstrad (both made in South Korea at much lower costs). When the attacking firm's product is comparable to the leaders, its lower price will cut into the leader's share. The leader at this point has several options:

■ **Maintain price.** The leader might maintain its price and profit margin, believing that (a) it would lose too much profit if it reduced its price; (b) it would not lose much market share; and (c) it could regain market share when necessary. The leader feels that it could hold on to good customers, giving up the poorer ones to the competitor. The argument against price maintenance is that the attacker gets more confident as its sales increase, the leader's sales force gets demoralized, and the leader loses more share than expected. The leader panics, lowers price to regain share, and finds it more difficult and costly than expected.

■ **Raise relative perceived quality.** The leader could maintain price but strengthen the value of its offer. It could improve its product, services, and communications. It could stress the relative quality of its product over that of the low-price competitor. The firm may find it cheaper to maintain price and spend money to improve its relative quality than to cut price and operate at a lower margin.

■ **Reduce price.** The leader might lower its price to the competitor's price. It might do this because (a) its costs fall with volume; (b) it would lose a lot of share because the market is price sensitive; and (c) it would be hard to rebuild market share once it is lost. This action will cut its profits in the short run. Some firms will reduce their product quality, services, and marketing communications to maintain profits, but this will ultimately hurt their long-run market share. The company should try to maintain the value of its offer as it cuts prices.

■ **Increase price and improve quality.** The leader might raise its price and introduce some new brands to bracket the attacking brand. Heublein, Inc., used this strategy when its Smirnoff's vodka, which had 23 percent of the American vodka market, was attacked by another brand, Wolfschmidt, priced at one dollar less a bottle. Instead of Heublein's lowering the price of Smirnoff by one dollar, it raised the price by one dollar and put the increased revenue into its advertising. Heublein set up another brand, Relska, to compete with Wolfschmidt and still another, Popov, to sell for less than Wolfschmidt. This strategy effectively bracketed Wolfschmidt and gave Smirnoff an even more elite image.

■ **Launch low-price fighter line.** One of the best responses is to add lower-price items to the line or to create a separate lower-price brand. This is necessary if the particular market segment being lost is price-sensitive, since it will not respond to arguments of higher quality.

The best response requires an analysis of the particular situation. The company under attack has to consider the product's stage in the life cycle, its importance in the company's product portfolio, the intentions and resources of the competitor, the price and value sensitivity of the market, the behavior of costs with volume, and the company's alternative opportunities.

An extended analysis of company alternatives is not always feasible at the time of a price change. The competitor may have spent considerable time in preparing this decision, but the company may have to react decisively within hours or days. About the only way to cut down price-reaction decision time is to anticipate possible competitors' price changes and to prepare contingent responses. Figure 17-8 shows a company price-reaction program to be used if a competitor cuts prices. Reaction programs for meeting price changes find their greatest application in industries where price changes occur with some frequency

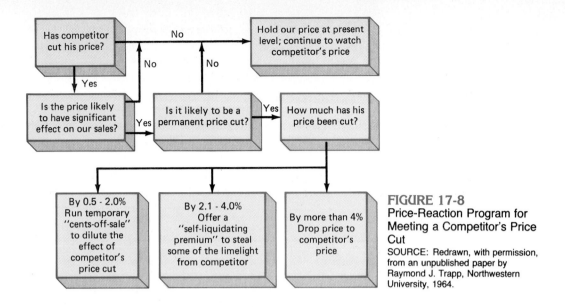

FIGURE 17-8
Price-Reaction Program for Meeting a Competitor's Price Cut
SOURCE: Redrawn, with permission, from an unpublished paper by Raymond J. Trapp, Northwestern University, 1964.

and where it is important to react quickly. Examples can be found in the meatpacking, lumber, and oil industries.

SUMMARY

In spite of the increased role of nonprice factors in the modern marketing process, price remains a critical element and is especially challenging in markets characterized by monopolistic competition or oligopoly.

In setting the price of a product, the company follows a six-step procedure. First, the company carefully establishes its marketing objective(s), such as survival, maximum current profit, maximum current revenue, maximum sales growth, maximum market skimming, or product-quality leadership. Second, the company determines the demand schedule, which shows the probable quantity purchased per period at alternative price levels. The more inelastic the demand, the higher the company can set its price. Third, the company estimates how its costs vary at different output levels and with different levels of accumulated production experience. Fourth, the company examines competitors' prices as a basis for positioning its own price. Fifth, the company selects one of the following pricing methods: markup pricing, target return pricing, perceived-value pricing, going-rate pricing, and sealed-bid pricing. Sixth, the company selects its final price, expressing it in the most effective psychological way, coordinating it with the other marketing-mix elements, checking that it conforms to company pricing policies, and making sure it will prevail with distributors and dealers, company sales force, competitors, suppliers, and government.

Companies adapt the price to varying conditions in the marketplace. One is geographical pricing, where the company decides on how to price to distant customers. A second is price discounts and allowances, where the company establishes cash discounts, quantity discounts, functional discounts, seasonal discounts, and allowances. A third is promotional pricing, where the company decides on loss-leader pricing, special-event pricing, cash rebates, low-interest financing, and psychological discounting. A fourth is discriminatory pricing, where the company establishes different prices for different customer segments, product forms, brand images, places, and times. A fifth is product-mix pricing, where the company decides on the price zones for several products in a product line and on the pricing of optional features, captive products, byproducts, and product bundles.

When a firm considers initiating a price change, it must carefully consider customers' and competitors' reactions. Customers' reactions are influenced by the meaning customers see in the price change. Competitors' reactions flow from either a set reaction policy or a fresh appraisal of each situation. The firm initiating the price change must also anticipate the probable reactions of suppliers, middlemen, and government.

The firm that faces a price change initiated by a competitor must try to understand the competitor's intent and the likely duration of the change. If swiftness of reaction is desirable, the firm should preplan its reactions to different possible price actions by competitors.

■ QUESTIONS

1. While tire-industry costs rose 4 percent, tire prices declined 7 percent. In the area of office personal computers, a striking new feature arises—a price tag of less than $1,000, down from the $3,000 price tag of three years ago. What factors common to both these products have driven down prices? How can companies gain higher margins in each of these industries?

2. Discount car dealers who have set prices at "$49 over invoice" have encountered long delivery delays and anonymous hate-mail. What factors have they ignored in developing their pricing strategy?

3. What is price elasticity? Differentiate between elasticity, inelasticity, long-run elasticity, and short-run elasticity. Provide examples from industry.

4. Under what circumstances would a manufacturer initiate price cuts?

5. In an effort to stimulate sales during a recessionary period, small-appliance manufacturers offered rebates, and auto makers offered low-interest-rate loans. What are the respective advantages and disadvantages of these two methods of price reduction?

6. Predatory pricing—pricing below costs to damage or destroy a competitor—is illegal. The Supreme Court ruled in the 1960s that total costs were the criteria for determining predatory pricing; in the 1970s, a *Harvard Law Review* article proposed that average variable costs be the level below which pricing would be considered predatory. What are the consequences for large and small companies for adoption of either test?

7. Armco, a major steel company, has developed a new process for galvanizing steel sheets so that they can be painted (previously not possible) and used in car-body parts to prevent rust. What factors should Armco consider in setting a price for this product?

8. A firm might set a low price on a product to discourage competitors from coming in. Are there any situations when a firm might deliberately want to attract competitors into a new market and set a high price for this reason?

9. Xerox developed an office-copying machine called 914. The machine was more expensive than competitive machines but offered the user superior copy and lower variable costs: 1 cent per copy as opposed to between 4 cents and 9 cents for competing processes. The machine cost $2,500 to produce, and management considered pricing it at either $3,500 or $4,500. How could management estimate unit sales at the two alternative price levels?

10. In principle, a reduction in price is tantamount to an increase in marketing effort. How can the price reduction be monetized into its equivalent in increased marketing effort?

11. Four companies, W, X, Y, and Z, produce electric can openers. Consumers were asked to allocate 100 points among the companies' products for each of four attributes. The results are shown below:

Importance Weight	Attribute	Company Products			
		W	X	Y	Z
0.35	Durability	30	15	40	15
0.15	Attractiveness	20	20	30	30
0.25	Noiselessness	30	15	35	20
0.25	Safety	25	25	25	25

An average electric can opener sells for $20. What should company W do about the pricing of its product if company Y charges $22?

■ FOOTNOTES

1 David J. Schwartz, *Marketing Today: A Basic Approach*, 3rd ed. (New York: Harcourt Brace Jovanovich, 1981), p. 271.

2 See "Segmentation Strategies Create New Pressure among Marketers," *Marketing News*, March 28, 1986, p. 1.

3 Thomas T. Nagle, *The Strategy and Tactics of Pricing* (Englewood Cliffs, N.J.: Prentice-Hall, 1987), Chap. 3. This is an excellent reference book for making pricing decisions.

4 John R. Nevin, "Laboratory Experiments for Estimating Consumer Demand—A Validation Study," *Journal of Marketing Research*, August 1974, pp. 261–68.

5 See Sidney Bennett and J. B. Wilkinson, "Price-Quantity Relationships and Price Elasticity under In-Store Experimentation," *Journal of Business Research*, January 1974, pp. 30–34.

6 Nagle, *Strategy and Tactics,* Chap. 11.

7 In summary:

$$Eqp = \frac{(Q_1 - Q_0)/\frac{1}{2}(Q_0 + Q_1)}{(P_1 - P_0)/\frac{1}{2}(P_0 + P_1)}$$

where:

Eqp = elasticity of quantity demanded with respect to a change in price

Q_0, Q_1 = quantity demanded per period before and after price change

P_0, P_1 = old and new price

Suppose a company lowers its price from $10 to $5, and its sales rise from 100 units to 150 units:

$$\frac{(150 - 100)/\frac{1}{2}(100 + 150)}{(\$5 - \$10)/\frac{1}{2}(\$10 + \$5)} = \frac{.40}{-.67} = -.60$$

Thus the demand elasticity is less than -1, or inelastic, and we know that total revenue will fall. Checking this, we note that the total revenue fell from $1,000 to $750.

8 Arnold C. Harberger, *The Demand for Durable Goods* (Chicago: University of Chicago Press, 1960), pp. 3–14.

9 For methods of estimating elasticity, see Leonard J. Parsons and Randall L. Schultz, *Marketing Models and Econometric Research* (New York: North-Holland, 1976).

10 "Supermarket 1984 Sales Manual," *Progressive Grocer*, July 1984.

11 See Daniel A. Nimer, "Pricing the Profitable Sale Has a Lot to Do with Perception," *Sales Management*, May 19, 1975, pp. 13–14.

12 Gary M. Erickson and Johny K. Johansson, "The Role of Price in Multi-Attribute Product-Evaluations," *Journal of Consumer Research*, September 1985, pp. 195–99.

13 George J. Szybillo and Jacob Jacoby, "Intrinsic versus Extrinsic Cues as Determinants of Perceived Product Quality," *Journal of Applied Psychology*, February 1974, pp. 74–78.

14 Paul W. Farris and David J. Reibstein, "How Prices, Expenditures, and Profits Are Linked," *Harvard Business Review*, November–December 1979, pp. 173–84.

15 Low-interest financing attracts customers to auto showrooms, but many do not buy when they learn that a large down payment is required; the loan must be paid back in thirty months instead of sixty months; the car price is not discounted much with this kind of loan; and the loan may apply only to expensive cars. See "Finance Deals Aren't Helping Sales of Autos," *Wall Street Journal*, March 17, 1983.

16 See Gerald J. Tellis, "Beyond the Many Faces of Price: An Integration of Pricing Strategies," *Journal of Marketing*, October 1986, pp. 146–60, here p. 155. This excellent article also analyzes and illustrates other pricing strategies.

17 For an excellent review, see Kent B. Monroe, "Buyers' Subjective Perceptions of Price," *Journal of Marketing Research*, February 1973, pp. 70–80.

18

Selecting
and Managing
Marketing Channels

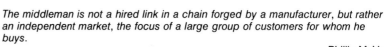

The middleman is not a hired link in a chain forged by a manufacturer, but rather an independent market, the focus of a large group of customers for whom he buys.

Phillip McVey

In today's economy, most producers do not sell their goods directly to the final users. Between them and the final users stand a host of marketing intermediaries performing a variety of functions and bearing a variety of names. Some intermediaries—such as wholesalers and retailers—buy, take title to, and resell the merchandise; they are called *merchant middlemen*. Others—such as brokers, manufacturers' representatives, and sales agents—search for customers and may negotiate on behalf of the producer but do not take title to the goods; they are called *agent middlemen*. Still others—such as transportation companies, independent warehouses, banks, and advertising agencies—assist in the performance of distribution but neither take title to goods nor negotiate purchases or sales; they are called *facilitators*.

Marketing-channel decisions are among the most critical decisions facing management. *The company's chosen channels intimately affect all the other marketing decisions.* The company's pricing depends on whether it uses mass merchandisers or high-quality boutiques. The firm's sales-force and advertising decisions depend on how much training and motivation the dealers need. In addition, the company's channel decisions *involve relatively long term commitments to other firms.* When an auto maker signs up independent dealers to sell its automobiles, it cannot buy them out the next day and replace them with company-owned outlets. When a drug manufacturer relies on independent retail druggists to sell its products, it must heed them when they object to its selling through mass-distribution outlets. Corey observed:

> A distribution system . . . is a key *external* resource. Normally it takes years to build, and it is not easily changed. It ranks in importance with key *internal* resources such as manufacturing,

research, engineering, and field sales personnel and facilities. It represents a significant corporate commitment to large numbers of independent companies whose business is distribution—and to the particular markets they serve. It represents, as well, a commitment to a set of policies and practices that constitute the basic fabric on which is woven an extensive set of long-term relationships.[1]

Thus there is a powerful inertial tendency in channel arrangements. Therefore management must choose channels with an eye on tomorrow's likely selling environment as well as today's.

In this chapter, we will answer the following questions: What is the nature of marketing channels? What decisions do companies face in designing, managing, evaluating, and modifying their channels? What trends are taking place in channel dynamics? In the next chapter we will examine marketing-channel issues from the perspective of retailers, wholesalers, and physical-distribution agencies.

THE NATURE OF MARKETING CHANNELS

Most producers work with marketing intermediaries to bring their products to market. The marketing intermediaries make up a *marketing channel* (also called trade channel or distribution channel). We will use Stern and El-Ansary's definition of a marketing channel:

Marketing channels can be viewed as sets of interdependent organizations involved in the process of making a product or service available for use or consumption.[2]

Why Are Marketing Intermediaries Used?
Why is the producer willing to delegate some of the selling job to intermediaries? The delegation means relinquishing some control over how and to whom the products are sold. The producer appears to be placing the firm's destiny in the hands of intermediaries.

Since producers could sell directly to final customers, they must feel that they gain certain advantages in using middlemen. These advantages are described below.

Many producers lack the financial resources to carry out direct marketing. For example, General Motors sells its automobiles through over ten thousand dealer outlets; even General Motors would be hard pressed to raise the cash to buy out its dealers.

Direct marketing would require many producers to become middlemen for the complementary products of other producers in order to achieve mass-distribution economies. For example, the Wm. Wrigley Jr. Company would not find it practical to establish small retail gum shops throughout the country or to sell gum door-to-door or by mail order. It would have to sell gum along with many other small products and would end up in the drugstore and grocery store business. Wrigley finds it easier to work through the extensive network of privately owned distribution institutions.

Producers who can afford to establish their own channels can often earn a greater return by increasing their investment in their main business. If a company earns a 20 percent rate of return on manufacturing and foresees only a 10 percent return on retailing, it will not want to undertake its own retailing.

Some producers, however, will set up a partially owned distribution system. Thus McDonald's owns over one-fourth of its total outlets. The advantage is that the company learns a lot about managing retail outlets and about the performance it can expect from operator-owned outlets. The disadvantage is that operator-owned outlets may resent the competition coming from company-owned outlets. Dual distribution often creates channel conflict.

The use of middlemen largely boils down to their superior efficiency in making goods widely available and accessible to target markets. Marketing intermediaries, through their contacts, experience, specialization, and scale of operation, offer the firm more than it can usually achieve on its own.

From the point of view of the economic system, the basic role of marketing intermediaries is to transform the heterogeneous supplies found in nature into meaningful goods assortments desired by people. According to Stern and El-Ansary:

> Intermediaries smooth the flow of goods and services . . . This procedure is necessary in order to bridge the discrepancy between the assortment of goods and services generated by the producer and the assortment demanded by the consumer. The discrepancy results from the fact that manufacturers typically produce a large quantity of a limited variety of goods, whereas consumers usually desire only a limited quantity of a wide variety of goods.[3]

Wroe Alderson summarized this by stating: "The goal of marketing is the matching of segments of supply and demand."[4]

Figure 18-1 shows one major source of the economies effected by the use of middlemen. Part (a) shows three producers, each using direct marketing to reach three customers. This system requires nine different contacts. Part (b) shows the three producers working through one distributor, who contacts the three customers. This system requires only six contacts. In this way, middlemen reduce the amount of work that must be done.

Marketing-Channel Functions and Flows

A marketing channel performs the work of moving goods from producers to consumers. It overcomes the critical time, place, and possession gaps that separate goods and services from those who would use them. Members in the marketing channel perform a number of key functions and participate in the following marketing flows:

■ **Information.** The collection and dissemination of marketing research information about potential and current customers, competitors, and other actors and forces in the marketing environment.

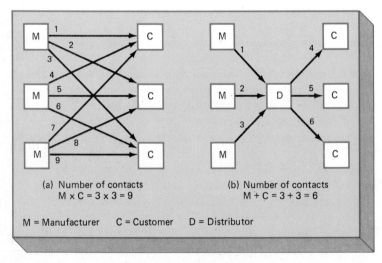

FIGURE 18-1
How a Distributor Effects an Economy of Effort

(a) Number of contacts
M × C = 3 × 3 = 9

(b) Number of contacts
M + C = 3 + 3 = 6

M = Manufacturer   C = Customer   D = Distributor

■ *Promotion.* The development and dissemination of persuasive communications about the offer designed to attract customers.

■ *Negotiation.* The attempt to reach final agreement on price and other terms of the offer so that transfer of ownership or possession can be effected.

■ *Ordering.* The backward communication of intentions to buy by the marketing-channel members to the manufacturer.

■ *Financing.* The acquisition and allocation of funds required to finance the carrying of inventory at any level of the marketing channel.

■ *Risk Taking.* The assumptions of risks in connection with carrying out the channel work.

■ *Physical Possession.* The successive storage and movement of physical products from raw materials to the final customers.

■ *Payment.* Buyers paying their bills through banks and other financial institutions to the sellers for the goods and services provided.

■ *Title.* The actual transfer of ownership from one marketing institution to another.

These functions and flow are listed in the normal order in which they arise between any two channel members. Some of these flows are *forward flows* (physical, title, and promotion); others are *backward flows* (ordering and payment); and still others move in *both directions* (information, finance, and risk taking). Five of these flows are illustrated in Figure 18-2 for the marketing of forklifts. If all of these flows were superimposed in one diagram, the tremendous complexity of even simple marketing channels would be apparent.

FIGURE 18-2
Five Different Marketing Flows in the Marketing Channel for Forklift Trucks

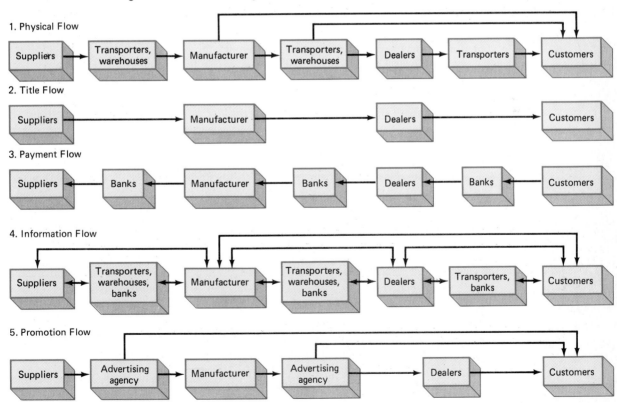

The question is not *whether* these functions need to be performed—they must be—but rather *who* is to perform them. All the functions have three things in common: They use up scarce resources; they can often be performed better through specialization; and they are shiftable among channel members. To the extent that the manufacturer performs the functions, the manufacturer's costs go up, and its prices have to be higher. When some functions are shifted to middlemen, the producer's costs and prices are lower, but the middlemen must add a charge to cover their work. If the middlemen are more efficient than the manufacturer, the prices faced by consumers should be lower. Consumers might decide to perform some of the functions themselves, in which case they would face still lower prices. The issue of who should perform various channel tasks is one of relative efficiency and effectiveness.

Marketing functions, then, are more basic than the institutions that at any given time perform them. Changes in channel institutions largely reflect the discovery of more efficient ways to combine or separate economic functions that must be carried out to provide meaningful assortments of goods to target customers.

Number of Channel Levels

Marketing channels can be characterized by the number of channel levels. Each middleman that performs some work in bringing the product and its title closer to the final buyer constitutes a *channel level*. Since the producer and the final consumer both perform some work, they are part of every channel. We will use the number of *intermediary levels* to designate the *length* of a channel. Figure 18-3(a) illustrates several consumer goods marketing channels of different lengths.

A *zero-level channel* (also called a *direct-marketing channel*) consists of a manufacturer selling directly to consumers. The three major ways of direct selling are door-to-door, mail order, and manufacturer-owned stores. Avon's sales representatives sell cosmetics to women on a door-to-door basis; Franklin Mint sells collectible objects through mail order; and Singer sells its sewing machines through its own stores.

A *one-level channel* contains one selling intermediary, such as a retailer.

A *two-level channel* contains two intermediaries. In consumer markets, they are typically a wholesaler and a retailer.

A *three-level channel* contains three intermediaries. For example, in the meatpacking industry, a jobber usually intervenes between the wholesalers and the retailers. The jobber buys from wholesalers and sells to the smaller retailers who generally are not serviced by the large wholesalers.

Higher-level marketing channels are also found but with less frequency. From the producer's point of view, the problem of attaining information and exercising control increases with the number of channel levels, even though the manufacturer typically deals only with the adjacent level.

Figure 18-3(b) shows common industrial marketing channels. The industrial goods manufacturer can use its sales force to sell directly to industrial customers. Or it can sell to industrial distributors who sell to the industrial customers. Or it can sell through manufacturers' representatives or its own sales branches directly to industrial customers, or use them to sell through industrial distributors. Thus zero, one, and two-level marketing channels are quite common in industrial goods marketing channels.

Channels normally describe a forward movement of products. One can also talk about *backward channels*. According to Zikmund and Stanton:

The recycling of solid wastes is a major ecological goal. Although recycling is technologically feasible, reversing the flow of materials in the channel of distribution—marketing trash through

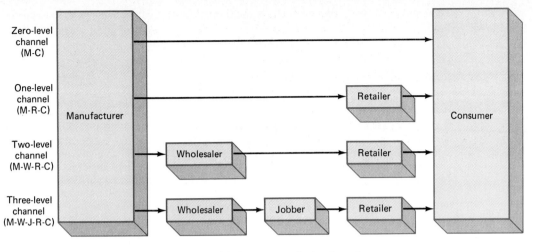

(a) Consumer marketing channels

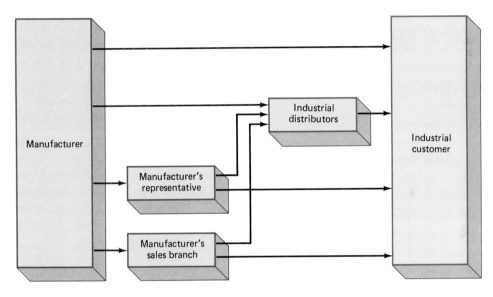

(b) Industrial marketing channels

FIGURE 18-3
Consumer and Industrial Marketing Channels

a "backward" channel—presents a challenge. Existing backward channels are primitive, and financial incentives are inadequate. The consumer must be motivated to undergo a role change and become a producer—the initiating force in the reverse distribution process.[5]

Several middlemen play a role in "backward" channels, including (1) manufacturers' redemption centers, (2) "Clean-up Days" community groups, (3) traditional middlemen such as soft-drink middlemen, (4) trash-collection specialists, (5) recycling centers, (6) modernized "rag and junk men," (7) trash-recycling brokers, and (8) central-processing warehousing. Using various backward channels, Reynolds Metal Company paid over $77 million in 1985 to retrieve over 7 billion used cans.

The concept of marketing channels is not limited to the distribution of physical goods. Producers of services and ideas also face the problem of making their output *available* and *accessible* to target populations. They develop "educational dissemination systems" and "health delivery systems." They must figure out agencies and locations for reaching a spatially distributed population:

> Hospitals must be located in geographic space to serve the people with complete medical care, and we must build schools close to the children who have to learn. Fire stations must be located to give rapid access to potential conflagrations, and voting booths must be placed so that people can cast their ballots without expending unreasonable amounts of time, effort, or money to reach the polling stations. Many of our states face the problem of locating branch campuses to serve a burgeoning and increasingly well educated population. In the cities we must create and locate playgrounds for the children. Many overpopulated countries must assign birth control clinics to reach the people with contraceptive and family planning information.[6]

Marketing channels also are used in "person" marketing. Before 1940, professional comedians could reach audiences through seven channels: vaudeville houses, special events, nightclubs, radio, movies, carnivals, and theaters. In the 1950s, television emerged as a strong channel, and vaudeville disappeared. Politicians also must find cost-effective channels—mass media, rallies, coffee hours—for distributing their messages to voters.[7]

CHANNEL-DESIGN DECISIONS

We will now examine several channel-decision problems facing manufacturers. In designing marketing channels, manufacturers have to struggle between what is ideal and what is available. A new firm typically starts as a local or regional operation selling in a limited market. Since it has limited capital, it usually uses existing middlemen. The number of middlemen in any local market is apt to be limited: a few manufacturer's sales agents, a few wholesalers, several established retailers, a few trucking companies, and a few warehouses. Deciding on the best channels might not be a problem. The problem might be to convince one or a few available middlemen to handle the line.

If the new firm is successful, it might branch out to new markets. Again, the manufacturer will tend to work through the existing intermediaries, although this might mean using different types of marketing channels in different areas. In the smaller markets, the firm might sell directly to retailers; in the larger markets, it might sell through distributors. In rural areas, it might work with general-goods merchants; in urban areas, with limited-line merchants. In one part of the country, it might grant exclusive franchises because the merchants normally work this way; in another, it might sell through all outlets willing to handle the merchandise. Thus the manufacturer's channel system evolves in response to local opportunities and conditions.

Designing a channel system calls for analyzing consumer needs, establishing channel objectives, identifying the major channel alternatives, and evaluating them.

Understanding what, where, why, when, and how consumers buy in the target market selected by the manufacturer is the first step in designing the marketing channel. The marketing functions or flows performed by members of a marketing channel can be expressed in terms of *service outputs*. Bucklin identified four service outputs:[8]

- **Lot size.** The lot size is the number of units that a consumer receives at any given delivery. The smaller the lot size, the greater the level of service provided by the marketing channel. Small lot size allows the consumer to buy only as much as needed for immediate consumption.
- **Waiting time.** Delivery or waiting time is the period during which the consumer must wait, after ordering, for receipt of the goods. Fast delivery times are preferred by consumers, as goods can be consumed immediately and future consumption need not be planned in advance.
- **Spatial convenience.** Spatial convenience or market decentralization is measured by the number and dispersion of retail outlets. Greater market decentralization means reduced transportation and search costs for the consumers.
- **Product variety.** The greater the breadth of assortment provided by a marketing channel to the consumer, the higher the service output level of that marketing channel.

To design the channel effectively, the designer must know not only the service output levels desired by the average consumer but also the aggregate demand function for each of the service outputs. Providing increased levels of service outputs means increased costs for the channel and higher prices for the consumer. The success of discount stores indicates that consumers are often willing to accept lower-service output levels if this translates into lower prices.

Establishing the Channel Objectives and Constraints

The channel objectives should be stated in terms of targeted service output levels. According to Bucklin, under competitive conditions, channel institutions should arrange their functional tasks so as to minimize total channel costs with respect to some desired level of service outputs.[9] Usually, several segments can be identified on the basis of differing service output levels that consumers demand. Effective channel planning means that the manufacturer should determine which market segments to serve and the best channels to use in each case. Each producer develops its channel objectives in the context of constraints stemming from products, intermediaries, competitors, company policies, the environment, and the level of service outputs desired by the consumers.

Product Characteristics

Perishable products require more direct marketing because of the dangers associated with delays and repeated handling. *Bulky* products, such as building materials or soft drinks, require channel arrangements that minimize the shipping distance and the number of handlings in the movement from producer to consumers. *Nonstandardized* products, such as custom-built machinery and specialized business forms, are sold directly by company sales representatives because middlemen lack the requisite knowledge. Products requiring installation and/or maintenance services are usually sold and maintained by the company or exclusively franchised dealers. *High unit value* products are often sold through a company sales force rather than through middlemen.

Middlemen Characteristics

Channel design reflects the strengths and weaknesses of different types of intermediaries in handling various tasks. For example, manufacturers' representatives are able to contact customers at a low cost per customer because the total cost is shared by several clients. But the selling effort per customer is less intense than if the company's sales representatives did the selling. In general, marketing intermediaries differ in their aptitude for handling promotion, negotiation, storage, contact, and credit.

Competitive Characteristics

Channel design is influenced by the competitors' channels. The producers may want to compete in or near the same outlets carrying the competitors' products. Thus food processors want their brands to be displayed next to competitive brands; and Burger King wants to locate next to McDonald's. In other industries, producers may want to avoid the channels used by competitors. Avon decided not to compete with other cosmetics manufacturers for scarce space in retail stores and established instead a profitable door-to-door selling operation.

Company Characteristics Company characteristics play an important role in channel selection. As subsequent channel modifications are costly and often not easily reversible, the overall long-run *goals* of the company should be considered when designing and selecting the marketing channel to be used. The company's *size* determines the size of its markets and its ability to secure desired dealers. Its *financial resources* determine which marketing functions it can handle and which to delegate to intermediaries. The company's *product mix* influences its channel pattern. The wider its product mix, the greater the company's ability to deal with customers directly. The greater the depth of the company's product mix, the more it might favor exclusive or selective dealers. The more consistent the company's product mix, the greater the homogeneity of its marketing channels. The company's *marketing strategy* will influence channel design. Thus a policy of speedy customer delivery affects the functions the producer wants intermediaries to perform, the number of final-stage outlets and stocking points, and the choice of transportation carriers.

Environmental Characteristics When *economic conditions* are depressed, producers want to move their goods to market in the most economical way. This means using shorter channels and dispensing with inessential services that add to the final price of the goods. *Legal regulations and restrictions* also affect channel design. The law has sought to prevent channel arrangements that ''may tend to substantially lessen competition or tend to create a monopoly.''

Identifying the Major Channel Alternatives Suppose a manufacturing company has defined its target market and desired positioning. It should next identify its major channel alternatives. A channel alternative is described by three elements: the *types of business intermediaries*, the *number of intermediaries*, and the *terms and mutual responsibilities of each channel participant*.

Types of Intermediaries The firm should identify the types of intermediaries available to carry on its channel work. Consider the following example:

A test equipment manufacturer developed an audio device for detecting poor mechanical connections in any machine with moving parts. The company executives felt that this product would sell in all industries where electric, combustion, or steam engines were used or manufactured. This meant such industries as aviation, automobiles, railroads, food canning, construction, and oil. The company's sales force was small, and the problem was how to reach these diverse industries effectively. The following channel alternatives came out of management discussion:

■ *Company sales force.* Expand the company's direct sales force. Assign sales representatives to territories and give them responsibility for contacting all prospects in the area. Or develop separate company sales forces for the different industries.

■ *Manufacturer's agency.* Hire manufacturer's agencies in different regions or end-use industries to sell the new test equipment.

■ *Industrial distributors.* Find distributors in the different regions and/or end-use industries who will buy and carry the new line. Give them exclusive distribution, adequate margins, product training, and promotional support.

Here is another example:

> A consumer electronics company decided to use its excess capacity to produce FM car radios. In considering channels of distribution, it came up with the following alternatives:
>
> ■ **OEM market.** The company could seek a contract with one or more automobile manufacturers to buy its radios for factory installation on original equipment. OEM stands for *original equipment manufacture*.
> ■ **Auto dealer market.** The company could sell its radios to various auto dealers for replacement sales when they service cars.
> ■ **Retail automotive parts dealers.** The company could sell its radios to the public through retail automotive parts dealers. It could reach these dealers through a direct sales force or through distributors.
> ■ **Mail-order market.** The company could arrange to have its radios advertised in mail-order catalogs.

Companies should also search for more innovative marketing channels. This happened when the Conn Organ Company decided to merchandise organs through department and discount stores, thus drawing more attention than organs had ever enjoyed in small music stores. A daring new channel was exploited when the Book-of-the-Month Club decided to merchandise books through the mails. Other sellers followed soon after with record-of-the-month clubs, candy-of-the-month clubs, and dozens of others.

Sometimes a company has to develop a channel other than the one it prefers because of the difficulty or cost of working with the preferred channel. The decision sometimes turns out extremely well. For example, the U.S. Time Company originally tried to sell its inexpensive Timex watches through regular jewelry stores. But most jewelry stores refused to carry them. The company looked for other channels and managed to get its watches into mass-merchandise outlets. This turned out to be a great decision because of the rapid growth of mass merchandising. Similarly, Avon chose to do door-to-door cosmetics selling as a result of not being able to break into regular department stores. It not only mastered door-to-door selling but made more money than most cosmetics firms that sold through department stores.

Number of Intermediaries   Companies have to decide on the number of middlemen to use at each channel level. Three strategies are available.

Intensive distribution   Producers of convenience goods and common raw materials typically seek *intensive distribution*—that is, stocking their product in as many outlets as possible. These goods must have place utility. Cigarettes, for example, sell in over one million outlets to create maximum brand exposure and consumer convenience.

Exclusive distribution   Some producers deliberately limit the number of intermediaries handling their products. The extreme form of this is *exclusive distribution*, where a limited number of dealers are granted the exclusive right to distribute the company's products in their respective territories. It often goes with *exclusive dealing*, where the manufacturer requires these dealers not to carry competing lines. Exclusive distribution is found to some extent in the distribution of new automobiles, some major appliances, and some women's apparel brands. Through granting exclusive distribution, the manufacturer hopes for more aggressive and knowledgeable selling and more control over intermediaries' policies on prices, promotion, credit, and various services. Exclusive distribution tends to enhance the product's image and allow higher markups.

Selective distribution   Between intensive and exclusive distribution stands *selective distribution*—the use of more than one but less than all of the intermediaries who are willing to carry a particular product. It is used both by established companies and by new companies seeking to obtain distributors by promising them selective distribution. The company does not have to dissipate its efforts over many outlets, including many marginal ones. It can develop a good working relation with the selected middlemen and expect a better than average selling effort. Selective distribution enables the producer to gain adequate market coverage with more control and less cost than intensive distribution.

Terms and Responsibilities of Channel Members

The producer must determine the conditions and responsibilities of the participating channel members. The main elements in the ''trade-relations mix'' are the *price policies*, the *conditions of sale*, the *territorial rights*, and the *specific services to be performed by each party*.

Price policy calls for the producer to establish a list price and schedule of discounts. The producer must be sure that discounts strike the middleman as equitable and sufficient.

Conditions of sale refer to the payment terms and to producer guarantees. Most producers grant cash discounts to their distributors for early payment. Producers may also extend guarantees to distributors regarding defective merchandise or price declines. A guarantee against price declines is used to induce distributors to buy larger quantities.

Distributors' territorial rights are another element in the trade-relations mix. Distributors want to know where the producer will enfranchise other distributors. They would also like to receive full credit for all sales taking place in their territory, whether or not these sales occurred through their personal efforts.

Mutual services and responsibilities must be carefully spelled out, especially in franchised- and exclusive-agency channels. For example, the McDonald's Company provides franchisees with a building, promotional support, a record-keeping system, training, and general administrative and technical assistance. In turn, franchisees are expected to satisfy company standards regarding physical facilities, cooperate with new promotional programs, furnish requested information, and buy specified food products.

Evaluating Major Channel Alternatives

Suppose a producer has identified several channel alternatives and wants to determine the one that would best satisfy the firm's long-run objectives. Each alternative needs to be evaluated against *economic*, *control*, and *adaptive criteria*. Consider the following situation:

> A Memphis furniture manufacturer wants to sell its line to retailers on the West Coast. The manufacturer is trying to decide between two alternatives:
>
> 1. One alternative calls for hiring ten new *sales representatives*, who would operate out of a sales office in San Francisco. They would receive a base salary plus commissions based on their sales.
> 2. The other alternative would use a San Francisco manufacturer's *sales agency* that has extensive contacts with retailers. The agency has thirty sales representatives, who would receive a commission based on their sales.

Economic Criteria

Each channel alternative will produce a different level of sales and costs. The first issue is whether more sales will be produced through a company sales force or through a sales agency. Most marketing managers believe that a company sales force will sell more. Company sales representatives concentrate entirely on the company's products; they are better trained to sell the company's products; they are more aggressive because their future depends on the company; they are more successful because customers prefer to deal directly with the company.

On the other hand, the sales agency could conceivably sell more than a company sales force. First, the sales agent has thirty sales representatives, not just ten. Second, the agency's sales force may be just as aggressive as a direct sales force. That depends on how much commission the line offers in relation to the other lines carried. Third, some customers prefer dealing with agents who represent several manufacturers rather than with salespersons from one company. Fourth, the agency has extensive contacts, whereas a company sales force would have to build them up from scratch.

The next step is to estimate the costs of selling different volumes through each channel. The cost schedules are shown in Figure 18-4. The fixed costs of engaging a sales agency are lower than those of establishing a company sales office. But costs rise faster through a sales agency because sales agents get a larger commission than company sales people.

There is one sales level (S_B) at which selling costs are the same for the two channels. The sales agency would be the preferred channel at any sales volume below S_B, and the company sales branch would be preferred at any volume higher than S_B. In general, sales agents tend to be used by smaller firms, or by larger firms in their smaller territories wherever the sales volume is too low to warrant a company sales force.

Control Criteria The evaluation must be broadened to consider control issues with the two channels. Using a sales agency poses more of a control problem. A sales agency is an independent business firm interested in maximizing its profits. The agent may concentrate on the customers who are the most important in terms of the assortment they buy rather than for their level of interest in the particular manufacturer's goods. Furthermore, the agent's sales force may not master the technical details concerning the company's product or handle its promotion materials effectively.

Adaptive Criteria Each channel involves some duration of commitment and loss of flexibility. A manufacturer using a sales agency may have to offer a five-year contract. During this period, other means of selling, such as direct mail, may become more effective, but the manufacturer is not free to drop the sales agency. A channel involving a long commitment should be greatly superior on economic or control grounds to be considered.

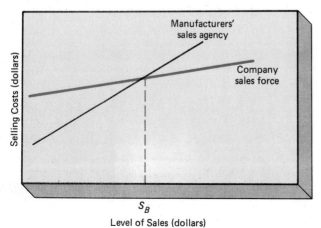

FIGURE 18-4
Break-Even Cost Chart for the Choice between a Company Sales Force and a Manufacturer's Sales Agency

CHANNEL-MANAGEMENT DECISIONS

After a company has chosen a channel alternative, individual middlemen must be *selected*, *motivated*, and *evaluated*. Also, channel arrangements must be modified over time.

Selecting Channel Members

Producers vary in their ability to attract qualified middlemen for the proposed channel. Some producers have no trouble recruiting middlemen. For example, Ford was able to attract twelve hundred new dealers for its ill-fated Edsel. In some cases, the promise of exclusive or selective distribution will draw a sufficient number of applicants.

At the other extreme are producers who have to work hard to line up the desired number of qualified middlemen. When Polaroid started, it could not get photographic-equipment stores to carry its new cameras and was forced to go to mass-merchandising outlets. Small food producers normally find it hard to get grocery stores to carry their products. Equipment manufacturers often find it hard to locate qualified distributors and dealers. (See Exhibit 18-1.)

EXHIBIT 18-1

Building a Distributor Team for Epson Products

Japan's Epson Corporation, a leading manufacturer of computer printers, was preparing to expand its product line to include computers. Not happy with its current distributors nor trusting their ability to sell to new types of retail outlets, Epson's general manager, Jack Whalen, decided to secretly recruit new distributors to replace the existing ones. Whalen hired Hergenrather & Company, a recruiting company, and gave the following instructions:

- ■ Search for applicants who had two-step distribution experience (factory to distributor to dealer) in either brown goods (TVs, etc.) or white goods (refrigerators, etc.).
- ■ The applicants would have to be CEO types who would be willing and able to set up their own distributorships.
- ■ They would be offered $80,000 yearly salary plus bonus, $375,000 to help them set up in business, each would add $25,000 of his own money, and each would get equity in the business.
- ■ They would handle only Epson products but could stock other companies' software. Each distributor would have a training manager and a fully equipped service center.

The recruiting firm had a hard time finding qualified and motivated prospects. Their want ads in the *Wall Street Journal* (which did not mention the company's name) pulled almost seventeen hundred letters, but mostly from unqualified people looking for jobs. Then the firm used the Yellow Pages to get the names of present distributors and phoned the second-in-command managers. It arranged interviews, and after much work produced a list of highly qualified individuals. Whalen interviewed them and chose the twelve most-qualified candidates for his twelve distributor areas. The recruiting agency was paid $250,000 for its recruiting effort.

The final step called for terminating Epson's existing distributors. These distributors had no inkling of this development, since the recruitment was conducted in secrecy. Jack Whalen gave them a ninety-day notice of the changeover. They were of course shocked, having worked with Epson as its first distributors. But they had no contracts. Whalen knew they lacked the ability to handle Epson's expanded computer product line and reach the required new distribution channels. He saw no other way to do this.

SOURCE: Arthur Bragg, "Undercover Recruiting: Epson America's Sly Distributor Switch," *Sales and Marketing Management*, March 11, 1985, pp. 45–49.

Whether producers find it easy or difficult to recruit middlemen, they should at least determine what characteristics distinguish the better middlemen. They will want to evaluate the middlemen's number of years in business, the other lines carried, growth and profit record, solvency, cooperativeness, and reputation. If the middlemen are sales agents, producers will want to evaluate the number and character of other lines carried and the size and quality of the sales force. If the middleman is a department store that wants exclusive distribution, the producer will want to evaluate the store's location, future growth potential, and type of clientele.

Motivating Channel Members

Middlemen must be continuously motivated to do their best job. The terms that lead them to join the channel provide some of the motivation, but these must be supplemented by training, supervision, and encouragement from the producer. The producer must sell not only through the middlemen but to them.

Stimulating channel members to top performance must start with the manufacturer understanding the middlemen's needs and wants. The key to understanding middlemen's needs is continuous, routine information collection through practices such as monitoring the middlemen, conducting market research studies, and establishing middlemen councils. According to McVey, manufacturers often criticize middlemen "for failure to stress a given brand, or for the poor quality of his salesman's product knowledge, his disuse of supplier's advertising materials, his neglect of certain customers (who may be good prospects for individual items but not for the assortment), and even for his unrefined systems of record keeping, in which brand designations may be lost."[10] However, these shortcomings from the manufacturer's point of view may be understandable from the middleman's point of view. McVey listed the following propositions to help understand middlemen:

> The middleman is not a hired link in a chain forged by a manufacturer, but rather an independent market. . . . After some experimentation, he settles upon a method of operation, performing those functions he deems inescapable in the light of his own objectives, forming policies for himself wherever he has freedom to do so. . . .

> [The middleman often acts] as a purchasing agent for his customers and only secondarily as a selling agent for his suppliers. . . . He is interested in selling any product which these customers desire to buy from him. . . .

> The middleman attempts to weld all of his offerings into a family of items which he can sell in combination, as a packaged assortment, to individual customers. His selling efforts are directed primarily at obtaining orders for the assortment, rather than for individual items. . . .

> Unless given incentive to do so, middlemen will not maintain separate sales records by brands sold. . . . Information that could be used in product development, pricing, packaging, or promotion-planning is buried in nonstandard records of middlemen, and sometimes purposely secreted from suppliers.[11]

Producers vary greatly in how they handle their distributor relations. We can distinguish three approaches: *cooperation*, *partnership*, and *distribution programming*.[12]

Most producers see the problem as finding ways to gain middlemen *cooperation*. They will use the carrot-and-stick approach. They will use such positive motivators as higher margins, special deals, premiums, cooperative advertising allowances, display allowances, and sales contests. At times they will apply negative sanctions, such as threatening to reduce the margins, slow down delivery, or terminate the relationship. The weakness of this approach is that the producer has not really studied the middlemen's needs, problems, strengths, and weaknesses. Instead the producer applies miscellaneous motivators based on crude stimulus-response thinking. McCammon notes that many manufacturer programs "consist of hastily improvised trade deals, uninspired dealer contests, and unexamined discount structures."[13]

More-sophisticated companies try to forge a long-term *partnership* with their distributors. The manufacturer develops a clear sense of what it wants from its distributors and what its distributors can expect in terms of market coverage, product availability, market development, account solicitation, technical advice and services, and market information. The manufacturer seeks an agreement from its distributors on these policies and may base compensation on their adhering to these policies. In one case the company, instead of paying a straight 25 percent sales commission, pays the following:

- Five percent for carrying the proper level of inventory
- Another 5 percent for meeting the sales quotas
- Another 5 percent for servicing the customers effectively
- Another 5 percent for proper reporting of customer-purchase levels
- Another 5 percent for proper accounts-receivables management

Distribution programming is the most-advanced arrangement. McCammon defines this as building a planned, professionally managed, vertical marketing system that incorporates the needs of both the manufacturer and the distributors.[14] The manufacturer establishes a department within the marketing department called distributor relations planning, and its job is to identify the distributors' needs and build up merchandising programs to help each distributor operate as optimally as possible. This department and the distributors jointly plan the merchandising goals, inventory levels, space and visual merchandising plans, sales-training requirements, and advertising and promotion plans. The aim is to convert the distributors from thinking that they make their money primarily on the buying side (through an adversary relation with the supplier) to seeing that they make their money on the selling side by being part of a sophisticated vertical marketing system.

Exhibit 18-2 describes the various mechanisms that progressive manufacturers use to convert their distributors into partners.

Evaluating Channel Members

The producer must periodically evaluate middlemen's performance against such standards as sales-quota attainment, average inventory levels, customer delivery time, treatment of damaged and lost goods, cooperation in company promotional and training programs, and middlemen services owed to the customer.

The producer typically sets sales quotas for the middlemen. After each period, the producer checks the sales-to-quota performance of each middleman. Diagnostic and motivational effort are then focused on underachieving middlemen.

Modifying Channel Arrangements

A producer must do more than design a good channel system and set it into motion. The system will require periodic modification to meet new conditions in the marketplace. Modification becomes necessary when consumer buying patterns change, market expands, product matures through the product life cycle, new competition arises, and innovative distribution strategies emerge.

This fact struck a large household-appliance manufacturer who had been marketing exclusively through franchised dealers and was losing market share. Several distribution developments had taken place since the original channel was designed:

Turning Industrial Distributors into Partners

Narus and Anderson interviewed several manufacturers who enjoyed excellent working relations with their distributors to discover the channel attitudes and practices that contributed to the successful relations. Here are some of the partner-building practices they found:

1. Timken Corporation (roller bearings) has its sales representatives make *multilevel calls* on distributors, including their general managers, purchasing managers, and sales personnel.

2. Square D (circuit breakers, switchboards) has its sales representatives spend a day with each distributor *"working the counter"* in order to understand the distributor's business.

3. Du Pont established a *Distributor Marketing Steering Committee*, which meets regularly to discuss problems and trends.

4. Dayco Corporation (engineered plastics and rubber products) runs an *annual weeklong retreat* with twenty young distributors' executives and twenty young Dayco executives interacting in seminars and outings.

5. Parker Hannifin Corporation (fluid power products) sends out an *annual mail survey* asking its distributors to rate the corporation's performance on key dimensions. It also informs its distributors about new products and applications through *newsletters and videotapes*. It collects and analyzes *photocopies of distributors' invoices* and advises distributors on how to improve their sales.

6. Cherry Electrical Products (electrical switches and electronic keyboards) appointed a distributor marketing manager who works with distributors to produce *formal distributor marketing plans*. The company also operates a *rapid response system* to distributor calls through assigning two inside sales people to each distributor.

These are a few of the ways that progressive manufacturers have successfully turned their distributors into working partners.

SOURCE: See James A. Narus and James C. Anderson, "Turn Your Industrial Distributors into Partners," *Harvard Business Review*, March–April 1986, pp. 66–71.

■ An increasing share of major-brand appliances were being merchandised through discount houses.

■ An increasing share of major appliances were being sold on a private-brand basis through large department stores.

■ A new market was developing in the form of volume purchases by tract home builders who preferred to deal directly with the manufacturers.

■ Door-to-door and direct-mail solicitation of orders was being undertaken by some dealers and competitors.

■ The only strong independent dealers were located in small towns, but rural families were increasingly making their purchases in large cities.

These developments led this manufacturer to undertake a major review of possible channel modifications.

Three levels of channel modification should be distinguished. The change could involve *adding or dropping individual channel members*, *adding or dropping particular market channels*, or *developing a totally new way to sell goods in all markets*.

Adding or dropping specific middlemen requires an incremental analysis. What would the firm's profits look like with and without this middleman? An automobile manufacturer's decision to drop a dealer would require subtracting the dealer's sales and estimating the possible loss or gain of sales to the manufacturer's other dealers.

EXHIBIT 18-3

Smart Companies Change Their Marketing Channels over the Product Life Cycle

No marketing channel can be trusted to remain competitively dominant over the whole product life cycle. Early adopters may be willing to pay for high value-added channels, but later buyers will switch to lower-cost channels. Thus small office copiers were first sold by manufacturers' direct sales forces, later through office equipment dealers, still later through mass merchandisers, and now by mail-order firms. Insurance companies that persist in using independent agents and auto companies that use independent dealers are facing competition from new lower-cost channels, and their reluctance to change may prove fatal in the long run.

Miland Lele developed the accompanying grid to show how marketing channels have changed for PCs and designer clothing at different stages in the product life cycle:

■ *Introductory stage.* Radically new products or fashions tend to enter the market through specialist channels (such as hobbyist shops, boutiques) that spot trends and attract early adopters.

■ *Rapid growth stage.* As buyers' interest grows, higher-volume channels appear (dedicated chains, department stores) that offer services but not as much as the previous channels offered.

■ *Maturity stage.* As growth slows down, some competitors move their product into lower-cost channels (mass merchandisers).

■ *Decline stage.* As the decline begins, even lower-cost channels emerge (mail-order houses, off-price discounters).

The earliest channels bear the problem of market creation; they are high cost because they must search for and educate buyers. They are followed by channels that must expand the market and offer sufficient services. In the maturity stage, many buyers want the costs to come down, and they patronize lower value-added channels. Finally, the remaining potential buyers can only be reached by creating extremely low value-added channels.

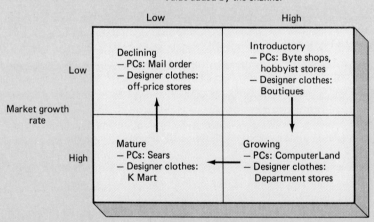

SOURCE: See Miland M. Lele, "Matching Your Channels to Your Product's Life Cycle," *Business Marketing*, December 1986, p. 64.

Sometimes a producer contemplates dropping all middlemen whose sales are below a certain amount. For example, International Harvester noted at one time that 5 percent of its dealers were selling fewer than three or four trucks a year. It cost the company more to service these dealers than their sales were worth. However, the decision to drop these dealers could have large repercussions on the system as a whole. The unit costs of producing trucks would be higher, since the overhead would be spread over fewer trucks; some employees and equipment would be idled; some business in these markets would go to competitors; and other dealers might become insecure. All of this would have to be taken into account.

The most difficult decision involves revising the overall channel strategy.[15] For example, an automobile manufacturer may consider replacing independent dealers with company-owned dealers; a soft-drink manufacturer may consider replacing local franchised bottlers with centralized bottling and direct sales. These decisions would require revising most of the marketing mix and would have profound consequences. (Exhibit 18-3 presents the argument for changing the channel at different stages of the product life cycle.)

CHANNEL DYNAMICS

Distribution channels do not stand still. New wholesaling and retailing institutions emerge, and new channel systems evolve. Here we will look at the recent growth of vertical, horizontal, and multichannel marketing systems and the way that these systems cooperate, conflict, and compete.

Growth of Vertical Marketing Systems   One of the most significant recent channel developments consists of *vertical marketing systems*, which have emerged to challenge *conventional marketing channels*. A conventional marketing channel comprises an independent producer, wholesaler(s), and retailer(s). Each is a separate business entity seeking to maximize its own profits, even if it is at the expense of maximizing the profits for the system as a whole. No channel member has complete or substantial control over the other members. McCammon characterizes conventional channels as "highly fragmented networks in which loosely aligned manufacturers, wholesalers, and retailers have bargained with each other at arm's length, negotiated aggressively over terms of sale, and otherwise behaved autonomously."[16]

A vertical marketing system (VMS), by contrast, comprises the producer, wholesaler(s), and retailer(s) acting as a unified system. Either one channel member owns the others or franchises them or has so much power that they all cooperate. The vertical marketing system can be dominated by the producer, the wholesaler, or the retailer. McCammon characterizes VMSs as "professionally managed and centrally programmed networks, preengineered to achieve operating economies and maximum market impact."[17] VMSs came into being to control channel behavior and eliminate the conflict that results from independent channel members pursuing their own objectives. They achieve economies through their size, bargaining power, and elimination of duplicated services. VMSs have become the dominant mode of distribution in the U.S. consumer marketplace, serving between 70 and 80 percent of the total market.

We will now examine three major types of VMSs, those shown in Figure 18-5.

Corporate VMS   A *corporate VMS* combines successive stages of production and distribution under single ownership. Vertical integration is favored by companies that desire a high level of control over the channels. Vertical integration can be achieved by backward or forward integration. As examples:

. . . Sherwin-Williams currently owns and operates over 2,000 retail outlets. . . . Sears reportedly obtains 50 percent of its throughput from manufacturing facilities in which it has

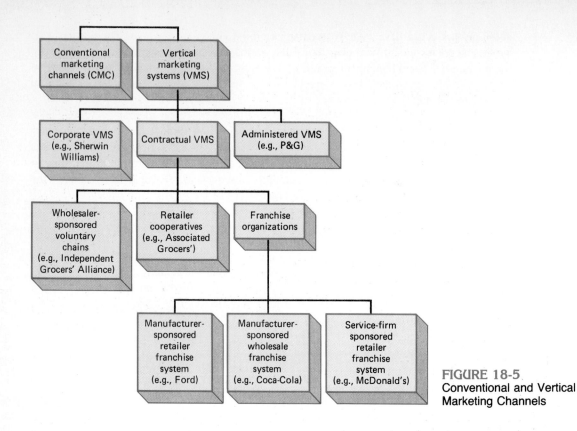

FIGURE 18-5
Conventional and Vertical
Marketing Channels

an equity interest. . . . Holiday Inns is evolving into a self-supply network that includes a carpet mill, a furniture manufacturing plant, and numerous captive redistribution facilities. In short, these and other organizations are massive, vertically integrated systems. To describe them as "retailers," "manufacturers," or "motel operators" oversimplifies their operating complexities and ignores the realities of the marketplace.[18]

Administered VMS An *administered VMS* coordinates successive stages of production and distribution not through common ownership but through the size and power of one of the parties. Manufacturers of a dominant brand are able to secure strong trade cooperation and support from resellers. Thus Kodak, Gillette, Procter & Gamble, and Campbell Soup are able to command unusual cooperation from their resellers in connection with displays, shelf space, promotions, and price policies.

Contractual VMS A *contractual VMS* consists of independent firms at different levels of production and distribution integrating their programs on a contractual basis to obtain more economies and/or sales impact than they could achieve alone. Contractual VMSs have expanded the most in recent years and constitute one of the most significant developments in the economy. Contractual VMSs are of three types.

Wholesaler-sponsored voluntary chains Wholesalers organize voluntary chains of independent retailers to help them compete with large chain organizations. The wholesaler develops a program in which independent retailers standardize their selling practices and achieve buying economies that enable the group to compete effectively with chain organizations.

Retailer cooperatives   Retailers may take the initiative and organize a new business entity to carry on wholesaling and possibly some production. Members concentrate their purchases through the retailer co-op and plan their advertising jointly. Profits are passed back to members in proportion to their purchases. Nonmember retailers may also buy through the co-op but do not share in the profits.

Franchise organizations   A channel member called a franchiser might link several successive stages in the production-distribution process. Franchising has been the fastest-growing and most interesting retailing development in recent years. Although the basic idea is an old one, some forms of franchising are quite new. Three forms of franchises can be distinguished.

The first is the *manufacturer-sponsored retailer franchise system*, exemplified by the automobile industry. Ford, for example, licenses dealers to sell its cars, the dealers being independent businesspeople who agree to meet various conditions of sales and service.

The second is the *manufacturer-sponsored wholesaler franchise system*, which is found in the soft-drink industry. Coca-Cola, for example, licenses bottlers (wholesalers) in various markets who buy its syrup concentrate and then carbonate, bottle, and sell it to retailers in local markets.

The third is the *service-firm-sponsored retailer franchise system*. Here a service firm organizes a whole system for bringing its service efficiently to consumers. Examples are found in the auto rental business (Hertz, Avis), fast-food service business (McDonald's, Burger King), and motel business (Howard Johnson, Ramada Inn). This type of franchising system is discussed further in Chapter 19.

Many independent retailers, if they have not joined VMSs, have developed specialty stores that serve market segments that are not attractive to the mass merchandisers. The result is a polarization in retailing between large vertical marketing organizations, on the one hand, and specialty independent stores, on the other. This development creates a problem for manufacturers. They are strongly tied to independent middlemen whom they cannot easily give up. But they must eventually realign themselves with the high-growth vertical marketing systems and have to accept less-attractive terms. Vertical marketing systems constantly threaten to bypass large manufacturers and set up their own manufacturing. *The new competition in retailing is no longer between independent business units but between whole systems of centrally programmed networks (corporate, administered, and contractual) competing against each other to achieve the best cost economies and customer response.*

Growth of Horizontal Marketing Systems   Another channel development is the readiness of two or more nonrelated companies to put together resources or programs to exploit an emerging marketing opportunity. Each company lacks the capital, know-how, production, or marketing resources to venture alone; or it is afraid of the risk; or it sees a substantial synergy in joining with another company. The companies may work with each other on a temporary or permanent basis or create a separate company. Adler calls this *symbiotic marketing*.[19] Here are several examples:

> Pillsbury and Kraft Foods Company set up an arrangement where Pillsbury makes and advertises its line of refrigerated dough products while Kraft uses its expertise to sell and distribute these products to the stores.
>
> H&R Block and Hyatt Legal Services formed a joint venture in which Hyatt's legal clinics are housed in H&R Block's tax preparation offices. Hyatt pays a fee for office space, secretarial assistance, and office equipment usage and enjoys a chance for accelerated market penetration through locating in H&R Block's nationwide office network. Meanwhile H&R Block benefits from renting its facilities, which would otherwise have a highly seasonal pattern.
>
> Coca-Cola Bottling Co. of New York and Joseph E. Seagram & Sons, Inc. formed a joint venture to produce and market a line of soft-drink mixers under the Seagram label.
>
> The Lamar Savings Bank of Texas arranged with Safeway Stores, Inc., to locate its savings offices and automated teller machines in Safeway stores. Lamar gained accelerated entry at a low cost, and Safeway was able to offer in-store banking convenience to its customers.
>
> Beecham Products, Inc., and Johnson & Johnson Company have jointly sponsored combined sales promotions of the former's Aqua-Fresh toothpaste and the latter's Reach toothbrush.

All said, symbiotic marketing arrangements have increased dramatically in recent years, and the end is nowhere in sight.[20]

Growth of Multichannel Marketing Systems

In the past, many companies sold to a single market or market segment and used a single channel to reach them. Some companies turned to *dual distribution*, which meant that they used two channels to reach one or two customer segments. Today, with the proliferation of customer segments and channel possibilities, more and more companies have adopted *multichannel distribution*. Weigand calls this *multimarketing*, which occurs when a single firm sets up two or more marketing channels to reach one or more customer segments.[21] Here are some examples:

> General Electric sells large home appliances through independent retailers (department stores, discount houses, catalog houses) and also directly to large housing-tract builders, thus competing to some extent with the retailers.
>
> IBM managed to put its new personal computers into twenty-five hundred stores in quick order by using a multichannel approach. Besides opening its own IBM Product Centers, it signed contracts with Sears, Computerland, and an assortment of other computer stores, office product dealers, and value-added resellers. It also sold its computers to colleges at heavy discounts, causing complaints from the retailers.
>
> McDonald's owns about one-fourth of its outlets, and they compete to some extent with those owned by its franchisers.
>
> Witco Chemical Company produces detergents under private labels for many major supermarket chains and also produces its own brand.
>
> Some insurance companies sell through outside agents, exclusive agents, and their own telemarketing and direct-mail systems.

The multimarketer gains volume with each new channel but also risks alienating its existing channels. Existing channels can cry "unfair competition" and threaten to drop the multimarketer if it does not limit the competition or recompense them in some way.

In some cases, the multimarketer's channels are all under its own ownership and control. For example, J. C. Penney operates department stores, mass-merchandising stores, and specialty stores. Tillman has labeled these *merchandising conglomerates* and defined them as "a multiline merchandising empire under central ownership, usually combining several styles of retailing with behind-the-scenes integration of some distribution and management functions."[22] Here there is no conflict with outside channels, but the merchandising conglomerate might face internal conflict over how much financial support each channel deserves. (See Exhibit 18-4 for the case for more multichannel retailing.)

EXHIBIT 18-4

The Case for Multichannel Retailing

Companies that persist in employing a single channel to sell different products to different customers will find themselves increasingly vulnerable to companies that build more appropriate channels. This can be illustrated with the *offering grid* shown in Figure (a) below.

The bottom of the grid shows products ranging from commodities to customized products; the vertical axis shows levels of distribution value-added service ranging from low to high. Thus pension fund management is located at the upper left: Pension funds are customized and require a high level of personal service, information, and execution. At the other extreme is Trade-Plus, a service of C. D. Anderson of San Francisco, which permits a person to trade directly at home using a personal computer; in this case, the product is extremely simple and there is hardly any value added by the channel.

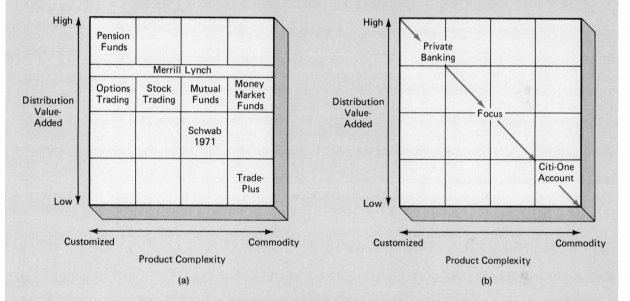

(a)   (b)

Now consider Merrill Lynch's offerings, which fall horizontally on the offering grid. Merrill Lynch offers several services through a fairly high value-added, full-service brokerage distribution channel consisting of its local office account executives and home office researchers. By sticking with only one channel, Merrill Lynch has allowed other competitors to appear, such as Charles Schwab & Company, which offers discount brokerage service. Schwab's customers phone Schwab's customer service representatives, who take orders but provide no investment advice or research.

The point is that each cell represents a potential opportunity if the demand is large enough. Companies that use only one channel for several products and customer groups will inevitably face increased competition. As customers become more knowledgeable about a service and as technology permits further mechanization, more channels will open up in the lower-right-hand cells of the grid, presenting competition to higher distribution value-added channels.

Citibank recognized this and has created the set of services shown in Figure (b). Private Banking consists of customized asset management services aimed at wealthy customers and delivered through personal bankers in gracious surroundings. Focus provides banking and investment services through an account officer who is available by phone. Citi-One Account Banking permits simple banking transactions to be executed through automated teller machines. Clearly, Citibank is building differentiated products and channels for different customer groups.

SOURCE: This discussion is adapted from *Distribution: A Competitive Weapon*, published in 1985 by The MAC Group, 1430 Massachusetts Avenue, Cambridge, Mass. 02138, pp. 14–18.

Roles of Individual Firms in a Channel

Vertical, horizontal, and multichannel marketing systems underscore the dynamic and changing nature of channels. Each firm in an industry has to define its role in the channel system. McCammon has distinguished five roles:[23]

- *Insiders* are members of the dominant channel who enjoy access to preferred sources of supply and high respect in the industry. They want to perpetuate the existing channel arrangements and are the main enforcers of the industry code.
- *Strivers* are firms seeking to become insiders. They have less access to preferred sources of supply, which can handicap them in periods of short supply. They adhere to the industry code because of their desire to become insiders.
- *Complementors* are not part of the dominant channel. They perform functions not normally performed by others in the channel, or serve smaller segments of the market, or handle smaller quantities of merchandise. They usually benefit from the present system and respect the industry code.
- *Transients* are outside the dominant channel and do not seek membership. They go in and out of the market and move around as opportunities arise. They have short-run expectations and little incentive to adhere to the industry code.
- *Outside innovators* are the real challengers and disrupters of the dominant channels. They develop a new system for carrying out the marketing work of the channel; if successful, they force major channel realignments. They are companies like McDonald's, Avon, and Holiday Inn, which doggedly develop new systems to challenge the old.

Another important channel role is that of *channel captain*. The channel captain is the dominant member of a particular channel, the one who leads it. For example, General Motors is the channel captain of a system consisting of a huge number of suppliers, dealers, and facilitators. The channel captain is not always a manufacturer, as the examples of McDonald's and Sears indicate. Some channels do not have a channel captain in that each firm proceeds on its own.

Channel Cooperation, Conflict, and Competition

Different degrees of cooperation, conflict, and competition can be found within and between marketing channels.

Channel cooperation is usually the dominant theme among vertical members of the same channel. The channel represents a coalition of dissimilar firms that have banded together for mutual advantage. Manufacturers, wholesalers, and retailers complement each other's needs, and their cooperation normally produces greater profits than each participant could have obtained individually. By cooperating, they can more effectively sense, serve, and satisfy the target market.

Channel conflict, however, often arises within the channel. Each member, in trying to maximize its self-interest, has the potential to hurt other members' interests. Conflict can arise for several reasons:

- *Goal incompatibility.* A manufacturer may want to pursue rapid growth through low price, but the dealers may want to pursue profitability through high margins.
- *Unclear roles and rights.* IBM sells personal computers to large accounts through its own sales force, and its licensed dealers are also trying to sell to large accounts. Territory boundaries, credit for sales, etc., are confused and causing conflict.
- *Differences in perception.* Distributors might think the manufacturer is trying to replace them when this is not the case.
- *Level of interdependence.* Exclusive dealers, such as auto dealers, are highly dependent on their manufacturers. The greater the interdependence between channel members, the greater the potential for conflict.

We can distinguish between horizontal and vertical channel conflict. *Horizontal intra-type conflict* describes conflict occurring between member firms at the same level of the channel. Some Ford car dealers in Chicago complain about other Ford dealers in the city being too aggressive in their pricing and advertising and stealing sales from them. Some Pizza Inn franchisees complain about other Pizza Inn franchisees cheating on the ingredients, maintaining poor service, and hurting the overall Pizza Inn image. In these cases, the *channel captain* must establish clear and enforceable policies and take quick action to control this type of conflict.

Vertical channel conflict is even more common and refers to conflicts of interest between different levels of the same channel. For example, General Motors came into conflict with its dealers some years ago in trying to enforce policies on service, pricing, and advertising. And Coca-Cola came into conflict with its bottlers who agreed to bottle Dr. Pepper.

Some amount of vertical channel conflict is inevitable, and the problem is not one of eliminating it but of managing it better. There are several mechanisms for conflict resolution:

- ■ *Channel captain leadership.* If one channel member acquires leadership and earns the trust of other members, it can set a tone that will reduce the potential for conflict and resolve conflicts more quickly.
- ■ *Superordinate goals.* Members may cooperate more fully when they recognize a common outside threat to their survival. Thus Chrysler and its dealers put aside their differences and adopted the superordinate goal of survival.
- ■ *Joint work.* Conflict is often lessened when channel members are able to meet more often, form advisory councils, and exchange personnel.
- ■ *Mediation and arbitration.* Administrative mechanisms such as mediation and arbitration procedures provide ways to resolve disputes when they happen.

Channel competition is another aspect of channel relations and describes the normal competition between firms and systems trying to serve the same target markets. *Horizontal intertype competition* occurs between competitors at the same channel level seeking sales in the same market. Thus department stores, discount stores, and catalog houses all compete for the consumer's appliance dollar. This competition should result in consumers' enjoying a wider range of choice of products, prices, and services. *Channel system competition* describes the competition between different whole systems serving a given market. For example, food consumers are served by conventional marketing channels, corporate chains, wholesaler-sponsored voluntary chains, retailer cooperatives, and food franchise systems. Each system will have some loyal followers, but the share of the different systems in the total food business will shift over time toward those systems that best meet consumer needs.

SUMMARY

Marketing-channel decisions are among the most complex and challenging decisions facing the firm. Each channel system creates a different level of sales and costs. Once a particular marketing channel is chosen, the firm must usually adhere to it for a substantial period. The chosen channel will significantly affect and be affected by the other elements in the marketing mix.

Middlemen are used when they are able to perform channel functions more efficiently than the manufacturers can. The most important channel functions and flows are information, promotion, negotiation, ordering, financing, risk taking, physical possession, payment, and title. These marketing functions are more basic than the particular retail and wholesale institutions that may exist at any time.

Manufacturers face many channel possibilities for reaching a market. They can decide on selling direct or using one, two, three, or more intermediary-channel levels. Channel design calls for determining the service outputs (lot size, waiting time, spatial convenience, and product variety), establishing the channel objectives and constraints, identifying the major channel alternatives (types and number of intermediaries, specifically intensive, exclusive, or selective distribution), and the channel terms and responsibilities. Each channel alternative has to be evaluated according to economic, control, and adaptive criteria.

Channel management calls for selecting particular middlemen and motivating them with a cost-effective trade-relations mix. The aim is to build a ''partnership'' feeling and joint distribution programming. Individual channel members must be periodically evaluated against their own past sales and other channel members' sales. Channel modification must be performed periodically because of the continuously changing marketing environment. The company has to evaluate adding or dropping individual middlemen or individual channels and possibly modifying the whole channel system.

Marketing channels are characterized by continuous and sometimes dramatic change. Three of the most significant trends are the growth of vertical, horizontal, and multichannel marketing systems. These trends have important implications for channel cooperation, conflict, and competition.

■ QUESTIONS

1. Describe the multichannel marketing systems used by record manufacturers. To what extent does each channel member participate in the marketing flows and functions discussed in the chapter?

2. Can any benefit be derived from applying channel management to service industries? How might the key functions and flows differ for a service industry?

3. ''The $260 billion auto-retailing industry is being transformed by new mega-dealers who each sell upwards of a dozen different brands of cars made by different manufacturers at up to thirty locations.'' If this trend becomes the norm, how will channel structures and relationships be affected? Who might become the channel captain?

4. When dealing with conflict, what is the goal of channel management? How might this goal be accomplished?

5. Suggest some alternative channels for (a) a small firm that has developed a radically new harvesting machine, (b) a small plastic manufacturer that has developed a picnic pack for keeping bottles and food cold, and (c) a tankless, instant water heater. What would be the advantages and disadvantages of each channel alternative?

6. ''In a battle between giants like Procter & Gamble and Safeway (supermarket chain) five years ago, P&G would have prevailed. Now Safeway can call the tune.'' What has caused the change in power?

7. Sears acquired Dean Witter Reynolds, the fifth-largest stock brokerage firm, in order to capitalize on the growing demand for financial services. Sears has opened financial service centers in its stores, offering money market funds, casualty and life insurance, credit cards, auto and boat installment loans, and so on. What forces are working for and against the success of such a venture?

8. In a market consisting of five producers and five customers, how many contacts would have to be made (a) without a middleman? (b) with a middleman? What are the general formulas?

9. Explain how the characteristics of (a) peaches and (b) cement affect the channels for them.

10. ''Middlemen are parasites.'' This charge has been made by many over the centuries. Is this likely to be the case in a competitive economic system? Why or why not?

11. There is often conflict between manufacturers and retailers. What does each party really want from the other, and why does this give rise to conflict?

◼ FOOTNOTES

1 E. Raymond Corey, *Industrial Marketing: Cases and Concepts* (Englewood Cliffs, N.J.: Prentice-Hall, 1976), p. 263.

2 Louis W. Stern and Adel I. El-Ansary, *Marketing Channels*, 2nd ed. (Englewood Cliffs, N.J.: Prentice-Hall, 1982), p. 3.

3 Ibid., p. 8.

4 Wroe Alderson, "The Analytical Framework for Marketing," *Proceedings—Conference of Marketing Teachers from Far Western States* (Berkeley: University of California Press, 1958).

5 William G. Zikmund and William J. Stanton, "Recycling Solid Wastes: A Channels-of-Distribution Problem," *Journal of Marketing*, July 1971, p. 34.

6 Ronald Abler, John S. Adams, and Peter Gould, *Spatial Organizations: The Geographer's View of the World* (Englewood Cliffs, N.J.: Prentice-Hall, 1971), pp. 531–32.

7 See Irving Rein, Philip Kotler, and Martin Stoller, *High Visibility* (New York: Dodd, Mead, 1987).

8 Louis P. Bucklin, *Competition and Evolution in the Distributive Trades* (Englewood Cliffs, N.J.: Prentice-Hall, 1972).

9 Louis P. Bucklin, *A Theory of Distribution Channel Structure* (Berkeley: Institute of Business and Economic Research, University of California, 1966).

10 Phillip McVey, "Are Channels of Distribution What the Textbooks Say?" *Journal of Marketing*, January 1960, pp. 61–64.

11 Ibid.

12 See Bert Rosenbloom, *Marketing Channels: A Management View* (Hinsdale, Ill.: Dryden Press, 1978), pp. 192–203.

13 Bert C. McCammon, Jr., "Perspectives for Distribution Programming," in *Vertical Marketing Systems*, ed. Louis P. Bucklin (Glenview, Ill.: Scott, Foresman, 1970), p. 32.

14 Ibid., p. 43.

15 For an excellent report on this issue, see Howard Sutton, *Rethinking the Company's Selling and Distribution Channels*, Research Report No. 885, Conference Board, 1986, 26 pp.

16 McCammon, "Perspectives for Distribution Programming," pp. 32–51.

17 Ibid.

18 Ibid., p. 45.

19 Lee Adler, "Symbiotic Marketing," *Harvard Business Review*, November–December 1966, pp. 59–71.

20 See P. "Rajan" Varadarajan and Daniel Rajaratnam, "Symbiotic Marketing Revisited," *Journal of Marketing*, January 1986, pp. 7–17.

21 See Robert E. Weigand, "Fit Products and Channels to Your Markets," *Harvard Business Review*, January–February 1977, pp. 95–105.

22 Bert C. McCammon, Jr., "Alternative Explanations of Institutional Change and Channel Evolution," in *Toward Scientific Marketing*, ed. Stephen A. Greyser (Chicago: American Marketing Association, 1963), pp. 477–90.

23 For an excellent summary of interorganizational conflict and power in marketing channels, see Stern and El-Ansary, *Marketing Channels*, Chap. 7.

19

Managing Retailing, Wholesaling, and Physical-Distribution Systems

When is a refrigerator not a refrigerator? . . . when it is in Pittsburgh at the time it is desired in Houston.

J. L. Heskett, N. A. Glaskowsky, R. M. Ivie

In the preceding chapter, we examined marketing intermediaries from the viewpoint of manufacturers who wanted to build and manage marketing channels. In this chapter, we view these intermediaries—retailers, wholesalers, and physical-distribution organizations—as requiring and forging their own marketing strategies. Some of these intermediaries are so large and powerful that they dominate the manufacturers who deal with them. Many are increasingly using modern strategic planning and marketing tools. They are measuring performance more on a return-on-investment basis than on a profit margin basis. They are segmenting their markets better and improving their market targeting and positioning. They are aggressively pursuing marketing expansion and diversification strategies.

We will ask the following questions about each sector (retailers, wholesalers, and physical-distribution firms): What is the nature and importance of this sector? What are the major types of organizations within this sector? What marketing decisions do organizations in this sector make? and What are the major trends in this sector?

RETAILING

Nature and Importance of Retailing

Retailing includes all the activities involved in selling goods or services directly to final consumers for their personal, nonbusiness use. Any organization that does this selling—whether a manufacturer, wholesaler, or retailer—is doing retailing. It does not matter *how* the goods or services are sold (by person, mail, telephone, or vending machine) or *where* they are sold (in a store, on the street, or in the consumer's home).

On the other hand, a *retailer* or *retail store* is any business enterprise whose sales volume primarily comes from retailing.

Retailing is one of the major industries in the United States. Retail stores constitute approximately 20 percent of all U.S. businesses, outnumbering manufacturing and wholesaling establishments and representing the third-largest source of employment in the nation, with over 14 million employees. The industry comprises over 1.5 million single-unit establishments and over 415,000 multiunit establishments, and it generated a total of approximately $1,300 billion in sales in 1984. The largest retailers and their sales in billions in 1985 were Sears Roebuck ($40.7), K-Mart ($22.4), Safeway Stores ($19.7), Kroger ($17.1), American Stores ($13.9), J. C. Penney ($13.7), Southland ($12.7), Federated Department Stores ($10.0), and Lucky Stores ($9.3).

Types of Retailers

Retail organizations exhibit great variety, and new forms keep emerging. Several classifications have been proposed. For our purposes, we will discuss (1) store retailers, (2) nonstore retailers, and (3) retail organizations.

Store Retailers

Consumers in a modern shopping center can shop in a wide variety of stores, including department stores, clothing boutiques, discount stores, fast-food outlets, service retailers such as travel agencies and brokerage firms, and so on. Upon driving out of the shopping mall, they will pass further types of stores, including supermarkets, convenience food stores, home improvement centers, warehouse stores, catalog showrooms, and factory outlets. Exhibit 19-1 describes the most important store types.

Retail store types, like products, pass through stages of growth and decline that can be described as the *retail life cycle*.[1] A retail store type emerges at some point in history, enjoys a period of accelerated growth, reaches maturity, and then declines. Older retail forms took many years to reach maturity, but newer retail forms reach their maturity much earlier. This is dramatically illustrated in Table 19-1. The department store took eighty years to reach maturity, whereas warehouse retail outlets, a more modern form, reached their peak in ten years.

The table also shows that some well-known store types (e.g., general stores and variety stores) have entered a stage of decline. This means that more units of these store types will be closed than opened in the coming years. Clearly, some well-located and well-run general stores and variety stores will survive because they serve their customers well and have adopted modern marketing and management practices. But as store types, they suffer competitive disadvantages in their operating costs and/or customer-value generating ability.

One reason that new store types emerge to replace old store types is given by the *wheel-of-retailing* hypothesis.[2] Conventional store types typically offer many services to their customers and price their merchandise to cover the cost. This provides an opportunity for new store forms to emerge—e.g., discount stores—which offer lower prices, less service, and less status but have lower operating costs. An increasing number of shoppers use the conventional stores for deciding what to buy and then drive to the discount stores to make the actual purchase. As these discount stores increase their market share, they offer more services and upgrade their facilities. Their increased costs, however, force them to raise their prices until they start to resemble the conventional outlets they displaced. As a consequence, they become vulnerable to newer types of low-cost, low-margin operations. This hypothesis explains the initial success and later troubles of department stores, supermarkets, and, more recently, discount stores.

EXHIBIT 19-1

Major Store Types

Here are brief descriptions of the most important store types.

Specialty Store   A specialty store carries a narrow product line with a deep assortment within that line. Examples of specialty retailers are apparel stores, sporting goods stores, furniture stores, florists, and bookstores. Specialty stores can be subclassified by the degree of narrowness in their product line. A clothing store would be a *single-line store*; a men's clothing store would be a *limited-line store*; and a men's custom-shirt store would be a *superspecialty store*. Some analysts contend that in the future, superspecialty stores will grow the fastest to take advantage of increasing opportunities for market segmentation, market targeting, and product specialization. Some of the successful current examples are Athlete's Foot (sport shoes only), Tall Men (tall-men's clothing), and The Gap (primarily jeans).

Department Store   A department store carries several product lines, typically clothing, home furnishings, and household goods, where each line is operated as a separate department managed by specialist buyers or merchandisers. Examples of well-known department stores are Bloomingdale's (New York), Marshall Field (Chicago), and Filene's (Boston). *Specialty department stores* can also be found, carrying only clothing, shoes, cosmetics, gift items, and luggage; examples are Saks Fifth Avenue and I. Magnin.

Many observers believe that department stores are in the declining stage of the *retail life cycle*. They point to the increased competition among department stores; the increased competition coming from other types of retailers, particularly discount houses, specialty-store chains, and warehouse retailers; and the heavy traffic, poor parking, and deterioration of central cities, which have made downtown shopping less appealing.

Department stores are waging a "comeback" war. Many have opened branches in suburban shopping centers, where there are better parking facilities and higher family incomes. Others are running more frequent sales to meet the discount threat. Still others are remodeling their stores, including "going boutique." Some are leasing departments to outsiders. Some are experimenting with mail-order and telemarketing. Some department stores are retrenching on the number of employees, product lines, and customer services, such as delivery and credit, but this strategy may hurt their major appeal, namely, better service.

Supermarket   A supermarket is a relatively large, low-cost, low-margin, high-volume, self-service operation designed to serve the consumer's total needs for food, laundry, and household maintenance products. Today there are over 30,500 supermarkets with annual sales over $2 million in operation, accounting for 72 percent of total grocery sales. Supermarkets earn an operating profit of only about 1 percent on their sales and 10 percent on their net worth.

Supermarkets have been hit hard by a number of innovative competitors, such as convenience food stores, discount food stores, and superstores. The food market is becoming more segmented, and no longer is it likely to be dominated by one major type of food retailer. Another challenge has been the rapid growth of out-of-home eating, with Americans now spending nearly 40 percent of their food budgets outside the food stores.

Supermarkets have moved in several directions to improve their competitiveness. They have opened *larger stores*, with today's selling space occupying approximately 25,000 square feet. Supermarkets carry a large *number and variety of items*, typically over 12,000 items. The largest increase has been in nonfood items, which now account for 25 percent of total supermarket sales. Many supermarkets are moving into prescriptions, appliances, records, sporting goods, hardware, garden supplies, and even cameras, hoping to find high-margin lines to improve profitability. Supermarkets are also *upgrading their facilities* through more expensive locations, larger parking lots, carefully planned architecture and decor, longer store hours and Sunday openings, and a wide variety of customer services, such as check cashing, restrooms, and background music. Supermarkets have also increased their *promotional budgets*. They have also moved heavily into *private brands* to reduce their dependence on national brands and increase their profit margins.

"Supermarketing" as a method of doing business has recently spread to other types of business, particularly in the drug, home improvement, toy, and sporting goods fields.

Convenience Store   Convenience food stores are relatively small stores that are located near residential areas, open long hours and seven days a week, and carry a limited line of high-turnover convenience products. Examples are Seven-Elevens and White Hen Pantries. Their long hours and their use by consumers mainly for "fill-in" purchases make them relatively high price operations. Yet they fill an important consumer need, and people seem willing to pay for the convenience. Convenience stores numbered 42,657 in 1984, with sales of about $20 billion.

Superstore, Combination Store, and Hypermarche *Superstores* are larger than the conventional supermarket, with 35,000 square feet of selling space, and they aim at meeting the consumers' total needs for routinely purchased food and nonfood items. They usually offer services such as laundry, dry cleaning, shoe repair, check cashing and bill paying, and bargain lunch counters. *Combination stores* represent a diversification of the supermarket store into the growing drug and prescription field. Combination food and drug stores average 55,000 square feet of selling space. *Hypermarches* are even larger than combination stores, ranging between 80,000 and 220,000 square feet. The hypermarche combines supermarket, discount, and warehouse retailing principles. Its product assortment goes beyond routinely purchased goods and includes furniture, heavy and light appliances, clothing items, and many other things. The basic approach is bulk display and minimum handling by store personnel, with discounts offered to customers who are willing to carry heavy appliances and furniture out of the store.

Discount Store A discount store sells standard merchandise at lower prices than conventional merchants by accepting lower margins and working on higher volume. A true discount store exhibits these elements: (1) the store regularly sells its merchandise at lower prices; (2) the store emphasizes national brands, so that low price does not suggest inferior quality; (3) the store operates on a self-service, minimum-facilities basis; and (4) the location tends to be a low-rent area, and the store draws customers from relatively long distances. In 1984, there were an estimated 8,738 discount stores, with almost $62.2 billion in sales.

In recent years, intense competition among discount houses and between discount houses and department stores has led many discount retailers to trade up. They have improved their decor, added new lines such as wearing apparel, added more services such as check cashing and easy returns, and opened new branches in suburban shopping centers, all leading to higher costs and forcing higher prices. Furthermore, department stores often cut their prices to compete with the discounters, with the distinction between the two growing progressively blurred.

Discount retailing has moved beyond general merchandise into specialty merchandise stores, such as discount sporting goods stores, discount electronics stores, and discount bookstores.

Warehouse Store A warehouse store is a no-frill, discount, reduced-service operation, which seeks to move high volume at low prices. One of its most interesting forms is the *furniture showroom warehouse* (such as Levitz or Wickes). Shoppers enter a football-field-size warehouse located in a suburban low-rent area and pass by a huge inventory of furniture piled in neat tiers. They enter a showroom containing approximately two hundred rooms of attractively displayed furniture. Customers make their selections and place orders with sales people. By the time the customer pays, leaves, and drives to the loading entrance, the merchandise is ready.

Catalog Showroom A catalog showroom applies catalog and discounting principles to a wide selection of high-markup, fast-moving, brand-name goods. These goods include jewelry, power tools, luggage, cameras, and photographic equipment. These stores have become one of retailing's hottest new forms, even posing a threat to the traditional discounter. Catalog showrooms issue four-color catalogs, often five hundred pages long, and supplement them with smaller seasonal editions. Each item's list price and discount price are shown. The customer can order an item over the phone and pay delivery charges or drive to the showroom, examine it firsthand, and buy it out of stock.

New store types emerge to meet widely different consumer preferences for service levels and specific services. Thus, in the past, most consumers purchased shoes in shoe stores where they were waited on by fitters. Today most shoes are bought in mass-merchandise outlets where consumers take them off the shelf, and an increasing number of shoes are purchased through the mail. It turns out that retailers in most product categories can position themselves as offering one of four levels of service:

■ *Self-service retailing.* Used in many retailing operations, especially for obtaining convenience goods and, to some extent, shopping goods. Self-service is the cornerstone of all discount

TABLE 19-1   The evolution of today's retail institutions

Institutional Type	Period of Fastest Growth	Period from Inception to Maturity (years)	Stage of Life Cycle	Representative Firms
General store	1800–1840	100	Declining	A local institution
Single-line store	1820–1840	100	Mature	Hickory Farms
Department store	1860–1940	80	Mature	Marshall Field's
Variety store	1870–1930	50	Declining	Morgan-Lindsay
Mail order house	1915–1950	50	Mature	Spiegel
Corporate chain	1920–1930	50	Mature	Sears
Discount store	1955–1975	20	Mature	K mart
Supermarket	1935–1965	35	Mature/declining	A&P
Shopping center	1950–1965	40	Mature	Paramus
Cooperative	1930–1950	40	Mature	Ace Hardware
Gasoline station	1930–1950	45	Mature	Texaco
Convenience store	1965–1975	20	Mature	Seven-11
Fast-food outlet	1960–1975	15	Late growth	Shoney's
Home improvement center	1965–1980	15	Late growth	Lowes
Super specialists	1975–1985	10	Late growth	The Limited
Warehouse retailing	1970–1980	10	Maturity	Levitz
Personal computer stores	1980–	?	Early growth	Computerland

SOURCE: J. Barry Mason and Hazel F. Ezell, *Marketing* (Plano, Tex.: Business Publications, 1987), p. 517.

operations. Many customers are willing to carry out their own locate-compare-select process to save money.

■ *Self-selection retailing.* Involves customers in finding their own goods, although they can ask for assistance. Customers complete their transactions by finding a salesperson to take the money for the item. Self-selection organizations have higher operating expenses than self-service operations because of the additional staff requirements.

■ *Limited-service retailing.* Provides more sales assistance because these stores carry more shopping goods, and customers need more information. The stores also offer services, such as credit and merchandise return privileges, not normally found in less-service-oriented stores and hence have higher operating costs.

■ *Full-service retailing.* Provides sales people who are ready to assist in every phase of the locate-compare-select process. Customers who like to be waited on prefer this type of store. The high staffing cost, along with the higher proportion of specialty goods and slower-moving items (fashions, jewelry, cameras), the more liberal merchandise-return policies, various credit plans, free delivery, home servicing of durables, and customer facilities such as lounges and restaurants, results in high-cost retailing.

By combining these different service levels with different assortment breadths, we can distinguish four broad positioning strategies available to retailers. They are shown in Figure 19-1.

1. Bloomingdale's typifies stores that feature a broad product assortment and high value added. Stores in this quadrant pay close attention to store design, product quality, service, and image. Their profit margin is high, and if they are fortunate enough to have high volume, they will be very profitable.

2. Tiffany typifies stores that feature a narrow product assortment and high value added. Such stores cultivate an exclusive image and tend to operate on a high margin and low volume.

3. Kinney Shoe typifies stores that feature a narrow line and low value added. Such stores,

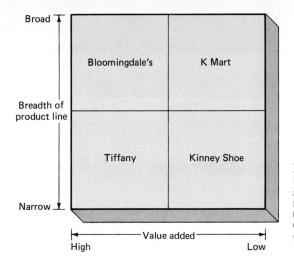

FIGURE 19-1
Retail Positioning Map
SOURCE: William T. Gregor and
Eileen M. Friars, "Money
Merchandising: Retail Revolution in
Consumer Financial Service"
(Cambridge, Mass.: The MAC Group,
1982).

often referred to as specialty mass merchandisers, appeal to price-conscious consumers. They keep their costs and prices low through designing similar stores and centralizing buying, merchandising, advertising, and distribution.

4. K-mart typifies stores that feature a broad line and low value added. They focus on keeping prices low so that they have an image of being a place for good buys. They make up for their low margin by achieving a high volume.

Non-Store Retailers   Although the overwhelming majority of goods and services are sold through stores, *nonstore retailing* has been growing much faster than store retailing, amounting to more than 12 percent of all consumer purchases. Some observers foresee as much as a third of all general-merchandise retailing being done through nonstore channels by the end of the century. Some predict the growth of *electronic shopping*, where consumers will order their goods using home computers and receive them or pick them up without stepping into stores. Here we will examine *direct marketing*, *direct selling*, *automatic vending*, and *buying service*.

Direct marketing   The Direct Marketing Association defines *direct marketing* as "an interactive system of marketing which uses one or more advertising media to effect a measurable response and/or transaction at any location." Direct marketers run advertisements describing their product, and the customer can write or call for it. The ordered merchandise is usually delivered by mail and paid for by a charge card. The direct marketer selects media vehicles that maximize the number of orders for a given advertising expenditure. The media are used to make the sale, not to create preferences and brand images as with general advertising. The following are the different forms that direct marketing has taken.

■ *Mail-order catalog.* Here the seller mails a catalog to a select list of customers and/or makes the catalog available on its premises. This approach is used by *general-merchandise* mail-order houses carrying a full line of merchandise. Sears is the industry giant, with nearly $3 billion in catalog operations, and it sends out 300 million catalogs annually. Recently specialty department stores, such as Neiman-Marcus and Saks Fifth Avenue, have begun sending catalogs to cultivate an upper-middle-class market for high-priced, often exotic, merchandise such as "his and her" bathrobes, designer jewelry, and gourmet foods. Several major corporations have also acquired or developed mail-order divisions. Xerox offers children's books; Avon sells women's apparel; W. R. Grace sells cheese; American Airlines offers luggage; General Foods offers needlework kits; and General Mills sells sports shirts. Some direct marketers offer an extension of the mail-order catalog by marketing their products through pretaped videocassettes. Consumers usually have to buy the videocassettes but are often given a free gift when they do so to make the offer attractive.

■ *Direct mail.* Direct-mail advertising is a $6-billion-a-year business. The direct marketer sends single mail pieces—letters, flyers, foldouts, and other "salesmen on wings"—to prospects whose names are on mailing lists of high-potential buyers of the product category. The mailing lists are purchased from mailing-list brokerage houses that can provide a list of names of people of almost any description—the superwealthy, mobile home owners, brand managers in North Dakota, and so on. Direct mail is increasingly popular because (1) it permits high customer target selectivity, (2) it can be personalized, (3) it is flexible, and (4) it permits ready testing of the effectiveness of different approaches. While the cost-per-thousand people reached is higher than with mass media, the people reached are much better prospects. Over 35 percent of Americans have responded to direct-mail ads, and the number is growing. Direct mail has proved very successful in promoting books, magazine subscriptions, and insurance and is increasingly being used to sell novelty and gift items, clothing apparel, gourmet foods, and industrial items. The major charities use direct mail to raise $31.9 billion, or over 80 percent of their total contributions.[3]

■ *Telemarketing.* Telemarketing has become a major direct marketing tool. In 1983, marketers spent more than $13.6 billion on telephone calls to help sell their products and services. Telemarketing blossomed in the late 1960s with the introduction of inward and outward Wide Area Telephone Service (WATS). With IN WATS, marketers can use toll-free 800 numbers to handle customer service and complaints, or to receive orders from television and radio ads, direct mail, or catalogs. With OUT WATS, they can use the phone to sell directly to consumers and businesses, generate or qualify sales leads, reach more-distant buyers, or service current customers or accounts. During January 1982, more than seven hundred people dialed an 800 number every minute in response to television commercials. The average household receives nineteen telephone sales calls each year and makes sixteen calls to place orders. Some telemarketing systems are fully automated. For example, automatic dialing and recorded message players (ADRMPs) can self-dial numbers, play a voice-activated advertising message, and take orders from interested customers on an answering-machine device or by forwarding the call to an operator. Telemarketing is used in business marketing as well as consumer marketing. For example, Raleigh Bicycles used telemarketing to reduce the amount of personal selling needed for contacting its dealers. In the first year, sales-force travel costs were reduced by 50 percent, and sales in a single quarter were up 34 percent.[4]

■ *Television marketing.* Television is being used in two different ways to market products directly to the ultimate consumer. Direct marketers buy 30- or 60-second spots on television and describe a product, and the customer can call a toll-free number and order the advertised item. Magazines, books, small appliances, records, and tapes are items with which this strategy works well. A newer method is an entire program on cable or a local television station devoted just to selling assorted merchandise. In a show called "Telephone Auction," a couple of salesmen display a product while a studio audience bids for it. The salesmen then dramatically offer the product to the audience and viewers at a fraction of the price bid for it. The product can be ordered by calling a toll-free number. Clothing, home appliances, stereo systems, wristwatches, and so on, are among the products sold.

■ *Other media marketing.* Magazines, newspapers, and radios are also used to make sales to customers. The person hears or reads about an offer and dials a toll-free number to place an order.

■ *Electronic shopping.* This can take two forms. Videotext systems permit consumers with interactive cable TV to order products displayed on their television screen by operating a small terminal. Alternatively, consumers can use personal computers to phone central data bases and compare various products being offered for sale. They can type in their orders along with their charge card numbers.

Today the direct marketing business is booming. The movement of women into the work force has substantially cut down on their available shoping time. Other factors have made shopping less pleasant: the higher costs of driving; traffic congestion and parking headaches; and the shortage of sales help and having to queue at checkout counters. In addition, many chain stores have dropped slower-moving specialty items, thus creating an opportunity for direct marketers to promote these items. Finally, the development of toll-free phone numbers and the willingness of direct marketers to accept telephone orders at night or on Sundays have boosted this form of retailing.

Direct selling Direct selling—which started centuries ago with itinerant peddlers—has burgeoned into a $9 billion industry, with over six hundred companies selling either *door-to-door*, *office-to-office*, or at *home sales parties*. The pioneers include the Fuller Brush Company (brushes, brooms, and the like), Electrolux (vacuum cleaners), Southwestern Company of Nashville (bibles), and World Book (encyclopedias). Door-to-door selling improved considerably with Avon's entry into the industry, with the concept of the homemakers' friend and beauty consultant—the Avon lady. Its army of nearly a million representatives worldwide produced over $2 billion in sales in 1985, making it the world's largest cosmetics firm and the number-one door-to-door marketer. Tupperware, on the other hand, helped popularize the home-sales-parties method of selling, in which several friends and neighbors are invited to a party in someone's home where Tupperware products are demonstrated and sold.[5]

Direct selling is expensive (the salespersons get a 20 to 50 percent commission), and there are the costs of hiring, training, managing, and motivating the sales force. The future of direct selling is somewhat uncertain, with more women at work during the day. The salesperson may well be replaced by electronic shopping in the future.

Automatic vending Automatic vending through coin-operated machines has been a major post–World War II growth area. By 1984 total sales had soared to $16.5 billion (1.3 percent of total retail trade). Automatic vending has been applied to a considerable variety of merchandise, including impulse goods with high convenience value (cigarettes, soft drinks, candy, newspapers, hot beverages) and other products (hosiery, cosmetics, food snacks, hot soups and food, paperbacks, record albums, film, T-shirts, insurance policies, shoeshines, and even fishing worms). Vending machines are found in factories, offices, large retail stores, gasoline stations, and even railway dining cars. According to the National Automatic Merchandising Association, over seven thousand machine operators in the United States operate more than one million machines.

Vending machines offer customers the advantages of twenty-four-hour selling, self-service, and unhandled merchandise. At the same time, automatic vending is a relatively expensive channel, and prices of vended merchandise are often 15 to 20 percent higher. Vendor costs are high because of frequent restocking at widely scattered locations, frequent machine breakdowns, and the high pilferage rate in certain locations. For the customer, the biggest irritations are machine breakdowns, out-of-stocks, and the fact that merchandise cannot be returned.

Vending machines are increasingly supplying entertainment services—pinball machines, slot machines, juke boxes, and the new electronic computer games. A highly specialized machine is the *automatic teller* that allows bank customers twenty-four-hour service on checking, savings, withdrawals, and transfer of funds from one account to another.

Buying service A buying service is a storeless retailer serving specific clienteles—usually the employees of large organizations such as schools, hospitals, unions, and government agencies. The organization's members become members of the buying service and are entitled to buy from a selective list of retailers who have agreed to give discounts to members of the buying service. Thus a customer seeking a video recording machine would get a form from the buying service, take it to an approved retailer, and buy the appliance at a discount. The retailer would then pay a small fee to the buying service. United Buying Service, for example, offers its nine hundred thousand members the opportunity to buy merchandise at "cost plus 8 percent."

Retail Organizations Although many retail stores are independently owned, an increasing number are falling under some form of corporate retailing. For example, shopping malls are increasingly populated with chain stores or franchised stores rather than independent stores. The five main types of corporate retailing are *corporate chains*, *voluntary chain and retailer cooperatives*, *consumer cooperatives*, *franchise organizations*, and *merchandising conglomerates*.

Corporate chain The chain store is one of the most important retail developments of the twentieth century. Gist has defined *chain store* as *two or more outlets that are commonly owned and controlled, sell similar lines of merchandise, have central buying and merchandising, and may use a similar architectural motif.*[6] Corporate chains have appeared in all types of retail operations: supermarkets and discount, variety, specialty, and department stores. In terms of product line, the corporate chains (when defined as having eleven or more units) are strongest in department stores (96 percent of the total sales volume of 1984), variety stores (84 percent), food stores (55 percent), drugstores (55 percent), shoe stores (49 percent), women's apparel (40 percent), and tire, battery, and auto and home supply stores (20 percent).

The success of corporate chains is based on their ability to achieve a price advantage over independents by moving toward high volume and lower margins. Chains achieve their efficiency in several ways. First, their size allows them to buy large quantities to take maximum advantage of quantity discounts and lower transportation costs. Second, chains are able to hire good managers and develop scientific procedures in the areas of sales forecasting, inventory control, pricing, and promotion. Third, the chains can integrate wholesaling and retailing functions, whereas independent retailers have to deal with many wholesalers. Fourth, the chains achieve promotional economies by buying advertising that benefits all of their stores and spreading the cost over a large volume. And fifth, the chains permit their units some freedom to meet variations in consumer preferences and competition in local markets.

Voluntary chain and retailer cooperative The chains triggered a competitive reaction from the independents, which began to form two types of associations. One is the *voluntary chain*, which consists of a wholesaler-sponsored group of independent retailers engaged in bulk buying and common merchandising. Examples include the Independent Grocers Alliance (IGA) in groceries, True Value in hardware, and Western Auto in auto supplies. The other is the *retailer cooperative*, which consists of a set of independent retailers who set up a central buying organization and conduct joint promotion efforts. Examples include Associated Grocers in groceries and ACE in hardware. These organizations achieved the needed merchandising economies and became effective in meeting the price challenge of the corporate chains.

Consumer cooperative A consumer cooperative (or co-op) is any retail firm owned by its customers. Consumer co-ops are started by community residents who feel that local retailers are not serving them well, either charging too high prices or providing poor-quality products. The residents contribute money to open their own store, and they vote on its policies and elect a group to manage it. The store may set its prices low or, alternatively, set normal prices with members receiving a patronage dividend based on their individual level of purchases.

Franchise organization A franchise organization is a contractual association between a franchiser (a manufacturer, wholesaler, or service organization) and franchisees (independent businesspeople who buy the right to own and operate one or more units in the franchise system). Franchise organizations are normally based on some unique product, service, or method of doing business, or on a trade name, or patent, or on goodwill that the franchiser has developed. Franchising has been prominent in fast foods, video stores, health/fitness centers, hair cutting, auto rentals, motels, travel agencies, real estate, and dozens of other product and service areas.[7]

The franchiser's compensation can consist of the following elements: an initial fee; a royalty on gross sales; rental and lease fees on equipment and fixtures supplied by the franchiser; a share of the profits; and sometimes a regular license fee. In a few cases, franchisers have also charged management consulting fees, but usually the franchisee is entitled to this service as part of the total package.

> One of the most successful franchise systems of all time is McDonald's. McDonald's charges franchisees an initial fee of $22,500 and receives a 3.5 percent service fee and a rental charge of 8.5 percent of the franchisee's monthly gross sales. It also requires its new franchisees to attend "Hamburger University" for three weeks to learn how to manage the business. The franchisees must also adhere to certain procedures in buying raw materials and in preparing and selling the product. In 1985, there were approximately 9,400 outlets in 45 countries with sales of $11.1 billion. McDonald's opens a new store every fifteen hours.

McDonald's and other fast-food franchisers are currently facing rising labor costs and food costs, forcing them to raise their prices to the customers. New competitors continue to emerge, popularizing ethnic foods, such as tacos and gyros. Some major franchisers are now opening units in smaller towns, where there is less competition. Others are moving into large factories, office buildings, colleges, and even hospitals. Others are experimenting with new products that they hope will appeal to the public and be profitable to the firm.

Merchandising conglomerate Merchandising conglomerates are free-form corporations that combine several diversified retailing lines and forms under central ownership, along with some integration of their distribution and management function.[8] Major examples include Federated Department Stores, Allied Stores, Dayton-Hudson, and F. W. Woolworth. For example, F. W. Woolworth, in addition to its variety stores, operates Kinney Shoe Stores, Afterthoughts (costume jewelry and handbag specialty stores), Herald Square Stationers, Frame Scene, and Kids Mart.[9] In the future, diversified retailing is likely to be adopted by more corporate chains. The major question is whether diversified retailing produces superior management systems and economies that benefit all the separate retail lines.

Retailer Marketing Decisions

Many retailers today are anxious to find new marketing strategies to attract and hold customers. In the past, they held customers by having special or unique assortments of goods, by offering greater or better services than competitors, and by offering store credit cards to enable their buyers to buy on credit. All of this has changed. Today many stores offer similar assortments: National brands such as Calvin Klein, Izod, and Levi are found not only in most department stores but in mass-merchandise outlets and in off-price discount stores. The national brand manufacturers, in their drive for volume, did not grant exclusives but put their branded goods everywhere. The result was that stores looked more and more alike; they became commoditized. In any city, a shopper could find many stores but only few assortments.

As for service differentiation among retailers, this too eroded. Many department stores cut down on their services and many discounters increased their services. Customers became smarter shoppers and more price-sensitive. They did not see the point of paying more for identical brands, especially when service differences were minimal or unimportant. Nor did they need to get credit from a particular store, as bank credit cards became increasingly accepted by all stores. For all these reasons, many retailers today are rethinking their marketing strategy.[10]

Retailers must make a number of decisions in designing their retailing strategy. Suppose a retailer wants to design a store for the "high service" segment of the market. Figure 19-2 illustrates a set of decisions made by the retailer to define its business. Note that the decision tree begins with selecting a target segment and positioning.

We will now examine more closely the marketing decisions faced by retailers in the areas of target market, product assortment and services, price, promotion, and place.

Target-Market Decision A retailer's most important decision concerns the target market. Should the store focus on upscale, midscale, or downscale shoppers? Do the target shoppers want variety, assortment depth, or convenience? Until the target market is defined and profiled, the retailer cannot make consistent decisions on product assortment, store decor, advertising messages and media, price levels, and so on.[11]

Too many retailers have not clarified their target market or are trying to satisfy too many markets, satisfying none of them well. Even Sears, which serves so many different people, must develop a better definition of which groups it will make its major target customers so that it can achieve more precision in its product assortment, prices, locations, and promotion with these groups.

Some retailers have defined their target markets quite well. Here are two prime examples whose founders are among the richest men in America:

Leslie H. Wexner borrowed $5,000 in 1963 to create The Limited Inc., which started as a single store targeted to young, fashion conscious, moderately affluent women. All aspects of the store—clothing assortment, fixtures, music, colors, personnel—were orchestrated to match the target consumer. He continued to open more stores, but a decade later his original customers were no longer in the "young" group. To catch the new "youngs," he started the Limited Express. Over the years, he started or acquired other targeted store chains, including Lane Bryant, Victoria's Secrets, Lerner's, and so on. Today The Limited operates twenty-four hundred stores in seven different segments of the market with sales of $2.4 billion in 1986.

Sam Walton and his brother opened the first Wal-Mart discount store in Rogers, Arkansas, in 1962. It was a big, flat, warehouse-type store aimed at selling everything from automotive supplies to small appliances to small-town America at the lowest possible prices. By 1985, Walton had opened more than 860 Wal-Marts stretching across twenty-two states. His secret: target small-town America, listen to the customers, treat the employees as partners, and keep a tight rein on expenses.

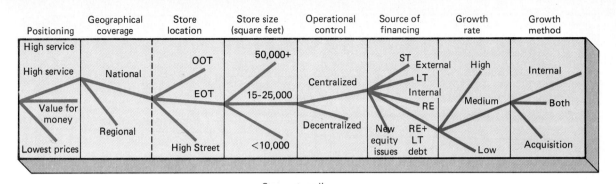

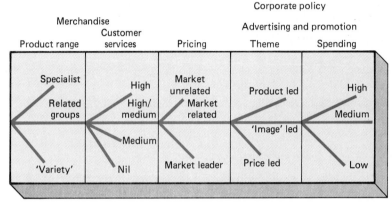

Corporate policy

Functional Area Policy

Key:
OOT — Out of town
EOT — Edge of town
ST — Short term
LT — Long term
RE — Retained earnings

FIGURE 19-2
A Retailing Decision Tree
SOURCE: See Derek Knee and David Walters, *Strategy in Retailing: Theory and Application* (Oxford: Philip Allan Publishers Limited, 1985), p. 7.

Retailers should carry out periodic marketing research to ensure that they are reaching and satisfying their target customers. Consider a store that seeks to attract affluent consumers but whose image is the one shown by the solid line in Figure 19-3. The store's image does not appeal to its target market, and it has to either serve the mass market or redesign itself into a "classier store." Suppose it decides on the latter. Some time later the store interviews customers again. The store image is now shown by the dashed line in Figure 19-3. The store has succeeded in realigning its image closer to its target market.

Product-Assortment-and-Services Decision   Retailers have to decide on three major "product" variables that help position their store to their target market, namely, product assortment, services mix, and store atmosphere.

The retailer's *product assortment* must match the shopping expectations of the target market. In fact, it becomes a key element in the competitive battle among similar retailers. The retailer has to decide on product assortment *width* (narrow or wide) and *depth* (shallow or deep). Thus in the restaurant business, a restaurant can offer a narrow and shallow assortment (small lunch counters), a narrow and deep assortment (delicatessen), a wide and shallow assortment (cafeteria), or a wide and deep assortment (large restaurants). Another product-assortment dimension is the quality of the goods. The customer is interested not only in the range of choice but also in the quality of the products.

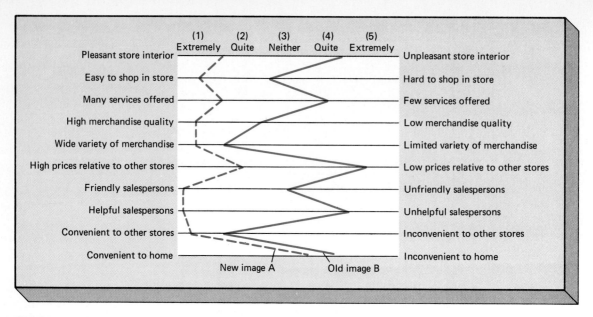

FIGURE 19-3
A Comparison Between the Old and New Image of a Store Seeking to Appeal to a Class
Market
SOURCE: Adapted from David W. Cravens, Gerald E. Hills, and Robert B. Woodruff, *Marketing Decision Making: Concepts and Strategy* (Homewood, Ill.: Richard D. Irwin, 1976), p. 234. © 1976 by Richard D. Irwin, Inc.

The retailer's real challenge only begins after defining the store's product assortment and quality level. There will always be competitors with similar assortments and quality. The challenge is to develop a product differentiation strategy. Wortzel suggests several product differentiation strategies for retailers:[12]

1. *Feature some exclusive national brands which are not available at competing retailers.* Thus Saks may get exclusive rights to carry the dresses of a well-known international designer.
2. *Feature mostly private branded merchandise.* Thus The Limited does its own designing of most of the clothes carried in its stores.
3. *Feature blockbuster distinctive merchandise events.* Bloomingdale's will run long shows featuring the goods of another country, such as India or China, throughout its store.
4. *Feature surprise or ever-changing merchandise.* Benetton changes some portion of its merchandise every month so that customers will want to drop in frequently. Loehmann's offers surprise assortments of distress merchandise, overstocks, and closeouts.
5. *Feature the latest or newest merchandise first.* The Sharper Image will lead other retailers in introducing the newest or latest electronic appliances from around the world.
6. *Offer merchandise customizing services.* Harrod's of London will make custom-tailored suits, shirts, and ties for customers, in addition to its ready-made men's wear.
7. *Offer a highly targeted assortment.* Lane Bryant carries goods for the mature, larger woman. Brookstone offers unusual tools and gadgets for the person who wants to shop in an "adult toy store."

Retailers must also decide on the *services mix* to offer customers. The old "mom and pop" grocery stores offered home delivery, credit, and conversation, services that today's supermarkets have completely eliminated. Table 19-2 lists some of the major services

TABLE 19-2   Typical Retail Services

Prepurchase Services	Postpurchase Services	Ancillary Services
1. Accepting telephone orders	1. Delivery	1. Check cashing
2. Accepting mail orders (or purchases)	2. Regular wrapping (or bagging)	2. General information
		3. Free parking
3. Advertising	3. Gift wrapping	4. Restaurants
4. Window display	4. Adjustments	5. Repairs
5. Interior display	5. Returns	6. Interior decorating
6. Fitting rooms	6. Alterations	7. Credit
7. Shopping hours	7. Tailoring	8. Rest rooms
8. Fashion shows	8. Installations	9. Baby-attendant service
9. Trade-ins	9. Engraving	
	10. COD delivery	

SOURCE: Carl M. Larson, Robert E. Weigand, and John S. Wright, *Basic Retailing* 2nd ed., (Englewood Cliffs, N.J.: Prentice-Hall, 1976), p. 384. Reprinted by permission of Prentice-Hall, Inc., Englewood Cliffs, N.J.

that full-service retailers can offer. The services mix is one of the key tools of nonprice competition for differentiating one store from another.

The *store's atmosphere* is a third element in its product arsenal. Every store has a physical layout that makes it hard or easy to move around. Every store has a "look"; one store is dirty, another is charming, a third is palatial, a fourth is somber. The store must embody a planned atmosphere that suits the target market and draws them toward purchase. A funeral parlor should be quiet, somber, and peaceful; and a discothèque should be bright, loud, and vibrating. The Banana Republic Travel & Safari Clothing stores work on the concept of "theater in retailing"; customers feel they are shopping in an African bazaar or hunting lodge. Supermarkets have found that varying the tempo of music affects the average time spent in the store and the average expenditures. Currently supermarkets are exploring ways to release aromas through sticker displays on store shelves to stimulate hunger or thirst. Some fine department stores vaporize perfume fragrances in certain departments. "Packaged environments" are designed by creative people who know how to combine visual, aural, olfactory, and tactile stimuli to produce the desired effect.[13]

Price Decision   The retailer's prices are a key positioning factor and must be decided in relation to the target market, the product-and-service assortment mix, and competition. All retailers would like to charge high markups and achieve high volumes, but usually the two do not go together. Most retailers fall into the *high-markup, lower-volume group* (fine specialty stores) or the *low-markup, higher-volume group* (mass merchandisers and discount stores). Within each of these groups, there are further gradations. Thus Bijan's on Rodeo Drive in Beverly Hills prices suits starting at $1,000 and shoes at $400, far in excess of the prices of fine department stores. At the other extreme, 47th Street Photo in New York City is a superdiscounter of well-known branded merchandise, pricing below even normal discounters and catalog houses.

Retailers must also pay attention to pricing tactics. Most retailers will put low prices on some items to serve as *traffic builders* or *loss leaders*. They will run storewide sales on some occasions. They will plan markdowns on slower-moving merchandise: for example, shoe retailers expect to sell 50 percent of their shoes at the normal markup, 25 percent at a 40 percent markup, and the remaining 25 percent at cost.

Promotion Decisions   The retailer must use promotion tools that support and reinforce its image positioning. Fine stores will advertise in magazines such as *Vogue* and *Harper's* and take out full-page tasteful newspaper ads. Discount retailers will place loud ads on radio, television, and newspapers touting low prices and specials. Differences will also occur in the use of sales people, sales promotion, and publicity. Fine stores will carefully train their sales people in how to greet customers, interpret their needs, and handle their doubts and complaints. Discounters will use less well trained sales people and use a whole range of sales promotion tools to generate traffic.

Place Decision   Retailers are accustomed to saying that the three keys to success in retailing are "location, location, and location." The retailer's choice of location is a key competitive factor in its ability to attract customers. For example, customers primarily choose the bank that is nearest to them. Department-store chains, oil companies, and fast-food franchisers are particularly careful in selecting locations. The problem breaks down into selecting regions of the country in which to open stores, then particular cities, and then particular sites. A supermarket chain, for example, may decide to operate in the Midwest and Southeast; within the Midwest, in the cities of Chicago, Milwaukee, and Indianapolis; and within Chicago, in fourteen locations, mostly suburban.

Large retailers must wrestle with the problem of whether to locate several small stores in many locations or larger stores in fewer locations. Generally speaking, the retailer should locate enough stores in each city to gain promotion and distribution economies. The larger the individual stores, the greater their trading area or reach.

Retailers have a choice of locating their stores in the central business district, a regional shopping center, a community shopping center, or a shopping strip.

> ■ *Central business districts* represent the oldest and most heavily trafficked city area, often known as "downtown." Store and office rents are normally high. But a number of downtowns, such as Detroit's, have been hit by a flight to the suburbs with resulting deterioration of downtown retailing facilities and a changing shopper composition.
>
> ■ *Regional shopping centers* are large suburban malls containing forty to over one hundred stores and drawing from a five- to ten-mile radius. Typically the malls feature one or two nationally known anchor stores such as Sears and Marshall Field's, and a great number of smaller stores, many of them under franchise operation. Malls are attractive because of generous parking, one-stop shopping, restaurants, and recreational facilities. Successful malls charge high rents but in return generate high traffic.
>
> ■ *Community shopping centers* are smaller malls with typically one anchor store and between twenty and forty smaller stores.
>
> ■ *Shopping strips* contain a cluster of stores serving a neighborhood's normal needs for groceries, hardware, laundry, and gasoline. They serve people within a five- to ten-minute driving range.

In view of the trade-off between high traffic and high rents, retailers must decide on the most advantageous locations for their outlets. They can use a variety of methods to assess locations, including traffic counts, surveys of consumer shopping habits, analysis of competitive locations, and so on.[14] Several models for site location have also been formulated.[15]

Retailers can assess the sales effectiveness of a particular store by looking at the following four indicators:

1. Number of people passing by on an average day
2. Percentage who drop in

3. Percentage of those dropping in who buy

4. Average amount purchased per sale

A store that is doing poorly may be in a poorly trafficked location; or not enough passersby drop in; or too many drop-ins browse but do not buy; or the buyers do not buy very much. Each can be remedied. Traffic is remedied by a better location; drop-ins are increased by better window displays and sales announcements; and the number buying and the amount purchased are largely a function of merchandise quality, prices, and salesmanship.

Trends in Retailing

At this point, we can summarize the main developments that retailers have to take into account as they plan their competitive strategies:

1. *New retail forms.* New retail forms constantly emerge to threaten established retail forms. A New York bank will deliver money to the customer's office or home. Adelphi College offers "commuter train classroom education" in which businesspeople commuting between Long Island and Manhattan can earn credits toward an M.B.A. American Bakeries started Hippopotamus Food Stores to allow customers to buy institutional-sized packages at savings of 10 to 30 percent. Domino's Pizza is set up to deliver pizza within thirty minutes anywhere in its area. Family First Casket Outlet sells caskets at discount prices ranging from $95 to $2,000.

2. *Shortening retail life cycles.* The life span of new retail forms is shortening because of the innovation speedup.

3. *Nonstore retailing.* Over the past decade, mail-order sales increased at twice the rate of in-store sales. The electronic age has significantly increased the possibilities for nonstore retailing. Consumers receive sales offers over their televisions, computers, and telephones to which they can immediately respond by calling a toll-free number.

4. *Increasing intertype competition.* Competition today is increasingly intertype or between different types of outlets. Thus we see competition between in-store and nonstore retailers. Discount stores, catalog showrooms, and department stores all compete for the same consumers.

5. *Polarity of retailing.* Increasing intertype competition has produced retailers positioning themselves on extreme ends of the number of product lines carried. High profitability and growth have been realized by both mass merchandisers such as K-Mart and specialty stores such as Radio Shack and Toys 'R' Us.

6. *Changing definition of one-stop shopping.* Specialty stores in "malls" are becoming increasingly competitive with large department stores as offering "one-stop shopping."

7. *Growth of vertical marketing systems.* Marketing channels are increasingly becoming professionally managed and programmed. As large corporations extend their control over marketing channels, independent small stores are being squeezed out.

8. *Portfolio approach.* Retail organizations are increasingly designing and launching new store formats targeted to different lifestyle groups. They are not sticking to one format such as department stores but are moving into a mix of businesses that appear promising.[16]

9. *Growing importance of retail technology.* Retail technologies are becoming critically important as competitive tools. Progressive retailers are using computers to produce better forecasts, control inventory costs, order electronically from suppliers, send electronic mail between stores, and even sell to customers within stores. They are adopting checkout-scanning systems, electronic funds transfer, in-store television, and improved merchandise-handling systems.

WHOLESALING

Nature and Importance of Wholesaling

Wholesaling includes *all activities involved in selling goods or services to those who buy for resale or business use.* A retail bakery selling pastry to a local hotel is engaged in wholesaling at that point. We will use the term *wholesalers*, however, to describe firms that are engaged primarily in wholesaling activity. It excludes manufacturers and farmers because they are engaged primarily in production, and it excludes retailers. About five million people are employed in some form of wholesaling, and wholesaling costs represent about 10 percent of every consumer dollar.

Wholesalers differ from retailers in a number of ways. First, wholesalers pay less attention to promotion, atmosphere, and location because they are dealing with business customers rather than final consumers. Second, wholesale transactions are usually larger than retail transactions, and wholesalers usually cover a larger trade area than retailers. Third, the government deals with wholesalers and retailers differently in regard to legal regulations and taxes.

Why are wholesalers used at all? Manufacturers could bypass them and sell directly to retailers or final consumers. The answer lies in several efficiencies that wholesalers bring about. First, small manufacturers with limited financial resources cannot afford to develop direct-selling organizations. Second, even manufacturers with sufficient capital may prefer to use their funds to expand production rather than carry out wholesaling activities. Third, wholesalers are likely to be more efficient at wholesaling because of their scale of operation, their wider number of customer contacts, and their specialized skills. Fourth, retailers who carry many lines often prefer to buy assortments from a wholesaler rather than buy directly from each manufacturer.

Thus retailers and manufacturers have reasons to use wholesalers. Wholesalers are used when they are more efficient in performing one or more of the following functions:

- **Selling and promoting.** Wholesalers provide a sales force enabling manufacturers to reach many small customers at a relatively low cost. The wholesaler has more contacts and is often more trusted by the buyer than is the distant manufacturer.
- **Buying and assortment building.** Wholesalers are able to select items and build assortments needed by their customers, thus saving the customers considerable work.
- **Bulk-breaking.** Wholesalers achieve savings for their customers through buying in carload lots and breaking the bulk into smaller units.
- **Warehousing.** Wholesalers hold inventories, thereby reducing the inventory costs and risks to suppliers and customers.
- **Transportation.** Wholesalers provide quicker delivery to buyers because they are closer than the manufacturer.
- **Financing.** Wholesalers finance their customers by granting credit, and they finance their suppliers by ordering early and paying their bills on time.
- **Risk bearing.** Wholesalers absorb some risk by taking title and bearing the cost of theft, damage, spoilage, and obsolescence.
- **Market information.** Wholesalers supply information to their suppliers and customers regarding competitors' activities, new products, price development, and so on.
- **Management services and counseling.** Wholesalers often help retailers improve their operations by training their salesclerks, helping with stores' layouts and displays, and setting up accounting and inventory-control systems. They may help their industrial customers by offering training and technical services.

A number of factors have contributed to wholesaling's growth over the years: the growth of larger factories located away from the principal users of the output; the growth of production in advance of orders rather than in response to specific orders; an increase in the number of levels of intermediate producers and users; and the increasing need for adapting products to the needs of intermediate and final users in terms of quantities, packages, and forms.

Types of Wholesalers	In 1982, there were 416,000 wholesaling establishments in the United States doing a total annual volume of $1,998 billion. The wholesalers fall into four groups, namely, *merchant wholesalers*, *brokers and agents*, *manufacturers' and retailers' branches and offices*, and *miscellaneous wholesalers* (see Exhibit 19-2).

Types of Wholesalers

In 1982, there were 416,000 wholesaling establishments in the United States doing a total annual volume of $1,998 billion. The wholesalers fall into four groups, namely, *merchant wholesalers*, *brokers and agents*, *manufacturers' and retailers' branches and offices*, and *miscellaneous wholesalers* (see Exhibit 19-2).

Wholesaler Marketing Decisions

Wholesalers, like retailers, must make decisions on their target market, product assortment and services, pricing, promotion, and place.

Target-Market Decision Wholesalers need to define their target markets and should not try to serve everyone. They can choose a target group of customers according to size criteria (e.g., only large retailers), type of customer (e.g., convenience food stores only), need for service (e.g., customers who need credit), or other criteria. Within the target group, they can identify the more-profitable customers and design stronger offers and build better relationships with them. They can propose automatic reordering systems, set up management training and advisory systems, and even sponsor a voluntary chain. They can discourage less-profitable customers by requiring larger orders or adding surcharges to smaller ones.

Product-Assortment-and-Services Decision The wholesalers' "product" is their assortment. Wholesalers are under great pressure to carry a full line and maintain sufficient stock for immediate delivery. But this can kill profits. Wholesalers today are reexamining how many lines to carry and are choosing to carry only the more-profitable ones. They are grouping their items on an ABC basis, with *A* standing for the most-profitable items and *C* for the least profitable. Inventory-carrying levels are varied for the three groups.

Wholesalers are also examining which services count most in building strong customer relationships and which ones should be dropped or charged for. The key is to find a distinct mix of services valued by their customers.

Pricing Decision Wholesalers usually mark up the cost of goods by a conventional percentage, say 20 percent to cover their expenses. Expenses may run 17 percent of the gross margin, leaving a profit margin of approximately 3 percent. In grocery wholesaling, the average profit margin is often less than 2 percent. Wholesalers are beginning to experiment with new approaches to pricing. They may cut their margin on some lines in order to win

---

EXHIBIT 19-2

Major Types of Wholesalers

The major types of wholesalers are *merchant wholesalers*, *brokers and agents*, *manufacturers' and retailers' branches and offices*, and *miscellaneous wholesalers*. They are described below.

Merchant Wholesalers Merchant wholesalers are independently owned businesses that take title to the merchandise they handle. In different trades they are called jobbers, distributors, or mill supply houses. They are the largest single group of wholesalers, accounting for over 60 percent of all wholesaling (in sales volume and in number of establishments). Merchant wholesalers can be subclassified into full-service wholesalers and limited-service wholesalers.

Full-Service Wholesalers Full-service wholesalers provide such services as carrying stock, maintaining a sales force, offering credit, making deliveries, and providing management assistance. They include two types: wholesale merchants and industrial distributors.

■ *Wholesale merchants.* Wholesale merchants sell primarily to retailers and provide a full range of services. They vary mainly in the width of their product line. *General-merchandise wholesalers* carry several merchandise lines to meet the needs of both general-merchandise retailers and single-line retailers. *General-line wholesalers* carry one or two lines of merchandise in a greater depth of assortment. Major examples are hardware wholesalers, drug wholesalers, and clothing wholesalers. *Specialty wholesalers* specialize in carrying only part of a line in great depth. Examples are health-food wholesalers, seafood wholesalers, and automotive-item wholesalers. They offer customers the advantage of deeper choice and greater product knowledge.

■ *Industrial distributors.* Industrial distributors are merchant wholesalers who sell to manufacturers rather than to retailers. They provide several services, such as carrying stock, offering credit, and providing delivery. They may carry a broad range of merchandise (often called a mill supply house), a general line, or a specialty line. Industrial distributors may concentrate on such lines as MRO items (maintenance, repair, and operating supplies), OEM items (original-equipment supplies such as ball bearings, motors), or equipment (such as hand and power tools, fork trucks). There are about twelve thousand industrial distributors in the United States, and their sales were more than $25 billion in 1974.

Limited-Service Wholesalers Limited-service wholesalers offer fewer services to their suppliers and customers. There are several types of limited-service wholesalers.

■ *Cash-and-carry wholesalers.* Cash-and-carry wholesalers have a limited line of fast-moving goods and sell to small retailers for cash and normally do not deliver. A small fish-store retailer, for example, normally drives at dawn to a cash-and-carry fish wholesaler and buys several crates of fish, pays on the spot, and drives the merchandise back to the store and unloads it.

■ *Truck wholesalers.* Truck wholesalers (also called truck jobbers) perform a selling and delivery function primarily. They carry a limited line of semiperishable merchandise (such as milk, bread, snack foods), which they sell for cash as they make their rounds of supermarkets, small groceries, hospitals, restaurants, factory cafeterias, and hotels.

■ *Drop shippers.* Drop shippers operate in bulk industries, such as coal, lumber, and heavy equipment. They do not carry inventory or handle the product. Once an order is received, they find a manufacturer, who ships the merchandise directly to the customer on the agreed terms and time of delivery. The drop shipper assumes title and risk from the time the order is accepted to its delivery to the customer. Because drop shippers do not carry inventory, their costs are lower, and they can pass on some savings to customers.

■ *Rack jobbers.* Rack jobbers serve grocery and drug retailers, mostly in the area of nonfood items. These retailers do not want to order and maintain displays of hundreds of nonfood items. The rack jobbers send delivery trucks to stores, and the delivery person sets up toys, paperbacks, hardware items, health and beauty aids, and so on. They price the goods, keep them fresh, set up point-of-purchase displays, and keep inventory records. Rack jobbers sell on consignment, which means that they retain title to the goods and bill the retailers only for the goods sold to consumers. Thus they provide such services as delivery, shelving, inventory carrying, and financing. They do little promotion because they carry many branded items that are highly advertised.

■ *Producers' cooperatives.* Producers' cooperatives are owned by farmer members and assemble farm produce to sell in local markets. Their profits are distributed to members at the end of the year. They often attempt to improve product quality and promote a co-op brand name, such as Sun Maid raisins, Sunkist oranges, or Diamond walnuts.

■ *Mail-order wholesalers.* Mail-order wholesalers send catalogs to retail, industrial, and institutional customers featuring jewelry, cosmetics, specialty foods, and other small items. Their main customers are businesses in small outlying areas. No sales force is maintained to call on customers. The orders are filled and sent by mail, truck, or other efficient means of transportation.

Brokers and Agents Brokers and agents differ from merchant wholesalers in two ways: They do not take title to goods, and they perform only a few functions. Their main function is to facilitate buying and selling, and for this they will earn a commission of anywhere from 2 to 6 percent of the selling price. Like merchant wholesalers, they generally specialize by product line or customer types. They account for 11.5 percent of the total wholesale volume.

Brokers The chief function of a broker is to bring buyers and sellers together and assist in negotiation. They are paid by the party who hired them. They do not carry inventory, get involved in financing, or assume risk. The most familiar examples are food brokers, real estate brokers, insurance brokers, and security brokers.

Agents Agents represent either buyers or sellers on a more permanent basis. There are several types.

■ *Manufacturers' agents.* Manufacturers' agents (also called manufacturers' representatives) are more numerous than other types of agent wholesalers. They represent two or more manufacturers of complementary lines. They enter into a formal written agreement with each manufacturer covering pricing policy, territories, order-handling procedure, delivery service and warranties, and commission rates. They know each manufacturer's product line and use their wide contacts to sell the manufacturer's products. Manufacturers' agents are used in such lines as apparel, furniture, and electrical goods. Most manufacturers' agents are small businesses, with only a few employees, who are skilled sales people. They are hired by small manufacturers who cannot afford to maintain their own field sales forces and by large manufacturers who want to use agents to open new territories or to represent them in territories that cannot support full-time sales people.

■ *Selling agents.* Selling agents are given contractual authority to sell a manufacturer's entire output. The manufacturer either is not interested in the selling function or feels unqualified. The selling agent serves as a sales department and has significant influence over prices, terms, and conditions of sale. The selling agent normally has no territorial limits. Selling agents are found in such product areas as textiles, industrial machinery and equipment, coal and coke, chemicals, and metals.

■ *Purchasing agents.* Purchasing agents generally have a long-term relationship with buyers and make purchases for them, often receiving, inspecting, warehousing, and shipping the merchandise to the buyers. One type consists of *resident buyers* in major apparel markets, who look for suitable lines of apparel that can be carried by small retailers located in small cities. They are knowledgeable and provide helpful market information to clients as well as obtaining the best goods and prices available.

■ *Commission merchants.* Commission merchants (or houses) are agents who take physical possession of products and negotiate sales. Normally they are not employed on a long-term basis. They are used most often in agricultural marketing by farmers who do not want to sell their own output and do not belong to producers' cooperatives. A commission merchant would take a truckload of commodities to a central market, sell it for the best price, deduct a commission and expenses, and remit the balance to the producer.

Manufacturers' and Retailers' Branches and Offices The third major type of wholesaling consists of wholesaling operations conducted by sellers or buyers themselves rather than through independent wholesalers. There are two types.

Sales Branches and Offices Manufacturers often set up their own sales branches and offices to improve inventory control, selling, and promotion. *Sales branches* carry inventory and are found in such industries as lumber and automotive equipment and parts. Sales offices do not carry inventory and are most prominent in dry goods and notion industries. Sales branches and offices account for about 9 percent of all wholesale establishments and 34 percent of all wholesale volume.

Purchasing Offices Many retailers set up purchasing offices in major market centers such as New York and Chicago. These purchasing offices perform a role similar to that of brokers or agents but are part of the buyer's organization.

Miscellaneous Wholesalers A few specialized types of wholesalers are found in certain sectors of the economy, such as agricultural assemblers, petroleum bulk plants and terminals, and auction companies.

important new customers. They will ask suppliers for a special price break when they can turn it into an opportunity to increase the supplier's sales.

Promotion Decision Most wholesalers are not promotion minded. Their use of trade advertising, sales promotion, publicity, and personal selling is largely haphazard. Personal selling is particularly behind the times in that wholesalers still see selling as a single salesperson talking to a single customer instead of a team effort to sell, build, and service major accounts. As for nonpersonal promotion, wholesalers would benefit from adopting some of the image-making techniques used by retailers. They need to develop an overall promotion strategy. They also need to make greater use of supplier promotion materials and programs.

Place Decision   Wholesalers typically locate in low-rent, low-tax areas and put little money into their physical setting and offices. Often the materials-handling systems and order-processing systems lag behind the available technologies. To meet rising costs, progressive wholesalers have been making time and motion studies of materials-handling procedures. The ultimate development is the automated warehouse. The orders are fed into a computer, and the items are picked up by mechanical devices and conveyed on a belt to the shipping platform, where they are assembled. This type of mechanization is progressing rapidly, and so is the mechanization of many office activities. Most wholesalers now use computers to carry out accounting, billing, inventory control, and forecasting.

> Grainger, a major distributor, developed a local inventory inquiry system to connect its 188 distribution branches. A Grainger branch can quickly locate whether items not in stock are available in another branch. This has greatly reduced customer response time and has boosted customer sales.

Trends in Wholesaling

Manufacturers always have the option of bypassing wholesalers or of replacing an inefficient wholesaler with a more dynamic one. Manufacturers' major complaints against wholesalers are as follows: They do not aggressively promote the manufacturer's product line, acting more like order takers; they do not carry enough inventory and therefore fail to fill customers' orders fast enough; they do not supply the manufacturer with up-to-date market and competitive information; they do not attract high-caliber managers and bring down their own costs; and they charge too much for their services.

Progressive wholesalers, on the other hand, are those who change their ways to meet the challenges of retail chain organizations, discount houses, and rising labor costs. They adapt their services to meet the needs of their suppliers and target customers. They recognize that in the long run the only rationale for their existence comes from increasing the efficiency and effectiveness of the entire marketing channel. To achieve this aim, they must constantly improve their services and/or reduce their costs.

> The large drug wholesaler, Foremost-McKesson, illustrates progressive wholesaling. Its survival depended upon becoming more cost effective than manufacturers' sales branches. The company proceeded to automate 72 of its warehouses, establish direct computer links with 32 drug manufacturers, establish a computerized accounts-receivable program for pharmacists, and provide drug stores with computer terminals for ordering inventories.[17]

Narus and Anderson interviewed leading industrial distributors and identified four ways in which they strengthen their relationships with manufacturers:[18]

1. They sought a clear agreement with their manufacturers about their expected functions in the marketing channel.
2. They gained insight into the manufacturers' requirements by visiting their plants and attending manufacturer association conventions and trade shows.

3. They fulfilled their commitments to the manufacturer by meeting the volume targets, promptly paying their bills, and feeding back customer information to their manufacturers.

4. They identified and offered value-added services to help their suppliers. (See Exhibit 19-3 for an excellent example.)

EXHIBIT 19-3 — Embracing the Marketing Concept in Industrial Distribution

Great Lakes Terminal & Transport, Inc. (GLT&T), a distributor of industrial chemicals and reinforced plastics, is based in Chicago and does business in thirty-five states. Louis Dehmlow, the firm's president, understands how to put the marketing concept into practice in industrial distribution. He recognizes and creatively finds ways to add value and/or reduce real costs for his suppliers and customers, the basic reason for an industrial distributor's existence.

An illustration is provided by his firm's response to the difficulties of a major chemical supplier in developing the market for a new product line of synthetic rubber. The supplier wanted to maintain a small sales force calling on only large-volume customers. Dehmlow felt that his distribution firm could cost-effectively prospect for smaller potential customers. He also realized that it would take considerable time, effort, and technical expertise to develop applications for the product. Fortunately, though, his firm had the needed technical expertise and could devote additional resources to acquire marketplace expertise.

Avoiding the usual term "functional *discount*," which had a negative connotation of getting something for seemingly doing nothing, Dehmlow negotiated an incremental "functional *allowance*" for market development of 3 percent (off the suggested resale price) and exclusive distribution rights for the areas in which GLT&T operated. For this functional allowance for market development, GLT&T offered to do the following: (1) assign two market specialists to the product line; (2) provide research lab support that developed custom compounds for specific customer applications; (3) train the twenty-person sales force to prospect for customer and product applications; (4) gather systematic information about applications; and (5) provide feedback on potential product-line modifications and extensions. This arrangement led to sales of over $7 million for this product line with prospects for continued growth.

Dehmlow has extended the value-added services concept in other ways. GLT&T does market research and development projects for several suppliers on a negotiated fee basis. GLT&T provides supplementary trucking services to both supplier and customer firms, thereby increasing the load factor of GLT&T trucks substantially above the industry norm. In summary, by embracing marketing and the concept of value-added services, Dehmlow's firm has achieved sales and profit growth competing in what many firms think of as a "commodity" industry.

SOURCE: Described to the author by James C. Anderson, Northwestern University, and James A. Narus, Case Western Reserve University, 1986.

An Arthur Andersen & Company study predicted several developments in the wholesaling industry.[19] Wholesaling companies will grow, primarily through acquisition, merger, and geographic expansion. Geographic expansion will require distributors to learn how to compete effectively over wider and more diverse areas. Wholesalers will be helped in this by the increased use of computerized systems; by 1990, over three-fourths of the wholesalers will use on-line order systems. Wholesalers will increasingly ship their merchandise using outside common and private carriers as they expand their geographic coverage. Foreign companies will increase their role in distribution to about 15 percent of total wholesale sales by 1990. Finally, the major source for executive and management training for wholesalers will be their own trade associations.

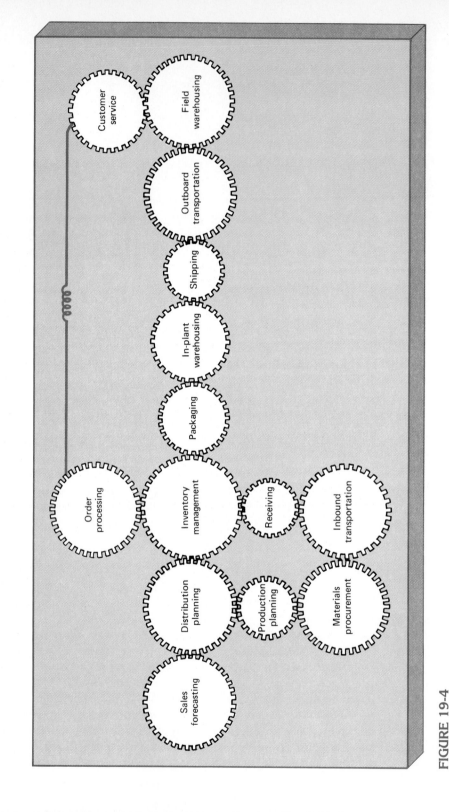

FIGURE 19-4
Major Activities Involved in Physical Distribution
SOURCE: Redrawn, with modifications, from Wendell M. Stewart, "Physical Distribution: Key to Improved Volume and Profits," *Journal of Marketing*, January 1965, p. 66.

PHYSICAL DISTRIBUTION

We are now ready to examine the organizations involved in physical distribution. Producers use these organizations to help them stock and move goods so that they will be available to customers at the right time and place. Customer attraction and satisfaction is highly influenced by the seller's physical-distribution capabilities and decisions. We will consider the nature, objectives, systems, and organizational aspects of physical distribution.

Nature of Physical Distribution

Physical distribution **involves planning, implementing, and controlling the physical flows of materials and final goods from points of origin to points of use to meet customer needs at a profit.**

A large number of tasks are involved in physical distribution, and they are shown in Figure 19-4. The first task is sales forecasting, on the basis of which the company schedules production and inventory levels. The production plans indicate the materials that the purchasing department must order. These materials arrive through inbound transportation, enter the receiving area, and are stored in raw-material inventory. Raw materials are converted into finished goods. Finished-goods inventory is the link between the customers' orders and the company's manufacturing activity. Customers' orders draw down the finished-goods inventory level, and manufacturing activity builds it up. Finished goods flow off the assembly line and pass through packing, in-plant warehousing, shipping-room processing, outbound transportation, field warehousing, and customer delivery and servicing.

Management has become concerned about the total cost of physical distribution, which exceeded $650 billion in this decade, or about 20 percent of the cost of goods reaching the final consumer. Considering that advertising only costs around 3 percent of sales, marketing executives would undoubtedly be well rewarded if they could help find ways to reduce physical-distribution costs. Lowered physical-distribution costs will permit lower prices or yield higher profit margins.

The main elements of total physical-distribution costs are transportation (46 percent), warehousing (26 percent), inventory carrying (10 percent), receiving and shipping (6 percent), packaging (5 percent), administration (4 percent), and order processing (3 percent). Experts believe that substantial savings can be effected in the physical-distribution area, which has been described as "the last frontier for cost economies" and "the economy's dark continent." Physical-distribution decisions, when uncoordinated, result in high costs. Not enough use is being made of modern decision tools for coordinating inventory levels, transportation modes, and plant, warehouse, and store locations.

Physical distribution is not only a cost, it is a potent tool in competitive marketing. Companies can attract additional customers by offering better service or lower prices through physical-distribution improvements. Companies lose customers when they fail to supply goods on time. In the summer of 1976, Kodak launched its national advertising campaign for its new instant camera before it had delivered enough cameras to the stores. Customers found that it was not available and bought a Polaroid instead.

Traditional physical-distribution thinking starts with goods at the plant and tries to find low-cost solutions to get them to customers. Marketers prefer *market logistics* thinking that starts with the marketplace and works backward to the factory. Here is an example of market logistics thinking:

German consumers typically purchase separate bottles of soft drinks. A soft-drink manufacturer decided to design and test a six-pack. Consumers responded positively to the convenience aspect of carrying a six-pack home. Retailers responded positively because the bottles could be loaded faster on the shelves, and more bottles would be purchased per occasion. The manufacturer designed the six-packs to fit comfortably on the store shelves. Then cases and pallets were designed for bringing these six-packs efficiently to the store's receiving rooms. Factory operations were redesigned to produce the new six-packs. The purchasing department let out bids for the new needed materials. Once implemented, this new packaging of soft drinks was an instant hit with consumers, and the manufacturer's market share rose substantially.

The Physical-
Distribution
Objective

Many companies state their physical-distribution objective as *getting the right goods to the right places at the right time for the least cost*. Unfortunately, this provides little actual guidance. No physical-distribution system can simultaneously maximize customer service and minimize distribution cost. Maximum customer service implies large inventories, premium transportation, and multiple warehouses, all of which raise distribution cost. Minimum distribution cost implies cheap transportation, low stocks, and few warehouses.

A company cannot achieve physical-distribution efficiency by asking each physical-distribution manager to minimize his or her own costs. Physical-distribution costs interact, often in an inverse way:

- The traffic manager favors rail shipment over air shipment whenever possible. It reduces the company's freight bill. However, because the railroads are slower, rail shipment ties up working capital longer, delays customer payment, and may cause customers to buy from competitors offering faster service.
- The shipping department uses cheap containers to minimize shipping costs. This leads to a high rate of damaged goods in transit and customer ill will.
- The inventory manager favors low inventories to reduce inventory cost. However, this policy increases stockouts, back orders, paperwork, special production runs, and high-cost fast-freight shipments.

Given that physical-distribution activities involve strong trade-offs, decisions must be made on a total system basis.

The starting point for designing the physical-distribution system is to study what the customers want and what competitors are offering. Customers are interested in several things: on-time delivery; supplier willingness to meet customer emergency needs; careful handling of merchandise; supplier willingness to take back defective goods and resupply them quickly; and supplier willingness to carry inventory for the customer.

The company has to research the relative importance of these services to customers. For example, service-repair time is very important to buyers of copying equipment. Xerox therefore developed a service-delivery standard that "can put a disabled machine anywhere in the continental United States back into operation within three hours after receiving the service request." Xerox runs a service division consisting of twelve thousand service and parts personnel.

The company must look at competitors' service standards in setting its own. It will normally want to offer at least the same level of service as competitors. But the objective is to maximize profits, not sales. The company has to look at the costs of providing higher levels of service. Some companies offer less service but charge a lower price. Other companies offer more service than competitors and charge a premium price to cover their higher costs.

The company ultimately has to establish physical-distribution objectives to guide its planning. For example, Coca-Cola wants to "put Coke within an arm's length of desire." Companies go further and define standards for each service factor. One appliance manufacturer has established the following service standards: to deliver at least 95 percent of the dealer's orders within seven days of order receipt; to fill the dealer's orders with 99 percent accuracy; to answer dealer inquiries on order status within three hours; and to ensure that damage to merchandise in transit does not exceed 1 percent.

Given a set of physical-distribution objectives, the company is ready to design a physical-distribution system that will minimize the cost of achieving these objectives. Each possible physical-distribution system implies a total distribution cost given by the expression

$$D = T + FW + VW + S \qquad (19\text{-}1)$$

where:

D = total distribution cost of proposed system

T = total freight cost of proposed system

FW = total fixed warehouse cost of proposed system

VW = total variable warehouse costs (including inventory) of proposed system

S = total cost of lost sales due to average delivery delay under proposed system

Choosing a physical-distribution system calls for examining the total distribution cost associated with different proposed systems and selecting the system that minimizes total distribution cost. Alternatively, if it is hard to measure S in (19-1), the company should aim to minimize the distribution cost $T + FW + VW$ of reaching a *target level of customer service*.

We will now examine the following major decision issues: (1) How should orders be handled? (*order processing*) (2) Where should stocks be located? (*warehousing*) (3) How much stock should be held? (*inventory*), and (4) How should goods be shipped? (*transportation*).

Order Processing   Physical distribution begins with a customer order. The order department prepares multicopy invoices and dispatches them to various departments. Items out of stock are back ordered. Shipped items are accompanied by shipping and billing documents with copies going to various departments.

The company and customers benefit when these steps are performed quickly and accurately. Ideally, sales representatives send in their orders every evening, increasingly through computer hookups. The order department processes these quickly. The warehouse sends the goods out as soon as possible. Bills go out as soon as possible. The computer is used to expedite the order-shipping-billing cycle.

Industrial engineering studies of how sales orders are processed can help shorten this cycle. Some of the key questions are: What happens when the company receives a customer purchase order? How long does the customer credit check take? What procedures are used to check inventory and how long does this take? How soon does manufacturing hear of new stock requirements? How long does it take for sales managers to get a complete picture of current sales?

Companies are making great progress in speeding up order handling, thanks to computers. General Electric operates a computer-oriented system that, upon receipt of a customer's order, checks the customer's credit standing and whether and where the items are in stock. The computer issues an order to ship, bills the customer, updates the inventory records, sends a production order for new stock, and relays the message back to the sales representative that the customer's order is on its way, all in less than fifteen seconds.

Warehousing Every company has to store its goods while they wait to be sold. A storage function is necessary because production and consumption cycles rarely match. Many agricultural commodities are produced seasonally, whereas demand is continuous. The storage function overcomes discrepancies in desired quantities and timing.

The company must decide on a desirable number of stocking locations. More stocking locations mean that goods can be delivered to customers more quickly. Warehousing costs go up, however. The number of stocking locations must strike a balance between customer service levels and distribution costs.

Some company stock is kept at or near the plant, and the rest is located in warehouses around the country. The company might own *private warehouses* and rent space in *public warehouses*. Companies have more control in owned warehouses, but they tie up their capital and face some inflexibility if desired locations change. Public warehouses, on the other hand, charge for the rented space and provide additional services (at a cost) for inspecting goods, packaging them, shipping them, and invoicing them. In using public warehouses, companies have a wide choice of locations and warehouse types, including those specializing in cold storage, commodities only, and so on.

Companies use storage warehouses and distribution warehouses. *Storage warehouses* store goods for moderate to long periods of time. *Distribution warehouses* receive goods from various plants and suppliers and move them out as soon as possible. For example, Wal-Mart Stores, Inc., a highly successful regional discount-store chain, operates four distribution centers. One center covers 400,000 square feet on a ninety-three-acre site. The shipping department loads fifty to sixty trucks daily, delivering merchandise on a twice-weekly basis to its retail outlets. This is less expensive than supplying each retail outlet from each plant directly.

The older multistoried warehouses with slow elevators and inefficient materials-handling procedures are receiving competition from newer single-storied *automated warehouses* with advanced materials-handling systems under the control of a central computer. The computer reads store orders and directs lift trucks and electric hoists to gather goods, move them to loading docks, and issue invoices. These warehouses have reduced worker injuries, labor costs, pilferage, and breakage and have improved inventory control.

Inventory Inventory levels represent another physical-distribution decision affecting customer satisfaction. Marketers would like their companies to carry enough stock to fill all customer orders immediately. However, it is not cost effective for a company to carry this much inventory. *Inventory cost increases at an increasing rate as the customer-service level approaches 100 percent.* Management would need to know by how much sales and profits would increase as a result of carrying larger inventories and promising faster order fulfillment times.

Inventory decision making involves knowing when to order and how much to order. As inventory draws down, management must know at what stock level to place a new order. This stock level is called the *order (or reorder) point.* An order point of twenty means reordering when the stock of the item falls to twenty units. The order point should be higher and higher the order lead time, the usage rate, and the service standard. If the order lead time and customer usage rate are variable, the order point should be set higher to provide a *safety stock.* The final order point should balance the risks of stockout against the costs of overstock.

The other decision is how much to order. The larger the quantity ordered, the less frequently an order has to be placed. The company needs to balance order-processing costs and inventory-carrying costs. Order-processing costs for a manufacturer consist of *setup costs* and *running costs* for the item. If setup costs are low, the manufacturer can produce the item often, and the cost per item is quite constant and equal to the running costs. If setup costs are high, however, the manufacturer can reduce the average cost per unit by producing a long run and carrying more inventory.

Order-processing costs must be compared with inventory-carrying costs. The larger the average stock carried, the higher the inventory-carrying costs. These carrying costs include storage charges, cost of capital, taxes and insurance, and depreciation and obsolescence. Inventory-carrying costs may run as high as 30 percent of inventory value. This means that marketing managers who want their companies to carry larger inventories need to show that the larger inventories would produce incremental gross profit that would exceed incremental inventory-carrying costs.

The optimal order quantity can be determined by observing how order-processing costs and inventory-carrying costs sum up at different possible order levels. Figure 19-5 shows that the order-processing cost per unit decreases with the number of units ordered, because the order costs are spread over more units. Inventory-carrying charges per unit increase with the number of units ordered, because each unit remains longer in inventory. The two cost curves are summed vertically into a total-cost curve. The lowest point on the total-cost curve is projected down on the horizontal axis to find the optimal order quantity Q^*.[20]

The growing interest in *just-in-time production methods* promises to change inventory-planning practices. Just-in-time production consists of arranging for supplies to come into the factory at the rate that they are needed. If the suppliers are dependable, then the manufacturer can carry much lower levels of inventory and still meet customer order fulfill-ment standards.

Transportation   Marketers need to take an interest in their company's transportation decisions. The choice of transportation carriers will affect the pricing of the products, on-time delivery performance, and the condition of the goods when they arrive, all of which will affect customer satisfaction.

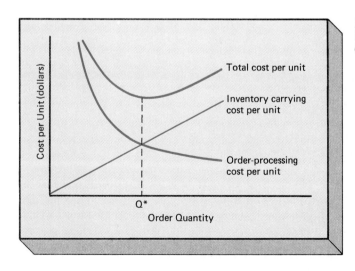

FIGURE 19-5
Determining Optimal Order Quantity

In shipping goods to its warehouses, dealers, and customers, the company can choose among the five transportation modes shown in Exhibit 19-4. In choosing a transportation mode for a particular product, shippers consider such criteria as *speed*, *frequency*, *dependability*, *capability*, *availability*, and *cost*. If a shipper seeks speed, air and truck are the prime contenders. If the goal is low cost, then water and pipeline are the prime contenders. Trucks stand high on most of the criteria, and this accounts for their growing share.

EXHIBIT 19-4

Five Major Transportation Modes

Rail   In spite of a shrinking share of total transportation, railroads remain the nation's largest transportation carrier, accounting for 30 percent of the nation's total cargo ton-miles. Railroads are one of the most cost-effective modes for shipping carload quantities of bulk products—coal, sand, minerals, farm and forest products—over long land distances. The rate costs for shipping merchandise are quite complex. The lowest rate comes from shipping carload rather than less-than-carload quantities. Manufacturers will attempt to combine shipments to common destinations to take advantage of lower carload rates. Railroads have recently begun to increase customer-oriented services. They have designed new equipment to handle special categories of merchandise more efficiently, provided flatcars for carrying truck trailers by rail (piggyback), and provided in-transit services such as diversion of shipped goods to other destinations en route and processing of goods en route.

Water   A substantial amount of goods move by ships and barges on coastal and inland waterways. Water transportation is very low in cost for shipping bulky, low-value, nonperishable products such as sand, coal, grain, oil, and metallic ores. On the other hand, water transportation is the slowest transportation mode and is dependent on climatic conditions.

Truck   Motor trucks have steadily increased their share of transportation and now account for 20 percent of total cargo ton-miles. They account for the largest portion of intracity as opposed to intercity transportation. Trucks are highly flexible in their routing and time schedules. They can move merchandise door to door, saving shippers the need to transfer goods from truck to rail and back again at a loss of time and risk of theft or damage. Trucks are an efficient mode of transportation for short hauls of high-value merchandise. Their rates are competitive with railway rates in many cases, and trucks can usually offer faster service.

Pipeline   Pipelines are a specialized means of shipping petroleum, coal, and chemicals from sources to markets. Pipeline shipment of petroleum products is less expensive than rail shipment, although more expensive than waterway shipment. Most pipelines are used by their owners to ship their own products, although they are technically available for use by any shipper.

Air   Air carriers transport less than 1 percent of the nation's goods but are becoming more important as a transportation mode. Although air freight rates are considerably higher than rail or truck freight rates, air freight is ideal where speed is essential and/or distant markets have to be reached. Among the most frequently air-freighted products are perishables (e.g., fresh fish, cut flowers) and high-value, low-bulk items (e.g., technical instruments, jewelry). Companies find that air freight reduces their required inventory levels, number of warehouses, and costs of packaging.

Shippers are increasingly combining two or more transportation modes, thanks to containerization. *Containerization* consists of putting the goods in boxes or trailers that are easy to transfer between two transportation modes. *Piggyback* describes the use of rail and trucks; *fishyback*, water and trucks; *trainship*, water and rail; and *airtruck*, air and trucks. Each coordinated mode of transportation offers specific advantages to the shipper.

For example, piggyback is cheaper than trucking alone and yet provides flexibility and convenience.

In choosing transportation modes, shippers can decide between private, contract, and common carriers. If the shipper owns its own truck or air fleet, the shipper becomes a *private carrier*. A *contract carrier* is an independent organization selling transportation services to others on a contract basis. A *common carrier* provides services between predetermined points on a schedule basis and is available to all shippers at standard rates.

Transportation decisions must consider the complex trade-offs between various transportation modes and their implications for other distribution elements such as warehousing and inventory. As the relative costs of different transportation modes change over time, companies need to reanalyze their options in the search for optimal physical-distribution arrangements.[21]

Organizational Responsibility for Physical Distribution

We see that decisions on warehousing, inventory, and transportation require the highest degree of coordination. A growing number of companies have set up a permanent committee composed of managers responsible for different physical-distribution activities. This committee meets periodically to develop policies for improving overall distribution efficiency. Some companies have appointed a vice-president of physical distribution, who reports to the marketing vice-president or manufacturing vice-president in most cases, or to the president. Here are two examples:

> The Burroughs Corporation organized the Distribution Services Department to centralize control over its physical-distribution activities. This department reported to the marketing vice-president because of the great importance Burroughs attached to good customer service. Within two and one-half years following the reorganization, the company achieved savings of over $2 million annually (on $200 million of sales), plus a higher level of service to field branches and customers.
>
> Heinz created a new department of coordinate stature with marketing and production, which was headed by a vice-president of distribution. Heinz felt that this arrangement would guarantee respect for the department, develop a greater degree of professionalism and objectivity, and avoid partisan domination by marketing or production.

The location of the physical-distribution department within the company is a secondary concern. The important thing is that the company coordinate its physical-distribution and marketing activities in order to create high market satisfaction at a reasonable cost.

SUMMARY

Retailing and wholesaling consist of many organizations designed to bring goods and services from the point of production to the point of use.

Retailing includes all the activities involved in selling goods or services directly to final consumers for their personal, nonbusiness use. Retailing is one of the major industries in the United States. Retailers can be classified in terms of store retailers, nonstore retailers, and retail organizations.

Store retailers include many types, such as specialty stores, department stores, supermarkets, convenience stores, superstores/combination stores/hypermarches, discount stores, warehouse stores, and catalog showrooms. These store forms have had different longevities and are at different stages of the retail life cycle. Depending on the wheel of retailing, some will go out of existence because they cannot compete on a quality, service, or price basis.

Nonstore retailing is growing more rapidly than store retailing. It includes direct marketing (mail-order catalog, direct mail, telemarketing, television marketing, electronic shopping), direct selling (door-to-door, party selling), automatic vending, and buying services.

Much of retailing is in the hands of retail organizations such as corporate chains, voluntary chain and retailer cooperatives, consumer cooperatives, franchise organizations, and merchandising conglomerates. More retail chains are willing to sponsor diversified retailing lines and forms instead of sticking to one form such as the department store.

Retailers, like manufacturers, must prepare marketing plans that include decisions on target markets, product assortment and services, pricing, promotion, and place. Retailers are showing strong signs of improving their professional management and their productivity, in the face of such trends as shortening retail life cycles, new retail forms, increasing intertype competition, new retail technologies, and so on.

Wholesaling includes all the activities involved in selling goods or services to those who are buying for the purpose of resale or for business use. Wholesalers help manufacturers deliver their products efficiently to the many retailers and industrial users across the nation. Wholesalers perform many functions, including selling and promoting, buying and assortment building, bulk-breaking, warehousing, transporting, financing, risk bearing, supplying market information, and providing management services and counseling. Wholesalers fall into four groups. Merchant wholesalers take possession of the goods and include full-service wholesalers (wholesale merchants, industrial distributors) and limited-service wholesalers (cash-and-carry wholesalers, truck wholesalers, drop shippers, rack jobbers, producers' cooperatives, and mail-order wholesalers). Agents and brokers do not take possession of the goods but are paid a commission for facilitating buying and selling. Manufacturers' and retailers' branches and offices are wholesaling operations conducted by nonwholesalers to bypass the wholesalers. Miscellaneous wholesalers include agricultural assemblers, petroleum bulk plants and terminals, and auction companies.

Wholesalers, too, must make decisions on their target market, product assortment and services, pricing, promotion, and place. Wholesalers who fail to carry adequate assortments and inventory and provide satisfactory service are likely to be bypassed by manufacturers. Progressive wholesalers, on the other hand, are adapting marketing concepts and streamlining their costs of doing business.

The marketing concept calls for paying increased attention to the physical-distribution concept. Physical distribution is an area of potentially high cost savings and improved customer satisfaction. When order processors, warehouse planners, inventory managers, and transportation managers make decisions, they affect each other's costs and demand-creation capacity. The physical-distribution concept calls for treating all these decisions within a unified framework. The task becomes that of designing physical-distribution arrangements that minimize the total cost of providing a desired level of customer service.

■ QUESTIONS

1. Discuss the environmental factors that facilitate the growth of nonstore retailing.
2. State who is being targeted by each of the following retailing strategies:
   a. "Big retailers adopt specialty stores' marketing tactics."
   b. "Retailers that target low-income shoppers are growing rapidly."
   c. "After Disney World and Epcot Center, the biggest tourist attraction in the greater Orlando area is the Belz Factory Outlet Mall."
3. The physical-distribution concept calls for treating a host of decisions within a unified framework that provides a desired level of customer service for a minimal cost. What does consumer service mean in the context

of physical distribution, and what is its relationship to the marketing concept?

4. A burgeoning market for discount direct-mail personal computers evolved in the 1980s despite the fact that manufacturers like IBM, Apple, and Hewlett-Packard refused to sell to such dealers. Given the additional fact that the product's complexity suggested the need for extensive technical and instructional support by the local retailer for the consumer, how do you account for such dramatic growth of the direct-mail discount business for personal computers?

5. In two of its San Diego outlets, Montgomery Ward opened "Law Store" booths that provide a one-shot consultation for a $10 fee. Customers are ushered to a telephone-boothlike enclosure, where operators connect them to a central office of lawyers who respond to queries over the telephone. Discuss the retailer marketing decisions for the "Law Store."

6. Wholesalers typically do not invest much in the promotional part of their marketing mix. Why has this been a weak area for wholesalers?

7. Does it follow that the company offering high customer service bears high physical-distribution costs in relation to sales?

8. What are the two inventory-production policy alternatives facing a seasonal producer?

9. A company's inventory-carrying cost is 30 percent. A marketing manager wants the company to increase its inventory investment from $400,000 to $500,000, believing this would lead to increased sales of $120,000 because of greater customer loyalty and service. The gross profit on sales is 20 percent. Does it pay the company to increase its inventory investment?

10. You are the marketing manager of a medium-sized manufacturing company. The president has just made the following statement: "The distribution activity is not a concern of the marketing department. The function of the marketing department is to sell the product . . . let the rest of the company handle production and distribution." How would you reply to this statement?

![icon] **FOOTNOTES**

1 William R. Davidson, Albert D. Bates, and Stephen J. Bass, "Retail Life Cycle," *Harvard Business Review*, November–December 1976, pp. 89–96.

2 Malcolm P. McNair, "Significant Trends and Developments in the Postwar Period," in *Competitive Distribution in a Free, High-Level Economy and Its Implication for the University*, ed. A. B. Smith (Pittsburgh: University of Pittsburgh Press, 1958), pp. 1–25. Also see the critical discussion by Stanley C. Hollander, "The Wheel of Retailing," *Journal of Marketing*, July 1960, pp. 37–42.

3 For an excellent text on direct-mail techniques, see Bob Stone, *Successful Direct Marketing Methods*, 3rd ed. (Lincolnwood, Ill.: Crain Books, 1984).

4 See Roy Voorhees and John Coppett, "Telemarketing in Distribution Channels," *Industrial Marketing Management*, 12 (1982), 104–12; and Joel Dreyfuss, "Reach Out and Sell Something," *Fortune*, November 26, 1984, pp. 127–28, 130, 132.

5 See "New Hustle for an Old Product," *Newsweek*, August 26, 1985, p. 48.

6 See Ronald R. Gist, *Marketing and Society: Text and Cases*, 2nd ed. (Hinsdale, Ill.: Dryden Press, 1974), p. 334.

7 See Ralph Raffio, "Double-Decker Franchising," *Venture*, November 1986, pp. 50–67.

8 See Rollie Tillman, "Rise of the Conglomerchant," *Harvard Business Review*, November–December 1971, pp. 44–51.

9 See "How They're Knocking the Rust Off Two Old Chains," *Business Week*, September 8, 1986, p. 44.

10 For a fuller discussion, see Lawrence H. Wortzel, "Retailing Strategies for Today's Mature Marketplace," *The Journal of Business Strategy*, Spring 1987, pp. 45–56.

11 See Roger D. Blackwell and W. Wayne Talarzyk, "Life-Style Retailing: Competitive Strategies for the 1980s," *Journal of Retailing*, Winter 1983, pp. 7–26.

12 Wortzel, "Retailing Strategies."

13 For more discussion, see Philip Kotler, "Atmospherics as a Marketing Tool," *Journal of Retailing*, Winter 1973–74, pp. 48–64; and "Beautiful Ways to Shop," *Newsweek*, November 10, 1986.

14 R. L. Davies and D. S. Rogers, eds., *Store Location and Store Assessment Research* (New York: John Wiley, 1984).

15 David L. Huff, "Defining and Estimating a Trading Area," *Journal of Marketing*, July 1964, pp. 34–38; David A. Gautschi, "Specification of Patronage Models for Retail Center Choice," *Journal of Marketing Research*, May 1981, pp. 162–74; and Avijit Ghosh and C. Samuel Craig, "An Approach to Determining Optimal Locations for New Services," *Journal of Marketing Research*, November 1986, pp. 354–62.

16 Also see Eleanor G. May, C. William Ress, and Walter J. Salmon, *Future Trends in Retailing* (Cambridge, Mass.: Marketing Science Institute, February 1985); and Louis W. Stern and Adel I. El-Ansary, *Marketing Channels* (Englewood Cliffs, N.J.: Prentice-Hall, 1982).

17 *Business Week*, December 7, 1981, pp. 115, 116, 118, 122.

18 James A. Narus and James C. Anderson, "Contributing as a Distributor to Partnerships with Manufacturers," *Business Horizons*, September–October 1987. Also see James D. Hlavecek and Tommy J. McCuistion, "Industrial Distributors—When, Who, and How," *Harvard Business Review*, March–April 1983, pp. 96–101.

19 Arthur Andersen & Co., *Future Trends in Wholesale Distribution: A Time of Opportunity* (Washington, D.C.: Distribution Research and Education Foundation, 1982), pp. 7–9.

20 The optimal order quantity is given by the formula $Q^* = \sqrt{2DS/I}$ where D = annual demand, S = cost to place one order, and I = annual carrying cost per unit. Known as the

economic-order quantity formula, it assumes a constant ordering cost, a constant cost of carrying an additional unit in inventory, a known demand, and no quantity discounts. For further reading on this subject, see Stephen F. Love, *Inventory Control*: *Mathematical Models* (New York: McGraw-Hill, 1979).

21 See the report prepared by A. T. Kearney, management consultants, entitled *Logistics Productivity*: *The Successful Companies* (National Council of Physical Distribution Management, 1984). Also see Ronald H. Ballou, *Basic Business Logistics*, 2nd ed. (Englewood Cliffs, N.J.: Prentice-Hall, 1987).

20 Designing Communication and Promotion Mix Strategies

People no longer buy shoes to keep their feet warm and dry. They buy them because of the way the shoes make them feel—masculine, feminine, rugged, different, sophisticated, young, glamorous, "in." Buying shoes has become an emotional experience. Our business now is selling excitement rather than shoes.
Francis C. Rooney

Modern marketing calls for more than developing a good product, pricing it attractively, and making it accessible to target customers. Companies must also communicate with their present and potential customers. Every company is inevitably cast into the role of communicator and promoter.

What is communicated, however, should not be left to chance. To communicate effectively, companies hire advertising agencies to develop effective ads; sales promotion specialists to design sales incentive programs; and public relations firms to develop the corporate image. They train their sales people to be friendly and knowledgeable. For most companies, the question is not whether to communicate but rather what to say, to whom, and how often.

A modern company manages a complex marketing communications system. The company communicates with its middlemen, consumers, and various publics. Its middlemen communicate with their consumers and various publics. Consumers engage in word-of-mouth communication with other consumers and publics. Meanwhile each group provides communication feedback to every other group.

The marketing communications mix (also called the promotion mix) consists of four major tools:

■ *Advertising.* Any paid form of nonpersonal presentation and promotion of ideas, goods, or services by an identified sponsor.
■ *Sales promotion.* Short-term incentives to encourage purchase or sale of a product or service.

TABLE 20-1   Some Common Communication/Promotion Tools

Advertising	Sales Promotion	Publicity	Personal Selling
Print and broadcast ads	Contests, games, sweepstakes, lotteries	Press kits	Sales presentations
Packaging—outer	Premiums and gifts	Speeches	Sales meetings
Packaging inserts	Sampling	Seminars	Telemarketing
Mailings	Fairs and trade shows	Annual reports	Incentive programs
Catalogs	Exhibits	Charitable donations	Salesmen samples
Motion pictures	Demonstrations	Public relations	Fairs and trade shows
House magazines	Couponing		
Brochures and booklets	Rebates		
Posters and leaflets	Low-interest financing		
Directories	Entertainment		
Reprints of ads	Trade-in allowances		
Billboards	Trading stamps		
Display signs	Tie-ins		
Point-of-purchase displays			
Audiovisual material			
Symbols and logos			

■ *Publicity.* Nonpersonal stimulation of demand for a product, service, or business unit by planting commercially significant news about it in a published medium or obtaining favorable presentation of it upon radio, television, or stage that is not paid for by the sponsor.

■ *Personal selling.* Oral presentation in a conversation with one or more prospective purchasers or the purpose of making sales.[1]

Within these categories are numerous specific tools, such as those listed in Table 20-1. At the same time, communication goes beyond these specific communication/promotion tools. The product's styling, its price, the package's shape and color, the salesperson's manner and dress—all communicate something to the buyers. The whole marketing mix, not just the promotional mix, must be orchestrated for maximum communication impact.

This chapter examines three major questions: How does communication work? What are the major steps in developing effective marketing communication? Who should be responsible for marketing communication planning? Chapter 21 deals with advertising; Chapter 22, with sales promotion and publicity; and Chapter 23, with the sales force.

THE COMMUNICATION PROCESS

Marketers need to understand how communication works. Some years ago, Lasswell said that a communication model will answer (1) who (2) says what (3) in what channel (4) to whom (5) with what effect.[2] Over the years, a communication model with nine elements has evolved, that shown in Figure 20-1. Two elements represent the major parties in a communication—*sender* and *receiver*. Another two represent the major communication tools—*message* and *media*. Four represent major communication functions—*encoding*, *decoding*, *response*, and *feedback*. The last element represents *noise* in the system. These elements are defined as follows:

- **Sender.** The party sending the message to another party (also called the source of communicator).
- **Encoding.** The process of putting thought into symbolic form.
- **Message.** The set of symbols that the sender transmits.
- **Media.** The communication channels through which the message moves from sender to receiver.
- **Decoding.** The process by which the receiver assigns meaning to the symbols transmitted by the sender.
- **Receiver.** The party receiving the message sent by another party (also called the audience or destination).
- **Response.** The set of reactions that the receiver has after being exposed to the message.
- **Feedback.** The part of the receiver's response that the receiver communicates back to the sender.
- **Noise.** Unplanned static or distortion during the communication process, resulting in the receiver's receiving a different message than the sender sent.

The model underscores the key factors in effective communication. Senders must know what audiences they want to reach and what responses they want. They must be skillful in encoding messages that take into account how the target audience usually decodes messages. The source must transmit the message through efficient media that reach the target audience. Senders must develop feedback channels so that they can know the receiver's response to the message.

For a message to be effective, the sender's encoding process must mesh with the receiver's decoding process. Schramm sees messages as essentially signs that must be familiar to the receiver. The more the sender's field of experience overlaps with that of the receiver, the more effective the message is likely to be. (See Figure 20-2.) "The source can encode, and the destination can decode, only in terms of the experience each has had."[3] This puts a burden on communicators from one social stratum (such as advertising people) who want to communicate effectively with another stratum (such as factory workers).

The sender's task is to get his or her message through to the receiver. There is considerable noise in the environment—people are exposed to several hundred commercial messages a day, aside from the other messages they attend to in their environment. Members of the audience may not receive the intended message for any of three reasons. The first is *selective attention* in that they will not notice all the stimuli. The second is *selective distortion* in that they will twist the message to hear what they want to hear. The third is *selective recall* in that they will retain in permanent memory only a small fraction of the messages that reach them.

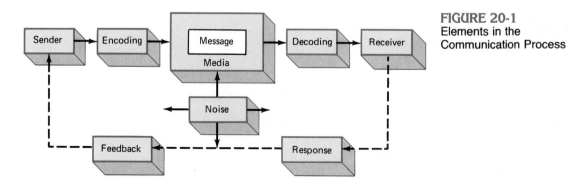

FIGURE 20-1
Elements in the
Communication Process

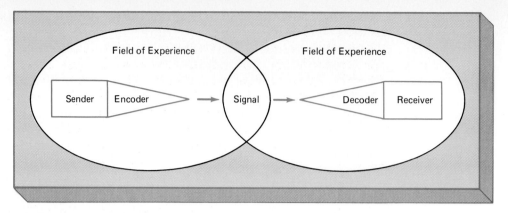

FIGURE 20-2
Elements Affecting Shared Meaning
SOURCE: Wilbur Schramm, "How Communication Works," in *The Process and Effects of Mass Communication* ed. Wilbur Schramm and Donald F. Roberts (Urbana: University of Illinois Press, 1971), p. 4.

The challenge to the communicator is to design a message that wins attention in spite of the surrounding distractions. Schramm suggested that the likelihood that a potential receiver will attend to a message is given by[4]

$$\text{Likelihood of attention} = \frac{\text{Perceived reward strength} - \text{Perceived punishment strength}}{\text{Perceived expenditure of effort}}$$

Selective attention explains why ads with bold headlines promising something, such as "How to Make a Million," along with an arresting illustration and little copy, have a high likelihood of grabbing attention. For very little effort, the receiver has an opportunity to gain a great reward.

As for selective distortion, receivers have set attitudes, which lead to expectations about what they will hear or see. They will hear what fits into their belief system. As a result, receivers often add things to the message that are not there (*amplification*) and do not notice other things that are there (*leveling*). The communicator's task is to strive for message simplicity, clarity, interest, and repetition, to get the main points across to the audience.

As for selective recall, the communicator aims to get the message into the receiver's long-term memory. Long-term memory is the repository for all the information one has ever processed. In entering the receiver's long-term memory, the message has a chance of modifying the receiver's beliefs and attitudes. But first the message has to enter the receiver's short-term memory, which is a limited-capacity store that processes incoming information. Whether the message passes from the receiver's short-term memory to his or her long-term memory depends on the amount and type of *message rehearsal* by the receiver. Rehearsal does not mean simple message repetition but rather the receiver's elaborating on the meaning of the information in a way that brings into short-term memory related thoughts previously stored in the receiver's long-term memory. If the receiver's initial attitude toward the object is positive and he or she rehearses support arguments, the message is likely to be accepted and have high recall. If the receiver's initial attitude is negative and the person rehearses counterarguments, the message is likely to be rejected but to stay in long-term memory. Counterarguing inhibits persuasion by making an opposing message available. Much of persuasion requires the receiver's rehearsal of his or her own thoughts. Much of what is called persuasion is self-persuasion.[5] If there is no rehearsal of arguments but simply discounting of the message, "I don't believe it," the receiver is still more susceptible to subsequent influence than the receiver who counterargues.

Communicators have been looking for audience traits that correlate with their degree of persuasibility. People of high education and/or intelligence are thought to be less persuasible, but the evidence is inconclusive. Women have been found to be more persuasible than men, although this is mediated by a woman's acceptance of the prescribed female role. Women who value traditional sex roles are more influenceable than women who are less accepting of the traditional roles.[6] Persons who accept external standards to guide their behavior and who have a weak self-concept appear to be more persuasible. Persons who are low in self-confidence are also thought to be more persuasible. However, research by Cox and Bauer showed a curvilinear relation between self-confidence and persuasibility, with those moderate in self-confidence being the most persuasible.[7] The communicator should look for audience traits that correlate with persuasibility and use them to guide message and media development.

Cartwright has outlined what must happen for a message to influence the behavior of another person:[8]

1. The "message" (that is, information, facts, and so on) must reach the sense organs of the persons who are to be influenced.
2. Having reached the sense organs, the "message" must be accepted as a part of the person's cognitive structure.
3. To induce a given action by mass persuasion, this action must be seen by the person as a path to some goal that he has.
4. To induce a given action, an appropriate cognitive and motivational system must gain control of the person's behavior at a particular point in time.

Fiske and Hartley have outlined some factors that moderate the effect of a communication:[9]

1. The greater the monopoly of the communication source over the recipient, the greater the change or effect in favor of the source over the recipient.
2. Communication effects are greatest where the message is in line with the existing opinions, beliefs, and dispositions of the receiver.
3. Communication can produce the most effective shifts on unfamiliar, lightly felt, peripheral issues, which do not lie at the center of the recipient's value system.
4. Communication is more likely to be effective where the source is believed to have expertise, high status, objectivity, or likability, but particularly where the source has power, and can be identified with.
5. The social context, group, or reference group will mediate the communication and influence whether or not it is accepted.

STEPS IN DEVELOPING EFFECTIVE COMMUNICATIONS

We will now examine the major steps in developing a total communication and promotion program. The marketing communicator must (1) identify the target audience; (2) determine the communication objectives; (3) design the message; (4) select the communication channels; (5) allocate the total promotion budget; (6) decide on the promotion mix; (7) measure the promotion's results; and (8) manage and coordinate the total marketing communication process.

Identifying the Target Audience

A marketing communicator must start with a clear target audience in mind. The audience may be potential buyers of the company's products, current users, deciders, or influencers. The audience may be individuals, groups, particular publics, or the general public. The target audience will critically influence the communicator's decisions on what is to be said, how it is to be said, when it is to be said, where it is to be said, and who is to say it.

The communicator should research the audience's needs, attitudes, preferences, and other characteristics so that they may be considered in setting the communication objectives. One of the most important things to establish is the audience's current *image* of the object (e.g., product, company).

Image Analysis

A major part of audience analysis is to assess the audience's current image of the company, its products, and its competitors. People's attitudes and actions toward an object are highly conditioned by *their beliefs about* the object. *Image is the set of beliefs, ideas, and impressions that a person holds of an object.*

It is important to measure the audience's image of the marketable object before any communication planning takes place. The first step is to measure the target audience's knowledge of the object, using the following *familiarity scale*:

Never	Heard	Know a	Know a	Know
heard of	of only	little bit	fair amount	very well

If most of the respondents circle the first two or three categories, then the company's task will be to build greater awareness.

Respondents who are familiar with the product should be asked how they feel toward it, using the following *favorability scale*:

Very	Somewhat	Indifferent	Somewhat	Very
unfavorable	unfavorable		favorable	favorable

If most of the respondents check the first two or three categories, then the organization must overcome a negative image problem.

The two scales can be combined to develop insight into the nature of the communication challenge. To illustrate, suppose area residents are asked about their familiarity and attitude toward four local hospitals, A, B, C, and D. Their responses are averaged and shown in Figure 20-3. Hospital A has the most positive image: Most people know it and like it. Hospital B is less familiar to most people, but those who know it like it. Hospital C is viewed negatively by those who know it, but fortunately not too many people know it. Hospital D is seen as a poor hospital, and everyone knows it!

Clearly, each hospital faces a different communication task. Hospital A must work at maintaining its good reputation and high community awareness. Hospital B must gain the attention of more people, since those who know it consider it a good hospital. Hospital C must find out why people dislike it and must take steps to improve its performance while keeping a low profile. Hospital D should lower its profile (avoid news), improve its quality, and then seek public attention again.

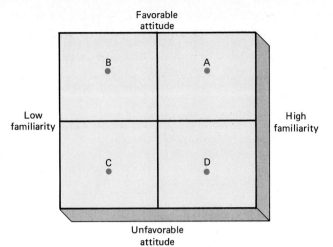

FIGURE 20-3
Familiarity-Favorability Analysis

Each hospital needs to go further and research the specific content of its image. The most popular tool for this is the *semantic differential*.[10] It involves the following steps:

1. **Developing a set of relevant dimensions.** The researcher asks people to identify the dimensions they would use in thinking about the object. People could be asked, "What things do you think of when you consider a hospital?" If someone suggests "quality of medical care," this would be turned into a bipolar adjective scale—say, "inferior medical care" at one end and "superior medical care" at the other. This could be rendered as a five- or seven-point scale. A set of additional dimensions for a hospital are shown in Figure 20-4.

2. **Reducing the set of relevant dimensions.** The number of dimensions should be kept small to avoid respondent fatigue in having to rate *n* objects on *m* scales. Osgood and his co-workers feel that there are essentially three types of scales:
   - Evaluation scales (good-bad qualities)
   - Potency scales (strong-weak qualities)
   - Activity scales (active-passive qualities)

FIGURE 20-4
Images of Three Hospitals (Semantic Differential)

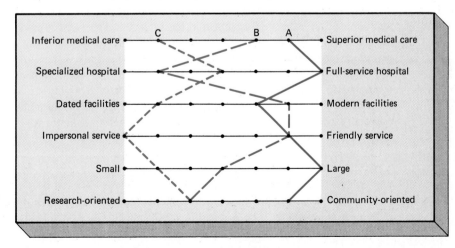

Using these scales as a guide, the researcher can remove redundant scales that fail to add much information.

3. ***Administering the instrument to a sample of respondents.*** The respondents are asked to rate one object at a time. The bipolar adjectives should be randomly arranged so as not to list all the unfavorable adjectives on one side.

4. ***Averaging the results.*** Figure 20-4 shows the results of averaging the respondents' pictures of hospitals A, B, and C (hospital D is left out). Each hospital's image is represented by a vertical "line of means" that summarizes how the average respondent sees that institution. Thus hospital A is seen as a large, modern, friendly, and superior hospital. Hospital C, on the other hand, is seen as a small, dated, impersonal, and inferior hospital.

5. ***Checking on the image variance.*** Since each image profile is a line of means, it does not reveal how variable the image actually is. If there were one hundred respondents, did they all see hospital B, for example, exactly as shown, or was there considerable variation? In the first case, we would say that the image is highly *specific*; and in the second case, highly *diffused*. An institution may not want a very specific image. Some organizations prefer a diffused image so that different groups can project their needs into this organization. The organization will want to check whether a diffused image is possibly the result of different subgroups rating the organization, with each subgroup having a highly specific image.

The marketers should now develop a picture of the *desired image* in contrast to the *current image*. Suppose hospital C would like the public to have a more favorable view of the quality of its medical care, facilities, friendliness, and so on. It is not aiming for perfection because the hospital recognizes its limitations. The desired image must be feasible in terms of the hospital's present image, facilities, and resources. Management must decide which image gaps it wants to close first. Is it more desirable to improve the hospital's image of friendliness (through staff training programs and the like) or the quality of its facilities (through renovation)? Each image dimension should be reviewed in terms of the following questions:

■ What contribution to the organization's overall favorable image would be made by closing that particular image gap to the extent shown?

■ What strategy (combination of real changes and communication changes) would help close the particular image gap?

■ What would be the cost of closing that image gap?

■ How long would it take to close that image gap?

An organization seeking to change its image must have great patience. Images are "sticky" and persist long after the organization has changed. Thus a hospital's medical care might have deteriorated, and yet it continues to be highly regarded in the public mind. Image persistence is explained by the fact that once people have a certain image of an object, they tend to be selective perceivers of further data. Their perceptions are oriented toward seeing what is consistent with their image. It will take highly disconfirming stimuli to raise doubts and open them to new information. Thus an image enjoys a life of its own, especially when people do not have continuous or new firsthand experiences with the changed object.

Determining the Communication Objectives

Once the target market and its characteristics are identified, the marketing communicator must decide on the desired audience response. The ultimate response, of course, is purchase. But purchase behavior is the end result of a long process of consumer decision making. The marketing communicator needs to know how to move the target audience from its present state to a higher state of readiness-to-buy.

The marketer may be seeking a *cognitive*, *affective*, or *behavioral* response from the target audience. That is, the marketer may want to put something into the consumer's mind, change the consumer's attitude, or get the consumer to undertake a specific action. Even here, there are different models of consumer-response stages. Figure 20-5 shows the four best-known *response hierarchy models*.

The *AIDA model* shows the buyer as passing through the stages of attention, interest, desire, and action. The *hierarchy-of-effects model* shows the buyer as progressing through awareness, knowledge, liking, preference, conviction, and purchase. The *innovation-adoption model* shows the buyer as passing through awareness, interest, evaluation, trial, and adoption. The *communications model* shows the buyer as progressing through exposure, reception, cognitive response, attitude, intention, and behavior. Most of these differences are semantic. All of these models assume that the buyer passes through a cognitive, affective, and behavioral stage, in that order.

We will work with the "hierarchy-of-effects" model and describe the six buyer-readiness states—awareness, knowledge, liking, preference, conviction, and purchase.

Awareness   If most of the target audience is unaware of the object, the communicator's task is to build awareness, perhaps just name recognition. This can be accomplished with simple messages repeating the name. Even then, building awareness takes time.

FIGURE 20-5
Response Hierarchy Models
SOURCES: (a) E. K. Strong, *The Psychology of Selling* (New York: McGraw-Hill, 1925), p. 9; (b) Robert J. Lavidge and Gary A. Steiner, "A Model for Predictive Measurements of Advertising Effectiveness," *Journal of Marketing*, October 1961, p. 61; (c) Everett M. Rogers, *Diffusion of Innovations* (New York: Free Press, 1962), pp. 79–86; (d) Various sources.

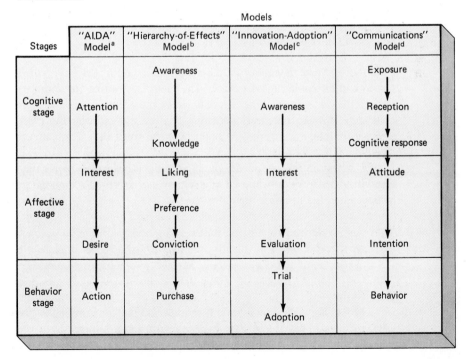

> Suppose a small Iowa college called Pottsville seeks applicants from Nebraska but has no name recognition in Nebraska. And suppose there were thirty thousand high school seniors in Nebraska who might potentially be interested in Pottsville College. The college might set the objective of making 70 percent of these students aware of Pottsville's name within one year.

Knowledge   The target audience might have company or product awareness but not know much more. Pottsville may want its target audience to know that it is a private four-year college in eastern Iowa with excellent programs in ornithology and thanatology. Pottsville College needs to learn how many people in the target audience have little, some, and much knowledge about Pottsville. The college may decide to build up product knowledge as its immediate communication objective.

Liking   If the target audience knows the object, how do they feel about it? If much of the audience looks unfavorably on Pottsville College, the communicator has to find out why and then develop a communications campaign to build up favorable feeling. If the unfavorable view is rooted in real inadequacies of the college, then a communication campaign will not do the job. The task requires improving the college and then communicating its quality. Good public relations call for ''good deeds followed by good words.''

Preference   The target audience might like the product but not prefer it to others. In this case, the communicator seeks to build consumer preference. The communicator will tout the product's quality, value, performance, and other attributes. The communicator can check on the campaign's success by remeasuring the audience's preferences after the campaign.

Conviction   A target audience might prefer a particular product but not develop a conviction about buying it. Thus some high school seniors might prefer Pottsville but not be sure they want to go to college. The communicator's job is to build conviction that going to college is the right thing to do.

Purchase   Some members of the target audience might have conviction but not quite get around to making the purchase. They may be waiting for additional information, plan to act later, and so on. The communicator must entice these consumers into taking the final step. Among purchase-producing devices are offering the product at a low price, offering a premium, offering an opportunity to try it on a limited basis, or indicating that it will soon be unavailable.

Determining the response sought is critical in developing a communication program. Exhibit 20-1 shows how the communicator can determine simultaneously both the target audience and the response sought.

Designing the Message   Having defined the desired audience response, the communicator moves to developing an effective message. Ideally, the message should get *attention*, hold *interest*, arouse *desire*, and elicit *action* (AIDA model). In practice, few messages take the consumer all the way from awareness through purchase, but the AIDA framework suggests the desirable qualities.

Formulating the message will require solving four problems: what to say (*message content*), how to say it logically (*message structure*), how to say it symbolically (*message format*), and who should say it (*message source*).

EXHIBIT 20-1

Determining the Target Audience and Sought Response

Communication objectives depend heavily on how many people already know about a product and may have tried it. Ottesen has developed a device called a *market map* to be used as a guide to choosing the target audience and eliciting the sought response. The market map is shown below:

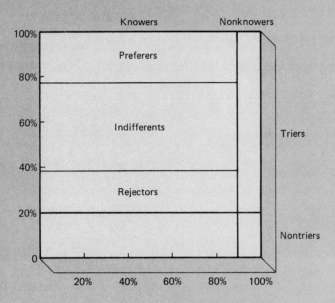

The horizontal dimension shows the current percentage of the market that know the brand, here 90 percent. The vertical dimension shows the percentage of the market that have tried the brand, here 80 percent. From these two measures, we know that the brand is mature. The knowers-triers further divide into those who prefer (23 percent), are indifferent (39 percent), and have rejected (18 percent) the brand. The knowers-nontriers can also be assumed to divide into those who have a positive, indifferent, and negative attitude toward the brand.

The task is to set communication objectives for this brand. Since 90 percent of the target market already know the brand, it would not make sense to build awareness in the remaining 10 percent. The 10 percent who do not know this brand consist of persons who are unaware of many things and probably do not have much income. It is expensive to reach these people and is seldom worth it.

What about getting more knowers-nontriers to try the product? That is a worthwhile objective and can best be accomplished through sales promotion (free samples, cents-off coupons, and so on) rather than through additional advertising or personal selling. Since 25 percent of the current triers prefer the brand, we cannot expect that more than 25 percent of the new triers will stay with the brand. The marketer should calculate whether achieving this number of new-trier preferers would be worth the cost of the sales promotion campaign.

Another plausible communication objective is to increase the proportion of triers who prefer this brand to other brands. This is difficult because consumer attitude is a function of how the consumer experiences the performance and price of the brand. If the company wants to increase preference, what is required is product improvement and lower prices rather than more advertising.

The following conclusions can be drawn about the three trier groups. Communication to those who already prefer the brand is usually not very productive unless there is high consumer forgetfulness or a high level of competitors' expenditure aimed at preferers. Communication directed to the rejectors is probably wasted because the rejectors are not likely to pay attention to the advertising and probably would not retry the brand. Communication directed to the indifferents will probably be effective in attracting some proportion of their purchases, especially if the advertising makes some strong point to this audience.

Message Content   The communicator has to figure out what to say to the target audience to produce the desired response. This has been variously called the *appeal*, *theme*, *idea*, or *unique selling proposition* (USP). It amounts to formulating some kind of benefit, motivation, identification, or reason why the audience should think about or investigate the product. Three types of appeals can be distinguished. *Rational appeals* appeal to the audience's self-interest. They show that the product will produce the claimed functional benefits. Examples would be messages demonstrating a product's quality, economy, value, or performance. It is widely believed that industrial buyers are most responsive to rational appeals. They are knowledgeable about the product class, trained to recognize value, and accountable to others for their choice. Consumers, when they buy certain big-ticket items, are also thought to gather information and carefully compare the alternatives. They will respond to quality, economy, value, and performance appeals.

Emotional appeals attempt to stir up some negative or positive emotion that will motivate purchase. Communicators have worked with *fear*, *guilt*, and *shame appeals* in getting people to do things they should (e.g., brushing teeth, taking an annual health checkup) or stop doing things they shouldn't (e.g., smoking, overimbibing, drug abuse, overeating). Fear appeals are effective up to a point, but if the audience anticipates too much fear in the message, they will avoid it. (See Exhibit 20-2.) Communicators also use positive emotional appeals such as *humor*, *love*, *pride*, and *joy*. Evidence has not established that a humorous message, for example, is necessarily more effective than a straight version of the same message. Humorous messages probably attract more attention and create more liking and belief in the sponsor, but humor may also detract from comprehension.[11]

Moral appeals are directed to the audience's sense of what is right and proper. They are often used to exhort people to support social causes, such as a cleaner environment, better race relations, equal rights for women, and aid to the disadvantaged. An example is the March of Dimes appeal: "God made you whole. Give to help those He didn't." Moral appeals are less often used in connection with everyday products.

Some advertisers believe that messages are maximally persuasive when they are moderately discrepant with what the audience believes. Messages that only state what the audience believes attract less attention and at best only reinforce audience beliefs. But if the messages are too discrepant with the audience's beliefs, they will be counterargued in the audience's mind and be disbelieved. The challenge is to design a message that is moderately discrepant and avoids the two extremes.

Message Structure   A message's effectiveness depends on its structure as well as its content. Hovland's research at Yale has shed much light on conclusion drawing, one-versus two-sided arguments, and order of presentation.

EXHIBIT 20-2

Do Fear Appeals Work?

Fear appeals have been studied more than any other emotional appeal, not only in marketing communications but also in politics and child rearing. For many years marketing communicators believed that a message's effectiveness increased with the level of fear produced. Actual study findings indicate that neither extremely strong nor extremely weak fear appeals are as effective as moderate ones in producing adherence to a recommendation. Ray and Wilkie explained the finding by hypothesizing two types of effects as fear increases:

> First, there are the facilitating effects that are most often overlooked in marketing. If fear can heighten drive, there is the possibility of greater attention and interest in the product and message than if no drive were aroused. . . . But fear also brings the important characteristic of inhibition into the picture. . . . If fear levels are too high, there is the possibility of defensive avoidance of the ad, denial of the threat, selective exposure or distortion of the ad's meaning, or a view of the recommendations as being inadequate to deal with so important a fear.

Of the 17 percent of all advertising that uses fear appeals, generally all exploit moderate- to low-level fears, usually fears concerning social disapproval and physical threats. Since many of our behaviors are performed to avoid the negative consequences of inaction, a moderate-level fear appeal is a logical motivator of consumer action.

Fear appeals often refer to negative consequences developed outside of the ad. When such fear appeals as "no caffeine," "no additives or preservatives," and "no sugar added" are used, only a few words are needed to cue the fear emotion, since other media have already sufficiently described the consequences of these appeals.

Source credibility also moderates fear appeals. When source credibility is high, a fear appeal induces attitude change. Only a highly credible, well-established advertiser should use fear appeals. American Express, a high-credibility source, uses the fear appeal in its campaign to admonish consumers to carry American Express traveler's checks.

Since different buyers have different levels of tolerance for fear appeals, the level of the fear message should be set differently for different market segments. Furthermore, if the fear message is to be effective, the communication should promise to relieve, in a believable and efficient way, the fear it arouses: otherwise buyers will ignore or minimize the threat.

SOURCES Michael L. Ray and William L. Wilkie, "Fear: The Potential of an Appeal Neglected by Marketing," *Journal of Marketing*, January 1970, pp. 55–56; Brian Sternthal and C. Samuel Craig, "Fear Appeals: Revisited and Revised," *Journal of Consumer Research*, December, 1974, pp. 22–34; John J. Burnett and Richard L. Oliver, "Fear Appeal Effects in the Field: A Segmentation Approach," *Journal of Marketing Research*, May 1979, pp. 181–90; and Lynette S. Unger and James M. Stearns. "The Use of Fear and Guilt Messages in Television Advertising: Issues and Evidence," in *1983 Educators' Proceedings*, ed. Patrick E. Murphy (Chicago: American Marketing Association, 1983), pp. 16–20.

Conclusion drawing is the question of whether the communicator should draw a definite conclusion for the audience or leave it to them. Some early experiments supported the greater efficacy of stating conclusions for the audience. Recent research, however, indicates that the best ads ask questions and allow viewers to come to their own conclusions.[12] Conclusion drawing may cause negative reactions in the following situations:

- If the communicator is seen as untrustworthy, the audience may resent the attempt to influence them.
- If the issue is simple or the audience is intelligent, they may be annoyed at the attempt to explain the obvious.
- If the issue is highly personal, the audience may resent the communicator's attempt to draw a conclusion.

Drawing too explicit a conclusion can limit a product's acceptance. If Ford had hammered away that the Mustang was for young people, this strong definition might have blocked other age groups who were attracted to it. *Stimulus ambiguity* can lead to a broader market definition and more spontaneous uses of certain products. Conclusion drawing seems better suited for complex or specialized products where a single and clear use is intended.

One- or two-sided arguments raises the question of whether the communicator should only praise the product or also mention some shortcomings. One would think that the best effect would be gained in one-sided presentations, which predominate in sales presentations, political contests, and child rearing. Yet the answer is not clear-cut. Here are some findings:[13]

■ One-sided messages work best with audiences that are initially predisposed to the communicator's position, and two-sided arguments work best with audiences who are opposed.

■ Two-sided messages tend to be more effective with better-educated audiences.

■ Two-sided messages tend to be more effective with audiences that are likely to be exposed to counterpropaganda.

Order of presentation raises the question of whether a communicator should present the strongest arguments first or last. In the case of a one-sided message, presenting the strongest argument first has the advantage of establishing attention and interest. This is important in newspapers and other media where the audience does not attend to the whole message. However, it means an anticlimactic presentation. With a captive audience, a climactic presentation may be more effective. In the case of a two-sided message, the issue is whether to present the positive argument first (*primacy effect*) or last (*recency effect*). If the audience is initially opposed, the communicator would be smart to start with the other side's argument. This will disarm the audience and allow concluding with his or her strongest argument. Neither primacy nor recency effect dominates in all situations, and more research is needed.[14]

Message Format   The communicator must develop a strong format for the message. In a print ad, the communicator has to decide on the headline, copy, illustration, and color. To attract attention, advertisers use such devices as key visuals, a payoff, image, demonstrations, testimonials, emotion, and music.[15] If the message is to be carried over the radio, the communicator has to carefully choose words, voice qualities (speech rate, rhythm, pitch, articulation), and vocalizations (pauses, sighs, yawns). The "sound" of an announcer promoting a used automobile has to be different from one promoting a quality mattress. If the message is to be carried on television or in person, then all of these elements plus body language (nonverbal clues) have to be planned. Presenters have to pay attention to their facial expressions, gestures, dress, posture, and hair style. If the message is carried

---

Color plays an important communication role in food preferences. When housewives sampled four cups of coffee that had been placed next to brown, blue, red, and yellow containers (all the coffee was identical, unknown to the housewives), 75 percent felt that the coffee next to the brown container tasted too strong; nearly 85 percent judged the coffee next to the red container to be the richest; nearly everyone felt that the coffee next to the blue container was mild and that the coffee next to the yellow container was weak.

by the product or its packaging, the communicator has to pay attention to color, texture, scent, size, and shape.

Message Source   Messages delivered by attractive sources achieve higher attention and recall. Advertisers often use celebrities as spokespeople, such as Michael Jackson for Pepsi-Cola, O. J. Simpson for Hertz, and Ed McMahon for Alpo dog food. Celebrities are likely to be effective when they personify a key product attribute. Thus O. J. Simpson is a good spokesman for Hertz because he is known for his speed. But what is equally important is that the spokesman has credibility. Messages delivered by highly credible sources are more persuasive. Pharmaceutical companies want doctors to testify about their products' benefits because doctors have high credibility. Antidrug crusaders will use ex-drug addicts to warn high school students against drugs because ex-addicts have higher credibility than teachers.

But what factors underlie source credibility? The three factors most often identified are expertise, trustworthiness, and likability.[16] *Expertise* is the specialized knowledge the communicator appears to possess, which backs the claim. Doctors, scientists, and professors rank high on expertise in their respective fields. *Trustworthiness* is related to how objective and honest the source is perceived to be. Friends are trusted more than strangers or sales people. *Likability* describes the source's attractiveness to the audience. Such qualities as candor, humor, and naturalness make a source more likable. The most highly credible source, then, would be a person who scored high on all three dimensions.

If a person has a positive attitude toward a source and a message, or a negative attitude toward both, a state of congruity is said to exist. What happens if the person holds one attitude toward the source and the opposite toward the message? Suppose a homemaker hears a likable celebrity praise a brand that she dislikes. Osgood and Tannenbaum posit that *attitude change will take place in the direction of increasing the amount of congruity between the two evaluations.*[17] The homemaker will end up respecting the celebrity somewhat less and respecting the brand somewhat more. If she encounters the same celebrity praising other disliked brands, she will eventually develop a negative view of the celebrity and maintain her negative attitudes toward the brands. The *principle of congruity* says that communicators can use their good image to reduce some negative feelings toward a brand but in the process may lose some audience regard.

Selecting the Communication Channels

The communicator must select efficient channels of communication to carry the message. Communication channels are of two broad types, *personal* and *nonpersonal*.

Personal Communication Channels   Personal communication channels involve two or more persons communicating directly with each other. They might communicate face to face, person to audience, over the telephone, or through the mails. Personal communication channels derive their effectiveness through the opportunities for individualizing the presentation and feedback.

A further distinction can be drawn between advocate, expert, and social channels of communication. *Advocate channels* consist of company sales people contacting buyers in the target market. *Expert channels* consist of independent persons with expertise making statements to target buyers. *Social channels* consist of neighbors, friends, family members, and associates talking to target buyers. This last channel, known as *word-of-mouth influence*, is the most persuasive in many product areas. Exhibit 20-3 illustrates how dentists can use the word-of-mouth effect to expand their client base.

Personal influence carries great weight, especially in the following two situations:

■ *Where the product is expensive, risky, or purchased infrequently.* Here buyers are likely to be high information seekers. They are likely to go beyond mass-media information and seek the opinions of knowledgeable and trusted sources.

■ *Where the product has a significant social status.* Such products as automobiles, clothing, and even beer and cigarettes have significant brand differentiation that implies something about user status or taste. Consumers are likely to choose brands acceptable to their groups.

Companies can take the following steps to stimulate personal influence channels to work on their behalf:

■ *Identify influential individuals and companies and devote extra effort to them.* In industrial selling, the entire industry may follow a single lead company in adopting new innovations. Early sales efforts should focus on this company.

■ *Create opinion leaders by supplying certain people with the product on attractive terms.* A new tennis racket may be offered initially to members of high school tennis teams at a special low price. The company would hope that these star high school tennis players would "talk up" their new racket to other high schoolers.

■ *Work through community influentials such as local disc jockeys, class presidents, and presidents of women's organizations.* When the Ford Thunderbird was introduced, invitations were sent to executives offering them a free car to drive for the day. Of the fifteen thousand who took advantage of the offer, only 10 percent indicated that they would become buyers while 84 percent said they would recommend it to a friend.

■ *Use influential people in testimonial advertising.* Pepsi-Cola paid Michael Jackson several million dollars to make Pepsi commercials; golf and tennis companies always use well-known players to endorse their equipment.

■ *Develop advertising that has high "conversation value."* Wendy's "Where's the Beef?" campaign (showing an elderly woman named Clara questioning where the hamburger was hidden in all that bread) and Burger King's "Search for Herb" (promising prizes to those who spotted Herb in a Burger King restaurant) both created high conversation value.[18]

Nonpersonal Communication Channels   Nonpersonal communication channels carry messages without personal contact or interaction. They include media, atmospheres, and events. *Media* consist of print media (newspapers, magazines, direct mail), broadcast media (radio, television), electronic media (audiotape, videotape, videodisc), and display media (billboards, signs, posters). Most of the nonpersonal messages we receive come through paid media.

Atmospheres are "packaged environments" that create or reinforce the buyer's leanings toward purchase or consumption of the product. Thus law offices are decorated with oriental rugs and oak furniture to communicate "stability" and "experience."[19] Department stores create comfortable purchase atmospheres for women's sportswear with trendy music and videos, bright colors, and lighting.

Events are occurrences designed to communicate particular messages to target audiences. Public relations departments arrange news conferences and grand openings to achieve specific communication effects on an audience.

Although personal communication is often more effective than mass communication, mass media may be the major way to stimulate personal communication. Mass communications affect personal attitudes and behavior through a *two-step flow-of-communication process.* "Ideas often flow from radio and print to opinion leaders and from these to the less active sections of the population."[20]

This two-step communication flow has several implications. First, the influence of mass media on public opinion is not as direct, powerful, and automatic as supposed. It is mediated by *opinion leaders*, persons who belong to primary groups and whose opinions are sought in one or more product areas. Opinion leaders are more exposed to mass media than those they influence. They carry messages to people who are less exposed to media, thus extending the influence of the mass media; or they may carry altered messages or none at all, thus acting as *gatekeepers*.

Second, the hypothesis challenges the notion that people's consumption styles are primarily influenced by a "trickle-down" effect from higher-status classes. To the contrary, people primarily interact within their own social class and acquire their fashion and other ideas from people like themselves who are opinion leaders.[21]

A third implication is that mass communicators would be more efficient by directing their messages specifically to opinion leaders, letting the latter carry the message to others. Thus pharmaceutical firms try to promote their new drugs to the most influential physicians first. More recent research indicates that both opinion leaders and the general public are affected by mass communication. Opinion leaders are prompted by the mass media to spread information, while the general public seeks information from the opinion leaders.

Communications researchers are moving toward a social-structure view of interpersonal communication.[22] They see society as consisting of *cliques*, small social groups whose members interact with each other more frequently than with others. Clique members are similar, and their closeness facilitates effective communication but also insulates the clique from new ideas. The challenge is to create more system openness whereby cliques exchange more information with each other and in the larger environment. This openness is helped by persons who function as liaisons and bridges. A *liaison* is a person who connects two or more cliques without belonging to either. A *bridge* is a person who belongs to one clique and who is linked to a person in another clique. Word-of-mouth communications flow most readily within cliques, and the problem is to facilitate communication between cliques and to create a diffusion network.

Establishing the Total Promotion Budget

One of the most difficult marketing decisions facing companies is how much to spend on promotion. John Wanamaker, the department store magnate, said: "I know that half of my advertising is wasted, but I don't know which half. I spent $2 million for advertising, and I don't know if that is half enough or twice too much."

Thus it is not surprising that industries and companies vary considerably in how much they spend on promotion. Promotional expenditures may amount to 30 to 50 percent of sales in the cosmetics industry and only 10 to 20 percent in the industrial machinery industry. Within a given industry, low- and high-spending companies can be found. Philip Morris is a high spender. When it acquired the Miller Brewing Company, and later the Seven-Up Company, it substantially increased total promotion spending. The additional spending at Miller's raised its market share from 4 to 19 percent within a few years.

How do companies decide on their promotion budget? We will describe four common methods used to set the total budget for any component, such as advertising.

Affordable Method

Many companies set the promotion budget at what they think the company can afford. One executive explained this method as follows: "Why it's simple. First, I go upstairs to the controller and ask how much they can afford to give us this year. He says a million and a half. Later, the boss comes to me and asks how much we should spend and I say 'Oh, about a million and a half.' "[23]

This method of setting budgets completely ignores the role of promotion as an investment and the immediate impact of promotion on sales volume. It leads to an uncertain annual promotion budget, which makes long-range market planning difficult.

Percentage-of-Sales Method

Many companies set their promotion expenditures at a specified percentage of sales (either current or anticipated) or of the sales price. A railroad company executive said: "We set our appropriation for each year on December 1 of the preceding year. On that date we add our passenger revenue for the next month, and then take 2 percent of the total for our advertising appropriation for the new year."[24] Automobile companies typically budget a fixed percentage for promotion based on the planned car price. Oil companies set the appropriation at some fraction of a cent for each gallon of gasoline sold under their own label.

A number of advantages are claimed for this method. First, the percentage-of-sales method means that promotion expenditures are likely to vary with what the company can "afford." This satisfies the financial managers, who feel that expenses should bear a close relation to the movement of corporate sales over the business cycle. Second, this method encourages management to think in terms of the relationship between promotion cost, selling price, and profit per unit. Third, this method encourages competitive stability to the extent that competing firms spend approximately the same percentage of their sales on promotion.

In spite of these advantages, the percentage-of-sales method has little to justify it. It uses circular reasoning in viewing sales as the cause of promotion rather than as the result. It leads to an appropriation set by the availability of funds rather than by the product opportunities in the market. It discourages experimenting with countercyclical promotion or aggressive spending. The dependence of the promotion budget on year-to-year sales fluctuations interferes with long-range planning. The method does not provide a logical basis for choosing the specific percentage, except what has been done in the past or what competitors are doing. Finally, it does not encourage building up the promotion budget by determining what each product and territory deserves.

Competitive-Parity Method   Some companies set their promotion budget to achieve *share-of-voice* parity with their competitors. This thinking is illustrated by the executive who asked a trade source: "Do you have any figures which other companies in the builders' specialties field have used which would indicate what proportion of gross sales should be given over to advertising?"[25] This executive believes that by spending the same percentage of his sales on advertising as his competitors, he will maintain his market share.

Two arguments are advanced for this method. One is that the competitors' expenditures represent the collective wisdom of the industry. The other is that maintaining a competitive parity helps prevent promotion wars.

Neither argument is valid. There are no grounds for believing that the competition knows better than the company itself what it should be spending on promotion. Company reputations, resources, opportunities, and objectives differ so much that their promotion budgets are hardly a guide. Furthermore, there is no evidence that budgets based on competitive parity discourage promotional wars from breaking out.

Objective-and-Task Method   The objective-and-task method calls upon marketers to develop their promotion budgets by defining their specific objectives, determining the tasks that must be performed to achieve these objectives, and estimating the costs of performing these tasks. The sum of these costs is the proposed promotion budget.

Ule showed how the objective-and-task method could be used to establish an advertising budget for a new filter-tip cigarette, Sputnik (name fictitious).[26] The steps are as follows:

1. *Establish the market-share goal.* The advertiser wants 8 percent of the market. Since there are 50 million cigarette smokers, the company wants to switch 4 million smokers to Sputnik.
2. *Determine the percent of the market that should be reached by Sputnik advertising.* The advertiser hopes to reach 80 percent (40 million smokers) with the advertising.
3. *Determine the percent of aware smokers that should be persuaded to try the brand.* The advertiser would be pleased if 25 percent of aware smokers, or 10 million smokers, tried Sputnik. This is because they estimate that 40 percent of all triers, or 4 million persons, would become loyal users. That is the market goal.
4. *Determine the number of advertising impressions per 1 percent trial rate.* The advertiser estimates that 40 advertising impressions (exposures) for every 1 percent of the population would bring about a 25 percent trial rate.
5. *Determine the number of gross rating points that would have to be purchased.* A gross rating point is one exposure to 1 percent of the target population. Since the company wants to achieve 40 exposures to 80 percent of the population, it will want to buy 3,200 gross rating points.
6. *Determine the necessary advertising budget on the basis of the average cost of buying a gross rating point.* To expose 1 percent of the target population to one impression costs an average of $3,277. Therefore, 3,200 gross rating points would cost $10,486,400 (= $3,277 × 3,200) in the introductory year.

This method has the advantage of requiring management to spell out its assumptions about the relationship between dollars spent, exposure levels, trial rates, and regular usage.

Alternatively, a manager may use a computer model, such as DEMON, to determine these same relationships. The DEMON model incorporates market structure variables to determine adequate budgets to stimulate product adoption or continued sales.[27]

The overall answer to how much weight promotion should receive in the total marketing mix (as opposed to product improvement, lower prices, more services, and so on) depends on where the company's products are in their life cycles, whether they are commodities or highly differentiable products, whether they are routinely needed or have to be "sold," and other considerations. In theory, the total promotional budget should be established where the marginal profit from the last promotional dollar just equals the marginal profit from the last dollar in the best nonpromotional use. Implementing this principle, however, is not easy.

Deciding on the Promotion Mix

Companies face the task of distributing the total promotion budget over the four promotion tools of advertising, sales promotion, publicity, and sales force. Within the same industry, companies can differ considerably in how they allocate their promotional budget. Avon concentrates its promotional funds on personal selling (its advertising is only 1.5 percent of sales), while Revlon spends heavily on advertising (about 7.0 percent of sales). In selling vacuum cleaners, Electrolux spends heavily on a door-to-door sales force, while Hoover relies more on advertising. Thus it is possible to achieve a given sales level with various mixes of advertising, personal selling, sales promotion, and publicity. (Exhibit 20-4 shows the promotional mix of business-to-business marketers.)

EXHIBIT 20-4

The Promotional Mix of Business-to-Business Marketers

Business Marketing magazine published a comprehensive study of the expenditure levels on major promotional tools by business-to-business marketers. It estimated that business-to-business marketers spent $91.5 billion in 1985, broken down as follows:

Advertising	$8.6	Business and consumer publications, radio and TV, directories, yellow pages, outdoor, and ad production
Direct marketing	30.9	Direct mail and telemarketing
Trade shows	21.0	Show costs and exhibitor travel and entertainment
Sales promotion	7.6	Collateral, audiovisual and point of sale
Incentives	15.1	Merchandise incentives, travel incentives and sweepstakes
Sales force management	5.9	Training and meetings
Public relations	2.4	Publicity

Companies are always searching for ways to gain efficiency by substituting one promotional tool for another as its economics become more favorable. Many companies have replaced some field sales activity with ads, direct mail, and telemarketing. Other companies have increased their sales promotion expenditures in relation to advertising, to gain quicker sales. The relative substitutability among promotional tools explains why marketing functions need to be coordinated in a single marketing department.

Designing the promotion mix is even more complicated when one tool can be used to promote another. Thus when McDonald's decides to run Million Dollar Sweepstakes in its fast-food outlets (a form of sales promotion), it has to take out newspaper ads to inform the public. When General Mills develops a consumer advertising/sales promotion campaign to launch a new cake mix, it has to also develop a campaign directed to the trade to win their support.

Many factors influence the marketer's choice of promotional tools. We will examine these factors in the following paragraphs.

Nature of Each Promotional Tool   Each promotional tool—advertising, personal selling, sales promotion, and publicity—has its own unique characteristics and costs. Marketers have to understand these characteristics in selecting them.

Advertising   Because of the many forms and uses of advertising, it is difficult to make all-embracing generalizations about its distinctive qualities as a component of the promotional mix. Yet the following qualities can be noted:[28]

- *Public presentation.* Advertising is a highly public mode of communication. Its public nature confers a kind of legitimacy on the product and also suggests a standardized offering. Because many persons receive the same message, buyers know that their motives for purchasing the product will be publicly understood.
- *Pervasiveness.* Advertising is a pervasive medium that permits the seller to repeat a message many times. It also allows the buyer to receive and compare the messages of various competitors. Large-scale advertising by a seller says something positive about the seller's size, popularity, and success.
- *Amplified expressiveness.* Advertising provides opportunities for dramatizing the company and its products through the artful use of print, sound, and color. Sometimes, however, the tool's very success at expressiveness may dilute or distract from the message.
- *Impersonality.* Advertising cannot be as compelling as a company sales representative. The audience does not feel obligated to pay attention or respond. Advertising is able to carry on only a monologue, not a dialogue, with the audience.

On the one hand, advertising can be used to build up a long-term image for a product (such as Coca-Cola ads), and on the other, to trigger quick sales (as in Sears' advertising a weekend sale). Advertising is an efficient way to reach numerous geographically dispersed buyers at a low cost per exposure. Certain forms of advertising, such as TV advertising, can require a large budget, while other forms, such as newspaper advertising, can be done on a small budget. Advertising may have an effect on sales simply through its presence. Consumers may believe a heavily advertised brand is one that offers ''good value''; otherwise, why would advertisers spend so much money backing a poor product?

Personal selling   Personal selling is the most effective tool at certain stages of the buying process, particularly in building up buyers' preference, conviction, and action. The reason is that personal selling, when compared with advertising, has three distinctive qualities:[29]

- *Personal confrontation.* Personal selling involves an alive, immediate, and interactive relationship between two or more persons. Each party is able to observe each other's needs and characteristics at close hand and make immediate adjustments.
- *Cultivation.* Personal selling permits all kinds of relationships to spring up, ranging from a matter-of-fact selling relationship to a deep personal friendship. Effective sales representatives will normally keep their customers' interests at heart if they want long-run relationships.
- *Response.* Personal selling makes the buyer feel under some obligation for having listened to the sales talk. The buyer has a greater need to attend and respond, even if the response is a polite ''thank you.''

These distinctive qualities come at a cost. A sales force represents a greater long term commitment than advertising. Advertising can be turned on and off, but the size of a sales force is more difficult to alter. In 1985, the average business-to-business sales call cost $230.[30] American firms spent over $172 billion on personal selling compared with $87.8 billion on advertising. This money supported over 8 million Americans who are engaged in sales work.[31]

Sales promotion   Although sales promotion tools—coupons, contests, premiums, and the like—are highly diverse, they have three distinctive characteristics:

- ■ *Communication.* They gain attention and usually provide information that may lead the consumer to the product.
- ■ *Incentive.* They incorporate some concession, inducement, or contribution that gives value to the consumer.
- ■ *Invitation.* They include a distinct invitation to engage in the transaction now.

Companies use sales promotion tools to create a stronger and quicker response. Sales promotion can be used to dramatize product offers and to boost sagging sales. Sales promotion effects are usually short run, however, and are not effective in building long-run brand preference.

Publicity   The appeal of publicity is based on its three distinctive qualities:

- ■ *High credibility.* News stories and features seem more authentic and credible to readers than ads do.
- ■ *Off guard.* Publicity can reach many prospects who might avoid sales people and advertisements. The message gets to the buyers as news rather than as a sales-directed communication.
- ■ *Dramatization.* Publicity has, like advertising, a potential for dramatizing a company or product.

Marketers tend to underuse product publicity or use it as an afterthought. Yet a well-thought-out publicity campaign coordinated with the other promotion-mix elements can be extremely effective.

Factors in Setting the Promotion Mix   Companies consider several factors in developing their promotion mix. These factors are examined below.

Type of product market   The effectiveness of promotional tools varies between consumer and industrial markets. The differences are shown in Figure 20-6. Consumer-goods companies normally devote most of their funds to advertising, followed by sales promotion, personal selling, and finally publicity. Industrial-goods companies devote most of their funds to personal selling, followed by sales promotion, advertising, and publicity. In general, personal selling is more heavily used with complex, expensive, and risky goods and in markets with fewer and larger sellers (hence, industrial markets).

While advertising is less important than sales calls in industrial markets, it still plays a significant role. Advertising can perform the following functions:

- ■ *Awareness building.* Prospects who are not aware of the company or product may refuse to see the sales representative. Furthermore, the sales representative may have to use up a lot of time describing the company and its products.
- ■ *Comprehension building.* If the product embodies new features, some of the burden of explaining them can be effectively undertaken by advertising.
- ■ *Efficient reminding.* If prospects know about the product but are not ready to buy, advertisements reminding them of the product would be much more economical than sales calls.

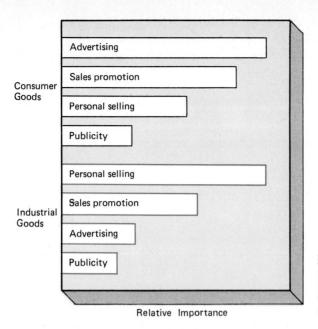

FIGURE 20-6
Relative Importance of Promotion Tools in Consumer versus Industrial Markets

- **Lead generation.** Advertisements carrying return coupons are an effective way to generate leads for sales representatives.
- **Legitimation.** Sales representatives can use tear sheets of the company's ads in leading magazines to legitimize their company and products.
- **Reassurance.** Advertising can remind customers how to use the product and reassure them about their purchase.

Advertising's important role in industrial marketing is underscored in a number of studies. Morrill showed in his study of industrial commodity marketing that advertising combined with personal selling increased sales 23 percent over what they were with no advertising. The total promotional cost as a percentage of sales was reduced by 20 percent.[32] Freeman developed a formal model for dividing promotional funds between advertising and personal selling on the basis of the selling tasks that each performs more economically.[33] Levitt's research also showed the important role that advertising can play in industrial marketing. (See Exhibit 20-5.) Lilien carried out a series of investigations in a project called ADVISOR in which he sought to determine and critique the practices used by industrial marketers to set their marketing communication budgets. (See Exhibit 20-6.)

Conversely, personal selling can make a strong contribution in consumer-goods marketing. Some consumer marketers play down the role of the sales force, using them mainly to collect weekly orders from dealers and to see that sufficient stock is on the shelf. The common feeling is that "sales people put products on shelves and advertising takes them off." Yet even here an effectively trained sales force can make three important contributions:

- **Increased stock position.** Persuasive sales representatives can influence dealers to take more stock and devote more shelf space to the company's brand.
- **Enthusiasm building.** Persuasive sales representatives can build dealer enthusiasm for a new product by dramatizing the planned advertising and sales promotion backup.
- **Missionary selling.** Sales representatives play a crucial role in signing up more dealers to carry the company's brands.

EXHIBIT 20-5

Role of Corporate Advertising in Industrial Marketing

Theodore Levitt sought to determine the relative contribution of the company's reputation (built mainly by advertising) and the company's sales presentation (personal selling) in producing industrial sales. Purchasing agents were shown filmed sales presentations of a new, but fictitious, technical product for use as an ingredient in making paint. The variables were the quality of the sales presentation and whether the salesperson came from a well-known company, a less-known but creditable company, or an unknown company. Purchasing-agent reactions were collected after seeing the films and again five weeks later. The findings were as follows:

1. A company's reputation improves the chances of getting a favorable first hearing and an early adoption of the product. Therefore, corporate advertising that can build up the company's reputation (other factors also shape its reputation) will help the company's sales representatives.
2. Sales representatives from well-known companies have an edge in getting the sale, if their sales presentations are adequate. If a sales representative from a lesser-known company makes a highly effective sales presentation, that can overcome the disadvantage. Smaller companies should use their limited funds to select and train good sales representatives rather than spend the money on advertising.
3. Company reputations have the most effect where the product is complex, the risk is high, and the purchasing agent is less professionally trained.

SOURCE Theodore Levitt, *Industrial Purchasing Behavior: A Study in Communication Effects* (Boston: Division of Research, Harvard Business School, 1965).

EXHIBIT 20-6

The Advisor Project Probes into How Industrial Marketers Set Their Marketing Expenditures— and How They Should Set Them

Professor Gary L. Lilien of M.I.T. directed a five-year study in the 1970s called the ADVISOR project, which examined how industrial marketers set their advertising budgets. ADVISOR ultimately consisted of two projects—ADVISOR 1 and ADVISOR 2.

ADVISOR 1

ADVISOR 1 was jointly sponsored by M.I.T. and the Association of National Advertisers. Data on various marketing factors were collected on sixty-six diversified industrial products from twelve cooperating companies. The study sought to develop marketing expenditure norms for industrial marketers. Industrial marketers tended to make a two-step decision in setting their advertising budgets. They decided, first, how much to spend on total marketing as a percentage of sales (the M/S ratio) and, second, how much to spend on advertising as a percentage of the marketing budget (the A/M ratio). When these ratios are multiplied, they give the A/S ratio, namely the advertising-to-sales ratio.

The data yielded the following norms:

	Advertising	A/S	M/S	A/M
Median:	$92,000	0.6%	6.9%	9.9%
Range for 50% of products:	$16,000–$272,000	0.1%–1.8%	3%–14%	5%–19%

Thus the average industrial company in the sample spent $92,000 on advertising each product, and in 50 percent of the cases this figure ranged from $16,000 to $272,000. The average industrial company spent only 0.6 percent of its sales on advertising; it budgeted about 7 percent of its sales for total marketing; and it budgeted about 10 percent of its total marketing budget for advertising. The table also shows the 50 percent ranges for each ratio.

A company could use this table to check whether its M/S and A/M ratios are within a 50 percent range of most companies. If one or both ratios are outside of the range, either too low or too high, then management should ask why. If good reasons cannot be found, the advertising and marketing budgets should be revised.

There could be good reasons for spending outside of the typical range. Lilien investigated a large number of factors suggested by marketing managers that would lead them to spend more or less than the normal amount on advertising and/or marketing. He found that six factors had a major influence on marketing budgets: stage in life cycle; frequency of purchase; product quality, uniqueness, and identification with the company; market share; concentration of sales; and growth rate of customers. Here are some findings:

- The M/S ratio fell as the product life cycle progressed.
- The higher the purchase frequency, the greater the A/M.
- The higher the product quality or uniqueness, the higher the A/M.
- The higher the market share, the lower the M/S.
- The higher the sales concentration (few customers accounting a high share of the purchases), the lower the M/S ratio.
- The higher the customer growth rate, the higher the M/S and A/M ratios.

Next ADVISOR investigated how industrial companies allocated their advertising budgets to the following four media:

- **Space:** trade, technical press, and house journals (41 percent)
- **Direct mail:** leaflets, brochures, catalogs, and other direct-mail pieces (24 percent)
- **Shows:** trade shows and industrial films (11 percent)
- **Promotion:** sales promotion (24 percent)

The numbers show the median percentage that industrial companies spent on each of the media. Lilien tested four variables that influence the allocation percentages that companies make to each media, namely, sales volume, life cycle, sales concentration, and number of customers. Here are some conclusions:

- The higher the sales volume, the more the use of shows and sales promotion and the less the use of space and direct mail.
- Products in later stages of the life cycle spend more on direct mail and less on sales promotion.
- The higher the sales concentration, the more the sales promotion and the less the use of trade shows.
- The greater the number of customers, the less the use of direct mail.

ADVISOR 2

ADVISOR 2 was launched subsequently with a twofold objective: to extend and verify the results of ADVISOR 1 and to determine the best level of spending and the best split of the spending between advertising and personal selling. Data were collected from 22 companies instead of 12 and covered 131 products instead of 66. When analyzed, the data confirmed the earlier ratios of A/S, A/M, and M/S. Several of the independent variables were confirmed and a few new variables were added to the analysis. ADVISOR 2 led to the building of some optimization models for setting marketing and advertising budgets.

SOURCES Gary L. Lilien and John D. C. Little, "The ADVISOR Project: A Study of Industrial Marketing Budgets," *Sloan Management Review*, Spring 1976, pp. 17–31, by permission of the publisher. Copyright © 1976 by the Sloan Management Review Association. All rights reserved; and Gary L. Lilien, "ADVISOR 2: Modeling the Marketing Mix Decision for Industrial Products," *Management Science*, February 1979, pp. 191–204. Copyright © 1979 The Institute of Management Science.

Push-versus-pull strategy The promotional mix is heavily influenced by whether the company chooses a push or a pull strategy to create sales. The two strategies are contrasted in Figure 20-7. A *push strategy* calls for using the sales force and trade promotion to push the product through the channels. The producer aggressively promotes the product to wholesalers; the wholesalers aggressively promote the product to retailers; and the retailers aggressively promote the product to consumers. A *pull strategy* calls for spending a lot of money on advertising and consumer promotion to build up consumer demand. If the strategy is effective, consumers will ask their retailers for the product, the retailers will ask their wholesalers for the product, and the wholesalers will ask the producers for the product. Companies differ in their predilection for push or pull. For example, Lever Brothers relies more heavily on push, and Procter & Gamble on pull.

Buyer-readiness stage Promotional tools vary in their cost-effectiveness at different stages of buyer readiness. Figure 20-8 shows the relative cost-effectiveness of three promotional tools. Advertising and publicity play the most important roles in the awareness stage, more than the role played by "cold calls" from sales representatives or sales promotion. Customer comprehension is primarily affected by advertising and personal selling. Customer conviction is influenced most by personal selling and less so by advertising and sales promotion. Closing the sale is predominantly influenced by personal selling and strong sales promotion. Reordering is also affected mostly by personal selling and sales promotion, and somewhat by reminder advertising. Clearly, advertising and publicity are most cost effective at the early stages of the buyer decision process, and personal selling and sales promotion are most effective at the later stages.

Product life-cycle stage The promotional tools also vary in their cost-effectiveness at different stages of the product life cycle. Figure 20-9 offers a speculative view of their relative effectiveness.

In the introduction stage, advertising and publicity have high cost-effectiveness, followed by sales promotion to induce trial and personal selling to gain distribution coverage.

In the growth stage, all the tools can be toned down because demand has its own momentum through word of mouth.

In the maturity stage, sales promotion, advertising, and personal selling all become more important, in that order.

In the decline stage, sales promotion continues strong, advertising and publicity are reduced, and sales people give the product only minimal attention.

FIGURE 20-7
Push-versus-Pull Strategy

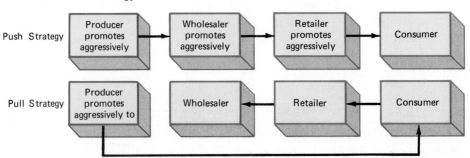

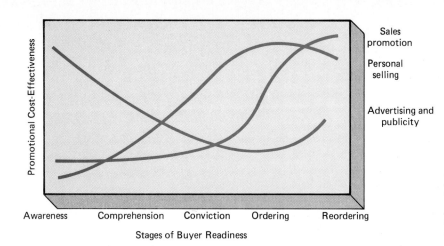

FIGURE 20-8
Cost-Effectiveness of
Different Promotional Tools
at Different Buyer-Readiness
Stages

Promotional Cost-Effectiveness

Awareness   Comprehension   Conviction   Ordering   Reordering

Stages of Buyer Readiness

Sales promotion

Personal selling

Advertising and publicity

Measuring Promotion's Results

After implementing the promotional plan, the communicator must measure its impact on the target audience. This involves asking the target audience whether they recognize or recall the message, how many times they saw it, what points they recall, how they felt about the message, and their previous and current attitudes toward the product and company. The communicator would also want to collect behavioral measures of audience response, such as how many people bought the product, liked it, and talked to others about it.

Figure 20-10 provides an example of good feedback measurement. Looking at brand A, we find that 80 percent of the total market are aware of brand A, 60 percent have tried it, and only 20 percent of those who have tried it are satisfied. This indicates that the communication program is effective in creating awareness, but the product fails to meet consumer expectations. On the other hand, only 40 percent of the total market are aware of brand B, only 30 percent have tried it, but 80 percent of those who have tried it are satisfied. In this case, the communication program needs to be strengthened to take advantage of the brand's satisfaction-generating power.

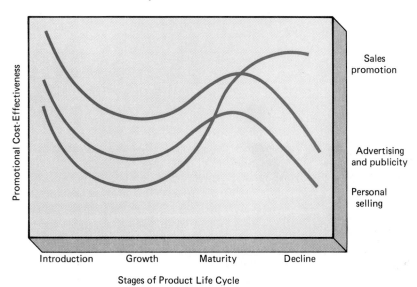

FIGURE 20-9
Cost-Effectiveness of
Different Promotional Tools
at Different Stages of Product
Life Cycle

Promotional Cost-Effectiveness

Introduction   Growth   Maturity   Decline

Stages of Product Life Cycle

Sales promotion

Advertising and publicity

Personal selling

FIGURE 20-10
Current Consumer States for Two Brands

Managing
and Coordinating
the Marketing
Communication
Process

The wide range of communication tools and messages available for reaching the target audience makes it imperative that they be coordinated. Otherwise the messages might be ill timed in terms of the availability of goods; they might lack consistency; or they might not be cost effective. Left alone, each manager of a communication resource will fight for more budget irrespective of the relative merits of each tool. The sales manager will want to hire two extra sales representatives for $80,000, while the advertising manager will want to spend the same money on a prime-time television commercial. Meanwhile the public relations manager feels that he or she can do wonders with more money for publicity. Little thought will be given to telemarketing and the direct-mail program unless they have their internal advocates.

Today some companies are moving toward the concept of *coordinated marketing communications*. This concept calls for

■ Appointing a marketing communications director who has overall responsibility for the company's persuasive communications efforts
■ Working out a philosophy of the role and the extent to which the different promotional tools are to be used
■ Keeping track of all promotional expenditures by product, promotional tool, stage of product life cycle, and observed effect, as a basis for improving further use of these tools
■ Coordinating the promotional activities and their timing when major campaigns take place

Coordinated marketing communications will poduce more consistency in the company's meaning to its buyers and publics. It places a responsibility in someone's hand—where none existed before—to unify the company's image as it comes through the thousand activities the company carries on. It leads to a total marketing communication strategy aimed at showing how the company and its products can help customers solve their problems.

SUMMARY

Marketing communications is one of the four major elements of the company's marketing mix. Marketers must know how to use advertising, sales promotion, publicity, and personal selling to communicate the product's existence and value to the target customers.

The communication process itself consists of nine elements: sender, receiver, encoding, decoding, message, media, response, feedback, and noise. Marketers must know how to get through to the target audience in the face of the audience's tendencies toward selective attention, distortion, and recall.

Developing the promotion program involves eight steps. The communicator must first identify the target audience and its characteristics, including the image it carries of the product. Next the communicator has to define the communication objective, whether it is to create awareness, knowledge, liking, preference, conviction, or purchase. Then a message must be designed containing an effective content, structure, format, and source. Then communication channels—both personal and nonpersonal—must be selected. Next the total promotion budget must be established. Four common methods are the affordable method, the percentage-of-sales method, the competitive-parity method, and the objective-and-task method. The promotion budget must be divided among the main promotional tools, as affected by such factors as push-versus-pull strategy, buyer-readiness stage, and product life-cycle stage. The communicator must then monitor to see how much of the market becomes aware and tries the product and is satisfied in the process. Finally, all the communications must be managed and coordinated for consistency, good timing, and cost-effectiveness.

■ QUESTIONS

1. Discuss the factors that may prevent someone from receiving *the* message intended by the communicator. What strategies can be employed to minimize this possibility?

2. You are faced with the following problems. Recommend an appropriate strategy and give reasons for your choice.
   a. The target audience for your product has reservations about it. What personal qualities would you recommend that the spokesperson for your message possess?
   b. State which appeal strategies would be the most effective for the following products or services and why: disposable diapers, detergent, cigarettes, seat belts, United Way, and life insurance.

3. A firm can choose to establish the size of its promotion budget on the basis of an arbitrary decision rule or a strategy-informed rule. What are the merits of each? Give examples.

4. Based on your understanding of the communication process, suggest some guidelines for the effective use of visual and verbal content in the creation of both print and broadcast advertising.

5. Lite Beer commercials by Miller were the most-often noticed, remembered, and liked ads on TV. Oscar Meyer commercials ranked twelfth on the list of most-remembered commercials. Can we claim that Miller ads were considerably more successful than Oscar Meyer ads? Why or why not?

6. Apply the four major tools in the marketing communication mix to professional sports teams.

7. The major mass media—newspapers, magazines, radio, television, and outdoor media—show striking differences in their capacity for dramatization, credibility, attention getting, and other valued aspects of communication. Describe the special characteristics of each media type.

8. Develop a set of thematic guidelines that laundry detergent companies might follow in preparing detergent ads aimed at upper-class, lower-class, and lower-middle-class homemakers in the 24 to 45 age bracket.

9. What types of consumer responses should be aimed at in communication strategies for the following products: legal services, frozen pizza, veterinarian services, sewing machines, pianos, telephone-answering services, hammers?

■ FOOTNOTES

1 These definitions, except for sales promotion, are from *Marketing Definitions: A Glossary of Marketing Terms* (Chicago: American Marketing Association, 1960). The AMA definition of *sales promotion* covered, in addition to incentives, such marketing media as displays, shows and exhibitions, and demonstrations that can better be classified as forms of advertising, personal selling, or publicity.

2 Harold D. Lasswell, *Power and Personality* (New York: W. W. Norton, 1948), pp. 37–51.

3 Wilbur Schramm, "How Communication Works," in *The Process and Effects of Mass Communication*, ed. Wilbur Schramm and Donald F. Roberts (Urbana: University of Illinois Press, 1971), p. 4.

4 Ibid., p. 32.

5 See Brian Sternthal and C. Samuel Craig, *Consumer Behavior, an Information Processing Perspective* (Englewood Cliffs, N.J.: Prentice-Hall, 1982), pp. 97–102.

6 See Alice H. Eagly, "Sex Differences in Influenceability," *Psychological Bulletin*, January 1978, pp. 86–116.

7 Donald F. Cox and Raymond A. Bauer, "Self-confidence and Persuasibility in Women," *Public Opinion Quarterly*, Fall 1964, pp. 453–66; and Raymond L. Horton, "Some Relationships between Personality and Consumer Decision-Making," *Journal of Marketing Research*, May 1979, pp. 233–46.

8 Dorwin Cartwright, "Some Principles of Mass Persuasion," *Human Relations*, 2 (1949), 253–67, here 255.

9 See John Fiske and John Hartley, *Reading Television* (London: Methuen, 1980), p. 79.

10 The semantic differential was developed by C. E. Osgood, C. J. Suci, and P. H. Tannenbaum, *The Measurement of Meaning* (Urbana: University of Illinois Press, 1957).

11 See Brian Sternthal and C. Samuel Craig, "Humor in Advertising," *Journal of Marketing*, October 1973, pp. 12–18; and John Koten, "After the Serious '70's, Advertisers Are Going for Laughs Again," *Wall Street Journal*, February 23, 1984, p. 31.

12 See James F. Engel, Roger D. Blackwell, and Paul W. Minard, *Consumer Behavior*, 5th ed. (Hinsdale, Ill: Dryden Press, 1986), p. 477.

13 See C. I. Hovland, A. A. Lumsdaine, and F. D. Sheffield, *Experiments on Mass Communication* (Princeton, N.J.: Princeton University Press, 1948), Vol. III, Chap. 8. For an alternative viewpoint, see George E. Belch, "The Effects of Message Modality on One- and Two-Sided Advertising Messages," in *Advances in Consumer Research*, ed. Richard P. Bagozzi and Alice M. Tybout (Ann Arbor: Association for Consumer Research, 1983), X, 21–26.

14 See Sternthal and Craig, *Consumer Behavior*, p. 282–84.

15 See Kenneth Roman and Jane Maas, *How to Advertise* (New York: St. Martin's Press, 1976), pp. 13–28.

16 Herbert C. Kelman and Carl I. Hovland, "Reinstatement of the Communication in Delayed Measurement of Opinion Change," *Journal of Abnormal and Social Psychology*, 48 (1953), 327–35.

17 C. E. Osgood and P. H. Tannenbaum, "The Principle of Congruity in the Prediction of Attitude Change," *Psychological Review*, 62 (1955), 42–55.

18 Also see Thomas S. Robertson, *Innovative Behavior and Communication* (New York: Holt, Rinehart & Winston, 1971), Chap. 9; and Peter H. Reingen and Jerome B. Kernan, "Analysis of Referral Networks in Marketing: Methods and Illustration," *Journal of Marketing Research*, November 1986, pp. 370–78.

19 See Philip Kotler, "Atmospherics as a Marketing Tool," *Journal of Retailing*, Winter 1973–74, pp. 48–64.

20 P. F. Lazarsfeld, B. Berelson, and H. Gaudet, *The People's Choice*, 2nd ed. (New York: Columbia University Press, 1948), p. 151.

21 See George P. Moschis, "Social Comparison and Informal Group Influence," *Journal of Marketing Research*, August 1976, pp. 237–44.

22 See Everett M. Rogers, *Diffusion of Innovations*, 3rd ed. (New York: Free Press, 1983).

23 Quoted in Daniel Seligman, "How Much for Advertising?" *Fortune*, December 1956, p. 123.

24 Albert Wesley Frey, *How Many Dollars for Advertising*? (New York: Ronald Press, 1955), p. 65.

25 Ibid., p. 49.

26 G. Maxwell Ule, "A Media Plan for 'Sputnik' Cigarettes," *How to Plan Media Strategy* (American Association of Advertising Agencies, 1957 Regional Convention), pp. 41–52.

27 See Robert D. Hisrich and Michael P. Peters, *Marketing Decisions for New and Mature Products: Planning, Development, and Control* (Columbus, Ohio: Chas. E. Merrill, 1984), p. 173.

28 See Sidney J. Levy, *Promotional Behavior* (Glenview, Ill.: Scott, Foresman, 1971), Chap. 4.

29 Ibid.

30 Result of a McGraw-Hill biennial survey reported in *Marketing News*, August 1, 1986, p. 1.

31 *Statistical Abstract of the United States*, 1986.

32 *How Advertising Works in Today's Marketplace: The Morrill Study* (New York: McGraw-Hill, 1971), p. 4.

33 Cyril Freeman, "How to Evaluate Advertising's Contribution," *Harvard Business Review*, July–August 1962, pp. 137–48.

21

Designing
Effective
Advertising Programs

*If you think advertising doesn't pay—we understand there are twenty-five
mountains in Colorado higher than Pike's Peak. Can you name one?*
The American Salesman

Advertising is one of the four major tools that companies use to direct persuasive communications to target buyers and publics. It consists of *nonpersonal or one-way forms of communication conducted through paid media under clear sponsorship*. In 1984, advertising ran up a bill of over $89 billion. The advertisers included not only commercial firms but museums, fund raisers, and various social-action organizations seeking to advertise their causes to various target publics. In fact, the thirty-fourth largest advertising spender is a nonprofit organization—the U.S. government.

Within the commercial sector, the top one hundred national advertisers account for approximately one-fourth of all national advertising. Procter & Gamble is the leading spender, accounting in 1984 for $872 million, or 6.2 percent of its total sales of approximately $14 billion. The other major spenders, in order, are General Motors ($764), Sears ($747), Philip Morris ($570), K-mart ($554), and General Foods ($450) (all figures in millions). Advertising as a percentage of sales is very low in the automobile industry (1.6); moderate in soft drinks (6.5), candy (6.6), and soap (7.5); and very high in perfumes (11.5) and phonograph records (22.5).

The advertising dollars support various media: magazine and newspaper space; radio and television; outdoor displays (posters, billboards, signs, skywriting); direct mail; novelties (matchboxes, pens, calendars); tear pads (car, bus); catalogs; directories (Yellow Pages); and circulars. And advertising has many purposes: long-term buildup of the organization's corporate image (*institutional advertising*), long-term buildup of a particular brand (*brand advertising*), information dissemination about a sale, service, or event (*classified advertis-*

ing), announcement of a special sale (*sale or promotional advertising*), and advocacy of a particular cause (*advocacy advertising*).

Although advertising is primarily a private-enterprise marketing tool, it is used in all the countries of the world, including socialist countries. Advertising is a cost-effective way to disseminate messages, whether it is to build brand preference for Coca-Cola all over the world or to motivate a developing nation's consumers to drink milk or to practice birth control.

Organizations obtain their advertising in different ways. In small companies, advertising is handled by someone in the sales or marketing department, who works with an advertising agency. Large companies set up their own advertising departments, whose managers report to the vice-presidents of marketing. The advertising department's job is to develop the total budget, approve advertising agency ads and campaigns, and handle direct-mail advertising, dealer displays, and other forms of advertising not ordinarily performed by the agency. Most companies use an outside advertising agency to help them create advertising campaigns and to select and purchase media.

In developing an advertising program, marketing managers must always start by identifying the target *market* and buyer *motives*. Then they can proceed to make the five major decisions in developing an advertising program, known as the five Ms:

■ What are the advertising objectives? (*mission*)
■ How much can be spent? (*money*)
■ What message should be sent? (*message*)
■ What media should be used? (*media*)
■ How should the results be evaluated? (*measurement*)

These decisions are further described in Figure 21-1 and in the following sections.

SETTING THE ADVERTISING OBJECTIVES

The first step in developing an advertising program is to set the advertising objectives. These objectives must flow from prior decisions on the target market, market positioning, and marketing mix. The market-positioning and marketing-mix strategies define the job that advertising must do in the total marketing program.

FIGURE 21-1
Major Decisions in Advertising Management

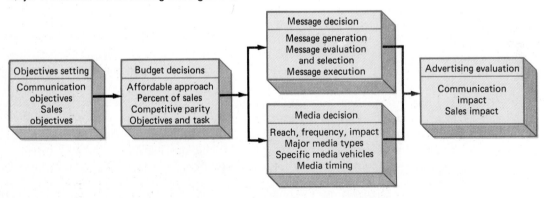

How a dirty old sneaker made living rooms livable.

When 3M first developed fluorochemicals, they did everything we expected... and a bit more. The bonus came when some spilled onto a tennis shoe and tests showed that part of the shoe just *couldn't* be easily soiled. It was the birth of "Scotchgard" Protector...the world's finest soil and stain repellent for carpet and fabrics.

It was another case of 3M people stretching their minds. Sharing technologies, probing, exploring. To make small ideas big ones, to make big ideas better.

It's an environment we encourage at 3M. To promote innovation. To make our people eager and able to respond to your needs. And it works wonders.

Let us demonstrate. Tell us of a business problem you have and watch how quickly we respond. Call Terry Baker at 800-328-3234. In Minnesota call 612-736-6772.

At 3M, one idea leads to another.

3M

This 3M ad dramatically indicates that what's good for rugs, upholsterery, and drapes—Scotchgard Fabric protector—works equally well on sneakers.   Courtesy of the 3M Company

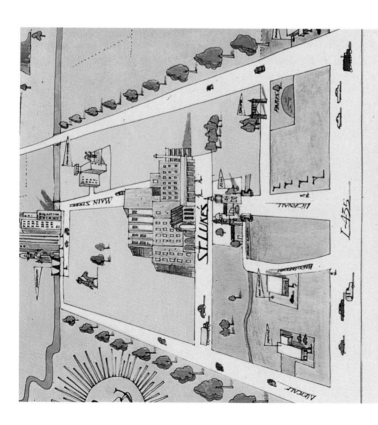

The Steelcase ad attracts attention by its brilliant colors.
Courtesy of Steelcase Inc.

This ad manages to position St. Luke's as a large and centrally located hospital in Kansas City and cleverly plays on such medical terms as "heart," "arteries," and "pulse" to suggest its services.
Courtesy of John Leifer Ltd. and St. Lukes Hospital, Kansas City

Private transportation the public can afford.

This Hyundai ad suggests to noncar owners that they really can afford a car . . . that the new Hyundai offers them private transportation at little more cost than public transportation.

Courtesy of Hyundai Motor America

This Virginia Slims ad suggests that cigarette smoking by women is a measure of their liberation.

Courtesy of Philip Morris, Inc.

As Elegant As a Swan.

A Unique Breed of Watch.

NOBILIA
CITIZEN

What trait distinguishes the Nobilia solid series? Could it be the supple bracelet? Perhaps the dazzling dials—in black and gold. Or maybe just the gentle bends that complete the effect. Whatever it is, you can be sure each watch is remarkably thin. And exceptionally accurate. Watch shown priced at $425.

This ad takes an ordinary watch and puts it into a dramatic context that borrows on the graceful qualities of a swan. Courtesy of Citizen Watch Co. of America, Inc. From the concept in the book Hanimals by Mario Mariotti. © by Fatatrac S.p.A., 1982

ADVERTISING MAKES THINGS COST MORE, RIGHT?

DRINKS 5¢ 3¢

DRINKS 5¢ 4¢

We admit it. Advertising has a tremendous impact on prices. But you may be surprised by what *kind* of impact.

In addition to being informative, educational and sometimes entertaining, advertising can actually lower prices.

It works like this: Advertising spurs competition which holds down prices. And since advertising also creates a mass market for products, it can bring down the cost of producing each product, a savings that can be passed on to consumers.

Moreover, competition created by advertising provides an incentive for manufacturers to produce new and better products.

Which means advertising can not only reduce prices, but it can also help you avoid lemons.

ADVERTISING
ANOTHER WORD FOR FREEDOM OF CHOICE.
American Association of Advertising Agencies

This ad aims to convince readers that the advertising industry actually lowers prices, using two appealing lemonade stand competitors to illustrate its point. Courtesy of American Association of Advertising Agencies

THE MERCEDES-BENZ OF TRUCKS

The competitive price of these diesel trucks will surprise you — but what won't surprise you is the same brilliant engineering as the world's most esteemed automobiles.

What other truck so articulates your pride in your business? Whatever your operation, whatever its size, there's a Mercedes-Benz built for your every in- and around-town trucking need. These are medium-duty trucks that earn their prestige by hard work and solid savings. That are assembled in America. Sold nationwide. Supported with parts and service like no other. Backed, as you expect, with the best warranty in their class.

To learn what makes these trucks so worthy of a name you've come to trust, call today for the name of your local Mercedes-Benz Truck Dealer.

1-800-367-2580
(In WA, call 1-800-537-3760)

MERCEDES-BENZ TRUCKS

This ad cleverly tells us that "Mercedes-Benz" of trucks is none other than . . . Mercedes Benz trucks.
Courtesy of Mercedes-Benz Truck Company, Inc.

Which copier fits best in your office?

Out there somewhere, hidden among the dozens of different copiers available today, is one that fits with the needs of your office.

And if it's your job to find it, we'd like to suggest that you begin your search at your Ricoh dealership.

You'll discover that Ricoh copiers come in all sizes and shapes, and offer a wide range of impressive capabilities. They also bring you some of the industry's brightest and most reliable technology. And best of all, they're incredibly friendly to the people who use them.

Innovations that make work easier and the office more efficient are abundant in Ricoh's world of copiers and other advanced office products.

That's why today, with so many copiers to choose from, it makes sense to consider Ricoh.

Because when it comes to performance, value and reliability, Ricoh copiers put it all together.

THE FRIENDLIEST NAME IN OFFICE AUTOMATION.

RICOH

COPIERS · FACSIMILE · PRINTERS · COPYBOARDS · CAMERAS
RICOH COMPANY, LTD., 15-5, Minami-Aoyama 1-chome, Minato-ku, Tokyo 107, Japan
RICOH CORPORATION, 5 Dedrick Place, West Caldwell, New Jersey 07006, U.S.A.
Phone 1-201-882-2000

This Ricoh ad uses the image of a company puzzle whose missing piece can be exactly filled in by a Ricoh copier. The ad makes many claims for Ricoh copiers, leaving the reader to determine which feature is most desirable. *Courtesy of the Ricoh Corporation*

The costliest perfume in the world.

This ad positions Joy as the costliest perfume—and by implication, the best perfume—in the world.
Courtesy of Jean Patou, Inc.

Ever wonder if the same people twisting your arm are also pulling your leg?

Whether out of pride, prejudice or desperation, everybody tells you their place is the place for you to locate your business.

But if you want to make an informed decision, you don't need the same old story. You need timely, meaningful information, intelligently prepared and presented.

That's the Maryland approach. We offer business more than you can imagine. So we can make a strong case for the Maryland move, with no arm-twisting or leg-pulling.

Just eye-opening facts.

To see if Maryland belongs on your list, contact Michael Lofton, Department of Economic and Community Development, Department 158, 45 Calvert Street, Annapolis, Maryland 21401. (301) 974-3514.

Maryland
More than you can imagine.

This ad attempts to position Maryland as having more to offer than any other state to businesses seeking new locations.
Courtesy of Maryland Department of Economic and Community Development

This New Balance ad uses long technical copy to imply that its running shoes are the best designed shoes in the world.

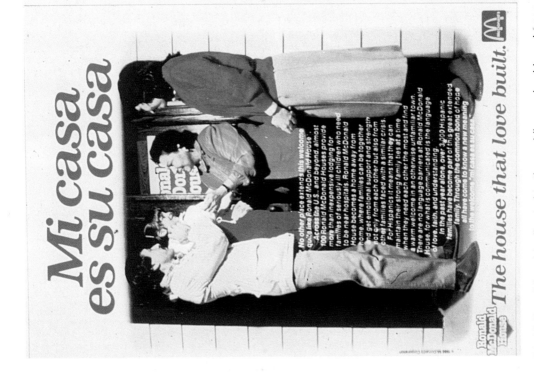

This McDonald's ad is directed to the rapidly growing hispanic population to convey that McDonald's is devoted to community service. Courtesy of McDonald's Corporation

Many specific communication and sales objectives can be assigned to advertising. Colley lists fifty-two possible advertising objectives in his well-known *Defining Advertising Goals for Measured Advertising Results.*[1] He outlines a method called DAGMAR (after the book's title) for turning advertising objectives into specific measurable goals. An *advertising goal* is a specific communication task and achievement level to be accomplished with a specific audience in a specific period of time. Colley provides an example:

> To increase among 30 million homemakers who own automatic washers the number who identify brand X as a low-sudsing detergent and who are persuaded that it gets clothes cleaner—from 10 percent to 40 percent in one year.

Note the four goal elements:

- **Target**: 30 million homemakers who own automatic washers
- **Communication objective**: the ability to identify brand X as a low-sudsing detergent and be persuaded that it gets clothes cleaner
- **Desired change**: from 10 to 40 percent
- **Time horizon**: one year

Advertising objectives can be classified as to whether their aim is to inform, persuade, or remind. Table 21-1 lists examples of these objectives.

Informative advertising figures heavily in the pioneering stage of a product category, where the objective is to build *primary demand*. Thus the yogurt industry initially had to inform consumers of yogurt's nutritional benefits and many uses.

Persuasive advertising becomes important in the competitive stage, where a company's objective is to build *selective demand* for a particular brand. Most of the advertising we view falls into this category. For example, Chivas Regal attempts to persuade consumers that it delivers status like no other brand of scotch. Some persuasive advertising has moved into the category of *comparison advertising*, which seeks to establish the superiority of one brand through specific comparison with one or more other brands in the product class.[2] Comparison advertising had been used in such product categories as deodorants, fast-food hamburgers, toothpastes, tires, and automobiles. The Burger King Corporation successfully

TABLE 21-1   Possible Advertising Objectives

To inform:	
Telling the market about a new product	Describing available services
Suggesting new uses for a product	Correcting false impressions
Informing the market of a price change	Reducing consumers' fears
Explaining how the product works	Building a company image
To persuade:	
Building brand preference	Persuading customer to purchase now
Encouraging switching to your brand	Persuading customer to receive a sales call
Changing customer's perception of product attributes	
To remind:	
Reminding consumers that the product may be needed in the near future	Keeping it in their minds during off seasons
Reminding them where to buy it	Maintaining its top-of-mind awareness

developed comparison advertising for its franchise when it battled McDonald's in a burger war over flame broiling versus frying hamburgers. Exhibit 21-1 describes some guidelines for creating successful comparison advertising.

EXHIBIT 21-1

Guidelines for Comparison Advertising

1. Identify but never disparage the brand leader.
2. The goal is primarily to gain increased attention from users of competitive brands or from those who regard a competitor as a quality standard.
3. Other brands can be named when your brand has a distinct advantage and when it takes time for others to counterattack.
4. Great care must be taken to avoid being misinterpreted as promoting the brand against which comparison is being made.
5. Comparisons are not helpful when a competitor could counterattack in an area where its brand is clearly superior on an important attribute.
6. Every effort must be made to leave the impression that the named competitor has not been deceiving the consumer.
7. The consumer must be able to verify the comparison and prove it to his or her satisfaction.

SOURCE Stanley J. Tannenbaum, *Comparative Advertising: The Advertising Industry's Own Brand of Consumerism* (Paper given at the 1976 annual meeting of the American Association of Advertising Agencies).

Reminder advertising is highly important in the mature stage of the product to keep the consumer thinking about the product. Expensive four-color Coca-Cola ads in magazines have the purpose not of informing or persuading but of reminding people to purchase Coca-Cola. A related form of advertising is *reinforcement advertising*, which seeks to assure current purchasers that they have made the right choice. Automobile ads will often depict satisfied customers enjoying some special feature of their new car.

The choice of the advertising objective should not be arbitrary but should be based on a thorough analysis of the current marketing situation. For example, if the product class is mature, and the company is the market leader, and if brand usage is low, the proper objective may be to stimulate more brand usage. On the other hand, if the product class is new, and the company is not the market leader, but its brand is superior to the leader, then the proper objective is to advertise the brand's superiority over the market leader.

DECIDING ON THE ADVERTISING BUDGET

After determining advertising objectives, the company can proceed to establish its advertising budget for each product. The role of advertising is to shift the product's demand curve upward. The company wants to spend the amount required to achieve the sales goal. But how does a company know if it is spending the right amount? If the company spends too little, the effect is insignificant and the company is, paradoxically, spending too much.

On the other hand, if the company spends too much on advertising, then some of the money could have been put to better use. Some critics charge that large consumer packaged goods firms tend to overspend on advertising, and industrial companies generally underspend on advertising:[3]

> Large consumer packaged goods companies use image advertising extensively and are uncertain about its effect, since it doesn't produce immediate sales. They overspend as a form of ''insurance'' against not spending enough. In addition, their advertising agency has a vested interest in convincing the company to put most of its promotional funds into advertising. Finally, the company gets low efficiency out of its dollars by doing too little front-end work (marketing research and strategic positioning) and too much back-end work (copy testing).

> Industrial companies rely heavily on their sales force to bring in orders. They do not spend enough on advertising to build customer awareness and comprehension. They underestimate the power of company-and-product image in preselling industrial customers.

A possible counterargument to the charge that consumer packaged goods companies spend too much is that advertising has a carryover effect that lasts beyond the current period. Although advertising is treated as a current expense, part of it is really an investment that builds up an intangible value called goodwill.

> A piece of capital equipment is treated as a depreciable asset, say over five years. If it weren't, the company might hesitate to buy it because it would require reporting a large loss in the first year. But when $5 million is spent on advertising to launch a new product, it must all be written off in the first year. But even if financial accounting principles do not allow treating part of advertising as an investment, the company should treat it as such in making managerial marketing decisions.

Four commonly used methods for setting the advertising budget were described earlier in Chapter 20, pages 604–06. We favored the *objective-and-task method* because it requires the advertiser to define the advertising campaign's specific objectives and then to estimate the costs of the activities needed to achieve these objectives. Here we will describe some specific factors that should be considered when setting the advertising budget:[4]

- ■ *Stage in the product life cycle.* New products typically receive large advertising budgets to build awareness and to gain consumer trial. Established brands usually are supported with lower budgets as a ratio to sales.
- ■ *Market share and consumer base.* High-market-share brands usually require less advertising expenditures as a percentage of sales to simply maintain their share. To build share by increasing the market or to take share from competitors requires larger advertising expenditures. Additionally, on a cost-per-impression basis, it is less expensive to reach consumers of a widely used brand than to reach consumers of low-share brands.
- ■ *Competition and clutter.* In a market with a large number of competitors and high advertising spending, a brand must advertise more heavily to be heard above the noise in the market. Even simple clutter in the market from advertisements not directly competitive to the brand creates a need for heavier advertising.
- ■ *Advertising frequency.* The number of repetitions needed to put across the brand's message to consumers also determines the advertising budget.
- ■ *Product substitutability.* Brands in a commodity class (e.g., cigarettes, beer, soft drinks) require heavy advertising to establish a differential image. Advertising is also important when a brand offers unique physical benefits or features.

Marketing scientists have built a number of advertising expenditure models that take into account these and other factors that bear on setting the advertising budget. One of the best early models was developed by Vidale and Wolfe.[5] Essentially the model called for a larger advertising budget, the higher the sales-response rate, the higher the sales-decay rate (i.e., the rate at which customers forget the advertising and brand), and the higher the untapped sales potential. On the other hand, this model leaves out other important factors, such as the rate of competitive advertising and the effectiveness of the company's ads.

John Little proposed an adaptive-control method for setting the advertising budget.[6] Suppose the company has set its advertising expenditure rate for the coming period based on its most current information on the sales-response function. It spends this rate in all markets except in a subset of $2n$ markets randomly drawn. In n of the test markets the company spends at a lower rate, and in the other n it spends at a higher rate. This will yield information on the average sales created by low, medium, and high rates of advertising that can be used to update the parameters of the sales-response function. The updated function is used to determine the best advertising expenditure rate for the next period. If this side experiment is conducted each period, advertising expenditures will closely track optimal advertising expenditures.[7]

DECIDING ON THE MESSAGE

Many studies of the sales effect of advertising expenditures neglect the message creativity factor. Some analysts argue that all large advertising agencies are equally creative, and therefore differences in individual campaigns "wash out." But it is precisely the differences in individual campaigns that advertisers seek. As William Bernbach observed: "The facts are not enough . . . don't forget that Shakespeare used some pretty hackneyed plots, yet his message came through with great execution." Consider the following:[8]

McDonald's spent $185.9 million on television in 1983, over twice the spending rate of its rival, Burger King. Yet viewers said they remembered Burger King ads better and preferred them to McDonald's.

The best-known and best-liked advertising on TV in 1983 was Miller Lite beer commercials showing sports figures and celebrities arguing over whether Miller's advantage was "great taste" or "less filling." This campaign outperformed all the other beer commercials even though several spent more money.

By leaving out the creative factor, a substantial part of market-share differences are unexplained. One study found that the effect of the creativity factor in a campaign is more important than the number of dollars spent. Only after gaining attention can a commercial help to increase the brand's sales.[9] Differences and variety in creative strategy are undoubtedly very important in advertising success.

Advertisers go through the following steps to develop a creative strategy: message generation, message evaluation and selection, and message execution.

Message Generation
In principle, the product's message (theme, appeal) should have been decided as part of developing the product concept; it expresses the major benefit that the brand offers. Yet even within this concept, there may be latitude for a number of possible messages. And over time, the marketer may want to change the message without even changing the product, especially if consumers are seeking new "benefits" from the product.

Creative people use several methods to generate possible advertising appeals. Many creative people proceed *inductively* by talking to consumers, dealers, experts, and competitors. Consumers are the major source of good ideas. Their feelings about the strengths and shortcomings of existing brands provide important clues to creative strategy. Leo Burnett advocates "in-depth interviewing where I come realistically face-to-face with the people I am trying to sell. I try to get a picture in my mind of the kind of people they are—how they use this product and what it is."[10] A leading hair-spray company carries out continuous consumer research to determine consumer satisfaction with existing brands. If consumers want stronger holding power, the company considers reformulating its product and using this new appeal.

Some creative people use a *deductive* framework for generating advertising messages. Maloney proposed one framework. (See Table 21-2.)[11] He saw buyers as expecting one of four types of reward from a product: *rational*, *sensory*, *social*, or *ego satisfaction*. And buyers may visualize these rewards from *results-of-use experience*, *product-in-use experience*, or *incidental-to-use experience*. Crossing the four types of reward with the three types of experience generates twelve types of advertising messages.

The advertiser can generate a theme for each of the twelve cells as possible messages for the product. For example, the appeal "get clothes cleaner" is a rational-reward promise following results-of-use experience; and the phrase "real gusto in a great light beer" is a sensory-reward promise connected with product-in-use experience.

How many possible ad themes should the advertiser create before making a choice? The more ads created, the higher the probability that the agency will develop a first-rate appeal. Yet the more time it spends creating ads, the higher the costs. There must be some optimal number of alternative ads that an agency should create and test for the client. Under the present commission system, typically 15 percent, the agency does not like to go to the expense of creating and pretesting many ads. In an ingenious study, Gross concluded that agencies generally create too few advertisement alternatives for their clients.[12] Gross estimates that advertising agencies spend from 3 to 5 percent of their media income on creating and testing advertising, whereas he estimates they should spend closer to 15 percent. He thinks agencies should devote a larger part of their budgets to finding the best ad and somewhat less to buying media. He even proposed that a company

TABLE 21-2

Examples of Twelve Types of Appeals

Types of Potentially Rewarding Experience with a Product	Potential Type of Reward			
	Rational	Sensory	Social	Ego Satisfaction
Results-of-Use Experience	1. Get clothes cleaner	2. Settles stomach upset completely	3. When you care enough to serve the best	4. For the skin you deserve to have
Product-in-Use Experience	5. The flour that needs no sifting	6. Real gusto in a great light beer	7. A deodorant to guarantee social acceptance	8. The shoe for the young executive
Incidental-to-Use Experience	9. The plastic pack keeps the cigarette fresh	10. The portable television that's lighter in weight, easier to lift	11. The furniture that identifies the home of modern people	12. Stereo for the man with discriminating taste

SOURCE: Adapted from John C. Maloney, "Marketing Decisions and Attitude Research," in *Effective Marketing Coordination*, ed. George L. Baker, Jr. (Chicago: American Marketing Association, 1961) pp. 595–618.

should hire advertising agencies to create advertisements, from which the best one would be selected.

Message Evaluation and Selection

The advertiser needs to evaluate the possible messages. A good advertisement normally focuses on one central selling proposition without trying to give too much product information, which dilutes the ad's impact. Twedt suggested that messages be rated on *desirability*, *exclusiveness*, and *believability*.[13] The message must first say something desirable or interesting about the product. The message must also say something exclusive or distinctive that does not apply to every brand in the product category. Finally, the message must be believable or provable.

For example, the March of Dimes searched for an advertising theme to raise money for its fight against birth defects.[14] Several messages came out of a brainstorming session. A group of young parents were asked to rate each message for interest, distinctiveness, and believability, assigning up to 100 points for each. (See Figure 21-2.) For example, "Five hundred thousand unborn babies die each year from birth defects" scored 70, 60, and 80 on interest, distinctiveness, and believability, while "Your next baby could be born with a birth defect" scored 58, 50, and 70. The first message outperformed the second and was preferred for advertising purposes.

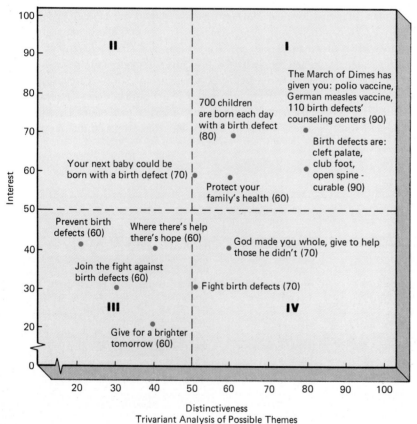

FIGURE 21-2
Advertising Message Evaluation
SOURCE: William A. Mindak and H. Malcolm Bybee, "Marketing's Application to Fund Raising, *Journal of Marketing*, July 1971, pp. 13–18.

Trivariant Analysis of Possible Themes

For pretesting to produce an accurate assessment of consumer opinion and purchase choice, a ''normal'' research setting should be created. A normal setting would possess these characteristics:[15]

1. Those individuals participating in the test are representative of the audience or market for the product.
2. The attention given to the advertisements tested is equivalent to regular advertising. The mere existence of the research can cause the respondents to pay more attention to the commercials.
3. The context of the test commercials is the same as the regular advertising. This implies use of the same medium, with the same form (color, content, and finish).

The advertiser should pretest with the hope of determining which appeal has the strongest behavioral impact. For example, the Washington State Apple Commission was trying to decide which advertising theme appealed more to housewives: One stressed the various *uses* of apples; the other stressed the *healthful* qualities of apples.[16] An experiment was conducted in seventy-two self-service food stores in six midwestern cities for sixteen weeks. The results showed that the apple-use theme significantly outperformed the other theme in promoting sales.

Message Execution
The message's impact depends not only on what is said but also on how it is said. The choice of headlines, words, and so on, can make a difference in the ad's impact (see Exhibit 21-2). Message execution can be decisive for those products that are highly similar, such as detergents, cigarettes, coffee, and beer. Execution is also gaining in importance for some industrial products that are becoming increasingly undifferentiated, such as pharmaceuticals in certain mature categories (antibiotics, etc.). Companies like Pfizer have launched aggressive campaigns designed to promote product image as well as quality. As Ogilvy and Mather, a major advertising agency, advocates, ''Every advertisement and commercial should contribute to the complex symbol which is the brand image.''

EXHIBIT 21-2

Relative Performance of Two Message Executions

Lalita Manrai created two proposed ads to test the effectiveness of different dimensions of an ad. The first ad carries the headline "A New Car," whereas the second asks, "Is This Car for You?" The second headline illustrates an advertising strategy called "labeling" in which the message recipient is labeled as the type of person who is interested in that type of product. Labeling is based on the belief that motivating the readers to associate message information with information about themselves creates a self-reference effect, which in turn enhances the persuasiveness of the communication.

The accompanying two ads also differ in that the copy in the first ad describes the car's features, whereas the second describes the car's benefits. Normally a reader should be more persuaded by an ad describing benefits rather than features.

In the test, the second ad far outperformed the first ad in terms of overall impression of the product, reader interest in buying the product, and likelihood of recommendation to a friend.

A NEW CAR.

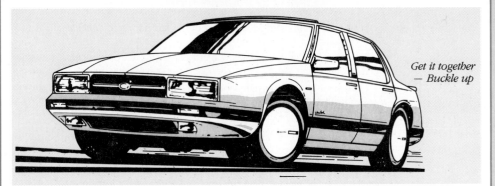

*Get it together
— Buckle up*

The new "CHEETAH" is made with extra thick galvanized steel – molded with careful attention to detail and extensively tested to ensure weather-proofing. This four door car comes equipped with newly designed shockabsorbers, a fuel efficient rotary engine and is fun to drive. You won't feel like selling it after a few years, but even if you did, its quality construction ensures that it will be a good used car. The car is easy to handle and stop. Accessories like air conditioning, stereo and contoured seats are standard – all this within a very reasonable sticker price. CHEETAH would be offered in a wide range of colors and finishes. It easily accomodates five people and we are backing it up with a 3 year warranty for major engine components.

IS THIS CAR FOR YOU?

**Decide for yourself to what extent the design of the car matches your needs
and to what extent it fits your lifestyle.**

*Get it together
— Buckle up*

The new "CHEETAH" is constructed to have a long body life – molded with careful attention to detail and eliminating any worries you may have about body defects and rust. You will find it very easy to get in and out of this car that is smooth to ride, gives an above average gas mileage and comes equipped with a sun roof. You won't feel like selling it after a few years but even if you did, you will get a very good resale value. The car has power brakes and standard accessories meant for luxury and relaxation – all this within a very reasonable sticker price. CHEETAH's many options also accomodate your preferences and tastes in styling. It is ideal for a family and if any major engine components need replacement within 3 years, we will bear the cost.

SOURCE Lalita Manrai, Ph.D. dissertation, "Effect of Labeling Strategy in Advertising: Self-Referencing versus Psychological-Reactance," (Northwestern University, 1987). Used with permission.

The advertiser usually prepares a *copy strategy statement* describing the objective, content, support, and tone of the desired ad. Here is the strategy statement for a Pillsbury product called 1869 Brand Biscuits:

> The *objective* of the advertising is to convince biscuit users that now they can buy a canned biscuit that's as good as homemade—Pillsbury's 1869 Brand Biscuits. The *content* consists of emphasizing the following product characteristics: they look like homemade biscuits; they have the same texture as homemade biscuits; and they taste like homemade biscuits. *Support* for the "good as homemade" promise will be twofold: (1) 1869 Brand Biscuits are made from a special kind of flour (soft wheat flour) used to make homemade biscuits but never before used in making canned biscuits, and (2) the use of traditional American biscuit recipes. The *tone* of the advertising will be a news announcement, tempered by a warm, reflective mood emanating from a look back at traditional American baking quality.

Creative people must now find a *style*, *tone*, *words*, and *format* for executing the message. All of these must work together and deliver a cohesive image and message. Since few people read body copy, the headline and graphic must summarize the selling proposition.

Any message can be presented in such different *execution styles* as the following:

- **Slice-of-life.** This shows one or more persons using the product in a normal setting. A family seated at the dinner table might express satisfaction with a new biscuit brand.
- **Lifestyle.** This emphasizes how a product fits in with a lifestyle. A Scotch ad shows a handsome middle-aged man holding a glass of Scotch in one hand and steering his yacht with the other.
- **Fantasy.** This creates a fantasy around the product or its use. Revlon's ad for Jontue features a barefoot woman wearing a chiffon dress. She comes out of an old French barn, crosses a meadow, and confronts a handsome young man on a white steed, who carries her away.
- **Mood or image.** This builds an evocative mood or image around the product, such as beauty, love, or serenity. No claim is made about the product except through suggestion. Many cigarette ads, such as those for Salem and Newport cigarettes, create moods.
- **Musical.** This uses background music or shows one or more persons or cartoon characters singing a song involving the product. Many cola ads have used this format.
- **Personality symbol.** This creates a character that personifies the product. The character might be *animated* (Jolly Green Giant, Pillsbury Doughboy, Mr. Clean) or *real* (Marlboro man, Morris the Cat.)
- **Technical expertise.** This shows the company's expertise and experience in making the product. Thus Hills Brothers shows one of its buyers carefully selecting the coffee beans, and Italian Swiss Colony emphasizes its many years of experience in winemaking.
- **Scientific evidence.** This presents survey or scientific evidence that the brand is preferred to or outperforms one or more other brands. For years Crest toothpaste has featured scientific evidence to convince toothpaste buyers of Crest's superior anticavity-fighting properties.
- **Testimonial evidence.** This features a highly credible, likable, or empathetic source endorsing the product. It could be a celebrity like O. J. Simpson (Hertz Rent-a-Car) or ordinary people saying how much they like the product.

The communicator must also choose an appropriate *tone* for the ad. Procter & Gamble is consistently positive in its tone; its ads say something superlatively positive about the product. Humor is avoided so as not to take attention away from the message. On the other hand, Volkswagen's ads for its famous "Beetle" typically took on a humorous and self-deprecating tone ("the Ugly Bug").

Memorable and attention-getting *words* must be found. The themes listed below on the left would have had much less impact without the creative phrasing on the right:[17]

THEME	CREATIVE COPY
7-Up is not a cola.	*"The Un-Cola"*
Let us drive you in our bus instead of driving your car.	*"Take the bus, leave the driving to us."*
Shop by turning the pages of the telephone directory.	*"Let your fingers do the walking."*
If you drink a beer, Schaefer is a good beer to drink.	*"The beer to have when you're having more than one."*
We don't rent as many cars, so we have to do more for our customers.	*"We try harder."*
Red Roof Inns offer inexpensive lodging.	*"Sleep cheap at Red Roof Inns."*

Creativity is especially required for headlines. There are six basic types of headlines: *news* ("New Boom and More Inflation Ahead . . . and What You Can Do About It"); *question* ("Have You Had It Lately?"); *narrative* ("They Laughed When I Sat Down at the Piano, but When I Started to Play!"); *command* ("Don't Buy Until You Try All Three"); 1-2-3 *ways* ("12 Ways to Save on Your Income Tax"); and *how-what-why* ("Why They Can't Stop Buying"). Look at the care exercised by airlines to find the right way to describe their planes as safe without mentioning safety: "The Friendly Skies of United" (United); "The Wings of Man" (Eastern); and "The World's Most Experienced Airline" (Pan American).

Format elements such as ad size, color, and illustration will make a difference in an ad's impact as well as its cost. A minor rearrangement of mechanical elements within the ad can improve its consumer attention-gaining power. Larger-size ads gain more attention though not necessarily by as much as their difference in cost. Four-color illustrations instead of black and white increase ad effectiveness and ad cost. By planning the relative dominance of different elements of the advertisement, optimal delivery can be achieved. New electronic eye-movement studies show that consumers can be led through an ad by strategic placement of the ad's dominant elements.

A number of researchers into print advertisements report that the *picture*, *headline*, and *copy* are important, in that order. The picture is the first thing the reader notices, and it must be strong enough to draw attention. Then the headline must be effective in propelling the person to read the copy. The copy itself must be well composed. Even then, a really outstanding ad will be noted by less than 50 percent of the exposed audience; about 30 percent of the exposed audience might recall the main point of the headline; about 25 percent might remember the advertiser's name; and less than 10 percent will have read most of the body copy. Ordinary ads, unfortunately, would not even achieve these results.

In 1982, an industry study about television and print advertising's ability to change brand preference listed the following characteristics for ads that scored above average in recall and recognition: innovation (new product or new uses), "story appeal" (as an attention-getting device), before-and-after illustration, demonstrations, problem solution, and the inclusion of relevant characters that become emblematic of the brand (these may be cartoon figures such as the Jolly Green Giant or actual people, who may or may not be celebrities).[18]

DECIDING ON THE MEDIA

The advertiser's next task is to choose advertising media to carry the advertising message. The steps are deciding on desired reach, frequency, and impact; choosing among major media types; selecting specific media vehicles; and deciding on media timing.

Deciding on Reach, Frequency, and Impact

Media selection is the *problem of finding the most cost-effective media to deliver the desired number of exposures to the target audience.* But what do we mean by the desired number of exposures? Presumably the advertiser is seeking a certain response from the target audience, for example, a certain level of *product trial.* Now the rate of product trial will depend, among other things, on the level of audience brand awareness. Suppose the rate of product trial increases at a diminishing rate with the level of audience awareness, as shown in Figure 21-3(a). If the advertiser seeks a product trial rate of (say) T^*, it will be necessary to achieve a brand awareness level of A^*.

The next task is to find out how many exposures, E^*, will produce a level of audience awareness of A^*. The effect of exposures on audience awareness depends on the exposures' reach, frequency, and impact:

- **Reach (R).** The number of different persons or households exposed to a particular media schedule at least once during a specified time period.
- **Frequency (F).** The number of times within the specified time period that an average person or household is exposed to the message.
- **Impact (I).** The qualitative value of an exposure through a given medium (thus a food ad in *Good Housekeeping* would have a higher impact than in the *Police Gazette*).

Figure 21-3(b) shows the relationship between audience awareness and reach. Audience awareness will be greater, the higher the exposures' reach, frequency, and impact. The media planner recognizes important trade-offs between reach, frequency, and impact. Suppose the media planner has an advertising budget of $1,000,000 and the cost per thousand exposures of average quality is $5. This means that the advertiser can buy 200,-000,000 exposures (= $1,000,000 ÷ $5/1,000). If the advertiser seeks an average exposure frequency of 10, then the advertiser can reach 20,000,000 people (= 200,000,000 ÷ 10)

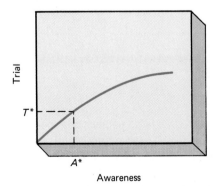

T^*

Trial

A^*

Awareness

(a) Relationship between product trial rate and audience awareness level

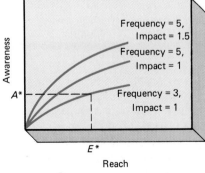

Frequency = 5, Impact = 1.5

Frequency = 5, Impact = 1

Awareness

A^*

Frequency = 3, Impact = 1

E^*

Reach

(b) Relationship between audience awareness level and exposure reach and frequency

FIGURE 21-3
Relationship between Trial, Awareness, and the Exposure Function

with the given budget. Now if the advertiser wants higher-quality media costing $10 per thousand exposures, the advertiser will be able to reach only 10,000,000 people unless it is willing to lower the desired exposure frequency.

The relationship between reach, frequency, and impact is captured in the following concepts:

■ ***Total number of exposures (E).*** This is the reach times the average frequency, that is, $E = R \times F$. This measure is referred to as the *gross rating points* (GRP). If a given media schedule reaches 80 percent of the homes with an average exoposure frequency of 3, the media schedule is said to have a GRP of 240 (= 80 × 3). If another media schedule has a GRP of 300, it is said to have more weight, but we cannot tell how this weight breaks up into reach and frequency.

■ ***Weighted number of exposures (WE).*** This is the reach times average frequency times average impact, that is, $WE = R \times F \times I$.

The media planning trade-off is as follows. With a given budget, what is the most cost-effective combination of reach, frequency, and impact? Reach is most important for achieving initial awareness of a new product, while frequency is more important for a complex product or for creating a brand image. Exhibit 21-3 details the situations where reach and frequency are most appropriate. Suppose the media planner is willing to use average-impact media. This leaves the tasks of deciding how many people to reach with what frequency. It would make sense to settle the issue of frequency first. How many exposures does an average member of the target audience need for the advertising to initiate behavior? Once this target frequency is decided, then reach will be determined.

EXHIBIT 21-3

Reach or Frequency?

REACH SITUATIONS	FREQUENCY SITUATIONS
New products	Strong competitors
Expanding category	Complex story
Flanker brand	Frequently purchased category
Strong brand franchise	Weak loyalty to brand
Undefined target market	Narrow target market
Infrequent purchase cycle	Consumer resistance to brand or category

SOURCE Adapted from Don E. Schultz, Dennis Martin, and William P. Brown, *Strategic Advertising Campaigns* (Chicago: National Textbook Company, 1984) p. 340.

Many advertisers believe that the target audience needs a large number of exposures for the advertising to work. Too few repetitions may be a waste, according to Lucas and Britt: "It can be reasoned that introductory advertisements make too weak an impression to initiate much interest in buying. Succeeding advertisements may sometimes be more effective by building up already established weak impressions to the action level."[19] Heavy introductory advertising may increase reach and frequency to the point that the impact may be sustained simply with maintenance-level advertising spending. Other advertising researchers doubt the value of multiple exposures. They feel that after people see the same ad a few times, they either act on it, get irritated by it, or stop noticing it. Krugman has made the case that three exposures to an advertisement may be enough:

> The first exposure is by definition unique. As with the initial exposure to anything, a "What is it?" type of cognitive response dominates the reaction. The second exposure to a stimulus . . . produces several effects. One may be the cognitive reaction that characterized the first exposure, if the audience missed much of the message the first time around. . . . More often, an evaluative "What of it?" response replaces the "What is it?" response. . . . The third exposure constitutes a reminder, if a decision to buy based on the evaluations has not been acted on. The third exposure is also the beginning of disengagement and withdrawal of attention from a completed episode.[20]

Krugman's thesis favoring three exposures has to be qualified. He means actual *advertising exposures*—i.e., the person seeing the actual ad three times. This should not be confused with *vehicle exposures*, namely, the number of times the person has been exposed to the vehicle carrying the ad. If only half the readers look at magazine ads, or if the readers only look at ads in every other issue, then the advertising exposure is only half of the vehicle exposures. Most research services only estimate vehicle exposures, not ad exposures. A media strategist would have to buy more vehicle exposures than three in order to achieve Krugman's three "hits."[21]

Another factor arguing for some advertising repetition is that of forgetting. The job of advertising repetition is partly to put the message back into memory. The higher the forgetting rate associated with that brand, product category, or message, the higher the warranted level of repetition.

Choosing Among Major Media Types

The media planner has to know the capacity of the major media types to deliver reach, frequency, and impact. The major advertising media are profiled in Table 21-3. The major media types, in order of their advertising volume, are *newspapers*, *television*, *direct mail*, *radio*, *magazines*, and *outdoor*. Each medium has certain advantages and limitations. Media planners make their choice among these media categories by considering several variables, the most important ones being the following:

- ▪ *Target-audience media habits.* For example, radio and television are the most effective media for reaching teenagers.
- ▪ *Product.* Women's dresses are best shown in color magazines, and Polaroid cameras are best demonstrated on television. Media types have different potentials for demonstration, visualization, explanation, believability, and color.
- ▪ *Message.* A message announcing a major sale tomorrow will require radio or newspapers. A message containing a great deal of technical data might require specialized magazines or mailings.
- ▪ *Cost.* Television is very expensive, whereas newspaper advertising is inexpensive. What counts, of course, is the cost-per-thousand exposures rather than the total cost.

Ideas about media impact and cost must be reexamined regularly. For a long time, television enjoyed the dominant position in the media mix, and other media were neglected. Then media researchers began to notice television's reduced effectiveness due to increased *commercial clutter*. Advertisers beamed shorter and more numerous commercials at the television audience, resulting in poorer audience attention and impact. Network television began losing audience to other media such as cable TV and videorecorders. Furthermore, television

TABLE 21-3
Profiles of Major Media Types

Medium	Volume in Billions (1986)	Percentage (1986)	Example of Cost (1986)	Advantages	Limitations
Newspapers	$25.2	29.0%	$27,099 one page, weekday Chicago Tribune	Flexibility; timeliness; good local market coverage; broad acceptance; high believability	Short life; poor reproduction quality; small "pass-along" audience
Television	19.7	22.6	$5,000 for thirty seconds of prime time in Chicago	Combines sight, sound, and motion; appealing to the senses; high attention; high reach	High absolute cost; high clutter; fleeting exposure; less audience selectivity
Direct mail	13.8	15.9	$1,190 for the names and addresses of 34,000 veterinarians	Audience selectivity; flexibility; no ad competition within the same medium; personalization	Relatively high cost; "junk mail" image
Radio	5.8	6.7	$650 for one minute of prime time in Chicago	Mass use; high geographic and demographic selectivity; low cost	Audio presentation only; lower attention than television; nonstandardized rate structures; fleeting exposure
Magazines	4.9	5.6	$84,000 one page, four-color in *Newsweek*	High geographic and demographic selectivity; credibility and prestige; high-quality reproduction; long life; good pass-along readership	Long ad purchase lead time; some waste circulation; no guarantee of position
Outdoor	0.9	1.0	$8,000 prime billboard cost per month in Chicago	Flexibility; high repeat exposure; low cost; low competition	No audience selectivity; creative limitations
Miscellaneous	16.7	19.2			
Total	$87.0	100.0%			

Miscellaneous media include media expenditures of the first six types that were not classified.

SOURCE: Columns 2 and 3 are from *Advertising Age*, May 12, 1986. Reprinted with permission. Copyright © 1986, Crain Communications, Inc.

advertising costs rose faster than other media costs. Several companies found that a combination of print ads and television commercials often did a better job than television commercials alone. This illustrates that advertisers must periodically review the different media to determine their best buys. Another reason for review is the emergence of new media, such as cable TV, videotext, and videorecorders.

Given the media characteristics, the media planner must decide on how to allocate the budget to the major media types. For example, in launching its new biscuit, Pillsbury might decide to allocate $3 million to daytime network television, $2 million to women's magazines, and $1 million to daily newspapers in twenty major markets.

Selecting Specific Media Vehicles Now the media planner chooses the specific media vehicles that would be most cost effective. The media planner faces an incredible number of specific media vehicles.

> In the magazine field, there are over four thousand special-interest magazines. This means that advertisers can easily reach special-interest groups but will find it hard to reach general-audience groups. *Look, Saturday Evening Post*, and other major general magazines have folded, and the only remaining large circulation magazines are *TV Guide* and *Reader's Digest*, both with 20 million circulation, and then *Time, Newsweek*, etc., with 4 million to 6 million circulation.
>
> In the television field, there are over 750 commercial and 200 public TV stations. Beyond this, there are thousands of program vehicles to consider. The favorites used to be prime-time network shows. Yet network TV, which reached 90 percent of homes during prime time in 1980, is now reaching only 76 percent of homes. The inroads are being made by cable and pay TV, videorecorders, compact disc players, computers, and other entertainment forms that at present offer little opportunity for advertising. Advertisers are experimenting with both old and new media to offset the decline of network TV.[22]
>
> In the radio field, there are nearly eight thousand radio stations, and in the newspaper field, over seventeen hundred daily newspapers. All of this spells a condition of extreme *media fragmentation*, which may allow advertisers to reach special-interest groups more effectively but raises the cost of reaching general audiences for such products as soaps, food products, and small appliances.

How does the media planner make choices among this rich array of media? The media planner relies on media measurement services that provide estimates of audience size, composition, and media cost. Audience size has several possible measures:

- **Circulation.** The number of physical units through which advertising is distributed.
- **Audience.** The number of people who are exposed to the vehicle. (If the vehicle has pass-on readership, then audience is larger than circulation.)
- **Effective audience.** The number of people with the target's characteristics who are exposed to the vehicle.
- **Effective ad-exposed audience.** The number of people with the target's characteristics who actually saw the ad.

The Cost-Per-Thousand Criterion Media planners calculate the *cost per thousand persons reached* by a particular vehicle. If a full-page, four-color advertisement in *Newsweek* costs $84,000 and *Newsweek's* estimated readership is 3 million people, the cost of reaching each one thousand persons is approximately $28. The same advertisement in *Business Week* may cost $40,000 but reach only 1 million persons, at a cost per thousand of $40. The media planner would rank the various magazines according to cost per thousand and favor those magazines with the lowest cost per thousand.

Several adjustments have to be applied to this initial measure. First, the measure should be adjusted for *audience quality*. For a baby lotion advertisement, a magazine read by one million young mothers would have an exposure value of one million, but if read by one million old men would have a zero exposure value. Second, the exposure value should be adjusted for the *audience attention probability*. Readers of *Vogue*, for example, pay more attention to ads than do readers of *Newsweek*. Third, the exposure value should be adjusted for the *editorial quality* (prestige and believability) that one magazine might have over another. Fourth, the exposure value should be adjusted for the magazine's ad placement policies and extra services (such as regional or occupational editions, lead time requirements, etc.).

Media planners are increasingly using more-sophisticated measures of media effectiveness and employing them in mathematical models for arriving at the best media mix.

Many advertising agencies use a computer program to select the initial media and then make further improvements based on subjective factors omitted in the model.[23] (See Exhibit 21-4.)

Deciding on Media Timing

The advertiser faces a macroscheduling problem and a microscheduling problem.

Macroscheduling Problem The advertiser has to decide how to schedule the advertising over the year in relation to seasonality and expected economic developments. Suppose 70 percent of a product's sales occur during the warm months of May to October. The firm has three options. The firm can vary its advertising expenditures to follow the seasonal pattern, to oppose the seasonal pattern, or to be constant throughout the year. Most firms pursue a policy of seasonal advertising. Yet consider this:

> Some years ago, one of the soft-drink manufacturers started to put more money into off-season advertising. This resulted in increased nonseasonal consumption of its brand while not hurting its brand's seasonal consumption. Other soft-drink manufacturers started to do the same, with the net result that a more-balanced consumption pattern occurred. The previous seasonal concentration had created a self-fulfilling prophecy.

EXHIBIT 21-4

Computer Models for Media Selection

Advertising researchers have built mathematical models for media selection, some of which are in active use by advertising agencies. Here are four types of models.

Linear programming Linear programming can be used to select the media mix that will maximize the number of effective exposures subject to a set of constraints. A linear-programming statement of the media-selection problem is shown below.

$$
\begin{aligned}
\text{Maximize:} \quad E = \ & 3{,}100X_1 + 2{,}000X_2 + 2{,}400X_3 \\
\text{Subject to:} \quad & 15{,}000X_1 + 4{,}000X_2 + 5{,}000X_3 \leq 500{,}000 \\
& 15{,}000X_1 \geq 250{,}000 \\
& X_1 \geq 0 \\
& X_1 \leq 52 \\
& X_2 \geq 1 \\
& X_2 \leq 8 \\
& X_3 \geq 6 \\
& X_3 \leq 12
\end{aligned}
$$

There are three media vehicles, X_1, X_2, X_3. Vehicle 1 gives 3,100 (in thousands) effective exposures per issue, vehicle 2 gives 2,000, and vehicle 3 gives 2,400. The media planner will seek to buy the number of issues of each vehicle that will maximize the total number of effective exposures, E. The media planner has an advertising budget of $500,000, which cannot be exceeded. Vehicle 1 costs $15,000 per issue, vehicle 2, $4,000, and vehicle 3, $5,000. Furthermore, the media planner wants to spend at least $250,000 on vehicle 1. Vehicle 1 puts out fifty-two issues a year, vehicle 2, eight issues, and vehicle 3, twelve issues. The media planner wants to buy at least one issue of vehicle 2 and six issues of vehicle 3.

A mathematical-solution technique is used to find the media mix. The limitations of this model are (1) linear programming assumes that repeat exposures have a constant marginal effect; (2) it assumes constant media costs (no discounts); (3) it cannot handle the problem of audience duplication; and (4) it does not schedule the ads.

Heuristic programming   This model selects media sequentially rather than simultaneously. The model selects the single best buy the first week. The remaining media choices are reevaluated to take into account audience duplication and potential media discounts. A second selection is made for the same week if the exposure rate for the week is below the *optimal* rate. The latter is a function of several marketing and media variables. This process continues until the optimal exposure rate for the week is reached, at which point new media choices are considered for the following week. This cycling process continues until the year's schedule is completed.[*]

The sequential procedure has the following advantages: (1) it develops a schedule simultaneously with the selection of media; (2) it handles the audience-duplication problem; (3) it handles the media-discount problem; and (4) it incorporates important variables such as brand-switching rates and multiple-exposure coefficients.

Simulation model   A simulation model estimates the exposure value of any given media plan. For example, the Simulmatics media model consists of 2,944 make-believe media users representing a cross section of the American population by sex, age, type of community, employment status, and education. Each person's media choices are determined probabilistically as a function of the person's socioeconomic characteristics and location. A particular media schedule is exposed to all the persons in this hypothetical population. The computer tabulates the number and types of people exposed. Summary graphs and tables are prepared at the end of the hypothetical year's run, and they supply a picture of the schedule's probable impact. The advertiser decides whether the audience profile and the reach and frequency characteristics of the proposed media schedule are satisfactory.

Simulation complements rather than competes with the preceding models. Its major limitations are (1) simulation normally does not include an overall effectiveness function; (2) it lacks a procedure for finding better schedules; and (3) the representativeness of the hypothetical population can be questioned.

MEDIAC   Little and Lodish created a model called MEDIAC.[†] MEDIAC handles in an analytical fashion a large number of marketing and advertising variables in the real media problem, such as market segments, sales potentials, exposure probabilities, diminishing marginal response rates, forgetting, seasonality, and cost discounts. MEDIAC asks questions, and the user supplies data and receives in a matter of seconds an optimal media schedule. The user can change the data inputs and note the effect on the media schedule.

Computerized media selection is an aid, not a substitute, for executive judgment. The plan is only a starting point, because the model cannot capture all the variables. The final media plan should be the joint product of the machine's ultralogical mind and people's imagination and judgment.

[*] See William T. Moran, "Practical Media Decisions and the Computer," *Journal of Marketing*, July 1963, pp. 26–30.
[†] John D. C. Little and Leonard M. Lodish, "A Media Planning Calculus," *Operations Research*, January–February 1969, pp. 1–35.

Forrester has proposed using his "industrial dynamics" methodology to test seasonal advertising policies.[24] He sees advertising as having a lagged impact on consumer awareness; awareness has a lagged impact on factory sales; and factory sales have a lagged impact on advertising expenditures. These time relationships can be studied and formulated mathematically into a computer-simulation model. Alternative timing strategies would be simulated to assess their varying impact on company sales, costs, and profits. Rao and Miller also developed a lag model to relate a brand's share to advertising and promotional expenditures on a market-by-market basis. They tested their model successfully with five Lever brands in fifteen districts relating share to dollars spent on TV, print, price-off, and trade promotions.[25]

Kuehn developed a model to explore how advertising should be timed for frequently purchased, highly seasonal, low-cost grocery products.[26] Kuehn showed that the appropriate timing pattern depends on the *degree of advertising carryover* and the *amount of habitual behavior in customer brand choice.* Carryover refers to the rate at which the effect of an advertising expenditure wears out with the passage of time. A carryover of 0.75 per month means that the current effect of a past advertising expenditure is 75 percent of its level last month, while a carryover of 0.10 per month means that 10 percent of last month's effect is carried over. Habitual behavior indicates how much brand holdover occurs independently of the level of advertising. High habitual purchasing, say 0.90, means that 90 percent of the buyers repeat their purchase of the brand regardless of the marketing stimuli.

Kuehn found that when there is no advertising carryover or habitual purchasing, the decision maker is justified in using a percentage-of-sales rule to budget advertising. The optimal timing pattern for advertising expenditures coincides with the expected seasonal pattern of industry sales. But if there is advertising carryover and/or habitual purchasing, the percentage-of-sales budgeting method is not optimal. It would be better to time advertising to lead the sales curve. The peak in advertising expenditures should come before the expected peak in sales, and the trough in advertising expenditures should come before the trough in sales. Lead time should be greater, the higher the carryover. Furthermore, the advertising expenditures should be steadier, the greater the extent of habitual purchasing.

Microscheduling Problem The microscheduling problem calls for allocating a set of advertising exposures over a short period of time to obtain the maximum impact. Suppose the firm decides to buy thirty radio spots in the month of September.

One way to classify the multitude of possible patterns is shown in Figure 21-4. The left side shows that advertising messages for the month can be concentrated in a small part of the month ("burst" advertising), dispersed continuously throughout the month, or dispersed intermittently throughout the month. The top side shows that the advertising messages can be beamed with a level frequency, a rising frequency, a falling frequency,

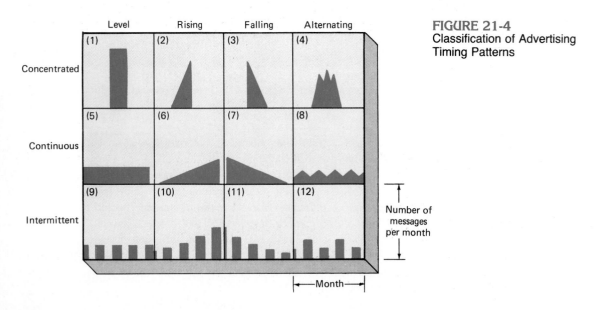

FIGURE 21-4
Classification of Advertising
Timing Patterns

or an alternating frequency. The advertiser's problem is to decide which distribution pattern would be the most effective.

The most effective pattern depends on the advertising communication objectives in relation to the nature of the product, target customers, distribution channels, and other marketing factors. Consider the following cases:

> A *retailer* wants to announce a preseason sale of skiing equipment. She recognizes that only certain people will be interested in the message. She thinks that the target buyers need to hear the message only once or twice. Her objective is to maximize the reach of the message, not the repetition. She decides to concentrate the messages on the days of the sale at a level rate but to vary the time of day to avoid the same audiences. She uses pattern (1).
>
> A *muffler manufacturer-distributor* wants to keep his name before the public. Yet he does not want his advertising to be too continuous because only 3 to 5 percent of the cars on the road need a new muffler at any given time. He chooses to use intermittent advertising. Furthermore, he recognizes that Fridays are paydays, so he sponsors a few messages on a midweek day and more messages on Friday. He uses pattern (12).

The timing pattern should consider three factors. *Buyer turnover* expresses the rate at which new buyers appear in the market; the higher this rate, the more continuous the advertising should be to reach these new buyers. *Purchase frequency* is the number of times during the period that the average buyer buys the product; the higher the purchase frequency, the more continuous the advertising should be. The *forgetting rate* is the rate at which the buyer forgets the brand; the higher the forgetting rate, the more continuous the advertising should be.

In launching a new product, the advertiser has to choose between ad continuity, concentration, flighting, and pulsing. *Continuity* is achieved by scheduling exposures evenly throughout a given period. But high advertising costs and seasonal variations in sales discourage continuous advertising. Generally, advertisers use continuous advertising in expanding market situations, with frequently purchased items, and in tightly defined buyer categories. *Concentration* calls for spending all the advertising dollars in a single period. This makes sense for a product that is sold in only one season or holiday. *Flighting* calls for advertising for some period, followed by a hiatus with no advertising, and then followed by a second flight. It is used when funding is limited, the purchase cycle is relatively infrequent, or with seasonal items. *Pulsing* is continuous advertising at low-weight levels reinforced periodically by waves of heavier activity. Pulsing draws upon the strength of continuous advertising and flights to create a compromise scheduling strategy. Those who favor pulsing feel that the audience will learn the message more thoroughly and money could be saved.

> Anheuser-Busch's research indicated that Budweiser could suspend advertising in a particular market and experience no adverse sales effect for at least a year and a half.[27] Then the company could introduce a six-month burst of advertising and restore the previous growth rate. This analysis led Budweiser to adopt a pulsing advertising strategy.

EVALUATING ADVERTISING EFFECTIVENESS

Good planning and control of advertising depend critically on measures of advertising effectiveness. Yet the amount of fundamental research on advertising effectiveness is appallingly small. According to Forrester:

I doubt that there is any other function in industry where management bases so much expenditure on such scanty knowledge. The advertising industry spends 2 or 3 percent of its gross dollar volume on what it calls "research," and even if this were really true research, the small amount would be surprising. However, I estimate that less than a tenth of this amount would be considered research plus development as these terms are defined in the engineering and product research departments of companies . . . probably no more than $\frac{1}{5}$ of 1 percent of total advertising expenditure is used to achieve an enduring understanding of how to spend the other 99.8 percent.[28]

Most of the measurement of advertising effectiveness is of an applied nature, dealing with specific ads and campaigns. Most of the money is spent by agencies on *pretesting* the given ad, much less is spent on *postevaluating* its effects. Many companies develop an advertising campaign, put it into the national market, and then evaluate its effectiveness. It would be better to put the campaign into one or a few towns first and evaluate what is happening before rolling a campaign throughout the country with a very large budget. One company tested its new campaign first in Phoenix. The campaign bombed, and the company saved all the money that it would have spent going national.

Most advertisers try to measure the *communication effect* of an ad, that is, its potential effect on awareness, knowledge, or preference. They would like to measure the *sales effect* but often feel it is too difficult to measure. Yet both can be researched.

Communication-Effect Research

Communication-effect research seeks to determine whether an ad is communicating effectively. Called *copy testing*, it can be done before an ad is put into actual media and after it is printed or broadcast.

There are three major methods of advertising pretesting. The first is a *direct rating method*, which exposes a consumer panel to alternative ads and asks them to rate the ads. These direct ratings are used to evaluate an ad's attention, read-through, cognitive, affective, and behavior strengths (see Figure 21-5). Although an imperfect measure of an ad's actual impact, a high rating indicates a potentially more effective ad. *Portfolio tests* allow a consumer to view and/or listen to a portfolio of advertisements, taking as much time as they need. Respondents are then asked to recall all the ads and their content, aided or unaided by the interviewer. Their recall level indicates an ad's ability to stand out and its message to be understood and remembered. *Laboratory tests* use equipment to measure

FIGURE 21-5
Rating Sheet for Ads

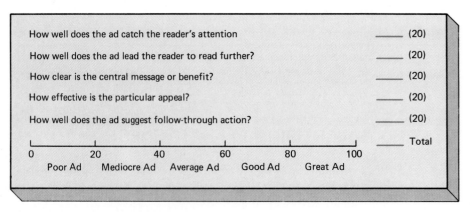

consumers' physiological reactions—heartbeat, blood pressure, pupil dilation, perspiration—to an ad. These tests measure an ad's attention-getting power but reveal nothing about the ad's impact on beliefs, attitudes, or intentions. (Exhibit 21-5 describes some specific advertising research techniques.)

Advertisers are also interested in measuring the overall communication impact of a completed advertising campaign. To what extent did the ad campaign increase brand awareness, brand comprehension, stated brand preference, and so on? Assuming that the advertiser had measured these levels before the campaign, the advertiser can draw a random sample of consumers in the target market after the campaign to assess the communication effects. If a company hoped to increase brand awareness from 20 percent to 50 percent of the target population, and only succeeded in increasing it to 30 percent, then something is wrong: The company is not spending enough, its ads are poor, or some other factor is missing.

Sales-Effect Research

Communication-effect advertising research helps advertisers assess the communication effects of an ad but reveals little about its sales impact. What sales are generated by an ad that increases brand awareness by 20 percent and brand preference by 10 percent?

The sales effect of advertising is generally harder to measure than the communication effect. Sales are influenced by many factors besides advertising, such as the product's features, price, and availability and competitors' actions. The fewer or more controllable these other factors, the easier it is to measure advertising's impact on sales. The sales impact is easiest to measure in mail-order situations and hardest to measure in brand or corporate-image-building advertising.

Companies are generally interested in finding out whether they are overspending or underspending on advertising. One approach to this question is to work with the following intuitive idea:

$$\frac{\text{Share of}}{\text{expenditure}} = \frac{\text{Share of}}{\text{voice}} = \frac{\text{Share of}}{\text{mind}} = \frac{\text{Share of}}{\text{market}}$$

In other words, a company's share of advertising expenditures produces a corresponding share of voice heard by consumers and therefore earns a corresponding share of their mind and ultimately of their buying actions. Peckham studied the relationship between share of voice and share of market for several consumer products over a number of years and typically found a one-to-one ratio for established products and a 1.5–2.0 to 1.0 ratio for new products.[29] Using this information, suppose we observed the following data for three well-established firms selling an almost identical product at an identical price:

	Advertising expenditure	Share of voice	Share of market	Advertising effectiveness
A	$2,000,000	57.1	40.0	70
B	1,000,000	28.6	28.6	100
C	500,000	14.3	31.4	220

Firm A spends $2,000,000 of the industry's total expenditures of $3,500,000; so its share of voice is 57.1 percent. Yet its share of market is only 40 percent. By dividing its share of market by its share of voice, we get an advertising effectiveness ratio of 70, suggesting that firm A is either overspending or at least misspending. Firm B is spending 28.6 percent of total advertising expenditures and has a 28.6 market share; the conclusion is that it is spending its money efficiently. Firm C is spending only 14.3 percent of the total and yet achieving a market share of 31.4 percent; the conclusion is that it is spending its money superefficiently and should probably increase its expenditures.

Researchers try to measure the sales impact through either historical or experimental analysis. The *historical approach* involves correlating past sales to past advertising expenditures on a current or lagged basis using advanced statistical techniques. Palda studied the effect of advertising expenditures on the sales of Lydia Pinkham's Vegetable Compound between 1908 and 1960.[30] He calculated the short-term and long-term marginal sales effects of advertising. The marginal advertising dollars increased sales by only fifty cents in the short term, seeming to suggest that Pinkham spent too much on advertising. But the long-term marginal sales effect was three times as large. Palda calculated the posttax marginal rate of return on company advertising to be 37 percent over the whole period.

Montgomery and Silk estimated the sales effectiveness of three communication tools used in the pharmaceutical industry.[31] A drug company spent 38 percent of its communication budget on direct mail, 32 percent on samples and literature, and 29 percent on journal advertising. Yet the sales-effects research indicated that journal advertising, the least-used communication tool, had the highest long-run advertising elasticity, here .365; samples and literature had an elasticity of .108; and direct mail had an elasticity of only .018. They concluded that the company spent too much on direct mail and too little on journal advertising.

Other researchers use *experimental design* to measure the sales impact of advertising. To determine whether they are overspending or underspending on advertising, they set aside some sales territories and instead of spending the normal percentage of advertising to sales, the company spends more in some and less in others. These are called *high-spending tests* and *low-spending tests*. If the high-spending tests produce substantial sales increases, it appears that the company has been underspending. If they fail to produce more sales and if low-spending tests do not lead to sales decreases, then the company has been overspending. These tests, of course, must be accompanied by good experimental controls and last sufficiently long to capture lagged effects of changed advertising expenditure levels.

Du Pont was one of the first companies to design advertising experiments. Du Pont's paint division divided fifty-six sales territories into high, average, and low market-share territories.[32] Du Pont spent the normal amount for advertising in one-third of the group; in another third, two and one-half times the normal amount; and in the remaining third, four times the normal amount. (See Figure 21-6.) At the end of the experiment, Du Pont estimated how much extra sales was created by higher levels of advertising expenditure. Du Pont found that higher advertising expenditure increased sales at a diminishing rate, and that the sales increase was weaker in Du Pont's high market-share territories.

Another approach to allocating an advertising budget geographically is to use a model that considers the differences between geographic areas in terms of their market size, advertising response, media efficiency, competition, and profit margins. Urban developed

FIGURE 21-6
Experimental Design for Testing the Effect of Three Levels of Advertising Expenditure on Market Share
SOURCE: From p. 166, *Mathematical Models and Marketing Management*, by Robert Buzzell. Boston: Division of Research, Graduate School of Business Administration, Harvard University, 1968. Reprinted by permission.

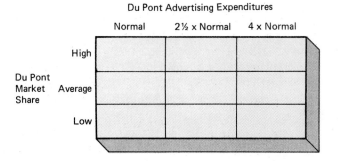

a media allocation model that relies upon these geographic measurements to help the firm in its allocation task.[33]

In general, a growing number of companies are striving to measure the sales effect of advertising expenditures instead of settling only for lower-order approaches such as testing ad recall or noting scores.

SUMMARY

Advertising—the use of paid media by a seller to communicate persuasive information about its products, services, or organization—is a potent promotional tool. American marketers spend over $89 billion annually on advertising, and it takes many forms (national, regional, local; consumer, industrial, retail; product, brand, institutional; and so on) designed to achieve a variety of objectives (immediate sales, brand recognition, preference, and so on).

Advertising decision making is a five-step process consisting of objectives setting, budget decision, message decision, media decision, and ad effectiveness evaluation. Advertisers should establish clear goals as to whether the advertising is supposed to inform, persuade, or remind buyers. The advertising budget can be established on the basis of what is affordable, as a percentage budget of sales, on the basis of competitors' expenditures, or on the basis of objectives and tasks; and more-advanced decision models are available. The message decision calls for generating messages, evaluating and selecting among them, and executing them effectively. The media decision calls for defining the reach, frequency, and impact goals; choosing among major media types; selecting specific media vehicles; and scheduling the media. Finally, campaign evaluation calls for evaluating the communication and sales effects of advertising before, during, and after the advertising.

QUESTIONS

1. "It is not important that the objectives and goals of an advertising campaign be stated. Management only needs to know that advertising's fundamental goal is to generate sales and profits." Discuss this statement. Say whether you agree or disagree with it. Give reasons for your position.

2. Choose two current advertising campaigns and develop what you think the objectives of each campaign might be. (Try to select campaigns that would suggest different objectives.) State your assumptions in your answer.

3. An executive recently recommended allocating advertising expenditures to various markets in proportion to sales in those markets. His reasons were as follows. In the absence of further company advertising, a fixed (but unknown) percentage of sales in each market would be lost to competitors. The role of advertising is to maintain the present level of customers. Therefore the promotional level in each market should be proportional to the sales level. Do you agree?

4. Examine current copies of two magazines (e.g., *Time* and *Ladies' Home Journal*). Classify the execution styles used by the full-page ads in each of these issues. Comment on differences of style, tone, and format

of the ads found in each magazine. What factors might contribute to these differences?

5. Discuss the strengths and weaknesses of both communication effects research and sales effects research. Assess the concerns that you have for each of the techniques used under these two research approaches.

6. Consumer protection is one of the major rationales used for regulating advertising around the world. What other global forces should be monitored for their potential impact on advertising regulation?

7. Advertisers often do research to test for the effectiveness of an ad before it is placed in the media. Suggest some principles that should be followed when testing ad copy.

8. Comparative advertising, in which an advertiser directly compares its product with that of a competitor who is identified by name, has been allowed by the FTC since 1972. What are some of the advantages and dangers in using this form of advertising?

9. Consider the following two statements: "The purpose of advertising is to create sales." "The purpose of advertising is to improve the buyers' disposition to-

ward the company's products.'' Which comes closer to the truth?

10. The advertising manager of a large firm asks the executive committee to approve a $100,000 increase in the advertising budget. She submits that this extra money will probably increase company sales by $500,000 over what they would otherwise be. What other information would you want in order to judge the budget request?

11. A canned-dog-food manufacturer is trying to choose between media A and B. Medium A has 10,000,000 readers and charges $20,000 for a full-page ad ($2 per 1,000). Medium B has 15,000,000 readers and charges $25,000 for a full-page ad ($1.67 per 1,000).

Is there any other calculation that might be made before assuming that B is the better medium?

12. A large oil company allocates its advertising budget to its territories according to current territorial sales. The advertising manager justifies using a constant advertising-to-sales ratio by saying that the company loses a certain percentage of its customers in each market each year and that advertising's most important job is to get new customers to replace them. What assumptions underlie this reasoning?

13. For many years, Hershey Foods did not advertise. In spite of this, its candy bar sales continued to grow. Does that suggest that companies with excellent products need little or no advertising?

▪ FOOTNOTES

1 See Russell H. Colley, *Defining Advertising Goals for Measured Advertising Results* (New York: Association of National Advertisers, 1961).

2 See William L. Wilkie and Paul W. Farris, ''Comparison Advertising: Problem and Potential,'' *Journal of Marketing*, October 1975, pp. 7–15.

3 For a good discussion, see David A. Aaker and James M. Carman, ''Are You Overadvertising?'' *Journal of Advertising Research*, August/September 1982, pp. 57–70.

4 See Donald E. Schultz, Dennis Martin, and William P. Brown, *Strategic Advertising Campaigns* (Chicago: Crain Books, 1984), pp. 192–97.

5 M. L. Vidale and H. R. Wolfe, ''An Operations-Research Study of Sales Response to Advertising,'' *Operations Research*, June 1957, pp. 370–81.

6 John D. C. Little, ''A Model of Adaptive Control of Promotional Spending,'' *Operations Research*, November 1966, pp. 1075–97.

7 For additional models for setting the advertising budget, see Gary L. Lilien and Philip Kotler, *Marketing Decision Making: A Model-Building Approach* (New York: Harper & Row, 1983), pp. 490–501.

8 See John Koten, ''Creativity, Not Budget Size, Is Vital to TV-Ad Popularity,'' *Wall Street Journal*, March 1, 1984, p. 25.

9 Ibid.

10 See ''Keep Listening to That Wee, Small Voice,'' in *Confessions of an Advertising Man* (Chicago: Leo Burnett Company, 1961), p. 61.

11 John C. Maloney, ''Marketing Decisions and Attitude Research,'' in *Effective Marketing Coordination*, ed. George L. Baker, Jr. (Chicago: American Marketing Association, 1961), pp. 595–618.

12 Irwin Gross, ''An Analytical Approach to the Creative Aspect of Advertising Operations'' (Ph.D. dissertation, Case Institute of Technology, November 1967).

13 Dik Warren Twedt, ''How to Plan New Products, Improve Old Ones, and Create Better Advertising,'' *Journal of Marketing*, January 1969, pp. 53–57.

14 See William A. Mindak and H. Malcolm Bybee, ''Marketing Application to Fund Raising,'' *Journal of Marketing*, July 1971, pp. 13–18.

15 See Robert D. Hisrich and Michael P. Peters, *Marketing Decisions for New and Mature Products* (Columbus, Ohio: Chas. E. Merrill, 1984), p. 379.

16 See Peter L. Henderson, James F. Hind, and Sidney E. Brown, ''Sales Effect of Two Campaign Themes,'' *Journal of Advertising Research*, December 1961, pp. 2–11.

17 L. Greenland, ''Is This the Era of Positioning?'' *Advertising Age*, May 29, 1972.

18 David Ogilvy and Joel Raphaelson, ''Research on Advertising Techniques That Work—and Don't Work,'' *Harvard Business Review*, July–August 1982, p. 14–18.

19 Darrell B. Lucas and Steuart Henderson Britt, *Measuring Advertising Effectiveness* (New York: McGraw-Hill, 1963), p. 218.

20 See Herbert E. Krugman, ''What Makes Advertising Effective?'' *Harvard Business Review*, March–April 1975, pp. 96–103, here p. 98.

21 See Peggy J. Kreshel, Kent M. Lancaster, and Margaret A. Toomey, ''Advertising Media Planning: How Leading Advertising Agencies Estimate Effective Reach and Fequency'' (Urbana: University of Illinois, Department of Advertising, January 1985), paper no. 20.

22 See ''As Network TV Fades, Many Advertisers Try Age-Old Promotions: They Switch to Direct Mail, Coupon and PR Ploys,'' *Wall Street Journal*, August 26, 1986, p. 1.

23 See Roland T. Rust, *Advertising Media Models: A Practical Guide* (Lexington, Mass.: Lexington Books, 1986).

24 See Jay W. Forrester, ''Advertising: A Problem in Industrial Dynamics,'' *Harvard Business Review*, March–April 1959, pp. 100–10.

25 See Amber G. Rao and Peter B. Miller, ''Advertising/Sales Response Functions,'' *Journal of Advertising Research*, April 1975, pp. 7–15.

26 See Alfred A. Kuehn, ''How Advertising Performance Depends on Other Marketing Factors,'' *Journal of Advertising Research*, March 1962, pp. 2–10.

27 Philip H. Dougherty, "Bud 'Pulses' the Market," *New York Times*, February 18, 1975.

28 Forrester, "Advertising," p. 102.

29 See J. O. Peckham, *The Wheel of Marketing* (Scarsdale, New York: privately printed, 1975), pp. 73–77.

30 Kristian S. Palda, *The Measurement of Cumulative Advertising Effect* (Englewood Cliffs, N.J.: Prentice-Hall, 1964), p. 87.

31 David B. Montgomery and Alvin J. Silk, "Estimating Dynamic Effects of Market Communications Expenditures," *Management Science*, June 1972, pp. 485–501.

32 See Robert D. Buzzell, "E. I. Du Pont de Nemours & Co.: Measurement of Effects of Advertising," in his *Mathematical Models and Marketing Management* (Boston: Division of Research, Graduate School of Business Administration, Harvard University, 1964), pp. 157–79.

33 See Glen L. Urban, "Allocating Ad Budgets Geographically," *Journal of Advertising Research*, December 1975, pp. 7–16.

22

Designing Sales Promotion and Public Relations Programs

Gifts are like hooks.

Martial (A.D. 86)

We despise no source that can pay us a pleasing attention.

Mark Twain

In this chapter, we turn to sales promotion and public relations. They are often viewed as playing a secondary role to the major tools of advertising and personal selling. Yet these tools can contribute strongly to marketing performance. Sales promotion and public relations are not well understood by marketing practitioners. Although some companies have created sales promotion departments, most companies lack a sales promotion manager and leave sales promotion decisions to product and brand managers. And most companies lack a product publicity director and must get help from the corporate public relations department. The recent difficult economic times, however, have led many firms to use these promotional tools more aggressively.

First we will examine sales promotion, and then public relations.

SALES PROMOTION

Sales promotion consists of a diverse collection of incentive tools, mostly short-term, designed to stimulate quicker and/or greater purchase of a particular product by consumers or the trade. Whereas advertising offers a *reason* to buy, sales promotion offers an *incentive* to buy. Sales promotion includes tools for *consumer promotion* (e.g., samples, coupons, cash refund offers, prices off, premiums, prizes, patronage rewards, free trials, warranties, demonstrations, contests); *trade promotion* (e.g., buying allowances, free goods, merchandise allowances, cooperative advertising, advertising and display allowances, push money, dealer sales contests); and *sales-force promotion* (e.g., bonuses, contests, sales rallies).

Sales promotion tools are used by most organizations, including manufacturers, distributors, retailers, trade associations, and nonprofit organizations. As examples of the last, churches often sponsor bingo games, theater parties, testimonial dinners, and raffles.

Rapid Growth of Sales Promotion

A decade ago, the *advertising-to-sales promotion ratio* was about 60:40. Today, in many consumer packaged goods industries, the picture is reversed, with sales promotion accounting for between 60 and 70 percent of the combined budget. Sales promotion expenditures have been increasing 12 percent per year compared with advertising's increase of 7.6 percent. Total sales promotion in all industries exceeded $85 billion in 1985.[1] And the fast growth rate is expected to continue.

Several factors contributed to the rapid growth of sales promotion, particularly in consumer markets.[2] Internal factors include the following: Promotion is now more accepted by top management as an effective sales tool; more product managers are qualified to use sales promotion tools; and product managers are under greater pressure to increase their current sales. External factors include the following: The number of brands has increased; competitors use promotions frequently; many brands are at parity; consumers are more deal oriented; the trade has demanded more deals from manufacturers; and advertising efficiency has declined because of rising costs, media clutter, and legal restraints.

The rapid growth of sales promotion media (coupons, contests, etc.) has created a situation of *promotion clutter*, similar to advertising clutter. There is a danger that consumers will start tuning out, in which case coupons and other media will weaken in their ability to trigger brand awareness or trial. Manufacturers will have to find ways to rise above the clutter, such as by offering larger coupon-redemption values or using more dramatic point-of-purchase displays or demonstrations.

Purpose of Sales Promotion

Sales promotion tools vary in their specific objectives. A free sample stimulates consumer trial, while a free management-advisory service cements a long-term relationship with a retailer.

Sellers use incentive-type promotions to attract new triers, to reward loyal customers, and to increase the repurchase rates of occasional users. New triers are of three types—users of another brand in the same category, users in other categories, and frequent brand switchers. Sales promotions often attract the brand switchers because users of other brands and categories do not always notice or act on a promotion. Brand switchers are primarily looking for low price, good value, or premiums. Sales promotions are unlikely to turn them into loyal brand users. Sales promotions used in markets of high brand similarity produce a high sales response in the short run, but little permanent share and user gain. In markets of high brand dissimilarity, sales promotions may alter market shares more permanently.

Sellers often think of sales promotion as designed to break down brand loyalty, and advertising as designed to build up brand loyalty. Therefore an important issue for marketing managers is how to divide the budget between sales promotion and advertising. Ten years ago marketing managers would decide what they needed to spend on advertising, and whatever was left they would put into sales promotion. Today marketing managers first estimate what they need to give to the trade, then what they need to give to consumers to drive in short-term volume, and whatever is left they will budget for advertising.

There is a danger, however, in letting advertising take a back seat to sales promotion. When a brand is price promoted too much of the time, the consumer begins to think of it as a cheap brand and often will only buy it on deal. No one knows when this happens, but probably there is risk in putting a well-known brand on promotion more than 30 percent of the time. Dominant brands use dealing infrequently, since most of it would only subsidize current users.

Most observers feel that dealing activities do not build long-term consumer franchise, as does advertising. Brown's study of twenty-five hundred instant coffee buyers concluded that

▪ Sales promotions yield faster responses in sales than advertising does.
▪ Sales promotions do not tend to yield new, long-term buyers in mature markets because they attract mainly deal-prone consumers who switch among brands as deals become available.
▪ Loyal brand buyers tend not to change their buying patterns as a result of competitive promotion.
▪ Advertising appears to be capable of increasing the ''prime franchise'' of a brand.[3]

There is also evidence that price promotions do not permanently build total category volume. They usually build short-term volume that is not maintained. Small-share competitors find it advantageous to use sales promotion because they cannot afford to match the large advertising budgets of the market leaders. Nor can they get shelf space without offering trade allowances or consumer trial without offering consumer incentives. Price competition is often used by a small brand seeking to enlarge its share, but it is less effective for a category leader whose growth lies in expanding the entire category.[4]

Prentice, however, divides sales promotion tools into two groups, those that are ''consumer-franchise building'' and those that are not.[5] The former imparts a selling message along with the deal, as in the case of free samples, coupons when they include a selling message, and premiums when they are related to the product. Sales promotion tools that are not consumer-franchise building include price-off packs, consumer premiums not related to a product, contests and sweepstakes, consumer refund offers, and trade allowances. Sellers should use consumer-franchise-building promotions because they reinforce the consumer's brand understanding.[6]

Sales promotion seems most effective when used together with advertising. ''In one study, point-of-purchase displays related to current TV commercials were found to produce 15 percent more sales than similar displays not related to such advertising. In another, a heavy sampling approach along with TV advertising proved more successful than either TV alone or TV with coupons in introducing a product.''[7]

Major Decisions in Sales Promotion

In using sales promotion, a company must establish the objectives, select the tools, develop the program, pretest the program, implement and control it, and evaluate the results. We will examine these steps in the following paragraphs.

Establishing the Sales Promotion Objectives

Sales promotion objectives are derived from broader *promotion objectives*, which are derived from more basic *marketing objectives* developed for the product. The specific objectives set for sales promotion will vary with the type of target market.

For *consumers*, objectives include encouraging purchase of larger-size units, building trial among nonusers, and attracting switchers away from competitors' brands. For *retailers*, objectives include inducing retailers to carry new items and higher levels of inventory, encouraging off-season buying, encouraging stocking of related items, offsetting competitive promotions, building brand loyalty of retailers, and gaining entry into new retail outlets. For the *sales force*, objectives include encouraging support of a new product or model, encouraging more prospecting, and stimulating off-season sales.

Selecting the Sales Promotion Tools

Many sales promotion tools are available to accomplish these objectives. The promotion planner should take into account the type of market, sales promotion objectives, competitive conditions, and cost effectiveness of each tool. Here is an example of determining the appropriate sales promotion tool given the situation and objective:

> A firm has launched a new product and achieved a 20 percent market share within six months. Its penetration rate is 40 percent (i.e., the percentage of the target market that purchased the brand at least once.) Its repurchase rate is 10 percent (the percentage of the first-time triers who repurchased the brand one or more times). This firm needs to create more loyal users. An in-pack coupon would be appropriate to build more repeat purchase. But if the repurchase rate had been high, say 50 percent, then the company should try to attract more new triers. Here a media-mailed coupon might be appropriate.

The main sales promotion tools are designed for consumer promotion, trade promotion, and business promotion.

Consumer Promotion Tools   The main consumer promotion tools include samples, coupons, cash refund offers, price packs, premiums, prizes, patronage rewards, free trials, product warranties, tie-ins, and point-of-purchase displays and demonstrations.

Samples are offers of a free amount or trial of a product to consumers. The sample might be delivered door to door, sent in the mail, picked up in a store, found attached to another product, or featured in an advertising offer. Sampling is the most effective and most expensive way to introduce a new product. For example, Lever Brothers had so much confidence in its new Surf detergent that it distributed free samples to four out of five American households at a cost of $43 million.

Coupons are certificates entitling the bearer to a stated saving on the purchase of a specific product. According to A. C. Nielsen:

> Over 180 billion coupons were distributed in 1985 at an average face value of 28 cents. They had a face value of over $50 billion. Consumers redeemed about 6.5 billion, or 3.6 percent, saving more than $4 billion on their shopping bills.

Some other data indicate that over 95 percent of packaged goods firms have used couponing. Furthermore, two-third of American consumers use coupons in their regular shopping. On the other hand, retailers are less happy, receiving only seven cents for each coupon turned in and waiting some time for reimbursement.[8]

Coupons can be mailed, enclosed in or on other products, or inserted in magazine and newspaper ads. The redemption rate varies with the mode of distribution, with newspaper coupons being redeemed about 2 percent of the time, direct-mail-distributed coupons about 8 percent of the time, and pack-distributed about 17 percent of the time. Several package goods companies are experimenting with computerized printers that automatically print out coupons at the cash register when certain products pass over the scanner. Coupons can be effective in stimulating sales of a mature brand and inducing early trial of a new brand. Experts believe that coupons should provide a 15 to 20 percent saving to be effective. P&G broke into the Pittsburgh market with its Folger brand by offering a thirty-five-cent *discount coupon* on a one-pound can mailed to area homes and a *coupon in can* for ten cents off.

Cash refund offers (or rebates) are like coupons except that the price reduction occurs after the purchase rather than at the retail shop. The consumer sends a specified ''proof of purchase'' to the manufacturer, who in turn ''refunds'' part of the purchase price by mail. Cash refunds have been used for major products such as automobiles as well as for packaged goods.

Price packs (also called cents-off deals) are offers to consumers of savings off the regular price of a product, flagged on the label or package. They may take the form of a *reduced-price pack*, which is single packages sold at a reduced price (such as two for the price of one), or a *banded pack*, which is two related products banded together (such as a toothbrush and toothpaste). Price packs are very effective in stimulating short-term sales, even more than coupons.

In some household goods categories, there has been so much dealing that it has increased the number of deal-prone consumers. A growing number of consumers just reach for the cheapest deal pack. Scott paper towels started to offer so many consumer deals that they were in danger of losing their ''good quality'' image.

Premiums (or gifts) are merchandise offered at a relatively low cost or free as an incentive to purchase a particular product. A *with-pack premium* accompanies the product inside (in-pack) or on (on-pack) the package. Quaker Oats ran a promotion where it inserted $5 million dollars of gold and silver coins in bags of Ken-L Ration dog food. The package itself, if a *reusable container*, may serve as a premium. A *free-in-the-mail premium* is an item mailed to consumers who send in a proof of purchase, such as a box top. A *self-liquidating premium* is an item sold below its normal retail price to consumers who request it. Manufacturers now offer consumers all kinds of premiums bearing the company's name: The Budweiser fan can order T-shirts, hot-air balloons, and hundreds of other items with Bud's name on them.[9]

Prizes are offers of the chance to win cash, trips, or merchandise as a result of purchasing something. Pepsi-Cola offered the chance to win cash by matching numbers under the bottle cap with numbers announced on television. A British cigarette company included a lottery ticket in each pack providing the chance to win up to $10,000 if the lottery ticket won. Sometimes the prize is a person, such as Canada Dry's offering the winner either $1 million or dinner with actress Joan Collins (cash won out in this case).[10]

Patronage rewards are values in cash or in other forms that are proportional to one's patronage of a certain vendor or group of vendors. Most airlines offer ''frequent flyer plans'' providing points for miles traveled that can be turned in for free airline trips. The Marriott Hotels adopted an ''honored guest'' plan that awards points for users of their hotels. Cooperatives pay their members dividends according to their annual patronage. Trading stamps also represent patronage rewards in that customers receive stamps in buying from certain merchants and can redeem them for merchandise at stamp redemption centers or through mail-order catalogs.

Free trials consist of inviting prospective purchasers to try the product without cost in the hope that they will buy the product. Thus auto dealers encourage free test drives to stimulate purchase interest.

Product warranties are an important promotional tool, especially as consumers become more quality-sensitive. When Chrysler offered a five-year car warranty, substantially longer than GM's or Ford's, customers took notice. They inferred that Chrysler quality must be good or else the company would be in deep trouble. And Sears' offer of a lifetime warranty on its auto batteries certainly screams quality to the buyers. Companies must make a number of decisions before featuring a warranty. Is the product quality high enough? Should the product quality be improved further? Can competitors offer the same warranty? How long should the warranty be? What should it cover (replacement, repair, cash)? How much should be spent to advertise the warranty so that potential consumers know about it and consider it? Clearly, companies must carefully estimate the sales-generating value against the potential costs of any proposed warranty program.

Tie-in promotions are becoming increasingly popular. In a tie-in promotion, two or more brands or companies team up on coupons, refunds, and contests to increase their pulling power. Companies pool funds with the hope of broader exposure, while several sales forces push these promotions to retailers, giving them a better shot at extra display and ad space.[11]

Point-of-purchase (POP) displays and demonstrations take place at the point of purchase or sale. A five-foot-high cardboard display of Cap'n Crunch next to Cap'n Crunch cereal boxes or at the end of an aisle is an example. Unfortunately, many retailers do not like to handle the hundreds of displays, signs, and posters they receive from manufacturers. Manufacturers are responding by creating better POP materials, tying them in with television or print messages and offering to set them up. The L'eggs pantyhose display is one of the most creative in the history of POP materials and a major factor in the success of this brand.

Trade Promotion Tools   More sales promotion dollars are directed to the trade (58 percent) than to consumers (42 percent)![12] Manufacturers seek four objectives in awarding money to the trade:

1. *Trade promotion can persuade the retailer or wholesaler to carry the brand.* Shelf space is so scarce that manufacturers often have to offer price-offs, allowances, buy-back guarantees, or free goods to get on the shelf, and once there, to stay on the shelf.
2. *Trade promotion can persuade the retailer or wholesaler to carry more than it normally carries.* Manufacturers will offer volume allowances to get the trade to carry more in their warehouses and stores. Manufacturers believe that the trade will work harder when they are "loaded" with the manufacturer's product.
3. *Trade promotion can induce the retailers to promote the brand through featuring, display, and price reductions.* Manufacturers may want an end-of-aisle display or increased shelf facings or price reduction stickers and obtain them by offering the retailers allowances paid on "proof of performance."
4. *Trade promotion can stimulate retailers and their sales clerks to push the product.* Manufacturers compete for retailer sales effort by offering push money, sales aids, recognition programs, premiums, and sales contests.

At the same time, manufacturers probably spend more on trade promotion than they would freely choose, as a result of the trade's growing power. The increased concentration of buying power in the hands of fewer and larger retailers has increased the trade's ability to demand manufacturers' financial support at the expense of consumer promotion and advertising. In fact, the trade has come to depend on promotion money from the manufacturers: It is estimated that grocery stores received $12.6 billion in 1984 from packaged goods manufacturers, three times as much as their entire reported profits. If this money were withdrawn, grocery prices would have to increase substantially. Nor can any individual competitor unilaterally stop offering trade allowances without losing channel support. In some countries, the retailers have become the major advertisers, using mostly the promotional allowances extracted from their suppliers.

Manufacturers use several trade promotion tools. Manufacturers may offer a *price-off* (also called off-invoice or off-list), which is a straight discount off the list price on each case purchased during a stated period of time. The offer encourages dealers to buy a quantity or carry a new item that they might not ordinarily buy. The dealers can use the buying allowance for immediate profit, advertising, or price reductions.

Manufacturers may offer an *allowance* (usually so much off per case) in return for the retailer's agreeing to feature the manufacturer's products in some way. An *advertising allowance* compensates retailers for advertising the manufacturer's product. A *display allowance* compensates them for carrying a special display of the product.

Manufacturers may offer *free goods*, which are extra cases of merchandise, to middlemen who buy a certain quantity or who feature a certain flavor or size. They may offer *push money*, which is cash or gifts to dealers or their sales force to push the manufacturer's goods. Manufacturers may offer free *specialty advertising items* to the retailers that carry the company's name, such as pens, pencils, calendars, paperweights, matchbooks, memo pads, ashtrays, and yardsticks.

Food retailers strongly prefer trade deals to consumer deals. They are unhappy about the amount of consumer deals they have to handle. According to Chevalier and Curhan:

> Retailers view promotional efforts initiated by manufacturers as encouraging profitless brand switching rather than increasing sales or profits. Manufacturers, on the other hand, complain that retailer-initiated promotions sometimes damage brand franchises which have been carefully and expensively nurtured over many years. Worse yet, manufacturers complain that retailers frequently take advantage of them by "absorbing" deals without passing their benefits along to consumers.[13]

As the number of competitive sales promotions have increased, friction has been created between the company's sales force and its brand managers. The sales force says that the retailers will not keep products on the shelf unless they receive more trade promotion money, while the brand managers want to spend their funds on consumer promotion and advertising.

Manufacturers have other problems with trade promotions. First, they find it difficult to police retailers to make sure that they are doing what they agreed to do. Retailers do not always convert the buying allowances into reduced prices for consumers, and they may not provide extra shelving or display even after receiving merchandise or display allowances. Manufacturers are increasingly insisting on proof of performance in paying these allowances.

Second, more retailers are doing "forward buying," namely, buying a greater quantity of the brand during the deal period than they can sell during the deal period. Retailers might respond to a 10 percent off-case allowance by buying a twelve or longer week supply. The manufacturer finds that it has to schedule more production than planned and bear the costs of extra work shifts and overtime.

Third, retailers are also doing more "diverting," namely, buying more cases than needed in a region in which the manufacturer offered a deal and shipping them to nondeal regions. Manufacturers are trying to handle forward buying and dealing by limiting the amount they will sell at a discount, or producing and delivering less than the full order in an effort to smooth production.[14]

Business Promotion Tools   Among the main business promotion tools are *conventions* and *trade shows*. Industry associations organize annual conventions and typically sponsor a trade show at the same time. Firms selling to the particular industry display and demonstrate their products at the trade show. Over fifty-six hundred trade shows take place every year, drawing approximately 80 million people. The participating vendors expect several benefits, including generating new sales leads, maintaining customer contacts, introducing new products, meeting new customers, selling more to present customers, and educating customers with publications, motion pictures, and audio-visual materials.[15] The Trade Show Bureau estimates that a sale generated by a trade show costs about $300, compared with $1,200 for a sale generated from a sales call.

Contests, sweepstakes, and games are another important set of tools. These devices give consumers, business customers, dealers, or sales forces the chance to win something—such as cash, trips, or goods—as a result of luck or extra effort. A *contest* calls for consumers to submit an entry—a jingle, an estimate, a suggestion—to be examined by a panel of judges who will select the best entries. A *sweepstake* calls for consumers to submit their names in a drawing. A *game* presents consumers with something every time they buy—bingo numbers, missing letters—which may or may not help them win a prize. A *sales contest* is a contest involving dealers or the sales force to induce them to redouble their sales efforts over a stated period, with prizes going to the top performers.

Developing the Sales Promotion Program

The marketer must make some additional decisions to define the full promotion program.

Size of Incentive The marketer has to determine how much to offer. A certain minimum incentive is necessary if the promotion is to succeed. A higher incentive level will produce more sales response, but at a diminishing rate. Some of the large consumer-packaged-goods firms have a sales promotion manager who studies the effectiveness of past promotions and recommends appropriate incentives to brand managers.

Conditions for Participation Incentives might be offered to everyone or to select groups. A premium might be offered only to those who turn in box tops or proof-of-purchase seals. Sweepstakes might not be offered in certain states or to families of company personnel or to persons under a certain age.

Distribution Vehicle for Promotion The marketer must decide how to promote and distribute the promotion program. A fifteen-cents-off coupon could be distributed in the package, store, mail, or advertising media. Each distribution method involves a different level of reach and cost.

Duration of Promotion If the sales promotion period is too short, many prospects will not be able to take advantage, since they may not be repurchasing at the time. If the promotion runs too long, the deal will lose some of its "act now" force. According to one researcher, the optimal frequency is about three weeks per quarter, and optimal duration is the length of the average purchase cycle.[16] Of course, the optimal promotion cycle varies by product category and even by specific product.

Timing of Promotion Brand managers need to develop calendar dates for the promotions. The dates will be used by production, sales, and distribution. Some unplanned promotions will also be needed and will require cooperation on a short notice.

Total Sales Promotion Budget The sales promotion budget can be developed in two ways. It can be built from the ground up, where the marketer chooses the individual promotions and estimates their total cost. The cost of a particular promotion consists of the *administrative cost* (printing, mailing, and promoting the deal) and the *incentive cost* (cost of premium or cents-off, including redemption costs), multiplied by the *expected number of units* that will be sold on the deal.

> Suppose a brand of after-shave lotion will be marked down $.09 for a limited period. The item regularly sells for $1.09, of which $.40 represents a contribution to the manufacturer's profit before marketing expense. The brand manager expects a million bottles to be sold under this deal. Thus the incentive cost of the deal will be $90,000 (= 0.09 × 1,000,000). Suppose the administrative cost is estimated at $10,000. Then the total cost is $100,000. In order to break even on this deal, the company will have to sell 250,000 (= $100,000 ÷ 0.40) more units than would have occurred over the same period without the deal.

In the case of a coupon deal, the cost would take into account the fact that only a fraction of the consumers will redeem the coupons. In the case of an in-pack premium, the deal cost must include the costs of procurement and packaging of the premium, offset by any price increase on the package.

The more common way to develop the sales promotion budget is to use a conventional percentage of the total promotion budget. For example, toothpaste may get a sales promotion budget of 30 percent of the total promotion budget, whereas shampoo may get 50 percent. These percentages vary for different brands in different markets and are influenced by the stages of the product life cycle and competitive expenditures on promotion.

Multiple-brand companies should coordinate their sales promotion activities, such as making single mailings of multiple coupons to consumers. Strang, in his study of company sales promotion practices, found three major budgeting inadequacies:[17]

▪ Lack of consideration of cost effectiveness.
▪ Use of simplistic decision rules, such as extensions of last year's spending, percentage of expected sales, maintenance of a fixed ratio to advertising, and the "left-over approach," where promotion gets what is left after advertising is set.
▪ Advertising and promotional budgets being prepared independently.

Pretesting the Sales Promotion Program

Although sales promotion programs are designed on the basis of experience, pretests should be conducted to determine if the tools are appropriate, the incentive size optimal, and the presentation method efficient. A survey by the Premium Advertisers Association indicated that fewer than 42 percent of premium offerers ever tested their effectiveness.[18] Strang maintains that promotions can usually be tested quickly and inexpensively and that some large companies test alternative strategies in selected market areas with each of their national promotions.[19]

Sales promotions directed at consumer markets can be readily pretested. Consumers can be asked to rate or rank different possible deals. Or trial tests can be run in limited geographical areas.

Implementing and Controlling the Sales Promotion Program

Implementation and control plans for each individual promotion should be established. Implementation planning must cover lead time and sell-in time. Lead time is the time necessary to prepare the program prior to launching it.

It covers initial planning, design, and approval of package modifications or material to be mailed or distributed to the home, preparation of conjunctive advertising and point-of-sale materials, notification of field sales personnel, establishment of allocations for individual distributors, purchasing and printing of special premiums or packaging materials, production of advance inventories and staging at distribution centers in preparation for release at a specific date, and finally, the distribution to the retailer.[20]

Sell-in time begins with the launch and ends when approximately 95 percent of the deal merchandise is in the hands of consumers, which may take one to several months, depending on the deal duration.

Evaluating the Sales Promotion Results

Evaluation is a crucial requirement, and yet, according to Strang, "evaluation of promotion programs receives . . . little attention. Even where an attempt is made to evaluate a promotion, it is likely to be superficial. . . . Evaluation in terms of profitability is even less common."[21]

Manufacturers can use four methods to measure sales promotion effectiveness. The most common method is to examine the *sales data* before, during, and after a promotion. Suppose a company has a 6 percent market share in the prepromotion period, which jumps to 10 percent during the promotion, falls to 5 percent immediately after the promotion, and rises to 7 percent in the postpromotion period. (See Figure 22-1.) The promotion evidently attracted new triers and also stimulated more purchasing by existing customers. After the promotion, sales fell as consumers worked down their inventories. The long-run rise to 7 percent indicates that the company gained some new users. If the brand's share returned to the prepromotion level, then the promotion only altered the time pattern of demand rather than the total demand.

Consumer panel data would reveal the kinds of people who responded to the promotion and what they did after the promotion.[22] If more information is needed, *consumer surveys* can be conducted to learn how many recall the promotion, what they thought of it, how many took advantage of it, and how the promotion affected their subsequent brand-choice behavior. Sales promotions can also be evaluated through *experiments* that vary such attributes as incentive value, duration, and distribution media. For example:

> A research firm called Information Resources has a balanced panel of twelve hundred households, each of which pays for its groceries with a special credit card containing its demographic profile. Each household's media habits are known, and the researchers can beam in special commercials and newspapers with special inserts to capture their response to different sales promotion offers.

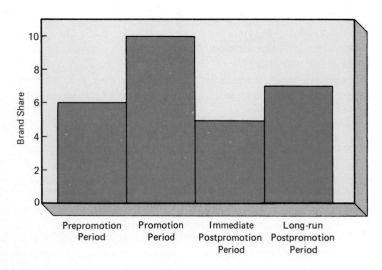

FIGURE 22-1
Effect of Consumer Deal on Brand Share

Beyond these methods of evaluating the results of specific promotions, management must recognize other potential costs and problems. First, promotions might decrease long-run brand loyalty by making more consumers deal-prone rather than advertising-prone. Second, promotions can be more expensive than they appear. Some are inevitably distributed to the wrong consumers (nonswitchers, always switchers, and the company's own customers who get a free subsidy). Furthermore, there are hidden costs of special production runs, extra sales-force effort, and handling requirements. Third, certain promotions irritate retailers, and they demand extra trade allowances or refuse to cooperate in the promotion.

In spite of these problems, sales promotion will continue to play a growing role in the total promotion mix. Its effective use will require defining the sales promotion objectives, selecting the appropriate tools, constructing the sales promotion program, pretesting it, implementing it, and evaluating the results.[23]

PUBLIC RELATIONS

Public relations (PR) is another important marketing tool. Until recently, however, it has been treated as a marketing stepchild. The public relations department is typically located at corporate headquarters; and its staff is so busy dealing with various publics—stockholders, employees, legislators, community leaders—that PR support for product marketing objectives tends to be neglected. PR departments perform the following five activities, most of which do not feed into direct product support:[24]

- *Press relations.* The aim of press relations is to place newsworthy information into the news media to attract attention to a person, product, or service.
- *Product publicity.* Product publicity involves various efforts to publicize specific products.
- *Corporate communications.* This activity covers internal and external communications and promotes understanding of the organization.
- *Lobbying.* Lobbying involves dealing with legislators and government officials to promote or defeat legislation and regulation.
- *Counseling.* Counseling involves advising management about public issues and company positions and image.

In addition, marketing managers and PR practitioners do not always talk the same language. One major difference is that marketing managers are much more bottom-line oriented, whereas PR practitioners see their job as disseminating communications. But this is changing in two ways. First, companies are calling for much more *market-oriented PR*. They want their PR department to manage all of their PR activities with a view to how these activities will contribute toward marketing the company and improving the bottom line. Second, companies are requiring their PR departments to set up a special section called *marketing PR* to directly support corporate/product promotion and image making. Thus marketing PR, like financial PR and community PR, would stand as a separate service to a corporate constituency, namely, the marketing department.

The old name for marketing PR was *publicity*, which was seen as the task of

> securing editorial space, as divorced from paid space, in all media read, viewed, or heard by a company's customers or prospects, for the specific purpose of assisting in the meeting of sales goals.[25]

But marketing PR goes beyond simple publicity. Marketing PR can contribute to the following tasks:

- **Assist in the launch of new products.** The amazing commercial success of Cabbage Patch Kids was due not so much to the paltry advertising budget of $500,000 but to clever publicity, including donating the dolls to children in hospitals, sponsoring Cabbage Patch Kids adoption parties for schoolchildren, and so on.
- **Assist in repositioning a mature product.** New York City had an extremely bad press in the seventies until the "I Love New York" campaign started to take root, bringing millions of additional tourists to the city.
- **Build up interest in a product category.** Companies and trade associations have used PR to rebuild interest in declining commodities such as eggs, milk, and potatoes and to expand consumption of such products as tea and orange juice.
- **Influence specific target groups.** McDonald's sponsors special neighborhood events in Hispanic and black communities for good causes and in turn builds up a good company image.
- **Defend products that have encountered public problems.** Johnson & Johnson's masterly use of PR was a major factor in saving Tylenol from extinction.
- **Build the corporate image in a way that projects favorably on its products.** Iaccoca's speeches and his autobiography helped project a whole new winning image for the Chrysler Company.

As the power of advertising weakens somewhat, due to rising media costs, increasing clutter, and smaller audiences, marketing managers are turning more to PR. In a survey of 286 *Advertising Age* subscribers who hold marketing management positions in U.S. companies, three-fourths reported that their companies were using marketing PR. They found it particularly effective in building awareness and brand knowledge, for both new products and established products. In several cases, it proved more cost effective than advertising. Nevertheless, it must be planned jointly with advertising. PR needs a larger budget, which may have to come from advertising.[26]

Marketing managers will need to acquire more skill in using PR resources. The Gillette company requires each brand manager to have a budget line for PR and to justify *not* using it if they do not. A brand manager will ask the PR professional how many cases would $100,000 for PR move. But this is a hard question to answer. PR is even more difficult to evaluate than advertising. Advertising is much more under the control of the company, and the measurement tools are better developed. Therefore PR people find it hard to recommend a budget level; much depends on coming up with good PR ideas and then convincing others that their impact would far exceed their cost.

Clearly, public relations can create a memorable impact on public awareness at a fraction of the cost of advertising. The company does not pay for the space or time in the media. It pays for a staff to develop and circulate the stories and manage certain events. If the company develops an interesting story, it could be picked up by all the news media and be worth millions of dollars in equivalent advertising. Furthermore, it would have more credibility than advertising. PR's results can sometimes be spectacular. Consider the following:

Promoting Paramount Pictures' *Saturday Night Fever* began months before its scheduled release. Robert Stigwood, the producer, issued the motion picture's sound track six weeks before the film's release. The records and tapes generated high-volume sales and received saturation radio play. When the film opened, moviegoers queued at the box office. Stigwood capitalized on America's fascination with celebrities by engineering a prime-time television "special" on the night of the Hollywood premiere of *Saturday Night Fever* to honor the film's star, John Travolta. The film's success was phenomenal. Stigwood's achievement was his ability to recognize a musical trend ("disco") and a talented performer (John Travolta) and to use publicity effectively to "hype" mass-market interest in the film.

Major Tools in Public Relations Public relations professionals have at least eight PR tools at their disposal, namely, news, speeches, events, public service activities, written material, audio-visual material, corporate identity media, and telephone information services. They are described below.

News One of the major tasks of PR professionals is to find or create favorable news about the company and/or its products or people. Sometimes news stories are inherent in the situation, and sometimes the PR person can suggest events or activities that would create news. News generation requires skill in developing a story concept and researching it extensively, much as a reporter does. But the PR person's skill must go beyond preparing news. Getting the media to accept press releases and attend press conference calls for marketing and interpersonal skills. A good PR media director understands the press's needs for stories that are interesting and timely, and for press releases that are well written and attention getting. The media director needs to cultivate as many news editors and reporters as possible. The more the press is cultivated, the more likely it is to give more and better coverage to the company.

Speeches Speeches are another tool for creating product and company publicity. Iacocca's charismatic talks before large audiences have helped to sell Chrysler's cars. Increasingly, company executives must field questions from the media or give talks at trade associations or sales meetings, and these can build or hurt the company's image. Some companies are carefully choosing their spokespersons and also using speech writers and coaches to help improve their delivery.

Events Companies can draw attention to new products or other company activities by arranging special events. These include news conferences, seminars, outings, exhibits, competitions, anniversaries, and so on, that will reach the target publics.

Public Service Activities Companies can improve public goodwill by contributing money and time to good causes. For example, in 1987 Procter & Gamble and Publishers' Clearing House jointly coordinated a promotion to aid the Special Olympics. Product coupons were included in the Publishers' Clearing House mailing, and Procter & Gamble donated ten cents per coupon redeemed to the Special Olympics program. In another example, B. Dalton Booksellers earmarked $3 million over a period of four years toward the fight against illiteracy. The company also encouraged its employees to participate in local programs as both tutors and board members.

Written Material Companies rely extensively on written materials to reach and influence their target markets. These include annual reports, brochures, articles, and company newsletters and magazines. Chrysler's annual report a few years ago was done almost as a sales brochure, showing and touting each new car to the stockholders. Brochures can play an important role in informing target customers about what a product is, how it works, and how it is to be assembled. Thoughtful articles written by company executives can draw attention to the company and its products. Company newsletters and magazines can help build up the company's image and convey important news to target markets. They should have an appearance and content that is consistent and supportive of the company's image.

Audio-Visual Material   Audio-visual material, such as films, slides-and-sound, and video and audio cassettes, are coming into increasing use as communication tools. The cost of audio-visual materials is usually greater than the cost of printed material, but so is the impact. They can provide high-impact product demonstrations and are likely to receive strong attention. In all cases, they should be put together with care; if they are done badly, they can impress the audience negatively rather than positively.

Corporate Identity Media   Normally a company's materials acquire separate looks, which causes confusion and misses an opportunity to create and reinforce a corporate identity. In an overcommunicated society, companies have to compete for attention. They should at least try to create a visual identity that the public immediately recognizes. The visual identity is carried by the company's permanent media—logos, stationery, brochures, signs, business forms, business cards, buildings, uniforms, and rolling stock. The corporate identity media become a marketing tool when they are attractive, distinctive, and memorable. The company should select a good graphic design consultant who will get management to identify the essence of the company, and then turn it into a concept backed by strong visual symbols.

Telephone Information Services   A newer PR tool is a telephone number through which prospects and customers can get information and better service from a company. Many hospitals, for example, use the telephone to provide health messages, offer on-the-spot counseling, and recommend physicians to people seeking one.

Major Decisions in Marketing PR

In considering when and how to use marketing PR, management should establish the marketing objectives, choose the PR messages and vehicles that will achieve the objectives, and evaluate the PR results.

Establishing the Marketing Objectives

Marketing PR can contribute strongly to the following objectives:

- *Build awareness.* PR can place stories in the media to bring attention to a product, service, person, organization, or idea.
- *Build credibility.* PR can add credibility by communicating the message in an editorial context.
- *Stimulate the sales force and dealers.* PR can help boost sales-force and dealer enthusiasm. Stories about a new product before it is launched will help the sales force sell it to retailers.
- *Hold down promotion costs.* PR costs less than direct-mail and media advertising. The smaller the company's promotion budget, the stronger the case for using PR to gain share of mind.

Specific objectives should be set for every PR campaign. The Wine Growers of California hired the public relations firm of Daniel J. Edelman, Inc., to develop a publicity campaign to convince Americans that wine drinking is a pleasurable part of good living and to improve the image and market share of California wines. The following publicity objectives were established: (1) develop magazine stories about wine and get them placed in top magazines (*Time, House Beautiful*) and in newspapers (food columns, feature sections); (2) develop stories about wine's many health values and direct them to the medical profession; and (3) develop specific publicity for the young adult market, college market, governmental bodies, and various ethnic communities. These objectives were refined into specific goals so that final results could be evaluated.

Choosing the PR Messages and Vehicles   The PR practitioner next identifies or develops interesting stories to tell about the product. Suppose a relatively unknown college wants more public visibility. The PR practitioner will search for possible stories. Do any faculty members have unusual backgrounds, or are any working on unusual projects? Are any new and unusual courses being taught? Are any interesting events taking place on campus? Usually this search will uncover hundreds of stories that can be fed to the press. The stories chosen should reflect the image this college wants.

If the number of stories is insufficient, the PR practitioner should propose newsworthy events that the college could sponsor. Here the challenge is to *create news* rather than *find news*. PR ideas include hosting major academic conventions, inviting celebrity speakers, and developing news conferences. Each event is an opportunity to develop a multitude of stories directed at different audiences.

Event creation is a particularly important skill in publicizing fund-raising drives for nonprofit organizations. Fund raisers have developed a large repertoire of special events, including *anniversary celebrations*, *art exhibits*, *auctions*, *benefit evenings*, *bingo games*, *book sales*, *cake sales*, *contests*, *dances*, *dinners*, *fairs*, *fashion shows*, *parties in unusual places*, *phonathons*, *rummage sales*, *tours*, and *walkathons*. No sooner is one type of event created, such as a walkathon, than competitors spawn new versions, such as readathons, bikathons, and jogathons.

For-profit organizations also use various events to call attention to their products and services. Humana, Inc., a hospital chain that had virtually no national name recognition in 1984, achieved 16 percent name recognition by the American public by February 1985 as a result of sponsoring a series of artificial heart implants that received national news coverage. Fuji Photo Film Company flew its blimp over the renovated Statue of Liberty during its massive celebration, scoring over its rival Kodak, which had mounted a permanent photo exhibit at the site. Anheuser-Busch sponsored a Black World Championship Rodeo in Brooklyn, attracting more than five thousand spectators.

PR practitioners are able to find or create stories on behalf of even mundane products. Here are two examples:

Some years ago the Potato Board decided to finance a publicity campaign to encourage more potato consumption. A national attitude and usage study indicated that many consumers perceived potatoes as too fattening, not nutritious enough, and not a good source of vitamins and minerals. These attitudes were disseminated by various opinion leaders, such as food editors, diet advocates, and doctors. Actually, potatoes have far fewer calories than most people imagine, and they contain several important vitamins and minerals. The Potato Board decided to develop separate publicity programs for consumers, doctors and dieticians, nutritionists, home economists, and food editors. The consumer program consisted of disseminating many stories about the potato for network television and women's magazines, developing and distributing *The Potato Lover's Diet Cookbook*, and placing articles and recipes in food editors' columns. The food editors' program consisted of food-editor seminars, conducted by nutrition experts.

One of the top brands of cat food is Star-Kist Foods' 9-Lives. Its brand image revolves around Morris the Cat. The advertising agency of Leo Burnett, which created Morris for its ads, wanted to make him more of a living, breathing, real-life feline to whom cat owners and cat lovers could relate. It hired a public relations firm, which then proposed and carried out the following ideas: (1) launch a Morris "look-alike" contest in nine major markets; (2) write a book called *Morris, an Intimate Biography*; (3) establish a coveted award called "The Morris," a bronze statuette given to the owners of award-winning cats at local cat shows; (4) sponsor an "Adopt-a-Cat Month," with Morris as the official "spokescat"; and (5) distribute a booklet called "The Morris Method" on cat care. These publicity steps strengthened the brand's market share in the cat food market.

Implementing the Marketing PR Plan   Implementing publicity requires care. Take the matter of placing stories in the media. A great story is easy to place. But most stories are less than great and may not get past busy editors. One of the chief assets of publicists is their personal relationship with media editors. Publicists are often ex-journalists who know many media editors and know what they want. Publicists look at media editors as a market to satisfy so that these editors will continue to use their stories.

Publicity requires extra care when it involves staging special events such as testimonial dinners, news conferences, and national contests. PR practitioners need a good head for detail and for coming up with quick solutions when things go wrong.

Evaluating the PR Results   PR's contribution is difficult to measure because it is used along with other promotion tools. If it is used before the other tools come into action, its contribution is easier to evaluate.

Exposures   The easiest measure of PR effectiveness is the number of *exposures* created in the media. Publicists supply the client with a clipping book showing all the media that carried news about the product and a summary statement such as the following:

> Media coverage included 3,500 column inches of news and photographs in 350 publications with a combined circulation of 79.4 million; 2,500 minutes of air time of 290 radio stations and an estimated audience of 65 million; and 660 minutes of air time on 160 television stations with an estimated audience of 91 million. If this time and space had been purchased at advertising rates, it would have amounted to $1,047,000.[27]

This exposure measure is not very satisfying. There is no indication of how many people actually read, heard, or recalled the message and what they thought afterward. There is no information on the net audience reached, since publications overlap in readership. Because publicity's goal is reach, not frequency, it would be useful to know the number of unduplicated exposures.

Awareness/comprehension/attitude change   A better measure is the change in product *awareness/comprehension/attitude* resulting from the PR campaign (after allowing for the impact of other promotional tools). For example, how many people recall hearing the news item? How many told others about it (a measure of word of mouth)? How many changed their minds after hearing it? The Potato Board learned, for example, that the number of people who agreed with the statement "Potatoes are rich in vitamins and minerals" went from 36 percent before the campaign to 67 percent after the campaign, a significant improvement in product comprehension.

Sales and profit contribution   Sales and profit impact is the most satisfactory measure, if obtainable. For example, 9-Lives sales increased 43 percent at the end of the "Morris the Cat" PR campaign. However, advertising and sales promotion had also been stepped up, and their contribution has to be allowed for. Suppose total sales have increased $1,500,000, and management estimates that PR contributed 15 percent of the total sales increase. Then the return on PR investment is calculated as follows:

Total sales increase	$1,500,000
Estimated sales increase due to PR (15%)	225,000
Contribution margin on product sales (10%)	22,500
Total direct cost of PR program	−10,000
Contribution margin added by PR investment	12,500
Return on PR investment ($12,500/$10,000)	125%

In the years ahead, we can expect more joint strategy planning of advertising, PR, and the other promotional tools. Major advertising agencies have recognized the growing leverage obtained from PR by recently acquiring major PR firms: For example, Young & Rubicam acquired Burson-Marsteller, and J. Walter Thompson acquired Hill and Knowlton. The acquired PR firms will benefit from the highly disciplined methods of the ad agencies, and the ad agencies will benefit from the expanded areas of creativity afforded by PR.

SUMMARY

Sales promotion covers a wide variety of short-term incentive tools designed to stimulate the consumer markets, the trade, and the organization's own sales force. Sales promotion expenditures now exceed advertising expenditures and are growing at a faster rate. Consumer promotion tools include samples, coupons, cash refund offers, price packs, premiums, prizes, patronage rewards, free trials, product warranties, tie-in promotions, and point-of-purchase displays and demonstrations. Trade promotion tools include price-off, advertising and display allowances, free goods, push money, and specialty advertising items. Business promotion tools include conventions/trade shows, and contests/sweepstakes/games. Sales promotion planning calls for establishing the sales promotion objectives, selecting the tools, developing, pretesting, and implementing the sales promotion program, and evaluating the results.

Public relations is another important communication/promotion tool. It has been the least-utilized tool, but it has great potential for building awareness and preference in the marketplace, repositioning products, and defending them. The major PR tools are news, speeches, events, public service activities, written material, audio-visual material, corporate identity media, and telephone information services. Public relations planning involves establishing the PR objectives, choosing the appropriate messages and vehicles, and evaluating the PR results.

■ QUESTIONS

1. What psychological and business factors have contributed to "promotion clutter"? How might a manager best respond to this problem?

2. What are the possible trade-offs a manager should consider when deciding between sales promotion and advertising strategies?

3. If top management were considering a proposal to establish a public relations department outside the marketing department, what would your response be to this proposal? Give reasons for the position you have taken.

4. Review three recent crises in business or government in which credibility was threatened. In each case, how was the damage to the entity's image managed from a public relations perspective? Can you suggest a strategy for damage control from these experiences?

5. what is meant by a "public"? Do organizations serve more than one public? If yes, say why and give examples. How might a public relations program be influenced by the existence of several publics?

6. Approximately 120 billion coupons were distributed by American manufacturers in one year. Only 5.4 billion were redeemed. What factors influence the rate of coupon redemption?

7. Companies annually spend over $6 billion a year on trade shows. What questions should marketing managers ask themselves when determining how much of the marketing budget to allocate to trade shows?

8. A major basketball team experienced a decline in home-game attendance. The team's owner decided to hire a marketer to stimulate attendance. What are some of the steps that can be taken?

9. Joe Pringle, a product manager at the XYZ Snacks Company, is concerned about falling sales in recent months. His inventory is high. He is contemplating a sales promotion to reverse the sales trend and reduce inventories. He is thinking of offering a case allowance to the trade. He expects sales to be 40,000 cases in the absence of promotion. The case price is $10, and the gross profit contribution is 40 percent. He is cur-

rently thinking of offering a $1/case allowance. He expects increased sales of 20,000 cases during the promotion period. The estimated cost of developing this promotion is $12,000. (a) Will he make a profit on this promotion? (b) What is the break-even sales increase that will justify this case allowance? (c) If he offers only a $.50/case allowance, he expects additional net sales of 12,000. Should he offer a $1/case or a $.50/case allowance?

10. Much of the public relations work done by business firms consists of miscellaneous and unrelated activities. Can you suggest an underlying public relations orientation a company could adopt that would provide a focus for many publicity activities?

11. Select a product or service and recommend which sales promotion tools should be used to build its consumer franchise.

■ FOOTNOTES

1 Kevin T. Higgins, "Sales Promotion Spending Closing in on Advertising," *Marketing News*, July 4, 1986, p. 8.

2 Roger A. Strang, "Sales Promotion—Fast Growth, Faulty Management," *Harvard Business Review*, July–August 1976, pp. 115–24, here pp. 116–19.

3 Robert George Brown, "Sales Response to Promotions and Advertising," *Journal of Advertising Research*, August 1974, pp. 33–39, here pp. 36–37.

4 F. Kent Mitchel, "Advertising/Promotion Budgets: How did We Get Here, and What Do We Do Now?" *Journal of Consumer Marketing*, Fall 1985, pp. 405–47.

5 See Roger A. Strang, Robert M. Prentice, and Alden G. Clayton, *The Relationship between Advertising and Promotion in Brand Strategy* (Cambridge, Mass.: Marketing Science Institute, 1975), Chap. 5.

6 Varadarajan, however, has argued effectively that all consumer-directed sales promotion tools possess "consumer franchise building" potential, if done correctly. See the appendix in P. Rajan Varadarajan, "Cooperative Sales Promotion: An Idea Whose Time Has Come," *Journal of Consumer Marketing*, Winter 1986, pp. 15–33.

7 Strang, "Sales Promotion," p. 124.

8 *Advertising Age*, September 15, 1985, p. 15.

9 For further reading, see Carl-Magnus Seipel, "Premiums—Forgotten by Theory," *Journal of Marketing*, April 1971, pp. 26–34.

10 For some recent new promotions, see "Firms Woo Jaded Consumers with Richer Sales Promotions," *Wall Street Journal*, May 29, 1986, p. 29.

11 See P. Rajan Varadarajan, "Horizontal Cooperative Sales Promotion: A Framework for Classification and Additional Perspectives," *Journal of Marketing*, April 1986, pp. 61–73.

12 *Advertising Age*, August 15, 1985, p. 19.

13 See Michel Chevalier and Ronald C. Curhan, *Temporary Promotions as a Function of Trade Deals: A Descriptive Analysis* (Cambridge, Mass.: Marketing Science Institute, 1975), p. 2.

14 See "Retailers Buy Far in Advance to Exploit Trade Promotions," *Wall Street Journal*, October 9, 1986, p. 35.

15 See Suzette Cavanaugh, "Setting Objectives and Evaluating the Effectiveness of Trade Show Exhibits," *Journal of Marketing*, October 1976, pp. 100–105.

16 Arthur Stern, "Measuring the Effectiveness of Package Goods Promotion Strategies" (Paper presented to the Association of National Advertisers, Glen Cove, N.Y., February 1978).

17 Strang, "Sales Promotion," p. 119.

18 Russell D. Bowman, "Merchandising and Promotion Grow Big in Marketing World, " *Advertising Age*, December 1974, p. 21.

19 Strang, "Sales Promotion," p. 120.

20 Kurt H. Schaffir and H. George Trenten, *Marketing Information Systems* (New York: Amacom, 1973), p. 81.

21 Strang, "Sales Promotion," p. 120.

22 See Joe A. Dodson, Alice M. Tybout, and Brian Sternthal, "Impact of Deals and Deal Retraction on Brand Switching," *Journal of Marketing Research*, February 1978, pp. 72–81. They found that deals generally increase brand switching, the rate depending on the type of deal. Media-distributed coupons induce substantial switching, cents-off deals induce somewhat less switching, and package coupons hardly affect brand switching. Furthermore, consumers generally return to their preferred brands after the deal.

23 For a more in-depth discussion, see Don E. Schultz and William A. Robinson, *Sales Promotion Management* (Chicago: Crain Books, 1982). For an excellent set of guidelines, see John W. Keon and Judy Bayer, "An Expert Approach to Sales Promotion Management," *Journal of Advertising Research*, June–July 1986, pp. 19–26.

24 Adapted from Scott M. Cutlip, Allen H. Center, and Glen M. Brown, *Effective Public Relations*, 6th ed. (Englewood Cliffs, N.J.: Prentice-Hall, 1985), pp. 7–17.

25 George Black, *Planned Industrial Publicity* (Chicago: Putnam's, 1952), p. 3.

26 Tom Duncan, *A Study of How Manufacturers and Service Companies Perceive and Use Marketing Public Relations* (Muncie, Ind.: Ball State University, December 1985).

27 Arthur M. Merims, "Marketing's Stepchild: Product Publicity," *Harvard Business Review*, November–December 1972, pp. 111–12.

23

Managing
the Sales Force

I don't know who you are.
I don't know your company.
I don't know your company's product.
I don't know what your company stands for.
I don't know your company's customers.
I don't know your company's record.
I don't know your company's reputation.
Now—what was it you wanted to sell me?

McGraw-Hill Publications

Robert Louis Stevenson observed that "everyone lives by selling something." In 1984, American firms spent approximately $172 billion on personal selling compared with $89 billion on advertising. Over 8 million Americans are employed in sales and related occupations. Sales forces are found in nonprofit as well as profit organizations. College recruiters are the university's sales-force arm for attracting new students. Churches use membership committees to attract new members. The U.S. Agricultural Extension Service sends agricultural specialists to sell farmers on using new farming methods. Hospitals and museums use fund raisers to contact and raise money from donors. Selling is one the world's oldest professions.

People who sell are called by various names: saleswomen and salesmen, sales representatives, salespersons, account executives, sales consultants, sales engineers, field representatives, agents, service representatives, and marketing representatives. The public tends to carry many stereotypes about sales representatives. "Salesman" may conjure up an image of Arthur Miller's pitiable Willy Loman in *Death of a Salesman* or Meredith Wilson's cigar-smoking, back-slapping joke-telling Harold Hill in *The Music Man*. Sales representatives are typically pictured as loving sociability—although many sales representatives actually dislike it. They are criticized for foisting goods on people—although buyers often search out sales representatives.

Actually the term *sales representative* covers a broad range of positions in our economy, where the differences are often greater than the similarities. McMurry devised the following classification of sales positions:[1]

1. **Deliverer.** Positions where the salesperson's job is predominantly to deliver the product (e.g., milk, bread, fuel, oil)
2. **Order taker.** Positions where the salesperson is predominantly an inside order-taker (e.g., the haberdashery salesperson standing behind the counter) or an outside order taker (e.g., the soap salesman calling on the supermarket manager)
3. **Missionary.** Positions where the salesperson is not expected or permitted to take an order but is called on only to build goodwill or to educate the actual or potential user (e.g., the medical "detailer" representing an ethical pharmaceutical house)
4. **Technician.** Positions where the major emphasis is placed on technical knowledge (e.g., the engineering salesperson who is primarily a consultant to the "client" companies)
5. **Demand creator.** Positions that demand the creative sale of tangible products (e.g., vacuum cleaners, refrigerators, siding, and encyclopedias) or of intangibles (e.g., insurance, advertising services, or education)

The positions range from the least to the most creative types of selling. The first jobs call for maintaining accounts and taking orders, while the latter require seeking prospects and influencing them to buy. Our discussion will focus on the more creative types of selling.

This chapter is divided into three parts. The first and second parts deal with several issues in designing and managing an effective sales force. (See Figure 23-1.) The third part deals with three aspects of effective personal selling, namely, salesmanship, negotiation, and relationship building.

DESIGNING THE SALES FORCE

Sales personnel serve as the company's personal link to the customers. The sales representative is the company to many of its customers and in turn brings back to the company much needed intelligence about the customer. Therefore the company needs to give its deepest thought to issues in sales-force design, namely, developing sales-force objectives, strategy, structure, size, and compensation.

FIGURE 23-1
Steps in Designing and Managing the Sales Force

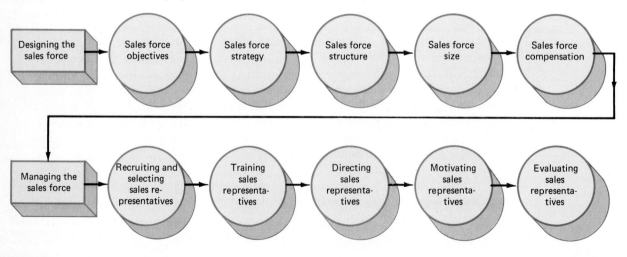

Sales-Force Objectives

Sales-force objectives must be based on the character of the company's target markets and the company's desired position in these markets. The company must consider the unique role that personal selling can play in the marketing mix to serve customer needs in a competitively effective way. Personal selling happens to be the most expensive contact and communications tool used by the company, costing companies an average of $230 a sales call in 1985.[2] Therefore it must be used sparingly. Personal selling is also the most effective tool at certain stages of the buying process, such as the buyer-education, negotiation, and sales-closing stages. It is important that the company carefully consider when and how to use sales representatives to facilitate the marketing task.

Companies set different objectives for their sales force, IBM's sales representatives are responsible for *selling*, *installing*, and *upgrading* customer computer equipment; AT&T sales representatives are responsible for *developing*, *selling*, and *protecting* accounts. Sales representatives perform one or more of the following tasks for their companies:

- *Prospecting.* Sales representatives find and cultivate new customers.
- *Communicating.* Sales representatives skillfully communicate information about the company's products and services.
- *Selling.* Sales representatives know the art of "salesmanship"—approaching, presenting, answering objections, and closing sales.
- *Servicing.* Sales representatives provide various services to the customers—consulting on their problems, rendering technical assistance, arranging financing, and expediting delivery.
- *Information gathering.* Sales representatives conduct market research and intelligence work and fill in call reports.
- *Allocating.* Sales representatives are able to evaluate customer quality and allocate scarce products during product shortages.

Companies often become more specific about their sales-force objectives and activities. One company advises its sales representatives to spend 80 percent of their time with current customers and 20 percent with prospects, and 85 percent of their time on established products and 15 percent on new products. If norms are not established, sales representatives tend to spend most of their time selling established products to current accounts and neglect new products and new prospects.

The sales representative's mix of tasks varies with the state of the economy. When widespread product shortages occurred in 1973, sales representatives in many industries found themselves with nothing to sell. Some observers jumped to the conclusion that sales representatives were redundant and could be retrenched. But this thinking overlooked the salesperson's other roles—allocating the product, counseling unhappy customers, communicating company plans on remedying the shortage, and selling the company's other products that were not in short supply

As companies increase their market orientation, their sales forces need to become more market-focused and customer-oriented. The traditional view is that sales people should worry about volume and sell, sell, sell and that the marketing department should worry about marketing strategy and profitability. The newer view is that sales people should know how to produce customer satisfaction and company profit. They should know how to analyze sales data, measure market potential, gather market intelligence, and develop marketing strategies and plans. Sales representatives need analytical marketing skills, and this becomes especially critical at the higher levels of sales management. Marketers believe that sales forces will be more effective in the long run if they are trained in marketing.

Sales-Force Strategy

Companies compete with each other to get orders from customers. They must deploy their sales forces strategically so that they are calling on the right customers at the right time and in the right way. Sales representatives can approach customers in several ways:

- ■ **Sales representative to buyer.** A sales representative talks to a prospect or customer in person or over the phone.
- ■ **Sales representative to buyer group.** A sales representative makes a sales presentation to a buying group.
- ■ **Sales team to buyer group.** A sales team (such as a company officer, a sales representative, and a sales engineer) makes a sales presentation to a buying group.
- ■ **Conference selling.** The sales representative brings resource people from the company to meet with one or more buyers to discuss problems and mutual opportunities.
- ■ **Seminar selling.** A company team conducts an educational seminar for a technical group in a customer company about state-of-the-art developments.

Thus the sales representative often acts as the "account manager" who arranges contacts between various people in the buying and selling organizations. Selling increasingly calls for teamwork, requiring the support of other personnel, such as *top management*, which is increasingly involved in the sales process, especially when *national accounts*[3] or *major sales*[4] are at stake; *technical people*, who supply technical information to the customer before, during, or after the purchase of the product; *customer-service representatives*, who provide installation, maintenance, and other services to the customer; and an *office staff*, consisting of sales analysts, order expediters, and secretaries.

Once the company decides on a desirable selling approach, it can use either a direct or a contractual sales force. A *direct (or company) sales force* consists of full- or part-time paid employees who work exclusively for the company. This sales force includes *inside sales personnel*, who conduct business from their office using the telephone and receiving visits from prospective buyers, and *field sales personnel*, who travel and visit customers. A *contractual sales force* consists of manufacturers' reps, sales agents, or brokers, who are paid a commission based on their sales.

Sales-Force Structure

The sales-force strategy will have implications for structuring the sales force. Sales-force structure is simple if the company sells one product line to one end-using industry with customers in many locations; the company would use a territorial-structured sales force. If the company sells many products to many types of customers, it might need a product-structured or market-structured sales force. These alternative sales-force structures are discussed below. (See Exhibit 23-1 for an example of the work involved in setting up a new sales force.)

Territorial-Structured Sales Force   In the simplest sales organization, each sales representative is assigned an exclusive territory in which to represent the company's full line. This sales structure has a number of advantages. First, it results in a clear definition of the salesperson's responsibilities. As the only salesperson working the territory, he or she bears the credit or blame for area sales to the extent that personal selling effort makes a difference. Second, territorial responsibility increases the sales representative's incentive to cultivate local business and personal ties. These ties contribute to the sales representative's selling effectiveness and personal life. Third, travel expenses are relatively small, since each sales representative travels within a small geographical area.

EXHIBIT 23-1

Building a Sales Force From Scratch: The Case of Wilkinson

Wilkinson Sword USA, the U.S. arm of the British company, had a 7.9 percent market share of the U.S. razor blade market in 1974, but its share had fallen to 0.7 percent by 1984. The parent company had cut down its U.S. advertising, preferring to spend the money in Europe, and U.S. sales had plummeted. In addition, Wilkinson USA did not have its own sales force but used manufacturers' reps for drugstores and brokers for food stores, with the result that its product had little push.

In 1984, the company was reorganized and president Norman R. Proulx was given a large budget to revive the company. He budgeted $23.5 million to run a two-year advertising campaign and used most of the rest of the budget to build a Wilkinson sales force for the first time. Ronald E. Mineo, Wilkinson's sales vice-president, proceeded to build a 34-person sales force by taking the following steps:

1. The first step was account identification. Wilkinson identified 25 leading chains in the food store, drugstore, and mass-merchandise business and established them as national accounts to be handled in Wilkinson's Atlanta headquarters by two national account managers. Then several regional accounts were identified and assigned to area sales managers. Finally, smaller accounts were assigned to sales representatives.

2. The second step was setting up geographical divisions. The country was partitioned into three divisions—East, West, and Central. Each division was sliced into roughly five areas, and each area further sliced into a few territories.

3. The third step was staffing the positions. Mineo said that "organizing is the easy part. The hard part is finding the people." He looked primarily for people with at least five years of selling experience in top health-and-beauty-aids companies. He offered a package at least as good as the competition's. It cost Wilkinson over half-a-million dollars in the first year's recruiting, training, salaries, bonuses, etc., to build the sales force.

4. The fourth step was hiring a vice-president of trade relations, who would be a critical appointment. Wilkinson also began hiring retail merchandisers to support the sales people by reducing out-of-stocks, building incremental facings and displays, and monitoring pricing.

Now that these steps are in place, we will learn in a few years if Wilkinson has achieved its goal of winning over 10 percent of the U.S. wet-shave market. Its ultimate goal is to become the number-two razor blade company in the United States. One of its managers said: "We've opened the doors. Now we need to kick the doors down."

SOURCE: Rayna Skolnik, "The Birth of a Sales Force," *Sales and Marketing Management*, March 10, 1986, pp. 42–44.

Territorial sales organization is supported by a hierarchy of sales management positions. Several territories will be supervised by a *district sales manager*; several districts will be supervised by a *regional sales manager*; and several regions will be supervised by a *national sales manager* or *sales vice-president*. Each higher-level sales manager takes on increasing marketing and administrative work in relation to the time available for selling. In fact, sales managers are paid for their management skills rather than their selling skills. The new sales trainee, in looking ahead at the career path, can expect to become a sales representative and then a district manager and, depending on his or her ability and motivation, may move to higher levels of sales or general management.

In designing a set of territories, the company seeks certain territorial characteristics: The territories are easy to administer; their sales potential is easy to estimate; they reduce total travel time; and they provide a sufficient and equitable workload and sales potential for each sales representative. These characteristics are achieved through decisions about the size and shape of territorial units.

Territory size   Territories can be designed to provide either *equal sales potential* or *equal workload*. Each principle offers advantages at the cost of some dilemmas.

Territories of *equal potential* provide each sales representative with the same income opportunities and provide the company with a means to evaluate performance. Persistent differences in sales yield by territory are assumed to reflect differences in ability or effort of individual sales representatives. Salespersons are encouraged to work at their top capacity.

But because customer density varies by territory, territories with equal potential can vary widely in size. The potential for selling drill presses in Chicago is larger than in several western states. A sales representative assigned to Chicago can cover the same sales potential with much less effort than the sales representative who sells in the Far West.

The sales representative assigned to the larger and sparser territory is going to end up with either fewer sales and less income for equal effort or equal sales through extraordinary effort. One solution is to pay the western sales representatives more compensation for the extra effort. But this reduces the profits on sales in the western territories. Another solution is to acknowledge that territories differ in attractiveness and assign the better or more senior sales representatives to the better territories.

Alternatively, territories could be designed to *equalize the sales workload*. Each sales representative can then cover his or her territory adequately. This principle, however, results in some variation in territory sales potentials. That does not concern a sales force on straight salary. But where sales representatives are compensated partly on their sales, territories will vary in their attractiveness even though their workloads are equal. A lower compensation rate can be paid to sales representatives in the territories with the higher sales potential, or the territories with the better potential can go to the higher performers.

Territory shape   Territories are formed by combining smaller units, such as counties or states, until they add up to a territory of a given sales potential or workload. They take into account the location of natural barriers, the compatibility of adjacent areas, the adequacy of transportation, and so forth. Many companies prefer a certain territory shape because this can influence the cost and ease of coverage and the sales representatives' job satisfaction. Most common are circular, cloverleaf, and wedge-shaped territories. Today companies can use computer programs to design sales territories that optimize on such criteria as compactness, equalization of workload or sales potential, and minimal travel time.[5]

Product-Structured Sales Force   The importance of sales representatives' knowing their products, together with the development of product divisions and product management, has led many companies to structure their sales force along product lines. Product specialization is particularly warranted where the products are technically complex, highly unrelated, or very numerous.

The mere existence of different company products, however, is not a sufficient argument for specializing the sales force by product. Such specialization may not be the best

---

For example, Kodak uses different sales forces for its film products and industrial products. The film products sales force deals with simple products that are intensively distributed, while the industrial products sales force deals with complex products that require technical understanding. As might be expected, the film sales force is paid a salary, while the industrial sales force earns more through a salary and commission plan.

course if the company's separate product lines are bought by the same customers. For example, the American Hospital Supply Corporation has several product divisions, each with its own sales force. It is possible that several sales representatives from the American Hospital Supply Corporation could call on the same hospital on the same day. This means that company sales personnel travel over the same routes, and each waits to see the customer's purchasing agents. These extra costs must be weighed against the benefits of more-knowledgeable product representation.

Market-Structured Sales Force   Companies often specialize their sales forces to serve different markets. Separate sales forces may be set up for different industries and even different customers. For example, IBM recently set up a separate sales office for finance and brokerage customers in New York, another for GM in Detroit, and still another for Ford in nearby Dearborn.

The most obvious advantage of market specialization is that each sales force can become knowledgeable about specific customer needs. At one time General Electric's sales representatives specialized in products (fan motors, switches, and so forth), but it later changed to specialization in industries, such as the air-conditioning industry and auto industry, because that is how customers saw the purchase of fan motors, switches, and so forth. A market-specialized sales force can sometimes reduce total sales-force costs. A pump manufacturer at one time used highly trained sales engineers to sell to both original-equipment manufacturers (who needed to deal with technical representatives) and jobbers (who did not need to deal with technical representatives). Later the company split its sales force and staffed the jobber sales force with lower-paid, less-technical sales personnel.

The major disadvantage of market-structured sales forces arises when the various types of customers are scattered throughout the country. This means extensive travel by each of the company's sales forces.

Complex Sales-Force Structures   When a company sells a wide variety of products to many types of customers over a broad geographical area, it often combines several principles of sales-force structure. Sales representatives may be specialized by territory-product, territory-market, product-market, and so on. A sales representative might then report to one or more line managers and staff managers. One of the most interesting developments is the growth of national account management divisions. (See Exhibit 23-2.)

Companies need to rethink their sales-force structure as the market and economic conditions change. Xerox is a good case in point:

Xerox managed several sales forces, the main one selling copier/duplicator equipment and others selling typewriters, printing systems, office systems, and so on. With the move to the electronic office, Xerox decided to collapse these different sales forces so that different Xerox sales people would not end up all calling on the same customers and confusing them with arguments for different office products and systems. Xerox divided the new sales force into four groups:

NAM's: national account managers serving major companies with dispersed multiple locations

MAM's: major account managers serving major accounts with one or two other accounts in the region

AR's: account representatives serving standard commercial accounts with potential of $5,000–10,000

MR's: marketing representatives serving all others

Each group faces a different selling cycle and is rewarded under a different compensation plan. In taking this step, Xerox put its sales force through a deep and long sales retraining program because each sales rep needed to learn how to represent all of Xerox's product lines to the customer.

EXHIBIT 23-2

National Account Management—What It Is and How It Works

When a company sells to many small accounts, it uses a traditional sales force, with each sales representative handling several accounts. If the company has a large account, this account is often assigned to a high-level sales manager. This large account is variously called a key account, a major account, or a house account. If this account is a large company with many divisions operating in many parts of the country and subject to many buying influences (such as Sears or General Motors), it is likely to be handled as a *national account* with a specific individual or sales team assigned to it. If the seller has several such accounts, it is likely to organize a *national account management* (NAM) *division*. The company will then sell its larger customers through this division and its smaller customers through its regular sales force. A company such as Xerox handles about 250 national accounts through its NAM division.

National account management is growing for a number of reasons. As buyer concentration increases through mergers and acquisitions, fewer buyers account for a larger share of a company's sales. Thus the largest 10 percent of accounts may account for more than 50 percent of a company's revenue. Another factor is that many buyers are centralizing their purchases of certain items instead of leaving those purchases to the local units. This gives them more bargaining power with the sellers. The sellers in turn need to devote more attention to these major buyers. Still another factor is that as products become more complex, more groups in the buyer's organization become involved in the purchase choice, and the typical salesperson may not have the needed authority or coverage to be effective in selling to the buyer.

In organizing a national account program, a company has to face a number of issues, including: how to select national accounts; how to manage them; how to develop, manage, and evaluate national account managers; how to organize a structure for national account management; and where to locate national account management in the organization.

Essentially a company wants its national account managers to be good at a number of things. They must be able to reach all the buying influences in the buyer's organization. They must be able to reach all the groups in their own organization—sales people, R&D staff, manufacturing people, and so on—to coordinate them in meeting the buyer's requirements. Thus national account managers link all the complex parts of their company with all the complex parts of the buying company. In many organizations they are, in fact, called "relationship managers."

SOURCES: For further discussion, see the working papers on National Account Management prepared by Benson P. Shapiro and Rowland T. Moriarty under the sponsorship of the Marketing Science Institute, Cambridge, Mass., published in 1980–83. Also see Philip Maher, "National Account Marketing: An Essential Strategy, or Prima Donna Selling?" *Business Management*, December 1984, pp. 38–45.

Sales-Force Size Once the company clarifies its sales-force strategy and structure, it is ready to consider sales-force size. Sales representatives are one of the company's most productive and expensive assets. Increasing their number will increase both sales and costs.

Most companies use the *workload approach* to establish sales-force size. This method consists of the following steps:

1. Customers are grouped into size classes according to their annual sales volume.
2. The desirable call frequencies (number of sales calls on an account per year) are established for each class. They reflect how much call intensity the company seeks in relation to competitors.
3. The number of accounts in each size class is multiplied by the corresponding call frequency to arrive at the total workload for the country, in sales calls per year.
4. The average number of calls a sales representative can make per year is determined.
5. The number of sales representatives needed is determined by dividing the total annual calls required by the average annual calls made by a sales representative.

Suppose the company estimates that there are one thousand A accounts and two thousand B accounts in the nation; and A accounts require thirty-six calls a year and B accounts require twelve calls a year. This means the company needs a sales force that can make sixty thousand sales calls a year. Suppose the average sales representative can make one thousand calls a year. The company would need sixty full-time sales representatives.

Sales-Force Compensation

To attract the desired number of sales representatives, the company has to develop an attractive compensation plan. Sales representatives would like income regularity, reward for above-average performance, and fair payment for experience and longevity. On the other hand, management would emphasize control, economy, and simplicity. Management objectives, such as economy, will conflict with sales representatives' objectives, such as financial security. It is understandable why compensation plans exhibit a tremendous variety, not only among industries but among companies within the same industry.

Management must determine the level and components of an effective compensation plan. The *level of compensation* must bear some relation to the "going market price" for the type of sales job and abilities required. For example, the average earnings of the experienced salesperson in 1985 amounted to over $30,000.[6] If the market price for sales people is well defined, the individual firm has little choice but to pay the going rate. To pay less would bring forth less than the desired quantity or quality of applicants, and to pay more would be unnecessary. The market price for sales people, however, is seldom well defined. For one thing, company plans vary in the importance of fixed and variable salary elements, fringe benefits, and expense allowances. And data on the average take-home pay of sales representatives working for competitive firms can be misleading because of significant variations in the average seniority and ability levels of the competitors' sales forces. Published data on industry sales-force compensation levels are infrequent and generally lack sufficient detail.

The company must determine the *components of compensation*—a fixed amount, a variable amount, expenses, and fringe benefits. The *fixed amount*, which might be salary or a drawing account, is intended to satisfy the sales representatives' need for some stability of income. The *variable amount*, which might be commissions, bonus, or profit sharing, is intended to stimulate and reward greater effort. *Expense allowances* enable the sales representatives to meet the expenses involved in travel, lodging, dining, and entertaining. And *fringe benefits*, such as paid vacations, sickness or accident benefits, pensions, and life insurance, are intended to provide security and job satisfaction.

Top sales management must decide on the relative importance of these components in the compensation plan. A popular rule favors making about 70 percent of the salesperson's total income fixed and allocating the remaining 30 percent among the other elements. But the variations around this average are so pronounced that it can hardly serve as a guide. Fixed compensation should have more emphasis in jobs with a high ratio of nonselling to selling duties and in jobs where the selling task is technically complex and involves teamwork. Variable compensation should have more emphasis in jobs where sales are cyclical or depend on sales-force initiative.

Fixed and variable compensation give rise to three basic types of sales-force compensation plans—straight salary, straight commission, and combination salary and commission. In one study, 28 percent of the companies paid straight salary, 21 percent paid straight commission, and 51 percent paid salary plus commission.[7] The advantages and disadvantages of each plan are described below.

Straight Salary   With this plan, sales representatives receive a fixed salary and an amount to cover expenses in performing various duties. Occasionally there will be additional compensation through discretionary bonuses or sales-contest prizes.

Management gains a number of advantages under a straight salary plan. The primary one is that management can alter sales duties without strong objection. Straight salary plans are also easier to explain and less costly to administer. They simplify the task of projecting the sales payroll for the coming year. Finally, by providing the sales force with a stable income, the straight salary plan may lead to higher sales-force morale and spirit.

The chief weakness of the straight salary plan is that it does not present the sales force with an incentive to do a better-than-average selling job. This puts a greater supervision burden on management to control, evaluate, and reward the performances of individual sales representatives. Other problems posed by straight salary plans are an inflexible selling-expense burden during business downswings; the danger that during upswings sales representatives on fixed salaries will not have sufficient incentive to exploit the increased business potential; thorny questions in salary adjustment for ability, rising living costs, and length of service; and the probability that the company will not attract or hold on to the more aggressive sales representatives.

Straight Commission   This plan pays sales representatives some fixed or sliding rate related to their sales or profit volume. They may or may not receive reimbursement for expenses incurred in performing the selling function. Straight commission plans are prominent in the selling of insurance and investment securities, furniture, office equipment, small office machines, and clothing and in the textile and shoe industries and in drug and hardware wholesaling.

The straight commission plan offers three advantages. First, it provides an incentive for sales representatives to work at maximum capacity. Second, it ties selling expenses more closely to current revenue. Third, management can set different commissions on different products and sales tasks, thereby influencing how the salespersons spend their time.

These advantages come at a substantial cost, however. Management encounters great resistance when it tries to get the sales force to do things that do not generate immediate income, such as following up leads, filling out reports, or providing customer service. The salesperson's financial stake in getting the sale may lead to high-pressure tactics or price discounting, which may damage customer goodwill. Straight commission plans are more costly to administer. Also they provide little security and cause morale to drop when sales fall through no fault of the sales force.

Management has several options regarding the commission base, commission rates, and the commission starting point. The *commission base* may be gross sales volume, net sales after returns, gross margins, or net profits. The *commission rates* may be identical for all sales or differentiated by customers and/or products; they may be constant with sales volume or vary in a progressive or regressive fashion. The *commission starting point* may be the first sale or sales over a minimum quota. For administrative simplicity, most companies base sales commissions on sales volume. But sales commissions based on sales volume fail to relate selling effort to product profitability. The payment of commissions on *gross margin* should do a superior job of motivating sales representatives to improve their product and customer mix and, therefore, company profits.[8]

Combination Salary and Commission   The great majority of firms pay a combination of salary and commission, in the hope of achieving the advantages of each while avoiding the disadvantages. The most common split is 70 percent salary and 30 percent commission. The combination plan is appropriate where sales volume depends on the sales representative's motivation and yet management wants some control over nonselling duties performed by the sales representative. The plan means that during downswings the company is not stuck with inflexible selling costs, and sales representatives do not lose their whole income.

Bonus   Many companies pay *bonuses* as a supplement or a substitute for commission-type incentives. Bonuses are noncontractual payments for extra effort, merit, or results. They reward sales representatives for performing tasks that are desirable but not rewardable through commissions, for example, preparing prompt reports, supplying useful selling ideas, and developing unusual product or market knowledge. The main problem with bonuses is that managerial judgment enters into their determination, and sales representatives can raise questions of fairness.

Other Costs   Besides salary, commission, and bonus, the company's selling costs include the following additional elements: *selling expenses* (travel, lodging, telephone, entertainment, samples promotion, and office and/or clerical expenses); *fringe benefits* (hospitalization insurance, life insurance, pension plan, association memberships, and moving expenses); *special incentives* (contests, service awards); and *staff backup costs* (cost of technical and customer-service people, sales analysts, computer time, and sales-training programs). Thus the cost of running a sales force adds up to much more than the direct compensation elements alone.

MANAGING THE SALES FORCE

Having established the objectives, strategy, structure, size, and compensation of the sales force, the company has to move to recruiting and selecting, training, directing, motivating, and evaluating sales representatives. Various policies and procedures guide these decisions.

Recruiting and Selecting Sales Representatives

Importance of Careful Selection   At the heart of a successful sales-force operation is the selection of effective sales representatives. The performance levels of an average and a top sales representative are quite different. One survey of over five hundred companies revealed that 27 percent of the sales force brought in over 52 percent of the sales. Beyond the differences in sales productivity are the great wastes in hiring the wrong persons. Of the sixteen thousand sales representatives who had been hired by the surveyed companies, only 68 percent still worked for the company at the end of the year, and only 50 percent were expected to remain throughout the following year.

The financial loss due to turnover is only part of the total cost. The new sales representative who remains with the company receives a direct income averaging around half of the direct selling cost. If he or she receives $20,000 a year, another $20,000 may go into fringe benefits, expenses, supervision, office space, supplies, and secretarial assistance. Consequently, the new sales representative needs to produce sales on which the gross margin at least covers the selling expenses of $40,000. If the gross margin is 10 percent, he or she would have to sell at least $400,000 for the company to break even.

What Makes a Good Sales Representative?   Selecting sales representatives would not be a problem if one knew what traits to look for. If effective sales representatives were always outgoing, aggressive, and energetic, these characteristics could be checked in applicants. But many successful sales representatives are introverted, mild mannered, and far from energetic. Successful sales representatives include men and women who are tall and short, articulate and inarticulate, well groomed and slovenly.

Nevertheless the search continues for the magic combination of traits that spells sure-fire sales ability. Numerous lists have been drawn up. McMurry wrote: "It is my conviction that the possessor of an *effective* sales personality is a *habitual 'wooer,' an individual who has a compulsive need to win and hold the affection of others.*"[9] McMurry listed five additional traits of the super salesperson: "a high level of energy, abounding self-confidence, a chronic hunger for money, a well-established habit of industry, and a state of mind that regards each objection, resistance, or obstacle as a challenge."[10]

Mayer and Greenberg offered one of the shortest lines of traits.[11] They concluded that the effective salesperson has at least two basic qualities: (1) *empathy*, the ability to feel as the customer does; and (2) *ego drive*, a strong personal need to make the sale. Using these two traits as criteria led to fairly good predictions of the subsequent performance of applicants for sales positions in three different industries.

How can a company determine the characteristics necessary for sales representatives in its industry? The job duties suggest some of the characteristics to look for. Is there a lot of paperwork? Does the job call for much travel? Will the salesperson confront a high proportion of rejections? The company should also examine the traits of its most successful sales representatives for possible clues.

Recruitment Procedures   After management develops its selection criteria, it must recruit. The personnel department seeks applicants by various means, including soliciting names from current sales representatives, using employment agencies, placing job ads, and contacting college students. As for college students, companies have found it hard to sell them on selling. Few students want to go into selling as a career.[12] The reluctant ones gave such reasons as "Selling is a job and not a profession," "It calls for deceit if the person wants to succeed," and "There is insecurity and too much travel." To counter these objections, company recruiters emphasize starting salaries, income opportunities, and the fact that one-fourth of the presidents of large U.S. corporations started out in marketing and sales.

Applicant-rating Procedures   Recruitment procedures, if successful, will attract many applicants, and the company will need to select the best ones. The selection procedures can vary from a single informal interview to prolonged testing and interviewing, not only of the applicant but of the applicant's family.[13]

Many companies give formal tests to sales applicants. Although test scores are only one information element in a set that includes personal characteristics, references, past employment history, and interviewer reactions, they are weighted quite heavily by such companies as IBM, Prudential, Procter & Gamble, and Gillette. Gillette claims that tests have reduced turnover by 42 percent and have correlated well with the subsequent progress of new sales representatives in the sales organization.

Training Sales Representatives

Many companies send their new sales representatives into the field almost immediately after hiring them. They are supplied with samples, order books, and a description of their territory. And much of their selling is ineffective. A vice-president of a major food company spent one week watching fifty sales presentations to a busy buyer for a major supermarket chain. Here is what he observed:

> I watched a soap company representative come in to the buyer. He had three separate new promotional deals to talk about with six different dates. He had nothing in writing. . . . After the salesman left, the buyer looked at me and said, "It will take me fifteen minutes to get this straightened out."
>
> I watched another salesman walk in to the buyer and say, "Well, I was in the area, and I want you to know that we have a great new promotion coming up next week." The buyer said, "That's fine. What is it?" He said, "I don't know. . . . I'm coming in next week to tell you about it." The buyer asked him what he was doing there today. He said, "Well, I was in the area."
>
> Another salesman came and said, "Well, it's time for us to write that order now . . . getting ready for the summer business." The buyer said, "Well, fine, George, how much did I buy last year in total?" The salesman looked a little dumbfounded and said, "Well, I'll be damned if I know. . . ."
>
> The majority of salesmen were ill prepared, unable to answer basic questions, uncertain as to what they wanted to accomplish during the call. They did not think of the call as a studied professional presentation. They didn't have a real idea of the busy retailer's needs and wants.[14]

It is true that training programs is costly. They involve large outlays for instructors, materials, and space; paying a person who is not yet selling; and losing opportunities because he or she is not in the field. Yet they are essential. Today's new sales representatives may spend a few weeks to several months in training. The median training period is twenty-eight weeks in industrial-products companies, twelve in service companies, and four in consumer-products companies.[15] Training time varies with the complexity of the selling task and the type of person recruited into the sales organization. In IBM, new sales representatives are not on their own for two years! And IBM expects its sales representatives to spend 15 percent of their time each year in additional training.

The annual sales-training bill for major U.S. corporations runs into multiple millions of dollars. Yet sales management sees training as adding more value than cost. Today's sales representatives are selling to more cost- and value-conscious buyers. Furthermore, they are selling technically complex products. The company wants and needs mature and knowledgeable sales representatives.

The training programs have several goals:

- ▪ *Sales representatives need to know and identify with the company.* Most companies devote the first part of the training program to describing the company's history and objectives, the organization and lines of authority, the chief officers, the company's financial structure and facilities, and the chief products and sales volume.
- ▪ *Sales representatives need to know the company's products.* Sales trainees are shown how the products are produced and how they function in various uses.
- ▪ *Sales representatives need to know customers' and competitors' characteristics.* Sales representatives learn about the different types of customers and their needs, buying motives, and buying habits. They learn about the company's and competitors' strategies and policies.

- **Sales representatives need to know how to make effective sales presentations.** Sales representatives receive training in the principles of salesmanship. In addition, the company outlines the major sales arguments for each product, and some provide a sales script.
- **Sales representatives need to understand field procedures and responsibilities.** Sales representatives learn how to divide time between active and potential accounts; how to use the expense account, prepare reports, and route effectively.

New methods of training are continually being explored. Among the instructional approaches are role playing, sensitivity training, cassette tapes, videotapes, programmed learning, and films on salesmanship and company products. There is no one way to evaluate the training results, but training departments need to collect as much evidence of improved sales performance as possible. There should be a measurable impact on such variables as sales-force turnover, sales volume, absenteeism, average sale size, calls-to-close ratio, customer complaints and compliments, new accounts per time unit, and volume of returned merchandise.

The substantial costs of company training programs raise the question of whether a company could do better by hiring experienced sales representatives away from other companies. The gain is often illusory, however, because the experienced salesperson is brought in at a higher salary. Some of the representatives' specific training and company experience is wasted when they transfer to other companies. Within some industries, companies tacitly agree not to hire sales personnel away from each other.

Directing Sales Representatives

New sales representatives are given more than a territory, a compensation package, and training—they are given supervision. Supervision is the fate of everyone who works for someone else. It is the expression of the employers' natural and continuous interest in the activities of their agents. Through supervision, employers hope to direct and motivate the sales force to do a better job. Exhibit 23–3 indicates that much work still needs to be done.

Companies vary in how closely they direct their sales representatives. Sales representatives who are paid mostly on commission and who are expected to hunt down their own prospects are generally left on their own. Those who are salaried and must cover definite accounts are likely to receive substantial supervision.

Developing Customer Targets and Call Norms

Most companies classify customers into A, B, and C accounts, reflecting the sales volume, profit potential, and growth potential of the account. They establish the desired number of calls per period on each account class. A accounts may receive nine calls a year; B, six calls; and C, three calls. The call norms depend on competitive call norms and expected account profitability.

The real issue is how much sales volume could be expected from a particular account as a function of the annual number of calls. Magee described an experiment where similar accounts were randomly split into three sets.[16] Sales representatives were asked to spend less than five hours a month with accounts in the first set, five to nine hours a month with those in the second set, and more than nine hours a month with those in the third set. The results demonstrated that additional calls produced more sales, leaving only the question of whether the magnitude of sales increase justified the additional cost.

Developing Prospect Targets and Call Norms

Companies often specify how much time their sales force should spend prospecting for new accounts. Spector Freight wants

EXHIBIT 23-3

How Efficiently Do Companies Manage Their Sales Force?

There is much evidence of inefficiency in the way companies manage their sales force. A survey of 257 "Fortune 500" companies revealed the following:

- 54 percent have not conducted an organized study of sales representatives' use of time, even though most respondents felt that time utilization represents an area for improvement.
- 25 percent do not have a system for classifying accounts according to potential.
- 30 percent do not use call schedules for their sales force.
- 51 percent do not determine the number of calls it is economical to make on an account.
- 83 percent do not determine an approximate duration for each call.
- 51 percent do not use a planned sales presentation.
- 24 percent do not set sales objectives for accounts
- 72 percent do not set profit objectives for accounts.
- 19 percent do not use a call report system.
- 63 percent do not use a prescribed routing pattern in covering territories.
- 77 percent do not use the computer to assist in time and territorial management.

SOURCE: Robert Vizza, "Managing Time and Territories for Maximum Sales Success," *Sales Management*, July 15, 1971, pp. 31–36.

its sales representatives to spend 25 percent of their time prospecting and to stop calling on a prospect after three unsuccessful calls.

Companies set up prospecting standards for a number of reasons. If left alone, many sales representatives will spend most of their time with current customers. Current customers are better-known quantities. Sales representatives can depend on them for some business, whereas a prospect may never deliver any business. Unless sales representatives are rewarded for opening new accounts, they may avoid new-account development. Some companies rely on a missionary sales force to open new accounts. (Exhibit 23-4 describes a model for estimating the value of a sales prospect.)

Using Sales Time Efficiently   Sales representatives need to know how to use their time efficiently. One tool is the *annual call schedule* showing which customers and prospects to call on in which months and which activities to carry out.

> Sales representatives of Bell Telephone companies plan their calls and activities around three concepts. The first is *market development*—various efforts to educate customers, cultivate new business, and gain greater visibility in the buying community. The second is *sales-generating activities*—direct efforts to sell particular products to customers on particular calls. The third is *market-protection activities*—various efforts to learn what competition is doing and to protect relations with existing customers. The sales force aims for some balance among these activities, so that the company does not achieve high current sales at the expense of long-run market development.

EXHIBIT 23-4

Estimating the Value of a Sales Prospect

Salespersons need a method to estimate the value of calling on different prospects in order to target the right accounts and use their time effectively. The method draws on investment theory, since call time will be invested in each prospect. First, the sales representative estimates the value of the prospect's business if the prospect were converted to a customer. The value of the prospect's business is seen as a discounted income stream lasting so many years. Specifically,

$$Z = \sum_{t=1}^{\bar{t}} \frac{mQ_t - X}{(1 + r)^t} \tag{23-1}$$

where:

Z = present value of the future income from a new customer

m = gross margin on sales

Q_t = expected sales from new customer in year t

X = cost of maintaining customer contact per year

r = company discount rate

t = a subscript for a year

$\bar{t}$ = number of years that this new customer is expected to remain a customer

Thus the sales representative estimates that if this prospect were converted to a customer, he would annually purchase from the company Q_t units with a profit per unit of m less a customer-contact cost (X) and that this last for t periods. Future income is discounted at an interest rate, r.

The next step is to consider the investment necessary to convert this prospect to a customer. The investment can be described as

$$I = nc \tag{23-2}$$

where:

I = investment in trying to convert the prospect to a customer

n = the number of calls to convert the prospect into a customer

c = cost per call

The number of calls to the prospects will influence the probability of conversion—that is,

$$p = p(n) \tag{23-3}$$

The value of the prospect's business should be scaled down by this probability. Putting the previous elements together, the following investment formula emerges for the value (V) of a prospect:

$$V = p(n) \sum_{t=1}^{\bar{t}} \frac{mQ_t - X}{(1 + r)^t} - nc \tag{23-4}$$

Thus the value of a prospect depends on the expected present value of the income stream less the investment cost in prospect conversion. Both the expected present value and the investment cost depend on the planned number of calls, n, upon the prospect. The planned or optimal number of calls can be found mathematically if the probability-of-conversion function is known.

The formula could be incorporated into a computer program. The sales representative would sit down at a terminal, type in estimates for each prospect regarding the expected volume of the prospect's business, the maximum probability of conversion, and so on, and receive back a ranking of all the prospects in order of their investment value along with the suggested number of calls to make on each.

Another tool is *time-and-duty analysis*. The sales representative spends time in the following ways:

- ■ *Travel.* In some jobs, travel time amounts to over 50 percent of total time. Travel time can be cut down by using faster means of transportation—recognizing, however, that this will increase costs. More companies are encouraging air travel for their sales force, to increase their ratio of selling to total time.
- ■ *Food and breaks.* Some portion of the sales force's workday is spent in eating and taking breaks.
- ■ *Waiting.* Waiting consists of time spent in the outer office of the buyer. This is dead time unless the sales representative uses it to plan or to fill out reports.
- ■ *Selling.* Selling is the time spent with the buyer in person or on the phone. It breaks down into ''social talk'' (the time spent discussing other things) and ''selling talk'' (the time spent discussing the company's products).
- ■ *Administration.* This is a miscellaneous category consisting of the time spent in report writing and billing, attending sales meetings, and talking to others in the company about production, delivery, billing, sales performance, and other matters.

No wonder actual face-to-face selling time may amount to as little as 25 percent of total working time![17] If it could be raised from 25 percent to 30 percent, this would be a 20 percent improvement. Companies are constantly seeking ways to use sales-force time effectively. Their methods take the form of training outside sales representatives in the use of ''phone power,'' simplifying the record-keeping forms, using the computer to develop call and routing plans, and supplying marketing research reports on customers.

To reduce time demands on their *outside sales force*, many companies have increased the size and responsibilities of their *inside sales force*. In a survey of 135 electronics distributors, Narus and Anderson found that an average of 57 percent of the sales-force members were inside sales people.[18] Managers gave as the reasons (a) the escalating cost of outside sales calls and (b) the growing use of computers and innovative telecommunications equipment. These managers think the proportion of inside sales-force members will reach two-thirds by 1990.

Inside sales people include three types. There are *technical support persons*, who provide technical information and answers to customers' questions. There are *sales assistants*, who provide clerical backup for the outside sales people. They call ahead and confirm appointments, carry out credit checks, follow up on deliveries, and answer customers' questions when they cannot reach the outside sales rep. And there are *telemarketers*, who use the phone to find new leads, qualify, and sell to them. A telemarketer can call up to fifty customers a day compared with the four that an outside salesperson can contact. They can be effective in the following ways:

- ■ Cross-selling compatible products
- ■ Upgrading orders
- ■ Introducing new company products
- ■ Opening new accounts and reactivating former accounts
- ■ Giving more attention to neglected accounts
- ■ Following up and qualifying direct-mail leads

The inside sales force frees the outside sales reps to spend more time selling to major accounts, identifying and converting new major prospects, placing electronic ordering systems in customers' facilities, and obtaining more blanket orders and systems contracts.

Meanwhile the inside sales people spend more time in checking inventory, following up orders, phoning smaller accounts, and so on. As might be expected, the outside sales reps are paid largely on an incentive compensation basis, and the inside reps on a salary or salary plus bonus pay.

Another dramatic breakthrough in improving sales-force productivity is made possible by the new technological equipment—desktop and laptop computers, videocassette recorders, videodiscs, automatic dialers, electronic mail, teleconferencing. The salesperson has truly gone "electronic." Not only is sales and inventory information transferred much faster, but specific computer-based decision support systems have been created for sales managers and sales representatives. Although usage is still far below potential, a recent study shows that the sales forces in one in five companies use their PCs for order entry, checking order status and inventory, and preparing forecasts. More companies are getting ready to use their PCs in territory management, account management, sales-call scheduling, and lead prospecting. Here are some results:

> Some companies with support systems report increases of 5 percent to 10 percent in a salesperson's selling time because of less travel and paperwork, better call planning, and more effective calls. At National Life Insurance, accumulating evidence suggests that agents' sales gains of as much as 50 percent may be attributable to their access to support systems that enable them to sell more effectively and see more clients per year.[19]

Motivating Sales Representatives

Some sales representatives will do their best without any special coaching from management. To them, selling is the most fascinating job in the world. They are ambitious and self-starters. But the majority of sales representatives require encouragement and special incentives to work at their best level. This is especially true of field selling, for the following reasons:

- ■ *The nature of the job.* The selling job is one of frequent frustration. Sales representatives usually work alone; their hours are irregular; and they are often away from home. They confront aggressive, competing sales representatives; they have an inferior status relative to the buyer; they often do not have the authority to do what is necessary to win an account; they lose large orders that they have worked hard to obtain.
- ■ *Human nature.* Most people operate below capacity in the absence of special incentives, such as financial gain or social recognition.
- ■ *Personal problems.* Sales representatives are occasionally preoccupied with personal problems, such as sickness in the family, marital discord, or debt.

The problem of motivating sales representatives has been studied by Ford, Walker, and Churchill.[20] The basic variables are shown below:

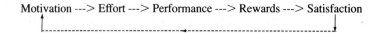

This says that the higher the salesperson's motivation, the greater his or her effort; greater effort will lead to greater performance; greater performance will lead to greater rewards; greater rewards will lead to greater satisfaction; and greater satisfaction will produce still greater motivation. Now it is important that the salesperson perceive and believe in these linkages. Thus:

1. *The sales managers must be able to convince the sales people that they can sell more by working harder or by being trained to work smarter.* But if sales are more determined by economic conditions or competitive actions, this linkage is somewhat undermined.

2. *The sales managers must be able to convince the sales people that the rewards for better performance are worth the extra effort.* But if the rewards seem to be set arbitrarily, or are too small, or of the wrong kind, this linkage is undermined.

The researchers went on to measure the order importance of the different possible rewards. The reward with the highest value was *pay*, followed by *promotion*, *personal growth*, and *sense of accomplishment* as a group. The least-valued rewards were *liking and respect*, *security*, and *recognition*. In other words, sales people are highly motivated by pay and the chance to get ahead and satisfy their intrinsic needs, and less motivated by needing strokes and security. But the researchers also found that the order of importance of motivators varied with the salespersons' demographic characteristics:

1. Financial rewards were mostly valued by older, longer-tenured sales people and those who had large families.

2. Higher-order rewards (recognition, liking and respect, sense of accomplishment) were more valued by young sales people who were unmarried or had small families and usually more formal education.

We discussed compensation as a motivator earlier. Here we will consider the role of sales quotas and some supplementary motivators.

Sales Quotas   Many companies set sales quotas for their sales representatives specifying what they should sell during the year and by product. Compensation is often related to the degree of quota fulfillment.

Sales quotas are developed in the process of developing the annual marketing plan. The company first decides on a sales forecast that is reasonably achievable. This becomes the basis for planning production, work-force size, and financial requirements. Then management establishes sales quotas for its regions and territories, which typically add up to more than the sales forecast. Sales quotas are set higher than the sales forecast in order to stretch the sales managers and sales people to their best effort. If they fail to make their quotas, the company nevertheless may make its sales forecast.

Each area sales manager divides the area's quota among the area's sales representatives. There are three schools of thought on quota setting. The *high-quota school* sets quotas higher than what most sales representatives will achieve but that are nevertheless attainable. Its adherents believe that high quotas spur extra effort. The *modest-quota school* sets quotas that a majority of the sales force can achieve. Its adherents feel that the sales force will accept the quotas as fair, attain them, and gain confidence. The *variable-quota school* thinks that individual differences among sales representatives warrant high quotas for some, modest quotas for others. According to Heckert:

> Actual experience with sales quotas, as with all standards, will reveal that sales representatives react to them somewhat differently, particularly at first. Some are stimulated to their highest efficiency, others are discouraged. Some sales executives place considerable emphasis upon this human element in setting their quotas. In general, however, good men will in the long run respond favorably to intelligently devised quotas, particularly when compensation is fairly adjusted to performance.[21]

Quotas can be set on dollars sales, unit volume, margin, selling effort or activity, and product type. Factors that influence the setting of sales quotas for individual sales persons are described in Exhibit 23–5.

EXHIBIT 23-5

Factors to Use in Setting a Variable Sales Quota

The variable-quota school will base sales quotas on a number of considerations, including the person's sales performance in the previous period, her territory's estimated potential, and a judgment of her aspiration level and reaction to pressure and incentive. Some propositions in this area are:

1. The sales quota for salesperson j at time t, Q_{jt}, should be set above her sales in the year just ending, $S_{j,t-1}$; that is,

$$Q_{jt} > S_{j,t-1}$$

2. The sales quota for salesperson j at time t should be higher, the greater the positive gap between the estimated sales potential of the salesperson's territory, S_{Pjt}, and her sales in the year just ending; that is,

$$Q_{jt} \sim (S_{Pjt} - S_{j,t-1})$$

3. The sales quota for salesperson j at time t should be higher, the more positively she responds to pressure, E_j; that is,

$$Q_{jt} \sim E_j$$

These three propositions can be combined in an equation for setting a salesperson's quota:

$$Q_{jt} = S_{j,t-1} + E_j (S_{Pjt} - S_{j,t-1})$$

Thus salesperson j's quota at time t should be at least equal to her actual sales in the previous period, plus some fraction, E_j, of the difference between estimated territorial sales potential and her sales last year; the more positively she reacts to pressure, the higher the fraction.

Supplementary Motivators   Companies use some additional motivators to stimulate sales-force effort. Periodic *sales meetings* provide a social occasion, a break from routine, a chance to meet and talk with "company brass," and a chance to air feelings and to identify with a larger group. Sales meetings are an important communication and motivational tool.[22]

Companies also sponsor *sales contests* to spur the sales force to a special selling effort above what would normally be expected. The awards could be cars, trips, fur coats, cash, or recognition. The contest should present a reasonable opportunity for enough sales people to win. If only a few can win or almost everyone can win, it will fail to spur additional effort. The sales contest period should not be announced in advance or else some salespersons will defer some sales to the beginning of the sales contest period; also some may pad their sales during the period with customer promises to buy that do not materialize after the sales contest period is over.

Evaluating Sales Representatives

We have been describing the *feed-forward* aspects of sales supervision—how management communicates what the sales representatives should be doing and motivates them to do it. But good feed-forward requires good *feedback*. And good feedback means getting regular information from sales representatives to evaluate their performance.

Sources of Information

Management obtains information about its sales representatives in several ways. The most important source is sales reports. Additional information comes through personal observation, customers' letters and complaints, customer surveys, and conversations with other sales representatives.

Sales reports are divided between *activity plans* and *writeups of activity results*. The best example of the former is the *salesperson's work plan*, which sales representatives submit a week or month in advance. The plan describes intended calls and routing. This report leads the sales force to plan and schedule their activities, informs management of their whereabouts, and provides a basis for comparing their plans and accomplishments. Sales representatives can be evaluated on their ability to "plan their work and work their plan." Occasionally management contacts individual sales representatives after receiving their plans to suggest improvements.

Companies are beginning to require their sales representatives to develop an annual *territory marketing plan* in which they outline their program for developing new accounts and increasing business from existing accounts. The formats vary considerably, some asking for general ideas on territory development and others asking for detailed volume and profit estimates. This type of report casts sales representatives into the role of market managers and profit centers. Their sales managers study these plans, make suggestions, and use them to develop sales quotas.

Sales representatives write up their completed activities on *call reports*. Call reports keep sales management informed of the salesperson's activities, indicate the status of the customers' accounts, and provide information that might be useful in subsequent calls. Sales representatives also submit *expense reports*, for which they are partly or wholly reimbursed. Additional types of reports that some companies require are reports on new business, reports on lost business, and reports on local business and economic conditions.

These reports supply the raw data from which sales managers can extract key indicators of sales performance. The key indicators are (1) average number of sales calls per salesperson per day, (2) average sales call time per contact, (3) average revenue per sales call, (4) average cost per sales call, (5) entertainment cost per sales call, (6) percentage of orders per hundred sales calls, (7) number of new customers per period, (8) number of lost customers per period, and (9) sales-force cost as a percentage of total sales. These indicators answer several useful questions: Are sales representatives making too few calls per day? Are they spending too much time per call? Are they spending too much on entertainment? Are they closing enough orders per hundred calls? Are they producing enough new customers and holding on to the old customers?

Formal Evaluation of Performance

The sales force's reports along with other reports and observations supply the raw materials for evaluating members of the sales force. Formal evaluation leads to at least three benefits. First, management has to develop and communicate clear standards for judging sales performance. Second, management is motivated to gather comprehensive information about each salesperson. And third, sales representatives know they will have to sit down one morning with the sales manager and explain their performance or failure to achieve certain goals.

Salesperson-to-salesperson-comparisons One type of evaluation is to compare and rank the sales performance of the various sales representatives. Such comparisons, however, can be misleading. Relative sales performances are meaningful only if there are no variations in territory market potential, workload, degree of competition, company promotional effort, and so forth. Furthermore, current sales are not the only success indicator. Management should be as interested in how much each sales representative contributes to current net profits; this requires examining each sales representative's sales mix of products sold and sales expenses. Even more important is finding out how satisfied the salesperson's customers are with his or her service.

Current-to-past-sales comparisons A second type of evaluation is to compare a sales representative's current performance with his or her past performance. This should provide a direct indication of progress. An example is shown in Table 23-1.

The sales manager can learn many things about John Smith from this table. Smith's total sales increased every year (line 3). This does not necessarily mean that Smith is doing a better job. The product breakdown shows that he has been able to push the sales of product B further than the sales of product A (lines 1 and 2). According to his quotas for the two products (lines 4 and 5), his success in increasing product B sales may be at

TABLE 23-1 Form for Evaluating Sales Representative's Performance

	Territory: Midland Sales Representative: John Smith			
	1983	**1984**	**1985**	**1986**
1. Net sales product A	$251,300	$253,200	$270,000	$263,100
2. Net sales product B	$423,200	$439,200	$553,900	$561,900
3. Net sales total	$674,500	$692,400	$823,900	$825,000
4. Percent of quota product A	95.6	92.0	88.0	84.7
5. Percent of quota product B	120.4	122.3	134.9	130.8
6. Gross profits product A	$ 50,260	$ 50,640	$ 54,000	$ 52,620
7. Gross profits product B	$ 42,320	$ 43,920	$ 55,390	$ 56,190
8. Gross profits total	$ 92,580	$ 94,560	$109,390	$108,810
9. Sales expense	$ 10,200	$ 11,100	$ 11,600	$13,200
10. Sales expense to total sales (%)	1.5	1.6	1.4	1.6
11. Number of calls	1,675	1,700	1,680	1,660
12. Cost per call	$ 6.09	$ 6.53	$ 6.90	$ 7.95
13. Average number of customers	320	324	328	334
14. Number of new customers	13	14	15	20
15. Number of lost customers	8	10	11	14
16. Average sales per customer	$ 2,108	$ 2,137	$ 2,512	$ 2,470
17. Average gross profit per customer	$ 289	$ 292	$ 334	$ 326

the expense of product A sales. According to gross profits (lines 6 and 7), the company earns more selling A than B. Smith may be pushing the higher-volume, lower-margin product at the expense of the more profitable product. Although he increased total sales by $1,100 between 1985 and 1986 (line 3), the gross profits on his total sales actually decreased by $580 (line 8).

Sales expense (line 9) shows a steady increase, although total expense as a percentage of total sales seems to be under control (line 10). The upward trend in Smith's total dollar expense does not seem to be explained by any increase in the number of calls (line 11), although it may be related to his success in acquiring new customers (line 14). There is a possibility, however, that in prospecting for new customers, he is neglecting present customers, as indicated by an upward trend in the annual number of lost customers (line 15).

The last two lines show the level and trend in Smith's sales and gross profits per customer. These figures become more meaningful when they are compared with overall company averages. If John Smith's average gross profit per customer is lower than the company's average, he may be concentrating on the wrong customers or may not be spending enough time with each customer. A look back at his annual number of calls (line 11) shows that Smith may be making fewer annual calls than the average salesperson. If distances in his territory are not much different from those of the average salesperson, this may mean he is not putting in a full workday, he is poor at planning his routing or minimizing his waiting, or he spends too much time with certain accounts.

Qualitative evaluation of sales representatives   The evaluation usually includes the salesperson's knowledge of the company, products, customers, competitors, territory, and responsibilities. Personality characteristics can be rated, such as general manner, appearance, speech, and temperament. The sales manager can also review any problems in motivation or compliance. The sales manager should check that the sales representative knows and observes the law. Each company must decide what would be most useful to know. It should communicate these criteria to the sales representatives so that they know how their performance is judged and can make an effort to improve it.

PRINCIPLES OF PERSONAL SELLING

We turn now from designing and managing a sales force to the purpose of a sales force, namely, to sell. Personal selling is an ancient art, which has spawned a large literature and many principles. Effective salespersons have more than instinct; they are trained in a method of analysis and customer management. Selling today is a profession that involves mastering and using a whole set of principles. There are many different styles of personal selling, some very consistent with the marketing concept and some antithetical to the spirit of the marketing concept. We will examine three major aspects of personal selling in the remainder of this chapter: salesmanship, negotiation, and relationship management.

Salesmanship   Today's companies spend hundreds of millions of dollars each year to train their sales people in the art of salesmanship. Over a million copies of books, cassettes, and videotapes on selling are purchased annually, with such tantalizing titles as *How to Outsell the Born Salesman, How to Sell Anything to Anybody, How Power Selling Brought Me Success in 6 Hours, Where Do You Go from No. 1?*, and *1000 Ways a Salesman Can*

Increase His Sales. One of the most enduring books is Dale Carnegie's *How to Win Friends and Influence People*.

All of the sales-training approaches try to convert a salesperson from being a passive *order taker* to being an active *order getter*. *Order takers* operate on the following assumptions: Customers know their needs; they would resent any attempt at influence; and they prefer salespersons who are courteous and self-effacing. An example of an order-taking mentality would be a Fuller brush salesman who knocks on dozens of doors each day, simply asking if the consumer needs any brushes.

In training salespersons to be *order getters*, there are two basic approaches, a *sales-oriented approach* and a *customer-oriented approach*. The first one trains the salesperson in *high-pressure selling techniques*, such as those used in selling encyclopedias or automobiles. The techniques include overstating the product's merits, criticizing competitive products, using a slick canned presentation, selling yourself, and offering some concession to get the order on the spot. This form of selling assumes that the customers are not likely to buy except under pressure, that they are influenced by a slick presentation and ingratiating manners, and that they will not be sorry after signing the order, or if they are, it doesn't matter.

The other approach trains sales personnel in *customer problem solving*. The salesperson learns how to listen and question in order to identify customer needs and come up with good product solutions. Presentation skills are made secondary to need analysis skills. This approach assumes that customers have latent needs that constitute company opportunities, that they appreciate good suggestions, and that they will be loyal to sales representatives who have their long-term interests at heart. The problem solver is a more compatible image for the salesperson under the marketing concept than the hard seller or order taker.

No sales approach works best in all circumstances. (See Exhibit 23-6.) Yet most sales-training programs agree on the major steps involved in any effective sales process. These steps are shown in Figure 23-2 and discussed below.[23]

Prospecting and Qualifying   The first step in the selling process is to identify prospects. Although the company may supply leads, sales representatives also need skill in developing their own leads. Leads can be developed in the following ways:

- Asking current customers for the names of prospects
- Cultivating other referral sources, such as suppliers, dealers, noncompeting sales representatives, bankers, and trade association executives
- Joining organizations to which prospects belong
- Engaging in speaking and writing activities that will draw attention
- Examining data sources (newspapers, directories) in search of names
- Using the telephone and mail to track down leads
- Dropping in unannounced on various offices (cold canvassing)

Sales representatives need skill in screening out poor leads. Prospects can be qualified by examining their financial ability, volume of business, special requirements, location, and likelihood of continuous business. The salesperson might phone or write to prospects before visiting to see if they are worth pursuing. All the leads that the company receives should be categorized:[24]

- **Hot lead.** Intends to buy within three months
- **Warm lead.** Intends to buy in three to twelve months

EXHIBIT 23-6

The Variety of Selling Styles and Buying Styles

Blake and Mouton distinguish various selling styles by examining two dimensions, the salesperson's *concern for the sale* and *concern for the customer*. These two dimensions give rise to the *sales grid* shown below, which describes five types of salespersons. Type 1, 1 is very much the order taker and 9, 1 is the hard seller. Type 5, 5 is a soft seller, while the 1, 9 is "sell myself." Type 9, 9 is the problem-solving mentality, which is most consistent with the marketing concept.

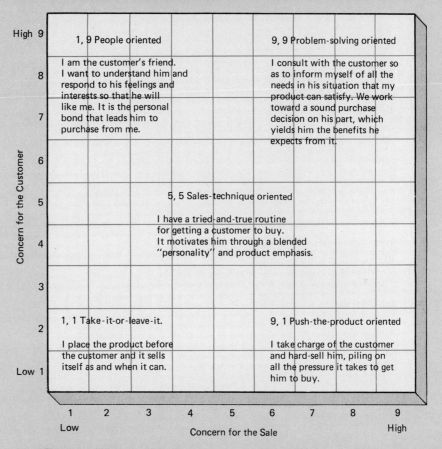

Blake and Mouton argue that no one type of sales style will be effective with all buyers. Buying styles are just as varied as selling styles. Buyers vary in their concern for the purchase and concern for the salesperson. Some buyers couldn't care less; some are defensive; some will only listen to salespersons from well-known companies.

The view that effective selling depends on matching the seller's style to the buyer's style means that salespersons should not be trained in only one style of selling. Evans sees selling as a *dyadic process*, where the outcome depends on the match of *buyer and seller characteristics* as well as on *buying and selling styles*. He found that people bought insurance from people very much like themselves in such factors as age, height, income, political opinions, religious beliefs, and smoking. What mattered was the perceived similarity more than the actual similarity. Evans proposed that insurance companies should hire all types of salespersons if they want to achieve broad market penetration. The only requirement is that they exhibit the intelligence and kinds of abilities effective in selling insurance. (See Franklin

B. Evans, "Selling as a Dyadic Relationship—a New Approach," *American Behavioral Scientist*, May 1963, pp. 76–79, at pp. 76 and 78. Also see Harry L. Davis and Alvin J. Silk, "Interaction and Influence Processes in Personal Selling," *Sloan Management Review*, Winter 1972, pp. 59–76; and Barton A. Weitz, Harish Sujan, and Mita Sujan, "Knowledge, Motivation, and Adaptive Behavior: A Framework for Improving Selling Effectiveness," Marketing Science Institute, Working Paper, November 1985.)

SOURCE: Robert R. Blake and Jane S. Mouton, *The Grid for Sales Excellence: Benchmarks for Effective Salesmanship* (New York: McGraw-Hill, 1970), p.4.

■ *Long-term potential.* No purchase intent within the next twelve months but is a definite prospect

■ *No potential.* Has no application for the product or is not a decision maker or influencer

Preapproach   The salesperson should learn as much as possible about the prospect company (what it needs, who is involved in the purchase decision) and its buyers (their personal characteristics and buying styles). The salesperson can consult standard sources (*Moody's*, *Standard and Poor*, *Dun and Bradstreet*), acquaintances, and others to learn about the company. The salesperson should set *call objectives*, which might be to qualify the prospect or gather information or make an immediate sale. Another task is to decide on the best *approach*, which might be a personal visit, a phone call, or a letter. The best *timing* should be thought out because many prospects are busy at certain times. Finally, the salesperson should give thought to an *overall sales strategy* for the account.

Approach   The salesperson should know how to meet and greet the buyer to get the relationship off to a good start. This involves the salesperson's appearance, the opening lines, and the follow-up remarks. The salesperson might consider wearing clothes similar to what buyers wear (for instance, in Texas the men wear open shirts and no ties); show courtesy and attention to the buyer; and avoid distracting mannerisms, such as pacing the floor or staring at the customer. The opening line should be positive, such as "Mr. Smith, I am Bill Jones from the ABC Company. My company and I appreciate your willingness to see me. I will do my best to make this visit profitable and worthwhile for you and your company." This might be followed by some key questions or by showing a display or sample to attract the buyer's attention and curiosity.

Presentation and Demonstration   The salesperson now tells the product "story" to the buyer, following the AIDA formula of getting *attention*, holding *interest*, arousing *desire*, and obtaining *action*. The salesperson emphasizes throughout customer benefits, bringing in product features as evidence of these benefits. A benefit is any advantage, such as lower cost, less work, or more profit for the buyer. A feature is a characteristic of a product, such as its weight and size. A common mistake in selling is to dwell on

FIGURE 23-2
Major Steps in Effective Selling

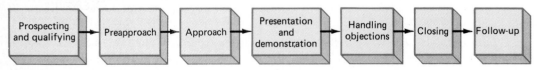

Prospecting and qualifying → Preapproach → Approach → Presentation and demonstration → Handling objections → Closing → Follow-up

product features (a product orientation) instead of customer benefits (a marketing orientation).

Companies use three styles of sales presentation. The oldest is the *canned approach*, which is a memorized sales talk covering the main points. It is based on stimulus-response thinking; that is, the buyer is passive and can be moved to purchase by the use of the right stimulus words, pictures, terms, and actions. Thus an encyclopedia salesperson might describe the encyclopedia as ''a once-in-a-lifetime buying opportunity'' and focus on some beautiful four-color pages of sports pictures, hoping to trigger desire for the encyclopedia. Canned presentations are used primarily in door-to-door and telephone selling.

The *formulated approach* is also based on stimulus-response thinking but identifies early the buyer's needs and buying style and then uses a formulated approach to this type of buyer. The salesperson initially draws the buyer into the discussion in a way that indicates the buyer's needs and attitudes. Then the salesperson moves into a formulated presentation that shows how the product will satisfy the buyer's needs. It is not canned but follows a general plan.

The *need-satisfaction approach* starts with a search for the customer's real needs by encouraging the customer to do most of the talking. This approach calls for good listening and problem-solving skills. It is well described by an IBM sales representative: ''I get inside the business of my key accounts, I uncover their key problems. I prescribe solutions for them, using my company's systems and even, at times, components from other suppliers. I prove beforehand that my system will save money or make money for my accounts. Then I work with the account to install the system and make it prove out.''[25]

Sales presentations can be improved with demonstration aids such as booklets, flip charts, slides, movies, audio and video cassettes and actual product samples. To the extent that the buyer can see or handle the product, he or she will better remember its features and benefits. During the demonstration, the salesperson can draw on five influence strategies:[26]

- **Legitimacy.** The salesperson emphasizes the reputation and experience of his or her company.
- **Expertise.** The salesperson shows deep knowledge of the buyer's situation and company's products, doing this without being overly ''smart.''
- **Referent power.** The salesperson builds on any shared characteristics, interests, and acquaintances.
- **Ingratiation.** The salesperson provides personal favors (a free lunch, promotional gratuities) to strengthen affiliation and reciprocity feelings.
- **Impression management.** The salesperson manages to convey favorable impressions of himself or herself.

Handling Objections   Customers almost always pose objections during the presentation or when asked to place an order. Their resistance can be psychological or logical. *Psychological resistance* includes resistance to interference, preference for established habits, apathy, reluctance to giving up something, unpleasant associations about the other person, tendency to resist domination, predetermined ideas, dislike of making decisions, and neurotic attitude toward money. *Logical resistance* might consist of objections to the price, delivery schedule, or certain product or company characteristics. To handle these objections, the salesperson maintains a positive approach, asks the buyer to clarify the objection, questions the buyer in a way that the buyer has to answer his or her own objection, denies the validity of the objection, or turns the objection into a reason for buying. The salesperson needs training in the broader skills of negotiation, of which handling objections is a part.

Closing Now the salesperson attempts to close the sale. Some sales people do not get to this stage, or do not do it well. They lack confidence or feel guilty about asking for the order or do not recognize the right psychological moment to close the sale. Salespersons need to know how to recognize closing signals from the buyer, including physical actions, statements or comments, and questions. Salespersons can use one of several closing techniques. They can ask for the order, recapitulate the points of agreement, offer to help the secretary write up the order, ask whether the buyer wants A or B, get the buyer to make minor choices such as the color or size, or indicate what the buyer will lose if the order is not placed now. The salesperson may offer the buyer specific inducements to close, such as a special price, an extra quantity at no charge, or a gift.

Follow-Up This last step is necessary if the salesperson wants to ensure customer satisfaction and repeat business. Immediately after closing, the salesperson should complete any necessary details on delivery time, purchase terms, and other matters. The salesperson should schedule a follow-up call when the initial order is received, to make sure there is proper installation, instruction, and servicing. This visit would detect any problems, assure the buyer of the salesperson's interest, and reduce any cognitive dissonance that might have arisen.

Negotiation

Salespersons who have stimulated customer interest in their product must now apply their negotiation skills. The two parties need to reach agreement on the price and the other terms of sale. Salespersons need to win the order without making concessions that will hurt profitability.

This section will focus on negotiation skills. These skills apply to dealing not only with customers but also with suppliers, middlemen, and ad agencies, store buying committees, other departments in the company, and various publics. We will define negotiation, describe some negotiation models, and examine the major decisions facing negotiators.

Negotiation Defined Marketing is concerned with exchange activities and the manner in which the terms of exchange are established. We can distinguish two general types of exchange: *routinized exchange*, where the terms are established by administered programs of pricing and distribution, and *negotiated exchange*, where price or other terms of exchange are set via bargaining behavior. Arndt has observed that a growing number of markets are coming under negotiated exchange, in which two or more parties negotiate long-term binding agreements (e.g., joint ventures, franchises, subcontracts, vertical integration). These markets are moving from being highly competitive to being highly "domesticated," that is, being less available to competitors.[27]

Although price is most frequently considered to be the object of negotiation activities, it is by no means the only one. Other objects of negotiation include time of contract completion; quality of goods or service offered; volume of goods sold; responsibility for financing, risk taking, promotion, and title; and safety of product with government agencies. The number of negotiation-related topics and parties is virtually unlimited.

We will use the terms *bargaining* and *negotiation* interchangeably. Bargaining has the following features:

■ At least two parties are involved
■ The parties have a conflict of interest with respect to one or more issues
■ The parties are at least temporarily joined together in a special kind of voluntary relationship

■ Activity in the relationship concerns the division or exchange of one or more specific resources and/or the resolution of one or more intangible issues among the parties or among those whom they represent

■ The activity usually involves the presentation of demands or proposals by one party and evaluation of these by the other, followed by concessions and counterproposals. The activity is thus sequential rather than simultaneous[28]

In these situations, the marketing managers must have negotiation skills if successful implementation of marketing strategies is to occur.

Bargaining/Negotiation Models and Paradigms   Bargaining has received attention in a variety of disciplines, including economics, applied mathematics, international relations, industrial relations, and social psychology. We will briefly describe the contribution of game theory, economics, social psychology, and experimental perspective.

Beginning with the work of von Neumann and Morgenstern, game theorists have examined the results of rational actors' strategies in situations involving interdependent decision making.[29] Game theory assumes that each actor has an objective (typically, loss minimization), and the payoffs depend on the decisions of his or her opponent. The major purpose of game theory is to describe the set of decision rules by which rational actors choose the best strategy. (For an example, see Chapter 4, 127–29.)[30]

Economists study the bargaining process through the concept of "bilateral monopoly." They see the process as a sequence of offers and counteroffers by the participants. They pay less attention to manipulative tactics, power, and bargaining skills of the participants.[31]

Social psychologists have studied the effect of several independent variables on bargaining effectiveness.[32] Rubin and Brown, in their exhaustive review of social-psychological studies on bargaining behavior, summarized the impact of four major variables—the structural context of bargaining, the behavioral predispositions of bargainers, the interdependence of bargainers, and the use of social-influence strategies—on bargaining effectiveness.[33] Bargaining effectiveness is usually measured by the number of cooperative or competitive choices made throughout the total number of trials and/or the magnitude of the outcomes obtained by the bargainers. The behavioral approach focuses on the concepts of power, tactical action, and bargaining settlements.[34]

Several models of the bargaining process have been published by experienced negotiators, who also offer courses to train executives in their approach to negotiation.[35] The experiential approach to the discussion of bargaining has the advantage of being based on firsthand experience in negotiation settings but lacks rigorous analysis.[36]

Marketers who find themselves in bargaining situations must make a number of decisions about when to negotiate and how to negotiate.

When to Negotiate   The question of when bargaining is an appropriate procedure for concluding a sale has been addressed in several ways. Lee and Dobler have listed the following instances when negotiation is appropriate for purchasing agents:

1. When many variable factors bear not only on price, but also on quality and service.
2. When business risks involved cannot be accurately predetermined.
3. When a long period of time is required to produce the items purchased.
4. When production is interrupted frequently because of numerous change orders.[37]

Young has developed a "bargainers' calculus," which mathematically demonstrates the point at which bargaining is an appropriate method of accomplishing objectives.[38]

For our purposes we will propose that bargaining is appropriate whenever the five definitional conditions are met (see pp. 690–91) and a *zone of agreement* exists.[39] A zone of agreement can be considered as the range of acceptable outcomes that exists simultaneously for all bargaining parties. This concept is illustrated in Figure 23-3. If two parties, say a manufacturer and one of its dealers, are negotiating a price, each privately establishes the threshold value that he or she needs. That is, the seller has a reservation price, s, which is the *minimum* he or she will accept. Any final-contract value, x, that is below s represents a price that is worse than not reaching an agreement at all. For any $x > s$, the seller receives a surplus. Obviously the seller (manufacturer) desires as large a surplus as possible while maintaining good relations with the buyer (dealer). Likewise the buyer has a reservation price, b, that is the *maximum* he or she will pay; any x that is above b represents a price that is worse than no agreement. For any $x < b$, the buyer receives a surplus. If the seller's reservation price is below the buyer's, that is, $s < b$, then a zone of agreement exists, and bargaining will determine where x will fall within the zone.

There is an obvious advantage in knowing or probabilistically assessing the other party's reservation price and in making one's own reservation price seem higher (for a seller) or lower (for a buyer) than it really is. However, the openness with which buyers and sellers reveal and use their reservation prices or otherwise practice strategic misrepresentation is often dictated by the personalities of the bargainers, the circumstances of the negotiation, and the expectation of future relations.

Formulating a Bargaining Strategy   Bargaining involves strategic decisions before bargaining begins and tactical decisions during the bargaining sessions.

> A bargaining strategy can be defined as a commitment to an overall approach that has a good chance of achieving the negotiator's objectives.

For example, some negotiators advise pursuing a "hard" strategy with opponents, while others maintain that a "soft" strategy yields more favorable results. Fisher and Ury propose still another strategy, that of "principled negotiation."[40] They claim that this strategy will result in outcomes favorable to its adopter regardless of the strategy selected by the other party. The strategy of principled negotiation is

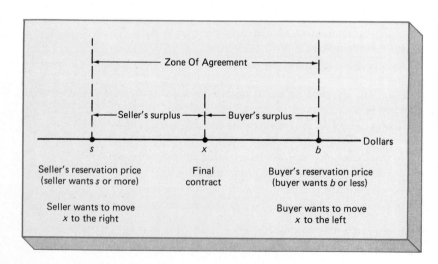

FIGURE 23-3
The Zone of Agreement
SOURCE: Reprinted by permission of the publishers from *The Art and Science of Negotiation*, by Howard Raiffa, Cambridge, Mass.: the Belknap Press of Harvard University Press, copyright © 1982 by the President and Fellows of Harvard College.

To decide issues on their merits rather than through a haggling process focused on what each side says it will and won't do. It suggests that you look for mutual gains wherever possible, and that where your interests conflict, you should insist that the results be based on some fair standards independent of the will of either side. The method of principled negotiations is hard on the merits, soft on the people.[41]

Similarly stated strategies have been referred to as ''win/win'' strategies, integrative bargaining, or using a strategy of flexible rigidity (flexible with respect to bargaining means, rigid with respect to goals). Exhibit 23-7 describes the four basic points of the principled negotiation strategy.

Bargaining Tactics During Negotiation
Negotiators use a variety of tactics when negotiating.

Bargaining tactics can be defined as maneuvers to be made at specific points in the bargaining process.

Threats, bluffs, last-chance offers, hard initial offers, and other tactics are discussed in both scholarly and ''how-to'' books. Many sources offer checklists of tactical do's and don'ts, such as ''Don't tip your hand too early'' and ''Do negotiate on home ground whenever possible.'' These lists of possible tactics are usually a shotgun blast of widely varied actions and are rarely consistent with a specific overriding bargaining strategy. (For a list of some classic tactics, see Exhibit 23-8.)

On the other hand, Fisher and Ury have offered some tactical advice that is consistent with their strategy of principled negotiation. Their first piece of tactical advice concerns what should be done if the other party is more powerful. The best tactic is to know one's BATNA—Best Alternative To a Negotiated Agreement. By identifying one's alternatives if a settlement is not reached, it sets a standard against which any offer can be measured. It protects one from being pressured into accepting unfavorable terms from a more powerful opponent.

Another tactic comes into play when the opposing party insists on arguing his or her position instead of his or her interests and attacks one's proposals or person. While the tendency is to push back hard when pushed against, the better tactic is to deflect the attack from the person and direct it against the problem. Look at the interests that motivated the opposing party's position and invent options that can satisfy both parties' interests. Invite the opposing party's criticism and advice (''If you were in my position, what would you do?'')

Another series of bargaining tactics concerns responses to opposition tactics that are intended to deceive, distort, or otherwise influence the bargaining to their own advantage. What tactic should be used when the other side uses a threat or a take-it-or-leave-it tactic or puts the other party on the side of the table with the sun in his or her eyes? To respond, a negotiator should recognize the tactic, raise the issue explicitly, and question the tactic's legitimacy and desirability—in other words, negotiate over it. Negotiating the use of the tactic follows the same principled negotiation procedure: Question the tactic, ask for the reasons why the tactic was used, suggest alternative courses of action to mutually pursue, suggest the principle behind the tactic as a negotiation rule. Finally, resort to one's BATNA if all else fails and terminate the negotiation until the other side ceases to employ these tricky tactics. Meeting these tactics by defending principles is more productive than counter-attacking with tricky tactics.

EXHIBIT 23-7

The Principled Negotiation Approach to Bargaining

In research known as the Harvard Negotiation Project, Roger Fisher and William Ury arrived at four points for conducting "principled negotiations" that have a high chance of concluding successfully for both parties. They are described below.

1. **Separate the people from the problem.** Because people, not machines, are conducting the face-to-face bargaining, it is easy for emotions to become entangled with the objective merits of the issue being negotiated. Framing negotiation issues in terms of the personalities involved rather than the interests of the parties can lead to ineffective bargaining. Negotiation deteriorates when it becomes a test of wills instead of a joint problem-solving activity. Separating the people from the problem first involves making accurate perceptions. Each party must understand empathetically the power of the opponent's viewpoint and try to feel the level of emotion with which they hold it. Second, emotions brought into or evolving out of negotiations should be made explicit and acknowledged as legitimate. Openly discussing emotions of both parties while not reacting to an emotional outburst helps keep negotiations from degenerating into unproductive name-calling sessions. Third, clear communications must exist between parties. Listening actively and acknowledging what is being said, communicating about problems rather than the opponent's shortcomings, and directly addressing interests rather than speaking first just to be heard are methods of improving the chances of jointly beneficial solutions by better communication techniques. In general, separating the people from the problem means looking at the issues side by side rather than face to face.

2. **Focus on interests, not positions.** The difference between positions and interests is that one's position is something one decided upon, while one's interests are what caused one to adopt the position. Thus a bargaining *position* may be that a contract must include a stiff penalty for late shipment; but the party's *interest* is to maintain an unbroken flow of raw materials. Reconciling interests works better because for every interest there usually exist several possible positions that could satisfy that interest. Also, opposing positions may hide shared and compatible interests (e.g., we want the predictability of a steady flow of orders, you want the security of an unbroken flow of raw materials). Making certain that interests are understood by all parties and then being flexible as to the means of achieving these interests, while negotiating firmly for the interests themselves, is an effective strategy. As Fisher and Ury state it:

   > Fighting hard on the substantive issues increases the pressure for an effective solution; giving support to the human beings on the other side tends to improve your relationship and to increase the likelihood of reaching agreement. It is the combination of support and attack which works; either alone is likely to be insufficient.[*]

3. **Invent options for mutual gain.** Inventing options for mutual gain involves searching for a larger pie rather than arguing over the size of each slice.[†] Developing options requires innovative thinking such as brainstorming sessions where judgment of options is undertaken only after many options have been invented. Looking for options that offer mutual gain facilitates the desirable condition of side-by-side bargaining and helps identify shared interests.

4. **Insist on objective criteria.** When an opposing negotiator is intransigent and argues his position rather than his interests, a good strategy is to insist that the agreement must reflect some fair objective criteria independent of the position of either side. This will help reach solutions on principle, not pressure. By discussing objective criteria instead of stubbornly held positions, neither party is yielding to the other; both are yielding to a fair solution. Such objective criteria may be market value, depreciated book value, competitive prices, replacement costs, wholesale price index, etc. This approach works best when each issue is seen as requiring a joint search for objective criteria, and each party is open to reason as to the standards best reflecting objectivity. Deviation from a fair, objective standard should be made only when a better one is offered, not because the opposing party is applying pressure, threats, or other means of imposing his will.

[*] Adaptation, Fisher and Ury, *Getting to Yes*, p. 57. Adapted by permission of Houghton Mifflin Company.
[†] For a discussion of the differences between integrative (larger pie) and distributive bargaining (size of slice), see Walton and McKenzie, *A Behavioral Theory of Labor Negotiation*. Also see Max H. Bazerman and Roy J. Lewicki, *Negotiating in Organizations* (Beverly Hills, Calif.: Sage Publications, 1983).

EXHIBIT 23-8

Some Classic Bargaining Tactics

Here are several standard bargaining tactics:

- **Acting Crazy.** Put on a good show by visibly demonstrating your emotional commitment to your position. This increases your credibility and may give the opponent a justification to settle on your terms.
- **Big Pot.** Leave yourself a lot of room to negotiate. Make high demand at the beginning. After making concessions, you'll still end up with a larger payoff than if you started too low.
- **Get a Prestigious Ally.** The ally can be a person or a project that is prestigious. You try to get the opponent to accept less because the person/object he or she will be involved with is considered "prestigious."
- **The Well Is Dry.** Take a stand and tell the opponent you have no more concessions to make.
- **Limited Authority.** You negotiate in good faith with the opponent, and when you're ready to sign the deal, you say, "I have to check with my boss."
- **Whipsaw/Auction.** You let several competitors know you're negotiating with them at the same time. Schedule competitors' appointments with you for the same time and keep them all waiting to see you.
- **Divide and Conquer.** If you're negotiating with the opponent's team, sell one member of the team on your proposals. That person will help you sell the other members of the team.
- **Get Lost/Stall for Time.** Leave the negotiation completely for a while. Come back when things are getting better and try to renegotiate then. Time period can be long (say you're going out of town) or short (go to the bathroom to think).
- **Wet Noodle.** Give no emotional or verbal response to the opponent. Don't respond to his or her force or pressure. Sit there like a wet noodle and keep a "poker face."
- **Be Patient.** If you can afford to outwait the opponent, you'll probably win big.
- **Let's Split the Difference.** The person who first suggests this has the least to lose.
- **Play the Devil's Advocate.** Argue against the opponent's proposal by stating, "Before I say yes or no, let's look at all the bad things that could possibly happen if we did what you want." This lets you show the opponent your better way of achieving his or her objectives without directly opposing the opponent's viewpoint.
- **Trial Balloon.** You release your decision through a so-called reliable source before the decision is actually made. This enables you to test reaction to your decision.
- **Surprises.** Keep the opponent off balance by a drastic, dramatic, sudden shift in your tactics in general. Never be predictable—keep the opponent from anticipating your moves.

SOURCE: From a list of over 200 tactics prepared by Professor Donald W. Hendon of the University of Hawaii in his seminar, "How to Negotiate and Win."

Relationship Management

The principles of personal selling and negotiation are *transaction oriented*, that is, their aim is to help marketers close a specific sale with a customer. There is a larger concept, however, that should guide the seller's dealings with customers, namely, that of *relationship management*. The seller who knows how to build and manage strong relationships with key customers will have plenty of future sales from these customers. Relationship management is a key skill needed by marketers.

Relationship management is most appropriate with those customers and publics who can most affect the company's future. For many companies, the top five or ten customers account for a disproportionate share of the company's sales. Sales people working with key customers must do more than call when they think customers might be ready to place orders. They should call or visit at other times, taking customers to dinner, making useful suggestions about their business, and so on. They should follow the fortunes of these key accounts, know their problems and opportunities, and be ready to serve them in a number of ways. This type of salesperson is often called a *relationship manager* (also called national account manager or customer manager).

The relationship manager represents the latest step in the evolution of the salesperson. Originally salespersons were *order takers*. Then they evolved into *order getters*, aggressively seeking business from purchasing agents. Later they evolved into *account representatives*, who dealt with a number of people in the buying organization who could influence purchases. Now they are evolving into *relationship managers*, who plan and service the entire relationship with the customers. Here are two examples:

> The marketing vice-president of an Atlanta construction firm has as a major account a large fast-food franchiser headquartered in New York. When he travels to New York, he always contacts the marketing vice-president of the fast-food franchising firm and takes him out to dinner or a show. He also invites this manager on skiing trips and golf outings. He rarely asks the fast-food franchiser for any business. Some people have called this LGD marketing: "lunch, golf, and dinner marketing."
>
> A major consulting firm observed that it had repeat business from certain clients and no repeat business from others. It discovered that some of its consultants were good at managing relationships and getting repeat business, and others were good at managing projects but not relationships. The consulting firm identified its key clients and made sure that consultants skilled in relationship building were assigned to them.

Relationship management will undoubtedly play an increasing role in the future. There are several factors. Companies are recognizing that they earn a higher return from getting repeat sales from current customers than from spending money to attract new customers. As customers become larger and fewer, each one counts more. Companies are recognizing more cross-selling opportunities with its current customers. More major companies are forming strategic partnerships to deal with global competition, and skilled relationship management is essential. And for the growing number of customers that buy large, complex products—such as cement factories, robotic equipment, and large computer systems—the sale is only the beginning of the relationship. Levitt sees a movement from product to augmented product to system orientation as being more characteristic of the future (see Table 23-2), and therefore requiring more skill in relationship marketing.[42] Barbara Jackson

TABLE 23-2   The Movement Toward Relationship Marketing

Category	Past	Present	Future
Item	Product	Augmented product	System contracts
Sale	Unit	System	System/time
Value	Feature advantage	Technology advantages	System advantages
Lead time	Short	Long	Lengthy
Service	Modest	Important	Vital
Delivery place	Local	National	Global
Delivery phase	Once	Frequently	Continuous
Strategy	Sales	Marketing	Relationship

SOURCE: Theodore Levitt, *The Marketing Imagination* (New York: Free Press, 1983), p. 116.

agrees, although she does not think relationship marketing is appropriate in all situations. (See Exhibit 23-9.)

Here are the main steps in establishing a relationship management program in a company:

- ■ *Identify the key customers meriting relationship management.* The company can choose the five or ten largest customers and designate them for relationship management. Additional customers can be added who show exceptional growth or who pioneer new developments in the industry, and so on.
- ■ *Assign a skilled relationship manager to each key customer.* The salesperson who is currently servicing the customer should receive training in relationship management or be replaced by someone who is more skilled in relationship management. The relationship manager should have characteristics that match or appeal to the customer.
- ■ *Develop a clear job description for relationship managers.* It should describe their reporting relationships, objectives, responsibilities, and evaluation criteria. The relationship manager is responsible for the client, is the focal point for all information about the client, and is the mobilizer of company services for the client. Each relationship manager will have only one or a few relationships to manage.
- ■ *Appoint an overall manager to supervise the relationship managers.* This person will develop job descriptions, evaluation criteria, and resource support to increase the effectiveness of this function.

EXHIBIT 23-9

When—and How—to Use Relationship Marketing

Barbara Bund Jackson argues that relationship marketing is not effective in all situations but is extremely effective in the right situations. She sees transaction marketing as more appropriate with customers who have a short time horizon and low switching costs, such as buyers of commodities. A customer buying steel can buy from one of several steel suppliers and choose the one offering the best terms. The fact that one steel supplier has been particularly attentive or responsive does not automatically earn it the next sale; its terms have to be competitive. Jackson calls these "always-a-share" customers.

On the other hand, relationship marketing investments pay off handsomely with customers who have long time horizons and high switching costs, such as buyers of office automation systems. Presumably the customer for a major system carefully researches the competing suppliers and chooses one to work with from whom it can expect good long-term service and state-of-the-art technology. Both the customer and the supplier invest a lot of money and time in the relationship. The customer would find it very costly and risky to switch to another vendor, and the seller would find that losing this customer would be a major loss. Jackson calls these "lost-for-good customers," and here relationship marketing has the greatest payoff.

In "lost-for-good" situations, the challenge is different for the in-supplier versus out-supplier. The in-supplier's whole strategy is to make switching difficult for the customer. The in-supplier will develop product systems that are incompatible with competitive products and will install proprietary ordering systems that facilitate inventory management and delivery. On the other hand, the out-supplier will design product systems that are compatible with the customer's system, are easy to install and learn, save the customer a lot of money, and promise to improve through time.

In summary, relationship marketing is not appropriate with all customers in that heavy relationship investments will not always pay off. But it is extremely effective with the right type of customers who get heavily committed to a specific system and expect consistent and timely service.

SOURCE: Barbara Bund Jackson, *Winning and Keeping Industrial Customers: The Dynamics of Customer Relationships* (Lexington, Mass.: Heath, 1985).

TABLE 23-3   Actions Affecting Buyer-Seller Relationships

Things Affecting Relationships	
Good Things	**Bad Things**
Initiate positive phone calls	Make only callbacks
Make recommendations	Make justifications
Candor in language	Accommodative language
Use phone	Use correspondence
Show appreciation	Wait for misunderstandings
Make service suggestions	Wait for service requests
Use "we" problem-solving language	Use "owe-us" legal language
Get to problems	Only respond to problems
Use jargon/shorthand	Use long-winded communications
Personality problems aired	Personality problems hidden
Talk of "our future together"	Talk about making good on the past
Routinize responses	Fire drill/emergency responsiveness
Accept responsibility	Shift blame
Plan the future	Rehash the past

SOURCE: Theodore Levitt, *The Marketing Imagination* (New York: Free Press, 1983), p. 119.

■ *Each relationship manager must develop long-range and annual customer-relationship plans.* The annual relationship plan will state objectives, strategies, specific actions, and required resources.

When a relationship management program is properly implemented, many subtle and not-too-subtle aspects of dealing with customers will change (see Table 23-3). In essence, the organization will begin to focus as much on managing its customers well as on managing its products well.

SUMMARY

Most companies use sales representatives, and many companies assign them the pivotal role in the marketing mix. Sales people are very effective in achieving certain marketing objectives. At the same time they are very costly. Management must give careful thought to designing and managing its personal-selling resources.

Sales-force design calls for decisions on objectives, strategy, structure, size, and compensation. Sales-force objectives include prospecting, communicating, selling and servicing, information gathering, and allocating. Sales-force strategy is a question of what types and mix and selling approaches are most effective (solo selling, team selling, and so on). Sales-force structure is a choice between organizing by territory, product, market, or some hybrid combination and developing the right territory size and shape. Sales-force size involves estimating the total workload and how many sales hours—and hence salespersons—would be needed. Sales-force compensation involves determining the pay level and pay components such as salary, commission, bonus, expenses, and fringe benefits.

Managing the sales force involves recruiting and selecting sales representatives and training, directing, motivating, and evaluating them. Sales representatives must be recruited and selected carefully to hold down the high costs of hiring the wrong persons. Sales-training programs familiarize new sales people with the company's history, its products and policies, the characteristics of the market and competitors, and the art of selling. Sales people need direction on such matters as developing customer and prospect targets and call norms and using their time efficiently through computer-aided information, planning and selling systems, and inside support sales people. Sales people also need encouragement through economic and personal rewards and recognition because they must make tough decisions and are subject to many frustrations. The key idea is that appropriate sales-force motivation will lead to more effort, better performance, higher reward, higher satisfaction, and therefore still more motivation. The last management step calls for periodically evaluating each sales person's performance to help him or her do a better job.

The purpose of the sales force is to produce sales, and this involves the art of personal selling. One aspect is salesmanship, which involves a seven-step process: prospecting and qualifying, preapproach, approach, presentation and demonstration, handling objections, closing, and follow-up. Another aspect is negotiation, the art of arriving at transaction terms that satisfy both parties. The third aspect is relationship management, the art of creating a closer working relation and interdependence between the people in two organizations.

◼ QUESTIONS

1. Discuss and evaluate the purpose of each of the following procedures used as standards for evaluation: salesperson-to-salesperson comparisons, current-to-past-sales comparisons, qualitative evaluations, and key indicators.

2. Describe the major variations in sales-force structure. Assume you had a sales force of eighty persons selling four major product groups to four types of retailers. How would the selling function be managed under each variation? What factors would you consider in evaluating each structure?

3. Apart from personal-selling skills, what other factors can help or hinder a salesperson's performance?

4. In what ways has the customer been viewed in the buying-selling transaction? What perspective does Leavitt say should form the buyer-seller transaction? What rights do you think customers would be entitled to under this concept?

5. What are some ways in which a microcomputer can be of help to a sales manager?

6. Select a bargaining situation between a marketing agent and another party (internal or external to the firm) and discuss how the principled-negotiation approach could be used to reach agreement for both parties successfully.

7. You are a member of a marketing team negotiating with a potential customer over a robotics system for her production line. The other party is attempting to use the "divide and conquer" tactic described in Exhibit 23-8. What is your response to this tactic?

8. A district sales manager voiced the following complaint at a sales meeting: "The average salesperson costs our company $40,000 in compensation and expenses. Why can't we buy a few less $40,000 full-page advertisements in *Time* magazine and use the money to hire more people? Surely one individual working a full year can sell more products than a one-page ad in one issue of *Time*." Evaluate this argument.

9. The text described some characteristics that might be looked for in sales representatives. What characteristics should be looked for in selecting district sales managers? What about the national sales manager?

10. A sales manager wants to determine how many sales calls per month the sales force should make to average-size accounts. Describe how an experiment might be set up to answer the question.

11. A sales manager is trying to figure out the most that should be spent to win a particular account. This account would produce sales of $10,000 a year, and the company is likely to retain it for at least four years. The company's profit margin on sales is 15 percent. The company wants its various investments to earn 8 percent. What is the most that the company should spend to win this account?

12. Suppose a salesperson can make 1,600 calls a year. If he or she has been writing $420,000 worth of business a year, how many calls can the salesperson make to a $10,000-a-year account without diluting the total business written during the year?

13. Describe several types of selling situations where a straight salary plan seems appropriate.

14. Should sales representatives participate in the establishment of sales quotas for their territories? What would be the advantages and disadvantages of their participation?

1 Adapted from Robert N. McMurry, "The Mystique of Super-Salesmanship," *Harvard Business Review*, March–April 1961, p. 114. For a study of other classifications, see William C. Moncrief III, "Selling Activity and Sales Postion Taxonomies for Industrial Salesforces," *Journal of Marketing Research*, August 1986, pp. 261–70.

2 Reported in *Marketing News*, August 1, 1986, p. 1.

3 Roger M. Pegram, *Selling and Servicing the National Account* (New York: Conference Board, 1972).

4 William H. Kaven, *Managing the Major Sale* (New York: American Management Association, 1971); Benson P. Shapiro and Ronald S. Posner, "Making the Major Sale," *Harvard Business Review*, March–April 1976, pp. 68–78; and Mack Hanan, *Key Account Selling* (New York: Amacom 1982).

5 Andris A. Zoltners and Prabhakant Sinha, "Sales Territory Alignment: A Review and Model," *Management Science*, November 1983, pp. 1237–56; and Leonard M. Lodish, "Sales Territory Alignment to Maximize Profits," *Journal of Marketing Research*, February 1975, pp. 30–36.

6 Joseph P. Vaccaro, "Compensation Should Suit Firm's Goals," *Marketing News*, November 8, 1985, p. 32.

7 Ibid.

8 See Ralph L. Day and Peter D. Bennett, "Should Salesmen's Compensation Be Geared to Profits?" *Journal of Marketing Research*, May 1964, pp. 39–43; John U. Farley and Charles B. Weinberg, "Inferential Optimization: An Algorithm for Determining Optimal Sales Commissions in Multiproduct Sales Forces," *Operational Research Quarterly*, June 1975, pp. 413–18; and V. Srinivasan, "An Investigation of the Equal Commission Rate Policy for a Multi-Product Salesforce," *Management Science*, July 1981, pp. 731–56. For an excellent review, see Anne T. Coughlan and Subrata K. Sen, "Salesforce Compensation: Insights from Management Science" (Cambridge, Mass.: Marketing Science Institute, March 1986), Report No. 81-107.

9 McMurry, "Mystique of Super-Salesmanship," p. 117.

10 Ibid., p. 118.

11 David Mayer and Herbert M. Greenberg, "What Makes a Good Salesman?" *Harvard Business Review*, July–August 1964, pp. 119–25.

12 John C. Crawford and James R. Lumpkin, "The Choice of Selling as a Career," *Industrial Marketing Management*, October 1983, pp. 257–61.

13 James M. Comer and Alan J. Dubinsky, *Managing the Successful Sales Force* (Lexington, Mass.: Lexington Books, 1985), pp. 5–25.

14 From an address given by Donald R. Keough at the twenty-seventh annual conference of the Super-Market Institute in Chicago, April 26–29, 1964.

15 "Double-Digit Hikes in 1974 Sales Training Costs," *Sales and Marketing Management*, January 6, 1975, p. 54.

16 See John F. Magee, "Determining the Optimum Allocation of Expenditures for Promotional Effort with Operations Research Methods," in *The Frontiers of Marketing Thought and Science*, ed. Frank M. Bass (Chicago: American Marketing Association, 1958), pp. 140–56.

17 "Are Salespeople Gaining More Selling Time?" *Sales and Marketing Management*, July 1986, p. 29.

18 James A. Narus and James C. Anderson, "Industrial Distributor Selling: The Roles of Outside and Inside Sales," *Industrial Marketing Management*, 15 (1986), 55–62.

19 See Conference Board, *Computers and the Sales Effort*, quoted in "Marketers and the PC: Steady as She Goes," *Sales and Marketing Management*, August 1986, pp. 53–55. Also see "Rebirth of a Salesman: Willy Loman Goes Electronic," *Business Week*, February 27, 1984, pp. 103–4.

20 Neil M. Ford, Orville C. Walker, Jr., and Gilbert A. Churchill, Jr., "Research Perspectives on the Performance of Salespeople: Selected Readings" (Cambridge, Mass.: Marketing Science Institute, September 1983), Report No. 83-107.

21 J. B. Heckert, *Business Budgeting and Control* (New York: Ronald Press, 1946), p. 138.

22 Richard Cavalier, *Sales Meetings That Work* (Homewood, Ill.: Dow Jones-Irwin, 1983).

23 Some of the following discussion is based on W. J. E. Crissy, William H. Cunningham, and Isabella C. M. Cunningham, *Selling: The Personal Force in Marketing* (New York: John Wiley, 1977), pp. 119–29.

24 Robert Hood, "Increase Sales by Decreasing the Number of Bad Leads," *Marketing News*, May 23, 1986, p. 18.

25 Mark Hanan, "Join the Systems Sell and You Can't Be Beat," *Sales and Marketing Management*, August 21, 1972, p. 44. Also see Mark Hanan, James Cribbin, and Herman Heiser, *Consultative Selling* (New York: American Management Association, 1970).

26 See Rosann L. Spiro and William D. Perreault, Jr., "Influence Use by Industrial Salesmen: Influence Strategy Mixes and Situational Determinants" (Unpublished paper, Graduate School of Business Administration, University of North Carolina, 1976).

27 Johan Arndt, "Toward a Concept of Domesticated Markets," *Journal of Marketing*, Fall 1979, pp. 69–75.

28 Jeffrey Z. Rubin and Bert R. Brown, *The Social Psychology of Bargaining and Negotiation* (New York: Academic Press, 1975), p. 18.

29 John von Neumann and Oscar Morgenstern, *Theory of Games and Economic Behavior* (Princeton, N.J.: Princeton University Press, 1944). For current applications, see Sridhar Moorthy, "Using Game Theory to Model Competition," *Journal of Marketing Research*, August 1985, pp. 262–82.

30 The following books have applied game-theoretic models to analyzing actual bargaining situations: John Dennis McDonald, *The Game of Business* (New York: Doubleday, 1975); and Thomas C. Schelling, *The Strategy of Conflict* (Cambridge, Mass.: Harvard University Press, 1960).

31 See Howard Raiffa, *The Art of Science of Negotiation* (Cambridge: Harvard University Press, 1982).

32 See, for example, R. E. Walton and R. B. McKenzie, *A Behavioral Theory of Labor Negotiations* (New York: McGraw-Hill, 1965).

33 See Rubin and Brown, *Social Psychology of Bargaining*, esp. Chap. 3.

34 Samuel B. Bacharach and Edward J. Lawler, *Bargaining: Power, Tactics, and Outcome* (San Francisco: Jossey-Bass, 1981).

35 See Herb Cohen, *You Can Negotiate Anything* (New York: Bantam Books, 1980); Gerard I. Nierenberg, *The Art of Negotiating* (New York: Pocket Books, 1984); and Chester L. Karrass, *The Negotiating Game* (Cleveland: World Publishing, 1970).

36 This literature lists the traits that effective negotiators should possess. The most important traits are preparation and planning skill, knowledge of subject matter being negotiated, ability to think clearly and rapidly under pressure and uncertainty, ability to express thoughts verbally, listening skill, judgment and general intelligence, integrity, ability to persuade others, and patience. See Karrass, *Negotiating Game*, pp. 242–44.

37 Lamar Lee and Donald W. Dobler, *Purchasing and Materials Management* (New York: McGraw-Hill, 1977), pp. 146–47.

38 Oran R. Young, ed., *Bargaining: Formal Theories of Negotiation* (Urbana: University of Illinois Press, 1975), pp. 364–90.

39 This discussion of zone of agreement is fully developed in Raiffa, *Art and Science of Negotiation*.

40 Roger Fisher and William Ury, *Getting to Yes: Negotiating Agreement without Giving In* (Boston: Houghton Mifflin, 1981).

41 Ibid., p. xii.

42 Theodore Levitt, *The Marketing Imagination* (New York: Free Press, 1983), Chap. 6, "Relationship Management," pp. 111–26.

Organizing
and Implementing
Marketing Programs

Success is a product of unremitting attention to purpose.

Benjamin Disraeli

Do your work with your whole heart and you will succeed—there is so little competition!

Elbert Hubbard

We now turn from the *strategic* and *tactical* sides of marketing to the *administrative* side to examine how firms organize, implement, and control their marketing activities. In this chapter, we will deal with marketing organization and implementation, and in the next chapter, with marketing control.

COMPANY ORGANIZATION

There is a growing view that companies need fresh concepts on how to organize their business and marketing in response to the significant changes that have occurred in the business environment in recent years. Advances in computers and telecommunications, the increase in global business and global competition, the greater purchasing sophistication of consumers and companies, the growing importance of service businesses, and several other forces are requiring companies to reconsider how to organize their business.

Figure 24-1 contrasts management's traditional view of how to relate the major business functions and the newer market-oriented view. The traditional view in Figure 24-1(a) holds that the research and development department (R&D) must take responsibility for searching for new-product ideas, screening them, and proposing the most promising ones to management. Bright ideas that achieve successful laboratory development and have a promising profit picture move to the design and engineering department (D&E), which works out the detailed character of the product and manufacturing process. The purchasing department then buys the necessary productive inputs, manufacturing makes the product, and marketing tries to sell it.

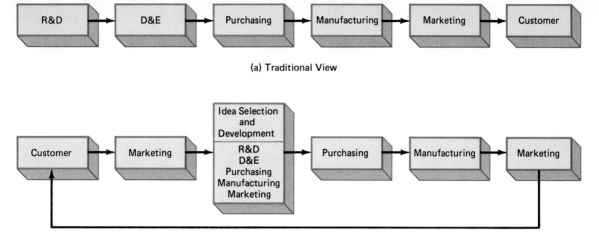

(a) Traditional View

(b) Market-oriented View

FIGURE 24-1
Two Views of Company Organization

Although the model sounds logical, it has several weaknesses.

1. R&D staff members often fall in love with new ideas way beyond the possible interest or purchasing power of customers. They tend to commit "the better mousetrap fallacy."
2. D&E often develops prototypes without consulting manufacturing, only to learn at a subsequent stage that manufacturing costs will be too high and some redesign work is necessary.
3. The manufacturing department may take some shortcuts that hurt quality or may resist adding features that marketing believes will help sell the product.
4. Marketing inherits a product to sell where it had minimum influence and yet is held responsible when the product doesn't sell well.
5. The customer is seen as the end of the process rather than the beginning, and little is done to collect and use customer feedback to improve the product and the process.

What is missing from the traditional model is the concept of starting with the customer and applying "teamwork" throughout the process of introducing successful products. Figure 24-1(b) presents a market-oriented view of the business flow process. Everything starts with the customer. The company's marketing department takes responsibility for collecting ideas from customers and other sources. Then all the functions participate in evaluating and selecting the better ideas and give inputs to R&D and D&E as the product is being developed. If the idea looks like a winner, purchasing assembles the resources, manufacturing makes the product, and marketing takes responsibility for selling it. Marketing watches the customers closely for their reactions and suggestions on improving the product.

The Japanese have further developed this view of the business process by adding the following concepts:

1. *Zero customer feedback time.* Customer feedback should be continuously collected after purchase to learn how to improve the product and its marketing.
2. *Zero product improvement time.* The company should take all the customer improvement ideas, evaluate them, and introduce the most valued and feasible improvements as soon as possible.

3. *Zero purchasing time.* The company should receive the required parts and supplies as needed through just-in-time arrangements with suppliers. By holding low inventories, the company can keep its costs low.
4. *Zero setup time.* The company should be able to manufacture any of its products as soon as they are ordered, without long delays in setup time.
5. *Zero defects.* The products should be of high quality and free from flaws.

In this context, we will now look at how the marketing department can be organized.

MARKETING ORGANIZATION

Marketing has evolved over the years from a simple sales function to a complex group of functions, not always well integrated either within itself or in its relationship with the nonmarketing functions of the firm. Questions abound concerning the relationship between marketing managers at headquarters and sales people in the field; about the future of brand management; about the need or lack of need for a corporate vice-president of marketing (as opposed to divisional marketing VPs); about marketing's relations to manufacturing, R&D, and finance; and so on. To gain an understanding of the complex issues, we will examine how marketing departments evolved in companies, how they are typically organized, and how they interact with other company departments.

The Evolution of the Marketing Department

The modern marketing department is the product of a long evolution. At least five stages can be distinguished, and companies can be found today in each stage.

Simple Sales Department   All companies start out with five simple functions. Someone must raise and manage capital (finance), hire people (personnel), produce the product or service (operations), sell it (sales), and keep the books (accounting). The selling function is headed by a sales vice-president, who manages a sales force and also does some selling. When the company needs some marketing research or advertising, the sales vice-president also handles those functions. This stage is illustrated in Figure 24-2(a).

Sales Department with Ancillary Marketing Functions   As the company expands to serve new types of customers or new geographical areas, it needs to strengthen certain marketing functions other than sales. For example, an East Coast firm that plans to open in the West will first have to conduct marketing research to learn about customer needs and market potential. If it opens business in the West, it will then have to do strong advertising to get its name and products known in the area. The sales vice-president will need to hire specialists to handle these activities on a more expert basis. The sales vice-president may also decide to hire a *marketing director* to manage these newer marketing functions. [Figure 24-2(b).]

Separate Marketing Department   The continued growth of the company increases the productive potential of investments in other marketing functions—marketing research, new-product development, advertising and sales promotion, customer service—relative to sales-force activity. Yet the sales vice-president normally continues to give disproportionate time and resources to the sales force. The marketing director will appeal for more resources but will usually get less than can be used effectively. Sometimes the marketing director will quit out of frustration.

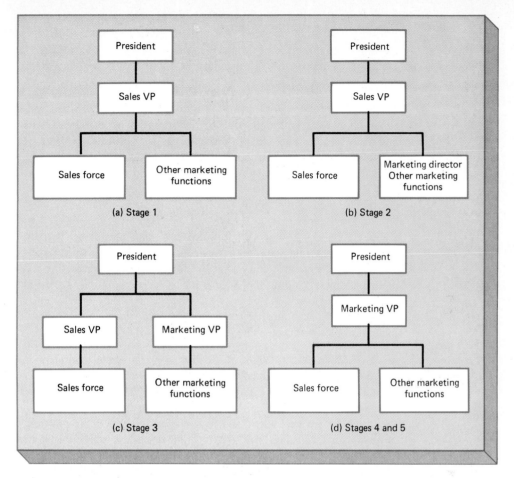

FIGURE 24-2
Stages in the Evolution of the Marketing Department

The company president will eventually see the advantage of establishing a separate marketing department that is independent of the sales vice-president. [See Figure 24-2(c).] The marketing department will be headed by a marketing vice-president, who reports, along with the sales vice-president, to the president or executive vice-president. At this stage, sales and marketing are separate functions in the organization and are supposed to work closely together.

This arrangement is used by many industrial companies. It has the advantage of permitting the company president to get a more-balanced view of company opportunities and problems. Suppose the company is losing sales and the company president asks the sales vice-president for solutions. The sales vice-president may recommend adding more sales people, raising sales compensation, running a sales contest, or providing more sales training, not to mention cutting the product's price so that it will be easier to sell. Then the company president asks the marketing vice-president for solutions. The marketing vice-president is less ready to suggest immediate price and sales-force solutions. The marketing vice-president will see the question more from the customer's point of view. Is the company going after the right customers? How do the target customers see the company and its products relative to competitors? Are there changes in product features, styling, packaging, services, distribution, other forms of promotion, and so on, that are warranted? In general, there will be more effort to understand the problem rather than going after it with a pure selling push.

Modern Marketing Department   Although the sales and marketing vice-presidents are supposed to work harmoniously, their relationship is occasionally characterized by rivalry and distrust. The sales vice-president resists letting the sales force become less important in the marketing mix; and the marketing vice-president seeks a larger budget for the non-sales-force functions. The sales vice-president tends to be short-run oriented and preoccupied with achieving current sales. The marketing vice-president tends to be long-run oriented and preoccupied with planning the right products and marketing strategy to meet the customers' long-run needs.

If there is too much conflict between sales and marketing, the company president may place marketing activities back under the sales vice-president, or instruct the executive vice-president to handle conflicts that arise, or place the marketing vice-president in charge of everything, including the sales force. The last solution is eventually chosen in many companies and forms the basis of the modern marketing department, a department headed by a marketing vice-president with subordinates reporting from every marketing function, including sales management. [See Figure 24-2(d).]

Modern Marketing Company   A company can have a modern marketing department and yet not operate as a modern marketing company. The latter depends on how the other company officers view the marketing function. If they view marketing as primarily a selling function, they are missing the point. Only when they see that all the departments are "working for the customer" and that marketing is the name not only of a department but of a company philosophy will they become a modern marketing company.

Ways of Organizing the Marketing Department

Modern marketing departments show numerous arrangements. All marketing organizations must accommodate to four basic dimensions of marketing activity: *functions*, *geographical areas*, *products*, and *customer markets*.

Functional Organization   The most common form of marketing organization consists of functional-marketing specialists reporting to a marketing vice-president, who coordinates their activities. Figure 24-3 shows five specialists: marketing administration manager,

FIGURE 24-3
Functional Organization

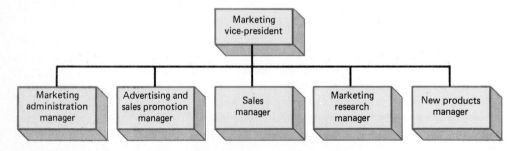

advertising and sales promotion manager, sales manager, marketing research manager, and new-products manager, respectively. Additional functional specialists might include a customer-service manager, a marketing-planning manager, and a physical-distribution manager.

If the number of functions reporting to the marketing vice-president becomes too large, they can be divided into major subgroups. At least two alternative groupings are found in practice:

1. *Service functions* (sales force, advertising, sales promotion, marketing research, customer services) vs. *program functions* (products, markets, customers, ventures)
2. *Planning functions* (strategic planning, product planning, marketing research, marketing projects) and *marketing communications* (sales force, advertising, sales promotion, public relations)

The main advantage of a functional marketing organization is its administrative simplicity. On the other hand, this form loses effectiveness as the company's products and markets grow. First, there is inadequate planning for specific products and markets, since no one has full responsibility for any product or market. Products that àre not favorites of various functional specialists get neglected. Second, each functional group competes to gain more budget and status vis-à-vis the other functions. The marketing vice-president has to constantly sift the claims of competing functional specialists and faces a difficult coordination problem.

Geographical Organization   A company selling in a national market often organizes its sales force (and sometimes other functions) along geographical lines. Figure 24-4 shows 1 national sales manager, 4 regional sales managers, 24 zone sales managers, 192 district sales managers, and 1,920 salespersons. The span of control increases as we move from

FIGURE 24-4
Geographical Organization

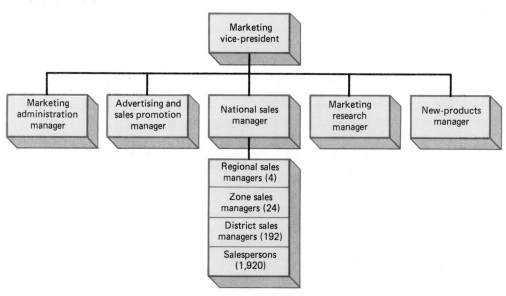

the national sales manager down toward the district sales managers. Shorter spans allow managers to give more time to subordinates and are warranted when the sales task is complex, the salespersons are highly paid, and the salesperson's impact on profits is substantial.

Several companies are now adding *local market specialists* to support the sales efforts in high-volume markets. The local market specialist for Cleveland, for example, would know Cleveland's situation in great detail and be able to help headquarters marketing managers adjust their marketing mix for Cleveland to take maximum advantage of the opportunities. The local market specialist would prepare the annual and long-range plan for winning in Cleveland and would act as liaison between the headquarters' marketing staff and the local sales force.

Product and Brand Management Organization Companies producing a variety of products and/or brands often establish a product or brand management organization. The product management organization does not replace the functional management organization but serves as another layer of management. The product management organization is headed by a products manager, who supervises several product group managers, who supervise product managers in charge of specific products. (See Figure 24-5.)

A product management organization makes sense if the products are quite different and/or if the sheer number of products is beyond the capacity of a functional marketing organization to handle.

Product management first appeared in the Procter & Gamble Company in 1927. A new company soap, Camay, was not doing well, and one of the young executives, Neil H. McElroy (later president of P&G), was assigned to give his exclusive attention to developing and promoting this product. He did it successfully, and the company soon added other product managers.

Since then many firms, especially in the food, soap, toiletries, and chemical industries, have established product management organizations. General Foods, for example, uses a

FIGURE 24-5
Product Management Organization

product management organization in its Post Division. There are separate product group managers in charge of cereals, pet food, and beverages. Within the cereal product group, there are separate product managers for nutritional cereals, children's presweetened cereals, family cereals, and miscellaneous cereals. In turn, the nutritional-cereal product manager supervises brand managers.[1]

The product manager's role is to develop product plans, see that they are implemented, monitor the results, and take corrective action. This responsibility breaks down into six tasks:

- Developing a long-range and competitive strategy for the product
- Preparing an annual marketing plan and sales forecast
- Working with advertising and merchandising agencies to develop copy, programs, and campaigns
- Stimulating interest in and support of the product among the sales force and distributors
- Gathering continuous intelligence on the product's performance, customer and dealer attitudes, and new problems and opportunities
- Initiating product improvements to meet changing market needs

These basic functions are common to both consumer- and industrial-product managers. Yet there are some differences in their jobs and emphases.[2] Consumer-product managers typically manage fewer products than industrial-product managers. They spend more time on advertising and sales promotion. They spend more time working with others in the company and various agencies and little time with customers. They are often younger and better educated. Industrial-product managers, by contrast, think more about the technical aspects of their product and possible design improvements. They spend more time with laboratory and engineering personnel. They work more closely with the sales force and key buyers. They pay less attention to advertising, sales promotion, and promotional pricing. They emphasize rational product factors over emotional ones.

The product management organization introduces several advantages. First, the product manager develops a cost-effective marketing mix for the product. Second, the product manager can react more quickly to problems in the marketplace than a committee of specialists can. Third, smaller brands are less neglected because they have a product advocate. Fourth, product management is an excellent training ground for young executives, for it involves them in almost every area of company operations. (See Figure 24-6.)

But a price is paid for these advantages. First, product management creates some conflict and frustration.[3] Typically, product managers are not given enough authority to carry out their responsibilities effectively. They have to rely on persuasion to get the cooperation of advertising, sales, manufacturing, and other departments. They are told they are "minipresidents" but are often treated as low-level coordinators. They are burdened with a great amount of "housekeeping" paperwork. They often have to go over the heads of others to get something done.

Second, product managers become experts in their product but rarely become experts in any functions. They vacillate between posing as experts and being cowed by real experts. This is unfortunate when the product depends on a specific type of expertise, such as advertising.

Third, the product management system often turns out to be costlier than anticipated. Originally, one person is appointed to manage each major product. Soon product managers are appointed to manage even minor products. Each product manager, usually overworked,

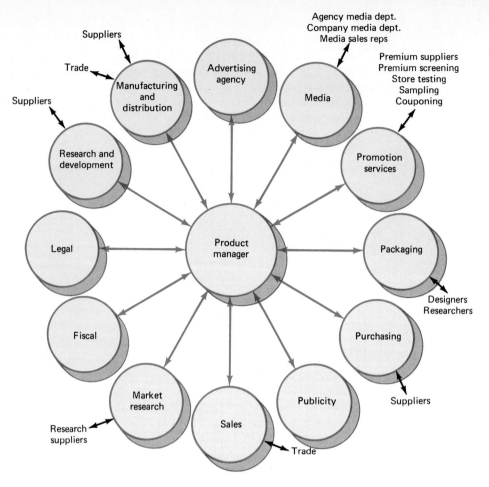

FIGURE 24-6
The Product Manager's Interactions
Adapted from "Product Managers: Just What Do They Think?" *Printers Ink*, October 28, 1966, p. 15.

pleads for and gets an *associate brand manager*. Later, both overworked, they persuade management to give them an *assistant brand manager*. With all these personnel, payroll costs climb. In the meantime, the company continues to increase its functional specialists in copy, packaging, media, sales promotion, market surveys, statistical analysis, and so on. The company becomes saddled with a costly structure of product management people and functional specialists.

Fourth, product managers tend to manage their brand for a short time. Either product managers move up in a few years to another brand or product, or they transfer to another company, or they leave product management altogether. Their short-term involvement with the product leads to short-term marketing planning and plays havoc with building up the product's long-term strengths.

Pearson and Wilson have suggested five steps to make the product management system work better:[4]

■ *Clearly delineate the limits of the product manager's role and responsibility for the product.* (They are essentially proposers, not deciders.)

■ *Build a strategy development and review process to provide an agreed-to-framework for the product manager's operations.* (Too many companies allow product managers to get away with shallow marketing plans featuring a lot of statistics but little strategic rationale.)

■ *Take into account areas of potential conflict between product managers and functional specialists when defining their respective roles.* (Clarify which decisions are to be made by the product manager, which by the expert, and which will be shared.)

■ *Set up a formal process that forces to the top all conflict-of-interest situations between product management and functional line management.* (Both parties should put the issues in writing and forward them to general management for settlement.)

■ *Establish a system for measuring results that is consistent with the product manager's responsibilities.* (If product managers are accountable for profit, they should be given more control over the factors that affect their profitability.)

A second alternative is to switch from a product-manager to a product-team approach. In fact, there are three types of product-team structures in product management. (See Figure 24-7.)

■ *Vertical product team.* This consists of a product manager, associate product manager, and product assistant. [See Figure 24-7(a).] The product manager is the leader and primarily deals with other executives to gain their cooperation. The associate product manager assists in these tasks and also does some paperwork. The product assistant does most of the paperwork and runs errands.

■ *Triangular product team.* This consists of a product manager and two specialized product assistants, one who takes care of (say) marketing research and the other, marketing communications. [See Figure 24-7(b).] This design is used at the Illinois Central Railroad, where various three-person teams manage different commodities. Also, the Hallmark Company uses a "marketing team" consisting of a market manager (the leader), a marketing manager, and a distribution manager.

■ *Horizontal product team.* This consists of a product manager and several specialists from marketing and other functions. [See Figure 24-7(c).] Thus the 3M Company divided its commercial tape division into nine business-planning teams, each team consisting of a team leader

FIGURE 24-7
Three Types of Product Teams

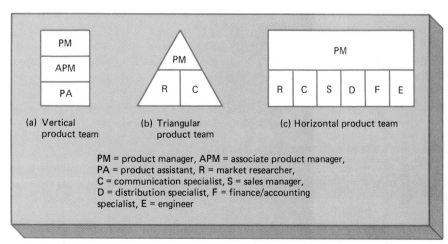

(a) Vertical product team   (b) Triangular product team   (c) Horizontal product team

PM = product manager, APM = associate product manager,
PA = product assistant, R = market researcher,
C = communication specialist, S = sales manager,
D = distribution specialist, F = finance/accounting
specialist, E = engineer

and representatives from sales, marketing, laboratory, engineering, accounting, and marketing research. Instead of a product manager's bearing the entire responsibility for product planning, he or she shares it with representatives from key parts of the company. Their input is critical in the marketing-planning process, and furthermore each team member can bring influence to bear in his or her own department. The ultimate step after a horizontal product team is organized is to form a product division around the product.

A third alternative is to eliminate product-manager positions for minor products and assign two or more products to each remaining product manager. This is feasible especially where two or more products appeal to a similar set of needs. Thus a cosmetics company does not need separate product managers, because cosmetics serve one major need—beauty—whereas a toiletries company needs different managers for headache remedies, toothpaste, soap, and shampoo, because these products differ in their use and appeal.

Product management systems are undergoing several important changes.[5] Exhibit 24-1 discusses current developments affecting the future of brand management.

EXHIBIT 24-1

What's the Future of Brand Management?

Brand management has become a well-established fixture in American consumer packaged goods companies. Yet the environment in which it was created and thrived is drastically altered today, and observers are questioning whether it provides the best system for managing brands in the new environment.

Today's brand managers are in a double bind: They are under great pressure to produce increased profits while being given less latitude for achieving them. Companies are wondering if they need all the layers of group brand managers, brand managers, associate brand managers, and assistant brand managers. Companies are facing three new environmental forces that are calling into question the whole concept of brand managers:

1. *Growing bargaining power of the distribution channels and growing importance of sales promotion.* The major distributors of consumer packaged goods—supermarket chains and mass merchandisers—are becoming more powerful and are demanding better terms from consumer packaged goods companies in exchange for scarce shelf space. These distributors are primarily interested in generating more store traffic, and they are pressing manufacturers for more trade deals. The heat is being felt by the manufacturers' sales forces, who tell the brand managers that they cannot get shelf space without more trade deals. The result is that the brand manager shifts more money into sales promotion and has less funds to build his or her brand franchise.

   Furthermore, the distributors are demanding more multibrand and multicategory promotion deals from each manufacturer. The distributors want customized multibrand deals that would enable them to distinguish their offers from competitors' offers. These deals have to be worked out at higher levels of management than the brand level. But the brand managers have to be taxed to support these deals, sometimes by giving up about 25 percent of their budget. The brand manager is being left with less control over his or her sales promotion funds.

   As sales promotion becomes more important, the manufacturers realize that they are not organized to handle it efficiently. Originally sales promotion was handled individually by each brand manager. Some companies later appointed a sales promotion specialist to help brand managers choose good premium and couponing schemes for consumer sales promotion. Meanwhile the company's sales force is heavily pressing for more trade promotion money. The question becomes, How much should be spent on sales promotion out of the total budget and how should this money be split between trade and consumer promotion? Unfortunately, the decisions are being made politically rather than rationally.

2. *Declining cost-effectiveness of mass advertising.* Brand managers are finding that they have less money to spend on advertising, the one tool they know best. Furthermore, mass advertising—particularly network television—is becoming less cost effective. There are fewer people watching

network television, and many of them are not interested in many products that are advertised. The money can be spent more effectively by studying category and brand interest levels market-by-market. But brand managers do not know the individual markets that well. Companies are increasingly developing local area marketing plans through other people rather than the brand managers.

3. **Declining level of customer brand loyalty.** Consumers have been exposed to so much dealing recently that a growing number are deal-prone rather than brand-prone. The consumers' evoked set of acceptable brands is increasing. As more consumers switch their brands each week depending on the deals, brand shares become more volatile. A brand's weekly or monthly market share means less and becomes less useful in deciding how much money to allocate to each brand. Higher levels of management have to decide how much in funds each brand should get based on more long-run criteria.

These developments are forcing consumer packaged goods companies to rethink how they should develop and manage their brands. There are two competing solutions:

1. **Changing the job description and the role of the brand manager.** One avenue of thought is that the brand manager should spend less time creating the promotion plans and become more involved in product improvement and production. Normally the brand manager has little time to think about creating flankers and brand extensions, and this has forced companies to appoint new-product specialists within brand or category groups to do this work. And the brand manager does not become very involved in knowing the production and logistics steps and how to find cost improvements. Therefore it might be argued that brand managers should have their responsibilities shifted more to product improvement and production/distribution efficiency concerns.

2. **Eliminating the brand management system.** Another avenue of thought is that a company should organize teams around major product categories such as snacks, dog foods, and cereals. Each team would be headed by a category manager and would consist of a marketing researcher, an advertising specialist, a sales promotion specialist, and a sales management specialist. This would reduce the number of middle managers and result in a leaner marketing organization.

If brand managers are eliminated, their counterparts in advertising agencies—namely, account executives—might also be eliminated. Many consumer packaged goods companies are pressing advertising agencies to lower their costs, especially considering the reduced effectiveness of mass advertising. These companies normally prepare their own brand marketing plans and simply want a good creative plan and media plan from their advertising agency. They wonder why they have to work through account executives and their assistants. Some companies are telling their advertising agencies they are going to pay less or else switch agencies, thus forcing these agencies to reconsider their own organizing patterns and the role of the account executives.

Making changes in the brand management system will not be easy. Everyone involved in brand management will fight changes, since these changes will destroy the normal climbing ladder in the organization. Any company that is rumored to be thinking about abandoning brand management will lose some of its best people before it can reorganize, and the transition will be difficult.

Yet changes are called for. The fact is that brand management is a sales-driven, not a market-driven, system. Brand managers are hired to get rid of the products as they come off the production line. They are not oriented toward spotting new customer groups and new needs and preparing new offers for these groups. They are narrowly focused on pushing out their brand to anyone and everyone.

SOURCE: Some of these observations were described to the author by Don E. Schultz of Northwestern University, coming from joint research conducted with Professor Robert Dewar, also of Northwestern.

Market Management Organization

Many companies sell their products to a diverse set of markets. For example, Smith Corona sells its electric typewriters to consumer, business, and government markets. U.S. Steel sells its steel to the railroad, construction, and public utility industries. When the customers fall into different user groups with distinct buying preferences and practices, a market management organization is desirable.

A market management organization is similar to the product management organization shown earlier in Figure 24-5. A *markets manager* supervises several *market managers* (also called market development managers, market specialists, or industry specialists). The market managers draw upon functional services as needed. Market managers of important markets may even have some functional specialists reporting to them.

Market managers are essentially staff, not line, people, with duties similar to those of product managers. Market managers develop long-range and annual plans for their markets. They must analyze where their market is going and what new products their company should offer to this market. Their performance is often judged by their contribution to market-share growth rather than to current profitability in their market. This system carries many of the same advantages and disadvantages of product management systems. Its strongest advantage is that the marketing activity is organized to meet the needs of distinct customer groups rather than focusing on marketing functions, regions, or products per se.

Many companies are reorganizing along market lines. Hanan calls these *market-centered organizations* and argues that "the only way to ensure being market-oriented is to put a company's organizational structure together so that its major markets become the centers around which its divisions are built."[6] Xerox has converted from geographical selling to selling by industry. The Mead Company has clustered its marketing activities around home building and furnishings, education, and leisure markets.

One of the most dramatic changes to market centeredness has occurred at the Heinz Company. Before 1964, Heinz was organized around a brand-management system, with separate brand managers for soups, condiments, puddings, and so on. Each brand manager was responsible for both grocery sales and institutional sales. Then in 1964, Heinz created a separate marketing organization for institutional sales because institutional sales were growing faster than grocery sales but were not as well understood by the brand managers. More recently Heinz created three broad market groups: groceries, commercial restaurants, and institutions. Each group contains further market specialists. For example, the institutional division contains market specialists for schools, colleges, hospitals, and prisons.

> The prison market manager's job is to visit prison kitchen managers and learn about their food needs and budgets. Then this manager proposes reformulations of Heinz ketchup, soup, mustard, and other products to make them cost effective and competitive with the offers of other suppliers. Thus Heinz will use a lower grade of tomato and will package its ketchup in bulk in order to compete for prison business, which happens to be a growth market!

Product Management/Market Management Organization Companies that produce many products flowing into many markets face a dilemma. They could use a product management system, which requires product managers to be familiar with highly divergent markets. Or they could use a market management system, which means that market managers would have to be familiar with highly divergent products bought by their markets. Or they could install both product and market managers, that is, a *matrix organization*.

Du Pont is a company that has done the latter.[7] (See Figure 24-8.) Its textile fibers department consists of separate product managers for rayon, acetate, nylon, orlon, and dacron; and also separate market managers for men's wear, women's wear, home furnishings, and industrial markets. The product managers have the responsibility for planning the sales and profits of their respective fibers. These product managers concentrate on improving their profits through finding more uses for their fiber. They contact the market managers and ask for an estimate of how much of their fiber can be sold in each market. The market managers, on the other hand, are more interested in meeting the needs of their market, rather than pushing a particular fiber. In preparing their market plan, they contact each product manager to learn about planned prices and availabilities of the different fibers. The final sales forecasts of the market managers and the product managers should add to the same grand total.

A product management/market management organization would seem desirable in a multiproduct, multimarket company. The rub is that this system is costly and conflictual. There is the cost of supporting a three-dimensional *matrix organization* (i.e., two layers of program management added to one layer of resource management). There are also questions about where authority and responsibility should reside. Here are two of many dilemmas:

■ *How should the sales force be organized?* Should there be separate sales forces for rayon, nylon, and each of the other fibers? Or should the sales forces be organized according to men's wear, women's wear, and other markets? Or should the sales force not be specialized?

■ *Who should set the prices for a particular product/market?* Should the nylon product manager have final authority for setting nylon prices in all markets? What happens if the men's wear market manager feels that nylon will lose out in this market unless special price concessions are made on nylon?

Most managers feel that only the more important products and markets would justify separate managers. Some are not upset about the conflicts and cost and believe that the benefits of product and market specialization outweigh the costs.[8]

Corporate/Divisional Organization   As multiproduct companies grow in size, they often turn their larger product groups into separate divisions. The divisions set up their own departments and services. This raises the question of what marketing services and activities should be retained at corporate headquarters.

Divisionalized companies have reached different answers to this question. Corporate marketing staffs follow one of four models:[9]

■ *No corporate marketing.* Some companies lack a corporate marketing staff. They don't see any useful function for marketing to perform at the corporate level. Each division has its own marketing department.

■ *Minimal corporate marketing.* Some companies have a small corporate marketing staff that performs a few functions, primarily (a) assisting top management with overall opportunity evaluation, (b) providing divisions with consulting assistance on request, (c) helping divisions that have little or no marketing, and (d) promoting the marketing concept to other departments of the company.

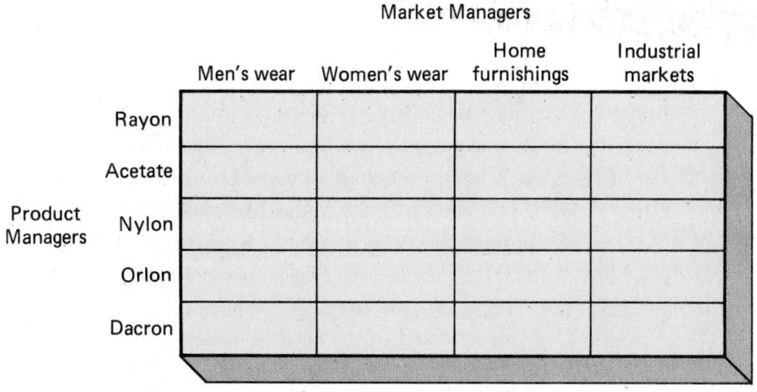

FIGURE 24-8
Product/Market Management System

■ *Moderate corporate marketing.* Some companies have a corporate marketing staff that, in addition to the preceding activities, also provides various marketing services to the divisions. The corporate marketing staff might provide specialized *advertising services* (e.g., coordination of media buying, institutional advertising, review of division advertising from an image standpoint, auditing of advertising expenditures), *sales promotion services* (e.g., companywide promotions, central buying of promotional materials), *marketing research services* (e.g., advanced mathematical analysis, research on marketing development cutting across divisional lines), *sales-administration services* (e.g., counsel on sales organization and sales policies, development of common sales-reporting systems, management of sales forces selling to common customers), and some miscellaneous services (e.g., counseling on marketing planning, hiring, and training of marketing personnel).

■ *Strong corporate marketing.* Some companies have a corporate marketing staff that, in addition to the preceding activities, participates strongly in the planning and control of divisional marketing activities.

The question arises as to whether companies are converging toward one of these models of the corporate marketing department. The answer is no. Some companies have recently installed a corporate marketing staff for the first time; others have expanded their corporate marketing department; others have reduced its size and scope; and still others have eliminated it altogether.

The potential contribution of a corporate marketing staff varies in different stages of the company's evolution. Most companies begin with weak marketing in their divisions and often establish a corporate marketing staff to bring marketing into the various divisions through education and supplying various services. Some members of the corporate marketing staff later join the divisions to head marketing departments. As the divisions become strong in their marketing, corporate marketing has less to offer them. Some companies decide that corporate marketing has done its job and eliminate the department.

A corporate marketing staff generally has three justifications. The first is to serve as a corporate focus for review and leadership of overall company marketing activities and opportunities. The second is to offer certain marketing services that could be provided more economically on a centralized basis than by being duplicated in the different divisions. The third is to take responsibility for educating divisional managers, sales managers, and others in the company on the meaning and implementation of the marketing concept.[10]

Marketing's Relations with Other Departments

In principle, business functions should mesh harmoniously to achieve the overall objectives of the firm. In practice, interdepartmental relations are often characterized by deep rivalries and misunderstandings. Some interdepartmental conflict stems from differences of opinion as to what is in the best interests of the firm, some from real trade-offs between departmental well-being and company well-being, and some from unfortunate departmental stereotypes and prejudices.

In the typical organization, each department has an effect on customer satisfaction through its activities and decisions. Under the marketing concept, all departments need to "think customer" and work together to satisfy customer needs and expectations. The marketing department must drive this point home. The marketing vice-president has two tasks: to coordinate the internal marketing activities of the company, and to coordinate marketing with finance, operations, and the other company functions, in the interests of the customers.

Yet there is little agreement on how much influence and authority marketing should have over other departments to bring about coordinated marketing. Generally speaking, the marketing vice-president must work through persuasion rather than authority.

This is well illustrated in the case of the marketing vice-president of a major European airline. His mandate is to build up his airline's market share. Yet he has no authority over other functions that affect customer satisfaction:

He can't hire or train the cabin crew (personnel department).

He can't determine the type or quality of food (catering department).

He can't enforce cleanliness standards on the plane (maintenance department).

He can't determine schedules (operations department).

He can't establish the fares (finance department).

What does he control? He controls marketing research, the sales force, and advertising and promotion. But he must work through the other departments to shape key factors that affect customer travel comfort.

Other departments may resist bending their efforts to meet the customers' interests. Just as marketing stresses the customer's point of view, other departments stress the importance of their tasks. Inevitably, departments define company problems and goals from their point of view. As a result, conflicts of interest are unavoidable. Table 24-1 summarizes the main differences in orientation between marketing and other departments. We will briefly examine the typical concerns of each department.

R&D   The company's desire for successful new products is often thwarted by poor working relations between R&D and marketing. In many ways, these groups represent two different cultures in the organization. The R&D department is staffed with scientists and technicians who pride themselves on scientific curiosity and detachment, like to work on challenging

TABLE 24-1   Summary of Organizational Conflicts Between Marketing and Other Departments

Department	Their Emphasis	Marketing's Emphasis
R&D	Basic research	Applied research
	Intrinsic quality	Perceived quality
	Functional features	Sales features
Engineering	Long design lead time	Short design lead time
	Few models	Many models
	Standard components	Custom components
Purchasing	Narrow product line	Broad product line
	Standard parts	Nonstandard parts
	Price of material	Quality of material
	Economical lot sizes	Large lot sizes to avoid stockouts
	Purchasing at infrequent intervals	Immediate purchasing for customer needs
Manufacturing	Long production lead time	Short production lead time
	Long runs with few models	Short runs with many models
	No model changes	Frequent model changes
	Standard orders	Custom orders
	Ease of fabrication	Aesthetic appearance
	Average quality control	Tight quality control
Finance	Strict rationales for spending	Intuitive arguments for spending
	Hard and fast budgets	Flexible budgets to meet changing needs
	Pricing to cover costs	Pricing to further market development
Accounting	Standard transactions	Special terms and discounts
	Few reports	Many reports
Credit	Full financial disclosures by customers	Minimum credit examination of customers
	Long credit risks	Medium credit risks
	Tough credit terms	Easy credit terms
	Tough collection procedures	Easy collection procedures

technical problems without much concern for immediate sales payoffs, and prefer to work without much supervision or accountability for research costs. The marketing/sales department is staffed with business-oriented persons who pride themselves on a practical understanding of the world, like to see many new products with sales features that can be promoted to customers, and feel compelled to pay attention to costs. Each group often carries negative stereotypes of the other group. Marketers see the R&D people as impractical, long-haired, sometimes mad-scientist types who do not understand business, while R&D people see marketers as gimmick-oriented hucksters who are more interested in sales than in the technical features of the product. These stereotypes get in the way of productive teamwork.

Companies turn out to be either technology-driven, market-driven, or balanced. In *technology-driven companies*, the R&D staff researches fundamental problems, looks for major breakthroughs, and strives for technical perfection in product development. R&D expenditures are high, and the new-product success rate tends to be low, although R&D occasionally comes up with major new products.

In *market-driven companies*, the R&D staff designs products for specific market needs, much of it involving product modification and the application of existing technologies. A higher ratio of new products succeed, but they represent mainly product modifications with relatively short product lives.

A *balanced technology- and market-driven company* is one in which effective organizational relations have been worked out between R&D and marketing to share responsibility for successful market-oriented innovation. The R&D staff takes responsibility not for invention alone, but for successful innovation. The marketing staff takes responsibility not for new sales features alone, but also for helping identify new ways to satisfy needs.

Gupta, Raj, and Wilemon concluded in a review of the literature that R&D-marketing integration is strongly correlated with innovation success.[11] Therefore a company should not choose between a technology focus and a market focus, but rather work on the best way to link and coordinate the two functions. There should be integration prior to the actual product development process, in jointly establishing priorities, goals, and schedules; integration during the product development process in all of its stages; and integration in the post-commercialization period to evaluate results and refine the new product further. R&D–marketing cooperation can be facilitated in several specific ways:[12]

- Joint seminars are sponsored to build understanding and respect for each other's goals, working styles, and problems.
- Each new project is assigned to an R&D person and a marketing person, who work together through the life of the project. R&D and marketing should jointly establish the goals of the marketing plan early in the project.
- R&D's participation continues into the selling period, including involvement in preparing technical manuals, participating in trade shows, carrying out some postintroductory marketing research with customers, and even doing some selling.
- Conflicts are worked out by higher management, following a clear procedure. In one company, R&D and marketing both report to the same vice-president.

Engineering Engineering is responsible for finding practical ways to design new products and new production processes. Engineers are interested in achieving technical quality, cost economy, and manufacturing simplicity. They come into conflict with marketing personnel when the latter want several models to be produced, often with product features requiring custom rather than standard components. Engineers see marketers as wanting "bells-and-whistles" on the products, rather than intrinsic quality. These problems are less pronounced in companies where marketing executives have engineering backgrounds and can communicate effectively with engineers.

Purchasing Purchasing executives are responsible for obtaining materials and components at the lowest possible cost and in the right quantities and quality. They see marketing executives pushing for several models in a product line, which requires purchasing small quantities of many inventory items rather than large quantities of a few items. They think that marketing insists on too high a quality of ordered materials and components. They dislike marketing's forecasting inaccuracy; it causes them to place rush orders at unfavorable prices and at other times to carry excessive inventories.

Manufacturing There are several potential conflicts between manufacturing and marketing. Manufacturing people are responsible for the smooth running of the factory to produce the right products in the right quantities at the right time for the right cost. They have spent their lives in the factory, with its attendant problems of machine breakdowns, inventory stockouts, and labor disputes and slowdowns. They see marketers as having little understanding of factory economics or politics. Marketers will complain about insufficient plant capacity, delays in production, poor quality control, and poor customer service. Yet marketers often turn in inaccurate sales forecasts, recommend product features that are difficult to manufacture, and promise more factory service than is reasonable.

Marketers do not see the factory's problems, but rather they see the problems of their customers, who need the goods quickly, who receive defective merchandise, and who cannot get factory service. Marketers seldom show enough concern for the extra factory costs involved in helping a customer. The problem is not only poor communication but an actual conflict of interest.

Companies settle these conflicts in different ways. In *manufacturing-driven companies*, everything is done to ensure smooth production and low costs. The company prefers simple products, narrow product lines, and high-volume production. Sales campaigns calling for a hasty production buildup are kept to a minimum. Customers on back order have to wait.

Other companies are *marketing-driven*, in that the company goes out of its way to satisfy customers. In one large toiletries company, the marketing personnel call the shots and the manufacturing people have to fall in line, regardless of overtime costs, short runs, and so on. The result is high and fluctuating manufacturing costs, as well as variable product quality.

Companies need to develop a *balanced manufacturing/marketing orientation* in which both sides codetermine what is in the best interests of the company. Solutions include joint seminars to understand each other's viewpoint, joint committees and liaison personnel, personnel exchange programs, and analytical methods to determine the most profitable course of action.[13]

Company profitability is greatly dependent on achieving successful manufacturing-marketing working relations. Marketers need to understand better the marketing implications of new manufacturing strategies—the flexible factory, automation and robotization, just-in-time production, quality circles, and so on. If the company wants to win through being the low-cost producer, this will call for one manufacturing strategy; if the company wants to win through excelling at high quality or high variety or high service, each of these calls for different manufacturing strategies. Thus manufacturing design and capacity decisions take their cues from the manufacturing targets set by marketing strategy with respect to planned output, cost, quality, variety, and service.

Manufacturing is also a tool of marketing after the product is produced. Before they choose a vendor, buyers often want to visit the plant to assess how well it is managed. Thus manufacturing personnel and plant layout become important marketing tools.

Finance   Financial executives pride themselves on being able to evaluate the profit implications of different business actions. When it comes to marketing expenditures, they feel frustrated. Marketing executives ask for substantial budgets for advertising, sales promotions, and sales force, without being able to prove how many sales will be produced by these expenditures. Financial executives suspect that the marketers' forecasts are self-serving. They think that marketing people do not spend enough time relating expenditures to sales and shifting their budgets to more profitable areas. They think that marketers are too quick to slash prices to win orders, instead of pricing to make a profit.

Marketing executives, on the other hand, often see financial people as controlling the purse strings too tightly and refusing to invest funds in long-term market development. They see all marketing expenditures as expenses rather than investments. Financial people seem overly conservative and risk averse, causing many opportunities to be lost. The solution lies in giving marketing people more financial training and giving financial people more marketing training. Financial executives need to adapt their financial tools and theories to support strategic marketing.

Accounting   Accountants see marketing people as lax in providing their sales reports on time. They dislike the special deals that sales people make with customers, because these require special accounting procedures. Marketers, on the other hand, dislike the way accountants allocate fixed-cost burdens to different products in the line. Brand managers may feel that their brand is more profitable than it looks, the problem being high overhead assigned to it. They would also like accounting to prepare special reports on sales and profitability by different channels, territories, order sizes, and so on.

Credit   Credit officers check out the credit standing of potential customers and deny or limit credit to the more doubtful ones. They think that marketers will sell to anyone, even to those from whom payment is doubtful. Marketers, on the other hand, often feel that credit standards are too high. They think that "zero bad debts" really means that the company lost a lot of sales and profits. They feel they work too hard to find customers to hear that they are not good enough to sell to.

Strategies
for Building
a Companywide
Marketing
Orientation

Only a handful of American companies—such as P&G, IBM, McDonald's—are truly marketing oriented. A much larger number of companies are sales oriented. These companies sooner or later experience some market shock. They may lose a major market, experience slow growth or low profitability, or find themselves facing more-sophisticated competitors.

These companies realized that they were weak in marketing and at a great disadvantage when competing against topflight marketing companies. Responding with traditional sales tactics was not enough. Sales managers want to react by spending more money and/or reducing prices. They think the answer lies in sales contests to get the sales force to work harder. But top management is becoming less confident in pure sales pressure. They want those responsible for sales to get smarter, not work harder. They want better analyses of

For years, General Motors prided itself on a marketing orientation and pointed to its huge sales volume and market share as evidence. However, as management witnessed the growing share of small foreign cars, they realized that they had not fully monitored the market and responded to consumer desires. They still have to learn how to design small cars with the quality and fuel economy that Americans have found in Japanese cars.[14]

In the early 1970s, American Telephone and Telegraph (AT&T) suddenly found itself facing keen competition in selling switchboards and ancillary telephone equipment. AT&T was totally unprepared to meet the new competition. They lacked marketing personnel and marketing muscle. They realized that they had been pushing sales when they should have been paying attention to changing market forces. They undertook a crash effort to acquire marketing know-how, with mixed results.[15]

American Hospital Supply Company enjoys a market leadership in the hospital-supplies business, based largely on its extensive distribution and sales coverage. It is now facing new sophisticated competitors, such as P&G, who are attacking its established markets. AHS is now committed to transforming itself from a sales-oriented company to a market-oriented company.

The Chase Manhattan Bank of New York has watched Citibank, its main competitor, make one smart marketing move after another, each time leaving Chase behind. Citibank has been systematically developing a marketing culture at the bank, while Chase has operated along traditional financial lines. Recently, Chase started a whole program to educate its officers in modern marketing thinking.

the changing forces in the marketplace; they want better marketing strategies and plans; they want products that meet new and emerging customer needs.

Top management's challenge is to convert the company from a sales-driven company to a modern market-driven company. Management has to take several steps to create a genuine marketing culture in their company.

Presidential Leadership The company president's leadership is a key prerequisite to establishing a modern marketing company. The vice-president of marketing cannot unilaterally direct other company officers to bend their efforts to serve customers. The company president must appreciate how marketing differs from sales, believe that marketing is a key to company growth and prosperity, and build marketing into speeches and decisions.

Marketing Task Force The president should appoint a marketing task force to develop a plan for bringing modern marketing practices into the company. The task force should include the president, the executive vice-president, the vice-presidents of sales, marketing, manufacturing, and finance, and a few other key individuals. They should examine the need for marketing, set objectives, anticipate problems in introducing it, and develop an overall strategy. For the next few years, this committee should meet periodically to measure progress and take new initiatives.

Outside Marketing Consultant The marketing task force would probably benefit from outside consulting assistance in building a marketing culture at the company. Consulting firms have considerable experience in the problems of, and approaches to, bringing marketing thinking into a company.

A Corporate Marketing Department A key step is to establish a corporate marketing department. This department should review each division's marketing resources and needs. Often the division's general manager does not understand marketing and confuses it with sales. The division's sales group is usually headed by a sales vice-president who is not marketing oriented. To appoint a marketing vice-president over this person would be asking for trouble. Alternatives might be to add the outside marketer to the division as the executive vice-president, or to add this person as a marketing vice-president on a level parallel to that of the sales vice-president, or to put this person in charge of the division's planning. Ultimately, each division will need a strong marketing vice-president if it wants to make marketing headway.

In-House Marketing Seminars   The new corporate marketing department should sponsor in-house marketing seminars for top corporate management, divisional general managers, marketing and sales personnel, manufacturing personnel, R&D personnel, and so on. The seminars should first be presented to the higher levels of management and move to lower levels. The marketing seminars should aim to change the marketing beliefs, attitudes, and behavior of various executive groups.

Hiring Marketing Talent   The company should consider hiring marketing talent away from leading marketing companies and also new M.B.A.'s receiving their degrees in marketing. When Citibank got serious about marketing some years ago, it hired away several brand managers from General Foods.

Promoting Market-Oriented Executives   The company should try to promote market-oriented individuals to positions as division managers. A large public-accounting firm is currently sending out signals that it will give preference to market-oriented partners for branch manager positions.

Installing a Modern Marketing-Planning System   An excellent way to train people to think marketing is to install a modern market-oriented planning system. The planning format will require managers to first think about the marketing environment, marketing opportunities, competitive trends, and other marketing issues. Then marketing strategies and the sales forecast can be developed on a hard-data marketing base.

The job of creating a marketing orientation throughout the company is an uphill and never-ending battle. The purpose is not to resolve every issue in favor of the customer, no matter what the cost, but rather to help the other managers see that customers are the foundation of the company's business.

Introducing Marketing in Nonbusiness Organizations

Most of the marketing examples in this book are drawn from the business sector. Starting in the 1970s, there has been a ''broadening of marketing'' to cover all organizations. All organizations have marketing problems and need marketing skills. The nonprofit and public sectors account for more than a quarter of the American economy and are in great need of management and marketing skills, especially with the recent cuts in federal aid.

Lovelock and Weinberg have identified several characteristics of the nonbusiness sector:[16]

■ **Multiple publics.** Nonbusiness organizations have two major publics to market to: *clients* and *donors*. The former pose the problem of *resource allocation* and the latter, the problem of *resource attraction*. In addition, other publics surround the nonbusiness organization, and these publics require marketing thought and planning. Thus a college directs marketing programs to prospective students, current students, parents of students, alumni, faculty, staff, local business firms, and local government agencies.

■ *Multiple objectives.* Nonbusiness organizations tend to pursue several objectives rather than one, such as profits. Nonfinancial objectives usually dominate. This makes the task of strategy formulation more difficult.

■ *Services and social behaviors rather than physical goods.* Most nonbusiness organizations produce services rather than goods, and many try to alter social behaviors. They therefore need to apply principles of services marketing and social marketing.

■ *Public scrutiny and nonmarket pressures.* Nonbusiness organizations are subject to close public scrutiny because they subsidized, tax exempt, and sometimes mandated into existence. They experience pressures from various publics and are expected to operate in the public interest. This means that their marketing activities will come under public scrutiny.

■ *Dual management.* Many nonprofit organizations contain professional managers as well as career specialists, and they often come into conflict. A hospital CEO must work with doctors, a museum's director must work with curators, and a threater manager must work with actors, etc. Often they don't agree on the organization's objectives or requirements.

Many nonbusiness organizations—colleges, hospitals, social service organizations, charities, museums, performing arts groups, churches, government agencies—are experiencing difficult times. They are losing clients, on the one hand, and finding it more difficult to raise public and private funds, on the other hand. Many are being forced to charge fees for formerly free services, or to raise their fees, or to start side businesses (e.g., gift shops, restaurants) to earn extra income. In the last case, commercial businesses are complaining about unfair competition from the nonprofits.

All of this has increased the interest of nonprofits in the subject of marketing. Where marketing at one time was alien to these organizations, many are now embracing it almost uncritically as a possible panacea to their problems. Many nonbusiness organizations initially think of marketing as synonymous with promotion. They think their problems will be solved by creating more advertising, sales promotion, trained sales personnel, and publicity. Consider what several colleges did when they discovered "marketing":

■ The admissions office at North Kentucky State University planned to release 103 balloons filled with scholarship offers; another college passed out promotional frisbees to high school students vacationing in Fort Lauderdale, Florida, during the Easter break.

■ St. Joseph's College in Rensselaer, Indiana, achieved a 40 percent increase in freshmen admissions through advertising in *Seventeen* and on several Chicago and Indianapolis rock radio stations. The admissions office also planned to introduce tuition rebates for students who recruited new students ($100 finder's fee), but this was canceled.

■ Bard College developed a same-day admission system for students who came to the campus and qualified.

■ Worcester Polytechnic Institute offered to negotiate credit for previous study or work experience to shorten the degree period.

There are several dangers in equating marketing with intensified promotion. Aggressive promotion can create negative reactions among the school's constituencies, especially the faculty, who regard hard selling as offensive. Also, hard promotion may turn off as many prospective students as it turns on. Aggressive promotion can attract the wrong students to the college—students who drop out when they discover they do not have the qualifications to do the work or that the college is not what it was advertised to be. Finally, this kind of marketing creates the illusion that the college has taken sufficient steps to reverse declining enrollment—an illusion that slows down the needed work on market definition and product improvement—the basis of all good marketing.

When a nonbusiness organization recognizes the need to adopt a thoroughgoing marketing orientation that includes all four Ps, it should appoint a marketing committee. The marketing committee's objectives are to identify the marketing problems and opportunities facing the organization, the major needs of various administrative units for marketing services, and the institution's possible need for a full-time director of marketing. As a part of this process, the marketing committee might be helped by a marketing consultant, who will point out some of the ways the organization can use marketing to improve its performance.

Eventually, the organization should consider adding a marketing director or a marketing vice-president. A marketing director occupies a middle-management position and primarily provides marketing services to others in the organization, such as marketing research, advertising, publicity, and product testing. The organization might ultimately appoint a marketing vice-president, who will have more authority and influence. A marketing vice-president not only coordinates and supplies marketing services but also is in a position to influence the vice-presidents of personnel, operations, and finance as to the importance of focusing their effort on satisfying the organization's customers. Thus in a college setting, the marketing vice-president would try to get the deans, faculty, maintenance people, food-service managers, and dormitory managers to see their task as promoting the well-being and satisfaction of the student body.

MARKETING IMPLEMENTATION

Having looked at how business and nonbusiness organizations handle the marketing function, we now turn to the question of how marketing personnel can effectively implement marketing plans. A brilliant strategic marketing plan will count for little if it is not implemented properly.

> *Marketing implementation* is the process that turns marketing plans into action assignments and ensures that such assignments are executed in a manner that accomplishes the plan's stated objectives.

Whereas strategy addresses the *what* and *why* of marketing activities, implementation addresses the *who*, *where*, *when*, and *how*. Strategy and implementation are closely related in that one ''layer'' of strategy implies certain tactical implementation assignments at a lower level. For example, top management's strategic decision to ''harvest'' a product in the decline stage of its life cycle must be translated into specific budgeting changes allocating fewer funds for marketing programs, directions to sales people to change their selling emphasis, a reprinting of price lists. Also, implementation has a feedback strategy in that anticipated difficulties in implementing a strategy may influence the choice of strategy.

Bonoma, in a study of the implementation problems of twenty-two organizations, identified four areas that can influence the effective implementation of marketing programs:[17]

- ▪ Skills in recognizing and diagnosing a problem
- ▪ Skills in assessing the company level where the problem exists
- ▪ Skills in implementing plans
- ▪ Skills in evaluating implementation results

We will examine these areas in the following paragraphs.

Diagnostic Skills　The close interrelationship between strategy and implementation can pose difficult diagnostic problems when marketing program results do not fulfill their expectations. Was the low sales rate the result of poor strategy or poor implementation? Moreover, is the issue to determine what the problem *is* (diagnosis) or what should be *done* about it (action)? For each problem, there are different sets of management "tools" and solutions.

Company Levels　Problems in marketing implementation can occur at any of three corporate levels.

One level is that of the *marketing functions* that must be performed in executing the marketing task—selling, licensing, advertising, new-product planning, channels of distribution, and so on. For example, how should the new-product-development function of a late entrant be organized in a high-loyalty market?

Another level is that of *marketing programs*—the synergistic blending of the marketing functions into a set of integrated activities. Pricing, promoting, and distributing a product line of oil filters to auto-parts retailers would exemplify a marketing program concern.

A third level of implementation is that of *marketing policies*. Here management is concerned with the directives that lead the marketing actors to understand what the organization stands for and does in marketing. Marketing leadership, as well as the more concrete variables of compensation, recruiting, training, and selling policies, communicates the marketing culture of the organization. The adoption of the societal marketing concept by company personnel in their dealings with customers, dealers, suppliers, and others requires clear marketing policies toward that end. Procter & Gamble is a good example of a company whose policies on handling customer complaints, developing new products, and so on, permeate all levels of operation. Bonoma found that marketing policies had the greatest impact on effective implementation, followed by the competence with which the marketing functions were executed. Therefore the successful implementation of marketing programs depends on establishing and implementing sound policies.

Marketing Implementation Skills　A set of skills must be practiced at each corporate "level"—functions, programs, policies—to achieve effective implementation. The four primary skills are allocating, monitoring, organizing, and interacting.

Allocating skills are manifested in the competence with which marketing managers budget time, money, and personnel to functions, policies, or programs. For example, allocating field sales personnel to geographical regions is a common problem facing industrial products companies. Determining how much money to spend on trade shows (functions level) or what warranty work to perform on "marginal" products (policies level) are other problems demanding allocation skills.

Monitoring skills consists of developing and managing a system of controls to give feedback on the results of marketing actions. Controls can be of four types: annual-plan control, profitability control, efficiency and strategic control. (See Chapter 25.) From an implementation standpoint, we are primarily concerned with the first three types of controls.

Organizing skills are concerned with specifying the structure of relationships among marketing personnel to accomplish corporate objectives. Managing the degree of centralization and formalization built into the system and also understanding the informal marketing organization are important prerequisites to the development of effective implementation procedures. The interaction of the informal and formal systems will influence the effectiveness of many implementation activities.

Interacting skills involve the manager's ability to get things done by influencing others. Marketers must not only be capable of motivating the organization's own people toward effectively implementing the desired strategy, they must also motivate outsiders—marketing research firms, ad agencies, dealers, wholesalers, agents—whose objectives may not exactly parallel those of the organization. Managing conflict within a channel of distribution, for example, demands a high level of interaction skill.

The frequency with which each problem area arises in an organization may be related to the firm's size, its market position, or the industry growth rate in which the firm competes. Excellence in marketing implementation requires management skill in each of the four areas (allocating, monitoring, organizing, interacting) at each of the three levels (functions, programs, policies).

Implementation-Evaluation Skills

Good performance in the marketplace does not necessarily prove that there was a good marketing implementation. It is difficult to use performance to differentiate between good strategy/poor implementation and poor strategy/good implementation. We can, however, do the spadework to evaluate a company's implementation effectiveness. Evidence of effective marketing implementation practice would include positive responses to the following questions:

- Is there a clear marketing theme, strong marketing leadership, and a culture that promotes and provokes excellence?
- Is there subfunctional soundness in the company's marketing activities? Are the selling function's distribution, pricing, and advertising well managed?
- Do the company's marketing programs integrate and deliver marketing activities in a focused fashion to various customer groups?
- How good is marketing management at interacting with (a) other marketing-related staff, like sales, (b) other functions in the company, and (c) the customers and trade?
- What monitoring efforts are used by management to inform itself about not only its own moves but also customer and prospect groups?
- How good is management at allocating time, money, and people to marketing tasks?
- How is management organized, both to do marketing tasks and to deal with customer interactions? Are there easily accessed ''organizational doors'' open to the customers and the trade?

Separating the effects of strategy and implementation on market results will always be a difficult task. But stressing the need for corporate excellence in both marketing implementation and strategic marketing planning will lead to improved overall performance.

SUMMARY

Companies must organize their various functions to produce customer-oriented teamwork early in the development of new products, rather than bring in marketing considerations only when the product is ready to be sold. This chapter examined how the marketing function is organized, how it relates to other company functions, and how marketing plans must be implemented in order to succeed in the marketplace.

The modern marketing department evolved through several stages. It stated as a sales department and later took on ancillary functions, such as advertising and marketing research. As the latter grew in importance, many companies created a separate marketing department to manage them. But the heads of sales and marketing occasionally disagreed, and eventually the two departments were merged into a modern marketing department headed by a marketing vice-president. A modern marketing department, however, does not automatically create a modern marketing company unless the other officers accept and practice a customer orientation.

Modern marketing departments are organized in a number of ways. The most common form is the functional marketing organization in which marketing functions are headed by separate managers reporting to the marketing vice-president. Another form is the product management organization in which products are assigned to product managers, who work with functional specialists to develop and achieve their plans. Another form is the market management organization in which major markets are assigned to market managers, who work with functional specialists to develop and achieve their plans. Some large companies use a product management and market management organization. Finally, multidivision companies usually operate a corporate marketing department and divisional marketing departments, with some variations as to the division of tasks.

Marketing must work smoothly with the other functions in a company. In its pursuit of customers' interests, marketing may come into conflict with R&D, engineering, purchasing, manufacturing, inventory, finance, accounting, credit, and other functions. These conflicts can be reduced when the company president commits the company to a customer orientation and when the marketing vice-president learns to work effectively with the other officers. Acquiring a modern marketing orientation requires presidential support, a marketing task force, outside marketing consulting help, a corporate marketing department, in-house marketing seminars, marketing talent hired from the outside and promoted inside, and a market-oriented marketing-planning system.

Those responsible for the marketing function must not only develop effective marketing plans but also implement them successfully. Marketing implementation is the process of turning plans into action assignments describing who does what, when, and how. Effective implementation requires skills in allocating, monitoring, organizing, and interacting at the level of marketing functions, programs, and policies.

■ QUESTIONS

1. Describe the various ways of organizing the marketing department. Discuss these designs in terms of their ability to respond to changing conditions.

2. Discuss the advantages and limitations of brand management as an organizational arrangement.

3. You have been asked to develop a marketing organizational design for a distributor of tankless water heater units ($100 million in sales). What kind of information would you need so that you might select an appropriate organizational design for the company?

4. What advantages and what problems do you anticipate in having a financial analyst as a member of the marketing department? What would be the purpose of such an appointment? How else might this purpose be achieved?

5. Choose a product or service and list some strategy-stage issues and some implementation-stage issues.

6. For the product or service discussed in question 5, indicate some specific problems of diagnosis and problems of action that could occur at the strategy and implementation stages.

7. For the product or service discussed in question 5, give an example of the problems that could arise at the function, program, and policy levels when implementing a marketing strategy.

8. In order to carry out a proposed national sales promotion, describe some of the departments whose efforts must be coordinated with those of the marketing department. Through what kind of planning device might these efforts be integrated?

9. Does it make organizational sense to combine the company's marketing department and public relations department under one vice-president?

10. A major airline's marketing department is now organized on a functional basis: advertising, field sales, customer services, and so on. The airline is considering setting up a route-manager organization, with a manager who would be assigned to each major route and would be to a route what a brand manager is to a brand. Do you think this is a good idea?

11. The General Electric Company does not have a corporate vice-president of marketing. Its vice-presidents

of marketing are found in various sectors, groups, and divisions. General Electric does have a corporate vice-president of strategic planning. Do you think a corporate vice-president of marketing should be added?

12. In large railroads, the operations department usually holds dominant power. The needs of freight customers are accorded less weight than achieving operational efficiency. Suggest a strategy for establishing a companywide marketing orientation.

13. Describe some industrial situations where local marketing specialists would be of particular assistance to a company.

■ FOOTNOTES

1 For details, see "General Food Corporation: Post Division," in *Organization Strategy: A Marketing Approach*, ed. E. Raymond Corey and Steven H. Star (Boston: Division of Research, Graduate School of Business Administration, Harvard University, 1971), pp. 201–30.

2 See Elmer E. Waters, "Industrial Product Manager . . . Consumer Brand Manager: A Study in Contrast," *Industrial Marketing*, January 1969, pp. 45–49.

3 See David J. Luck, "Interfaces of a Product Manager," *Journal of Marketing*, October 1969, pp. 32–36.

4 Andrall E. Pearson and Thomas W. Wilson, Jr., *Making Your Organization Work* (New York: Association of National Advertisers, 1967), pp. 8–13.

5 See Richard M. Clewett and Stanley F. Stasch, "Shifting Role of the Product Manager," *Harvard Business Review*, January–February 1975, pp. 65–73; Victor P. Buell, "The Changing Role of the Product Manager in Consumer Goods Companies," *Journal of Marketing*, July 1975, pp. 3–11; "The Brand Manager: No Longer King," *Business Week*, June 9, 1973; Joseph A. Morein, "Shift from Brand to Product Line Marketing," *Harvard Business Review*, September–October 1975, pp. 56–64; and Thomas D. Giese and T. M. Weisenberger, "Product Manager in Perspective," *Journal of Business Research*, 10 (1982), 267–77.

6 Mark Hanan, "Reorganize Your Company around Its Markets," *Harvard Business Review*, November–December 1974, pp. 63–74.

7 For details, see Corey and Star, *Organization Strategy*, pp. 187–96.

8 See B. Charles Ames, "Dilemma of Product/Market Management," *Harvard Business Review*, March–April 1971, pp. 66–74.

9 See Watson Snyder, Jr., and Frank B. Gray, *The Corporate Marketing Staff: Its Role and Effectiveness in Multi-Division Companies* (Cambridge, Mass.: Marketing Science Institute, April 1971).

10 For further reading on marketing organization, see Nigel Piercy, *Marketing Organization: An Analysis of Information Processing, Power and Politics* (London: George Allen & Unwin, 1985); Robert W. Ruekert, Orville C. Walker, and Kenneth J. Roering, "The Organization of Marketing Activities: A Contingency Theory of Structure and Performance," *Journal of Marketing*, Winter 1985, pp. 13–25; and Tyzoon T. Tyebjee, Albert V. Bruno, and Shelby H. McIntyre, "Growing Ventures Can Anticipate Marketing Stages," *Harvard Business Review*, January–February 1983, pp. 2–4.

11 Askok K. Gupta, S. P. Raj, and David Wilemon, "A Model for Studying R&D–Marketing Interface in the Product Innovation Process," *Journal of Marketing*, April 1986, pp. 7–17.

12 See William E. Souder, *Managing New Product Innovations* (Lexington, Mass.: Heath, 1987), Chaps. 10–11; and William L. Shanklin and John K. Ryans, Jr., "Organizing for High-Tech Marketing," *Harvard Business Review*, November–December 1984, pp. 164–71.

13 See Benson P. Shapiro, "Can Marketing and Manufacturing Coexist?" *Harvard Business Review*, September–October 1977, pp. 104–14.

14 See J. Patrick Wright, *On a Clear Day You Can See General Motors* (New York: Avon Books, 1979), esp. Chap. 8.

15 Bro Uttal, "Selling Is No Longer Mickey Mouse at A.T.&T.," *Fortune*, July 17, 1978, pp. 98–104. Also see AT&T Marketing Men Find Their Star Fails to Ascend as Expected: Manufacturing Experts Win Early Rounds in the Clash of Corporate Cultures," *Wall Street Journal*, February 13, 1984, p. 1.

16 Christopher H. Lovelock and Charles B. Weinberg, *Marketing for Public and Nonprofit Managers* (New York: John Wiley, 1984), pp. 31–37.

17 Thomas V. Bonoma, *The Marketing Edge: Making Strategies Work* (New York: Free Press, 1985). Much of this section is based on Bonoma's work.

25

Evaluating and Controlling Marketing Performance

Having lost sight of our objective, we redoubled our efforts.

Old Adage

If anything can go wrong, it will.

Murphy's Law

The marketing department's job is to plan and control marketing activity. Because many surprises will occur during the implementation of marketing plans, the marketing department has to engage in continuous monitoring and control of marketing activities. Marketing control systems are essential to make sure the company operates efficiently and effectively.

In spite of the need for effective marketing control, many companies have inadequate control procedures. This conclusion was reached in a private study of seventy-five companies of varying sizes in different industries. The main findings were:

- ■ Small companies have poorer controls than large companies. They do a poorer job of setting clear objectives and establishing systems to measure performance.
- ■ Fewer than half of the companies know the profitability of their individual products. About one-third of the companies have no regular review procedure for spotting and deleting weak products.
- ■ Almost half of the companies fail to compare their prices with competition, to analyze their warehousing and distribution costs, to analyze the causes of returned merchandise, to conduct formal evaluations of advertising effectiveness, and to review their sales-force call reports.
- ■ Many companies take four to eight weeks to develop control reports, and they are often inaccurate.
- ■ Marketing control, however, is far from being a single process.

Four types of marketing control can be distinguished (Table 25-1).

TABLE 25-1   Types of Marketing Control

Type of Control	Prime Responsibility	Purpose of Control	Approaches
I. Annual-plan control	Top management Middle management	To examine whether the planned results are being achieved	Sales analysis Market-share analysis Sales-to-expense ratios Financial analysis Attitude tracking
II. Profitability control	Marketing controller	To examine where the company is making and losing money	Profitability by: product territory customer group trade channel order size
III. Efficiency control	Line and staff management Marketing controller	To evaluate and improve the spending efficiency and impact of marketing expenditures	Efficiency of: sales force advertising sales promotion distribution
IV. Strategic control	Top management Marketing auditor	To examine whether the company is pursuing its best opportunities with respect to markets, products, and channels	Marketing-effectiveness rating instrument Marketing audit

In *annual-plan control* marketing, personnel check ongoing performance against the annual plan and take corrective action when necessary. *Profitability control* consists of efforts to determine the actual profitability of different products, territories, end-use markets, and trade channels. *Efficiency control* involves searching for ways to improve the impact of different marketing tools and expenditures. *Strategic control* consists of periodically examining whether the company's basic strategies are well matched to its opportunities. We now turn to these four types of marketing control.

ANNUAL-PLAN CONTROL

The purpose of annual-plan control is to ensure that the company achieves the sales, profits, and other goals established in its annual plan. The heart of annual-plan control is *management by objectives*. Four steps are involved. (See Figure 25-1.) First, management must set monthly or quarterly goals in the annual plan as benchmarks. Second, management must monitor its performance in the marketplace. Third, management must determine the causes of any serious performance deviations. Fourth, management must take corrective action to close the gaps between its goals and performance. This may require changing the action programs or even changing the goals.

This model of control applies to all levels of the organization. Top management sets certain sales and profit goals for the year. These goals are elaborated into specific goals for each lower level of management. Thus each product manager is committed to

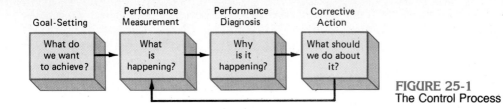

Goal-Setting	Performance Measurement	Performance Diagnosis	Corrective Action
What do we want to achieve?	What is happening?	Why is it happening?	What should we do about it?

FIGURE 25-1
The Control Process

attaining specified levels of sales and costs. Each regional and district sales manager and each sales representative is also committed to specific goals. Each period, top management sees the results and can ascertain where any shortfalls occurred and seek to find out why they occurred.

Managers use five tools to check on plan performance: sales analysis, market-share analysis, marketing expense-to-sales analysis, financial analysis, and customer-attitude tracking.

Sales Analysis

Sales analysis consists of measuring and evaluating actual sales in relation to sales goals. There are two specific tools in this connection.

Sales-variance analysis measures the relative contribution of different factors to a gap in sales performance. Suppose the annual plan called for selling 4,000 widgets in the first quarter at $1 per widget, or $4,000. At quarter's end, only 3,000 widgets were sold at $.80 per widget, or $2,400. The sales performance variance is $1,600, or 40 percent of expected sales. The question arises; How much of this underperformance is due to the price decline and how must to the volume decline? The following calculation answers this question:

$$\text{Variance due to price decline} = (\$1.00 - \$.80)(3,000) = \$\ 600 \quad 37.5\%$$

$$\text{Variance due to volume decline} = (\$1.00)(4,000 - 3,000) = \frac{\$1,000}{\$1,600} \frac{62.5\%}{100.0\%}$$

Almost two-thirds of the sales variance is due to a failure to achieve the volume target. The company should look closely into why its expected sales volume was not achieved.[1]

Micro-sales analysis may provide the answer. *Micro-sales analysis* looks at specific products, territories, and so fourth, that failed to produce their expected share of sales. Suppose the company sells in three territories and expected sales were 1,500 units, 500 units, and 2,000 units, respectively, adding up to 4,000 widgets. The actual sales volume was 1,400 units, 525 units, and 1,075 units, respectively. Thus territory 1 showed a 7 percent shortfall in terms of expected sales; territory 2, a 5 percent surplus; and territory 3, a 46 percent shortfall! Territory 3 is causing most of the trouble. The sales vice-president can check into territory 3 to see which hypothesis explains the poor performance: Territory 3's sales representative is loafing or has a personal problem; a major competitor has entered this territory; or GNP is depressed in this territory.

Market-Share Analysis

Company sales do not reveal how well the company is doing relative to competitors. Suppose a company's sales increase. This could be due to improved economic conditions wherein all companies gained. Or it could be due to improved company performance in relation to its competitors. Management needs to track its market share. If the company's market share goes up, the company is gaining on competitors; if it goes down, the company is losing relative to competitors.

These conclusions from market-share analysis, however, are subject to certain qualifications:[2]

- ■ **The assumption that outside forces affect all companies in the same way is often not true.** The U.S. surgeon general's report on the harmful consequences of cigarette smoking caused total cigarette sales to falter but not equally for all companies. Companies with a reputation for better filters were hurt less.

- ■ **The assumption that a company's performance should be judged against the average performance of all companies is not always valid.** A company's performance should be judged against that of its major competitor or competitors in its strategic group.

- ■ **If a new firm enters the industry, then every existing firm's market share may fall.** A decline in a company's market share may not mean that the company is performing any worse than other companies. A company's share loss will depend on the degree to which the new firm hits the company's specific markets.

- ■ **Sometimes a market-share decline is deliberately engineered by a company to improve profits.** For example, management may drop unprofitable customers or products to improve its profits.

- ■ **Market share can fluctuate for many adventitious reasons.** For example, the market share can be affected by whether a large sale is made on the last day of the period or at the beginning of the next period. Not all shifts in market share have marketing significance.

The first step in using market-share analysis is to define which measure(s) of market share will be used. Four different measures are available.

- ■ **Overall market share.** The company's overall market share is its sales expressed as a percentage of total industry sales. Two decisions are necessary to use this measure. The first is whether to use unit sales or dollar sales to express market share. Any changes in unit market share reflect volume changes among competitors, whereas changes in dollar market share reflect a combination of volume and price changes.

    The other decision has to do with defining the total industry. For example, suppose Harley Davidson wants to measure its share of the American motorcycle market. If motor scooters and motorized bikes are included, then Harley Davidson's market share will be lower, since it does not produce these. The issue hinges on whether consumers perceive lighter cycles to be highly substitutable for standard motorcycles.

- ■ **Served market share.** The company's served market share is its sales expressed as a percentage of the total industry sales in the served market. Its served market is the market that would be interested in the company's offering and is reached by the company's marketing effort. If Harley Davidson only produces and sells expensive motorcycles on the East Coast, its served market share would be its sales as a percentage of the total sales of expensive motorcycles sold on the East Coast. A company's served market share is always larger than its overall market share. A company could have close to 100 percent of its served market and yet a relatively small percentage of the overall market. A company's first task is to try to get the lion's share of its served market. As it approaches this goal, it should add new product lines and territories to enlarge its served market.

- ■ **Relative market share (to top three competitors).** This involves expressing the company's sales as a percentage of the combined sales of the three largest competitors. For example, if this company has 30 percent of the market, and the next two largest competitors have 20, and 10 percent, then this company's relative market share is 50 percent ($=30/60$). If each of the three companies had 33⅓ percent of the market, then the company's relative market share would be 33 percent. Relative market shares above 33 percent are considered to be strong.

- ■ **Relative market share (to leading competitor).** Some companies track their sales as a percentage of the leading competitor's sales. A relative market share greater than 100 percent indicates a market leader. A relative market share of exactly 100 percent means that the firm is tied for the lead. A rise in the company's relative market share means that it is gaining on its leading competitor.

After choosing which market-share measure(s) to use, the company must find the necessary data. Overall market share is normally the most available measure, since it requires only total industry sales, and these are often available in government or trade association publications. Estimating served market share is harder in that the company will have to keep track of its served market, which will be affected by changes in the company's product line and geographical market coverage, among other things. Estimating relative market shares is still harder because the company will have to estimate the sales of specific competitiors, who guard these figures. The company has to use indirect means, such as learning about competitors' purchase rate of raw materials or the number of shifts they are operating. In the consumer-goods area, individual brand shares are available through syndicated store and consumer panels.

The final requirement is to be able to interpret market-share movements correctly. Market-share analysis, like sales analysis, increases in value when the data are disaggregated along various dimensions. The company might watch the progress of its market share by product line, customer type, region, or other breakdowns.

A useful way to analyze market-share movements is in terms of the following four components:

$$\begin{matrix} \text{Overall} \\ \text{market} \\ \text{share} \end{matrix} = \begin{matrix} \text{Customer} \\ \text{penetration} \end{matrix} \times \begin{matrix} \text{Customer} \\ \text{loyalty} \end{matrix} \times \begin{matrix} \text{Customer} \\ \text{selectivity} \end{matrix} \times \begin{matrix} \text{Price} \\ \text{selectivity} \end{matrix} \qquad (25\text{--}1)$$

where:

Customer penetration is the percentage of all customers who buy from this company.

Customer loyalty is the purchases from this company by its customers expressed as a percentage of their total purchases from all suppliers of the same products.

Customer selectivity is the size of the average customer purchase from the company expressed as a percentage of the size of the average customer purchase from an average company.

Price selectivity is the average price charged by this company expressed as a percentage of the average price charged by all companies.

Now suppose the company's dollar market share falls during the period. Equation (25-1) provides four possible explanations:

- ■ The company lost some of its customers (lower customer penetration).
- ■ Existing customers are buying a smaller share of their supplies from this company (lower customer loyalty).
- ■ The company's remaining customers are smaller in size (lower customer selectivity).
- ■ The company's price has slipped relative to competition (lower price selectivity).

By tracking these factors through time, the company can diagnose the underlying cause of market-share changes. Suppose that at the beginning of the period, customer penetration was 60 percent; customer loyalty, 50 percent; customer selectivity, 80 percent; and price selectivity, 125 percent. According to (25-1), the company's market share was 30 percent. Suppose that at the end of the period, the company's market share fell to 27 percent. In checking, the company finds customer penetration 55 percent, customer loyalty at 50 percent, customer selectivity at 75 percent, and price selectivity at 130 percent. Clearly, the market-share decline was due mainly to a loss of some customers (fall in customer penetration) who normally made larger-than-average purchases (fall in customer selectivity). The manager can now investigate why these customers were lost.

Marketing Expense-to-Sales Analysis

Annual-plan control requires making sure that the company is not overspending to achieve its sales goals. The key ratio to watch is *marketing expense-to-sales*. In one company, this ratio was 30 percent and consisted of five component expense-to-sales ratios: *sales force-to-sales* (15 percent); *advertising-to-sales* (5 percent); *sales promotion-to-sales* (6 percent); *marketing research-to-sales* (1 percent); and *sales administration-to-sales* (3 percent).

Management needs to monitor these marketing-expense ratios. They will exhibit small fluctuations that can well be ignored. But fluctuations in excess of the normal range are a cause for concern. The period-to-period fluctuations in each ratio can be tracked on a *control chart* (Figure 25-2). This chart shows that the advertising expense-to-sales ratio normally fluctuates between 8 and 12 percent, say ninety-nine out of one hundred times. In the fifteenth period, however, the ratio exceeded the upper control limit. One of two hypotheses can explain this occurrence:

■ **Hypothesis A:** The company still has good expense control, and this situation represents one of those rare chance events.

■ **Hypothesis B:** The company has lost control over this expense and should find the cause.

If hypothesis A is accepted, no investigation is made to determine whether the environment has changed. The risk in not investigating is that some real change may have occurred, and the company will fall behind. If hypothesis B is accepted, the environment is investigated at the risk that the investigation will uncover nothing and be a waste of time and effort.

The behavior of successive observations even within the control limits should be watched. Note that the level of the expense-to-sales ratio rose steadily from the ninth period onward. The probability of encountering six successive increases in what should be independent events is only one out of sixty-four.[3] This unusual pattern should have led to an investigation sometime before the fifteenth observation.

When an expense-to-sales ratio gets out of control, disaggregative data are needed

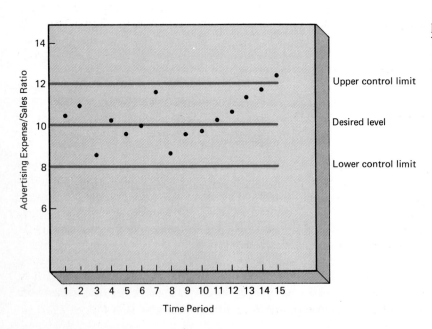

FIGURE 25-2
The Control-Chart Model

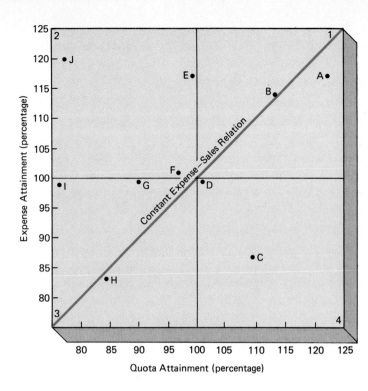

FIGURE 25-3
Comparison of Expense and
Revenue Deviations by
District

SOURCE: Adapted from D. M.
Phelps and J. H. Westing, *Marketing
Management*, 3rd ed. (Homewood,
Ill.: Richard D. Irwin, Inc., 1968), p.
754. © 1968 by Richard D. Irwin, Inc.

to track down the problem. An *expense-to-sales deviation chart* can be used. Figure 25-3 shows the performances of different sales districts in terms of their sales-quota attainment and expense attainment in percentages. For example, district D achieved its sales quota close to the expected expense level. District B exceeded its quota, and its expenses are proportionately higher. The most troubling districts are in the second quadrant. For example, district J achieved less than 80 percent of its quota, and its expenses are disproportionately high. The next step is to prepare a chart for each deviant district showing sales representatives' standings. Within district J, for example, the poor performance might be associated with a few sales representatives.

Financial
Analysis

The expenses-to-sales ratios should be analyzed in an overall financial framework to determine how and where the company is making its money. Marketers are increasingly using financial analysis to find profitable strategies and not just sales-building strategies.

Financial analysis is used by management to identify the factors that affect the company's *rate of return on net worth*.[4] The main factors are shown in Figure 25-4, along with some illustrative numbers, for a large chain-store retailer. The retailer is earning a return on net worth of 12.5 percent. Many retailers would argue that this is too low and that retail organizations need at least a 15 percent return to fully satisfy their profit requirements. Some successful retailers routinely earn over 20 percent.

Next we notice that the return on net worth is the product of two ratios, the company's *return on assets* and its *financial leverage*. To improve its return on net worth, the company must either increase the ratio of its net profits to its assets or increase the ratio of its assets to its net worth. The company should analyze the composition of its assets (i.e.,

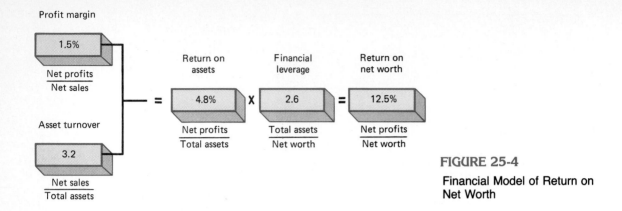

Profit margin

FIGURE 25-4

Financial Model of Return on Net Worth

cash, accounts receivable, inventory, and plant and equipment) and see if it can improve its asset management.

The return on assets is the product of two ratios, namely, the *profit margin* and the *asset turnover*. The profit margin seems low, while the asset turnover is more normal for retailing. The marketing executive can seek to improve performance in two ways: (1) to increase the profit margin by increasing sales or cutting costs; and (2) to increase the asset turnover by increasing sales or reducing the assets (e.g., inventory, receivables, etc.) that are held against a given level of sales.[5]

Customer-Attitude Tracking

The preceding annual-plan control measures are largely financial and quantitative in character. They are important but not sufficient. Needed are qualitative measures that provide early warnings to management of impending market-share changes. Alert companies set up systems to monitor the attitudes of customers, dealers, and other marketing-system participants. By monitoring changing levels of customer preference and satisfaction before they affect sales, management can take earlier action. The main customer-attitude tracking systems are:

■ *Complaint and suggestion systems.* Market-oriented companies record, analyze, and respond to written and oral complaints that come from customers. The complaints are tabulated, and management attempts to correct whatever is causing the most frequent types of complaints. Many retailers, such as hotels, restaurants, and banks, provide suggestion cards to encourage customer feedback. Market-oriented companies try to maximize the opportunities for consumer complaining so that management can get a more complete picture of customer reactions to their products and services.[6]

■ *Customer panels.* Some companies run panels consisting of customers who have agreed to communicate their attitudes periodically through phone calls or mail questionnaires. These panels are more representative of the range of customer attitudes than customer complaint and suggestion systems.

■ *Customer surveys.* Some companies periodically send out questionnaires to a random sample of customers to evaluate the friendliness of the staff, the quality of the service, and so on. The customers answer these questions on a five-point scale (very dissatisfied, dissatisfied, neutral, satisfied, very satisfied). The responses are summarized and go both to local managers and to higher-management levels, as illustrated in Figure 25-5. Local managers see how the various components of their service were rated in the current period compared to the last period, to the average of all the local units, and to the standard. This system improves the staff's motivation to provide good customer service in the knowledge that their ratings will go to higher management.[7]

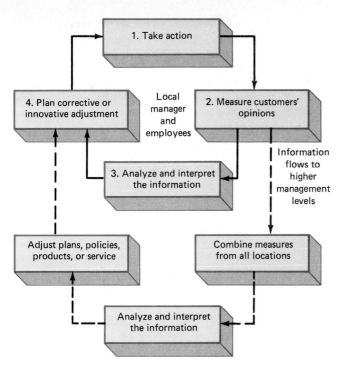

1. Local managers and employees serve customers' needs on a daily basis, using locally modified procedures along with general corporate policies and procedures.

2. By means of a standardized and locally sensitive questionnaire, determine the needs and attitudes of customers on a regular basis.

3. Comparing financial data, expectations, and past attitude information, determine strengths and weaknesses and their probable causes.

4. Determine where and how effort should be applied to correct weaknesses and preserve strengths. Repeat the process by taking action—Step 1—and maintain it to attain a steady state or to evolve in terms of customer changes.

5. A similar process can take place at higher levels, using aggregated data from the field and the existing policy flows of the organization.

FIGURE 25-5
A Consumer-Survey Feedback System
SOURCE: Arthur J. Daltas, "Protecting Service Markets with Consumer Feedback," *Cornell Hotel and Restaurant Administration Quarterly*, May 1977, pp. 73–77.

Corrective Action   When performance starts deviating too much from the plan's goals, management needs to undertake corrective action. Consider the following case:

> A large fertilizer company's sales were lagging behind its goals. The industry was marked by excess capacity and rampant price cutting.

In its efforts to cope with the situation, the company adopted increasingly drastic actions:

1. *Production cutting.* The company ordered cutbacks in production.
2. *Price cutting.* The company began to cut its prices selectively.
3. *Increased pressure on sales force.* The company put more pressure on its sales force to meet their quotas. The sales representatives started "beating down" doors, pressuring customers to buy more or to buy before the end of the year.
4. *Fringe expenditure cutting.* The company cut the budgets for personnel hiring and training, advertising, public relations, charities, and research and development.
5. *Personnel cuts.* The company began to lay off, retire, or fire personnel.
6. *Bookkeeping adjustment.* The company undertook some fancy bookkeeping to produce a better picture, including changing the depreciation base, recording purchases as capital items rather than as expenses, selling some company assets for leaseback, and recording sales to phantom buyers.

7. *Investment cutting.* The company began to cut its investment in plant and equipment.
8. *Selling property.* The company decided to sell some of its product lines to other companies.
9. *Selling the company.* The company started to consider selling out or merging with another company.

PROFITABILITY CONTROL

Here are some disconcerting findings from a recent study by the MAC Group:[8]

- We have found that anywhere from 20 to 40 percent of an individual institution's products are unprofitable, and up to 60 percent of their accounts generate losses.
- Our research has shown that in most firms, more than half of all customer relationships are not profitable, and 30 to 40 percent are only marginally so. It is frequently a mere 10 to 15 percent of a firm's relationships that generate the bulk of its profits.
- Our profitability research into the branch system of a regional bank produced some surprising results . . . thirty percent of the bank's branches were unprofitable.

Besides annual-plan control, companies need to measure the profitability of their various products, territories, customer groups, trade channels, and order sizes. This information will help management determine whether any products or marketing activities should be expanded, reduced, or eliminated.

Methodology of Marketing-Profitability Analysis

We will illustrate the steps in marketing-profitability analysis with the following example:

> The marketing vice-president of a lawn mower company wants to determine the profitability of selling its lawn mower through three types of retail channels: hardware stores, garden supply shops, and department stores. Its profit-and-loss statement is shown in Table 25-2.

Step 1: Identifying the functional expenses   Assume that the expenses listed in Table 25-2 are incurred to sell the product, advertise it, pack and deliver it, and bill and collect for it. The first task is to measure how much of each expense was incurred in each activity.

TABLE 25-2   A Simplified Profit-and-Loss Statement

Sales		$60,000
Cost of goods sold		39,000
Gross margin		$21,000
Expenses		
Salaries	$9,300	
Rent	3,000	
Supplies	3,500	
		15,800
Net profit		$ 5,200

TABLE 25-3

Mapping Natural Expenses into Functional Expenses

Natural Accounts	Total	Selling	Advertising	Packing and Delivery	Billing and Collecting
Salaries	$ 9,300	$5,100	$1,200	$1,400	$1,600
Rent	3,000	—	400	2,000	600
Supplies	3,500	400	1,500	1,400	200
	$15,800	$5,500	$3,100	$4,800	$2,400

Suppose that most salary expense went to sales representatives and the rest went to an advertising manager, packing and delivery help, and an office accountant. Let the breakdown of the $9,300 be $5,100, $1,200, $1,400, and $1,600, respectively. Table 25-3 shows the allocation of the salary expense to these four activities.

Table 25-3 also shows the rent account of $3,000 as allocated to the four activities. Since the sales representatives work away from the office, none of the building's rent expense is assigned to selling. Most of the expenses for floor space and rented equipment are in connection with packing and delivery. A small portion of the floor space is used by the advertising manager and office accountant.

Finally, the supplies account covers promotional materials, packing materials, fuel purchases for delivery, and home-office stationery. The $3,500 in this account is reassigned to the functional uses made of the supplies. Table 25-3 summarizes how the natural expenses of $15,800 were translated into functional expenses.

Step 2: Assigning the functional expenses to the marketing entities The next task is to measure how much functional expense was associated with selling through each type of channel. Consider the selling effort. The selling effort is indicated by the number of sales made in each channel. This is found in the selling column of Table 25-4. Altogether 275 sales calls were made during the period. Since the total selling expense amounted to $5,500 (see Table 25-4), the selling expense per call averaged $20.

Advertising expense can be allocated according to the number of ads addressed to the different channels. Since there were 100 ads altogether, the average ad cost $31.

The packing and delivery expense is allocated according to the number of orders placed by each type of channel; this same basis was used for allocating billing and collection expense.

TABLE 25-4

Bases for Allocating Functional Expenses to Channels

Channel Type	Selling	Advertising	Packing and Delivery	Billing and Collecting
	No. of Sales Calls in Period	No. of Advertise-ments	No. of Orders Placed in Period	No. of Orders Placed in Period
Hardware	200	50	50	50
Garden supply	65	20	21	21
Department stores	10	30	9	9
	275	100	80	80
Functional expense	$5,500	$3,100	$4,800	$2,400
No. of units	275	100	80	80
Equals	$20	$31	$60	$30

Step 3: Preparing a profit-and-loss statement for each marketing entity A profit-and-loss statement can now be prepared for each type of channel. The results are shown in Table 25-5. Since hardware stores accounted for one-half of total sales ($30,000 out of $60,000), this channel is charged with half the cost of goods sold ($19,500 out of $39,000). This leaves a gross margin from hardware stores of $10,500. From this must be deducted the proportions of the functional expenses that hardware stores consumed. According to Table 25-4, hardware stores received 200 out of 275 total sales calls. At an imputed value of $20 a call, hardware stores have to be charged with a $4,000 selling expense. Table 25-4 also shows that hardware stores were the target of 50 ads. At $31 an ad, the hardware stores are charged with $1,550 of advertising. The same reasoning applies in computing the share of the other functional expenses to charge to hardware stores. The result is that hardware stores gave rise to $10,050 of the total expenses. Subtracting this from the gross margin, the profit of selling through hardware stores is only $450.

This analysis is repeated for the other channels. The company is losing money in selling through garden supply shops and makes virtually all of its profits in selling through department stores. Notice that the gross sales through each channel are not a reliable indicator of the net profits being made in each channel.

Determining the Best Corrective Action

It would be naive to conclude that garden supply shops and possibly hardware stores should be dropped in order to concentrate on department stores. The following questions would need to be answered first:

- To what extent do buyers buy on the basis of the type of retail outlet versus the brand? Would they seek out the brand in those channels that are not eliminated?
- What are the trends with respect to the importance of these three channels?
- Have company marketing strategies directed at the three channels been optimal?

On the basis of the answers, marketing management can evaluate a number of alternative actions:

- *Establish a special charge for handling smaller orders to encourage larger orders.* This move assumes that small orders are a cause of the relative unprofitability of dealing with garden supply shops and hardware stores.
- *Give more promotional aid to garden supply shops and hardware stores.* This assumes that the managers of these stores could increase their sales with more training or promotional materials.

TABLE 25-5   Profit-and-Loss Statements for Channels

	Hardware	Garden Supply	Dept. Stores	Whole Company
Sales	$30,000	$10,000	$20,000	$60,000
Cost of goods sold	19,500	6,500	13,000	39,000
Gross margin	$10,500	$ 3,500	$ 7,000	$21,000
Expenses				
Selling ($20 per call)	$ 4,000	$ 1,300	$ 200	$ 5,500
Advertising ($31 per advertisement)	1,550	620	930	3,100
Packing and delivery ($60 per order)	3,000	1,260	540	4,800
Billing ($30 per order)	1,500	630	270	2,400
Total expenses	$10,050	$ 3,810	$ 1,940	$15,800
Net profit (or loss)	$ 450	$ (310)	$ 5,060	$ 5,200

- **Reduce the number of sales calls and the amount of advertising going to garden supply shops and hardware stores.** This assumes that some costs can be saved without seriously reducing sales to these channels.
- **Do nothing.** This assumes that current marketing efforts are optimal and either that marketing trends point to an imminent profit improvement in the weaker channels or that dropping any channel would reduce profits because of repercussions on production costs or on demand.
- **Don't abandon any channel as a whole but only the weakest retail units in each channel.** This assumes that a detailed cost study would reveal many profitable garden shops and hardware stores whose profits are concealed by the poor performance of other stores in these categories.

In general, marketing-profitability analysis indicates the relative profitability of different channels, products, territories, or other marketing entities.[9] It does not prove that the best course of action is to drop the unprofitable marketing entities, nor does it capture the likely profit improvement if these marginal marketing entities are dropped.

Direct versus Full Costing

Like all information tools, marketing-profitability analysis can lead or mislead marketing executives, depending on the degree of their understanding of its methods and limitations. The example showed some arbitrariness in the choice of bases for allocating the functional expenses to the marketing entities being evaluated. Thus the "number of sales calls" was used to allocate selling expenses, when in principle "number of sales man-hours" is a more accurate indicator of cost. The former base was used because it involves less record keeping and computation. These approximations may not involve too much inaccuracy, but marketing executives should perceive this judgmental element in determining marketing costs.[10]

Far more serious is another judgmental element affecting profitability analysis. The issue is whether to allocate *full costs* or only *direct and traceable costs* in evaluating the performance of a marketing entity. The example above sidestepped this problem by assuming only simple costs that fit in with marketing activities. But the question cannot be avoided in the actual analysis of profitability. Three types of costs have to be distinguished:

- **Direct costs.** These are costs that can be assigned directly to the marketing entities that give rise to them. For example, sales commissions are a direct cost in a profitability analysis of sales territories, sales representatives, or customers. Advertising expenditures are a direct cost in a profitability analysis of products to the extent that each advertisement promotes only one company product. Other direct costs for specific purposes are sales-force salaries, supplies, and traveling expenses.
- **Traceable common costs.** These are costs that can be assigned only indirectly, but on a plausible basis, to the marketing entities. In the example, rent was analyzed in this way. The company's floor space was needed for three different marketing activities, and an estimate was made of how much floor space supported each activity.
- **Nontraceable common costs.** These are costs whose allocation to the marketing entities is highly arbitrary. Consider "corporate image" expenditures. To allocate them equally to all products would be arbitrary because all products do not benefit equally from corporate image making. To allocate them proportionately to the sales of the various products would be arbitrary because relative product sales reflect many factors besides corporate image making. Other typical examples of difficult-to-assign common costs are management salaries, taxes, interest, and other types of overhead.

There is no controversy concerning the inclusion of direct costs in marketing cost analysis. There is a small amount of controversy concerning the inclusion of traceable common costs. Traceable common costs lump together costs that would change with the scale of marketing activity and costs that probably would not change in the near future. If the lawn mower company drops garden supply shops, it is likely to continue to pay the same rent for contractual reasons. In this event, its profits would not rise immediately by the amount of the present loss in selling to garden supply shops ($310). The profit figures are more meaningful when traceable costs can be eliminated.

The major controversy concerns whether the nontraceable common costs should be allocated to the marketing entities. Such allocation is called the *full-cost approach*, and its advocates defend it on the grounds that all costs must ultimately be imputed in order to determine true profitability. But this argument confuses the use of accounting for financial reporting with the use of accounting to provide a quantitative basis for decision making and profit planning. Full costing has three major weaknesses:

- The relative profitability of different marketing entities can shift quite radically when an arbitrary way to allocate nontraceable common costs is replaced by another. This weakens confidence in the tool.
- The arbitrariness demoralizes managers, who feel that their performance is judged adversely.
- The inclusion of nontraceable common costs may weaken efforts at real cost control. Operating management is most effective in controlling direct costs and traceable common costs. Arbitrary assignments of nontraceable common costs may lead them to spend their time fighting the arbitrary cost allocations rather than managing their controllable costs well.

EFFICIENCY CONTROL

Suppose a profitability analysis reveals that the company is earning poor profits in connection with certain products, territories, or markets. The question is whether there are more efficient ways to manage the sales force, advertising, sales promotion, and distribution in connection with these poorer-performing marketing entities.

Sales-Force Efficiency

Sales managers at each level—regional, district, and area—should keep track of the following key indicators of sales-force efficiency in their territory:

- Average number of sales calls per salesperson per day
- Average sales-call time per contact
- Average revenue per sales call
- Average cost per sales call
- Entertainment cost per sales call
- Percentage of orders per 100 sales calls
- Number of new customers per period
- Number of lost customers per period
- Sales-force cost as a percentage of total sales

An analysis of these statistics will raise such useful questions as the following: Are sales representatives making too few calls per day? Are they spending too much time per call? Are they spending too much on entertainment? Are they closing enough orders per hundred calls? Are they producing enough new customers and holding on to the old customers?

When a company starts investigating sales-force efficiency, it can often find a number of areas for improvement. General Electric was able to reduce the size of one of its divisional sales forces without any sales loss after discovering that sales representatives were making too many calls on customers. When a large airline found that its sales representatives were both selling and servicing, they transferred the servicing function to lower-paid clerks. Another company conducted time-and-duty studies and found ways to reduce the ratio of idle-to-productive time.

Advertising Efficiency

Many managers feel that it is almost impossible to measure what they are getting for their advertising dollars. But an effort should be made to keep track of at least the following statistics:

- ■ Advertising cost per thousand target buyers reached by media category and media vehicle
- ■ Percentage of audience who noted, saw/associated, and read most for each print media vehicle
- ■ Consumer opinions on the ad content and effectiveness
- ■ Before-after measures of attitude toward the product
- ■ Number of inquiries stimulated by the ad
- ■ Cost per inquiry

Management can undertake a number of steps to improve advertising efficiency, including doing a better job of positioning the product, defining advertising objectives, pretesting messages, using the computer to guide the selection of advertising media, looking for better media buys, and doing advertising posttesting.

Sales Promotion Efficiency

Sales promotion includes dozens of devices for stimulating buyer interest and product trial. To improve sales promotion efficiency, management should record the costs and sales impact of each sales promotion. Management should watch the following statistics:

- ■ Percentage of sales sold on deal
- ■ Display costs per sales dollar
- ■ Percentage of coupons redeemed
- ■ Number of inquiries resulting from a demonstration

If a sales promotion manager is appointed, that manager can analyze the results of different sales promotions and advise product managers on the most cost-effective promotions to use.

Distribution Efficiency

Management needs to search for distribution economies. Several models are available for improving inventory control, warehouse locations, and transportation modes. Improvement of local delivery costs is also possible, as the following example shows:

Wholesale bakers face increased competition from chain bakers. They are especially at a disadvantage in the physical distribution of bread. The wholesale bakers must make more stops and deliver less bread per stop. Furthermore, the driver typically loads each store's shelf, while the chain bakery leaves the bread at the chain's unloading platform to be placed on the shelf by store personnel. This led the American Bakers' Association to investigate whether more efficient bread-handling procedures were achievable. A systems engineering study was conducted. The bread delivery operation was studied in minute detail from the time of truck loading to the time of shelving. As a result of riding with the drivers and observing procedures, the engineers recommended several changes. Economies could be secured from more scientific routing; from a relocation of the truck's door from the back of the trailer to the driver's side; and from the development of preshelved racks. These economies were always available but not recognized until competitive pressure increased the need for improved efficiency.

STRATEGIC CONTROL

From time to time, companies must undertake a critical review of their overall marketing effectiveness. Marketing is an area where rapid obsolescence of objectives, policies, strategies, and programs is a constant possibility. Each company should periodically reassess its overall approach to the marketplace. Two tools are available, namely, a *marketing-effectiveness rating review* and a *marketing audit*.

Marketing-Effectiveness Rating Review

Here is an actual situation.

> The president of a major industrial-equipment company reviewed the annual business plans of various divisions and found several divisional plans lacking in marketing substance. He called in the corporate vice-president of marketing and said:
>
> > I am not happy with the quality of marketing in our divisions. It is very uneven. I want you to find out which of our divisions are strong, average, and weak in marketing. I want to know if they understand and are practicing customer-oriented marketing. I want a marketing score for each division. For each marketing-deficient division, I want a plan for improving its marketing effectiveness over the next few years. I want evidence next year that each marketing-deficient division is making progress toward a marketing orientation.
>
> The corporate marketing vice-president agreed, recognizing that it was a formidable task. His first inclination was to base the evaluation of marketing effectiveness on each division's performance in sales growth, market share, and profitability. His thinking was that high-performing divisions had good marketing leadership and poor-performing divisions had poor marketing leadership.

Actually, marketing effectiveness is not necessarily revealed by current marketing performance. Good results may be due to a division's being in the right place at the right time, rather than having effective marketing management. Improvements in that division's marketing might boost results from good to excellent. Another division might have poor results in spite of excellent marketing planning. Replacing the present marketing managers might only make things worse.

The marketing effectiveness of a company or division is reflected in the degree to which it exhibits five major attributes of a marketing orientation: *customer philosophy*, *integrated marketing organization*, *adequate marketing information*, *strategic orientation*, and *operational efficiency*. Each attribute can be measured. Table 25-6 presents a *marketing-effectiveness rating instrument* based on these five attributes. This instrument is filled out by marketing and other managers in the division. The scores are then summarized.

The instrument has been tested in a number of companies, and very few achieve scores within the superior range of 26 to 30 points. The few include well-known master marketers such as Procter & Gamble, McDonald's, IBM, and General Electric. Most companies and divisions receive scores in the fair-to-good range, indicating that their own managers see room for marketing improvement. The scores of each attribute indicate which elements of effective marketing action need the most attention. Divisional management can then establish a plan for correcting its major marketing weaknesses.[11]

Customer Philosophy

A. *Does management recognize the importance of designing the company to serve the needs and wants of chosen markets?*

Score

0 ☐ Management primarily thinks in terms of selling current and new products to whoever will buy them.

1 ☐ Management thinks in terms of serving a wide range of markets and needs with equal effectiveness.

2 ☐ Management thinks in terms of serving the needs and wants of well-defined markets chosen for their long-run growth and profit potential for the company.

B. *Does management develop different offerings and marketing plans for different segments of the market?*

0 ☐ No.

1 ☐ Somewhat.

2 ☐ To a good extent.

C. *Does management take a whole marketing system view (suppliers, channels, competitors, customers, environment) in planning its business?*

0 ☐ No. Management concentrates on selling and servicing its immediate customers.

1 ☐ Somewhat. Management takes a long view of its channels although the bulk of its effort goes to selling and servicing the immediate customers.

2 ☐ Yes. Management takes a whole marketing systems view recognizing the threats and opportunities created for the company by changes in any part of the system.

Integrated Marketing Organization

D. *Is there high-level marketing integration and control of the major marketing functions?*

0 ☐ No. Sales and other marketing functions are not integrated at the top and there is some unproductive conflict.

1 ☐ Somewhat. There is formal integration and control of the major marketing functions but less than satisfactory coordination and cooperation.

2 ☐ Yes. The major marketing functions are effectively integrated.

E. *Does marketing management work well with management in research, manufacturing, purchasing, physical distribution, and finance?*

0 ☐ No. There are complaints that marketing is unreasonable in the demands and costs it places on other departments.

1 ☐ Somewhat. The relations are amicable although each department pretty much acts to serve its own power interests.

2 ☐ Yes. The departments cooperate effectively and resolve issues in the best interest of the company as a whole.

F. *How well-organized is the new product process?*

0 ☐ The system is ill-defined and poorly handled.

1 ☐ The system formally exists but lacks sophistication.

2 ☐ The system is well-structured and professionally staffed.

Adequate Marketing Information

G. *When were the latest marketing research studies of customers, buying influences, channels, and competitors conducted?*

0 ☐ Several years ago.

1 ☐ A few years ago.

2 ☐ Recently.

H. *How well does management know the sales potential and profitability of different market segments, customers, territories, products, channels, and order sizes?*

0 ☐ Not at all.

1 ☐ Somewhat.

2 ☐ Very well.

TABLE 25-6 Continued

I. What effort is expended to measure the cost effectiveness of different marketing expenditures?

0 ☐ Little or no effort.

1 ☐ Some effort.

2 ☐ Substantial effort.

Strategic Orientation

J. What is the extent of formal marketing planning?

0 ☐ Management does little or no formal marketing planning.

1 ☐ Management develops an annual marketing plan.

2 ☐ Management develops a detailed annual marketing plan and a careful long-range plan that is updated annually.

K. What is the quality of the current marketing strategy?

0 ☐ The current strategy is not clear.

1 ☐ The current strategy is clear and represents a continuation of traditional strategy.

2 ☐ The current strategy is clear, innovative, data-based, and well-reasoned.

L. What is the extent of contingency thinking and planning?

0 ☐ Management does little or no contingency thinking.

1 ☐ Management does some contingency thinking although little formal contingency planning.

2 ☐ Management formally identifies the most important contingencies and develops contingency plans.

Operational Efficiency

M. How well is the marketing thinking at the top communicated and implemented down the line?

0 ☐ Poorly.

1 ☐ Fairly.

2 ☐ Successfully.

N. Is management doing an effective job with the marketing resources?

0 ☐ No. The marketing resources are inadequate for the job to be done.

1 ☐ Somewhat. The marketing resources are adequate but they are not employed optimally.

2 ☐ Yes. The marketing resources are adequate and are deployed efficiently.

O. Does management show a good capacity to react quickly and effectively to on-the-spot developments?

0 ☐ No. Sales and market information is not very current and management reaction time is slow.

0 ☐ Somewhat. Management receives fairly up-to-date sales and market information; management reaction time varies.

2 ☐ Yes. Management has installed systems yielding highly current information and fast reaction time.

Total Score

The instrument is used in the following way. The appropriate answer is checked for each question. The scores are added—the total will be somewhere between 0 and 30. The following scale shows the level of marketing effectiveness:

0–5 = None	16–20 = Good
6–10 = Poor	21–25 = Very good
11–15 = Fair	26–30 = Superior

The Marketing Audit Those companies and divisions that discover marketing weakness through applying the marketing-effectiveness rating review should undertake a more thorough study known as a *marketing audit*.[12]

We define *marketing audit* as follows:

A *marketing audit* is a *comprehensive, systematic, independent,* and *periodic* examination of a company's—or business unit's—marketing environment, objectives, strategies, and activities with a view to determining problem areas and opportunities and recommending a plan of action to improve the company's marketing performance.

Let us examine the marketing audit's four characteristics:

- **Comprehensive.** The marketing audit covers all the major marketing activities of a business, not just a few trouble spots. It would be called a functional audit if it covered only the sales force, or pricing, or some other marketing activity. Although functional audits are useful, they sometimes mislead management as to the real source of its problem. Excessive sales-force turnover, for example, may be a symptom not of poor sales-force training or compensation but of weak company products and promotion. A comprehensive marketing audit usually is more effective in locating the real source of the company's marketing problems.

- **Systematic.** The marketing audit involves an orderly sequence of diagnostic steps covering the organization's marketing environment, internal marketing system, and specific marketing activities. The diagnosis is followed by a corrective-action plan involving both short-run and long-run proposals to improve the organization's overall marketing effectiveness.

- **Independent.** A marketing audit can be conducted in six ways: (1) self-audit, (2) audit from across, (3) audit from above, (4) company auditing office, (5) company task-force audit, and (6) outsider audit. Self-audits, where managers use a checklist to rate their own operations, may be useful, but most experts agree that the self-audit lacks objectivity and independence.[13] The 3M Company has made good use of a corporate auditing office, which provides marketing audit services to divisions on request.[14] Generally speaking, however, the best audits are likely to come from experienced outside consultants, who have the necessary objectivity and independence, broad experience in a number of industries, some familiarity with this industry, and the undivided time and attention to give to the audit.

- **Periodic.** Typically, marketing audits are initiated only after sales have turned down, sales-force morale has fallen, and other company problems have occurred. Ironically, companies are thrown into a crisis partly because they failed to review their marketing operations during good times. A periodic marketing audit can benefit companies in good health as well as those in trouble. "No marketing operation is ever so good that it cannot be improved. Even the best can be made better. In fact, even the best *must* be better, for few if any marketing operations can remain successful over the years by maintaining the status quo."[15]

Marketing Audit Procedure A marketing audit starts with a meeting between the company officer(s) and the marketing auditor(s) to work out an agreement on the objectives, coverage, depth, data sources, report format, and the time period for the audit. A detailed plan as to who is to be interviewed, the questions to be asked, the time and place of contact, and so on, is carefully prepared so that auditing time and cost are kept to a minimum. The cardinal rule in marketing auditing is, Don't rely solely on the company's executives for data and opinion. Customers, dealers, and other outside groups must be interviewed. Many companies do not really know how their customers and dealers see them, nor do they fully understand customer needs.

When the data-gathering phase is over, the marketing auditor presents the main findings and recommendations. A valuable aspect of the marketing audit is the process that the managers go through to assimilate, debate, and develop new concepts of needed marketing action.

Components of the Marketing Audit The marketing audit consists of examining six major components of the company's marketing situation. The six components are described below, and the major auditing questions are listed in Table 25-7.

TABLE 25-7   Components of a Marketing Audit

Part I. Marketing-Environment Audit

MACROENVIRONMENT

A. Demographic
1. What major demographic developments and trends pose opportunities or threats to this company?
2. What actions has the company taken in response to these developments and trends?

B. Economic
1. What major developments in income, prices, savings, and credit will affect the company?
2. What actions has the company been taking in response to these developments and trends?

C. Ecological
1. What is the outlook for the cost and availability of natural resources and energy needed by the company?
2. What concerns have been expressed about the company's role in pollution and conservation, and what steps has the company taken?

D. Technological
1. What major changes are occurring in product technology? In process technology? What is the company's position in these technologies?
2. What major generic substitutes might replace this product?

E. Political
1. What laws are being proposed that could affect marketing strategy and tactics?
2. What federal, state, and local actions should be watched? What is happening in the areas of pollution control, equal employment opportunity, product safety, advertising, price control, and so forth, that affects marketing strategy?

F. Cultural
1. What is the public's attitude toward business and toward the products produced by the company?
2. What changes in consumer and business lifestyles and values have a bearing on the company?

TASK ENVIRONMENT

A. Markets
1. What is happening to market size, growth, geographical distribution, and profits?
2. What are the major market segments?

B. Customers
1. How do customers and prospects rate the company and its competitors on reputation, product quality, service, sales force, and price?
2. How do different customer segments make their buying decisions?

C. Competitors
1. Who are the major competitors? What are their objectives and strategies, their strengths and weaknesses, their sizes and market shares?
2. What trends will affect future competition and substitutes for this product?

D. Distribution and Dealers
1. What are the main trade channels for bringing products to customers?
2. What are the efficiency levels and growth potentials of the different trade channels?

E. Suppliers
1. What is the outlook for the availability of key resources used in production?
2. What trends are occuring among suppliers in their pattern of selling?

F. Facilitators and Marketing Firms
1. What is the cost and availability outlook for transportation services?
2. What is the cost and availability outlook for warehousing facilities?
3. What is the cost and availability outlook for financial resources?
4. How effective are the company's advertising agencies and marketing research firms?

G. Publics
1. What publics represent particular opportunities or problems for the company?
2. What steps has the company taken to deal effectively with each public?

TABLE 25-7 Continued

Part II. Marketing-Strategy Audit

A. Business Mission
1. Is the business mission clearly stated in market-oriented terms? Is it feasible?

B. Marketing Objectives and Goals
1. Are the corporate and marketing objectives stated in the form of clear goals to guide marketing planning and performance measurement?
2. Are the marketing objectives appropriate, given the company's competitive position, resources, and opportunities?

C. Strategy
1. Is management able to articulate a clear marketing strategy for achieving its marketing objectives? Is the strategy convincing? Is the strategy appropriate to the stage of the product life cycle, competitors' strategies, and the state of the economy?
2. Is the company using the best basis for market segmentation? Does it have sound criteria for rating the segments and choosing the best ones? Has it developed accurate profiles of each target segment?
3. Has the company developed a sound positioning and marketing mix for each target segment? Are marketing resources allocated optimally to the major elements of the marketing mix—i.e., product quality, service, sales force, advertising, promotion, and distribution?
4. Are enough resources or too many resources budgeted to accomplish the marketing objectives?

Part III. Marketing-Organization Audit

A. Formal Structure
1. Does the marketing officer have adequate authority over and responsibility for company activities that affect the customer's satisfaction?
2. Are the marketing activities optimally structured along functional, product, end-user, and territorial lines?

B. Functional Efficiency
1. Are there good communication and working relations between marketing and sales?
2. Is the product management system working effectively? Are product managers able to plan profits or only sales volume?
3. Are there any groups in marketing that need more training, motivation, supervision, or evaluation?

C. Interface Efficiency
1. Are there any problems between marketing and manufacturing, R&D, purchasing, finance, accounting, and legal that need attention?

Part IV. Marketing-Systems Audit

A. Marketing Information System
1. Is the marketing intelligence system producing accurate, sufficient, and timely information about marketplace developments with respect to customers, prospects, distributors and dealers, competitors, suppliers, and various publics?
2. Are company decision makers asking for enough marketing research, and are they using the results?
3. Is the company employing the best methods for market and sales forecasting?

B. Marketing Planning Systems
1. Is the marketing planning system well conceived and effective?
2. Is sales forecasting and market potential measurement soundly carried out?
3. Are sales quotas set on a proper basis?

C. Marketing Control System
1. Are the control procedures adequate to ensure that the annual-plan objectives are being achieved?
2. Does management periodically analyze the profitability of products, markets, territories, and channels of distribution?
3. Are marketing costs periodically examined?

TABLE 25-7 Continued

D. New-Product-Development System	**1.** Is the company well organized to gather, generate, and screen new-product ideas?
	2. Does the company do adequate concept research and business analysis before investing in new ideas?
	3. Does the company carry out adequate product and market testing before launching new products?

Part V. Marketing-Productivity Audit

A. Profitability Analysis	**1.** What is the profitability of the company's different products, markets, territories, and channels of distribution?
	2. Should the company enter, expand, contract, or withdraw from any business segments and what would be the short- and long-run profit consequences?
B. Cost-Effectiveness Analysis	**1.** Do any marketing activities seem to have excessive costs? Can cost-reducing steps be taken?

Part VI. Marketing-Function Audits

A. Products	**1.** What are the product-line objectives? Are these objectives sound? Is the current product line meeting the objectives?
	2. Should the product line be stretched or contracted upward, downward, or both ways?
	3. Which products should be phased out? Which products should be added?
	4. What is the buyers' knowledge and attitudes toward the company's and competitors' product quality, features, styling, brand names, etc? What areas of product strategy need improvement?
B. Price	**1.** What are the pricing objectives, policies, strategies, and procedures? To what extent are prices set on cost, demand, and competitive criteria?
	2. Do the customers see the company's prices as being in line with the value of its offer?
	3. What does management know about the price elasticity of demand, experience curve effects, and competitors' prices and pricing policies?
	4. To what extent are price policies compatible with the needs of distributors and dealers, suppliers, and government regulation?
C. Distribution	**1.** What are the distribution objectives and strategies?
	2. Is there adequate market coverage and service?
	3. How effective are the following channel members: distributors, dealers, manufacturers' representatives, brokers, agents, etc.?
	4. Should the company consider changing its distribution channels?
D. Advertising, Sales Promotion, and Publicity	**1.** What are the organization's advertising objectives? Are they sound?
	2. Is the right amount being spent on advertising? How is the budget determined?
	3. Are the ad themes and copy effective? What do customers and the public think about the advertising?
	4. Are the advertising media well chosen?
	5. Is the internal advertising staff adequate?
	6. Is the sales promotion budget adequate? Is there effective and sufficient use of sales promotion tools such as samples, coupons, displays, sales contests?
	7. Is the publicity budget adequate? Is the public relations staff competent and creative?
E. Sales Force	**1.** What are the organization's sales-force objectives?
	2. Is the sales force large enough to accomplish the company's objectives?
	3. Is the sales force organized along the proper principles of specialization (territory, market, product)? Are there enough (or too many) sales managers to guide the field sales representatives?

TABLE 25-7 Continued

4. Does the sales-compensation level and structure provide adequate incentive and reward?
5. Does the sales force show high morale, ability, and effort?
6. Are the procedures adequate for setting quotas and evaluating performances?
7. How does the company's sales-force compare to competitors' sales forces?

- ▆ *Marketing-environment audit.* This audit calls for analyzing major macroenvironment forces and trends in the key components of the company's task environment: markets, customers, competitors, distributors, and dealers, suppliers, and facilitators.
- ▆ *Marketing-strategy audit.* This audit calls for reviewing the company's marketing objectives and marketing strategy to appraise how well these are adapted to the current and forecasted marketing environment.
- ▆ *Marketing-organization audit.* This audit calls for evaluating the capability of the marketing organization implementing the necessary strategy for the forecasted environment.
- ▆ *Marketing-systems audit.* This audit involves examining the quality of the company's systems for analysis, planning, and control.
- ▆ *Marketing-productivity audit.* This audit calls for examining the profitability of different marketing entities and the cost effectiveness of different marketing expenditures.
- ▆ *Marketing-function audits.* These audits consist of in-depth evaluations of major marketing-mix components, namely, products, price, distribution, sales force, advertising, promotion, and publicity.

Example of a Marketing Audit[16] O'Brien Candy Company is a medium-sized candy company located in the Midwest. In the past two years, its sales and profits have barely held their own. Top management feels that the trouble lies with the sales force; they do not "work hard or smart enough." To correct the problem, management plans to introduce a new incentive-compensation system and hire a sales-force trainer to train the sales force in modern merchandising and selling techniques. Before doing this, however, they decide to hire a marketing consultant to do a marketing audit. The auditor conducts a number of interviews with management, customers, sales representatives, and dealers and examines various data. Here is what the auditor finds:

- ▆ The company's product line consists primarily of eighteen products, mostly candy bars. Its two leading brands are in the mature stage of their life cycles and account for 76 percent of total sales. The company has looked at the fast-developing markets of chocolate snacks and candies but has not made any moves yet.
- ▆ The company recently researched its customer profile. Its products appeal especially to lower-income and older people. Respondents who were asked to assess O'Brien's chocolate products in relation to competitor's products described them as "average quality and a bit old-fashioned."
- ▆ O'Brien sells its products to candy jobbers and large chains. Its sales force call on many of the small retailers reached by the candy jobbers, to fortify displays and provide ideas; its sales force also call on many small retailers not covered by jobbers. O'Brien enjoys good penetration of small retailing, although not in all segments, such as the fast-growing restaurant area. Its major approach to middlemen is a "sell-in" strategy: discounts, exclusivity contracts, and stock financing. At the same time O'Brien does not do too well in penetrating the various chains. Its competitors rely more heavily on mass consumer advertising and store merchandising and are more successful with the large chains.
- ▆ O'Brien's marketing budget is set at 15 percent of its total sales, compared with competitors' budgets of close to 20 percent. Most of the marketing budget supports the sales force, and

the remainder supports advertising; consumer promotions are very limited. The advertising budget is spent primarily in remainder advertising for the company's two leading products. New products are not developed often, and when they are, they are introduced to retailers by using a "push" strategy.

■ The marketing organization is headed by a sales vice-president. Reporting to the sales vice-president is the sales manager, the marketing research manager, and the advertising manager. Having come up from the ranks, the sales vice-president is partial to sales-force activities and pays less attention to the other marketing functions. The sales force is assigned to territories headed by area managers.

The marketing auditor concluded that O'Brien's problems would not be solved by actions taken to improve its sales force. The sales-force problem was symptomatic of a deeper company malaise. The auditor prepared and presented a report to management consisting of the findings and recommendations shown in Table 25-8.

TABLE 25-8   Summary of Marketing Auditor's Findings and Recommendations for O'Brien Candy Company

Findings

The company's product lines are dangerously unbalanced. The two leading products accounted for 76 percent of total sales and have no growth potential. Five of the eighteen products are unprofitable and have no growth potential.

The company's marketing objectives are neither clear nor realistic.

The company's strategy is not taking changing distribution patterns into account or catering to rapidly changing markets.

The company is run by a sales organization rather than a marketing organization.

The company's marketing mix is unbalanced, with too much spending on sales force and not enough on advertising.

The company lacks procedures for successfully developing and launching new products.

The company's selling effort is not geared to profitable accounts.

Short-Term Recommendations

Examine the current product line and weed out marginal performers with limited growth potential.

Shift some marketing expenditures from supporting mature products to supporting the more recent ones.

Shift the marketing-mix emphasis from direct selling to national advertising, especially for new products.

Conduct a market-profile study of the fastest growing segments of the candy market and develop a plan to break into these areas.

Instruct the sales force to drop some of the smaller outlets and not to take orders for under twenty items. Also, cut out the duplication of effort of sales representatives and jobbers calling on the same accounts.

Initiate sales-training programs and an improved compensation plan.

Medium-to-Long-Term Recommendations

Hire an experienced marketing vice-president from the outside.

Set formal and operational marketing objectives.

Introduce the product manager concept in the marketing organization.

Initiate effective new-product-development programs.

Develop strong brand names.

Find ways to market its brands to the chain-stores more effectively.

Increase the level of marketing expenditures to 20 percent of sales.

Reorganize the selling function by specializing sales representatives by distribution channels.

Set sales objectives and base sales compensation on gross profit performance.

SOURCE: Adapted with permission from Dr. Ernst A. Tirmann, "Should Your Marketing Be Audited?" *European Business*, Autumn 1971.

THE MARKETING CONTROLLER CONCEPT

We have examined how an outside marketing auditor can contribute to strategic control. Some companies have established inside positions known as *marketing controllers* to monitor marketing expenses and activities. Marketing controllers are persons working in the controller office who have specialized in the marketing side of the business. In the past, controller offices concentrated on watching manufacturing, inventory, and financial expenses and did not include staff that understood marketing very well. The new marketing controllers are trained in finance and marketing and can perform a sophisticated financial analysis of past and planned marketing expenditures. A survey by Goodman showed that

> large sophisticated companies, such as General Foods, Du Pont, Johnson & Johnson, Trans World Airlines, and American Cyanamid, have all instituted financial control positions which directly oversee advertising and, in some selected cases, merchandising policies. The major functions of these individuals are to verify advertising bills, ensure the optimization of agency rates, negotiate agency contracts, and perform an audit function regarding the client's agency and certain of the suppliers.[17]

Goodman feels that this step is in the right direction and advocates an even fuller role for the marketing controller. The marketing controller would

- Maintain record of adherence to profit plans
- Maintain close control of media expense
- Prepare brand managers' budgets
- Advise on optimum timing for strategies
- Measure the efficiency of promotions
- Analyze media production costs
- Evaluate customer and geographic profitability
- Present sales-oriented financial reports
- Assist direct accounts in optimizing purchasing and inventory policies
- Educate the marketing area to financial implications of decisions

The Nestlé Company took a step in this direction when a specific segment of the controller operation was made available for marketing planning and control. Marketing-service analysts were assigned to each of Nestlé's six marketing divisions to work for the marketing head. They carried out diverse assignments designed to improve marketing efficiency and performance. Their reports proved helpful, and the position served as a training ground for future general managers because of their exposure to marketing, production, and finance.

The marketing controller position is desirable, particularly in organizations where marketing is still oriented toward sales rather than profits. The marketing controller can help analyze how and where the company is making its money. As future marketing managers acquire greater financial training, they can do more of this work themselves, with marketing controllers providing primarily a monitoring function of marketing expenditures.

SUMMARY

Marketing control is the natural sequel to marketing planning, organization, and implementation. Companies need to carry out four types of marketing control.

Annual-plan control consists of monitoring the current marketing effort and results to ensure that the annual sales and profit goals will be achieved. The main tools are sales analysis, market-share analysis, marketing expense-to-sales analysis, financial analysis, and customer-attitude tracking. If underperformance is detected, the company can implement several corrective measures, including cutting production, changing prices, increasing sales-force pressure, and cutting fringe expenditures.

Profitability control calls for determining the actual profitability of the firm's products, territories, market segments, and trade channels. Marketing-profitability analysis reveals the weaker marketing entities, although it does not indicate whether the weaker units should be bolstered or phased out.

Efficiency control is the task of increasing the efficiency of such marketing activities as personal selling, advertising, sales promotion, and distribution. Managers must watch certain key ratios that indicate how efficiently these functions are being performed.

Strategic control is the task of ensuring that the company's marketing objectives, strategies, and systems are optimally adapted to the current and forecasted marketing environment. One tool, known as the marketing-effectiveness rating instrument, profiles a company's or a division's overall marketing effectiveness in terms of customer philosophy, marketing organization, marketing information, strategic planning, and operational efficiency. Another tool, known as the marketing audit, is a comprehensive, systematic, independent, and periodic examination of the organization's marketing environment, objectives, strategies, and activities. The purpose of the marketing audit is to determine marketing problem areas and recommend a corrective short-run and long-run action plan to improve the organization's overall marketing effectiveness.

A growing number of companies have established marketing controller positions to monitor marketing expenditures and develop improved financial analyses of the impact of these expenditures.

■ QUESTIONS _____

1. In what ways are the "planning" and "control" of marketing strategy similar and in what ways are they different?

2. There are four types of marketing control. Compare and contrast their objectives and purposes. How does each contribute to assessing the marketing effectiveness of the firm?

3. Discuss any major problems that confront attempts to control and evaluate marketing activities.

4. What reasons can you offer to justify doing a marketing audit for a very successful manufacturer and distributor of power boats designed for the upscale end of the market?

5. In many instances, marketing control requires comparison of a performance measure with an established standard of measurement. Suggest some steps that marketing managers could take to establish a performance standard.

6. What are the relative advantages and disadvantages of consumer attitudes tracking when compared with other annual plan control approaches?

7. Do you foresee a professional marketing auditing association that would license practitioners on the model of professional certified public accountants? Why or why not? Do you think it is a good idea?

8. A sales manager examined his company's sales by region and noted that the East Coast sales were about 2 percent below the quota. To probe further, the sales manager examined district sales figures. He discovered that the Boston sales district within the East Coast region was responsible for most of the underachievement. He then examined the individual sales of the four sales people in the Boston sales district. This examination revealed that the top salesman, Roberts, had filed only 69 percent of his quota for the period. Is it safe to conclude that Roberts is loafing or having personal problems?

9. Suppose a company's market share falls for a couple of periods. The marketing vice-president, however, refuses to take any action, calling it a random walk. What does he mean? Is he justified?

10. Company XYZ produces five products, and its sales people represent the full product line on each sales call. In order to determine the profit contribution of each product, sales representatives' costs (salary, commission, and expenses) have to be allocated among the five products. How should this be done?

11. A large manufacturer of industrial equipment has a salesperson assigned to each major city. Regional sales managers supervise the sales representatives in several cities. The chief marketing officer wants to evaluate the profit contribution of the different cities. How might each of the following costs be allocated to the cities: (a) billing, (b) district sales manager's expenses, (c) national magazine advertising, (d) marketing research?

12. A company conducts a marketing cost study to determine the minimum-size order for breaking even. After finding that size, should the company refuse to accept orders below it? What issues and alternatives should be considered?

13. The idea of treating the marketing department as a profit center raises some difficult problems. Name them and suggest possible solutions.

14. What is the difference between the job of a marketing auditor and that of a marketing controller?

■ FOOTNOTES

1 For further discussion, see James M. Hulbert and Norman E. Toy, ''A Strategic Framework for Marketing Control,'' *Journal of Marketing*, April 1977, pp. 12–20.

2 See Alfred R. Oxenfeldt, ''How to Use Market-Share Measurement,'' *Harvard Business Review*, January–February 1969, pp. 59–68.

3 There is a $\frac{1}{2}$ chance that a successive observation will be higher or lower. Therefore the probability of finding six successively higher values is given by $(\frac{1}{2})^6 = \frac{1}{64}$.

4 Alternatively, companies need to focus on the factors affecting *shareholder value*. The goal of marketing planning is to take the steps that will increase shareholder value. Shareholder value is the *present value* of the future income stream created by the company's present actions. *Rate-of-return analysis* usually focuses on only one year's results. See Alfred Rappaport, *Creating Shareholder Value* (New York: Free Press, 1986), pp. 125–30.

5 For additional reading on financial analysis, see Peter L. Mullins, *Effective Financial Management for Wholesaler-Distributors* (Washington, D.C.: National Association of Wholesaler-Distributors, 1979); and Peter L. Mullins, *Measuring Customer and Product Line Profitability* (Washington, D.C.: Distribution Research and Education Foundation, 1984).

6 See Claes Fornell, ''Complaint Management and Marketing Performance'' (Unpublished paper, Graduate School of Management, Northwestern University, Evanston, Ill., October 1978).

7 For an application to a hotel chain, see Arthur J. Daltas, ''Protecting Service Markets with Consumer Feedback,'' *Cornell Hotel and Restaurant Administration Quarterly*, May 1977, pp. 73–77.

8 The MAC Group, *Distribution: A Competitive Weapon* (Cambridge, Mass., 1985), pp. 20, 22.

9 For another example, see Leland L. Beik and Stephen L. Buzby, ''Profitability Analyses by Market Segments,'' *Journal of Marketing*, June 1973, pp. 48–53.

10 For common bases of allocation, see Charles H. Sevin, *Marketing Productivity Analysis* (New York: McGraw-Hill, 1965).

11 For further discussion of this instrument, see Philip Kotler, ''From Sales Obsession to Marketing Effectiveness,'' *Harvard Business Review*, November–December 1977, pp. 67–75.

12 See Philip Kotler, William Gregor, and William Rodgers, ''The Marketing Audit Comes of Age,'' *Sloan Management Review*, Winter 1977, pp. 25–43.

13 However, useful checklists for a marketing self-audit can be found in Aubrey Wilson, *Aubrey Wilson's Marketing Audit Checklists* (London: McGraw-Hill (U.K.) Limited, 1982); and Mike Wilson, *The Management of Marketing* (Westmead, Eng.: Gover Publishing, 1980).

14 Kotler, Gregor, and Rodgers, ''Marketing Audit Comes of Age,'' p. 31.

15 Abe Shuchman, ''The Marketing Audit: Its Nature, Purposes, and Problems,'' in *Analyzing and Improving Marketing Performance*, ed. Alfred Oxenfeldt and Richard D. Crisp (New York: American Management Association, 1950), Report No. 32, pp. 16–17.

16 This case is adapted with permission from the excellent article by Dr. Ernst A. Tirmann, ''Should Your Marketing Be Audited?'' *European Business*, Autumn 1971, pp. 49–56.

17 Sam R. Goodman, *Increasing Corporate Profitability* (New York: Ronald Press, 1982), Chap. 1.

Company Index

A

A&P (Great Atlantic & Pacific Tea Company), 75, 225, 468, 558
ACE hardware, 562
Acorn (C.A.C.I.), 269
Advertising Checking Bureau, 106, 112
Alabe Products, 288
Allen-Bradley Company, 244, 414
Allied Stores, 563
American Airlines, 109–14, 120, 560
American Bakeries, 569
American Bakers Association, 743
American Brands, Inc., 378
American Can Company, 37
American Cyanamid Company, 378, 753
American Express Company, 463
American Hospital Supply Corp., 104, 213, 669, 721
American Marketing Association, 11
American Oil, 152
American Stores, 555
Amtrak, 30
Anheuser-Busch, Inc., 173, 465, 470, 637, 649, 659
Apple Computer Company, 2, 135, 163, 194, 321, 341, 408, 457
Arm & Hammer Baking Soda, 320–21, 350, 360
Armour & Company, 469
Armstrad computers, 524
Armstrong Cork Company, 326

Armstrong Rubber Company, 35
Arthur Andersen & Company, 575
AT&T (American Telephone & Telegraph Co.), 24, 155, 321, 381, 665, 721
Atari, 16, 337
Athlete's Foot sport shoes, 556
Atlas typewriters (disguised name), 66–75
Avis, Inc., 314, 321, 330, 338, 547
Avon Products, Inc., 23, 135, 537, 550, 559–61

B

Banana Republic Travel & Safari Clothing, 567
Bang & Olufsen, 462
Bantam Books, 377
Baskin-Robbins Ice Cream, 377
Bausch & Lomb, 252
Bean, L. L., Inc., 20
Beatrice Foods (BCI Holding Corp)., 405
Beecham, 3, 30, 239, 292, 304, 548
Bell Industries (Laboratories), 156, 412
Bell regional communications companies, 321, 667
Benetton, 566
BERI surveys, 389
Bic Corporation, 135
Bissell Company, consumer preference measurements, 422–24
Black & Decker Mfg. Company, 401–2
H & R Block, 479, 547

Bloomingdale's, 556, 558, 559, 566
Blue Bell, Inc., 104
BMW automobiles, 455, 460
Boeing Company, 155, 281, 320, 378
Book-of-the-Month Club, 537
Borden, Inc., 157, 225, 464
Boston Consulting Group (BCG), 40–41, 43, 62, 247, 311
Bowmar calculators, 357, 456–57
Braniff Airways, Inc., 483
Bristol-Myers Company, 323, 366, 407
British Petroleum, 378
Brookstone Company, 566
Bulova Watch Company, 386
Burger King Corporation, 17, 321, 489, 536, 547, 602, 619, 622
Burke Marketing Services, 112
Burnett, Leo, Company, 362, 623, 659
Burroughs Corporation, Distribution Services, 583
Burson-Marsteller public relations, 661

C

Calvin Klein, 466, 564
Campbell Soup Company, 287, 327, 357, 395, 407, 466, 467, 546
Canada Dry, 649
Canon, 57, 490–91
Capitol Records, 377
Carrier Corp., 39
Case, J. I., 230, 328, 332

Caterpillar, Inc., 23, 38, 59, 215, 389
Charles Schwab, 483, 549
Chase Econometric, 273
Chase Manhattan Corporation, 314, 721
Cherry Electrical Products, 543
Chesebrough-Ponds, 471
Christian Dior, 465
Chrysler Corporation, 1, 155, 214, 285, 324, 460, 649, 657
Ciba-Geigy, 381, 396
Citicorp (Citibank), 27, 314, 484, 486, 549, 721, 722
Cluster Plus, Donnelley M.I.S., 269
CMC International, 388
Coca-Cola Company, 29, 238, 302, 305, 314, 319, 321, 322, 340, 357, 378, 380, 391, 394, 397, 402, 434–35, 471, 547, 548, 551, 579, 607, 618, 620
Colgate-Palmolive Company, 239, 292, 294, 334, 337, 407, 432, 467
Columbia Pictures, 39
Computer Technology Corp., 156
Computerland, 548, 558
Concorde Airline, 407, 435
Conn Organ Company, 537
Continental Illinois NB & T Company, 27
Control Data Corp., 156, 378
Corning Glass Works, 381
CPC International, Inc., 378, 407
Cray Research, 252
Cross, A. T., 394, 395
Curtis Candy Company, 291

D

Daimler-Benz, 384
Dalton Booksellers, 657
Data General Corp., 455
Data Resources, 273
Datsun, 61, 462
Dayco Corporation, 543
Dayton-Hudson Corp., 563
DEC computers, 328–29
Deere & Company, 23, 328, 332, 378, 455, 465
Defense Department, 229
Del Monte Corp., 248, 327
Delta Air Lines, Inc., 1, 23, 59, 486
Diamond Crystal Salt, 339
Digital Equipment Corp., 156, 455
Direct Marketing Association, 559
Disney, Walt, Productions, Disneyland, 309–10, 463, 466, 486, 488
Domino's Pizza, 569
Dow Chemical Company, 24, 37, 155, 378, 411
Doyle Dane Bernbach, 161
Dr Pepper, 551
du Pont de Nemours, E. I., 15, 37, 139, 156, 214, 246, 290, 320, 407, 429, 497–98, 506, 543, 641, 714–15, 753

E

Eastern Airlines, 628
Eastman Kodak Company, 16, 155, 214, 225, 230, 322, 338, 378, 415, 471, 491, 516–17, 524, 546, 577, 659, 668
Edelman, Daniel J., Inc., 658
Edison Brothers, 303

Electrolux, 397, 561, 606
Electrophonic, 78
Elgin National Watch Company, 14
Encyclopedia Britannica, 39
Endicott Johnson, 415
Epson Corporation, 540
Exxon Corp., 378, 397

F

Fairchild Camera and Instrument Corp., 60, 349
Family First Casket Outlet, 569
Federated Department Stores, 555, 563
Fiberglas, 468
Filene's Department Store, 556
Firestone Tire & Rubber Companys, 378, 466
Fleischmann, 510
Ford Motor Company, 2–3, 34, 38, 58, 61, 174, 202, 214, 235, 248, 251, 279–80, 284–85, 288, 290–91, 322, 324, 378, 457, 540, 547, 551, 600, 602, 649
Foremost-McKesson, 574
47th Street Photo (N.Y.C.), 567
Franklin Mint, 532
Freightliner, 58
Frigidaire, 468
Frito-Lay (PepsiCo), 1
Fuji Photo Film Company, 321, 338, 524, 659
Fujitsu, 252, 381
Fuller Brush Company, 561

G

Gallup & Robinson, Inc., 639
Gap, The, 556
General Electric Company (GE), 23, 29, 35, 39, 40, 43–46, 51, 62, 78, 219, 240, 248, 271, 334, 349, 447, 451, 453, 467, 486, 548, 579–80, 669, 742–44
General Foods Corp., 23, 122, 248, 287–88, 363–64, 380, 395, 396, 407, 410, 428–29, 560, 617, 708–9, 722, 753
General Mills, Inc., 84, 122, 327, 411, 560, 606
General Motors (GM) Corp., 4, 5, 15, 19, 22, 29, 35, 52, 59, 61–62, 160, 215–17, 235, 251, 279, 282, 284–85, 289, 290–91, 302, 303, 319, 321, 325, 327, 342, 381, 389, 397, 455–57, 459, 463, 469, 477, 505, 516, 518, 529, 550, 551, 617, 649, 669, 670, 721
Genesco, Inc., line brands, 467
Georgia-Pacific Corp., 327
Gerber Products Company, 38, 144, 145, 389, 483
Giant Foods, Inc., 28
Gillette Company, 248, 249, 319, 321, 333, 334, 377, 378, 394, 524, 546, 656, 674
Good Housekeeping, 422–23
B. F. Goodrich Company, 466
Goodyear Tire & Rubber Company, 34, 155, 209, 230, 378, 395, 466
Gould Corp., 244, 408
W. R. Grace, 560
W. W. Grainger, 574
Great Lakes Terminal & Transport, Inc. (GLT&T), 575

GTE (General Telephone & Electronics Corp.), 381
Gucci's, 387, 397, 466
Gulf Oil Corp., 389

H

Hallmark cards, 357, 380, 711
Hamm, 470–71
Harley Davidson, 1, 24, 217, 456, 466, 732
Harris Trust & Savings Bank (Chicago), 27, 484
Harrod's of London, 566
Hart Schaffner & Marx, 465
Heidrick and Shruggles, Inc., 2
H. J. Heinz Company, 174, 325, 327, 336, 338, 339, 396, 466, 467, 714
Helena Rubinstein, 145
Helene Curtis Industries, 335
Hendry Corporation, 286
Hergenrather & Company, 540
Hershey Foods Corporation, 136–42, 164, 170
Hertz Corp., 314, 321, 331, 338, 547, 601, 627
Hesston, 328
Heublein, 472, 524
Hewlett-Packard Company, 1, 21, 241, 301, 342, 456–57
Hill and Knowlton, 661
Hills Brothers, 627
Hippopotamus Food Stores, 569
Hitachi, 3
Hoffman-LaRoche, 398
Holiday Corporation (Holiday Inns), 39, 549, 550
Homart, 467
Honda Motor Company, LTD, American, 135, 190, 235, 259, 285, 340, 377, 469
Honeywell, Inc., 156, 335, 458
Hoover Vacuum Cleaner Company, 606
Howard Johnson Company, 547
J. L. Hudson, 494
Humana, Inc., 659
Hunt's Foods, 325, 336, 338, 339, 407
Hyatt Hotel, 480
Hyatt Legal Services, 548

I

IBM (International Business Machines) Corporation, 2, 18, 21, 23, 59–60, 66–68, 106, 155, 175, 185, 188–90, 194, 252, 296, 302, 303, 319, 321, 322, 328–31, 334, 335, 338, 378, 383, 386, 401, 402, 446–48, 455, 460, 465, 520, 524, 548, 550, 665, 669, 674, 675, 689, 720, 744
Illinois Central Railroad, 711
Independent Grocers Alliance (IGA), 562
Information Resources, Inc., 119, 654
International Harvester Company, 1, 24, 57, 58, 75, 217, 328, 497
International Hough Company, 388
International Minerals and Chemicals, 39
Italian Swiss Colony, 627
ITT (International Telephone & Telegraph) Corp., 378

J

Jerold Panas, Young & Panners, Inc., 416
Jewel Food Stores, 322–23, 464, 521
Johnson & Johnson, 144, 145, 252, 335, 393, 410, 548, 656, 753
Johnson, S. C., & Son, 334

K

K mart Corp., 135, 451, 555, 558, 559, 569, 617
Kasle Steel, 216
Kellogg Company, 378, 380, 467
Kerrybrook Clothing, 467
Kinney Shoe Stores (F. W. Woolworth), 558–59, 563
Kodak (see Eastman Kodak)
Komatsu Construction, 332
Kraft Foods Company, 248, 397, 471, 548
Kroger Company stores, 555

L

Lamar Savings Bank of Texas, 548
Lamborghini, 383
Lane Bryant, 566
Leading Edge Computers, 524
L'eggs, 471, 650
Lever Brothers, 239, 407, 612, 635
Levi Strauss & Company, 60, 135, 468, 564
Life Savers, 469
Lilly, Eli, & Company, 155
The Limited, Inc., 2, 135, 558, 564, 566
Lincoln Electric, 221
Lipton Tea, 377
Little, Arthur D., management consulting, 318
Litton Industries, 405
Lockheed Corp., 273
Loehmann's, 566
Lucky Stores, Inc., 555

M

MAC Group, 549
Mack Trucks, 58
I. Magnin department stores, 556
Magnavox Consumer Electronics, 78, 80
Market Facts, Inc., 112
Market Research Corporation of America, 106, 112
Marriott Corp., 21, 23, 486, 649
Mars Candy Co., 140
Marshall Field, 415, 556, 558, 568
Martin, Jeffrey, Inc., 366
Massey-Ferguson, Inc., 332
Mattel Company, 395
Max Factor & Company, 402
Mayo Clinic, 484
Maytag Company, 240
Mazda automobiles, 16, 159, 462
McDonald's Corporation, 1, 23, 37, 59–60, 135, 148, 174, 280, 319, 321, 331, 378, 380, 387, 394, 395, 402, 437, 481, 486, 489, 529, 536, 538, 547, 548, 550, 563, 606, 619–20, 622, 656, 720, 744

McDonnell-Douglas Corp., 155, 281
McGraw-Hill Research, 272
MCI Communications, 321
McKinsey & Company, 59, 387, 509
Mead Corporation, 104, 714
Mennen, 407
Mercedes-Benz, 3, 58, 235, 280, 285, 325, 328, 338, 377, 378, 449, 459
Merck & Company, Inc., 155, 412
Merrill Lynch & Company, 549
MGM/United Artists Communications, 463
Michelin Tire Company, 34–35, 321, 330
Micrin, 429
Microelectronics, 156
Midas Muffler, 491
Miller Brewing Company, 135, 293–94, 333, 336, 338, 470, 604, 622
Miller, Herman, 462, 490
Minnetonka, Inc., 180
Minolta, 398
Missouri-Pacific Railroad, 39
Mitsubishi, 378, 459
Mobil Corporation, 378
Monsanto Company, 396
Montgomery Ward, 271, 319, 330
Morton's Salt, 192, 339
Motorola, Inc., 321, 459

N

National Automatic Merchandising Association, 561
National Bureau of Economic Research, 271
National Cash Register Company, 396
National Lead, 272
Navistar International, 58
Neiman-Marcus, 559
Nestlé, 30, 140, 290, 377, 753
Nielsen Company, A. C., 106, 107, 147, 226, 243, 268, 350, 648
Nikon Company, 448
Nippon Steel, 378
Nissan Motor, 285
Nixdorf, 30
Norelco, 377
Northwest Airlines, 325–26

O

O'Brien Candy Company, 751–52
Ogilvy and Mather, 625
Olivetti Corporation of America, 66, 68, 381, 385
Opinion Research Corporation, 272
Osborne computers, 357
Osco Drug Stores (Jewel Stores), 323
Oster blenders, 459

P

PACCAR trucks, 58
Pan Am World Airways, 378, 628
Panasonic Company, 78, 516
Paramount Pictures Corp., 656
Parker Hannifin Corporation, 105, 543
Patio Foods, 433

Penney Company, J. C., 17, 248, 466, 491, 548, 555
Pennwalt Corporation, 272
Penthouse, 319
People's Express, 483, 518
PepsiCo, Inc. (Pepsi-Cola), 2, 152, 235, 305, 314, 321, 330, 339, 340, 360, 384, 385, 434, 601, 602, 649
Perdue Farms, 22, 448
Perrier water, 377
Pfizer Inc., 156, 625
Philip Morris Companies, Inc., 135, 326, 350, 604, 617, 627
Philip Gloeilampenfabrieken, 378
Philips Industries, 3, 380
Phillips Petroleum Company, 468
Piedmont Aviation, 37
Pierre Cardin, 4, 465
Pillsbury Company, 547, 632, 637
Pizza Inn, 551
Playboy Enterprises, Inc., 135, 319, 463
Polaroid Corp., 338, 413, 437, 498, 540, 577, 631
Porsche, 280, 314, 466
Potato Board (PR), 659, 660
Premium Advertisers Association, 653
PRIZM, 269
Procter & Gamble Company (P&G), 23, 29, 107, 108, 135, 173, 193, 239, 292, 319, 321, 331, 365–66, 371–372, 380, 399, 449, 452, 461, 464, 465, 467, 469, 546, 612, 617, 627, 657, 674, 708, 720, 721, 725, 744
Prudential, 296, 674
Publishers' Clearing House, 657
Purex Corporation, 366

Q

Quaker Oats Company, 84, 139, 396, 436, 464, 468–69, 521, 649

R

Radford Community Hospital, 482
Radio Shack, 243, 569
Raleigh Bicycles, 560
Ralston Purina Company, 465
Ramada Inns, Inc., 547
RCA Corp., 156, 334, 349, 407, 415, 458
Red Roof Inns, 627
Rent-a-Wreck, Inc., 342
Revlon, Inc., 39, 248, 252, 430, 446, 606
Reynolds Pen, 357
R. J. Reynolds Industries, Inc., 326
Reynolds Metal Company, 533
Russell Reynolds Associates, 2
Rheingold Brewing Co., 218, 407
Rolex Watches, 341
Rolls-Royce, 458, 460–61
Royal Dutch-Shell Group, 378
Royal Typewriter Company, 68

S

Saatchi & Saatchi, 394
Safeway Stores, Inc., 548, 555

Saks Fifth Avenue, 377, 556, 559
SAMI (Selling Areas-Marketing, Inc.), 107, 112
SAS (Scandanavian Airlines), 22, 23
Schaefer Brewing Co., 293, 628
Schering-Plough Corp., 252
Joseph Schlitz Brewing Company, 294, 470
Schwinn Company, 397
SCM Corporation, 515
Scotch Tape, 468
Scott Paper Company, 407, 469, 649
Seagram & Sons, Joseph E., 548
Sealed Air Corporation, 448
Sears, Roebuck, 37, 51, 152, 240, 271, 319, 342, 391–92, 455, 458, 466, 467, 482, 491, 548, 550, 555, 558, 559, 564, 568, 617, 649, 670
Seiko, 325, 336
Seven-Up Company, 314, 470, 604, 628
Shakey's, 437
Sharper Image, The, 566
Sherwin-Williams Company, 545
Siemens, 378
Signal Companies, 155
Simmons Market Research Bureau, 112
Sindlinger & Company, 272
Singapore Airlines, 483
Singer Company, 24, 75, 149–50, 532
Sloane-Kettering Institute, 484
Smith Corona, 68, 713
Sony Corporation, 3, 36, 78, 80, 135, 237, 377, 387, 394
Southland Corporation, (7–11 stores) 135, 555, 557, 558
Southwestern Company, 561
Sperry Corporation, 156
Sperry-New Holland Company, 328
SRI International, 184
Sprint, 321
Square D, 543
Standard Oil Company, 39
Starch Pretesting Service, 639
Steelcase Inc., 296
Strategic Planning Institute, 327, 460, 489
Suntory Liquors, 289
Survey Research Center, 271

Swift & Company, 396, 468
Swissair, 486

T

Tall Men Shops, 556
Texaco Inc., 558
Texas Instruments Inc. (TI), 13–14, 54, 60, 135, 241, 244, 325, 330, 349, 407, 456–57, 497, 501–3
3M Company, 1, 19, 37, 333, 411, 491, 711–12, 747
Thompson, J. Walter, 661
Tiffany and Company, 494, 558, 559
Timken Corporation, 543
Toshiba Corporation, 3, 321
Toyota Motors, 30, 61, 235, 284, 285, 306, 381
Toys 'R' Us, 569
Trade-Plus, 549
Transitron, 60, 349
Travelers Corporation, 106
True Value Hardware, 562
Tupperware, 561
TWA (Trans World Airlines), 378, 753
Typetronic, 68

U

Unilever, 3, 30, 38, 378
Uniroyal, Inc., 35, 37
United Buying Service, 562
U.S. Bureau of Labor Statistics, 147
U.S. Gypsum, 521
U.S. Postal Service, 30
U.S. Time Company, 291–92, 338, 537
United Technologies Corporation, 155

V

Victor Talking Machine Company, 415 (see also RCA)
Videotext, 560

Volkswagen, 61, 280, 284, 285, 301, 377, 627
Volvo, Inc., 30, 58, 61, 285, 378

W

Wal-Mart Stores, Inc., 564, 580
Wanamaker, John, 494, 604
Warner Electric Brake and Clutch, 412
Warner-Lambert Company, 402, 429
Wendy's, 314, 602
Western Auto, 562
Westinghouse Electric Corp., 248, 326, 330, 400, 411
Wharton Econometric, 273
Whirlpool Corporation, 143, 240, 465
White Hen Pantries, 557
White Motor Corp., 58
Wide Area Telephone Service (WATS), 560
Wilkinson Sword USA, 667
Witco Chemical Company, 548
F. W. Woolworth & Company, 493, 563
World Book Encyclopedia, 561
Wm. Wrigley Jr., 529
Wrangler Womenswear, 104

X

Xerox Corporation, 24, 39, 67, 319, 333, 338, 357, 378, 402, 456, 483, 559, 669, 714

Y

Yamaha, 339, 340
Yankelovich, Skelly & White, 160
Young & Rubicam, 661

Z

Zenith Electronics Corporation, 24, 77–83, 88, 97, 243, 398, 518

Name Index

A

Aaker, David A., 621, 643 *n*3
Abell, Derek F., 39, 40, 61, 64 *nn*12, 13, 20, 91
Abler, Robert A., 463, 474 *n*6
Abler, Ronald, 534, 553 *n*6
Abrams, Bill, 161, 172 *n*30
Achenbaum, Alvin A., 433, 444 *n*27
Ackerman, Martin, quoted, 347
Ackoff, Russell L., 87, 100 *n*5; 265, 277 *n*4
Adams, John S., 534, 553 *n*6
Adler, Lee, 547, 553 *n*19
Aguilar, Francis Joseph, 105, 132 *n*5
Albrecht, Karl, 19, 32 *nn*18, 19, 20; 476, 493 *n*1
Alderson, Wroe, 530, 553 *n*4
Alexander, Ralph S., 221, 364, 376 *n*21
Alford, Charles L., 413, 444 *n*12
Alpert, Mark L., 191, 200, 207 *n*30
Alsop, Ronald, 174, 206 *n*4
Alter, Stewart, 174, 206 *n*5
Ames, B. Charles, 296, 316 *n*13; 715, 728 *n*8
Amstutz, Arnold E., 124, 133 *n*29
Anderson, James C., 105, 132 *n*7; 221, 232 *n*21; 574, 575, 585 *n*18; 679, 700 *n*18
Anderson, M. J., Jr., 328, 345 *n*11
Andreasen, Alan R., 30, 32 *n*26; 284, 316 *n*2
Ansoff, H. Igor, 46–47, 64 *n*16; 347, 348, 375 *n*1
Arbeit, Stephen P., 280, 316 *n*1

Arndt, Johan, 690, 700 *n*27
Arnold, John E., 413, 443 *n*10
Arpan, Jeffrey S., 386, 403 *n*4
Ashcraft, Laurie, 180
Assael, Henry, 191, 207 *n*25
Athos, Anthony G., 59, 64 *n*18
Austin, Nancy, 1, 31 *n*2
Ayal, Igal, 386, 403 *n*6; 393, 404 *n*11

B

Bacas, Harry, 143, 172 *n*9
Bacharach, Samuel B., 691, 701 *n*34
Backhaus, Klaus, 222, 232 *n*22
Bagozzi, Richard P., 600, 616 *n*13
Bailey, Earl L., 407, 443 *n*3
Ballachey, Egerton L., 190, 207 *n*24
Ballou, Ronald H., 583, 586 *n*21
Banting, Peter G., 490, 493 *n*17
Barksdale, Hiram C., 481, 493 *n*8
Bartlett, Christopher A., 400, 404 *n*15
Bass, Frank M., 127, 133 *n*31; 294, 316 *n*11; 426, 676, 700 *n*16
Bass, Stephen J., 555, 585 *n*1
Bates, Albert D., 555, 585 *n*1
Bateson, John E. G., 476, 493 *n*1
Bauer, Raymond A., 161, 172 *n*31; 201, 207 *n*37; 591, 616 *n*7
Bayer, Judy, 655, 662 *n*23
Bayes, Barry L., 203, 207 *n*42
Behrens, William W., III, 144, 151, 172 *nn*7, 13

Beik, Leland L., 741, 755 *n*9
Belch, George E., 600, 616 *n*13
Belk, Russell W., 284, 316 *n*2
Bell, David E., 263, 277 *n*2
Bell, Martin L., 28, 32 *n*23; 289, 316 *n*6
Bennett, Peter D., 672, 700 *n*8
Bennett, Sidney, 500, 527 *n*5
Benson, Lissa, 28, 32 *n*24
Berelson, Bernard, 188, 207 *n*22; 603, 616 *n*20
Bernbach, William, 622
Bernett, Amanda, 114, 133 *n*12
Berning, Carol K., 204, 207 *n*47
Bernstein, Peter W., 184
Berry, Leonard L., 476, 479, 482, 484–85, 493 *nn*1, 5, 10, 15
Best, Roger J., 273, 278 *n*12
Bettman, James R., 194, 207 *n*27
Biggadike, Ralph, 344
Bishop, William S., 210, 232 *n*3
Black, George, 655, 662 *n*25
Blackwell, Roger D., 116, 133 *n*13; 194, 207 *n*28; 564, 585 *n*11; 599, 616 *n*12
Blake, Robert R., 687–88
Blattberg, Robert, 425, 444 *n*21
Bloom, David E., 150, 172 *n*12
Bloom, Paul N., 143, 329, 345 *n*15; 482, 493 *n*11
Bonoma, Thomas V., 295, 296, 316 *n*13; 724, 725, 728 *n*17
Booz, Allen & Hamilton surveys, 328, 345 *n*13; 405–6, 408–9, 412, 443 *nn*1, 2, 8
Borch, Fred J., 17, 32 *n*16

Borden, Neil H., Jr., 225, 233 *n*25
Boulding, Kenneth, 151
Bowman, Russell D., 653, 662 *n*18
Boyd, Harper W., Jr., 90, 100 *n*8; 185, 200, 206 *n*16; 207 *n*34; 429, 444 *n*25; 447, 474 *n*1
Boyle, Peter, 211, 232 *n*7
Bragg, Arthur, 540
Bramel, Dana, 202, 207 *n*41
Brinberg, David, 179, 206 *n*9
Britt, Steuart Henderson, 457, 474 *n*4; 630, 643 *n*19
Brooks, John, 181, 206 *n*13
Brown, Bert R., 691, 700 *n*28, 701 *n*33
Brown, George H., 294, 316 *n*12
Brown, Glen M., 655, 662 *n*24
Brown, James R., 209, 232 *n*2
Brown, Rex V., 127, 133 *n*31
Brown, Robert George, 647, 662 *n*3
Brown, Sidney E., 625, 643 *n*16
Brown, William P., 621, 630, 643 *n*4
Bruning, Edward R., 123, 133 *n*19
Bruno, Albert V., 716, 728 *n*10
Bucklin, Louis P., 534–35, 542, 553 *nn*8, 9
Buell, Victor P., 388, 404 *n*8; 712, 728 *n*5
Bultez, Alain V., 124, 133 *n*23
Burdick, Richard K., 213, 232 *n*10
Burnett, John J., 599
Butler, Rhett W., 307
Buzby, Stephen L., 741, 755 *n*9
Buzzell, Robert D., 227, 233 *n*30; 327, 330, 345 *nn*9, 10; 350, 355, 375 *nn*5, 15, 16, 17; 414, 444 *n*14; 641, 644 *n*32
Bybee, H. Malcolm, 624, 643 *n*14

C

Cacioppo, John R., 200, 207 *n*34
Calder, Bobby J., 188, 207 *n*23
Cannon, Hugh M., 269
Canton, Irving D., 482, 493 *n*14
Cardozo, Richard N., 222, 233 *n*24; 295, 296, 316 *n*13
Cardwell, John J., 98, 100 *n*13
Carlson, Chester, 415
Carlzon, Jon, 22, 23
Carman, James M., 621, 643 *n*3
Carnegie, Dale, 686
Carson, Rachel, 142, 151, 172 *n*14
Cartwright, Dorwin, 591, 616 *n*8
Catry, Bernard, 332, 345 *n*18
Cattin, Philippe, 124, 133 *n*21
Cavalier, Richard, 700 *n*22
Cavanaugh, Richard E., 343, 346 *n*28
Center, Allen H., 655, 662 *n*24
Chevalier, Michel, 332, 345 *n*18; 651, 662 *n*13
Choate, Robert, 142
Chou, Ya-Lun, 274, 278 *n*13
Churchill, Gilbert A., Jr., 211–12, 232 *n*8; 680, 700 *n*20
von Clausewitz, Carl, 322, 345 *n*4
Clayton, Alden G., 647, 662 *n*5
Clemons, Eric K., 217
Clewett, Richard M., 712, 728 *n*5
Clifford, Donald K., 343, 346 *n*28
Cohen, Herb, 691, 701 *n*35
Cohen, Joel B., 198, 207 *n*33
Cohen, William A., 239
Coleman, Richard P., 178, 289, 316 *n*6

Colley, Russell H., 619, 643 *n*1
Comer, James M., 674, 700 *n*13
Cook, Victor, 350, 351, 375 *nn*4, 6
Cooper, Arnold C., 328, 345 *n*12
Coppett, John, 560, 585 *n*4
Corey, E. Raymond, 528–29, 553 *n*1; 708–9, 714, 728 *nn*1, 7
Cox, Donald F., 201, 207 *n*37; 591, 616 *n*7
Cox, William E., Jr., 350, 351, 375 *n*9
Craig, C. Samuel, 568, 585 *n*15; 591, 598, 599, 600, 616 *nn*5, 11, 14
Cravens, David W., 566
Crawford, C. Merle, 350, 375 *n*9
Crawford, John C., 674, 700 *n*12
Cribbin, James, 689, 700 *n*25
Crisp, Richard D., 747, 755 *n*15
Crissy, William J. E., 306–7, 317 *n*24, 686, 700 *n*23
Crosby, Philip B., 330, 345 *n*16
Cross, James, 221
Crutchfield, Richard S., 190, 207 *n*24
Cunningham, Isabella C. M., 686, 700 *n*23
Cunningham, William H., 686, 700 *n*23
Curhan, Ronald C., 651, 662 *n*13
Cutlip, Scott M., 655, 662 *n*24

D

Dalkey, Norman, 273, 277 *n*12
Daltas, Arthur, Jr., 736, 737, 755 *n*7
Davidson, William R., 555, 585 *n*1
Davies, R. L., 568, 585 *n*14
Davis, Harry L., 180, 206 *n*12; 688
Davis, Robert T., 90, 100 *n*8
Davis, Stanley M., 60, 64 *n*19; 282
Dawson, Leslie M., 28, 32 *n*24
Day, Ellen, 492, 493 *n*19
Day, George S., 44, 46, 64 *n*15
Day, Ralph L., 202, 203, 207 *n*40; 303, 317 *n*20; 672, 700 *n*8
Deal, Terrence E., 60, 64 *n*19
Dehmlow, Louis, 142
Dempsey, William A., 220, 232 *n*18
Denenberg, Herbert S., 142
Derrick, Frederick W., 182
Dewar, Robert, 713
Dhalla, Nariman K., 371, 376 *n*26
Dichter, Ernest, 186, 206 *n*19; 214, 232 *n*13
Dickinson, Roger A., 226, 233 *n*29
Dietvorst, Thomas F., 204, 207 *n*47
Dillon, William R., 123, 133 *n*19
Dizard, John W., 384
Dobler, Donald W., 691, 701 *n*37
Dodson, Joe A., 654, 662 *n*22
Dolan, Robert J., 332, 345 *n*17
Donnelly, James H., Jr., 203, 207 *n*46; 483, 493 *n*13
Dorfman, Robert, 96, 100 *n*10
Dougherty, Philip H., 637, 644 *n*27
Douglas, Susan P., 402, 404 *n*16
Dowst, Somerby, 217
Doyle, Peter, 367
Dreyfuss, Joel, 560, 585 *n*4
Drucker, Peter F., quoted, 16, 32 *n*15; 37, 61, 64 *n*8; 74, 100 *n*2; 134, 161, 172 *nn*1, 32
Dubinsky, Alan J., 674, 700 *n*13
Duncan, Tom, 656, 662 *n*26
Dunphy, Dermot, 448
Dychtwald, Ken, 174, 206 *n*3

E

Eagly, Alice H., 591, 616 *n*6
Ehrlich, Paul R., 151
Eiglier, Pierre, 476, 493 *n*1
Eisenhower, Dwight D., quoted, 65
El-Ansary, Adel I., 529–30, 550, 553 *nn*2, 23; 569, 585 *n*16
Ely, E. S., 2, 3, 32 *nn*5, 6
Emerson, Ralph Waldo, quoted, 32 *n*11
Emery, Albert W., quoted, 234
Emery, C. William, 28, 32 *n*23
Engel, Ernest, 151
Engel, James F., 194, 207 *n*28; 599, 616 *n*12
Enis, Ben M., 332, 345 *n*17
Eovaldi, Thomas L., 158, 172 *n*27; 211, 232 *n*4
Erickson, Gary M., 511, 527 *n*12
Evans, Franklin B., 291, 316 *n*7; 687–88
Ezell, Hazel F., 558

F

Fahey, Lian, 402
Faris, Charles W., 211, 218, 232 *nn*6, 17
Farley, John U., 201, 207 *n*35; 672, 700 *n*8
Farris, Paul W., 511, 527 *n*14; 619, 643 *n*2
Feick, Lawrence F., 179, 206 *n*9
Feinstein, Selwyn, 119, 133 *n*14
Feldman, Laurence P., 28, 32 *n*23; 366, 376 *n*25
Fenn, Dan H., Jr., 161, 172 *n*31
Ferber, Robert, 96, 100 *n*9
Fern, Edward F., 209, 232 *n*2
Festinger, Leon, 202, 203, 207 *nn*41, 43
Finch, Peter, 104, 132 *n*4
Fishbein, Martin, 198, 201, 207 *nn*33, 36
Fisher, Roger, 692–94, 701 *nn*40, 41
Fisk, George, 28, 32 *n*24
Fiske, John, 591, 616 *n*9
Flax, Steven, 248–49
Fogg, C. David, 332, 345 *n*18
Forbis, John L., 509
Ford, Henry, 14
Ford, Neil M., 680, 700 *n*20
Fornell, Claes, 357, 736, 755 *n*6
Forrester, Jay W., 130, 133 *n*34; 635, 637–38, 643 *n*24, 644 *n*28
Foster, David, 337
Foster, George, 239, 255 *n*5
Fourt, Louis A., 426
Fox, Richard J., 492, 493 *n*19
Fram, Eugene H., 105, 132 *n*6
Freeman, Cyril, 609, 616 *n*33
Frey, Albert Wesley, 71, 100 *n*1; 219, 604, 605, 616 *nn*24, 25
Frey, John B., 357–58, 375 *n*18
Friars, Eileen M., 559
Frons, Marc, 435
Fu, Marilyn Y. C., 386, 403 *n*4
Fuld, Leonard M., 234, 255 *n*1

G

Gafin, Arniram, 201, 207 *n*37
Galbraith, John Kenneth, 142
Gale, Bradley T., 327, 345 *n*9
Gardner, Burleigh, 302, 317 *n*19
Garreau, Joel, 147–49

Gaskin, S. P., 323
Gatignon, Hubert, 442, 444 *n*34
Gaudet, H., 603, 616 *n*20
Gautschi, David A., 568, 585 *n*15
Gelb, Betsy D., 435
Gelb, Gabriel M., 435
George, William R., 481, 483, 493 *nn*8, 13
Ghosh, Avijit, 568, 585 *n*15
Giddy, Ian H., 380, 403 *n*3
Giese, Thomas D., 712, 728 *n*5
Gilbert, J., 180
Gilly, Mary C., 203, 207 *n*45
Gilman, Hank, 174, 206 *n*3
Gist, Ronald R., 562, 585 *n*6
Glaskowsky, N. A., 554
Golanty, John, 425, 444 *n*21
Goldman, Arieh, 252, 253, 399, 404 *n*14
Goldstein, Matthew, 123, 133 *n*19
Goldstucker, Jac L., 350, 375 *n*5
Gonik, Jacob, 273, 277 *n*11
Goodman, Charles S., quoted, 208
Goodman, Sam R., 753, 755 *n*17
Gordon, William J. J., 414–15
Gould, Peter, 534, 553 *n*6
Graf, Franklin H., 226, 233 *nn*26, 27
Graham, John L., 210, 232 *n*3
Gray, Frank B., 715, 728 *n*9
Green, Paul E., 197, 200, 207 *n*32; 422, 424, 523
Greenberg, Herbert M., 674, 700 *n*11
Greenland, Leo, 157, 172 *n*26; 628, 643 *n*17
Greer, Thomas V., 30, 32 *n*27
Gregor, William T., 559, 746, 747, 755 *nn*12, 14
Greyser, Stephen A., 143
Groeneveld, Leonard, 222, 232 *n*22
Gronroos, Christian, 482, 493 *nn*9, 12
Gross, Irwin, 623, 643 *n*12
Gubar, George, 182
Gupta, Askok K., 718, 728 *n*11
Guzzardi, Walter, Jr., 218, 232 *n*16

H

Haire, Mason, 121, 133 *n*16
Haley, Russell J., 292, 434, 444 *n*28
Hall, William G., 432, 444 *n*26
Hall, William K., 58
Hamelman, Paul W., 365, 376 *n*22
Hamermesh, Richard G., 328, 345 *n*11; 350, 375 *n*7
Hanan, Mark, 415, 444 *n*18; 666, 689, 700 *nn*4, 25; 714, 728 *n*6
Hansen, Richard W., 203, 207 *n*45
Harberger, Arnold C., 501, 527 *n*8
Harding, Murray, 214, 232 *n*13
Harper, Marion, quoted, 101
Harrell, Steve, 35, 64 *n*5
Harrigan, Kathryn Rudie, 238, 255 *n*2; 365, 376 *nn*23, 24
Harris, Brian F., 475 *n*8
Harris, Catherine L., 132 *n*3
Harris, J. E., 328, 345 *n*11
Hartley, John, 591, 616 *n*9
Hartley, William D., 399, 404 *n*13
Harvey, Michael G., 427, 444 *n*22
Hauser, John R., 124, 133 *n*22; 323
Heany, Donald F., 327, 345 *n*9
Heckert, J. B., 681, 700 *n*21
Heenan, D. A., 389
Heiser, Herman, 689, 700 *n*25

Helmer, Olaf, 273, 277 *n*12
Henderson, Bruce, 247–48, 255 *n*8
Henderson, Peter L., 625, 643 *n*16
Hendon, Donald W., 179, 206 *n*8; 695
Henion, Karl E., II, 153, 172 *n*17
Hensel, James S., 116, 133 *n*13
Hertz, David B., 428, 444 *n*24
Herzberg, Frederick, 186, 187, 206 *n*21
Heskett, J. L., 554
Higgins, Kevin T., 646, 662 *n*1
Hill, Richard, 221
Hills, Gerald E., 566
Hind, James F., 625, 643 *n*16
Hindin, Russell, 211, 232 *n*5
von Hippel, Eric, 321, 345 *n*3; 412, 414, 421, 443 *n*9; 444 *n*14
Hirschman, Albert O., 203, 207 *n*44
Hirshman, Elizabeth, 181, 206 *n*14
Hise, Richard T., 365, 376 *n*22
Hisrich, Robert D., 605, 616 *n*27; 625, 643 *n*15
Hlarac, T. E., Jr., 133 *n*23
Hlavacek, James D., 296, 316 *n*13; 574, 585 *n*18
Holbrook, Morris, 181, 206 *n*14
Hollander, Stanley C., 555, 585 *n*2
Honomichi, Jack, 435
Hood, Robert, 686, 700 *n*24
Hopkins, David S., 407, 410, 443 *nn*3, 7
Hormer, La Rue T., 45
Hornby, William H., 26, 32 *n*22
Horton, Raymond L., 591, 616 *n*7
Hostage, G. M., 480, 493 *n*6
Houston, Franklin S., 28, 32 *n*23
Hovland, Carl I., 598, 600, 601, 616 *nn*13, 16
Howard, John A., 191, 194, 196, 201, 207 *nn*25, 28, 29, 35
Howell, Charles D., 103, 132 *n*2
Huff, David L., 568, 585 *n*15
Hughes, G. David, 434, 444 *n*28
Hulbert, James M., 731, 755 *n*1

I

Iacocca, Lee, 2–3, 656
Ivancevich, John M., 203, 207 *n*46
Ivie, R. M., 554

J

Jackson, Barbara Bund, 696–97
Jackson, Donald W., Jr., 213, 232 *n*10
Jacoby, Jacob, 204, 207 *n*47
James, John C., 487
Jatusripitak, Somkid, 393, 402, 404 *n*11
Jobs, Steve, 2
Johanson, Jan, 393, 404 *n*10
Johansson, Johny K., 511, 527 *n*12
Johnson, S. C., 47, 64 *n*16
Jones, Conrad, 47, 64 *n*16
Jones, Michael H., 210, 232 *n*3

K

Kalwani, Manohar U., 286, 316 *n*3
Kanuk, Leslie Lazar, 175, 206 *n*7
Kaplan, Robert M., 433, 444 *n*27

Karass, Chester L., 691, 701 *nn*35, 36
Kassarjian, Harold H., 185, 206 *n*17
Katz, Elihu, 441, 444 *n*33
Katz, Gerald M., 124, 133 *n*22
Kaven, William H., 666, 700 *n*4
Kearney, A. T., 583, 586 *n*21
Keefer, Bill, 412
Keegan, Warren J., 395, 404 *n*12
Keeney, Ralph L., 263, 277 *n*2
Keith, Janet E., 213, 232 *n*10
Keith, Robert J., 17, 32 *n*16
Kelly, Eugene J., 71, 100 *n*1
Kelman, Herbert C., 601, 616 *n*16
Kennedy, Allan A., 60, 64 *n*19
Kennedy, Gavin, 386, 403 *n*4
Keon, John W., 655, 662 *n*23
Keough, Donald R., 675, 700 *n*14
Kerin, Roger A., 427, 444 *n*22
Kernan, Jerome B., 609, 616 *n*18
Killing, J. Peter, 392, 404 *n*9
Kindel, Stephen, 174, 206 *n*5
Kinnear, Thomas C., 112, 122, 133 *nn*11, 18; 179, 206 *n*9
Klompmaker, Jay E., 434, 444 *n*28
Knee, Derek, 565
Kobrin, Stephen, 389
Koiki, Hisao, 340
Koopman-Iwerna, Agnes M., 187, 207 *n*21
Korenman, Sander D., 150, 172 *n*12
Koten, John, 598, 616 *n*11; 622, 643 *n*8
Kotler, Philip, 13, 30, 32 *n*26; 87, 100 *nn*6, 7; 131, 133 *n*35; 137, 141, 172 *n*3, 4; 202, 207 *n*38; 263, 277 *n*2; 282, 322, 329, 345 *n*5, 15; 365, 366, 376 *nn*22, 25; 385, 402, 437, 444 *n*30; 463, 474 *n*6; 482, 493 *n*11; 534, 553 *n*7; 567, 585 *n*13; 603, 616 *n*19; 622, 643 *n*7; 744, 746, 747, 755 *nn*11, 12, 14
Kovacic, Mary L., 123, 133 *n*19
Kraar, Louis, 389
Krech, David, 190, 207 *n*24
Kreshel, Peggy J., 631, 643 *n*21
Krugman, Herbert E., 193, 207 *n*26; 631, 643 *n*20
Kuehn, Alfred A., 303, 317 *n*20; 636, 643 *n*26
Kurland, Mark A., 234, 246, 255 *n*1

L

La Barbera, Priscilla A., 202, 207 *n*39
Lambin, Jean-Jacques, 87, 100 *n*4
Lancaster, Kent M., 631, 643 *n*21
Land, Edwin H., 413
Landon, E. Laird, Jr., 203
Langeard, Eric, 476, 493 *n*1
Larson, Carl M., 567
Lasswell, Harold D., 588, 616 *n*2
Lavidge, Robert J., 129, 133 *n*33; 432, 444 *n*26; 595
Lawler, Edward J., 691, 701 *n*34
Lazar, William, 71, 100 *n*1
Lazarfeld, Paul F., 441, 444 *n*33; 603, 616 *n*20
Learner, David B., 124, 133 *n*28
Lee, Lamar, 691, 701 *n*37
Lehmann, Donald R., 133 *nn*10, 17; 221, 232 *n*20
Leigh, Thomas W., 124, 133 *n*21
Leighton, David S. R., 404 *n*8
Lele, Miland M., 491, 493 *n*18; 544

Leonard, Stew, 1–2
Lepisto, Lawrence, 181, 206 n14
Lerreche, Jean-Claude, 124, 133 n27
Levinson, Horace C., 120, 133 n15
Levitt, Theodore, 17, 32 n8; 38, 64 n10;
  259–60, 277 n1; 320, 345 n2; 339, 346
  n26; 351, 375 n10; 394–95; 420, 444
  n20; 447, 448, 474 n2; 477, 489, 493
  nn3, 16; 609, 610, 696, 698, 701 n42;
  quoted, 446, 476, 477
Levy, Sidney J., 13; 137, 172 n3; 185, 206
  nn15, 16; 302, 317 n19; 447, 474 n1;
  607, 616 nn28, 29
Liddell-Hart, B. H., 322, 336, 337, 345 n4,
  346 nn22, 25
Lilien, Gary L., 1, 87, 100 n7; 131, 133
  n35; 263, 277 n2; 609–11; 622, 643 n7
Lincoln, John W., 415, 444 nn16, 17
Linda, Gerald, 269
Linfield, Alane E., 182
Little, Arthur D., 46, 318, 345 n1
Little, John D. C., 124, 133 nn23, 25, 26;
  263, 277 n2; 611, 622, 635, 643 n6
Lodish, Leonard M., 124, 133 nn24, 25; 635
Lonsdale, Ronald T., 294, 316 n11
Love, Stephen F., 581, 586 n20
Lovelock, Christopher H., 476, 493 n1; 722,
  728 n16
Lublin, Joann S., 145, 172 n10
Lucas, Darrell B., 630, 643 n19
Luce, R. Duncan, 129, 133 n32
Luck, David J., 709, 728 n3
Lumpkin, James R., 674, 700 n12
Lumsdaine, A. A., 600, 616 n13

M

Maas, Jane, 600, 616 n15
MacKay, David B., 124, 133 n21
Magee, John F., 676, 700 n16
Maher, Philip, 670
Maidique, Modesto A., 412, 443 n8
Maloney, John C., 623, 643 n11
Manoochehri, G. H., 217
Manrai, Lalita, 625–26
Mantrala, Murali K., 202, 207 n38
Markin, Rom J., 196, 207 n29
Marriott, Bill, Jr., 21
Marschner, Donald C., 96, 100 n11
Martilla, John A., 487
Martin, Dennis, 621, 630, 643 n4
Maslow, Abraham, 186, 187, 206 n20; 373
Mason, Joseph Barry, 304, 317 n23; 413,
  444 n12; 558
Mathews, H. Lee, 222, 232 n22
May, Eleanor G., 569, 585 n16
Mayer, David, 674, 700 n11
Mazursky, David, 202, 207 n39
Mazze, Edward M., 365, 376 n22
McAlister, Leigh, 197, 207 n32
McCammon, Bert C., Jr., 541, 542, 548,
  550, 553 nn13, 14, 16, 22, 23
McCann, John M., 131, 133 n35
McCarthy, E. Jerome, 71, 100 n1
McCormick, Ernest J., 480
McCuistion, Tommy J., 574, 585 n18
McDonald, John Dennis, 691, 700 n30
McElroy, Neil H., 708
McFarlan, F. Warren, 217
McGinniss, Joseph, 16, 32 n14
McIntyre, Shelby H., 716, 728 n10

McKelvy, Natalie, 303, 317 n21
McKenzie, R. B., 691, 700 n32
McKitterick, John B., 17, 32 n16
McLaughlin, Robert L., 274, 278 n13
McMurray, Robert N., 663–64, 674, 700
  nn1, 9, 10
McNair, Malcolm P., 555, 585 n2
McVey, Phillip, quoted, 528; 541, 553 nn10,
  11
Meadows, Dennis L., 144, 151, 172 nn7, 13
Meadows, Donella H., 144, 151, 172 nn7,
  13
Mehta, Nitin T., 509
Meidan, Arthur, 124, 133 n24
Merims, Arthur M., 660, 662 n27
Mickwitz, Gosta, 362, 375 n20
Miller, Peter B., 635, 643 n25
Mindak, William A., 141, 172 n4; 624, 643
  n14
Miniard, Paul W., 194, 198, 207 nn28, 33;
  599, 616 n12
Mitchel, F. Kent, 647, 662 n4
Mitchell, Arnold, 162, 172 n33; 184
Mitchell, Paul, 211, 232 n7
Moncrief, William C., III, 663–64, 700 n1
Monroe, Kent B., 521, 527 n17
Montgomery, David B., 106, 124, 125, 133
  nn27, 30; 226, 233 n28; 641, 644 n31
Moore, Thomas, 269
Moore, William L., 252, 255 n11
Moorthy, Sridhar, 691, 700 n29
Moran, William T., 635
Morein, Joseph A., 712, 728 n5
Morgenstern, Oscar, 691, 700 n29
Moriarty, Rowland T., 215, 232 n15; 670
Morrill, John E., 609, 616 n32
Morrison, Donald G., 286, 316 n3
Moschis, George P., 179, 206 n10; 603, 616
  n21
Mossman, Frank H., 306–7, 317 n24
Mouton, Jane S., 687–88
Mueller, Robert W., 226, 233 n26, 27
Muller, Eitan, 352–53
Mullins, Peter L., 736, 755 n5
Murphy, Patrick E., 182, 599
Mushashi, Miyamoto, 322, 345 n4
Myers, James H., 197, 200, 207 n30

N

Nader, Ralph, 61, 142
Naert, Philippe A., 124, 133 n23
Nagle, Thomas T., 499, 500, 527 nn3, 6
Naisbitt, John, 163–64
Naor, Jacob, 30, 32 n28
Narayana, Chem L., 196, 207 n29
Narus, James A., 105, 132 n7; 221, 232
  n21; 543, 574–75, 585 n18; 679, 700
  n18
von Neumann, John, 691, 700 n29
Nevin, John R., 500, 527 n4
Nicosia, Francesco M., 194, 207 n28
Nierenberg, Gerald I., 691, 701 n35
Nimer, Daniel A., 511, 527 n11

O

Oberdick, Larry E., 123, 133 n19
Ogilvy, David, 628, 643 n18
Ohmae, Kenichi, 387

O'Keefe, Frank R., Jr., 35
Oliver, Richard L., 599
Olson, Jerry C., 179, 206 n11
O'Meara, John T., Jr., 418, 444 n19
Osborn, Alex F., 413, 414, 443 n11; 444
  n15
Osgood, C. E., 593, 601, 616 nn10, 17
O'Shaughnessy, John, 221, 232 n20
Ostrom, Lonnie L., 222, 233 n23
Ottesen, Otto, 598
Oxenfeldt, Alfred R., 252, 255 n11; 732,
  747, 755 nn2, 15
Ozanne, Urban B., 211–12, 232 n8

P

Packard, David, 21
Packard, Vance, 142
Page, Albert L., 215, 232 n15; 366, 376 n25
Palda, Kristian S., 275, 278 n15; 640–41,
  644 n30
Panas, Jerold, 416
Panat, Charles, 155, 172 n21
Parasuraman, A., 365, 376 n22; 484–85,
  493, n15
Parsons, Leonard J., 501, 527 n9
Pascale, Richard Tanner, 59, 64 n18
Patel, Peter, 46, 64 n15
Pearson, Andrall E., 710, 728 n4
Peckham, J. O., 640, 644 n29
Pegram, Roger M., 666, 700 n3
Perdue, Frank, 22, 448
Perlmutter, Howard V., 402, 404 n16
Perreault, William D., Jr., 689, 700 n26
Peters, Michael P., 605, 616 n27; 625, 643
  n15
Peters, Thomas J., 1, 2, 31 nn1, 2; 59, 64
  n18
Peterson, Esther, 28
Petre, Peter, 174, 206 n3
Petty, Richard E., 200, 207 n34
Phillips, Michael B., 116, 133 n13
Piercy, Nigel, 716, 728 n10
Plimpton, Linda, 179, 206 n9
Plummer, Joseph T., 183
Pol, Louis G., 144, 172 n5
Polli, Rolando, 350, 351, 375 nn4, 6
Pope, N. W., 488
Popper, Ed, 77, 100 n3
Porter, Michael E., 57, 64 n17; 238, 245,
  251, 252, 255 nn3, 4, 7, 9, 10; 299,
  308–10, 315, 317 nn5, 16, 25; 322,
  328, 345 nn6, 13, 15; 386, 403 n5
Posner, Ronald S., 666, 700 n4
Prentice, Robert M., 647, 662 n5
Price, Linda L., 179, 206 n9
Punj, Girish, 123, 133 n20

Q

Quelch, John A., 466

R

Raffio, Ralph, 563, 585 n7
Raia, Ernest, 217
Raiffa, Howard, 129, 133 n32; 691, 692,
  700 n31, 701 n39
Rainwater, Lee P., 178

Raj, S. P., 718, 728 *n*11
Rajaratnam, Daniel, 548, 553 *n*20
Randers, Jorgen, 144, 151, 172 *nn*7, 13
Rankin, Deborah, 29, 32 *n*25
Rao, Amber G., 635, 643 *n*25
Raphaelson, Joel, 628, 643 *n*18
Rappaport, Alfred, 735, 755 *n*4
Ray, Michael L., 200, 207 *n*34; 599
Reibstein, David J., 511, 527 *n*14
Reid, Stan, 393, 404 *n*11
Reilly, Ann, 159, 172 *n*28
Rein, Irving J., 15, 32 *n*13, 534, 553 *n*7
Reingen, Peter H., 609, 616 *n*18
Rejans, Adrian B., 125, 133 *n*30
Resnik, Alan J., 304, 317 *n*23
Ress, C. William, 569, 585 *n*16
Revson, Charles, quoted, 445, 446
Reynolds, William H., 354, 375 *n*12
Richman, Barry M., 418
Ricks, David A., 386, 403 *n*4
Ries, Al, 234, 255 *n*1; 313–15; 469, 475 *n*9
Ring, L. Winston, 201, 207 *n*35
Ringer, Jurgen F., 103, 132 *n*2
Rink, David R., 350, 375 *n*9
Roach, John D. C., 328, 345 *n*13
Roberto, Eduardo, 144, 172 *n*8
Roberts, Alan A., 302, 303, 317 *nn*17, 22
Roberts, Donald F., 589–90, 616 *n*3
Robertson, Thomas S., 185, 206 *n*17; 442, 444 *nn*29, 34; 609, 616 *n*18
Robinson, William T., 357
Robinson, Dwight E., 354, 375 *n*13
Robinson, Patrick J., 211, 218, 232 *nn*6, 17
Robinson, S. J. Q., 46, 64 *n*15
Robinson, William A., 655, 662 *n*23
Rodgers, Frank "Buck," 2, 32 *n*3
Rodgers, William, 746, 747, 755 *nn*12, 14
Roering, Kenneth J., 332, 345 *n*17; 716, 728 *n*10
Rogers, D. S., 568, 585 *n*14
Rogers, Everett M., 203, 207 *n*43; 439–41, 444 *nn*31, 32; 595; 603, 616 *n*22
Roman, Kenneth, 600, 616 *n*15
Rooney, Francis C., quoted, 587
Rosenbloom, Bert, 541, 553 *n*12
Rothe, James T., 28, 32 *n*24, 427, 444 *n*22
Rothschild, William E., 242, 243, 245, 255 *n*6
Rubin, Jeffrey Z., 691, 700 *n*28, 701 *n*33
Ruckert, Robert W., 716, 728 *n*10
Rummel, R. J., 389
Rust, Roland T., 634, 643 *n*23
Ryans, John K., Jr., 718, 728 *n*12

Salancik, Gerald R., 160, 172 *n*29
Salmon, Walter J., 569, 585 *n*16
Sammon, William L., 234, 246, 255 *n*1
Sasieni, Maurice, 95
Sasser, W. Earl, 481, 493 *n*7
Schaffir, Kurt H., 653–54, 662 *n*20
Schelling, Thomas C., 691, 700 *n*30
Scherer, F. M., 236
Schiedt, Marsha A., 212, 232 *n*9
Schiffman, Leon G., 123, 133 *n*19; 175, 206 *n*7
Schoeffler, Sidney, 327, 345 *n*9
Schramm, Wilbur, 589–90, 616 *nn*3, 4
Schultz, Donald E., 621, 630, 643 *n*4; 655, 662 *n*23; 713

Schultz, Randall L., 124, 133 *n*27; 501, 527 *n*9
Schwartz, David J., 494, 527 *n*1
Scredon, Scott, 435
Scully, John, 2
Seipel, Carl-Magnus, 649, 662 *n*9
Seligman, Daniel, 604, 616 *n*23
Sen, Subrata K., 672, 700 *n*8
Sevin, Charles H., 741, 755 *n*10
Sexton, Donald E., Jr., 87, 100 *n*4
Shanklin, William L., 718, 728 *n*12
Shapiro, Benson P., 215, 232 *n*15; 295, 296, 316 *n*13; 453, 474 *n*3; 666, 670, 700 *n*4; 719, 728 *n*13
Sheffet, Mary Jane, 185, 206 *n*17
Sheffield, F. D., 600, 616 *n*13
Sheth, Jagdish N., 191, 194, 196, 201, 207 *nn*25, 28, 29, 35
Shiskin, Julius, 274, 278 *n*13
Shocker, Allan D., 432, 444 *n*26
Shostack, G. Lynn, 476, 493 *n*1
Shuchman, Abe, 747, 755 *n*15
Shugan, Steve M., 323
Silk, Alvin J., 432, 444 *n*26; 641, 644 *n*31; 688
Silk, Steven B., 350, 375 *n*7
Singh, Ravi, 322, 345 *n*5
Sinha, Prabhakant, 124, 133 *n*24; 668, 700 *n*5
Sirgy, M. Joseph, 185, 206 *n*18
Skolnik, Rayna, 667
Smith, A. B., 555, 585 *n*2
Smith, Lee, 15, 32 *n*12
Smith, Wendell P., 302, 317 *nn*17, 18
Smythe, Robert J., 296, 297, 317 *n*14
Snickle, Ken, 174, 206 *n*4
Snyder, Watson, Jr., 715, 728 *n*9
Souder, William E., 718, 728 *n*12
Spiro, Rosann L., 179, 206 *n*11; 689, 700 *n*26
Spitalnic, Robert, 234, 246, 255 *n*1
Sproles, George B., 354, 375 *n*14
Srinivasan, V., 672, 700 *n*8
Stanton, William J., 532–33, 553 *n*5
Staples, William A., 182
Star, Steven H., 708–9, 714, 728 *nn*1,7
Stasch, Stanley F., 712, 728 *n*5
Stearns, James M., 599
Steele, Alfred N., 340
Steiner, Gary A., 129, 133 *n*33; 188, 207, *n*22; 595
Steiner, Peter O., 96, 100 *n*10
Stern, Arthur, 652, 662 *n*16
Stern, Louis W., 158, 172 *n*27; 211, 232 *n*4, 529–30, 550–53 *nn*2, 23; 569, 585 *n*16
Sternthal, Brian, 116, 133 *n*13; 200, 206 *n*23; 591, 598, 599, 600, 616 *nn*5, 11, 14; 654, 662 *n*22
Stevenson, Robert Louis, quoted, 663
Stevenson, Thomas H., 215, 232 *n*15
Stewart, David W., 123, 133 *n*20
Stewart, John B., 361, 375 *n*19
Stoller, Martin, 534, 553 *n*7
Stone, Bob, 268, 277 *n*7; 560, 585 *n*3
Stonich, Paul J., 97, 100 *n*12
Strang, Roger A., 465, 475 *n*8; 646, 647, 653, 654, 662 *nn*2, 5, 7, 17, 19, 21
Strong, E. K., 595
Strong, Edward C., 200, 207 *n*34
Stumpf, Robert V., 310
Suci, C. J., 593, 616 *n*10
Sujan, Harish, 688

Sujan, Mita, 688
Sultan, Ralph G. M., 327, 345 *n*9
Summers, John O., 124, 133 *n*21
Suss, Warren H., 229, 233 *n*32
Sutton, Howard, 545, 553 *n*15
Swan, John E., 212, 232 *n*9; 350, 375 *n*9
Sweeney, James K., 388, 403 *n*7

T

Talarzyk, W. Wayne, 564, 585 *n*11
Tannenbaum, P. H., 593, 601, 616 *nn*10, 17
Tannenbaum, Stanley J., 620
Tauber, Edward M., 413, 414, 444 *nn* 12, 13
Taylor, James R., 112, 122, 133 *nn*11, 18
Taylor, James W., 201, 207 *n*37
Taylor, Mark B., 469, 475 *n*10
Tellis, Gerald J., 350, 375 *n*9; 517, 527 *n*16
Thierry, Henk, 187, 206 *n*21
Thomas, Dan R. E., 478
Thomas, Robert J., 436, 444 *n*29
Thomopoulos, Nick T., 275, 278 *n*14
Tigert, Douglas J., 294, 316 *n*11
Tillman, Rollie, 563, 585 *n*8
Tirmann, Ernst A., 751–52, 755 *n*16
Toffler, Alvin, 134, 155, 172 *nn*2, 19, 20; 340
Toomey, Margaret A., 631, 643 *n*21
Torrance, George W., 201, 207 *n*37
Toy, Norman E., 731, 755 *n*1
Trapp, Raymond J., 525
Trawick, Frederick T., 212, 232 *n*9
Trenten, George, 653–54, 662 *n*20
Trout, Jack, 234, 255 *n*1; 313–15; 469, 475 *n*9
Tsu, Sun, 322, 345 *n*4
Turney, Peter B. B., 304, 317 *n*23
Twedt, Dik Warren, 107, 108, 132 *n*8; 293; 624, 643 *n*13
Tybout, Alice M., 200, 207 *n*23; 600, 616 *n*13; 654, 662 *n*22
Tyebjee, Tyzoon T., 716, 728 *n*10

U

Ule, G. Maxwell, 605, 616 *n*26
Unger, Lynette S., 599
Upah, Gregory D., 160, 172 *n*29
Urban, Glen L., 124, 133 *n*22; 432, 444 *n*26; 642, 644 *n*33
Ury, William, 692–94, 701 *nn*40, 41
Uttal, Bro, 24, 32 *n*21; 343, 346 *n*27; 721, 728 *n*15

V

Vaccaro, Joseph P., 671, 700 *nn*6, 7
Varadarajan, P. "Rajan," 548, 553 *n*20; 647, 650, 662 *nn*6, 11
Venkatesh, Alladi, 174, 206 *n*6
Verdoorn, P. J., 96, 100 *n*9
Vernon, Raymond, 380, 403 *nn*2, 3
Vidale, M. L., 622, 643 *n*5
Viswanathan, R., 365, 376 *n*22
Vizza, Robert, 677
Voorhees, Roy, 560, 585 *n*4

W

Walker, Orville C., Jr., 680, 700 *n*20; 716, 728 *n*10
Walters, David, 565
Walton, R. E., 691, 700 *n*32
Walton, Sam, 564
Wanamaker, John, quoted, 604
Ward, Scott, 77, 100 *n*3
Wasson, Chester R., 349, 354, 367, 375 *nn*3, 11
Waterman, Robert H., Jr., 1, 31 *n*1, 59, 64 *n*18
Waters, Elmer E., 709, 728 *n*2
Weber, John A., 363–64, 367
Webster, Frederick E., Jr., 208, 213, 214, 232 *nn*1, 11, 12, 14
Weigand, Robert E., 548, 553 *n*21; 567
Weinberg, Charles B., 106; 672, 700 *n*8; 722, 728 *n*16
Weisenberger, T. M., 712, 728 *n*5
Weiss, Doyle L., 87, 100 *n*4
Weitz, Barton A., 688
Wells, Louis T., Jr., 380, 403 *n*2
Wells, William D., 182, 184
Welt, Leo G. B., 384
Westfall, Ralph, 291, 316 *n*8; 425, 444 *n*25

Wexner, Leslie H., 564
Whalen, Jack, 540
Wheeler, Elmer, 446
Whittle, Jack W., 282
Wiedersheim-Paul, Finn, 393, 404 *n*10
Wiersema, Frederik D., 330
Wieters, C. David, 222, 233 *n*23
Wilemon, David, 718, 728 *n*11
Wilkie, William L., 599, 619, 643 *n*2
Wilkinson, J. B., 500, 527 *n*5
Wilson, Aubrey, 247, 755 *n*13
Wilson, David T., 222, 232 *n*22
Wilson, Mike, 247, 755 *n*13
Wilson, Thomas W., 710, 728 *n*4
Wind, Yoram J., 197, 200, 207 *n*32; 208, 211, 213, 214, 218, 232 *nn*1, 6, 11, 14, 17; 295, 296, 310, 316 *n*13; 402, 404 *n*16; 422, 424
Winer, Leon, 56
Wittink, Dick R., 124, 133 *n*21
Wolfe, H. R., 622, 643 *n*5
Woo, Carolyn Y., 328, 345 *n*12
Wood, Wally, 116, 133 *n*13
Woodlock, Joseph N., 426
Woodruff, Robert B., 566
Woodside, Arch G., 211, 232 *n*7
Wortzel, Lawrence H., 179, 206 *n*11; 566, 585 *nn*10, 12

Wright, J. Patrick, 721, 728 *n*14
Wright, John S., 350, 375 *n*5; 567
Wright, Robert V. L., 318, 345 *n*1

Y

Yale, Jordan P., 339, 345 *n*2; 351, 375 *n*9
Yankelovich, Daniel, 291, 316 *n*10; 432, 444 *n*26
Young, Shirley, 291, 316 *n*9
Younger, Michael, 46, 64 *n*15
Yuspeh, Sonia, 371, 376 *n*26

Z

Zaltman, Gerald, 437, 444 *n*30
Zeithaml, Valarie A., 483–85, 493 *nn*13, 15
Zemke, Ron, 19, 32 *n*18, 19, 20; 476, 493 *n*1
Zif, Jehiel, 386, 403 *n*6
Zikmund, William G., 532–33, 553 *n*5
Zirger, Billie Jo, 412, 443 *n*8
Zoltners, Andris A., 124, 133 *nn*24, 27
Zufryden, Fred S., 124, 133 *n*22

Subject Index

A

Accountants, company, 720
Action programs, marketing plan, 77, 83
Ad response, electronic market research, 119
Advertising, 607–12, 614, 617–42
  deception in, 152; defined, 587; in direct marketing, 559–60; efficiency control of, 743; functions of, 608–9; industrial marketing role, 609–11; low-involvement buyers, 192–93; in marketing mix, 72–75, 618, 647; -to-sales promotion ratios, 646–47; selling concept and, 15–16; strategy statement of, 82; types of, 617–20
Advertising, comparison, 620
Advertising agencies, 138, 139, 587, 618, 622–25, 634
Advertising budget, 96–98, 604–7, 611, 618, 629–34, 641, 642
  decided for each product, 620–22; See also Advertising expenditures—budget
Advertising copy, creative wording, 628
Advertising copy testing, 638–39
Advertising expenditures, 95–98, 169, 604–8, 610–12, 614, 617, 618, 620, 632–37, 640–42, 646
  budget for, 96, 620–22, 629–34, 641–42; models for, 621–22
Advertising goal, 619
Advertising manager, 11, 74
Advertising (message) pretesting, 625, 638–39, 642

Advertising theme rating and testing, 624–25
Advisor, 610–11
Age group populations, U.S., 145, 181
Agent middlemen, 137–38, 528, 572, 573
AIDA message model, 595, 596
Allowances, manufacturer, 651
Analytical marketing system, 103, 122–31
Annual plan control, 75, 730–38, 753–54
Antimerger Act of 1950, 158
Antitrust legislation, 157, 159, 328
Appeals, message, 598, 599
Atmospheres, 567, 603
Attack strategies, market challenger, 333–39
Attitude and buying behavior, 189–90, 295
Attributes, product/brand (see Product attribute)
Audience message-target (receiver), 589–99, 629–33, 635–37
Audience response, desired, 294–98, 631–33
Audience target (see Target audience)
Audit, company-performance, 747–52
  departmental strength/weakness, 54–55
Augmented product, 446–47
Automatic vending, 561
Automobile industry:
  car design change, 18, 28, 61–62, 149, 153, 164, 282–86, 354; sales by, 617, 625–27
Automobile Information Disclosure Act of 1958, 158
Available market, 258, 259

B

Backward integration, 47–48
Bank marketing, 26–27
Bargaining and negotiation, 690–95
Bargaining strategy/tactics, 692–93
Barter transactions, 7, 384
Bayesian (statistical) decision theory, 127
Behavioral segmentation, 287, 291–95
Beliefs and buying behavior, 189–96
Benefit segmentation, 291–93
Birthrate (U.S.), 144–45
Blanket contracts, 222
Boston Consulting Group (BCG) growth share matrix, 40–43, 62
  new competitive advantage matrix, 311–12
Brainstorming, 414
Brand, ideal, 199
Brand, manufacturer-owned or licensed name, 465–66
Brand, private label, 465–67, 556
Brand awareness, sales-effect research, 613–14, 636, 639, 640
Brand beliefs and image, 197–201
Brand-celebrity congruity, 601
Brand comparison advertising, 619–20
Brand competition, 140–42, 620
Brand development index, 267, 268
Brand differentiation and choice, buying decision, 191–92, 196–99, 202, 303–4
Brand extension, 469
Brand familiarity or conviction, 192–94, 196
Brand loyalty, 294, 465, 646–67, 713

Brand management system, 541, 645, 651, 708–14
Brand name, 463–69, 472
Brand name, family or individual, 467–69, 474
Brand preference, 140–42, 178–79, 193, 198–202, 466–68, 470, 471, 618, 619
Brand promotion, 646–48, 653
Brand repositioning, 470–71
Brand switching, 125, 193, 646, 647, 655
Branding, advantages listed, 463–65
Branding, logical-flow diagram, 129
Brands:
benefit segmentation from, 292–93; life cycle of, 350, 360, 362, 372, 406; of market leaders, 193, 319, 321, 330–32, 466, 467; of product items, 463–71
Breakeven chart, 505–6
Brokers, 572–73
Brochures and written material, company, 657, 658
Budget-to-sales ratio, 71, 73
Budgets, 46, 71, 83, 656 (see also Advertising budget; Research & development; Sales budget; Sales promotion)
Business economics research, company, 108
Business functions, traditional vs market-oriented, 702–3
Business level, organizational, 35
Business market (see Industrial market)
Business mission and scopes, 37–38, 49, 50, 57
Business promotion, 651–52
Business strategic planning, 35, 49–63, 65, 66 (see also Strategic planning)
Business strength and weakness analysis, 52–55
Business success factor of marketing, 1–3, 51
Business-unit identification and definition, 38–40
Business units, marketing departments, strategic planning relationship, 66, 67
Buy back arrangement, 384
Buy classes, 211
Buyflow, 222–23
Buy grid framework, 218
Buy phases, 218
Buyer, disjunctive or conjuctive, 199–200
Buyer, price change reactions, 521–22
Buyer and seller:
Levitt on, 17; price dispute between, 494
Buyer market, 16
Buyer readiness, 294–95
stages of, 594–96, 612, 613
Buyer role, 191
Buyers, industrial, 209–22
Buyers, organizational, 68–69, 208, 209
Buying, 3, 4, 7, 9, 15–16, 636–37
Buying, industrial, 210–24
Buying behavior, 191–93
Buying center, 213
Buying decision involvement, high or low, 191–94
Buying decision process:
of consumers, 175, 190–205; of government, 228–30; research methods, 193–94; by resellers, 225, 277
Buying decisions, organizational:
by industrialists, 208, 209, 211–24; of resellers, 225–27
Buying intentions surveys, 270–72

Buying patterns, 24
"Buying Power, Annual Survey of" (Sales Management), 267
Buying service, retail, 562

C

Calls, sales representative, 683, 729, 741–43
Carriers, common and private, 575, 583
Cash cow (growth-share cell), 41–43
Cash-flow statement, projected, 425, 427
Cash refund (rebate), 648–49
Casual-analysis diagram, 129–30
Catalog showroom, 557
Category development index, 267–68
Causal analysis diagram, 128–30
Celebrity messages, 601
Census tracts, 268
Central business districts, 568
Chainstores, wholesaler-sponsored, or corporate, 546–47, 562–63
Channel captain (firm), 550
Channel conflict and cooperation, 550–51
Channels, distribution, 14, 108, 166–68, 342, 528–52, 554, 712, 726 (see also Marketing channels)
Child Protection Act of 1966, 158
Children, goods and services, 145
Clayton Act of 1914, 157, 158
Closing the sale, 690
Cluster analysis, 123
Colleges, promoted or marketed, 722–24
Combination store, 557
Commerce Business Daily (U.S. Government Printing Office), 229–30
Commercial transactions, 7
Commercialization, 436–37
Commission, salesperson, straight or combined, 672–73
Commodity-type products, 448, 495
Common Market (EEC), 382
Common Market, Central American (CACM), 382
Communication and promotion programs, total, 591–615
Communication channels, personal and nonpersonal, 601–3
Communication-effect and copy research, 591, 638–39
Communication mix, 587–88 (see also Promotional mix)
Communication model, 588–90, 595
Communication process, 588–91
Company, competitor-centered, 252–54
Company, customer-centered, 253–54
Company, divisionalized, and headquarters marketing, 715–16
Company, traditional business, 702–4
Company demand (function), 259, 261–64
Company forecast, 263–64
Company image (set) or target audience, 592–94
Company marketing channel, 536–40
Company marketing decisions, input-output map, 166, 170
Company marketing environment, 134–71, 702
Company orientations toward the marketplace, 13–28
Company strengths and weaknesses, 52–53, 80

Company survival and pricing, 497
Competition:
in channels, 550, 551; federal regulation of, 156–57, 159; management process for, 68–71, 76; overseas, recent, 33–34, 159, 391
Competitive advantage, 51, 54, 359–60, 388
product positioning and, 308, 310–13
Competitive equilibrium, 247–48
Competitive offense and counteroffense, 325–26, 332
Competitive position, business portfolio, 43–45, 318–19
Competitive-parity promotion expenditures, 605
Competitive situation, marketing plan, 78
Competitive strategies, 2–3, 65, 157
in channels, 535–36
Competitors, 235–55, 359, 391, 412, 731
in company microenvironment, 136, 139–41; pricing/offers of, 503–11, 514–17; reactions to changes, 518, 522–25; reaction profiles of, 247–48; rival companies selected as, 250–52; strategies identified, 239–41, 535–36
Competitors, strong vs weak, and other polarities, 250–52
Complaints, customer (consumer), 19, 142, 412, 736
Computer models:
for media vehicle selection, 634–36; planning profit by, 84, 90–93; for profit-projections, 90–93
Concentrated marketing, 301
Concept development positioning and testing, 418–20
Conclusion-drawing, communicator-message, 598–600
Conjoint analysis, 123–24, 422–24
Conjunctive model of consumer choice, 199
Constant-budget line, 93–95
Consulting firms, 138, 721
Consumer-adoption, new product, 439–42
Consumer Affairs, U.S. Office of, 159
Consumer awareness advertising, 635, 656
Consumer behavior, 173–90
Consumer confidence measure, 271–72
Consumer co-op, 563
Consumer credit and debt, 150–51
Consumer decision-making:
brand-choice sets in, 196–98; in buying process, 190–205
Consumer expenditure patterns, 151
Consumer evaluation procedure, buying decision, 197–201
Consumer-franchise-building, sales promotion, 647
Consumer-goods classification, 449–50, 621
Consumer Goods Pricing Act of 1975, 158
Consumer information sources, 195–96
Consumer interest level, 257, 258
Consumer markets, 68, 139–40, 173–75
analysis of, 173–90, 205; segmentation of, 286–95
Consumer orientation, 25
Consumer preference, product concept, 419–20, 422, 423, 429–30
Consumer Product Safety Act of 1972 (Commission), 158, 159
Consumer roles, buying decision, 190–91

Consumer surveys and panel data, 654
Consumer testing, new product, 429–30
Consumer-want satisfaction, 5–6, 27, 28
    See also Customer satisfaction
Consumerism (movement), 142–43, 152, 157–60
Consumers, final, and wholesaling, 570
Contact methods, 117–18
Contests, promotional, 652
Contingency plan, marketing plan control, 83
Contract manufacturing, 391–92
Contraction (strategic withdrawal), segment, 326–27
Control chart, expense-sales ratio, 734
Control responsibilities, annual plan, 75, 76
Controls, annual plan, 75, 76, 730–38, 753–54
Controls, marketing plan monitoring, 77, 83
Convenience goods, 449, 451
Convenience store, 556–57, 558
Coordinated marketing, 17–18, 19–22
Copyright, 463
Copy testing, 638
Core product-benefit, 446–47
Corporate headquarters, 35, 36, 65
Corporate identity, visual, 658
Corporate marketing, 715–16
Corporate mission, 36–38
Corporate responsibility research, 108
Corporate retail organizations, 562–63
Corporate strategic plan, 35–49, 62
Cost estimation:
    new products and profits, 425, 427–28, 431–32; for production and curve-pricing, 501–3, 525
Costing, full or direct, marketing profitability analysis, 741–42
Cost-plus pricing, 504–5
Costs, physical distribution, 577–84
Costs, product and profit projection, 90–93
Countertrade and counterpurchase, 384
County and City Data Book, 112
Coupons (sales promo), 646, 648, 649, 653
Creativity methods, 412–15
Creative strategy, advertising message, 622–24, 627, 628
Credit, 151, 514, 720
Critical-path (network-planning diagram, 129
Cross-elasticity of demand, 235
Cross-impact analysis, 271
Cues, 189
Cultural factors and environment, 160–64, 175–77, 385–86
Current market demand estimation, 264–70
Current marketing situation, 77–79
Current profit, maximum, and price, 497
Customer-attitude tracking, 736–37
Customer complaints, 19, 142, 412, 736
Customer groups of market segment, 50, 69–70, 259
Customer needs, 1–5, 50, 69
Customer orientation, 18–19, 22–25, 69, 252–54
Customer resistance, 689
Customer satisfaction, 17–27, 31, 482, 665, 737
    key to customer retention, 18–19, 25; market definition of, 33, 38, 39; post-purchase behavior and, 192, 194, 202–4
Customer segment profile, 296–98
Customer service, 103–5

Customer-service managers, 11, 707
Customer target, 12, 30, 50, 71, 136, 182, 370, 484, 490, 532, 564–65, 676, 706
    See also Target market
Customer value analysis, 250
Customers:
    in company microenvironment, 136, 139, 141, 143; identification of, 37–38; point of view of, 18–19; relationship-manager with, 695–98; sales representative link to, 664–66, 677, 685, 686; *See also* Consumers
Customized marketing, 281–82

D

DAGMAR, 619
Data, marketing-results or happenings-intelligence, 102, 105
Data, primary or secondary research source, 111–15, 121
Data analysis, marketing research, 119
Data collection, 118–19
Dealers (*see* Retailers)
Death of a Salesman (Miller), 663
Decision models, optimization-type, 122, 125–27, 129, 131, 523–24
Decision support system, 122–31
Decision-tree diagram, 128, 130, 564, 565
Decline stage, market, 362–66, 372, 612
Defender model, 322, 323
Defense Department, 229
Defense strategies, market leader, 321–27
Defining Advertising Goals for Measured Advertising Results (Colley), 619
Delphi method, 87, 273
Demand, 3–4, 8, 13, 31, 256–70, 319
    decline in, 24; for industrial goods, 210; measurement of, 256–64; price determined by, 499–501; states of, 12–13, 189, 480–81
Demand management, 12, 13
Demand/technology life cycle, 347–49
    demarketing, 12–13
Demographic consumer-market segmentation, 10, 283, 287–90, 292
Demographic environment, 143–50
Demographic industrial market segmentation, 295–98
DEMON model, 605
Department store, 555, 556, 558, 562, 564, 568
Descriptive models, analytical system, 124–25
Design decisions, 462–63
Design and engineering (D&E) department, 702–3, 718–19
Determinance model of consumer choice, 200
Deterministic model, 131
Differential calculus (decision-optimization model), 126
Differentiated marketing, 303–4
Direct-mail advertising, 560
Direct marketing, retailer forms, 559–62
Direct selling to home or office, 561
Discount stores, 535, 555, 557, 558, 562, 564
Discounts and allowances, 513–14, 520, 650–51, 672
Discriminant analysis, 123
Discrimination, learning, 189

Discriminatory pricing, 515
Disjunctive model of consumer choice, 200
Disneyland and theme parks, 309–10, 463, 486, 488
Dissonance reducing, 192, 204–5
Distortion, selective (perception), 188, 189
Distribution, dual or multichannel, 548, 549
Distribution, intensive, exclusive dealing, or selective, 537–38
Distribution, physical, 36, 82, 355, 359, 528–30, 538, 576–84
Distribution channels, 14, 108, 166–68, 342, 528–52, 554, 712, 726 (see also Marketing channels)
Distribution channels, foreign, 398–99
Distribution costs, total, 579
Distribution efficiency, 743
Distribution expenditures in mathematical programming decisions, 126–27
Distribution firms, 136
Distribution programming, 541, 542
Distribution situation, current, 79
Distribution system, 528–29
Distribution team, 540
Diversification growth strategy, 35, 46, 47, 49, 62
Divestiture, portfolio model (plan), 41
Divorce rate, U.S., 146
Dog (growth-share cell), 42, 43, 66
Door-to-door retailing, 561
Drive, stimulus, 189
DROP-error, GO-error, 415
Drop shoppers, 572
Drug industry technology R&D, 154–56
Dumping, foreign market, 398
Dun's Market Identifiers, 266
Durable goods, 449
Dynamic mathematics model, 130–31

E

Early adopter theory, 439
Economic circumstance and product choice, 181–82
Economic environment, 150–51, 214
    of foreign market, 382–83
Education and work force demand, 147, 149
Efficiency control, 75, 730, 742–43, 754
Elasticity, 500–501
Electronic market research, ad-response, 119
Embargo, 381
Emotional appeals, 598
Employment transaction, 7
Encoding and decoding messages, 588–89
Encirclement attack, 336–37
Encyclopedia of Associations, 112
Energy costs, 153, 154, 159
Engineering and design, 428, 702–3, 718–19
Environment (external), 66, 68, 135
    forecasting, 270, 271; threat analysis, 49–52
Environment (internal), 142, 748
    strength and weakness within, 49, 52–54
Environment (physical), 151–54
Environmental movement impact, 151–54
Environmental protection, governmental, 153–54, 158

Environmental Protection Agency (EPA), 158, 159, 249
Equal Credit Opportunity Act of 1975, 158
Ethnic (nationality) groups, 149, 173–74, 176
European Economic Community (EEC) (Common Market), 382
Events marketing, 603
Exchange, 6–9, 30–31
Exclusive distribution and dealing, 537
Executive promotions, 722
Executive summary, marketing plan, 77–78
Expectancy value model of consumer choice, 198–200
Expenditures:
    for advertising (see Advertising expenditures); consumer pattern changes, 151; and market-orientation process, 24, 720–21; of marketing mix, 85–88, 90–93, 95–99; of new product introduction/promotion, 355–56, 359; for promotion, 604–6
Expense-to-sales analysis, 734–35
Expenses, functional, in profitability analysis, 738–40
Experience curve, 502–3
Experimental research, subject group, 114, 118
Experimental sales-response estimation method, 87, 196
Expert opinion, 271
Exponential smoothing, time-series, 274
Export, 378, 380–83, 386, 388, 392, 393, 398, 399
Export, active, 390, 399
Export, direct or indirect, 389–91
External and internal marketing, 21–22, 49–54, 101, 112, 134, 135
Eye cameras, research, 115–16

F

Facilitators, 528
Factor analysis, 123
Fads, consumer, 28, 253, 254
Fair Credit Reporting Act of 1970, 158
Fair Debt Collection Practice Act of 1978, 158
Fair Packaging and Labelling Act of 1960, 473
Family:
    buying behavior, 179–80; changes in America, 145–46, 149; life-cycle stages of, 181
Fashion, 353–54
Fast-food industry, criticized, 28
Fear appeals, 598
Features decisions, 461–62
Federal Cigarette Labeling Act of 1967, 158
Federal civilian buying establishment, 228
Federal Food and Drug Act of 1906, as amended, 157
Federal government agency buying expenditures, 227–30
Federal Trade Commission (FTC) Act of 1914, 157–59, 514
Feedback-system diagram, 130
Financial analysis, annual plan, 735–36
Financial intermediaries, 139
Financial objectives, marketing plan, 81, 720
Firm, dominant, strategies of, 318–30
Focus group interviewing, 113–14

Food and Drug Administration (FDA), 156, 159, 429
Food retailing, trade deals, 651 (see also Supermarkets)
Forecast experts, 273
Forecasting, 261, 263–64
    of demand and sales, 270–75, 719
Forecasting, corporate, long- and short-range, 85, 90, 107, 108, 124
Foreign competition, 1, 3, 34, 377–78, 380–81, 401–2
Foreign firms entering home markets, 377–78
Foreign markets (consumers), 139, 377–403 passim
Foreign product invasion (1970s), 33–34
Forestry products, 152, 155
Fortune on intelligence techniques of competitors, 248–49
Fortune 500, sales force efficiency, 677
Fortune 1000 CEOs, marketing backgrounds, 2, 315
Forward integration, 47–48
Four Ps, 71–72, 75
Fragmented industry market, 407
    and competitive advantage, 311–12
Franchise systems, sponsored, 546, 547, 563
Franchised dealers, 534, 542–43, 545
Freudian motivation theory, 186
Functional-relationship diagram, 130
Future demand estimation, 270–76
Future profit potential, 34, 46
Future Shock (Toffler), 134, 155

G

Game plan (broad strategy), 34–35, 42–45, 71, 75, 82
Game theory, decision alternatives, 127, 129
Gatekeepers, 213
General Agreement on Tariffs and Trade (GATT), 382
General Services Administration, 230
Generics and national brands, 464–67
Geocoding systems, 268, 269
Geographical markets, 400, 607, 707–8
    industrial buyers in, 209–10, 224
Geographical market segments:
    and population shift, 146–50, 176, 259, 286–88; rollout strategy for, 437
Geographical segmentation regions, 259, 286–88, 342
Geographical territory, sales force structure, 666–69, 683
Ghost shoppers, 106
Global markets (industries), 13, 238, 377–402
Goal formation, strategic planning, 49, 55–57, 75, 400, 402
Goals, annual plan, 730–38 passim
    deviation from, 737
Goods, durable and nondurable, 449
Goods, sought and unsought, 15, 38, 151, 450
Goods and services:
    in definitions, 7, 449–51, 530, 554, 569; industrial buyers of, 208–11, 213, 218; in the market, 10, 151, 174, 445, 554, 583; offer mix of, 477, 479, 482; resale market, 224–27
Government market, 227–30

Graphical models, analytical system, 87, 128–30
Gross contribution margin (per unit), 84–85
Growth and opportunities, product, 41–47, 352, 358–59
Growth-share matrix, portfolio (evaluation) model, 40–43, 45, 46, 62, 66
Growth stage, 358–59, 371
Guerrilla action, competitive, 325, 337, 339

H

Habitual buying, 192–93, 636
Hard-sell, 15, 16, 17
Harvest/divest objective, SBU, 42, 44, 45
Headlines, 628
Heavy users, 293, 439
Heuristic model, decision, 125
Hierarchy-of-effects model, 595
Hispanic consumers, 173–74
Historical database, sales, 87, 88, 90
Horizontal integration strategies, 48–49
Horizontal marketing systems, 547–48, 550
Households, nonfamily, 146
Humorous appeals, 598
Hypermarche, 557

I

IBM personal computer, purchasing, psychological factors, 175, 185, 188–89, 194, 322, 524, 550
IBM Way, The (Rodgers), 2
Idea, product, 445–46
Idea generation, 412–15
Idea screening, 415–18
Ideal brand model of consumer choice, 199
Image (brand), 418, 625
Image (company), current, 592–94
Image pricing, 515
Import markets, 377–81, 386, 390–93
In Search of Excellence: Lessons from America's Best-Run Companies (Peters & Waterman), 1, 59
Income, disposable personal, 150–51
Income distribution, foreign, 383
Income per capita, real or money, 150, 151
Income segmentation, and as demographic variable, 289–90
Index method, 266–68
Industrial buying, 210–24
Industrial competition, 235–36
Industrial damage, environmental, 151–54
Industrial distributors, 532, 575
Industrial goods, 434–36, 450–51, 532
Industrial market(ing):
    advertising role in, 609–11; and buyer behavior, 209–24; segmentation of, 295–96
Industrial product (goods), market testing, 434–36
Industrial product managers, 709
Industry attractiveness, 40–46
Industry entry and exit barriers, 238
Industry structure, competitive, 236–39, 311–12, 382–83
Influencer, 191, 213
Information advertising, 619
Information center, company, 106
Information search, consumer, 195–96
Innovation-adoption model, 595

Innovation process, described, 439–42 (*see also* Product innovation; Service innovation)
Institutional buying market, 228
Institutional loyalty, 161
Integration, vertical, 238, 240
Integrative growth strategies, 48–49
Intelligence-gathering systems:
　for competition, 234, 248–50; external environment scanning, 50–51, 68–69, 112
Intensive growth, 46–48
Interest, consumer (buyer), 257, 258
Intermediaries (*see* Marketing intermediaries; Middlemen)
Internal marketing microenvironment, 21–27, 101, 112, 136, 482
Internal reports system, 103–5
International marketing, 30, 377–402
Interstate Commerce Commission, 159
Interview, focus group, 113–14
Interview, personal, arranged or mail intercept, 117–19
Interview, telephone, 117–19
Introduction stage, 355–58
Inventory and stock level, 580–81
Inventory control, wholesale, 574, 577, 579–81, 583
Invest/grow objective, SBU, 43–45
Investment, direct, foreign, 392
Investment opportunities and technology, 154, 159, 408–9, 428
Investment portfolio management, 34
Iso-sales curves, 94
Issues analysis, marketing plan, 80–81

J

Japan:
　in global markets, 163, 377–80, 386, 387, 401–2; U.S. competitor goals compared, 242–43; world marketer champs, 401–2
Jobbers, 571, 572, 669
Joint ventures, foreign market, 392
Judgmental sales-response estimation method, 87–89
Just-in-time (JIT) production, 62, 216–17, 401, 581, 719

L

Labeling functions, 142–43, 472–74
Labor force and education, 147
Laboratory test markets, 431–32
Law of demand, 86
Leads, sales, 686, 688
Learning and buying behavior, 189
Leasing, 211
Legal-political foreign environment, 383–84
Legislation, 156–60
Lexicographic model of consumer choice, 200
Licensing, brand name, 465–66
Licensing, international market, 391–92
Life-cycle stage, psychological, 181, 288
Lifestyle and buyer behavior, 178, 182–85, 290
Life-way groups, 162
Limits to Growth, The (Meadows et al.), 144, 151
Linear and nonlinear math model, 130

A. D. Little portfolio model, 46
Lobbying (PR), 655
Logical-flow diagram, 128–29
Long-term contracts, 215–16
Looping, logical-flow diagram, 129
Loss leaders, 567
Loyalty status (*see* Brand loyalty)

M

Macroenvironment, company, 50, 136, 143–63, 386
　audit of, 747, 751; marketing plan, 78, 79; in marketing system, 165–71
Macromodel, descriptive, 124
Macroscheduling, advertising, 634–36
Magazines, 631–33
Magnuson-Moss Warranty/FTC Improvement Act of 1975, 158
Mail order, 556, 558–60, 572
Management:
　of product support services, 489–92; of service industries, 482–92 passim, 707
Management-by-objectives, 730
Managers:
　in company organization, 21–23, 74, 75, 706–8; marketing-effectiveness rating by, 744–46; in marketing tasks, described, 11–13, 136–37, 618, 704–16 passim
Manufacturers:
　complaints about wholesalers, 574–75; as retailers, 546, 547, 554
Manufacturing-driven companies, 719–20
Market(s), 9–10
　defined, 9, 257; measures and measurable types of, 257–58
Market, latent, 370
Market attractiveness, 43–45, 51, 52
Market broadening or myopia, 326
Market-buildup method, 265–66
Market-centered organizations, 714
Market challenger attack-strategies, 193, 330–41
Market challenger strategies, 330–39
Market coverage strategies, 301–2
Market demand, 256–70, 319
　defined, 259–60; *See also* Demand
Market demand, current, estimated, 264–70
Market demand, future, estimated, 270–76
Market demand (response) function, 260–61
Market development strategy, 47–48
Market diversification, 326
Market emergence stage, 370–71
Market entry, 343, 344, 371
　by international trade, 389–93, 400, 402; market pioneer, 356–58; timing of, 436
Market evolution concept and stages, 369–74
Market expansion, total, and firm dominance, 319–21, 356, 358–59
Market focus, 17, 18
Market follower strategies, 339–41
Market followers, 332, 339–41
Market forecasts, 261, 263–64, 270–75, 719
Market growth rate, 144
　in game plan strategy, 82; in portfolio evaluation, 40–50
Market growth stage, 358–59, 371
Market leader:
　pricing by cutting into, 499, 524–25; strategies of, 319–30, 339, 341
Market logistics thinking, 577–78

Market management system, 708, 713–16
Market manager, 11, 13
　role in organization, 713–16; tasks of, 45–46
Market map, 597
Market niche(r) strategies, 35, 58, 342–44, 370, 371
Market nicher strategies, 342–43
Market leader strategies, 319–30
Market opportunity analysis, 66–69
Market opportunity index, 267–68
Market orientation (focus), 24, 702–3
　obstacles to, 24–28; strategies for building, 720–24
Market-oriented definition, 38–39
Market partitioning theory, 286
Market penetration strategy, 47, 48, 258, 439, 497
Market pioneer and product life-cycle, 356–58
Market potential, 260, 261
　in current-demand estimation, 264–66
Market response function, 260
Market segment, 35, 65, 96, 162, 308
　branding in, 465, 470–71; consumer groups of, 173–74; evaluation and selection of, 298–308; invasive targeting of, 305–6; operating in more at once, 304–5; regional "nations" of North America, 147–49
Market segmentation, 69–70, 280–98, 315
　formal procedure in, 283–86; variables in: consumers, 286–95; industrials, 295–96
Market share, overall, analysis, 731–33
Market share:
　in portfolio evaluation models, 41–43, 45–47
Market shares:
　analytical measures of, 732–33; expansion of, 327–30, 401; leader defense of, 321–27, 524–25; and counteroffensive, 325–27; price cuts to gain, 518, 522–24; research/selection for, 69–71, 243–44
Market situation data, marketing plan, 78
Market size, defined, 257–59
Market strategy statement, new product, 420–21
Market-specialized sales force, 669
Market targeting, 280, 298–308
Market testing, new product, 409, 430–36
Market testing, sales forecast, 273, 434, 436
Marketers, 7–11, 24, 26, 134
　consumer behavior understood by, 174–75, 179, 181, 184–85, 187, 190; defined, 10–11, 152
Marketing:
　analysis and planning in, 27; business sector growth of, 29; control and monitoring of activities, 729–54; core concepts in, 3–11; defined, 3; innovation in, 27, 34–35; management backgrounds in, 2; multinational practice of, 30; nonprofit organizations using, 29–30, 722–24; principles forgotten fast in, 27
Marketing, differentiated, undifferentiated and concentrated, 302–4
Marketing, interactive (service), 482–83
Marketing audit, 746–52
Marketing channel levels, 532–33
Marketing channels, 14, 166–68, 342, 528–52, 554, 712, 726
　alternatives, major, 534, 536–40; conflict

Marketing channels (*continued*)
  or cooperation, 550–51; design decisions, 534–39; members: selecting and stimulating, 540–42, 544–45; trade-relations mix of, 538; producer decisions, 540–45; *See also* Distribution
Marketing company, modern, 706, 721, 722
Marketing concept, 1, 2, 17–28, 31, 65
Marketing consulting firms, 138, 721
Marketing control systems, 729–52
Marketing controller concept, 753, 754
Marketing decisions, 122–31 passim, 523, 528
Marketing department:
  evolution of, 704–13; functions of, 26–27, 704–6, 715–18, 721–22, 725, 729; relation to other departments, 716–20; strength and weakness of, 54–55
Marketing director, 30, 704–5
Marketing effectiveness, 75–76, 744
Marketing-effectiveness rating review, 744–46
Marketing efficiency studies, 75 (*see also* Efficiency control)
Marketing environment, 49–54, 68, 105, 134–71, 259–60
  meaning of, 134–36; strategy and system relative to, 164–71; of trading abroad, 381–86; *See also* Environmental threat
Marketing expenditure functions, 86–88 (*see also* Expenditures)
Marketing expense ratios, monitored, 734–35
Marketing flows and functions, 530–33
Marketing functions, 704–8, 725, 727
  ancillary to sales, 704; audit of, 750–51; learning stages of, 26–27
Marketing implementation process, 724–26
Marketing Information Guide, 112
Marketing information systems, 68, 76, 102–5
Marketing information types, 101–2
Marketing intelligence system, 103, 105–6
Marketing intermediaries, 135, 136, 137–38, 528, 535–38
  producer delegation to, 529–30; *See also* Middlemen
Marketing management:
  assessing SBUs, 39, 40, 43, 45–48; described, 11–13, 618, 655; process of, 66–76
Marketing mix, 71–74, 308, 341, 445, 618
  interactions to be watched, 95–98; modification, product maturity, 361–62; optimization of, 93–95, 99; pricing and, 395–96, 511, 518–20; profit level in, 84–92, 99, 329–30
Marketing mix, worldwide, standardized or customized, 393–95, 398
Marketing-mix variables, 95–96, 329
Marketing network, 9
Marketing objectives, plan statement, 81–82
Marketing organization, 704–24
  audit of, 749, 751
Marketing plan, 35, 65, 722
  implementation of, 74–76, 724–26; sections in, 76–83; simulator of, 90
Marketing planning decisions, 13
Marketing productivity audit, 750, 751
Marketing profitability analysis, 75, 738–40
  See also Profitability
Marketing programs, 702–26

Marketing research, 11, 30, 82, 101–3, 107–22, 131, 134, 174–75, 244, 530
  company department scope of, 107–8, 121; deficiencies of, 121–22; evolving techniques (1910–1980), 108, 110; plan development, 111–18; problem definition and objectives, 109–11; target population, 68–71, 116, 117
Marketing research firms, 107, 108, 138, 432, 435
Marketing service agencies, 138–39
Marketing skills:
  implementation of, 725–26; in nonbusiness organizations, 722–24
Marketing strategy, 71–76, 134, 318–44, 437
  audit of, 749, 751; for challengers, 330–40; defined, 71; environment and system interaction with, 164–71; for followers, 340–41; for leader firms, 319–30; in marketing plan, 77, 82–83; for service firms, 481–89
Marketing system:
  audit of, 749, 751; strategy and environment interaction with, 164–71
Marketing vice-president, functions, 11, 20, 22, 24, 74–75, 705, 706, 716, 721, 724
Marketplace, changing, 32
Marketplace, consumers buying up seven Os, 173–75
Markets, blocked (megamarketing), 385
Markets, customer, 68, 139–40 (*see also* Consumer markets)
Markov-process model, 124, 125
Markups, retailer, 404–5, 567
Marriage, U.S. age of, 145
Mass advertising, 712–13
Mass marketing, 279, 280, 370, 439
Mass markets, 149, 370
Mathematical models, analytical system, 130–31
Mathematical programming, decision model, 126–27
Matrix organization, 714–15
Maturity stage, 359–62, 371–72
McKinsey seven-S framework, 59–61
Meat Inspection Act of 1906, 157
Mechanical research measuring devices, 115–16
Media, advertising, 588–89, 629–37
Media clutter, 631, 646
Media firms, 138
Megamarketing, 385
Megatrends: Ten New Directions Transforming Our Lives (Naisbitt), 163–64
Megatrends, macroenvironmental world and United States forces, 143–64
Memory, long-term or short-term, 590–91
Merchandising conglomerate, 563
Merchant (middlemen) wholesalers, 138, 528, 548, 571–72, 584
Mergers, 159
Message, advertising:
  in communication process, 588–91; creative generation of, 622–24; design of, 596–601; evaluation (rating) of, 624–25; frequency beamed, 636–37
Message execution, ad, 625–28
Message format, 600–601, 628
Message rehearsal, 590–91
Message source credibility, factors, 601
Messages, one- or two-sided, 600

Microanalytic model, descriptive, 124
Microbehavioral model, 124
Microenvironment, company, 135–43, 170
Micromarket trend, 149–50
Microscheduling, advertising, 636–37
Middlemen, 137–38, 399, 528, 530, 532–35, 537, 540–45
  motivation of, 541–42; number limits of, 537–38, 540; *See also* Agent middlemen; Merchant middlemen
Military buying, 229
Miller-Tydings Act of 1937, 157
Minimax criterion, game theory, 127, 129
Mission statement, business, 37–38, 49, 50
Missionary sales force, 211
Model-bank, operations research, 124–31
Monetary transaction, 7
Monopoly, 237, 264
Moody's Manual, 112
Moral appeals, 598
Morphological analysis, new product, 413
Morrill Study, 609
Motivation theories and buying behavior, 185–88
Motivational research, Dichter's, 186
Motive, stimulus object, 189
Multibrand decision, 469
Multifactor portfolio matrix, General Electric, 43–46, 63
Multimarketing, 548–49
Multinational corporations:
  commercial cover agreements, 399–400; new competition for, 30, 378, 387, 392, 398, 399; strategies of, 243, 378–79, 392–403 passim
Multiple regression analysis, 122–23
Music Man, The (Wilson), 663

N

National account management and customer relationship, 669, 670, 695–98
National Association of Purchasing Managers (NAPM), 210
National Commission on Consumer Finance, 158
National Environment Policy Act of 1969, 158
National Traffic and Safety Act of 1956, 142, 158
Need(s), market/consumer, 3–6, 9, 10, 17–18, 23, 30, 31, 39, 102, 144, 686
  buying psychology of, 185–88, 195, 197, 291, 686–90; in demand-technology lifecycle, 347–48; identification: new product development, 407, 412–14; segment gap: challenger attack on, 335–36; of services, 478, 534–35
Need set, 5, 8
Needs-hierarchy process, 373
Negotiation and bargaining, 8, 690–95
Network-planning (critical-path) diagram, 129
New product concepts and development, 15, 48, 49
New product characteristics, 441–42
New product development, 74, 320, 405–42, 655, 665
  audit of, 750; business analysis during, 421–28; commercialization in, 436–38, 495, 648; failure rate in, 407–8, 413, 415,

New product development (*continued*) 431; packaging and labeling, 471–73; profit-projection program on, 90–93
New product failure rate, 407–8
New product idea generation, 412–15, 418
  screening of, 415–16, 417–18
New product introduction and distribution, 355–58, 495, 648, 656
New product level and life-cycle, 320, 352–53, 355–56, 358, 360, 407
News stories and press releases, PR, 657–60
New task purchase, 211–12
New users and uses, 320–21
Niche(r) strategies, 35, 58, 342–44, 359, 370, 371
Nonprofit/nonbusiness sectors, 722–24

O

Objections, handling, 689
Objective-and-task promotion budget, 605–6, 621
Objectives, company:
  set for advertising, 618–20; control procedures over, 75; of market challengers, 333; set for market targeting, 300–301; in marketing plan, 77, 80–82; set for marketing research, 110–11; for price-setting, 496–99; set for sales force, 665; sales-promotion-marketing for, 647; set for strategic business unit, 33–35, 46, 55–57
Objectives, competitors, 241–43
Observation, research, 113, 120
Occasion segmentation, 291
Occupation and consumption, consumer, 181
Office equipment field, management, 66–75
Office of Management and Budget, 228, 229
Oil demands, 153
Older consumers, 174
Oligopolies, 237–38
Open-bid buying, 230
Opinion leaders, mass media, 179, 603
Opportunities, company, 33, 34, 46, 51–53
Opportunity and threats analysis, marketing plan, 77, 79–81, 160
Optimization models, decision, 125, 126
Order getter or taker, sales, 686, 696
Order processing, 579–81
Order-routine specification, 222
Order-shipping-billing cycle, 103, 579–80
Organizational arrangements, new product work, 408–12, 702–3
Organizational buying, defined, 208
Organizational buying markets, analyzed, 208–31
Organizational marketing, 11–13, 68–69, 76, 208–9
  competing concepts of activity, 13–28
Organized resistance, customer, 24–26
Outdoor advertising, 632
Overfull demand, 12

P

Packaging and design, 471–73
Partnership, producer-distributor, 542, 543
"Parts and service" business, 491
Passion for Excellence, A (Peters), 1

Penetration strategy, 258, 356, 358
People-based services, and staffing, 477–80
People's relationships and cultural values, 161–63
Perceived risk, 201–2
Perceived-value pricing, 506–7
Percentage-of-sales promotion expenditures, 604
Perception, motivated buyer, 188–89
Personal buying decisions, 181–85
Personal communication and influence, 441, 601–3, 609, 685–99
Personal selling, 588, 606–10, 665, 685–95
Personality:
  brand-consumer segmentation, 290–91; buying behavior and, 185
Persuasibility, audience, 591
Persuasive advertising, 619–20
Physical distribution, 577–83
Physical environment, 151–54
PIMS, 327–30, 460
Planning, 65–96
Point-of-purchase (POP) display, 432, 650
Political/legal environment, 156–60
Pollution, environmental, 151–54
Population growth, world, 144
Population shifts and North American geographic segments, 146–49
Portfolio evaluation models, 40–46
Positioning, 13, 27, 70–71, 82, 140, 280, 308–16, 419, 618
  defined, 27, 308, 314, 315–16; four Cs of, 141; for price, 495–96; *See also* Product positioning
"Positioning Era, The" (Ries & Trout), 314–15
Postpurchase satisfaction or dissatisfaction, 192, 194, 202–5
Potential market, 257
Postpurchase services, 567
Premiums, 646, 649, 516
President of company, 721
Prestige-goods strategy, 338
Pretests, ad message, 625, 638–39, 642
Pretests, sales promotion, 653
Price(s), 74, 82, 102, 397–98, 421, 494–526
  adapting of, 512–17; meanings of, 494–95
Price changes response and initiation, 517–25
Price cuts, 517–18, 522–25, 737
Price-discount strategy, 513–14
Price elasticity of demand, 500–501, 525
Price escalation, foreign market, 397–98
Price increases, 518–22
Price-off (discount), 650–51
Price packs, 649
Price promotion, 646–50
Price sensitivity, 499–500
Price-setting, 495–511
Pricing, 495–517, 528
  retailer decision on, 567; wholesaler decision on, 571, 573
Pricing, by-product, 517
Pricing, captive-product, 516–17
Pricing, discriminating, 515
Pricing, geographic, 512–13
Pricing, going-rate, 507–8, 510
Pricing, markup, 504–5, 567
Pricing, optional feature, 516
Pricing, perceived value, 506–9
Pricing, product-bundling, 517
Pricing, product-line, 516

Pricing, product-mix, 516–17
Pricing, promotional, 514–15
Pricing, psychological, 510–11
Pricing, sealed bid, 510
Pricing, target return, 505–6
Pricing, two-part, 517
Pricing policies, company, 511
Principled negotiation strategy, 693–94
Private label brands, 465–67, 556
Prizes and rewards, promotional, 649
Problem definition, marketing research, 109–11
Producer cooperatives, 572
Producer (industrial) market, 209–24 (*see also* Industrial market)
Product, 74, 532
  decisions on each item, 458–73; terms and definitions of, 5, 74, 445–47, 535; *See also* New product development
Product accessibility (place), 74
Product acquisition, 405
Product assortment, retailer, 565–66
Product assortment building, 570, 571
Product attribute, new, 372–73, 413, 424
Product attribute, salient, 197–201, 458–63
Product attribute, tangible, 458–63
Product choice set, 5, 186, 194, 196–98, 200, 257 (*see also* Purchasing decisions)
Product classification, 448–51
Product concept, organizational, 14–15, 31
Product concept (idea), measuring, 418–24, 428
Product copies (knockoffs), 341
Product cost, 13–14
Product decisions, 445–72
Product decline, 352, 362, 364–66, 368, 369, 724
Product design, 462–63
Product development, new (*see* New product development)
Product development strategy, 47, 48, 160
Product differentiation, 341–47 passim
Product dissatisfaction, 202–4
Product family, 447
Product growth, 358–59, 368, 369
Product hierarchy, 447–48
Product idea rating, 416–18, 420
Product improvement, quality or feature, 360, 361
Product innovation/imitation, 339, 411
  and retaliation, 339–41, 354, 439; *See also* New product development
Product level, organizational, 35
Product life cycle (PLC), 45, 73, 179, 347–54, 355–65, 366–74, 544
  on foreign markets, 379–81, 395–96; sales estimate by, 421, 424, 425; stages and shape of curve, 349–54, 366–69, 374
Product line, 452–58
  defined, 452–53; item-number length of, 454–57; strategy options for, 82, 453–58; stretching of, 455–57
Product line, new or existing, 406, 447, 452–58
Product-line specialist (niche), 342
Product management system, 708–15
Product manager, 11, 143, 707
  role of, 645, 708–12, 714–15
Product-market battlefield, 239, 242
Product market (expansion) grid, 47, 69–70
Product/market life cycle, 73, 347–74

Product markets, 10
Product maturity stage, 352, 359–64, 368, 369
Product mix decisions, 448, 451–52
Product-oriented definition, 38–39
Product positioning, 280, 308–16, 420
  maps of, 70–71, 419; *See also* Positioning
Product proliferation, 338
Product quality, 14–15, 459–61
Product research, company, 108
Product safety, 141–43, 154
Product situation data, marketing plan, 78, 79
Product-structured sales firms, 668–69
Product substitution, 235, 621
Product support servicing, 489–92
Product team structures, 711–12
Product usage rate, 293–94
Product-use test, 435
Product value analysis, cost reduction, 219
Product variety marketing, 279–80
Production concept, marketing organization, 13–14
Production level and accumulation, 501–3
Products and services, 4, 5, 74, 482, 490
  (*see also* Product support servicing)
Profit-and-loss planning base, 90, 740
Profit and sales equation, 84–85, 89
Profit Impact of Market Strategy (PIMS), 327–30, 460
Profit optimization (maximization), 75, 95, 168, 241–42
  marketing mix for, 85–90, 99
Profit-projection, long-run, 90–93
Profitability, 17–19, 21–24, 28, 75, 155, 333, 460, 484, 495, 719
  control and analysis, 729, 730, 738–42, 754; pretax return-on-investment, 327–30, 333; projection of, 45–46, 69
Profit-and-loss statement, 79, 83, 738
Profitability ratio of competitor, 245–46
Promotion, product, 74, 82, 355–56, 359, 531, 568, 646–47, 650
Promotional budgets, 604–6, 652–53
Promotional mix, 587–88
  budget for, 604–7, 609–11; in marketing strategy, 71–73; of wholesaler, 573–74
Promotional mix, business-to-business, 606–15
Promotional pricing, 514–15, 568
Promotional strategy, foreign trade, 396–97
Proof-of-purchase redemptions, 648–49, 652
Prospect, sales, 10, 676–78, 686, 688
Psychographic consumer market segmentation, 287, 290–92
Psychological factors, buyer, 185–90
Public-action committees (PACs), 159–60
Public interest, societal marketing, 28
Public interest groups, 159–60
Public opinion gatekeepers and leaders, 603
Public relations (PR), 141, 161, 587, 655–61
  media, messages and vehicles in, 657–60
Public service goodwill, PR, 657
Publicity, 588, 608
Publics, company environment, listed, 136, 141–43
Purchase frequency, 637
Purchasing, industrial, 215–16, 226
Purchasing decisions, 175–205 passim, 719
  evaluation stage, 201–2
Purchasing department, 136, 215, 573, 719
Push-versus-pull strategy, promotional, 612

Q

Quality decisions, 459–61
Quality is Free (Crosby), 330
Quantity discount, 513
Question mark (growth-share cell), 41–43
Questionnaire, executive information needs, 104–5
Questionnaires, marketing research, 108, 114–17, 736
Questions, closed- and open-end, 114–15
Queuing models, descriptive, 124, 125
Quota, 263, 381, 681–82

R

Racial population-change, 149, 176
Rack jobbers, 572
Rating scales, 429–30
Reagan, Ronald, administration, and deregulation, 159
Real-income and money income growth, U.S., 150, 151
Rebates (refund offers), 514, 648–49
Rebuy, industrial purchase, 211–13
Reciprocity, 211
Recruitment procedures, 674
Reference groups, influences, 177–80
Reinforcement, 189
Relationship management, 695–98
Relationship marketing, 8–9
Remarketing, 12
Reminder advertising, 619, 620
Repeat and replacement sales, 425
Research and development (R&D), 49, 59, 82, 152, 156, 320, 321
  budgets high for, 155–56; company marketing and, 717–18; of new product, 406, 408, 411, 425, 428–29, 717; in traditional model, 702–4
Research objectives, 109–11
Research-subject contact methods, 117–18
Reseller market, 209, 224–27
Resistance to marketing, 24–27
Resources, infinite, and finite renewable and nonrenewable, 151–54
Resources, product, 5, 9, 10, 11, 33, 34, 37, 144, 722
Retail services mix, 566–67
Retail stores, 568–69
Retailer cooperatives, 547, 562–63
Retailers, 557–59
  classified, 555–63; marketing decisions (strategies), 564–69
Retailing, 399, 532, 533, 547, 554–69, 647
  trends in, 569
Retention, selective (perception), 189
Return on net worth, rate, financial analysis, 735–36
Revenue, current maximum, and pricing, 497
Rewards, product-use-experience (ad appeal), 623–24
Risk taking, 201–2
Robinson-Patman Act of 1936, 157, 225
Role, buyer behavior, 180–81
Rollout market entry, 437

S

S-shaped curve, PLC, 349–51, 354, 374
Sales, first-time, new products, 424–26

Sales agency as channel alternative, 538–39
Sales analysis, annual plan, 108, 731
Sales and Marketing Management, 267, 278
Sales and profit equation, 84–85, 89, 90, 97, 169
Sales branches, 573
Sales budget, 263–64
Sales concept selling, 15–16
Sales contests, 652
Sales decline, 24
Sales department functions, 704, 705
Sales-effect advertising research, 640–42
Sales estimation, business analysis, 421–25
Sales force (people), 11, 21, 22, 24, 75, 82, 83, 86, 136, 609, 651, 663
  audit of, 750–52; in company MIS systems, 103–5; compensation of, 671–73; design of, 664–73, 715; efficiency control of, 742–43; forecast estimates/intelligence brought by, 272–73, 664; selection of, 538–39, 673–74; strategy-structuring of, 666; training of, 675–76
Sales force, outside or inside, 679–80
Sales forecasting, 107, 124, 136, 270, 273–75, 421, 424–26
Sales growth, 24, 497
Sales managers, responsibilities and functions, 11, 74, 104, 136, 664–67, 671, 681, 683, 684, 706–8, 716
Sales presentation, 688–89
Sales projections, new business plan, 45–46
Sales promotion, 82, 608, 645–55, 661, 712
  action program of, 82, 83; use with advertising, 646–47, 653; budget for, 604–6, 652–53; efficiency improvement of, 743; evaluation methods, 654–55
Sales quota, 263, 681–82
Sales reporting/information system, 103–4
Sales reporting, salesperson activity, 683
Sales representatives (salespersons), 663, 665–66, 668–85
  motivating of, 680–83; performance evaluation, final, 683–85; supervision of, 676–80; tasks of, 665–66; traits sought for, 674
Sales-response, average and marginal, 96–97
Sales-response function, 85–87, 168
Sales revenue, 82
Sales territory, 666–69, 683
Sales-variance research, 731
Sales vice-president, functions, 704–6, 721–22
Sales volume (Q), marketing-mix strategy, 82, 83, 85–89
Sales-wave research, 431
Salesmanship, 685–86
Samples, promotional (trial), 646, 648
Sampling, marketing research, 108, 110, 114, 116–18, 120
Satisfiers and dissatisfiers, Herzberg's, 187–88
Saving trends, consumer, 150–51, 181–82
SBU (strategic business units), 36–63 passim
Scenarios, 271
Scientific method, 114, 120
Scope, business mission, 37–38, 50
Sealed-bid pricing, 510
Segment (*see* Market segment; Market segmentation)
Segment analysis, detailed, 306–8
Segmentation; Segmentating (*see* Market segmentation)
Selective distortion and attention, 589–90

Selective distribution, 538
Selectivity/earnings objective, SBU, 44, 45
Self-concept and buying choice, 185
Self service, 557–58
    in packaging, 471
Sellers number determining industry struc-
    ture, 236–38
Selling, 2, 11, 15–16, 31, 665, 685
Selling, high pressure, 686
Selling, personal, 588, 606–10, 665, 685–95
Selling/calling-time controls, 677–78
Selling concept, 15–16, 31, 588
Semantic differential, 593–94
Seminars, marketing, in-house, 435, 657,
    722
Served market, 258
Service, defined, and classified, 477–78
Service channels, 534
Service differentiation, 483–84
Service innovation, 483–84
Service outputs, consumer needs, 534–35
Service quality managing, 482–86
Service pre-sale and post-sale, 490–92
Services:
    characteristics of industry, 478–81; as
    product, 445–46, 449; terminologies of, 4–
    5
Services, industrial, 476–89
Services, product support, 489–92
Services, wholesaler, 571
Seven O's of market buying, 174
Sex segmentation, 288–89
Sexes, megatrends, 145–46, 149
Shelf space, 467
Shell directional policy model, 46
Sherman Antitrust Act of 1890, 157
Shopping center (retail), 555, 558, 568
Shopping goods, 449
Silent Spring (Carson), 151
Simulated store technique (laboratory test
    markets), 431–32
Skimming strategies, new product, 355–56,
    495–99
Small Business Administration, 229
Social audit, 161
Social class stratification, 177, 178, 290
Social/cultural environment, 160–63
Social roles and reference groups, 177–81
Societal marketing concept, 28, 31
Soft-drink industry, 28
Specialist functions, organization, 707–9,
    714
Specialist roles and niche, 342–43 (see also
    Niche strategies)
Specialization, product market, 399, 668,
    669
    segments of, 301, 302, 311–19, 321
Specialty goods, 449–50
Specialty shops, 556, 558–59, 562
Spending or saving, 181–82 (see also Saving
    trends)
Stages in buying decision process, 194–204
Stalemated industry, competitive advantage,
    311–12
Star (growth-share cell), 41, 42
Static math model, 130–31
Statistical Abstract of the U.S., annual, 112
Statistical bank, analytical system, 122–24
Statistical (Bayesian) decision theory, 127
Statistical demand analysis, 275
Status, consumer behavior, 180–81

Stimuli-response, consumer, 174–76, 188,
    189, 195
Stimuli-response model, 175–76
Stochastic model, 131
Stock level, inventory, 579–81
Storage, warehousing, 579, 580–81
Store atmosphere, 567
Store features, 566
Stores, combination food and drug, 557
Stores, retail, described, 555–59
STP (segmenting/targeting/positioning) mar-
    keting, 279, 313
Strategic alliances, 387
Strategic business unit (SBU), 36, 38–63
    passim, 65, 66
    characteristics of, 40–41
Strategic control, organization, 730, 744–52,
    754
Strategic groups, 239–41, 250
Strategic planning, 33–63, 65, 66
Strategic planning programs and implementa-
    tion, 49, 59–60, 65
Strategic withdrawal (contraction), market
    segment, 326–27
Strategy, game plan, 34–35, 71, 75,
    82
    assignment of, 42–45
Strategic formation, 49, 57–58
Strategy statement, marketing plan, 82–83
Strengths and weaknesses, company, 52–53
    analysis of, 80; competitors assessed, 243–
    47, 250–52
Styling decisions, 462–63
Style and fashion cycles, 353–54
Subcultural values, 160
Suburb, termed, 149
Success factors, 51
Supermarkets, 555–58, 567, 568–69
Super segments, 305
Super store, 557
Suppliers:
    buying center selection of, 219–22; in
    company environment, 135–37, 139; dis-
    tribution requirements, 578, 580–81; in-
    dustrial buying, 209, 211, 214, 216–17,
    224, 451
Suppliers, prime or secondary, 221–
    22
Supplies, operating or maintenance, 451
Supply and demand, 480–81, 530
Survey of Current Business (National Bureau
    of Economic Research), 271
Surveys, marketing research, 107–
    20 passim, 736
Sweepstakes, 650, 652
Symbiotic marketing, 547–48
Synectics (W. J. J. Gordon), 414–15
Synchromarketing, 12
Systems buying and selling, industrial, 212–
    14

T

Target audience, 589–99
    media exposure of, 629–33, 635–37; pro-
    motional impact on, 613–14
Target customer (see Customer target)
Target (served) market (TM), 11–13, 18, 27,
    30, 46, 51, 82
    budget allocation to, 96–97; buying behav-
    ior of, 173; defined, 258; environment:

Target (served) market (continued)
    supplier-customer chain, 136, 139, 141,
    160–62, 170–71, 532, 534; research and
    selection for, 66, 67, 69–72, 76, 435, 437;
    retailer decision of, 564–65; wholesaler
    decision of, 571; See also Customer target
Target marketing, 290, 432, 439 (see also
    Market segmentation; Market targeting;
    Product positioning; Target markets)
Tariff, 381–82, 398
Technological environment, 154–56
Technological leapfrogging, new product,
    337
Technology-defined business, 39
Technology-driven companies, 718
Telemarketing, 560
Telephone Company Interstate (disguised
    name), hierarchy of objectives, 55–57
Telephone information services, PR, 658
Territory, sales representative, 666–69, 683
Test marketing, 432–36
Test markets, 273, 409, 432–36
Testing products, 429, 435
Third Wave, The (Toffler), 155
Threats and opportunities, marketing, 77,
    79–80, 160
Tie-in promotion, 650
Time-and-duty analyses, 679
Time-series analysis, sales, 273–75
Toy Safety Act of 1984, 158
Trade channel, 529 (see also Marketing
    channels)
Trade marketing mix, 169
Trade-off analyses, 424
Trade promotion, 645, 650–51
Trade shows and conventions, 435, 651–52,
    656, 657
Trademark, 463
Trading, international, 377–78, 381–
    82
Trading stamps policy, 158–59
Transaction marketing, 7–9
Transfer, 7
Transportation and delivery, 138, 581–83
Trend extrapolation, 271
Trend Report (Naisbitt), 163
Truck jobbers, 572
Truth-in-advertising, 142
Truth-in-lending, 141, 142
Truth-in-Lending Act of 1968, 158
Triad Power (Ohmae), 387
Trucking (carriers), 582–83
Turnkey solution, 212
TV ads, 560
    to passive-information recipients, 192–93
Typewriters, marketing management process,
    66–75

U

Undifferentiated marketing, 302–3
Unemployment rate, and real income, 150
Unit pricing, 142
U.S. Census Bureau, 147, 268
U.S. Industrial Outlook, 112
Usage-rate segmentation, 293–94
User, new, 320–21
User group in new markets, 47–49, 320
Utility (time, place, quantity, assortment), 5,
    138

V

Valve analysis, 219, 251
Value, product, 5–7, 30
Value chain, firm activities, 310–11
Values, 160–63
Variables, marketing problem, 122–24, 129
Variety-seeking buying behavior, 193
Verbal models, analytical system, 129
Vertical marketing systems (VMS), 342–43, 545–47, 550
Volume industry, 311–12
Voluntary chains, 546–47

W

Wants (consumer), 3–4, 6, 8, 17, 30, 31, 101, 102, 412
Warehouse store, 555, 557, 558
Warehousing and storage, 138, 570, 577, 580, 583
Warranties, product, 649–50
Wheeler-Lea Act of 1938, 158
Wholesalers:
  classified, 571–73; functions, 570, 571
Wholesalers, cash-and-carry, 572
Wholesaling, 532, 533, 546–47, 554, 569–76
  locating for handling and processing orders, 574; trends in, 574–75

Women, married, in workforce, 146
Word-of-mouth channel of influence, 601–3
Workload, sales force size, 670
Work plan, sales representative, 683

Y

Yankelovich Monitor, 160–61

Z

Zero-based budgeting, 97
ZIP-code centers, 268